Guide to William Bartram's Travels

Guide to

William Bartram's
TRAVELS

Following the Trail of America's First Great Naturalist

Brad Sanders

Fevertree Press

Copyright © 2002 by Brad Sanders
Fevertree Press
www.fevertreepress.com
189 Hidden Hills Lane, Athens, Georgia
All rights reserved

Design, composition, cartography, and photography are by the author.

The paper in this publication meets established guidelines for permanence and durability.

ISBN 0-9718763-0-4
Library of Congress Control Number: 2002091596

Publisher's Cataloging-in-Publication

Sanders, Brad, 1951–
    Guide to William Bartram's travels : following the trail of America's first great naturalist / Brad Sanders. —1st ed.
    p. cm.
    Includes bibliographical references and index.
    LCCN 2002091596
    ISBN 0-9718763-0-4

    1. Bartram, William, 1739–1823—Journeys—Southern States. 2. Southern States—Description and travel. 3. Southern States—History—Colonial period, ca. 1600–1775. 4. Natural history—Southern States—Guidebooks. I. Title. II. Title: William Bartram's travels

F213.S36 2002   917.504'3
                          GBI02-200383

While the author has spent years in the preparation of this book it is inevitable that errors remain in the text. Establishments may change their operating hours, facilities may cease operation, and new facilities may open after the printing of this book. The author welcomes the addition of new information and corrections related to historical figures, events, and spelling.

On the cover: Fern Hammock Springs, Ocala National Forest, Marion County, Florida. This photograph has been manipulated in Adobe PhotoShop® to increase color saturation.

dedicated to the memory of

Melissa Williams

Stars burn brightest before they fade

Acknowledgments

In the course of my travels during the last eight years I have been aided by numerous people and institutions. First, I would like to thank the staff of Hargrett Rare Book and Manuscript Library at the University of Georgia whose facilities and assistance were most important to this research. Invaluable assistance was provided by the Library of Congress, the Clements Library of the University of Michigan, the Georgia Department of Archives, the South Carolina Department of Archives & History, the South Carolina Historical Society, and Alabama Department of Archives and History.

I have sought the advice of many historians and scientists: Dr. Louis DeVorsey, historical geographer; Chad Braley of Southeastern Archaeological Services; Mike Price of Armstrong College; George Rogers, retired historian from Georgia Southern University; Elliott Edwards, long time president of the Bartram Trail Conference; Martha Wolf of the Historic Bartram's Garden; John Winterhawk Johnson, spiritual leader of the Eastern Creeks; Sylvia Flowers of Ocmulgee National Monument; and Dr. Dan Patillo, biologist at Western Carolina University. Special thanks are due Linda Chafin for getting me started in pursuit of William Bartram and teaching me a little botany.

Thanks to the North Carolina Bartram Trail Society, the Bartram Trail Conference, the Georgia Botanical Society, the Florida Trail Association, the Coastal Georgia Land Trust, and the Broad River Watershed Association. Particular thanks go to the Nature Conservancy and the Audubon Society in each of the seven states for protecting our natural heritage.

I could have accomplished little without the encouragement and moral support of many friends; Chris Sobek and Barbara Benson who hike with me; Georgeanne Olive and Elizabeth Bloemer who ride with me to obscure places; Larry and Deborah Davis who photograph with me; Maria and Scott Center who entertain me in Savannah; Pilar Pages, spiritual advisor; Claudia and Joseph Ammons; Tracy, Brook and Steve Statham; Ann and Steen Harvey; Peggy Linston, Pat Flannagan, Van and Mary Strickland, Don Chapman, Gene Weeks, and John and Sandy Lott. Of course I must thank my parents, Robert and Ruth Sanders, who keep wanting to know when this book will be finished.

Then, there are the fellow Bartram enthusiasts; Rosie Rotwein, Chuck Spornick, Lawrence Hettrick, Debbie Cosgrove, Burt Kornegay, Ian Macfie, Tom and Gisela Gresham, Lee Fox, and Kathryn Braund.

I have met many wonderful people on my travels; Walter and Lucy Parlange of New Roads, Louisiana; Dot Shields of Thomson, Georgia; Marie Reade of Charleston; Jim Smith of Uchee, Alabama; and the staff members of the Monroe County, Alabama, Chamber of Commerce who let me buy books on credit, "just send us a check when you get home." There are many people at the many visitor centers and chambers of commerce where I stopped for information and everyone was friendly and helpful. The South is truly the land of hospitality.

Darcie
December 30, 1991–September 29, 1999

The reader is advised that there are inherent dangers in many outdoor activities. The inclusion of recreational areas or mention of any outdoor recreational activity in this book does not imply any guarantee of safety. People who are engaged in outdoor recreation must be prepared, skilled, and equipped for the activity.

The Southeastern United States contains subtropical and temperate climates that support populations of biting and stinging insects which may be present even during winter months. There are venomous reptiles that may be present in a variety of habitats. Hiking, climbing, and boating are activities that carry a risk of injury or even death if not approached with caution and preparation. Weather can be unpredictable, sudden, and severe and the reader is advised to be prepared for any eventuality. Many roads mentioned in this guide are unpaved and are therefore hazardous during wet weather.

The maps in this publication are intended as illustrations for the text and are not intended to show accuracy regarding distances. Readers are advised to refer to official United States government maps when necessary. The inclusion of descriptions of private property in this book does not grant the reader access to that private property. The reader is advised to be aware of boundaries between public and private property and to respect the rights of owners.

Brad Sanders and the Fevertree Press will not accept any responsibility for injury, damage to property, or legal issues arising from persons engaged in travel or outdoor recreation.

Contents

Index to the Maps	viii
Introduction	xi
1. William Bartram	1
2. Savannah	11
Historic Savannah	22
3. Georgia Coast	28
4. An Uninhabited Wilderness	40
5. Savannah River	54
6. Augusta	60
Historic Augusta	73
7. Great Buffalo Lick	77
8. Upper Savannah River	91
9. East Florida	96
10. Upper St. Johns River	108
11. New Smyrna	117
12. Alachua	122
13. Suwannee River	130
14. Charleston	135
Historic Charleston	151
15. The Lowcountry	158
16. The Upcountry	170
17. Cherokee Lower Towns	178
18. Old Stecoe	189
19. Cherokee Middle Towns	195
20. Cherokee Overhill Towns	203
21. The Great Trading Path	208
22. The Sand Hills	219
23. Lower Creek Towns	226
24. Upper Creek Towns	238
25. The Mobile & Pensacola Path	250
26. Mobile	256
Historic Mobile	264
27. Pensacola	266
Historic Pensacola	271
28. Gulf Coast	273
29. Lake Pontchartrain	281
30. Mississippi River	288
31. Santee	298
32. Long Bay	308
33. Cape Fear	312
Wilmington	321
34. Home Again	323
Appendix A. Timeline	325
Appendix B. Publications about John & William Bartram	332
Appendix C. Organizations	333
Appendix D. Historical Names for Rivers & Islands	334
Bibliography	335
Index	341

Historical Maps

A Map of Virginia, North Carolina, South Carolina, and Georgia: Comprehending the Spanish Provinces of East and West Florida by Joseph Purcell, 1788 x

Map of Georgia from Savannah to Augusta by Archibald Campbell, 1780 10

Sketch of the Country between River Altamaha and Musqueta Inlet, Containing Part of Georgia and East Florida 41

A Map of the Ceded Lands by Philip Yonge, 1773 78

A Map of South Carolina, c. 1779 by Henry Mouzon 136

A New Map of the Cherokee Nation by Thomas Kitchin, 1760 196

Detail of *A Map of West Florida, Part of East Florida, Georgia and Part of South Carolina* by John Stuart and Joseph Purcell, 1780 219

Detail of *A map of the Southern Indian District of North America* by Joseph Purcell, 1780 274–275

Index to the Maps

Numbers indicate pages where maps of the Bartram Trail are located in this book

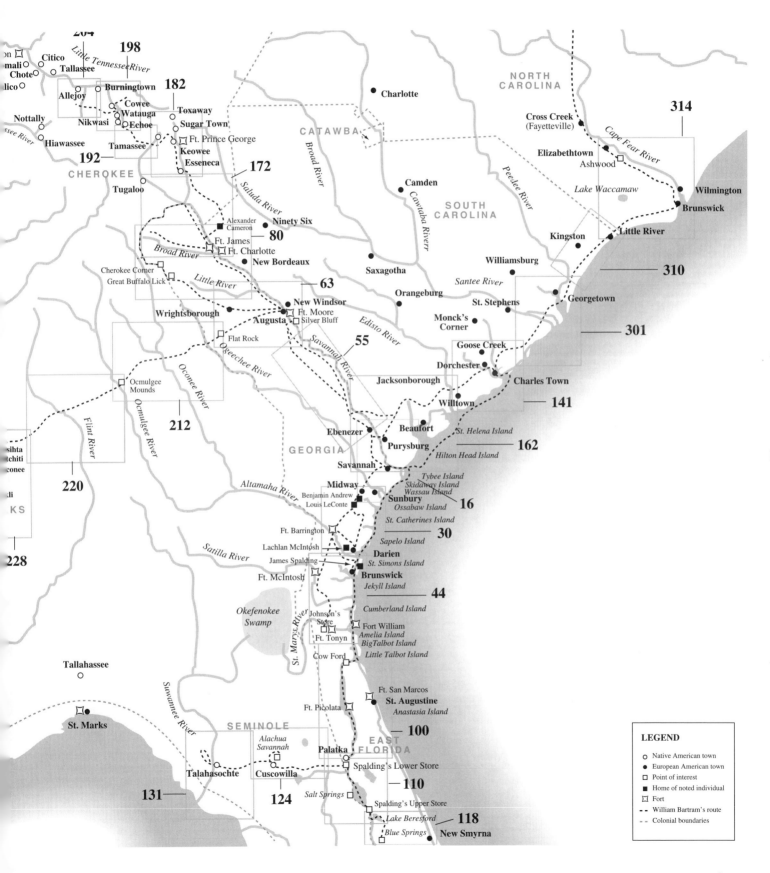

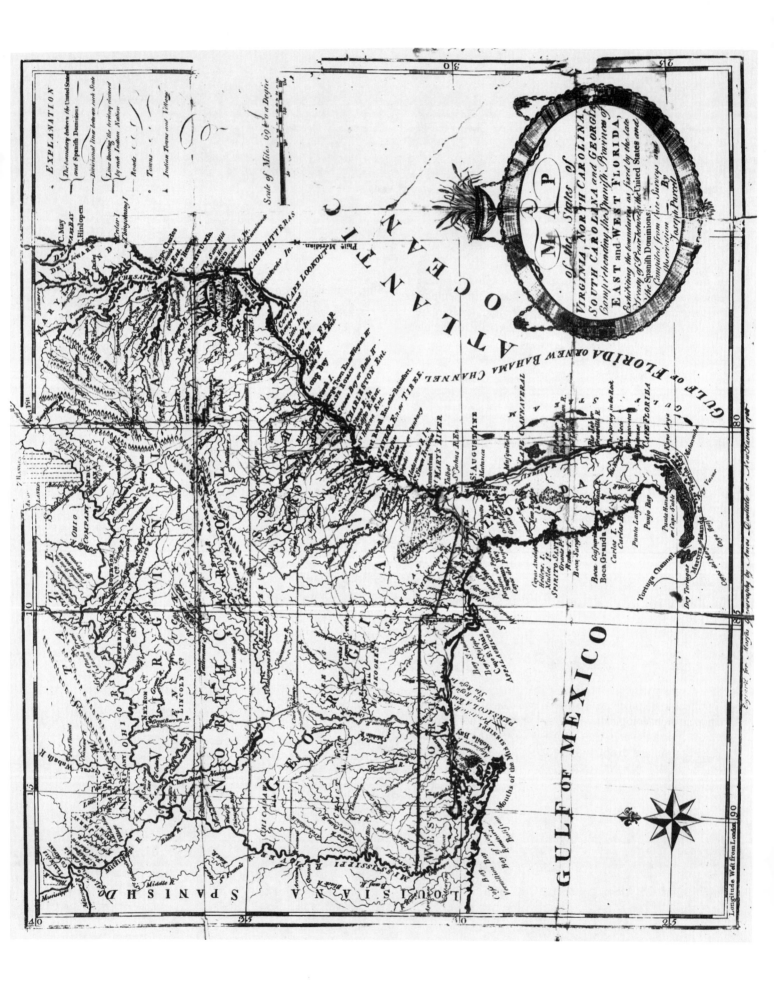

Introduction

I have always been a little uncomfortable with one of the arguments used to sway public opinion and influence political policy regarding habitat and species protection. It is often suggested that within a forest might lie cures and medicines yet unknown and if we lose those plants we might never know what they offer to the health and well-being of humankind. In a civilized world it is not believed that a human life is no more important to the balance of the Earth than a bear, a yew, a moss, a fish, or any non-human species. But, emphasizing the pharmaceutical and economic potential of natural resources implies that other species exist primarily for the pleasure and health of humans and it trivializes their inherent value. Isn't this precisely how resources have traditionally been managed, or mismanaged? Species are protected and encouraged that benefit human economy and others are allowed to exist only because of benign neglect.

Considering the fact that there are now six billion humans on the earth there are few places that plant and animal species can exist apart from human geography. Plants and animals in the wild can be hunted to extinction, they can be domesticated and farmed, or they can occupy a niche within the human habitat; but they can no longer live outside the sphere of human influence because humans are now changing the earth on a scale once accomplished only by climatic and geologic forces.

Much of our Southern natural environment was forever changed because cotton was so profitable. So much so that the forests and the very soil itself were sacrificed to produce cotton and earn much needed cash. I grew up in the South and the paradigm has been always production, profit, and return; not integrity, ecology, and sustainability. A modern concept of environmental stewardship is becoming more widely accepted and although many acres of environmentally significant habitat have been preserved in the South during the last century there continues to be much destruction. Soapstone Ridge near Atlanta, an archaeologically important site, could not be protected against the pressures of suburban housing developers. The beautiful and exotic Florida Scrub is being bulldozed and replanted with orange trees. People with means covet the Sea Islands and hammocks for their vacation retreats.

Within the writings of William Bartram we witness the contradictory elements of the practical and the transcendental need to know nature. While he exulted in the beauty and grandeur of nature for nature's sake, Bartram also said that he was searching for plant productions that might be of benefit to fellow humans. On the very first page of the introduction to the *Travels* he wrote,

Men and manners undoubtedly hold the first rank—whatever may contribute to our existence is also of equal importance, whether it be found in the animal or vegetable kingdoms: neither are the various articles, which tend to promote the happiness and convenience of mankind, to be disregarded.[1]

But, he then goes on to say,

This world, as a glorious apartment of the boundless palace of the sovereign Creator, is furnished with an infinite variety of animated scenes, inexpressibly beautiful and pleasing, equally free to the inspection and enjoyment of all his creatures.[2]

and for William Bartram he sees in nature the work of God,

Perhaps there is not any part of creation, within the reach of our observations, which exhibits a more glorious display of the Almighty hand, than the vegetable world. Such a variety of pleasing scenes, ever changing, throughout the seasons, arising from various causes and assigned each to the purpose and use determined.[3]

During a time when the natural landscape was expected to serve an economic purpose and little more, William Bartram's voice presaged modern nature writing for he began to see all things in nature as being good and necessary in their own right and he derived spiritual benefit from studying nature. It may have been his contact with the Creeks, Cherokees, and Seminoles that lead Bartram to begin viewing humans as subjects of nature rather than masters of it. While he acknowledged that humans are a part of the landscape and like other animals are subject to the laws of survival, unnecessary excess and arrogance offended Bartram. While traveling through Alabama he was indignant when his traveling companions killed a wolf puppy they discovered…

we had not proceeded far before our people roused a litter of young wolves, to which giving chase we soon caught one of them, it being entangled in high grass, one of our people caught it by the hind legs and another beat out its brains with the but of his gun,—barbarous sport![4]

William Bartram, traveling in a vast and unsettled wilderness, could not have been moved to promote the preservation of nature for he could not conceive of what would happen to it in

Facing page: A Map of Virginia, North Carolina, South Carolina and Georgia: Comprehending the Spanish Provinces of East and West Florida, *by Joseph Purcell, 1788. Reproduced from the Collections of the Library of Congress.*

1. William Bartram, *Travels through North and South Carolina, Georgia, East and West Florida, the Cherokee Country, the Extensive Territories of the Muscogulges or Creek Confederacy, and the Country of the Chactaws*; Philadelphia, 1791, ix.
2. Ibid.
3. Ibid.
4. Ibid., 396

the years after his passing. It was to be another hundred years before Americans, alarmed at the rate of clear-cutting, began protecting their forests. Another writer and naturalist of a mind with Bartram, John Muir, would begin a movement to preserve the natural landscape, not for future production, but for the simple beauty and pleasure of having it and walking in it. If William Bartram was alive and writing today he might be a powerful voice for the preservation of the natural world not simply because it is beneficial to us, or gives us pleasure, or because nature is beautiful, but also because it is our moral duty as God's stewards.

William Bartram was the first great American naturalist and he was the transition between a tentative colonial scientific community dominated by European minds to an American science characterized by self-confidence, boldness, and a peculiar relationship to the natural world that has produced numerous environmental movements, the world's first national park system, the science of Ecology, and a burgeoning market for outdoor gear. William Bartram, as the first observer of the Southern landscape and pioneer of American nature writing ought to be the symbol of environmental preservation in the Southeast.

Retracing William Bartram's Travels

Although I was born in Atlanta and raised in rural Georgia, I did not have a proper admiration for my own region. Many years ago when I graduated from college I thought that eventually I would migrate northward, like so many literary and artistic Southerners before me. But, I stayed and I began to realize that I could not live away from family and friends—perhaps because the clannish nature of my Scottish heritage was too strong. I had to acknowledge that, regardless of my pretensions, I was bound to the people and land of the Southeast, heart and soul. It took William Bartram, an outsider, to help me see the Deep South as a land of exotic beauty worthy of protection and admiration. He lead me out into the landscape to travel the back roads and byways, into swamps, marshes, mountains, and forests. I have learned more botany, geology, biology, climatology, and ecology than I ever dreamed I would.

I began reading William Bartram's *Travels* in 1991, coincidentally the bicentennial anniversary of its publication. I was familiar with William Bartram and the work of the Bartram Trail Conference in preserving his memory, but I had not known just how extensive had been his travels nor how often his path and mine had crossed throughout my life. As I read I was intrigued that I had been to many of the places Bartram described and traveled many of the same paths that he traveled, but I had not seen what he saw. I spent my early years living near Omaha, Georgia, which lies just downriver from the site of Yuchi, visited by William Bartram in the summer of 1775. As a child I visited cousins in Fernandina, where Bartram met Mr. Egan at Lord Egmont's plantation. When we visited my grandfather near Sarasota we would take US-441 and as we passed through Paynes Prairie I always wondered "What is this place?" As a teenager I lived near Stephens, Georgia, which lies on Bartram's route from the Great Buffalo Lick to Cherokee Corner. As an adult I have loved traveling to the mountains and my route from Clayton to Franklin is the same as that traveled by William Bartram in 1775. Now I call Athens home, which is where Bartram viewed the North Oconee River as he traveled with the survey party in the New Purchase in June, 1773.

I began to follow roads that appeared to approximate Bartram's route. At first I did this close to home, then I began to venture farther and farther away; to the coast of Georgia, to Charleston, Palatka, Montgomery, and Mobile. I began photographing the places that I visited and had the idea of making a visual documentary of the Bartram Trail. On my way home from a trip to Charleston I had the idea that I should write and publish a simple guide, including maps, to help people who were also interested in retracing Bartram's *Travels*. As I learned more about William Bartram and the colonial Southeast, I became more interested in telling the whole story and my little guide grew from thirty-six pages to over three-hundred. What was to be a cursory guide to Bartram's *Travels* became ever more detailed as I learned more about the cultural and natural history of the Southeast. I began to see this guide as a way to tell the story of the region and promote an appreciation for our remaining natural areas as well as popularize the life and travels of William Bartram.

There have been several vexing problems confronting scholars when recreating William Bartram's trail through the seven states bordering the Gulf and Atlantic coasts. One is a lack of modern landmarks that can be related back to colonial times. William Bartram rode through land that, although crisscrossed by trails, was uninhabited wilderness. There were few settlements, monuments, or outstanding physical features mentioned that could help us identify his route. Another problem arises from William Bartram's inaccurate estimation of distances. Francis Harper, in *The Travels of William Bartram: Naturalist Edition*, found that at times when Bartram wrote of a number of yards he should have said feet. Sometimes Bartram overestimated the distance traveled. Harper also documented Bartram's notorious sloppiness regarding dates and made corrections in the *Naturalist Edition*. In this guide I have used Harper's corrected chronology rather than Bartram's dates in the *Travels*. However, the organization of chapters in this guide follow the order of the *Travels*. Another problem is that so much of the land through which Bartram traveled is now privately owned and much altered.

I have interpreted parts of the trail differently from other scholars and have explained this within the text. There are several important instances worth mentioning. On his route from Fort Charlotte, South Carolina, to the Lower Creek Towns I believe that William Bartram reached the Lower Creek Trading Path closer to Augusta rather than passing through Wrightsborough. On his travels between Augusta and Savannah I believe that Bartram's route was close to the Savannah River, except possibly during his first trip to Augusta in May 1773. I have accepted the research of Rowell Bosse and Charles Moore in the Bartram Trail Conference *Heritage Report* that suggests Bartram crossed the Nantahala Mountains at Burningtown Gap rather than at Wayah Gap as outlined by Francis Harper. It must be remembered that sections of the Bartram Trail are open to debate and what is presented here is one person's interpretation.

What is important is that William Bartram will become a guide for others who want to learn more about the natural world around us. Get out, travel, and enjoy!

William Bartram

What, in his day, drew criticism to William Bartram's *Travels* are qualities that today attract us to his writing and have made his book popular reading for over two centuries. He was an impassioned observer of nature as well as skilled scientist and for that he was faulted by some for not holding to a strictly scientific text. But, the *Travels* was more than botanical observation, it was possibly the first of a modern style of nature writing that combined scientific observation, travel information, adventure, and personal impressions. William Bartram was one of the first modern Americans in that he had a spiritual relationship with nature, concern for animal welfare, and he was tolerant of other cultures. The *Travels* combined science and poetry in what Thomas Carlyle characterized as "a floundering kind of eloquence." His florid and embellished style of writing was not in vogue during the early nineteenth century, so he was dismissed by some as being quaint and archaic. Some of his style must be attributed to his Quakerism and some to his times, but today it draws us more sensibly into the scenes he painted with words. His writing described the Southern wilderness that would change forever just a few years after his visit.

John Bartram

The study of William Bartram cannot begin without mention of his father, John, America's first native-born naturalist and creator of the first garden in North America devoted exclusively to the collection, display, and propagation of native plants. He was William's teacher as well as his concerned and loving father. John was a better scientist than his son but he was an uneven and often inelegant writer. The father was a confident, sociable, and practical man, successful at all to which he turned his attention. The son was an artist whose temperament and sensitivity ensured his failure as a merchant and planter but great success as America's first environmental writer and naturalist.

John Bartram was born near Philadelphia on May 3, 1699. His mother died when he was only two and he was raised by his grandmother. John's father, William I, moved with his new wife and children to North Carolina in 1709. He was killed by Indians and his wife and children, William II and Elizabeth, were abducted. They were later ransomed and returned to Philadelphia. William II, the uncle of William III, the botanist, returned to North Carolina as an adult and settled on the Cape Fear River where he was visited often by his nephew.

John Bartram was blessed with a natural intellect and curiosity. He became a successful farmer and self-taught botanist. This humble Quaker farmer eventually came to correspond with the learned men of America and England and carried on a brisk business supplying native American plants to the collectors on the European continent. Linnaeus called him "the greatest natural botanist in the world" and used John Bartram's specimens to name many common North American plants.

John Bartram began collecting interesting plants and flowers around the time his first wife, Mary Maris, died in 1727. He bought the property that is now the Bartram Garden in Philadelphia in 1728 and started his famous garden on a five-acre plot between the house and the Schuylkill River. His interest in plants was due in no little part to his interest in medicine for at the time pharmacy and botany were inseparable.

In 1732 John Bartram began a correspondence with Peter Collinson, a wealthy Quaker merchant of London who had a keen interest in botany, especially new and unusual plants. Collinson became Bartram's agent in Europe, supplying the American with books, advice, and money while trading Bartram's seeds and plants to wealthy collectors. Patrons of John Bartram included Sir Hans Sloane, whose collections helped start the British Museum; Robert James, Baron Petre; the Earls of Bute, Leicester, and Lincoln; the Dukes of Argyle, Richmond, Norfolk, Marlborough, and Bedford; Queen Ulrica of Sweden, and Carl Linnaeus, who developed the modern system of classification. John Bartram entered the intellectual society of Philadelphia, then the largest and most prosperous city in North America, and became close friends with Benjamin Franklin. Together they founded the American Philosophical Society in 1743.

John Bartram made his first botanical expedition in 1736 when he traveled to the swamps of New Jersey to collect white cedar and then traveled up the Schuylkill River in the fall of that year. He traveled to Virginia in 1737 and in 1738 and while exploring the Susquehannah River he found ginseng, not known to exist in North America before then. He then traveled often to New Jersey and to remote areas of Pennsylvania, to New York, to the Catskill Mountains in 1741, and to Onondago in the Iroquois Confederation in 1743. His fourteen-year-old son, William, accompanied him to the Catskills in 1753 and again in 1754 where they met Dr. Alexander Gar-

Above: William Bartram, painted by Charles Wilson Peale, c. 1808
Used by permission of Independence National Historical Park

John Bartram's Correspondents

Mark Catesby (1682–1749) author of *Natural History of Carolina, Florida and the Bahama Islands*. Catesby was one of the first illustrators to combine plant and animal species in association. See page 68.

John Ellis (1710–1766), English naturalist, member of the Royal Society of London, friend of Peter Collinson, and correspondent of Linnaeus.

Carl Linnaeus (1707–1778), Swedish botanist, creator of modern systematic botany, and author of *Systema naturae* and *Species plantarum*.

John Clayton (1693–1773) was an official in Gloucester County, Virginia. His collections were used by Johann Gronovius to prepare *Flora Virginica*, published in 1739. Linnaeus based many of his descriptions of American plants on the collections of Clayton. The Clayton herbarium is one of the important historical collections in the Natural History Museum in London.

Jan Frederick Gronovius (1690–1760), botanist of Leiden, Holland. Gronovius was one of the first practitioners of the Linnaean system of plant classification. He used John Clayton's work as the basis for publishing *Flora Virginica*.

Sir Hans Sloane (1660–1753) was a physician and naturalist practicing in London. He began collecting plants while working in Jamaica and published his discoveries in a two-volume set on the natural history of Jamaica. His extensive library and large herbarium was the basis for creating the British Museum.

Johann Jacob Dillenius (1687–1747) was a German physician who emigrated to England in 1721. He was hired to work with William Sherard on his botanical encyclopedia and later published works of his own. His herbarium is preserved at Oxford University.

James Logan (1674–1751) came to Pennsylvania as personal secretary to William Penn. He was thereafter involved in the government of Pennsylvania. He was an amateur naturalist and corresponded with Hans Sloane and Peter Collinson.

Martha Logan (c. 1704–1779) ran a school at Wando River, South Carolina, and was an avid gardener. In 1752 she wrote the first gardening calender in America and ran a nursery business at Trott's Point. Her garden was visited by John Bartram in 1760 and the two exchanged seeds and plants until his death.

Dr. Alexander Garden (1728–1792), physician of Charleston who supplied plants to Linnaeus. See page 153.

Cadwallader Colden (1688–1776), was first a physician then lieutenant governor of New York. He was the first to use the Linnaean system of taxonomy in North America. He sent upwards of 400 plants to Linneaus. His daughter Jane was an expert in the Linnean system and an artist.

Benjamin Franklin (1706–1790) was possibly the most famous man of his time. Franklin was a printer, writer, civic leader, statesman, diplomat, inventor, and scientist. He was a lifelong friend of John Bartram and together they founded the American Philosophical Society.

Peter Collinson (1694–1768), John Bartram's friend and agent in London, Peter Collinson was a Quaker and wool draper whose primary trade was with the colonies. He was an avid plant collector and established a famous garden at his home in Peckham, Surrey. Collinson and Bartram began corresponding in 1733 and continued until Collinson's death. Through Collinson John Bartram's plants found their way into the major gardens of England and Bartram was introduced to his European correspondents.

Dr. John Fothergill (1712–1780) was a London physician who began corresponding with John Bartram in 1743. His enthusiasm for collecting plants grew from his interest in medicines. Fothergill funded William Bartram's travels in the South in 1773–1776.

Thomas Lamboll (1694–1774) **and Elizabeth Lamboll** (1725?–1770), residents of Charleston who helped create interest in gardening in that city. See page 151.

Henry Laurens (1724–1792), Charleston businessman and planter who became president of the Continental Congress. See page 157.

---

den at the home of Dr. Cadwallader Colden. Father and son traveled to New England in 1754. John made his first trip to the South in 1759 where he was hosted in Charleston by Dr. Alexander Garden and Thomas and Elizabeth Lamboll. He traveled to the Cape Fear River in North Carolina to visit his brother William and went to North Carolina again in 1761 with his sons Moses and William.

Britain obtained Florida, Canada, and Illinois at the end of the French and Indian War and requests were made for John's presence on several expeditions into the new territories. He hoped to accompany Henry Bouquet to the upper Mississippi, but unrest among the Indians in that region ended plans for the expedition. Peter Collinson helped John gain an appointment as botanist to King George III in 1765. Bartram's first official duty as Royal botanist was to explore the new colony of East Florida and report on the soil and plants. He and William traveled in Georgia and Florida from July 1765 to April of the following year.

Peter Collinson died in 1768. He had corresponded with his friend, John Bartram, for thirty-six years although the two never met. Dr. John Fothergill offered to take over as Bartram's agent in England although he would not be able to devote as much time as had Collinson. Most of the routine business was handled by Fothergill's nephew, James Freeman. John's years of collecting and travel through the frontiers of the colonies were rewarded by his election to the Royal Academy of Sciences in Stockholm.

John turned over the business of his nursery to son Johnny in 1771 and retired from collecting. During the years 1773 through 1776 John had to worry about William, then on his famous travels in the Southern colonies. William was not a dependable correspondent and his parents had to learn of his whereabouts and well-being through Dr. Chalmers, Dr. Fothergill, and the Lambolls. John was delighted when William returned home unexpectedly in January, 1777, and took vicarious pleasure in hearing the details of his son's adventures and discoveries.

John's other children were not so troublesome as William. John, Jr., was a steady and sensible young man who was entrusted to take over the nursery business. Moses was first a sea captain and then joined brother Isaac at his apothecary business in Philadelphia. James and Benjamin became farmers in Darby. Daughters Ann, Elizabeth, and Mary all married well, but we know little of their lives. John Bartram died September 22, 1777, and is buried in an unmarked grave in Darby Friends Burial Ground.

William Bartram's Early Years

William Bartram was born on February 9, 1739, in Kingsessing, Pennsylvania, now part of Philadelphia. His parents were John Bartram and Ann Mendenhall and his twin sister was Elizabeth. Beginning in 1752, William attended the Philadelphia Academy, later to become the College of Philadelphia. He studied with the leading classical scholars then living in the American colonies, which served him well when he wrote the *Travels*. He often used classical references in describing the beauty and awful power of nature.

William was exposed to the best scientific minds of the New World from an early age. Philadelphia was home to Bartram friends James Logan, Joseph Breintnall, and Benjamin Franklin. Beginning at fourteen years of age, William traveled with his father on botanical expeditions and met such notable persons as Cadwallader Colden; Jane Colden, botanical artist; Henry Laurens, statesman; and Alexander Garden, physician and botanist. The Bartram home was visited by Peter Kalm (student of Linnaeus), General Henry Bouquet, and Hector St. John de Crèvecoeur.

William showed an inclination toward botany and a talent for drawing. His father had in his library a copy of Mark Catesby's *Natural History of Carolina*, given to John by Catesby himself, which must certainly have inspired the young Bartram to pursue his interest as a botanical artist. Peter Collinson circulated William's drawings among his circle of correspondents, including Linnaeus, J. F. Gronovius, Lord Bute, Dr. Fothergill, and famous botanical artist C. D. Ehret.

John Bartram became concerned about his son's ability to earn a living and set about seeking a trade for his sixteen-year-old son. William rejected an offer from Benjamin Franklin to learn the printing trade. John declined an offer to study medicine under Dr. Garden for he believed William was interested only in learning the botany. His father suggested surveying and Collinson suggested engraving. William eventually entered into a profession for which he was less suited than any of the others, he became an apprentice merchant in Philadelphia. In 1761 he left Philadelphia and went to the Cape Fear River in North Carolina to operate a store at his uncle's plantation, Ashwood. He was not very successful and we might assume that his heart was elsewhere for he spent all available time botanizing and drawing. William was still at Ashwood when John wrote of his appointment as Royal Botanist and the planned trip to East Florida. He asked William to settle his business and prepare to join him.

The Bartram's Travel to Florida in 1765

John Bartram sailed to Charleston, arriving on July 8, 1765. He visited old friends in Charleston, then traveled to his brother's home, Ashwood, on the Cape Fear River north of Wilmington. Father and son left Ashwood on August 6 and traveled to Brunswick, where they visited with Governor William Tryon. They then traveled to Little River and along the beach at Long Bay and spent the evening in Georgetown on August 12. They followed the King's Road from Georgetown, the same road that William would travel ten years later. They remained in Charleston from August 15 through August 28. During that time they visited Dr. Garden, Superintendent John Stuart, and Henry Laurens. On rainy days John arranged his collections and organized his journal while William made drawings.

The Bartrams traveled to Georgia, crossing the Savannah River at Purrysburg, and arrived in Savannah on September 4 where they visited James Habersham and Governor James Wright. The Bartrams traveled up the Savannah River to Shell Bluff, Silver Bluff, and Augusta. The end of September was spent in and around Savannah and on September 30 they finally set out for Florida, traveling overland on the King's Road. They explored the Altamaha River around Fort Barrington where they discovered Ogeechee lime, Franklinia, and fevertree. They crossed the St. Johns River on October 10 and arrived in Saint Augustine the next day. They dined with Governor James Grant and several gentlemen from South Carolina, who we might assume were John and James Moultrie and William Drayton, who were officials in the colonial government of East Florida.

The Bartrams stayed in Saint Augustine until the middle of November, John being ill much of the time from malaria. William used the time to explore Anastasia Island and the surrounding countryside. They traveled with the governor and officials to Picolata for the conference with the Creeks where a treaty was signed on November 18. They set out again from Saint Augustine on December 19 to search for the head of the St. Johns River.

As they traveled upriver they stopped at several places that William would revisited in 1774—Picolata, Rollestown, Murphy Island, Spalding's Lower Store, Mount Hope at Beecher Point, Mount Royal at Fruitland Cove, Spalding's Upper Store, Blue Springs, and Salt Springs. They ascended the St. Johns as far as they could before it broke into myriad branches and became choked with reeds. This was due west of Titusville near the southeast corner of Volusia County. They turned back around the middle of January 1766.

The trip to Georgia and East Florida ruined William for any possible future success as a businessman. He had become enamored with Florida and chose to stay and take a land grant near the mouth of Six Mile Creek just north of Picolata where he intended to grow rice and indigo. To finance his venture he borrowed against his inheritance, doing so against his father's strong advice to the contrary. John left Saint Augustine on March 17 and returned to Charleston.

Henry Laurens assisted John in choosing several slaves to be sent from Charleston. During the summer of 1767 Laurens toured Florida seeking land and business opportunities and he stopped by Picolata to see the young Bartram. William was ill, his crops were doing poorly, and his slaves were rebellious. Never a robust person and having a gentle nature, William was not to have any more success at building a plantation than he had at being a merchant. Laurens wrote to John that he should urge William to abandon Picolata, even at a loss.[1] Laurens took the liberty of sending provisions to William including rum and wine to lift his spirits.

William disposed of his property then spent several months as an assistant to William De Brahm, surveyor general for Florida. He helped De Brahm run the lines for the New

---
1. This letter is on display in the library of the American Philosophical Society in Philadelphia.

Smyrna colony that was being developed south of Saint Augustine. William was shipwrecked off the coast in late 1766 and was feared lost by his family until word came from Charleston in April 1767 that he was alive and well. He returned to Philadelphia that summer.

William entered the mercantile business again in Philadelphia after working as a farmhand for awhile. During that period he began receiving commissions for drawings from Collinson, Fothergill, and others. In 1770 he was again failing at business and disappeared suddenly when one of his creditors threatened him. No one knew where he was until several months later when word arrived from North Carolina that he was at his Uncle William's home. Unfortunately his beloved Uncle William and his aunt died about this time and were followed shortly in death by their son Bill, who had recently finished his medical training in Philadelphia. Ashwood had always been a refuge for William and it must certainly have seemed very lonely now, but he at least was able to finish some of his commissioned drawings.

While William was in North Carolina Dr. Fothergill proposed that William make an expedition to Florida for the purpose of collecting new plants and seeds and making drawings. Perhaps the good doctor, being less conventional in his concern for the young botanist's career than either John Bartram or Peter Collinson, hoped to help William fulfill his dreams and at the same time satisfy his own passion for natural history. A letter from Fothergill in October 1772 gives William detailed instructions for collecting, preserving, and shipping specimens as well as preparing the drawings. William was to be paid £50 per annum, plus expenses and remuneration for the drawings. Although this sum is only $75 in today's money, it was the income of an average middle-class worker in the eighteenth century. William returned to Philadelphia in the winter of 1772 to prepare for his journey.

The Travels

During the next four years William Bartram traveled throughout the recently settled and frontier parts of the Southeast. Not only did he discover new plants, his excellent mind and trained eye also turned to the observation of birds, reptiles, and geography. He lived among the Seminoles, traveled to the Cherokee and Creek nations, and recorded their customs and history. He met danger in the wilderness against an intrepid Seminole, a hungry wolf, belligerent alligators, violent storms, and illness. He traveled for extended periods of time alone either on horseback or by boat and on foot. He met the most important people of the day living in Georgia, South Carolina, and East and West Florida. Everyone who met William Bartram delighted in his company and assisted him in his quest even if they found his mission somewhat baffling.

According to Henry Laurens, William was "of a tender and

Dr. Daniel Solander

Dr. Daniel Solander studied at the University of Upsala, Sweden, where he won the particular notice of Linnaeus. He left Sweden to become a librarian at the British Museum. He later became secretary to Sir Joseph Banks and accompanied him on Captain Cook's voyage in the Pacific. Solander was engaged by Dr. Fothergill to catalogue the plants collected by William Bartram and prepare their descriptions for publication. Unfortunately Solander died on May 16, 1782, after a dissipated life in London without completing much of the work. Bartram's dependence on others to complete his botanical work in faraway London led him to encourage younger scientists in America to become versed in the modern taxonomic method and publish their findings at home before publishing in Europe.

delicate frame of body and intellect." It is surprising that a man of slight build, lacking the physical vigor of his father and the aggressive nature needed to be successful in business, would accept and carry out an assignment of such physical and emotional challenge. Yet he often traveled alone with only his horse and gun and met the challenges he encountered.

The account of his journey of discovery was published in 1791 as *Travels through North & South Carolina, Georgia, East & West Florida, the Cherokee Country, the Extensive Territories of the Muscogulges, or Creek Confederacy, and the Country of the Chactaws; Containing an Account of the Soil and Natural Productions of Those Regions, Together with Observations on the Manners of the Indians*, now simply known as the *Travels*. It was a new kind of nature writing that combined scientific observation with lyrical descriptions of the natural world, including the humans who inhabited it. His use of a common, as well as scientific vocabulary, made his work accessible to a much larger reading public. Bartram alternated his lists and descriptions of species with passages of story and anecdote, punctuated with moments of tension and adventure to keep the reader's interest engaged. Bartram draws us into the scene by addressing us directly and at times he changes to the present tense so that we participate in the experience with him as we sense his breathless excitement.

He placed some events out of chronological sequence if it suited the flow of his narrative, which has caused some confusion when scholars have tried to recreate his route. Bartram was so casual about time that he got some of his dates off by months, others by as much as a year. The dates and true sequence of Bartram's movements were sorted out by Francis Harper and reported in *The Travels of William Bartram: Naturalist's Edition*. Harper also expertly identified Bartram's scientific names with specific plants, an important accomplishment since most of Bartram's names have not been adopted into usage.

William Bartram, being a devout Quaker, viewed nature as the perfect handiwork of God. This led him to value all that existed in nature, even to pleading for the life of a giant rattlesnake discovered by his camping party on Sapelo Island. The events of nature were as they should be, neither good nor bad, but right. William's sensitivity, Quakerism, and artistic nature caused him to view nature in a more personal and holistic sense than in distinct parts as was more common to the scientific minds of the Age of Enlightenment. William Bartram's profession of admiration and awe at the beauty of nature were incomprehensible to many of his age who took a more utilitarian approach to the landscape. Had William been more rational and less intuitive he could have been more successful at business, but then we would not have the *Travels*.

Still, being a Quaker and a man of the times, William Bartram believed in the benefits of civilization and part of his goal was to discover new plants that would benefit humans. The paradox in the *Travels* is that the wilderness as seen and admired by Bartram could not last with the coming of civilization. The historical value of Bartram's work is that he gives us a glimpse of the South as a lost paradise.

The *Travels* caught the imagination of armchair travelers, scientists, philosophers, and poets on both sides of the Atlantic, especially the Romantic writers. Coleridge and Wordsworth borrowed from Bartram's descriptions of subtropical Florida and the near-wild Indians who exemplified man in his natural state. The *Travels* influenced the next generation of scientists and writers in America. Henry David Thoreau read Bartram and was influenced by the synthesis of science and poetry found in the *Travels*.

William Bartram and Native Americans

William Bartram's observations on the Southeastern Indians are an invaluable resource for modern historians but have not often been presented as an important part of his legacy. His writings demonstrate that he, indeed, was a man ahead of his times. His enlightened view of Native Americans is revealed early in the *Travels*, at the end of his introduction,

> ... I shall now offer such observations as must necessarily occur, from a careful attention to, and investigation of the manners of the Indian nations; being induced, while travelling among them, to associate with them, that I might judge for myself whether they were deserving of the severe censure, which prevailed against them among the white people, that they were incapable of civilization.
>
> In the consideration of this important subject it will be necessary to enquire, whether they were inclined to adopt the European modes of civil society? Whether such a reformation could be obtained, without using coercive or violent means? And lastly, whether such a revolution would be productive of real benefit to them, and consequently beneficial to the public?[2]

Bartram was not a government official, missionary, or trader, nor did he covet the Indian lands. He, therefore, had the luxury of befriending the Indians, especially the Muscogulges, on their own terms. He was welcomed into their homes and was affected by their unprejudiced and generous hospitality. William's concern for fellow humans was a part of his Quaker faith; but, his fair and impartial judgement of people was most certainly an innate part of his character. Although he applied his judgement universally and without bias, he was still a part of European culture and desired that the Native Americans become civilized in the manner of his own people.

One criticism of William Bartram's writings about Native Americans was that he was overly indulgent and portrayed them in a romantic, golden light; praising the admirable qualities of native culture while dismissing or justifying controversial traits. There are several things that can be said in Bartram's defense. He was trying to understand the Native Americans in the context of their own culture and without European preconceptions, a concept that was lost among the ethnocentric readers of his day. In fact, it was well into this century that European-Americans ceased treating Native Americans as misguided children who needed civilizing and began to appreciate their rich culture. Bartram was writing for an audience that he knew would be prejudiced and hostile to his opinions and by not touching on very controversial subjects he could temper passions. Most importantly, William Bartram's judgement of people was rarely unfavorable; he could be either brief or full of approbation regarding a person's character, but never disparaging. Any misgiving or disapproval he may have had of others did not play out in his writing and were kept close to his heart.

William's tutor at the Philadelphia Academy was Charles Thomson, secretary of the Continental Congress until 1780. Thomson was an adopted member of the Delaware Tribe and his Indian name was "Truth Teller" because of his fair treatment and admiration of American Indians. This undoubtedly had more influence on the character of William Bartram than did the feelings of William's own father. John Bartram was not an admirer of the Indian because his parents had been killed in the Tuscarora War in North Carolina, and he thought Indians the antithesis to civilized man. William Bartram, on the other hand, came to admire and befriend the native peoples he met in the Southeast and he remains one of the earliest authorities on the colonial history and customs of the Creek, Cherokee, and Seminole Indians. His observations of Native American culture in the Southeast remain a primary source for a period in which written accounts are lacking. He helped refute the notion that the Indians were simple and primitive. He was one of the first to see the complex symbolism and structure in their society.

William Bartram's Later Years

William Bartram returned home in January 1777 in time for him to spend a few months with his father before John died. William continued to live at the Bartram home after his father's death and worked in the horticultural business with brother Johnny. William undoubtedly spent his time with the plants while Johnny tended to the business of running the garden.

William worked on the manuscript for the *Travels* and had a manuscript ready in 1783; but, it was not published until 1791. In 1787 he wrote to Benjamin Smith Barton, then studying in Scotland, that he had not yet decided on publishing and doubted the merit of his story. Bartram wrote that he had been

---

Retracing Bartram's Travels

A number of eminent scientists were inspired to retrace William Bartram's travels in the South. Those who did so and the year in which they accomplished this are:

Moses Marshall	1803
Thomas Nuttall	1815
William Baldwin	1817
William Maclure, Titian Peale, George Ord and Thomas Say	1818
Major John Eatton LeConte	1822
John James Audubon	1832
Sir Charles Lyell	1845

---

2. William Bartram, *Travels through North and South Carolina, Georgia, East and West Florida, the Cherokee Country, the Extensive Territories of the Muscogulges or Creek Confederacy, and the Country of the Chactaws*; Philadelphia, 1791, xxiii.

thinking of making another Southern journey to gather more material for his book, but had been handicapped by his long recovery after a fall from a cypress that broke his right leg. Because he took so long to publish, other botanists received credit for naming plants that were discovered by Bartram. Even before the wider world became aware of William Bartram his fame among the learned, especially those with a taste for botany, spread quickly and many people visited the botanist at his home in Kingsessing.

He was offered a position as lecturer in botany at the University of Pennsylvania in 1782, but declined due to his health problems. During the Constitutional Convention held at Philadelphia in 1787 he was visited by Alexander Hamilton, James Madison, John Rutledge, George Mason, and George Washington. Thomas Jefferson developed a special affection for William and continued to correspond with him for many years. Jefferson asked William to join one of the western expeditions; although which one was never stated, it might have been the Red River Survey of 1804 or the Pike Expedition of 1805. Bartram declined all offers of travel for he had lost most of the sight in one eye from his illness while traveling in West Florida, and he was no longer a young man.

When the *Travels* became available to the reading public on both sides of the Atlantic, William Bartram became the grand old man of American natural science. William Bartram's greatest achievement after the publication of the *Travels* was that of advisor to a younger generation of naturalists and as proponent of a uniquely American scientific community. Through his contact with naturalists, he encouraged a younger generation to collect, name, and publish their species in American publications.

He did not escape criticism, however, to which he was always sensitive because it called into question his elemental integrity as a naturalist and Christian. He was accused of being too favorable in his portrayal of the Native Americans. His account of battling alligators on the St. Johns River was doubted by many who had never even seen an alligator and thought the story embellished. Others said his prose was too pompous and florid. One reviewer wrote "Many rhapsodical effusions might, we think, have been omitted, with advantage to the work."[3]

Let us return to Bartram's alligators and his description of two males fighting over territory,

> *Behold him rushing forth from the flags and reeds. His enormous body swells. His plaited tail brandished high, floats upon the lake. The waters like a cataract descend from his opening jaws. Clouds of smoke issue from his dilated nostrils. The earth trembles with his thunder. When immediately from the opposite coast of the lagoon, emerges from the deep his rival champion. They suddenly dart upon each other. The boiling surface of the lake marks their rapid course, and a terrific conflict commences. They now sink to the bottom folded together in horrid wreaths. The water becomes thick and discoloured. Again they rise, their jaws clap together, re-echoing through the deep surrounding forests. Again they sink, when the contest ends at the muddy bottom of the lake, and the vanquished makes a hazardous escape, hiding himself in the muddy turbulent waters and sedge on a distant shore. The proud victor exulting returns to the place of action. The shores and forests resound his dreadful roar, together with the triumphing shouts of the plaited tribes around, witnesses of the horrid combat.*[4]

The vivid description of this dreadful encounter moves beyond prose or storytelling; it verges on poetry because of Bartram's sensitivity to remembered images.

William Bartram was also criticized for not being more systematic in his cataloguing of plants and animals. This is a legitimate criticism because he was not an accomplished taxonomist. However all collectors in North America at this time depended upon their European counterparts to create taxonomic descriptions and verify names. Dr. Solander had been hired by Dr. Fothergill to do just this for William's collections, but the work was never finished due to the death of both doctors and Bartram's names did not find their way into publication until the *Travels* was published in 1791. Therefore, in most cases William either did not receive credit for the approved names or his own names were rejected by the scientific commissions governing scientific nomenclature. He must have felt shackled by this dependency on European authorities and was compelled to encourage his followers to become more independent. As a patriot William Bartram believed America deserved her own community of professional scientists.

In 1786 an advertisement was issued to solicit subscriptions for an edition of the *Travels* that would contain a catalogue of plants with descriptions. Unfortunately, this edition never materialized and when the *Travels* was finally published in 1791 it was without the catalogue. By that time other collectors had published descriptions of many of Bartram's plants. Among the botanists who have been given credit for naming Bartram discoveries was his own cousin, Humphrey Marshall.

William was a modest man who sought no attention or accolades; he was content to serve as advisor to others and let his work stand for the benefit of man and the glory of God. He did, however, insist on being given credit for discovering and naming *Franklinia alatamaha*.

Epilogue

Once he returned from his travels in the South, William Bartram, the indefatigable traveler, never ventured outside the environs of Philadelphia during the remainder of his life. His health had been compromised by his illness on the Gulf Coast or he may have been content with his duties at the Bartram Garden. When Johnny died, the business went to his daughter Ann and her husband Robert Carr. William continued to live with his niece and work in the Garden. On the morning of July 22, 1823, after writing a description of a plant, he arose to go to the garden. William died of a burst blood vessel only a few steps from the door among his beloved plants. His study at the Bartram Garden is arranged as it might have looked on that morning.

The Bartrams introduced over two hundred native plants into the horticultural trade and at the Bartram Garden they propagated nearly 4,000 species. The Garden was preserved by Andrew Eastwick, who purchased the property in 1850. The city of Philadelphia bought the Garden in 1891. William Bartram's drawings are currently located in three collections:

---

3. The Universal Asylum and Columbian Magazine; Philadelphia, April, 1792, 266.

4. William Bartram, *Travels*, 116.

the library of the Earl of Darby, the Natural History Museum Botany Department Library in London, and the American Philosophical Society. His specimens are in the collection of the Natural History Museum in London.

William Bartram's Circle of Acquaintance

William Bartram quickly became the best-known American naturalist in the years following the completion of his journey of discovery through the South. After the appearance of the *Travels*, Bartram became known to an ever widening audience of readers on both sides of the Atlantic. He was visited by the leading statesmen and academics of his day, including many delegates during the years Congress met in Philadelphia. Following are some of the people who corresponded or visited with William Bartram.

André Michaux (1746–1802). Michaux came to Charleston in 1786 to collect trees to replenish the forests of France that were depleted by a century of wars. He lived in America for almost ten years and established two gardens, one at Charleston and another at Trenton, New Jersey. Michaux visited William Bartram on several occasions and retraced some of the same territory covered by Bartram. A number of plants observed, described, or drawn by Bartram are attributed to Michaux, including flame azalea and lesser rosebay. André's son, François, admired William and even lived at the Bartram home for an extended period in 1807. François published *North American Sylva*, which was begun by his father and was the most complete description of American trees for many years. William's *Bignonia bracteate*, commonly known as fevertree, was named *Pinckneya pubens* by the young Michaux in honor of his friend Colonel Charles Cotesworth Pinckney of Charleston.

Benjamin Smith Barton (1766–1815) was a teacher, America's first academic botanist, and author of *The Elements of Botany*, the first American textbook on botany. He made specimen collections for his herbarium at the Bartram Garden and used William's drawings in his textbook. Barton tutored Meriwether Lewis in botany in preparation for the expedition to the Louisiana Purchase.

Alexander Wilson (1766–1813) published the first great book of American ornithology and was William Bartram's best-known student. Wilson was a Scottish immigrant who took a teaching post near the Bartram Garden. He became intrigued by William's *Travels* and descriptions of American birds, at the time the most complete list of native birds. Wilson became friends with William in 1803 and received much encouragement and instruction from the elder naturalist. In 1808 Wilson published *American Ornithology, or the Natural History of the Birds of the United States*.

Thomas Nuttall (1786–1859) studied botany in Philadelphia with Benjamin Smith Barton and William Bartram. He collected plants in the Rocky Mountains and the Pacific Coast and went on to become professor of botany at Harvard.

Thomas Say (1787–1834) was William Bartram's great-nephew and the first authority on American conchology and entomology. He retraced much of William Bartram's travels in 1818 while on an expedition for the American Academy of Natural Sciences. Other members of the expedition included George Ord, Titian Peale, and William Maclure.

John James Audubon (1785–1851) produced one of the world's great works of natural science, *The Birds of America*. Audubon visited William Bartram at the Bartram Garden and Audubon's former assistant, Joseph Mason, worked as an illustrator for the Bartrams for several years. Audubon was influenced by Bartram's disciple, Alexander Wilson, and met Wilson several times.

Constantine Rafinesque (1783–1840) was born near Constantinople and immigrated to the United States as a young man. He was a pioneer in the study of American fishes and taught botany at Transylvania College in Kentucky. He was a prolific writer and examined areas of anthropology, linguistics, geology, sociology, poetry, and is the translator of the *Walam Olum*, a Lenape Indian document. Rafinesque was one of the most eccentric and interesting characters in American science. He had an interesting encounter when he lodged at the home of Audubon in Henderson, Kentucky, when he was awakened in the night by bats that flew in an open window. Rafinesque destroyed Audubon's favorite violin trying to kill the bats. In his later years Rafinesque lived in Philadelphia where he visited William Bartram.

Sir Charles Lyell (1797–1875). The great British geologist read the *Travels* and retraced much of William Bartram's route when he visited America in 1845 although he never met the botanist. Of particular interest to him were the petrified trees that Bartram saw on the Mississippi River. In his book, *Principles of Geology*, he mentioned the Mississippi Delta as an illustration of the Theory of Uniformity, which says that all geological phenomena is the result of existing forces working uniformly over time. Lyell's protegé was Charles Darwin, who applied his mentor's principles to living creatures in developing his theory of the origin of species.

Humphrey Marshall was John Bartram's first cousin and author of *Arbustum Americanum* (1785). He received credit for naming some of William Bartram's discoveries because the *Travels* was not published until six years after *Arbustum Americanum*.

Moses Marshall, nephew of Humphrey Marshall, was the last to see Franklinia in the wild during a trip to the Altamaha River in 1803.

Caspar Wistar (1761–1818). Wistar was professor of chemistry and physiology at the College of Philadelphia beginning in 1789. He was elected president of the American Philosophical Society in 1815. Wistar corresponded with explorer Alexander von Humboldt and botanist François Michaux.

William Baldwin (1779–1819). Baldwin learned botany from Moses Marshall and Benjamin Smith Barton and became a physician in Wilmington, Delaware. As a naval surgeon he was able to collect plants from South America, particularly Buenos Aires. He contracted tuberculosis and sought the mild coastal air of St. Marys, Georgia, to restore his health. He explored East Florida in 1816–1817 and retraced parts of William Bartram's route. He was surgeon and botanist for an expedition on the Missouri River when he died.

William Darlington (1782–1863) was a physician in Philadelphia who had learned botany from Benjamin Smith Barton and was a close friend of William Baldwin. In 1849 he wrote *Memorials of John Bartram and Humphrey Marshall*.

Dr. Benjamin Rush (1745–1813). Benjamin Rush was a physician in Philadelphia who gained a considerable reputation for treating yellow fever patients during the epidemic of 1793. He was a writer of medical and philosophical subjects and was one of the first to write about diseases of the mind and to identify alcoholism as a disease. He became an ardent patriot, was a signer of the Declaration of Independence, a member of the Constitutional Convention, treasurer of the U.S. Mint, and vice-president of the American Philosophical Society.

Chronology of William Bartram's Travels

William Bartram got his dates confused by the time he wrote the *Travels*. Toward the end of the book he was off by as much as a year. Additionally, he included some events out of sequence in the book if it made literary sense to do so. For example, his trip up the Altamaha River can be dated by the eclipse he witnessed on April 31, 1776, yet he included his description of the event at the beginning of the book as occurring Spring 1773. The dates included in this chronology are taken from Francis Harper's *Bartram's Travels: Naturalist Edition* and do not necessarily follow the events as they appear in the *Travels*.

1773

March 31	Arrived in Charleston and stayed with Thomas and Elizabeth Lamboll at #19 King Street.
April 11 or 12	Arrived in Savannah.
April 16	Traveled to Midway and stayed with Benjamin Andrew. In a few days he continued to Darien where he stayed with Lachlan McIntosh and family.
Late April	Visited Brunswick.
May 3	Returned to Savannah.
May 5	Visited Ebenezer.
May 9	Crossed Savannah River to Silver Bluff, home of George Galphin.
May 16–19	Visited the Quaker community of Wrightsborough.
June 7	The survey party left Augusta.
June	The party traveled to the Great Buffalo Lick, the Cherokee Line, and followed the boundary of the New Purchase to the Tugaloo and Savannah rivers.
Mid-July	Returned to Savannah.
Winter	Remained in the Savannah area and coastal Georgia.

1774

March	Traveled from Savannah to Darien and Frederica, then by boat to Cumberland Island.
Early April	Visited with Stephen Egan on Amelia Island.
Mid-April	Purchased a boat at Cow Ford (Jacksonville) and began his voyage up the St. Johns River to Spalding's Lower Store near present-day Palatka.
Late April	Traveled to Cuscowilla (Micanopy) and Alachua Savannah (Paynes Prairie) then returned to the Lower Store in early May. In his report to Dr. Fothergill Bartram placed the trip to Alachua before the trip up the St. Johns River, however in the *Travels* he placed it after.
Mid-May	Traveled up the St. Johns River to Spalding's Upper Store at present day Astor. He continued upriver and had his famous battle with alligators in Lake Dexter at the mouth of Mud Creek. He traveled as far as Blue Springs near Orange City then returned to the Lower Store in early June. The trip upriver is a composite of two separate trips, one in May and June and the other in August and September.
Mid-June	Traveled again to Alachua Savannah and on to Talahasochte on the Suwannee River (near Chiefland).
August–September	Bartram made a second voyage up the St. Johns River.
Nov. 10	Returned to Broughton Island and Darien.

1775

March 25	Returned to Charleston.
April 22	Left Charleston and traveled up the west side of the Savannah River to Augusta.
Early May	Traveled from Augusta to Fort James on the Broad River.
May 10	Left Fort James and crossed the Savannah River. He traveled through what is now Abbeville County and stayed several days with Alexander Cameron.
May 15	Arrived at Seneca.
May 19	Left Fort Prince George on the Keowee River, then crossed the Oconee Mountains at Oconee State Park, crossed the Chatooga River, and passed through present-day Clayton, Georgia, then known as Old Stekoa.
May 22	Arrived at Cowee, north of Franklin, North Carolina. He spent a day exploring the Cowee Mountains.
May 24	Traveled along Iotla Creek and crossed the Nantahala Mountains at Burningtown Gap. After crossing the Nantahala River he met the great Cherokee leader, Attakullakulla.
May 30	Arrived back at Fort Prince George.
Early-June	Arrived again at Fort James and explored the Broad River.
June 22	Left Fort James and traveled down the Savannah River, stopping first at a plantation near New Bordeaux, where he joined a party of traders bound for the Creek Nation. They followed the Lower Creek Trading Path from a point west of Augusta.
June 27	Camped at Flat Rock.
July 1	Arrived at Rock Landing on the Oconee River, just south of Milledgeville.
July 3	Crossed the Ocmulgee River at Ocmulgee Mounds.
July 5	Crossed the Flint River at the site of the Old Creek Agency.
July 11	Arrived at Yuchi Town on the Chattahoochee River at the mouth of Uchee Creek. Visited Apalachicola a few miles south.
July 13	Traveled west along the south side of Uchee Creek, through Tuskegee and to Talasi just south of the present-day town of Talassee.
July 19	Traveled through the prairies in southern Montgomery County.
July 20	Passed near present-day Pintlala.
July 21	Passed near Greenville, through Fort Deposit and traveled the Pensacola and Mobile Path that is now the boundary between Monroe and Conecuh counties.
July 26	Arrived at Major Farmar's plantation.

1775 continued

July 30 or 31	Arrived in Mobile.
August 5	Sailed up the Mobile River to the Tombigbee River.
Mid-August	Explored present-day Baldwin county.
Sept. 3	Sailed to Pensacola.
Sept. 4 & 5	Visited Pensacola.
Sept. 6	Returned to Mobile.
Sept. 7	Became ill upon his return to Mobile yet he sailed from Mobile and stayed on the Pearl River for several days at the home of the Frenchman who owned the boat in which they traveled.
Mid-Sept.	Arrived at the Pearl River plantation of Mr. Rumsey and stayed several weeks while he recuperated from his illness. Bartram explored the extreme southeastern part of St. Tammany Parish as his health improved.
Mid-October	Crossed lakes Pontchartrain and Maurepas, sailed up the Amite River, and Bayou Manchac (then known as Iberville River).
Oct. 21	Bartram saw the Mississippi River from Fort Bute on Bayou Manchac.
Oct. 27	Explored north of Baton Rouge in company of William Dunbar. They traveled to Pointe Coupee on October 28.
Nov. 10 (?)	Departed Baton Rouge.
Nov. 16	Arrived again in Mobile.
Nov. 27	Departed Mobile.
Dec. 4	Arrived on the Tallapoosa River northeast of Montgomery. Visited Fort Toulouse, Muklasa, Tuckabatchee, Kolomi, and Atasi.

1776

Jan. 2	Left the Upper Creek Towns.
Jan. 14–18	stayed in Augusta.
Late Jan.	Arrived in Savannah.
Spring & Summer	Remained on the Georgia coast. Evidence shows that Bartram was engaged in gathering intelligence for Gen. Lachlan McIntosh. As tensions with England mounted, an invasion from Florida was feared. It was during this time that he had an encounter with the intrepid Seminole near the St. Marys River.
July 31	Bartram's account of sailing up the Altamaha River is out of place in the *Travels* and actually took place at this time. Francis Harper used the eclipse of the moon as his point for correctly dating this event.
Late Oct.	Departed Darien for Savannah.
Early Nov.	Departed Savannah for Charleston.
Early Dec.	Arrived at Ashwood on Cape Fear River.
Mid Dec.	Departed Ashwood.
Dec. 25	Traveled through Georgetown, Maryland.

1777

Very early Jan. Arrived home in Philadelphia.

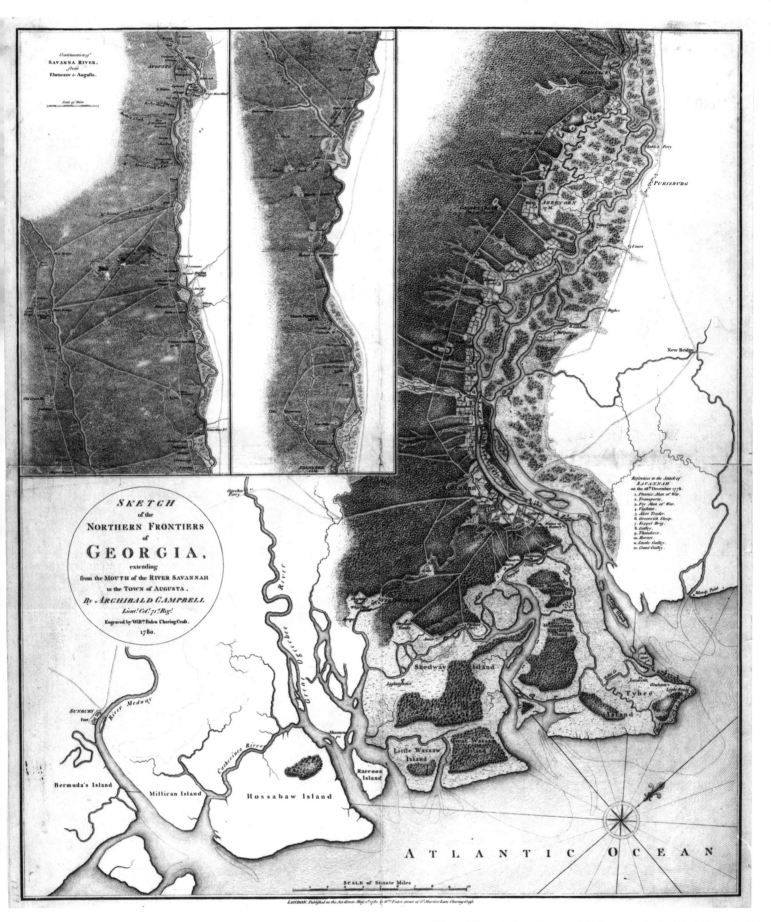

Map of Georgia from Savannah to Augusta, by Archibald Campbell
Courtesy of Hargrett Rare Book & Manuscript Library/ University of Georgia Libraries

2

Savannah

The Savannah River was called Rio Dulce by early Spanish explorers. Lucas Vásquez de Ayllón attempted to settle a colony on the upper coast of South Carolina, probably at Winyah Bay, in August 1526. Finding the area unsuitable the colony moved south within the month and established the settlement of San Miquel de Gualdape. The most current historical research now suggests that the first European colony north of Mexico was made on the coast of Georgia, either at Sapelo Sound or the mouth of the Savannah River. The people were resettled in late September, too late to plant crops. The weather turned unseasonably cold in October and Ayllón became ill and died on October 18. Neighboring Indians became tired of the drain on their food supplies and slew the Spaniards who had come to live with them. Facing starvation, mutiny, and Indian attack the settlers decided to abandon San Miquel de Gualdape and the last of them were evacuated in November 1526.

Jean Ribault explored the Southeastern coast in the spring of 1562, he entered the Savannah River and named it Riviere Grande. At that time the Savannah River was the vague boundary between the Guales on the coast of Georgia and the Cusabos on the lower coast of South Carolina. After Governor Menéndez de Avilés established greater Florida in the late 1560s the Savannah River lay within an uninhabited area between the Spanish provinces of Escamaçu to the north and Guale to the south. Santa Elena, on Parris Island, was abandoned in 1587 and the capital of Florida was moved to Saint Augustine. The Spanish thereafter concentrated their energies in Florida south of the Savannah River. Occasionally, priests crossed the river to minister to the few Christian Indians living at Santa Elena Island.

During the decade of the 1660s there came into the Savannah river region two forces that were to spell the beginning of the end for the Spanish in present-day Georgia. The Westoes (Chichimecos to the Spanish) invaded the upper Savannah River and in 1661 began raiding towns on both sides of the

Ebenezer Creek

river and on the coast. Christian as well as pagan Indians sought refuge among the Spanish missions of Guale and Mocama. Coinciding with this turmoil was the appearance of English traders and explorers in 1663 and the founding of Charleston in 1670. The mission towns in Guale suffered from devastating raids by the Westoes in 1680 and raids by the pirate Grammont in 1683. By 1685 all the Spanish missions and Christian Indians had been withdrawn to south of the St. Marys River. The English forged an alliance with the Savannahs and drove the Westoes from the Savannah River in 1681. The region was now open to the English and their Indian allies.

That part of South Carolina that lay between the Savannah and Altamaha Rivers became a proprietary grant to Sir Robert Montgomery in 1717 with the stipulation that he settle the area. This colony was to be called the Margravate of Azilia with Montgomery as the Margrave. Because Savannah and Jerusalem lie near latitude 32°N it was believed that Georgia could produce the same products as the Near East. Claiming that Eden could be reproduced again in the New World, Montgomery issued tracts in England extolling the healthfulness and productiveness of the land. But, he was unable to begin any settlements and gave up his grant in 1719. His idea was revived in 1730 by a group of reformists who envisioned a Utopian colony for debtors and the underemployed where they might begin life anew. They named the colony Georgia, after King George II, a political move calculated to generate Royal interest and support. Parliament was interested in establishing a presence to negate Spanish claim to the area and provide a military buffer against a Spanish invasion of South Carolina.

On January 13, 1733, 112 colonists aboard the *Ann* arrived off the coast of South Carolina. Governor Robert Johnson and the Trustees agreed that the colonists should not land and see Charleston least they be tempted to remain. James Edward Oglethorpe, the representative of the Trustees in America, presented the charter of the colony to Johnson, and Johnson in turn promised all possible assistance to the Georgians. On January 20 the passengers landed at Port Royal and lodged at the military barracks three miles south of Beaufort. The South Carolina General Assembly resolved to give the Georgia colonists 105 head of cattle, five bulls, twenty sows, four boars, twenty barrels of rice, a marine patrol, and the assistance of Colonel William Bull. Oglethorpe and Bull preceded the colonists to Georgia and chose Yamacraw Bluff on the Savannah River as the site for the town of Savannah. A half-mile upriver was Yamacraw Town and north of there was the trading house of John and Mary Musgrove.

The settlers were divided into three groups; one to clear land for planting, one to construct a fort and palisades, one to clear land where the town lots would be. On February 9 Oglethorpe and Bull laid out Johnson Square, several streets, and forty lots. The first house was begun on that day by Thomas Milledge, James Goddard, Noble Jones, William Bull, and several Carolinians. Oglethorpe was held in high regard by the settlers and they worked for him with enthusiasm.

Through his interpreter, Mary Musgrove, Oglethorpe negotiated an agreement with Tomochichi, Mico (headman) of the Yamacraws. On May 21, 1733, the Creeks signed a treaty of alliance, friendship, and commerce with the Georgians and allowed them the right to settle the coast as far as the tide ebbed and flowed. The town of Yamacraw and the islands of Ossa-

James Edward Oglethorpe

James Edward Oglethorpe was born December 22, 1696, in Godalming, Surrey. The Oglethorpe family were Jacobites, supporting the restoration of the exiled James Stuart (James II) to the throne of England. Oglethorpe's mother, Eleanor, was Irish born and known among Jacobite circles as Old Fury. Her energy and ambition were passed on to her children.

Oglethorpe entered Corpus Christi College at Oxford University in 1714. The next year James III lost his attempt to regain the throne to George Hanover (George I), a protestant German prince and grandson of James I. Oglethorpe followed his brothers and sisters to France and there he became aide-de-camp to Prince Eugene of Savoy. After visiting his sisters in France, and his brother Theophilus and James Stuart III in Italy, Oglethorpe returned to England in 1719. In 1722 he broke with his family and announced that he would run for Parliament as a supporter of George I, not as a Jacobite supporter of the Stuarts. He was elected and took his seat in Parliament in October, 1722.

Owing to his family's participation in the opposition, Oglethorpe remained a silent member of Parliament. He built his career by being an energetic and able member of numerous committees that looked into the affairs of sailors, soldiers, debtors, issues of public safety, and prison conditions. In his office as chairman of the committee to report on the condition of the prisons, Oglethorpe came into contact with Reverend Dr. Thomas Bray, founder of the Society for the Propagation of the Gospel in Foreign Parts and the Society for the Promotion of Christian Knowledge. Two of Dr. Bray's associates were members of Oglethorpe's committee, Lord John Perceval, who became the First Earl of Egmont, and James Vernon. By his work Oglethorpe gained a reputation as a humane and honest man in a time when public office was used to line private pockets.

In 1730 these men and their associates began formulating plans for the utopian colony of Georgia. Oglethorpe chose to settle the new colony personally and was the sole representative of the Trustees in America. Many of the first Georgians were unsuited to self-government and the tasks required to build a new country. Their situation was made more precarious because they settled on a frontier bordered by England's enemy, Spain. Therefore, Oglethorpe's management was of necessity paternalistic and at times despotic.

Oglethorpe returned to England in 1743 to answer charges of financial misconduct. He was vindicated and reimbursed for his expenses in administering the government of Georgia. He married Elizabeth Wright the following year and did not return to Georgia. Oglethorpe commanded a regiment during the Jacobite Uprising in 1745. He was accused by the Duke of Cumberland (always suspicious of Oglethorpe) for having been indifferent in his pursuit of the enemy. Oglethorpe faced court martial and was acquitted, but he was never again allowed a command though he rose to be the highest ranking general in the British Army. He lost his seat in Parliament in 1754.

James Oglethorpe was a close friend of Sir Hans Sloane and a trustee of Sloane's estate. Oglethorpe was one of the moving forces in the creation of the British Museum in 1759, which used the Sloane collection as a foundation. As he grew older General Oglethorpe became the darling of the literary society of London that included Samuel Johnson, Oliver Goldsmith, Sir Joshua Reynolds, and Edmund Burke. During the years leading up to the Revolution Oglethorpe was among the moderates lead by William Pitt who sought a conciliatory approach to dealing with the rebellious colonies. On June 4, 1785, Oglethorpe visited John Adams, now the minister to England from the United States of America, and offered him a warm welcome. James Edward Oglethorpe died on June 30, 1785,

baw, Sapelo, and St. Catherines were reserved for the Creeks. The Yamacraws desired Christian education and instruction in English and writing. Oglethorpe organized two companies of Indian warriors, headed by Tuscaney and Skee. The terms of trade with the Creeks were fair and the personal friendship between Oglethorpe and Tomochichi was important in preserving peace during the tentative early years of Georgia.

On July 7 a day of thanksgiving was observed. This day marked the naming of streets, wards, and tithings; offices were filled, and a court was established. However, disease, the deaths of thirty to forty settlers, and the heat of that first summer left the colonists in a contentious mood. Oglethorpe blamed these troubles on rum smuggled from South Carolina and ordered all spirits destroyed. Still, by the middle of July half the colony was sick.

On July 11 an unauthorized ship arrived, containing Dr. Samuel Nunes Ribeiro and Portuguese Jews. Dr. Nunes went to work among the sick of Savannah, refusing pay for his service. His prescriptions of cold baths, cooling drinks, and other soothing treatments seemed to work, and Oglethorpe wrote that none died who followed his instruction. However, some colonists believed the sickness came from drinking river water and things improved when the public well was finished.

In March 1734 Protestants from Salzburg arrived in Savannah and were settled upriver on Ebenezer Creek. In May Oglethorpe, Tomochichi, his wife Senauchi, nephew Toonahowi, and several Creeks sailed for England. While in England Tomochichi had his portrait painted, dined with King George II, and was presented to Parliament.

Oglethorpe returned to Georgia in early 1736 with two ships of settlers that included John and Charles Wesley, Moravians, and more Salzburgers. Highlanders had preceded Oglethorpe to Darien on the Altamaha River. Frederica was laid out just south of the Georgia boundary on the inland passage as the primary defense against the Spanish in Florida. Other defenses were established at the south end of Saint Simons and Cumberland islands. In the same year, Oglethorpe instructed that a town named Augusta be laid out at a crossing point on the Savannah River, 150 miles above Savannah.

Oglethorpe's time was increasingly spent on military affairs. He returned to England in January 1737 and was made Commander-in-Chief of the South Carolina and Georgia military forces and named Colonel of a regiment that he raised. He returned to Georgia in October 1738. In 1739 the War of Jenkins' Ear started a conflict between England and Spain. It then merged with the War of Austrian Succession, or King George's War as it was known in America. In the late spring of 1740 Oglethorpe carried out his first invasion of Florida. The Siege of Saint Augustine lasted for over a month and was abandoned in late July. This was the low point of Oglethorpe's career and he lost credibility among the Royal governors. In the summer of 1742 the feared and expected Spanish invasion of Georgia materialized. Many Georgians evacuated their homes and became refugees in South Carolina. The Georgians and their Creek allies met the Spanish on Saint Simons Island and routed them at the Battle of Bloody Marsh. This victory ended Spanish threats to the British colonies. Oglethorpe made another unsuccessful attempt to capture Saint Augustine in March 1743.

When Oglethorpe left the colony in 1743 no one had the

The Government of Colonial Georgia

The chief executive for the colony of Georgia was the royal governor, who was appointed by the King. His advisors were the Royal Council, who were chosen from the wealthiest and most influential men of the colony and they constituted the Upper House of the General Assembly. The nineteen members of the Lower House, or Commons House of Assembly, were elected from men who owned at least 500 acres of land. Members of the Commons were elected by propertied men who held at least fifty acres of land. The property qualifications were abandoned in favor of income requirements because there were influential men in Savannah whose wealth was not tied to real estate.

The Commons House of Assembly was convened or adjourned at the pleasure of the royal governor and any legislation passed by them was subject to his veto. The royal governor might request instructions from Parliament on whether to accept or reject laws passed by the Commons.

The courts were dominated by the Court of Appeals, which was composed of members of the Royal Council. Beneath the Court of Appeals was a general court, a chief justice and associate justices, and a court of admiralty. On the local level were courts of justices of the peace.

authority or strength of character to effectively administer its affairs. William Stephens had been secretary for the Trustees in the colony and was appointed president. His age prevented him from exercising the duties of his office effectively so Henry Parker, as vice-president, took on many responsibilities. Ultimate authority still resided with the Trustees in far-off London. After the Treaty of Aix-la-Chapelle in 1748 brought a period of peace, financial support for the military and the colony was reduced, leading to a severe economic recession. The population of the colony declined to below a thousand and the economy verged on bankruptcy.

By 1750 restrictions on land, rum, and slaves were weakened to encourage people to move into Georgia. Parliament refused further funds for the Trustees and on June 23, 1752, the Trustees gave up their charter to the King. The first royal governor was John Reynolds, a naval officer who became unpopular due to his greed and arrogance. He alienated the Creeks by his indifference at a time when they were being heavily courted by the French in Louisiana. He served in the office from October 1754 to October 1756 and was then recalled. Reynolds was appointed vice admiral in the British navy and served during the Revolution.

Reynolds was replaced by Henry Ellis, a scholar, gentleman, and explorer. Ellis was elected a Fellow of the Royal Society after the publication of his scientific account of the 1746 search for the Northwest Passage. Governor Ellis arrived in Savannah in the winter of 1757 to great expectations. He was a conscientious and capable leader, immediately setting about restoring the economy of the colony and the friendship of the Creeks. Although he was successful and well liked in the colony he resigned in 1760, claiming health problems due to the excessively hot climate.

The next governor was James Wright, a former attorney general and agent for South Carolina. Governor Wright became an enthusiastic booster for Georgia. Under his leadership inspection standards were established to guarantee the quality of products shipped from the colony, and an agent, William Knox, was engaged to represent Georgia in London. In 1751 the population of Georgia stood at 2,300. The beginning of royal government brought a period of prosperity to the colony, so that when William Bartram arrived in Savannah in 1773 the population had increased to 33,000, due in large part to the policies of Wright's government.

Wright remained popular with much of the population outside the Savannah vicinity until the outbreak of the Revolution, because of his effectiveness in obtaining new land for settlers. Although he worked to keep Georgia within the British Empire, his primary concern was for the well-being of the colony. Wright proved to be the most capable colonial governor in America during his tenure.

The Coming of Revolution

The French and Indian War, also known as the Seven Years War and the War for Empire, had been a costly affair for Great Britain. Many in Parliament felt it only fair that the colonies help bear the burden of their own defense. For this purpose the Stamp Act was enacted in 1765 to raise money for a standing army in North America. The law required that all legal documents and printed matter in the colonies carry a stamp purchased from the government. The law was met with widespread resistance and was repealed the following year. James Wright was the only Royal governor to enforce the Stamp Act, an accomplishment that brought him into conflict with the radical element in Savannah.

Parliament attempted a moderate approach with the passage of the Townshend Revenue Act on July 2, 1767. This act placed an import duty on glass, paper, paint, and tea. The colonies again resisted on the grounds that taxes could be levied only by elected representatives and the Americans had no representatives in Parliament. As England attempted to levy tax from the colonies, resistance began to grow in the coastal cities and prosperous colonies. There arose among the gentry an opposition party called Whigs. In Georgia the Whig party was centered in Savannah among the well-to-do and educated, and among the Congregationalists of Midway. On Christmas Eve in 1768 Noble Wimberly Jones pushed through the Assembly a bill opposing the Townshend Acts. In response Governor Wright dissolved the Assembly. When Jones was again elected speaker of the Lower House of Assembly (Commons) in 1771 he was rejected by Governor Wright. The Assembly issued a resolution objecting to the governor's abuse of power and they were again dissolved.

Noble Wimberly Jones, John Houstoun, Archibald Bullock, and George Walton sponsored a meeting at Peter Tondee's Tavern on August 10, 1774, and there began active participation in the Revolution. Eight resolutions were drawn up condemning the British occupation of Boston, demanding equal rights as British citizens, opposing deportation to England for trial, opposing taxation without representation, and establishing correspondence with the other colonies. They did not choose to send delegates to the First Continental Congress because all of the Georgia parishes were not represented. The Sunbury radicals did sent Dr. Lyman Hall to represent St. John's Parish at the Congress. He took with him two hundred barrels of rice and cash for the unfortunate citizens of Boston.

In January, 1775, Noble Wimberly Jones called together the First Provincial Congress. They assembled in the Government House and were careful to inform Governor Wright of the proceedings. They pointedly made a distinction between their opposition to Parliament and their continuing loyalty to the king. The Assembly also met at the same time and Governor Wright advised working within legal channels to address their grievances. His closest advisors, James Habersham and the elderly Noble Jones, were at an age that they could not influence governmental affairs as they once had. Their sons, however, were energetic and ardent patriots whose course of action eventually led to independence for Georgia.

On February 15, 1775, the Georgia patriots held their Sugar Party. They seized molasses and sugar that had been confiscated for nonpayment of the import tax. One of the sailors on guard was thrown in the Savannah River and drowned and the customs inspector, James Edgar, was tarred and feathered. On May 11, upon hearing of fighting at Lexington, Massachusetts, Noble W. Jones, Joseph Habersham, Edward Telfair, and other Whigs broke into the Filature and stole gunpowder that they shipped to Boston patriots. Jones left a receipt for the gunpowder. On June 11 the Council of Safety was formed.

On July 7, 1775, the Second Provincial Congress elected delegates to the Second Continental Congress—Noble Wimberly Jones, Archibald Bulloch, John Houstoun, Reverend John J. Zubly, and Dr. Lyman Hall. Archibald Bulloch was elected president of the new provincial government and did not attend. Zubly left the Continental Congress when talk turned to separation from England. He was forced to leave Georgia as patriotic fervor escalated and his property was confiscated. In March a unit of the South Carolina militia commanded by Colonel Stephen Bull crossed the Savannah River to help strengthen the Whigs control of Savannah. Tories were forced to leave the city.

The first armed vessel of the Georgia Navy was *Liberty*, a converted trading schooner that carried ten guns and a crew of fifty. On July 8, 1775, the crew captured the British ship *Phillippa*, landed her at Cockspur Island, and confiscated guns and powder destined for the Florida loyalists. On January 18, 1776, Joseph Habersham, on orders from the Council of Safety, arrested Governor Wright. The governor and his council members were paroled to their homes and instructed to not leave town. Several weeks later, Wright slipped out of town and took refuge on the *Scarborough* anchored at Cockspur Island.

In the summer of 1776 Lachlan McIntosh lead a raid into Florida in an attempt to breakup loyalists strongholds and prevent guerrilla attacks on the Altamaha frontier. His success caused the members of the Council of Safety to become over confident and they recommended an attempt to take Saint Augustine, against the advice of Major General Charles Lee. The campaign was hastily planned and poorly provisioned. The men had to live off the land and became bogged down by swamps and heat. The invasion was abandoned when Lee was reassigned to the North. A second invasion of Florida took place in the spring of 1777. A dispute between President Button Gwinnett and General Lachlan McIntosh as to the rightful command of the campaign lead to both being recalled to Savannah and Colonel Samuel Elbert was placed in command. Lack of coordination between sea and land forces, lack of provisions, and the heat of the season caused the expedition to lose momentum. Elbert finally abandoned the effort and returned to Savannah.

In the spring of 1778 Continental soldiers along with Georgia and South Carolina militia made an expedition to Florida in an attempt to dislodge the British army from Saint Augustine. The campaign once again deteriorated before reaching the St. Johns River owing to conflict and lack of coordination among the Georgia and Continental commanders. This time there was the added problem of an outbreak of malaria and dysentery. Elijah Clark's troops made it as far as Alligator Creek Bridge on the Nassau River where a surprise attack drove them back. Nothing was accomplished by any of these invasions except the retaliation of the British Army that came later in the year.

The Siege of Savannah

As the British invasion of Georgia approached, disputes between Governor John Houstoun, George Walton, and General Howe caused the American defenses in Savannah to remain unprepared. On December 29, 1778, Lieutenant Colonel Archibald Campbell and his British troops literally walked into Savannah as General Howe and the Americans slipped across to South Carolina. Patriots who could not swim were trapped at the site of Yamacraw Town and killed or captured. Patriot leaders fled to Charleston or upriver to Augusta, except Mordacai Sheftall who was captured at Yamacraw. When Charleston fell to the British, Noble W. Jones was captured and imprisoned in Saint Augustine. Governor Wright returned the following summer and resurrected a loyalist government.

In September, 1779, French ships commanded by Comte d'Estaing began gathering near the mouth of the Savannah River and on the 12th French troops came ashore. Within two days Count Kasimir Pulaski had moved his cavalry across the river above Savannah and General Benjamin Lincoln was in place with the American Continental Army. On September 16 Comte d'Estaing approached the city and asked Genera Augustine Prevost to surrender. Granted a 24-hour truce Prevost pretended to consider the terms he would seek for surrender. During the night new troops from Beaufort slipped across the river into Savannah.

Both sides then began frantically building fortifications. On October 3 d'Estaing began a five-day bombardment; then on the 9th the allied forces launched an unsuccessful and brief assault on the British. The French and Americans suffered high casualties during the second most bloody day of fighting in the Revolution. That day d'Estaing abruptly announced that he would lift the siege and set sail because of the impending hurricane season. This left the ground forces little choice but to retreat. Savannah became a garrison town with little commerce or civilian population.

After General Cornwallis surrendered at Yorktown the British command in New York decided to reinforce their army in Charleston and ordered Savannah evacuated. James Wright and several thousand Loyalists left Savannah with the British troops on July 11, 1782. Thomas Brown and the East Florida Rangers headed south to Saint Augustine. James Jackson entered Savannah with the Georgia Army and the Patriot leaders immediately returned to Savannah to set up a permanent government.

Comte d'Estaing has been assigned responsibility for the failure of the siege although at the time he effectively deflected blame. He was among the nobles guillotined after the French Revolution. Fighting with the French at Savannah were Haitian troops, including Henri Christophe who later lead the revolution in Haiti.

William Bartram's Travels around Savannah

William Bartram arrived in Savannah on either the 12th or 13th of April, 1773. His first item of business was to visit Governor James Wright at the governor's mansion on St. Julian Square (now Telfair Square). During his visit in Savannah he met Benjamin Andrew of Midway. It is possible that Bartram lodged at the boardinghouse of Mrs. Cuyler on Bay Street, because her establishment was frequented by many members of the Assembly. Bartram may have also been the guest of James Habersham, whom he had met in 1765. Habersham's home was located on Johnson Square at Bull and Bryan streets, but it seems likely that Bartram would have made mention of such a meeting. Bartram bought a horse on April 15 and left Savannah the following day. He returned to Savannah on May 3.

During his travels William Bartram spent the winter of 1773–1774 in Savannah and the coast of Georgia. On his return from Louisiana, Bartram reached Savannah in January 1776 and spent most of that year on the coast of Georgia. He left Savannah in early November 1776 as he began his journey home. His first evening was spent several miles north of Savannah at the home of Jonathan Bryan, located at the site of the Georgia State Docks in Garden City.

Sites

1. Springfield is the seat of Effingham County and is located near the site of the first Salzburger settlement of Old Ebenezer. The Old Ebenezer historical marker is located on GA-21 at Log Landing Road, south of Springfield. Many streets and roads retain the German names of original Salzburg families. The Effingham County courthouse was at five different locations before being moved to Springfield. The present 1908 courthouse features a dome modeled after Thomas Jefferson's Monticello.

Old Jail Museum contains memorabilia and history of Effingham County. The Museum displays fossils from the Savannah River banks, Native-American artifacts, everyday Colonial items, and memorabilia of the Confederacy. The Museum is operated by the Historic Effingham Society. Located in the Old Jail on the Courthouse Square in Springfield. Open on Sundays only, 2 p.m.–5 p.m.

2. Ebenezer Creek, a Georgia Wild and Scenic River, is a unique backwater creek, meaning the depth of the slow-moving stream is due to its being impounded by the larger volume of water in the Savannah River. Naturalists believe that a sill of sand across the mouth of Ebenezer Creek also keeps water level high. Ebenezer is so slow moving that canoeing upstream is almost as easy as going downstream. The Old August Road, over which William Bartram traveled, crossed Ebenezer Creek a little above its mouth.

Ebenezer Creek has cut a steeply banked channel. The water level can fluctuate as much as eight feet during the year but because it is contained within high banks Ebenezer Creek does not have a wide floodplain swamp. The attraction for naturalists visiting Ebenezer Creek are the dwarf cypress trees that are found in the creek for several miles upstream from the mouth. These very old, but relatively small trees are supported by buttresses that reach diameters of eight to twelve feet. The lower section of the creek is noted for its beautiful tupelo swamp of 100-foot trees.

There are weekend homes located occasionally along the course but no extensive development. Homeowners wave and give advice and directions to passing canoeists. The Ebenezer Creek Greenway is working to preserve the quiet beauty and integrity of this historic stream. Boat access is from Log Landing Road off GA-21, Long Bridge Road off Wylly Road, and at Ebenezer Landing near the Salzburger Museum.

3. Bethany was a German community located to the north of Ebenezer Creek founded in 1751 by William De Brahm. De Brahm became surveyor general of Georgia and directed the construction of the Charleston fortifications and Fort Loudon. As surveyor general of Florida he employed William Bartram at Saint Augustine in 1766.

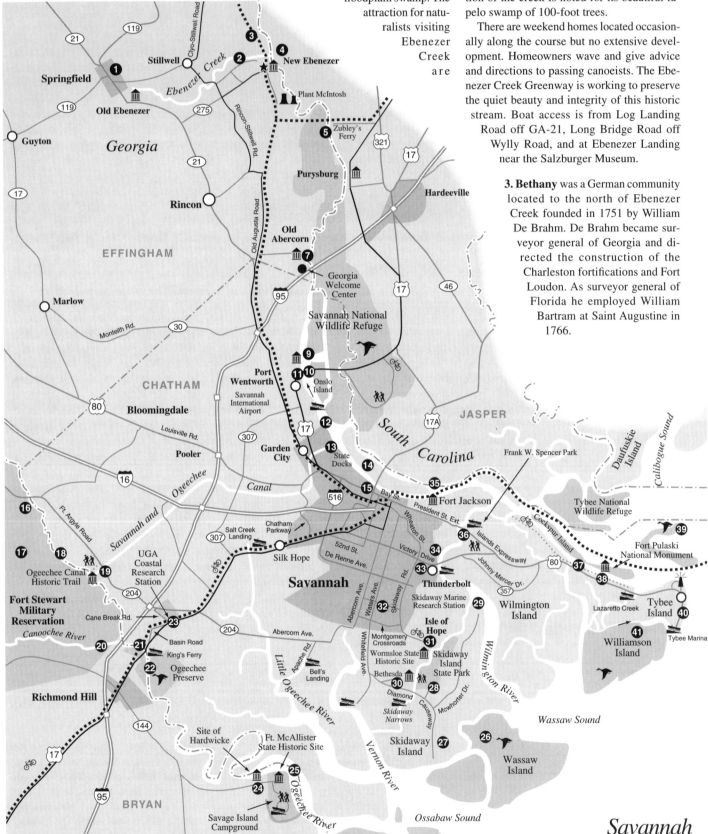

Savannah

4. New Ebenezer. The Society for the Propagation of the Gospel in Foreign Parts arranged for Protestants from Salzburg, Austria, to emigrate to the new colony of Georgia. It was believed their sober habits and industry would benefit the colony economically and they would serve as a positive influence on the idle settlers of Savannah. The original settlement, near Springfield, proved to be an unhealthy place and in 1736 the people moved to the Red Bluff overlooking the Savannah River at the mouth of Ebenezer Creek. The Salzburgers quickly became prosperous owing to their habits of frugality and hard work. While silk culture was abandoned in Savannah the Salzburgers continued to produce silk up until the outbreak of the Revolution. In good years they shipped as much as 2,000 pounds of raw silk to England in return for much needed currency.

The death of their spiritual leader, Martin Bolzius, and the destruction of many homes during the Revolution lead to the disintegration of the close-knit Ebenezer community. The inhabitants moved to other parts of Effingham County, particularly around Springfield. When Luigi Castiglioni visited in 1785 there were only five families remaining at New Ebenezer. Today it is the site of the Salzburger Cemetery, Jerusalem Church, the Salzburger Museum, and the New Ebenezer Family Retreat Center. If the museum is open, inquire about walking through the retreat center, which is built on the old town lots and streets of Ebenezer.

Jerusalem Church is the mother church for the Lutheran Salzburg descendants of Georgia. Completed in 1770, it was built of bricks made and fired at Ebenezer. Some of the bricks in the church wall retain the fingerprints of the women and children who carried the bricks to the building site.

Salzburger Museum. This modern brick building occupies the site of Georgia's first or-

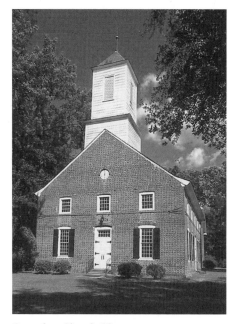
Jerusalem Church, Ebenezer

phanage. Reverend George Whitefield probably got the idea for his Bethesda orphanage while visiting the Salzburgers at Ebenezer. Artifacts from the first settlers and subsequent generations are on display. Genealogical information is available and descendants may register with the Salzburger Society. A bookstore contains books and pamphlets about the history of Germans in Georgia and the Ebenezer community.

Nature Trail. New Ebenezer sits above one of the unique Savannah River bluffs that harbors an interesting plant community containing a mixture of coastal and piedmont plants. Even plants more common in the mountains, like flame azalea, may be found in these bluff plant communities. In April one finds flame azalea in bloom, a full two months earlier than on the Bartram Trail at Wayah Bald in North Carolina. The entrance to the hiking trail is directly across the road from the retreat building (the *No Trespassing* sign is meant as a warning for hunters and not historians). Directly across the road from the Bartram historical marker is a sunken portion of the colonial Augusta Road that William Bartram traveled from Savannah to Ebenezer.

5. Zubly's Ferry (also Zubley). See Chapter 18, the Lowcountry.

6. Old Augusta Road. The Indian path from Savannah to Savannah Town became the Augusta Road when Augusta was established. Sections are still in use today.

7. Abercorn was a short-lived settlement on the river north of Savannah. Because Oglethorpe chose town sites based on military rather than civic considerations, settlements were not always successful. Abercorn suffered from disease, a lack of good farm land, and was abandoned within a few years.

8. Savannah National Wildlife Refuge. See Chapter 18, the Low Country.

9. Mulberry Grove was the home of General Nathanael Greene and his wife Catherine, and where Eli Whitney invented the cotton gin. Mulberry Grove occupied the site of Joseph's Town, an early Native-American settlement and was later the plantation of Lieutenant Governor John Graham. The property was confiscated by the provincial government and awarded to General Greene for his service in the Revolution. Greene died in 1786 after he and Catherine visited a neighbor on a hot day and General Greene complained of the heat.

Eli Whitney came south to tutor the Greene children and began developing his idea for a cotton engine when he saw the slaves laboriously picking the seeds from cotton bolls by

Legend

1. Springfield
2. Ebenezer Creek
3. Bethany
4. New Ebenezer
   Jerusalem Church
   Salzburger Museum
   Nature Trail
5. Zubly's Ferry
6. Old Augusta Road
7. Abercorn
8. Savannah National Wildlife Refuge
9. Mulberry Grove
10. Houlihan Bridge
11. Musgrove Trading Post
12. Savannah River
13. Brampton
14. Hutchinson Island
15. Pipe Makers Creek, Moravian Village and Irene Indian Mound
16. Fort Argyle
17. Fort Stewart Military Reservation
18. Ogeechee River
19. Savannah-Ogeechee Barge Canal Museum and Nature Center
20. Canoochee River
21. Kings Ferry
22. Ogeechee River Preserve
23. Coastal Gardens, University of Georgia Coastal Extension Center
24. Hardwicke
25. Fort McAllister State Historic Site
26. Wassaw Island National Wildlife Refuge
27. Skidaway Island
28. Skidaway State Park
29. Skidaway Institute of Oceanography
30. Bethesda Orphanage
31. Wormsloe State Historic Site
32. Chatham County Garden Center & Botanical Gardens
33. Thunderbolt
34. Bonaventure Cemetery
35. Fort Jackson
36. Oatland Island Educational Center
37. Savannah to Tybee Rails to Trails
38. Fort Pulaski National Monument
39. Tybee National Wildlife Refuge
40. Tybee Island
41. Williamson Island

Whitefield Chapel at Bethesda Home for Boys

hand. Catherine Greene married the manager of the Greene's plantations, Phineas Miller, who became a business partner in the company of Whitney & Miller that manufactured cotton gins. The invention was a success but the partners failed to reap their expected fortunes due to the number of various designs of gins that soon appeared on the market.

The original buildings were destroyed during the Civil War and the property is now owned by Georgia Ports Authority. Preservation organizations are trying to obtain the property for a historical and interpretative site.

10. Houlihan Bridge, built in 1925, was the first permanent route across the lower Savannah River.

11. Musgrove Trading Post. The home of John and Mary Musgrove was located on property now owned by Dixie Crystals Refinery. Mary was a mestizo whose Creek name was Coosaponakesee. She was the niece of Emperor Brim, a principle chief of the Creeks in the early eighteenth century. Some said her father was Henry Woodward. She served the office of Oglethorpe's interpreter during his years in Georgia. After Oglethorpe returned to England and John Musgrove died, Mary moved her trading house to the Altamaha River. She married Thomas Bosomworth, whose influence caused her to become involved in a near war with the Georgians. She claimed her position as Queen of the Creeks and threatened war if she did not receive payment for her service to the colony and for lands now occupied by Georgians. She was given her back pay and the Saint Catherines Island, making her the wealthiest and largest landowner in the colony.

12. Savannah River. Jean Ribault named this stream Rivièr Grande; the Spanish called it Rio Dulce. When the English came to Carolina in 1670 it was called Westabou, River of the Westoes. In 1681 the Westoes were driven away by the Savannahs, a branch of the Shawnees, who had recently moved to the upper Savannah River. They founded Savannah Town on the west bank below the falls which became an important trade center. The river was thereafter known as Savannah River.

13. Brampton was the plantation home of Jonathan Bryan. In early November 1776, when he left Savannah for the last time, William Bartram accompanied Jonathan Bryan to Brampton. Bartram spent the evening with the Bryans and began his long trip home to Philadelphia the next day. Brampton was located between Garden City and the Savannah River below Pipemakers Creek; the site is now occupied by the Georgia State Docks. Brampton Plantation became the Bryans' residence in 1765 and is named for the Bryan ancestral English home. The plantation cemetery is located on Brampton Road.

Bryan was responsible for some of the friction between the English and the Seminoles that preceded and delayed Bartram's travel to Florida in 1774. Bryan tried to lease or buy all of the northern part of East Florida but was thwarted by the intercession of Governor Tonyn and the outbreak of the Revolution. The scheme aroused the ire of the young Seminole warriors.

Bryan was very wealthy and possibly the largest landowner in the colony of Georgia. He was a native of the Beaufort Precinct from near Pocotaligo, South Carolina. As a captain of the coastal patrol, he accompanied Oglethorpe and the first Georgia colonists to Yamacraw Bluff. In South Carolina Jonathan and his brother Hugh Bryan were harshly criticized for evangelizing among the slaves. Reverend Johann Martin Bolzius wrote of visiting the Brampton plantation in 1742 and noted that Bryan's neighbors complained that his slaves did nothing but pray and sing and neglect their work. The Bryan slaves could not have neglected their work too much for Bryan's plantation became very prosperous.

Bryan moved to Georgia about 1750 when the prohibition against slavery was lifted. He became a member of both the Governor's Council and Commons House of Assembly in Georgia. He became an ardent patriot, member of the Provincial Congress, and the first to promote a boycott of British goods. Bryan was captured by the British in 1778

William Gerard De Brahm

William De Brahm was born in Germany in 1717 to a family of minor nobility. He became a Protestant in 1740 and emigrated with his wife to Ebenezer in 1751. De Brahm had been trained as a military engineer and was soon called upon to inspect the dilapidated fortifications at Charleston. He became Joint Surveyor of Land in Georgia in 1754 and soon became Surveyor General and the state cartographer. He also held office as justice of the peace and tax collector.

De Brahm was appointed Surveyor General for South Carolina in 1755 to replace the deceased George Hunter. The French and Indian War created an urgent need to repair the Charleston fortifications and construct a fort among the Cherokees to check French influence and intrigue. There arose a disagreement between De Brahm and Captain Raymond Demere over supervision of construction and the design for Fort Loudon. Demere denounced De Brahm to Governor Lyttleton and the Assembly, which damaged De Brahm's reputation in South Carolina.

De Brahm was appointed Surveyor General for the Southern District in 1764 with the charge to make a general survey of East Florida so the British government could make decisions regarding settlement in the newly acquired colony. His office made surveys and recorded plats of land grants. William Bartram worked with De Brahm for a short period in 1766 and probably helped with the survey of the New Smyrna township. De Brahm was at odds with Governor James Grant who believed that the surveyor general's office came under his direct jurisdiction, while De Brahm believed that he answered to the Board of Trade and the Crown. Grant listed numerous grievances against De Brahm and suspended him in 1770. The next year De Brahm went to London to answer the charges against him and was reinstated.

He outfitted a schooner, the *Cherokee*, to aid in his survey of the East Florida coast. When he returned to Charleston in September 1775 the ship was pressed into service by the patriots. De Brahm refused to give up allegience to the king and sailed to England in 1777 to avoid the Revolution. He was in poor health thereafter and did not work again as an engineer or surveyor. He wrote religious essays and became a Quaker. He moved to Philadelphia around 1791 and died in 1799.

William De Brahm made the first scientific maps of the Southeast and was the first to describe the character of the Gulf Stream. He had an inquiring, methodical, and observant mind and his writings tell us a great deal about the eighteenth century South, including agriculture, slavery, Native Americans, commerce, and natural phenomena.

when they seized Savannah and he lived for the next two years aboard a prison ship. He was exchanged in 1781 and died in Georgia in 1788.

First African American Baptist Church was organized at the Bryan plantation in 1773 by a white preacher, Abraham Marshall, and a slave, Jesse Peter. The first pastor was Andrew Bryan, a slave of Jonathan Bryan who was either freed or had bought his freedom. His skill as an orator brought phenomenal growth to the church. Members of the congregation came from up and down the river by boat to hear Reverend Bryan preach. The congregation bought land in Yamacraw Village and erected their first church in 1788. First Bryan Baptist Church still meets on the site at 559 West Bryan Street.

14. Hutchinson Island was cleared in the early days of the colony for pasture to support the Trustees' cattle. The first murder among the colonists occurred here in 1734. William Wise was the first settler on Hutchinson Island and the caretaker of the Trustees' cattle. When Wise became sick he was given two indentured servants, Richard White and Alice Riley, to care for him and the cattle until his recovery. White strangled the elderly Wise with his own neckerchief and Riley shoved his head into a bucket of water for good measure. White was captured by Joseph Fitzwalter, the gardener, but escaped and recaptured. Riley was found to be pregnant upon her later apprehension. Both were hanged, Riley not for two months until she had delivered her child. Certainly the stuff of history at times reads better than fiction.

Rice was grown on Hutchinson Island beginning in the mid-eighteenth century. The Savannah International Trade and Convention Center is located on Hutchinson Island, directly across the river from the historic Savannah Riverfront. A residential community and golf course are part of present development plans. The Coast Guard station is located at the east end of the island.

15. Pipe Makers Creek, Moravian Village, and Irene Indian Mound. The Yamacraws reserved lands for their use that extended from Pipe Makers Creek to Palachucola Bluff, about forty miles upriver. Their primary settlement was at Pipe Makers Creek just west of Savannah. The area has since been called Yamacraw.

The **Moravians** were a group of Austrian Protestants who settled just north of Savannah near Pipe Makers Creek. Their religious policy forbade them to bear arms; therefore, they engendered resentment among their neighbors during the wars with Spain. They settled their debts and moved to Pennsylvania.

The **Irene Mound** dates to the Mississippian period, 1300 to the late 1400s. It is located on Georgia Ports Authority property and is one of the significant mound sites on the coast, although it has been eroded by the river. Mounds were smaller nearer the coast and all of the Savannah River sites were abandoned by the time of Spanish exploration because the river had by that time become a buffer zone between separate chiefdoms.

16. Fort Argyle was the first post of defense built in Georgia by Oglethorpe. It was located where an Indian path crossed the Ogeechee River near GA-204. The site is located on Fort Stewart property.

17. Fort Stewart Military Reservation contains significant areas of longleaf pine-wire grass habitat and wetlands. There are populations of endangered red-cockaded woodpeckers and Georgia plume. The Nature Conservancy and Georgia Botanical Society occasionally organize field trips to Fort Stewart through the naturalists who work on base.

18. Ogeechee River. The Ogeechee rises in the Piedmont just outside the city limits of Union Point in Greene County. It was the northwestern boundary of Georgia prior to the Revolution.

In 1778, the wives of Georgia loyalists serving with Thomas Brown and the East Florida Rangers built huts along deserted stretches of the Ogeechee River as a haven for their husbands when they operated close to Savannah. These men had left their farms in the capable hands of their wives, planning to return home once the fighting was over and the rebels had been defeated.

19. Savannah-Ogeechee Barge Canal Museum and Nature Center. The Savannah River was once connected to the Ogeechee River by the Savannah-Ogeechee canal, which opened to traffic in 1831. Although long unused, parts of the tow path have been reopened for hiking and as a heritage trail. The canal is 16.5 miles long. The visitor area is located at 681 Fort Argyle Road, 2.3 miles west of I-95. Open 9 a.m.–5 p.m. every day.

20. Canoochee River is a blackwater tributary of the Ogeechee River. Because the Canoochee runs through the Fort Stewart military reserve and other sparsely populated areas it is a pristine and beautiful river for canoeists.

21. King's Ferry is the historic Ogeechee River crossing of the King's Road. It is now a modern county park with recreational facilities, including a boat and canoe launch. US-17 at the Ogeechee River.

22. Ogeechee River Preserve. The Nature Conservancy has a conservation easement of nearly 4,000 acres of bottomland swamp along the lower Ogeechee River. This property is located both above and below the King's Ferry bridge in Richmond Hill and is accessible by boat. The bottomland hardwood swamp is in pristine condition with dense growth of many indigenous trees, including Ogeechee lime, discovered by John and William Bartram at this site in 1765.

23. Coastal Gardens, University of Georgia Coastal Extension Center. The Coastal Gardens began as a USDA plant introduction station and was acquired by the University of Georgia in 1983. The center is best known for its collection of over 100 varieties of bamboo. The gardens also contain rare trees, 150 varieties of roses, 225 varieties of daylilies, turf grasses, hibiscus, and herbs. There are experimental vegetable and flower displays, and a comprehensive expansion program is being completed. Located at the corner of Canebrake Road and US-17. Open everyday.

24. Hardwicke was one of Georgia's dead towns until its recent revival. Governor Reynolds chose the site of Hardwicke to be the capital of Georgia in order to remove the government from his detractors in Savannah. The lack of funds and Reynolds' departure from the colony prevented any development and the seat of government remained in Savannah.

25. Fort McAllister State Historic Site protects a Confederate earthen fort on the south side of the Ogeechee River. A picnic area is located on the banks of the river near the fort. Camping, hiking, and a boat ramp are available on Savage Island, connected to the park by a mile long causeway. Savage Island is bounded by the Ogeechee River on the north and by marshes on all other sides. The park is located on GA-144 Spur east of Richmond Hill and is open 7 a.m.–10 p.m. daily. The historic site is open on a more restricted schedule. Admission.

26. Wassaw Island National Wildlife Refuge. Wassaw Island was first settled in 1866 by George Parsons and retains more of its original habitat than any of the Sea Islands. The Cabretta Research Project on Wassaw Island is one of the most important organizations doing research on loggerhead turtles. It is a joint effort of the Savannah Science Museum, U.S. Fish and Wildlife Service, and the Wassaw Island Trust. The refuge is open for day use and special hunts. It contains 2,500 acres and six miles of undeveloped beach. The Wassaw Island Foundation retains a small piece of property that is not open to the public. Accessible by boat. Contact the Department of Natural Resources for more information.

Maritime forest, Skidaway Island State Park.

27. Skidaway Island. The first English settlers on Skidaway were Thomas and Lucy Mouse. It is one of Georgia's developed barrier islands but much of it is state property and is available for public visitation.

28. Skidaway State Park. Located on the marshes of Skidaway Narrows, this 533-acre state park contains coastal habitats accessible by nature trails. Visitors may walk through a salt barren, along dikes in the salt marsh, over sloughs, through spartina and maritime forests. The park has an excellent campground located under a live oak forest.

Available facilities include a visitor center, camping, picnic area, playground, nature programs, and hiking trails. Located just off Diamond Causeway as it enters Skidaway Island. The park is open daily from 7 a.m.–10 p.m.

29. Skidaway Institute of Oceanography. This complex of research facilities includes the University of Georgia Marine Extension Center and the Skidaway Institute of Oceanography. The Extension Center provides educational outreach and the Institute is the research center. The Institute has a visitor center, twelve aquariums, and exhibits for the public. A nature trail begins behind the visitor center. Open 8 a.m.–5 p.m., Monday–Friday. The nature trail is open dawn to dusk, daily.

30. Bethesda Orphanage, now Bethesda Home for Boys, was founded by Reverend George Whitefield and was his most beloved lifelong accomplishment. A renowned preacher, Reverend Whitefield accepted the post of minister for the Church of England in Georgia rather than live a comfortable life installed in a wealthy church in London. Upon arriving in Georgia in 1737 his energy and enthusiasm brought many back to the church. After visiting the orphanage at Ebenezer he was inspired to build his own orphan house. Whitefield obtained a grant of 500 acres south of Savannah in 1739 and set about raising funds to construct the buildings. He preached up and down the Atlantic Seaboard and brought back substantial sums of money with which to build his dream. He was considered an upstart by the Anglican establishment who attempted to limit his influence in Anglican strongholds like Charleston. He enjoyed much success among the average citizens.

A telling story of Whitefield's power as a speaker and spiritualist is found in the *Autobiography of Benjamin Franklin* when Franklin wrote:

> *I happened soon after to attend one of his sermons, in the course of which I perceived he intended to finish with a collection, and I silently resolved he should get nothing from me. I had in my pocket a handful of copper money, three or four silver dollars, and five pistoles in gold. As he proceeded I began to soften, and concluded to give the coppers. Another stroke of his oratory made me asham'd of that, and determin'd me to give the silver; and he finish'd so admirably, that I empty'd my pocket wholly into the collector's dish, gold and all.*[1]

1. *The Autobiography of Benjamin Franklin.* Collier Books, New York, 1962.

In Franklin's defense, it was not frugality that predisposed him to resist Whitefield but his belief that it would be wiser and less expensive to build the orphanage in Pennsylvania and have Whitefield send the orphans there rather than build on the frontier.

Construction of the orphanage was a boon to Savannah for it brought steady work for the craftsmen and hard cash to the infant colony. In November of 1740 sixty-one children were moved to Bethesda. There they worked and learned skills that would make them useful members of society. It was at Bethesda that Peter Tondee learned carpentry. Others who passed through the doors of Bethesda were the future Governor John Milledge and General Lachlan McIntosh. John and William Bartram visited Bethesda in 1765.

After the death of Whitefield in 1770 the orphanage went in trust to the Countess of Huntington who enlarged and revived Bethesda. The original building burned to the ground after a lightning strike in May 1773 and the orphanage was closed in 1805.

The Union Society was organized in 1750 by Peter Tondee, Richard Milledge, Benjamin Sheftall, and others. The Society took as its mission the encouragement of trade, protection of skilled-craft professions, and charitable work around Savannah. When Bethesda was closed the Society carried on work in behalf of orphans and eventually bought Bethesda in 1854.

31. Wormsloe State Historic Site. Wormsloe is the home of Noble Jones and his descendants, established in 1736 on the Isle of Hope. Jones was one of the original colonists who accompanied Oglethorpe on the *Ann*. He was the colony's surveyor, physician, and carpenter. He also served in the militia, as assistant to the president of the colony, constable, Indian agent, and member of the Council. The fortified plantation also served as a marine base from which to patrol the coast for Spanish spies and guard Jones Narrows. The Narrows was once the inland waterway to Savannah but has silted up since the Intracoastal waterway was dredged nearby. The tabby house that is the centerpiece of the historic site was finished in 1745. Noble Jones remained loyal to the king while his son, Noble Wimberly Jones, became a patriot. Noble Jones died in 1775 before he could see the Revolution tear his colony apart.

The interpretative trail features the paintings of Mark Catesby and identifies plants and natural habitats encountered along the trail. Just off the trail is the Colonial Life Area, demonstrating the everyday life of servants and colonists of modest means. The single room daub and wattle hut is surrounded by a fenced living compound containing tools and animal shelters.

Located at 7601 Skidaway Road. Open from

9 a.m.–5 p.m., Tuesday–Saturday and from 2–5:30 p.m. on Sunday. Closed on Mondays except major holidays.

Noble Wimberly Jones was a patriot and member of the Tondee Tavern enclave that brought the Revolution to Georgia. He was a member of the Provincial Congress and was elected to the Second Continental Congress but did not attend due to his father's illness. Jones was captured at the fall of Charleston and imprisoned in Saint Augustine. He was a correspondent of Benjamin Franklin and founded the Georgia Medical Society in 1804.

32. Chatham County Garden Center & Botanical Gardens. The Chatham County Gardens cover ten acres and contain displays of roses, perennials, vegetables, and herbs. The visitor center is a farm house built in the 1840s. The Gardens are operated by the Savannah Area Garden Clubs. Located at 1388 Eisenhower Drive, between Waters Avenue and Skidaway Road. Open 10 a.m.–2 p.m., Monday through Friday.

33. Thunderbolt was settled during the first year of the colony of Georgia. The name comes from a blasted tree at the site when the town was surveyed. The Thunderbolt residential area overlooks the Wilmington River and is home to a fleet of shrimp boats.

34. Bonaventure Cemetery. John Muir spent a night in Bonaventure Cemetery when he arrived in Savannah on his first long walk. Bonaventure features beautiful monumental architecture and a view of the marshes of Wilmington River.

35. Fort Jackson is the oldest existing brick fort in Georgia, though not the oldest fortification site. An earthen rampart was built at the site in 1775 to protect Savannah from invasion by sea. That fort was abandoned because of the high incidence of malaria. This left the Savannah River unguarded and allowed the British to take the city in 1778. Construction on the present brick fortification was begun in 1808 and named for Revolutionary war hero and Georgia governor James Jackson. Fort Jackson became a Confederate fort during the Civil War and was the base for the ironclad *Georgia* that patrolled the Savannah River.

Visitors to Fort Jackson have impressive views of Savannah and the Savannah River. Every ship ascending the river must pass the fort. Located off President Street Extension on Fort Jackson Road. Open everyday, 9 a.m.–5 p.m. Admission.

36. Oatland Island Educational Center is operated by the Chatham County School District and is used as an environmental education center. Visitors can see plants and animals native to Georgia's coastal habitats as well as farm animals. Nature trails lead through maritime forest and salt-marsh. Although facilities and programs are geared to visiting school children, the public may visit from 8:30 a.m.–5 p.m., Monday through Friday. Special programs are held on Saturdays from October through May. The center is closed on major holidays.

37. Savannah to Tybee Rails to Trails. The old Savannah to Tybee Railroad bed has been converted into a biking trail. The trail follows the railroad grade with the banks of the Savannah River on one side and salt marsh on the other. The trail is being constructed in sections and will eventually connect downtown Savannah to downtown Tybee. Presently, the main entrance is located at Fort Pulaski.

38. Fort Pulaski National Monument. Fort Pulaski was completed in 1847 to guard the approach to Savannah and is still in remarkable condition. It was built on Cockspur Island where two previous forts had been constructed, Fort George in 1761 and Fort Greene in 1795. Fort Pulaski was named for Count Kasimir Pulaski who died at the siege of Savannah during the Revolution and is celebrated with a special day each October. Robert E. Lee was one of the commanders overseeing the construction of Fort Pulaski. Engineers used inverted arches below ground to support the weight of the massive seven-feet-thick walls.

The monument includes 5,600 acres of salt marsh surrounding Cockspur Island. The high ground on Cockspur was created in part during the construction of Fort Pulaski and the subsequent dredging of the Savannah River. Three hiking trails and the Savannah to Tybee Bike Trail provide an excellent opportunity to enjoy nature in the salt marsh.

The entrance to Fort Pulaski is located on Tybee Road. Open 8:30 a.m.–5:30 p.m. daily with extended hours from Labor Day to Memorial Day. Closed on Christmas Day. Admission.

39. Tybee National Wildlife Refuge. See Chapter 18, the Lowcountry.

40. Tybee Island has been a resort for Savannahians for nearly two centuries. Sites to see are the Tybee Light House, and the Tybee Museum at Fort Screven. Tybee is a Yuchi word for salt.

Tybee Lighthouse. The first Tybee lighthouse was built by Oglethorpe in 1736, the present lighthouse dates from 1867 and is now a museum. The admission fee allows visitors to climb the stairs once they have toured the museum. At 154 feet the lighthouse offers an impressive view of the seacoast and Savannah River. Located on the north end of Tybee Island.

Tybee Museum is located at old Fort Screven and features the history of the Island from colonial times. Open from 10 a.m. Operating hours for the museum and lighthouse vary throughout the year. Admission.

40. Tybee Island Marine Science Center. The Center features an aquarium of local marine animals. There are a touch tank for children and a of shell exhibit. Located at the Fourteenth Street parking area. Open 9 a.m.–4 p.m., Monday through Saturday, and 1–4 p.m. on Sunday. Closed on weekends during winter.

Tybee Visitor Center. Second Avenue and US-80 on Tybee Island.

41. Williamson Island is a testament to the dynamic nature of Georgia's coast. In 1957 there was only a sand bar here but by 1976 Williamson Island had grown to 250-acres. It has since reduced in size and migrated westward.

Counties

Effingham County is named for Thomas Howard, Third Earl of Effingham who resigned his commission rather than participate in a war against the American colonies. Effingham County was formed from St. Mathews Parish in 1777.

Chatham County is named for William Pitt, Earl of Chatham, and was formed in 1777. It was originally Christ Church Parish. Pitt was the most popular member of Parliament in the colonies because of his support of American interests and rights.

Bryan County was formed from parts of Chatham and Effingham Counties in 1793 and is named for Jonathan Bryan, patriot, member of the Council of Safety and Provincial Congress.

Historic Savannah

The 2.2 square-mile Savannah Historic District is one of the largest in the nation. Oglethorpe's original town plan included a grid of streets and alleys surrounding open public squares and is still considered one of the most effective urban designs today. Savannah has always had a livable in-town district that encourages people to walk their neighborhoods. The first streets were named for South Carolinians who contributed to the maintenance of the Georgia colony during the lean early years. The naming of the squares is indicative of the advance of Savannah's growth for they reflect the events of the day. Twenty-one of Oglethorpe's twenty-four planned squares were built.

Colonial Squares

Ellis. The original city market was in Ellis Square, named for Royal Governor Henry Ellis. The destruction of the old market to make way for a parking deck was a catalyst for the establishment of the Historic Savannah Foundation and the movement to save the historic structures of the city.

Johnson. Named for Governor Robert Johnson of South Carolina, who helped the Georgia colonists during the trying first year. This was the first of Savannah's squares, laid out in 1733 by James Oglethorpe and Colonel William Bull. The lots surrounding Johnson Square contained the Trustees' Store, the church, public oven, and house for strangers. The Declaration of Independence was read here on August 10, 1776. William Bartram was on the Georgia coast at the time and though he tells little of his comings and goings during that summer we cannot doubt that he knew of the events brewing in Savannah. At the center of the square lies the grave and monument to General Nathanael Greene.

Reynolds. A statue of John Wesley is the centerpiece of Reynolds Square. This square was named for Royal Governor John Reynolds who served from October 1754 to October 1756 when he was recalled by the Trustees.

Telfair (originally St. James). The Royal governor's house stood at St. James Square on the site now occupied by the Telfair Museum. Upon his arrival in Savannah William Bartram visited with Governor James Wright.

Wright. Laid out in 1733 and named for Royal Governor James Wright. Wright Square was originally named Egmont Square for John Perceval, Earl of Egmont, a Trustee of Georgia. Tomochichi is buried in the center of the Square. Due to a mistake as to the location of the great Yamacraw leader's grave, a monument to William Gordon was erected in 1883. Gordon was the first president of the Central Railroad and Banking Company. The monument to Tomochichi is in the southeast corner of Wright Square.

Oglethorpe is named for Georgia's founder, James Edward Oglethorpe.

Post-Revolutionary Squares

Franklin. Honors Benjamin Franklin.

Warren. Named for General Joseph E. Warren who was killed at the Battle of Bunker Hill.

Washington. Named for General and President George Washington.

Liberty. Honors the liberty of the recently independent United States and the fervent patriotism of the Midway Congregationalists.

Columbia. During colonial times Bethesda Gate was located at what is now Columbia Square. This gate was one of six entrances through the palisade into Savannah. Columbia Square is named for the feminine symbol of America.

Greene. Named for Revolutionary General Nathanael Greene of Rhode Island who settled at Mulberry Grove Plantation north of Savannah after the war.

Orleans. Named for the Battle of New Orleans, January 8, 1814.

Chippewa. Commemorates the 1815 Battle of Chippewa in Canada. The statue of James Oglethorpe dominates the center of the square.

Crawford. Named for William H. Crawford, member of the General Assembly of Georgia, U.S. Senator, Ambassador to France from 1813–1815, Secretary of the Treasury from 1815–1825, candidate for the Presidency in 1823, and Judge of the Northern Circuit of Georgia until his death in 1834.

Pulaski. Named in honor of Count Kasimir Pulaski who died at the siege of Savannah in 1779.

Madison. Honors President James Madison and contains the statue of Sergeant William Jasper, South Carolina patriot who fell at the siege of Charleston in 1779.

Lafayette. Named in honor of General Lafayette who fought in the American Revolution.

Troup. Named for Governor George Troup.

Chatham. Named for Chatham County and William Pitt, the Earl of Chatham.

Monterey. Named for the Battle of Monterey in 1846.

Calhoun. Named for John C. Calhoun, defender of States Rights and popular senator from South Carolina.

Telfair Square and the Telfair Museum, site of the colonial governor's mansion.

Legend

1. Riverfront Plaza Bartram Trail Marker
2. Factor's Walk
3. Oglethorpe's landing
4. Customs House
5. Cotton Exchange
6. Ships of the Sea Museum
7. Trustees Garden
8. Pirates' House, Old Herb Shop
9. Filature Site
10. Assembly House site
11. Trustees' Store site
12. Christ Episcopal Church
13. James Habersham's Home
14. The Old Market
15. First African Baptist Church
16. Yamacraw Town
17. Tondee's Tavern site
18. Abigail Mini's Tavern
19. Lutheran Church of the Ascension
20. Colonial Governor's Mansion
21. Tomochichi
22. Independent Presbyterian Church
23. Colonial City Limits
24. Colonial Park Cemetery
25. Bethesda Gate
26. Savannah History Museum & Visitors Center
27. Historic Railroad Shops
28. Jones Street
29. Beach Institute
30. Temple Mickve Israel
31. Georgia Historical Society
32. Forsyth Park
33. King-Tisdell Cottage

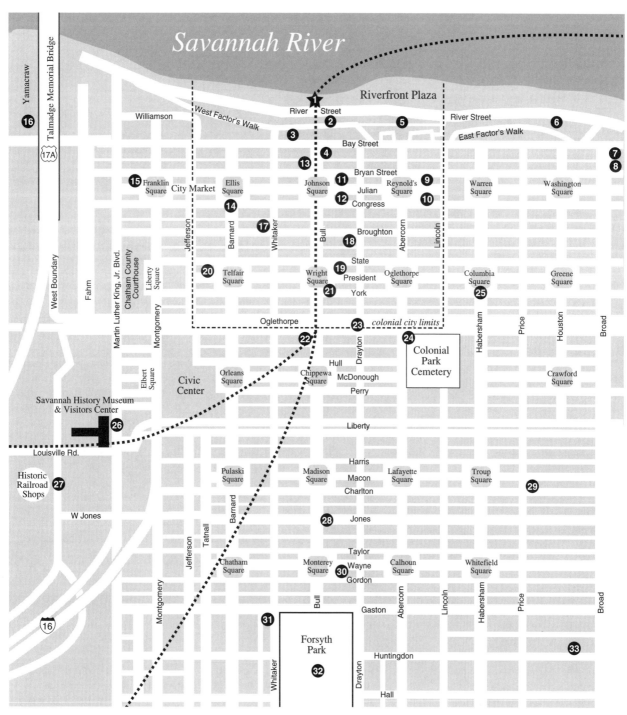

Savannah

Whitefield. Honors George Whitefield, the greatest English orator of his day, Episcopal minister in colonial Georgia, founder of Bethesda Orphanage, and one of the founders of Methodism.

Sites

1. Riverfront Plaza. A promenade, benches, and a view of the river make this park on River Street a not-to-be-missed attraction on every tourist's itinerary. James Edward Oglethorpe and the early colonists first stepped on Georgia soil at this site as did William Bartram and countless early settlers and adventurers. An outdoor festival is held in the plaza on the first Saturday of each month.

Bartram Trail Marker, River Front Plaza, commemorates William Bartram's arrival in Savannah in April 1773.

2. Factor's Walk was constructed to bridge the space from the second floor of the riverfront businesses to the top of the bluff, allowing businessmen and clients to avoid the traffic moving to and from the wharves. A factor was a broker who arranged for the sale of products, most notably cotton. In the early days of the Southeastern ports a factor also purchased imported goods for his clients. Planters sent cotton to their factor in Savannah and brought back European crystal and Northern furniture. The streets and warehouses on the riverfront are built of stones brought from New England and Europe as ship's ballast.

3. Oglethorpe's landing is commemorated by a historical marker on the west side of City Hall. A stone bench marks the spot where the tent was pitched that protected the colonists and their supplies while they built their houses. The City Exchange stood at the site of the present City Hall from 1799 to 1904.

4. Customs House. The U.S. Customs House occupies the site of Oglethorpe's quarters during the spring of 1773 and scene of John Wesley's first sermon in Georgia. The Customs House was built in 1852. Directly across the street are cannons presented to Savannah by George Washington.

5. Cotton Exchange. The last few decades of the 19th century were prosperous times for Savannah when it became one of the world's leading cotton ports. The Cotton Exchange in Savannah was built in 1887 as the business center for the city's cotton factors. A fall in cotton prices at the end of the century sent Savannah into a period of decline.

Savannah Cotton Exchange

6. Ships of the Sea Museum. The Museum contains collections of models that represent seagoing ships from the earliest times. Located on River Street. Open 10 a.m.–5 p.m. daily except Thanksgiving, Christmas, New Years, and St. Patrick's Day. Admission.

7. Trustees' Garden. Within a month of arriving at the site of Savannah the colonists had begun work on the Trustees' Garden. This ten-acre experimental garden was conceived by Sir Hans Sloane and was the first agricultural experiment station in America. It was used to determine plants suited to the climate and soil of Georgia and as a nursery to propagate and disperse the plants to the citizens. During the years that the Garden was in operation the gardeners planted hemp, flax, olives, cochineal, indigo, tea, ginger, hops, quinine, sesame, and medicinal plants. Upland cotton and peaches were first planted in America at the Trustees Garden.

The Trustees employed Dr. William Houston to gather plants for the Garden, but he died while collecting in Jamaica. A Mr. Wilson was then employed but was captured by the Spanish and did not reach Georgia. Joseph Fitzwalter was the first gardener but he became involved in a dispute with Martin Amatis over control of the Garden. Amatis was responsible for establishing the silk industry, including propagating thousands of mulberry trees to feed the silkworms. The Trustees decided in favor of Amatis and Fitzwalter left for South Carolina to pursue a life of the woods, to whose bounty and pleasures he had become attached.

Amatis was a petty and contentious man and was removed from the garden by Oglethorpe. Amatis destroyed the silk machinery and went to South Carolina where he soon died. Fitzwalter was brought back to the Garden. He put the Garden back in shape again, and continued to experiment with vegetables and fruits.

The Garden did not fulfill its promising function because the Trustees, in distant London, favored the pursuit of wine and silk production over other agricultural industries. They allowed market needs in England to blind them to the realities of soil and climate conditions in Savannah. The mercantilist economies of Europe needed colonies to provide products that could not be grown or manufactured at home and this meant principally tropical productions.

In 1755 Governor Reynolds noted the failure of the Garden and asked for the property, which he received. The Trustees' Garden then became a residential area. Ramparts were built and the area became known as Trustee' Garden Battery. It was renamed Fort Wayne in 1784 to honor Revolutionary hero, General Anthony Wayne.

8. Pirates' House, Old Herb Shop. The main part of the Pirates' House Restaurant was built in 1753 and since that time has been the source of many stories and legends. It was a favorite rendezvous for sailors and pirates in the mid-eighteenth century. There is a rumor of a hidden tunnel through which drugged sailors were spirited to the docks and forced to complete a ship's crew. They awoke the next day at sea with no option but to volunteer for service. The Pirates' House is supposed to be the inspiration for the tavern in Robert Louis Stevenson's *Treasure Island*. It sits upon land that was once the Trustees' Garden and the herb house was once thought to have been built in 1734 as the residence for the gardener, but it was probably built in the mid-nineteenth century.

9. Filature Site. The Filature was the building that housed the work space and machinery for silk manufacture. It was located on Reynolds Square between Bryan and St. Julian Streets and was the third filature structure, replacing the first that burned in 1758. The new Filature was built by Peter Tondee and Benjamin Goldwire in the same year for £114. A great ball was held in the long room during the visit of George Washington in May, 1791. The Filature was used as city hall, a hospital, school, boarding house, and theater before being destroyed by a fire in 1839.

10. Assembly House site. The seat of colonial government was located on Reynolds Square between St. Julian and Duke Streets. The building was begun as the second filature but was converted to the new Assembly House in 1754 after the original Council House collapsed. President Archibald Bulloch read the Declaration of Independence to the public on August 10, 1776 in front of the Assembly House.

11. Trustees' Store site. During the years that Georgia was governed by the Trustees the store was used to disperse food and supplies to the colonists as they struggled to begin life in the New World. It was not intended that the Georgians should become dependent on the store, but many were unskilled at farming and, at best, were unfamiliar with the crops that would succeed in the subtropical weather. The store was supposed to become self-supporting but was mismanaged by the keeper, Thomas Causton, and closed by the Trustees in 1738.

12. Christ Episcopal Church, the first church of the colony of Georgia, was established in 1733. Early pastors included John Wesley and George Whitefield. The present church dates from 1838.

13. James Habersham's Home was located at the corner of Bryan and Bull Streets on the northwest of Johnson Square. Habersham was visited by John and William Bartram on September 4, 1765. He introduced the Bartrams to Governor James Wright.

Governor James Wright

James Wright was born in London in 1716 and moved to Charleston around 1730. He studied law in London and was appointed Attorney General upon his return to South Carolina. In 1757 he was appointed agent for South Carolina and returned again to London. In 1760 he was appointed Lieutenant Governor of Georgia. When Governor Henry Ellis resigned his position, Wright was given the governorship.

Although he is remembered for his loyal opposition to the patriots and American independence, Wright's greatest legacy is that he guided Georgia through a period of growth and prosperity. He arrived in Savannah near the end of the French and Indian War when the Treaty of Paris removed the French and Spanish threat to the colony. Wright and John Stuart, Superintendent of Indian Affairs, maintained peace with the Creeks, which allowed settlers on the newly purchased lands to enjoy long periods of unmolested industry. Although the immediate effect was a series of border skirmishes between Creeks and settlers, they were of short duration. During his tenure, Georgia increased in area by over threefold. The Purchase of 1773, which is described in the *Travels*, was the special project of Wright. He was made a baronet while in England securing permission for the land purchase made at the 1773 Treaty of Augusta.

James Wright went against current convention of making large land grants to wealthy landowners and speculators. He encouraged immigration of yeoman farmers and their families. He believed the security and prosperity of the colony was best served by communities of small farms on the frontier worked by the owners and defended by the citizens. Larger land grants were given on the coast where the rice and indigo planters were establishing new plantations. Governor Wright himself was one of the colony's largest landowners, with 26,000 acres in eleven plantations. His material investment in Georgia meant Wright approached affairs with an eye to long-term results. He established ports at Sunbury, Brunswick, and St. Marys to encourage settlement and investment in the southern part of the colony.

Governor Wright enjoyed the support and cooperation of the Assembly. He was possibly the most competent Royal governor in the American colonies during the period leading up to the Revolution. Unlike many other governors, James Wright worked with his council and assembly to increase representation and services in the newly settled parishes. Wright, however, followed the letter of the law regardless of his views. Even though he understood American sentiment in the early days of the coming confrontation with England the governor always supported the Crown and Parliament. His steadfast adherence to instructions from London lead him into escalating confrontation with the Commons House of Assembly, which was becoming more radicalized. Fearing for his safety, Wright fled Savannah on February 11, 1776.

Savannah was captured by the British in March 1779 and James Wright returned to Savannah in July. Despite his pleas for more troops in Georgia, Wright was never to receive enough support to completely recapture the frontier of Georgia. After the British surrender at Yorktown, General Anthony Wayne and Continental troops were dispatched to Georgia where they put the British on the defensive. The British evacuation of Savannah was ordered in May 1782 and Governor Wright left with the troops on July 10. He died in London on November 20, 1785, and is buried in the north cloister of Westminster Abbey.

Sir James Wright
Courtesy of the Georgia Department of Archives and History

14. The Old Market. The old city market for Savannah was located in Ellis Square. The Historic Savannah Foundation was born out of the controversy surrounding the sale of this Square for construction of a parking deck.

15. First African Baptist Church was organized in December 1773 at Brampton Plantation and is thought to be the oldest Black congregation in the country. The congregation first occupied the site of the present First Bryan Church before moving to the present location on Franklin Square at #23 Montgomery Street. The present church building dates from 1861.

16. Yamacraw Town was the Creek village of Tomochichi's people. They separated from the Creeks for some unknown reason and moved among the Apalachicolas on the Savannah River then moved to Yamacraw Bluff (present-day Savannah). During Tomochichi's life, the Yamacraws lived at the site now occupied by the south end of the Talmadge Memorial Bridge. Upon his death in 1739, the Yamacraws moved back among the Creeks and became absorbed into their towns.

17. Tondee's Tavern site. It is possible that William Bartram dined at Tondee's Tavern in the spring of 1773 and there he met the leading men of Georgia, including Benjamin Andrew. The Tavern was at the northwest corner of Broughton and Whitaker and the famous Long Room was immediately adjacent. Peter and Lucy Mouse Tondee began operating the Tavern at their home around 1770. It was the scene of meetings of the Union Society, the Council of Safety, the Provincial Congress, and served as headquarters for the British army during the occupation of Savannah. Lucy continued to operate the Tavern after the death of Peter in 1775 until her own death in 1785. The Tavern burned in the fire of 1796.

The Long Room was the largest dining facility in colonial Savannah and the scene of many banquets and public meetings. The Liberty Boys rallied at the Tavern on July 27, 1774, upon hearing news of the closing of the port of Boston. The first organized meeting of patriots was held on August 10 with Peter Tondee presiding as door sentinel to prevent unauthorized people from entering. When news of fighting at Lexington reached Savannah, the patriots met at Tondee's Tavern on May 10, 1775, and severed formal allegience to England. The first meeting of the Georgia Provincial Congress was held at the Tavern on July 4, 1775.

Peter Tondee died at the Tavern on October 27, 1775, in the midst of preparations for the coming conflict with England. Otherwise his name would have been much more prominent among the important revolutionaries who helped win independence. The Council of Safety continued to meet at Tondee's Tavern every Monday at 10 a.m. Following the Revolution the Assembly reconvened at Tondee's Tavern and organized the permanent government of the newly independent state.

18. Abigail Mini's Tavern was the other popular gathering place in Savannah. She often was called upon to cater official meetings and gatherings.

19. Lutheran Church of the Ascension. Reverend Martin Bolzius conducted services in Savannah on April 12, 1741, and the Church of the Ascension dates from that first sermon. The property on Wright Square was purchased in 1771 and the present building dates from 1844.

20. Governor's Mansion. On their visit to Savannah in 1865, John and William Bartram were invited to dine with Governor Wright. The governor's mansion then stood at the northwest corner of St. James Square, now Telfair Square. The lot is now occupied by the Telfair Museum.

21. Tomochichi was the mico, or headman, of the Yamacraws. He and his people welcomed the new English colonists who arrived in Georgia in 1733 and made a place for them near their own village. Tomochichi was reportedly very old when he met Oglethorpe yet he was regal, dignified, eloquent, and renowned for his wisdom. We know more about Tomochichi than most other Native Americans in the Southeast during the colonial period because of his association and friendship with Oglethorpe. Tomochichi can rightly be called the co-founder of the colony of Georgia.

In 1734 Tomochichi, his family, and advisors traveled to England with Oglethorpe. They were presented to Parliament and King George II. Tomochichi won the affection of the Earl of Egmont, who wrote about the mico in his journals. Tomochichi told the Earl that, though the Yamacraws were simple and less worldly than the English, they were certainly happier. He was baffled by the large, substantial houses and wondered why anyone would build a home that would last longer then the life of the builder. Like other Native Americans, the concept of personal property was foreign to Tomochichi. He was displeased by the stratification of British society into upper and lower classes and was eager to return to Georgia. Tomochichi died on October 5, 1739, at an estimated age of ninety-seven and is buried in Wright Square. His grave lies in the center of the Square beneath the Gordon Monument, therefore, the monument to Tomochichi is located in the southeast corner of the square.

Tomochichi's nephew, Toonahowi, continued as a valued ally to Georgia. He participated in the Georgia invasion of Florida in 1740 and was in the vanguard of the assault that repulsed the Spanish at the Battle of Bloody Marsh. He was killed near Saint Augustine in 1743 when his warriors ambushed a party of Spanish horsemen.

The Yamacraws, like the Seminoles later in the century, were formed of disaffected members of several Lower Creek towns and remnants of the Yamassees who wished to disassociate themselves from their radical kinsmen. They chose Tomochichi as their leader, owing to his wisdom and natural abilities of leadership. They settled on the Savannah River in 1732 and were the only Native American town of any size on the Atlantic coast of Georgia when Oglethorpe arrived the next year. Tomochichi and the Yamacraws were exiled from the Lower Creeks although there is nothing in the records to indicate their offense. It seems likely that the estrangement was political rather than criminal for Tomochichi was highly regarded by other Creek leaders. His star rose with the settling of Savannah and the improvements in trade introduced by his association with Oglethorpe.

22. Independent Presbyterian Church was founded in 1755. The present building dates from 1890 and is a replica of the structure that stood from 1815–1819.

23. Colonial City Limits. The limit of developed streets and squares extended to Oglethorpe Avenue, though houses and farms extended to East Broad Street to the east, West Boundary to the west, and beyond the gates to the south. Oglethorpe Avenue was laid out in 1801 as South Broad.

24. Colonial Park Cemetery contains the graves of General Lachlan McIntosh and his wife Margery, James Spalding, General Samuel Elbert, Georgia's first printer James Johnston, William Scarbrough, promoter of the first trans-Atlantic steamship, and the Habershams.

25. Bethesda Gate was where Bethesda Road entered the colonial city. John and William Bartram would have passed this way when they visited Bethesda Orphanage in 1765.

26. Savannah History Museum & Visitors Center. Savannah's history from 1773 to the present day is exhibited in the old Central of Georgia passenger station. General information for tourists is available at the Visitors Center, located in the same building.

Operated by the Coastal Heritage Society. 303 Martin Luther King, Jr. Boulevard. There is an admission fee for the Museum; the Visitors Center is free.

27. Historic Railroad Shops. This collection of thirteen brick antebellum shops is the oldest existing railroad complex in the country. The growth and wealth of Savannah was boosted by the building of railroads to bring cotton from the interior of the state. Located north of Martin Luther King Boulevard and just west of the Savannah History Museum & Visitors Center. Open 10 a.m.–4 p.m., Monday–Saturday and on Sunday from Noon–4 p.m. Admission.

28. Jones Street. This street of restored nineteenth century town houses is shaded by live oaks and is one of the most beautiful streets in the South.

29. Beach Institute. The Beach Institute African-American Cultural Center was established in 1865 as a school for newly freed slaves. It is now a showcase for African-American arts and crafts. 502 E. Harris Street. Open noon–5 p.m., Tuesday through Sunday.

30. Temple Mickve Israel was established in 1733. It is the oldest Reform Jewish Congregation in the United States and the third oldest synagogue in America. The first members were Spanish and Portuguese Jews escaping persecution in their homeland. They arrived in Savannah aboard the *William* and *Sarah* in July 1733, bringing with them the Torah that is in the present temple. Among the group was Dr. Samuel Nunes Ribeiro who began treating the numerous Savannahians suffering from dysentery and malaria. Since the Trustees did not expressly forbid Jews from immigrating to the Georgia colony, Oglethorpe hoped to seek forgiveness rather than permission for allowing them to enter.

Although many Jewish immigrants moved to South Carolina or farther north, the Sheftalls remained in Savannah and became a prominent family. During the Revolution, Mordecai Sheftall and his son, Sheftall Sheftall, were members of the Committee of Safety and fought with the Continental Troops in Georgia.

31. Georgia Historical Society, founded in 1839. Historical documents, books, and maps are housed in the library of the Georgia Historical Society. Located at the northeast corner of Gaston and Bull Streets.

32. Forsyth Park is especially beautiful in spring when the azaleas are in bloom. The fountain is one of Savannah's most recognizable icons. Located near the fountain is a fragrant garden for visually impaired visitors.

33. King-Tisdell Cottage. This 1896 cottage houses the King-Tisdell Foundation and Museum of African-American History. It is located at 514 E. Huntington Street. Open noon–4:30 p.m., Tuesday through Friday and 1–4 p.m. on Sundays.

Itinerary

North to Ebenezer

Miles	Directions
	Begin at the Savannah Visitor Center, turn right onto MLK Boulevard then make an immediate right onto Louisville Road
.8	Right onto East Lathrop, the make an immediate left on Augusta Avenue
1.4	Left on West Bay Street/US-17
.8	Right onto Burnsed Boulevard (US25/21 North)
.1	Left on US-21N
6.5	Historical marker for Mulberry Grove Plantation
3.7	Turn right at the historical marker for Abercorn and make an immediate left on Old Augusta Road
.5	Keep right through the intersection at the Effingham County sign
4.6	Right on Fort Howard Road
2.6	Right on Rincon-Stillwell Road
1.5	Right on Ebenezer Road
3.0	New Ebenezer

South to Midway

	Begin at Bay Street and Whitaker, travel south on Whitaker Street
1.7	Right on 37th Street
2.3	Left on Ogeechee Road (becomes Atlantic Coast Highway/US-17)
10.7	Entrance to Coastal Gardens and UGA Coastal Research Center
1.9	Cross the Ogeechee River
15.5	Midway Church

Georgia Coast

Guale (pronounced *Wallie*) was the name of the coastal Chiefdom and Spanish province lying between the Ogeechee and Altamaha rivers. The native people living there were Muskhogean-speaking, their mico (headman) was also named Guale, and their principal town was on Saint Catherines Island. After removing the French threat to Spanish Florida in 1565, Menéndez de Avilés reconnoitered the coast and established garrisons where he could find allies among the native people. In 1568 he invited the Jesuits to establish missions among the friendly tribes and to use their "civilizing" influence to turn the natives into good Spanish subjects and converts to the Catholic faith. Missions strung from Santa Elena (Beaufort) to Saint Augustine served the Christian Indians for almost a hundred years. In the 1660s the Spanish were forced to move their mission towns ever closer to St. Augustine because of a series of attacks by enemy tribes, pirates, and Carolinians. By 1685 all Christian Indians were living south of the St. Marys River. The Yamassees, having only recently sought refuge among the Guale people, had not been fully transformed to the Christian faith. They thought it more expedient to seek the protection of the English and they moved to South Carolina to the place that still bears their name.

Thus this land was left deserted and eventually other Muskhogean Indians moved in, most notably the Yamacraws who settled at the first high bluff on the Savannah River. The English wanted to occupy this area as a buffer to protect the valuable colony of South Carolina and in 1721 they built Fort Prince George at the mouth of the Altamaha River. In 1733 Parliament allowed the creation of the Georgia colony between the Savannah and Altamaha rivers. In January 1734 General James Oglethorpe built Fort Frederica on Saint Simons Island which, being just south of the Altamaha River, was located in de facto Spanish territory. In 1735 General James Oglethorpe traveled to England and returned with disenfranchised Scottish Highlanders of the McIntosh clan and settled them on the Altamaha River. They named their community Darien and they proved to be the hardiest Europeans to settle in Georgia. Not only did they survive, they prospered and helped reduce further threat of invasion by leading the attack that led to the defeat of the Spanish force at Bloody Marsh.

In 1754 Congregationalists from Dorchester, South Carolina, founded Midway. They brought with them a strong sense of independence, a distrust of the British government, and a strong ethic of work and prosperity. When Georgia became a Royal Colony and slavery was legalized in 1752 the tidal regions of the rivers were turned into rice plantations. There was an influx of planters and money from South Carolina, creating a period of prosperity and growth for Midway, Sunbury, and Darien.

This region of the Georgia Coast was devastated by General Prevost's British troops as they marched toward Savannah in

Shrimp boats at Darien

1778. They burned Midway Church, plantation homes, and crops they could not carry off. The Lachlan McIntosh home was burned during the British invasion. His crops had been destroyed in 1776 by foraging Continental soldiers and Georgia volunteers and he was forced to move his family to Savannah in September, 1776 because they could not survive the winter on the plantation. After the Revolution, planters returned to the coast and the area became an important rice-growing region, especially in the Altamaha delta.

William Bartram's Travels on the Georgia Coast

William Bartram left Savannah on April 16, 1773, traveled south on the King's Road, now closely followed by US-17, and crossed the Ogeechee River at King's Ferry. He arrived at Sunbury later in the day. He attended service at Midway Church where he heard the Reverend William Piercy preach.[1] The next morning he crossed, not Saint Catherines Sound as he wrote, but more probably a narrow part of Dickinson and Jones creeks where they come near one another. He spent the day on Colonels Island, possibly at the invitation of Benjamin Andrew who owned property there. Bartram mistakenly names Ossabaw as St. Helena Island.

On April 18 Bartram proceeded southward on the King's Road. He stayed with Benjamin Andrew at his rice plantation on Peacock Creek, about a half-mile mile north of the intersection of US-17 and Barrington Ferry Road. Bartram's route then followed Barrington Ferry Road. Just south of LeConte-Woodmanston, Bartram turned to the east and became lost in either Big Mortar Swamp or Bull Town Swamp. Beyond Jones Road the old Barrington Ferry Road is now incorporated into pine plantations.

At South Newport William stayed with Donald McIntosh Bain during a storm. Bartram continued on to Sapelo Bridge, now Eulonia, where he delivered a letter from Governor Wright to Mr. Baillie. This was probably Robert Baillie who was married to Ann McIntosh, the only sister of the McIntosh boys. Baillie was commander of the garrison at Fort Barrington and became a Tory during the Revolution. Bartram's route was then generally along US-17 to Darien where he was hosted by Lachlan McIntosh and family who lived on Cathead Creek north of Darien. The route from Darien to Fort Barrington is the same today as it was for Bartram. On April 24 or 25 he left Darien following GA-251 (River Road), he kept straight on Cox Road then traveled along the unpaved Barrington Road to Fort Barrington on the banks of the Altamaha River.

William Bartram spent a great deal of time on the Georgia coast during the fall and winter of 1773–1774, the winter of 1774–1775, and most of 1776. In August, 1776 he moved with the McIntosh family to Savannah.

[1] The *Report to Dr. John Fothergill* differs from the *Travels* in that Bartram wrote that he attended service at Midway before going to Sunbury.

Sites

1. Ocean Highway and the Coastal Georgia Land Trust. In 1736 General James Oglethorpe directed Walter Augustine and a Mr. Tolme to cut a road from Savannah to Darien. The road would facilitate a quick response in case of Spanish attack and encourage settlement. The present US-17 closely follows the original road, occasionally deviating only a few hundred feet from the colonial route. The Atlantic Coastal Highway, US-17, was completed in 1927 and was the first important tourist route to Florida. In Georgia it is known as Ocean Highway. The Coastal Georgia Land Trust is working to establish a collection of cultural and natural trails based along US-17. The goal of this monumental project is to connect Ocean Highway to historic sites and areas of natural and recreational interest with an emphasis on alternative modes of transportation—boating, bicycling, pedestrian, and equestrian. The Bartram Trail will be a major component of the master plan.

2. Hardwicke was laid out by Governor Reynolds and was to be the capital of Georgia, hoping to remove the government from his detractors in Savannah. He resigned before anything came of the town.

3. Fort McAllister State Historic Site is a well preserved Civil War earthwork fortification overlooking the tidal portions of the Ogeechee River. The park has a campground, nature trails, and boat ramp on Savage Island. The park is open 7 a.m.–10 p.m daily, while the historic site is open 9 a.m.–5 p.m. Tuesday–Saturday. To reach the Park from US-17 in Richmond Hill take GA-144 and GA-144 Spur to the end. Admission.

4. Ossabaw Island Heritage Preserve is owned by Georgia and held as a preserve for scientific, educational, and natural research. Special permission from the State Department of Natural Resources or the Ossabaw Foundation is required for visitation. Ossabaw Island covers 11,800 acres and has 9.5 miles of beach.

5. Hall's Knoll. Although Dr. Lyman Hall owned a plantation just north of Midway he lived in Sunbury. The Knoll is now owned by the Liberty County Historical Society, which had plans to create a nature preserve.

Lyman Hall was born in Connecticut and became a Congregationalist minister. He moved south to Dorchester, South Carolina, then to Midway with other Congregationalists. There he became the most noted physician in the area. Hall was an official member of the Second Continental Congress and an unofficial member of the First Continental Congress and the only representative from Georgia. He was a signer of the Declaration of Independence. When the British seized Savannah and invaded the countryside, Hall fled to Connecticut with his family and his home was burned in 1782. He returned when Savannah was released by the British and was elected Governor in 1783. He later lived in Burke County at Shell Bluff above the banks where John and William Bartram discovered fossilized oyster shells.

Hall was buried first at Shell Bluff, then his remains were reinterred in Augusta alongside those of George Walton beneath the Signer's Monument. The original gravestone from Shell Bluff was sent to Wallingford, Connecticut, where Hall was born, and placed in the town cemetery.

6. Midway is so named because it is midway between Savannah and Darien. Nearby Medway River is named for the river in England in the district that was home to many of the original Puritans who emigrated to Massachusetts. Midway was founded by Congregationalists, descendants of the Massachusetts Puritans, who had settled at Dorchester, South Carolina, just north of Charleston. When the area around Charleston became overcrowded and the lands diminished in productivity, the community looked to Georgia for a new home. The Midway Society received 40,000 acres of land in 1754 which was organized into St. John's Parish.

In Savannah the Hot Heads of the Revolution tended to be the sons of the colony's wealthy and established society. Not so in Midway where patriotism was more universally embraced. These descendants of the Puritan

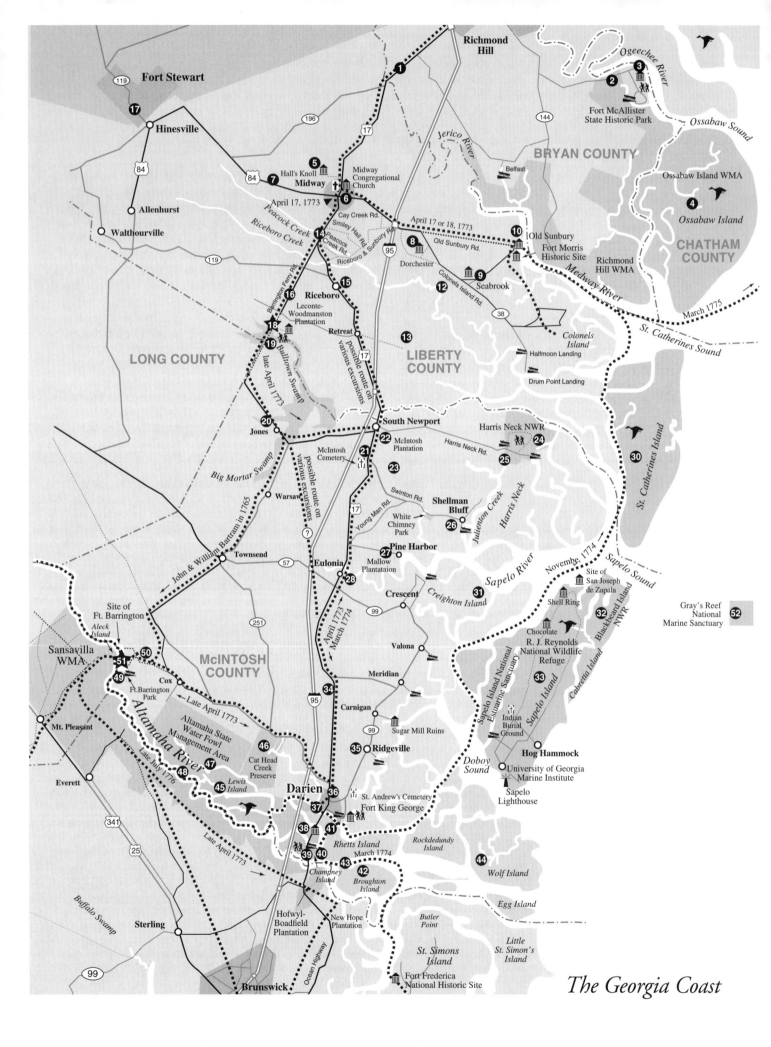

Independent Sect who emigrated from England to Massachusetts in the 1630s were independent in spirit and action, having practiced their doctrine in the New World for well over a century. Georgia's First Provincial Congress failed to send delegates to the First Continental Congress and in disgust St. John's Parish asked to be annexed to South Carolina. When that request was denied, the Parish sent Dr. Lyman Hall as their own delegate. Among their revolutionaries were Dr. Lyman Hall and Button Gwinnett, Brigadier Generals James Screven and Daniel Stewart, and Colonel John Baker.

Midway Congregational Church. According to his report to Dr. Fothergill, William Bartram attended services at Midway Church where he heard Reverend William Piercy, director of Bethesda Orphanage. Because William left Savannah on April 16 he probably attended Church at Midway on April 18, a Sunday. He must have attended services at Midway on more than one occasion for he also heard the Reverend John Osgood preach. Osgood lead the move of the Congregationalist community from Dorchester, South Carolina, to Midway in 1754. Osgood preached his last sermon on May 5, 1773, and died on August 2, 1773. He was revered by his flock and is honored by a historical marker at his grave in the Midway cemetery. The Church that Bartram visited was burned by the British in 1778. The present building dates from 1792.

Midway Cemetery. The graves of many important persons from the early history of the Georgia Coast rest here: Louis LeConte, General James Screven, General Daniel Stewart, Governor Nathan Brownson, Reverend John Osgood, and many of the original citizens of Midway.

Midway Museum and Visitors Center. The design of the Midway Museum building is based on a drawing sketched by Basil Hall when he travelled on the coast in 1828. It is typical of raised cottage homes built in the area during that time. Located on US-17 just north of Midway Church. Open 10 a.m.–4 p.m, Tuesday–Saturday and 2–4 p.m. on Sunday. Closed on Monday and Holidays.

Button Gwinnett Historical Marker. William Bartram may very well have met Button Gwinnett either during his stay in Savannah or while visiting Midway. Gwinnett was mortally wounded in a duel with Lachlan McIntosh and has the distinction of owning the most valuable autograph in America due to its rarity caused by his public life being cut short.

Button Gwinnett was born in Down Hatherly, Gloucestershire, England, in 1735 and became a merchant in Bristol as a young man. He settled in Savannah in the 1760s and operated a mercantile business for a short time. He purchased Saint Catherines Island from Thomas Bosomworth, husband of Oglethorpe's interpreter, Mary Musgrove. Gwinnett was not successful as a planter and sold most of Saint Catherines Island for £5,250 to settle his debts but retained his house. He then devoted himself to political affairs, possibly due to the influence of his friend Dr. Lyman Hall. Gwinnett became speaker of the Georgia As-

Colonial Coast Birding Trail

The Georgia Department of Natural Resources is promoting birdwatching on the coast by marking a series of eighteen public sites that have excellent birding opportunities. The sites are:

Fort Pulaski National Monument
Tybee Island North Beach
Skidaway Island State Park
Savannah-Ogeechee Canal
King's Ferry on the Ogeechee River
Fort McAllister State Historic Site
Melon Bluff Nature Preserve
Harris Neck National Wildlife Refuge
Altamaha Wildlife Management Area
Hofwyl-Broadfield State Historic Site
Saint Simons Island East Beach
Jekyll Island North End
Jekyll Island Causeway
Jekyll Island South End
Crooked River State Park
Cumberland Island National Seashore
Okefenokee National Wildlife Refuge

Legend

1. Ocean Highway and the Coastal Georgia Land Trust
2. Hardwicke
3. Fort McAllister State Historic Site
4. Ossabaw Island Heritage Preserve
5. Hall's Knoll
6. Midway
   Midway Congregational Church
   Midway Cemetery
   Midway Museum and Visitors Center
   Button Gwinnett Historical Marker
7. Dorchester Academy
8. Dorchester
9. Seabrook Village
10. Fort Morris Historic Site
11. Sunbury
12. Melon Bluff Nature Preserve
13. Liberty County
14. Benjamin Andrew
15. Riceboro
16. Barrington Ferry Road
17. Fort Stewart
18. LeConte-Woodmanston Plantation
19. Bull Town Swamp
20. Jones
21. McIntosh Family Cemetery
22. Donald McIntosh Bain
23. McIntosh Family
24. Harris Neck NWR
25. Gullah/Geechee
26. Shellman Bluff
27. Mallow (McIntosh Plantation)
28. Sapelo Bridge
29. McIntosh County
30. Saint Catherines Island
31. San Miguel de Gualdape
32. Blackbeard Island NWR
33. Sapelo Island
    Hog Hammock
    Shell Ring
    Chocolate
    UGA-Marine Research Institute
34. Presbyterian Meeting House
35. Ridgeville
36. Darien
    Old Tabby Ruins
    Oglethorpe Oak
    Highlander Monument
    St. Andrew's Cemetery
    Fort King George
37. Lachlan McIntosh
    John McIntosh
38. Fanny Kemble
39. Ansley-Hodges Memorial Marsh Project
40. Champney River Park
41. General's Cut
42. Broughton Island
43. Altamaha River
44. Wolf Island NWR and Wilderness Area
45. Lewis Island State Natural Area
46. Cathead Creek Nature Preserve
47. Buffalo Swamp
48. Altamaha State WMA
49. Barrington Park on Harper Lake
50. Discovery of Franklinia and fevertree
51. Fort Barrington
52. Gray's Reef National Marine Sanctuary

Midway Church and cemetery

sembly, member of the Council of Safety, president of the Executive Council, delegate to the Second Continental Congress, and signer of the Declaration of Independence. He contributed significantly to the creation of Georgia's first permanent constitution in 1777.

Gwinnett became jealous of the commission given to Lachlan McIntosh and McIntosh became indignant for having to rescue Gwinnett in his failed attempt to take Saint Augustine and East Florida. Gwinnett and his friends tried to paint Lachlan's brother John as lacking in patriotic devotion, McIntosh called Gwinnett "a scoundrel and a lying rascal" on the floor of the Assembly. A challenge was issued by Gwinnett and accepted by McIntosh. A duel was fought on May 16, 1777, with both men receiving balls in the thigh. McIntosh recovered but Gwinnett died of an infection that was blamed on the incompetence of his doctor, corroborated by the fact that Mrs. Gwinnett brought prosecution against the physician who had attended her husband. Button Gwinnett's name has become more widely known than it otherwise might have because his signature, being in short supply, commands such a high price. Gwinnett's signature sold for $28,500, a record for any Signer's signature. The location of his grave is not known, but, he is remembered by a marker in Colonial Cemetery.

7. Dorchester Academy was founded after the Civil War to educate freed slaves. In the early part of this century the school had eight buildings and 300 students. It was closed in the 1940s when a new consolidated school was built. Dr. Martin Luther King, Jr., retreated here in preparation for the 1963 Birmingham civil rights campaign. Dorchester Academy is today a community center and museum with several special events held each year. Located two miles from Midway on US-84.

8. Dorchester was the fourth community to bear the name of the original home of the Puritans, Dorchester, England. There is also Dorchester, Massachusetts (1630) and Dorchester, South Carolina (1695). Grants to land in the Dorchester, Georgia area were made to Congregationalists on July 11, 1752. The center of religious and social life for citizens centered around Midway, but the distance from outlying plantations lead to the establishment of Dorchester about 1843. It was built on high ground halfway between Midway and Sunbury and the church was built in 1854. Dorchester is another deserted town, its decline beginning with the destruction and impoverishment caused by the Civil War.

9. Seabrook Village. During the days of the large rice plantations the coast of Georgia was a de facto African country. Most whites lived away from the fields and the miasmas they believed hung over the stagnant water. The cultivation of rice by gangs of slaves created a large, isolated population of blacks. During the Civil War the white population deserted the coastal plantations of Georgia and South Carolina, many never to return. The former slaves were left to form communities and earn a livelihood as best they could. Sherman, by decree, made all the Sea Islands a separate state for freed slaves. Although the order was later rescinded, this region remained a separate cultural state. Blacks received small parcels of land and were able to survive off the bountiful gardens and tidal creeks and produce a little extra for trade.

The best-known product of the isolation of these coastal African-American communities is the Geechee dialect, a mixture of African and English that developed out of the need for speakers of many languages to communicate with one another. Geechee communities existed on Saint Simons Island, Sapelo Island, and in isolated communities on the coastal mainland between Brunswick and Savannah. In South Carolina the African derived dialect and culture is called Gullah (see page 34).

Seabrook Village is a recreation of an actual rural African-American community that existed from 1870 to about 1930. The village includes authentic buildings, demonstrations, and oral history events. The Annual Seabrook Celebration is held at the end of October and Old Timey Day is the last Sunday of February. Open 10 a.m.–5 p.m, Tuesday through Saturday.

10. Fort Morris Historic Site. Fort Morris is named for Captain Thomas Morris, a commander of the Georgia Continental Artillery, and was renamed Fort Defiance during the War of 1812. Fort Morris was constructed on the site of a Guale Indian village and was to protect Sunbury and Saint Catherines Sound from the British. Benjamin Andrew was the supervisor of construction.

Colonel Mark Prevost and Colonel L. V. Fuser made an attempt to capture the fort in November 1778 but failed. During the siege there were McIntoshes inside and outside the fort, demonstrating the complex nature of the Scottish relationship to Great Britain and the fact that the Revolution was also a civil war. Midway Church and plantations were burned as the British marched back to Florida. Fort Morris was taken by the British in January, 1779 soon after their successful campaign against Savannah.

Fort Morris State Historic Site has a primitive camping area, nature trails, picnic area, and a museum. To reach Fort Morris State Historic Site from Midway follow GA-38, Colonels Island Road, and Ft. Morris Road. Open 9 a.m.–5 p.m., Tuesday through Saturday and 9:30 a.m.–5:30 p.m. on Sunday and legal holidays. Admission.

11. Sunbury. All that remains of this once bustling seaport is the cemetery. The town of Sunbury was laid out around 1758 in 496 lots on lands owned by Mark Carr, James Maxwell, Kenneth Baillie, John Elliott, Grey Elliott, and John Stevens—all citizens of Midway. The name is from the Saxon language and means a sunny place or a sunny town. Sunbury is also the name of a town in England on the Thames

River. Extensive wharves were built and Sunbury became a port of entry in 1761, closely rivaling Savannah for maritime commerce during the time of Bartram's visit. It was always closely connected to the wealth and business of the Midway community. Most of the leading citizens of the area had a lot and house in Sunbury. James Spalding and partner Roger Kelsall owned one of the major wharves.

Sunbury was occupied by the British during the Revolution. The disruption and destruction caused by the occupation were exacerbated by yellow fever and hurricanes, causing Sunbury to decline. In 1797 the courthouse was moved to Riceboro and by 1848 there was little left of this once successful rival to Savannah. The history of Sunbury is exhibited at Fort Morris Historic Site.

From Midway Church Follow GA-38, Colonels Island Road, and Sunbury Road to Sunbury Historic Site. Continue on Sunbury Road after it becomes dirt to reach Sunbury Cemetery. Old Sunbury Road returns to Midway.

12. Melon Bluff Nature Preserve. This is a unique natural area in that it was developed privately by the family that owns the land. The preserve contains 5,000 acres of natural marsh and maritime forest. Amenities include a bed & breakfast, hiking, kayaking, festivals, birding, and nature study. 2999 Islands Highway, east of Midway (three miles from exit 13, I-95).

13. Liberty County. The Georgia Assembly created Liberty County from St. John's, St. Phillip's, and St. Andrew's parishes in 1777 and named it for the patriotic fervor of the citizens. McIntosh and Long counties were later carved from the original Liberty County. Rice helped make this the most prosperous section of Georgia prior to the outbreak of the Revolution. Many plantations were burned by the British, causing many families to seek land in newer sections of the state after the war's end.

The citizens of St. John's Parish, being impatient with Savannah, sent Dr. Lyman Hall to the First Continental Congress independently of the Georgia Provincial Congress. He took with him to Philadelphia rice and £50 for relief of the Boston patriots.

14. Benjamin Andrew, 1730–1790, was one of the original settlers of Midway and an ardent patriot. Benjamin Andrew moved from Pon Pon District, South Carolina, to Midway in 1754. He established a rice plantation halfway between Midway and Riceboro, on Peacock Creek about two miles from Midway Church. He was visited by William Bartram at his home and the two men rode about the plantation to view the fields. Andrew also had a summer home on Colonels Island, which was probably also visited by Bartram.

Inez Stevens grinds corn at Seabrook Village

Andrew was a member of the Provincial Congress, President of the Executive Council in 1777, member of the Continental Congress in 1780, and he supervised the construction of Fort Morris. After the Revolution, he continued to live in Liberty County and was the associate justice. Andrew was a member of the Georgia House of Representatives and died on the floor of the House in Augusta on December 16, 1790.

He may have lived in Lincoln County sometime in the early 1790s. If he is the Benjamin Andrew of Lincoln County, his land was located on Mill Creek, a few miles below the mouth of the Broad River. Although Andrew was an important figure during the late Colonial and Revolutionary periods, we know little about his personal life other than that his wife was named Elinor.

15. Riceboro was settled on the Savannah-Darien road near where it crossed the North Newport River and was named for the principal product of the area. As the inland part of Liberty County became settled, it became increasingly inconvenient for citizens to travel to Sunbury for legal business. Therefore the courthouse was moved to the bridge at North Newport River and was named Riceborough. When the courthouse was later moved to Hinesville the coming of the railroad kept Riceboro from dying. Captain Basil Hall and his wife Margaret visited Riceboro in 1828. His sketch of one of the homes is the model for the Midway Museum and Visitors Center.

16. Barrington Ferry Road. The Savannah to Saint Augustine Road branched off the Savannah-Darien Road near present-day Riceboro. It crossed the Altamaha River at Fort Barrington and was known locally as the Barrington Ferry Road. This stretch of straight, sandy road was trod many times by Georgians in their attempts to dislodge first the Spanish then the British from East Florida.

17. Fort Stewart. Interestingly, some of the best-preserved natural areas in the South are on military bases. Fort Stewart is the largest military base east of the Mississippi River and encompasses many thousands of acres of pine land and river swamp, including a long stretch of the Canoochee River. The Nature Conservancy has completed a botanical inventory for Fort Stewart and has catalogued a number of endangered and rare species. There are several colonies of Georgia plume (*Elliottia racemosa*) and the sand hills are home to gopher tortoises, both species were first described by William Bartram. Additionally, there are several species thought to be extinct in Georgia or out of their range at Fort Stewart. Such large tracts of land that receive relatively little disturbance and are fire maintained are extremely valuable to the biodiversity of the coastal plain. Since Fort Stewart is an active military base the lands are not open to the public except during organized field trips.

18. LeConte-Woodmanston Plantation. Woodmanston Plantation was established by John Eatton LeConte of New York in 1760 as an extensive upland rice plantation. LeConte used gravity fed water stored in a pond rather than tidal energy to flood the rice fields. The Fort Barrington road ran across the dike of the pond and the fields were east of the road. The famous gardens of *Camellia Japonica* and bulbs were established by his son Louis and were well known during the early part of the nineteenth century, drawing visitors from around the country and Europe. Louis became well known for his knowledge of coastal botany and was a correspondent of William Baldwin and Asa Gray. The Woodmanston Plantation gardens were featured in *English Gardener Magazine* in 1832.

Another son, John Eatton II, lived in Philadelphia but he did extensive research in natural history on numerous trips back home and became the leading authority on Georgia natural history. It was he who questioned some of William Bartram's observations and wrote in 1830 that Bartram was "much laughed at in Georgia." However, in 1854, after a trip to Florida where he verified Bartram's observations he changed his mind and wrote that "Mr. Bartram was a man of unimpeached integrity and veracity, of primeval simplicity of manners and honesty unsuited to these times, when such virtues are not appreciated." John Eatton II introduced the LeConte pear to Woodmanston, a cross between a sand pear and the French dessert pear. LeConte's sparrow is named for him. His son, John Lawrence, in turn, became a leading entomologist.

Louis' sons, John and Joseph, became physicians, then professors at the University of Georgia, University of South Carolina, and University of California. John LeConte became the first president of the University of California at Berkeley. Joseph was a nationally known geologist, a charter member of the Sierra Club, and close friend of John Muir. Mount LeConte in the Great Smoky Mountains National Park is named for these eminent brothers.

The LeConte descendants held Woodmanston during the 1800s though they lived elsewhere. Eventually, the house disappeared and the gardens and rice fields returned to forest. In 1977 the Jones family and the Brunswick Pulp and Paper Company deeded sixty-four acres of the original house and garden site to the Garden Club of Georgia. The botanical garden is being restored and there are plans for a rice-growing demonstration. Two of the gardens will reproduce John Louden's design for a Circular Garden and a Mingled Garden. A hiking trail makes a loop along the remnant of a rice dike and travels around the rice demonstration area into Bull Town Swamp. The gardens are open on weekends from 9 a.m.–5 p.m. on Saturday and 2–5 p.m. on Sunday, April through Labor Day. Admission.

Contact the LeConte-Woodmanston Foundation, P.O. Box 179, Midway, GA 31320.

19. Bull Town Swamp. William Bartram lost his way in Bull Town Swamp as he traveled along the Fort Barrington Ferry Road.

20. Jones Community. The book, *Children of Pride*, is based upon the correspondence of the Jones family of Liberty County during the period leading into the Civil War.

21. McIntosh Family Cemetery. West side of US-17 between South Newport and Eulonia.

22. Donald McIntosh Bain was a cousin of Lachlan McIntosh and lived near South Newport. He was the "venerable gray-headed Caledonian" with whom William sought refuge during a storm.

23. McIntosh Family. While botanizing on the coast William Bartram often stayed with Lachlan McIntosh and his family at Darien. During his travels up the Savannah River and to the New Purchase in 1773 his companion was Lachlan's son, John.

This family was the second and third generation of the Highland McIntosh clan and associated families who came with John McIntosh Mohr to settle Darien and serve under Oglethorpe. The youngest son, Lewis, was killed by an alligator while swimming in the

Fort King George, Darien, Georgia

Altamaha River soon after the clan settled Darien. John Mohr was captured at Saint Augustine and sent to prison in Spain.

John Mohr lived to an ancient age due, as he believed, to his habit of drinking buttermilk every day and nothing stronger. His son Lachlan was an important figure in the early history of the state of Georgia. Other sons and grandsons were active in the American cause and entered public service.

This family is too extensive, too confusing (with names being repeated in each generation) and too accomplished to be treated here. There are numerous accounts of McIntosh family history in the Darien Library.

24. Harris Neck National Wildlife Refuge is unique in that it is one of the few coastal national wildlife refuges with a driving trail. Water birds and ducks winter here in the several ponds. There is a fishing pier and boat ramp. The entrance is located on GA-131 east of US-17. Open sunrise to sunset, daily.

Harris Neck was a Gullah community founded by former slaves. The United States government confiscated the land surrounding the Harris Neck community in 1942 to use as an air station. The inhabitants were moved, many unwillingly, off the Neck and although the federal government promised to return the land after the end of the war, it was instead incorporated into Harris Neck National Wildlife Refuge in 1962.

25. Gullah. McIntosh County has recently become culturally connected to the West African nation of Sierra Leone by a song sung by Harris Neck resident Mary Moran. It is a funeral song passed down through the generations since the eighteenth century by Ms. Moran's family and is still sung in the Mende language of Sierra Leone. She had no idea of the meaning of the words until it was translated for her.

Gullah/Geechee. The African-American dialects of the Sea Islands are known as Gullah in South Carolina and Geechee in Georgia. This dialect is derived from a combination of English and West African languages that was the product of members of numerous tribes living and working together in isolation on the coastal rice plantations. The names probably derive from tribal names of the African Rice Coast, also known as the Biafran Bight. Gullah is possibly derived from the Gola tribe and Geechee from the Kissi tribe, both of Sierra Leone. The connection of Geechee with nearby Ogeechee River, where there were several large rice plantations, is probably a mere coincidence. Slaves who had a knowledge of rice cultivation were valued over others; therefore, many Africans brought to the colonial Southeast were related in language and customs even if they spoke differing dialects.

The rice plantations of the Antebellum South were isolated African communities because the white families refused to live near the fields from April until frost for fear of disease. The slaves blended their dialects and traditions of their homeland with minimal influence from white European culture. After the Civil War many of the rice plantations were abandoned by their white owners and former slaves became landowners, again in communities with little outside influence. Tourism and vacation communities are mostly a modern occurrence on the coast and the old black communities have been slowly broken up by development and economic migration. However, there are a few communities remaining — Sapelo Island, Harrington on Saint Simons Island, Seabrook, and Harris Neck on the Georgia coast; Pin Point and Sand Fly near Savannah; Daufuskie Island and Saint Helena Island in South Carolina, and sections of Charleston County.

26. Shellman Bluff is a popular fishing-camp town reminiscent of earlier days on the coast. It is a charming village, far from upscale, and has a fine view of the marsh. End of Shellman's Bluff Road.

27. Mallow Plantation is the home of the father of William McIntosh, the noted Creek statesman. The property contains the gravesite and historical marker for Captain William McIntosh, father of General William McIntosh and Roderick McIntosh, both who became leaders of the Creek Nation.

28. Sapelo Bridge (Eulonia) was at one time the county seat for Liberty County.

29. McIntosh County is named for the family that founded Darien in 1736 and dominated the political and social life of the area for the next century. It was created out of Liberty County in 1793 from the area coinciding with the original parish of St. Andrew, patron saint of Scotland.

30. Saint Catherines Island was originally named Guale for the local mico, or chief, and

Rice mill ruins, Butler Island

was the capital of Guale Province. In 1565 Pedro Méndez de Avilés established Mission Santa Catalina de Guale on the island, which eventually included a thousand Indian converts. The French traded with the Guale Indians for sassafras, which was used in perfume, medicines, and as a refreshing drink. The Spanish missions suffered from several internal Indian uprisings and harassment from other tribes. The grave of Mary Musgrove, Oglethorpe's Indian interpreter and assistant, is on Saint Catherines Island. She received the Island in payment for her services to the young colony of Georgia. Under the influence of her third husband, Reverend Thomas Bosomworth, she had herself named Queen of the Creek Indians and marched to Savannah, demanding land and money for payment of services she had rendered to the colony. Bartram said he explored Saint Catherines but it was really Colonels Island that he visited.

Button Gwinnett purchased the island in 1765 and his home is still used today by the Saint Catherines Island Foundation. The island is now a refuge for endangered species where healthy and viable populations are maintained by a cooperative effort between the Foundation and the New York Zoological Society.

31. San Miguel de Gualdape was the first European settlement north of the Caribbean, established in 1526 by Lucas Vásquez de Ayllón. It was thought until recently to have been at Winyah Bay, South Carolina. New scholarship, however, places the colony on the coast of Georgia, possibly at Creighton Island on the Sapelo River. Other scholars believe that San Miguel de Gualdape was at the mouth of the Savannah River.

Although no archaeological research has been done on Creighton Island, William De Brahm surveyed the island in the 1750s and found ditches and embankments that were more similar to European fortifications than Native-American. Sapelo Sound has the third-deepest natural harbor on the east coast, which would make it a favorable site for a colony.

In 1525 Lucas Vásquez de Ayllón sailed with five ships and 500 people and attempted first to settle at Winyah Bay, but stayed only a short time before moving south to the Georgia coast. Like many subsequent attempts at establishing settlements, the colonists suffered from hunger, fevers, and disillusionment. After the untimely death of Ayllón, the remaining colonists sailed for Cuba. A hurricane sank one of the ships and only about a hundred colonists survived to reach Cuba.

32. Blackbeard Island National Wildlife Refuge. Blackbeard Island was reputedly one of the hideouts of the famous pirate Edward Teach, also known as Blackbeard. It was acquired by the federal government in the early nineteenth century as one of the naval live oak preserves. There are hiking trails and an exhibit kiosk. Access is by boat only and no vehicles are allowed. Open from sunrise to sunset except for two weeks during special hunts. Access may be arranged by commercial operators in Shellman's Bluff.

33. Sapelo Island was called Sapala by the Guale Indians and was the site of the Mission of San Joseph de Sapala, located on the north end of the island. Some of the earliest pottery in North America has been found on Sapelo Island. Thomas Spalding, son of James Spalding, became the owner of Sapelo Island in 1802 and began his extensive Sea Island cotton and sugar plantation. The South End House was built for Thomas Spalding in 1810 by Roswell King, who later became the overseer for the Butlers.

Sapelo is the only undeveloped barrier island that people can easily visit, although only for a day because reservations are required for any visit not arranged through the Welcome Center in Darien. The McIntosh County Welcome Center operates tours on Wednesdays and Saturdays, September through May and on Fridays, June through August. Contact the Welcome Center at (912) 437–6684 or stop by the office in Darien (at the bridge on US-17).

Lodging may be arranged with several bed and breakfasts operated by residents of Hog Hammock. Phone numbers may be obtained through the McIntosh County Welcome Center and from the internet. Group camping is available on Cabretta Island by contacting the Georgia Department of Natural Resources at (912) 485–2251.

If you stay in Hog Hammock remember that you are a guest in a close-knit community and, though the islanders depend on tourists for income, they have private lives and private property. Accommodations are comfortable but simple and you will have to take food for breakfast and lunch, but you will have miles of beach and dirt roads all to yourself.

Hog Hammock is an African-American community where land has been passed from generation to generation since the coastal islands were given to the freed slaves by Gen-

Ruins of Chocolate on Sapelo Island

eral Sherman. The inhabitants of Sapelo were relocated here from around the island when their land was bought by R. J. Reynolds.

Shell Ring. Most shell mounds were probably kitchen middens that eventually also served the purpose as a lookout spot, being slightly higher than the surrounding flat, low land. The Sapelo Shell Ring, however, is open in the middle, indicating that it was a ceremonial site or possibly a fortress against attack.

Chocolate. These tabby ruins are what remains of a plantation mansion, barns, and a sugar house. Thought by some to be a corruption of *chatelet*, the name appears as Chocolate on deeds from 1797, so it must have been an intentional name given by an early owner. In 1789 a group of French investors, escaping the revolution at home, bought Sapelo Island and incorporated the Sapelo Company. They raised cattle, corn, and cotton. In 1793 the company dissolved and Christophe Poulain Dubignon used the proceeds from his shares to purchase Jekyll Island. His son became a prominent Georgian and member of the legislature. The Chocolate tract on Sapelo was bought by Edward Swarbreck who built the buildings.

UGA-Marine Research Institute. There is a small nature museum at the Marine Institute that demonstrates the dynamics of a salt marsh estuary and has numerous marine animals on display. The University of Georgia Marine Institute performs research in the Sapelo National Estuarine Sanctuary. There are hiking trails from the Institute that lead to Nanny Goat Beach and Sapelo Lighthouse.

34. Presbyterian Meeting House. The first Presbyterian meeting house for the Scottish settlers of Darien was located off US-17 between Eulonia and Darien (the building no longer exists).

35. Ridgeville is a beautiful residential community first settled by local planters seeking relief from heat and mosquitoes. In Ridgeville live oaks have the right of way as the road winds around their massive trunks.

36. Darien. General James Oglethorpe sent Captain Hugh Mackay and Captain George Dunbar to Scotland in 1735 to find settlers for the Altamaha River to form a first line of defense against Spanish incursions from the south. John McIntosh Mohr lead McDonalds, Mackays, Morrisons, Dunbars, Baillies, Cuthberts, and Sutherlands to the infant Georgia colony. In Scotland they had become disenfranchised for supporting the Jacobean Uprising. England passed punitive laws forbidding them to hold office, serve as military officers, or occupy important jobs. Scots were even forbidden to wear kilts and play golf until those privileges were restored for their service to

Lachlan McIntosh

Lachlan McIntosh was eight years old when his family came to Georgia from Scotland. The family, being Highlanders, were very closely bound. When the youngest child, Lewis, was killed by an alligator while swimming in the Altamaha River the other children drew closer together and remained a tightly knit family and business unit well into the nineteenth century. John Mohr, Lachlan's father, was captured during the attack on Saint Augustine and imprisoned in Spain. During that time Lachlan, then thirteen, and his young sister, Anne, were sent to Reverend Whitefield's orphanage at Bethesda while their mother and the other children sought refuge at Fort Palachacola on the Savannah River.

Upon leaving Bethesda, Lachlan spent a brief period in the military at Frederica and a few years helping the family. During the hard times in Georgia, he moved to Charleston where he worked for the next eight years. He entered Charleston society, met and married Sarah Threadcraft and made many acquaintances that would benefit him throughout his life. Henry Laurens became his mentor and closest friend outside the McIntosh family. That friendship gave Lachlan access to credit and advice that helped him build one of the largest rice plantations on the Georgia coast. His most important property was General's Island, in the Altamaha River at Darien. He also became agent and overseer for Laurens' plantations on Broughton Island.

During the Revolution Lachlan McIntosh, his relatives, and associates were the voices of conservatism in the patriot movement. This is an ironic turn of events that the Scots were the reasonable and cautious party while the Midway patriots,

General Lachlan McIntosh. Courtesy of Hargrett Rare Book & Manuscript Library/ University of Georgia Libraries

descendents of sober Puritans, were the impatient and impulsive Hotheads. The tension between conservative and radical Whigs lead to the famous duel between Lachlan McIntosh and Button Gwinnett, resulting in the death of Gwinnett. McIntosh was transferred to the northern theater of the war and spent the winter with Washington at Valley Forge. When he returned to Georgia he was at the siege of Savannah and was captured at the fall of Charleston. He was exchanged in early 1782.

The war left McIntosh financially strapped and he slowly fell deeper and deeper into debt. He lived his last years in Savannah and held the post of naval officer for the port of Savannah. He died in Savannah on February 20, 1806, and is buried with his wife in Colonial Cemetery. Much of Lachlan McIntosh's correspondence is preserved at the University of Georgia Library and the Georgia Historical Society.

King George III during the Revolution.

Idle and restless Highlanders willingly sailed for Georgia and proved to be the most resilient, resourceful, and dependable of the groups who settled in Georgia. Indeed very few Highland Scots died upon reaching Georgia, whereas the mortality among German and English colonists could be twenty to forty percent during the first year of seasoning. It could be that the harsh living conditions in the Scottish Highlands had sorted out the weak from the strong prior to emigration. The Earl of Egmont remarked that the Darien Scots had the good sense to plant their crops first and then build houses whereas the people of Savannah did the reverse and suffered for it. The Highlanders were also great timber cutters.

In early 1736 Oglethorpe settled the Highland families on the first high bluff on the north side of the Altamaha River. The new town was modeled on the Savannah plan and named Darien in honor of the failed Scottish colony on the Isthmus of Panama (still remembered in the name of the eastern most province of Panama). That Central American colony was the idea of William Paterson, founder of the Bank of England, and financed by him. He lost his fortune in the venture but was later reimbursed by the government.

Oglethorpe refused the cot and tent that

were prepared for him during the settling of Darien, choosing instead to sleep with the Highlanders on the ground wrapped in plaid against the winter cold. This act of solidarity and subsequent attentions endeared the governor to the Darien settlers.

Fort Darien was built on the site of the present day McIntosh County Visitor Center at the bridge on US-17. Many men were killed or taken prisoner during Oglethorpe's siege of Saint Augustine in 1740. Darien was left weakened and fearful of an imminent Spanish attack and the town was deserted as families sought safety closer to Savannah. After the Spanish army was turned back at Bloody Marsh the people returned to Darien but the close knit community was forever changed as families began to live on independent plantations.

It is ironic that in 1782 Georgia banned Scots from entering the state. The Scots who immigrated immediately preceding the Revolution were predominantly Lowland Scots who tended to be devoted to a monarchy, due to their vested interest in the exiled James III and service in the British Army. Other Scots had little love for England, as was the case with the independent-minded, disenfranchised Highlanders and the Ulster Scots.

There is a commemorative marker at the McIntosh County Court House honoring the contributions of the Highland Scots to the success of the young Georgia Colony.

Old Tabby Ruins, c. 1810–1830, are the remains of riverfront warehouses and stores. Located on the river at the US-17 bridge.

Oglethorpe Oak. This stump is the remains of the live oak that sheltered General Oglethorpe's tent. He endeared himself to the Highlanders by refusing his bed and sleeping on the ground amongst the people and wrapped in the plaid.

Highlander Monument. Erected in 1936 to honor the 155 Scottish Highlanders who founded Darien in January 1736 and aided in the defense of Georgia. Several hundred descendants of the original settlers still reside in McIntosh County.

St. Andrew's Cemetery. Original Spalding family cemetery.

Fort King George. At Fort King George State Historic Site visitors can see the panorama of five centuries of coastal history. The reconstructed blockhouse of Fort King George (1721) offers a bird's-eye view of the marsh and Lower Bluff Creek, once the North Branch of the Altamaha but since diminished in size. This low bluff overlooking the Altamaha River delta is also the site of a pre-colonial Indian village, the Spanish mission Santo Domingo de Talaje, a British military cemetery (1721–1727), ruins of a nineteenth century sawpit, and a twentieth-century steam powered sawmill—a span of 500 years. The site of the Span-

Early nineteenth century tabby warehouse ruins, Darien

ish mission Santo Domingo de Talaje was located on the grounds of the visitor center.

Colonel John Barnwell convinced the Board of Trade in London to build a fort on the Altamaha River to protect the southernmost settlements of South Carolina from Spanish harassment and French incursions on the Indian trade. The fort was garrisoned with his Majesty's 41st Independent Company, known as the Invalid Regiment because its members were older veterans. Many died of disease or from encounters with Indians and the survivors suffered greatly from loneliness, boredom, and drunkenness. In 1727 the soldiers were called to Port Royal.

The reconstructed fort compound will eventually contain outbuildings including barracks, hospital, kitchen, and a replica of a coastal supply boat.

Located on Fort King George Street one mile east of the McIntosh County Visitor Center. Open Tuesday through Saturday from 9 a.m.–5 p.m. and on Sunday from 2–5:30 p.m. Closed on Mondays, Thanksgiving, Christmas, and New Year's Day.

37. Lachlan McIntosh lived north of Darien on Cathead Creek. It is obvious from William Bartram's writing and letters that he held Lachlan in high regard and was always welcomed among the McIntosh family. During the late summer and fall of 1773 and most of 1776, when William noted simply that he spent the season in the low country between Carolina and East Florida, he undoubtedly spent many of those days at the McIntosh home.

John McIntosh (1757–1792) was the youngest son of Lachlan and Sarah McIntosh. He traveled with William Bartram in the summer of 1773 to Augusta and the New Purchase. He managed his family's rice plantations after the Revolution.

38. Fanny Kemble spent a year on Butler Island, one of her husband's rice and cotton plantations, and at Hampton (Butler Point) on Saint Simons Island. She wrote of her experience in *A Journal of a Residence on a Georgia Plantation in 1838–1839*. Kemble was a popular British actress who married Pierce Mease Butler when she toured America. Butler inherited plantations in Georgia from his grandfather, Major Pierce Butler. Fanny accompanied her husband when he came south to check on his property and put his business in order. Her candid accounts of the antebellum South and life on a slave plantation are notable in that she was thrust into this world without prior knowledge or preparation for its extreme contrast to her native England.

Unlike many of the professional travelers of that period, Kemble lived among the white planters and their slaves for an extended period of time and was able to write an inside view of the world of a large plantation and personal accounts of the local gentry, many of whom are prominent in Georgia history. She found little to like about the plantation system and the people who lived in and around Darien although she loved walking in the fields and boating on the Altamaha. She wrote beautiful descriptions of her outings and the natural surroundings of the Butler plantation. The overseer of the Butler plantations was Roswell King, who earned no kind words from Fanny. King moved to the newly ceded Cherokee Nation in the 1830s and founded Roswell, Georgia.

Site of Fort Barrington on the Altamaha River

Fanny and Pierce were divorced in 1849, due in part to their differences on the issue of owning slaves; she lost custody of her children and returned to England. Her journal was not published until 1863 when she became appalled that England supported the Confederacy for economic reasons and ignored the issue of slavery.

39. Ansley-Hodges Memorial Marsh Project is located within the Altamaha Wildlife Management Area. This project includes an observation tower overlooking a converted ricefield that is home to seventeen species of resident ducks. Located west of US-17 on Champney Island.

40. Champney River Park has a boat ramp, fishing pier, and restrooms. East side of US-17 on Champney Island.

41. General's Cut. A legend of many years standing had General James Oglethorpe chopping this shortcut through General's Island with his sword in a single day. The canal was dug during Oglethorpe's residence in Georgia to facilitate communication between Frederica and Darien. The cut is probably named for General's Island, which in turn is named for General Lachlan McIntosh who owned it for many years.

42. Broughton Island was one of Henry Laurens' Georgia plantations. William Bartram sailed to Broughton Island when he departed Florida in November 1774. Laurens was a friend of Dr. Fothergill and graciously agreed to take William Bartram's botanical collection onboard one of his ships bound for England with a shipment of rice. William then sailed with Laurens to Sunbury.

43. Altamaha River. Called the Amazon of the Southeast, the Altamaha River discharges the second greatest amount of water into the Atlantic—second only to the Chesapeake. Its many miles of cypress and gum floodplain add to the effect of a wide and mysterious river. It was once thought that name of the Altamaha River was derived from the ancient province of Tama, which was visited by De Soto and was believed to have been located in the forks of the Ocmulgee and Oconee rivers. The name then became Altama, meaning *the way to Tama*. However the Spanish called the river Rio de Talaje and Rio de Isabella. The Altamaha River undoubtedly takes its name from the Yamassee chief and town of the same name that was located on the Oconee River south of Milledgeville during the earliest historical period. The Oconee River was originally called Altamaha.

The Altamaha River Bioreserve is a conservation easement made by agreement with Georgia Pacific, International Paper, The Nature Conservancy, and the State of Georgia. It contains 1,300 acres of land and protects a thirty-five-mile scenic greenway along the river. There are 125 rare or endangered plants and animals that are found along this section of the river. There are eleven species of mussels found in the river, seven of which are found nowhere else. The short-nosed sturgeon and swallow-tailed kite are now protected by the greenway buffer.

In part I, chapter V, of the *Travels*, Bartram made a trip up the Altamaha River through …

> *Magnolian groves, from whose tops the surrounding expanse is perfumed, by clouds of incense, blended with the exhaling balm of the Liquid-amber, and odours continually arising from circumambient aromatic groves of Illicium, Myrica, Laurus, and Bignonia.*[1]

44. Wolf Island National Wildlife Refuge and Wilderness Area includes Wolf Island, Egg Island, and Little Egg Island. This area is tidal salt marsh and low dunes. Only about 135 acres of the 5,000 acres is high ground. Wolf Island NWR is an important nesting area for terns and other marine birds and is closed to human activity.

45. Lewis Island State Natural Area. Lewis Island contains one of the largest remaining virgin cypress stands in the Southeast and is home to a grove of thousand-year old trees. Although the area is underwater for part of the year, a hiking trail is maintained by the Department of Natural Resources that may be found during the dry summer months. Access to Lewis Island is by boat and the trail is located one-fourth mile southeast of the intersection of Studhorse Creek and Pico Creek.

46. Cathead Creek Nature Preserve. As a part of their Altamaha River Bioreserve project, the Nature Conservancy of Georgia purchased this tract of land on Cathead Creek.

47. Buffalo Swamp Natural Heritage Preserve is a property of the Georgia Department of Natural Resources, containing nearly 6,000 acres of bottomland along the Altamaha River. The purchase was made in 1992 as part of the Preservation 2000 program to protect important natural areas. The tract has been incorporated into the Altamaha State Waterfowl Management Area.

48. Altamaha State Waterfowl Management Area includes 26,000 acres of marsh, swamp, and bottomland forest. The Altamaha area is the second-largest waterfowl management area east of the Mississippi and is refuge for many species, including alligators and bobcats. The management area includes the historic Altamaha River islands that were the center of rice growing in Georgia. The office and information kiosk are located on US-17 on Butler Island.

1. William Bartram, *Travels through North and South Carolina, Georgia, East and West Florida, the Cherokee Country, the Extensive Territories of the Muscogulges or Creek Confederacy, and the Country of the Chactaws*; Philadelphia, 1791, 47.

49. Barrington Park on Harper Lake. This McIntosh County park is a popular fishing and boating spot on weekends. Overnight camping is allowed, although there are no facilities. Boat ramp and access to the Altamaha River.

50. Discovery of Franklinia and fevertree. Somewhere along Barrington Road near the edge of a sand ridge, John and William Bartram discovered the Franklinia tree on October 1, 1765. It was not in bloom that late in the year so William did not see the flowers until July 1776, when he also would have seen fevertree, *Pinckneya pubens*, in bloom. In Part III, Chapter IX of the *Travels*, Bartram gave his description of the Franklinia and named it for his friend Benjamin Franklin. His voyage up the Altamaha would have occurred on July 31, 1776, since the eclipse of the moon he witnessed can be fixed at that date. Pinckneya, also know locally as fevertree, was named by F. A. Michaux in honor of his friend, Thomas Pinckney.

51. Fort Barrington was built as a defense against Spanish and Indian attack from Florida. It was renamed Fort Howe during the Revolution and was burned by Thomas Brown and his East Florida Rangers on March 13, 1778. Fort Barrington was named for Colonel Joshiah Barrington who owned a plantation at Sansavilla Bluff. He was an English nobleman and a relative of James Oglethorpe. The Barrington Ferry was still in use in the early twentieth century.

52. Gray's Reef National Marine Sanctuary. Gray's Reef is what marine biologists call a live bottom. It is an outcropping of limestone ledges and troughs that support an array of invertebrates, including anemone, coral, and sponges living on the rock. Swimming in and out of these immobile residents are sea cucumbers, urchins, crab, lobsters, shrimp, squids, octopus, and sea snails. With such a variety of animal life it is no wonder that Gray's Reef also attracts loggerhead turtles and over 150 species of fish. In summer months tropical species arrive—queen angelfish, butterflyfish, cocoa damsel, and cardinalfish.

University of Georgia anthropologists have made dives searching for prehistoric human settlements on the Ice-age coast. Divers have found mammoth bones near a drowned river channel at Gray's Reef, a sign that humans were almost certainly hunting in the area.

Gray's Reef is administered by the National Oceanic and Atmospheric Administration for research and education purposes. The reef is a popular fishing spot for bonito, amberjack, snapper, mackerel, and black sea bass. The abundance of marine life and the beauty of the limestone outcrop and reef life make this a favorite diving site.

Itinerary

To Darien

Miles	Directions
	Begin at King's Ferry Park on the Ogeechee River and travel south on US-17
.1	Cross the Ogeechee River
15.5	Left on Martin Road in Midway
1.3	Left on GA-84, Islands Highway
3.5	Right on Colonels Island Road
3.0	Left on Trade Hill Road
.6	Entrance to Seabrook Village
.2	Left on Fort Morris Road
2.0	Entrance to Fort Morris
.5	Sunbury Monument, left on Old Sunbury Road
4.8	Sunbury Road becomes paved
4.7	Left on US-17
2.5	Right on Barrington Ferry Road
4.0	The road becomes dirt after crossing Brier Bay Road
1.0	Entrance to LeConte-Woodmanston
2.9	Left on paved road, Jones Road
8.8	Right on US-17
7.4	Cross Sapelo River
12.5	Darien visitor center and Altamaha River

Fort Barrington

Miles	Directions
	Go back north from downtown Darien and turn left on River Road (GA-251)
4.4	Keep straight on Cox Road
3.4	Keep Left
2.1	Left on Barrington Road (dirt)
3.1	Left to Barrington Park, straight to Fort Barrington Site (private)
	Return to the Cox road and turn left
3.7	Right, keep on the paved road
4.7	Left on GA-57
3.8	Fort Barrington historical marker
10.4	Old Barrington Road historical marker. This was the main overland route to Florida.
3.3	Cross Doctor's Creek
4.0	Left on US-301 and cross the Altamaha River to Jesup

Counties

Bryan, named for Jonathan Bryan, a member of the Governor's Council, patriot, and Georgia's largest landowner.

Liberty, named to honor the patriotic spirit of the citizens of Midway and Sunbury.

McIntosh, named in honor of the McIntosh family who settled Darien.

An Uninhabited Wilderness

The first permanent Spanish settlement in La Florida was established in 1565 when Governor Menéndez drove the French protestants from the St. Johns River and founded Saint Augustine. Spain realized that a presence must be established or lose the territory to rivals. The Spanish approach to occupation was a military and religious presence, relying upon the native population to form their citizenry because Spain had difficulty finding colonists willing to leave their homeland and move to an unknown wilderness. The pacification and conversion of the Atlantic coastal tribes began in earnest with the arrival of the Franciscans in 1573.

The Guale missions were established in an area ranging from Ossabaw Island south to Saint Simons Island. The Guale towns were members of the large Muskhogean linguistic family. The part of Guale stretching from Sapelo Island to Saint Simons and up the Altamaha River was known as the Asao-Talaxe Chiefdom. Between Guale and Saint Augustine was the territory of Mocama, speaking an eastern dialect of the Timucuan language, which included the two principal tribes of Tacatacura and Saturiwa. The principal Mocama missions were San Pedro de Mocama on Cumberland Island, Santa Maria and San Felipe on Amelia Island, and San Juan del Puerto on Saint George Island.

After the founding of Charleston, raids by the Carolinians and their Indian allies forced the Spanish to move the Guale and Mocama missions south of the St. Marys River. By the beginning of the eighteenth century there were no missions north of the St. Johns River nor any Indian towns between there and the Savannah River. This abandoned area became a buffer zone between the Spanish and Carolinians, but with the founding of Georgia in 1733 the English steadily and repeatedly encroached upon the region.

In a treaty with Spain in 1670 the English were allowed lands they already occupied north of Port Royal, and territory south of there was to be Spanish land. The English began to appropriate Spanish territory, first by building Fort King George, then by creating the colony of Georgia on land between the Savannah and Altamaha rivers. James Oglethorpe tried to extend the claim to the St. Johns River with an invasion of Florida in 1740 and the construction of forts on Cumberland and Fort George islands. When the attack on Saint Augustine failed, Oglethorpe had to content himself with remaining at the Altamaha River. Frederica was founded on Saint Simons Island, with one toe over the line, as a guard against attack from the south. Fort Frederica was one of the largest and most expensive forts built by the British in North

Okefenokee Swamp

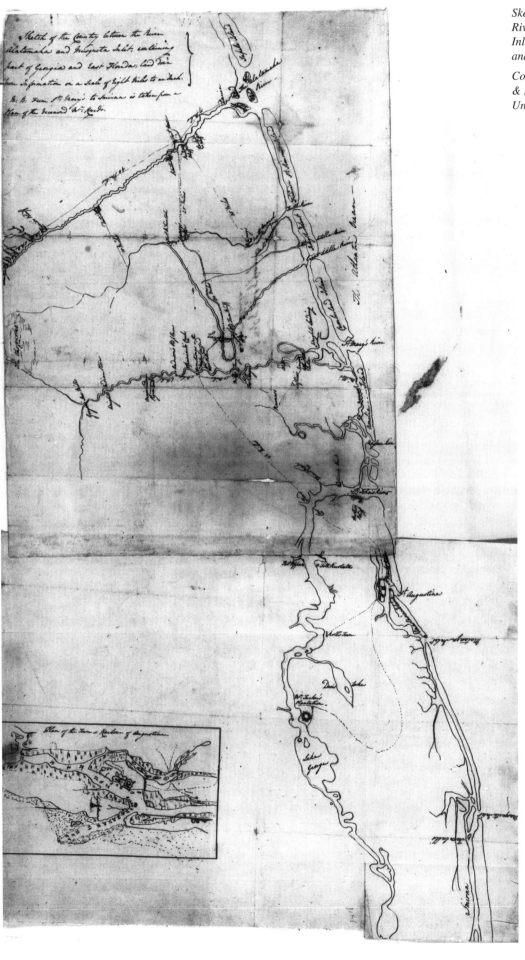

Sketch of the country between the River Altamaha and Musqueta Inlet, containing part of Georgia and East Florida

Courtesy of Hargrett Rare Book & Manuscript Library/ University of Georgia Libraries

America due to its position as guardian of the southern gate. The town flourished while Oglethorpe governed the colony and the fort was garrisoned. When Oglethorpe returned to England in 1743 and the garrison was disbanded, Frederica lost its reason for existence and much of its livelihood. The town declined rapidly in the following years.

After the humiliating defeat at the Battle of Bloody Marsh in 1742, Spain did not pursue her claim to this contested land between the Altamaha and St. Marys rivers. England and Spain entered a period of relative peace that lasted almost seventeen years. In order to maintain the peace, England tried to keep this land as a buffer zone and forbade settlement south of the Altamaha, a policy that was violated repeatedly. New Hanover was an illegal settlement on the Satilla River thirty miles from its mouth, settled by political outcasts and adventurers lead by Edmund Gray and Ephraim Alexander. They operated a store at the settlement and attracted a number of questionable characters, known as Gray's Gang, who operated outside the law. Governor Reynolds examined the region in 1755 and reported that settlers were ascending the Satilla River by the boatload. In 1756 a Spanish delegation was sent into the area, carrying orders for the settlers to remove from the territory.

When Henry Ellis became governor of Georgia he discovered that Saint Augustine was attempting to attract the business of New Hanover to the St. Johns River, which would give Spain stronger influence and claim to this disputed territory. In response Ellis issued a trading license to Ephraim Alexander and allowed the removal of the store to a site near present-day St. Marys. England feared not only that Spain might be offended by this settlement of English-speaking people but that the Creeks might be continually stirred up by these ungoverned frontiersmen. Ellis was reprimanded by the Board of Trade for violating the neutrality of the Altamaha-St. Johns region. Commissioners were sent to disband the settlements and order the inhabitants to leave. They made a pretense of disbanding then returned once the authorities were gone. Elsewhere in the Southeast the Creek Nation was an effective wedge between the Spanish and English in the east and the French and English in the west.

At the conclusion of the French and Indian War Spain and France lost all their land east of the Mississippi River and land grants were made in these new British lands. Before the Treaty of Paris was ratified South Carolina made land grants south of the Altamaha River claiming it as a part of the original Carolina grant. Georgia governor James Wright protested and was supported by London. Georgia then began granting land and settlers began to move legally into the trans-Altamaha region. Rice plantations were established on the Satilla River and Sea Island cotton was grown on island plantations.

After fighting the costly French and Indian War, England sought to prevent further conflict between the Native Americans and British colonists. The Royal Proclamation of 1763 established the boundaries between Indian nations and the area reserved for colonial settlement. The northern boundary of East Florida was set at the St. Marys River. The Indian Boundary Line ran from the Altamaha River just east of Jesup and Doctortown to the St. Marys River at Folkston. South Georgia finally had a fixed boundary and was organized into Saint David's, Saint Patrick's, Saint Thomas,' and Saint Mary's Parishes. In 1777 the first two parishes became Glynn County and the second two parishes became Camden County.

This section of Georgia was officially added to the colony in 1763 and was at the time still thinly settled. Governor Wright's brother, Jermyn, was one of the largest landowners with a home at Scrubby Bluff. Colerain became an important crossing place of the St. Marys River when the new Indian boundary was surveyed. Trader's Hill became an important commercial center at the head of navigation on the St. Marys River which lead to the decline of Colerain.

According to the original agreement between South Carolina and the Trustees of Georgia, the Trustees were allowed the land between the Savannah and Altamaha rivers. South Carolina therefore still claimed all land between the Altamaha and the St. Marys rivers. The issue was settled at the Beaufort Conference in 1787 when South Carolina gave up this claim and in return Georgia gave up claim to what is now Oconee County, South Carolina.

William Bartram's Travels in South Georgia

William Bartram's description of his travels south of the Altamaha River is a composite of several trips. The trip to Brunswick was in April 1773 but the trip to the St. Marys River was most likely made in the summer of 1776.[1] On the first visit south of the Altamaha Bartram visited Colonel Henry Laurens' plantation. Laurens acquired Broughton Island and New Hope Plantation in 1763 and had well-established rice plantations.

The King's Road to Saint Augustine crossed the Altamaha River just downstream of Fort Barrington. In later times the ferry crossed at the site of Fort Barrington. The site of the fort is on private property north of the old road. Part of the site has been eroded by the river. The road then turned slightly north upon landing on the opposite shore and followed the present Howard Road through Sansavilla Wildlife Management Area. This road became the Old Post Road, forming the county line between Brantley and Glynn Counties. One evening Bartram stopped at a cowpen, probably Carney's Cowpen, which was shown on old maps as lying at the head waters of the North Branch of Turtle River.

South of US-82 much of the old Saint Augustine Road (Old Post Road) is now unpaved and follows the sand ridge east of the upper Satilla River. Francis Harper makes the case for Bartram's route as crossing at Owen's Ferry on the Satilla and King's Ferry on the St. Marys River. A map titled *A Sketch of the Country between the River Altamaha to Musqueta Inlet*, located at the Hargrett Library, indicates that the King's Road crossed the St. Marys River farther upstream near present-day Folkston. James Ward extensively researched the King's Road through Florida and determined that it did indeed cross at Camp Pinckney and White Sand Landing, just a mile east of Folkston.[2]

---

1. *Travels in Georgia and Florida, 1773–74: A Report to Dr. John Fothergill*, by William Bartram. Annotated by Francis Harper. Philadelphia: The American Philosophical Society, 1943.
2. In an article for the *Time-Union and Journal* of Jacksonville, dated October 7, 1973, Ward described in detail the history of the King's Road, its present location, and its importance in the settlement of East Florida.

But, John and William Bartram traveled to East Florida in 1765, a year before the King's Road was begun. Indeed, most of the road was not completed until the 1770s. Because William had a penchant for retracing familiar roads, he undoubtedly followed the same route from Owen's Ferry to King's Ferry that he and his father had traveled previously. When Britain gained possession of Florida a store was established at Mill's Ferry, later known as King's Ferry, and it was this store that William Bartram visited in the *Travels*. Fort Tonyn was built just downriver from the store.

In March 1774 William Bartram visited James Spalding at Frederica. In April Bartram embarked on his much-anticipated trip to Florida. He traveled the Intracoastal Waterway from Saint Simons Island to Fort William on Cumberland Island. His baggage was sent forward while he waited for the recent Seminole uprising to subside. Fort William was located on the south end of Cumberland Island in the vicinity of the Dungeness ruins.

William Bartram landed on the north end of Amelia Island in early April 1774 near where Fort Clinch now stands. He traveled south, crossing Egan's Creek and passing through Old Fernandina to Lord Egmont's plantation where modern Fernandina is now located. Bartram was entertained by Egmont's agent, Stephen Egan, who rode with him around the island, viewing the plantation and shell mounds. They sailed from Amelia Island through Kingsley Creek (Amelia Narrows) and probably down South Amelia River to Nassau Sound (Fort George Sound) and camped on the north end of Big Talbot Island. They followed Sawpit and Sister Creeks to the St. John's River and then on to present-day Arlington.

Bartram noted the inland passage that lies between the islands and mainland and extending along the Atlantic and Gulf coasts, a protected navigational route that is now the Intracoastal Waterway. In November 1774 William Bartram again passed through the inland passage as he returned from East Florida. He stopped at Frederica and called upon James Spalding. He then joined Henry Laurens at Broughton Island and arranged for his collections to be shipped to Dr. Fothergill.

In 1776 Bartram spent the greater part of the year in Darien and on the Georgia coast. He was possibly acting as a spy for

View of the Altamaha River from Lower Sansavilla Bluff

Colonel Lachlan McIntosh during part of the time. Fort Tonyn was located a little east of present-day King's Ferry and it may be that Bartram's excursion to the St. Marys River was for the purpose of gaining intelligence about British preparations. During this trip he encountered the intrepid Seminole. After his frightful encounter with the Seminole he continued on to the St. Marys River and crossed at King's Ferry. Bartram described the dwarf pawpaw (his *Annona*) and lady lupine (*Lupinus villosus*) on these trips south of the Altamaha.

According to George Ord in his *Biographical Sketch of William Bartram* (1832) Bartram was offered a lieutenancy but declined because the purpose of the military operation, an invasion from Florida, did not materialize. Francis Harper, in the *Naturalist's Edition of Bartram's Travels*, speculated that Bartram was without his gun at the St. Marys River because he wanted to emphasize the peaceful nature of his ramblings and not draw suspicion to himself, for he was never without his gun otherwise. A letter from William Bartram to Secretary of War Henry Knox reveals that Bartram was indeed present during a battle at the St. Marys River on May 29, 1776 when Continentals and Georgia militia attempted to disperse the Florida loyalists.

Sites

1. Sansavilla Wildlife Management Area includes historic Aleck Island and Upper and Lower Sansavilla Bluffs. The Bluffs extend three miles along the Altamaha River from Aleck Island to Alecks Creek. Lower Sansavilla Bluff offers a breathtaking view of the Altamaha River. The old Savannah to Saint Augustine Road crossed from Harper Lake just below Fort Barrington, turned north on the west side of the river, then followed the present-day Howard Road. One can still follow an old path into the swamp where Howard Road ends and the old road descends to the bottomland.

Sansavilla is a corruption of Santa Isabel, the Spanish name for the Altamaha River and the name of a mission that was located in the area. Mary Musgrove, interpreter for James Oglethorpe, had a trading post here. Aleck Island is named for Captain Aleck, a Creek Indian who lived among Georgians and was instrumental in maintaining good relations between the two people during the mid-eighteenth century. He established his home near Sansavilla when the 1763 boundary of Georgia was moved westward to the mouth of Penholloway Swamp.

Sansavilla WMA is nearly 20,000 acres, half planted pine and half hardwood bottomland. The land is owned by Brunswick Pulp and Paper. There is an information kiosk near the entrance at Mt. Pleasant.

From US-341 north, after crossing the railroad tracks turn right for Lower Sansavilla or turn left to Upper Sansavilla. There is a boat ramp and picnic area at the upper bluff.

2. Brunswick Pulp and Paper, Tyler WMA. The old Savannah to Saint Augustine Road passed through the southeastern portion of this property now owned by Brunswick Pulp and Paper. Access is from a dirt road on the north side of the Old Post Road.

Brunswick Pulp and Paper, Harrington WMA. This tract lies on the Old Post Road.

3. Altamaha Park is a Glynn County park with boat ramp, store, and picnic area. There are weekend cottages and mobile homes owned by locals. The ruins of the infamous river houses, outlawed by the Georgia legislature

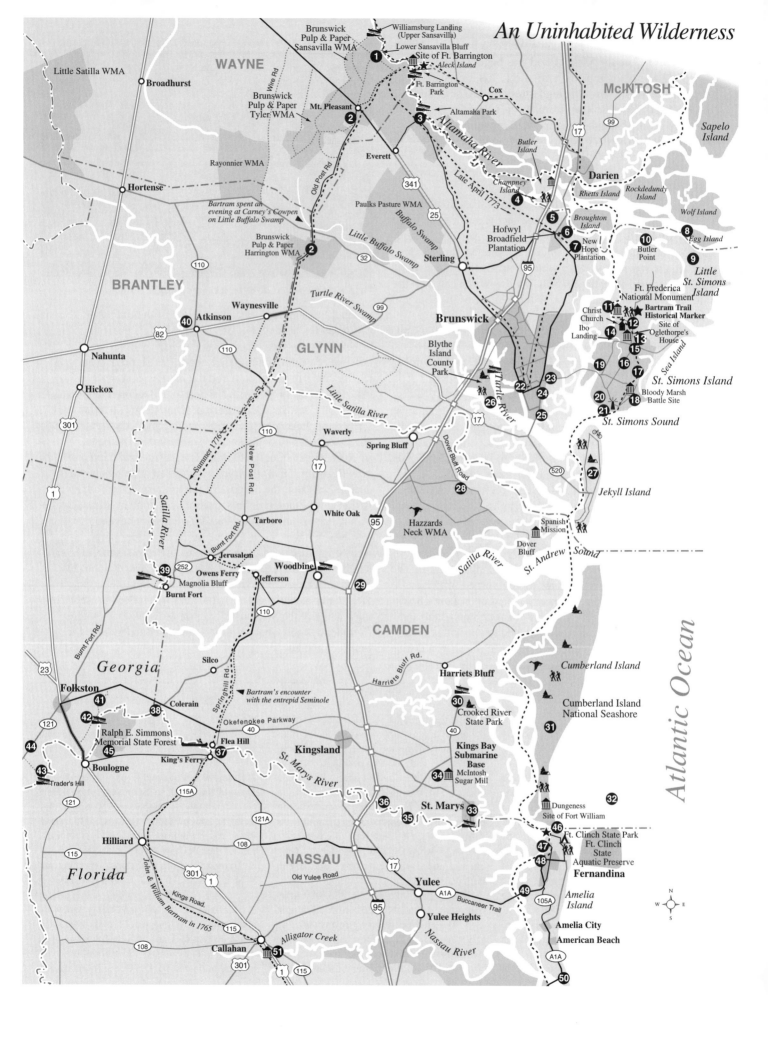

and abandoned, were still visible in recent years.

4. Hopeton was possibly the most famous plantation of the Altamaha River rice empire. It was begun by John Couper and James Hamilton and became the estate of James Hamilton Couper. The elder Couper was mentioned often in Fanny Kemble's book because she found him to be the most interesting and pleasant of her acquaintances in Georgia. The younger Couper was a pioneer in cottonseed oil extraction and sugar production from ribbon cane. He was a scientific farmer and his plantation attracted agriculturalists from around the South. Sir Charles Lyell visited Couper during his southern travels in 1845. Couper was involved in the organization of the Brunswick Canal and discovered the bones of extinct mammals during the excavation, including giant sloth, mastodon, American horse, and elephant. He was a naturalist and supplied fossils and freshwater mussels from the Altamaha region to the museums in Philadelphia and London.

5. Life in the Wild Park. Jim Fowler, the well-known television personality and native son, is creating a 1,800-acre wildlife park. The park will be divided in two sections. One tract east of I-95 will preserve natural habitat and feature native animals and plants. Another section west of I-95 will feature exotic animals. Fowler also plans to create cultural and historical exhibits around the Native Americans and colonial settlers who lived along the Altamaha River. Because this park lies astride one of William Bartram's routes, it is fitting that it will feature fauna that once roamed the coastal area, such as bison, wolves, and panthers.

6. Hofwyl-Broadfield Plantation was the last operating rice plantation on the Georgia coast, changing to a dairy operation in 1915. In 1773 Broadface Plantation was owned by Lachlan McIntosh. William Brailsford bought the property in 1806 and renamed it Broadfield. One of the modern owners, James Dent, demonstrated that malaria was transmitted by mosquito rather than by miasma rising from the stagnant waters. He had read of experiments in Italy pointing to the mosquito as vector, so in 1903 he screened the windows of his home and remained the entire summer season in safety. This made a deep impression on concerned friends and neighbors because most people of means moved to summer homes near the beaches or in upland pine forests during hot weather.

The Dent family descendants gave the land to the state in 1973 to preserve the cultural history of one of Georgia's longest continually operated plantations. A nature trail passes through old pastures to a boardwalk built into the old rice fields. Located on US-17 south of the Altamaha River. Open 9 a.m.–5 p.m., Tues-

The Rice Plantations

Rice fields are flooded several times during the growing season to help control weeds. The early rice plantations, during the first half of the eighteenth century, were built on inland creeks and used impounded water to flood the fields. An example of this type of rice field may be seen at LeConte-Woodmanston Plantation. During the 1750s the technology using tidal energy to flood rice fields was perfected and plantations were established on the Ogeechee and Savannah rivers and on the Altamaha River islands.

It was well known that sickness lurked in the rice fields for whites during summer. For that reason planters and their families withdrew to high, inland summer homes or moved to the islands. April 1 was moving day and families returned with the frost. When the owner or his overseer had to visit fields during the summer they always made sure to be away from the fields by dark. The malaria carrying Anopheles mosquito avoids the heat of the day and is more active at dusk and twilight and in the shade of the forests.

Legend

1. Sansavilla WMA
2. Tyler WMA
3. Altamaha Park
4. Hopeton
5. Life in the Wild Park
6. Hofwyl-Broadfield Plantation
7. New Hope Plantation
8. Egg Island
9. Little Saint Simons Island
10. Hamilton, Butler Point
11. Fort Frederica National Monument
12. Oglethorpe's House
13. Christ Church
    Wesley Woodland Walk
14. Ebo Landing
15. Harrington
16. Sea Island Cotton
17. Military Road
18. Bloody Marsh Battle Site
19. Gascoigne Bluff
20. Retreat Plantation
21. Saint Simons Island
    The Sea Island Festival
    Museum of Coastal History
22. Brunswick
23. Golden Isles Visitor Center
24. Overlook Park
25. Georgia Department of Natural Resources
    Coastal Regional Headquarters
    Earth Day Nature Trail
26. Blythe Island Regional Park
27. Jekyll Island
    Welcome Center
    Clam Creek Picnic Area and Bicycle Trail
    Millionaire's Village
    South Dunes Picnic Area
    Saint Andrew Picnic Area
28. Hazzards Neck WMA
29. Satilla River
30. Crooked River State Park
31. Cumberland Island National Seashore
32. Right whales
33. St. Marys
    Cumberland Island National Seashore Museum
34. McIntosh Sugar Mill
35. St. Marys River
36. Wright's Fort
37. King's Ferry
    Fort Tonyn
38. Colerain
39. Burnt Fort
    Magnolia Bluff
40. Fort McIntosh
41. Camp Pinckney Park
42. White Sand Landing
43. Trader's Hill
44. Okefenokee Swamp
    Suwannee Canal National Recreation Area
    Stephen Foster State Park
    Laura S. Walker State Park
    Obediah's Okefenok
45. Ralph E. Simmons Memorial State Forest
46. Fort Clinch State Park
47. Old Fernandina
48. Historic Downtown Fernandina
49. Amelia Island
50. Amelia Island State Recreation Area
51. Battle of Alligator Creek Bridge

An Uninhabited Wilderness

Ruins of the barracks and magazine at Fort Frederica, Saint Simons Island

day through Saturday and 2–5:30 p.m. on Sunday, closed on Mondays, Thanksgiving, Christmas, and New Year's Day. Admission.

7. New Hope Plantation was established in 1763 by Henry Laurens. Laurens, like many patriots, used his own money to finance his public office then lost much of his property during the British occupation. He put his Broughton Island and New Hope properties up for sale in 1787; but they did not sell, so the properties went to his heirs who sold them in the nineteenth century.

8. Egg Island receives its name from the large number of nests found on the island. It is a rookery for numerous species of marine and shore birds.

9. Little Saint Simons Island was one of the Butler Sea Island Cotton Plantations although there were no structures on the island. The hands traveled to and from Butler's Point by boat to work the fields. Little Saint Simons Island is now privately owned and encompasses nearly 10,000 acres of barrier island with very little development. The present owners keep the island in its natural state and it has become a favorite birding site. They operate a resort that emphasize the natural history of the barrier islands.

10. Hamilton, at Butler Point, was one of the Butler Plantations described by Fanny Kemble in *Journal of a Residence on a Georgia Plantation in 1838–1839*. The Plantation was established by Pierce Butler, an Irish officer who came to America with the British army. He resigned his office and married into the powerful Middleton family of Charleston. He served in Congress during the Constitutional Convention and was senator from South Carolina several terms. He established three plantations in Georgia on the Altamaha River and was the strictest and most efficient planter in the region. His slaves were isolated whereas other owners allowed their slaves to visit outlying plantations and attend church service. Butler's wealth and connections brought such visitors as Sir Charles Lyell and Aaron Burr. His property went to his nephew, who took the name of his uncle as a condition of inheritance.

11. Fort Frederica National Monument. The town of Frederica was built in 1736 at the site of an old Indian field on Saint Simons Island and was named for the Frederick Lewis, Prince of Wales, son of George II and father of George III. The finer homes of Frederica were built of brick in the style of Georgian England. The town of Frederica flourished during the years that James Oglethorpe lived in Georgia and the British regiment was stationed there. At its peak the town reached a population of 500 and had a lively trade. When William Bartram visited James Spalding Frederica had been abandoned, save for the Spaldings. Bartram was wrong in saying that Frederica was the first town built by the English in Georgia. Fort Frederica commanded a bend in the Frederica River where a ship sailing up the river had to expose her sides to British guns. Frederica is located at the end of Federica Road on Saint Simons Island. Open 8 a.m.–5 p.m. daily.

12. Oglethorpe's House. Just behind Oglethorpe Memorial Gardens on Frederica Road is a historical marker for the site of General James Oglethorpe's house. It was situated just off the military road and was the only dwelling that he owned while he lived in the colony. At the time of William Bartram's visit the property was owned by James Spalding.

13. Christ Church was the third church established in Georgia and was a missionary branch of Christ Church, Savannah. This was Charles Wesley's first assignment as an ordained minister and his trial by fire. He was offended by the crude customs of the military post and in turn was rejected by the soldiers. The present church building was finished in 1879 and its setting beneath the aged and gigantic live oaks is one of the sublime spots on the coast.

Wesley Woodland Walk lies directly across Frederica Road from Christ Church. The trail winds through a wet maritime forest and swamp to a formal garden and memorial to Reverend Charles Wesley, Secretary for Indian Affairs, hymn writer, and leader in the evangelical movement that became Methodism. This is where Wesley walked and prayed during his trying times at Frederica.

14. Ebo Landing, on Dunbar Creek, was a landing point for slave ships and camp where the human cargo was quartered until sold. The Ebo (Igbo) gained a reputation as not being desirable slaves for they would rather die than submit to involuntary servitude. This landing received its name for the members of that tribe who willingly walked into the river and drowned. Dunbar Creek is named for one of Oglethorpe's officers and an early resident of Saint Simons Island. Follow Sea Island Road from Gascoigne Bluff, as it crosses Dunbar Creek look north to see Ebo Landing, now private property.

15. Harrington is a community of African-Americans who have held title to their land since the sea islands were given to them after the Civil War. It is located on the original land grant to Captain Raymond Demere, called Harrington Hall.

16. Sea Island Cotton, *Gossypium Barbadense*, was first grown on Saint Simons Island from seed sent from Anguilla, West Indies. In 1787 Nicholas Turnbull and James Spalding made the first plantings. Spalding's seed was sent by his former partner, Roger Kelsall, lately of Little Exuma and a former loyalist merchant from Sunbury. There had been a cotton boom in the Bahamas but the sandy soils wore out

James Spalding

James Spalding was born in County Perth, Scotland, and was an heir to the barony of Ashantilly. He came to Charleston in the early 1760s with hopes of earning enough money to regain his mortgaged ancestral home. He entered the Indian trade in the newly acquired lands in south Georgia and East Florida. His first partner was Donald Mackay and then in 1768 he formed a business with Roger Kelsall of Beaufort, South Carolina. They established trading houses from Sunbury to the Upper St. Johns River.

Spalding was married to Margery McIntosh, daughter of William McIntosh and niece of Lachlan McIntosh. At one time the Spaldings owned James Oglethorpe's house and made it their temporary home before moving to Retreat Plantation.

James Spalding was opposed to the British regulations that stifled the economy of the colonies but he sought redress as a loyal subject. In 1776 he was labeled a threat to the liberties of the colony due to his lack of patriotic zeal and imprisoned for two weeks. Upon release he moved to East Florida where he spent the remainder of the Revolution as a neutral. He was among the forty-two individuals found guilty of high treason and had his property confiscated in 1778.

When the Floridas were returned to Spain at the end of the Revolution, Spalding petitioned to return to Georgia and have his name stricken from the confiscation list. Because he had not opposed the patriots and was not an active loyalist he was granted permission to return to Georgia. But, he had to accept restrictions on voting and holding office for fourteen years, and he had to pay a twelve percent tax on his property. Two years later he was granted full civil rights and soon became the wealthiest man in Glynn County.

James Spalding was a commissioner for building the courthouse for Glynn County and served as Justice of the Inferior Court of Glynn County. He died in 1794 and is buried in the McIntosh vault in Colonial Cemetery in Savannah. Margery McIntosh Spalding is buried at St. Andrews Cemetery in Darien.

At the time of William Bartram's visit in early April 1774, the Spaldings had a new baby boy named Thomas, born March 25 of that year. Thomas Spalding became the owner Sapelo Island and was a member of the Georgia Assembly. He was a well-respected writer of agricultural treatises and a biographer of James Oglethorpe.

Hooded Pitcher-plant, Sarracenia minor, *is a Bartram discovery that is common in wet areas on the coast of Georgia. Its habitat has been reduced due to fire suppression and the proliferation of pine plantations in this century. In the* Travels *Bartram mistakenly placed it at Pensacola, where it does not grow naturally.*

quickly. Seeds probably reached more than one friend in America from exiled Tories during the 1780s and 90s for there are several stories about first plantings. Sea Island cotton has a long fiber, called staple or lint, and brought premium prices due to its high quality and ease of spinning. Sea Island cotton reached the Southeastern coast just as the new spinning machines in England's textile mills created a hungry demand for fibers. Acreage of Sea Island cotton was limited to the coastal islands of Georgia and South Carolina.

17. Military Road. Fort Frederica and Fort Saint Simons were connected by a military road built by soldiers and citizens of Federica in three days during September 1738. Oglethorpe wisely routed it away from the Frederica River so troop movements could not be observed by ships lying in the river.

18. Bloody Marsh Battle Site. War between Spain and England broke out in 1739. Called the War of Jenkins' Ear, it was as more about the slave trade and English occupation of Spanish claims than it was about Mr. Jenkins' severed ear. Oglethorpe took the war to Florida in early 1740, capturing Fort Picolata, Fort San Francisco de Poppa, and Saint Augustine but failing to take Castillo de San Marcos. He lost favor among the South Carolinians who believed the failure lay entirely with Oglethorpe's leadership.

The inevitable Spanish retaliation came in July 1742, as ships and 2,000 troops from Cuba descended upon the Georgia coast. Oglethorpe, his regiment, Darien Scots, and Indian allies faced the enemy alone because neighboring South Carolina lacked faith in the general's ability to withstand a larger, more organized force. South Carolina hesitated in sending assistance until after Spanish ships had appeared off the coast of Georgia. When the Spanish sailed into Saint Simons Sound the Georgians abandoned Fort Saint Simons, retreated to Frederica, and a dispatch was sent to South Carolina announcing the long-expected invasion was underway.

The Spanish troops landed at Gascoigne Bluff and marched toward Frederica. The ships lay about, unable to ascend the river without exposing their sides to the cannons at Fort Frederica. The Spanish troops were ambushed by British Regulars and Georgia militia within a mile of town and retreated southward to open area. The Americans continued retreating toward Frederica, except the rear guard, which turned back and secreted themselves in the woods. Another body of Spanish soldiers advanced but believed the enemy was in full retreat and had already returned to Fort Frederica. Thinking themselves out of harm's way, the Spanish soldiers stopped at the edge of a marsh to rest and prepare meals. The tenacious Highlanders and Creeks surprised them at their leisure. The ensuing battle completely routed and confused the Spaniards, who were all either killed, wounded, or captured. Hearing the sound of battle Oglethorpe rushed to the scene, arriving when it was over.

By a ruse Oglethorpe got false information into the Spanish fort in the form of a letter to a French deserter who was implicated as a double agent. The letter indicated a large American troop strength, impending aid from South Carolina, and a British attack on Havana. When three ships of the South Carolina navy appeared off the coast the Spanish believed significant reinforcements were indeed on the way and they withdrew to Saint Augustine, half-heartedly firing on Fort William as they passed Cumberland Island.

James Oglethorpe, with only 650 men, had repulsed an army of 2,000 Spaniards with fifty boats. The news of the Spanish repulsion swept through the colonies and all manner of assistance and congratulations were offered. For good measure Oglethorpe invaded Florida in August, marched around Castillo de San Marcos, and along the St. Johns River in a show of impunity. Florida Governor Montiano was recalled and court-martialed.

Gathering sap for turpentine, Ware County, Georgia

The Highlanders were lead by Hugh MacKay and Lieutenant Sutherland, the Yamacraws by Toonahowi (Tomochichi's nephew), and the militia from Savannah was lead by Noble Jones. General Oglethorpe and Captain Raymond Demere commanded the 42nd Regiment of British regulars.

Much has been made of the importance of this battle. Some historians have said that it determined the language of the continent. It is indeed a fact that the Spanish planned to sweep the English from Georgia and possibly South Carolina and with that done they might have continued up the coast, but it seems doubtful that they could have overwhelmed the larger colonies to the north. With this remarkable victory James Oglethorpe did indeed reduce the threat of another Spanish invasion and he vindicated himself among his Carolina neighbors.

19. Gascoigne Bluff was the home of Captain James Gascoigne, the British naval officer who escorted the first Georgia settlers across the Atlantic. Ship repairs were made at the bluff from the earliest days of the colony. There is an open meadow and public garden at Gascoigne Bluff next to Torras Parkway. Coming from Brunswick, turn left on Sea Island Road immediately upon entering Saint Simons Island, cross Demere Road and turn left on Hamilton Road, then left again on Arthur J. Moore Road. The park is at the end of the road.

20. Retreat Plantation was the home of James Spalding, who was a partner with Roger Kelsall of Beaufort in the firm of Kelsall & Spalding. Their trading company owned the stores on the St. Johns River where William Bartram made his headquarters.

Live oak timbers from Retreat plantation were milled and shipped from Gascoigne Bluff for building the USS Constitution.

21. Saint Simons Island is the most developed island on the Georgia coast south of Tybee. Upon arriving on Saint Simons Island, go downtown and purchase a copy of *A Naturalist's Guide to Saint Simons Island* by Taylor Schoettle. This book contains excellent observations on the natural history of salt marshes and the Sea Islands. Visitors can use it to tour St. Simons' unique and accessible natural areas. Schoettle describes how the Sea Islands grow and change from the influence of Georgia's unusually high tide. There are several areas for beach access, including Massingale Park and any street perpendicular to Kings Way and Ocean Boulevard.

Saint Simons Island was possibly called Guadalquini by the original inhabitants, the people of Guale. The Guale town of Talaxe and Mission San Domingo were moved to the north end of Saint Simons Island from its original site at Fort King George when they were devastated by the Chichimeco (Westo) in 1661. The town of Guadalquini, Mission San Buenaventura de Guadalquini, and Mission San Simón were located on the south end of the island, though not all at the same time. The French called Saint Simons Isle de la Loire and the Spanish called it Isla de Guadalquini. James Oglethorpe later built Fort Saint Simons near the present-day lighthouse. In 1736 Oglethorpe built the Ft. Frederica to guard against invasion from the south.

The Sea Island Festival is held the third weekend of each August at Neptune Park in downtown Saint Simons. This African-American cultural festival features the foods and music unique to the Gullah communities of South Carolina and the Geechee of Georgia. Storytelling, singing, and the West African cultural connection are highlights of the weekend. The Georgia Sea Island Singers and the McIntosh Shouters are popular performers. Visitors can purchase sweetgrass baskets, quilts, West African crafts, smoked mullet, stuffed crab, and sweet potato pie.

The Museum of Coastal History is housed in the Saint Simons lighthouse keeper's cottage. From the lighthouse visitors have a rare view of the coast from above the tree line. The Museum contains exhibits of Saint Simons history, a bookstore, and gift shop. Open 10 a.m.–5 p.m., Tuesday through Saturday and 1:30–5 p.m. on Sunday during summer. Closed on Monday and major holidays. Hours are 1–4 p.m. from Labor Day to Memorial Day. Admission.

Neptune Park was the property of Neptune Small, a freedman of the King family who once owned Retreat Plantation. Neptune accompanied two of the King sons to war in the 1860s. He retrieved the body of Henry King when he was killed at Fredericksburg and brought it home to Saint Simons Island. After the war Small was given the land that is now Neptune Park, the Saint Simons Island Visitor Center, and the Saint Simons Library. The Sea Island Festival is held at Neptune Park the third weekend of each August. It is a favorite place to watch shrimp boats, sunrises, and sunsets. Parking is at the end of Mallory Street in the business district.

22. Brunswick. Yes, Brunswick stew is named for Brunswick, Georgia, where it was first

The replica of Endeavour, *Captain Cook's research ship, at anchor in the Turtle River at the Brunswick docks*

served over a hundred years ago. The iron stew pot that cooked the first pot of Brunswick Stew is on display at the Visitors Center. No barbecue is complete without it and there are as many recipes as there are barbecue chefs.

Brunswick was laid out in 1771 on the Savannah plan and the streets still retain their original pre-Revolutionary names. Brunswick is named for Braunsweig, Germany, the ancestral home of King George III and the royal Hanovers. Many streets in the historic district still bear the names of their colonial and British honorees—the Duke of Gloucester, Duke of Richmond, Earl of Halifax, Earl of Egmont, Governors Reynolds and Ellis.

Governor James Wright believed that Brunswick was destined to become the capital someday. The growth of the town was interrupted because many of the early landowners were Tories and fled to England or Florida during the war. Brunswick is the westernmost port on the eastern seaboard, nestled in the curve of the Georgia Bight, and has the nation's largest shrimping fleet.

Mary Ross Waterfront Park is a good place to watch shrimp boats and sunsets. Visiting ships dock here, such as the replica of Captain Cook's *Endeavour* which visited Brunswick in March 1998. Located at the end of Gloucester Street on the waterfront.

23. Golden Isles Visitor Center. Located at the intersection of US-17 and Fernando Torras Causeway, and Exit 8 of I-95.

24. Overlook Park views the extensive salt marshes where Sidney Lanier was inspired to write his poem, the *Marshes of Glynn*. The nearby Lanier Oak is where he supposedly sat as he wrote the poem. The twice daily tide creates a soup of detritus and decaying organic matter that feeds the young shrimp, crabs, and fish. They enjoy the protection of the marsh before maturing and heading to sea. Oyster beds are visible near the park.

25. Georgia Department of Natural Resources Coastal Regional Headquarters. The new building for the DNR Coastal Headquarters has brochures, posters, and information available for people interested in crabbing, shrimping, and fishing. Exhibits on the natural history of the coast are planned for the future. Turn left from US-17 at Sidney Lanier Bridge. Open 8 a.m.–4:30 p.m., Monday through Friday, closed on holidays.

The **Earth Day Nature Trail** is located at the DNR Coastal Regional Headquarters and is a must for anyone interested in learning about the extensive salt marsh surrounding Brunswick. The trail winds through a maritime hammock where blinds allow the hiker to observe herons, egrets, and sanderlins as they hunt for dinner. From the end of the boardwalk, one can walk onto the salt barren, a unique habitat of salty, sandy land that becomes relatively dry at low tide. Here one finds the salt tolerant plants like glasswort, saltwort, and saltgrass living on soil four times more saline than seawater. The trail is open whenever the DNR Coastal Headquarters is open.

26. Blythe Island Regional Park. This county park is located near Brunswick, Jekyll, and Saint Simons islands. There are tent and RV sites, a camp store, laundry, free boat ramp, picnic area, trails, docks, and educational programs. Located on Turtle River, take GA-303 north of US-17. Admission.

27. Jekyll Island was named for Sir Joseph Jekyll, Master of the Rolls, who contributed money to the Trustees for the establishment of Georgia. It was known to the Spanish as Isla de Ballenas, meaning Island of Whales. After the settlement of Georgia a Major Horton made his home at the north end of the island. Much of Jekyll Island became the property of Poulain du Bignon, formerly of the Sapelo Island Syndicate, in the later part of the eighteenth century. The Jekyll Island Club bought the island in 1886 and the State of Georgia bought it in 1947. It is now one of the most popular state parks in Georgia.

Welcome Center. Jekyll Island Causeway.

Clam Creek Picnic Area and Bicycle Trail. Nature walks lead by the Docents of the University of Georgia Marine Extension Service take place on Mondays, except holidays, 9:30 a.m.

Millionaire's Village. In 1886 the Jekyll Island Club, a syndicate of millionaires, bought Jekyll Island and the members built winter homes. These families represented a significant portion of America's wealth of the day. The homes purposefully had no kitchens. Families gathered at the community dining hall to eat meals together which helped foster the social life of the island.

South Dunes Picnic Area. Nature walks led by the Docents of the University of Georgia Marine Extension Service take place on Tuesdays, except holidays, 9:30 a.m.

St. Andrew Picnic Area. Nature walks lead by the Docents of the University of Georgia Marine Extension Service take place on Wednesdays, except holidays, 9:30 a.m.

28. Hazzards Neck WMA. This pine plantation is owned by Georgia DNR and Brunswick Pulp and Paper. Turn left on Dover Bluff Road from US-17, go 5.8 miles to the entrance.

29. The Satilla River was called Rivière Somme by the early French explorer Jean Ribault. We don't know the Spanish name but the sound between Cumberland and Jekyll Island

Colonial Names in Brunswick

Albany Street is named for Edward Hanover, Duke of York and Albany, brother of King George III.

Amherst Street is named for Jeffrey Amherst, commander of British troops in North America.

Dartmouth Street is named for William Legge, Second Earl of Dartmouth, Secretary of State to King George III, and president of the Board of Trade. He was a close friend of John Wesley and Dr. John Fothergill.

Egmont Street is named for John Perceval, Lord Egmont, first president of the Board of Trustees for Georgia.

Ellis Street is named for Henry Ellis, Royal Governor of Georgia and member of the British Royal Society.

George Street is named for George William Frederick Hanover, King George III.

Gloucester is named for William, Duke of Gloucester, brother to King George III.

Halifax Square is named for George Montagu Dunk, Earl of Halifax.

Hanover Square is named for the Royal family and their German ancestral home.

Hillsborough Square is named for Wills Hill, Earl of Hillsborough, British Secretary of State when Brunswick was surveyed.

London Street is named for the city of London.

Newcastle Street is named for Thomas Pelham, Duke of Newcastle, Prime Minister of England.

Prince Street is named for George Augustus Frederick Hanover, Prince of Wales, oldest son of King George III.

Reynolds Street is named for Royal Governor John Reynolds.

Richmond Street is named for the Charles Lennox, Duke of Richmond.

Union Street is named in honor of the union of England and Scotland.

Wolfe Street is named for Major General James Wolfe, who was killed during the Battle of Quebec.

Wright Square is named for Royal Governor James Wright.

James Seagrove

James Seagrove was the first federal agent to the Creek Nation, appointed in 1790. In the fall of 1793 he made a diplomatic trip to Tuckabatchee and succeeded in preventing a war between the Creeks and the United States.

James Seagrove was probably born in Ireland and came to New York before the Revolution where he was involved in a mercantile business and land speculation on the Hudson River. He came to Georgia in 1785 and married Anne Zubly Bard, the daughter of Reverend John Joachim Zubly and widow of Peter Bard. They settled in St. Marys and had a cotton plantation at Point Peter. Seagrove was a member of the state legislature and State Constitutional Convention. His last years were troubled by debts and unsuccessful land speculation. He died in 1812.

was named Barra de Ballenas. The mission period, 1565–1685, the Satilla River was the dividing line between the provinces of Guale to the north and Mocama to the south. The Satilla is Georgia's premier blackwater river and remains remarkably wild. French ships ascended the Satilla and St. Marys rivers to replenish their water stores, the tannic acid in the tea-colored water kept it from spoiling on long ocean voyages. The French also carried on an extensive sassafras trade well into the mission period. Canoe and boat access is on US-82, US-84, US-301, GA-15, US-17 at Woodbine and GA-252 at Burnt Fort. For more information contact Southeast Georgia Regional Development Center, 3395 Harris Road, Waycross, GA 31503.

Satilla River Park, US-17 Bridge on the Satilla River. The old railroad bed in downtown Woodbine has been converted into a beautiful park with access to the river.

Magnolia Bluff, though privately owned, is well known for its forest of large magnolia and beech trees growing on the wet river slope.

30. Crooked River State Park is popular with local communities for its access to Crooked River and saltwater fishing. There is a short nature trail that begins at the campground. Located at the end of GA-40 Spur. Open 7 a.m.–10 p.m. daily.

31. Cumberland Island National Seashore. Cumberland Island was the northernmost part of the Timucuan province that extended into Florida and down the St. Johns River. Cumberland Island was called Isla San Pedro and was the site of the mission San Pedro Puturiba on the north end and San Pedro de Mocama at the south end. The Timucuan name for Cumberland Island may have been either Puturiba or Mocama. Another possible name suggested is Tacatacuru, the name of the cacique.

The story is told that Toonahowi, Tomochichi's nephew, was surveying the coast with Oglethorpe and wanted to change the island's name from San Pedro to Cumberland in honor of his friend, the Duke of Cumberland. The Duke had given Toonahowi a gold watch during his visit to London in 1734. William Han-

over, Duke of Cumberland, was the son of George I and was honored by the English by having the flower Sweet William named for him. He was reviled in Scotland because he defeated Charles Edward Stewart at the Battle of Culloden and broke the Highland Clans. He ordered his army to kill any surviving Clansmen soldiers who could be found. His army then proceeded to pacify the Highlands by killing untold numbers, including women and children, for merely being Scottish. In Scotland a plant called Stinking Willy is named after the Duke of Cumberland.

Oglethorpe had several fortifications constructed on Cumberland Island. Fort William was at the south end and was visited by William Bartram in 1774. With the threat of Spanish invasion removed after 1742 Cumberland Island was settled by planters. In 1786 General Nathanael Greene purchased Dungeness on the south end but died very soon afterward. Catherine Greene sold Mulberry Grove above Savannah and moved to Cumberland Island after the death of her husband.

In 1818 General Richard Henry Lee, Revolutionary War patriot and father of Robert E. Lee, became ill during a return trip from Cuba. The ship arranged to stop at Cumberland Island where the daughter of Lee's old friend General Green resided and there he died. In 1913 his body was moved from Cumberland Island to Lexington, Virginia, to lie beside his son. The Carnegie family bought the southern end of the island and built a magnificent home at Dungeness. When the mansion burned it was not rebuilt and the ruins remain today as one of the islands noted landmarks.

32. Right whales calve off the shores of the Georgia and Florida barrier islands from December through February, then return north to their feeding grounds in summer. The presence of the whales lead the Spanish to name Jekyll Island Isla de Ballenas, Island of Whales.

33. St. Marys is named for the river though there was also a Spanish Mission named Santa Maria near the present town. Local lore says that some early settlers of the area were French Acadian refugees who found their way to the area after the Revolution. The signs on the historic trail are also written in Braille, the only such trail in the Southeast. Botanist William Baldwin lived and worked in St. Marys in 1811, where he sought relief from his tuberculosis.

Cumberland Island National Seashore Museum. This museum features information and the history of Cumberland Island. Osborne Street in downtown St. Marys.

34. McIntosh Sugar Mill was believed to be the ruins of a Spanish mission until recent years. It was built by John Houston McIntosh about 1825 and was first a sugar mill then served as a starch factory during the Civil War. The machinery for the sugar operation was driven by cattle. It is interesting that the history of this expansive tabby ruin could be forgotten in less than seventy-five years. Located behind Memorial Park on GA-40 Spur.

35. St. Marys River was named Rivière Seine by Ribault when he explored the Southeastern coast looking for a place to plant a French colony. The St. Marys River probably received its name from the Mission of Santa Maria located on Amelia Island, though the river was called Rio de San Pedro by the Spanish. The St. Marys River begins in the Okefenokee Swamp, flows through the bottom of Trail Ridge, then along the east side of the ridge, and enters the Atlantic Ocean between Amelia and Cumberland islands. The river flows through a region of white sand with occasional limestone outcrops. The St. Marys River Canoe Trail begins at GA-23/121 and ends at US-1.

36. Wright's Fort was a fortification built about 1774 by Jermyn Wright near his home at Scrubby Bluff on the St. Marys River. Wright owned extensive property on both sides of the St. Marys. Loyalists sought refuge there during several patriot invasions of East Florida. Scrubby Bluff is located on the Georgia side of the St. Marys River at the I-95 bridge.

37. King's Ferry is named for a local family and not for the King of England. It appeared on the colonial maps as Mill's Ferry. King's Ferry became a thriving river town during the nineteenth century as lumbering grew in importance. King's Ferry rapidly declined after the Mizell Saw Mill closed in 1912 and the last scheduled riverboat service ended in 1916. On the Georgia side of the river lies the community of Flea Hill, which is private with no public river access. There are two Bartram Trail markers at the intersection of Springhill Road and Okefenokee Parkway, just north of Flea Hill.

Fort Tonyn was constructed near King's Ferry at the outbreak of the Revolution in 1776. Fort Tonyn was a fortified post at the trading station of Roger Kelsall. Colonel Lachlan McIntosh invaded the St. Marys region with a force of Georgia militia and Continental soldiers in the summer of 1776 but failed to take Fort Tonyn. The fort became the headquarters for Thomas Brown and the East Florida Rangers as they harassed the southern frontier of Georgia. Elijah Clark invaded Florida again in the spring of 1778 and as he crossed the St. Marys River the Rangers abandoned Fort Tonyn. It was burned sometime that same year.

38. Colerain doesn't exist today but has remained on state maps since the very early 1800s. It probably started as an Indian village prior to the Revolution. James Armstrong and James Seagrove received grants totaling 43,000 acres in this section of St. Thomas Parish on December 1, 1786. In 1787 James and Robert Seagrove, James Armstrong, and Noble Hardee opened a mercantile business at Colerain to trade with the Creeks and Seminoles. The road from Savannah to Saint Augustine crossed near Colerain after the completion of the King's Road and was the only land route north from East Florida.

From June 16–29, 1796 the **Treaty of Colerain** between the United States and the Creeks was held at Colerain on the St. Marys River. It reaffirmed the Treaty of New York as well as the previous treaties of Shoulderbone Creek, Galphinton, and the 1783 Treaty of Augusta. The treaty defined the new boundaries between Georgia and the Creek Nation. The new boundary extended Georgia to the Oconee River in the northwest and from the mouth of Penholloway Creek on the Altamaha River to Colerain. The Colerain conference was attended by Benjamin Hawkins, Andrew Pickens, Governor James Jackson of Georgia, and Creek headmen. Fushatchee Micco was the spokesman for the Creeks.

Governor Jackson read a long list of property stolen or destroyed by Creeks that was worth $110,000 and then demanded restitution. The Big Warrior remarked that "I can fill up more paper than Jackson has done, with a list of similar outrages of the Georgians upon my People." Jackson believed that Seagrove had influenced the Creeks to refuse to cede the land between the Oconee and Ocmulgee rivers. After the conference the two men became bitter enemies and eventually fought a duel. Seagrove was removed from office in 1796 by his political enemies who felt he had betrayed the interests of white Georgians.

Fort Pickering was garrisoned by the federal government sometime in the early 1790s. The United States established a trading post, called a factory, there in 1796 to oversee trade with the Creeks in Georgia and Florida. The factory was moved to Fort Wilkinson at Milledgeville in 1797. Little remains of Fort Pickering today but a stone monument erected by the DAR.

39. Burnt Fort. No one knows which fort was burned to give this community its name. Some have thought the ruins were what remained of New Hanover, the settlement founded by Edmund Gray, but there is no hard evidence to support that theory. The Revolutionary-era Fort McIntosh was farther up the Satilla River. This stretch of the St. Marys River is one of the most beautiful spots in South Georgia.

Magnolia Bluff lies immediately upriver from Burnt Fort and is considered an excellent example of a displaced botanical community. The bluff forest is composed of mature magnolias and beeches.

40. Fort McIntosh was built by the Georgia army in December 1776 when loyalists and rangers began raiding between the St. Marys River and Altamaha River. Colonel William McIntosh was in charge of defending the southern part of Georgia and built Fort McIntosh on the Satilla River not far from the Savannah to Saint Augustine Road. The fort was located eighty yards from the river and thirty miles south of Fort Howe (the Revolutionary name for Fort Barrington).

Colonel Louis V. Fuser, Thomas Brown, and Daniel McGirth lead a force of British regulars and Florida Rangers against the fort on February 14, 1777. The next afternoon Captain Richard Winn surrendered the fort and negotiated a guarded retreat to Fort Howe. During the night Winn discovered that his British escort had deserted. Fearing that this was a prelude to an Indian ambush he roused his men and struggled through thirty miles of swamp to avoid the watched roads and Indian trails. They reached the safety of Fort Howe the next morning. Fort McIntosh was burned and never rebuilt.

40. Camp Pinckney Park. Captain Thomas Pinckney supposedly camped near here while on an expedition against the Lower Creeks and the fort constructed a few years later was named Camp Pinckney. It may be that the fort was named for Pinckney because he negotiated the treaty with Spain that established the Georgia-Florida boundary and not because he ever visited the spot. There was a trading post nearby called "Armstrong's on the Upper Cowford," which was probably property of James Armstrong, a business partner of James Seagrove. The first turpentine camp in Georgia operated near Camp Pinckney. The town of Centerville grew up around the site of the fort as a stop on the Savannah-Saint Augustine stage. The community of Centerville had disappeared by the end of the nineteenth century. A boat ramp and picnic area are now open to visitors. The park may be reached by Camp Pinckney Road from US-1 south of Folkston or GA-40 east of town.

41. White Sand Landing, opposite Camp Pinckney Park, was an important crossing of the St. Marys River during the late colonial period and was the most important overland road from Georgia to East Florida.

42. Trader's Hill is located at the head of navigation on the St. Marys River and was the most important commercial center in the lower part of Georgia during the very early nineteenth century. It began as a trading post around 1755 and was the site of Fort Alert in the mid-1790s. It was made the seat of government for newly formed Charlton County in 1854. Trader's Hill declined after the county government was moved to Folkston in 1901. The old ferry landing is now a county park with facilities picnicking, camping, fishing, and a boat ramp. Located seven miles south of Folkston off GA-23 at the end of Tracy Road.

43. Okefenokee Swamp. Bartram's stories of a mysterious race of Indians inhabiting the great Okefenokee Swamp may not have been far from fanciful, for near the Chesser Homestead there is a mound that yielded the bones of seven-foot humans. The Chesser Family themselves figured prominently in Francis Harper's important work on the pioneers of the swamp, *Okefenokee Album*. If you visit the Homestead on a weekend you can visit with Chesser descendents who work for the park service, keeping the house in order and tending the vegetable garden. The best-known inhabitant of the Okefenokee Swamp is, of course, Pogo Possum, the great American political and social commentator created by Walt Kelly.

The Okefenokee Swamp is one of America's greatest natural treasures. Its biology and botany are unparalleled for variety and abundance of species and the mysterious beauty of the landscape is haunting. The Suwannee and St. Marys rivers both rise within the swamp and flow in opposite directions, Suwannee to the Gulf and St. Marys to the Atlantic.

In addition to being the greatest authority on William Bartram, Francis Harper was also a biologist for Cornell University and did research in the Okefenokee in the second decade of this century. His book, *Okefenokee Album*, tells the human story of the swamp and dispels many of the myths that paint the inhabitants as being isolated and anachronistic. They did not speak King James English as one author has written nor were they completely removed from outside contact.

Harper's brother, Roland, made the first botanical survey of the Okefenokee in 1902 and in 1919 completed a second survey with Francis. The brothers grew up in Americus, Georgia, and made their early trips to the swamp by train.

Okefenokee Swamp is eighteen miles wide

and thirty-eight miles long, covering over 400,000 acres. It formed in a depression when a saltwater lagoon was cut off from the sea by Trail Ridge as the ocean retreated. Trail Ridge extends seventy-five miles from the Satilla River east of Waycross to Starke, Florida. The Okefenokee averages only eight to twelve feet deep in the open areas but most of the swamp is wet prairie, peat bog, and cypress islands. The islands of high ground that support trees are called houses. Floating mats of vegetation that float lead the Indians to call this area the land of the trembling earth. Although the exact meaning of the word Okefenokee is debated, we have at least settled on one of the seventy-seven documented spellings. Fire has historically kept the Okefenokee from becoming completely filled with peat and forest, but the Suwannee Sill keeps water level constant now and fire is uncommon. As time goes by this may mean that the Okefenokee will slowly fill up and become a vast cypress wetland, then in time return to pine forest.

Suwannee Canal National Recreation Area is the east entrance to the Okefenokee Swamp and is reached from GA-23/121 south of Folkston. The Okefenokee Wildlife Refuge visitor center is located at the Recreation Area, there is an automobile drive, and several nature trails. The most popular trail at the Suwannee Canal area is the boardwalk to the observation tower. The concession has canoes and jon-boats for rent.

Stephen Foster State Park is the western entrance to the Okefenokee National Wildlife Refuge. There is a nature center, boardwalk, canoe rental, and campground. Located at the end of GA-177, off US-441 south of Fargo.

Laura S. Walker State Park is located northeast of Okefenokee NWR and southeast of Waycross between US-1 and US-82. Facilities include camping, fishing, boating, and hiking trails.

Obediah's Okefenok is a historical park built around the homestead of Obediah Barber, one of the original pioneers. Nature trails, twenty buildings dating from the mid-nineteenth century, educational programs, and a native wildlife zoo make Obediah's Okefenok an excellent place to begin a tour of the Okefenokee.

Okefenokee Park is located on the north side of Okefenokee NWR near Waycross and is a private, nonprofit park featuring tours and wildlife exhibits.

44. Ralph E. Simmons Memorial State Forest. This preserve, formerly named St. Marys River State Forest, is located on the south side of the St. Marys River, contains over 3,000 acres of land, and almost seven miles of riverbank. The forest protects several endangered and rare plants, including purple Baldwina, William Bartram's ixia, orchids, and pitcher plants. It is also home to the endangered gopher tortoise. Year-round activities include hiking, canoeing, wildlife observation, primitive camping in designated areas, fishing, horseback riding, and bicycling. Seasonal hunting is allowed. Access is from several dirt roads off Lake Hampton Road. Information is available from the kiosk on Pigeon Creek Road.

45. Fort Clinch State Park was built beginning in 1847. It was occupied by Confederate forces when the Civil War began and was taken by U.S. troops in 1861. It was decommissioned in 1898. Fort Clinch became one of Florida's first state parks when it opened in 1938.

There are two short hiking trails and the longer, ten-mile Fort Clinch Historic Trail that leaves the park, crosses Egans Creek, passes through Old Fernandina and the historic district, then loops back to Fort Clinch. The park is reached by Fort Clinch Road from A1A. The grounds are open 8 a.m.–sundown daily. The fort and visitor center are open 8 a.m.–5 p.m. daily.

46. Old Fernandina. Laid out in 1811, Old Fernandina was the last town platted by the Spain in the Western Hemisphere. In 1675 the Franciscans had established a village at this site and sometime between 1736 and 1742 General James Oglethorpe built a fort and es-

---

Itinerary

Brunswick

There is no crossing of the Altamaha River between Darien and Jesup; therefore this itinerary will begin at Doctortown on the south side of the Altamaha on US-25/82/301, just north of Jesup. The first portion of this itinerary is not shown on the map.

Miles	Directions
	Begin at Doctortown on the Altamaha River and travel south on US-25/82/301 toward Jesup
3.2	Left at the first intersection, continue on US-25
2.5	Left on US-25/341
4.6	Historical marker for the Indian boundary established by the 1763 Treaty of Augusta, surveyed in 1768
1.2	Left on paved road
4.8	Turn right at the intersection with dirt road (left for Paradise Park at Upper Sansavilla Bluff, 1.5 miles)
3.5	Left on dirt road
2.0	Intersection with a dirt road (left for Lower Sansavilla Bluff, .9 mile to the bluff)
1.6	Dead end at Howard Road, continue right
	The road to the left is a possible remnant of the old road from Barrington Ferry. One can park and walk to the floodplain and follow an old path through the bottomland to Aleck's Island
4.2	Left on US-24/341
3.8	Left on Altamaha Park Road
3.0	Right on Pennick Road, unpaved (or continue straight .5 mile to Altamaha Park)
3.0	Pavement begins
6.7	Left on Old Jesup Road
1.5	Left on US-341
.7	Left on GA-99
7.2	Right on US-17
.15	Entrance to Hofwyl-Broadfield Plantation State Historic Site
1.05	New Hope Plantation, established 1763 by Henry Laurens
11.9	Right on Gloucester Street in Brunswick
1.0	Right on Newcastle Street, US-25
24.0	Arrive at Old Post Road in Mt. Pleasant

Continued on next page

tablished a Highland regiment here. This area was a buffer zone between Georgia and Florida and did not prosper until the United States gained control of Florida.

47. Historic Downtown Fernandina. There is a historical marker at the end of Centre Street that commemorates William Bartram's visit to Amelia Island. The first cross-Florida railroad was built by Henry Flagler from downtown Fernandina to Cedar Key.

48. Amelia Island was named for the sister of King George II when Oglethorpe occupied the island in 1735. When Florida came into British possession in 1765 Lord Egmont established a plantation here with the town of Egmont near where Old Fernandina is today.

49. Amelia Island State Recreation Area is nestled against developed areas of Amelia Island on the south end of the island. This small, 200-acre, recreational area offers opportunities for hiking, horseback riding, and fishing. Natural habitats include beaches, salt marsh, and maritime forest. Located on FL-A1A, eight miles south of Fernandina Beach.

50. Battle of Alligator Creek Bridge was fought in spring 1778 and was a defeat for the Georgia and Carolina patriots during their last invasion of East Florida. Elijah Clark and the patriot forces were in pursuit of Thomas Brown and the East Florida Rangers. Near the head of the Nassau River at present-day Callahan, they unknowingly passed by British regulars. At the bridge where the King's Road crossed Alligator Creek the Rangers turned and caught the patriots between the Rangers and the regulars. The Americans, weakened by sickness and disputes among their officers, were routed. This was the last time that the Georgians tried to take East Florida from the loyalists.

Counties

Glynn County is one of the original counties created by the Georgia Constitution of 1777 and is named for John Glynn, a member of Parliament sympathetic to the American cause. Glynn county was formed from St. David's and St. Patrick's Parishes.

Camden County was created by the Constitution of 1777 and honors Charles Pratt, Earl of Camden, Chief Justice and Lord Chancellor of England. Camden was previously the parishes of St. Thomas and St. Mary's.

Nassau County was created in 1899 and is named for the Nassau River and Nassau Sound. Nassau is a duchy in western Germany and the name was brought to the area by English settlers during the reign of George III.

Itinerary

St. Marys River

	Begin Old Post Road in Mt. Pleasant and travel south
9.7	Historical marker for the Old Post Road, cross GA-32
6.1	Right on US-82
2.1	Left on Brantley-168 in Waynesville
.5	Left at fork
3.6	Left on GA-110
1.1	Right on New Post Road at the sign for Mt. Zion Church
	At 2.4 miles detour right on Kings Bay Road then travel .3 miles to Old Post Road, gated property of Union Camp; this was the actual road traveled by Bartram
5.2	Right on Incachee Road at the 4-way stop
4.8	Right on the paved road
.8	Left on Old Post Road, note green Bartram Trail sign
2.6	Road becomes paved
	Note Old Post Road on the right at 1.8 miles after pavement begins
4.5	Cross Burnt Fort Road and continue on Owen's Ferry Road
	Turn right and travel 4.3 miles to the Satilla River at Burnt Fort
.2	Road becomes dirt, note Green Bartram Trail sign
2.2	Left at Ivanhoe Plantation, the old road continued straight to the Satilla River
1.0	Right on Maryfield Plantation Road
1.9	Right on Refuge Road
3.1	Right on US-17, cross the Satilla River and enter Woodbine
1.2	Right on GA-110
3.9	Right on paved road at Westlight Baptist Church sign (Old Jefferson Highway)
1.0	Road ends at the Satilla River, turn around.
.5	Right on Old National Highway
3.0	Right on GA-110
2.6	Left on Springhill Road
6.4	Intersection Okefenokee Parkway, GA-40
	Bartram's route continued straight to the ferry on the St. Marys River and crossed to King's Ferry

At this point travelers may continue east to Kingsland, St. Marys, Cumberland Island, and US-17 to Nassau County to begin the East Florida portion of the Bartram Trail. An alternative is to travel west on the Okefenokee Parkway to Folkston, visit the Okefenokee National Wildlife Refuge then take US-1/301 from Folkston to Callahan, Florida, then A1A to Fernandina.

Savannah River

The land between Ebenezer Creek and Augusta was virtually uninhabited in 1763, except for several small Yuchi villages. The area was ceded by the Creeks in 1763 and officially opened for settlement by Europeans. The Yuchis had lived in the section between Brier Creek and Ebenezer Creek with towns at Mt. Pleasant on the Savannah River and Old Town on the Ogeechee. They moved westward about 1751 to the Flint and Chattahoochee rivers. The Ebenezer Salzburgers looked longingly to the fertile land lying north of them. When this territory became available at the end of the French and Indian War, it was quickly settled and became Saint Georges Parish. William Gerard De Brahm organized the settlement of Bethany, just north of Ebenezer Creek. By the time William Bartram traveled through the area there were farms scattered along the length of Savannah Road and Quaker Road and cow pens in the uninhabited areas.

Saint George Parish was renamed Burke County in 1777 to honor Edmund Burke who promoted American rights in Parliament. These new plantations and farms were barely settled when the Revolution began and brought devastation. It has been estimated that a third of the Americans were patriots, a third were loyalists, and a third were neutral. Saint George Parish was no exception and saw a great deal of bipartisan violence. After the fall of Savannah and Augusta, the loyalist government controlled all of Georgia save the extreme upper parts of Wilkes County. One of the worst defeats for the American forces in the South was the defeat of General Ashe at the Battle of Brier Creek. In the summer of 1781 fortune turned against the loyalists when generals Elijah Clark and Andrew Pickens swept the Tories and British army from the frontier.

William Bartram's Travels to Augusta

As he traveled north from Ebenezer in 1773 William Bartram may have taken the Quaker Road (GA-24) which diverged to the left from the Augusta Road about nine miles due east of Sylvania. The right-hand road, now called River Road, followed closer to the Savannah River and was Bartram's route in April 1775, for he said that he kept near the river as he embarked on his journey to the Cherokee Nation. John Bartram wrote in his journal of September 8, 1765, that they kept about a mile from the river as they traveled to Augusta. On their re-

Silver Bluff, South Carolina

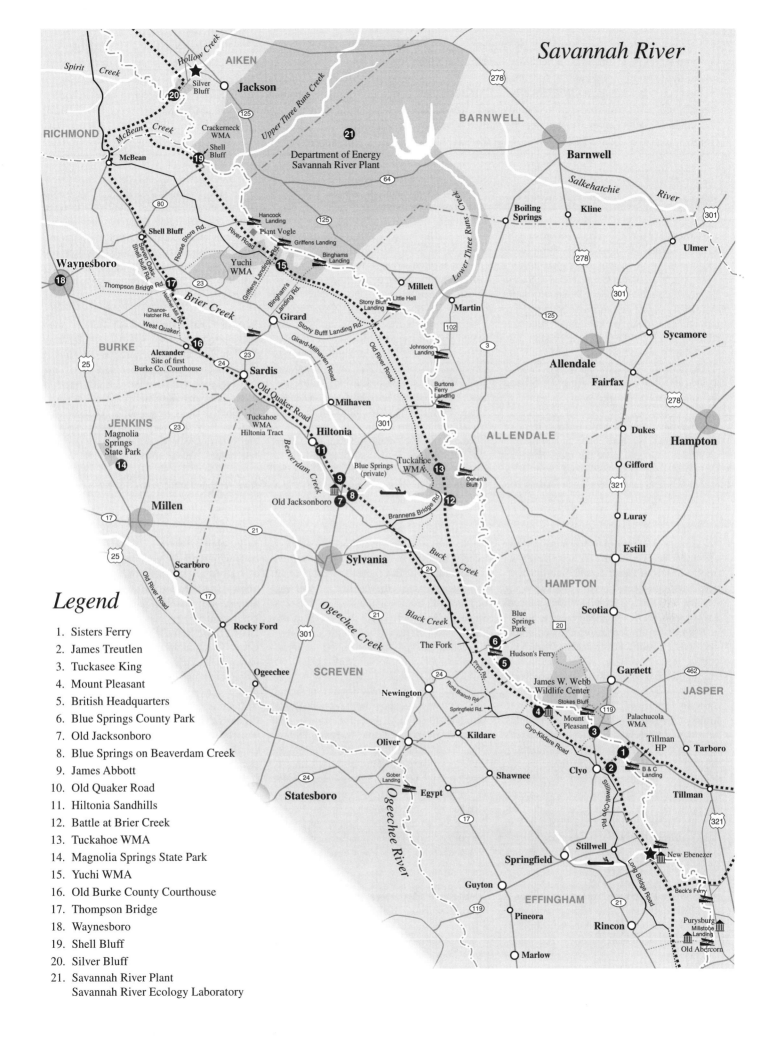

turn to Savannah the Bartrams went by way of one of George Galphin's cowpen, somewhere near Waynesboro, and then followed the Quaker Road back to Savannah.

On each trip to Augusta William crossed McBean Creek, then turned east through the bottomlands, and crossed the Savannah River at Silver Bluff. There he visited with George Galphin for several days.[1] Bartram crossed the Savannah River again at the site of Old Fort Moore (Sandbar Ferry) and arrived at Augusta on May 14, 1773. He visited Augusta again in April 1775 on his trip to the Cherokee Nation and in January 1776 on his return from the Mississippi River. It is assumed that on his trips back to Savannah he also went by Silver Bluff.

1. *Report to Fothergill.*

Sites

1. Sisters Ferry. William Bartram crossed the Savannah River at Three Sisters Ferry as he traveled from Charleston to Augusta in April 1775. The bluff on the Georgia side of Sisters Ferry is the southernmost of the unique bluffs that harbor plants of a northern affinity. Here one will find mountain laurel and flame azalea intermixed with plants of the coastal plain. The ferry operated until 1921.

The Historical marker for Sisters Ferry is located at the intersection of Sisters Ferry Road and Clyo-Stilwell Road.

2. Governor James Treutlen was a member of Jerusalem Church at Ebenezer and the first governor of Georgia after the adoption of the Constitution of 1777. Little is known of his early life and his death remains a mystery. He was born in Austria and arrived in Georgia with the Salzburg immigrants on March 12, 1734. He became a teacher at New Ebenezer, Justice of the Peace, Surveyor of Roads, and the owner of 12,000 acres of land. He won the seat as first governor of Georgia over Button Gwinnett. Treutlen placed a bounty of $500 for the capture of William Henry Drayton as an enemy of the state. Drayton had come to Savannah to petition for the absorption of Georgia into South Carolina but hurriedly left when the bounty became effective.

Though he was prominent in state government from 1775 to the end of his term as governor in January 1778, he disappeared from history after that. The story has been told that he was murdered by Tories while visiting his family who had taken refuge in Orangeburg District, South Carolina and was buried on the spot. However, stories handed down by his slaves tell that South Carolina Tories crossed the river and killed him at his home, then cut him up and buried him in the yard. His son later retrieved the body and moved it to the family cemetery. Sisters Ferry Road passes through his former estate.

3. Tuckasee King Landing is a fine example of a bluff containing plants of the coastal plain and mountains intermixed in the same habitat. On the cool, steep banks near the boat ramp, one may find wild ginger and hepatica or explore the swamp of bald cypress and tupelo. Tuckasee King Landing is unique in that it is easily accessible and remains in a fairly natural state.

This site has been known as Tuckasee King since the earliest days of English inhabitation. It was named for a Yuchi village located nearby whose leader was named Tuckasee. The Carolinians, not understanding the complex nature of leadership among the Southeastern Indians, called all important leaders a "King." The first seat of government for Effingham County was at Tuckasee King. The first Baptist Church in Georgia was established there in 1767 by Reverend Benjamin Stirk of Euhaw, South Carolina. Reverend Edward Botsford succeeded him in 1770 and expanded the Baptist Church in Georgia.

Removal of the county government caused Tuckasee King to begin its decline. In 1855 an elderly couple traveling from Mexico were passing through on their return to their former home. The man became ill and died at the Tuckasee King Stagecoach station. The woman became ill but recovered and continued on her journey home. Soon the station operator became ill and sent his family away. He died as did his father who had come to care for him. It was determined that the disease was Mexican Leprosy and the few remaining buildings at Tuckasee King were burned to prevent the spread of the disease.

Tuckasee King is located on the Savannah River near Clyo just north of GA-119.

4. Mount Pleasant was a trading post and Yuchi Indian village on the Savannah River. Mount Pleasant and Palachacola, on the east side of the river, were visited by Baron Philipp Georg Friederich Von Reck in May 1736. Von Reck kept a journal and illustrated it with watercolors of a busk (ceremonial dance), the Yuchi village, and New Ebenezer. These sketches have been published in *Von Reck's Voyage* and are our earliest images of the infant colony of Georgia. Mount Pleasant existed as a Native-American town until as late as 1760.

5. British Headquarters. General Augustine Prevost bivouacked his 4,000 British Regulars at Hudson's Ferry in February 1779. They built a redoubt on the south side of the mouth of Ferry Creek and from there completed the subjugation of the Georgia frontier. Prevost concealed the movements of 1,500 of his troops as they moved north on March 1. At Brier Creek they encircled General Ashe and his force of Continentals and North Carolina militia. The Americans were defeated with 150 dead, 170 captured, and their army effectively dispersed. The rest of Georgia lay open to the British.

6. Blue Springs County Park. This is often thought to be the Blue Springs mentioned by William Bartram in his report to Fothergill, but that spring is located on Beaverdam Creek near Old Jacksonboro. The divergence of the Augusta Road and Old Quaker Road, known as the Fork, was located a little north of Blue Springs Park. The park is primarily a weekend getaway with private dwellings and mobile homes. The springs are open for swimming and there is a boat ramp on the Savannah River. Located at the end of Blue Spring Road.

7. Old Jacksonboro. The courthouse for Screven County was originally located at Jacksonboro. This town lives in infamy for early writers traveling through Georgia told of a race of one-eyed men known as *gougeurs*, known for fighting, drinking, and general meanness. It was common practice to try to mutilate one's opponent in a fight. Louis Le Clerc Milfort, traveling from Savannah to the Creek Nation in the early 1780s, told of children picking up eyeballs and putting them in teacups on Sunday morning after a Saturday night frolic.

There is a local legend that the evangelist Lorenzo Dow placed a curse upon the town when he was threatened by a mob of local citizens whom he had denounced for immorality. He was taken in and protected by Seaborn Goodall. Dow's curse foretold the end of the town and sure enough the only building left in Jacksonboro today is the Goodall House where he was offered sanctuary.

8. Blue Springs on Beaverdam Creek. This is the Blue Springs that was mentioned by John Bartram in his account of traveling through Georgia in 1765. This Blue Springs is located on private property and is not accessible to the public. It is about a half-mile downstream from the bridge at Jacksonboro.

9. James Abbott was a noted artist and naturalist who sold his specimens and watercolors to collectors in Europe. He spent much of his time in Screven County around Jacksonboro, Thompson Bridge, and along the Savannah River. He is not so well known today because he did not publish a book of his work as did William Bartram, Alexander Wilson, and John James Audubon. He was the first important student of American insects and was an authority on birds of the Southern coast. Many of his descriptions and drawings were included in European scientific publications.

John Abbott corresponded with the noted naturalists of his day. He exchanged specimens with his friends Stephen Elliott, William Baldwin, and John Eatton LeConte. He was visited by Alexander Wilson in 1809 and advised him on the birds of the Savannah River. Abbott continued to send bird specimens to Wilson and, later, George Ord in Philadelphia. He sent a small package of his collections to William Bartram by way of their mutual friend Wilson. In 1818 Abbott met Titian Peale when Peale traveled through Savannah with George Ord, William Maclure, and Thomas Say as they retraced William Bartram's travels. Abbott died in Bulloch County sometime after 1840 and is buried in an unmarked grave in the McElveen family cemetery near Arcola.

10. Old Quaker Road. The Quaker Road from Savannah to Wrightsborough opened in 1769 and today coincides with GA-24 as far as Waynesboro.

11. Hiltonia Sandhills. William Bartram noted the successive sand hills that are arranged parallel to the coast and cut across river courses. These are dunes and sand bars of the ancient coast lines. As you near Hiltonia, notice that the hills beside the highway support turkey oaks, an indication of deep, well drained sand. In summer you will see hairy false foxglove in bloom; it has sticky leaves and grows in association with the roots of turkey oaks.

> *We now rise a bank of considerable height, which runs nearly parallel to the coast, through Carolina and Georgia: the ascent is gradual by several flights or steps, for eight or ten miles, the perpendicular height whereof, above the level of the ocean, may be two to three hundred feet (and these are called the sand-hills)* ...[1]

12. Battle of Brier Creek. An American force under General John Ashe was surprised and routed by Lieutenant Colonel Mark Prevost on March 3, 1779. Many of the militia deserted and of 1,500 militia and Continentals only 450 were able to rejoin Benjamin Lincoln in South Carolina. This disaster brought the entirety of Georgia under loyal control, except for the backcountry of Wilkes County.

[1]. William Bartram, *Travels*, 30.

George Galphin

George Galphin was born in Scotland, the son of a flax weaver, and arrived in Georgia about 1739. He built a trading post at a historical crossing on the Savannah River called Silver Bluff. Galphin engaged in trade at Coweta and was very influential among the Lower Creeks. He owned hundreds of packhorses and employed men who ranged across Georgia and Alabama. Galphin and James Adair supplied the Chickasaws with guns and powder in 1754 and encouraged them to resist the French.

George Galphin was one of the traders who was to be reimbursed by land sales in the New Purchase. His payment was approved at £9,791, but he was never paid because the Revolution began soon after Parliament ratified the 1773 treaty. Congress appointed Galphin Commissioner for Indian Affairs in the Southeast. Galphin was a political enemy of Alexander Cameron and worked to dilute his influence among the Creeks. Henry Laurens credited Galphin with keeping the Creeks from forming an alliance with the British during the Revolution. Galphin died at Silver Bluff on December 2, 1780.

It was written by James Adair that George Galphin had three families—white, black, and Indian. We do know from his will that he had four wives and mistresses with whom he had children. Mina and Sappho were African, Nitshukey and Metawney were Indian, and Rachel Dupree was white. Metawney was Creek and had two sons, John and George Galphin. They followed their father in the trading business, establishing themselves at Galphinton across the Ogeechee River from Louisville. John seems to have moved within White or Creek society as it suited his needs. After many years of petition the heirs of George Galphin received $245,000 from Congress in 1848 for the unpaid debt related to the New Purchase. Many of his descendants still live in Georgia and South Carolina.

One of Galphin's cowpens was on the Ogeechee River where Queensborough was laid out, later the site of Louisville. George Galphin's copy of Adair's History of the American Indians is in the Charleston library.

13. Tuckahoe WMA. The Tuckahoe Wildlife Management Area contains 15,000 acres, including 10,000 acres of lowlands along Savannah River and Brier Creek. Naturalists have the opportunity to view a variety of wildlife and plant species. William Bartram would have passed through Tuckahoe WMA in April 1775 while enroute to Augusta. From GA-24, turn right on Brannen's Bridge Road.

Hiltonia Tract. From Hiltonia follow GA-24 2.7 miles, then left on Hurst Road. Travel for .7 miles then turn left on Mt. Pleasant to the entrance.

14. Magnolia Springs State Park is the site of a Civil War prison camp, built near the springs for access to fresh water. Today the park adjoins the Millen National Fish Hatchery and Aquarium and is a popular recreational area for the local communities. There are facilities for family outings, including playgrounds, picnic shelters, a lake for boating and fishing, and tent and trailer camping sites. There are two nature trails. Open 7 a.m.–10 p.m. daily. Located on US-25 north of Millen.

15. Yuchi Wildlife Management Area. Yuchi WMA is composed of old cotton fields that are now planted in pines. Located east of GA-24 between Girard and Shell Bluff. The kiosk is located on Old River Road.

16. Old Burke County Courthouse. Burke County was formed by the Georgia Provincial Congress in 1777 and the courthouse was established on the Quaker Road, now the community of Alexander. Within a few years the Courthouse was moved to the site of the county jail where Waynesboro is today.

17. Thompson Bridge, across Brier Creek, was known as Odom's Ferry in the eighteenth century. It connected the Quaker Road with Savannah Road.

18. Waynesboro is the county seat for Burke County, the courthouse being moved there during the Revolution. The Battle of Burke County Jail took place in January 1779 west of downtown on McIntosh Creek. The town was laid out in 1783 and named for General "Mad" Anthony Wayne. There are historical markers in downtown Waynesboro celebrating Shell Bluff, the town of Waynesboro, and Burke County. A granite marker in front of the BP-Amoco station, opposite the Burke County Museum, commemorates President Washington's visit to Waynesboro in 1791.

Burke County Museum. The history of Burke County and Waynesboro is the focus of the Burke County Museum, but there are also exhibits on the prehistoric people and geology of the area. Interesting features of Burke County history are the cotton era and the famous Burke County bird dogs.

536 Liberty Street (US-25). Open 10 a.m.–5 p.m., Monday through Friday.

19. Shell Bluff was visited by John and William Bartram in 1765 and is where they discovered fossils of giant oysters, *Crassostrea gigantissima*, which grew to two feet. Shell Bluff became the home of Dr. Lyman Hall after the Revolution, an estate named Montville. He died there in 1790 and was buried on the bluff overlooking the Savannah River. His remains were later relocated to Signer's Monument in Augusta. To reach Shell Bluff follow GA-80 past where it ends at GA-23. There is a historical marker beside the road at the bluff. The road continues down the bluff onto the flood plain and ends at a private residence. Land on both sides of the road is private.

20. Silver Bluff is the site of a very ancient ford of the Savannah River where a branch of the Lower Creek Trading Path crossed. It became the home and trading post of George Galphin, trader to the Creeks. The site of George Galphin's store and residence was on the bluff near where the present-day boat landing.

Galphin immigrated from Ireland in 1750 and quickly became one of the most prominent Indian traders. The royal presents were distributed from Galphin's store which gave him unparalleled influence among the Creeks. Canoes and barges worked the river from Silver Bluff to Savannah and up to Augusta. George Galphin was respected by the Indians with whom he traded because of his fairness. He had a cowpen and trading post at Old Town near the Ogeechee River, which appears on several colonial maps. Galphin's cowpen on the Ogeechee River was to become the town of Queensborough which was reserved for Irish immigrants. Louisville was laid out near the old site of Queensborough following the Revolution. In 1765 John and William Bartram traveled with George Galphin to one of his cowpens, probably near the present town of Waynesboro.

Galphin's fortified home was named Fort Galphin by the Americans. The fort was captured by the British during their conquest of the Savannah River and Augusta and was renamed Fort Dreadnought. On May 21, 1781 Major John Rudolph lured the British garrison from the fort. Elijah Clark and his Continentals rushed in and subdued the few remaining guards. The Americans confiscated a large depot of supplies bound for the British Indian allies and captured 126 British regulars and loyalists. The capture of Fort Galphin weakened the British position in Augusta and contributed to the American recapture of the city.

For many years Silver Bluff was thought to be the site of the town of Cofitachiqua, but it is now accepted that it was in the interior of South Carolina and that De Soto crossed the Savannah River north of Augusta. Silver Bluff is now a wildlife refuge owned by the Audubon Society. The walls of Galphin's home were still standing in the latter part of the last century and his grave is near the home site.

Silver Bluff Plantation Sanctuary. The former plantation of George Galphin forms part of a 3,000-acre tract of pine plantations and croplands that includes virgin hardwood forests and bottomland swamp. A unique program developed by the Audubon Society demonstrates ways timber and crops can be produced profitably while encouraging wildlife and preserving environmental values and natural beauty. Thirty acres of ponds have become a rookery for endangered wood storks. Located at 4542 Silver Bluff Road, Jackson, South Carolina.

21. Savannah River Plant. The nuclear reactors and facilities at the Savannah River Plant were built to provide fissionable fuel for the nuclear arms industry. When the facilities were completed in 1956, Barnwell County began calling itself the Atomic Capital of the World. Over the years accidental and incidental contamination of the area with tritium and other radioactive wastes has raised concerns among environmentalists, health officials, and biologists. Contaminants have shown up in the local fish. The legacy of the Cold War arms race are these sites where radioactive wastes were inadequately stored in corroding drums.

The first time I traveled SC-125, I found the signs unsettling: *Restricted Highway, No Stopping Next 20 Miles*. The secrecy surrounding the operations at the Savannah River Plant and other weapons facilities meant that accidents and mishandling of wastes went unreported until the late 1980s. The Savannah River Plant ceased operation in 1988 but the cleanup and containment of the leftover wastes will continue for decades and cost as much as $25 billion.[2]

Savannah River Ecology Laboratory. Ecological research at the Savannah River Site was begun in 1951 by Dr. Eugene Odum of the University of Georgia. In 1972 the 300-square-mile Savannah River Plant was designated America's first National Environmental Research Park. Current research is divided into three divisions: Biogeochemical Ecology, Wetlands Ecology, and Wildlife Ecology and Toxicology.

It would seem that there is nothing left in the Piedmont to discover, after two centuries of settlement and farming. But, biological systems at the Savannah River Plant Reservation are showing a remarkable amount of biodiversity as witnessed by Upper Three Runs Creek. During a time when other waterways have received runoff contaminated with pesticides, petroleum by-products, and construction sediment, streams within the Savannah River Site are free from such outside influences.

Upper Three Runs Creek remains a pristine stream that has the distinction of containing more species of life than any other waterway in North America. Biologists believe that it is an example of what many streams in the South were like in the past. Over five-hundred species of insects have been found in Upper Three Runs Creek and its tributaries, some are new species and some are more common to the Appalachian mountains.

The effects of an on-site nuclear plant and the release of warm water from cooling towers have been major research projects on Three Runs Creek. Radioecology research studies the effects of radiation on individual organisms and ecosystems. The science of Genotoxicology studies the effect of environmental contaminants on DNA. Additionally, scientists have been able to study large-scale ecological succession in the old cotton fields.

Savannah River Ecology Laboratory has a well established Environmental Outreach and Education Division that provides information for the general public and special programs for students and teachers.

Counties

Screven County was formed from Effingham in 1793 and named for General James Screven who died during the fighting near Midway Church in November 1778. Salzburgers founded the settlement of New Gottingen near Burton's Ferry which was abandoned by 1758. Colonel Mark Prevost overwhelmed the American forces of General Ashe at the Battle of Brier Creek.

Burke County was created from St. Georges Parish by the Constitution of 1777. It is named for Edmund Burke who was the most outspoken champion of equal and fair treatment of the American colonies in Parliament. During the Proprietary Period from 1733–1752 this area was known as Halifax District.

During the Revolution the jail for Burke County was located at present-day Waynesboro. The courthouse was built where the little community of Alexander is today, then it was moved to Waynesboro sometime before 1779. At the old courthouse a road diverged from the Quaker Road, crossed Brier Creek at Thompson's Bridge, and joined Savannah

---

2. Tom Horton, "Savannah River: the Deadly Cleanup," *Outdoor Life*; April, 1992.

Road at McBean Creek. A major Revolutionary War battle took place near the jail when Colonel John Twiggs defeated the East Florida Rangers of Colonel Thomas Brown and Daniel McGirth in January 1779. Brown and the Rangers were with Archibald Campbell as his troops marched toward Augusta. They were given permission to attempt the rescue of local loyalists who were imprisoned at the jail.

Itinerary

Begin in Ebenezer, return on GA-275 to the first intersection and take a right on Long Bridge Road.

Miles	Directions
2.7	Right on Springfield-Stillwell Road (becomes Clyo-Springfield Road)
9.0	Historical marker for Sister Ferry
	Clyo-Stillwell Road becomes 4th Street in Clyo, right on Marion, then a sharp left, cross GA-119 and begin Clyo-Kildare Road
10.1	Right on Old Augusta Road
2.5	Left on Runs Branch Road
3.3	Right on the Hudsons Ferry Road then right on Newington Road (GA 24)
16.4	Right on Pine Grove Inn Road, which becomes Brannen Bridge Road
2.4	Tuckahoe Kiosk on Greenwood Church Road
9.8	Cross Burton's Ferry Road (US-301) and continue straight on Old River Road
	It is one mile to the Savannah River and Georgia welcome center by turning east here on US-301.
6.9	Keep straight at stop
3.9	Intersection with Stony Bluff Landing Road
7.6	Intersection with Brigham's Landing Road, primitive camping available
2.2	Intersection with Griffin Landing Road
1.9	Information kiosk for Yuchi WMA
.4	Road becomes unpaved
1.0	Keep left
10.3	Intersection of River Road and GA-80
	Turn right for Shell Bluff, it is two miles to Shell Bluff and Montville, Lyman Hall's plantation
7.0	Right on Spur-56
.1	Cross McBean Creek

Savannah River

Augusta

The oldest pottery yet found north of Mexico, dating to 2,500 years ago, has been unearthed at Stallings Island in the Savannah River. Stallings Island lies north of Augusta, just downriver from the Stevens Creek Dam. Inhabitation of Stallings Island began about 4,500 years ago. Later, a large chiefdom existed in the upper Savannah River during the Mississippian era but the mounds built by these people have not survived the annual spring floods. The area was abandoned about 1450, possibly due to years of poor harvest and growing political instability. The De Soto expedition found little food and no inhabitants living between the chiefdom of Ocute on the Oconee River north of Milledgeville and Cofitachequi at Camden, South Carolina. By that time the upper Savannah River had become a buffer zone between these two chiefdoms.

In the early years of South Carolina several native tribes established themselves on the Savannah River, where several trading paths crossed the river, seeking the protection of the English and trade opportunities. The most powerful tribe in the Carolina interior were the Westoes (Chichimecos to the Spanish). Henry Woodward encountered the Westoes at the upper reaches of navigation of the Savannah River. They had been supplied with guns by Virginia traders and were the most formidable force of Indians in the province of Carolina. The river was first named for the Westoes, but about 1680 a group of Shawnees, known as the Savannahs, settled on the river near Beech Island and drove the Westoes away. The Savannahs remained there until just prior to the Revolution when they moved to the Chattahoochee River.

The Westoes lived between the Savannah and Saluda rivers during the 1670s. They controlled the slave trade with

Heggie's Rock Preserve

Charleston and are responsible for the destruction of the Spanish missions of Guale and Apalachee. They became too bold and reckless for the comfort of the English and they blocked easy trade with tribes beyond the Savannah River. In 1780 the Carolinians and Indian allies, particularly the Savannahs, made war against the Westoes and dispersed them. The remnants of the tribe sought refuge among the Creeks.

The Yamassee War of 1715 convinced other tribes to put more distance between themselves and the English and many towns moved farther west. A band of Chickasaws, weary of war with the French, moved from their homeland in northern Mississippi and settled near Fort Moore. Around 1757 they moved across the Savannah River to New Savannah Town. About 1775 they left the area, moving first to Kasihta, then returning to their homeland.

The fall line of the Savannah River was a choice site for Georgia to establish a trade center and the town of Augusta was laid out by Roger de Lacy in 1735. Yuchis and Apalachees settled north of Augusta. South of Augusta were Shawnees at Savannah Town. In 1751 the first Quakers settled in Georgia on land purchased from the Yuchis. Little is known about the history of this community but their settlement is still remembered in the name of Quaker Springs in Martinez. The springs unfortunately are now covered over by the Washington Highway at the entrance to Quaker Springs Apartments. About 1754 the infamous Edmund Gray and his followers, claiming to be Quakers, settled between Augusta and Little River. Their community was to be called Brandon, although it is uncertain that a town was ever laid out. Gray, a member of the Lower House of Assembly, ran afoul of Governor Reynolds and was removed from the Assembly. Gray and his followers soon left the area, moved south of the Altamaha River, and founded New Hanover in the buffer zone between British Georgia and Spanish Florida.

Land surrounding Augusta was legally unavailable for European settlement until the 1763 Congress of Augusta closed the French and Indian War in the South. The congress was attended by Governor James Wright of Georgia, Governor Thomas Boone of South Carolina, Governor Arthur Dobbs of North Carolina, Lieutenant Governor Francis Fauquier of Virginia, and Superintendent of Indian Affairs John Stuart. Representatives of the Catawba, Cherokee, Chickasaw, Choctaw, and Creek nations were present. The congress established for the first time actual boundary lines between the Southeastern tribes and the British colonies.

Before 1763 the upper boundary between Georgia and the Creeks ran from near Ebenezer to Fort Barrington on the Altamaha River. The new boundaries were extended to the Ogeechee River in the west; the Lower Creek Trading Path, Brier Creek, and Williams Creek in the northwest; and Little River to the north of Augusta. The fertility of the new land attracted settlers, most notable were the Quakers at Wrightsborough. Queensborough on the Ogeechee River was reserved for Irish immigrants. The lower part of this new territory was organized into St. George's Parish and the upper part, including Augusta, became St. Paul's Parish.

The 1773 Treaty of Augusta opened land west of Wrightsborough and north of the Little River. The first settlers were from the North Carolina and South Carolina Piedmont.

Crackers

Native-born white Georgians and their descendents who settled north Florida are known as *Crackers*. Though the name can now be borne without stigma, much as *Cajun* can be proudly worn in Louisiana, Cracker was once a term of derogation, denoting a person of low birth, uneducated, and possessing of crude social behavior. It is commonly thought that the term Cracker refers to the skill with which Georgia mule drivers used their whips. However, Cracker is a word of much older origin, coming from the British Isles where it has meant exactly what it means today—an uncouth, unsophisticated, and crude jokester. In other words, a Redneck!

There were many vagrant families who were displaced and set loose on the frontier as a result of the Revolution. Honest, prosperous citizens were in danger of predation from these Crackers, so the Carolinas and Virginia went to war on these plunderers and forced them to seek refuge in the frontiers of Georgia.

Louis Le Clerc Milfort described Crackers in Franklin County and at Tugaloo, Georgia, who were also called *Gougers* for their habit of gouging out the eyes of their opponents during a fight. Anything was allowed in battle and combatants went at one another with claws, teeth, and spurs—the intention was to maim and disfigure as much as to dishonor. The Crackers were independent minded and lived outside the government, preferring to live by hunting and planting enough tobacco to trade for powder and whiskey, and they were continually on the move. Their character was a result of several generations of living on the frontier where there was no government, schools, and very few churches. Their culture was based in the rough-and-tumble world of scraping a living from raw land in the face of the threat of Indian attack. They were known as braggarts, jokesters, and intemperate citizens who served no man.

Milfort wrote:

I have traveled through the sixteen states of the United States of America, and everywhere I have met deceitful and hypocritical men who are proud and haughty in success, and vile and base in adversity. Americans consider themselves the foremost people in the world; they are so dishonest that it may happen that they sell to several persons at the same time lands which do not belong to them. I witnessed that in the hinterland of Georgia where I saw several buyers appear with equal claim to take possession of the same land.[1]

Indeed this short of chicanery is what lead to the Yazoo Fraud.

Crackers have their origins in the Celtic borderlands of the British Isles, where the name originates. They were removed from civilized society, uneducated, and retained their clannish political alliances. Although the motto of the state of Georgia is "Wisdom, Justice, and Moderation" the Crackers were certainly not given to moderation. They were fond of whiskey, brawling, and sexuality—then just as readily they turned their section of the South into the Bible Belt, honoring their other heritage as good Scots Presbyterians. They embraced the new Baptist and Methodist evangelical preachers. In defense of Southerners, the Cracker character was not confined only to the South. Witness the braggadocio of the indomitable Mike Fink (also of Celtic heritage), the most famous of the Ohio boatmen.

For a historical explanation of the origins of the Cracker personality see Grady McWhiney's *Cracker Culture: Celtic Ways in the South.*

1. Louis Le Clerc Milfort, *Memoirs or a Quick Glance at My Various Travels and My Sojourn in the Creek Nation*, translated and Edited by Ben C. McCary; the Beehive Press, Savannah, 1959.

The Augusta Canal

When the Provincial Congress in Savannah was organized and sent delegates to the Continental Congress, residents of Wrightsborough and the communities on Little and Broad rivers published a petition in the *Georgia Gazette* condemning the bold action of the Liberty Boys. The Georgians in the upper part of the state were not inclined to find offense with the King or Parliament since the British army (where they were available) protected settlers from Indian attack, the King had given them their land, and the interior inhabitants of the South had little in common with the coastal gentry.

During the early part of 1774, while Savannah Whigs were meeting at Tondee's Tavern to protest British policy, the Augusta region was in danger of war with the Lower Creeks. It was Royal Governor James Wright whose diplomacy prevented hostility, not the Committee of Safety. However, many of these petitioners later became ardent patriots in response to Tory atrocities and British-instigated Indian raids. They helped keep newly formed Wilkes County in the hands of patriots throughout the conflict. Among the dissenters who later turned patriot were James and William Few, Elijah Clark, John Dooly, and Baptist preacher Daniel Marshall.

St. Paul's Parish was renamed Richmond County in 1777 to honor Charles Lennox, Duke of Richmond, for his support of the American cause. When Savannah was captured by the British army, Whigs organized a new government in Augusta, called a convention, and elected William Glascock as president. For the first time the government was controlled by representatives from the frontier instead of wealthy coastal planters. Soon, dispersed members of the government reassembled and named themselves the Supreme Executive Council with John Wereat as President.

After securing British control of Savannah, Lieutenant Archibald Campbell marched north and captured Augusta in February 1779, but was forced to withdraw two weeks later due to increasing American strength gathering in the South Carolina Piedmont. On June 8, 1780, Lieutenant Colonel Thomas Brown returned to Georgia with the King's Carolina Rangers and took the town of Augusta. The British built Fort Cornwallis in September on the site of the earlier Fort Augusta. A type of peace settled over Georgia and South Carolina with the British in control, the Creeks remaining neutral, and the Cherokees brought back into alliance with the British.

On September 14, 1780, Elijah Clark and sixty irregular troops attacked Augusta, besieging the town for four days until loyalist reinforcements arrived on the South Carolina side of the river. Clark and his troops retreated first to the Little River then to the Broad River and across the Savannah. In the wake of Clark's action British troops and loyalist militia bore down on Wilkes County requiring an oath to the crown or suffer eviction from the state. Clark and his army retreated into the Watauga District of North Carolina (now northeastern Tennessee) with their families. Some of Clark's men joined the Overmountain army that defeated Ferguson at King's Mountain.

In May 1781 combined forces of Lieutenant Colonel Harry Lee, General Andrew Pickens, and Lieutenant Colonel Elijah Clark besieged Fort Cornwallis at Augusta. Realizing a direct assault would be futile and costly, the Americans built a Mayhem Tower, thirty-feet tall, constructed of logs, and filled with earth and rubble. With only one six-pound gun, Lee was able to demolish the interior of the fort and effect the surrender of Brown on June 5, 1781. With the withdrawal of the British and

Legend

1. New Bordeaux
2. Hickory Knob State Resort
3. Baker Creek State Park
4. McCormick
5. Bethany & Liberty Hill
6. Savannah River Scenic Highway
7. Elijah Clark State Park
8. Price's Store
9. Lincoln County Historical Park
10. Graves Mountain
11. Stevens Creek
12. Hamilton Branch State Park
13. Sumter National Forest, Edgefield District
14. Edgefield
15. Stevens Creek Heritage Preserve
16. Burks Mountain
17. Uchee Creek
18. Heggie's Rock
19. Kiokee Baptist Church
20. Old Columbia County Courthouse
21. William Few
22. Site of Brandon on the Little River
23. Mistletoe State Park
24. The Rocks
25. Flowing Wells Spring
26. Quaker Springs
27. Savannah Rapids Park
28. Thomas Brown
29. Augusta Canal
30. Savannah Bluffs Heritage Preserve
31. North Augusta Greenway
32. Riverview Park
33. Hamburg Railroad
34. Fort Moore
35. Phinizy Swamp
36. New Savannah Town
37. Redcliffe Plantation State Park
38. Dearing
39. Stagecoach Road
40. The Rock House
41. Wrightsborough

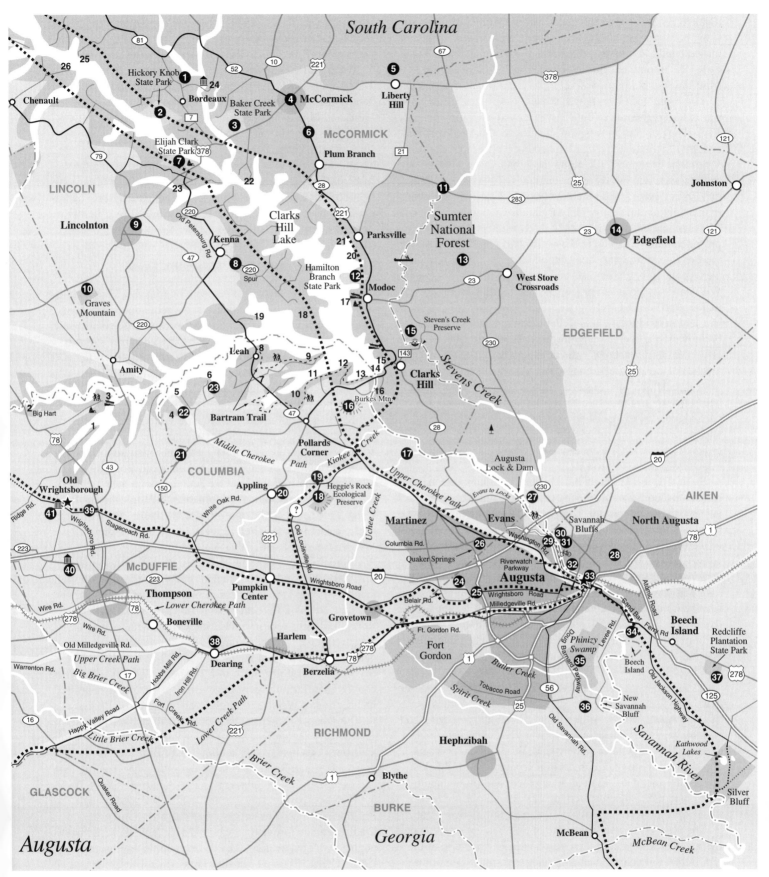

loyalists from Augusta the upper part of Georgia returned to Whig control. Daniel McGirth, though a professed loyalist, turned bandit and harassed the countryside of Georgia, especially Richmond and Burke counties, as his rangers robbed from loyalist and patriot alike.

The capital of Georgia was moved to Augusta following the war and remained there until it was moved to Louisville in 1795. The population was now concentrated in the Piedmont and growing. After 1784 and the end of war, a large number of Virginians began to settle along the Broad River. These new settlers were leaving the worn-out lands of the older sections of Virginia, having seen the new Georgia lands while serving in the Continental Army. The Virginians were generally more educated and cosmopolitan than the North Carolinians who preceded them. This led to the rise of two opposing factions in the early government of the state of Georgia. The Virginians were prone to be Federalists and looked to James Jackson and William Crawford as their leaders. The North Carolinians rallied around Elijah Clark.

Land in the Piedmont is richer than the land in the Coastal Plain, which attracted many farmers. At the end of the eighteenth century tobacco was the dominant cash crop in the upper reaches of Georgia, being more suited to small farms than to large plantations, and Augusta became the most important tobacco market in the nation for a brief period. Tobacco was packed into large barrels, an axle was run through the heads, and the barrels were rolled to market in Augusta by mule. The easiest roads to town were along the ridges and they became known as the tobacco roads.

Soon after Eli Whitney built his first cotton engine in 1793, he established a manufacturing facility in Augusta. Cotton fever spread throughout the state, especially in the fertile Piedmont counties. Cotton displaced tobacco as the economic base of the region and Augusta became the world's largest inland cotton market. Broad River cotton was shipped from Petersburg to Augusta on Petersburg boats. These boats were built long and narrow to navigate the shoals and the Augusta Canal. Competition between Charleston and Savannah for the lucrative cotton shipping market caused leaders of both towns to build railroads to the interior of their states. When the railroad was built from Charleston to Hamburg (North Augusta) it was the longest in the world.

As tobacco and cotton exhausted the land, families took up new lands farther west, necessitating a series of treaties with the Native Americans. Although articles about preserving soil fertility began to appear in the early 1800s it was easier and cheaper to simply move to new land. Wealthier landowners could buy and hold large tracts in reserve as their old fields wore out. This meant that, although there was often uncultivated land in the older settled regions of Georgia and South Carolina, they were unavailable to farmers of modest means.

The urge to migrate was a trait of Southerners often noted by travelers who visited the Deep South. The opening of the rich prairies of central Alabama set loose a great migration from the upper Piedmont in the 1820s. Some of those who moved to Alabama were small farmers looking for a better life for their families and some were sons of wealthy planters from the older sections of the Carolinas and Virginia who were seeking their fortune. The organizers of the first government in Alabama were men from Hancock, Wilkes, Oglethorpe, Richmond, and Elbert Counties in Georgia; Abbeville, Anderson, Spartanburg, and Greenville counties in South Carolina.

When Peruvian guano became commercially available in 1858 land long in cultivation, or abandoned, could be renewed. This coincided with the lack of new desirable lands in Alabama and Mississippi becoming available. Railroads, fully realizing the value of maintaining cotton production where their lines existed, carried guano at a reduced rate.

One must not visit the Augusta area without hiking the levee of the Augusta Canal on a spring morning to admire this beautiful, free-flowing section of the Savannah River. The upper Savannah was once an incredibly beautiful river before it became a series of engineered lakes.

William Bartram's Travels about Augusta

William Bartram arrived in Augusta on May 14, 1773. While the congress with the Cherokees and Creeks was being held, Bartram occupied his days with excursions in the countryside surrounding Augusta, particularly up the Savannah River to the rapids where he found the shoals spider lily, *Hymenocallis coronaria*, and the lesser rosebay, *Rhododendron minus*.

Bartram visited Wrightsborough from May 16–19, although he does not mention this in the *Travels*. If we are to trust Bartram (who was notoriously inaccurate with distances), he said in his report to Dr. Fothergill that he missed his original road some five or six miles from Augusta and found himself at the Rocks. If this is the case, on his way to Wrightsborough he must have followed the Trading Path to a point near Grovetown where a side road joined with Wrightsborough Road. This could be the point where his return took a different route, which was definitely by way of the present-day Wrightsborough Road.

There is another possibility. His route to Wrightsborough may have followed the original Wrightsborough Road through Quaker Springs, which was built in 1769. Today the route corresponds to GA-232 (Columbia Road) and Old Stagecoach Road. Bartram's return to Augusta was by the new Wrightsborough Road, just opened in 1773. The two roads came together near the present intersection of White Oak Road and Stagecoach Road just north of I-20 on the Columbia-McDuffie county line. Bartram spent the evening at the Rocks near the intersection of Wrightsborough Road and Jackson Road.

The Treaty of Augusta was concluded on June 3 and the survey party set out from Augusta on June 7. There seems to have been two main roads leading west from Augusta, the Wrightsborough Road and the Trading Path. The Trading Path is present-day US-78. Old maps show the Lower Creek Trading Path as crossing Butler Creek, which Wrightsborough Road does not do. The survey party must have followed the Trading Path to Grovetown where they joined the Wrightsborough Road. That evening they camped on the headwaters of Uchee Creek. The next day they crossed Kiokee Creek and in the evening arrived at Wrightsborough where they stayed until June 21. There has been some confusion about the route the survey party took from Augusta to the Great Buffalo Lick. Bartram's Report to Dr. Fothergill would indicate that they traveled the Lower Cherokee Trading Path to the headwaters

Chigoe Branch, Fort Gordon Recreation Area, Columbia County

of the Ogeechee River, present-day Union Point. He obviously confused the Ogeechee River with Little River.

In mid-July, upon completing the survey of the newly ceded lands, the party returned to Augusta along the west side of the Savannah River. Marion Hemperly noted an unusual feature of the Upper Cherokee Trading Path in that it stayed close to the river, crossing near the mouth of each stream rather than taking an easier route along a ridge. The later wagon trail was known as the Petersburg Road, one of the tobacco roads to Augusta.

William Bartram was again in Augusta in early May, 1775 enroute to Cherokee Country. He traveled from Augusta to Fort James along the Upper Cherokee Path. After returning from Cherokee Country he lingered at Fort James and made excursions along the Broad River during the middle of June. He joined Indian traders at Fort Charlotte who were bound for the Creek Nation. They left Fort Charlotte on June 22, 1775 and the day's travel found them near Bordeaux where they stayed with Jean Louis de Mesnil du St. Pierre at his plantation overlooking the Savannah River. The next day they stopped at another plantation on the Savannah near Plum Branch. The company of traders was completed and they set off, crossing the river at one of three places, Price's Ferry or farther downstream at Middleton's Ferry or Fury's Ferry.

Fort Charlotte was captured by South Carolina Rangers just three weeks after Bartram's departure. Edward Cashin, in his book *William Bartram and the American Revolution on the Southern Frontier*, makes a compelling argument that Bartram's journey to the Gulf Coast conveniently kept him out of sight as the storm of revolution was brewing in South Carolina and Georgia. Certainly Bartram's friendship with Alexander Cameron and John Stuart and his recent journey into Cherokee Country would look suspicious in light of a British sponsored Cherokee uprising.

The path that Bartram and the traders took through Richmond County is problematic due to lack of detail both in Bartram's account and in the early maps. Old maps indicated the most important trails yet the landscape was crisscrossed with numerous lesser trails of which we will never be acquainted. For this reason this itinerary from Bordeaux to the Lower Path is arbitrary. Although Francis Harper thought the trading caravan might have gone by way of Wrightsborough, it is only conjecture. Bartram and the traders probably started out on the Lower Creek Path rather than the Upper Creek Path, as Harper believed, and it would seem plausible that they entered the Lower Path nearer to Augusta, possibly at Harlem or Dearing. Hinton's 1779 map of Georgia shows a road from New Bordeaux to a crossing of the Savannah River just above the mouth of Little River then crossing Little River at Brandon, now a dead town or possibly never built. From there travelers could have gone by way of Wrightsborough and turned south on the Quaker Road to reach the Lower Creek Trading Path.

If the trading party crossed at Middleton's Ferry their route would have been along Burks Mountain Road, through Pollards Corner, then through Appling and on to the Lower Path, a route where settlements already existed. If they crossed at Fury's Ferry their route would have followed closely to the present-day Belair Road.

The shoals on the Savannah River at the Augusta Lock and Dam

Clarks Hill Lake

Clarks Hill Lake is the largest man-made lake in the eastern United States and was completed in 1954. This was the first step in containing the free flow of the upper Savannah River, a once beautiful and large Piedmont river. The lake has 1,200 miles of shoreline and covers 70,000 acres. The Army Corps of Engineers manages a total of 150,000 acres, much of which is open to the public.

In 1991 the lake was renamed J. Strom Thurmond Lake and Dam. While South Carolina honored their longtime senator, Georgians did not accept the change. Ironically Georgians keep tradition by using the name that honors a town in South Carolina.

Clarks Hill sites are indicated on the map by numbers without a circle.

1. Little River Boat Ramp. This is an excellent place for a leisurely canoe trip. The boat ramp is near the upper limit of the lake so one can paddle into the Clarks Hill Lake or go up the Little River and back with ease. US-78.

2. Big Hart Campground. Boat ramp, picnic area, RV hookups, beach, camping, playground, bathhouse, and hiking trail.

3. Holiday County Park. Boat ramp, picnic area, campground. From US-378 take Metasville Road to Goat Pasture Road, the park is at the end of the road.

4. Raysville Campground. Boat ramp, RV hookups, bathhouses. GA-43, south side of Little River.

5. Amity Recreation Area. Boat ramp, picnic area, shelters, pier, beach, playground, and restrooms. Off GA-43, north side of Little River.

6. Clay Hill Campground. Boat ramp, RV hookups, bathhouse. End of Clay Hill Road

7. Winfield Campground. Boat ramp, beach, camping, RV hookups, playground, and bathhouse. From GA-150 take Mistletoe State Park Road to Winfield Road

8. Fort Gordon Recreation Area. Boat ramp, picnic area, campground, RV hookups, playground, bathhouse, and hiking trails. Off GA-47.

9. Ridge Road Campground. Boat ramp, campground, RV hookups, beach, playground and bathhouse. Located on Ridge Road off GA-47.

10. Wildwood County Park. Boat ramp, picnic area, campground, RV hookups, beach, playground, bathhouse and hiking trails. GA-47.

11. Petersburg Campground. Observation tower, boat ramp, campground, RV hookups, beach, playground, and bathhouse. Part of the Bartram Trail through Petersburg Campground is wheelchair accessible. Located at the end of Petersburg Road off US-221.

12. Lake Springs Recreation Area. Boat ramp, picnic area, pier, playground, beach, restrooms, and hiking trail. Located off US-221 near the dam.

13. West Dam Recreation Area. Picnic area, pier, playground, beach, and restrooms. On US-221, west end of the dam.

14. Visitor Center and Strom Thurmond Dam. Take the sidewalk to the center of the dam for an excellent view of the Savannah River and surrounding hills. The visitor center has exhibits on local history from earliest settlement dating from 10,000 years ago. Recreational information for the area is available. Located at the west end of the dam on US-221. Open 8 a.m.–4:30 p.m. daily October through March, and 8 a.m.–8:30 p.m. April through September. Closed on Thanksgiving, Christmas, and New Year's Day.

15. Clarks Hill Park. Boat ramp, picnic area, playground, beach, and restrooms. Located on US-221, east end of the dam.

16. Below Dam Recreation Area. Boat ramp, picnic area, pier, and restrooms.

17. Modoc Campground. Boat ramp, campground, RV hookups, beach, playground, bathhouse, and hiking trails.

18. Bussey Point Campground. Boat ramp, picnic area, hiking trails. Located on GA-220 Spur. **Bussey Point Wildlife Management Area** was crossed by the Upper Cherokee Path, though it has long since disappeared under the plow. Although hunts are scheduled at Bussey Point WMA for part of the year the area is open for hiking and picnicking during the rest of the year.

19. Cherokee Recreation Area. Boat ramp and restrooms. Located just off US-47.

20. Parksville Wayside Park. Picnic area. US-221 in Parksville.

21. Parksville Recreation Area. Boat ramp, playground, beach, and restrooms.

22. Hawe Creek Campground. Boat ramp, campground, RV hookups, and bathhouse. Located on County Road 124 off US-378.

23. Soap Creek County Park. Boat ramp, picnic area, beach. GA-220.

24. Long Cane Creek. Boat ramp and picnic area. From SC-28 east of Long Cane Creek follow County Road 276 to 277.

25. Leroy's Ferry Campground. Boat ramp, primitive camping. From Willington follow signs, County Road 196 to 135 and 366.

26. Hester's Ferry Campground. Boat ramp, campground, RV hookups, playground, and bathhouses. From GA-79 follow GA-44 to Hester's Ferry Road.

27. Bartram Trail. The Bartram Trail at Clarks Hill Lake was developed on Army Corps of Engineers land, constructed and maintained by local Boy Scout troops. The original hiking trail was almost forty miles long but some sections have fallen into disuse. Most visitors to Clarks Hill Lake are interested in fishing and boating, but this trail has beautiful and peaceful sections, especially the Keg Creek Loop. Other sections remaining in good condition are at Fort Gordon Recreation Area and Wildwood Park. The trail sections near Thurmond Dam are well used and maintained. About four miles of the trail near the West Dam were paved due to heavy use and is an excellent trail for the handicapped. The trail crosses rolling, wooded hills, rocky streams, and gives occasional views of coves in the lake.

Access points for the trail are at both ends of the bridge over Keg Creek, GA-104; the main road from 194 to Fort Gordon Recreation Area, end of Ridge Road; Wildwood Park; Petersburg Campground; Lake Springs Recreation Area; and West Dam.

Sites

1. New Bordeaux was settled in 1764 by Huguenots from the south of France. A town was laid out in the Hillsborough Township and named for Bordeaux, France, but the settlers soon moved into desirable farmland on the Little River (South Carolina), Savannah River, and Long Cane Creek. The first wine shipped from South Carolina was produced at the plantation of Monsieur St. Pierre, who was visited by William Bartram on June 22, 1775. André Michaux was disappointed with Augusta and the hospitality available there but was very pleased with the generosity and reputation of his countrymen in New Bordeaux, South Carolina. A granite cross marks the site of the Huguenot church, located on a dirt road off Huguenot Parkway, east from SC-7.

One of the Huguenot descendants was James Petigru, the only member of the South Carolina legislature to vote against secession. His now famous statement was "South Carolina is too small to be a republic and too large to be an insane asylum."

2. Hickory Knob State Resort Park. The Guillebeau House at Hickory Knob is the only house known to remain from the original French Huguenot settlement of New Bordeaux. It was built by Andre Guillebeau who arrived in Charleston in 1764. The log structure was moved to Hickory Knob State Park, restored, and is available to guests for lodging and special events.

Hickory Knob is a resort park and provides facilities for conferences, skeet shooting, tennis, archery, and a championship golf course. It also has boating, fishing, camping, and two nature trails. Open daily, 6 a.m.–9 p.m., April through September; 6 a.m.–6 p.m during the remainder of the year. From US-378 follow CR-7 and CR-421 to Hickory Knob Park.

3. Baker Creek State Park. Amenities include Wild Mint Nature Trail, Baker Creek Hiking Trail, horse trails, camping, bath house, picnic area, boat ramp, swimming area and playground. Open daily, 6 a.m.–9 p.m., April through September; 6 a.m.–6 p.m., October through March. US-378 three miles west of McCormick.

4. McCormick was the site of a gold rush in 1851. The town is named for Cyrus McCormick, the inventor of the reaping machine and owner of one of the local gold mines. The town was built on land donated by McCormick and rests above old gold mine tunnels. The turn-of-the-century downtown has been restored and features an antique district, restaurants, and businesses catering to the local rural community.

5. Bethany and Liberty Hill, part of Londonderry Township, was settled by German Palatines in 1765. The first Liberty Pole in South Carolina was raised there.

6. Savannah River Scenic Highway begins as SC-28 in McCormick County, South Carolina, then becomes US-81 at Long Cane Creek. This scenic automobile route passes through the charming towns of Clarks Hill, Plum Branch, McCormick, Mt. Carmel, Calhoun Falls, and on to Anderson. The southern part of the highway near Modoc and Clarks Hill parallels the railroad, originally Savannah Valley Railroad built in the 1880s. The tracks follow an ancient trail that was used by the Cherokees and Augusta traders.

7. Elijah Clark State Park. Soon after the 1773 Treaty of Augusta, settlers began to move into the New Purchase from North and South Carolina. Elijah Clark,[1] John Dooly, and their families were among the first settlers, coming from North Carolina in 1775. Although virtually illiterate, Clark was one of Georgia's prominent patriots, a general in the Georgia Militia, victor at the Battle of Kettle Creek, and president of the short-lived Trans-Oconee Republic. Clark, Colonel John Dooly, and Stephen Heard were the defenders of Wilkes County, the only part of Georgia to remain out of British control. Clark was a stubborn and tireless fighter for the American cause yet he apparently maintained a gentlemanly approach to what was essentially a cruel civil war in the backcountry, for in a letter to Cornwallis he suggested that both sides take measures to ensure the safety and property of neutral parties.

The Clark family settled first on Red Lick Creek is western Wilkes County, probably about 1773. Their home was destroyed by Tories in 1778 and they moved to the Savannah River. Following the Revolution, Clark received a plantation as a gift from Georgia in

---

1. Elijah Clark's son, John, became governor of Georgia from 1819 to 1823. Their name has sometimes been spelled Clarke.

Dot Shields welcomes visitors to the Elijah Clark Memorial

gratitude for his part in the defense of the state. The land was located at present-day Hesters Ferry and had been confiscated from Thomas Waters. Clark became prominent in state politics and his son John became governor. John Clark was embroiled in the factionalism that dominated the government of Georgia in the early nineteenth century.

Never known for restraint Elijah Clark was involved in several colorful events. He was given a commission by Citizen Genet to raise an army for an invasion of Florida. That enterprise having failed and being filled with the republican spirit, Clark and associates formed the Trans-Oconee Republic in 1793. It was to be located in Indian territory on the west side of the Oconee River in present-day Morgan, Jasper, Putnam, Jones, and Baldwin counties and was outside the legal boundaries of Georgia and the United States. The Republic erected two forts, Advance and Defiance, near trails crossing the river. Unlike the British who preceded them, the Trans-Oconee Republic government meant to simply take the land by occupation rather than by treaty. President Washington directed Governor Mathews to arrest Clark; that being accomplished there could be no jury found that would sit in judgement of the popular colonel, so he was freed and later elected to the Georgia legislature.

Elijah Clark State Park contains a replica of Clark's home. The house is constructed of logs, two pens separated by a dog trot, and a detached kitchen. It is a fine example of the substantial log homes built on the frontier and is filled with furnishings and implements common during the early days of the American Republic. The Fall Pioneer Rendezvous is held the second weekend of each October. A reproduction of the Philip Younge map of the Ceded Lands (the New Purchase) is displayed in the main room.

8. Price's Store is the oldest operating rural general store in Georgia. Listed on the National Register of Historic Places, Price's sells everything from candy to hardware to fishing gear. Follow Ashmore-Barden road from GA-47 for four miles, then right on Double Branch Road for one mile. Open Monday through Saturday from 6:30 a.m.–7 p.m.

9. Lincoln County Historical Park. The park features a restored doctor's home and one of the oldest hand-operated cotton gins in existence. The park also contains outbuildings and a restored nineteenth century carriage. Located at 147 Lumber Street, Lincolnton.

10. Graves Mountain can be seen from the GA-47 bridge over the Little River, a distance of ten miles. This little mountain is the remnant of a pyroclastic plume where gases and effluent condensed and solidified within the throat of a volcano. This occurred during the time when the island arc chain of volcanoes that became the Piedmont arose in the proto-Atlantic Ocean around 500–700 million years ago. In modern times Graves Mountain was mined for rutile and rhyolite. It is currently fenced and off limits to visitors. US-378 west of Lincolnton.

11. Stevens Creek has a population of the protected rocky shoals spider lily, first described by William Bartram. This colony of lilies is located on private property south of the SC-283 bridge, east of Plum Branch. They are easily viewed from the bridge.

12. Hamilton Branch State Park. Camping, picnic area, playground, boat ramp. Open daily, 6 a.m.–9 p.m., April through September; 6 a.m.–6 p.m. for the remainder of the year. Located on US-221 south of McCormick.

13. Sumter National Forest, Edgefield District. In 1936 the U.S. government established Sumter National Forest and began buying worn-out and abandoned cotton land that had been plundered of timber, game, and soil. The Forest Service and the Civilian Conservation Corps planted trees, arrested erosion, and began building recreational facilities at Lick Fork Lake and Parson's Mountain. Although there are areas of exceptionally diverse forest and rich woods filled with spring wildflowers, much of this worn-out land is in pine plantations. Although not as interesting to the botanist as virgin forest, the land at least has a rest from the destructive farming practices of the past and provides habitat for game animals that

Mark Catesby

Mark Catesby (1682–1749) was the first botanist to explore and collect plant specimens from the Southern frontier outside of Virginia. His legacy is the beautifully illustrated three-volume collection of drawings and descriptions, *The Natural History of Carolina, Florida, and the Bahamas*. He was the first artist to illustrate animals and plants in association and to pose his animals in action. His paintings influenced William Bartram and John James Audubon, both of whom were much better artists.

Mark Catesby completed much of his work before the Linnean system of classification was generally accepted and as a result many of the Catesby names have not been retained. His observations of the geology, plants, animals, and Indians of the South Carolina frontier predate William Bartram by half a century and remain a valuable source for studying the world of the colonial South.

Mark Catesby was raised in the town of Sudbury in Suffolk, England. He was a self-taught artist and became interested in botany at an early age. He traveled to Virginia in 1712 to visit his sister, Elizabeth, who was married to Dr. William Cocke of Williamsburg, a prominent figure in the colonial government. In Virginia Catesby was befriended by William Byrd II who taught him about native American plants. Catesby made extended expeditions around Virginia during the next seven years and returned to England in 1719 where he began showing his drawings.

William Sherard helped secure financial support to send Catesby back to the American colonies. The interest and support of South Carolina's first royal governor, Francis Nicholson, influenced Catesby to travel to Charleston where he landed on May 3, 1722. During the next three years he traveled about the Lowcountry and up the Savannah River to Fort Moore.

Mark Catesby returned to London in 1726. He took a position in Thomas Fairchild's nursery and began to seek subscribers for his planned book. He was supported in his project by Sir Hans Sloane and other prominent men of the Royal Society. Peter Collinson lent him money and gave him access to his garden at Peckham, Surrey, which was filled with plants sent by John Bartram. Catesby completed his book in sections of twenty plates, the first section was presented to the Royal Society in 1729 and the last, an appendix, was completed in the spring of 1747. After 1730 he worked with the noted artist Georg Ehret, who influenced Catesby to use a greater range of values and to add form to his images. During these years Catesby corresponded with botanists in Europe and in the American colonies. Catesby was the go-between for John Clayton and J. F. Gronovius, who published *Flora Virginica*.

Mark Catesby was elected a fellow of the Royal Society on April 26, 1733 and later sponsored General James Oglethorpe for membership. Mark Catesby died on December 23, 1749 and is buried at St. Luke's Church, St. Luke's Parish.

had disappeared until being reintroduced in this century.

Turkey Creek Hiking Trail. Twenty miles. This trail has beautiful sections that pass through climax forests and north-facing slopes reminiscent of mountain terrain. As you hike along Stevens Creek imagine that many now-flooded tributaries of the Savannah River once looked much like this in Bartram's day. The trail is in two sections. The north section runs from SC-283 to the junction of Turkey Creek and Stevens Creek. The south section travels from FS632-A south to SC-23.

Lick Fork Lake Recreation Area. Horn Creek Trail is a six-mile loop from Lick Fork Lake. From Edgefield follow SC-23, turn left on SC-230 then left on CR-263 after a half mile.

14. Edgefield was created in 1785 as the courthouse for Edgefield District. The area has been known for the potters who lived and worked there in the nineteenth century. Pottersville is a museum commemorating the utilitarian ware made at the site; located at the intersection of US-25 and SC-430. Edgefield is also well known for the Antebellum homes, especially Oakley Park which contains memorabilia of the South. The Old Edgefield District Archives contain useful documents for historians and genealogists. The Wild Turkey Center located on US-25 is the headquarters of the National Wild Turkey Federation and has an exhibition area devoted to the noble bird.

15. Stevens Creek Heritage Preserve. Nestled on a steep north-facing slope of Stevens Creek this preserve has one of the most spectacular wildflower displays in the Piedmont. Flowering in April are bloodroot, trout lily, and shooting stars. The Florida gooseberry grows there in the only known place outside of the few sites in Florida. The forest is old growth white oak, American ash, and bitternut hickory. Webster's salamander, a protected and rare species found at Stevens Creek, is found only in McCormick and Edgefield counties. Naturalists believe that Stevens Creek Heritage Preserve is a botanical relic of the Pleistocene age and that much of the Piedmont looked like this during the last glacial period. A hiking trail allows access from CR-88, it continues through the preserve, and loops back along the banks of Stevens Creek. Open during daylight hours.

16. Burks Mountain has been an important local landmark since earliest settlement. It is a geologic formation known as a serpentine barren, due to the lack of nutrients in the parent rock and resulting soil. Serpentine rock is rich in magnesium and is not common this far south of Maryland. The vegetation is stunted and sparse. Michael Godfrey, in the Sierra Club's *Guide to the Piedmont*, noted that what looks like an abandoned field on serpentine rock is really a climax plant community. This is private property but may be viewed from Burks Mountain Road, off US-47 just south of Pollards Corner.

17. Uchee Creek. The Yuchis (or Uchees) moved from eastern Tennessee about 1661 to the Savannah River around Augusta. In the early 1700s another band of Yuchis moved farther down the Savannah River where they settled between Ebenezer Creek and Brier Creek, with their main settlement at Mt. Pleasant. Other towns spread into the frontier west of Augusta during the time when Augusta was the capital of the Indian trade and attracted many small bands of Indians. These Yuchis gave their name to the Ogeechee River.

18. Heggie's Rock. William Bartram's description of the Flat Rock is the earliest mention of the unique botanical community found on the granite outcrops of the Piedmont. Granite outcrops are common in the Piedmont from Lancaster, South Carolina, to Auburn, Alabama. The greatest occurrences are in the area around Atlanta, Sparta, and Elberton in Georgia. In Atlanta and in Pickens County, South Carolina, one finds great dome-shaped outcrops called monadnocks, the best known example being Stone Mountain, Georgia.

These are the basement rock of the ancient mountain chain that was eroded into the present Piedmont. Where molten magma wells up into existing rock, it cools into a harder, more durable rock that erodes more slowly than the surrounding countryside. These *plutons* eventually become exposed and, given time, may become large monadnocks like Stone Mountain.

Heggie's Rock near Appling in Columbia County is not only one of the most beautiful and largest granite outcrops in the Southeast, it is also a botanical wonderland without equal.

Early morning scene on the Old Wrightsborough Road, McDuffie County

A mountain species, rock spike moss, is found there growing in large mats. A species of quill wort is found in only one pool at Heggie's Rock and nowhere else. The rare amphianthus, or pool sprite, is common in the vernal pools here. The spring wildflower display in early April is startling with green mosses, bright red diamorpha, and yellow southern ragwort.

Heggie's Rock is owned by the Nature Conservancy and has had to be fenced and gated due to abuse by adventurers on bicycles and ATV's. Call the Nature Conservancy's Atlanta office to check for availability of field trips.

19. Kiokee Baptist Church, 1772. Old Kiokee Church is located near the intersection of Kiokee Lane and US-221 near Appling. Kiokee Church is the oldest existing Baptist Church in Georgia and was organized in 1772 by **Reverend Daniel Marshall**. The memorial to Reverend Marshall is built on the site his farm on Kiokee Lane just east of Kiokee Creek. Marshall was ordered to leave Georgia for preaching without permission but answered his antagonists with the question "whether it be right to obey God or man?"

Old Kiokee Baptist Church is open during daylight hours.

20. The Old Columbia County Courthouse in Appling dates from 1812 and is the oldest continually used courthouse in the state.

21. William Few was a Revolutionary War soldier, Georgia statesman, and signer of the Constitution. The site of Few's home is on GA-150 near the Columbia-Wilkes county line. He is buried in the yard of St. Paul's Church in downtown Augusta.

22. Brandon on the Little River. The first Quakers in Georgia settled north of Augusta at the township of Brandon, which appears on old maps but may never have been built. Tensions with the Indians forced them to retreat to Augusta. Edmund Gray, professing the Quaker religion, settled there but left with his followers (known as Gray's Gang) when he was denied a seat in the Assembly. They went south of the Altamaha and founded New Hanover on the Satilla River in the neutral area between Georgia and Florida. Governor Ellis forced them out but they reassembled after making a pretense of dispersing.

23. Mistletoe State Park was named for Mistletoe Junction, known for its abundance of mistletoe. The attractions of the park are the recreational amenities—beach, Clarks Hill Lake, boat ramps, camping, picnic area, and hiking trails.

24. The Rocks. William Bartram took refuge at the Rocks as he returned to Augusta from Wrightsborough. He mistook the white rocks for the faint candlelight of a farm house. The rocks are now gone, victims of urban development. They were located just north of the Wrightsborough Road near Jackson Road.

25. Flowing Wells Spring. A number of springs, or flowing wells, occur in the Augusta area. One of the most popular is the Flowing Wells Spring on Wrightsborough Road near the site of the Rocks. The Spring is protected by a house and a pipe diverts water for public use.

26. Quaker Springs no longer exists but was a well-known spring on the old Quaker Road that was built in 1769. Its name remains today as a street and apartment complex in Martinez just off GA-232, the Columbia Road.

27. Savannah Rapids. The rapids, or falls, of the Savannah River stretch for much of the length of the Augusta Canal. The upper end of the rapids has been an important crossing for humans and animals for thousands of years.

Savannah Rapids Park. The Park provides access to Augusta Canal Lock and Dam Park and the levee. The Park is located at the end of Evans to Locks Road and is open during daylight hours. Each March Columbia County holds the Savannah Rapids Spring Festival where recreational services offered by various organizations are exhibited. Entertainment and crafts are also features of the festival.

28. Thomas Brown was a recent immigrant living near New Richmond at the opening of the Revolution. He was a vocal loyalist and ridiculed the American cause during a toast. He was captured by patriots on August 1, 1775, and taken to Augusta where he was tarred, feathered, and badly burned. Brown was taken to a nearby plantation for confinement and care. His guard called for a doctor to tend his wounds then allowed Brown to escape. Brown fled to South Carolina where he allied himself with Thomas Fletchall and the loyalists. He then moved to Saint Augustine and organized refugee loyalists into the East Florida Rangers. Brown offered their services to Governor Tonyn and was given the rank of lieutenant colonel. Brown's associate was the notorious Daniel McGirth, a former South Carolina Regulator. Brown became a bitter enemy of the patriots due to his harsh treatment at their hands.

The East Florida Rangers served as spies, scouts, hunters, and guerillas for regular army operations. They exemplified the fact that the Revolution was a civil war as much as it was a war of independence. They raided the empty lands between the Altamaha River and East Florida. Their wives in Georgia built rude huts along the Ogeechee River for their husbands refuge when raiding among the settled parts of Georgia. Brown and the Rangers were with Prevost at the capture of Savannah. On June 8, 1780, Brown and his troops, renamed the Royal Carolina Rangers, took Augusta and occupied Fort Cornwallis until June of the following year.

After the war Brown settled in the Bahamas for nearly twenty years then spent his last years as a wealthy sugar planter on St. Vincent.

29. Augusta Canal. The Augusta Canal was opened in 1846 to carry goods around the rapids of the Savannah River. The canal is nine miles long and ends in Augusta at 13th Street. The canal also provided water power for mills and municipal water for home use and

Rocky shoals spider lily, Hymenocallis coronaria

firefighting. Boats going upstream provided people of Augusta with pleasure excursions and the locks became a popular place for picnics and dances.

In 1976 the Augusta Bartram Trail Bicentennial Committee and associated organizations built the Bartram Memorial Trail on the towpath of Augusta Canal. The part of the trail along the canal was a wilderness trail and five miles of trail in town was a historical trail. The Bartram Trail did not become popular enough to keep it from becoming overgrown and it fell to the fate underused trails suffer in many urban areas, the wrong sort of people began using it for the wrong sort of activities.

In 1990 the city of Augusta closed the locks because of safety concerns and began restoring the trail and Lock and Dam Park. Construction of Savannah Rapids Pavilion at the locks has helped bring people to the park again by providing parking, restrooms, and a sense of permanence. The towpath is now a popular hiking and bicycling trail for families and sports enthusiasts. On spring and fall weekends hundreds of people are out on the towpath. Unfortunately, the trail is no longer called the Bartram Memorial Trail.

Today the Augusta Canal has a canoe trail beginning at the locks and ending at Meadow Garden. The most popular section of the hiking trail is from the locks to the waterworks parking area. An interesting feature to look for are the squatters houses on the riverside of the towpath, relics of a time when the property was abandoned.

Augusta Canal was designated a National Heritage Area in 1996. Plans call for a nature trail on the south side of the canal, a Petersburg boat interpretative area, a connecting trail along the river from the waterworks to Riverwalk, an exhibit at the Confederate Powder Works, and an industrial museum at the old Enterprise Mill. Plans also include the restoration of the Old Second Level and creation of an ecumenical park. When all is completed the Augusta Canal will be one of the premier urban recreation areas in the South.

Information and maps are available at the Cotton Exchange, corner of Eighth and Reynolds streets.

30. Savannah Bluffs Heritage Preserve was established to protect the rocky shoals spider lily, relict trillium, yellowwood, and a disjunct population of bottlebrush buckeye (discovered by William Bartram on the Chattahoochee River). The steep rocky slopes of the Piedmont blend into Coastal Plain where palmetto and Spanish moss grow at the lower end of the thousand foot river front.

From SC-230 in North Augusta go north to Plantation Road, just before I-20. Turn left and follow Plantation Road to Plantation Drive, keep left and the street becomes Savannah Barony in a recently built subdivision. Turn onto the powerline right-of-way and park. Signs and a gate mark the entrance to the hiking trail. Open during daylight hours.

31. North Augusta Greenway. The first three-mile phase of the Greenway was opened in 1997 and travels from Riverview Park north along an old railroad bed to end at Martintown Road. It is paved and relatively flat, accessible to all non-motorized activities. Eventually the trail will cover eight miles along the Savannah River through North Augusta. Significant plants along the trail are coral honeysuckle, atamasco lily, ferns, magnolias, Florida clover, and phlox. The largest colony of the endangered relict trillium grows along the Greenway. From Georgia Avenue in downtown North Augusta follow West Buena Vista until it ends at Georgetown Road, turn left and go to Riverview Park. The trail head is to the right of the Activity Center.

32. Riverview Park. Boat ramp and access to North Augusta Greenway. Follow West Buena Vista from Georgia Avenue in downtown North Augusta, then left on Georgetown Road.

33. Hamburg Railroad. When the railroad from Charleston to Hamburg was completed in 1833 it was the longest line in the world at 138 miles. It was constructed to take the Upcountry cotton shipping business away from Augusta and Savannah. At first the builders did not plan to cross the river with track but the Augusta cotton market was so important that it became necessary to extend the line across the Savannah. Hamburg was therefore eclipsed by Augusta and did not begin to grow until it became a resort in the late nineteenth century. The community was incorporated as North Augusta in 1906.

34. Fort Moore was built in 1717 in the aftermath of the Yamassee War. It was named for General James Moore and occupies the site of Old Savannah Town, a Shawnee village. The fort was abandoned in 1766 and by the time Bartram visited the site in 1773 little was left of the fort because the bluff had been eroded by spring freshets.

In 1723 a band of Chickasaws, tiring of conflict with the French, moved from their home in Mississippi to Fort Moore. They were deeded their land by South Carolina but by the 1760s they had moved across the Savannah River to New Savannah Town because the South Carolina side had became settled by whites. Before the Revolution the Chickasaws moved back to their homeland in Mississippi.

35. Phinizy Swamp Nature Park is only a step away from downtown Augusta but is teeming with wildlife including such elusive creatures as bobcats, alligators, and otters. Phinizy Swamp is a nature preserve and learning environment encompassing 1,100 acres. The Park is operated by the Southeastern Natural Sciences Academy and is adjacent to **Phinizy Swamp Wildlife Management Area**. The entire ecosystem protects over 7,000 acres of wetland.

To reach Phinizy Swamp take Bobby Jones Expressway (I-520) to exit 10, travel south on Doug Bernard Parkway one mile to Lock and Dam Road. The entrance is one-half mile on the left. The Park is open from dawn to dusk on Saturday and Sunday, closed on Christmas Day.

36. New Savannah Town. Shawnees (Shawano or Sowanoka) who were living in the eastern part of Tennessee were being displaced as the Cherokees as they expanded their territory in the seventeenth century. In 1674 two Shawnee men who had recently been to Saint Augustine met Henry Woodward at a Westo town in the upper part of South Carolina. These two men enticed their people to move from the Cumberland River to the Savannah River. They drove the Westoes away in 1681 and remained on the Savannah River at Beech Island until about 1707 when they began to rejoin their relatives in Pennsylvania and Kentucky. Some settled across the river south of Augusta at New Savannah Town. The last of the Shawnees moved to the Coosa River about 1725. The Savannah River takes its name from an English pronunciation of their name.

37. Redcliffe Plantation State Park. The plantation house was built in 1857 by James Hammond, governor of South Carolina, and is the centerpiece of the park. There is also a picnic area and Redcliffe Trail.

38. Dearing is located near the fork of the Upper and Lower Creek Trading Paths. In a little

Wrightsborough Methodist Church, constructed in 1810, marks the heart of the old town of Wrightsborough

book titled *A History of Dearing, McDuffie County, Georgia from 1850 to 1904*, the author, A. J. Taylor, tells of the rough times in the mid-1800s. He describes the drinking and fighting that took place on Saturday afternoons. It was a grisly business—eyes gouged out, ears bitten off, and staggering drunkenness. The religious revival that swept the nation in the 1840s brought churches to the area and religious conversion lead men to abandon the bottle and fisticuffs.

39. Stagecoach Road. This old thoroughfare was at one time the stage route from Augusta to Washington and Athens. It was built on the original colonial road from Augusta to Wrightsborough.

39. The Rock House is the only remaining home from the early Quaker settlement of Wrightsborough. It was built about 1784 by Thomas Ansley and is patterned after the houses of the Delaware River Valley.

4. Wrightsborough. In 1767 Joseph Maddock and Jonathan Sell petitioned for a grant of land in Georgia and subsequently brought 124 Quaker families from Orange County, North Carolina to the frontier near Augusta. The reasons for leaving North Carolina were related to Governor Tryon's harsh taxes, unfair seizure of property in lieu of unpaid taxes, tensions caused by the Regulator movement, and a possible schism within the Quaker meeting at Hillsboro. The land grant was part of an Indian land cession in 1763 and a reserve of 12,000 acres was created for the Quakers.

In 1770 additional land was obtained and in this new grant a thousand-acre section was laid out into a town and named for Governor James Wright. The early road to Wrightsborough from Augusta was what is now Stagecoach Road and GA-232 by way of Quaker Springs. In 1773 the present Wrightsborough Road was opened and the first meetinghouse was built. Wrightsborough was not so much a compact town at first but a collection of family farms scattered throughout the larger township.

When William Bartram visited Wrightsborough the town proper had about twenty houses and must have presented a pleasing contrast to the normal settlement patterns prevalent in Georgia at the time. The Quakers were frugal, industrious, educated, and they formed a close-knit community. They grew a greater variety of produce than did the typical Southern farmer—fruits, vegetables, berries, honey, flax, grain, cattle, sheep, horses, and various fowl. They built gristmills on the numerous creeks.

During the Revolution the Quakers at Wrightsborough were caught between the Whigs and Tories, both sides resented and distrusted them because of their pacifism. Quakers were exempted from military service but had to pay an extra twenty-five percent tax. Yet, there were Quaker men who served the patriot cause. They were dismissed from meeting during the war, then accepted again once their service ended if they confessed their misconduct. Many Quakers sought refuge in Savannah when Whigs vented their anger by plundering from those who had not joined the patriot cause.

A greater threat to the Quaker community of Wrightsborough came with the invention of the cotton gin in 1793 and the increased presence of slaves because the Quakers' industriousness was degraded by the presence of a large pool of cheap labor. Quakers had universally rejected slavery in 1774, then, in 1802, Quaker prophet Zachariah Dicks visited Wrightsborough and urged his brethren to remove themselves from among slaveholders and leave Georgia. He predicted a civil war that would take place within the lives of the youngest generation, a war that would bring about the slaughter of Quakers. By 1806 not a practicing Quaker was left in Georgia, most having moved to Ohio. Some renounced their faith in the Society of Friends and remained in Georgia.

Wrightsborough continued on as a town. The present Methodist church was built in 1810 to serve all faiths. Wrightsborough had a post office, woolen mill, stores, newspaper, tavern, and Wrightsborough Academy. The town was incorporated in 1837. The Georgia Railroad was built through Thomson in 1833, helping that town grow at the expense of Wrightsborough. The Civil War disrupted life and took the lives of many young men. In this century people left Wrightsborough to find work in other towns. The arrival of the boll weevil and loss of the cotton gin to a fire in the 1920s destroyed the last industry in the town. Today what is left is the church and about a half-dozen homes.

From Thomson go north on US-78 and turn left on Stagecoach Road, or follow Old Wrightsborough Road from US-78 in Thomson.

Counties

Aiken County, SC. Named for one of the directors of the Charleston-Hamburg Railroad.

Columbia County, GA. Organized in 1790 and named for the feminine symbol of America.

Edgefield County, SC, was created in 1785 out of the Ninety Six District and named for the town of Edgefield.

McDuffie County, GA, was organized in 1870 and named for George McDuffie, statesman of South Carolina.

Richmond County, GA, is one of Georgia's original counties organized by the Assembly in 1777. Named for Charles Lennox, Duke of Richmond, a friend of the American colonies.

Warren County, GA, is named for General Joseph Warren who was one of the first Americans killed at the Battle of Bunker Hill. Organized in 1793.

Lincoln County, GA, was created in 1796 out of Wilkes County and named for Revolutionary War hero General Benjamin Lincoln.

McCormick County, SC, is named for Cyrus McCormick, the inventor of the reaping machine and an investor in the gold fields of South Carolina. He donated the land for the town of McCormick. The county was organized in 1916 from parts of Abbeville, Greenwood, and Edgefield counties.

Itinerary

Savannah to Augusta

Begin Old Savannah Road (GA-56) at McBean Creek

Miles Directions
- 14.0 Right on US-25
- 0.3 Left on Savannah Road
- 0.8 Savannah Road becomes Twiggs Street after the intersection with M. L. King Boulevard
- 0.8 Downtown Augusta

Excursion to Wrightsborough

Begin at St. Paul's Episcopal Church and travel South on Sixth Street

Miles Directions
- .4 Keep right on Twiggs Street
- 1.1 Right on Wrightsborough Road
- 7.9 Flowing Wells Spring
- 6.5 Right on GA-223, still Wrightsborough Road
- 12.0 Right on Whiteoak Road
- 1.0 Left on Stagecoach Road
- .4 Left on Stagecoach Road
- 10.4 Wrightsborough

Excursion to Fort James

Begin at St. Pauls Episcopal Church and travel west on Reynolds Street

Miles Directions
- 1.3 Left on Fifteenth Street
- .1 Right on Broad Street
- 1.7 Right on Washington Road, GA-28
- 4.5 Right on Old Petersburg Road
- 2.3 Right on Old Evans Road
- 1.3 Right on Washington Road
- 10.5 Pollards Corner, keep straight on Ga-47
- 7.2 Cross Little River
- 5.2 Right on GA-220
- 2.1 Left on Old Petersburg Road, GA-220
- 6.6 Left on US-378
- .4 Right on Bethany Church Road
- 4.8 Right on GA-79

Return from Keowee

Begin at the Intersection of US78/SC28 in McCormick

Miles Directions
- 20.0 Right on US-221
- 7.7 Intersection at Pollards Corner
- 5.3 Right on White Oak Road
- 7.3 Right on GA-223

To the Creek Nation

Because William Bartram ended his return trip from the Creek Nation at Augusta in the winter of 1775, the itinerary for this trip will begin in downtown Augusta at St. Paul's Episcopal Church and travel south on Sixth Street

Miles Directions
- .4 Keep right on Twiggs Street
- 1.3 Right on Martin Luther King Boulevard, US-78/278
- 1.7 Martin Luther King Boulevard becomes Milledgeville Road
- 4.6 Left on Fort Gordon Highway, US-78
- 7.8 Right on Old Augusta Berzilia Road
- .1 Left on Old Augusta Berzilia Road
- 5.1 Right on Fort Gordon Highway, US-78
- 6.5 Left on Hobbs Mill Road in Dearing
- 5.5 Left
- .3 Right on Fort Creek Road
- .3 Cross GA-17 and begin Happy Valley Road

Historic Augusta

Governor James Oglethorpe directed that a fort and town be built on the Savannah River at a point where trading paths crossed the falls of the river. He ws inspired by Samuel Eveleigh of Charleston who applied for 250 acres at a place called Kenyon's Bluff. Eveleigh promised to build a fort and wanted a five-year monopoly on the deerskin trade. Oglethorpe feared that the South Carolina trade was poorly controlled and that the Indian allies of the English might be pushed to seek better terms among the French in Louisiana. He quickly saw the advantage of building his own fort at the bluff. The site for the fort was selected by Kennedy O'Brien and Roger de Lacy and the first warehouse in Augusta was built by O'Brien. Oglethorpe visited Augusta only once, in 1739.

Georgia law required any trader working west of the Savannah River to obtain a license and to adhere to Georgia regulations. These regulations created fixed and fair prices, abolished rum as a trade item, and provided an avenue for legal redress of complaints by the Indians. Oglethorpe rightly saw that amicable relations with the Creeks was necessary for the survival of the young Georgia colony. South Carolina objected and had her agents in London argue against the Georgia regulations, but to no avail. Upstart Georgia had the temerity to impound Charleston rum from boats headed up the Savannah River.

The new fort on the upper Savannah would help control the Indian trade in Georgia territory and draw business away from Fort Moore, which lay directly across the river in South Carolina. Indeed, the traders of South Carolina abandoned Fort Moore and moved across the river where they dominated the business of early Augusta. Construction on the fort and lot surveys were begun in 1737 by Roger de Lacy. The new frontier city was named Augusta in honor of Augusta of Saxe-Gotha, the new wife of Frederick Louis, Prince of Wales, and mother of King George III. The original town plan called for forty lots surrounded by a commons. Forty years later, at the outbreak of the Revolution, Augusta was a community of scattered homesteads and farms along the river instead of a discrete and compact city. In 1776 Augusta contained about a hundred houses, a considerable town in a vast frontier. In March 1776 the provincial government moved to Augusta.

Augusta was the most important town on the Southeastern frontier at the end of the colonial period, owing her success to the Indian traders who operated their far-flung businesses from Augusta warehouses. Among the businessmen who helped make Augusta the center of the Indian trade in the Southeast were Samuel Brown, George Curry, Kennedy O'Brien, Joseph Pavey, Lachlan McBean, Lachlan McGillivray, and George Galphin. Each spring a trade fair was held that filled the city with thousands of Indians and adventurers. These successful traders enlisted subcontractors to carry goods into the Indian towns and act as their agents. These men often lived among the Indians for part of the year, marrying and raising children. They were a vital link between the Native Americans and the European economy. The success of the Scots in the Indian trade was due in no small part to common cultural traits—such as clan loyalty, a warrior class, living close to the earth, and a

Site of Fort Augusta, located behind St. Paul's Episcopal Church at the Augusta levee

reputation for being hot-blooded. For good reason the Scots were called *White Brother to the Cherokee*.

At the end French and Indian War a congress was held in Augusta on November 5, 1763, where the English informed the Creeks, Choctaws, and Chickasaws that they could no longer look to the French for aid. In attendance were the governors of North and South Carolina, Virginia, and Georgia and 800 representatives of the Southern tribes. New boundaries were delineated between Indian and English land, and the Indian trade was open to all comers who could get a license. Soon the unethical business practices that had lead to the Yamassee War in 1715 reappeared after years of careful control by the governor and the powerful Augusta traders. The borders of Georgia were pushed to the Little River in the north and the Ogeechee River in the west.

White settlement beyond the Appalachians was forbidden by the Royal Proclamation of 1763. Migration was thus diverted southward and many new settlers appeared in the Piedmont of Georgia and South Carolina. New tensions arose as the Indian trade practices worsened and barely civilized frontier whites settled on Indian land. The more lawless among the whites committed atrocities against Indians, including murder and the theft of livestock.

Another congress was held at Augusta in 1773 in which the Creeks and Cherokees agreed to sell land in exchange for retiring their debts to the Augusta traders. William Bartram awaited the conclusion of the meeting and traveled with the survey party into the New Purchase.

Augusta was the unofficial end of the Great Wagon Road over which settlers poured into the Georgia Piedmont when the French and Indian War ended. Following the Revolution Augusta became the capital of Georgia from 1785 to 1795. Tobacco was the staple of the economy after the Revolution and Augusta was made an inspection and warehousing site for the leaf being shipped from the Piedmont. Very soon after Eli Whitney built his cotton engine in 1793, gins and cotton fields appeared in the Piedmont and Augusta became the second-largest inland cotton market after Memphis. The volume of

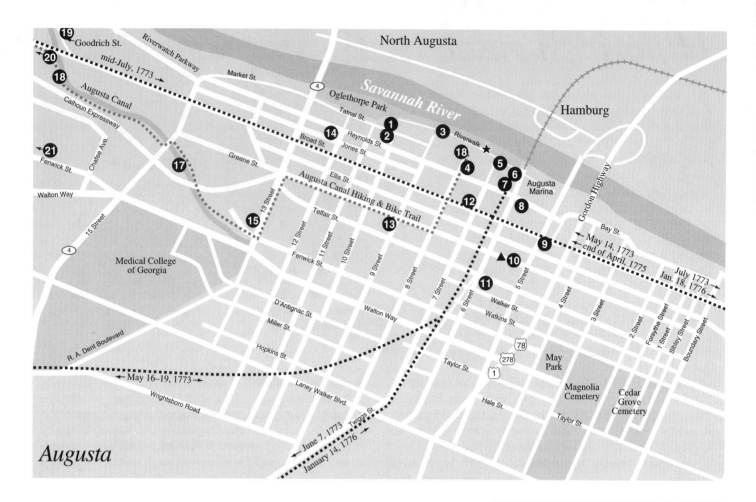

cotton arriving in Augusta was so great that it was temporarily stored in the streets until it could be shipped. Cotton drove the building of the first railroads in the South and Augusta became a railroad town when the Hamburg Railroad was extended across the river from South Carolina in 1833.

Today Augusta has a vibrant economy with a mix of manufacturing, nearby Fort Gordon, several colleges including the Medical College of Georgia, regional recreational facilities, and the Masters Golf Tournament.

Sites

1. Morris Museum of Art. The Morris Museum is the only art museum devoted entirely to the art and artists of the South. The collection spans the last two centuries and includes functional pieces as well as folk and high art. One of the ten galleries is devoted to Southern landscape painting during the last 150 years. Located at Tenth Street and Riverwalk. Tuesday through Saturday, 10 a.m.–5:30 p.m.; Sunday, 12:30–5:30. Admission.

2. Historic Augusta, Inc., dedicated to the preservation of Augusta's history. Information on tours and historic sites is available at the office located at 111 Tenth Street.

3. Riverwalk. The levee between Fifth and Tenth streets has become a popular promenade since its development in 1987. The Riverwalk has displays on the history of the Savannah River and Augusta. At the south end of Riverwalk are the railroad bridge and marina. There are two levels, bankside and top of the levee. The lower walk contains landscaped areas of native plants. The Bartram Trail historical marker is located on the lower walk near the Eighth Street entrance.

4. The Cotton Exchange Welcome Center. The Cotton Exchange was built in 1886 when Augusta was the world's second-largest inland cotton market, after Memphis, Tennessee. At one time there were over two hundred members of the exchange, today there are only three. In addition to tracking prices for cotton and other commodities, the Cotton Exchange became a sort of unofficial men's club where members played checkers, cards, and bet on sports events—women and children were not allowed in the Exchange.

Legend

1. Morris Museum of Art
2. Historic Augusta, Inc.
3. Riverwalk
4. The Cotton Exchange Welcome Center
5. Fort Discovery
6. Site of Fort Augusta
7. Saint Paul's Episcopal Church
8. Augusta-Richmond County Museum
9. Haunted Pillar
10. Signers Monument
11. Old Medical College
12. *The Augusta Chronicle*
13. Augusta-Richmond County Public Library
14. Springfield Baptist Church
15. Meadow Garden
16. Lucey Laney Museum
17. Augusta Canal
18. Bartram Trail
19. Confederate Powder Works
20. Ezekiel Harris House
21. Richmond County Historical Society collections

The Welcome Center contains ongoing exhibits on cotton farming and the ginning process. There are many locally collected artifacts such as plows, fertilizer, and cotton scales. Of particular interest is the forty-five-foot chalkboard where cotton prices were posted. It was uncovered during renovation and has figures dating from the early part of this century.

32 Eighth Street, (706) 724–4067. Open Monday through Saturday, 9 a.m.–5 p.m., and Sundays, 1–5 p.m.

5. Fort Discovery is the National Science Center's interactive science and technology center andy is one of the premier science and technology learning centers in the nation. Exhibits involve hands-on experiments in gravity, power generation, computer technology, imaging and perception, electronics, robotics, and space technology. The Teacher Resource Center and NSC programs promote math and science education. Enter from Riverfront Science Plaza on Riverwalk. Open Monday through Saturday from 10 a.m.–6 p.m., Sundays from 12–6 p.m. Closed on Thanksgiving and Christmas. Admission.

6. Site of Fort Augusta. The Saint Andrew's cross behind Saint Paul's Episcopal Church marks the site of Fort Augusta, built in 1737, and the origins of the city of Augusta.

7. Saint Paul's Episcopal Church. The present church was built in 1916 and is the fourth building on this site. The first church was built in 1750 at the edge of Fort Augusta and became the mother church for Saint Paul's Parish. Eighteenth-century graves that lie within the churchyard include William Few, patriot and signer of the Constitution.

8. Augusta-Richmond County Museum. The imposing new museum brings together many exhibits that feature the natural and cultural history of the Augusta area. Beginning with the creation of the earth, exhibits tell of the earth's formations and the era of dinosaurs. The human era begins with the first inhabitants of 4,500 years ago, and include portrayals of the cultures of Native Americans, European discovery and settlement, Revolutionary conflict, cotton era, Civil War, and modern technology. The aquarium contains species of the Savannah River and a Petersburg boat is on display. Located at 560 Reynolds Street, corner of Sixth Street. Open Tuesday through Saturday, 10 a.m.–5 p.m. Closed major holidays. Admission.

9. Haunted Pillar. This pillar is all that remains of the old Lower Market where Augustans sold produce, livestock, and slaves in the early nineteenth century. When a preacher was barred from preaching at the market he

The Deerskin Trade

Native Americans were eager to obtain the manufactured goods brought by Europeans. They used deerskins to trade for metal knives, guns, woven cloth, mirrors, scissors, hoes, and axes. The deerskins were in high demand in Europe for the leather was very soft and comfortable to wear. The natural balance between the Indians and their environment was strained as deer were hunted, not for food, but for their skins alone and the population began to plummet.

The deerskin trade also upset the traditional economic structure of the Southern tribes and their clans. Historically all property resided with the women as well as final authority over selection of leaders. The deerskin trade elevated the role of the husband and warrior. Their position soon supplanted that of the women as the source of the economic base and the women lost much of the power that they traditionally held.

put a curse on the building, predicting that it would be destroyed by a great wind but for one pillar. This came to pass in 1878. Stories since then account for the deaths of people who have attempted to disturb or move the pillar. Two men who tried to move the pillar during a street-widening project were supposedly struck by lightning and killed. Alhough many doubt that there is any real merit to the curse, there are many who avoid the pillar and it is now a popular tourist attraction. Corner of Fifth Street and Broad.

10. Signers Monument. Beneath the obelisk in the middle of the 500 block of Greene Street lie the remains of Lyman Hall and George Walton, signers of the Declaration of Independence. The monument honors all three Georgia signers, but the location of Button Gwinnett's grave in Savannah is unknown.

11. Old Medical College was built in 1835 for the Georgia Medical Society and was one of the first medical colleges in the U.S. It is now used for social events and is open for tours by appointment. 598 Telfair Street.

12. The *Augusta Chronicle* is the oldest operating newspaper in the South. It began as the *Augusta Gazette* in August 1785. Through several name changes, mergers, and owners, the newspaper has not missed a publication date since the yellow fever epidemic of 1839. The *Augusta Chronicle* is the first newspaper to put its entire data base online. Visitors can use the internet to search the archives back to 1918. Located at 725 Broad Street.

13. Augusta-Richmond County Public Library. Greene and Ninth Street.

14. Springfield Baptist Church was organized in 1787 and has held services at this location since that time. It is one of the oldest black congregations in the nation and the current building dates from 1801. The founder, Jesse Peters, was educated in the ministry by Reverend Abraham Marshall of Kiokee Baptist Church. The Augusta Baptist Institute was organized at Springfield Church in 1867 and later became Morehouse College in Atlanta. The Georgia Equal Rights Association was organized at Springfield Baptist Church in 1866. 114 Twelveth Street, tours by appointment only.

15. Meadow Garden (c. 1791) is the historic home of George Walton. Walton came to Augusta around 1769 and represented Saint Paul's Parish in the provincial congress. He was elected president of the Council of Safety and a delegate to the Continental Congress where he became the youngest signer of the Declaration of Independence. After the Revolution he was elected Chief Justice and twice governor of Georgia. Walton was a political enemy of Lachlan McIntosh and was responsible for much of the general's political problems during his military service. Walton was visited by George Washington during the president's southern tour in 1791. Meadow Garden was the first historic preservation project in Georgia.

Located at Thirteenth Street and Walton Way. Open Monday through Friday, 10 a.m.–4 p.m. Admission.

16. Lucey Laney Museum. Lucey Craft Laney started the first kindergarten for blacks in Augusta, the first nurses' training for blacks, and the Haines Institute where thousands of young blacks received their education.

1116 Phillip Street, (706) 724–3576, tours by appointment.

17. Augusta Canal. The Augusta Canal was built to bring water to Augusta for drinking and as a power source. Several nineteenth-century mills can be seen from the tow path hiking trail, one of the loveliest trails in the Piedmont. The canoe, hiking, and bicycling trail end at Thirteenth Street. Other sections of Level Two and Level Three of the Canal may be renovated and flooded in the future.

18. Bartram Trail. A green marker on Cotton Row at Riverwalk indicates the beginning of the Bartram Memorial Trail that was established in 1976. The original route was along the levee, but construction of Riverwatch Parkway has closed that section at the north end of Riverwalk. The new trail is now called the Augusta Canal Trail. It starts (or ends) at Riverwalk and Eighth Street, follows Eighth Street then right on Greene, left on Twelveth, then Fenwick Street to the Canal Basin and the levee. Maps are available at the Cotton Exchange.

19. Confederate Powder Works. All that remains of the powder works building is the 168-foot chimney, now a memorial to the Confederate soldiers who lost their lives in the Civil War. The original site contained twenty-six buildings, was the largest powder works in the world when completed, and was the only permanent structure built and completed by the Confederate States government. The buildings were torn down in the late eighteenth century to make way for Sibley, King, Enterprise, and Sutherland mills—all still standing.

20. Ezekiel Harris House (1797). Ezekiel Harris was a prominent tobacco merchant. He built his house outside Augusta in Harrisburg, a town that was expected to compete economically with Augusta for the tobacco trade. The house is notable for its eclectic use of styles. 1822 Broad Street. Admission.

21. Richmond County Historical Society collections are held at the Reese Library at Augusta College. 2500 Walton Way.

Indian Paths

During the second half of the eighteenth century Augusta was the center for the Southeastern Indian trade. Many important trails that carried pack horses, traders, and hunters to and from Augusta were famous in their day and continued to be used as wagon roads. Towns grew up along these trails and their routes are today major highways.

Hightower (Etowah or Itawa) Trail, also known as the Lower Cherokee Path, passed through Dearing, Camak, Crawfordville, Union Point, and Greensboro.

Middle Cherokee Path. This trail ran from Augusta across the Little River to Washington, Lexington, Crawford, and crossed the Oconee River at Athens. From there it traversed Hall County to north of Atlanta and on to Chattanooga. It was an important route to the western Tennessee towns and became part of the Cherokee Federal Highway that brought access to such far-away places as Knoxville and Nashville.

Upper Cherokee Path. This was the route that the New Purchase survey party followed from Tugaloo back to Augusta in July 1773. The trail ran from Augusta up the west side of the Savannah River very close to the banks. From the junction of the Tugaloo and Seneca rivers at present-day Hartwell, the trail ran up the western side of the Tugaloo to meet other important trails at a place called the Dividings, which is now the site of Clayton, Georgia.

Lower Creek Trading Path. Hightower Trail and the Lower Creek Trading Path forked at Dearing. The Lower Path then followed the county line between Warren-Glascock and Hancock-Washington through Linton and crossed the Oconee River at Rock Landing below Milledgeville.

Oakfuskie, Upper Creek Path. The Oakfuskie Path diverged from the Lower Creek Path a little east of Harlem. The two paths ranged up to fifty miles apart before coming together again in the Creek Towns on the Alabama River. Near Sweetwater Creek the Hightower Trail branched northward from the Oakfuskie Trail. The Oakfuskie Trail continued through Warrenton and over the Ogeechee River at Latimore's Mill just above Mayfield. It crossed the Oconee above Milledgeville at Shoulderbone Creek.

The Cotton Kingdom

Cotton, more than any other feature of the landscape, was to dominate the commerce and minds of the South to such an extent that one cannot think of the Old South without visions of fields of pure white fiber.

During the colonial period Parliament viewed the colonies as producers of raw materials and consumers of English manufactured goods. Regulations prevented the colonists from entering into manufacturing that competed directly with English businesses. This helped create a state-of-mind in the colonies that favored the production of raw materials on a large scale while discouraging industrial innovation.

In populous New England local artisans found steady work supplying the prosperous farmers. In the sparsely settled South the easiest way to prosperity was through agriculture since large amounts of cheap land was readily available. Southern colonists supplied England with lumber, naval stores, beef, rice, tobacco, and indigo. Tobacco was the most profitable crop until 1793 when Eli Whitney built the first practical cotton engine. The new British textile mills created a sharply increased demand for cotton and prices soared. At the end of the eighteenth century cotton planting soared. Shipments from the South increased from five-million pounds in 1793 to 225 million in 1825.

Cotton cultivation required labor, always in short supply in the South, and gave a boost to the institution of slavery at a time when it seemed to be on the wane. Cheap land, slave labor, and cotton fever helped develop the character of the Antebellum South. Slave labor and cotton built most of the large plantation homes across the cotton belt. The need to get cotton to market was the impetus for building the early railroads and improving public roads. The first railroad in North America was the Charleston-Hamburg line, built to draw the cotton trade from the Piedmont of Georgia and South Carolina to Charleston. Savannah soon followed with a railroad building boom of her own and became the largest cotton port in the Antebellum United States.

Even after the Civil War brought freedom to American slaves, the switch to sharecropping continued to keep poor blacks and whites planting, chopping, and picking cotton. The dependence on one crop continued to dominate the Southern economy until the boll weevil spread across the region in the 1920s. Today in Enterprise, Alabama, there is a monument to the boll weevil—acknowledging its role in forcing the South to develop a modern and more varied economy.

Great Buffalo Lick

During the colonial period there were few inhabitants in the Georgia Piedmont outside the Savannah River Valley. In prehistoric times there was a chiefdom centered at Shoulderbone Creek in Hancock County with its northern territory at Scull Shoals on the Oconee River. In the wake of the De Soto expedition it seems that the native people left the area then returned in the 18th century, lured by trade with Charleston. Spanish coins dated 1718 have been found in Greene County. Due to a lack of specie even the English colonists used Spanish coins, the most common form of currency in the New World. When William Bartram arrived, the Georgia Piedmont was a Creek hunting reserve crisscrossed by trails and there were a few cowpens scattered throughout the area.

During the French and Indian War, which lasted roughly from 1753 to 1760, settlers avoided the turbulent frontier of western Pennsylvania and turned southward. All along the Piedmont in North and South Carolina the frontier was filling up with settlers who kept testing the limits of the vague borders between the colonies and the Indian nations. This was a concern to Parliament and British officials in America for they hoped that further conflicts with the Native Americans could be avoided, especially considering the costly war just concluded against the French and their Indian allies. For that reason a Royal Proclamation Line was established in 1763 that set the legal limits of European settlement. Quite often what made the difference between a patriot and a loyalist early in the Revolution was whether one felt that their interests had been served by the King who gave land and protection, or disserved by Parliament who protected the Indian lands from white encroachment.

Stephens, Georgia, is situated on the Great Ridge and within a few miles of the Great Buffalo Lick

There was a growing sentiment on the frontier that the business interests of the wealthy traders and status quo was being protected at the expense of opportunities for the average farm family. The wealthy landowners in the settled parts of the Southern colonies had benefited by the influx of poor settlers into the interior, for those very frontiersmen were a barrier between the gentry and the Indians.

In the early 1770s white settlers began crossing the Savannah River from South Carolina and moving north from Augusta to settle illegally in the region that was to become known as the New Purchase. In 1773 Governor James Wright was made aware that the Cherokees were trying to sell this land to traders in Augusta in order to settle their debts, which had become substantial. Parliament had forbade private individuals from buying Indian land or settling west of the Proclamation Line. Wright therefore took charge of the negotiations and approached the Creeks about also retiring their debts with a sale of land. The Creeks were not so enthusiastic because their debts were negligible. The treaty was signed in Augusta in early June and the boundary was surveyed. William Bartram joined the survey party that marked the northern boundary and his account in the *Travels* is the only written record of that event.

The newly ceded land was called the New Purchase by Governor Wright and was incorporated into Saint Paul's Parish. That summer two Cherokee youths were brutally murdered by Hezekiah Collins near the Broad River. News of the deaths of their kinsmen set the Cherokees on edge. Young Creeks, who were angry over the land sale, attacked Wrightsborough on December 16 and killed the William White family. Creeks and Cherokees together attacked Sherrill's Fort on January 14, 1774. A band of Georgians then attacked a group of Cowetas as they were traveling from Tugaloo and killed Big Elk. Several white settlers were killed at St. Joseph's Bay in Florida and it appeared a general war was about to erupt. Superintendent John Stuart imposed a ban on trade with the Creeks and Seminoles. It took another six months to reestablish peace along the frontier.

Elijah Clark was the nominal leader of the earliest settlers to take up land in the New Purchase. He and fellow North Carolinians entered Georgia in 1774 and built their homes on the Broad River north of Fort James. During the Revolution Colonel George Mathews entered the Broad River area searching for Tories. He took note of the fertility of the region and purchased land at Goose Pond on the south side of the Broad River. After the war ended he went home to Virginia and returned in 1784 with some of his neighbors—Meriwether, McGehee, Gilmer, Barnett, Marks, Taliaferro, Pope, Davenport, Moore, and Bradley. During the next ten years settlers from Virginia, South Carolina, and North Carolina poured into the Broad River Valley and spread out along the creek bottoms north and south of the river.

The New Purchase was renamed Wilkes County in 1777 by the Provincial Congress. When Savannah and Augusta fell to British troops and loyalist militia in early 1779, the provincial government retreated to the frontier of Wilkes County and resistance was kept alive by Elijah Clark, John Dooly, and Stephen Heard. The Provincial government was held for a time at Fort Heard, now Washington. In late 1780 the loyalists attempted to extend their authority over Wilkes County. Whig families were spirited to the mountains of North Georgia and the upper parts of North and South Carolina until Wilkes and Richmond counties were returned to Whig control in May 1781.

The Broad River Valley became the most populous section of Georgia by the end of the eighteenth century and in the early 1800s was the center of learning and political power for a brief period. Political rivalry in the area came to dominate state politics and formed two camps, Virginians and Carolinians.

Elbert County was created in 1790, Oglethorpe County was formed from Wilkes in 1793, Madison was created in 1811, and in 1825 Taliaferro was created from portions of several counties. The Treaty of Hopewell in 1785 added land that became the original Franklin County, which was further subdivided into Clarke, Jackson, Banks, and Hall counties. By the Treaty of Augusta in 1783, the Treaty of Galphinton in 1785, and at Shoulderbone Creek in 1786, various Creek headmen signed papers to cede all land east of the Oconee River. Georgia organized Washington County from this cession in 1784 then divided it into numerous counties including Greene and Hancock. The dividing line between these two new counties of Franklin and Washington was a continuation of the Cherokee Line from Cherokee Corner.

Bounty land for Revolutionary War soldiers was reserved in Franklin County. Among those claiming land were Lachlan McIntosh, 290 acres on the Oconee River; Colonel Benjamin Cleveland, 200 acres at the confluence of the Tugaloo and Seneca Rivers; and George Walton, 400 acres in Franklin County. In 1784 a grateful Georgia legislature granted 20,000 acres in newly organized Franklin County to Count D'Estaing, the French admiral who blocked the evacuation of the British army from Yorktown. The D'Estaing grant was purchased by wealthy French merchant, Michael Gavin, who settled in Athens in the early 1800s.

Until 1803 lands were distributed by the headright system whereby each claimant received a specified number of acres for each dependent. The land was surveyed (or not as was often the case) by the system of metes and bounds. These irregular lots were bounded by physical features—a rock, tree, creek, road, or other property lines. Land seekers often ran their property boundary around the good land and avoided the poor land. In the new counties of Franklin and Washington more land was granted than there was land available. The people to first claim their grants, pay the fees and taxes became landowners, leaving latecomers out of luck. Speculators and unscrupulous surveyors caused confusion with duplicate warrants and under-the-table deals. The failure of this system in meeting the demands of orderly settlement lead to the land lottery system in Georgia, where the new counties were surveyed into regular sections and lots prior to sale. A similar system was adopted by the federal government, called the Public Land Survey System, and was used as new lands in the west were opened for settlement.

A Map of the Ceded Lands drawn by Philip Yonge in 1773
Reprinted by permission of the Public Record Office in Kew, England

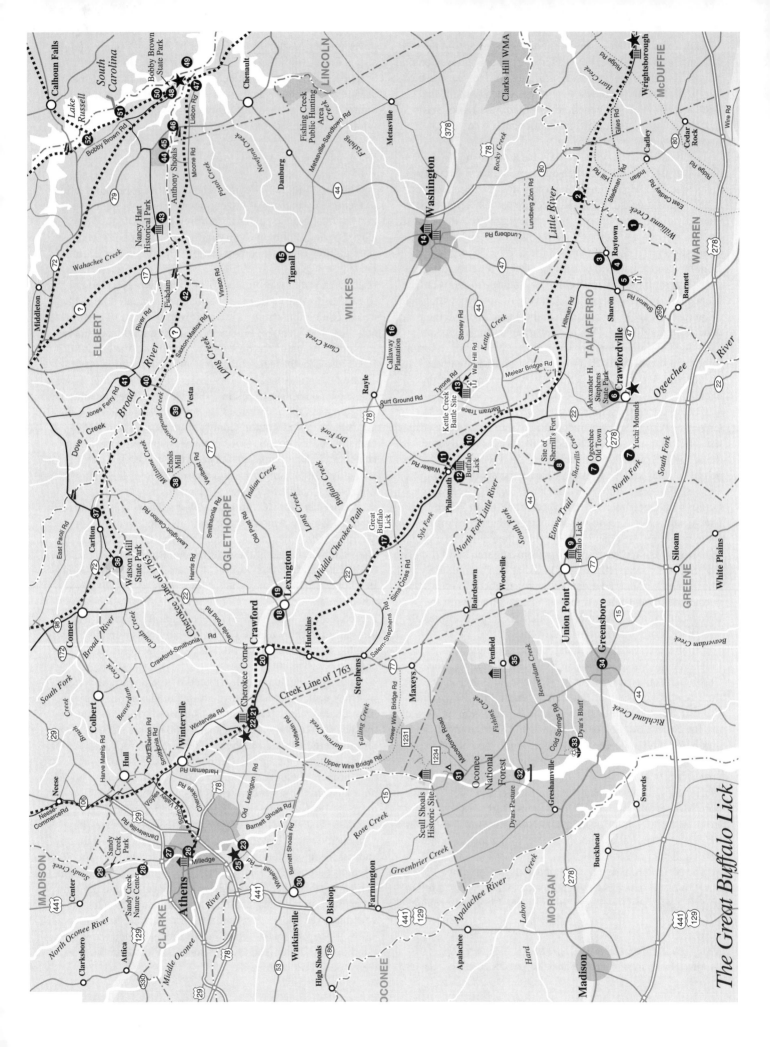

Legend

1. Williams Creek
2. Colonsay
3. Robert Grier
4. First Catholic Church in Georgia
5. Raytown-Sharon Garden Club
6. Alexander H. Stephens State Park
7. Yuchi Mounds/Ogeechee Old Town
8. Site of Sherrill's Fort
9. Buffalo Lick Monument
10. The Immense Forest
11. Philomath
12. Francis Harper's Buffalo Lick
13. Kettle Creek Battle Site
14. Washington
    Mary Willis Library
    Washington Wilkes Museum
    Heard's Fort
15. North Wilkes Museum
16. Callaway Plantation
17. Great Buffalo Lick
18. Lexington
    Shaking Rock Park
19. Goodness Grows Nursery
20. William H. Crawford
21. Cherokee Corner
22. Bartram Trail Roadside Park
23. Whitehall
24. State Botanical Garden of Georgia
25. University of Georgia
    UGA Libraries
    Institute of Ecology
    Museum of Natural History
    Herbarium
    Oconee Forest Park
    Garden Clubs Founders Garden
26. Athens
    Athens Welcome Center
    Downtown Athens Tree Trail
    The Tree that Owns Itself
    Georgia Railroad
    Ben Burton Park
    Memorial Park
    North Georgia Garden and Nursery Trail
27. North Oconee River Greenway
28. Sandy Creek Nature Center
29. Sandy Creek Park
30. Watkinsville
    Eagle Tavern
31. Oconee National Forest
    Scull Shoals Archaeological Site
    Scull Shoals Historic Site
    Oconee River Recreation Area
32. Cofaqui
    Dyars Pasture
33. Dyers Bluff
34. Burning of Greensboro
35. Penfield Academy
36. Watson Mill State Park
37. Fork Creek Roadside Park
38. Echols Mill
39. Meriwether Lewis
40. GA-77 Bridge & River Access
41. Elbert County Environmental Forest
42. Broad River Settlers
43. Nancy Hart Historical Park
44. Anthony Shoals
45. Factory Ruins
46. Broad River Camp
47. Site of Lisbon
48. Fort James
    Petersburg
    Bobby Brown State Park
    Great Wagon Road
49. Fort Charlotte
50. Indian Mounds
51. Russell Dam
52. Shuck Pen Eddy

The New Purchase

The Treaty of Augusta between Georgia and the Cherokee and Creek nations was concluded on June 3, 1773. In return for dissolving their debt to traders in Augusta the Cherokees gave up lands in the Piedmont north and west of Augusta and the Creeks turned over all claim to land east of the Ogeechee River. The Creeks were brought into the negotiations because of a dispute over the land lying between the Little River and Broad River, claimed by both the Creeks and Cherokees. Individuals were forbidden to buy land directly from the Indians so the purchase became an international affair. Cessions made by the two Indian nations totaled over two million acres.

During the French and Indian War the Cherokees fell deep into debt because their hunters were fighting with the British rather than collecting deerskins, the currency of the frontier trade. The general decline in deer population due to overhunting also aggravated their credit problem. The Creeks had also fallen into debt, although not to the extent of the Cherokees. Credit extended to the two nations by the traders in Augusta eventually totaled £40,000 pounds, an enormous sum for a day when most people might earn, at best, a couple hundred pounds per year. The creditors were George Galphin; James Jackson & Co.; Martin Campbell & Son; Goodgion, Rae, Whitefield & Co.; Edward Barnard; James Grierson; James Spalding & Co.; and Edward Keating.

In return for paying off the Augusta traders, Georgia received lands in the Piedmont bounded by the Little River on the South, the high ridge dividing the Oconee River from the Broad River was the boundary on the west, and then a line running northeasterly from Ila to Hartwell was the northern limit. This newly acquired land became part of Saint Paul's Parish and contained 674,000 acres. In 1777 the Provincial Legislature named this county in honor of John Wilkes, a member of Parliament who supported the right of freedom of the press. At the time the cession was commonly called the New Purchase and out of it were created the modern counties of Lincoln, Elbert, Wilkes; most of Hart, Madison, Oglethorpe, Taliaferro, and the Winterville section of Clarke.

The Cherokees used this area as a hunting ground and the only whites in the area were the Quakers in Wrightsborough and Carolinians in the Savannah River valley north of Augusta. Governor Wright advertised the land for sale at modest prices in the hopes that it would be settled by the best sort of families, those with the means to pay rather than the uncivilized and destitute Crackers who had engendered so much disgust among the Indians.

On June 7, 1773, Colonel Edward Barnard (not Barnet as Bartram wrote) left Augusta to survey the new boundary with an entourage of Indian chieftains, surveyors, land speculators, and other interested persons totaling about eighty in number. The Creeks were lead by Young Warrior; the name of the Cherokee leader is lost to history. Unfortunately Barnard's report is also lost, although a copy of a map drawn by Philip Yonge is preserved in the archives of the Public Record Office in Kew, England. Fortunately William Bartram was invited by Superintendent of Indian Affairs John Stuart to accompany the survey party and he wrote of his observations in the *Travels*. The official surveyors were Edward Barnard, William Barnard, Le Roy Hammond, Joseph Purcell, and Philip Yonge.

The official description of the boundaries is as follows:

To begin at the place where the Lower Creek Path intersects Ogguechee River, and along the main branch of said river to the source of the southernmost branch of said river and from thence along the ridge between the waters of Broad river and Occonee river up to the Buffaloe Lick, and from thence in a straight line to the tree marked by the Cherokees near the head of a branch falling into the Occonee river, and from thence along the said ridge twenty miles above the line already run by the Cherokees, and from thence across to Savannah river by a line parallel with that formerly marked by them.

William Bartram's Travels in the New Purchase

The survey party traveled from Augusta to Wrightsborough where they purchased provisions. Upon leaving Wrightsborough, they followed the Middle Cherokee Trading Path and crossed William's Creek a little above its mouth with Little River. Ironically some of William Bartram's Mendenhall cousins would obtain land nearby in the 1790s. The home they built still stands today. The path did not follow a ridge but ran near the Little River and crossed the North and South forks of Little River just above their junction. On the ridge dividing the Broad River basin from the Little River, now delineated by GA-22, Bartram entered the immense forest where he saw trees of awesome diameter.

> *To keep within the bounds of truth and reality, in describing the magnitude and grandeur of these trees, would, I fear, fail of credibility: yet, I think I can assert, that many of the black oaks measured eight, nine, ten, and eleven feet diameter five feet above the ground, as we measured several that were above thirty feet girt, and from hence they ascend perfectly straight, with a gradual taper, forty or fifty feet to the limbs...*[1]

This level ridge continues on to the Great Buffalo Lick,[2] the location of which has been the subject of a long-time debate. The only description of the New Purchase comes from Bartram's *Travels*, which is not at all precise as to locations and distances. Any descriptions made by the surveyor, Colonel Edward Barnard, or any of the survey party are lost if any ever existed. If we are to believe Bartram, the Great Buffalo Lick was located near the headwaters of the Ogeechee River. Indeed a granite marker was placed on US-278 one mile east of Union Point in the 1930s, near the headwater of the North Fork of the Ogeechee River.

In the late 1940s Dr. Francis Harper made an extended trip south to retrace Bartram's *Travels*. T. G. McFie of Taliaferro County took Harper to a likely place on the old Indian trail near Philomath that he thought was the site of the Great Buffalo Lick. The Bartram Trail Conference erected a wooden sign on GA-22 just south of Philomath commemorating the site.

The Eleazar Early map of Georgia, published in 1818, shows the Great Lick as lying between the headwaters of Buffalo Creek and Dry Creek in Oglethorpe County. In recent years the map of the New Purchase drawn by Philip Yonge has been rediscovered at the Public Record Office in England. It clearly shows the trails and three buffalo licks, only one of which is called the Great Buffalo Lick and it is not in either of the two places that have been identified with markers. Dr. Louis DeVorsey's recent research has determined that the Great Buffalo Lick is located on GA-22 near Buffalo Creek.

It is curious that mention of such a notable physical feature of the landscape has not survived in local lore. My own family has lived within several miles of this place for 150 years and no one has ever heard of it. Also curious is Bartram's statement that,

> *It is the common opinion of the inhabitants, that this clay is impregnated with saline vapours ...*[3]

Indians had not lived in the area since the early part of the eighteenth century and whites had been disallowed settlement west of Williams Creek, so, who were the inhabitants? Bartram says that horned cattle, horses, and deer were fond of licking the clay so there must have been whites running their cattle on Indian lands. This was probably an itinerant venture with no permanent settlement. The frontier of the South was often first occupied by herds of cattle held in *cowpens* and looked after by cowboys. The cattle were branded for identification, since they were free roaming. These cowboy customs were taken to Texas in the 1830s by Southerners and there blended with the culture of the Spanish vaquero.

Bartram said that they followed a straight path to the marked tree at the Cherokee Line, known today as Cherokee Corner. The Yonge map, however, shows a meandering route that dodged around stream heads. This route today follows the old railroad bed from Stephens to Crawford and then to Winterville. It was probably near Winterville that Bartram made his excursion to the Oconee River where the trading path crossed at Cedar Shoals, later the site of Athens Manufacturing Company. This meant that he probably viewed the North Oconee River from the Carr's Hill section of Athens.

1. William Bartram, *Travels*, 37.
2. In his report to Dr. Fothergill Bartram refers to the site as the Great Buffalo Lick, in the *Travels* it is simply called Buffalo Lick.
3. William Bartram, *Travels*, 39.

Sites

1. Williams Creek was the western boundary of the Wrightsborough township. It was also the western boundary of Georgia until the Treaty of Augusta in 1773 when the line was moved westward to the Ogeechee River.

2. Colonsay. This private residence lies very near the old trail that William Bartram and the survey party traveled. Ironically, it was built by cousins of Bartram, the Mendenhals, in the 1790s and the original structure still stands. It is the home of the late T. G. McFie who was Francis Harper's guide in Taliaferro County.

3. Ray's Place (Raytown) was a popular resort for Washington society at the beginning of the nineteenth century and is the oldest community in Taliaferro County. The community grew up around the intersection of Double Wells Stage Road and Wrightsborough Road. The parents and grandparents of Jefferson Davis owned plantations in the Raytown community in the early 1800s.

4. Robert Grier, founder of *Grier's Almanac*, grew up near Raytown. In 1807 he published the *Georgia and South Carolina Almanack*, which was later named after its founder. A historical marker is located at the farm where he grew up.

5. First Catholic Church in Georgia. The community of Sharon was settled in the early 1800s by Irish immigrants who built the first Catholic Church in Georgia. Catholics were banned from entering the colony during the colonial period because it was thought they would be sympathetic to the Spanish and French. The cemetery still exists and a monument in the form of an altar commemorates the early settlers.

The **Raytown-Sharon Garden Club** was organized in 1903 and was the second Garden Club organized in Georgia.

6. Alexander H. Stephens State Park encompasses the estate and home of Alexander H.

Stephens, vice-president of the Confederate States and governor of Georgia. His home, Liberty Hall, was built in 1875 and is furnished with many original pieces of furniture. The park contains 1,200 acres, two lakes, a campground, and several hiking trails. Next to the Stephens home is the Confederate Museum containing artifacts and exhibits related to the Civil War. Located just north of the Taliaferro court house. Open daily, 7 a.m.–10 p.m. Liberty Hall and the Confederate Museum are open 9 a.m.–5 p.m., Tuesday through Saturday; 2–5 p.m. on Sunday. Closed Mondays, except when Monday falls on a legal holiday.

7. Yuchi Mounds/Ogeechee Old Town. The Yuchis (also Uchee and Yuchee) lived in eastern Tennessee during the seventeenth century. They moved south in several migrations to the Savannah and Ogeechee Rivers south of Augusta, the last being after the Yamassee War. They were befriended by the Kasihtas and moved to the Chattahoochee River in 1729. There they were visited by William Bartram in 1775. Ogeechee possibly means "River of the Yuchis."

8. Site of Sherrill's Fort. Sherrill's Fort was the fortified home of William Sherrill. Creeks and Cherokees attacked Sherrill's Fort on January 14, 1774, killing seven people. William White and his family had been killed in Wrightsborough on December 25, 1773. The settlers withdrew to the Savannah River, fearful of further attack. This was worst period of a general rise in tensions between Creeks and Georgians caused by the cession of the New Purchase.

9. Buffalo Lick Monument. The CCC erected a monument near the headwaters of the Ogeechee River in Greene County in the 1930s. Many people have thought that this was the likely site of the Great Buffalo Lick for Bartram said that,

> A large cane swamp and meadows, forming an immense plain, lie S. E. from it; in this swamp I believe the head branches of the great Ogeeche river take their rise.[2]

He had confused the Ogeechee River with the Little River. The marker is located on US-278 one mile east of Union Point.

10. Bartram's Immense Forest was located on the trail after crossing the North Fork Little River. The forest would have been traversed by GA-22 southeast of Philomath.

11. Philomath was originally named Woodstock but because that name was already taken the community had to choose a new

2. Ibid., 39.

Mule Day at Callaway Plantation is one of the most popular festivals in the region

name when the post office was established. Alexander H. Stephens was given the honor of naming the community and he chose Philomath, which means *love of knowledge*, for the town's reputation as a seat of learning. Philomath indeed owes its very existence to the pursuit of learning. Wealthy local plantation owners built an academy for their children's education and homes so families could gather during the school session. These families had two homes, one at the plantation and one in town for the benefits of society and education.

Although Jefferson Davis' cabinet had been dismissed in nearby Washington the remnants of his entourage traveled on to Philomath and gathered at the home of Captain John Daniel. There they furled the flag and paid off the bodyguard, the last official act of the Confederate government.

12. Francis Harper's Buffalo Lick. Francis Harper, researching the Bartram Trail in the late 1940s, concluded that Bartram's Buffalo Lick was immediately south of Philomath on an old trail that was still visible at the time. The Bartram Trail Conference erected a wooden sign on GA-22 to mark the site. This sign is about a quarter-mile east of town, but there is little to see today because the site has overgrown with pines and brambles.

13. Kettle Creek Battle Site. While the majority of Georgia was reoccupied by the British military in the early part of 1779, Wilkes County remained in patriot hands. Upon the fall of Augusta to loyalists many families of Wilkes fled to South Carolina or north to the mountains. The British presence brought renewed strength to the Tories who began to administer the Oath to the remaining citizens and burned homes of those who had fled. The Patriots placed themselves under the command of Colonel John Dooly and Elijah Clark. They joined forces with Andrew Pickens at Fort Charlotte and followed the loyalist militia into Georgia and caught up with them at Kettle Creek.

In the early morning of February 14, 1779, the loyalists were surprised as they prepared breakfast and began a retreat. Elijah Clark believed a nearby hill to be the key to victory and rushed to occupy it. The Battle of Kettle Creek lasted for almost two hours. The Loyalists retreated in confusion and Boyd died of wounds during the withdrawal and was buried at War Hill. Some of the local Tories fled to Florida and some retreated to Augusta with the British, the notorious Daniel McGirth being among them.

The nature of the Revolution as a civil war is illustrated by the fact that Andrew Pickens and the loyalist commander James Boyd were acquaintances prior to the conflict. Pickens called upon the wounded Boyd and offered him all possible aid. Boyd, knowing death was near, requested two loyalists to attend his body in burial and then gave Pickens a gold broach to deliver to Mrs. Boyd.

Seventy of the Tories were captured, tried for treason, and seven were hanged. Until that time important prisoners were traded, but after the Battle at Kettle Creek they were hanged in increasing numbers. This was possibly a response to Tarleton's excesses in South Carolina.

The Kettle Creek monument and Revolutionary War cemetery is open during daylight hours. From Crawfordville follow GA-22 north, turn right on GA-44, left on Stoney Road, left on Tyrone Road then left on War Hill Road.

14. Washington was named for General George Washington in 1780 while he was commander of the Continental Army and is the first city named in his honor. Today Washington is known for its beautiful Antebellum homes. In May 1865, Jefferson Davis officially dissolved the Confederate government at the Heard House, now the site of the Wilkes County courthouse. The Civil War figures largely in the history of Washington for it was also the home of Robert Toombs, Secretary of State for the Confederate States and one of the few who never took an oath of allegiance to the United States.

Mary Willis Library. In addition to having an excellent collection of local and Southern history, the library is also home to the Bartram Trail Library system that supports smaller local libraries. Mary Willis Library was the first free public library in Georgia, established in 1888.

Washington Wilkes Museum. The Museum is housed in the 1835 Semmes House. The first floor is a house museum while the second floor houses an extensive Civil War collection and exhibits on the rise of the plantation system. 308 East Robert Toombs Avenue. Open Tuesday through Saturday, 10 a.m.–5 p.m. and on Sunday, 2–5 p.m. Closed on Monday, Thanksgiving, Christmas, and New Year's Day. Admission.

Dr. Louis DeVorsey (l) and Chad Braley (r) inspect the site of the Great Buffalo Lick in Oglethorpe County

Heard's Fort. When Georgia was returned to royal government by the British occupations of Augusta and Savannah, the provincial government was moved to Heard's Fort in February 1780. At the time, the darkest moment of the Revolution in Georgia, the only Whig territory was Wilkes County on the frontier. With many of the state's leaders in prison or in exile it was left to the citizens of Wilkes to hold the line.

The government seat for Wilkes County was established at Heard's Fort, renamed Fort Washington. In the same year the city of Washington was chartered at Heard's Fort. Fort Washington Park is located behind the Wilkes County courthouse. The John Nelson Stone was placed in the park from its original site six miles south of Washington. It was carved in 1792 and includes a plat of the 1775 land grant of which John Nelson was obviously so proud.

15. North Wilkes Museum, Tignall. The Museum focuses on the history of the Broad River Valley and the original Wilkes County. Exhibits tell the story of the human inhabitants from prehistoric times. Maps show locations of early homes, churches, and forts. William Bartram's travels and description of the Broad River are prominently featured. The museum is located above the library in the old bank building and is open during library hours, Monday through Thursday from 4–5:30 p.m.

16. Callaway Plantation is a museum of a successful Antebellum plantation. Five historic buildings are preserved, including the brick Callaway mansion and the boyhood home of Governor George Rockingham Gilmer. The mansion contains period furniture donated by local families. An herb garden, vegetable garden, and cotton patch are tended during the growing season. The pioneer log cabin dates from 1785. As the settlers' economic condition improved, they built larger dwellings similar to the four-room Federal Plainstyle home that sits in front of the cabin. The Callaway Plantation was a gift from the family that has farmed the surrounding lands since the 1790s.

One of the most popular events in the area is the Annual Mule Day Festival where the sober, strong, and steady animals are given their deserved honors. During the festival visitors can watch craftsmen make soap, tar, oak baskets, and syrup. There is old-time music, plowing demonstrations, and stock-dog demonstrations. Located on US-78 west of Washington.

17. Great Buffalo Lick. The great lick visited by William Bartram was located in Oglethorpe County between Philomath and Lexington, a half-mile south of Buffalo Creek and a few hundred feet north of GA-22. Although the Great Lick was one of the important features of the area during colonial times, knowledge of its location was lost through time. Dr. Louis De Vorsey has recently established the exact location of the lick by using original land plats located in the Georgia Surveyor General's office. No vestige of the lick is present today and the site is now a pine plantation.

While the survey party camped at the Great Buffalo Lick there arose a controversy over the accuracy of the survey instruments used to determine the new boundary line. Young Warrior claimed that the surveyor was taking in too much land and insisted on determining the line themselves. From this point a party including Bartram, Colonel Edward Barnard, and the Cherokees went north to Cherokee Corner and then to the Tugaloo River. The other party, which included Young Warrior and the Creeks, traveled south to survey down the Ogeechee River.

18. Lexington was the metropolis of the Broad River area until supplanted by Athens. As early as 1774 North Carolina settlers had established themselves on Long Creek near the present site of Lexington. This was only a year after the Treaty of Augusta formally opened up the land for settlement. Life on the frontier was tenuous due to frequent Indian raids. When Oglethorpe County was formed in 1793 the courthouse was established at its present location and the town was named Lexington to honor the town in Massachusetts where the Revolutionary War began. After the war ended the population grew and new wealth arrived with tobacco and cotton cultivation. Oglethorpe County was known for the culture, education, and republican spirit of her citizens. Lexington was the home of governors George Mathews, George Gilmer, Stephen Upson, and Wilson Lumpkin.

The first large mercantile store outside of Augusta was built in Lexington by Ferdinand Phinizy whose descendants include writer Walker Percy and historian Phinizy Spalding. Francis Meson left his estate for the establishment of an academy. Meson Male Academy opened in 1808 and eventually drew students from the entire state. The education of girls began in 1810. The first Presbyterian Theological Seminary in Georgia was established in Lexington at the Presbyterian Manse. It was moved to Columbia, South Carolina, then to Decatur, Georgia, where it operates today as Columbia Theological Seminary. When the railroad was built in the 1830s the station for Lexington was built three miles from town and became the town of Crawford.

The courthouse is an example of Richardsonian-Romanesque architecture and was completed in 1887. The granite, bricks, and lumber used in its construction were all manufactured in Oglethorpe County.

Shaking Rock Park. Outcroppings of granite boulders are common in the Georgia Piedmont. One of the most unusual gatherings of rocks is at Shaking Rock Park in Lexington. One boulder weighs twenty tons and is balanced atop another. The Park takes its name from the fact that this behemoth once could be rocked by a single person, but no longer. The Park contains several very large trees and is adjacent to a beautiful beaver pond (privately owned). To the north of the Park, also on private property, one can see the remains of a nineteenth-century blue granite quarry. Turn onto Shaking Rock Park Road from US-78 in downtown Lexington.

19. Goodness Grows Nursery is a major grower and developer of native perennials. Many native shrubs and trees are also available for sale. Open 9 a.m.–5 p.m., Monday through Saturday and on Sundays from 1–5 p.m.

20. William Harris Crawford was born in Virginia in 1772 and came to Wilkes County, Georgia, while young. He was educated at Dr. Waddel's school at Willington, South Carolina. He was admitted to the bar and practiced law at Lexington until he was elected to the General Assembly of Georgia, then to the U.S. Senate in 1806. He was ambassador to France from 1813–1815, Secretary of War from 1815–1816, and Secretary of the Treasury from 1816–1825.

His height and countenance lead Napoleon to call Crawford, "the most regal man in my entire court." While campaigning for the presidency in 1823 he suffered a stroke caused by an overdose of lobelia that left him partially paralyzed. None of the candidates received enough votes for a majority, so the election was determined by the House of Representatives. The House chose John Quincy Adams for president, with Andrew Jackson second, Crawford third, and Henry Clay fourth. From 1827 until his death in 1834, Crawford was Judge of the Northern Circuit of Georgia. The grave of Crawford is on the property of his former home, Woodlawn, located off US-78 west of Crawford.

21. Cherokee Corner was the site of the Treaty Tree, which marked the western end of a boundary line between Cherokee lands to the north and white settlements to the south and east. It was at this point that the line intersected the Middle Cherokee Trading Path. The line ran from there to the present-day southern boundary of Greenville County, South Carolina, and coincides exactly with the Anderson-Abbeville county line. The marker for Cherokee Corner is located on US-78 about 150 feet west of the site of the Treaty Tree.

22. Bartram Trail Roadside Park. A small park on US-78 and Bartram Trail historical marker commemorates William Bartram's visit to the Cherokee Corner. The park occupies the approximate site of the surveyors' camp on Moss Creek at the most western part of the boundary of Georgia. Picnic tables and benches on Moss Creek provide a rest area for travelers.

23. Whitehall grew up around the Athens Manufacturing Company textile mill (later named the Georgia Factory) established in 1829. The original mill was the second to be built in the South and was in continuous use until it closed in 1988. It has now been converted into studio apartments with the exterior of the historic structures left intact. Across the river from the mill is Whitehall Bluff (private), a montane environment harboring disjunct populations of mountain leucothoe, mountain laurel, and galax growing at one of its most southern sites.

24. State Botanical Garden of Georgia. The Garden encompasses 313 acres along the Middle Oconee River. It has hiking trails, vegetable gardens, a pitcher-plant bog, the International Garden, Dunson Native Garden, Galle Native Azalea Garden, physic and herb garden. A recently completed master plan will establish more gardens for magnolias, oaks, home landscape plants, children's gardens, aquatic plants, and a Japanese garden. The conservatory has a collection of tropical plants, a bookstore, and café. The national headquarters of the Garden Clubs of America is located at the State Botanical Garden of Georgia.

The Botanical Garden is the home of the

The Broad River as seen from the GA-281 bridge, the Broad River Heritage Preserve is seen on the left bank of the river just below the bridge

Georgia Endangered Plant Propagation Network. The garden studies and propagates ten endangered native plants and distributes them to associated organizations. The plants include torreya, Georgia plume, purple pitcher-plant, pink lady's slipper, persistent trillium, hairy rattleweed, mountain scullcap, mat forming quillwort, and smooth purple coneflower.

The International Garden features the plant explorers, including the Bartrams, and plant discoveries of the New World. A Bartram Trail historical marker is located on the entrance road and commemorates William Bartram's visit to the Oconee River at Athens.

South Milledge Avenue. Open 8 a.m.– 8 p.m., April through September, and until 5 p.m., October through March.

25. University of Georgia. Due to the energies of Abraham Baldwin, the Georgia Legislature adopted the Charter for the University of Georgia on January 27, 1785, the first public university in America though not the first to open its doors. The institute was called Franklin College of Arts and Sciences but classes did not begin until sixteen years later.

Abraham Baldwin served as the president of a university that existed only on paper. In 1801 a committee traveled to the edge of the frontier and selected a place to build the college. The site chosen for the University was a hill overlooking the Cedar Shoals on the North Oconee River. This was north of the frontier settlement of Watkinsville and well away from the tavern that might inspire the students to neglect their studies. The new college would be situated near clean water and healthful breezes. The legislature endowed the college with 5,000 acres of land.

Joshiah Meigs became president late that same year when Baldwin was elected to the United States Senate. The first students arrived in September 1801. Classes were held outdoors when weather permitted or in the president's home until a log building was finished. The first permanent building, now called Old College, opened in 1806. A section of the college's land was laid out in lots for the town of Athens.

Meigs was a believer in science and pure knowledge, which put him at odds with the conservative trustees. He resigned as president and continued as lecturer in philosophy, mathematics, and chemistry. The college went into a decline and closed in 1818. Dr. Moses Waddel became president in 1819. He brought stability to the institution and raised the enrollment to a hundred students.

Libraries. The University of Georgia has one of the largest library systems in the country and has several significant collections of interest to Bartram enthusiasts. The Georgia Room contains many volumes of Georgia history and regional natural history, including out of print books related to the Bartrams. The Hargrett Rare Book Room contains the *Memorials of John Bartram & Humphrey Marshall* by William Darlington and an original edition of Catesby's *Natural History of Carolina, Florida and the Bahama Islands*. The University of Georgia Map Room is the most extensive in the Southeast.

Rocky shoals spider lilies in bloom at Anthony Shoals on the Broad River

Institute of Ecology. Founded by Dr. Eugene Odum, the Institute of Ecology is known worldwide for its pioneering research and teaching of ecology, a relatively new science. There are displays in the lounge that promote the Institute's current projects and a reading rack of ecology-related publications. The grounds of the Ecology Building are of interest to naturalists for they are landscaped with native plants—grasses, yaupon, wax myrtle, pines, and oakleaf hydrangea.

Georgia Museum of Natural History. The University's Museum of Natural History currently exists primarily for education and research purposes and is distributed in many locations around campus. The Georgia legislature has designated the Museum to be the state museum of natural history, which will eventually be housed in a new facility. The collections contain artifacts and specimens of archaeology, botany, geology, mycology, and zoology. Tours are available by arrangement for educational groups. Located on East Campus Drive at Cedar Street.

Herbarium. The botanical herbarium at the Museum of Natural History contains 22,000 specimens of vascular plants collected in Georgia and the Southeast. In addition to being a prominent research facility the Herbarium staff responds to numerous identification inquiries each year. The University of Georgia Herbarium is the largest in the Southeast.

Oconee Forest Park. This sixty-acre forest is 100 years old and was once part of the University of Georgia School of Forest Resources research facilities. The state champion scarlet oak is located on Birdsong Creek in the forest. There are 1.5 miles of hiking trails, an off-road bike trail, fifteen-acre Lake Herrick, and an off-leash area for dogs to play. Located within the UGA Recreation Sports Area at the intersection of College Station Road and East Campus Road. Open during daylight hours.

Garden Clubs of America Founders Garden. The first Garden Club was organized in Athens in 1891. The old headquarters of the Georgia Garden Clubs is surrounded by formal gardens and walkways shaded by large oaks. The Gardens are open during daylight hours. Located on North Campus.

University of Georgia Visitor Center, Four Towers Building, located on College Station Road between East Campus Road and the Athens Bypass.

26. Athens is named for the center of arts and learning of classical Greece. The town grew up around the University of Georgia and occupies the site where two Cherokee paths crossed the Oconee River. One was the Middle Cherokee Path from Augusta to Etowah that crossed the North Oconee River at Cedar Shoals, the probable place where Bartram viewed the river. The other trail came south from Tugaloo and was an extension of the Virginia Path. The shoals are located just downstream of the US-78 bridge over the North Oconee River.

Athens became the center of learning for Antebellum Georgia and many noted families made Athens their home. The Federal Road began in Athens when it opened in 1811 and ended at Fort Stoddert on the Alabama River near Mobile.

Athens Welcome Center. Information and an orientation film about Athens and Clarke County are available at the Church-Waddel-Brumby House. The Brumby House is the oldest surviving home in Athens, built in 1820, and is furnished as a house museum. The garden contains traditional herbs and native flowers. Located at 280 E. Dougherty Street in downtown. Open Monday through Saturday, 10 a.m.–5 p.m., and on Sundays, 2–5 p.m.

Downtown Athens Tree Trail. This urban nature trail makes a circuit through downtown and features a variety of trees that grow in Athens. Native trees include southern magnolia, pin oak, redbud, chaste tree, willow oak, Darlington oak, pecan, walnut, dogwood, American elm, scarlet oak, and green ash. Non-native trees that thrive in Athens include dawn redwood, crepe myrtle, Japanese maple, sweet olive, Chinese elm, and yoshino cherry. Clayton Street is lined with Athens' adopted tree, the gingko. On the north side of the academic building on the University of Georgia campus are descendants of yews brought from the home of James Oglethorpe in Essex, England. Maps are available at the Welcome Center.

The Tree that Owns Itself. William Jackson so loved an oak that provided shade and beauty for his home that he deeded a piece of his property to the tree. Although this might be legally challenged, no one has ever done so. The tree has even dictated the route of Finley Street, which narrows to one lane as it passes the tree. The present tree is a descendant of the original and occupies an eight-foot diameter lot. Located at the intersection of Dearing and Finley Streets.

The Georgia Railroad was organized in Athens in March 1834 at the home of James Camak. With three manufacturing mills in Athens, the business leaders were eager to improve transportation to Augusta and Savannah. The roads of the day were so bad that wagons carrying textiles and machinery became mired in mud. The first section of the railroad extended from Augusta to Crawfordville in 1838, then to Greensboro in 1839. The rails finally reached Athens in 1841 by way of the ridge from Union Point to Crawford to Winterville. Passenger service was five cents a mile.

Ben Burton Park occupies a picturesque section of the Middle Oconee River with spectacular shoals surrounded by a hardwood forest. Located on Mitchell Bridge Road.

Memorial Park covers seventy-two acres and contains a hardwood forest, lake, playground, hiking trails and a small zoo that features native animals. Located at 293 Gran Ellen Drive.

North Georgia Garden and Nursery Trail is a collection of specialty nurseries that sell native and unusual plants for Southern gardens. Several nurseries have been featured in national publications. Information is available at the Athens Welcome Center.

86 • *Great Buffalo Lick*

27. North Oconee River Greenway. The Greenway connects Sandy Creek Park north of Athens with downtown Athens and the University of Georgia. The trail will eventually extend downriver to Whitehall. The Greenway is a recreational trail for hiking and bicycling. As it passes through downtown Athens, it becomes a historical trail with displays and exhibits related to the history of Athens and includes mention of William Bartram's visit to the Oconee River.

28. Sandy Creek Nature Center. The Nature Center is located on 225 acres of land between Sandy Creek and the North Oconee River. It is a wildlife sanctuary and outdoor education center. The numerous trails connect river floodplain, pine uplands, marsh, and hardwood forest. Trails are open during daylight hours. The gate and office is open daily 8 a.m.–5 p.m., Monday–Friday; and on Saturdays from 12–5 p.m., March through mid–November.

29. Sandy Creek Park. Lake Chapman is the focus of Sandy Creek Park. While this park is primarily used for picnicking and sports, there is a lakeside trail and the four-mile long Cook's Trail that connects to Sandy Creek Park. The trail crosses a beaver swamp and follows the floodplain of Sandy Creek.

Located off US-441 North. Park hours are from 7 a.m.–10 p.m., April 1 through September 30, closed on Wednesdays. From October 1 through March 31, the hours are 7 a.m.–7 p.m., Thursday through Sunday, closed on Monday, Tuesday, and Wednesday.

30. Watkinsville was originally known as Big Spring. It was chosen as the county seat of Clarke County in 1802 and was incorporated as Watkinsville in 1806. When the county seat was moved to Athens the citizens of the lower part of Clarke County petitioned the legislature to create a new county. Oconee County was created in 1875 and the seat remained at Watkinsville.

Eagle Tavern (c. 1800). Watkinsville might have been the site for the University of Georgia but for the presence of Eagle Tavern. As early as 1801 Eagle Tavern was a stagecoach stop in the frontier settlement of Big Spring. The tavern provided meals and lodging for travelers as well as spirituous libation. Upstairs rooms were reserved for stage passengers, while other travelers could sleep on the public room floor for the price of a drink. The two-over-two plain-style building was renovated in the 1950s. It is now the welcome center for Oconee County and is furnished with period pieces. Located on Main Street in Watkinsville, across from the courthouse. Open 9 a.m.–5 p.m., Tuesday through Friday, and from 2–5 p.m. on Saturdays. Closed on Sunday and Monday.

Rhododendron minus, *the lesser rosebay or Piedmont rhododendron, is found along the banks of the Broad River*

31. Oconee National Forest. Established in 1959, the Oconee National Forest contains 109,000 acres of old cotton land. Indeed, Greene County was one of the most degraded farming areas of the Piedmont. The forest and the Piedmont National Wildlife Refuge encompass a considerable portion of the central Georgia Piedmont and provide unimpeded habitat for wildlife. Lake Oconee has become a popular resort and recreation area. The forest also has pine plantations and two forest experiment stations. Significant archaeological sites are located at Scull Shoals and the inundated Dyars Mound Site. The district ranger's office is at 349 Forsyth Street in Monticello.

Scull Shoals Archaeological Site. This site contains two small earthen mounds built on the Oconee River floodplain. Scull Shoals was the center of a chiefdom during the Mississippian Period (1000 A.D. to DeSoto's arrival) that controlled the upper Oconee River. Indian Mound Trail starts at the end of FS-1231A.

Scull Shoals was Georgia's first industrial city. Settlers came as early as 1784 but their stay was tenuous until Fort Clark was built in 1794 to protect against Indian raids. Scull Shoals had Georgia's first paper mill and one of the first cotton factories was built there in 1834. Governor Peter Early built his home nearby. At the height of the town's prosperity there were around 500 inhabitants. The brick walls of the office are all that remain today. Turn left on Macedonia Church Road after crossing the river going south on GA-15, turn left on FS-1234, then left on FS-1231. A hiking trail to the site begins at the recreation area at the GA-15 bridge.

Oconee River Recreation Area. Camping, hiking, and picnicking facilities are available at the recreation area. Scull Shoals Trail begins there and follows the banks of the river for a mile to the Scull Shoals historic site. Water and restrooms are provided. Located on GA-15 at the Oconee River.

32. Cofaqui was one of the subordinate towns to the paramount chiefdom of Ocute, located at Shoulderbone Creek in present-day Hancock County. The De Soto expedition arrived here on April 12, 1540 and left the next day. The site of the town was possibly at the Dyar Site now flooded by Lake Oconee.

Dyars Pasture. Hiking and birdwatching are popular activities at Dyars Pasture Conservation Area. From US-278 turn right on Greshamville Road, right on Copeland Road, then right on the unpaved road to Dyars Boat Ramp.

33. Dyers Bluff. This rich woods bluff contains a spring flower display of shooting stars, lousewort, Catesby trillium, wild azalea, atamasco lilies, mayapple, and an uncommon plant named *Lithospermum tubarosum*. From GA-15 turn left on Cold Springs Road, right on FS-1274, then left on FS-1274A. Park and follow the trail to the wildlife opening. The bluff is to the west of the wildlife opening.

Watson Mill Bridge State Park

34. Burning of Greensboro. With the 1786 Treaty of Shoulderbone Creek leaders ceded all land east of the Oconee River. The next year disaffected warriors crossed the river, attacked and burned the town of Greensboro, killing thirty-one inhabitants. At the time it was the worst massacre of civilians in the United States.

35. Penfield Academy was founded by the Georgia Baptist Association at Penfield in 1833 and began as a manual school for the training of students of the ministry. It later became Mercer Institute and was moved to Macon in 1871 where it was renamed Mercer University. Several of the original buildings remain in Penfield, including a dormitory and the chapel. Located on Boswell Road in Penfield.

36. Watson Mill State Park. One of the most beautiful settings in the Piedmont is found at Watson Mill, which features a covered bridge, dam, and shoals on the South Fork of the Broad River. A nature trail leads to the ruins of the water-driven power plant that supplied electricity to the mill complex. The covered bridge, built in 1885, is the longest in the state at 228.6 feet. The park has facilities for picnicking, hiking, camping, canoeing swimming, and horse trails. From Colbert go south on GA-22 then left on Covered Bridge Road. Open 7 a.m.–10 p.m. daily.

37. Fork Creek Roadside Park. This unmarked roadside picnic area is on the south side of GA-72 just before the bridge at the Carlton city limits east. The hillside on the opposite bank of Fork Creek is a north-facing slope and is covered with mountain laurel. Because adjacent land is private, hiking is restricted to the small area of the park, yet the view is exceptional in early May when the mountain laurel is in bloom.

38. Echols Mill was once an excellent example of a large granite outcrop although much of it has now been quarried. It contains many of the plants endemic to the Piedmont outcrops and one rare plant, American pillwort, in a disjunct population. Echols Mill is located on Millstone Creek and is crossed by county road 212 (private property).

39. Meriwether Lewis came from Virginia to the Goose Pond area of Oglethorpe County with his mother, Lucy Meriwether, and his stepfather, John Marks. Meriwether was at least ten years of age when they moved, about 1784 or 1785. Like most of the people who settled on the Broad River, the family prospered and Meriwether was sent back to Virginia for his education. Lucy later returned to Albemarle County, Virginia, when her husband died.

Lewis became personal secretary to his boyhood friend, President Thomas Jefferson. Lewis was chosen by Jefferson to lead an expedition to explore the Louisiana Purchase because he had a knowledge of botany, mineralogy, astrology, and he was dependable, honorable, and thorough.

The official transfer of the upper Louisiana Territory was held at St. Louis on March 8, 1804. Lewis and his co-commander, William Clark, began their voyage up the Missouri River in May 1804, and returned to St. Louis on September 23, 1806, after having reached the Pacific Ocean at the mouth of the Columbia River.

Meriwether Lewis became governor of the Louisiana Territory and died under mysterious circumstances at Grinder's Stand in Tennessee while traveling to Washington. Evidence strongly suggests that he committed suicide because he occasionally suffered from depression and he had fallen on hard times, but some believe he was murdered.

40. GA-77 Bridge, unpaved river access. Downstream from the bridge is a large granite outcrop at water's edge, a favored spot from which to view the river.

41. Elbert County Environmental Forest. The marked nature trail takes visitors through pine upland, lowland hardwood forest, and an abandoned granite quarry. Lichen-covered granite boulders along the ridges, some of imposing size, are typical of the lower Broad River Valley. The Elbert County Board of Education, the Elbert County Cooperative Extensive Service, Resource Investment, Inc., and the Elbert County board of Commissioners sponsor the project.

42. Broad River Settlers. Governor George Rockingham Gilmer was born near Fishdam on the Broad River and wrote of his ancestors and the first settlers in the Broad River Valley in his book *Sketches of Some of the Early Settlers of Upper Georgia, of the Cherokees and of the Author*. The rich lands of Wilkes County attracted settlers from Virginia, where good tobacco land was fast becoming scarce, and from North Carolina. By the census of 1810 there were 45,000 people living in the Broad River region, making it the most populous area of the state. It also became the source of political energy during the first two decades of the nineteenth century.

43. Nancy Hart Historical Park. Nancy Hart was six feet tall, muscular, and courageous; known to all as Aunt Nancy. She was a spy for the patriots and a deadly shot. During the Revolution she captured six Tories who had invaded her home by getting them drunk then taking their guns. Hart County, Georgia is named for her and is the only county in Georgia named for a woman.

Sometime before 1794 Benjamin and Nancy Hart moved to Brunswick, Georgia, and owned property in town. When her husband died in late 1801 Nancy moved to Clarke County, Alabama, to live with her son, John, on the Tombigbee River. The Harts then moved to Kentucky where they lived out their years and are buried in a family cemetery ten miles from Henderson.

A replica of Aunt Nancy's cabin is built on the site of her home and incorporates the original chimney stones. The park is operated by the Georgia D.A.R. and contains a display homestead herb garden, picnic pavilions, and short walking paths. The gate is not always open so park and walk in to see the cabin and garden. Don't be frightened by the black snake that lives in the rocks of the chimney.

44. Anthony Shoals. The rare and endangered rocky shoals spider lily grows at Anthony Shoals. A fishing trail guides hikers through vegetation that is more common in mountain foothills. Remains of the raceway for Burton Mill are visible at the upper end of the shoals. The Anthony Shoals area is maintained by the U.S. Army Corps of Engineers. Anthony Shoals is located 1.5 miles from GA-79 by boat. Anthony Shoals can also be reached by taking Anthony Shoals Road from Broad River Road (CR-193.

45. Factory Ruins. The brick ruins of Hopewell Factory are located on the north side of the Broad River at Anthony Shoals. They are reached by a dirt road from GA-79, just north of the bridge.

46. Broad River Camp. Camping and boat launch on the Broad River. Operated by the U.S. Army Corps of Engineers. Located on GA-79

47. Site of Lisbon. The town of Lisbon flourished briefly in the early 1800s and declined along with Petersburg. The site is on the south side of the mouth of the Broad River.

48. Fort James was built in 1773 upon the completion of the Treaty of Augusta and named for Governor James Wright. It provided a garrison to protect the frontier and became the destination for settlers immigrating from North and South Carolina along the Great Wagon Road.

Petersburg was originally named Dartmouth after the Earl of Dartmouth, who promoted the New Purchase. The town grew up below the site of Fort James and by 1800 was the third largest town in Georgia and the shipping port for tobacco grown in the Broad River Valley. Long Petersburg boats were used to navigate the shoals downriver as they carried tobacco to market at Augusta.

Bobby Brown State Park is located at the confluence of the Broad and Savannah Rivers. The park contains the sites of Fort James, mentioned in the *Travels*, and Petersburg, once the third largest town in Georgia.

The 1.9-mile hiking trail is named Bartram Trail. Pioneer camping, trailer hookups, boat ramp, fishing, and concession. Open 7 a.m.– 10 p.m. daily. Located at the end of Bobby Brown Park Road.

The Great Wagon Road, also known as the Piedmont Road in the South, brought settlers from Pennsylvania into the Carolinas. It started at Philadelphia and ran westward through Lancaster, York, and Gettysburg. From there it passed through the Shenandoah Valley, broke through the Blue Ridge Mountains at Roanoke, and passed through Charlotte and Camden to end at Augusta. After the New Purchase was opened for settlement in 1773 the road shifted northward to pass through Newberry and deposited immigrants at Fort James.

49. Fort Charlotte occupied a hill on the South Carolina side of the Savannah River opposite Fort James. The patriots captured Fort Charlotte on July 12, 1775 and moved the ammunition to Ninety Six. The town of Vienna grew up near the site of Fort Charlotte.

50. Indian Mounds. The mounds described by William Bartram were at Remberts Bottom, now covered by Lake Russell. Archaeological displays and information about the mounds and village sites on this section of the Savannah River are located at the Russell Dam Visitor Center.

51. Russell Dam. The visitor center for Russell Dam is on the Georgia side of the Savannah River just off Bobby Brown Park Road. The history of the upper Savannah River region is told in an attractive exhibit room. Open 8 a.m.–4:30 p.m. weekdays and 8 a.m.–1 p.m. on weekends. An overlook and picnic area are located on the east side of the River off SC-81

52. Shuck Pen Eddy Boat Ramp. William Bartram crossed the Savannah River near this point on May 10, 1775. Shuck Pen Eddy is near the lower end of historic Trotter Shoals and Goat Island, now inundated.

Counties

Clarke County. When Clarke County was formed in 1801 the county seat was established at Watkinsville. The seat of government was moved to Athens in 1871 causing the citizens of Watkinsville to petition for a separate county, which was named Oconee and Watkinsville was once again a county seat. Clarke County is named for Elijah Clark.

Oglethorpe County. Organized in 1793 and named for the founder of Georgia, General James Edward Oglethorpe.

Taliaferro County. Organized in 1825 and named for Colonel Benjamin Taliaferro (pronounced Tollifer). The Taliaferros are descendants of an Italian family that immigrated to Virginia. Colonel Taliaferro moved to Wilkes County after the Revolution and took up land on the south side of the Broad River, ten miles from the Savannah River. He was a member of Congress and as president of the Georgia senate refused to vote for the Yazoo Act. For this display of integrity he was made Judge of the Superior Court while the careers of his opponents languished.

Wilkes County was formed into a governmental unit by the adoption of the state constitution on February 5, 1777. It was named for John Wilkes, member of Parliament who opposed the military solution taken by the ad-

Itinerary

Miles	Directions
	Begin in Wrightsborough and travel west on Wrightsborough Road
2.6	Left on Giles Road
2.3	Left on GA-80
.1	Right on Stedman Road (may be impassable during wet weather, in which case follow GA-80, Highway 223, and US-278 to Crawfordville)
1.9	Cross Indian Hill Road
3.6	Left on Raytown Road
3.7	Right on GA-47 in Sharon
2.6	Left on Hillman Road
8.7	Right on GA-22
1.5	Cross Little River
6.9	Historical marker for Buffalo Lick
5.1	Left on Sims Cross Road
	The site of the Great Buffalo Lick is approximately .7 mile northwest of this intersection
4.6	Keep straight onto Salem Road at the intersection
2.8	Right on GA-77 in Stephens
4.6	Keep left at the Fork
1.9	Left on US-78 in Crawford
4.6	Cherokee Corner
1.0	Right on Walter Sams Road
.5	Keep left at the fork
1.5	Keep right at the fork onto Dunlap Road
1.3	Left on Arnoldsville Road/South Main Street
3.1	Left on Athens Road then an immediate right onto Moores Grove Road
1.3	Right on Old Elberton Road
.3	Left on Pittard Road
1.4	Right on Hull Road/GA-72
.2	Left on Harve Mathis Road
1.2	Right on Danielsville Road/US-29
.8	Left on GA-106 (Fortson Store Road)
.9	Cross the intersection and begin Sanford Road
.5	Right on Smith Road (becomes Old Ila Road)
1.0	Cross GA-106 and begin Willis Glenn Road
.3	Keep left at the fork for Old Ila Road
.8	Left on Diamond Hill-Neese Road
.2	Neese Community

Oconee River

	Begin at the intersection with Moores Grove Road and travel west on Spring Valley Road
3.6	Keep straight on Winterville Road
.9	Right on Lexington Road, US-78
1.0	Right on Poplar Street
	Immediate left for access to the North Oconee River Greenway

ministration of Lord Frederick North's government. Wilkes was also the publisher of *The North Briton*, the opposition paper to the North government and the rampant corruption in British government. Wilkes County included all of the New Purchase and was later divided into Elbert, Lincoln, Madison, Oglethorpe, and Warren counties. During the Antebellum period the cotton planters of Wilkes County were among the wealthiest in the state.

Upper Savannah River

Artifacts discovered by archaeological investigation prior to the completion of Richard Russell Dam show that the upper Savannah River valley has seen human habitation since at least 8,000 B.C. Gregg Shoals has been inhabited throughout the entire range of human occupation of North America. The visitor center at Russell Dam has on display a Clovis point dating from 12,000 years ago that was uncovered at Rucker's Bottom Mound. Other artifacts found at that site include Palmer and Savannah points from the archaic period and fishing net weights from the woodland period. The Beaverdam Mound site at the mouth of Beaverdam Creek, near Heardmont, turned up ancient pottery bowls that are also on display at the Russell Dam Visitor Center.

Hernando De Soto found the Savannah River valley completely uninhabited when his army passed through in 1540. There were no towns between Ocute on the Oconee River in Georgia and the town of Cofitachequi at Camden, South Carolina. Although this region had an extensive chiefdom during the early Mississippian period, drought may have cleared the Savannah River Valley of population by the sixteenth century. The area then became an acknowledged buffer zone between the chiefdoms of Ocute and Cofitachequi.

The Upper Cherokee Trading Path was opened in 1740 and linked Augusta to the towns on the upper Savannah River. There were few settlers north of Augusta and the region between Little River and the Cherokee town of Tugaloo was virtually uninhabited when the survey party ran the line for the New Purchase. In 1773 Fort James was built in the fork of the Broad River and Savannah River to provide protection for settlers and house the land office. Colonel Edward Barnard was the commander of the garrison at Fort James. He died in June 1775 during the time that William Bartram was exploring the area.

Georgia Guidestones

When William Bartram traveled to Fort James in 1775 new farms were scattered along the Savannah River. Among the new settlers were the Clarks, the Doolys, and related families from North Carolina. After the war ended many families from Virginia and North Carolina moved into the region as did families from coastal Georgia whose property had been destroyed.

William Bartram's Travels in the New Purchase

June, 1773. The New Purchase survey party traveled from Augusta to the marked tree at Cherokee Corner. After leaving Cherokee Corner the survey party passed through Winterville and followed the ridge between the North Oconee and Broad rivers. This route is now approximated by GA-106. The travelers crossed the Broad River a little upstream of its junction with the Hudson River. Although the Yonge map of the New Purchase indicates a slightly meandering course to the Savannah River, other maps show the line to be straight. In the *Travels* Bartram incorrectly said that they marked a corner tree at the confluence of Little River and Savannah River, he obviously meant the Tugaloo River and Savannah River. However, the early boundary seems to have been fixed at the mouth of Lightwood Log Creek. Bartram returned to Augusta by the Upper Cherokee Path that ran along the west bank of the Savannah River.

May 1775. Bartram traveled from Augusta to Fort James over the Upper Cherokee Path. There he was befriended by Dr. Francis Begbie, the surgeon of the garrison, and together they explored up the Savannah River. The mound described by Bartram was Rembert's Mound which was 1.5 miles downstream from the present-day Russell Dam. It had almost disappeared by the time Francis Harper visited the site in 1940. Captain Rembert excavated the mound in 1848 and discovered human remains, pottery, tools, and points.

William Bartram's description of his exploration of the Broad River is frustratingly brief. He says simply that he made collections and observations "which were extended to a considerable distance in the environs of Dartmouth." We can assume that William Bartram explored a goodly portion of southeastern Elbert County. He crossed the Savannah River on May 10 bound for Cherokee Country.

June 1775. Bartram returned from the Cherokee Nation in early June and learned that a company of traders were organizing an expedition to West Florida. This was the opportunity that Bartram sought, to travel to the Creek Nation and beyond to the Mississippi River. While at Fort James in June he made,

> *little botanical excursions towards the head of Broad river, in order to collect some curiosities which I had observed thereabouts, which being accomplished ...*[1]

He possibly traveled up the ridge on the north side of the Broad River on a path shown on the Yonge map. This would have taken him through Elberton and Bowman. This path branched off from another trail that paralleled the south side of the Broad River. He would have crossed the Broad River somewhere near Bell's Ferry (GA17 bridge). Did Bartram stay close to the trails or did he descend to the river lands on side trips? If only we knew more!

1. William Bartram, *Travels*, 373.

Sites

1. King Hall Mill on Mill Shoal Creek is one of the most interesting geologic and botanical sites in the area. The mill is gone and the property is now in private hands but it has always been a favorite place for picnics. Mill Shoal Creek makes a bend in a rock basin and crashes over ledges of gneiss as it makes its way to the Broad River.

2. Broad River Heritage Preserve. Georgia's Rivercare 2000 program had a particular interest in acquiring property on the Broad River and the Broad River Heritage Preserve remains one of the few public properties on the river. The Broad River Land Trust helped organize the purchase, which it called the Human Tract after the family that once owned it. The entrance to the preserve is on the east side of GA-281 about one-half mile from the north end of the bridge.

Among the plants found at the preserve are fringe tree, black cohosh, whorled coreopsis, climbing hydrangea, Carolina silverbell, witch hazel, cucumber tree, Solomon's seal, bloodroot, styrax, trillium, wild azalea, and lesser rosebay. An unusual find is wild columbine, which is more common in soils less acid than is normally found in the Piedmont.

The Broad River has headwaters in Habersham County, midway between Cornelia and Toccoa. Its course is one of the least developed of any Piedmont river in the South, which has helped keep it relatively clean and unpolluted. The Broad River valley was the most populous region of Georgia in the waning days of the eighteenth century and provided many of the state's leaders in the post-Revolutionary era, including several governors and one ambassador to France, William H. Crawford.

3. US-29 Bridge. This bridge crosses the Hudson River near where William Bartram and the Edward Barnard survey party crossed. There is a path to the riverbank.

4. Victoria Bryant State Park contains 406 acres on Rice Creek. The nature trail along the creek is a lesson in microclimates; with the cool north facing south side harbors montane plants while the hot and dry south facing north side is much more like the Piedmont. Activities include hiking, camping, fishing, picnicking, swimming, and golf. Located on GA-327 just north of US-29. Open 7 a.m.–10 p.m., daily. Admission.

5. Center of the World. West of Hartwell on GA-59 is the site of the Center of the World, an important gathering and ceremonial place for the Cherokees.

6. Hart State Park includes Beech Bluff Nature Trail, store, boat ramp, camping, picnic area, and playground. Open daily from 7 a.m.–8 p.m. during peak season and 7 a.m.–6 p.m. during the off season. Hours are longer from Friday through Sunday during peak season and Friday only during the off season. Located off US-29 just east of Hartwell.

7. Hartwell Dam Visitor Center. Intersection of US-29 and GA-181. Open daily except Christmas and New Year's Day. Weekend hours vary throughout the year.

Watsadler Campground is located just west of the Hartwell Dam Visitor Center.

8. Georgia Guidestones. On a high hill just north of Elberton, not far from where William

Upper Savannah River

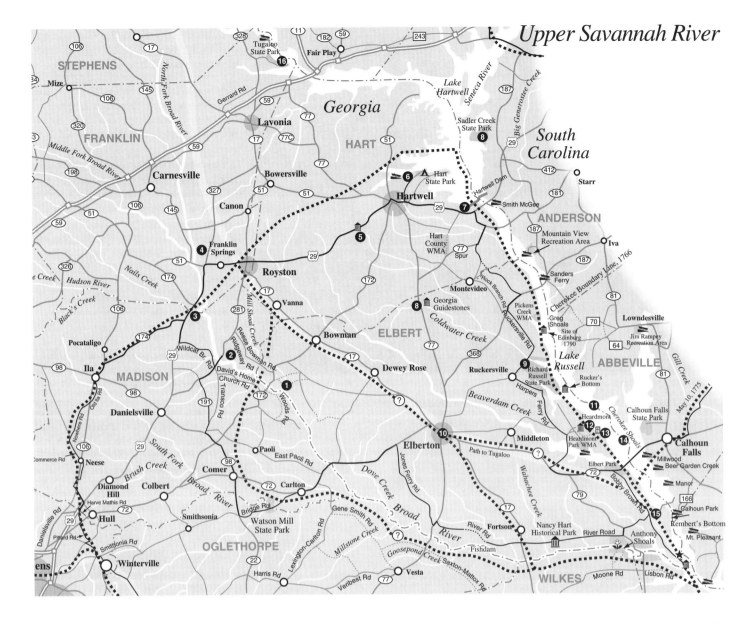

Bartram traveled, are the Georgia Guidestones. They are nineteen-feet tall and are built of native granite. In twelve languages they are inscribed with this message:

- Maintain humanity under 500 million in perpetual balance with nature
- Guide reproduction wisely, improving fitness and diversity
- Unite humanity with a living new language
- Rule passion, faith, tradition and all things with tempered reason
- Protect people and nations with fair laws and just courts
- Let all nations rule internally, resolving external disputes in a world court
- Avoid petty laws and useless officials
- Balance personal rights with social duties
- Prize truth, beauty, love, seeking harmony with the infinite
- Be not a cancer on the earth, leave room for nature, leave room for nature

9. Richard Russell State Park. One of the Southeast's most important paleo-Indian sites, Rucker's Bottom, is inundated by Lake Russell at Richard Russell State Park. This site was excavated in 1980 prior to the completion of the lake and the artifacts may be seen on display at the Russell Dam Visitor Center. Russell State Park has camping, hiking, picnicking, swimming, boat ramp, and fishing. Located on Ruckersville Road, off GA-77. Open 8 a.m.–dark, daily. Admission.

10. Elberton was chosen by Stephen Heard as the site of the courthouse for the newly created Elbert County in 1790. Elberton is now known as the granite capital of the world.

Elberton Granite Museum. Learn how granite is quarried and cut at this unique museum. Exhibits include samples of granite, granite-working tools, and a beautiful photographic exhibit of the granite industry in the first half of the twentieth century. Information about the Georgia Guidestones is available at

Legend

1. King Hall Mill
2. Broad River Heritage Preserve Broad River
3. US-29 Bridge
4. Victoria Bryant State Park
5. Center of the World
6. Hart State Park
7. Hartwell Dam Visitor Center
8. Georgia Guidestones
9. Richard Russell State Park
11. McCalla Island Mounds
10. Elberton
12. Heardmont
13. Old Dan Tucker
14. Cherokee Shoals
15. Richard B. Russell Dam
16. Tugaloo State Park

King Hall Mill, Elbert County, Georgia

Itinerary

Broad River Day Trip

Miles	Directions
	Begin at the Fort James monument at Bobby Brown State Park and travel north on Bobby Brown State Park Road
4.7	Left on Brad Dixon Road
2.0	Left on GA-79
.5	Right on River Road
6.2	Nancy Hart Historical Park
1.7	Cross Nancy Hart Highway (GA-17) and continue on River Road
1.7	Pavement ends *River Road is treacherous during wet weather for the next 1.8 miles*
5.3	Left on Lexington Highway (GA-77), immediate right on Jones Ferry Road
.6	Entrance to Elbert County Environmental Forest
5.9	Left on US-72
5.5	Cross Broad River
2.1	Roadside Park on the left
2.1	Left, cross the railroad tracks, and turn right on South Railroad Avenue
1.6	Enter Watson Mill Bridge State Park
3.5	Right on GA-22
3.0	Left on US-72 in Comer
.1	Right on GA-98
2.6	Keep straight on GA-98 at Gholston Stand Crossroads
1.3	Right on GA-191
4.4	Right on GA-281
1.8	Cross Broad River
.3	Parking for Broad River Natural Area Go back across Broad River
1.8	Right on Old Wildcat Bridge Road
1.5	William Bartram Trail marker at Camp Kiwanis
2.7	Right on US-29
2.6	Cross Hudson River
.6	Cross Broad River

the museum. Located on GA-72 just west of downtown. Open 2–5 p.m. from January 15 through November 15.

11. McCalla Island Mounds. McCalla Island originally known as Heard's Island, was the site of several Mississippian Mounds. The island is now inundated by Lake Russell.

12. Heardmont was the plantation of Stephen Heard after the Revolution and was the most elegant home in the area. Heard was born in Ireland and immigrated first to Virginia with his family during the French and Indian War then to Georgia in the 1770s. Heard was elected President of the Executive Council in February 1780 upon the death of President George Wells, who was killed by James Jackson in a duel. In 1781 Heard was named governor of a government in exile. After the war he was involved in local political affairs and helped choose the site for Elberton. Heardmont is a ten acre park surrounding the hill where his home stood. He is buried in the family cemetery at the top of the hill.

13. Old Dan Tucker. Reverend Daniel Tucker was known for his warmth, charm, and friendship towards all people. He was so well liked by the local black population that he became the subject of a well-known folk song …

Old Dan Tucker was a grand old man
He washed his face in a frying pan
He combed his hair with a wagon wheel
And died with a toothache in his heel

Dan Tucker's grave is at the end of a hiking trail on Old Dan Tucker Cemetery Road. The walk is well worth the effort. The gravestones are obviously of local manufacture for the carver had to cram the letters together as he reached the edge of the stone. Though I have heard the call of the Whippoorwill every summer of my life I have seen this elusive creature only once, and that was in 1997 at Dan Tucker's grave.

14. Cherokee Shoals was one of the most important crossings of the upper Savannah River since prehistoric times. The shoals are now inundated by Lake Russell.

15. The Richard B. Russell Dam is located at the lower end of historic Trotters Shoals. The visitor center has excellent exhibits on the human settlement of the area from the paleo-Indian period 10,000 years ago to the present. Artifacts from the archaeological excavations are on display in the museum. Located off Bobby Brown State Park Road. Open 8 a.m.– 5 p.m.

Rembert's Bottom. The site of the mound visited by William Bartram, is just downriver from the Richard Russell Dam at Rembert's

Bottom. The mounds were washed away earlier in this century and the site is now underwater.

Gregg Shoals. Artifacts found at this site have established a record of continual occupation by humans throughout the entire range of North American inhabitation.

Rucker's Bottom. A Clovis point has established paleo-Indian inhabitation to at least 8,000 B.C. Other artifacts have been retrieved from the Archaic and Woodland periods.

Beaverdam Mound is located at the mouth of Beaverdam Creek in the Heardmont Park area. A small bowl from this mound is on display at the Russell Dam Visitor Center.

16. Tugaloo State Park. Facilities include cottages, fishing, boat ramps, picnic area, and two nature trails. To reach the park take GA-17 north from I-85, then east on Garrard Road and north on GA-328 to the park. Open daily. Admission.

Counties

Hart County, Georgia, is named for Nancy Hart who captured Tories at her home on the Broad River in present Elbert County. Hart County was created in 1853.

Elbert County, Georgia, is named for Revolutionary War General Samuel Elbert and was created in 1790.

Itinerary

Route of the 1773 Survey Party through the New Purchase

Miles	Directions
	Begin at the intersection of US-29 and GA-106, travel west on GA-106 (Fortson Store Road)
.9	Cross the intersection and begin Sanford Road (GA-106 turns right)
.5	Right on Smith Road (becomes Old Ila Road)
1.0	Cross GA-106 and begin Willis Glenn Road
.3	Keep left at the fork for Old Ila Road
.8	Left on Diamond Hill-Neese Road
.2	Cross GA-106 and begin Neese-Commerce Road
1.4	Right on Nowhere Road
2.3	Keep left on Old Ila Road at the fork
1.1	Cross GA-106 and continue Old Ila Road
2.0	Right on GA-106
.6	Ila
.8	Right on GA-174
7.0	Left on US-29
1.1	Cross Hudson River
.6	Cross the North Fork of the Broad River
6.1	Downtown Royston
10.2	Historical marker for *Ah weh li Alohee*, Cherokee council ground
2.7	Right on Howell Street in Hartwell
.6	Right on Franklin Street (US-29)
.7	Intersection with Ridge Road and access to Hart State Park
5.3	Hartwell Lake Office, visitor center, boat ramp and recreation area
	Right at this point on Smith-McGee Road (GA-181)
1.3	Right on St. James Road
2.8	Cross Cokesbury Highway
.6	Left on Turner Road
2.7	Left on Monticello Road
2.9	Right on GA-368
1.5	Left on Ruckersville Road
4.7	Entrance to Richard Russell State Park
1.4	Left on Harper's Ferry Road
4.6	Left
2.2	Intersection with Heardmont Road. *Left for the graves of Governor Stephen Heard and Old Dan Tucker* Harper's Ferry Road becomes Pearle Mill Road.
3.0	Left on Calhoun Falls Road (GA-72)
6.0	Right on Bobby Brown State Park Road
3.4	Intersection with Russell Dam Road *Take a left for the visitors center and a view of the dam*
.5	Intersection with Brad Dixon Road
4.6	Bobby Brown State Park and the site of Fort James

East Florida

The first Europeans to see the coast of North America were possibly John Cabot and his sailors. In 1498 they were sailing the north Atlantic under the patronage of King Henry VII of England, in search of a passage to the Far East. After exploring Newfoundland they sailed southward, possibly as far as Florida, before returning to England. This voyage became the proof for England's later claim to the land north of the Florida peninsula. Florida appeared on the 1511 map drawn by Peter Martyr and was named Biminy.

Juan Ponce de León, governor of Puerto Rico landed on the Florida coast on Easter Sunday 1513. His ships may have reached landfall north of Saint Augustine or farther south near Melbourne Beach. He named this new land Florida for the day of discovery, *Pascua Florida*, and for the flowers in bloom. His claim included all of eastern North America. De León was given the governorship and instructed to colonize Florida. León was also the first to notice the northerly flowing ocean current just offshore of Florida. It did not take long for the Spanish treasure ships to take advantage of the Gulf Stream to shorten the return trip to Europe. Ponce de León was wounded in 1521 in a battle with Indians while building a village at Charlotte Harbor and died in Cuba. It is certain that Spanish slavers had visited the Florida coast before Ponce de León, which explains the source of the hostility that he met in the native Floridians and the presence of Spanish words among the Calusas.

The next significant exploration of East Florida was by the French, not the Spanish. Spain had given up trying to occupy Florida after several disastrous attempts in South Carolina and on the Gulf Coast. Jean Ribault, under the sponsorship of Admiral Gaspard de Coligny, explored the St. Johns River in May 1562. He named it Rivière May and erected a monument before sailing north through the inland passage of Georgia. He entered a large and protected bay that he named Port Royal. Ribault established a garrison at Port Royal and named it Charlesfort, after Charles IX of France, and the colony was named Carolina. He returned to France, then in the grips of the first of a series of religious wars between Protestants and Catholics. Ribault, a Huguenot, escaped to England where he interested some Englishmen in attempting a colony in Florida. Ribault was arrested while in London and held in prison for a year. Meanwhile, in North America, the Charlesfort garrison mutinied and killed their captain, Albert de la Pierria. They then built boats and set sail for France. They were picked up by an English ship and delivered home.

When peace was reestablished in France Admiral Gaspard de Coligny engaged René de Laudonnière to complete the task of establishing a French Protestant colony in Florida. Laudonnière reached the St. Johns River on June 22, 1564 with 300 colonists and commenced building Fort Caroline. One of the colonists was Jacques Le Moyne, an artist who had been commissioned to make a report on the new land. His drawings have been lost but Theodore de Bry published etchings of the originals, the first illustrations of Native Americans and their culture.

Some of the colonists deserted Fort Caroline, stole two ships and began pirating on the Atlantic Coast, which alerted the Spanish to the French presence in Florida. Pedro Menéndez de Avilés became Adelantado of Florida just as news of the French colony reached Spain. A French colony so close to the Gulf Stream shipping lane was a threat to Spanish treasure ships and Menéndez was ordered to seek out the interlopers and disperse them. He entered a fine harbor on September 7, 1565, and named it San Agustín, for it was the feast day of the saint. Fort Caroline had recently been reinforced by Ribault and 500 new French colonists. However, on September 10 Ribault and 600 soldiers and sailors departed the St. Johns River, leaving the French settlement in a weakened condition. Ribault hoped to entrap the Spanish at Saint Augustine and defeat them before further reinforcements could arrive from Cuba, but a hurricane drove his ships toward the south and wrecked them off the coast of Matanzas Inlet. Menéndez seized the opportunity and immediately set out overland for the French settlement. The Spanish force caught Fort Caroline by surprise and killed nearly half of the French who remained. Some of the French were able to escape by swimming to a ship anchored in the river. Among the sixty survivors who were able to return to Europe were René de Laudonnière and Jacques le Moyne.

Governor Menéndez renamed the fort San Mateo and in-

Ribault Monument overlooking the St. Johns River

Black Rock Beach, Talbot Islands State Park

stalled a garrison. He returned to Saint Augustine to discover that Ribault and a number of his men had survived and were on the coast to the south. Menéndez set out with a small force and encountered the French as they traveled up the coast. Upon learning of the fate of Fort Caroline, the French surrendered to Menéndez and were promised fair treatment. The Spanish bound the French in groups of ten as they were ferried across Metanzas Inlet and then murdered all but a few who professed to be Catholics. Over 300 French Huguenots were killed among the sand dunes south of Saint Augustine and the place has since been named Matanzas, which means *place of slaughter* in Spanish. One group of 170 French, deciding to take their chances with the Indians rather than the Spaniards, went further south and built a fort. When this group finally surrendered to Menéndez they were promised safe passage back to Europe and this time the Spanish governor kept his word.

Menéndez set up forts along the Atlantic and Gulf coasts to protect the Spanish claim to Florida. He sent Juan Pardo from Santa Elena to explore the interior and establish forts. In August 1567, Dominique de Gourgues and his Saturiwa allies attacked Fort San Mateo in retaliation for the execution of French Protestants.

Spain considered abandoning Florida but decided instead to strengthen her military presence by establishing missions to Christianize the Indians and making allies of them. A string of fifty-two missions was established along the Atlantic coast and across north Florida. The number of missions, and Spanish influence, grew despite occasional revolts and repeated disturbances. A new danger to Spanish control of Florida came with the founding of Charles Town in 1670. The Indians of Santa Elena and Guale became dissatisfied with their Spanish patrons and were attracted to the English in South Carolina by trade, particularly the trade in guns. By 1686 the missions north of the St. Marys River had been abandoned. Governor James Moore and a band of Carolinians destroyed the remaining missions north of Saint Augustine and burned much of the city but failed to take Castillo de San Marcos. By 1708 all missions outside Saint Augustine had been destroyed or abandoned.

The founding of Georgia in 1733 was further cause for concern among the Spanish. James Oglethorpe built forts on islands still claimed by Spain and invaded Florida on two occasions. After the War of Jenkins' Ear, Spain and England agreed to leave the land between the St. Johns and Altamaha Rivers unoccupied.

British Florida

Spain entered into war against England at the very end of the Seven Years War just as France was ready to capitulate. British forces attacked and captured Havana, Cuba. The First Treaty of Paris, 1763, included a provision for Britain to receive

Florida in exchange for giving up Havana. Not all of the members of the British government were happy to get a land of swamps and sandy pine barrens in exchange for the jewel of the Caribbean, but England was now indisputable master of North America east of the Mississippi River and had removed both French and Spanish threats to her colonies.

The British organized the Florida peninsula into East Florida and the Gulf Coast west of Apalachicola River became West Florida; the fourteenth and fifteenth colonies. Saint Augustine remained the capital of East Florida. James Grant was named the governor and was considered a good choice for he had fought and defeated the Cherokees in 1761 and was familiar with the Southeastern Indians. He had also been involved in the siege of Havana. With an infant colony and no inhabitants, Grant had to invite such men to settle in Florida who could maintain a skeletal government and assist in attracting more settlers to an empty land. Among the officials of the new government were James and John Moultrie of South Carolina; John Stuart, Superintendent of Indian Affairs for the Southern District; Dr. John Turnbull, founder of New Smyrna; William Drayton of South Carolina; and William Gerard De Brahm, Surveyor General of Georgia.

Brown pelican

The Bartrams' 1765 exploration of Florida was a result of John Bartram's appointment as botanist to the King and a directive to report on the soil, climate, and vegetation of East Florida. They Bartram's were at the Indian congress, hosted by Governor Grant at Fort Picolata, when the boundary for East Florida was established. The line ran from the mouth of the Oklawaha River to the forks of Black Creek, near Middleburg in Duval County, then to the St. Mary's River near Trader's Hill. From the mouth of the Oklawaha River the boundary followed the St. Johns River south to an indefinite point, but for all practical purposes there was little activity by European settlers below this point the founding of New Smyrna, which did not last.

Interest in the new colonies lead to several significant reports on the natural history of Florida. The most important were Bernard Romans' *Concise Natural History of East and West Florida*, 1775; Dr. William Stork's *Account of East-Florida, 1766,* which also contained John Bartram's Florida journal; William Roberts' *Account of the First Discovery, and Natural History of Florida*; Captain Philip Pittman's *Present State of the European Settlements on the Mississippi*; and William Gerard De Brahm's unpublished *Report of the General Survey in the Southern District of North America*; and, of course, William Bartram's *Travels*.

Land was granted by the head-right system whereby the head of a household received a hundred acres of land plus fifty acres for each family member and servant. Former soldiers and sailors could receive bounty lands according to years of military service. Additionally, large grants of 10,000 to 20,000 acres were granted to persons of wealth who were expected to bring colonists and create a settlement at their own expense. There were attempts to establish Utopian or cooperative settlements in East Florida at Rollestown and New Smyrna. The dissolution of Rollestown was mentioned by Bartram. The Greek, Italian, and Minorcan immigrants of New Smyrna sought refuge in Saint Augustine.

Bernard Romans estimated that a family emigrating from the middle colonies to Florida would need $2,500 for transportation, tools, livestock, fees, building materials, slaves, and living expenses during the period of settlement when income was not forthcoming. The financiers of the colonies and settlements in North America rarely saw any profit on their investment. Indeed, most saw a steady drain on their purses.

James Grant was popular with the citizens of East Florida for he always ruled by example—advancing money to workers, subscribing to the building of the road to New Smyrna, beginning a plantation, and by numerous acts of kindness to individuals that demonstrated his real interest in the welfare of the colony. He was willing to yield where circumstance and reason required rather than cling to petty prerogative. He was a *bon vivant* and of apparent good nature. However, he was criticized by the leading citizens for not calling together an assembly. Grant left Florida in 1771 but the new governor, Patrick Tonyn, did not arrive until March 1774. Meanwhile, John Moultrie acted as interim governor.

Tonyn was everything Grant was not—the new governor was confrontational, authoritarian, dishonest, and suspicious. He distrusted William Drayton, the Chief Justice for East Florida, and suspected him of patriot sympathies. Drayton was suspended and returned to his relatives in South Carolina where after the Revolution he became the first Judge of the United States District Court for South Carolina. Turnbull also fell out of favor with Tonyn. The governor allowed the New Smyrna colony to disperse by not forcing the indentured settlers to return as was required by law. Turnbull moved to Charleston during the British occupation and remained to become a founding member of the South Carolina Medical Society.

A scheme by Georgian Jonathan Bryan and associates to lease five million acres in East Florida was one of the causes of tensions between the Seminoles and whites that preceded Bartram's visit in 1774. The speculators had arranged with a few Creek leaders for the lease of land owned by Seminoles. The Seminoles were understandably displeased with designs on their land. Additionally, whites were legally forbidden to arrange the sale or lease of lands as individuals. Governor Tonyn and Superintendent John Stuart moved quickly to block the land grab but the coming of the Revolution solved the problem for them.

After July 1776 there was no turning back from war, and

Florida, being vulnerable, expected an invasion from Georgia and South Carolina. In addition to the British regular troops there was soon operating in Florida, a militia, the South Carolina Royalists, the Royal North Carolina Regiment, and the East Florida Rangers. The Rangers were controversial because they were under the command of Tonyn, a civilian official, rather than Major Mark Prevost, the military commander in East Florida. The Ranger's guerilla war in Georgia was denounced by the patriots but they served the British cause well. Their leader, Thomas Brown, was a Tory who had been tarred and feathered and driven from his home near Augusta. He appeared in Florida in 1776 and by the end of the year had organized, with Daniel McGirth, a company of 130 Rangers and had received the rank of lieutenant colonel. The Rangers served as spies, scouts, hunters, and guerillas for regular army operations. They also carried out numerous cattle raids into Georgia.

It was this new threat that may have lead William Bartram to join General Lachlan McIntosh's forces. Bartram's brief reference to spending the summer of 1776 in revisiting the hinter parts of Georgia and the border of East Florida may conceal a part of his history he was reluctant to reveal. There is good evidence that he supplied intelligence to his friend Lachlan McIntosh.

A military party from Florida captured Fort McIntosh on the Satilla River in February 1777. Georgia retaliated that spring with a failed attempt to invade Florida. In March 1778, the East Florida Rangers and Indian allies burned Fort Barrington. In June 1778 General Howe and Colonel Samuel Elbert marched to the border with intentions of invading Florida. An advance force under General James Screven and Elijah Clark was turned back at the Battle of Alligator Creek Bridge on June 30. The forces of East Florida under Major Mark Prevost marched north to join General Henry Clinton and Lieutenant Colonel Archibald Campbell in the capture of Savannah. In November 1778, they reached Midway, looted the community, and burned the meeting house.

The Revolution in Florida was primarily a war between Georgia patriots and Florida loyalists. The British occupation of Savannah in 1778 and Charleston in 1780 removed one threat to East Florida, but the Spanish capture of Pensacola in 1781 brought another. Saint Augustine had become a haven for loyalists escaping the Revolution and in 1782 the city was filled with 13,000 refugees evacuating Charleston and Savannah when those cities were returned to the Americans. The population previous to this time was only 1,000 whites and 3,000 Blacks. The economic future for East Florida looked bright for a moment with this influx of new inhabitants and capital.

However, the Second Treaty of Paris that was concluded on September 19, 1783, returned East Florida (and Minorca) to Spain in exchange for Britain being allowed to keep Gibraltar. A new Spanish government lead by Governor Manuel de Zéspedes took control of East Florida on July 12, 1784. The British inhabitants had eighteen months to settle their affairs and leave or become Spanish citizens. Most British citizens of Florida emigrated to the Bahamas, Nova Scotia, Jamaica, and a few disappeared into the interior of the continent. The Greek, Italian, and Minorcan inhabitants of Saint Augustine universally accepted the new government and remained.

Jacksonville and the St. Johns River

William Bartram's Travels in East Florida

William Bartram accompanied his father to East Florida in 1765 when John explored this recently acquired British territory as royal botanist to King George. William's return in 1774 must have been a bittersweet experience filled with nostalgia and apprehension. He failed to mention the year he spent as a novice planter near Picolata on the St. Johns River, an enterprise at which he failed miserably.

William fell in love with Florida during the 1765 expedition and set his heart on becoming a rice planter. He persuaded his father to help him choose the land, purchase slaves, seeds, and tools. John argued against such a course for he rightly judged William to lack the constitution and temperament to make it through the first few backbreaking years until he could make his plantation profitable.

Henry Laurens visited William while on his tour of East Florida in June 1766, and wrote to John that William was sick with a fever, the land was poorly situated and promised to be unproductive. Laurens had taken the liberty to have provisions sent from Charleston and he urged John to advise William to dissolve his holdings and abandon his notion of becoming a rice planter. William did so with relief but was shipwrecked off New Smyrna when he sailed from Florida. He then spent several more months in Saint Augustine working as a draftsman for William De Brahm, the surveyor general.

On his second expedition to Florida in early April 1774, William Bartram landed on the north end of Amelia Island, near where Fort Clinch now stands. He traveled south, crossing Egan's Creek and passing through Old Fernandina to Lord Egmont's plantation where modern Fernandina now stands. Bartram was entertained by Egmont's agent, Stephen Egan, who rode with him about the entire island, observing the plantation and Indian mounds. The shell mounds Bartram saw are shown on a 1770 map by De Brahm, but they have since been mined for their shell to pave roads.

William and Mr. Egan sailed from Amelia Island through the Intracoastal Waterway. Their route was through Kingsley Creek (*Amelia Narrows*) and down South Amelia River to Nassau Sound (*Fort George Sound*). They made a pleasant camp on the north end of Big Talbot Island where they roasted oysters. They followed Sawpit and Sister creeks to the St. Johns River and on to present-day Arlington where Bartram

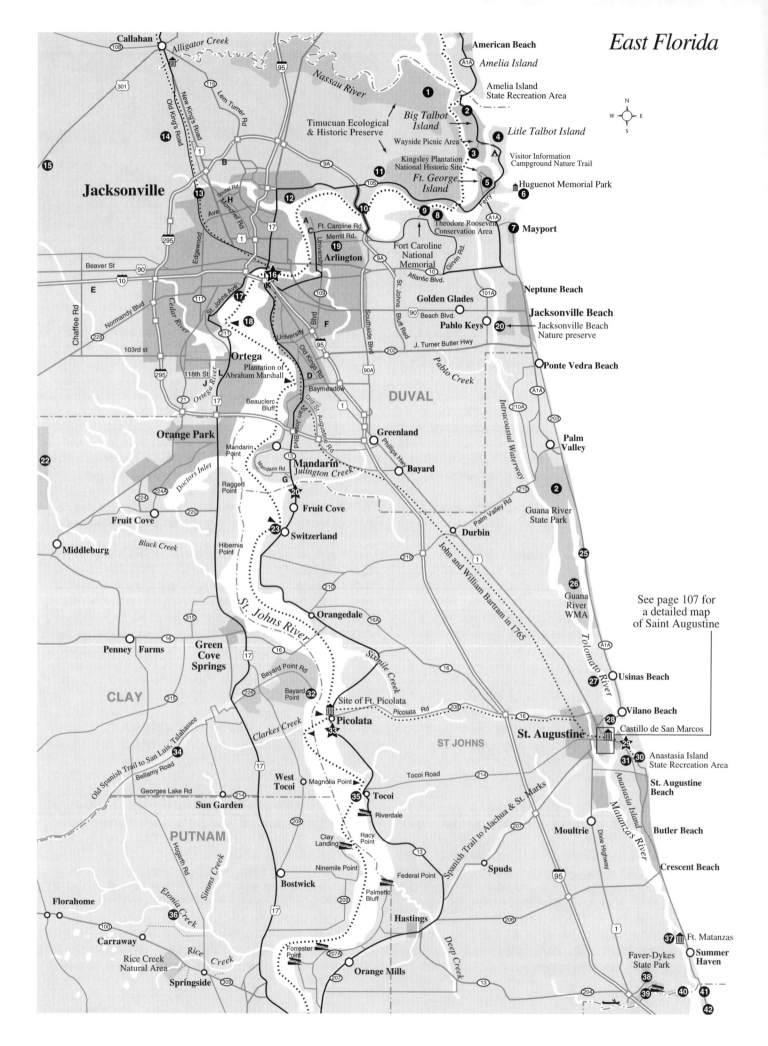

purchased a little sailboat. Bartram noted that a passage existed between the islands and mainland that extended from Virginia along the Atlantic and Gulf coasts. This protected navigational route is now the Intracoastal Waterway.

Upon leaving the Cow Ford (Jacksonville), Bartram made his first camp in the vicinity of Ortega on the west bank of the St. Johns River at Sadler Point (this is mentioned in the report to Dr. Fothergill). It was mid-April 1774 and the growing season was well underway. With the approach of hot summer weather storms also come to full flower such as the one that caused Bartram to seek shelter early in the afternoon. I myself have met with several storms on each trip along the St. Johns when the sun gives way to darkness and drenching rain in the course of fifteen minutes, then just as quickly the sun returns.

The second night Bartram was a guest of Abraham Marshall at his plantation, Satonia, near Goodby Creek on the east shore. The third night found Bartram at the plantation of Francis Philip Fatio at Switzerland. There he received information concerning the recent disturbances at Spalding's Stores. The depredations had been caused by young, hot-headed warriors, but the wiser and older chiefs were reluctant to jeopardize trade and they sought to restore peace. Bartram paused the next day at Fort Picolata then crossed the river to the mouth of Clarke's Creek and camped. Being kept ashore by a strong wind the next day he embarked late and crossed the river to Tocoi Creek and camped just north of the present community of Tocoi.

Bartram then kept to the west bank or *Indian shore*, the river being the division between Indian country on the west bank and English land on the east. The Indian village he observed was on the bluff where Palatka now stands, a fine prospect for a town now just as it was in 1774. Bartram was entertained there with a watermelon feast just before he departed Florida.

Sites

1. Timucuan Preserve. This 46,000-acre preserve protects environmental and archaeological treasures and is located in the extensive wetlands between the Nassau and St. Johns rivers. Most of the preserve is accessible only by boat.

2. Big Talbot Island is part of the larger Talbot Islands GEOpark and may be explored by several hiking trails.

Blackrock Trail. This short trail winds through maritime forest to reach Blackrock Beach where soft, unconsolidated black rocks and downed trees line the beach.

3. BEAKS is an acronym for Bird Emergency Aid and Kare Sanctuary. BEAKS sponsors educational programs for schools and communities. They teach bird-rescue classes throughout Florida and maintain a response unit that works at oil spills throughout the Southeast. The headquarters on Big Talbot Island has a number of birds that have been rescued and rehabilitated. The grounds are open Tuesday–Sunday from noon until 4 p.m. Located at the south end of Big Talbot Island on Macintosh Road.

4. Little Talbot Island is well known for its beach and dune complex. The desert-like dunes are extraordinarily beautiful but please don't walk over them, they are fragile. The campground has a nature trail and there is canoe access to the same salt marsh that William Bartram sailed.

Simpson Creek Trail passes through the salt marsh along a natural ridge.

5. Fort George Island was called Alimacani by the Timucuans. It is the most southern of the large sea islands that stretch from Charleston to the mouth of the St. Johns River. The Spanish established the mission of San Juan del Puerto on the island in 1587 and gave the name San Juan to Fort George Island and the river. Oglethorpe built Fort St. George on the island in 1736 and the English thereafter referred to the island by that name. Florida State Recreation and Parks has published a guide to the island that includes a driving tour. Guides to the Saturiwa Trail are available at the Talbot Islands State Park and from the kiosk at the Ribault Club House located on the east road.

San Juan del Puerto Mission was located just south of the Kingsley Plantation on San Juan Creek. It was built in the village of Saturiwa, a Timucuan people, and was destroyed by Carolinians in 1702.

Legend

1. Timucuan Preserve
2. Big Talbot Island
3. BEAKS
4. Little Talbot Island
5. Fort George Island
   San Juan del Puerto Mission
   Saturiwa Trail
   Kingsley Plantation
   Rollins Bird & Plant Sanctuary
   Mount Cornelia
6. Huguenot Park
7. Mayport
   Kathryn Abbey Hanna Park
8. Theodore Roosevelt Area
9. Fort Caroline National Memorial
10. Yellow Bluff Fort State Historical Site
11. E. Dale Joyner Nature Preserve
12. Jacksonville Zoological Gardens
13. King's Road
14. American Forests Famous & Historic Trees, Inc.
15. Cary State Forest
16. Cow Ford (Jacksonville)
    Black Heritage Trail
    Museum of Science and History
    Friendship Park
    Jacksonville Historical Center
    Southbank Riverwalk
    Jacksonville parks
17. Cummer Art Museum
18. St. Johns River
19. Tree Hill
20. Jacksonville Beach Wildlife Refuge
21. Bartram Memorial Highway
22. Jennings State Forest
23. Switzerland
24. Diego Plains
25. Guana River State Park
26. Guana River WMA
27. Stokes Landing Conservation Area
28. Fort Mose
29. Anastasia Island Coquina Quarry
30. Anastasia Island State Recreation Area
31. Saint Augustine Alligator Farm
32. Bayard Point Conservation Area
33. Picolata
34. Old Spanish Trail
35. Tocoi
36. Etonia Creek
37. Fort Matanzas
38. Faver-Dykes State Park
39. Pellicer Creek Aquatic Preserve
40. Princess Place Preserve
41. Marineland
42. Washington Oaks State Gardens

Saturiwa Trail is named for the Timucuan Chief Saturiwa and the tribe of the same name who befriended the French at Fort Caroline.

Kingsley Plantation. Zephaniah Kingsley's father was a Tory during the Revolution and took over the confiscated business of Daniel De Saussure when the British occupied Beaufort in 1780. He was banished from South Carolina in 1782 and went first to Nova Scotia then to Florida where he acquired Fort George Island. His son Zephaniah Kingsley moved to Fort George Island in 1814 with his wife, Ana Madgigine Jai, a Senegalese African, and their three children. They accumulated more than 32,000 acres of land in north Florida and more than 200 slaves.

When the United States purchased Florida in 1821 the new American territorial laws were not as liberal toward blacks as were the Spanish. To escape the atmosphere of repression and intolerance, the Kingsleys moved to Haiti in 1837.

The plantation passed through several owners before being bought by the Florida Park Service in 1989. The Kingsley Plantation home dates from 1798 and is open to the public.

Rollins Bird & Plant Sanctuary was donated to the state by Rollins College in 1950.

Mount Cornelia is the highest point on the Atlantic Coast south of the Outer Banks, sixty-five feet above sea level. It was once believed that Mount Cornelia was built by James Oglethorpe as a military defense during the Georgia invasion of Florida, but it is most likely a large beach dune remnant.

6. Huguenot Memorial Park is located at Ward's Bank, a sand spit at the entrance to the St. Johns River. This is a popular birding spot in winter. It is also the first land touched by French colonists in North America. Turn left at the yellow blinking light on Hecksher Drive (FL-105), just after leaving Little Talbot Island and before Fort George Island.

7. Mayport is named for the River May, the French name of the St. Johns River, and is one of the oldest fishing communities in the U.S.

Kathryn Abbey Hanna Park, in Mayport, has miles of hiking trails through maritime forest for naturalists and beaches for vacationers. There are campsites, concessions, bike and boat rental. Located on Mayport Road (A1A). Open 8 a.m.–sunset, daily. Admission.

8. Theodore Roosevelt Area. Obtain maps of hiking trails and a schedule of ranger-guided nature hikes from Fort Caroline National Memorial. National Park Service, 12713 Fort Caroline Road, Jacksonville, FL 32225.

9. Fort Caroline National Memorial. The site of the first French colony in North America is protected by Fort Caroline National Memorial.

Fort Caroline National Memorial

La Caroline was to be a commercial venture and a refuge for French Huguenots. The French community was destroyed by the Spanish in 1565 and the fort became a Spanish garrison.

The French fort has been reconstructed on the low banks of the St. Johns River. A replica of the Ribault Monument overlooks the St. Johns River from a high bluff to the east. Located on Fort Caroline Road which may be reached from Monument Road or St. Johns Bluff Road. Open daily, 9 a.m.–5 p.m. Admission.

10. Yellow Bluff Fort State Historical Site, New Berlin Road. The site of this Civil War earthen fort is open to the public, although it has not been developed. The ramparts are still visible.

11. E. Dale Joyner Nature Preserve at Pelotes Island includes several salt marsh islands in the St. Johns River. There are several Timucuan shell middens that support some interesting tropical plants at the northern end of their range. There are two hiking trails. This preserve is open only to groups by reservation. Call Florida Power and Light Company, (902) 751–7700.

12. Jacksonville Zoological Gardens. The Jacksonville Zoo has many exotic animals that one would expect to find at a first-class zoo in addition to native animals living in their natural habitat. The Florida Wetlands area features bobcats, black bears, Florida panther, and a reproduction of a Timucuan village. Located off Hecksher Drive. Open 9 a.m.–5 p.m., Monday through Sunday and until 8 p.m. on Friday and Saturday in the summer. Admission.

13. King's Road was the main thoroughfare along the Southeastern coast. The King's Road crossed the St. Mary's River at King's Ferry, Nassau County, then it crossed in later years at Camp Pinckney. The road from King's Ferry to Saint Augustine was improved in 1766 by subscription. Its modern equivalent would be CR-115A to Hilliard, CR-115 to Callahan, US-1 and Old King's Road to cross the St. Johns River in downtown Jacksonville. From there it followed Old Saint Augustine, King's Road, and US-1 to Saint Augustine. In 1765 John and William Bartram traveled the King's Road from Savannah to Saint Augustine.

14. American Forests Famous & Historic Trees, Inc. propagates and sells trees of historical significance, including trees of the Bartram Garden. These trees are the direct offspring of the parent trees from seed and cuttings collected from historic sites such as Elvis Presley's Graceland, the Washington Mall, homes of the presidents, historic gardens, and the last surviving Rambo apple planted by John "Appleseed" Chapman. Although the main offices for American Forests are in Washington, D.C., the Famous & Historic Trees section is located in Jacksonville at 8555 Plummer Road. Information and a catalogue are available from the American Forests web site.

15. Cary State Forest. This 3,400 acres of pine land has several hiking trails and a wildlife observation tower. Located on US-301. Open daily.

16. Cow Ford (Jacksonville) was an old fording place on the St. Johns River. The narrowness of the river at this point made it a convenient crossing place for the King's Road. Jacksonville was founded at the Cow Ford in 1822 and named for Andrew Jackson, territorial governor of Florida.

Black Heritage Trail. This collection of sites allows visitors to trace the history of blacks in Jacksonville. The trail includes American Beach, Catherine Street Fire Station, Kingsley Plantation, Masonic Temple, Mt. Zion A.M.E. Church, Bethel Baptist Institutional Church, Edward Waters College, Olustee Battlefield, and Edwin Stantin School. Information is available at the visitors centers in Jacksonville and the beaches.

Museum of Science and History. This excellent regional museum contains a planetarium, aquarium, aviary, and a native plant garden. The exhibits tell the story of the St. Johns River and Jacksonville. A special exhibit displays artifacts from the wreck of the *Maple Leaf* and contains personal items from three regiments of occupying Union soldiers. The museum is located on the riverfront on Museum Circle. Hours are 10 a.m.–5 p.m., Monday through Friday; 10 a.m.–6 p.m. on Saturday and 1 p.m.–6 p.m. on Sunday. Closed on New Year's Day, Christmas, and Thanksgiving. Admission.

Friendship Park is located on the St. Johns River at the Museum of Science and History.

Jacksonville Historical Center. The story of the Jacksonville area is told in exhibits that begin with the Timucuan Indians and the time before European contact. Located on Southbank Riverwalk behind the Museum of Science and History. Open daily 12–5 p.m.

Southbank Riverwalk follows the south banks of the St. Johns River for 1.2 miles in downtown Jacksonville.

Jacksonville parks. Jacksonville is a city of parks and there are over 200. The following parks are keyed to the map on Page 100. Parks are open daily from sunrise to sunset and are free to the public.

A. Arlington Lions Club Park. Boardwalk, nature trails, picnic area, boat ramp and manatee education exhibit. 4322-1 Richard Denby Gatlin Road.

B. Bethesda Park. Handicap accessible boardwalk, nature trail, and fishing pond. 10790 Key Haven Road.

C. Blue Cypress Park. Hiking access to the St. Johns River. 4012 University Boulevard North.

D. Camp Tomahawk. Nature trails and picnic area. 8419 San Ardo Road.

E. Crystal Springs Road Park. Nature trails and picnic area. Crystal Springs Road east of Chaffee Road and south of I-10.

F. Lovelace Park. Nature trails and picnic area. 6401 Barnes Road.

G. Mandarin Park. Nature trails, nature center, observation pier, boardwalk, and picnic area. 14780 Mandarin Road.

H. Lonnie C. Miller, Sr. Regional Park. Nature trails and picnic area. Moncrief Road at Soutel Drive.

I. Ortega Stream Valley Park.

J. Ringhaver Park. Nature trails, picnic area, and children's playscape. 5198 118th Street.

K. Treaty Oak at Jessie Ball Dupont Park. Boardwalk, picnic areas, and information kiosks. 1123 Prudential Drive, between Flagler Street and the Main Street exit from I-95.

L. Westside Regional Park. Nature center, wildlife observation tower, picnic areas, nature trails, and bike trails. 7000 Roosevelt Boulevard.

17. Cummer Museum of Art & Gardens. The Cummer Museum's permanent collection contains works of Western art that span 4,000 years. The Museum also hosts national and regional touring exhibitions. The grounds contain formal English and Italian gardens with a view of the St. Johns River. The gardens were begun in 1903 by Ninah May Holden Cummer, a founder and first chair of the Garden Club of Florida. Located at 829 Riverside Avenue. Open Tuesday and Thursday, 10 a.m.–9 p.m.; Wednesday, Friday, and Saturday, 10 a.m.–5 p.m.; and on Sunday from noon to 5 p.m. Closed on Monday and major holidays. Admission.

18. St. Johns River. The river known to the Timucuans as Welaka was called River May by the French and Rio San Mateo by the Spanish. Sometime in the seventeenth century it became known as Rio San Juan, possibly named for the mission San Juan del Puerto on Fort George Island. The St. Johns River is brackish as far upriver as Palatka and is characterized as marine estuary, providing habitat for fresh water and salt water plants and animals. The River has its source near Melbourne and flows 318 miles to the Atlantic at Mayport. It varies in width from a few hundred yards to three miles, sometimes becoming lake-like.

The St. Johns River was created when the sea retreated during the Pleistocene epoch and land was built up east of the central Florida uplands. The river was a series of lagoons that have remained as lakes and wide stretches of the river. It carries little sediment, has neither river floodplain nor delta, and is bordered along much of its length by steep banks and bluffs. It is a slow, blackwater river with a descent of only one inch per mile and is one of the few major rivers in North America to flow northward. Because the St. Johns has such a low gradient the tide affects the river as far as Lake George and has a tide of three feet as far upriver as Palatka. Lake George and Crescent Lake are flat-bottomed, shallow lakes that were formed from Pamlico-era estuaries of 12,000–100,000 years ago.

Spanish explorers may have sailed the St. Johns River as early as the 1520s but the French lead by Ribault were the first to give it significant attention when they named it River May and established their Protestant colony at Fort Caroline. This fort was within the chiefdom of Saturiwa, a grand and noble leader revered by his people. One of Laudonnière's lieutenants, Ottigny, was sent up the St. Johns River to explore the interior of the new French colony. He may have reached as far as Palatka where he encountered other Timucuan Indians. The French enterprise galvanized the

Gaillardia in bloom on Anastasia Island

Spanish to action, to protect and make good their claim to *la Florida* and led to the founding of Saint Augustine. This first river of North America may well be the least known and appreciated of our great rivers, though it is certainly one of the most exotic and romantic.

19. Tree Hill. The Jacksonville Nature Center is located at Tree Hill, a forty-acre property in the heart of Arlington. The center has a learning laboratory, classroom, meeting room, and gift shop to serve the local education community. Interactive exhibits feature the local wildlife and natural history of the Jacksonville area. Tree Hill has three hiking trails, an organic garden, butterfly garden, and a wildlife-viewing area. Located at 7152 Lone Star Road. Open 8:30 a.m.–5 p.m., Monday through Saturday. Admission.

20. Jacksonville Beach Wildlife Refuge. Located in Jacksonville Beach on the Intracoastal Waterway, accessible by boat.

21. Bartram Memorial Highway. FL-13 was designated the Bartram Memorial Highway by the Florida legislature. The historical marker is located on the south side of Julington Creek.

22. Jennings State Forest is noted for the variety of natural ecosystems contained within its 21,000 acres. Visitors may explore the forests and wetlands by hiking numerous trails and canoeing the streams and creeks. Located north of CR-218 and reached by Nolan Road and Longhorn Road, by Long Branch Road from CR-217, on the north; and Old Jennings Road from CR-21 from the east.

23. Switzerland. New Switzerland, the plantation of Francis Philip Fatio of Bern, was located at the present-day community of Switzerland. William Bartram lodged with Fatio and commented on his garden that contained a greater variety of plants than was commonly found on Florida plantations. His primary cash crop was indigo. Fatio, unlike most of the British Floridians, remained in Florida during the Second Spanish Period and became a leading citizen. His descendants still live in Florida.

24. Diego Plains, Palm Valley, was the site of a plantation owned by Diego Spinoza who built a private stockade called Fort Diego. During the siege of Saint Augustine, General Oglethorpe garrisoned the fort with his Georgia Highlanders.

25. Guana River State Park was once believed to be the site where Ponce de León landed on Easter Sunday, 1592, but new research indicates that it may have been farther south, possibly near Melbourne Beach. Guana comes from the Timucuan word for *River of Palms*. There are 2,400 acres on Guana River and adjoining beaches. Recreational activities include saltwater fishing, bicycling, boating, and hiking. Open 8 a.m.–sunset. Highway A1A Ponte Vedra Beach.

26. Guana River WMA protects marshes, hammocks, and archaeological sites of the Guana and Tolomato rivers. The Guana River Shell Ring dates from 4,000–3,500 years ago. The management area is an extremely productive and popular saltwater fishing area. The wetlands and ponds support wood storks, roseate spoonbills, white and glossy ibis, and all the common water birds. Several roads and trails provide access for naturalists to the interior marshes and pine flatwoods. More nature trails, a wood stork interpretive center, and observation towers are being constructed. A fire management program provides open pine woods for natural beauty and wildlife habitat. Seasonal hunts are held from October 11–December 8, so hikers and naturalists should take precaution during this period. The entrance is from Guana River State Park, Highway A1A, Ponte Vedra Beach.

27. Stokes Landing Conservation Area was established to preserve water quality along the Tolomato River Basin and serve as an outdoor classroom. There are hiking and biking trails, an observation platform, canoe launch, fishing, and primitive camping by special permit. From US-1 heading north of Saint Augustine Airport turn right on Venetian Boulevard, right on Old Dixie Road, then left on Lakeshore Drive.

28. Fort Mose was known to the Spanish as Gracia Real de Santa Teresa de Mosé (pronounced Moh Say). It was founded in 1738 as a settlement for slaves who escaped South Carolina and were given their freedom by the Spanish in Florida. Governor Manuel de Montiano established a fort at the Mose community the same year and garrisoned it with an African militia. Mose was truly an international community with representatives of many West African tribes, mulattos, and Native Americans.

During Oglethorpe's invasion of Florida in 1740, the Darien Highlanders and South Carolina Militia were surprised early one morning and defeated at Mose. Colonel John Palmer of Beaufort was killed during the battle. His death and Oglethorpe's failure to take San Marcos caused an outcry in the South Carolina Assembly and a loss of support for the Georgia governor. When Florida was ceded to the British in 1763 the entire community of Mose moved to Cuba.

29. Anastasia Island Coquina Quarry. Coquina blocks used for constructing Castillo de San Marcos were quarried in the historic coquina beds located near the entrance to Anastasia State Recreation Area. When James Oglethorpe and his Georgia Rangers besieged Saint Augustine in 1740 they set up their artillery on Anastasia and bombarded San Marcos for twenty-eight days, but to little effect because of the strength of the coquina walls. The Cross & Sword Amphitheater is located in another nearby quarry.

30. Anastasia Island State Recreation Area has four miles of beach to please vacationers. Salt Run lagoon is the place to see wading birds and to try your hand at sailboarding. In summer the interdunes are carpeted with brightly colored gaillardia in bloom. A campground is nestled among the live oaks and there is a boardwalk to the beach.

31. Saint Augustine Alligator Farm and Zoological Park is the oldest continuously operated tourist attraction in Florida, beginning in 1890. During the devastating and uncontrolled slaughter that fed the skin market for leather goods, the alligator population in Florida and Georgia plummeted. By World War II half of all alligators remaining in Florida were living at the Saint Augustine Alligator Farm. In addition to being instrumental in preserving the species, research on the habits and physiology of the alligator continue to be an important aspect of the Alligator Farm's mission. All twenty-two species of crocodilians are represented at Saint Augustine Alligator Farm as well as exotic birds and monkeys. Located on A1A on Anastasia Island. Admission.

32. Bayard Point Conservation Area. Seven miles of river frontage, hardwood wetlands, pine flatwoods, and sandhill ridges make Bayard Point a naturalist's delight. The area north of Bayard Point Road is closed to hunting and has several trails for hiking, biking, and horseback riding. Primitive camping is allowed in the section west of CR-209.

33. Picolata was the site of a Timucuan village and the mission of San Diego de Salamototo. The Spanish built Fort Picolata at the present-day town of Picolata and Fort San Francisco de Poppa on the west bank at Bayard Point. In 1740 Oglethorpe and his Georgia Rangers captured both forts on the St. Johns River when England and Spain commenced hostilities during the War of Jenkins' Ear. These two forts guarded the ferry of the overland route from Saint Augustine to Pensacola. In 1765 John and William Bartram attended the Indian Congress at Fort Picolata when the boundary between the Indian and English land was determined. The fort was abandoned in 1769.

William became enamored with tropical Florida and stayed to become an indigo planter. He drew on his inheritance to purchase tools and land. Henry Laurens helped John Bartram purchase six slaves in Charleston. When Laurens visited the young botanist at the Picolata plantation in August of 1766 he had an unhappy report to send to John Bartram. Laurens found William situated on poor land with slaves who were unmanageable (possibly due to William's natural lack of forcefulness) and William had a fever. Laurens took it upon himself to send wine and provisions to Picolata and advised John to gently release his son from the expectations of succeeding at the doomed project.

It is uncertain what William did once he disposed of his plantation at Picolata. From different sources we gather that for a short time he was at Saint Augustine and in the employ of William Gerard De Brahm, surveyor general of Florida. William was shipwrecked off the coast of Florida while enroute to Philadelphia and returned to Saint Augustine for a few months before re-embarking for home.

We must agree with Francis Harper that it is curious and significant that William made no reference to his residence, and failures, at Picolata in the *Travels*. Rather than stay the night, he crossed the river to camp.

By 1823, when Charles Vignoles published his *Observations upon the Floridas*, most of the blockhouse of Picolata had fallen down. Now the site of the old fort has been completely reclaimed by the river.

34. Old Spanish Trail was the main overland route from Saint Augustine to Tallahassee and Pensacola. It then continued on along the Gulf of Mexico to Texas and Mexico. Beyond Tallahassee the trail was mostly wilderness and little traveled because such a trip was easier and safer by water. The section from Saint Augustine to Tallahassee became the Bellamy Road in the early 1800s.

35. Tocoi (also Tocoy) was mentioned as a Christian Indian town in a Spanish paper of 1602.

36. Etonia Creek is well known to Florida Trail hikers. Etonia Ravine is a 40-foot deep canyon that harbors more northern plants such as tuliptree, dogwood, and native azaleas. The Florida panther has been sighted there.

37. Fort Matanzas was built on Rattlesnake Island in 1569 to guard Matanzas Inlet and was originally a simple wooden tower. The present fortress dates from 1740–1742 and is built of coquina. Matanzas means *slaughter* because in 1565, by deceit, Governor Menéndez systematically executed over 300 French Huguenots among the dunes on the east side of Matanzas Inlet. Among the unfortunates was Jean Ribault who had erected the stone monument at La Caroline and founded the unsuccessful French colony of Charlesfort at Port Royal. When France again attempted to establish a North American colony she looked northward to Canada, to put as much distance as possible between Acadia and Spanish Florida.

Fort Matanzas is an excellent place to view wildlife and observe a variety of natural habitats, including dunes, beach, maritime hammock, scrub, and marsh. There is a free ferry from the parking area on A1A.

38. Faver-Dykes State Park has several nature trails, camping, and boat access to Pellicer Creek. The park is seldom crowded and has a beautiful longleaf pine forest. 1000 Faver-Dykes Road, Saint Augustine, FL 32086

39. Pellicer Creek Aquatic Preserve protects the floodplain of Pellicer Creek from US-1 to Matanzas River and is a designated canoe trail.

40. Princess Place Preserve protects 1,435 acres at the confluence of Pellicer Creek and Matanzas River. Located on Old King's Road 1.5 miles after the beginning of the unpaved road. Open 11 a.m.–5 p.m., Friday through Sunday.

41. Marineland is Florida's oldest marine park and continues to feature live aquatic shows. Highway A1A south of Saint Augustine. Open 9 a.m.–5:30 p.m. daily. Admission.

42. Washington Oaks State Gardens is the site of Belle Vista Plantation and Florida's first commercial orange grove. It is now a horticultural garden with plantings of roses, camellias, azaleas, and tropical plants surrounding natural springs. The largest outcropping of coquina rock in the world can be seen along the shore.

Saint Augustine

Saint Augustine was founded in 1565 by Pedro Menéndez de Avilés on the feast day of Saint Augustine. At that time Spain had not been able to establish a long-lasting presence in Florida, which to them meant all of the mainland north of the Gulf of Mexico. When French Huguenots attempted to settle on the St. Johns River in 1562 Spain became alarmed at the danger posed to her treasure ships that sailed off the coast of Florida. Governor Menéndez destroyed the French colony and began a settlement at Saint Augustine. He discovered that ships could sail against the strong Gulf Stream by keeping close to the Florida coast. This made Saint Augustine strategic in the defense of the Spanish shipping lanes.

Saint Augustine grew slowly and was always a military town with most of the inhabitants on the government payroll and most of the food and supplies coming from Cuba. With very little presence other than Saint Augustine the Spanish were always vulnerable to attack from French, English, Indians, and pirates. Sir Francis Drake burned the city on June 6, 1586. Drake commanded the largest fleet yet seen in the west-

Saint Augustine, replica of the Old Government House

ern Atlantic and the Spanish withdrew in the face of overwhelming English superiority. The English looting lasted for seven days.

During the first hundred years there was always a threat from the freebooters and privateers cruising the Caribbean. In 1702 the Spanish and their Indian allies attempted to rout the

English from the area of Santa Elena but were turned back. Governor Moore of South Carolina then attacked Saint Augustine but could not take Castillo de San Marcos. In 1703 Moore attacked the Apalachee Province and destroyed many of the missions. The Chichimecos (Westoes), Uchisees (Creeks), and Chiluques began raiding the Guale Province causing the missions and Christian Indians to retreat southward.

With the creation of Georgia in de facto Spanish territory came a new and greater threat. During the War of Jenkin's Ear, General James Oglethorpe invaded Florida in 1740, building forts on Amelia and Fort George islands and burning Fort Picolata. Later in the year he attacked Saint Augustine and occupied the town but failed to take Castillo de San Marcos.

When the Spanish flag over Castillo de San Marcos was replaced by the British flag in 1763 nearly all of the 3,046 Spanish inhabitants of Saint Augustine emigrated to Cuba and Mexico. The Christian Indians also went to Cuba, thus Florida was virtually uninhabited until the British and Seminoles moved in. At the onset of the Revolution the population of East Florida, the fourteenth colony, numbered only about 1,000 white citizens, 2,000 Seminoles, and a larger number of African slaves. Saint Augustine continued to be the seat of government and the largest city in East Florida. There was little patriot sentiment for a revolution in Florida due to its dependence on support from Parliament. Thus, Saint Augustine and Pensacola became strongholds for loyalist refugees. Many illustrious Southern patriots were imprisoned at Saint Augustine, including Arthur Middleton, Edward Rutledge, and Thomas Heyward of South Carolina who were all signers of the Declaration of Independence.

Refugees from Georgia included William Panton and partner John Leslie, and James Spalding. After the Treaty of Paris, Panton and Leslie won the concession for Indian trade in Spanish East and West Florida and moved to Pensacola in 1785. James Spalding returned to Georgia and became a leading citizen of Glynn County. Charles McLatchy operated the Spalding stores on the St. Johns River and at Alachua. He built his own store at St. Marks. Most Florida Tories moved to the Bahamas, greatly increasing its population and importance in the Caribbean. Others went to England or Jamaica. Some of the native Georgians quietly moved to the north side of the St. Marys River or moved farther into the western lands. Thomas Brown emigrated first to the Bahamas for nearly twenty years and then spent his last years as a wealthy sugar planter on Saint Vincent.

Sites in Saint Augustine

1. Fountain of Youth Archaeological Park is located on the site of the Indian Village, Seloy, and was the site of Saint Augustine during its first year. This park commemorates the landing of Ponce de León on Easter in 1513 and the naming of Florida. Features include a planetarium, natural spring, and Christian Indian burial ground. Open 9 a.m.–5 p.m. daily. Admission.

2. Mission de Nombre de Dios was the first mission established in Florida by the Spanish and the last to be abandoned when Catholic Indians were withdrawn from the abandoned missions at the beginning of the eighteenth century. The monumental cross north of Castillo San Marcos commemorates the first mass celebrated in Saint Augustine when Don Pedro Menéndez de Avilés landed in 1565.

3. Saint Augustine Visitor's Center. Located at the corner of Castillo Drive and San Marco Boulevard.

4. Castillo de San Marcos was begun in 1672 and finished in 1695. It was the last of several structures to occupy the site and certainly the most imposing. The walls are coquina, a natural stone of compacted shell that was mined at the quarries on Anastasia Island. The need for such a fortress was due to extensive privateering along the coast of Florida by England, France, and Holland during the seventeenth century. The new British colonies to the north gave impetus to the construction and, indeed, no invaders ever took the fort, although Saint Augustine was occupied several times. Runaway slaves from South Carolina were offered freedom in Saint Augustine if they converted to Catholicism and remained to work on the fortress. San Marcos is a National Monument of the National Park Service. Located in downtown Saint Augustine. Open 8:45 a.m.–4:45 p.m. Admission.

Castillo de San Marcos, Saint Augustine

5. Old City Gates. The gate through the old city wall is located at the intersection of San Marco Avenue with Orange and St. George streets. The Cubo Defense Line ran westward from Castillo de San Marcos to the San Sebastian River and was completed in 1721 during the office of Governor Antonio de Benavides. The ramparts were built of palmetto walls filled with sand. The Cubo Line was soon rebuilt with masonry and was the wall in which the surviving gates were built. The Rosario Line protected Saint Augustine on the west and south. Current archaeological research is determining the location of the original walls that surrounded and protected the city.

6. Spanish Quarter Museum is a living history museum that includes demonstrations of colonial skills and scenes from daily life. Located on Saint George Street in the historic district. Open 9 a.m.–5 p.m. daily. Admission.

7. Government House is built on the foundation of the original government house where all the colony's official business was transacted. The building now houses the Museum of Historic Saint Augustine. Located on 48 King Street at Plaza de la Constitution. Open 10 a.m.–4 p.m., daily. Admission.

8. Cathedral Basilica of Saint Augustine. The Cathedral was built in 1797 during the Sec-

Legend

1. Fountain of Youth Archaeological Park
2. Mission de Nombre de Dios
3. Saint Augustine Visitor's Center
4. Castillo de San Marcos
5. Old City Gates
6. Spanish Quarter Museum
7. Government House
8. Cathedral Basilica of Saint Augustine
9. Plaza de la Constitution
10. Oldest House
11. Leitner Museum
12. Museum of Weapons and Early American History

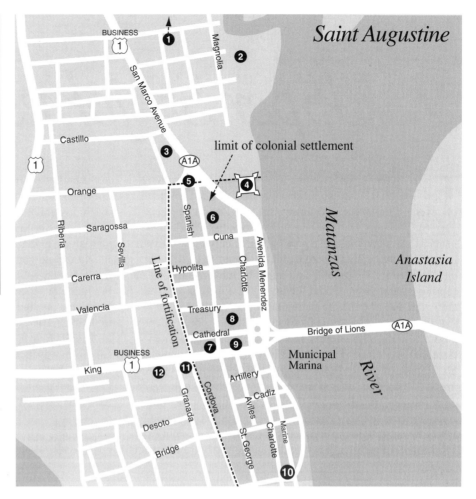

ond Spanish Period. Located on Cathedral Street facing Plaza de la Constitution.

9. Plaza de la Constitution marks the center of the original plan for Saint Augustine. The Spanish government issued a decree in the sixteenth century that all towns be laid out around a central square. The plaza was the center of the social life of colonial Saint Augustine and a popular recreation area. The Plaza is the site of contains numerous historical markers.

10. Oldest House. The Oldest House occupies the site of an earlier and simpler thatched structure that may have been built as early as 1600. The tabby floor and coquina walls of the first floor of the present structure date from 1702, the year Saint Augustine was burned by South Carolina troops. Since then the home has been occupied continuously and altered by succeeding inhabitants through the several national periods. The surrounding grounds have a garden of native plants, a British garden, the Albert Manucy Hall Museum, the Museum of Florida's Army, a research library, and a museum store. Located at 14 Saint Francis Street. Open 9 a.m.–5 p.m. daily. Admission.

11. Leitner Museum. The Leitner Museum is housed in the former Alcazar Hotel. The collection contains examples of American, European, and Oriental art; antiques, crystal, and exhibits of natural history. Located at the corner of King and Granada streets. Open 9 a.m.–5 p.m. daily. Admission.

12. Museum of Weapons and Early American History. This collection contains items dating from 1500 and includes artifacts of Native American and colonial settlement in addition to the historical weapons. Located at 81C King Street. Open 8:30 a.m.–5 p.m. daily. Admission.

Itinerary

Miles	Directions
	Begin in downtown Folkston and travel south on US-17
4.3	Cross St. Marys River
9.4	Left on A1A in Yulee
11.8	Left on Centre Street to Historic Downtown Fernandina
0.7	Bartram Trail Marker at the end of Centre Street at the marina
4.7	Return by A1A and turn left on Amelia Island Parkway
15.0	Entrance to Little Talbot Island State Park
3.6	Entrance to Huguenot Memorial Park (A1A becomes Hecksher Drive)
1.0	Entrance to Fort George Island
0.6	Entrance to Mayport Ferry (A1A continues on the south side of the St. Johns River in Mayport)
14.7	Left on US-1/17
5.9	Cross the St. Johns River at Main Street Bridge
.4	Right on FL-13, Museum Circle
.1	Left on San Marcos Boulevard
1.5	Right on Hendricks Avenue, FL-13
7.9	FL-13 becomes San Jose Boulevard
5.3	Cross Julington Creek
4.4	Enter Switzerland
18.1	Picolata
6.5	Tocoi Point
	Return to Jacksonville by US-17 on the west side of the St. Johns River

Upper St. Johns River

It was on the upper St. Johns River at the entrance to Stagger Mud Lake that the most celebrated, and controversial, event of the *Travels* occurred—the alligator battle (see page 6). The story was disbelieved by a number of naturalists, many of whom had not seen an alligator or only those alligators living near civilization where they had learned to be timid of men with guns. The rational and scientific mind had trouble accepting Bartram's emotional literary style, although poets certainly did not. Major John Eatton LeConte remarked in 1830 that Bartram was "but little of a naturalist, and very frequently incorrect in his observations. Bartram is much laughed at in Georgia." After having traveled in Florida, LeConte renounced his former opinion and verified Bartram's credibility. He wrote in 1854, "Mr. Bartram was a man of unimpeached integrity and veracity, of primeval simplicity of manners and honesty unsuited to these times, when such virtues are not appreciated." James Spalding said the account of the alligators was not exaggerated and Francis Harper, working in the Okefenokee Swamp in the early part of the twentieth century, heard stories from the old-timers that further verified Bartram's story.

An insight to the personality of William Bartram can be found in the account of Henry Wansey's visit to the Bartram Garden on June 9, 1794. He wrote, "One of my companions joking the old gentleman about the alligators that he had formerly fought with, he became so reserved, that we could get but little conversation from him."[1] We can well imagine William's opinion of the armchair travelers, ensconced safely in their libraries, who doubted his veracity.

The St. Johns River narrows dramatically south of Palatka. Charlotia was located on the east bank of the river about where the Florida Power & Light Putnam Plant now stands between East Palatka and San Mateo. There is a roadside park on the west side of US-17 and a historical marker commemorating

1. *Henry Wansey and his American Journal 1794*, edited by David J. Jeremy; American Philosophical Society, 1970, P. 112.

Upper St. Johns River

William Bartram's visit to Charlotia. Bartram learned that the goods from the store and his own property were stowed at Murphy Island. After inspecting his chest Bartram proceeded to Spalding's Lower Store at Stokes Landing, south of Palatka. This was to be his residence and office for much of his time in Florida.

William Bartram's account of his trip on the St. Johns River is a composite of two separate excursions, one at the end of May and the other at the end of August 1774. The first mentioned landmark after leaving the Lower Store was Mount Hope at Beecher Point on the north end of Little Lake George. In the evening the company of travelers stopped at Mount Royal near Fort Gates Ferry and Fruitland Cove. Archaeological exploration of Mount Royal unearthed a copper medallion similar to one found in Oklahoma, which demonstrates the extent of Native American trade. Bartram told of three islands in Lake George, but today there are only two. The largest, Drayton Island, was where the travelers found safe harbor.

The next day Bartram crossed Lake George and camped at Zinder Point, on the east side of the mouth of the St. Johns River as it enters Lake George. He explored the woods and savannahs nearby and when he returned he found his companions fishing for *trout* (largemouth bass). Bartram arrived at Spalding's Upper Store the next day, located in the present-day town of Astor. The store at Volusia later became a part of the Panton & Leslie trading empire and was moved to the east side of the river. The disturbance that delayed Bartram from traveling to Florida in 1774 was the looting of the Upper Store by Seminoles. The emissaries to the towns at Alachua and the Suwannee River were empowered to discuss the payment of damages and reopening of trade in the aftermath of this event.

Ascending the river from the Upper Store, Bartram's Indian companion deserted him at the end of the first day. Bartram gives the first description of the royal palm from this section of the St. Johns River, but several subsequent hard freezes have eliminated them this far north. Bartram camped at Idlewilde Point and there battled the alligators. He was the first naturalist to describe the mating habits of the American alligator. His description of the anhinga, also called snake bird or water turkey, are among the first and most complete.

His next camp was at Mosquito Grove, a half-mile below the mouth of Horseshoe Mud Lake in Alexander Springs Wilderness area. There he spent a sleepless night watching for alligators, swatting mosquitoes, and being awakened by the screeches of owls. This was one of the few times that Bartram admitted to fatigue and misery. Everyone who aspires to emulate William Bartram must spend a night on the ground in Florida, in the open, near a river, in the middle of summer. It is misery, indeed!

Storm on the St. Johns River at Riverdale, St. Johns County

The next evening Bartram chose Saint Francis Bluff for his camp and found the next morning that he was at a Yamassee burying ground. The Yamassee warriors had been slain in battle with Creeks. After a restful night he explored the banks of the river, first stopping about a half mile south of the FL-44 bridge.

Bartram stopped at a bluff near Hontoon Landing despite warnings in the air of an approaching storm. Before he could cross Lake Beresford the storm arrived with violent force, whipping trees and snapping branches. Unable to stay within the confines of the river, Bartram had little choice but to enter the lake and tie up in the open near its banks. Thunderstorms are common in Florida in summer but this one was obviously more powerful than normal. When Bartram arrived at Lord Beresford's plantation, near Beresford Station in DeLand, his papers and collections were soaked and the inhabitants were greatly surprised that he had survived the storm unhurt. Bartram spent a few days at the plantation and took a side-trip to Blue Springs, which he had visited in 1765 with his father. Bartram made a digression in his narrative to tell of his visiting New Smyrna while employed as an assistant to William Gerard De Brahm, surveyor general for Florida.

On his return from the first upriver trip in May William Bartram visited Salt Springs (his Six-Mile Springs). In his report to Dr. Fothergill, Bartram wrote of another trip upriver in August. On his return in late August or early September he visited Silver Glen Springs (his Johnson's Springs).

The state of Florida has been aggressive in acquiring lands for conservation and public recreation. The counties along the St. Johns and Oklawaha rivers contain numerous county parks and conservation areas in addition to the state and national holdings. This is a naturalist's paradise any time of the year.

Sites

1. Palatka–Navair Rail to Trail. This long trail will follow the old railroad bed from Palatka to Navair, just southeast of Lake City in Columbia County.

2. Rice Creek Natural Area is located on eighteenth-century rice fields along Rice Creek. The hiking trail follows the old dikes through cypress and gum swamps. Even in early spring it can be uncomfortable on a warm, humid day but hikers are rewarded with a beautiful display of swamp iris that thrive there. Rice Creek Natural Area is located about five miles west of Palatka on FL-100 on Georgia Pacific Property. A spur trail connects to the Florida National Scenic Trail.

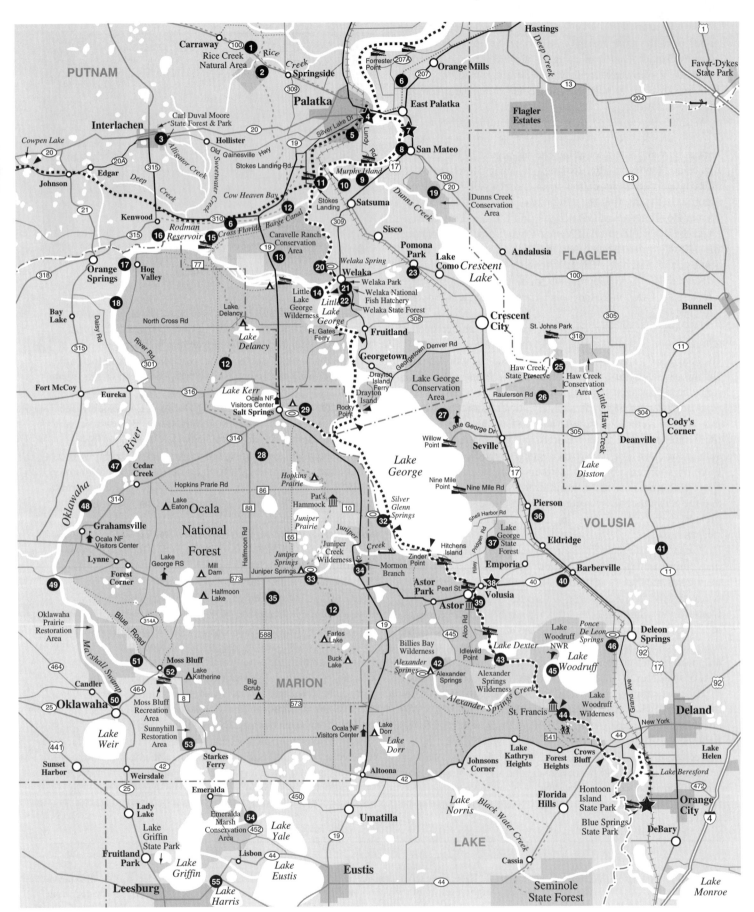

Upper St. Johns River

3. Carl Duval Moore State Forest & Park is comprised of two separate parcels on each side of FL-20 just east of Interlachen. The forest has several picnic areas and hiking trails running through pine upland and bay swamps. The southern parcel adjoins Alligator Creek and is accessible from FL-20 by way of Twin Lakes Road.

4. Palatka. The Indian Village that William Bartram noted as he ascended the St. Johns River stood on the bluff at Palatka. The original name was either Pilaklikaha or Pilotaikita, meaning *crossing over*. It later became Pilatka Vaca, a mixture of Indian and Spanish words that means *cow's crossing*. This crossing of the river was where the Alachua Ferry was later established on the road from Saint Augustine to Alachua. This bluff was included in a Spanish land grant made in the seventeenth century to Don Tomas Menéndez Marquéz, a wealthy citizen of Saint Augustine.

The modern town of Palatka began in 1820 when James Marver and two friends named Hines and Woodruff established a trading post on the site of the former Indian village. Several trails crossed the St. Johns River at that point and gave the enterprise easy access to trade. A U.S. military post was established at Palatka during the Second Seminole War. Palatka became the gateway to the upper St. Johns River when steamboats began service in 1829.

The Putnam County economic base is a mix of steel and concrete manufacturing, forest products, vegetable farming, cut flowers and ferns, and sport fishing. Within an easy drive are the Ocala National Forest, several wildlife refuges, and numerous Florida conservation areas. Palatka is a bit of the real Florida where nature and history lovers can have a wonderful time. Because of its location Palatka should be headquarters for the Bartram traveler just as it was for William Bartram himself.

To reach the riverfront park, turn south onto either Memorial Parkway or Second Avenue from US-17.

Putnam Historic Museum. 100 Madison Street in Palatka. Open 2 a.m.–5 p.m., Tuesday, Thursday, and Sunday.

Florida Sandhill Cranes

Ravine Gardens State Park. The ravines were created by spring water flowing from the high river bluff. There are many native plants in the Park but most of the gardens were planted by the WPA during the 1930s and contain a variety of subtropical landscape plants. Nature trails wind around the rim of the ravines and the spring-fed stream below. The most popular time to see Ravine Gardens is during the Palatka Azalea Festival at the end of March. The Bartram Trail historic marker is at the entrance to the gardens at 1600 Twigg Street. Open 8 a.m.–sunset, the loop road at the rim is open to cars only from 9 a.m.–4 p.m. Admission.

5. St. Johns Loop Trail will begin in Palatka and connect the downtown business district with the outlying natural areas along the St. Johns River. Numerous local agencies have been involved in the planning and creation of the trail, which will eventually include an environmental education center. The south entrance is open at Buckman Lock with access to the Florida Trail

6. Palatka–Saint Augustine Rail to Trail. This rail to trail conversion follows the general route of the historic Spanish trail from Saint Augustine to Palatka.

7. Charlotia (Rollestown) was established by Denys Rolle in 1764 as a utopian community. He sought to reform and rehabilitate the prostitutes and fallen women of London by sending them to Florida, far from temptation and close to good hard work. Later arrivals included beggars, vagrants, and debtors. They were not farmers, nor were they accustomed to demanding physical labor and many soon drifted to Georgia, South Carolina, and Saint Augustine, where we assume some attempted to reclaim their former careers. The lack of law

Legend

1. Palatka–Navair Rail to Trail
2. Rice Creek Natural Area
3. Carl Duval Moore State Forest & Park
4. Palatka
   Putnam Historic Museum
   Ravine Gardens State Park
5. St. Johns Loop Trail
6. Palatka–Saint Augustine Rail to Trail
7. Charlotia (Rollestown)
8. San Mateo
9. Murphy Island
10. Buffalo Bluff
11. Spalding's Lower Store
12. Florida National Scenic Trail
13. Caravelle Ranch Conservation Area
14. Little Lake George Wilderness
15. Rodman Campground
    Rodman Spillway
16. Kenwood Campground
17. Orange Springs Recreation Area
18. Cross Florida Greenway
19. Dunns Creek Conservation Area
20. Welaka
21. Beecher Springs Trail
22. Mud Spring Trail, Welaka State Forest
23. Pomona Park
24. Crescent City
25. Haw Creek Preserve
26. Haw Creek Conservation Area
27. Lake George Conservation Area
28. Ocala National Forest
29. Salt Springs
30. Hopkins Prairie
31. Pat's Hammock
32. Silver Glen Springs
33. Juniper Springs
34. Mormon Branch
35. Big Scrub
36. Lake George County Conservation Area
37. Lake George State Forest
38. Volusia
39. Spalding's Upper Store
40. Pioneer Settlement for the Creative Arts
41. Candace R. Strawn-Lake Dias County Park
42. Alexander Springs Wilderness Area
43. The Celebrated Alligator Battle
44. Saint Francis
45. Lake Woodruff WMA
46. DeLeon Springs
47. Gore's Landing River Trailhead
48. Oklawaha River
49. Marion County Parks & Recreation Headquarters
50. Marshall Swamp Trailhead
51. Oklawaha Prairie Restoration Area
52. Moss Bluff Recreation Area
53. Sunny Hill Restoration Area
54. Emeralda Marsh Conservation Area
55. Lake Harris Conservation Area

enforcement gave Rolle no way to retrieve those who ran from their indenture. In their defense the people who colonized Rollestown were not allowed land of their own, but worked in the common fields and for the common good. There was also fever that took its toll on the health of the settlement.

Denys Rolle was a member of Parliament from a noble family of Devonshire. John Bartram met Rolle in Philadelphia in 1761 and prevailed upon him to deliver a letter to Thomas Lamboll in Charleston.

When William Bartram visited Rollestown there was no one left but the blacksmith and his wife. In 1823 Charles Vignoles reported that no buildings stood and only foundation pits and an avenue of trees indicated that a town had existed. The land is now the Florida Power & Light Putnam Plant located on the east side of US-17. A Bartram Trail historical marker is on the west side of the highway at the roadside park.

8. San Mateo (marker). Fort San Mateo was located at this site on the St. Johns River. It was the refuge for the Spanish when Sir Francis Drake attacked and burned Saint Augustine in 1583.

9. Murphy Island. William Bartram's trunk was stored on Murphy Island during the Indian raid on Spalding's Upper Store, the keeper of the Lower Store having been warned of the attack. Bartram had sent the trunk from Savannah ahead of his own departure.

10. Buffalo Bluff was mentioned by Bartram in the *Travels* and later became an American settlement with a path to Saint Augustine.

11. Spalding's Lower Store, Stokes Landing, was one of the stores of Spalding & Kelsall of Frederica, Georgia, and was managed by Charles McLatchy. The Lower Store was William Bartram's headquarters and where he prepared and shipped many of his collections to London. While Bartram was at the Lower Store the Long Warrior and his entourage threw a *frolick* and exhibited much drunkenness and licentiousness. Prior to decamping the young warriors prevailed upon Bartram to kill a rattlesnake and then proclaimed Puc-Puggy a true and brave friend of the Seminole. Upon Spalding's death his business holdings were bought by William Panton of Pensacola and became part of Panton, Leslie & Co.

A season's work for a deer hunter was forty pounds of skins. At the Spalding stores in Florida prices in deerskins were;

   1 lb. ... 40 musket balls or 5 strings of beads
   5 lbs. ... a gingham shirt
   18 lbs. ... a gun
   60 lbs. ... a saddle

Tar Flower, Befaria racemosa

12. The Florida National Scenic Trail. The St. Johns Loop Trail will begin in Palatka and connect the downtown business district with the outlying natural areas along the St. Johns River, including the Cross Florida Greenway and Florida National Scenic Trail. The south entrance is open at Buckman lock with access to the Florida Trail. Hikers on the Florida Trail must cross the lock between the hours of 8 a.m. and 5 p.m. daily when the lock master is on duty to open the gate.

13. Caravelle Ranch Conservation Area was established as part of the restoration of the Oklawaha and St. Johns River, and for protection of wildlife and archaeological sites. Recreational opportunities include hiking, horseback riding, bird-watching, hunting, boating, and fishing. Some activities are restricted during seasonal hunts. The entrance is on US-19 between the Cross Florida Greenway and Oklawaha River.

14. Little Lake George Wilderness is located on Little Lake George and the Oklawaha River. It contains 2,500 acres of wetlands.

15. Rodman Campground provides access to Rodman Reservoir and the Florida National Scenic Trail. Campground, boat ramp, restrooms, picnic area, fishing, and bird watching.

Rodman Spillway. Recreational access on the Oklawaha River, with a boat ramp, picnic area, restrooms, fishing, bird watching, and access to the Florida National Scenic Trail provided.

16. Kenwood Campground. Recreational access to Rodman Reservoir. Camping, picnic area, boat ramp.

17. Orange Springs Recreation Area. Recreational access to Oklawaha Lake. Boat ramp, fishing, restrooms, picnic area, and bird watching. Highway 315 northeast of Orange Springs.

18. Cross Florida Greenway. The Cross Florida Barge Canal is an idea that had been considered since the early nineteenth century, but construction on an actual canal to connect the Atlantic shipping lanes with the Gulf of Mexico was not begun until 1930. It has been stopped and started several times. Appropriations were halted in the early 1970s and the canal was officially cancelled in 1986. The land that had been purchased is being turned into the Cross Florida Greenway. It contains 70,000 acres of land and extends 110 miles along a corridor still rich in native flora and fauna. Numerous equestrian, bicycle, and hiking trails are planned.

The **Rodman Reservoir** was constructed as part of the Cross Florida Barge Canal project and is maintained by the Army Corps of Engineers as a recreation area. There is a strong movement to remove the Rodman Dam, return the Oklawaha River as a free-flowing stream, and let the river bottom renew itself. There are few large tributaries to the St. Johns River; the Oklawaha is the most significant and the withdrawal of its nutrients has had an effect on the water quality of the Lower St. Johns. Engineered lakes do not act like natural lakes, such as Lake George and Woodruff. Man-made lakes have continual problems with excess vegetation and oxygen levels. But Rodman Reservoir is popular with local boaters and fishermen and supports a wide variety of wildlife that might be discouraged by a change to a wetland. Rodman Dam is south of Palatka on US-19, turn right on Rodman Road after crossing the Cross Florida Greenway.

19. Dunns Creek Conservation Area. The floodplain of Dunns Creek was purchased for the CARL program (Conservation and Recreation Lands). Recreational activities include canoeing, hunting, wildlife viewing, horseback riding, bicycling, and hiking on the old Tram Road. Enter at Tram Road, three miles from US-17 on FL-100, south of San Mateo.

20. Welaka is an Indian name originally spelled Ylacco, meaning *river* or possibly *chain of lakes*. Welaka was once called Mount Tucker after Lord Tucker who had a land grant there during the British period. **Welaka National Fish Hatchery** raises game fish for the coastal freshwater rivers of Alabama, Georgia, and Florida. There is an aquarium stocked with native fish, amphibians, and reptiles. An observation tower and a nature trail allow visitors to observe waterfowl. The aquarium is open 7 a.m.–4 p.m. everyday, and the hatchery is open 7 a.m.–4 p.m. Monday through Friday.

21. Beecher Springs Trail, University of Florida Research & Education Center, west of CR-309 between Welaka and Fruitland.

22. Mud Spring Trail is a new trail, one of many recently constructed nature trails in Putnam County, and lies within **Welaka State Forest**. There is a 1.7-mile nature trail to Mud Spring and another trail for biking. Located on CR-309 south of Welaka.

23. Pomona Park is named for Pomona, the Roman goddess of fruits and vegetables.

24. Crescent City is the center of a nursery industry that grows over eighty percent of the world's ferns for the nursery trade.

25. Haw Creek Preserve provides a protective buffer for the Crescent Lake floodplain.

26. Haw Creek Conservation Area provides opportunities for boating, canoeing, fishing, hiking, and camping. The Flagler County Tract is reached by taking Flagler 305 to 318 then 2007 to the entrance. The Volusia County Tract is reached by taking Raulerson Road east from US-17.

27. Lake George Conservation Area. Lake George supports crab, shrimp, and other marine life even though it is beyond the reach of tidal influence. The numerous springs issuing from the limestone strata of the Ocala Ridge wash mineral salts into Lake George. Though not nearly as saline as seawater, it is salty enough to support salt tolerant species. The conservation area contains many hiking trails that wander through pine upland and hardwood wetlands. Lake George Conservation Area provides an extensive wildlife corridor for many species of animals including black bear, bald eagles, gopher tortoise, bobcats, osprey, and otter. Access is from US-17 on Lake George Drive, Georgetown-Denver Road and Nine Mile Road.

28. Ocala National Forest is the oldest national forest east of the Mississippi River, established in 1908. The forest occupies a high sand ridge called the Ocala Ridge and encompasses a biological ecosystem long known to locals as the Big Scrub. Ecological environments that one may observe are desert-like scrub, pine flatwoods, longleaf pine-turkey oak, hardwood hammock, springs, and riverine swamp. The central part of Ocala National Forest is an extensive Pleistocene dune field created by the coming and going of ocean beaches. During glacial periods the climate was much drier and dunes formed along the estuary that was to become the St. Johns River. From there they migrated westward and southwestward. White sand indicates the remains of windblown dunes and beige sands occur in areas deposited by sea water.

Hopkins Prairie, Ocala National Forest

An excellent view of this relic dune system is best seen on FL-19 between Juniper Creek and Salt Springs, especially at the intersection of Hopkins Prairie Road. As you leave FL-19 and climb the hill on Hopkins Prairie Road take a moment to turn around and look across Lake George, it is evident just how high the central part of the Ocala National Forest is relative to the land east of Lake George. Underlying the Ocala Ridge is Ocala Limestone, the oldest exposed rock in Florida and almost a mile thick in places. At each side of the Ocala Ridge, where the limestone is nearer the surface, numerous springs issue into the St. Johns and Oklawaha rivers. The water in these springs and the spring runs remains at a constant temperature year-round, between 72 and 74 degrees Fahrenheit.

Ocala National Forest contains large areas of scrub, economically marginal land with stunted vegetation growing on deep sand hills. There are occasional islands of longleaf pine. Sand pine is adapted to this wet desert environment. It often has a curved trunk and does not grow very large, making it unsuitable for lumber. In the 1930s sand pine became useful as pulpwood for manufacturing paper and today the forest service has large sections devoted to pine plantation.

Ocala National Forest is a beautiful and mysterious place. William Bartram was the first to describe the unique environment of the scrub and undoubtedly spent many hours exploring the wilderness that is now Ocala National Forest.

29. Salt Springs was a favored spot for William Bartram. During his 1765 visit with his father the younger Bartram discovered yellow anise, *Illicium parviflorum*, at Salt Springs. Although the spring has been developed and is surrounded by a walkway, it is still a pleasant spot. The four-mile spring run is an easy and beautiful canoe trip. A mile south of the recreation area the Salt Springs Trail meanders through hardwood hammock to an observation deck overlooking Salt Springs Run. Another trail connects to the Florida National Scenic Trail. One of the Ocala National Forest visitor centers is located on FL-19 in the community of Salt Springs.

30. Hopkins Prairie is an excellent place to observe migratory birds in winter and watch sunrises and sunsets anytime of the year. The campground has toilets but no other amenities. The Florida National Scenic Trail passes through the edge of the campground.

31. Pat's Hammock was once a farm and was visited by Marjorie Rawlings as she gathered stories from the local people. Remnants of the homestead are still visible.

32. Silver Glen Springs is a popular recreation area that is often crowded on weekends. On his trip downstream from the Upper Store, Bartram camped near the mouth of Silver Glen Springs on his second day out. During the night he awoke to find that a wolf had skillfully stolen his cooked fish, which hung over his head. Bartram wondered if it would not have been of more benefit to the wolf to have taken him for food rather than

> *... espying the fish over my head, with the greatest of caution and silence rear up and take them off the snags one by one, then make off with them, and that so cunningly as not to waken me until he had fairly accomplished his purpose?* [1]

1. William Bartram, *Travels*, 157.

Hontoon Island State Park

33. Juniper Springs is probably the most popular recreation area of the Ocala National Forest. Although there are usually crowds of people at the spring boil the spring run trail is not so crowded and the canoe trail weaves through an extraordinarily beautiful section of the Juniper Springs Wilderness Area. The Florida Trail also passes through the recreation area. Juniper Springs Recreation Area was developed in the 1930s by the Civilian Conservation Corps for swimming, camping, hiking, and picnicking. The visitor center sells locally made jams and jelly and has information on local wildlife.

34. Mormon Branch. At a point where the sandy forest service road crosses Mormon Branch there is a grove of Atlantic white cedars, one of the southernmost stands of this majestic tree. The yellow anise, Illicium parviflorum, grows wild among the cedars. The swamp of Mormon Branch contains several other rare species that have drawn the attention of botanists—flaccid quillwort and large-flowered grass-of-Parnassus.

35. Big Scrub, FL-40 west of Juniper Springs, represents the type of humid desert that Bartram passed through on his travels from Spalding's Store to Alachua. It was in a similar area west of Deep Creek, between Rodman Reservoir and Interlachen, that William Bartram discovered the scrub jay and described the gopher tortoise. The scrub of Ocala National Forest is the largest of its kind, extending thirty-five miles from north to south and fifteen miles wide. These well drained, deep sandy soils retain little moisture for plants to utilize. Vegetation is sparse, stunted, and adapted to dry conditions. The soil is poor due to the paucity of humus and loss of minerals to leaching.

The plants of the Big Scrub tend to be evergreen shrubs and deep-rooted trees and there is little herbaceous ground cover. Seasonal fires typical of flatwoods and savannahs are rare in the scrub due to lack of fuel buildup on the ground. When fire occurs it is much more intense and destructive because it will become a crown fire in the tops of the sand pine. The shrubs, however, will sprout back from roots and the seeds of sand pine are released to generate a new stand of trees. Typical plants of the Big Scrub are sand pine, myrtle oak, Chapman oak, sand live oak, Florida rosemary, scrub palmetto, turkey oak, bear grass, and devilwood. Animals that call the scrub home are gopher tortoise, scrub jay, scrub lizard, sand skink, and indigo snake.

36. Lake George County Conservation Area, located east of Lake George. Call (904) 736–5927, ext. 2719 for information and permission to explore the conservation area.

37. Lake George State Forest has hiking and horse trails, and seasonal hunts. Access from FL-40 or Riley Pridgen Road.

38. Volusia. Hernando Fontaneda was a captive of the Timucuans about 1545 and he placed the town of Maiaca at the present site of Volusia. In 1657 mission San Salvador de Mayaca was built on the shell mounds near Volusia. In 1680 Fort Antonio de Anacape was built at Maiaca as part of the series of forts erected in response to English and French designs on Florida. The Yamassees replaced the Maiacans on the Upper St. Johns by force. In 1697 the Yamassees themselves were driven away and many returned to South Carolina. The christianized Maiacans were either absorbed or exterminated by tribes invading from the north. In 1722 a faction of Yuchis, as English allies, conquered the Maiaca area. The name *Volusia* may be derived from the Yuchi language.

When steamboats began service on the St. Johns River in 1831 the timber shipments grew to such an extent that the U.S. government sent the schooners Sylph and Spark to protect the live oak forests in Mosquito County (now Volusia, Orange, and counties southward), timber that was needed for shipbuilding.

The American town of Volusia was laid out in 1834. The history of Volusia from 1558 is told in the Volusia Museum through historic land documents and artifacts from the Native American and Spanish inhabitants of the area.

39. Spalding's Upper Store was located at Astor on the west side of the St. Johns River. James and Roger Kelsall began building trading stores in East Florida in 1763 when it became a British colony and were joined in business by James Spalding of Frederica, Georgia. The manager in Florida was Charles McLatchy, who became a friend of William Bartram. The business was taken over by one of Spalding's later business partners, William Panton, and became part of the Panton, Leslie & Co. trading empire of Pensacola.

A historical marker located under a large live oak on the east side of the river commemorates the settlement of Volusia County. Several publications and De Brahm's survey place the store on the west side of the river immediately south of Astor, but early U.S. survey maps clearly show it on the east side. The store may possibly have been moved by Panton, Leslie & Co. when they acquired the business.

40. Pioneer Settlement for the Creative Arts. Rural life in Volusia County is depicted in this collection of historic buildings, shops, and turpentine still from the turn of the century. During special occasions local artisans demonstrate the crafts that were essential to the survival and growth of rural communities. The farm has a collection of animals that were important to the early settlers. Travel west on FL-40 in Barberville, left on Volusia 3, then an immediate right. Open 9 a.m.–3 p.m., Monday through Friday and 9 a.m.–1 p.m. on Saturday, closed on Sunday. Admission.

41. Candace R. Strawn-Lake Dias County Park. Boat ramp on Lake Dias, camping, picnicking, playground, and pavilion. Located on FL-11.

42. Alexander Springs Wilderness Area. Alexander Springs is one of the premier natural springs in the U.S. and the largest on government property, producing seventy-five million gallons per day. Alexander Springs issues from a basin sprinkled with springs and lakes. Alexander Springs, like other inaccessible areas in this region of part water and part earth, was never heavily developed or altered by humans so that many native and disjunct plants may be found there. Bartram's crying bird, the limpkin, is found in the wilderness area as is the coontie, a cycad that is a primitive bridge between ferns and palms.

Although the spring boil area is developed for swimming, picnicking, and camping, the spring run remains a pristine and exotic landscape much as it appeared during Bartram's time. The spring run is sixteen miles to the St. Johns River and is a very popular and scenic canoe trip.

Alexander Springs Wilderness Trail is twelve miles, beginning at River Forest Campground and ending at FL-445. It is unmarked through the wilderness area.

43. The Celebrated Alligator Battle. The most memorable, and controversial, event of the Travels was Bartram's alligator battle (see page 6). The battle took place at the mouth of Stagger Mud Lake.

44. Saint Francis was once a thriving shipping town but railroads took the river traffic and brought about the demise of the town. William Bartram made a camp just south of Saint Francis on the ridge between the St. Johns River and Saint Francis Dead River. When he awoke the next morning he found to his surprise that he had slept in the burial ground of slain Yamassee warriors. Ten miles of trails begin at River Forest Group Camp, just off Highway 42. The trails cross a variety of habitats—river swamp, oak hammock, pine flatwoods, scrub, and a pristine spring.

45. Lake Woodruff WMA encompasses 19,000 acres of freshwater marsh, swamp, and upland hammock, including two nature trails for hikers. Sandhill cranes, limpkins, bald eagles, egrets, herons, ibis, manatees, and many species of ducks may be seen in winter and moorhen and rails nest in summer. Vultures roost on Tick Island in October. William Bartram was the first to describe the limpkin, which is uncommon today and restricted to freshwater marsh and swamps where their favorite food, apple snails, are found. Lake Woodruff WMA Headquarters, 4490 Grand Avenue, DeLeon Springs. The public area is one mile west of the headquarters on Mud Lake Road.

Itinerary

Miles	Directions
	Begin US-17 in East Palatka and travel south
2.2	Bartram Trail historical marker, roadside park and site of Rollestown
8.5	Right on FL-309 in Satsuma
6.8	Mud Spring Trail entrance, Welaka State Forest
2.0	Beecher Run Nature Trail
4.8	Right, then left in Georgetown *Drayton Island Ferry is immediately on the right*
2.4	Left on Georgetown-Denver Road
6.3	Keep straight ahead at Junction Road after crossing the railroad tracks *becomes Denver Road after a sharp right turn*
1.9	Right on Old US-17
2.3	Right on US-17
21.9	Right on Rhetta Street in DeLeon Springs
0.1	Left on Grand Avenue
0.7	Intersection with Mud Lake Road *1.1 miles to Lake Woodruff NWR*
6.1	Cross New York Avenue (FL-44) *left for downtown DeLand*
0.6	Old New York Avenue *Right to Hontoon Road and Hontoon Landing, approximately 4.8 miles … or left for downtown DeLand, 3 miles … or straight ahead on Beresford Road South until it intersects with Beresford Road West for a view of Lake Beresford and the approximate location of Beresford Plantation continue on Beresford Road West to US-17, approximately 3 miles, and turn right; or from downtown DeLand, follow FL-44 and US-17 to Orange City*
6.0	Right on French Avenue West in Orange City
2.3	Enter Blue Springs State Park *Return by US-17 through DeLand to Barberville, left on FL-40*
6.9	Bartram Trail Marker *A stone marker under the live oak commemorates the Spalding/Panton store and the beginnings of Volusia County*
9.5	Right on FL-19
6.7	Silver Glen Springs
21.2	Parking for Caravelle WMA walk-in
3.5	Keep right on FL-19
1.9	Buckman Lock Road and entrance to Cross Florida Greenway
3.8	Right on Penial Road
0.5	Intersection with Stokes Landing Road *Turn right on Stokes Landing Road to reach the site of Spalding's Lower Store*
0.5	Right on Silver Lake Road
3.1	Right on Twigg Street
0.3	Left on South Fifteenth Street, then an immediate right on River Street
1.0	Memorial Parkway and St. Johns River

46. DeLeon Springs State Recreation Area may have been one of the springs visited by Juan Ponce de León as he searched for the Fountain of Youth and the spring is named for him. This popular park provides a picnic area, canoe launch with access to Lake Woodruff NWR, and a nature trail. The springs were visited by Jean James Audubon. Go west on Ponce De León Boulevard from US-17 as you enter the town of DeLeon Springs. Admission.

Chuck Lennon Park. Picnic area, nature trail, and playground located at 5000 Greenfield Dairy Road, next to DeLeon Springs State Recreation Area.

47. Gore's Landing River Trailhead. Access to Oklawaha River, boat ramp, canoe trail, restrooms, and primitive camping. East on Daisy Road from Highway 315.

48. Oklawaha River is being restored to its natural beauty by the state of Florida through a series of land acquisitions. It historically contained more extensive marshes and swamps than the St. Johns River but sections of the Oklawaha were compromised by canals and ditching. There has been recent discussion to remove the Rodman Dam and let the Oklawaha River return to its natural state.

49. Marion County Parks & Recreation Headquarters. Highway 314 at the Oklawaha River.

50. Marshall Swamp Trailhead. Hiking and equestrian trails, restrooms, and parking area. Highway 314 at the Oklawaha River. The other end of the trail is located at the intersection of Highways 25 and 464.

51. Oklawaha Prairie Restoration Area provides habitat for sandhill cranes, gopher tortoise, bobcats, and many wading birds. Access is by appointment only due to restoration activity. Call St. Johns River Water Management District at (904) 329–4404. The entrance is at the intersection of Blue Road and Highway 314A.

52. Moss Bluff Recreation Area is a Marion County Recreation area that has a boat launch, picnic area, and fishing. Highway 464 near the intersection with 324A

53. Sunny Hill Restoration Area will return a nine-mile portion of the Oklawaha River floodplain to its natural state. Restoration has attracted bears, bobcats, ospreys, and river otters back to the area. Access is from FL-42 at the Oklawaha River and from Forest Service Road 8 two miles further east.

54. Emeralda Marsh Conservation Area preserves about half of the 10,000 acres designated as a National Natural Landmark. Emeralda Marsh is an important winter home for waterfowl, sandhill cranes, wood storks, and limpkins. Activities include hiking, bicycling, canoeing, horseback riding, fishing, and seasonal hunting. Access is from FL-452, south of 44 in Ocala National Forest.

55. Lake Harris Conservation Area is small at 411 acres but is an excellent place to view waterfowl, wading birds, and alligators. Hiking, boat ramp, picnicking. Access from Sleepy Hollow Road off US-441.

11

New Smyrna

William Bartram described the colony of New Smyrna though he did not venture that far south during the period of his *Travels*. He did visit New Smyrna in 1766 after abandoning his plantation at Picolata. William De Brahm was surveyor general for East Florida and employed Bartram as a draftsman when the New Smyrna land was surveyed. Bartram's ship was wrecked off New Smyrna Beach as he sailed for home in the winter of 1766. Nothing is known of William during this time, no doubt owing to the embarrassing nature of his failure as a planter in Florida and the habit of Quaker modesty. His own parents were ignorant of his whereabouts and well-being until a letter arrived from Thomas Lamboll in April, 1767 reporting that William was alive and well in Saint Augustine. William returned to Philadelphia in the fall of 1767, much to the relief of his family.

In January, 1766 John and William Bartram reached their southernmost point on the St. Johns River, due west of Titusville, before becoming confused by the numerous meandering channels and lakes.

Sites

1. River Forest Recreation Area. Camping, picnic area, fishing, restrooms, and hiking trail. Intersection of FL-42 and FL-44.

2. Ed Stone Park. River access to the St. Johns River along one of its most attractive sections. The park has picnic facilities, boat ramps, restrooms, and fishing piers.

3. Lake Beresford Greenway will follow the east side of Lake Beresford and will provide hikers with views of the Lake Beresford and access to the site of Lord Beresford's plantation. Lord Beresford's land was located on the east side of the lake near the north end.

4. DeLand is called the Athens of Florida for its significant cultural history and position as an important seat of learning. DeLand is the home of **Stetson University**, founded in 1883 by John Stetson, the hat manufacturer. Stetson is the oldest private university in Florida and provides much of the cultural atmosphere for the city. Stetson University is listed in the National Register of Historic Places. For a town of its size DeLand has a surprising number of museums, including the **African American Museum of the Arts**, 325 Clara Avenue; **Cultural Arts Center/the DeLand Museum of Art**, 600 North Woodland Boulevard; and **Gillespie Museum of Minerals**, 234 East Michigan Avenue.

The **West Volusia Historical Society** and its research library is housed in the DeLand House Museum at 137 West Michigan Avenue. Open 12 a.m.–4 p.m., Tuesday through Saturday, closed on Sunday and Monday.

DeLand Area Public Library, 130 East Howry Avenue. Open 10 a.m.–6 p.m. on Monday and Wednesday; 10 a.m.–8 p.m., Tuesday and Thursday; 10 a.m.–5 p.m., Friday; and 9 a.m.–5 p.m. on Saturday. Florida archives are located on the second floor.

Early morning in the hammock at Blue Springs State Park

5. Hontoon Island State Park is an island park of over a thousand acres accessible only by boat. Visitors park at the entrance on River Ridge Road and take the free ferry across the St. Johns River to the park. The special features are an eighty-foot observation tower and a shell mound. The park has extensive hiking trails and a forest of mature live oaks and palmetto. A replica of a 600-year-old wooden owl totem found at Hontoon Island is on display. The original totem is the largest prehistoric artifact found in Florida. Open 8 a.m.–sunset, everyday. Admission.

6. Blue Springs State Park is an important Bartram site for both John and William visited there in January 1766 and William returned in 1774. This is an important winter refuge for manatees and a popular swimming spot. The Thursby House was built on a Timucuan shell mound and became an important landing during riverboat days. Oranges were shipped from Orange City before the groves were killed by freezes in the late 1800s. The first settlement at Orange City was in 1775 but

117

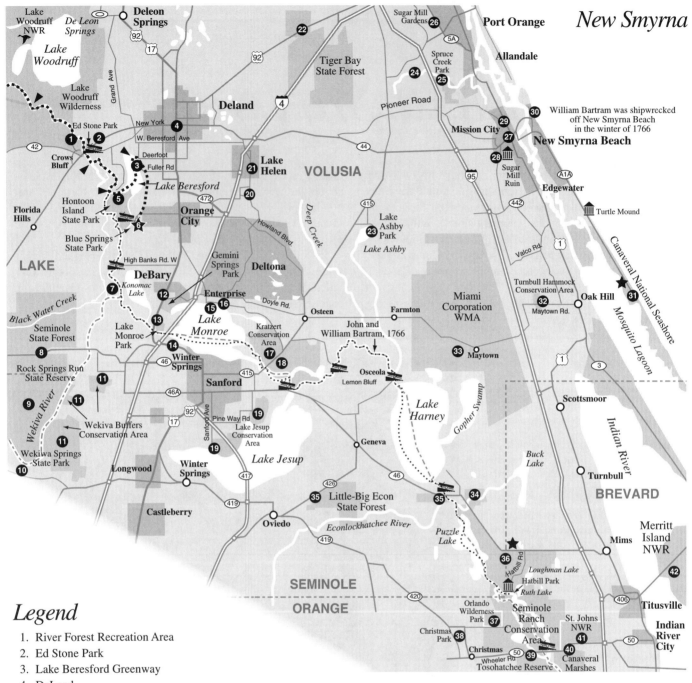

Legend

1. River Forest Recreation Area
2. Ed Stone Park
3. Lake Beresford Greenway
4. DeLand
   The West Volusia Historical Society
   DeLand Area Public Library
5. Hontoon Island State Park
6. Blue Springs State Park
7. Lower Wekiva River State Reserve
8. Seminole State Forest
9. Rock Springs Run State Reserve
10. Wekiwa Springs State Park
11. Wekiva Buffer Conservation Area
12. Gemini Springs Park
13. Lake Monroe Park
14. Central Florida Zoo
15. Riverfront Park
16. Green Springs
17. Kratzert Conservation Area
18. Lake Monroe Conservation Area
19. Lake Jesup Conservation Area
    Lake Jesup County Park
20. Cassadega
    Seneca Park
    Lake Colby County Park
21. Asa Gray Park
22. Tiger Bay State Forest
23. Lake Ashby Park
24. Spruce Creek Preserve
    Spruce Creek Canoe Trail
25. Spruce Creek Park
26. Sugar Mill Gardens
27. New Smyrna
28. Sugar Mill Ruins Historic Site
29. King's Road
30. Smyrna Dunes Park
31. Canaveral National Seashore
    Turtle Mound
32. Turnbull Hammock Conservation Area
33. Miami Corporation Wildlife Management Area
34. South Lake Harney Conservation Area
35. Little-Big Econ State Conservation Area
36. Seminole Ranch State Conservation Area
37. Orlando Wilderness Park
38. Christmas Park
39. Tosohatchee State Reserve
40. Canaveral Marshes Conservation Area
41. St. Johns National Wildlife Refuge
42. Merritt Island National Wildlife Refuge

it wasn't until 1856 that the permanent community began to grow.

There is an excellent boardwalk that winds through a dense hammock beside the spring run and overlooks the spring boil. There is a boat ramp on the St. Johns River, several hiking trails, canoe rentals, picnicking, cabins, and a campground. Located at the end of French Avenue in Orange City. Admission.

7. Lower Wekiva River State Reserve is bounded on the east by Wekiva River and on the west by Black Water Creek and has one mile of frontage on the St. Johns River. The Reserve contains a variety of habitats and wildlife. The entrance is from north of FL-46, five miles west of Sanford.

8. Seminole State Forest. Thirteen thousand acres of mixed hardwood, pine flatwoods, scrub, and freshwater marsh. There are fifteen miles of hiking trails. Access is from FL-46. Permit required for camping and canoeing. The office is at 9610 CR-44, Leesburg.

9. Rock Springs Run State Reserve. Nearly nine thousand acres of former timber and farm land is being restored. Hunting is allowed during the fall. During the remainder of the year hiking, canoeing, wildlife observation, and camping are permitted. Rock Springs Run Reserve contains pine flatwood, freshwater marsh, scrub and hardwood swamp. The reserve is home to the scrub jay, limpkin, gopher tortoise, and black bear. Access is from CR-433 off FL-46.

10. Wekiwa Springs State Park. The Wekiva River has its headwaters at Wekiwa Springs State Park. The park contains almost seven thousand acres of diverse habitat, including river swamp, pine flatwoods, and pine scrub. The park has thirteen miles of trails, an eight-mile horse trail and a sixteen-mile canoe trail to the St. Johns River. Campsites, picnic area, and swimming are available. Wildlife is abundant. Located on Wekiva River Road. Open 8 a.m.–sunset daily.

11. Wekiva Buffer Conservation Area protects the floodplain of Wekiva and Little Wekiva rivers and contains 2,342 acres bounded by the two rivers. The southern parcel contains the Sabal Point Audubon Wildlife Sanctuary. Permitted recreational activities include wildlife observation, hiking, fishing, canoeing, biking, and picnicking. Wildlife is abundant. Access is from Wekiva River Road, turn north into Sabal Point Development and proceed to Wilderness Drive. Information is available from Wekiwa Springs State Park.

12. Gemini Springs Park is the newest addition to the public spaces of Volusia County. The park has horse trails, a nature trail, canoeing on DeBary Bayou, boat launch, picnic area, and bicycling. Located at 37 Dirksen Drive, east of US-17, DeBary.

13. Lake Monroe Park borders the St. Johns River adjacent to US-17. Boat ramp, boardwalk, camping, nature trail, picnicking, and fishing dock.

14. Central Florida Zoo is fast becoming one of Central Florida's top attractions. The Central Florida Zoo was begun in 1923 and was moved to the present location in 1975 where it covers 109 acres of native Florida habitat. The Zoo features exotic animals including endangered primates, cats, reptiles, amphibians, ungulates, and birds. The Central Florida Zoo participates in the Species Survival Plan and has a breeding program for ten endangered animals. Located at 1755 N.W. Highway 17/92 at I-4, exit 52. Open daily, 9 a.m.–5 p.m., except Thanksgiving and Christmas.

15. Riverfront Park. Located between Lakeshore Drive and Lake Monroe. Boat ramp and picnic area.

16. Green Springs. This thirty-six-acre park includes hardwood hammock, archaeological sites, the spring, and spring run. Located on Green Springs Road north of Enterprise Osteen Road in Enterprise.

17. Kratzert Conservation Area. This floodplain and wetland conservation area preserves water quality along the shores of Lake Monroe and the St. Johns River. Hiking, birding, bicycling, and horseback riding are permitted activities; primitive camping is available by permit. Endangered wood storks and sandhill cranes are often sighted. The entrance is on Reed Ellis Road off FL-415, or Enterprise-Osteen Road from US-17.

18. Lake Monroe Conservation Area is east of Kratzert Conservation Area and adjacent to Highway 415.

19. Lake Jesup Conservation Area. This conservation area of 2,473 acres is divided into two tracts containing mostly wet prairie and some hardwood hammock. The northern tract is accessible from FL-46 and Cameron Drive or from FL-417 by Pine Way Road. This parcel is contiguous with the Seminole County Expressway Authority restoration project on the north end of Lake Jesup.

The southern portion of the conservation area lies astride the Seminole County Expressway and is being restored as mitigation for the expressway construction. **Lake Jesup County Park** is located in the southern end of the conservation area at the end of Sanford Avenue.

20. Cassadega was established in 1875 as a spiritualist camp by seer George Colby. The site he chose was already known to him through séance. It is still home to many psychics and lecturers in spiritual matters of far ranging interest. Meetings are held at the A. J. Davis Hall.

Seneca Park and the Mae Graves Ward Gazebo. Located at Spirit Pond, this park is designed to be a quiet and meditative retreat. There are nature trails to Spirit Pond and Lake Colby. Located off CR-4139 on Stevens Street.

Lake Colby County Park. Picnic area, pavilion, and nature trail. 1099 Massachusetts Street.

21. Asa Gray Park is named for the distinguished botanist and is the botanical garden of the Lake Helen Garden Club. Located at Hopkins Hall, corner of Main Street and Euclid Avenue in Lake Helen.

22. Tiger Bay State Forest (also known as Tomoka Wildlife Management Area) is named for the large bay swamp that it surrounds. The forest contains 11,000 acres and includes a large portion of wet forest habitat and numerous roads suitable for hiking. US-92 east of DeLand. The entrance is located at the end of Wildlife Drive, near the county prison.

23. Lake Ashby Park. Boat ramp, boardwalk, nature trail, picnic area, restrooms, and playground. 4150 Boy Scout Road, off FL-415.

24. Spruce Creek Preserve offers tours of the Backwood Nature Trail and historic buildings on Wednesday and Saturday. Canoe and boat trips are available on Saturday. The preserve is a combination of river hammock and old growth longleaf pine owned by the Nature Conservancy. Located on Taylor Road two miles west of I-95. Admission.

Spruce Creek Canoe Trail. Travel west on FL-421, Taylor Road, then south on Airport Road to Spruce Creek.

25. Spruce Creek Park features a boardwalk, fishing, camping, nature trail, and picnicking. 6250 S. Ridgewood Avenue, Port Orange.

26. Sugar Mill Gardens. Twelve acres of botanical gardens contain the ruins of an eighteenth century sugar mill. 950 Sugar Mill Road, off FL-51 (Nova Road), Port Orange.

27. New Smyrna. Although William Bartram did not visit the Mosquito River and settlement at New Smyrna during his *Travels*, a description of the area from an earlier visit was included in the Introduction and Chapter 7. The town of New Smyrna was a Utopian project of Dr. Andrew Turnbull and was composed of Greek, Italian, and Minorcan immigrants. Turnbull's wife was from Smyrna, Turkey, and Turnbull himself had spent time in the eastern Mediterranean. His plan was to populate the settlement with people of a similar climate who could raise citrus and semitropical products.

In August 1768, 1,403 indentured people arrived at New Smyrna. As always the first years were difficult due to disease and dependence on provisions from benefactors. The colony prospered briefly but by the late 1770s there were complaints of severe working conditions with little promise of an independent life. A committee presented their complaints to Governor Tonyn and sought refuge in Saint Augustine. Governor Tonyn was legally obligated to return them to New Smyrna, but he thought it more expedient to offer protection and asylum rather than have them fly on to Georgia or South Carolina and join the patriots. Many of the indenture contracts expired in 1777 and the New Smyrna colonists preferred to pursue their lives elsewhere. At one time half the population of Saint Augustine were Greek descendants of New Smyrna colonists. There are several archaeological ruins remaining from the eighteenth century structures.

William Bartram was employed by William De Brahm, surveyor general of East Florida, when the lands for New Smyrna were surveyed. In November 1766, William sailed from New Smyrna for Philadelphia but was shipwrecked off Mosquito Bar and returned to Saint Augustine. He finally reached Philadelphia in the fall of 1767. The spacious Indian mound he saw near the town of New Smyrna is now called **Turtle Mound** and is located at Canaveral National Seashore.

28. Sugar Mill Ruins Historic Site preserves the remains of the mill destroyed by Seminoles in 1835. The first sugar cane in Florida was grown at New Smyrna. 600 Mission Road, off FL-44.

29. King's Road is the southernmost part of the great colonial highway along the Southeastern coast. The road from Saint Augustine to New Smyrna was cleared in the late 1760s and was funded by subscription.

30. Smyrna Dunes Park is a popular birding area among the dunes at Ponce de León Inlet. This is a nesting area in summer and home for migratory birds in winter. The park has a boardwalk and observation tower. From New Smyrna take FL-44 east to A1A, then north on Peninsula Avenue. The park entrance is at the end of the road.

Blue Springs

31. Canaveral National Seashore includes Mosquito Lagoon and twenty-four miles of the adjoining Atlantic beaches. The lagoon is a winter home for manatees, the beaches are a nesting area for sea turtles, and more than a hundred islands provide a winter home for numerous bird species. Mangrove reaches its northern limit on the Atlantic at the Indian River.

Bartram's **Turtle Mound** is located on A1A and is reached by a nature trail and boardwalk. It is thought to be the largest shell mound in North America at fifty feet in height and covering two acres. Turtle Mound was built between 800 and 1400 A.D. Canaveral Seashore and adjacent Merritt Island NWR were formed from lands acquired by NASA. Outdoor activities permitted at Canaveral National Seashore are hiking, camping by permit, fishing, canoeing, and boating. The north entrance and visitor center is located at the end of A1A. There are two Bartram historical markers in Canaveral National Seashore. One commemorates his visit to Mosquito Lagoon and the other his discovery of zebra butterfly.

32. Turnbull Hammock Conservation Area is a forested wetland and helps protect water quality for the Indian River. Activities include hiking, bird-watching, bicycling, and photography. Seasonal flooding creates a challenge for visitors. From US-1 turn west on Maytown Road.

33. Miami Corporation WMA. This very large wildlife management area contains 52,000 acres, has two hunt camps and a number of unimproved roads. Access is from Maytown Road.

34. South Lake Harney Conservation Area contains important habitat surrounding Cabbage Slough. The spring-fed water of this area is saline enough to support marine species. Birds sighted in the Conservation Area are sandhill cranes, bald eagles, osprey, roseate spoonbills, wood storks, and other waterfowl. Recreational activities include hiking, canoeing, fishing, and bird watching. Located on FL-46 just east of the St. Johns River.

35. Little-Big Econ State Conservation Area protects a significant portion of the blackwater Econlockhatchee River and supports abundant wildlife. Canoe access to the river is available and a spur trail connects to the Florida Trail. Camping and horseback riding are allowed by permit. Access is from FL-426, FL-429, and Snowhill Road.

36. Seminole Ranch State Conservation Area is a large tract, nearly 29,000 acres, and protects twelve miles of the St. Johns River and its floodplain. The salinity of the small lakes is one-third that of seawater and supports marine species not found elsewhere in the St. Johns River. Activities enjoyed in the conservation area include fishing, canoeing, hiking, bird watching, bicycling, horseback riding, and primitive camping.

Seminole Ranch is the farthest point on the St. Johns River reached by John and William

Bartram on January 12, 1766. They became confused by the numerous braided channels of the St. Johns River. They found dry land at Baxter Mound and believed they had reached the headwaters of the river. Baxter Mound is located in Seminole Ranch west of Hatbill Road.

Seminole Ranch is reached from FL-46 by Hatbill Road and from FL-420 north of Christmas by Wheeler Road.

37. Orlando Wilderness Park contains an artificial wetland designed to treat wastewater. Hiking trails follow dikes around lagoons populated with numerous waterfowl species. The area is closed October–January for hunting. Located on Wheeler Road, off FL-420, Fort Christmas Road, north of Christmas.

38. Christmas Park. Fort Christmas Museum is a replica of the 1837 fort built during the Second Seminole War. It contains artifacts from the early settlement of the area. Open 10 a.m.–5 p.m. Tuesday through Sunday. Located on FL-420, Fort Christmas Road, two miles north of FL-50, Orlando Road.

39. Tosohatchee State Reserve contains areas of pine uplands, hammocks, cypress swamps, marsh, and nineteen miles of frontage on the St. Johns River. There are several mounds indicating the Timucuans lived there. Tosohatchee Reserve is accessible by several dirt roads and hiking trails. Recreational activities include hiking, canoeing, primitive camping, horseback riding, and fishing. Hunting is allowed at certain times. Access is by Taylor Road from Orlando Road, FL-50.

40. Canaveral Marshes Conservation Area protects and restores the floodplain on the east side of the St. Johns River from FL-50 to Lake Poinsett. Access to the northern tract is from FL-50 through the Great Outdoors Resort.

41. St. Johns National Wildlife Refuge was established to protect the dusky seaside sparrow which was unfortunately declared extinct in 1990. The Refuge covers a little more than 6,000 acres, protects salt-marsh adjacent to the St. Johns River, and provides habitat for migratory birds. Access is by special permit from the Merritt Island NWR office in Titusville.

42. Merritt Island National Wildlife Refuge is a popular birding site with more than 300 species inhabiting the area. Loggerhead sea turtles nest beginning in May. Visitors have access to trails, an observation tower, and wildlife drive. Located along FL-406 and FL-402. The visitor center is located on FL-402 and is open Monday through Friday.

Alachua

Gainesville was the site of the Spanish mission San Francisco de Potano and the town of the Potanoes, a powerful Timucuan tribe. The French of Fort Caroline assisted their allies, the Utinas, in a war against the Potanoes in 1565. The bruised Potanoes moved from Orange Lake to a site in the southeastern part of San Felasco Hammock State Preserve. Some years later the Spanish retaliated against Potano depredations by driving them from Alachua. The Potanoes were allowed to return in 1602 when they asked for a mission to be established in their town. The Potanoes took part in the revolt against the Spanish in 1656

European diseases caused the Timucuan population to decline sharply. Bubonic plague struck in 1613, smallpox in 1649, yellow fever in 1653, measles in 1659, and an unknown epidemic in 1675. Colonel James Moore executed the first raid against the Spanish mission towns of central Florida in 1702. Over the next twenty years South Carolina and Creek allies destroyed the missions and caused the Spanish to move the Christian inhabitants to Saint Augustine and the coastal missions. This left the northern part of Florida virtually uninhabited. Disaffected Creeks began moving into this vacuum in the 1740's and called themselves Seminoles, from cimarroné, the Spanish name for a wild cow.

The Seminoles

The Spanish government was desirous of settling the interior of Florida to protect its frontier and to contain the English. Saint Augustine sent agents into the Creek towns with an invitation to take up the empty lands abounding with game. Ahaya, the Cow

Downtown Micanopy

Keeper, was likely one of Oglethorpe's Creek allies when the Georgians attacked Saint Augustine in 1740. It may have been then that Ahaya decided to move his people to Florida.

Another explanation of the origins of the Seminoles is found in General Thomas Woodward's *Reminiscences*. J. G. Klinck wrote in a letter to the *Montgomery Mail* that when the Creeks waged war against the Yamassees in Florida many young Creek warriors took Yamassee women for wives. Creek law required the young women to stay outside the nation for a year of purification. Before their time was up the young Creek warriors decided to remain in Florida and create a new nation with their new wives.

The Oconees were the nucleus of those Creeks who separated from the other towns and became Seminoles. Their disaffection may have been due to the fact that they were a Hitchiti-speaking people and were considered lesser members of the Creek Confederacy. The Oconees had once lived at Rock Landing on the Oconee River south of Milledgeville, Georgia in the late seventeenth century. The Oconees probably had lived earlier on the Chattahoochee River but moved eastward on the Great Trading Path to be closer to the commercial activity emanating from Augusta. Around 1715, in the aftermath of the Yamassee War, the Oconees moved back to the Chattahoochee River. In Florida they gathered about them remnants of declining tribes, disenchanted Creeks, and runaway slaves. Their numbers were later augmented by Red Sticks who fled Alabama after the Creek War of 1813–1814. Thus, there arose two divisions of the Seminoles distinguished by language, Hitchiti and Muskogee, with leaders coming from the Oconee/Hitchiti line.

When King Payne was chief of the Seminoles in the nineteenth century the villages began to appear more like plantations than traditional Creek villages. With the decrease of the deer population the Seminoles turned to the cattle trade and prospered during the second Spanish period.

In the early 1800s the Seminole plantations were the target of border ruffians. The Georgia Militia led by Colonel Daniel Newnan attacked Payne's Town during the Patriot War of 1812. The Georgians were repulsed by King Payne, his brother Bowlegs, 200 warriors, and their black allies. Payne was wounded and died soon after. Tennessee volunteers raided through north Florida in early 1813 and caused a great deal of destruction. Seminoles began to move deeper into Florida and away from the Americans.

During the Second Seminole War of 1835, the great Osceola won the admiration of whites, blacks, and Indians for his struggle to hold on to his people's land. Most Seminole people were moved to Oklahoma when the war ended in 1845 but a significant number escaped south to the Everglades where their descendants live today.

The black Seminoles were a band of runaway slaves who became associated with the Seminoles of Paynes Prairie. Many slaves found an opportunity for escape during the Revolution when coastal plantations were abandoned by their owners as the British approached. The slaves naturally sought refuge in Florida where the Spanish opposed slavery and promised freedom. The former slaves, knowing the white man's language and customs, became an invaluable business partner in the Seminole cattle trade. In return, the blacks received freedom,

Paynes Prairie

protection, respect, and economic opportunity. The British and Americans assumed that they were slaves of the Seminoles and this assumption was turned to advantage by the Seminoles and their black friends to prevent slave catchers from operating in their country. Whatever the status of blacks living among Native Americans in other parts of Florida and the Southeast, the blacks of Paynes Prairie were not owned by the Seminoles. Though there was intermarriage and cooperation, the Seminoles and blacks maintained separate towns. The original black Seminole town was located about where US-441 crosses the south rim of Paynes Prairie.

The Arredondo Grant encompassed a large area of land surrounding Paynes Prairie and Gainesville. This grant was made on December 17, 1817, during the second Spanish period, to the commercial firm of Don Fernando de la Maza Arredondo and Son of Havana. They subdivided the property and several companies were formed with the purpose of attracting colonists to the area. Settlers from Georgia and South Carolina were drawn to Alachua County beginning in the 1820s when Florida became a U.S. territory. The settlement of Hog Town was renamed Gainesville when it became the county seat of Alachua County in 1853.

William Bartram's Travels to Alachua

Maps of territorial Florida show trails that approximate the route that Bartram would have taken on his trip to Alachua Savannah and Talahasochte. Although the old Spanish trails were beginning to disappear at the time of Bartram's visit, we can assume that during the second Spanish period and at the beginning of American ownership of Florida these trails were revived because the desirable land for plantations and settlements were the same as they had always been. Francis Harper thought that the trail from Micanopy to the crossing on the Suwannee River went northwest to near Lake Kanapaha and joined the old Spanish trail to St. Marks. This seems to be an out-of-the-way route for Bartram to take, especially because the early maps show a more direct trail going southwest from Micanopy around Levy Lake and Kanapaha Prairie then almost in a straight line to Old Town, on the Suwannee River.

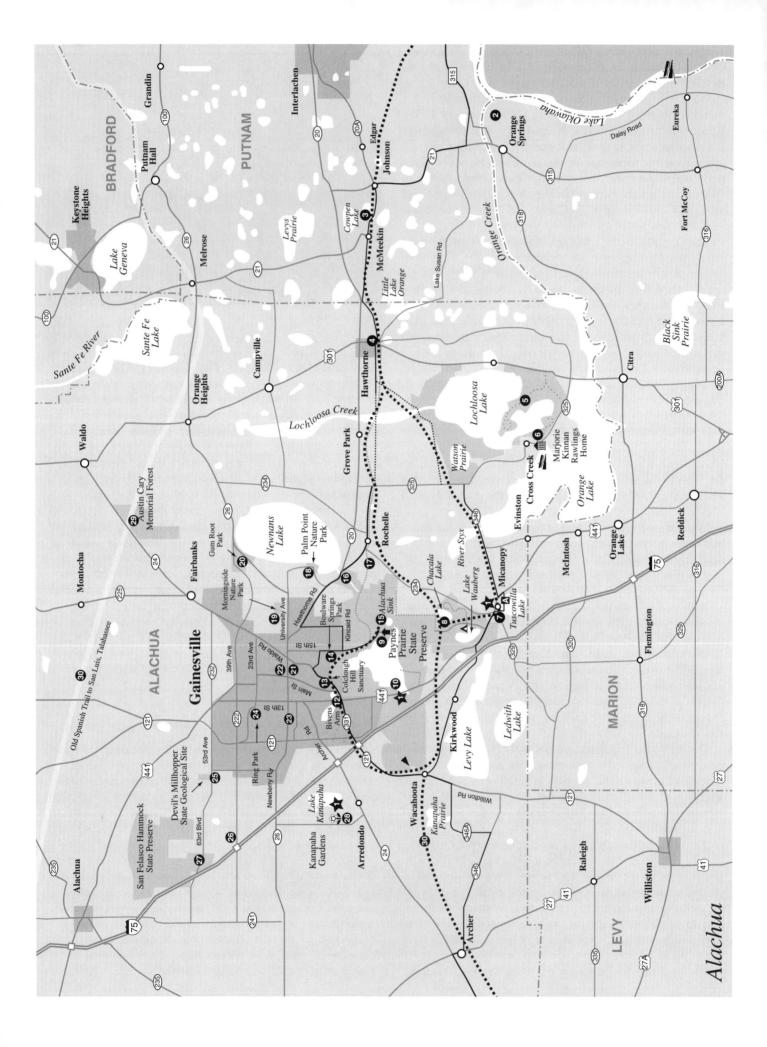

Bartram's traveling party would have reached the St. Marks Trail somewhere near Bronson. It seems more likely that the beautiful little lake where Bartram and the traders made their camp was Kanapaha Prairie or some other of the numerous lakes in the area and not Lake Kanapaha as Francis Harper believed. During wet weather Kanapaha Prairie would have been a lake and the sinks and rock outcrops that Bartram mentioned are very common in the entire region now contained within Alachua County.

The dreary, solitary desert that Bartram encountered the next day is the rolling sand hills of western Alachua County located around and north of Archer. These are the remains of ancient beach dunes formed when the Gulf of Mexico extended farther inland. Here we find specially adapted plants that are endemic to the Florida Sandhills, most common is the Florida rosemary. The Seminole town of Talahasochte was located north of Manatee Springs in the area of Andrews Wildlife Management Area.

Sites

1. Bartram Trail historical markers are located at Paynes Prairie, Lake Kanapaha, Micanopy, and Newberry. Bartram's visit is also acknowledged in the state historical marker on North Johnson Street in Hawthorne.

2. Orange Springs Recreation Area provides recreational access to Lake Oklawaha. Boat ramp, fishing, restrooms, picnic area, and bird watching. Located at FL-315 and Orange Creek.

3. Cowpen Lake is Bartram's Halfway Pond and is located halfway between Palatka and Micanopy (Cuscowilla). It lies north of FL-20A, four and a half miles west of the intersection with FL-21.

4. Hawthorne prospered as a station at the intersection of the Peninsular Railroad and the Florida Southern Railroad. The colonial trading path that William Bartram traveled passed through Hawthorne and crossed Little Orange Creek.

> *We gently descended again over sand ridges, crossed a rapid brook (Little Orange Creek), rippling over the gravelly bed, hurrying the transparent waters into a vast and beautiful lake (Johnson Lake), through a fine fruitful orange grove, which magnificently adorns the banks of the lake to a great distance on each side of the capes of the creek.*[1]

1. William Bartram, *Travels*, 178.

River Styx, Lochloosa Wildlife Management area

5. Lochloosa Conservation Area surrounds about eighty percent of Lake Lochloosa shoreline with adjacent parcels protecting Cross Creek, Lochloosa Creek, and River Styx. The entire Lochloosa Conservation Area covers 10,333 acres. There are four hiking trails, three boat launches, and numerous birdwatching areas. An information kiosk is located on CR-325 just south of the Marjorie Kinnan Rawlings home. Wildlife sightings might include bald eagles, wood storks, sandhill cranes, and black bears.

6. Marjorie Kinnan Rawlings State Historic Site preserves the home of the author of the *Yearling* and winner of the Pulitzer Prize for fiction. The Rawlings home is an unpretentious Cracker-style house with oranges, lemons, and grapefruit growing in the backyard. She worked at her typewriter on the spacious,

Legend

1. Bartram Trail historical markers
2. Orange Springs Recreation Area
3. Cowpen Lake
4. Hawthorne
5. Lochloosa Conservation Area
6. Marjorie Kinnan Rawlings State Historic Site
7. Micanopy
8. Paynes Prairie State Preserve
9. Ranchero de la Chua
10. Observation Deck, US-441
11. Interstate 75 Rest Area
12. Bivens Arm Nature Park
13. Colclough Hill Audubon Sanctuary
14. Boulware Springs Park
15. Alachua Sink
16. Prairie Creek Conservation Area
17. Gainesville to Hawthorne Rail Trail
18. Palm Point Nature Park
19. Morningside Nature Park
20. Gum Root Conservation Area
21. Matheson Historical Center
22. The Thomas Center
23. University of Florida
    Lake Alice Wildlife Sanctuary
    Florida Museum of Natural History
    Samuel P. Harn Museum of Art
24. Alfred A. Ring Park
25. Devil's Millhopper State Geological Site
26. Sante Fe College Teaching Zoo
27. San Felasco Hammock Preserve
28. Kanapaha Gardens
29. Austin Cary Memorial Forest
30. The Old Spanish Trail

Marjorie Kinnan Rawlings Historic Site in Cross Creek

screened veranda where she could feel the weather and catch the scent of orange blossoms. Rawlings drew inspiration for her characters from the farmers who lived in the area between Micanopy and Ocala.

Located on Alachua 325 at Cross Creek between Lochloosa and Orange Lakes. Open 10–11:30 a.m. and 1–4:30 p.m. Tours are on the half hour and limited to ten people. Closed Tuesdays and Wednesdays. Admission.

7. Micanopy is built at the site of the Indian town of Cuscowilla and is one of the oldest towns in Florida. The village that Bartram visited was just east of present-day downtown Micanopy about 300 yards north of Tuscawilla Lake where a stream enters the lake. The people of Cuscowilla were a branch of the Oconee Indians who had emigrated from the Chattahoochee River at Omaha, Georgia in the mid-eighteenth century. During the time of Bartram's visit their headman was Ahaya, the Cow Keeper. His brother and war chief was Long Warrior.

Ahaya and his people once lived on the edge of Payne's Prairie but moved to Tuscawilla Lake around 1770 to escape the mosquitoes and smell of decaying fish. Another reason may have been to escape the spirit of a murdered warrior who was killed by the son of Long Warrior. In a drunken rage he killed a friend with a broken liquor bottle and the horrified townspeople moved soon after. The town consisted of about thirty buildings and a large herd of cattle rounded up from the strays left by Spanish ranchers. They were the nucleus of the Seminole tribe and eventually drew into their sphere the small tribes of Florida and the refugees and malcontents of the Upper and Lower Creek towns.

Leadership passed to Ahaya's son, King Payne, who became wealthy from his large herds of cattle and horses. The success of the Seminoles in the cattle trade brought about the demise of their traditional community, a town built around a central square. Payne's community was more like a plantation than a town. Colonel Daniel Newnan and the Georgia Militia attacked Payne's Town in 1812 in an attempt to take Florida and keep it out of British hands. The Seminoles defeated the Georgians but King Payne was wounded and died.

Micanopy was a descendant of Cow Keeper and nephew of Payne. He was headman of the Paynes Prairie Seminoles during the Second Seminole War but deferred military leadership to Osceola. Micanopy moved to Olkahumpka in Lake County then in 1838 he was deported to Oklahoma.

The American settlement of Wanton was built on the site of Cuscowilla in 1821 and was renamed Micanopy. Charles Vignoles writes in 1823 that Micanopy was the hub of numerous paths radiating in all directions.

Micanopy Historical Society Museum. NE Cholokka Boulevard, one block south of US-441 in Micanopy. Open on Wednesday, Friday, Saturday, and Sunday from 1–4 p.m. Admission.

8. Paynes Prairie State Preserve is the celebrated **Alachua Savannah** that so delighted William Bartram and was treasured above all places he explored in his travels. The site of the trading post is near a spring at Chacala Lake. The preserve is named for the Seminole Chief Payne who died during the Georgia invasion of Florida in 1812.

Paynes Prairie is a large basin formed when underground limestone dissolved and collapsed. For part of the year it is covered with wet prairie and at other times it is dry enough for the park service to burn. Because fire is a natural ecological agent it keeps the savannah from becoming shrubby and helps the prairie retain its historical appearance. The management at Paynes Prairie has attempted to reestablish the natural habitat of the savannah as it appeared to William Bartram. They have used his descriptions as their guide, even bringing in herds of buffalo, Spanish cattle, and horses. Paynes Prairie is a major wintering home for hundreds of greater sandhill cranes. There is a small population of non-migrating Florida sandhill cranes that may be seen any time of year.

The bison herd at Paynes Prairie is perhaps the most popular and best-known feature of the preserve. Getting a glimpse of them is a rare and exciting event. The herd once numbered about thirty but an outbreak of bovine brucellosis forced the park service to sell the infected individuals for slaughter. The herd is now rebounding from this setback. American bison never ranged the Southeast in the great numbers that were found in the Midwest and the newly arrived Europeans quickly hunted them to extinction. The woodland bison of the east were smaller than their western relatives.

The entrance to Paynes Prairie is located on US-441 north of Micanopy. Open 8 a.m.–sunset, everyday. The visitor center is open 8 a.m.–5 p.m. daily.

9. Ranchero de la Chua was a large and successful Spanish ranch that operated from 1646 to 1705. Chua is a Timucuan word for sinkhole, which are numerous in the area. The ranch was once owned by Thomas Menéndez Marquéz, a relative of Governor Menéndez de Avilés. Cattle were driven to the Suwannee River and shipped to Cuba or to St. Augustine where they fed the garrison at Castillo de San Marcos. The ranch was abandoned when South Carolinians and Creeks began raiding isolated Spanish settlements in the early eighteenth century. The site of the ranch headquarters was on the north rim where the Florida Park Service regional office is now located.

Some cattle and horses were left behind and grew into the herds that William Bartram saw grazing on the lush grass of Alachua Savannah. Spanish horses were brought to the New World in slings aboard ships to prevent injury. At Saint Augustine they were unloaded with hoists. The horses at Paynes Prairie are descended from these original Spanish horses and have free range of the preserve. They can be seen often at Bolen's Bluff. The Spanish cattle were of the long-horned Andalusian breed. The Paynes Prairie herd is located west of US-441.

In 1817 the company of Don Fernando de la Maza Arredondo and Son of Havana was granted a large tract of land that included Paynes Prairie. The Arredondos subdivided the land and companies were formed for the purpose of luring settlers from the United States.

10. Observation Deck, US-441. A Bartram Trail historical marker commemorates William Bartram's visit to Alachua Savannah. There is a parking area for a boardwalk to the savannah.

11. Interstate 75 Rest Area. Snakes became so numerous at this rest area that a barrier wall was constructed to keep them away from the travelers. The barrier is a whimsical serpentine wall complete with masonry snake eyes.

12. Bivens Arm Nature Park is mentioned in the *Travels*,

> ... on the way [we] were constrained to wade a mile or more through the water, though at a little distance from us it appeared as a delightful meadow, the grass growing through the water, the middle of which, however, when we came up, proved to be a large space of clear water almost deep enough to swim our horses ...[2]

Alachua Sink at low water

The extensive growth of grass hid the fact that this meadow was mostly fresh water, forcing Bartram's party to wade across to the high ground on the opposite side. Today Bivens Arm is a beautiful urban preserve where quotes from noted nature writers enhance the pleasure of a walk through the marsh. A 1,200-foot boardwalk winds through the wetland and has several observation decks and benches. 3650 South Main Street, just north of Williston Road. Open 9 a.m.–5 p.m. everyday.

13. Colclough Hill Audubon Sanctuary was a prehistoric village site now owned by the Florida Audubon Society. William Bartram crossed Colclough Hill as he traveled around Alachua Savannah. From Williston Road turn left onto SW 32nd Way, turn right onto SW First Way, keep right on SW First Way to the sanctuary entrance at the end of the street.

14. Boulware Springs Park is the site of the spring where Gainesville began in 1854. There is a nature trail and the Gainesville-Hawthorne Trail begins there. Located on SE Fifteenth Street. Open dawn to dusk everyday.

15. Alachua Sink is located on the north rim of Paynes Prairie and is one of the places of special mention in Bartram's *Travels*. In 1881 the sink became clogged and Paynes Prairie became a lake with steamboats cruising from the north to south shore. Just as quickly in 1891 the sink opened and the lake drained almost overnight. Access is from the North Rim Interpretative Center, SE Fifteenth Street, or Boulware Springs Park, also on SE Fifteenth Street.

16. Prairie Creek Conservation Area was created to help protect the waterway from Newnans Lake through Paynes Prairie to River Styx and Orange Lake. The state of Florida designated Orange and Lochloosa lakes as Outstanding Florida Waters and sought to protect the water systems that flow to them. Prairie Creek is a small conservation area but there is a short hiking trail and the Gainesville-Hawthorne Trail crosses through it parallel to FL-20. Access is from FL-20 east of Prairie Creek, parking is available at the commercial fish camp. Information is available from Paynes Prairie State Preserve.

17. Gainesville to Hawthorne Rail Trail begins at Boulware Springs Park, passes through Paynes Prairie, Prairie Creek, Lochloosa Wildlife Management Area, and ends seventeen miles later in Hawthorne. The trail is built on an old railroad bed that roughly follows the Spanish Lachua Trail. William Bartram and the traders entered this path when they left the trading post at Paynes Prairie and returned to Palatka. Open 8 a.m.–sunset daily.

18. Palm Point Nature Park is located on the western bank of Newnans Lake. It is small and undeveloped but has facilities for picnicking, birdwatching, fishing, and has a native plant habitat. Lakeshore Drive, two miles north of FL 20. Open 8 a.m.–sunset, everyday.

19. Morningside Nature Park has a homestead farm that illustrates the subsistence lifestyle of the early Cracker settlers who moved south from Georgia. The garden features heirloom plants and the barnyard has a very friendly milk cow in residence. Morningside Park is a wildlife sanctuary and has over seven miles of nature trails that enter several ecosystems—cypress dome, marsh, savannah, and longleaf pine-turkey oak forest. The forest is fire managed to promote the growth of wildflowers and wiregrass and to attract the animals that are dependent on the open pine flatwoods. Second only to Paynes Prairie, Morningside Nature Park is the best public area for visitors to see native Florida landscape in Gainesville.

Open 9 a.m.–5 p.m. daily. 3540 East University Avenue.

20. Gum Root Conservation Area is a classic Southern hardwood swamp and is important in protecting and filtering the water that flows into Newnans Lake, Prairie Creek, and Orange Lake. There are several hiking trails, a birdwatching area at the lake, and a canoe launch. Access to the state-owned portion is from FL-26 at Newnans Lake. The information kiosk for the Gainesville city property is located on NW 27th Avenue immediately after turning off FL-26, on the right.

21. Matheson Historical Center houses such Floridiana as postcards and prints as well as a historical collection of books and maps. There is an excellent exhibition hall devoted to the history of Gainesville, beginning with the prehistoric inhabitants and including a kiosk devoted entirely to William Bartram. There is a research library and archives of Alachua

2. Ibid., 200.

County. Sweetwater Park is being developed on the Matheson property and the three adjoining blocks. There is a native plant garden surrounding the center. 513 East University Avenue. Open 10 a.m.–4 p.m. Monday through Saturday. Admission.

22. The Thomas Center has exhibits of local history, art, and period furnishings in a historical house and gardens. 306 NE Sixth Street. Open 8 a.m.–5 p.m., Monday–Friday, and 1–4 p.m. on Saturday and Sunday.

23. The University of Florida was created in 1905, being formed from the union of two existing institutions—Florida Agricultural College and East Florida Seminary. The University has since grown into a major, prestigious university with a student body of over 40,000. William Bartram's visit to Alachua is remembered in the name of Bartram Hall, which is adjacent to the Florida Museum of Natural History office building.

Lake Alice Wildlife Sanctuary is located within the campus grounds of the University of Florida and is home to a number of urban alligators. There is an orientation kiosk for the hiking trails and gardens located at the west end of Museum Road. The map on display at the kiosk shows ambitious plans for an herb and native plant garden.

Florida Museum of Natural History is the largest natural history museum in the South and one of the top ten facilities in the country. The Museum of Natural History carries out extensive archaeological research and houses a large collection of fossil plants, shells, insects, fish, vertebrate, and invertebrate animals. The anthropological collection is the largest in the Southeast. Florida natural environments and history are featured in permanent exhibition halls. Special events showcase Native-American dances and music, and lectures by noted scientists. Powell Hall, the new Education and Exhibition Center of the museum, is located at the intersection of SW 34th Street and Hull Road.

Located at the corner of Museum Road and Newell Drive on the University of Florida campus. Open 10 a.m.–5 p.m. Monday–Saturday; 1–5 p.m. on Sundays and holidays, closed on Christmas Day.

Samuel P. Harn Museum of Art has collections of American paintings, African and pre-Columbian artifacts, and contemporary art. Located at Hull Road and SW 34th Street, University of Florida campus. Open 11 a.m.–5 p.m. Tuesday–Friday; 10 a.m.–5 p.m. on Saturday; and 1–5 p.m. on Sunday. Closed Monday and holidays. Admission.

24. Alfred A. Ring Park is located in the hilly land surrounding Glen Springs Run and Hogtown Creek. The most important feature for visitors is the Emily S. Ring Wildflower Garden and Lily Pool. The entrance is on NW 22nd Street just south of NW 23rd Avenue. Open dawn–sunset, everyday.

25. Devil's Millhopper State Geological Site provides a cutaway view of Florida's geologic past. This funnel-shaped limestone sink is 120 feet deep and 500 feet across with several spring-fed waterfalls that add interest and beauty. The microclimate supports a lush growth of ferns and temperate plants.

Florida rests on limestone, which is easily dissolved by the weak acid of rainwater. Underground caverns form where the limestone is dissolved and carried away in solution by groundwater. The cavern becomes larger over time and the ceiling collapses, forming a sinkhole. These sinkholes can occur over much of Florida but they are particularly numerous in Alachua County. William Bartram described a near accident when he endeavored to reach some curious plants and realized that the ground under his feet was hollow.

> ... observing chasms through the ground, I quickly drew back, and returning again with a pole with which I beat in the earth, to my astonishment and dread appeared the mouth of a well through the rocks, and I observed the water glimmering at the bottom.[3]

Devil's Millhopper is located at 4732 Millhopper Road. Open 9 a.m.–sunset, daily; 9 a.m.–5 p.m. from October 1 through March 30. Guided nature walk at 10 a.m. on Saturdays. Admission.

26. Sante Fe College Teaching Zoo is home to a variety of animals from Africa, Asia, Australia, Europe, and the Americas. This unique college-based teaching zoo is the only one of its kind in the country. 3000 NW 83rd Street, exit 77 from I-75. Open 9 a.m.–2 p.m. Saturday and Sunday, by appointment only during the week.

27. San Felasco Hammock Preserve. This 6,500-acre preserve covers the repertoire of north Florida natural habitats with eighteen biological communities represented. San Felasco is a mispronunciation of San Francisco. The site of the Spanish Mission San Francisco de Potano is believed to have been near the southeastern corner of the preserve's boundaries. There are two hiking trails, one is a half mile and one is eight-miles long. There are guided hikes and overnight camping expeditions on a regular schedule. Parking is found on FL-232 just east of the I-75 overpass (no exit). Open 8 a.m.–sunset, daily. Obtain information from Devil's Millhopper State Geological Site.

28. Kanapaha Gardens is noted for its herb garden, one of the largest in the Southeast. There are also hummingbird, bamboo, vine, and bog gardens. There are many rare and unusual plants from around the world collected there and a nursery offers plants for sale. The entrance to Kanapaha Gardens was part of the old Indian trading path that traveled to the Suwannee River and Saint Marks. The Bartram historical marker commemorating William Bartram's trip from Alachua to Talahasochte stands in the azalea garden near the edge of Lake Kanapaha.

Located off FL-24 one mile west of I-75 at 4625 SW 63rd Boulevard. Open 9 a.m.–5 p.m. Monday, Tuesday, and Friday; 9 a.m.–sunset Wednesday, Saturday and Sunday. Closed on Thursday. Admission.

29. Cary State Forest encompasses 3,400 acres of pine land and has several hiking trails and a wildlife observation tower. Located on US-301. Open daily.

30. The Old Spanish Trail from Saint Augustine became the Old Bellamy Road. It crossed the St. Johns River at Picolata and passed through the present community of Melrose, crossed the Sante Fe River north of High Springs, and continued past Ichetucknee Springs to Tallahassee. The trail from Picolata to Alachua would be close to the present route of FL-20, FL-20A, and Alachua 346 to Micanopy. Another branch from Palatka went northwest to meet the Spanish Trail near Melrose. The **St. Marks Trail** was a continuation of the Alachua Trail from Palatka to Paynes Prairie, passing north of Bronson, north of Chiefland, and crossing the Suwannee River at the site of the Indian Village of Talahasochte, between Manatee Springs and Fanning Springs. Paynes Prairie was a hub for paths crisscrossing Florida. Charles Vignoles reported in 1823 that trails from there led in all directions; to Volusia, Saint Augustine, Picolata, Palatka, St. Marks, Tallahassee, Tampa Bay, and Lake Weir.

Counties

Alachua County was created in 1824 and is named for Ranchero de La Chua.

---

3. William Bartram, *Travels*, 245.

Itinerary

Palatka to Paynes Prairie

Begin in downtown Palatka and travel west on Reid Street/US-17

Miles	Directions
.6	Left on FL-20
2.6	Left on FL-19
8.9	Right on CR-310
7.7	Right on CR-315, Grand Avenue
4.0	Left on Middleton Street at Interlachen Middle School, becomes Strickland Street
1.6	Left on FL-20A, McMeekan Road
4.1	Intersection of McMeekan Road and FL-21 in Johnson
2.5	Left on Old Hawthorn/McMeekan Road
3.0	Left on SE-Second Avenue, becomes Myrtle Avenue in Hawthorne
2.0	Right on US-301/Center Street
.1	Left on West Lake Avenue/CR20A
1.4	Left on dirt road at the Gainesville-Hawthorne Rail to Trail sign, SE 200 Drive
.3	Cross the Gainesville-Hawthorne Trail
2.7	Right at intersection
4.0	Left on CR-325
1.2	Right on CR-346
5.3	Left on US-441
.3	Right on East Cholokka Boulevard/SE 165 Avenue
.8	Right on NE Cholokka Boulevard in downtown Micanopy
.4	Left on US-441
1.1	Entrance to Paynes Prairie State Preserve

Around Paynes Prairie

Leave Paynes Prairie and turn right on US-441

.3	Left on SE Wacahoota Road
6.3	Right on Williston Road/FL-121
2.4	Keep straight on FL-331 at intersection, still Williston Road
2.2	Intersection of Williston Road and US-441, keep straight on Williston Road *The entrance to Bivens Arm Nature Preserve will be immediately on the left*
2.2	Right on SE Fourth Street, which curves and becomes 22nd Avenue
.9	Right on SE Fifteenth Street/Kincaid Road
1.1	Entrance to the north rim of Paynes Prairie, curve becomes SE 40th Avenue
.9	Left on SE 27th Street
2.1	Right on Hawthorne Road/FL-20
4.0	Right on Rochelle Road/CR-2082
1.2	Right on CR-234 for Micanopy

To Talahasochte

Leave Paynes Prairie and turn right on US-441

.3	Left on SE Wacahoota Road
6.3	Left on Williston Road/FL-121
2.2	Right on CR-346A/SW 137th Avenue
3.8	Right on CR-346/High Street
5.5	Right on US-27/41, University Avenue *Immediate left on Main Street, right at the depot onto Magnolia Street*
.6	Left on FL-24
9.7	Enter Bronson

Suwannee River

Hernando De Soto's army crossed the Suwannee River near Dowling Park on September 23, 1539 and encountered the Apalachee Indians living between the Aucilla and Apalachicola rivers. The Apalachee tribe gave their name to the interior of La Florida and to the mountains beyond. During the early seventeenth century Spanish missions extended in a gentle arc from San Francisco de Potano near Gainesville to Sabacola at the confluence of the Chattahoochee and Flint Rivers. The greatest part of the Indian population of north-central Florida during the seventeenth century lay north and west of the Suwannee River.

The entire region was abandoned at the beginning of the eighteenth century due to repeated attacks by South Carolina and her Indian allies. In 1704 the Apalachee towns were completely destroyed by Colonel James Moore and 1,300 Apalachees were resettled near Augusta. The remaining Apalachees moved to Mobile and sought the protection of the French. The Oconees began moving into north Florida around 1750 and established themselves at Alachua Savannah, but a branch town also settled on the Suwannee River at Old Town. The Suwannee River Oconees later moved to the east side of the river and built Talahasochte. William Bartram visited Talahasochte and Old Town in the summer of 1774. Kolomi Indians moved from southwest Georgia to Old Town in 1778.

Creek Indians moved to the region in even greater numbers during the Second Spanish Period, 1784–1821, as the United States whittled away at their Alabama lands. Old Town became known as Bowlegs Town when the Hitchiti Chief Bowlegs (Istaapaopoya) relocated there from Alachua after the 1814 Patriot War. North Florida became the refuge for Red Sticks defeated during the Creek War of 1813–1814. The Seminoles were pushed southward during the First Seminole War in 1818.

When the United States gained possession of East and West Florida in 1821 Governor Andrew Jackson divided the territory into two counties, Escambia and St. Johns, with the

Spring boil at Manatee Springs State Park

Legend

1. Watermelon Pond
2. Alligator Hole
4. Manatee Springs State Park
3. Andrews WMA
5. Fanning Springs Recreation Area
6. Nature Coast Trail Dixie-Levy-Gilchrist Greenway
7. Suwannee River
8. Old Town
9. Cummer Sanctuary
10. Lower Suwannee River NWR
11. Levy County Campground
12. Cedar Key Scrub State Reserve
13. Waccassassa Bay State Preserve
14. Cedar Key Cedar Key State Museum
15. Cedar Keys NWR
16. Gulf Hammock WMA
17. Big Bend Saltwater Paddling Trail
18. Ichetucknee Springs State Park
19. Santa Fe River
20. Ginnie Springs
21. Poe Springs County Park
22. River Rise State Preserve
23. O'Leno State Park
24. St. Marks Trail

Suwannee River

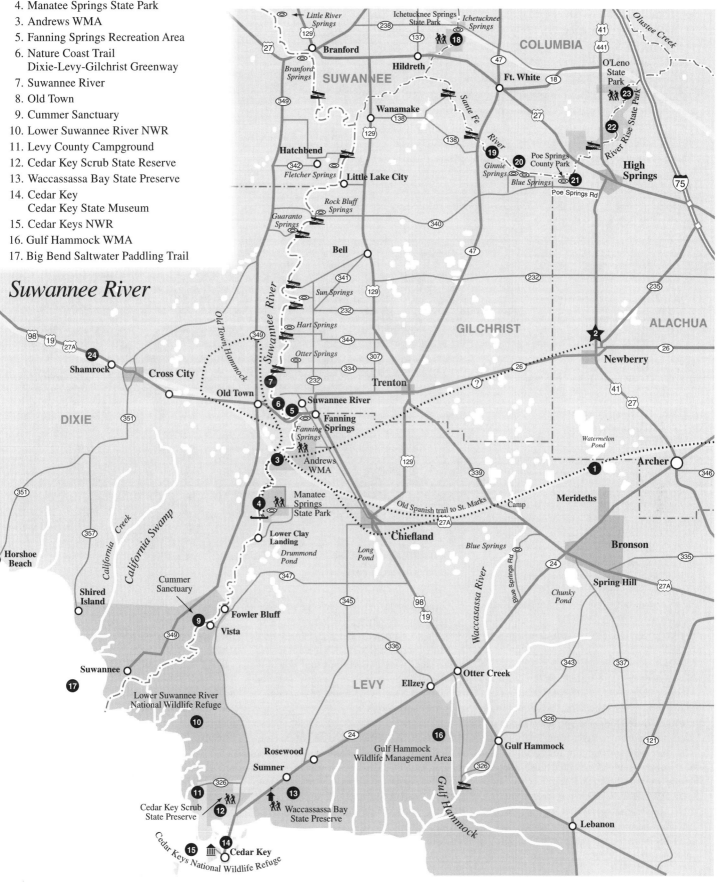

boundary at the Suwannee River. The lower Suwannee River began to be settled by Americans in the 1820s at the close of the First Seminole War and steamboats began plying the river in the 1830s. The Florida Railroad reached Cedar Key in 1861 and provided transportation to Fernandina. John Muir ended his Thousand Mile Walk at Cedar Key in 1867. The lower Suwannee counties remained sparsely populated even late into the twentieth century. The area has become popular in recent decades as a place for weekend homes.

An arc from High Springs to Newberry to Archer encompasses a high, dry sandhill region that marks the ancient western coastline of Florida. This area represents what is known in the Southeast as a wet desert. Plentiful rainfall drains through the deep sand so quickly that only xeric plants can survive. There we find aromatic plants such as juniper and Florida rosemary. This habitat, known as Florida Scrub, is home to endangered fauna such as the scrub jay and gopher tortoise. The geological area Bartram described as limestone riddled by crevasses and holes is called karst.

William Bartram's Travels to the Suwannee River

William Bartram accompanied a delegation of traders to the Suwannee River in June, 1774. Their purpose was to re-establish trade with the town of Talahasochte, although John Stuart had imposed a ban on trade with the Creeks and Seminoles. There are three accounts of this excursion left by Bartram: the *Travels*; the *Report to Dr. Fothergill*; and a letter to Lachlan McIntosh dated July 15, 1774.

The trail from Alachua Savannah to Talahasochte on the Suwannee River has not been identified in modern times but seems to be in a generally straight or gently curving line from the vicinity of Micanopy and Kanapaha Prairie. It later became the Andrew Jackson Highway when Florida became an American territory. There is no lake in the vicinity of Archer today that is named General's Pond. Francis Harper believed that it was the present-day Watermelon Pond.

Sites

1. Watermelon Pond may have been the traders' campsite on their return trip to Alachua when Bartram and his companions visited the Bird Isle. Bartram was awakened that night by the noise of his companions battling a menacing alligator. Follow US 42/27 south from Newberry (north from Archer), turn west on SW 46th Avenue, then left on SW 250th Street to Watermelon Pond and the boat ramp.

2. Alligator Hole (Blue Sink near Newberry). If this was the Alligator Hole visited by Bartram, then it is much farther from Talahasochte than Bartram indicated. Francis Harper explored the area in 1940 and believed that the Blue Sink answered to Bartram's description of the Alligator Hole. There are so many sinks in this part of Florida that we will probably never identify with much assurance the one visited by Bartram.

The historical marker for Bartram's sink is located north of Newberry on US-41/27 and marks nearby Blue Sink, which is privately owned.

Cedar Key Scrub Preserve

4. Manatee Springs State Park is a first magnitude spring and has a beautiful spring run that flows to the Suwannee River. William Bartram visited Manatee Springs on a day trip down the Suwannee River from Talahasochte. The park land surrounding the spring is predominantly hammock and sand hills. Along the spring run and Suwannee River is a cypress swamp. Look for wild pine, *tillandsia setacea*, an epiphyte that grows in clumps on tree branches and is close to its northern limit at Manatee Springs. Manatees visit the springs in winter because the water temperature remains constant throughout the year, providing warmth during cold spells. Bartram saw the skeleton of a manatee there that the Indians had killed and eaten. Manatees are not so common as they were in Bartram's time due to the numbers killed by motor boats and other modern hazards. Open year-round from 8 a.m. to sunset. Admission.

3. Andrews Wildlife Management Area includes one of the largest hardwood hammocks remaining in Florida. Three Florida champion trees live there—persimmon, Florida maple, and bluff oak. Andrews also has two national champions, basswood and winged elm. There are six nature trails in Andrews WMA; maps are available from the information kiosk at the entrance on Levy 211 north of Chiefland.

Talahasochte. The site of the Seminole village Talahasochte is located on the banks of the Suwannee River at Ross Landing within Andrews WMA. The headman of Talahasochte was the White King.

5. Fanning Springs State Recreation Area. This popular recreation area has a nature trail, picnic area, swimming area, and springs. Manatees visit frequently in winter.

6. Nature Coast Trail is a four mile multipurpose trail. It loops the town of Fanning Springs and crosses the Suwannee River on a refurbished railroad trestle. Access is from Fanning Springs State Recreation Area.

Dixie-Levy-Gilchrist Greenway. This work in progress will follow thirty-one miles of the old railroad bed from Cross City to Fanning Springs. From there the trail will fork with one branch going south to Chiefland and the other to Trenton. The ambitious plans include the creation of Fanning Springs Historical Park that will contain a replica of Fort Fanning, a Seminole village, history museum, and education center.

7. Suwannee River. William Bartram spoke of the clarity of the water in the Suwannee River, but that is a rare occurrence. Bartram may have seen the river during a time when the dark water was diluted by an abundance of rain or an increase in the volume of fresh spring water entering the river There are reports that during dry spells, when the water draining from cypress swamps is diminished, clear spring water makes up a greater part of the volume of the Suwannee River and it runs clear.

The Suwannee River rises in the Okefenokee Swamp. It is 235 miles long and is the second largest watershed in Florida. There are eighty springs that discharge fresh water into the Suwannee. The name Suwannee may be derived from the name of an Indian princess or it may be from *sawani*, the Creek word for "echo." It is probably a corruption of San Juanito, the Spanish name for the river. The Timucuans called the Suwannee *Guasaca Esqui*, "River of Reeds." De Soto called it "River of Deer."

There is a great deal of romance connected to the Suwannee River, conjuring up images of exotic plants and tropical birds. Much of this is due to Stephen Foster's song about a river he never saw. He used the Suwannee River in "Old Folks at Home" because the name had the right number of syllables and resonance.

Nearby camping facilities are at Fanning Springs, Guaranto Spring, Gilchrist County Recreational Area, and Otter Springs.

8. Old Town was an earlier site of the Seminole town of Talahasochte before it was moved to the east side of the Suwannee River. Bartram saw the vestiges of the old fields.

9. Cummer Sanctuary. Bottom hardwood forest, pine flatwoods, and sandhill communities owned by the Nature Conservancy. A nature trail is accessible from the parking lot off Vista Camp Road.

10. Lower Suwannee River National Wildlife Refuge was established to protect one of the largest undeveloped river deltas in the country and to provide wildlife habitat in the extensive cypress swamps and estuary. In addition to the 250 species of birds that have been observed in the refuge there are black bears, turkeys, otters, and alligators. The rich and isolated coastal waters are frequently visited by bottlenose dolphins and manatees. Entrances to the refuge are off Levy 347 and at the end of Dixie 357. Camping is not permitted in the refuge but is available at the Levy County Campground and at Shired Island. The hiking trail along the Suwannee River is just south of Fowler's Bluff. The refuge and coastal waters are open year-round, the office is open Monday through Friday from 7:30 a.m.–4 p.m.

11. Levy County Campground. Boat ramp and camping. Located on CR-326.

12. Cedar Key Scrub State Reserve. Although this 4,000-acre preserve contains such diverse habitat as salt marsh and pine flatwoods, it is the Florida Scrub that is most interesting. It protects specially adapted plants and the Florida scrub jay—first described by William Bartram. The Scrub habitat occurs throughout Florida on ancient sea and river dunes of deep, well-drained sand. They are likened to deserts but in truth they should be called humid deserts for there is no lack of rain here. The deep sand allows the rain water to percolate rapidly downward out of reach of roots. Areas of Florida Scrub have been greatly reduced by development and agriculture with few sites remaining that are in their natural state.

Extensive hiking trails at Cedar Key Scrub Reserve give the public an opportunity to explore this fascinating and endangered ecosystem. Animals endemic to the Scrub are the Florida scrub jay and gopher tortoise. Distinctive plants are Florida rosemary, Chapman oak, sand live oak, gopher apple, and staggerbush. Coontie, a native cycad, is easily found in the Reserve, although it is becoming increasingly uncommon throughout Florida. With almost 5,000 acres protected the reserve includes much more than the Scrub—there are salt marshes, islands, and freshwater ponds.

Open during daylight hours, closed during special hunts. Located on FL-347 near Cedar Key. Contact Cedar Key Scrub State Reserve, P.O. Box 187, Cedar Key, FL 32625.

13. Waccassassa Bay State Preserve is primarily undisturbed wetlands accessible only by boat. The pristine salt marsh provides a breeding area for fish and shellfish. Migratory birds have made the preserve an important feeding stop. Red mangrove is at its northern limit in the southern end of Waccassassa Bay Preserve. There are numerous islands scattered through the salt-marsh that give this area its particular beauty. These islands are dominated by typical upland hammock plants—wax myrtle, Southern red cedar, palmetto, live oak, and yaupon. The large amount of publicly owned and preserved habitat in the lower Suwannee River and Gulf Hammock area have made it possible for such mammals as Florida panther, black bear, bobcat, and fox to find a home and prosper. Access by boat is from CR-326 near the town of Gulf Hammock, CR-40A near Yankeetown, and at Cedar Key.

The Waccassassa Bay State Preserve headquarters is on FL-24 between Rosewood and Cedar Key.

14. Cedar Key was settled by people attracted by the industries that extracted the resources of the once extensive Gulf Hammock—cedar for pencils, sabal palm for fiber, pines for turpentine and lumber. The Florida Railroad reached Cedar Key in 1861, bringing economic growth and a connection with the interior of Florida. Until then all goods came and went by sea. Each of the industries declined, first lumbering, then the oyster beds were overworked, larger ships needed deeper ports, and sabal fiber was replaced by plastics.

Cedar Key is unlike other coastal towns in Florida and more like old Florida before the appearance of chain restaurants, high-rise hotels, shopping malls, and retirement villages. Cedar Key is not yet a well-known destination, except for those who have gone out of their way exploring to see what's at the end of the road. Cedar Key is located at the center of an area known as the Nature Coast, so named for the recreational opportunities found in the wildlife management areas, preserves, and sanctuaries rather than in theme parks and water slides.

Cedar Key State Museum depicts the colorful history of Cedar Key from its settlement in the 1840s. The museum contains one of the most complete shell collections in the country. The grounds are landscaped with local native plants—coontie, live oak, sabal palm, sand pine, and wax myrtle.

Cedar Key State Museum is located at 1710 Museum Drive in Cedar Key. Open 9–12 a.m. and 1–5 p.m., closed Tuesday and Wednesday.

15. Cedar Keys National Wildlife Refuge is composed of twelve islands surrounding the town of Cedar Key, including four that are designated National Wilderness Areas. Cedar Keys is one of the largest nesting areas in Florida. The highest elevation on the west coast of Florida is at Seahorse Key where an ancient sand dune rises to fifty-two feet. The interior of the islands are closed to humans, but the beaches are open to the public for exploring. Seahorse Key is closed completely during March and June. Cedar Keys NWR is accessible by boat and prohibited activities includes camping, hunting, pets, fires, and other man-made disturbances.

16. Gulf Hammock Wildlife Management Area is adjacent to Waccassassa Bay State Reserve and serves as a natural buffer to Waccassassa Bay. Gulf Hammock is a corporate-owned and managed forest that allows public access through special agreement with the state. There are numerous dirt roads in the area. Access is from US-98 south of Lebanon Station.

17. Big Bend Saltwater Paddling Trail is the first designated water trail in Florida. It begins at Saint Marks Lighthouse and ends at the Suwannee River. The Big Bend is Florida's least developed coastal area. It extends from the Suwannee River to Saint Marks and receives fewer storms and less rough water than other parts of the Gulf Coast. This region is sparsely populated and abounds in wildlife that take advantage of the extensive salt marshes and tidal creeks of the Big Bend Aquatic Preserve.

Information concerning access points, camping, and maps are available from the Florida Department of Environmental Protection, Office of Greenways and Trails, 325 John Knox Road, Woodcrest Office Park, Building 500, Tallahassee, FL 32303. (904) 488–3701.

18. Ichetucknee Springs State Park is a 2,241-acre recreation area with a variety of habitats—sand hills, hammocks, river swamp, and nine springs. Ichetucknee Springs was designated a National Natural Landmark in 1972 and is a first magnitude spring. There are ruins of a Spanish mission at Mission Springs and Native Americans left sand mounds in the area. Limpkins may be seen in the park feeding on apple snails. This bird was first described by William Bartram and is not nearly so common as it once was due to loss of habitat and a decrease in the population of the apple snails, an indication of decreased water quality across Florida.

Ichetucknee is a day-use area that offers canoe access to the Ichetucknee River, picnicking, and nature trails. Located four miles northwest of Fort White, follow FL-47 then FL-238. Open 8 a.m.–sunset everyday.

19. Santa Fe River arises from Santa Fe Lake and forms the northern border of Alachua County. It is canoeable from O'Leno State Park.

20. Ginnie Springs is a commercial recreation resort that has nature trails and canoe access to the Santa Fe River. It is a popular cave-diving destination. Ginnie Springs has great appeal for families with its variety of facilities—playground, picnic pavilion, grills, RV campsites, and swimming area.

21. Poe Springs County Park has a nature trail, boat access to the Santa Fe River, picnic area, and swimming. Poe Springs is the largest spring in Alachua County and has been a popular retreat since the turn of the century. Poe Springs Park consists of 197 acres with two springs and bluffs on the Santa Fe River. Located three miles west of High Springs on Alachua 340. Open 8 a.m.–sunset. Admission.

22. River Rise State Preserve is a unit of Open Lands Florida which provides public access to significant natural areas, though not developed as a park or recreation area. River Rise Preserve is contiguous to O'Leno State Park, where visitors may obtain information and pay user fees. Access is from US-441 north of High Springs.

23. O'Leno State Park is the site of the dead town of Leno and has hiking trails to the river sink, where the Santa Fe River disappears underground. One trail crosses the river on a suspension bridge; another trail loops a limestone outcrop. O'Leno State Park, like many parks and preserves in this area of Florida, contains several distinct ecological habitats which include sinkholes, hardwood hammocks, riverine swamp, and sand hills. The historic Bellamy Road (c. 1826) passes through the park. O'Leno is a full-service park with camping and equipped cabins. Enter from US-441 six miles north of High Springs. Admission.

24. Saint Marks Trail was established by the Spanish in the seventeenth century to connect Saint Marks to Saint Augustine.

Counties

Dixie County was created in 1921 and is named for the Old South.

Gilchrist County was created in 1925 and was the last county created in Florida. It is named for Albert W. Gilchrist, the twentieth governor of Florida.

Levy County was created in 1845 and named for David Levy Yulee, the first United States senator from Florida, president of the Florida Railroad, and owner of a large plantation on the Homosassa River.

Itinerary

Miles	Directions
	Begin in Archer and travel west on FL-24 to Bronson
9.7	Right on Hathaway Avenue (US-27A) in Bronson
13.1	Left on FL-345 South (SE Fourth Avenue)
1.2	Right on SW First Street in Chiefland, which becomes NW Twelfth Drive and parallels the Seaboard Coast Line tracks
1.8	Left for Manatee Springs State Park on Manatee Springs Road (FL-320)
7.3	Enter Manatee Springs State Park return to Twelfth Drive (CR-207) and turn left *CR-207 is intermittently dirt and becomes Old Fanning Road*
5.3	Left on NW 160th Street/River Landing Road for Andrews WMA (turn at the concrete plant)
2.0	Right on Suwannee River Road
.2	Arrive at the Suwannee River
	The town of Talahasochte was in this section of Andrews WMA
	The Bartram historical marker for the Blue Sink is 1.4 mile north of Newberry on US-27/42, Newberry is twenty-four miles from Fanning Springs

14

Charleston

The coast of Charleston County between the Cooper and Santee rivers was inhabited by Sewee Indians in the seventeenth century. The Cusabos lived between the Cooper and Savannah rivers and comprised a half-dozen component tribes. The Sewees spoke a Siouan language and the Etiwans on the Cooper River spoke a Muskhogean language. It is unclear whether the Cusabos were related to the Muscogees or Hitchitis. The first contact between the native people and Europeans came when Francisco Gordillo, sailing for Lucas Vásquez de Ayllôn, explored the coast of South Carolina in 1521. Somewhere between Charleston Harbor and Winyah Bay, Gordillo's crew lured a group of Indians aboard ship, then hoisted anchor and sailed to Santo Domingo where the captives were sold as slaves. Ayllôn interceded with Governor Diego Columbus to have the slaves freed. Among those unfortunates was a young Indian who was christened and named Francisco. He told Ayllôn of his native home of Chicora, which became the Spanish name of the province north of Santa Elena. The Spanish name for Charleston Harbor was San Jorge.

Because the coastal tribes were less organized and weaker than inland tribes, they welcomed the protection of the English and the manufactured goods they could provide, especially guns. The Kiawahs lived on the coast near present-day Charleston and it was their cacique who urged the English to settle on the Kiawah River (Ashley River) rather than at Port Royal. Coastal tribes were in decline when the English arrived due to disease brought by the French and Spanish. They continued to decline from smallpox, alcohol, and economic subservience to the English. English slave traders fostered enmity between tribes because the resulting wars provided them with a supply of captives for the slave trade.

In early Charleston it was the custom for successful whites to retain an Indian to supply the household with wild game. The Indian was paid in goods and powder and received status from this wealth. South Carolinians began preying on weak tribes and enemies of their Indian allies as a source for slaves, and an Indian slave trade flourished during the first half-century of the colony. Captured Indian women were sold to white landowners, because they were accustomed to working in the fields, and the men were executed or shipped to the Caribbean sugar cane

Early morning on the Battery

135

A Map of South Carolina, *c. 1779*, after Henry Mouzon
Courtesy of the Hargrett Rare Book & Manuscript Library/University of Georgia

Colonial garden at Magnolia Gardens, this small enclosed garden is thought to be the oldest formal garden in America, dating from the very early 1700s

plantations or to New England. Many characteristics of Southern cooking and gardening formed during the time when Indians, Africans, and whites intermingled on the frontier plantations. Trade in Indian slaves subsided when African slaves became readily available.

Colonization

The first English attempt at settling the region south of Virginia was in a grant of land to Sir Robert Heath in 1629. He named the grant Carolana in honor of Charles I of England and it lay between parallel 31° to 36° latitude. The success of the Virginia, Maryland, and Massachusetts colonies diverted settlers, money, and energy away from the southern venture and the English civil war disrupted further efforts at colonization until the Restoration of Charles II to the throne. During the Cromwell years following the war, English exploration and colonization efforts had languished, and Charles hoped to spur new interest in North America by crating a new colony. The Lords Proprietors were a group of men who supported Charles II in his return to the throne of Britain and were rewarded with the Heath grant in 1663. They honored the king by Latinizing his name and calling the new colony Carolina. The Carolina colony originally included present North and South Carolina and was governed from London by the Lords Proprietors.

William Hilton explored the coast of Carolina in 1663, searching for suitable land for a company of New Englanders who were desirous of moving south. Hilton later explored the Port Royal area for the benefit of Peter Colleton and the Company of Barbadian Adventurers, who were also seeking new opportunities.

William Yeamans, working with another group of Barbadians, made an agreement with the Lords Proprietors in 1665 for a settlement at Port Royal. Robert Sanford made the first exploratory voyage in June 1666, searching for a suitable site at Port Royal. However, the Lords Proprietors were slow to provide support for the colony and it was several years before a settlement was attempted.

The surgeon sailing with Sanford was Dr. Henry Woodward who chose to remain behind when the ship sailed so that he might learn the native language. Woodward not only learned to communicate with the Carolina tribes, he became the first and most influential English trader south of Albemarle Sound. Woodward traveled through the upper part of South Carolina and as far as the Chattahoochee River establishing alliances and trade relations. He became the nemesis of the Spanish in Saint Augustine, who saw their influence in the Savannah and Chattahoochee river valleys waning.

The colony of Carolina was finally realized when the Lords Proprietors were galvanized to action by the energy of Lord Anthony Ashley Cooper, soon to be the first Lord Shaftesbury. The colony became his pet project and due to his efforts money and arrangements were made to send the first colonists to Port Royal. In August 1669, three ships and a hundred colonists left England and sailed for Barbados where they were joined by their governor, William Sayle. They then sailed for Carolina and reached Port Royal in March 1670. The Cacique of Kiawah was visiting the area and persuaded the English to choose a place farther north. The people of Kiawah, being harassed by the Westoes, desired the protection of the English.

Ninety-three English colonists arrived on the *Carolina* in April 1670, at Albemarle Point, known today as Charles Towne Landing. Another ship, the *Port Royal,* was wrecked in Bermuda. The *Three Brothers* was blown off course and landed in Virginia, eventually reaching Carolina at the end of May. Among the settlers were twenty-nine masters and sixty-three indentured servants. The colonists carried with them the Fundamental Constitutions of Carolina, the document of government created by Lord Anthony Ashley Cooper and John Locke. The most important clause of the constitution was the guarantee of religious freedom, a feature that was to figure in the colony's success at attracting settlers.

During the first year many colonists became sick while adjusting to the hot, humid climate. The Spanish appeared in the harbor, intent on dispersing the settlement, but were driven away by a storm. With such an inauspicious beginning no one would have thought that fifty years later Charleston would be one of North America's premier cities and the Queen City of the South.

In 1679 the Lords Proprietors instructed the Carolinians to lay out a town at White Point and move the offices of government across the river to the new site of Charles Towne. The advantages of the new location were pleasant ocean breezes, a good harbor, and high, healthy land that was easily fortified. By the turn of the century defensive walls and bastions had been built around the city, making Charleston one of only two walled cities in America.

A policy of religious tolerance attracted new immigrants to South Carolina and the Proprietors began advertising this advantage

South Carolina Population

	1685	1775	2000
Indian	10,000	500	13,718
White	1,400	71,600	2,695,560
Black	500	107,300	1,185,216
Hispanic			95,076
Asian			36,014

Source: Charleston Museum exhibit and U.S. Census Bureau.

Saint Andrews Parish Church, 1706

more widely. The first group of French Protestants, or Huguenots, arrived in April 1680. When in 1685 Louis XIV revoked the Edict of Nantes, which guaranteed freedom of worship to French Protestants, many Huguenots left their homeland for Charleston.

Charleston's population was augmented by Barbadian planters looking for new land and an escape from their overcrowded island. The families of Barbados were mostly from the upper classes of England, expatriate Royalists, and Parliamentarians who fled during the Cromwell years. In Carolina they fully expected to receive all the rights due them as Englishmen of the ruling class. The Barbadian settlers could easily pay their own way, which relieved the Lords Proprietors of the burden of dipping into their own purses. Among the Barbadian Adventurers were Edward Middleton, Thomas Drayton, and Robert Daniel. The aristocratic Barbadians soon dominated the government and society of Carolina. They were bon vivants, independent, ostentatious, Anglican, and imperialistic. These were all characteristics that became associated with the Lowcountry aristocracy of the Southeast. They were aggressive in business affairs and intended to be rich even if it meant using slave labor or trading with pirates.

The Fundamental Constitutions drafted by Cooper and Locke organized government around an elite society based on property. Like Parliament it was a balance between democratic, popular society and an aristocratic society. The largest tracts of land, baronies of 12,000 acres, were granted to landgraves and caciques. Precincts of 12,000 acres were set aside to divide among commoners. Only property owners could vote and eligibility for office was dependent on the size of a man's estate. Although it was never adopted in full the concept of government by the largest landowners was attractive to those who would benefit by such an arrangement. In 1682 the Proprietors amended the Constitution to increase the power of the Assembly and allow that body to create landgraves. It also allowed that land could be purchased outright rather than obtained through quit rents.

In the same year the southern part of Carolina was divided into three counties. Berkeley included Charles Town and had boundaries from Sewee on the northeast to Stono River on the southwest and thirty-five miles inland from the coast. Colleton County lay south of Berkeley and occupied the section between Stono River to Combahee River and thirty-five miles inland. Craven County was bounded on the southwest by Sewee River, then twenty-three miles along the coast and in a straight line thirty-five miles northwest inland. Granville County was later created between the Combahee and Savannah rivers. The Church Acts of 1704 and 1706 established ten parishes and designated that a church be built in each using public funds.

Within thirty years of its founding Charleston had a population of 2,000 and was a bustling seaport shipping deerskins, lumber, tar, beef, pork, rice, and Indian slaves. Growth continued despite the fact the city was fast gaining a reputation as an unhealthy place for Europeans. From the summer of 1697 to the winter of 1699 Charleston experienced an epidemic of smallpox, an earthquake, a devastating fire, an epidemic of yellow fever, and a hurricane. At the beginning of the eighteenth century Charleston was still a frontier town with Indians and sailors roaming the streets, deer and bobcats north of Broad Street, and drinking was the favorite entertainment.

The fortunes made by the wealthy families of Charleston bred a local aristocracy. At the beginning of the eighteenth century the Goose Creek Faction, allied with their neighboring Huguenots, gained control of the government. In 1704 they passed a law establishing the Church of England as the official church of South Carolina and restricted public office to Anglicans. Although the law was disallowed in 1706 the Church of England did become the official church. Although other religions were allowed freedom of worship and the right to hold office, only the Church of England was financially supported by public funds. The spirit of religious tolerance attracted many people to South Carolina where Anglicans, Anabaptists, Presbyterians, Huguenots, Jews, Congregationalists, and Quakers found a home. The number and variety of churches has earned Charleston the nickname of *Holy City*.

The early history of South Carolina is defined by trade and relations with the native population. For many years Carolina hugged the coast where small tribes were soon displaced or destroyed by disease. The interior of the colony was dominated by larger and more aggressive tribes. The easy profits and lack of regulations among the traders lead to abuses that came to anger the Indians.

On April 15, 1715, the Yamassees attacked settlements in present-day Beaufort County, killing nearly a hundred people including trader Thomas Nairne. The Yamassees were soon joined by Creeks, Choctaws, and Catawbas. Charleston could muster less than a thousand militiamen and was saved only by the entry of the Cherokees into the war in early 1716 as allies of the Carolinians. At the end of the war the countryside beyond the

---

The Lords Proprietors

Anthony Ashley Cooper, *First Earl of Shaftesbury, Lord High Chancellor,* and author of the Habeas Corpus Act

General George Monk, *Duke of Albemarle*

Edward Hyde, *Earl of Clarendon*

John Berkeley, *Baron of Stratton*

Sir William Berkeley, *governor of Virginia*

William, *Earl of Craven*

Sir George Carteret

Sir John Colleton, *planter of Barbados*

Indigo

The dye that is familiar to all Americans as the blue in blue jeans was historically derived from the indigo plant native to India. The deep blue dye has been a valued trade product for thousands of years. The varieties of *Indigofera* grown in the South were *tinctoria* and *anil* and the first indigo was grown as early as 1622 in Virginia. Eliza Lucas experimented with indigo seed sent to her by her father George Lucas, governor of Antigua, and she succeeded in producing a top-quality crop in 1742. By 1744 she had enough seed to distribute to her neighbors.

Indigo became an important cash crop because it could be grown where rice could not. Production rose from just six pounds shipped by Eliza and Judge Charles Pinckney in 1744 to 216,000 pounds in 1750. In 1770 shipments to England reached a million pounds annually. Indigo reached the price of a dollar a pound and was as good as cash in Georgetown. Parliament offered a bounty on American indigo to encourage production in British colonies. Indigo lost its importance in the South Carolina economy when the bounty was lost during the Revolution and Britain turned to India for her supply.

Indigo seed was planted soon after the last frost in early March and was cut once in early July and again in August when the plants were in bloom. Cut indigo was handled carefully so as not to remove the powdery coating on the leaves. The plants were placed in vats of water and allowed to ferment. The liquid was drained into another vat and beaten until it foamed. Lime water was added to precipitate the solid matter. The "indigo mud" was turned into cloth bags and allowed to dry to a paste. The paste was spread out to dry further before being cut into bricks.

Though natural indigo dye was replaced by chemical dyes in the late nineteenth century, interest in natural dyes is increasing because their manufacture and use is often less harmful to the environment.

---

walls of Charleston lay devastated and abandoned. Over four hundred Carolinians had lost their lives.

The Catawbas, a large group of Siouxian-speaking people, occupied the region of the upper Catawba River. Although they joined with the Yamassees in war they afterward became the most constant allies to the Carolinians but were greatly weakened by European diseases. They were one of the few Indian tribes to side with the Americans during the Revolution. South Carolina set aside a reservation of fifteen miles square for the Catawbas in 1763. The Catawba Reservation today has been reduced in size and is located on the upper Catawba River near Rock Hill.

In 1718 piracy on the Southeastern coast reached its peak when Edward Teach, also known as Blackbeard, blockaded Charleston Harbor and took hostages from the city. His ransom was nothing more than several chests of medicine. The indignant and exasperated merchants of Charleston outfitted two ships under the command of William Rhett and pursued the pirates. Although Teach eluded them the gentleman pirate Stede Bonnet was captured at Cape Fear and brought to Charleston for trial. He soon escaped, possibly with the help of local citizens who would be embarrassed by his testimony. Pirates again appeared at Charleston's harbor but this time the governor and volunteers met them with four armed merchant vessels and overwhelmed them in a four-hour battle at sea. Bonnet was recaptured on Sullivan's Island and was hung that fall at White Point. In all forty-nine pirates were captured, tried, and hung. They were buried below the high tide line at White Point where their bones are now covered by the stately homes of the Battery.

In 1719 the Carolinians, dissatisfied with the Proprietary government's inability to provide protection and support, asked that the Crown take control of the colony. The Carolinians had come to realize that they had only themselves to rely upon and they therefore intended to govern themselves. They declared themselves independent of control by the Proprietors and declared the Assembly to be the legitimate government of Carolina. Governor Robert Johnson opposed the new government so the Assembly elected General James Moore, Jr., as acting governor. Johnson returned to England and thus ended the first revolution in South Carolina. General Francis Nicholson became the first royal governor in 1721.

The rise of rice cultivation on the coast of South Carolina created a large demand for African slaves. By 1720 the population of blacks surpassed that of whites in South Carolina. Fears of an insurrection became real on September 9, 1739, when slaves on plantations along the Stono River revolted. They battled with the South Carolina militia at Parkers Ferry on the Edisto River and were defeated. The Assembly passed the Negro Act in 1740 that severely restricted freedom of movement for slaves. Laws making it a crime to teach slaves to read and write endeavored to keep blacks culturally as well as physically enslaved. The Stono Rebellion was the largest slave revolt in Colonial America.

As the upper parts of South Carolina began to be settled the Charlestonians were unwilling to give up power and were reluctant to tax themselves. At times bread might be taxed in South Carolina but not slaves. All government and legal affairs had to be transacted in Charleston, which presented a great hardship for poor Piedmont farmers. The Regulator Movement grew out of the frustration with the coastal gentry's hold on power and their unwillingness to allow courts and representation in the backcountry.

Revolution comes to South Carolina

One of the circumstances that aggravated the tensions between Parliament and the American colonies was the general ineptness and pettiness of the royal governors. Often the governors and assembly clashed over the question of who held ultimate power and the governors did not hesitate to exercise their prerogative to dissolve the assembly if things did not go their way. In South Carolina the governors prior to the Revolution were unable or unwilling to work with their assemblies. This had been a problem since the founding of the colony because of the power and influence of the independent-minded Barbadians. When Governor Lyttleton dismissed William Wragg from the Governor's Council it became a point of honor for native Carolinians to refuse a seat on the council. It was filled instead with men selected by the king, many of whom remained loyal during the Revolution. The Governor's Council therefore lost real power and legitimacy as a governing body. In 1760 Governor Lyttleton mishandled Cherokee diplomacy so badly that it lead to war and created new controversies.

Thomas Boone dissolved the assembly in 1762 because he disagreed with the method of election for the representatives. The assembly members then refused to interact with the governor and excluded his salary from the budget. Boone was replaced with native son, Lieutenant Governor William Bull.

The Stamp Act of 1765 and the Townshend Acts of 1768 galvanized the quest for American, or rather Carolinian, rights in Charleston. The patriot cause divided into two camps. The radical element was represented by the city's craftsmen, Christopher Gadsden, Thomas Lynch, Rawlins Lowndes, John and Edward Rutledge, and James Parsons. The conservative element included very wealthy merchants and planters—Henry Laurens, William Henry Drayton, Charles Pinckney, William Wragg, and Peter Manigault. It must be noted that, although their means differed, their goals were the same.

Governor Lord Charles Montagu dissolved the Assembly in 1768 because that body resolved to correspond with the other colonies in an effort to have the Townshend Acts rescinded. Citizens met outside the halls of legislature and formed a committee to promote the nonimportation of British goods until the Townshend Acts were removed. One resolution called for non-signers of the nonimportation agreement to be regarded as unfriendly to the cause of American rights and boycotted as well.

Parliament's *Additional Instruction* to Governor Bull on April 14, 1770 declared that the South Carolina Commons House of Assembly did not have sole authority to raise taxes. It further declared that no funds could be appropriated without the consent of the governor and Council. This last instruction was in response to a gift of public money for the defense of John Wilkes and the right to freedom of speech. King George's attempt to reassert the royal prerogative aggravated the strained relationship between the colonies and Parliament, though many continued to profess loyalty to the king down to the opening shots of the war.

In 1772 Governor Montagu moved the Assembly to Beaufort in the hopes of diluting the power of his Charleston opposition, but this affront propelled them to new levels of energy and attendance remained high. Having failed in his scheme Montagu dissolved the assembly and moved it back to Charleston. In 1773 the Commons House of Assembly declared that the Governor's Council had no legislative authority.

The delegates to the First Continental Congress were Henry Middleton, John Rutledge, Edward Rutledge, Thomas Lynch, and Christopher Gadsden. Henry Middleton was chosen president of Congress in October 1774. On January 11, 1775 the First Provincial Congress of South Carolina was convened at the Old Exchange. That spring rumors reached Charleston that the British were inciting the Cherokees to attack the frontier settlements. Superintendent John Stuart was accused of sedition and fled first to Tybee Island then to Saint Augustine. That summer South Carolina got a new governor, Lord William Campbell, who was married to Sarah Izard of Charleston. With the news of fighting in Massachusetts came news that reinforcements for the British Army were enroute to the colonies. The South Carolina militia seized the gunpowder and artillery at Fort Johnson. The infant

Legend

1. Edisto River Canoe and Kayak Trail
2. Willtown
3. ACE Basin National Wildlife Refuge
4. Edisto Island
5. Edisto Beach State Park
6. Savannah Highway
7. Dungannon Plantation
8. Deveaux Bank Heritage Preserve
9. Beachwalker County Park
10. Charleston Tea Plantation
11. Angel Oak Park
12. Bird Key-Stono Heritage Preserve
13. Folly Beach County Park
14. Grave of Sammy Smalls, Porgy
15. Fort Johnson
16. James Island County Park
17. Wappoo Cut
18. Eliza Lucas Pinckney
19. Clemson University Urban Research and Demonstration Center
20. Clemson University Coastal Research & Education Center & USDA Vegetable Laboratory
21. USDA Center for Forested Wetlands Research, Southeast Forest Experiment Station
22. Charles Towne Landing
23. Ashley River
24. Saint Andrews Parish Church
25. Colonel William Washington
26. Drayton Hall
27. Magnolia Gardens & Audubon Swamp
28. Middleton Place
29. Ten Mile
30. Michaux's Garden
31. General William Moultrie
32. Otranto
33. Ralph Izard Wannamaker Park
34. Saint James Goose Creek Parish Church
35. Goose Creek
36. Thorogood
37. Old Dorchester State Park
38. Summerville
39. Edisto Indian Tribe
40. Cooper River Rice Plantations
41. Cainhoy
42. Palmetto Islands County Park
43. Boone Hall
44. Snee Farm, Charles Pinckney National Historic Site
45. Christ Episcopal Church
46. Sweetgrass Basket Stands
47. Mount Pleasant Museum on the Common Shem Creek Maritime Museum
48. Sullivan's Island Fort Moultrie
49. Fort Sumter National Monument

South Carolina and Georgia navies seized ships carrying gunpowder and appropriated it for their militias. South Carolina was now at war with England.

The Commons House of Assembly last met on August 28, 1775. When Governor Campbell fled Charleston, on September 15 the Second Provincial Congress became the legislative body of South Carolina with the Council of Safety acting as an executive committee.

In March 1776, the Provincial Congress of South Carolina drafted a constitution and established the General Assembly. The Assembly elected John Rutledge president, Henry Laurens vice-president, and William Henry Drayton chief justice of South Carolina. Even then many members still hoped that reconciliation with Parliament might be brokered.

In June 1776, Commodore Peter Parker anchored at Five Fathom Hole in Charleston Harbor. With Parker sailed Sir Henry Clinton, Lord Cornwallis, and British troops. Clinton offered a pardon for all who would renew allegiance to the king. Rather than capitulate, the militia in South Carolina was mobilized to protect Charleston against an invasion. On June 28 the bombardment of Sullivan's Island fort commenced but accomplished little. The British force then unsuccessfully attacked Fort Moultrie. Meanwhile in Philadelphia the Continental Congress was preparing the Declaration of Independence. Signers for South Carolina were Thomas Heyward, Jr., Thomas Lynch, Jr., Arthur Middleton, and Edward Rutledge.

The winter of 1780 found Lord Cornwallis and Sir Henry Clinton again in Charleston. Having failed to decisively win the northern colonies they turned their attention to the southern colonies where there was a much larger proportion of loyalists and sympathizers.

The Fall of Charleston

The British hoped to regain the Southern colonies with a large military presence and organized loyalist governments. It was believed that patriot resistance would wither with time since only a third of the population were ardent patriots. The British fleet arrived at Charleston in early February 1780 and blockaded the harbor. They fortified James Island, entered Charleston Harbor, and began a bombardment that lasted two months. As the situation worsened Governor Rutledge and the council escaped to Jacksonborough. On April 13 the British, having completed the encirclement of Charleston, unleashed a devastating barrage upon the city.

General Benjamin Lincoln, not one to make hasty decisions, hesitated to evacuate the Continental Army until all avenues had been closed. Lincoln sent his terms of surrender and evacuation to General Henry Clinton, which were rejected. In light of the desperate nature of the American position Clinton demanded complete surrender. When Fort Moultrie was surrendered on May 5 any hope that remained with the Americans evaporated. Lincoln capitulated and surrendered on May 12.

Prominent citizens were arrested and required to sign an Oath of Loyalty to the king in order to obtain parole. Military officers were sent to prison ships and government officials were sent to Saint Augustine. Henry Laurens was captured at sea enroute to the Netherlands in September 1780 and imprisoned in the Tower of London. He was exchanged for Lord Cornwallis and released on December 31, 1781.

Believing the end of resistance had arrived many American soldiers chose parole and signed the Oath of Loyalty. Among the signers of the Oath were Andrew Pickens and Andrew Williamson. When Clinton required that paroled Rebels take up arms for the king and join the loyalist militia, Pickens and others returned to the patriot cause but Williamson adhered to his oath and became a loyalist. Francis Marion, recuperating at his home on the Santee River, escaped being captured and continued to harass the British from his hideouts in Hell Hole Bay, Four Holes Swamp, and the swamps near Georgetown. Thomas Sumter did the same in the Upcountry.

On August 4, 1781, Colonel Isaac Hayne was hanged in Charleston for violating his parole. The order to hang captured rebels and a requirement that paroled soldiers fight for the Crown galvanized new resistance among the patriots and radicalized many moderates and neutrals. Renewed patriot resistance in the Upcountry of South Carolina and victories at Cowpens and King's Mountain brought General Nathanael Greene into control of much of the interior of the state. With Cornwallis in pursuit of Greene through North Carolina and Virginia, the British garrison at Charleston was virtually imprisoned within the city. The British force left Charleston on December 14, 1782, six months after Parliament voted to end the war. The delay was due to the necessity of evacuating more than 9,000 loyalists.

South Carolinians quickly resurrected their government, but the Lowcountry aristocracy had lost their position of power. The inland patriots rightly expected increased representation in government and equal treatment in the application of laws. The Assembly elected to move the capital to the center of the state, a move that was resisted by many of the powerful Lowcountry representatives. The controversy was finally decided in 1788 when a fire destroyed the State House in Charleston and the city of Columbia was laid out as the new capital.

Charleston continued to prosper as a port for exporting rice and sea island cotton and magnificent fortunes were made. In the 1830s local businessmen invested in the nation's first railroad in an attempt to draw the cotton business to Charleston and away from Savannah. As population spread out away from the coast and railroads brought cargo to other seaports, Charleston went into a period of economic decline just prior to the Civil War though it continued to be a cultural center.

John Bartram in Charleston

John Bartram first visited Charleston in the spring of 1760. He was again in Charleston in July 1765 as he embarked on his expedition to Georgia and Florida. He arrived in Charleston on July 7 and went straightway to the home of Dr. Alexander Garden. In the evening he visited Mr. Hopton and Colonel Henry Laurens at their homes near Charleston. The next day he visited the Lambolls, with whom he was a friend and correspondent. He accompanied Dr. Garden up the Charleston Neck and stopped at Windsor Hill, the home of General William Moultrie (then a major). On July 9 Bartram rode with John Deas about his plantation at Thorogood to view the indigo and corn fields.

On July 14 Bartram accompanied Mr. Hopton to his plantation called Starved Gut Hall on the Wando River. He left that day for the Cape Fear River to get William, who would accompany him to Florida. They returned to Charleston in mid-August and departed for Florida a week later.

William Bartram's Travels in Charleston

William Bartram arrived in Charleston on March 31, 1773. During the next ten days he visited Dr. Lionel Chalmers and Colonel John Stuart, Superintendent for Indian Affairs. William left by ship for Savannah on April 11 or 12. Ships sailed close to shore, keeping land in sight, so Bartram would have seen the South Carolina sea Islands. He returned to Charleston on March 25, 1775, aboard one of Henry Laurens' boats. He stayed with Mary Lamboll Thomas while he prepared his collections for shipping.

After consulting with the learned citizens of Charleston, William decided it was time to visit the Cherokee Nation. Bartram's advisors must have included Henry Laurens, Lionel Chalmers, and Dr. Alexander Garden. Bartram left Charleston on April 22, 1775 for the Cherokee Nation. He traveled up Charleston Neck along Dorchester Road and crossed the Ashley River just below Drayton Hall. He traveled west on Bees Ferry Road and Savannah Road. Bartram returned to Charleston in late November 1776 over the same road and again stayed with Mary Thomas. When he began his journey home to Philadelphia in December 1776 Bartram traveled up Charleston Neck and crossed the Cooper River to Daniel Island. He followed Clements Ferry Road and Dickerson Road along the north side of Wando River.

Sites

1. Edisto River Canoe and Kayak Trail. The Edisto River is one of the premier blackwater rivers in America. Much of its length is undeveloped and unpopulated. The beginning of the designated trail is at US-21 near the Bamberg-Colleton county line and ends at Givhans Ferry. Another access point is Colleton State Park at the midway point. Information is available from any of the state parks located near the river or from the Edisto River Canoe and Kayak Trail Commission, PO Box 1763, Walterboro, SC 29488.

2. Willtown. John and William Bartram strayed from the Savannah Road when they traveled through the Lowcountry in 1765 and found themselves at Willtown, where they spent the night in the corn crib at a local plantation. Willtown was settled in the late 1600s as South Carolina's second city and first Indian trading post. In 1715 Willtown became an early target in the Yamassee War. At one time Willtown contained approximately eighty structures but fell into decline by the middle of the eighteenth century. The property was then incorporated into a plantation and is now the site of several private homes. Charleston County maintains a public boat ramp at Willtown Bluff. Visit the Charleston Museum for exhibits on the history and archaeology of Willtown.

3. ACE Basin National Wildlife Refuge consists of two disjunct parcels. The Edisto Unit is located north of the Intracoastal Waterway and east of the Edisto River. The Combahee Unit is north of US-17 on the Combahee River and adjacent to Cuckolds Creek. Both units contain hiking trails and opportunities for fishing and wildlife observation. Entrance to the Edisto Unit is from CR-55 and CR-346. The office for the refuge is in Hollywood.

Grave of Osceola, Fort Moultrie National Historic Site, Sullivan's Island

4. Edisto Island has been inhabited for many thousands of years. It is named for the Kusso (Cusabo) Indian town that occupied the island when the English arrived. The name has also appeared as Edistaw and Edistow. Indigo and rice were grown in the area during the early eighteenth century. At the end of the century sea island cotton became the dominant crop and was of such a superior quality that local legend says French lacemakers contracted for each crop even before it was planted. The Edisto Island Museum contains exhibits on the history of human habitation of the island. The natural history room contains fossils and specimens of local plants and animals. Located on SC-174 on Edisto Island. Open 1–4 p.m., Tuesday, Thursday, and Saturday. Admission.

5. Edisto Beach State Park. This barrier island park contains a large area of salt marsh and beaches. A nature trail leads to Spanish Mount where the second oldest pottery remains in South Carolina have been found. Hiking, camping, kayaking, canoeing, fishing, swimming, picnicking, and boat ramp. Located at the southern end of SC-174 on Edisto Island. Open 6 a.m.–10 p.m. during summer and 8 a.m.–6 p.m. during the rest of the year.

6. US-17 west of Charleston is named **Savannah Highway** and follows closely the colonial road from Charleston to Jacksonborough. Older sections are called Old Jacksonborough Road. This road was opened in the very early 1700s and became part of the King's Road that stretched from Wilmington, North Carolina to New Smyrna, Florida.

7. Dungannon Plantation. This preserve provides a feeding and roosting area for wood storks, great egrets, anhingas, and great blue herons. It is the second largest wood stork rookery in South Carolina. Wood storks were not common in South Carolina until recent years. It is believed they are spreading north from Florida where they have lost habitat to development.

8. Deveaux Bank Heritage Preserve is a shore bird breeding preserve. Closed to visitation from April through August.

9. Beachwalker County Park. Picnic area, showers, restrooms, snack bar, and beach access. Follow Bohicket Road to Kiawah Island. The park is on the right just before the Kiawah Island gate. Hours vary during the season, closed November through March. Admission.

10. Charleston Tea Plantation. America's only tea plantation grows on Johns Island near Rockville. They produce the *American Classic* brand of tea that is organically grown and free of pesticides. The first tea plants (*Camellia sinensis*) grown in America were planted at Middleton Gardens Plantation by André Michaux about 1789. Charleston Tea Plantation is located at 6617 Maybank Highway one mile from Rockville on Wadmalaw Island. Open for visitors at various times during the year.

11. Angel Oak Park. This impressively large live oak is one of the oldest in South Carolina although no one knows just how old it is. If its estimated age of 1,400 years is accurate then the Angel Oak is the oldest living tree east of the Mississippi River. Charleston County purchased the tree and surrounding property in 1991 and opened it as a public park. From US-17 go east on Bohicket Road then right on Angel Oak Road.

12. Bird Key-Stono Heritage Preserve. This small island protects South Carolina's largest brown pelican rookery. Closed to visitation from April through August.

13. Folly Beach County Park. Picnic shelters, bathrooms, parking, and beach access. West end of Ashley Avenue on Folly Beach.

14. Grave of Sammy Smalls, "Porgy." Samuel Smalls, also known as Goat Cart Sammy, was the model for the character of Porgy in Dubose Heyward's novel *Porgy and Bess* and George Gershwin's classic American opera. Smalls lived in the tenements on Cabbage Row, which became Catfish Row in the novel. He was a cripple and well known for his incorrigible nature. He later lived on James Island and is buried at James Island Presbyterian Church on Fort Johnson Road.

15. Fort Johnson occupied the site of an earlier fort at Windmill Point and was constructed in the early 1740s. The ruins of Fort Johnson are near the Marine center buildings. The area is now owned by the College of Charleston and the Medical College of South Carolina. The Marine Biology Research Station complex includes the Marine Biological Laboratory, South Carolina Marine Research Laboratory, and National Fisheries Center.

The first American flag to replace a British flag was raised at Fort Johnson in September 1775. This flag was designed by William Moultrie and held a white crescent on a field of blue. Following the patriot victory at the Battle of Sullivan's Island a palmetto tree was added and the flag was adopted as the state flag of South Carolina. The fort at Sullivan's Island was built of spongy palmetto ramparts filled with sand. British cannon balls could do little damage because they bounced off the palmetto walls and rolled away.

André Michaux

André Michaux, the eminent and indefatigable French botanist, came to America in 1785 in search of beneficial plants for the French government. He especially wanted trees because France had depleted her forests during the wars of the eighteenth century. He found the southern forests held more than twice the species of trees as all of Europe.

Michaux had earlier traveled in Persia in 1782 and 1783 and collected plant specimens to ship to France. Upon his return he was commissioned to travel to America, newly independent of Britain. His instructions stipulated that he gather seeds, establish a nursery near New York, and ship transplants to the Park of Rambouillet near Paris. He arrived in America in 1785 and established his first garden near Hackensack, New Jersey.

In June 1786 Michaux met William Bartram for the first time when he traveled in Pennsylvania and Virginia. Michaux longed to visit the South and on September 21, 1786, he made his first visit to Charleston. He returned in 1787 to establish a second garden near Charleston on 111 acres he purchased near the Ten Mile road marker north of Charleston. This plantation became his headquarters and was known locally as the French Garden. From there he explored Appalachia, Florida, Canada, Kentucky, Ohio, Missouri, and the Bahamas. Exotic species introduced from Michaux's Garden to America were ginkgo, *Ginkgo biloba*; varnish tree, *Firmiana platanifolia*; tallow tree, *Stillingia sebifera*; mimosa, *Albrizzia julibrissin*; crepe myrtle, *Lagerstoremia indica*; and *Camellia Japonica*.

André Michaux was a devoted patriot and welcomed the French Revolution though it meant his financial support became even more tenuous. Upon hearing of the success of the Revolution he sang the *Marseillaise* from a mountain top in North Carolina. Michaux was commissioned by Citizen Genet to explore the western territory, which had once been part of French Louisiana. Michaux's trip west of the Appalachians in the summer of 1793 was cut short by Genet's censure by President Washington and Congress. Michaux continued to travel at his own expense and returned to France in 1796 nearly bankrupt.

Michaux was shipwrecked off the coast of Holland and lost several journals, but his collections were saved and are preserved today in the Museum National D'Histoire Naturelle, Laboratore de Phanerogamie in Paris. The new Republican French government would not finance a return to America. Michaux was sent instead to the East Indies and died on Madagasgar on November 13, 1802 of a sudden illness.

André Michaux is credited with teaching the Appalachian settlers the value of ginseng and how to prepare it for the Chinese market. He is considered the authority on twenty-six genera and 188 species of plants. His best-known discovery in South Carolina was Oconee bells, *Shortia galacifolia,* on the upper Keowee River.

Michaux's son and traveling companion, François, was wounded in an eye by a stray bullet in 1789 and sent back to France for medical care. He returned to America in 1802 after his father's death to dispose of the properties in New Jersey, Charleston, and in upstate South Carolina. François traveled through the new states west of the Appalachians and completed the work started by his father, *The North American Sylva*. He visited William Bartram at Philadelphia and was a houseguest for several weeks. François was one of two paying passengers on the first run of Robert Fulton's steamboat during a trip to New York.

François Michaux donated his father's journals to the American Philosophical Society. The journals were published in French in 1889.

16. James Island County Park. Shelters, fishing, camping, nature trails, cottage rentals, canoe and kayak rentals. Located on Riverland Drive, off Maybank Highway. Open at 8 a.m. and closes at various times during the year. Admission.

17. Wappoo Cut was authorized by the Governor's Council in 1712. It connected Stono River with Wappoo Creek, thus providing inland navigation for the planters. Wappoo Cut was dug ten-feet wide and six-feet deep. Other cuts were built along the coast south of Charleston and were a precursor to the Intracoastal Waterway.

18. Eliza Lucas Pinckney (1722–1793). Eliza Lucas ran her father's plantation on Wappoo Creek when she was only seventeen. About 1740 she began experimenting with indigo cultivation and perfected a method for making the dye. She learned much about the rendering of indigo dye from her neighbor André DeVeaux. Eliza promoted the indigo industry by freely giving away seeds and growing information to coastal planters.

Eliza Lucas married Charles Pinckney and moved with him to London when he became South Carolina's agent. When Charles died Eliza ran Belmont Plantation until it was destroyed during the Revolution. Belmont was located between Charleston and North Charleston in the narrowest section of the Neck. Their daughter, Harriott, married Colonel Daniel Horry and became mistress of Hampton Plantation on the Santee River. George Washington detoured from the Old Georgetown Road on May 1, 1791 to breakfast at Hampton. He was certainly compelled by the prospect of keeping company with the sophisticated Eliza Pinckney, a brilliant conversationalist, and his desire to offer an office to one of her sons. Eliza and Washington became friends and he served as a pallbearer at her funeral. She died on May 16, 1793 in Philadelphia where she had gone for medical care and is buried at St. Peter's Church.

Eliza's son Thomas became the first American minister to Great Britain after the Revolution. He helped negotiate the 1795 Treaty of San Lorenzo, also known as the Pinckney Treaty, which reopened trade relations with Spain. The Pinckney Treaty established the boundary between Florida and the U.S. and allowed the U.S. access to the Mississippi River. He was governor of South Carolina from 1787–1789.

Another son, General Charles Cotesworth Pinckney (not to be confused with his cousin Governor Charles Pinckney) was a patriot, member of the Constitutional Convention, minister to France, and long involved in South Carolina government. He was an unsuccessful candidate for vice-president in 1800 and ran unsuccessfully for president in 1804 and 1808. François Michaux named the fevertree, *Pinckneya pubens,* in honor of his friend General Pinckney.

19. Clemson University Urban Research and Demonstration Center. Just east of the Clemson Coastal Research Education Center is a demonstration area for urban gardens. Some of the plants include blackberry lily, eucalyptus, hollies, roses, verbena, daylilies, and native perennials. The Clemson Coastal Arboretum is adjacent to the garden. Open during daylight hours.

20. Clemson University Coastal Research & Education Center & USDA Vegetable Laboratory is part of the Clemson University research and extension system. There are no public facilities.

21. USDA Center for Forested Wetlands Research, Southeast Forest Experiment Station. The center provides no exhibits or facilities for visitors but brochures and some information are available to the public.

Diseases and Medicine

Yellow fever and malaria were brought to the Southeast from Africa by way of the Caribbean and both diseases were spread throughout the population by mosquitoes. Malaria could return sporadically for many years. Yellow fever first appeared in Charleston in 1699 and those who survived were immune to further outbreaks. Dysentery was also common among new arrivals who had to adjust to new microbes. Their first summer was the most critical time for Europeans in the Southern colonies and the first year was known as the *seasoning period*. The mortality rate could reach over fifty percent for new arrivals.

Colonists soon understood the fact that disease was more prevalent near stagnant water and they began to avoid swamps. Summer resorts were established on the sea islands and, after the Revolution, inland pine forests where there was little standing water. It was thought that bad air carried disease causing miasma while clean, pine-scented or salt air was healthy. In the nineteenth century those who could afford to do so retreated to the foothills in upstate South Carolina. Charleston, open to prevailing sea breezes, was relatively healthy except during general epidemics.

Medical care was relatively ineffective regardless of wealth, except in the comfort provided to the wealthy as they died. In fact, the poor yeoman farmer who could only afford homegrown herbal remedies was much better off. There were two schools of medicine in the eighteenth century, one based on traditional botanical treatment and the other based on heroic treatments such as bloodletting and explosive laxatives.

Some remedies were actually counterproductive to the cure of the patient, such as in the case of bloodletting to rid the body of *bad humours*. One remedy that was truly effective was the use of Peruvian Bark, or *Cinchona ledgeriana* and *Cinchona succirubra,* for the prevention of malaria. Cinchona is the source of quinine, a bitter alkaloid that has strong antiviral and antibacterial properties and reduces fever. The British began to use quinine water, or tonic water, throughout their tropical and subtropical colonies and added a little sugar and gin to make it palatable.

22. Charles Towne Landing. The site of the first settlement of Charles Town at Albemarle Point is now Charles Towne Landing historical park. Points of interest are the settlers' village, a replica of the sailing ship *Adventure*, and archaeological evidence of buildings and fortification. The park has a popular zoo of native animals, including alligators, American bison, otters, raccoons, elk, white tail deer, ducks, black bears, and cougars. There is a nature trail near the parking area and eighty acres of native landscape. Located on Old Towne Road, off SC-171. Open daily, 9 a.m.–5 p.m., September through May; 9 a.m.–6 p.m., June through August. Closed December 24 and 25. Admission.

23. The Ashley River was called Kiawah by the Native Americans and San Jorge by the Spanish. It was named by the English for Lord Anthony Ashley Cooper, First Earl of Shaftesbury, one of the proprietors and the most ardent supporter of the Carolina colony. William Bartram crossed the Ashley River on a ferry just south of Drayton Hall.

24. Saint Andrew's Parish Church (1706) is the oldest surviving church in South Carolina. 2604 Ashley River Road.

25. Colonel William Washington was a cousin to George Washington. He came to Charleston during the Revolution and stayed after the war ended to become a successful rice planter. In 1782 he married Jane Reily Elliott, who owned the estate of Sandy Hill, near Ravenel. His tomb is located off Davidson Road (Highway 317).

26. Drayton Hall was built by John Drayton between 1738 and 1742. It is considered one of the finest examples of Georgian-Palladian architecture in America and has remained unaltered since its construction. André Michaux was a frequent visitor to Drayton Hall when it was the home of Dr. Charles Drayton in the late eighteenth century. When the botanist's horse died on one visit Dr. Drayton supplied him with another. Upon returning home to his garden, Michaux sent the Doctor's horse back laden with rare plants.

The Draytons ceased using the building as a primary residence and came only on weekends for a number of years. They never made modern improvements to the structure, not even wiring it for electricity. Located on SC-61, Ashley River Road. Open 10 a.m.–4 p.m., March through October; and 10 a.m.–3 p.m., November through February. Admission.

27. Magnolia Gardens and Audubon Swamp Gardens. Magnolia Gardens is the ancestral home of the Draytons since the end of the seventeenth century. The parterre garden called

Flowerdale is supposed to date from the late 1600s, possibly making it the oldest existing formal garden in America. Much of what we see today was built by Reverend John Grimke-Drayton in the 1840s and 1850s. He opened the garden up to the public in 1870 and it has been a popular destination since. The beautiful white bridge that arches over the cypress lagoon is one of the most photographed spots in South Carolina.

Audubon Swamp is a sixty-acre cypress and tupelo swamp approached by boardwalks and dikes. It is filled with wildlife, especially waterfowl. Native plants are combined with horticultural plantings such as spring bulbs and azaleas. The grounds contain a wildlife refuge, nature trails, observation tower, petting zoo, and numerous gardens. Located on Ashley River Road. Admission.

28. Middleton Place is renowned for its formal landscaped gardens that were laid out about 1741. The first camellias brought to America were planted at Middleton Place by André Michaux. The mansion is gone but the stables and gardens are restored. Middleton Place was the home of Henry Middleton, first president of the Continental Congress, and his son Arthur Middleton, signer of the Declaration of Independence. The single remaining structure was built in 1755 and became the principal residence after the main house was burned during the Civil War. The library contains first editions by Catesby and Audubon. The epicenter of the great 1886 Charleston earthquake was at Middleton Plantation. Located on Ashley River Road, Highway 61. Open 9 a.m.–5 p.m. daily. Admission.

29. Ten Mile. The path from Charleston to Goose Creek and beyond was once marked by stone mile markers. There was a tavern at the ten-mile marker that became known as Ten Mile Tavern. André Michaux owned land and built his garden at Ten Mile.

30. Michaux's Garden. André Michaux was dispatched to America by the French government in 1785 to search for new plants. He was particularly interested in finding useful trees to replenish the forests of France that had been cutover to supply timber for the numerous military conflicts of the eighteenth century. Michaux established a garden near Hackensack, New Jersey, and in 1787 he built another one north of Charleston that included 120 acres purchased with his own funds. Michaux's collections were propagated and cultivated at his two gardens before being shipped to Park de Rambouillet near Paris. He spent most of his time in America at his garden in Charleston.

The French Garden, as it came to be known, was once part of the Arthur Middleton estate and Michaux became closely acquainted with the Middleton family. The oldest camellias and crepe myrtles in America are at Middleton Place where they were planted by André Michaux himself. Michaux's son François returned to South Carolina in 1802 and sold the Charleston garden property to J. J. Himely. On February 8, 1803, the property was conveyed to the Agricultural Society of South Carolina who held it until 1820. All deeds mention it as the French Garden, property of France, not of Michaux.

The site of this important botanical garden was north of the intersection of US-78 and Remount Road in North Charleston, lying on and east of the railroad tracks. The station of the South Carolina Railroad called Ten Mile Hill was located on this tract about one-half mile east of the Michaux residence and garden site. The French Garden was owned by the Agricultural Society of South Carolina until 1820. After that the property was owned by a number of people until it was acquired by the U.S. government during World War II. When it became surplus property in 1946 the Garden Club and Dr. Kenneth Hunt of Charleston College began an effort to preserve a part of the original property as a memorial to André Michaux. The plans were never realized and the area is now a trailer park and the suburban neighborhood of Hanahan.

31. General William Moultrie (1730–1805) lived at Windsor Hill, located in the vicinity of present Pepperhill and Windsor Hills neighborhoods (north of Ashley Phosphate Road on the Berkeley-Charleston County line). John Bartram visited him at Windsor Hill on July 8, 1765 in company with Dr. Alexander Garden.

Thomas Walter

Thomas Walter was a Charleston merchant and planter who is remembered today as the author of *Flora Caroliniana*. Walter's *Flora* was published in London in 1788 and was the first publication of American flora to use the Linnean system of plant classification. Because he was the first to publish, some of the plants described by William Bartram in the *Travels* carry the name of Walter.

Thomas Walter was born about 1740 in Southampton, Hampshire, England. He arrived in Charleston some time prior to 1769 and established a mercantile business. He began to purchase land in the surrounding parishes and eventually owned a total of 4,500 acres. After the death of his wife, Anne Lesesne, in 1769 he became interested in botany and began traveling in South Carolina collecting plants. He established himself in Berkeley County on the Santee River in 1787 where he built a botanical garden.

When South Carolina broke with England Walter was appointed a member of the Committee of Continental Association, Deputy Paymaster of the Militia, and after the war he was a member of the Santee Canal Company. Although Walter was acquainted with the society surrounding Goose Creek he apparently did not know Dr. Alexander Garden, the other noted botanist of Charleston. Walter probably did not meet William Bartram either.

John Fraser met Thomas Walter in late 1786 very soon after Fraser's brief travels with André Michaux. Fraser added his collection of plants to that of Walter's and helped complete the *Flora Caroliniana*. Fraser carried the specimens and manuscript on his return to England where the book was published in 1788. Walter honored his friend in the name of Fraser magnolia (Bartram's *Magnolia auriculata*). Walter's herbarium is located today in the Botany Department of the Museum of Natural History in London.

Thomas Walter died on January 17, 1789, and is buried in Berkeley County at the site of his botanical garden. There are no signs of the garden remaining today but the grave was restored in 1931 and is open to the public. From SC-45 on the north side of Lake Moultrie, go west on CR-31, then a sharp right, remaining on CR-31. This road dead-ends into Wilson's Landing. Take the dirt road on the right to the grave site.[1]

Walter described and named eighty-eight plant species that are valid today, all collected within fifty miles of Charleston. A few of the significant plants that are attributed to Walter include;

spruce pine, *Pinus glabra*
pine lily, *Lilium catesbaei*
yellow-eyed grass, *Xiris caroliniana*
showy lady slipper, *Cypripedium reginae*
turkey oak, *Quercus laevis*
Fraser magnolia, *Magnolia fraseri*
sweet pitcher-plant, *Sarracenia rubra*
hooded pitcher-plant, *Sarracenia minor*
tall meadow beauty, *Rhexia alifanus*
catalpa, *Catalpa bignonioides*
floating bladderwort, *Utricularia inflata*
dog fennel, *Eupatorium compositifoliu*
river cane, *Arundinaria gigantea*
Solomon's seal, *Polygonatum biflorum*
goat's beard, *Aruncus dioicus*
staggerbush, *Lyonia feruginea*

1. *Thomas Walter, Carolina Botanist*, David H. Rembert. Museum Bulletin Number 5, South Carolina Museum Commission, Columbia, 1980.

Moultrie was a major of the South Carolina militia having entered military service as a captain in the Cherokee War in 1760. During the early days of the Revolution he was a member of the Provincial Congress and General Assembly. Moultrie was chosen by the Council of Safety to command the army at Sullivan's Island. From their hastily built fort, Moultrie's forces successfully repulsed Sir Henry Clinton's infantry and Peter Parker's ships. He was then promoted to Brigadier-General of the Continental Army. Moultrie was captured at the fall of Charleston and was exchanged in 1782, along with other prisoners, for General Burgoyne. After the war he served two terms as governor. William Moultrie was buried first at Windsor Hill then his remains were moved to Fort Moultrie. His grave marker was moved to Saint James Goose Creek Church.

32. Otranto was the country home and plantation of Dr. Alexander Garden. He was a correspondent of John Bartram and the two became friends during Bartram's Charleston visit in 1765. Garden purchased this property in 1771 from John Moultrie, who became lieutenant governor of East Florida. Otranto was previously owned by Arthur Middleton who had operated an indigo plantation there. Originally known as *Yeshoe*, the Gardens named the plantation *Otranto* after the novel by Horace Walpole, *The Castle of Otranto*.

Upon the outbreak of the Revolution the Gardens returned to England, but their son, also named Alexander, remained in America and was given title to the plantation. Young Alex, a patriot, became a major in the Continental Army and served as an aide-de-camp under Nathanael Greene. He built the present home around 1790. That house still stands and the Otranto property is now the Otranto subdivision. The indigo vats that were built by Middleton have been moved to Bushy Industrial Park on SC-503 and are the oldest existing indigo apparatus in South Carolina. Major Alexander Garden II is the author of *Anecdotes of the Revolution*.

33. Ralph Izard (1741–1804) was a descendent of one of South Carolina's earliest French settlers. He was educated in England where he became a friend of Edmund Burke, who opposed Parliament's radical approach to the dispute with the colonies. Izard, along with Benjamin Franklin and Arthur Lee, was delegated to Parliament to petition against unfavorable laws targeted at the colonies. He was later appointed by Congress as minister to the Duke of Tuscany.

During the Revolution Izard was a commander in Nathanael Greene's army. After the war he served in the U.S. Senate. His son entertained General Lafayette at Charleston in 1825.

The Izard plantation was called the Elms and was located between US-78 and US-52 in an area still known as the Elms. The Izard townhouse on Broad Street still stands and is in excellent condition.

Wannamaker Park is located on part of the Izard family's Elms Plantation and borders Goose Creek Reservoir. The park contains over a thousand acres of woodland and wetlands. Amenities include picnic areas, hiking and biking trails, canoeing, playground, and meeting facilities. Located on US-78 about a half-mile north of the intersection of US-52. Opens at 9 a.m. and closes at varying times during the year. Admission.

34. Saint James Goose Creek Parish Church, 1719. The parish church of Saint James Goose Creek was spared by the occupying British army because it bears the Royal Coat of Arms of Great Britain over the chancel. Located off Goose Creek Road, near the intersection of US-78 and US-52. Signs direct visitors to the church.

35. Goose Creek was settled as early as 1672 by John Yeamans and fellow planters from Barbados. Goose Creek included the area centered around the modern town of Goose Creek and the rich lands along the Goose Creek waterway. This creek possibly earned its name from the graceful bends in the river that are reminiscent of a goose's neck. The community was originally called the Parish of Saint James, Goose Creek, and was created in 1706. Early settlers included the families of Edward and Arthur Middleton, George Chicken, the Moultries, Izards, Mazycks, Maurice Moore, and Governor James Moore.

Barbados was the possession of Edward Howard, second Earl of Carlisle. Although management of the colony was subordinate to the proprietor, an elective form of government was established with representatives chosen by landowners. The Barbadians therefore became use to a level of democracy not known in England. The growth of large sugar cane plantations and the investment required in slaves forced small farmers to look elsewhere for economic opportunity. The first Barbadians arrived in Charleston in 1671 and most settled on Goose Creek.

These Barbadians differed from the common English immigrant in that they were experienced planters. They favored a slave economy and the privileges of a landed class system, they were loyal Anglicans, and they were experienced in self-government. They were also fond of leisure, food and drink, and they were not given to moderation.

The Barbadians were experienced colonists and they had money, two advantages that helped them dominate the economic and political life of early South Carolina. There arose two factions in early Charleston politics, one of which became known as the Goose Creek Faction. Their opposition was composed mostly of dissenters of the Church of England who supported the Proprietors.

In 1680 the Goose Creek families were joined by Huguenots fleeing persecution and religious wars in France. Among the French families were Gaillard, St. Julien, Marion, Prioleau, and Bonneau.

36. Thorogood was the plantation of John Deas. John Bartram and Dr. Alexander Garden visited Deas at Thorogood on July 8, 1765. They toured his fields of indigo and corn and saw an artificial fish pond built in a worn out rice field. The property was named for Joseph Thorogood who was the original grantee.

37. Old Dorchester State Park. Dorchester, South Carolina was founded in 1696 by a group of Puritans from Windsor, Connecticut. Their new home was named after the first Puritan settlement in Massachusetts, which in turn was named after one of their hometowns in England. Dorchester lay on the trading path to the Indian nations and was at the head of navigation on the Ashley River. Dorchester prospered and the Puritans, known as the Congregationalists, became leaders in early South Carolina.

The Congregationalists tended to settle close together and on smaller tracts of land than their Church of England neighbors. The sickly nature of the area and loss of fertile farmland started the decline of Dorchester. Thus some of the congregation desired to move to a more "capacious and healthful environment." Because they were loathe to separate their society most agreed to move to Midway, Georgia, where they acquired 22,400 acres of land. A total of forty-eight families made the migration with Reverend Osgood in 1754.

The park has a picnic area, nature trail, and river access for canoeing and fishing. Located on SC-642 north of Charleston. Open 9 a.m.– 6 p.m., Thursday through Monday.

38. Summerville was a popular nineteenth century resort for Lowcountry inhabitants seeking a respite from summer diseases. Downtown Summerville is on the National Register of Historic Places.

Summerville-Dorchester Museum. Located at 100 East Doty Avenue, Summerville. Open 2–5 p.m., Wednesday through Sunday.

39. Edisto Indian Tribe. The Edistos are the descendents of the Kusso (Cussabo) and Natchez but have adopted the name Edisto because of modern convenience. The Kusso were living on the upper Ashley River in present Dorchester County at the end of the seventeenth century. The Kusso and English maintained friendly relations in the beginning, but tensions began to grow as Indians were abused and cheated by the traders.

The Natchez were a powerful tribe living on the Mississippi River but were dispersed by the French and Choctaws in 1730. Many joined the Upper Creeks but a small group went to South Carolina and settled in Colleton County near the Kussos. In the nineteenth century a small group of Indians were living in the Four Holes Swamp area of Dorchester County and their descendants are the modern Edisto Tribe. Contact Edisto Indian Tribal Council, 1125 Ridge Road, Ridgeville, SC 29472.

40. Cooper River Rice Plantations. The Cooper River was one of the greatest rice-producing areas in the American colonies. At the height of the rice era plantations lined both sides of the river. Many of the homes have disappeared and smaller plantations became incorporated into larger ones. There remain today a number of the most successful of the colonial plantations. On the east side of the river are the plantations of Middleburg, c. 1697; Silk Hope, c. 1690, the home of Governor Sir Nathaniel Johnson; Rice Hope; Mepkin, c. 1762, home of Henry and Eleanor Laurens; and North Chacan. On the west side of the river are Mulberry Plantation, c. 1714; Lewisfield, 1767; and Bluff Plantation, 1710.

The first commercial rice mill was built by Jonathan Lucas at Middleburg Plantation. Rice cultivation dropped dramatically after the Civil War, yet there were still 9,000 acres in production at the beginning of the twentieth century, producing six million pounds of rice annually.

The colonial chapels built for the convenience of the far-flung faithful are still standing; Pompion Hill Church, c. 1763; Strawberry Chapel, c. 1725; Biggins Church, c. 1756 (in ruins); and Saint Stephens Episcopal Church, c. 1768.

41. Cainhoy, on the Wando River, has existed as a town since before 1735 and was an important ferry site. It was settled by French Huguenots and Scots Presbyterians.

42. Palmetto Islands County Park. This Charleston County park has an excellent boardwalk on the marsh and a fifty-foot observation tower. The playground and Splash Island are popular with local children. Facilities include canoe rental, playground, fishing dock, snackbar, and pool. Located off US-17, follow Long Point Road past Snee Farm, turn right on Needlerush Parkway. Admission.

43. Boone Hall plantation was a land grant to Major John Boone, one of the original settlers of South Carolina. The plantation grew to nearly 12,000 acres but is now only 738. Boone Hall is known for its alley of live oaks, its large pecan grove, and intact slave quarters. Located off US-17 north of Mount Pleasant. Open 9 a.m.–5 p.m. daily, except Christmas and Thanksgiving. Hours are longer from April 1 through Labor Day. Admission.

44. Snee Farm, Charles Pinckney National Historic Site. Charles Pinckney was born to a prominent Huguenot family, the son of Colonel Charles Pinckney and Frances Brewton. He became one of the leading patriots of South Carolina and was imprisoned aboard a British ship after the fall of Charleston. After the Revolution he was a leading statesman in the early government of the United States. Pinckney represented South Carolina at the Constitutional Convention and is credited with being the primary author of that document when he was only thirty years old. He was governor of South Carolina for four terms, U.S. senator, U.S. representative, and Thomas Jefferson's minister to Spain.

The plantation dates from a land grant made in 1698. Charles Pinckney inherited Snee Farm in 1782 and lived there with his wife, Mary Eleanor Laurens, until 1817. George Washington took breakfast at Snee Farm on the morning of May 2, 1791, but Governor Pinckney was still in Charleston making preparations for the president's visit. The National Park Service conducts archaeological research on the twenty-eight acres and has converted the farmhouse into a museum that illustrates life on a colonial coastal plantation.

Located on Long Point Road, off US-17. Hours are 9 a.m.–5 p.m., Thursday through Monday.

45. Christ Episcopal Church, 1725. The original church was a wooden structure built in 1706 and burned in 1725. The brick church was built that year then burned by the British, rebuilt, and burned again by Federal Troops. Located on Old Georgetown Highway

46. Sweetgrass Basket Stands. The famous Charleston sweetgrass baskets are made from spartina, cord grass, bulrush, longleaf pine needles, and palmetto. The preferred material is sweetgrass, *Muhlenbergia filipes*, because it is soft, pliable and has a pleasant fragrance. The baskets are patterned after the types of baskets made on the west coast of Africa and brought to South Carolina three centuries ago by the slaves who worked the rice fields.

The baskets are still made by African-American artisans who pass their skill to each succeeding generation. Basket making has become such an important cottage industry among Charleston County African Americans that they have formed an association and the state has set aside sweetgrass preserves so that the raw materials will not become scarce. A plantation was established in Jasper County where sweetgrass is cultivated for the basket makers. Most of the basket makers have stands along US-17 east of Mount Pleasant. They sell their baskets in downtown Charleston at the City Market and at the important tourist sites.

47. Mount Pleasant dates to 1680 when Florentia O'Sullivan received a grant for more than 200 acres of land in the area. Mount Pleasant receives its name from Jacob Motte's plantation. He built a home in 1755 that still stands at 111 Hibben Street (not open to the public). The town of Mount Pleasant dates from 1808.

Museum on the Common. The history of the East Cooper River area and Hurricane Hugo (1989) are featured exhibits. 217 Lucas Street in Mount Pleasant. Open 10 a.m.–5 p.m., Monday through Saturday.

Shem Creek Maritime Museum exhibits the maritime history of Charleston and a master boat builder is on the premises. Located on Shem Creek at 514 Mill Street, Mt. Pleasant. Open 10 a.m.–5 p.m., Monday through Saturday.

48. Sullivan's Island is named for Florentia O'Sullivan who received a land grant that included Mount Pleasant. A cannon on Sullivan's Island was fired to let the city know when a ship passed the bar into the Charleston Harbor. For many years a sentry post was located on Sullivan's Island to warn of approaching Spanish, British, or Federal troops, and pirates. The slave quarantine station was located on Sullivan's Island during colonial days. In the 1790s when Charleston regained its prosperity after the Revolution, Sullivan's Island became a summer resort for townspeople escaping the fevers and heat of the city.

Fort Moultrie. The South Carolina militia built a fortress of palmetto logs on the southern end of Sullivan's Island at the site of present-day Fort Moultrie. The first patriot victory was won on June 28, 1776 when Admiral Peter Parker's ships were battered by cannon fire from the palmetto fort. During the battle Sergeant William Jasper raised the South Carolina flag on the ramparts despite the danger.

Osceola was imprisoned at Fort Moultrie and died there on January 30, 1838. His grave is at the entrance to the fort. General William Moultrie's remains were moved from his home at Windsor Hill and reburied at Fort Moultrie.

Visitors to Fort Moultrie are treated to a fine view of Charleston harbor. The surrounding dunes and beach are a well-known birding site. Open daily, 9 a.m.–6 p.m. in spring and summer and until 5 p.m. during fall and winter.

49. Fort Sumter National Monument. Any student of the Civil War knows Fort Sumter, where the first shots of that conflict were fired.

Fort Sumter was built on a man-made island in Charleston Harbor.

Counties

Berkeley. Though organized in 1882, the name Berkeley dates from the founding of the colony of Carolina. Charleston was the county seat of the first Berkeley County. At the time there were only three counties in South Carolina, Craven in the northeast, Berkeley centered around Charleston, and Colleton in the southwest.

Charleston. The city of Charleston was located in the original Berkeley County, one of three counties created in 1682. The counties had little political purpose because there was little local government and most power was centered in Charleston. Beginning in 1721 church parishes also served as election districts. New judicial districts were created in 1769 in response to the increased need for courts in the backcountry. The Charleston District included all of the original Berkeley and Colleton counties. The state constitution of 1785 created thirty-four counties in the state and Charleston District became Charleston County. Colleton County was created out of Charleston District in 1800 and Berkeley County was created from it in 1882.

Dorchester. Created in 1897 from Colleton and Berkeley counties. It is named for the Dorchester community.

Sites in Berkeley County

Middleburg Plantation, c. 1697. The oldest existing plantation house in South Carolina is the 1699 structure at Middleburg Plantation. It was built by Benjamin Simons, a French Huguenot. Jonathan Lucas, Jr., married Simons' granddaughter Lydia. Lucas and his father, the engineer Jonathan Lucas, Sr., built the first toll rice mill in South Carolina at Middleburg in 1799.

Huger, 1735. This community is named for the Huger Family (pronounced Hewgee or Ugee).

Mepkin Plantation and grave of Henry Laurens. Mepkin was the plantation home of Henry Laurens beginning in 1762 when he purchased the property from the Colleton family. Though John and William Bartram visited Laurens during their visit to Charleston in 1765, we don't know if they visited Mepkin. However, William probably visited Mepkin during his longer stay in Charleston in 1775, especially when we consider the kindness extended to him when Henry Laurens toured Florida in 1766.

Itinerary

Miles   Directions

Traveling southwest to the Edisto River

   Begin at White Point Garden and travel North on Meeting Street

.2   Cross Lamboll Street

.3   Cross Tradd Street

.1   Cross Broad Street

.1   Cross Chalmers Street

1.0   Charleston Museum on the right and the Charleston Visitor Center on the left

.5   Left lane for US-52N, Meeting Street, follow US-52 N to Cosgrove Avenue

4.7   Left on Cosgrove avenue, SC-7

2.7   Right on Sam Rittenberg Boulevard

1.8   Right on Ashley River Road, SC-171

3.4   St. Andrews Parish Church

.7   Left on Bees Ferry Road

4.8   Right on US-17

6.1   Right on Old Savannah Road

2.9   Cross SC-165, road becomes dirt

3.9   Right on US-17

.2   Left on Old Jacksonborough Road

5.3   Right on Parkers Ferry Road

.2   Left on US-17

3.0   Edisto River

Traveling northeast to the Santee River

   Begin at the Visitor Center and travel north on Meeting Street

.3   Right for US-17N to Mount Pleasant

2.4   Coleman Boulevard (right for downtown Mount Pleasant)

6.4   Christ Church

1.0   Sweetgrass basket stands

.3   Left on SC-41N

9.1   Right on Highway 100, Wambaw Creek Road

1.4   Enter Francis Marion National Forest, the route is now called Halfway Creek Road

4.2   Right on Guerin's Bridge Road (unmarked paved road)

   Immediate left on FS-202, Willow Hall Road, 8.7 miles to Hwy-133/1032 near Awendaw

The Laurens' home at Mepkin Plantation was destroyed by the British during the Revolution. Laurens built a second home and retired to Mepkin after the Revolution. The property remained in the Laurens family until 1916. The graves of Henry and Eleanor Laurens and their son John are located in the family cemetery on the grounds of Mepkin Abbey overlooking the Cooper River. Visitors check in at the gate but admission is free to see the gardens. Located off SC-402, River Road, on Mepkin Abby Road. Open 9 a.m.–4:30 p.m.

Cypress Gardens is a modern garden, laid out in the 1920s. The gardens contain 250 acres located at Dean Hall Plantation on the Cooper River. The gardens include planted and landscaped areas, a natural wetland and a reconstructed rice field. There are two nature trails and the wetlands may be explored by rented flat bottom boats. Located on Cypress Garden Road, off US-52. Open 9 a.m.–5 p.m., daily. Admission.

Dennis Wildlife Center carries out wildlife research for the surrounding state lands. The lobby of the administration building contains an interesting exhibit of fish and bird's eggs collected by eighteenth century naturalist William Elliott. The hatchery at the Dennis Cen-

Charleston • 149

ter is the world's largest producer of striped bass.

Moncks Corner grew up at the intersection of two important early roads in the mid-eighteenth century. This section of land was included in the barony of Lord Peter Colleton. His grandsons, John and Peter, settled in South Carolina and sold part of the land to Thomas Monck in 1735. A community of stores and a tavern grew up at the crossroads, but by the end of the Revolution the town had almost disappeared. When the railroad was built the town began to grow again and was chosen as county seat of Berkeley County in the 1890s.

Berkeley County Museum. This excellent regional museum covers 12,000 years of cultural and natural history. The collections contain artifacts from Native American settlements, the Revolution, and the Antebellum era. Local hero General Francis Marion is given a prominent place in the historical exhibits. Located at the entrance to Santee Canal State Park in Moncks Corner. Open 9 a.m.–5 p.m., Monday through Saturday and from 1–5 p.m. on Sunday. Admission.

Old Santee Canal State Park. The nation's first canal was the Santee Canal, which began operation in 1800. It connected the Santee with the Cooper River by way of Biggins Creek to bring products to Charleston from inland plantations. The state park preserves the Biggin Creek section of the canal. Santee Canal State Park is a wildlife paradise and may be canoed or hiked. There are extensive hiking trails and boardwalks into the wetlands. Biggins Creek cuts through limestone, which outcrops along the trails and harbors plants adapted to alkaline conditions. The Interpretative Center features the history of the area and explains how the canal was constructed. Located on Stony Landing Road in Moncks Corner. Open 9 a.m.–6 p.m. daily in summer and until 5 p.m. in winter. Admission.

Francis Marion National Forest, Witherbee Ranger District. Located on Copperhead Road, Highway 125, near the intersection with Witherbee Road, Highway 171, just north of Huger.

Tomb of Francis Marion. Francis Marion was born at Cordes Plantation near Mepkin Abbey but moved to Winyah Bay at an early age. After the Revolution he settled in present Berkeley County. His grave is located on Belle Isle Plantation Road off SC-45 on the north side of Lake Moultrie.

Four Holes Swamp/Francis Beidler Forest is the largest virgin bald cypress and tupelo forest in America. Four Holes Swamp is a slow flowing black water stream that is sixty-two miles long. Some of the giant cypresses are 1000 years old. The boardwalk is 1.5 miles long and provides easy access into the swamp. The visitor center has a slide show and information on the natural history of Four Holes Swamp and the forest. The forest is saved and protected by the Audubon Society and the Nature Conservancy. Located north of Charleston off US-178 near Harleyville, exit 177 on I-26. Open 9 a.m.–5 p.m., Tuesday through Sunday. Closed on Monday, Thanksgiving, December 24 and 25, New Year's Eve, and New Year's Day. Admission.

Historic Charleston

During the Colonial period, Charleston was the only city in the Southeast of any size and cosmopolitan aspirations. She has been called the *Queen City of the South* by some and the *Holy City* by others, because of the number of churches in the historic district. Here is how Charleston looked to Adam Hodgson in February, 1820:

> On entering the city, we seemed to be transported into a garden. Orange trees laden with ripe oranges, peach trees covered with blossoms, and flowering shrubs of a description which I had been accustomed to see only in hot-houses, gave me impressions similar to those which I suppose you experienced on visiting some of the cities on the Mediterranean.[1]

With a history of hurricanes, earthquake, fire, disease, and sieges by pirates, Indians, Spanish, British, and Federal forces it is a wonder there are so many historical structures left in Charleston. Significantly, two homes visited by William Bartram still stand, the John Stuart House at 106 Tradd Street and the Thomas and Elizabeth Lamboll House at 19 King Street. Colonial homes that William Bartram would have seen as he walked about Charleston are too numerous to mention here, only the most significant properties will be addressed.

1. Adam Hodgson, *Letters from North America Written During a Tour in the United States and Canada*, Vol. I., 1824. Quoted from an original edition in the University of Georgia Library.

Sites

1. White Point Gardens and the Battery. White Point received its name from the mounds of oyster shells found by the early colonists. Stately homes began to appear at White Point in the 1770s as Charleston experienced a period or prosperity. The park and garden were planted in the 1830s. The Battery is so named because fifteen guns were placed there during the War of 1812.

2. The Thomas & Elizabeth Lamboll House. William Bartram lodged at the home of Mary Lamboll Thomas, 19 King Street, during his last visit in Charleston in December, 1776. She was the daughter of Thomas and Elizabeth Lamboll and had inherited the home when her father died in October 1774. William probably had stayed with Thomas Lamboll in the same house when he arrived in Charleston earlier in April 1773.

Elizabeth Lamboll was the first Charlestonian to plant a garden in the European fashion, combining food crops and flowers, and is credited with creating a gardening craze among the gentry. Thomas planted the first Chinaberry trees in South Carolina. The Lambolls were correspondents of John Bartram and exchanged plants with him, beginning their friendship during John's first visit to Charleston in 1760. The Bartrams stayed with the Lambolls during their expedition to the South in 1765. Peter Collinson in London remonstrated the elder Bartram for going about the gardens with Mrs. Lamboll in the heat of the day. He wrote;

> I wish thou may temper they zeal with prudence, but I do not think it an instance of it, when thou and Mrs. Lamboll rambled in the intense heat of a midday sun.[2]

2. William Darlington, *Memorials of John Bartram and Humphrey Marshall*, 1849. Used with the permission of the University of Georgia Library.

The Lamboll House was at the time separated from Lamboll's wharf by the garden, now occupied by a block of houses between Lamboll Street and South Battery Street. After his return to Philadelphia William Bartram and Mary Thomas continued to correspond and she sent him a box of plants in 1785. In a letter dated July 15, 1786, William thanked her for shipping a trunk he had left in her care when he departed Charleston nearly a decade earlier, no doubt delayed by the war. The Lambolls also owned a plantation on James Island that the Bartrams visited in 1765. The Lamboll House is now a bed and breakfast.

3. Miles Brewton House, 27 King Street. This home was completed in 1769 and is known as one of the nation's finest High Georgian-style buildings. The original owner, Miles Brewton, was one of Charleston's leaders and a wealthy merchant. When Brewton and his family were lost at sea in 1775 the house passed to his sister, Rebecca Motte. This house became British headquarters during the Revolution and was occupied by Sir Henry Clinton, Lord Rawdon, and Lord Cornwallis.

4. George Eveleigh's House, 39 Church Street. This home was built by George Eveleigh in 1743. Eveleigh was one of the most successful merchants in the Indian trade and operated a store in Augusta.

5. Governor Campbell's Residence. Though a wealthy colony, South Carolina never built a residence for the royal governors. The governors had to arrange lodging for themselves, an example of the troubled relationship between Charleston and royal authority. The home at No. 34 Meeting Street was built about 1760 by the Bull family and was the residence of the last royal governor, Lord William Campbell. He fled Charleston on the night of September 14, 1775, seeking refuge on the *Tamar* anchored in Charleston Harbor. The house was later owned by the Huger family. Francis

Thomas & Elizabeth Lamboll House

Kinloch Huger is remembered for his unsuccessful attempt to rescue the Marquis de Lafayette from an Austrian prison in 1794. Lafayette was entertained by the Hugers in this house during his American tour of 1825.

6. First Baptist Church, 61 Church Street. This is the oldest Baptist congregation in the South, founded in 1682 by Baptists led by William Screven from Kittery, Maine. The present church was built in 1822.

The **Baptists** were an evangelical group who believed that people must go through an emotional conversion from *sinner* to *saved* in order to become a true Christian and gain a place with God in the hereafter. They opposed slavery during the eighteenth century and eschewed many popular forms of pleasure. The ascetic Baptists were therefore looked upon with suspicion by worldly Anglicans and viewed with disdain by reasonable Presbyte-

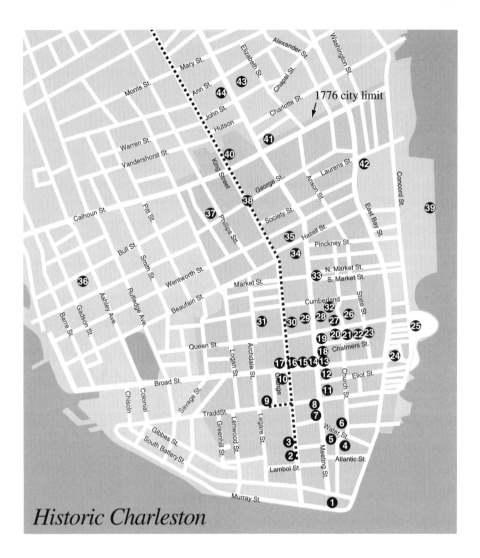

Historic Charleston

Legend

1. White Point Gardens and the Battery
2. The Thomas Lamboll House
3. Miles Brewton House
4. George Eveleigh's House
5. Governor Campbell's Residence
6. First Baptist Church
7. Historic Charleston Foundation
8. First Presbyterian Church
9. The John Stuart House
10. Historic Charleston Reproduction Shop
11. Heyward-Washington House
12. St. Michael's Episcopal Church
13. City Hall Gallery
14. South Carolina State House
15. Dr. David Ramsay
16. Dr. Alexander Garden
17. Dr. John Lining
18. Fireproof Building, South Carolina Historical Society
19. Historic Charleston Foundation Preservation Society
20. Dock Street Theater
21. The French Protestant Church
22. Dr. Lionel Chalmers
23. Old Slave Mart
24. Old Exchange and Provost Dungeon
25. Waterfront Park
26. Saint Philip's Episcopal Church
27. Thomas Elfe House
28. Circular Congregation Church
29. Gibbes Museum of Art
30. Charleston Library Society
31. Saint Johns Lutheran Church
32. Old Powder Magazine
33. City Market
34. Saint Mary's Catholic Church
35. Congregation Beth Elohim
36. Avery Research Center for African-American History and Culture
37. College of Charleston
38. King Street
39. South Carolina Aquarium
40. Marion Square and Old City Gate
41. Emanuel A.M.E. Church
42. Henry Laurens House
43. Charleston Museum
44. Charleston Visitor Center

rians and Congregationalists. Baptist preachers need only be called by God and they need not have any formal training in religious matters. This helped them flourish in the backcountry where the Presbyterians and Anglicans languished due to a lack of properly trained or willing ministers.

7. Historic Charleston Foundation, located in the Nathaniel Russell House, 51 Meeting Street. Open 10 a.m.–5 p.m., Monday through Saturday and on Sunday, 2–5 p.m.

8. First Presbyterian Church, 53 Meeting Street, was organized in 1731 by Scottish immigrants. The present church was built in 1814.

9. The John Stuart House. John Stuart built the house at 106 Tradd Street in 1772 at a cost of £2,350. William Bartram visited John Stuart at his home in April 1773. The house was confiscated by the Revolutionary government after Stuart fled to Charleston. It was used by the South Carolina military establishment until the fall of Charleston to the British. Stuart's son, Lieutenant General Sir John Stuart, failed to reclaim the property after the war and the house was sold at auction. The Stuart House is a well-known masterpiece of architectural proportions and is currently a private residence.

10. Historic Charleston Reproduction Shop, 105 Broad Street. Reproductions of historical wallpaper, fabric, furniture, and accessories are available through the reproduction shop.

11. Heyward-Washington House. This perfectly preserved colonial townhouse was built in 1772 by Daniel Heyward, father of Thomas Heyward, signer of the Declaration of Independence. Thomas lived in this house during the Revolution. While Heyward was imprisoned in Saint Augustine, British officers took over the home for their personal use. The house was rented for President George Washington during his visit in 1791. The Heyward House is unusual in that all the original structures are intact, including the privy and detached kitchen. It is furnished with authentic eighteenth century furniture manufactured in Charleston and the garden is planted in the style of the period. 87 Church Street. Open 10 a.m.–5 p.m., Monday through Saturday and 1–5 p.m. on Sunday.

Dr. Alexander Garden

In a letter to John Ellis dated July 15, 1765, Dr. Alexander Garden wrote:

He tells me that he is appointed King's Botanist in America. Is it really so? Surely John is a worthy man; but yet to give the title of King's Botanist to a man who can scarcely spell, much less make out the characters of any one genus of plants, appears rather hyperbolical. Pray how is this matter? Is he not rather appointed or sent, and paid, for searching out the plants of East and West Florida, and for that service only to have a reward and his expenses: Surely our King is a great King! The very idea of ordering such a search is noble, grand, royal.[1]

Dr. Garden was a competent botanist and might have been a little disappointed or jealous of the attention given to John Bartram. Garden was university educated and a correspondent with the leading intellectuals of Britain, advantages lacking in the self-educated Bartram. Despite his comment, Garden and Bartram were friends and carried on a lively correspondence for years.

Dr. Garden came to Charleston in the spring of 1752 to work with Dr. William Rose. Garden began to correspond with learned men in England and Europe as a way to combat the intellectual isolation of South Carolina. Soon after his arrival in South Carolina he traveled to Florida and the Blue Ridge Mountains. During his second summer he traveled to New York where he met Cadwallader Colden, the most accomplished scientist working in America at the time. Garden took over the practice of Dr. Lining and thereafter had little time to travel.

Dr. Garden sent to his correspondents in London numerous plants that were given names and descriptions. Among the plants he introduced to the European naturalists are Carolina silverbell, gordonia, cyrilla, and yellow-wood. He helped identify the class of amphibians known as *Sirenidae*. He befriended Henry Ellis while the future Georgia governor was in Charleston and continued a correspondence with Ellis after he returned to London and became a fellow of the Royal Society.

The Gardens bought Yesho Plantation at Goose Creek and renamed it *Otranto*. There they grew indigo and Dr. Garden could collect and cultivate native plants. The Gardens left America for England in 1783 as the Revolution came to a close. Dr. Garden appeared before the Loyalist's Commission on behalf of many of the exiled Charleston families. He was elected a regular member of the Royal Society. He toured the continent in 1788 where he was received among the scientific community with affection. Dr. Garden died on April 15, 1791.

The Gardens' son, Alex, was a patriot and remained in America. He was more impulsive than his father and lacked the business acumen to build on his father's success. Young Alex had to sell parts of Otranto to remain solvent.

Dr. Alexander Garden is remembered today in the name of the popular Southern landscape plant—Gardenia.

1. *Diary of a Journey through the Carolinas, Georgia, and Florida*; John Bartram. Annotated by Francis Harper. Transactions of the American Philosophical Society, New Series, Vol. XXXIII, Part I, December, 1942.

Dr. Alexander Garden's home was located at 98 and 100 Broad Street, Charleston. The remains of an outbuilding are incorporated in this structure.

12. Saint Michael's Episcopal Church is the oldest church building in Charleston, completed in 1761. George Washington worshipped at Saint Michael's in 1791. Located at the corner of Meeting and Broad streets.

13. City Hall Gallery, 80 Broad Street, contains a portrait gallery of national and local leaders, including a portrait of George Washington by John Trumbull. Open 9 a.m.–5 p.m., Monday through Friday.

14. The South Carolina State House stood on the northwest corner of Broad and Meeting streets, an area known as the Four Corners of Law. The State House was completed in 1756 and burned on February 5, 1788. The 1786 decision by the legislature to move the capital inland was still controversial in Charleston but the loss of the State House facilitated the move. The old State House lot was chosen as the site for a new courthouse building.

15. Dr. David Ramsay lived at 92 Broad Street in a home built around 1740. He studied medicine under Dr. Benjamin Rush in Philadelphia. Dr. David Ramsay was a physician in the Continental Army and imprisoned in Saint Augustine after the fall of Charleston. Ramsay came to Charleston in 1773, married Martha Laurens, daughter of Henry Laurens, entered South Carolina politics, was a member of the Continental Congress and the state legislature. He was an early proponent of sterilizing drinking water and smallpox inoculation. Ramsay is the author of a well-known history of South Carolina and the Revolutionary War. Dr. Ramsay was murdered by a madman on the streets of Charleston in 1815. It is possible that Ramsay was one of the "gentlemen of that city, eminent for the promotion of science and encouraging merit and industry" who encouraged William Bartram to visit the Indian nations in 1775.

16. Dr. Alexander Garden lived on a lot that included the present 98 and 100 Broad Street. The Gardens were loyalists and gave up the property when they left during the 1782 British evacuation of Charleston. The home was reclaimed by Alexander, Jr., who was a patriot and veteran. The Garden house was demolished in the early nineteenth century and the present structure at 98 Broad Street was built by Dr. Henry Frost about 1835 as an office. The rear portion of the present building may have been an outbuilding of the Gardens' residence.

17. Dr. John Lining was one of America's first formally educated physicians. His medical practice was taken over by Dr. Alexander Garden so that Lining could devote his time to scientific experiments. Lining's home still stands at 106 Broad Street and is thought to be the oldest frame building surviving in Charleston. It was built about 1695 and served as his office and pharmacy.

18. Fireproof Building, South Carolina Historical Society, 100 Meeting Street. The Historical Society maintains their archives and reading research room in the Fireproof Building. This building was constructed between 1822 and 1827 to house county records and was the first fireproof building in the country. It was designed by native son, Robert Mills, one of the nation's first professional architects and the designer of the Washington Monument.

John Stuart house, 106 Tradd Street

John Stuart

John Stuart was one of the most powerful men in the Southeast during the interim of the French and Indian War and the opening of the Revolution. As Superintendent of Indian Affairs for the Southern Department he was intimately involved with forming Indian policy, controlling trade, and determining the boundary lines dictated by the Royal Proclamation of 1763. Though much of his correspondence is preserved there is little written of his personal life and there are no portraits of him. We know that he suffered from gout and was overweight later in life, indicating that he enjoyed eating and drinking to excess. The house he built in Charleston in 1772 still stands at 106 Tradd Street and is one of the most noted structures in the city.

John Stuart was born in Inverness in 1718 of the Kincardine branch of the royal Stuart family. His father was a successful merchant and a Jacobite. John was sent to London to further his education in 1735. He joined the navy in 1740 and circumnavigated the globe with George Anson's privateering expedition against Spain. Stuart's share of the Anson expedition made him a small fortune, several thousand pounds compared to his annual salary of £100. He then sailed for South Carolina, arriving in Charleston in the spring of 1748 where he set himself up as a merchant in partnership with Patrick Reid. They established another store in Beaufort that was operated by John's younger brother, Francis. The company of Stuart & Reid did not prosper and Stuart became bankrupt upon the death of Reid. During this time John Stuart married his wife, Sarah. Her family connections are not known though she was probably a native South Carolinian.

John Stuart became involved in civic matters and local society. He was elected to the Commons House of Assembly in 1754, was a member of the Charleston Library Society, the Saint Andrews Society, and tax assessor for Saint Philip's Parish. Stuart was appointed captain in the South Carolina Provincial Army in 1756 and served with Demere at Fort Loudon. There he demonstrated his talent for Indian diplomacy. When Fort Loudon surrendered to the Cherokees Stuart was purchased from his captor by Attakullakulla, the headman of Chota, and spirited off to Virginia.

Stuart was appointed Superintendent of Indian Affairs for the Southern Department on January 5, 1762, but did not receive his documents and instructions until a year later. He enjoyed an annual salary of £600 and began to grow more prosperous from his increased land holdings. As Superintendent, Stuart spent considerable time among the Cherokees where it was rumored that he had a wife and a son and that their descendents are members of the Bushyhead family.

Stuart's position as Superintendent of Indian Affairs and his loyalist sentiment brought him into conflict with some powerful enemies at the opening of the Revolution. In May 1775, he was accused of inciting the Southeastern Indians to attack backcountry farms. Although it is not known how much of the Indian disturbance can actually be attributed to Stuart, he nevertheless felt it expedient to leave Charleston. He went first to his plantation near Beaufort, then to Savannah, and finally Saint Augustine. He then moved his office to Pensacola, where he died on March 21, 1779 after an illness of two years. The location of his grave is not known though it may be in Saint Michael's Cemetery, which was in use at least by 1778.

19. Historic Charleston Foundation Preservation Society, 108 Meeting Street. This visitors center contains exhibits on the architecture of Charleston and the efforts to preserve historical structures. A display contains architectural details rescued from demolished buildings. The bookstore has an excellent selection of local and state history. Open 10 a.m.–5 p.m., Monday through Saturday and 2–5 p.m. on Sunday.

20. Dock Street Theater, 135 Church Street. The wealth and love of pleasure that was characteristic of eighteenth century Charleston led to the creation of America's first theater. One of the first plays written and produced in America was *The Orphan,* performed at Shepheard's Tavern in Charleston. The success of the play lead to a drive to build a permanent theater. The Dock Street Theater opened its first season in 1736 with a performance of *The Recruiting Officer.* Today performances are held in the reconstructed New Dock Street Theater. Queen Street was once known as Dock Street because a creek flowed by the theater.

21. The French Protestant Church, 136 Church Street, dates from 1687 when Huguenots arrived in Charleston, fleeing persecution in Catholic France. The present church was built in 1845 and is the fourth one on this site.

22. Dr. Lionel Chalmers was a prominent Charleston physician. He was educated in Edinburgh and came to South Carolina in 1735 at age twenty and was associated with Dr. Lining for a time. Although he was a leading citizen and patron of the sciences, little is known about Chalmers' personal life.

Chalmers published *Essay on Fevers* in London in 1768, which may have been the impetus for his correspondence with Dr. Fothergill.

Chalmers published *An Account of the Weather and Diseases of South Carolina* in 1776, which dealt primarily with illnesses and treatments of children. He is thus considered a pioneer of pediatric medicine.

Dr. Chalmers acted as Dr. Fothergill's agent in sponsoring William Bartram's botanical expedition in the South. Chalmers dispensed the funds and kept up a correspondence with Bartram, who was a casual correspondent. Dr. Chalmers' memorial appeared in the *South Carolina Gazette* on May 12, 1777.

Dr. Chalmers was the son-in-law of Martha Logan (1704–1781). Logan was one of Charleston's well-known eighteenth century horticulturists and a correspondent of John Bartram. She wrote the first gardening almanac in America, which was published in Charleston from 1751 until 1818.

The Chalmers home was on the north side of Chalmers Street (then Union Alley) between State and Church streets. The house burned in the fire of 1778 along with 250 other houses, the library, and museum. Chalmers Street is one of the few remaining streets in Charleston paved with ballast stones. Empty ships arrived in port laden with stones to keep the vessel from riding too high in the water. In Charleston and Savannah, where there is a noticeable lack of naturally occurring rocks and stones, the discarded ballast was used for paving and construction.

23. Old Slave Mart. Slaves were displayed and auctioned on the streets in front of the Exchange for many years. In 1856 a city ordinance forbade slave sales on public property so the business moved to yards and buildings about the city. One such slave market was at No. 6 Chalmers Street. The Old Slave Mart was an African-American museum of arts and history. It was recently closed but may reopen in the future.

24. Old Exchange and Provost Dungeon. The Exchange was constructed in 1771 at Half Moon Battery on the site of the old Council Chamber. The customs offices and jail were located in the new building. The Declaration of Independence and Constitution were announced from the steps of the Exchange. The legislature met in the Exchange during the debates on ratifying the Constitution. American patriots were imprisoned there during the Revolution and a ball was held for George Washington in 1791. Located at 122 East Bay Street at Broad Street. Open 9 a.m.–5 p.m. daily. Admission.

25. Waterfront Park occupies a quarter mile of the Cooper River along Concord Street. The park has picnic tables and benches for the unhurried tourist or the harried Charleston worker. Open 6 a.m. to midnight.

The Old Exchange

26. Saint Philip's Episcopal Church, 146 Church Street. Established in 1670, Saint Philip's is the mother church of South Carolina. The original church was located at the site of Saint Michael's and was then part of the Church of England. The first building at the present site was constructed in 1724 and was the church William Bartram would have seen on his walks about Charleston. That church burned in 1835 and was replaced by the present building, finished in 1838. Many South Carolinians are buried at Saint Philip's church, including John C. Calhoun; Charles Pinckney, signer of the Constitution; Edward Rutledge, signer of the Declaration of Independence, president, and governor of South Carolina; and Dubose Heyward, author of *Porgy and Bess*.

27. Thomas Elfe House (1760), 54 Queen Street. The Elfe House was the home of Charleston's premier cabinetmaker during the colonial period. The house remains in its original condition with interior decoration unchanged. Open 10 a.m. until noon. Admission.

The home of Dr. Lionel Chalmers was located on present-day Chalmers Street, in the middle of the far side of the street in this view

28. Circular Congregation Church, 150 Meeting Street, was organized in 1681 by Congregationalists from New England. The Congregationalists built a unique circular church on this site in 1806, which burned in 1861. The present church was built in 1891.

29. Gibbes Museum of Art, 135 Meeting Street. The Gibbes Museum collections include portraits of well-known South Carolinians and landscapes of South Carolina by native artists. Open 10 a.m.–5 p.m., Tuesday through Saturday, and 1–5 p.m. on Monday and Sunday. Admission.

30. Charleston Library Society was founded in 1748 and the third oldest library in America. Library Society members were closely associated with the founding of the College of Charleston and the Charleston Museum. Located at 164 King Street.

31. Saint Johns Lutheran Church was organized in 1734 by German immigrants. The present building was built in 1817. Located at the corner of Clifford and Archdale Streets.

32. Old Powder Magazine, 79 Cumberland Street. The Magazine was constructed in 1713 and held the powder and arms for the militia. It is the oldest public building in South Carolina. The Magazine has been renovated by the Historic Charleston Foundation and contains exhibits on the history of the city.

Open 10 a.m.–5 p.m., Monday through Saturday and 1–5 p.m. on Sunday.

33. City Market is built on land set aside in 1788 for a public market. The first building was constructed about 1806 and housed the city's butchers. There are now three buildings that house restaurants, shops, and a flea market. Located on South Market Street. Open 9 a.m.–5 p.m.

34. Saint Mary's Catholic Church, 89 Hasell Street. The Catholic Church was late coming to the southern colonies. Despite laws allowing religious freedom, Catholics were not often tolerated and were even banned from Georgia where it was feared they might ally themselves with French or Spanish invaders. Saint Mary's is the Mother Church of the Dioceses of Georgia, North and South Carolina. The church was established in 1789 and the present church was built in 1839.

35. Congregation Beth Elohim, 90 Hasell Street. The Reform Society of Israelites founded Reform Judaism in Charleston in 1824. Jews were attracted to Charleston from the earliest days because of religious freedom and economic opportunity. The first congregation was organized in 1749 and the present synagogue was constructed in 1840, to replace an earlier structure destroyed by fire. It is the oldest synagogue in continuous use in the United States.

Open to the public 10 a.m.–noon, Monday through Friday.

36. Avery Research Center for African-American History and Culture, located at the College of Charleston, 125 Bull Street. The Avery Center contains archives and exhibits of the Gullah history of coastal South Carolina. The Avery Institute was one of the most prestigious private African-American schools in America in the nineteenth century.

Tours are available 2–4 p.m., Monday through Friday. The research area is open 12–5 p.m., Monday through Saturday.

37. College of Charleston is the oldest municipal school in the country, founded in 1770. The land was set aside for educational purposes in 1724 and the main building was built in 1828. Located at St. Phillips and George streets.

38. King Street was the major thoroughfare on the Charleston peninsula and it followed the highest ground. Vendors coming into town to sell their produce and wares set up along the road. As the city grew, King Street developed into the principal commercial district. North of town it was also known as the New Broad Path.

39. South Carolina Aquarium. The new South Carolina aquarium will certainly become one of the top attractions in Charleston. The galleries contain exhibits that re-create aquatic habitats from open ocean to secluded mountain ravines. The exhibits portray each habitat with related species, including plants, amphibians, reptiles, birds, and mammals. The Atlantic Ocean exhibit has a great ocean tank and sandy sea floor aquarium. The Coast Exhibit contains salt marsh and estuary. The Coastal Plain Exhibit has re-creations of brown water and black water swamps. The South Carolina Aquarium is the only aquarium to re-create a living Carolina Bay. The Piedmont exhibit shows life among the river shoals and the popular recreational lakes. The Mountain Forest exhibit has a ravine and cascade replete with mountain plants and birds. There is a special exhibit, Shifting Shorelines, that follows the changing coast line of South Carolina during the past 100 million years.

The South Carolina Aquarium is located on Charleston Harbor at the end of Calhoun Street. Hours are 9 a.m.–7 p.m., July through August; 9 a.m.–5 p.m., September through October and March through June; 10 a.m.–5 p.m., November through February. Admission.

40. Marion Square and Old City Gate. Charleston was one of the few fortified cities built in America. During the middle of the eighteenth century William De Brahm was employed to build new fortifications for the growing city. Part of the original city gate may be seen at Marion Square.

The Charleston Single House

A unique style of townhouse developed in Charleston early in the eighteenth century. It is two or three floors, one room deep with two rooms on each floor. The house is oriented perpendicular to the street on a short side. The west or south side of the house has a covered porch, called a *piazza* in Charleston, to shade the rooms from the sun and provide an outdoor room in pleasant weather. The back of the house usually has few windows to preserve privacy among the closely spaced buildings. The street end of the piazza is usually enclosed with an attractive door opening onto the porch. The main entrance to the home is in the center of the first floor piazza.

---

41. Emanuel A.M.E. Church, 110 Calhoun Street, was founded in 1791. Denmark Vesey laid plans for the slave rebellion at Emanuel Church. The present church was built in 1891.

42. Henry Laurens House. The Laurens' home was located in fashionable Ansonboro at the southeast corner of East Bay and Laurens streets. He moved to this house in 1764 and employed an English gardener named John Watson to design and care for a four acre garden planted on reclaimed marshland. There the Laurens planted exotic trees and fruits gathered from many foreign lands and Henry experimented with new crops. Tending the garden was one of Eleanor Laurens greatest joys. The Laurens were visited by John and William Bartram in 1765 and we can assume that William visited them while in Charleston during his travels in the 1770s. The house was destroyed in 1916.

43. Charleston Museum, 360 Meeting Street, is the oldest museum in the nation, founded in 1773 as a part of the College of Charleston. The museum's collections portray the cultural history of Charleston, African-Americans in South Carolina, indigenous crafts, and the natural history of the coast. The museum also owns the Joseph Manigault House and the Heyward-Washington House. The natural history collections date back to the founding of the museum. The Charleston Museum has an archaeological program that operates throughout the coastal area. Open 9 a.m.–5 p.m., Monday through Saturday, and from 1–5 p.m. on Sunday. Admission.

44. Charleston Visitor Center is located in the old South Carolina Railway Freight Depot, the site where railroading began in America. The Hamburg Railroad started there and was the longest railroad in the world when it was completed in 1833. The first locomotive was the famous *Best Friend of Charleston* and it provided the first regular passenger service in America. A full-sized replica of the Best Friend of Charleston is located next-door to the Visitor Center. Displays of Charleston's historic district and unique architecture are on exhibit. Information, maps, and parking are available to visitors. Tickets for events such as the Spoleto Festival, the Charleston Symphony, and theatrical events may be purchased at the Visitor Center.

375 Meeting Street. Open 8:30 a.m.–5:30 p.m. each day except Thanksgiving, Christmas, and New Year's Day. Closing time is 5:00 p.m. From November through March.

Henry Laurens

Henry Laurens was a wealthy merchant, successful planter, member of the Commons House of Assembly, president of the Continental Congress, and a founder of the College of Charleston. Though wealthy and shrewd in business, Henry Laurens was known for his kindness to those in need. He often helped people avoid debtors prison and was a benefactor to sailors and the sick. He was always ready to help young men at the beginning of their careers, as he did Lachlan McIntosh.

The Laurens were avid gardeners. Eleanor Laurens developed a four-acre garden on East Bay Street in 1755, renowned for its collection of plants from around the world. Her collection was no doubt assisted by her husband's far-reaching business contacts. They hired a professional English gardener, John Watson, to oversee the plantings.

Henry Laurens was born March 6, 1724, in Charleston, the oldest son of Jean and Esther Laurens. The Laurens were Huguenots from a respected family named Laurent of Rochelle, France. Henry Laurens was sent to London in 1744 to apprentice to James Crokatt, which ended when an expected partnership did not materialize. Laurens' father died in 1747 and young Henry took over the responsibility of settling his estate and entered into partnership with George Austin. He married Eleanor Ball in the summer of 1750. They had twelve children, four of whom reached adulthood. The fourth child, John, was the first to survive infancy.

Laurens business was that of factor and importer/exporter. He dealt in rum, deerskins, rice, indigo, slaves, coffee, sugar, and the indentures of servants. He gave up the trade in imported slaves because of the abuses and cruelty he witnessed, although he had made a great deal of money at it. He did, however, continue to advise friends in the business of slavery. In the early 1760s he purchased two plantations and hired overseers, including his brother-in-law John Coming Ball. From 1764 he began to reduce his active participation in business due to the demands of his plantations.

During the time that he was expanding his business as a planter he bought lands in Georgia—Broughton Island, New Hope, a town lot in Brunswick, and land on the Turtle River. He toured Georgia and Florida during the summer of 1766, taking stock of his holdings in the former and looking for new opportunities in the latter. While in Florida he looked in upon the newly established rice and indigo planter at Picolata on the St. Johns River, William Bartram. It was not a pretty sight. William was weak from illness and his slaves were uncooperative. Laurens had wine and food sent to the desperate William and wrote to John Bartram that he should urge his son to abandon the scheme and sell out.

Laurens was a colonel in the South Carolina militia during the invasion of the Cherokee Nation in the summer of 1761. He and Thomas Middleton parted as a result of disputes arising from the Cherokee War. The affair also divided Laurens from his lifelong friend Christopher Gadsden. Still, these men were able to put aside enough of their enmity to effectively form a revolutionary government a few years later.

Henry Laurens was first elected to the South Carolina Commons House of Assembly in 1757. He was a well respected, but conservative, legislator. He remained quiet and watchful during the uproar over the Stamp Act, noting that patience and working through proper legal channels was an appropriate way to effect change. He also noted that the radical approach would inevitably bring about a revolution.

Laurens' own revolutionary spirit developed from a disgust with the myriad petty intrigues and high-handed interferences into business and government by the king's appointed officials. Two of Laurens' ships were confiscated in 1767 under the pretense that their cargo had not been properly bonded, but it soon became obvious that it was an attempt by some of the king's appointed officials to line their pockets with the resulting fines. His confrontation with Judge Egerton Leigh galvanized Laurens defense of American rights. However, as a conservative, Laurens disapproved of mob rule and violence and urged lawful and economic resistance as well as petition to effect change.

Eleanor died in 1770, which deeply affected Henry for they had been very close and deeply devoted to one another. Laurens retired from his mercantile business to attend to his properties and his children's education. He lived in England from 1771 to 1774 while overseeing the education of his sons. During that time he was able to closely watch the activities of Parliament and work for the rights of South Carolina. He also acquired a disrespect for the English gentry and the corruption of the ruling class.

Upon returning to Charleston he was elected to the First Provincial Congress held in January 1775. The General Committee, with Laurens as President, was charged with the government of South Carolina. He then succeeded to the presidency of the Provincial Congress when Charles Pinckney resigned. Under the constitution adopted on March 26, 1776, Henry Laurens was chosen vice-president of the General Assembly. South Carolina elected Laurens to the Continental Congress in early 1777 and on July 21 of that year he joined the Congress in Philadelphia.

On November 1 Henry Laurens was unanimously elected president of the Second Continental Congress, an office he held until December 1778. His tenure saw trying times for the new republic, the Conway Cabal tried to unseat Washington, defeats for the American forces, Congress reduced as members returned home to assist their own states in defense, and his own breach with Christopher Gadsden; but, he also saw France enter the war as an ally to the Americans. Though widely admired and trusted, his office was not without controversy due to the strong personalities of the men with whom he worked and the jealousy of each state

Henry Laurens
Reprinted with the permission of the South Carolina Department of Archives and History

for maintaining its own sovereignty. He resigned the presidency in late 1778 and became a regular member of Congress.

Henry Laurens was elected in November 1779, to engage a diplomatic mission to Holland seeking a treaty of commerce and a loan of $10,000,000. Laurens' ship was captured off the coast of Newfoundland on September 3. Among the papers he retained was a draft of the treaty of amity and commerce which the British ministry cited in the declaration of war on Holland.

Laurens was taken to England and imprisoned as a traitor in the Tower of London. British authorities attempted to persuade him to take up the king's cause, which he resisted, and though offered escape and pardon he steadfastly refused to leave under circumstances that would imply guilt. Edmund Burke began working for his release and in December 1781, Laurens was exchanged for Lord Cornwallis.

As Laurens was about to sail for home, he received orders to join the peace commission in Paris. He had earlier declined to participate, believing his presence was surperfluous to the work already done by John Jay, John Adams, Thomas Jefferson, and Benjamin Franklin. He therefore arrived at the end of negotiations and contributed little to the document. He made several trips to London to negotiate particular articles of the treaty and was absent when the final document was signed.

Upon returning home to Charleston in 1784, Laurens retired from public life to Mepkin on the Cooper River. His children continued to be a source of pleasure. His daughter Martha married Dr. David Ramsay and Mary Eleanor married Charles Pinckney. Henry Laurens gained two sons-in-law with whom he could be proud and vicariously participate in building a new state and nation. Martha was herself a noted scholar and taught herself Latin and Greek. She attended to the education of her sons and could probably have contributed much more to the intellectual society of Charleston but for the fact she was a woman, wife, and mother.

Henry Laurens died December 8, 1792, at Mepkin and was one of the first European Americans to be cremated.

The Lowcountry

The region between Charleston and the Savannah River was known as the province of Escamaçu during the sixteenth century. They inhabitants were Muskhogean-speaking Indians and included the tribes of Ashepoo, Combahee, Edisto, Escamaçu, Hoya, Kiawah, Kusso, Toupa, Mayon, Orista, Stalame, Stono, Wando, Wimbee, Witcheough. Collectively they were known as the Cusabos.

The first Europeans to see the Southeastern coast were the members of the Pedro Salazar Expedition of 1514 and 1516. Pedro Quexos made a voyage along the coast in 1521 and gave the name *La Punta de Santa Elena* to a point of land, possibly Tybee Island, which became a landmark that indicated entry into the country of Santa Elena to the north. In 1561 Angel de Villefañe explored the coast and sailed into the harbor of Santa Elena (Port Royal). One of many hurricanes that were to plague the Spanish wrecked two of his ships and killed twenty-six men. This prevented Villefañe from leaving a settlement as planned.

Jean Ribault built the settlement of Charlesfort, named for King Charles IX, on Parris Island in 1562 and named the harbor Port Royal. The colony was sponsored by Admiral Gaspard de Coligny who hoped to create a refuge for Huguenot protestants. An American colony would give France an important position in competing with Spain for trade and international prestige as well as a claim on the new lands in North America. Ribault left a garrison and sailed for France for more supplies.

Ribault was detained in France because of the religious civil war and did not return for two years. A fire at Charlesfort destroyed a great portion of the precious supplies. The French settlement at Port Royal, like so many early attempts at colonization, failed due to lack of food and conflict with local Indians who had grown weary of supplying the Europeans. Captain Albert de la Pierria resorted to harsh measures in order to maintain discipline, prompting the soldiers to rebel and murder him. The Frenchmen built a boat and using their clothing for sails set out for France in April 1563. They continued to have bad luck at sea when they became becalmed. Almost

Site of Santa Elena, first capital of La Florida, located on Parris Island, South Carolina

starving, they voted to draw lots for one to give up his life to feed the others. They were picked up near land by an English ship and returned to France.

Cuban governor Mazariego sent Captain Don Hernando de Manrique Rogas to search out and destroy the French colony at Port Royal. He arrived in May 1564, too late to find the French, but he destroyed the fort and the stone monument left by Ribault. The second French attempt at colonizing Florida was La Caroline on the St. Johns River, which met with disaster at the hands of Governor Menéndez de Avilés in 1565. In order to improve and protect the Spanish claim to Florida, Menéndez established Fort San Felipe near the ruined Charlesfort in the summer of 1566. The Spanish called the province Santa Elena, which became the frontier of Florida. The Spanish showed little interest in establishing a presence any further north because the Gulf Stream, and the Spanish treasure ships, turned eastward into the Atlantic at this latitude.

From Santa Elena Captain Juan Pardo explored the upper part of South Carolina, into the North Carolina mountains, and into western Georgia in 1567. Father Juan Rogel established a Jesuit mission at Santa Elena in 1569 but had little success with the Indians. Governor Menéndez died in 1574 and Florida was mismanaged for the next few years. Captain Solis antagonized the Indians of Santa Elena to the point of rebellion by the unprovoked murders of several chiefs. On June 17, 1576, the Escamaçus killed a party of Spanish soldiers who came demanding food then they laid siege to Fort San Felipe. They forced the evacuation of the remaining Spanish inhabitants and burned the fort. The rebellion quickly spread south to Guale on the Georgia coast and the Timucuans in northeast Florida.

After the uprising subsided in 1577 Florida Governor Pedro Menéndez Marqués built on Parris Island a new fort, named Fort San Marcos. Captain Gutierrez de Miranda was in command of Spain's northernmost outpost and enjoyed a decade of relative peace. The Council of the Indies decided that it would be better to concentrate Spanish defenses in one location; therefore Fort San Marcos at Santa Elena was abandoned in 1587 in favor of Saint Augustine. When the Jesuits expanded their missions in the early seventeenth century it was to the west and north along the Georgia coast but not reaching to Santa Elena. This left the coast north of the Savannah River open to English trespass.

The Spanish made the same mistake as had the French, populating New World settlements with more soldiers than farmers and artisans. The Spanish emphasized the military nature of their settlements as a way to protect shipping and control the native population. The natural resources they desired were gold and silver rather than timber, fiber, and food. A garrison was not a colony and soldiers were not often capable of, or inclined toward, self-sufficiency. On the other hand, colonists were not willing to immigrate to a howling wilderness where they were continually exposed to danger while they built shelters and cleared land.

If Fort Caroline had not been so soon destroyed by the Spanish it is certain that qualified French colonists would have emigrated to Florida. However, the French turned their attention to Canada, well away from the Spanish. The success of the English in settling Carolina was due to their success in attracting a large number of working-class citizens who were in-

Wood storks, Jasper County, South Carolina

terested in founding farms and establishing trades. A century after the failure of Charlesfort and Fort Caroline, French Protestants were again looking for a home but this time it was among the English in Carolina rather than among their Catholic cousins in Canada.

British Colonization

William Hilton, in the service of the Company of Barbadian Adventurers, explored the Southeastern coast in search of suitable land for the Barbadians to develop. He reached Port Royal on August 10, 1663 and explored the area for several weeks. The Proprietors of Carolina commissioned Robert Sanford to explore the coast in 1666. He arrived at Port Royal in July of that year and was welcomed by the Kiawah and Escamaçu Indians.

Nisquesalla, the cacique of the Escamaçu, wanted his nephew to return to England and learn English. Dr. Henry Woodward offered to remain in Port Royal and learn the Indian language. He was captured by the Spanish the following year and taken to Saint Augustine. When the English privateer Robert Searles besieged Saint Augustine, Woodward escaped and joined him. Searles' ship was wrecked and Woodward was picked up by the first fleet of colonists bound for Carolina. Woodward was the first citizen of the Carolina colony and developed the English-Indian trade south of Virginia.

The original destination for the Carolina colonists who founded Charleston was Port Royal. However, the Sewees and Kiawahs convinced them that it was too dangerous that far south because the area had recently been devastated by the Westoes and was uncomfortably close to the Spanish garrison at Saint Augustine. They invited the English to settle among their people farther up the coast. Of course there was an advantage for the Kiawahs and Sewees to have English protection and trade so close at hand.

In 1682 a group of Scottish nobles led by Lord Cardross approached the Proprietors with a proposal to establish a settlement of Scottish protestants in Carolina. Scottish Covenanters had opposed the return of Charles II to the throne and suffered for it when he succeeded in 1660. In retaliation he attempted to subordinate the Presbyterians to the Church of England. In October of 1682 Lord Cardross engaged a ship and crew to reconnoiter the coast of South Carolina for a suitable location to make a settlement. When the *Carolina Merchant* arrived at Port Royal in November 1684, she carried Lord Cardross, William Dunlop, Robert Montgomery, paying passengers, indentured servants, and banished protestant rebels—149 passengers in all.

The colonists settled a little south of the present town of Beaufort and called their settlement Stuart Town. They soon alienated the Charleston power structure by claiming the Indian trade in their area and they provoked a Spanish attack by raiding missions and Timucuan villages in Florida. Retaliation came on August 17, 1689. The Spaniards burned the town although most of the inhabitants escaped. The Spanish sortie then sailed north to destroy Charleston but the fleet was scattered by a storm, the first of several that were to save Charleston from invasion. Lord Cardross and some of the Stuart Town settlers returned to Scotland, others moved to Charleston.

English settlers soon populated the tidewater south from Charleston. Newcomers included the families of John (Tuscarora Jack) Barnwell, Joseph and Thomas Parmenter, Thomas Nairne, Joseph Bryan, Hugh and Katherine Bryan, John and Elizabeth Palmer, William Bray, John Cochran, Joseph Morton, John Bull, Burnaby Bull, and William and Mary Bull. The area south of the Edisto River was cattle country until the appearance of rice plantations. Herds could be easily contained on necks of land in this well-watered region and were fed in the savannahs that remained green year round. The Yamassee War destroyed the cattle industry but many old cowpens developed into working plantations.

It became imperative to protect the southern frontier of Carolina during the tensions of Queen Anne's War, 1702–1713, when Spain and France were allied against England. A fort was built in 1703 at Port Royal where the deep harbor could accommodate ships of war. The garrison developed into a settlement and trading post. In 1711 the Lords Proprietors directed that a port and town be surveyed at Port Royal and a highway be built from there to the Ashepoo River. The new town was to be named for Proprietor Henry Somerset, second duke of Beaufort.

The Yamassees moved from central Georgia to the South Carolina coast about 1684 to be closer to the English trade. In 1707 the Assembly set aside a reservation for the Yamassees that lay between the Combahee and Savannah Rivers. The Yamassee towns were Altamaha, Pocosabo, Ocute, Salkehatchee, Euhaw, Huspa, Tomatly, Chechesee, and Tuscage. Scottish immigrants were settled at Port Royal and with the Yamassees they guarded the Southern frontier of Carolina. The Yamassees, however, were angered by abuses they suffered at the hands of the English traders and in 1715 went to war against Carolina. The conflict soon involved most of the Muskhogean tribes of the Southeast and threatened the existence of Charleston.

To provide further protection on the southern border of the colony the English government instructed John Barnwell to build Fort King George on the Altamaha River in 1721, effectively pushing the Carolina border farther south. After the Yamassee War subsided, South Carolina built Fort Palachacola on the Savannah River and created a marine patrol to guard against invasion. The Port Royal inhabitants were not totally free from Yamassee attacks until 1728 when Colonel John Palmer invaded Florida with the militia and Indian allies. They attacked the Yamassee village near Castillo de San Marcos and weakened the Yamassees to the point that they never regained the strength to make war. By the end of the eighteenth century the Yamassees had ceased to exist as a separate tribe and were absorbed by the Creeks and Seminoles.

The first township created in South Carolina was Purrysburg, established on the Savannah River in 1732. The largest number of settlers arrived in 1734. Savannah was settled in 1733 and the Beaufort District became closely associated with the colony of Georgia. The relationship was mutually beneficial because the Carolinians supplied provisions during the lean early years and the Georgians provided a patrol against Spanish and Indian attack from the south. When the defeat of the Spanish force at Bloody Marsh removed any further threat of invasion from Florida the citizens of Beaufort acknowledged that Oglethorpe had done more for their security than had Charleston.

A period of peace during mid-century allowed the Beaufort area to prosper. Rice plantations were established along inland swamps and indigo was planted on high ground. Both crops brought money and slaves to the Lowcountry. Many of the prominent and wealthy families of South Carolina established new plantations in the Beaufort District. They took up large tracts of the best land but there were numerous smaller landowners who had enough land to live comfortably. After the transition to tidal rice cultivation the coast became a land of slaves living on very large and isolated plantations owned by a few families. This locked out the planter of modest means who had to look for land farther inland or in Georgia.

The Revolution

Members of the Provincial Congress from the Beaufort District included Colonel Stephen Bull, John Bull, Thomas Rutledge, Daniel DeSaussure, Daniel Heyward, Jr., Thomas Heyward, Isaac Motte, Thomas Middleton, Cornelius Dupont, Gideon Dupont, Colonel Benjamin Garden, John Joyner, John Barnwell Jr., Philotheos Chiffelle, John Ward, and William Williamson.

When the Continental Congress issued an embargo on all trade with Great Britain. The South Carolina delegates, all being from Charleston, were successful in having rice exempted from the embargo because it would create a hardship for the colony. The Beaufort area, in contrast, depended on indigo for income. Beaufort soon became rife with smuggling in and out of the colony with a backdoor through Savannah, which was not yet completely in Whig control. As patriot power increased loyal Beaufort citizens left the colony. Beaufort merchant Roger Kelsall became a colonel in the East Florida Rangers and Fort Tonyn was built at his trading post on the St. Mary's River. Henry Stuart joined his brother John in exile in Florida as did Charles Shaw, prominent merchant and overseer of John Stuart's Lady's Island plantation.

Once the British secured Savannah they turned their attention northward. Major General Benjamin Lincoln was stationed at Purrysburg to keep British troops contained south of the Savannah River and Beaufort was guarded by Fort Lyttleton at Spanish Point. Captain De Treville spiked his guns and abandoned Fort Lyttleton when British ships sailed into the

Beaufort River. Although reinforcements were coming from Charleston, that intelligence had not yet reached Captain De Treville. General William Moultrie reached Beaufort two days later to take the town back from the British. The Americans and British met on February 2, 1779, near the Marine Corps Air Station on the present-day Trask Highway. The Americans, mostly militia, won the engagement but because they were out of ammunition they dared not pursue the retreating British. As the British retreated to their ships they were harassed by Captain John Barnwell's light cavalry and stragglers were captured. Although Beaufort was safe for the time being, the plantations of Saint Helena and Hilton Head lay in ruins and the inland sea route was open to the British and privateers.

In May, General Augustine Prevost crossed the Savannah River and pushed Moultrie back, forcing him to retreat to Charleston. The British, Tories, and the notorious Colonel Daniel McGirth laid waste to plantations and churches. Prevost pursued Moultrie to Charleston but retreated through the sea islands to Beaufort when Lincoln's army arrived. Slaves from destroyed plantations attached themselves to the British force. Most of the slaves were abandoned on Otter Island where many died of sickness and starvation, others were taken to the Caribbean and sold into slavery again.

That September the British garrison at Beaufort, commanded by Lieutenant Colonel John Maitland, reinforced the British in Savannah at the eleventh hour and kept the Georgia capital from falling to the Americans and French. The British departure, however, opened the way for the Americans to reoccupy Beaufort that November. The new American commander was Francis Marion, stationed at Sheldon. As the British prepared to take Charleston in early 1780 General Ferguson and Colonel Banastre Tarleton secured the Beaufort district then they joined Sir Henry Clinton at Charleston. During the next year the Revolution was kept alive in the Beaufort district by the guerrilla activities of Colonel William Harden, Francis Marion's counterpart in the southern part of the state.

Anarchy reigned in the Beaufort District in 1781 and 1782 because there was no government, army, or effective militia. Old scores and hatreds stemming from the war were settled by murder. The leading Tory from Beaufort was Andrew Deffeaux, Jr., who made a daring siege on Nassau and recaptured Bermuda from the Americans and Spanish. He stole slaves from the ravaged plantations around Beufort and took them to Bermuda. In 1780 Colonel Banastre Tarleton confiscated every horse on Port Royal Island and the British and American armies slaughtered cattle for food. The war ended with the Lowcountry in shambles.

New Prosperity

During the last decade of the eighteenth century tidal rice plantations were expanded and long staple sea island cotton was planted on the islands, replacing indigo as the cash crop. Sea island cotton was like white gold for the planters. For a number of years demand at the new textile mills in England and New England easily outstripped the supply of cotton. The price of cotton averaged about thirteen cents per pound in 1790 and sixty-three cents in 1818. The fortunes made with cotton helped Beaufort fashion itself into a smaller version of Charleston where Sea Island planters could resort to their town houses for society. Beaufort had one of the highest per capita incomes of American cities during the early antebellum period. Towns in Jasper, Beaufort, and Colleton counties developed in open pine uplands where planters could escape the sickness of the rice fields in summer.

The islands and east side of the lower Savannah River, being lower than the Georgia side, became one of the important rice producing regions in the nineteenth century. From the river front offices in Savannah one could see rice fields stretching eastward to the horizon in present-day Jasper County. Most of those rice fields have been incorporated into the Savannah National Wildlife Refuge. The large rice plantations were developed by wealthy and prominent men because the investment required in land and slaves excluded farmers of modest means. In fact, most rice plantations were operated by hired managers and the owners attended to their political and business careers in Charleston and Savannah. Rice was grown on the Tullafinny, Pocotaligo, Coosawhatchie, and Combahee rivers and in the Great Swamp on New River. The only rice grown today on the Atlantic Coast is in southern Jasper County at Turnbridge Plantation.

Rice and sea island cotton cultivation required large amounts of labor and spurred the importation of slaves from the Congo and Angola. The isolated plantations were populated by communities of Africans who developed their own culture known as Gullah. Significant Gullah communities grew up on Daufuskie, Saint Helena, and Hilton Head islands and remain there today where they have yet to be displaced by resort developments.

Upland farmers were not so wealthy as the rice planters but they compensated by diversifying their crops and businesses. They grew produce and upland cotton, and operated mercantile businesses and sawmills. When new Indian lands were opened in the west the population declined as families sought good cotton land elsewhere.

William Bartram's Travels in the Lowcountry

The Bartrams dined at George Alison's on September 2, 1765, and we assume that William also stopped there on his way to the Cherokee Nation in 1775. The road from Alison's to Purrysburg is as straight now as it was then. John Bartram wrote in his diary that …

> *"we travailed 7 mile on A causway as straight as posible & as even as A bowling green I believe no roads is finer to travail then ye carolinas mostly shaded with lofty pines oaks tupelo or liquid amber."*[1]

The Purrysburg Road was constructed from Coosawhatchie Bridge to the Savannah River about 1736.

When William Bartram traveled with his father in 1765 they met with their only true lack of hospitality in all their travels near Willtown. A planter refused to put them up for the evening, even for money, but the Bartrams were allowed to sleep in a dilapidated shed after much pleading. Ironically, the

---

1. John Bartram, *Diary of a Journey Through the Carolinas, Georgia, and Florida: From July 1, 1765, to April 10, 1766*, edited by Francis Harper. Transactions of the American Philosophical Society; Philadelphia, 1942.

modern Hardeeville is known as a center of hospitality because of the concentration of motels and restaurants springing up along I–95.

When William returned to South Carolina in 1773 he traveled from Charleston to Savannah by boat on April 11 or 12. On his return from Florida in March 1775 he again arrived in Charleston by boat. When William Bartram traveled to the Cherokee Nation in 1775 his route followed US-17 from Jacksonboro to Pocotaligo. He crossed Coosawhatchie Bridge then followed SC-462 and Highway 13 to Ridgeland. He spent the evening of April 24, 1775 near Ridgeland at a private home. The route from Ridgeland was a straight line to Tillman then Highway 119 to Three Sisters Ferry on the Savannah River. He arrived at Sisters Ferry on April 25 and ate lunch at the ferry house. When William left Savannah on his return home in November 1776 he crossed the Savannah River at Zubly's Ferry near Purrysburg. From there he followed the Purrysburg Road to Ridgeland and retraced his earlier route to Charleston.

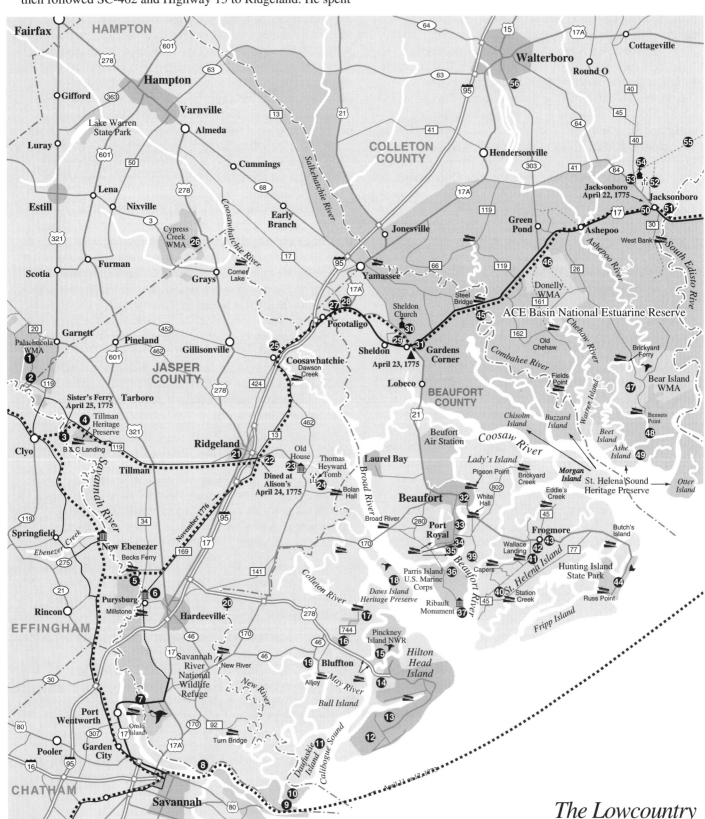

The Lowcountry

Sites

1. Palachucola Wildlife Management Area. Recent additions have brought the total land holdings for Palachucola WMA to almost 6,000 acres. It now adjoins the James Webb Nature Center and contains significant wetlands. Stokes Bluff Landing offers a fine view of the Savannah River. For maps and information visit the Webb Center. The entrance to the office is located on Highway 20 three miles west of Garnett.

James Webb Nature Center. The Webb Center provides a number of recreational opportunities for outdoor enthusiasts, including hiking, birding, canoeing, fishing, and hunting during specified periods. The Webb Center offers educational programs in management of natural resources. Land was purchased in 1941 and includes property with titles dating back to the early 1700s. Most of the center is upland pine forest with about twenty-five percent in river floodplains dominated by old-growth cypress and tupelo. Six thousand acres provide a haven for wildlife, especially birds.

The Savannah River Swamp Trail begins at Bluff Lake and reaches the banks of the Savannah River. It may be impassable in wet weather.

2. Palachacola. This bluff of the Savannah River has been called Palachacola (with numerous spellings) since the earliest maps of the area were drawn. The name is a corruption of Apalachicola, which is Choctaw for "People of the Ruling Place." The Apalachicolas were a Hitchiti-speaking people who were recorded as living originally on the lower parts of the Chattahoochee River. The Spanish made several attempts to establish a mission among the Apalachicolas and applied their name to the river and all the tribes of the area, including Muskoghean-speaking tribes farther upriver.

A band of Apalachicolas moved to the Savannah River to take advantage of the trade emanating from Charleston. They may have also been seeking the protection of the English for they had been attacked by the Muscogees in 1706. They were allied with the Yamassees and in the aftermath of the Yamassee War of 1715 most Apalachicolas returned to their ancestral home at the confluence of the Chattahoochee and Flint rivers. By the mid-eighteenth century they had moved north to what is now Russell County, Alabama. One legend says that a treaty between the Apalachicolas and Muscogees was the foundation for the Creek Confederacy.

When the Apalachicolas left the Savannah River the Yuchis moved in and lived at Palachacola and at Mt. Pleasant across the river. South Carolina constructed a palisaded fort at Palachacola in 1723 and established a garrison commanded by Lieutenant William Bellinger. In 1740, during the War of Jenkins' Ear, families from the Altamaha River settlements sought refuge at Fort Palachacola because of the impending Spanish invasion.

3. Sisters Ferry was originally called Three Sisters Ferry. William Bartram dined at the ferry on April 25, 1775, then crossed over into Georgia. Sisters Ferry Road on the Georgia side ends at Clyo.

4. Tillman Heritage Preserve. This 953-acre heritage preserve is a sand ridge formed by the Savannah River during the Pleistocene era. The natural communities are longleaf pine and wiregrass, mixed bottomland hardwood, and cypress-tupelo. Georgia Pacific donated the land to the Nature Conservancy who then transferred it to the South Carolina Wildlife and Marine Resources Department. This is the only preserve in South Carolina devoted to preserving the gopher tortoise and its habitat. Fire is important in keeping the longleaf pine-wiregrass environment free of turkey oaks and promoting new plant growth that the tortoise feed upon.

The gopher tortoise was first described by William Bartram:

> *The dens, or caverns, dug in the sandhills, by the great land-tortoise, called here Gopher, (Testudo Polyphemus) present a very singular appearance: these vast caves are their castles and diurnal retreats, from whence they issue forth in the night in search of prey. The little mounds, or hillocks of fresh earth thrown up in great numbers in the night, have also a curious appearance.*[1]

> *The first signs of this animal's existence, as we travel Southerly, are immediately after we cross the Savanna River. It is to be seen only on the high dry Sandhills.*[2]

1. William Bartram, *Travels*, 18.
2. Ibid., 180

Legend

1. Palachucola Wildlife Management Area
   James Webb Nature Center
   Savannah River Swamp Trail
2. Palachacola
3. Sisters Ferry
4. Tillman Heritage Preserve
5. Old Zubly's Ferry
6. Purrysburg
7. Savannah River National Wildlife Refuge
8. Carolina Gold Rice
9. Tybee National Wildlife Refuge
10. Turtle Island Wildlife Management Area
11. Daufuskie Island
12. Sea Pines Forest Preserve
13. Hilton Head Island
14. Green Shell Enclosure
15. Pinckney Island National Wildlife Refuge
16. Victoria Bluff Heritage Preserve
17. Waddell Mariculture Center
18. Daws Island Heritage Preserve
19. Bluffton
20. Great Swamp Wildlife Management Area
21. Ridgeland
    Blue Heron Nature Trail
    Pauline Pratt Webel Museum
    Pratt Memorial Library
22. Grahamville
23. Old House
24. Thomas Heyward Grave
25. Coosawhatchie
26. Cypress Creek Wildlife Management Area
27. The Yamassees
28. Thomas Nairne
29. Oyotunji
30. Old Sheldon Church
31. Gardens Corner
32. Beaufort
33. Fort Lyttleton
34. Fort Frederick
35. Stuart Town
36. Parris Island
37. Ribault Monument
38. Port Royal
39. Lady's Island
40. Saint Helena Island
41. Saint Helena Episcopal Chapel of Ease
42. Penn Center
43. Frogmore
44. Hunting Island State Park
45. Combahee Ferry
46. Donnelley Wildlife Management Area
47. Bear Island Wildlife Management Area
48. ACE Basin
49. Saint Helena Island Heritage Preserve
50. Jacksonborough
51. Edisto Nature Trail
52. Isaac Hayne Tomb
53. Bethel Presbyterian Church
54. Pon Pon Chapel of Ease Ruins
55. Battle of Parkers Ferry
56. Colleton County Museum

Gopher tortoise

The deep burrows of the gopher tortoise are extensive and support a number of other species, including lizards, mice, rabbits, and a tick that is parasitic only on the tortoise. Many insects seek refuge from the dry, hot sand in the recesses of the cool, damp burrows. The rare indigo snake and gopher tortoise often live together in the same burrow. The gopher tortoise has no prey, except humans, as Bartram says and they are complete herbivores.

The entrance to the Tillman Preserve is located on Highway 119. Open from dawn to dusk except during scheduled hunts. For a map and information visit the James Webb Nature Center in Garnett.

5. Old Zubly's Ferry. The old ferry landed passengers at a site just below Ebenezer now occupied by the McIntosh power plant. Zubly is a Salzburg German name made prominent by Reverend Johann Joachim Zubly, a Georgia delegate to the Second Continental Congress. He was, however, against complete separation from England and left the Congress. The times did not allow for moderation and he was forced to leave Georgia. His daughter, Ann, married James Seagrove, the trader and Indian agent of Colerain on St. Marys River. After the Revolution she tried to obtain compensation for her father's confiscated property.

6. Purrysburg (also Purysburg). Jean Pierre Purry established a colony of French and Swiss protestants in 1732 on a bluff overlooking the Savannah River at a site that was formerly a Yamassee village. Purry envisioned gradual settlement of the land between the Savannah and Mississippi rivers and proposed that the new country be called Georgia, after the King of England who had granted the land for the settlement.

Though it boasted a population of almost 900 at one time, Purrysburg failed to prosper due to the prevalence of disease. Many immigrants, weakened by the hot climate, died of malaria and dysentery during their first year in South Carolina. There were boon times during the Trustee Government when rum was outlawed in Georgia. Intemperate Georgians would ferry across the Savannah River to engage in liquid merriment. If it is true that it was whiskey that settled the West, and not Colt pistols, we might speculate that it was rum that made life bearable on the frontier of the Southeast.

The sandy soil was not very fertile and many inhabitants of Purrysburg left for Savannah, Beaufort, and Charleston. Hardeeville supplanted Purrysburg in the late eighteenth century as the commercial center of the area. The site of Purrysburg is commemorated by a stone monument near the intersection of Highways 34 and 203.

Purry died in 1736 and the town quickly dispersed. The French and German families entered the mainstream of South Carolina politics and culture to become leaders. The names of Huguenin, Jeanneret, Zerdier, deBeaufain, Bugnion, Holzendorf, Mayerhoffer, and Zubly became well known. Purry's son Charles became an important merchant in Beaufort and was murdered by his slaves in 1754. Charles and his wife had no children so the Purry name did not survive in South Carolina. The other son, David, became a successful banker and philanthropist in Portugal.

7. Savannah River National Wildlife Refuge. The Savannah River National Wildlife Refuge is a formidable natural area with 26,000 acres of land, including 13,000 acres of bottomland cypress/tupelo swamp, and twenty-five miles of dikes open to hiking and biking. The old rice fields provide a perfect habitat for waterfowl and alligators. The vastness of the impounded rice fields makes the Refuge an ideal place to view sunsets. To the south one has a view of the Savannah docks and industrial district along the Savannah River.

There is a four-mile automobile tour named the Laurel Hill Wildlife Drive. It begins on the south side of US-17. Near the entrance there is a self-serve visitor's kiosk where maps, information, and public restrooms are available. The drive is open until a half-hour after dusk and the gates close automatically. The impoundments on the north side of US-17 are open to hunting during designated times, the south side is closed to hunting at all times.

8. Carolina Gold Rice. The grain that built many fortunes in colonial South Carolina is still being grown at Turnbridge Plantation, although in minuscule quantities compared to the ship loads that once sailed from South Carolina. Their rice is available only through Holy Trinity Episcopal Church in Ridgeland, call (803) 726–3743. By the early 1800s rice was grown on the east side of the Savannah River from below Savannah to north of present

Dr. Henry Woodward

Robert Sanford sailed the coast of South Carolina in 1666 and made contact with the coastal Indians of Port Royal, who desired an English presence for protection against the Westoes and Spanish. Among those sailing with Captain Sanford was the remarkable Dr. Henry Woodward. When it was arranged that the local chief's nephew would return to England with Captain Sanford, Woodward agreed to stay behind as collateral for the young Indian's safe return.

Woodward learned the language and ways of his hosts, but he was captured by the Spanish when they heard that the English were trying to establish a presence in their northern territory. Woodward was taken to Saint Augustine where he soon won the trust and kindness of his captors. When the English pirate Robert Searles plundered Saint Augustine in 1668 Henry Woodward sailed with him to the Antilles. Woodward signed on as ship's surgeon and was shipwrecked while bound for England. He survived and reached Nevis. The first group of English colonists and Barbadian planters bound for Carolina made a call at Nevis and added Dr. Woodward to their venture.

Henry Woodward established the English-Indian deerskin trade in the Carolina colony. He made alliances with the fierce Westoes on the Savannah River and the Muscogees on the Chattahoochee. He was a constant aggravation to the Spanish who watched their influence in the distant parts of Santa Elena and Apalachee begin to erode. Woodward taunted the Spanish with sarcastic notes left behind as he disappeared into the forest at the approach of their soldiers. When he became ill at Coweta in 1686 he was carried by Indians on a stretcher all the way to Charleston where he soon died. To the Indians of the interior Henry Woodward must have appeared almost divine in his ability to produce brightly colored cloth, guns, axes, kettles, knives, and pretty glass beads that could be had in exchange for readily available deerskins.

Henry Woodward's plantation was located on the Ashepoo River and his descendants continued to live in the Beaufort area for many years

day US-17. Many of those old rice fields have been incorporated into the Savannah National Wildlife Refuge.

9. Tybee National Wildlife Refuge. This small, 100-acre island is home to terns, pelicans, egrets, herons, and seagulls. It is accessible only by boat.

10. Turtle Island Wildlife Management Area contains 1,700 acres of salt marsh and maritime forest and is accessible only by boat. Turtle Island is a small but unspoiled barrier island.

11. Daufuskie Island. Gullah is still spoken on Daufuskie Island because there is no bridge to the mainland and the island has had limited interaction with the outside world. Daufuskie Island was planted in Sea Island cotton until the boll weevil arrived earlier this century and many land owners had to sell their plantations. Oyster canning was an important industry after World War II but pollution from the Savannah River has caused the oyster beds to decline. There is a ferry to Daufuskie from Hilton Head Island and private boats can dock at New River Landing on the southwest end of the island. If you go to Daufuskie, remember that its communities are private property. Beaches and roads, of course, are public property.

12. Sea Pines Forest Preserve. A two-mile hiking trail from the preserve parking area leads to one of the largest shell rings in the Southeast. It is 150 feet in diameter and several feet deep. Access to the shell ring and forest preserve is located at the end of William Hilton Parkway. Visitors must pay a fee at the gate to Sea Pines Plantation. The preserve is located off Greenwood Drive.

13. Hilton Head Island is named for William Hilton, the Puritan ship captain who in 1661 explored the Southeastern coast from Cape Fear to the Satilla River. He was employed by Barbadian planters who were seeking new land. Hilton Head is one of the largest of the Sea Islands and remained relatively isolated until development began in 1956. Now it is one of the best-known resort complexes in the country and little remains of its natural habitat. Hilton Head Island, like most Sea Islands, has been inhabited for thousands of years by humans who have found plentiful game and seafood. As you enter Hilton Head look on the right for the scenic view preserved by the local land trust.

Hilton Head Museum. 100 William Hilton Parkway, Hilton Head Island.

14. Green Shell Enclosure. This very large shell ring is dated from the Irene phase of the Mississippian Period, c. 1300 A.D.

Carolina Gold rice at Turnbridge Plantation, Jasper County, South Carolina

15. Pinckney Island National Wildlife Refuge. In 1734 Charles Pinckney (husband of Eliza Lucas Pinckney) acquired the islands that make up this refuge. Upon his death the island went to his son, Charles Cotesworth Pinckney (1746–1825). The younger Pinckney was an officer of the Revolution, member of the Constitutional Convention, minister to France, candidate for the presidency, and a friend of François Michaux. The Georgia fevertree, a Bartram discovery, was named *Pinckneya pubens* by Michaux in his honor of C. C. Pinckney. He practiced law in Charleston after the Revolution and was a founder of the Charleston Museum. He developed a Sea Island cotton plantation on Pinckney Island after retiring from public life in 1801. He began to experiment with unusual and exotic plants and built a nursery. He also experimented with animal breeding and chemistry.

Inhabitation of Pinckney Island by native Americans began 12,000 years ago. Pinckney Island is 4,053 acres with creeks and salt marsh making up sixty-seven percent of the area. There are fourteen miles of trails for hiking and bicycling that are closed to motorized traffic. The trails lead along salt marsh, through upland pines, and to bluffs overlooking the creeks. The freshwater ponds are havens for snowy egrets, herons, ospreys, ibis, and wood storks. Visitor parking and an information kiosk are located on the north side of US-278. An available brochure has educational information on the dynamics of the salt marsh and the importance of fire in maintaining pine lands. Open year-round during daylight hours.

16. Victoria Bluff Heritage Preserve. More typical of Florida than South Carolina this preserve has a botanical community of saw palmetto and pines. Rusty lyonia is found in South Carolina only there and the best population of rare pond spice (*Litsea aestivalis*) in the country grows at Victoria Bluff in wet shallow depressions. Access to parking and the hiking trail is by way of Sawmill Creek Road north of US-278 and is marked by a diamond-shaped game management sign. The preserve is open year round. There is a two-week archery season for deer in November and another in December when the preserve should be avoided by hikers.

Stephen Elliott

Stephen Elliott (1771–1830) was one of South Carolina's eminent naturalists and a native of Beaufort. He was born to the wealthy Elliott and Barnwell families and married Esther Habersham, granddaughter of James Habersham of Georgia. Elliott graduated from Yale with honors in 1791 and returned to Beaufort to manage the family plantations in South Carolina and Georgia. He was a founder of Beaufort College and the Beaufort Library Society and as a state representative Elliott was one of the authors of the Free School Act that helped establish public education in South Carolina. He became the president of the Bank of South Carolina in 1812 and gave up the planter's life. While living in Charleston he was a member of the board of trustees of the College of Charleston and professor of natural history at the Medical College of South Carolina. Obviously a man of boundless energy he helped found the Literary and Philosophical Society and the *Southern Review*.

Elliott had a keen interest and ability in natural history and began collecting botanical specimens while living in Beaufort. He published *Botany of South Carolina and Georgia* in 1821, which established him as the most important botanical scholar in the South during his lifetime. His name is honored in one of William Bartram's discoveries, *Elliottia racemosa*, or Georgia plume. Elliott collected his specimen of *Elliottia* near Waynesboro in Burke County, Georgia, in 1808. It was named by Henry Muhlenberg in 1810 while Bartram's specimen lay forgotten in the British Museum.

17. Waddell Mariculture Center is one of the largest research facilities in the world devoted to marine agriculture. Located on Sawmill Creek Road north of US-278.

18. Daws Island Heritage Preserve. Daws Island contains four Late Archaic period shell rings and twenty-three archaeological features that date from 10,000 B.C. to A.D. 500. Public entry is by guided tour only. Call the Heritage Trust Archaeologist at (803) 734-3753 for tours.

19. Bluffton. Planters from the surrounding area built summer homes on this high bluff overlooking the May River where southeastern breezes kept mosquitoes and malaria in check. The botanist Dr. Joseph Mellichamp lived at Bluffton and is buried at St. Luke's Church.

20. Great Swamp Wildlife Management Area. Great Swamp is the lowlands of the New River and was one of the Lowcountry's rice-producing areas in the early nineteenth century. It contains 3,098 acres with access on Highway 141 east of Hardeeville.

21. Ridgeland was originally known as Gopher Hill for the number of gopher tortoises in the area. Ridgeland grew up as a railroad town and as a railroad depot the town prospered and engulfed the nearby community of Grahamville.

Blue Heron Nature Trail. The city of Ridgeland, the local Soil and Water Conservation District, Jasper County, and local organizations cooperatively built this excellent urban nature preserve. The gardens contain plants that attract butterflies, hummingbirds, and songbirds. Display beds feature plant selections suited to the soil and climate of the South Carolina Coastal Plain. As the trail leaves the formal garden area it encounters habitats filled with native plants and trees. The park contains outdoor classrooms, boardwalks and a nature center. Blue Heron Nature Trail is a half-mile long and connects to the walking tour of Ridgeland, totaling five miles. Located just off SC-336 between downtown Ridgeland and I-95. Follow the access road past the Comfort Inn.

Pauline Pratt Webel Museum. On display are dioramas of agricultural life in the Lowcountry and artifacts from pre-European inhabitation and the colonial period. One of the more interesting historical items was the discovery of jug wells used to collect pure water by sinking large, porous clay jars into saturated soil. Located at 123B East Wilson Street.

Pratt Memorial Library, 123A Wilson Street. The gardens at the library were designed by Richard K. Webel, a nationally known landscape architect. Maps, books, and portraits relating to Lowcountry history are on view.

22. Grahamville. During the Colonial are the settlement of Grahamville grew up at the intersection of Savannah Road and the road to the Euhaw Settlement. When William Bartram passed through there the community consisted of Alison's Tavern and the crossroads. John and William Bartram stayed at George Alison's tavern in 1765 and we can assume that William stopped again during his *Travels*. There was probably at least a tavern and public inn at the crossroads, yet Washington had to detour to White Hall where Thomas Heyward lived in order to find suitable lodgings.

Euhaw Baptist Church was organized in 1751 on nearby Euhaw Creek. The first pastor was Reverend William Tilly who became a follower and friend of Reverend George Whitefield. The Euhaw Baptist Church helped establish Baptist churches in lower South Carolina and Georgia. The present church was built in 1905 at Grahamville because many of the congregation had moved to town.

23. Old House. Plantations grew up along Euhaw Creek where rice could be grown. The ruin of this plantation house gives the community its name. It is owned by the Historic Charleston Foundation and is posted against trespassing without permission.

24. Thomas Heyward Grave. The tomb of Thomas Heyward, Jr., signer of the Declaration of Independence, is in a private cemetery overlooking the marsh. The oak-lined avenue to the Heyward family cemetery is noted by a historical marker on SC-268 at Old House. Heyward served as a judge and first president of the Agricultural Society of South Carolina. His White Hall mansion was built in the 1780s of brick and tabby and burned shortly after the conclusion of the Civil War. The ruins are still visible at the intersection of SC-462 and SC-268. It is marked by an entrance gate and a double avenue of live oaks. Heyward entertained George Washington at his home on the evening of May 11, 1791.

25. Coosawhatchie is named for the Kusso Indians who lived in the area during the seventeenth century. The community of Coosawhatchie grew up at the bridge over the Coosawhatchie River on the site of an earlier Indian village. The road from Pocotaligo to Purrysburg was opened in the 1730s and the bridge was built about 1750. Nearly all travelers going south crossed at the bridge and several businesses were established to take advantage of the commercial traffic. Daniel and David De Saussure built a store there in the 1760s.

Coosawhatchie became the county seat of Beaufort County in 1788 because of the difficulty of traveling to and from Beaufort according to the tide on the Coosaw River. An elegant two-story courthouse designed by William Jay was built in 1816 but, unfortunately, does not survive today. The county government were later moved to Gillisonville to avoid malaria and fevers were so prevalent in Coosawhatchie. While supervising the defense of the Charleston-Savannah Railroad Robert E. Lee bought a horse at Coosawhatchie for $200. He changed the horse's name from Greenbriar to Traveller.

26. Cypress Creek Wildlife Management Area. 4,605 acres of creek swamp and upland. North of Grays just off US-278 on CR-55.

27. The Yamassees. The first mention of the Yamassees seems to be in the province of Altamaha, recorded in the narratives of Hernando de Soto. Altamaha lay on the Oconee River near Milledgeville and it is the name of the traditional capital of the Lower Yamassees. By the late 1600s they had moved to the Apalachee region near Tallahassee and among the Guale on the Georgia Coast. The Yamassees became dissatisfied with their Spanish patrons and around 1685 moved to the lower parts of South Carolina onto land given them by the English. During the Yamassee War they suffered more than other participants and many withdrew again to the protection of the Spanish in Saint Augustine where they became an indentured people. The Florida Yamassees were absorbed into the Seminole Nation and the Yamassees on the Apalachicola River joined with the Upper and Lower Creeks. Some of the Upper Creek Yamassees migrated to the Yamacraw Bluff on the Savannah River with their Chief, Tomochichi.

Pocotaligo was the principal town of the Yamassee Indians and the epicenter of the Yamassee War in 1715. The war began on the morning of April 15, 1715 with the murders of Agent Thomas Nairne and his deputies. More than ninety English traders, planters, and their families were killed that day and the uprising soon spread to all other native tribes including the Catawbas, Cheraws, Santees, Congarees, and Waterees in South Carolina; and the Creeks and Choctaws in Alabama. Homes were burned as well as the fledgling town of Beaufort. The war lasted a year and devastated the countryside, forcing whites from the frontier and into the safety of Charleston. Farms languished and crops went unplanted. Ninety of the one hundred White traders working in South Carolina had been executed by the Yamassees.

The hostilities grew out of legitimate resentment over slaving, ill-treatment of Indian women, and corrupt business practices that left the Indian families continually in debt. Emperor Brim of the Creeks became the driving force behind this war that threatened to wipe out the young colony of Carolina. An alliance between Carolina, the Cherokees, and the

Chickasaws defused the tensions and the war quickly died down without much more bloodshed except for sporadic and punitive raids. By the end of the first year of the war the Creeks began to weary of the disruption to trade caused by the incessant raids and the Creeks themselves turned against the Yamassees. The war officially ended with a treaty concluded in June 1718, although the Yamassees in Florida continued raiding South Carolina until 1721. Without the aid of the Cherokees the English could probably have been driven from Charleston.

As a result of the ineffectiveness of the Proprietors to protect the colony, Carolinians petitioned to become a Crown Colony and place themselves under the protection of the king. In 1729 Parliament bought the shares of all Proprietors but Lord Granville, whose tract remained little inhabited for years due to difficulty in obtaining outright land ownership.

Oyotunji, an African village in Sheldon, South Carolina

28. Thomas Nairne was one of the first European settlers on Saint Helena Island. Nairne was a trader and in 1708 made an expedition into the Creek and Choctaw territory as far as the Mississippi River. He became the Indian agent for South Carolina and was the first to feel the wrath of the Yamassee War in 1715. Though he had worked on behalf of the Yamassees to protect their trading interests and prevent trespassers onto their reservation Nairne and his deputies were attacked the morning after a conference with the Yamassees, who had appeared to have been appeased. He was tortured and burned to death by *petite feu*, where splinters of fat pine wood are inserted into the skin and set afire.

29. Oyotunji. This authentic African village was built in 1970 and is dedicated to the re-establishment of the Yoruba culture and religion. Shops and monthly festivals introduce visitors to the art, ceremonies, history, and spiritual beliefs of the people who inhabit the ancient kingdoms of Yoruba. These kingdoms are located in Nigeria, Southern Dahomey, Togoland, and parts of Ghana. Festivals celebrate the ancient gods—Oshun, goddess of love; Ifa, god of destiny; Obatala, patron god of the village. Located on US-17 in Sheldon. Open daily from 10 a.m. to dusk. Admission.

30. Old Sheldon Church is named for the English ancestral home of the Bull family and was the parish church of Prince William Parish. It was constructed from 1745–1755 and was one of the finest buildings in the South at the time but it is now in ruins. It was the first building constructed in America to use a classic Greek temple form. The church was burned by the British in 1799 as they marched to Beaufort after taking Savannah. It was rebuilt then burned again by Federal troops during the Civil War. William Bull, Sr., died in 1755 and is buried at the altar within the interior of the church. He assisted Oglethorpe in laying out the streets of Savannah and was governor of South Carolina from 1737–1743.

31. Gardens Corner is named for the Garden family whose name appears on the 1775 Mouzon map. This was probably Colonel Benjamin Garden, no relation to Dr. Alexander Garden. It was a crossroads community then as it is now.

32. Beaufort was created as a port of entry by direction of the Lords Proprietors in 1711. Intermittent war with the Yamassees prevented the growth of Beaufort and the lower parishes. It was not until hostilities with the Yamassees ended in 1721 that Beaufort began to prosper. The Historic Beaufort Foundation is located on the first floor of the John Mark Verdier House on Bay Street.

Beaufort Arsenal Museum is housed in the Arsenal at 713 Craven Street. Fossils, Native American and colonial artifacts are exhibited and local crafts are for sale. Admission.

North Street Aquarium features marine life of the sounds and salt marsh of the Southeastern coast. 609 North Street.

33. Fort Lyttleton was built on the site of Stuart Town at Spanish Point to guard the Beaufort River during the Revolution. The fort was destroyed by the American garrison in January 1779, to prevent it falling into the hands of a British naval force lying in the Beaufort River. Fort Marion was built on the site after the Revolution.

34. Fort Frederick was built between 1726 and 1740 by South Carolina and was barely finished before it fell into disrepair. The waning of the Yamassees and the establishment of the buffer colony of Georgia removed most threats of invasion and reduced the importance of a fortification at Port Royal. The tabby ruins are located on the Beaufort River at the U.S. Naval Hospital in Port Royal.

35. Stuart Town is the site of the 1684 Scottish settlement founded by Lord Cardross. The town was destroyed by the Spanish on August 17, 1689.

36. Parris Island. The first U.S. Marine Corps post was established on Parris Island in 1891 as an attachment to the naval station. In 1915 complete command was transferred to the U.S. Marine Corps and the recruiting station was transferred from Norfolk, Virginia to Parris Island. Now the entire island is under the jurisdiction of the Marine Corps. Extensive archaeological projects have been completed on the early Indian, French, and Spanish heritage. The Parris Island Museum exhibits artifacts and history of the Native Americans and European colonial attempts in the Port Royal area.

Open 10:00 a.m.–4:30 p.m. Monday through Sunday. Closed Thanksgiving, Christmas, and New Year's Day. Free admission.

37. Ribault Monument. Located near the site of Charlesfort on Parris Island this monument commemorates the founding of the first French colony in North America in 1562. The monument is actually built at the site of the Spanish Fort San Marcos, dating from 1576. The French village was a little north of the monument.

38. Port Royal. Port Royal Sound and the Beaufort River offered protection for ships and settlers in early attempts to colonize Carolina. The Spanish began exploring the area as early as 1514 and named the area Santa Elena. Lucas Vásquez Ayelles de Ayllôn entered St. Helena Sound in 1521 to capture Indian slaves. To the native Americans the area was known as Chicora, which extended northward to Charleston.

The French claim to North America dated from the 1524 voyage of Giovanni de Verrazzano who sailed for Francis I. In 1562 Jean Ribault explored the River May (St. Johns) and then sailed north along the coast of Georgia. He found an excellent harbor he named Port Royal and decided to leave a garrison of twenty-seven men. They built a fort on Parris Island and named the settlement Charlesfort, after their king. Ribault returned to France for supplies and reinforcements but civil strife in France prevented his timely return. The French soldiers at Charlesfort soon wore out their welcome with the native inhabitants who came to see the Europeans as shiftless freeloaders, continually begging for food and offering little help. The French commander Albert de la Pierria became so overbearing that the garrison killed him and chose a new leader. The inhabitants of Charlesfort became so discouraged they returned to France in a ship built with their own hands and outfitted with sails made of clothing. They were becalmed for a month before reaching the coast of England and had to eat one of their crew to survive.

In 1566 Florida Governor Pedro Menéndez de Avilés established Fort San Felipe on Parris island in order to assert the Spanish claim to the area. It became the capital of Florida and priests established missions at Santa Elena. In 1576 the governor directed Juan Pardo to seek an overland route from Santa Elena to Mexico. Fort San Felipe was attacked and destroyed by local Indians and was abandoned by the Spanish authorities in favor of Saint Augustine, which was better suited for the protection of the treasure ships following the Gulf Stream.

The missions in the Port Royal and Saint Helena area were subordinate to Guale and never as strong as the missions on the Georgia coast. After the Westo invasion in 1661 the Spanish retreated south of the Savannah River. The first English colonists bound for Carolina in 1670 bypassed Port Royal because of the historical Spanish presence in the area. After Saint Augustine, the Port Royal area has the longest history of European presence in the United States.

39. Lady's Island was named for the wife of the original owner. Later, John Stuart owned a 1,500-acre plantation at the southern end of Lady's Island that also included Gibbes, Cat, and Cane Islands. This profitable plantation was confiscated after Stuart fled the colony in 1775. His brothers Henry and Francis ran a mercantile business in Beaufort at the corner of Bay and Carteret streets. Henry was also involved with overseeing John's indigo plantations on Lady's Island. Francis Stuart's son, Dr. James Stuart, became an American patriot.

Sheldon Church

40. Saint Helena Island. Today Saint Helena Island is noted as one of the remaining Gullah communities and is largely undeveloped.

41. Saint Helena Episcopal Chapel of Ease. Throughout the coastal parishes of South Carolina chapels of ease were built in areas that were remote from the main parish church. The chapel of ease on Saint Helena Island dates from 1748. A fire in 1886 left it in ruins with only the tabby walls standing. It is located on Land's End Road.

42. Penn Center. The planters of the Sea Islands fled their coastal plantations during the occupation by Federal Troops at the end of the Civil War. Their property was confiscated and turned over to the former slaves who were then paid to grow Sea Island cotton. The first school for blacks was established by missionaries in a prefabricated building shipped from Philadelphia. This school became known as the Penn School and operated from 1862 to 1953. The building was renamed the Penn Center and was used for community services and as a conference center. The 1963 march on Selma was organized by Dr. Martin Luther King at the Penn Center. Located on Land's End Road.

43. Frogmore was once the plantation of William Bull, Jr. He was lieutenant governor of South Carolina and a loyalist during the Revolution. He left the state in 1777 and died in England. The slaves of Frogmore developed a large Gullah community that became well known for its witch doctors and Frogmore Stew.

44. Hunting Island State Park. Hunting Island is so named because it was always a hunting preserve, even at the beginnings of the colony, because the uneven nature of the land made it unfit for planting. André Michaux explored Hunting Island on April 25–26 and May 13, 1787 and Alexander Wilson explored the area in 1809. A group of planters jointly owned the island in later years to use for their private hunting parties. Hunting Island is now one of the most beautiful state parks in the Southeast with four miles of beach and many acres of maritime forest. The bleached oaks and fallen pines at the north end are especially haunting in the early morning. The beach is eroding at the north end and the forest is slowly being toppled onto the beach. There is a delightful boardwalk through the salt marsh and hammocks. Camping sites and cabins are available. US-21 on Saint Helena Island. Admission.

45. Combahee Ferry. This ferry was the important crossing of the lower Combahee River during colonial times. It began operation in 1715 and was licensed by the assembly to Joseph Bryan, father of Hugh and Jonathan Bryan. He was allowed to charge extra due to the expense of maintaining the causeway through the marsh. A bridge was built in 1741 but it was not maintained and fell down by the early 1750s. William Bull's Newbury Plantation was on the west side of the Combahee where the ferry landed. The Combahee River is named for the Combahee Indians.

46. Donnelley Wildlife Management Area. In addition to the many opportunities to view wildlife the Donnelley area also has two hiking trails. The entrance is located on US-17 just past the intersection with SC-303. Open 8 a.m.–5 p.m., Monday through Saturday except during hunts. Information is available at the kiosk on the Main Road one-half mile from the entrance.

47. Bear Island Wildlife Management Area. 11,000 acres including 4,400 acres of waterfowl marshland. Follow CR-26 south from US-17 east of Green Pond.

48. ACE Basin. ACE stands for the three rivers—Ashepoo, Combahee, and Edisto. A consortium of private and public landowners has cooperated in protecting and preserving the natural splendor of this large system of estuaries, tidal marshes, and islands. The combined holdings of 350,000 acres provides an immense area of diverse ecosystems, forming a haven for native wildlife, including many endangered and threatened species. Conservation agreements with private landowners allow for continued traditional land use that is consistent with habitat protection but restricts development for commercial purposes. Organizations and agencies that have helped create the ACE Basin initiative are the South Carolina Wildlife and Marine Resources Department, the U.S. Fish & Wildlife Service, Ducks Unlimited, The Nature Conservancy, and numerous individuals. Information is available at Donnelley WMA and from the Nature Conservancy of South Carolina.

49. St. Helena Sound Heritage Preserve contains Big, Warren, Ashe, Beet, and Otter islands and covers 7,536 acres of sensitive marsh and pristine estuary. Access is by water only.

50. Jacksonborough. The South Carolina General Assembly convened at Jacksonborough on January 18, 1782 after the surrender of Charleston. At Jacksonborough they were protected by the Continental Army of General Nathaneal Greene. Since the fall of Charleston there had been a general state of anarchy and civil war in the countryside. Governor Rutledge hoped to bring order and law back to South Carolina but the mood turned punitive and the principal business of the assembly turned to the confiscation of loyalist properties and banishment of Tories.

51. Edisto Nature Trail. This excellent and easily hiked trail circles through an old rice field and includes a boardwalk on the edge of the Edisto River. The first section of the trail follows the bed of the old King's Road, exactly the route taken by William Bartram and his faithful horse. The parking area is adjacent to US-17 at the west end of the Edisto River bridge. The trail was built by the Colleton County Historical and Preservation Society and Westvaco Corporation. They have printed an excellent guide to the natural areas and plants along the trail and have included a list of the botanical names of local plants.

52. Isaac Hayne Tomb. During the occupation of Charleston the British executed Isaac Hayne for violating his parole as a prisoner of war. His death galvanized anti-British sentiment on the coast much as Tarleton's excesses in the Upcountry unified and radicalized the Piedmont patriots.

53. Bethel Presbyterian Church, 1728. Bethel was one of the first Presbyterian churches built in South Carolina. When their church burned in 1886 the congregation moved to Walterboro. The old cemetery is located at the intersection of SC-64 and Highway-40. It includes the grave of Captain Dent who was once the commander of the *Constitution*.

54. Pon Pon Chapel of Ease Ruins, 1753. The Pon Pon Chapel was established to serve Saint Bartholomew's Parish. It burned in 1801, was rebuilt and became known as Burnt Church. The brick walls still stand on Old Parkers Ferry Road. Pon Pon was an early name for the Edisto River.

55. Battle of Parkers Ferry, August 30, 1781. Francis Marion dashed across South Carolina to the aid of Colonel Harden, who was the only remaining opposition to the British in the southern part of the colony. A British force operating in the area had confiscated rice and was crossing the Edisto River at Parkers Ferry. Marion lay in ambush for them on the Parkers Ferry causeway and forced them to retreat to Charleston. This victory helped boost patriot moral in the wake of Colonel Isaac Hayne's execution. The British remained confined to Charleston and the surrender of Cornwallis at Yorktown soon brought the war to an end.

56. Colleton County Museum. Colleton County is one of the three original counties of the Carolina colony, being named in 1682. The museum tells the story of the area from prehistory to the present day and includes artifacts of the Native Americans and the colonial era. Located in the Old Jail on Jeffries Street in Walterboro. Open 10 a.m.–1 p.m. and 2–5 p.m., Tuesday through Friday.

Counties

Beufort was formed in 1769 as Beufort Judicial District and is named for Henry, Duke of Beufort.

Colleton was one of three original counties and was named for Lord Proprietor Sir John Colleton. It was recreated in 1880.

Hampton was created from Beufort in 1878 and is named for Governor Wade Hampton.

Jasper was created from Hampton and Beufort in 1912 and is named for Sergeant William Jasper

Itinerary

Miles	Directions
	Begin at Westvaco Edisto Nature Trail, west side of the Edisto River bridge
.6	Jacksonborough, keep left on US-17
6.3	Cross Ashepoo River
10.6	Cross Combahee River
6.4	Old Sheldon Church, one mile to the right
1.0	Entrance to Oyotunji in Sheldon
3.0	Keep left
2.1	Cross I-95, take a right then an immediate left onto the local road *Do not follow US-17 and I-95*
4.8	Left on SC 462 in Coosawhatchie
.3	Cross I-95
3.1	Right on SSR-13
5.7	Right on SC-336
2.2	Enter Ridgeland *SC-36 becomes SSR-119 in Tillman*
19.4	Left on US-321
4.1	Intersection of US-321 and Clyo-Kildare Road

The Upcountry

When George Hunter made his survey of the Charleston-Keowee Path in 1730 there were few native people living in the Piedmont of South Carolina, the tribes having been absorbed by either the Creeks or Catawbas. In 1729 South Carolina became a royal colony, instead of proprietary, and the government began encouraging development of the interior. Settlement began to spread up from the coast and by mid-century the backcountry pioneers of Virginia, Pennsylvania, and North Carolina began to come down through the Piedmont.

In North Carolina and Virginia, Americans had settled to the edge of the Blue Ridge and crossed over into the Great Valley. As available land became scarce people turned south along the Piedmont and crossed over into South Carolina. Land in the Piedmont was much more desirable to small farmers than land in the Coastal Plain. By 1760 the entire backcountry of South Carolina had 7,000 whites and 300 black slaves. Thus the Coast and Piedmont regions of South Carolina were settled, while the intervening land in the upper Coastal Plain remained thinly inhabited. Many of the families in the Piedmont were descendants of Ulster Scots, or Scots Irish as they came to be known in this country.

The French and Indian War created a great deal of hardship for Americans living on the frontier of Pennsylvania and Virginia. Settlers of Scottish, English, and German heritage began moving south—away from the terror of the guerilla war on the Virginia and Pennsylvania frontier. In the northern colonies the best land was already taken by earlier immigrants or held in large reserves by the elite families. During the 1760s Virginians and North Carolinians began to flood into the Ninety Six District of South Carolina.

The Great Wagon Road brought settlers from the western parts of Virginia and Pennsylvania through the present towns of Lynchburg, Greensboro, Charlotte, Camden, and Augusta. Ninety Six became an important trading center at the intersection of the Wagon Road and the Charleston-Keowee Path. In 1751 the northwestern boundary between South Carolina and the Cherokee Lower Towns was established at Long Cane Creek. A few years later South Carolina called the Little River "North Fork of Long Cane Creek" with an eye to taking in more land. The first settlements in the Long Cane area were made by Virginians—the Calhouns and Pickens.

After the conclusion of the French and Indian War the Proclamation of 1763 forbade whites settling beyond an established line. A section of the Proclamation Line was surveyed as the boundary between the Cherokee Lower Towns and South Carolina, which today corresponds exactly with the Abbeville-Anderson county line.

As the interior of South Carolina became settled there arose a great need for courts, government offices, and schools. Although the population steadily increased in upper South Carolina people still had to travel to Charleston for all legal matters. A landowner might travel all the way to the capital to obtain land warrants only to find that someone else had beat him to it. Although there were petitions from these Piedmont settlements requesting the right to elect representatives, to build courthouses, churches, schools, and an increase in the taxable rate of their lands to provide for these, the assembly was disinterested in their needs. In 1767 the strongest petition was prepared by the Reverend Charles Woodmason. It intimated that 4,000 men were ready to march to Charleston to demand satisfaction. The Assembly was then moved to have the Upcountry representatives arrested and the petition burned.

In the absence of established law the citizens were forced to use extralegal means. Thus the Regulator movement in South Carolina arose to arrest and punish the bandits who took advantage of a judicial vacuum. The response of the government in Charleston was to arrest the leaders and break up the movement. Among the leaders of the Regulators were men who would become prominent in the Revolution as soldiers for both sides: Thomas Fletchall, Thomas Sumter, Moses Kirkland, Richard Richardson, and Patrick Calhoun.

Governor Bull commissioned Joseph Coffell (or Scophol), a man of dubious character, to organize an Upcountry militia sympathetic to the Assembly and loyal to the King. Coffell was supposed to arrest twenty-five targeted Regulators, but his followers, the Scopholites, began harassing the backcountry settlements by ransacking farms while the owners tended to legal business in Charleston. The Regulators hurried back to protect their families and homes. Civil war was averted when representatives of the Assembly brought news that Coffell's commission was rescinded. In November 1769 King George approved an act establishing new courts in Beaufort, Camden, Cheraw, Georgetown, Orangeburg, and Ninety Six. The whole affair left a deep distrust of the coastal gentry among the Upcountry citizens, a distrust that was to figure greatly in the upcoming conflict with England. The Scopholites, having been disenfranchised in South Carolina, joined the loyalist army in East Florida.

In August 1775 William Henry Drayton and Reverend William Tennent began their campaign to win the Upcountry over to the patriot cause at Ninety Six. At rallies they sought signatures for the Agreement on Association and Nonimportation and organized militia companies. As a matter of diplomacy the ambassadors used the term *Upcountry* rather than the more common and demeaning *Backcountry*. There were pockets of settlers who vowed to fight for their king, especially the Germans of Saxagotha and the Baptists.

The inhabitants of interior South Carolina had little in common with the wealthy planters and merchants of the coast and

British soldiers defend their position at Ninety Six National Historic Site

indeed retained a great deal of resentment lingering from the campaigns against the Regulator movement. Upcountry settlers had obtained their land from the King and the taxes and tariffs opposed by the gentry meant little to people who could ill afford the luxuries upon which the taxes were levied. As elsewhere in the South the Revolution in South Carolina was a civil war between Tories and Whigs.

Command of patriot militia groups was awarded by the Provincial Congress of South Carolina and command of loyalist militia was granted by Royal Governor William Campbell. Those who supported the king followed Thomas Fletchall, Robert Cunningham, and Moses Kirkland. The patriots organized under Colonel Richard Richardson, Thomas Sumter, and Andrew Williamson. During the winter of 1775 the Whigs consolidated their support in the Upcountry, and the loyalists lost heart and submitted. They signed affidavits that they would not take up arms against the provincial government. Thomas Brown and Daniel McGirth fled to Saint Augustine and Moses Kirkland repented from his prison cell in Philadelphia.

The most important factor in converting fence-sitters to the American cause was the British-sponsored Cherokee attacks on Upcountry settlements. Alexander Cameron was held responsible for inflaming the Cherokees and turning them away from their alliance with South Carolina, and John Stuart was implicated with him. On July 1, 1776, in concert with the arrival of British ships off Charleston, the Cherokees swept down on the back settlements of the Carolinas, Georgia, and Virginia. By the end of July over a thousand militiamen under the command of Major Williamson had assembled at the border near DeWitt's Corner. The Indian threat had united Tories and Whigs who had six months earlier opposed one another in a near civil war. The South Carolina provincial army set out to subdue the Lower Towns and capture Alexander Cameron.

Cameron escaped but the Lower Towns were burned and never rebuilt.

After the British capture of Augusta, Savannah, and Charleston, General Cornwallis moved his headquarters to Camden, South Carolina and began consolidating loyalist support in the Piedmont. The Whigs of Ninety Six were isolated in their resistance and therefore General Andrew Williamson surrendered to Richard Pearis in June of 1780. The Whig militia were paroled and the entirety of South Carolina was brought under martial rule. Whigs then organized on the upper border between the Carolinas under command of colonels William Hill, Samuel Watson, and William Bratton. They formed a government in exile and elected Thomas Sumter as Brigadier General, they then joined forces with General Rutherford and his North Carolinians. The loyalists were defeated in the Piedmont at King's Mountain in October 1780 and at Cowpens in January 1781; the British had Pyrrhic victories at Guilford Courthouse in February 1781 and at Eutaw Springs in August. When Cornwallis began his march to Virginia in April the relentless activity of Green, Pickens, Sumter, and Marion and their forces kept the remaining British troops confined to Charleston for the remainder of the war.

William Bartram's Travels in South Carolina

Leaving Fort James on May 10, 1775, Bartram followed a path north and crossed the Savannah River near Shuck Pen Eddy. He passed through Calhoun Falls and on to Alexander Cameron's home on Penny Creek, crossing swollen streams along the way. The weather was rainy and Bartram stayed with Cameron for a few days. When Francis Harper completed his important research in the late 1940s he thought that Bartram probably entered the Keowee Path at some point and followed it through present-day Pendleton to the Cherokee town of Sen-

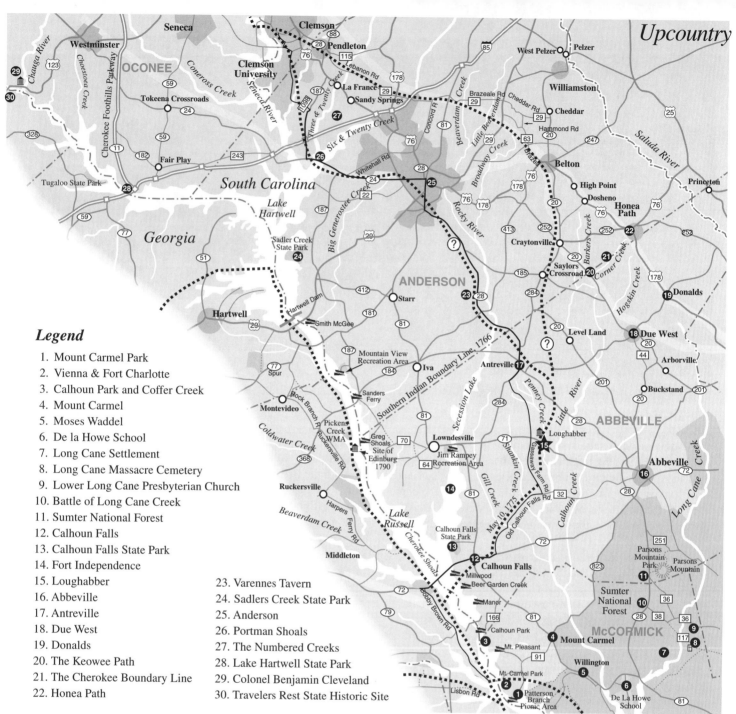

Upcountry

Legend
1. Mount Carmel Park
2. Vienna & Fort Charlotte
3. Calhoun Park and Coffer Creek
4. Mount Carmel
5. Moses Waddel
6. De la Howe School
7. Long Cane Settlement
8. Long Cane Massacre Cemetery
9. Lower Long Cane Presbyterian Church
10. Battle of Long Cane Creek
11. Sumter National Forest
12. Calhoun Falls
13. Calhoun Falls State Park
14. Fort Independence
15. Loughabber
16. Abbeville
17. Antreville
18. Due West
19. Donalds
20. The Keowee Path
21. The Cherokee Boundary Line
22. Honea Path
23. Varennes Tavern
24. Sadlers Creek State Park
25. Anderson
26. Portman Shoals
27. The Numbered Creeks
28. Lake Hartwell State Park
29. Colonel Benjamin Cleveland
30. Travelers Rest State Historic Site

eca. This would have been a route through Due West, Belton, then arcing around the east side of Anderson and on through Pendleton. This seems a circuitous route in an area that must have been crisscrossed by numerous paths, some certainly a more direct route to Seneca. The Keowee Path, being the most important path through the Upcountry, was depicted on all maps but that does not imply that it was the only route.

Twelve years later André Michaux followed a route that is well documented in his journals and we might assume that his path would closely follow that of William Bartram. Indeed, the French botanist consulted with Bartram before coming south. Michaux visited General Andrew Pickens at Hopewell, now Abbeville. He traveled through the central part of Anderson County and crossed Deep Creek at Porter Shoals, below the confluence of Three & Twenty Creek and Six & Twenty Creek. He followed high ground from there to Fort Rutledge, at the old town of Seneca. Michaux's route followed what was to become known as the General's Road leading from Pickens' old Hopewell to his new Hopewell on the Seneca River. It would be likely that General Pickens cut this road for his own convenience, so this road must have followed an older path. Antreville lay on this route and was an important Cherokee spa known as the Temple of Health.

Other evidence for a more direct route from Cameron's plantation to Seneca is found in the journal of Thomas Griffiths during his expedition to the Cherokee Nation in January 1768 in search of clay for Wedgewood. During his return trip he stayed with Reverend Daniel Hammerer on Little River, and at Mathew Edward's on Long Cane, and Major Williamson's Whitehall Plantation on Turkey Creek. This route seems to lie parallel to the Charleston-Keowee Path and halfway between it and the Savannah River.

Bartram returned to Dartmouth and Fort James and made his exploration of the Broad River in the middle of June. He crossed the river to Fort Charlotte and made his rendezvous with the traders. They left Fort Charlotte and reached the home of Monsieur St. Pierre at Bordeaux on June 22, 1775.

Sites

1. Mount Carmel Park. Camping facilities and boat ramp. Located at the end of CR-91.

2. Vienna & Fort Charlotte. Fort Charlotte was built in 1766 of native stone and named in honor of the Queen, wife of George III. Dr. John Murray and Andrew Williamson were the contractors. Fort Charlotte was to be a replacement for Fort Moore as settlement had shifted northward.

The first military action of the Revolutionary War in South Carolina took place on July 12, 1775 when patriots under Major James Mayson demanded the surrender of Fort Charlotte. William Bartram had been at the Fort but departed just three weeks earlier. In his report to East Florida Governor Patrick Tonyn, Thomas Brown noted that Fort Charlotte was the key to controlling the Upcountry and from there Georgia and North Carolina could be secured by the British and loyalists. After the Revolution the fort was abandoned and the town of Vienna took its place but failed to match its European namesake in growth, commerce, or elegance. An old and often impassable dirt road branches off from CR-337 at Mt. Carmel Park and passes through the old town site. Little is left of the town but some fence posts and an acre of *vinca major*.

3. Calhoun Park and Coffer Creek. Calhoun Park has a boat ramp but no facilities. It does provide access to beautiful Coffer Creek. The stream winds around boulders and cascades over rock outcrops. In April the stream side is sprinkled with bluets, rue anemone, hepatica, trillium, and spiderwort.

4 Mount Carmel, National Register of Historic Places. This attractive little town still has two thriving stores, one of which has been in operation for over a hundred years. Fort Boone was built nearby in 1760 to protect the Long Cane Settlement during the Cherokee war.

5. Moses Waddel and the Willington Academy. Dr. Moses Waddel opened the Willington Academy in 1804. He instructed such noted men as William H. Crawford, George Gilmer, Augustus Longstreet, James Petigru, and John C. Calhoun. Waddel was the president of the University of Georgia from 1819 to 1829 and is buried in the Old Athens Cemetery on North Campus of the University.

Willington is almost gone although the storefronts remain and the community is listed as one of South Carolina's endangered places. Oriental red spider lilies (*Lycoris*) were first planted in this country near Willington and became a popular Southern garden plant.

6. De la Howe School and Forest. The de la Howe School for the Blind is built on the lands of Lethe Plantation, the home of Dr. John de la Howe. De la Howe died without heirs and left his land to the state of South Carolina.

De la Howe came to Charleston around 1765. He obtained his first land grant in the Long Cane district in 1770 and moved there around 1785. Very little is known of this benefactor though he was an important citizen of the area. This is unfortunate because several facts that are known point to an interesting and intriguing life. De la Howe's farm, Lethe, is named for the mythical river in Hades where souls drank to forget their earthly troubles before entering the afterlife.

De la Howe left his wife in Charleston and moved to Long Cane Creek with Rebekah Woodin, who may have been a spiritual and intellectual friend rather than his mistress. Rebekah died in 1788 and John died in 1797. Although his will stipulated that his estate be used for the support of a school it seems that was not accomplished until the 1820s. The present school buildings date from the 1890s.

There is a 120-acre tract of old growth forest on Little River in the south part of the school's property, now designated a National Natural Landmark. There is very little virgin forest left in the Piedmont and this is one of the better known and protected stands. The tomb of John de la Howe and Rebekah Woodin is at the end of the road that passes through the school campus. Stop at the information center for directions and permission since the gate to the forest is closed at times.

John De la Howe Interpretive Forestry Trail. This one-mile trail loops through the De la Howe forest and is the first phase of an environmental education center. Located east of the John de la Howe barn on SC-81. A brochure is available at the de la Howe school offices.

7. Long Cane Settlement. The Calhouns and Pickens were among the first settlers in this part of South Carolina, arriving in the late 1750s. In 1754, South Carolina gained more land than the Cherokees intended to sell by calling Little River the North Branch of Long Cane Creek, the latter being the actual boundary set by the treaty.

8. Long Cane Massacre Cemetery is the burial site of the settlers killed by the Cherokees on February 1, 1760. Cherokee warriors attacked the Long Cane area during the Chero-

---

Whigs and Tories

American Whigs were synonymous with the patriots and Tories with the loyalists. The Whigs believed in the principles of self-government, balances and checks on ministerial powers, and they favored a break with England. When Britain attempted to strengthen Royal authority over the colonies in the 1760s and weaken the colonial legislatures, Whig ideology became radicalized. The Tories believed that the king remained the sovereign and they supported the suppression of the American rebels. Although there were many Tories who agreed with the Whigs that American colonists were being denied their full rights as British citizens they were unwilling to give up allegiance to their native country. The American Tory party disappeared with the loyalist refugees who fled the country following the conclusion of the war.

The Whig and Tory political parties had their roots in Britain around 1679 when the Whigs opposed the ascension of catholic James II to the throne. The Whigs came to support the authority of Parliament as the ultimate governing body in Great Britain and they urged tolerance of dissenters. They were also great promoters of commercial and industrial growth. The Tories, who supported James II, were monarchists and believed in the authority of the Church of England. The Glorious Revolution of 1688 removed James from the throne and established the Whigs as the dominant party for the next century and a half. The Whigs promoted Parliamentary reform in the nineteenth century while the Tories sought to preserve the status quo. Peelite Conservatives, reforming Whigs, and Free Traders formed the Liberal Party in 1859 and supported William Gladstone in his successful bid as Prime Minister. High Tories and High Whigs evolved into the Conservative Party during the 1860s and resisted the extension of democratic reforms, particularly home rule for Ireland. Members of the Conservative Party are still called Tories today.

kee War and killed twenty-three white settlers including Catherine Calhoun, grandmother of John C. Calhoun. From SC-28 follow CR-38, CR-117 and CR-141.

9. Lower Long Cane Presbyterian Church, organized 1771. There has been no break in services at the church since the entire congregation immigrated to South Carolina from Newry, Ireland. The present building was constructed in 1856. Located on CR-38.

10. Battle of Long Cane Creek, December 12, 1780. Reenactments are held each October. Junction of SC-28 and CR-38.

11. Sumter National Forest, Long Cane District

Long Cane Scenic Area. This 700-acre tract of the Long Cane District of Sumter National Forest is not managed for timber or wildlife. Natural succession and processes are allowed to progress without human intervention. The Long Cane Horse Trail crosses the area and passes by the largest shagbark hickory in South Carolina.

Parson's Mountain Lake Recreational Area. The recreational facilities at Parson's Mountain Lake were built by the CCC in the mid-1930s. A hiking trail and a motorcycle trail lead to the top of Parson's Mountain. Camping, picnicking, boating, swimming, restrooms, and hiking trails. Follow SC-28 to CR-251 south of Abbeville.

12. Calhoun Falls was founded in the 1890s by the Western Carolina Land and Improvement Company. It was laid out at the intersection of the Charleston & Western Carolina and SAL Railroads. Today its economy depends on the textile mill and recreational opportunities provided by Lake Russell. The information center for Calhoun Falls and Lake Russell is in the old filling station at the intersection of Cox Street and Savannah Street (SC-72). Calhoun Falls Library is located on Tugaloo Street, which runs parallel to Savannah Street.

13. Calhoun Falls State Park. This is a new and rather modern recreation park with camping, marina, boat ramp, pier, playgrounds, beach, and bathhouse. For hikers and botanists there are the Blue Hole Nature Trail and Cedar Bluff Nature Trail. Open daily.

14. Fort Independence began as a fortified homestead built by Captain Robert Anderson. It was purchased by South Carolina in 1777 and garrisoned with patriots. Tories burned Fort Independence in 1779. It was located on Rocky River five miles south of Lowndesville. The site was excavated by archaeologists prior to the flooding of Lake Russell and was found to have been inhabited since the Archaic period.

Alexander Cameron

Considering Alexander Cameron's importance in the history of Cherokee affairs and the Revolution in South Carolina, little is known about Bartram's host at Loughabber. Cameron was a native of Scotland from a family of modest background and was related to John Stuart through Stuart's wife. Cameron came to Georgia with Oglethorpe's 42nd Regiment in 1738. He joined a South Carolina regiment in 1749 and from 1762 to 1763 he was in the garrison at Fort Prince George. For his military service Cameron claimed 2,000 acres of land in the Long Cane area where he had relatives. This bounty land became the Loughabber estate.

Cameron was known as Scotchie to the Cherokees, with whom he was a trusted friend. His wife, Molly, was the daughter of an Estatoe warrior. Their three children, George, Susanna, and Jane were educated in England. Because of his standing among the Cherokees of the Lower Towns, Cameron was enlisted as an ambassador to maintain their friendship following the Cherokee War of 1760–1761. He noted with surprise the good will that the Cherokees maintained toward whites despite their mistreatment by traders and trespasses by white hunters and settlers.

In 1768 Cameron became Deputy Superintendent for the Western Division of the Southern District for Indian Affairs. In the same year and again in 1770 there were conferences at Loughabber. He was present at other Indian conferences that set boundaries between the Cherokees and neighboring states. Cameron's son, George, was granted by the Cherokees a tract of land above the boundary line. This gave the Cherokees access to one of the routes to Charleston and maintained an open path by keeping settlers out of the area. John Stuart was very displeased with the gift although Cameron insisted that it was not his idea but that of Cherokee leaders. This land now includes Golden Grove community, south of Greenville, at the fork of Saluda River and Grove Creek.

At the time of Bartram's visit to Loughabber during May 10–15, 1775, Cameron was being implicated in the British plot to raise the Cherokees against the Americans. In September Cameron left Loughabber for Keowee and from there he instigated the Cherokee attacks on the frontier settlements of Georgia and North and South Carolina. Although the South Carolina Assembly tried to win his allegience, Cameron was a committed loyalist and became the most wanted man in South Carolina due to his role in the frontier warfare and his policy of taking no prisoners. His combined Cherokee and Tory regiment made attacks on the frontier settlements in July 1776, but the Cherokees made no distinction between loyalist and patriot. Cameron, therefore, helped drive many loyalists, save the most radical, into the arms of the patriots.

In August, 1776 Colonel Andrew Williamson was ordered to punish the Cherokees and capture Cameron. As he passed through the Long Cane Settlement he burned Loughabber then went on to Seneca where his rangers engaged Cameron and Dragging Canoe in battle. At the time the Cherokees were divided in their relationship to South Carolina. Attakullakulla and Oconostota agreed to give Cameron over to the Americans for a £100 bounty but Cameron left for Pensacola before they could attempt his capture. Dragging Canoe and his followers separated themselves from the Middle and Overhill towns. They founded new settlements near present-day Chattanooga and called themselves Chickamaugas. They became the most radical and warlike band of Cherokees and remained allied to Cameron and the British.

When John Stuart died in 1777 the office of superintendent was divided between Thomas Brown and Alexander Cameron. Cameron was assigned the western office for the Creeks and Choctaws and Brown was given the position of deputy superintendent for the Cherokees even though Cameron had spent more than fifteen years among the Cherokees. Due to his age, illness, unfamiliarity with the Muskhogean Tribes, and lack of support from General Campbell while in Pensacola, Cameron resigned and retired to British-occupied Savannah where he owned a house. He died in Savannah on December 27, 1781, and is probably buried in Colonial Cemetery.

It is ironic that William Bartram became a friend of both Alexander Cameron and George Galphin and spoke well of each, although the two men were bitter enemies.

15. Loughabber. The home of Alexander Cameron was on Penny Creek north of SC-71. William Bartram stayed at Loughabber from May 10 to May 15, 1775. Loughabber contained approximately 2,600 acres, 2,000 of which were granted for service in the French and Indian War.[1]

---

1. Memorial Book ix, 131, Historical Commission of South Carolina.

Coffer Creek at the Russell Dam

16. Abbeville was founded in 1785 and named by Dr. John de la Howe in honor of the local Huguenots whose home was Abbeville in northern France. The land was originally owned by General Andrew Pickens. He sold this land for the county courthouse when he moved to Hopewell on the Seneca River.

Abbeville has a historical walking tour that includes the Opera House, one of the finest of its kind for a town of this size. The first secession meeting and the last meeting of the Confederate Council of War were both held in Abbeville.

The library is located one block from the downtown square on South Main Street. It has a South Carolina historical section and a permanent exhibition of Native-American crafts from around the country. There is an excellent map of the Lower Cherokee Towns on display. The Abbeville Museum is located in the old jail on Poplar Street, but the hours of operation are limited. There are two authentic log cabins and a garden behind the museum. Abbeville Books, located in the mall on the north end of the square, specializes in regional authors, history, and maps.

17. Antreville was once a Cherokee gathering place known as the Temple of Health.

18. Due West. This charming town boasts the oldest private college in South Carolina, Erskine College, founded in 1839 by the Associate Reformed Presbyterian Church. The library contains archives and publications related to the history of the region. The town of Due West got its name from nearby DeWitt's Corner where a trading post was located and the peace treaty of 1777 was signed. The Cherokee-South Carolina boundary line as stipulated by the Proclamation of 1763 was run in 1766 and passed through DeWitt's Corner. It is little wonder that DeWitt became Due West, for the name has been written numerous ways over the last two centuries. Variations include Devises, DeWisse, Devittes, Jewettes, and Dewettes.

19. Donalds is the site of Boonesborough, one of the original settlements of the Long Cane District. It was surveyed in 1761 and settled by Ulster-Scots. It was later renamed for the Donald family.

20. The Keowee Path was the trade route from Charleston to the Cherokee Nation, also known as the Charleston-Keowee Path. It crossed the Cherokee-South Carolina boundary at DeWitt's Store on Corner Creek. As the frontier became settled the road moved eastward and followed present-day US-178 through Donalds and Honea Path, an easier route for wagons.

21. The Cherokee Boundary Line. The Proclamation of 1763 created a boundary between Indian land and British colonies that was to be the limit of legal settlement for European Americans. The old Indian Line in South Carolina was surveyed in 1766 and forms the present boundary between Anderson and Abbeville counties.

22. Honea Path has baffled historians with the origin of its name. In old documents it is referred to as Honey Path and it is unclear when the name was changed. One story relates that honea means path in Cherokee and that they had a habit of repeating, or doubling, words for emphasis. Another story tells that there were many bee hives in the area and the Cherokees, being fond of honey, called the trail the Honey Path, later corrupted to Honea Path. Still another story says a railroad agent named Honea changed the name from Honey when it was time to name the station. What is certain is that Honea Path was on the Old Charleston Wagon Road that was built on the high ridge east of the Keowee Path.

The Honea Path Massacre. 45,000 textile workers participated in the United Textile Workers National General Strike from September 1–22, 1934. On Labor Day private security guards fired upon strikers at Chiqoula Mills in Honea Path, killing six. The General Strike was the largest strike in American history and the Chiquola massacre was one of the most infamous cases of violence in American labor relations. Abuses of worker rights by management, increasing violence, and the growing unrest among American workers during 1934 to 1937 lead to the enactment of the National Labor Relations Act, the Fair Labor Standards Act, and the Child Labor laws.

23. Varennes Tavern began operating soon after the Revolution. The name is taken from Varennes, France, the native home of the original owner.

The Scotch-Irish

Ulster in Northern Ireland was England's second colony, established in 1610, three years after the founding of Jamestown, Virginia. The northern Irish lords were finally defeated in 1603 and the confiscated lands were granted to English and Scottish gentry and protestants were encouraged to resettle in Northern Ireland. Lowland Scots were the largest number of immigrants, owing to the poor quality of land in Scotland, and many moved across the channel after the official invitation was issued by King James in March 1609. The Scots blended with the native Irish with whom they had a common language and culture. However, the Irish were predominantly Catholic and the Scots were Protestant, which prevented total assimilation of the two groups. The Ulster-Scots began leaving Northern Ireland in the early 1700s when the enclosure laws and changing land tenure laws made life uncertain.

In America they found a paradise where they could farm, hunt, and worship as they pleased. In America they chose to settle on the frontier where land was free or cheap, and far from the tidewater English gentry. The Ulster-Scots were independent, aggressive, and hardy—setting the tone for the American frontier. They were accustomed to self-government and elections in their Presbyterian churches and on the frontier they had to create their own governmental institutions. Fighting the Indians for a place to farm was no different from fighting the Irish for land in Ulster.

By 1776 there were a quarter million Ulster-Scots in America and they formed a large part of the Revolutionary forces. They lead the vanguard of settlement down through the Shenandoah Valley and into the Piedmont and mountains of the South. These Ulster-Scots were first known as Ulster-Irish and Northern Irish but they came to be known as Scotch-Irish after the great wave of Catholic Irish immigration in the nineteenth century created a prejudice among Americans for anything *Irish*.

24. Sadlers Creek State Park. Pine Grove Nature Trail, camping, boat ramp, picnic area, and playground. Open daily, 6 a.m.–9 p.m., April–September; 7 a.m.–6 p.m. (8 p.m. on Friday), October–March. Located off SC-187 on Sadlers Creek Road.

25. Anderson is on the route of an old path to Tugaloo that branched off the Charleston-Keowee Path. Another historic route was the General's Road that ran from Abbeville to General Andrew Pickens' home at Hopewell on the Seneca River. In 1826 Pendleton District was divided into Pendleton and Anderson counties and the stagecoach stop on the General's Road near the center of Anderson County was chosen for the new courthouse. Anderson is called the Electric City for it was the first municipality in the Deep South to electrify. Anderson pioneered long distance transmission of electricity from the old power plant at Portman Shoals. Because of this pioneering effort, Anderson has been at the center of industrial growth in South Carolina since the turn of the century.

Anderson County Museum. Located at the Anderson Public Library on the corner of Greenville and McDuffie Streets. Open Monday through Friday, 10 a.m.–4 p.m.

26. Portman Shoals. Anderson's first electric-generating plant was built at High Shoals on Rocky River in 1894. In 1897 a plant was built at Portman Shoals on Deep Creek, making Anderson the first city in the South to have a steady supply of electricity and earning it the nickname of the Electric City. The section of Six & Twenty Creek between its junction with Three & Twenty Creek and the Seneca River was called Deep Creek before Lake Hartwell flooded the streams. André Michaux crossed there on June 7, 1787 enroute to the Keowee River.

27. The Numbered Creeks. Creeks flowing into the Seneca River are numbered going south from Keowee. The origin of their names is found in a story about Cateechee, a slave girl among the Cherokees whose Creek name was Issaqueena. She had fallen in love with Allen Francis, a white trader at Ninety Six. One day she overheard plans that the Cherokees planned to attack the post at Ninety Six. She escaped during the night to carry warnings to Francis and his people. As she traveled she marked the streams as she went—One Mile, Six Mile, Twelve Mile, Eighteen Mile, Three and Twenty, and Six and Twenty. The inhabitants of Ninety Six were prepared for the attack and repulsed the warriors when they arrived.

Itinerary

Miles Directions

	Begin at the Fort James monument in Bobby Brown State Park and travel north
9.0	Right on Calhoun Falls Highway, GA-72
4.8	Through the traffic light at SC-81 in Calhoun Falls
.1	Next right on SC-72, Savannah Street
1.5	Left on Old Calhoun Falls Road, SC-32
6.8	Left on Gassoway Farm Road, CR-63
3.8	Right on SC-71
.9	Bartram Trail Marker commemorating William Bartram's visit to Alexander Cameron's Loughabber plantation.
.9	Return north on SC-71 and turn right on CR-63 (Brownlee Road)
2.3	Right on Flat Rock Road
.9	Cross CR-72
1.4	Left on SC-28
18.0	Keep straight on Business SC-28
3.5	Downtown Anderson
2.7	Left on Woodcrest Drive
.7	Keep straight on Whitehall Road
5.2	Right on SC-24
3.2	Right on SC-187
7.3	Left on US-76, Clemson Highway
.7	Right on SC-28, South Mechanic Street
1.1	Enter Pendleton, keep straight on North Mechanic Street
4.7	Right on US-76
.2	Left on Perimeter Road
.3	South Carolina Botanical Gardens

28. Lake Hartwell State Park. This popular recreation park has facilities for camping, fishing, a boat ramp, picnic area, and a nature trail. Located off SC-11 one-half mile north of Exit-1 of I-85. Open daily.

29. Colonel Benjamin Cleveland Monument. Benjamin Cleveland was an uneducated frontiersman, friend of Daniel Boone, and the hero who led the charge against the British at King's Mountain. After the Revolution Cleveland settled at the forks of the Tugaloo and Chauga rivers and became a prominent local citizen. He was remembered by his neighbors for his size, he allegedly weighed upwards of 400 pounds.

17. Traveler's Rest State Historic Site. The Deveraux Jarrett estate and Traveler's Rest Inn were established in the early 1800s at the junction of the Unicoi Turnpike and the Federal Road. The town of Tugaloo was located at this strategic river crossing in the eighteenth century and was the principal town of the Cherokees in northeast Georgia. Jarrett's empire included a grist mill, sawmill, store, inn, post office, tanyard, smokehouse, cotton gin, tavern, and toll bridge. George Featherstonhaugh was a visitor at Traveler's Rest in the 1830s and wrote of it in his book *Trip up the Minay Sotor*. The Inn is a national historic landmark, noted for its ninety-foot long porch.

Located just off US-123 at the Tugaloo River on Old Church Road. Open Monday–Saturday, 9 a.m.–5 p.m. and on Sunday from 2 p.m.–5 p.m. Admission.

Counties

Abbeville County, South Carolina, is named for Abbeville, France, and was created in 1785.

Anderson County, South Carolina, is named for Revolutionary War General Robert Anderson and was created in 1826 when Pendleton District was divided into Anderson and Pickens counties.

Greenwood County

Whitehall, the home of Andrew Williamson, was at the center of activity for the Whig Militia of Ninety Six. General Andrew Williamson was a patriot and early leader of the provincial militia. When Charleston was surrendered by General Lincoln and the loyalist militia in the backcountry combined with the Florida Rangers to take back the interior of South Carolina, Williamson and the militia of Ninety Six felt that their position was hopeless. On June 10, 1780 delegates signed the treaty of peace on behalf of the people living on the south side of the Saluda River and promised to not take up arms against the King's army.

Greenwood is the ninth largest city in South Carolina and the seat of Greenwood County. It is the home of the South Carolina Festival of Flowers each June.

Park Seed Company. George W. Park and his descendants have supplied seeds to Southern gardeners since moving to Greenwood in 1924. Today they are involved in extensive research and development of new varieties and hybrids, many developed for the special growing conditions of the Southeast. Visitors can buy seeds and plants at the company's outlet store. The highlight of a trip to Greenwood is visiting the demonstration gardens at Park headquarters on Cokesbury Road. Each June Park's holds a special visitor's day on the weekend of the South Carolina Festival of Flowers.

Ninety Six National Historic Site. The Ninety Six Historic Site preserves the site of the original settlement and the Star Fort. Ninety Six was an important trading post and seat of Ninety Six District. It was strategically located at the intersection of the Charleston Road, Hard Labor Road, and Island Ford Road. In 1746 Governor Glenn held a conference at Ninety Six with Cherokee headmen, lead by Connacorte (Old Hop). As a result of this talk the Cherokees remained allies to South Carolina during the French and Indian War. During the Cherokee War of 1760–1761 Ninety Six was attacked twice.

Ninety Six was made the seat of government in 1769 when the district began to be settled after peace with the Cherokees was re-established. The first permanent resident of the area was Robert Gouedy who in 1751 moved his trading operation from Great Telico to Ninety Six. The district of Ninety Six later became the counties of Abbeville, Anderson, Edgefield, Greenwood, Laurens, and McCormick.

The first land battle in the South took place at Ninety Six on November 18, 1775, when loyalists under Major Joseph Robinson attacked the patriots commanded by Major Andrew Williamson. The siege lasted for two days until both sides agreed upon a truce and withdrew. The British built the Star Fort at Ninety Six in 1780. The next year General Nathanael Greene, Colonel Harry Lee, and 1,000 patriots besieged the fort with extensive zigzagging siege lines and a rifle tower. The siege trenches and parallels were designed by Thaddeus Kosciuszko, Greene's engineer. The siege lasted for twenty-eight days in May and June of 1781. Greene and the patriots withdrew in the face of superior numbers when Lord Rawdon marched from Charleston with reinforcements. Two weeks later the loyalists abandoned Ninety Six.

Earthen banks of the British Star Fort and the patriot's siege trenches are still visible. The Park Service has reconstructed the patriot's Stockade Fort and the Rifle Tower. The main hiking trail takes visitors on a tour of the historic sites and a side trail follows the old Charleston-Keowee Path. The visitor center has exhibits about the village of Ninety Six, Revolutionary War engagements, and an excellent selection of books for sale.

Each fall a heritage festival is held that includes the rare opportunity to see a Revolutionary encampment and battle re-enactment. Colonial crafts are demonstrated by re-enactors who have taken the persona of a historical figure, such as village doctor, Indian trader, or tinsmith. The excitement is heightened by roving bands of Cherokees and British soldiers. In April there is a Revolutionary War encampment during odd years and a French and Indian War encampment during even years.

Ninety Six was burned when the British withdrew and a new town named Cambridge grew up nearby after the war. When the district was subdivided into counties and the seat of government was moved the town died. The present town of Ninety Six is built on the railroad line about two miles west of the park. It was the site of the first Fourth of July celebration in South Carolina when the day's festivities offered barbecue, whisky, and oration. Dr. Benjamin E. Mays was born near Ninety Six in 1894. He was a force in the early Civil Rights Movement, author, educator, and president of Morehouse College from 1940–1967.

The name of Ninety Six was in use by 1730 when George Hunter marked the spot on his map of the Charleston-Keowee Trading Path. There are two stories about the origin of this unusual name. The first is that Hunter reckoned that this pleasant camp site was ninety-six miles from Keowee. Another explanation is that travelers encountered two groups of streams flowing in a direction opposite the other streams. Most streams along that section of the path flow east to the Saluda River but travelers encountered a group of nine streams and then a group of six streams flowing west to the Savannah–*nine and six* was corrupted to Ninety Six.

Ninety Six National Historic Site is two miles south of the town of Ninety Six on SC-248. Open 8 a.m.–5 p.m., daily except Christmas, New Year's Day, and Thanksgiving.

Cherokee Lower Towns

The Cherokees arrived in the Southern Appalachians some time in the fourteenth or fifteenth century and made the valleys of the mountains their home. With plenty of food, a good climate, and refuge from enemies the Cherokees flourished and became the second-largest nation in the eastern United States.

As their population increased the Cherokees slowly took up more and more hunting grounds and began building towns along the rivers throughout their territory. When the Spanish entered the area in the early 1500s the Cherokees claimed 40,000 square miles. Their towns spilled over into the Piedmont of Georgia and South Carolina. The towns located in the upper part of present-day South Carolina were called the Lower Towns or the Underhill Towns. The principal town of the Lower Cherokees was Keowee. Recent work by Charles Hudson disputes the previous idea that De Soto passed through the Lower Towns; instead they probably entered the mountains farther north. Juan Pardo's expedition of 1566 may have passed through the Lower Towns.

Soon after Charleston was established the Carolinians took up trade with the Cherokees. Being closer to the English the Lower Towns were the first Cherokees to have traders, and the first to be attacked in time of war. The Cherokees obtained their first guns about 1700, after their neighbors to the east and south already had them. Colonel Maurice Moore, Colonel George Chicken, Eleazer Wigan, and Robert Gilcrest traveled to the Cherokee towns in December 1715 and secured the alliance of the Cherokees during the Yamassee War. The Cherokees announced their decision to join the Carolinians by assassinating a deputation of Creeks at Tugaloo Town. The English immediately gained 5,000 fighting men and turned the tide of the war in their favor.

The Cherokees asked that a fort be built in the Lower Towns. They hoped the presence of an English garrison would intimidate the Creeks and renegade Indians who caused trouble by raiding whites and Cherokees alike. The presence of a fort and garrison also helped regulate trade and keep whites from squatting on Cherokee land and poaching their game. Attakullakulla was the spokesman for the Cherokees at the treaty in 1753 when Governor Glenn agreed to purchase land and build Fort Prince George at Keowee Town.

The French and Indian War created turmoil in the western part of Virginia and Pennsylvania and caused the movement of settlement to shift southward down the Piedmont through North and South Carolina. In the late 1750s communities sprang up on Long Cane Creek, at the Saluda River, Ninety Six, and Camden in South Carolina. As new settlers arrived some took advantage of vacant land that was on the boundary or even within Cherokee land. The Cherokees called these new arrivals *Virginians* and they had a greater dislike for them than for the English and Scots of South Carolina with whom they traded. Though families like the Calhouns and Pickens were educated and devout Presbyterians there were other Virginians who were a rough frontier breed, often illiterate and unchurched from several generations of living on the edge of civilization. Sophisticated whites called them *Crackers*. Their culture stood somewhere between that of the Indians and the English. They showed no compunction about taking what they wanted from the Indians, or even from whites, and they were prone to as much violence as the ungovernable young Cherokee warriors. Their ranks included a disproportionate number of the descendants of Scottish immigrants from the Ulster Plantations of Northern Ireland.

The Cherokee War began in the closing moments of the French and Indian War. In 1758 as Cherokee gunmen returned

Oconee Bells photographed at Devil's Fork State Park, Oconee County, South Carolina

from service as allies to the English they were attacked and arrested for taking food and horses as they passed through the back parts of Virginia. They had seen white soldiers do the same without incident during the war and thought it their due for aiding the English. Young warriors retaliated by attacking white settlements in the South Carolina Upcountry. Like most Indians of the Southeast, the Cherokees practiced retribution against groups of people rather than individuals.

Governor Lyttleton mishandled the whole affair, possibly escalating his response and the resulting war for personal political gain and glory. In late 1759 Lyttleton demanded that twenty-four Cherokees be delivered up for execution to pay for the deaths of white settlers, then he took hostage twenty-two headmen who had come to Charleston to negotiate peace. Two of the headmen were allowed to return with Lyttleton's demands, and the rest of the hostages were transferred to Fort Prince George. The Cherokees were justifiably incensed by this treatment of their diplomats. Even Attakullakulla, who had worked diligently to avoid war, could no longer restrain his people.

In February 1760, Oconostota lured Captain Cotymore from Fort Prince George and killed him. The English soldiers fell upon their Cherokee prisoners and killed everyone, this was almost all of the headmen of the Lower Towns. Cherokee warriors retaliated by attacking the frontier settlements, including Long Cane where fifty settlers were killed as they tried to reach Augusta. Lyttleton was appointed governor of Jamaica and left South Carolina that spring.

In April 1760, Colonel Archibald Montgomery led a combined force of troops from the Carolinas and Virginia into Cherokee country and burned Estatoe, Kulsage, and Keowee. The Middle Towns would not accept peace so Montgomery marched to the Little Tennessee River where he won a Pyrrhic victory near present-day Otto. The British and South Carolinians withdrew their wounded with difficulty and Montgomery returned to New York.

In March 1760, the Cherokees began a siege of Fort Loudon. John Stuart escaped only by the aid of Attakullakulla. In the spring of 1761 South Carolina again sent troops into the Lower and Middle Towns under command of Colonel James Grant. They laid waste to the towns and caused the weak and starving Cherokees to sue for peace.

The Cherokees, instigated by Alexander Cameron and Richard Pearis, attacked the frontier settlements from Virginia to Ninety Six in July 1776. That August Major Andrew Williamson's Ninety Six Militia Regiment, aided by volunteers from North Carolina, marched into the Cherokee Lower Towns to subdue and punish the Cherokees. The Americans were attacked at Seneca, but the following morning they crossed the river and burned the town. They proceeded to burn crops and every village in the Lower Towns. Neighboring Georgia and North Carolina coordinated attacks on Cherokee towns on their frontiers. The Cherokees sought peace and signed a treaty at De Witt's Corner on May 20, 1777, in which they gave up any claim to land in present day South Carolina, except the extreme northwestern section.

When the lower parts of Georgia and South Carolina were returned to British control in 1780 the Cherokees joined the

Hanover House and the Heirloom garden at the South Carolina Botanical Gardens in Clemson

British and attacked frontier settlements. They were again defeated by coordinated efforts of the Americans. The strength of the Lower Towns was so weakened that they were abandoned. The inhabitants sought refuge among the Cherokee Middle and Valley Towns. The land above the Cherokee boundary line was ceded in the Treaty of Hopewell in 1785 and formed into Pendleton District.

Many of the early settlers of Pendleton District were of Scotch-Irish heritage and were veterans of the Revolution claiming their bounty land. In the early 1800s wealthy South Carolinians from the coast began building resort homes in the area. The Pendleton Farmer's Society did much to improve the productivity of farmers throughout the state and encouraged manufacturing in the piedmont region. Old Pendleton District lies astride the I-85 commercial corridor from Atlanta to Raleigh where the textile-based economy is now being replaced by high-tech industry.

Bartram's Travels

It is possible that William Bartram arrived at Seneca by a more direct route than the well-known Charleston-Keowee Path. If he traveled by a route taken a decade later by André Michaux, he would have crossed Six and Twenty Creek at Portman Shoals. Bartram said he traveled "forty-five miles through an uninhabited wilderness." The upper part of Long Cane Creek was already inhabited so he may not have gone northward to the Keowee Path from Loughabber but headed northwestward toward the future site of Anderson. There was almost certainly an existing path that later became the General's Road, the route from Abbeville through Anderson to Pendleton.

After crossing Six and Twenty Creek he traveled along the ridge lying to the east of the Seneca River and reached Seneca Town on the east bank of the river where Clemson University is located. Bartram's path from Seneca to Fort Prince George seems to have been also along the east side of the river if we

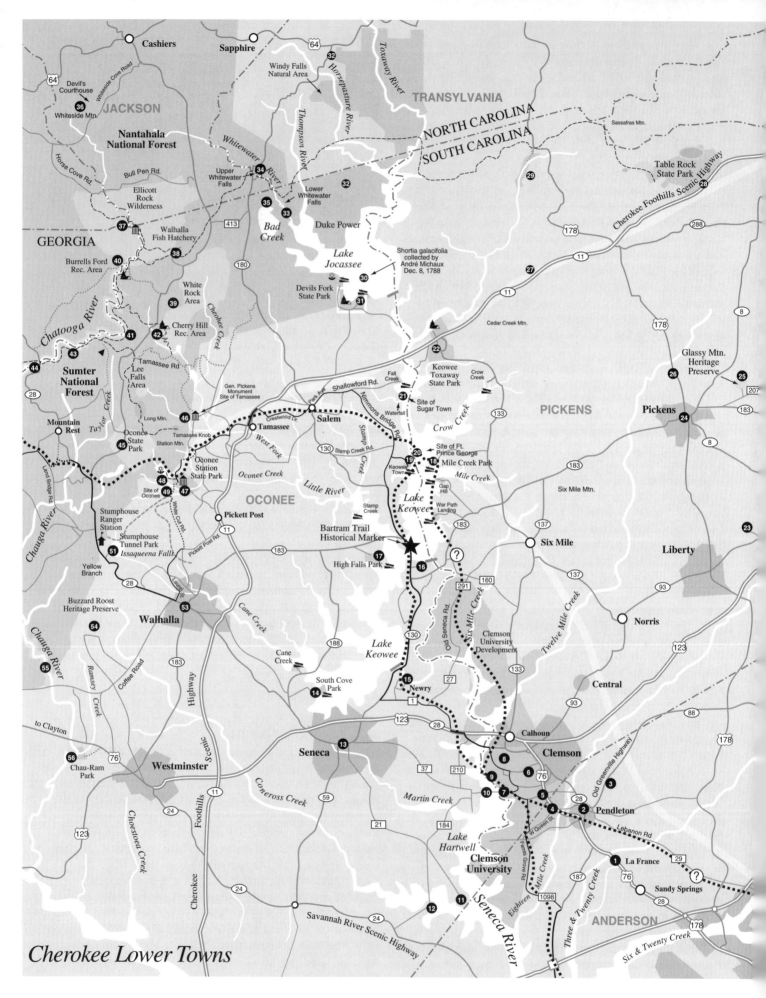

take Bartram's writing literally, though others have opted for a path on the west side of the river.

From Fort Prince George William Bartram crossed to the west bank and entered the Virginia path near Salem. The trail made an arc through Tamassee School and Oconee Station and crossed Station Mountain. The abandoned town he saw was Chauga, in the forks of the Village Creek at the head of Chauga River.

Sites

1. LaFrance is the site of the oldest operating textile mill in South Carolina, originally known as Pendleton Factory. The community was originally called Autun, probably named for the city in France.

2. Pendleton. The Charleston-Keowee Path passed through Pendleton. When this section of South Carolina was ceded by the Cherokees in 1785 wealthy Low Country aristocrats began to resort in Pendleton District during the summer months. The town of Pendleton was created as the county seat of Pendleton District in 1790 and it became a center of culture and learning in the Upcountry. The Pendleton Farmer's Society was organized in 1815, a lending library was started in 1811, the Male Academy was started in 1825, and the Pendleton Female Academy opened in 1827.

Pendleton District Historical, Recreational and Tourism Commission is housed in Hunter's Store (1850). Located on the town square. Open Monday through Friday, 9 a.m.–4:30 p.m. Closed on holidays.

Farmers Hall (c. 1826) was to be the courthouse for Pendleton District, However, division of the district into counties while the courthouse was under construction made the towns of Pickens and Anderson the new county seats. The **Pendleton Farmer's Society** took over the building, finished it, and used it for their meetings. The society was organized in 1815 and was one of the first and most influential agricultural societies in the nation. The purpose of the society was to educate farmers and publish agricultural information. The annual Pendleton Fair began about 1818 and became a popular event at a time when most men of means and education were also involved in agriculture. The building now houses a restaurant. Located on the town square in Pendleton.

James Beamer House. James Beamer was the leading trader at Eastatoe and a patriot during the Revolution. His home was moved to Pendleton during the construction of Lake Keowee.

Pendleton Library. Mechanic Street south of the town square.

Miller's Weekly Messenger was published by John Miller in Pendleton from 1795 until his death in 1807. Miller was one of the owners of the *London Evening Post* from 1769 to 1780 and helped establish the idea that the press should not only report the events but editorialize and investigate. He was brought to trial in a libel case for publishing the famous *Letters of Junius,* which criticized official corruption in the British Parliament, judicial system, and ministries of government. This case brought to public attention the rights of freedom of the press and the role of the press in public debate. The letters were written by John Wilkes who became a hero to the American cause of freedom.

Miller lost his press and property and then joined in publishing *The London Courant.* He again ran afoul of the government and the king for opposing the war with the American colonies. He was imprisoned for one year for an allegedly untrue paragraph about the Russian ambassador. He decided to emigrate to America where the freedoms he espoused were more universally supported. Miller arrived in Philadelphia in January 1783, and was immediately invited by the South Carolina delegates at the Continental Congress to come to Charleston and become the state printer. He started the *South Carolina Gazette and General Advertiser* on December 1, 1785, then sold it a year later.

Legend

1. LaFrance
2. Pendleton
   Pendleton District Historical,
     Recreational & Tourism Commission
   Farmers Hall
   James Beamer House
   Pendleton Library
   Miller's Weekly Messenger
3. The Mavericks
4. Pendleton District Agriculture Museum
5. Old Stone Church
6. South Carolina State Botanical Garden
   Hanover House
7. Hopewell-Keowee Monument
   Treaty of Hopewell
8. Clemson
   Clemson University
   John C. Calhoun
   Fort Hill
   Robert M. Cooper Library
   Clemson City Library
   Clemson Visitors Center
   Clemson Park and Recreation Area
9. Site of Seneca and Fort Rutledge
10. Robert Anderson
11. Oconee Point
12. Coneross Park
13. Lunney Museum
14. South Cove County Park
15. Newry
16. Duke Power Keowee-Toxaway Center
17. High Falls Park
18. Mile Creek Park
19. Keowee
20. Fort Prince George
21. Sugar Town (Kulsage)
22. Keowee-Toxaway State Park
23. Golden Creek Mill
24. Pickens County Museum
25. Glassy Mountain Heritage Preserve
26. Hagood Mill
27. Cherokee Foothills Scenic Highway
28. Table Rock State Park
29. Eastatoe Creek Heritage Preserve
30. Lake Jocassee
    Bad Creek Visitors Center
31. Devils Fork State Park
32. Blue Ridge Escarpment & Gorges
    Windy Falls Natural Area
33. Lower Whitewater Falls
34. Upper Whitewater Falls
35. Coon Branch Natural Area
36. Whiteside Mountain
37. Ellicott Rock Wilderness
38. Walhalla Fish Hatchery
39. White Rock Scenic Area
40. Burrell's Ford Recreation Area
41. Foothills Trail
42. Cherry Hill Recreation Area
43. Chatooga River Trail
44. Russell Homestead
45. Oconee State Park
46. General Pickens Monument
    Tomassee
47. Oconee Station State Park
48. Station Cove Botanical Area
49. Oconee Town
50. Blue Ridge Railroad Historical Trail
51. Stumphouse Tunnel
    Isaqueena Falls
52. Sumter National Forest
53. Walhalla
54. Buzzard Roost Heritage Preserve
55. Chauga River Scenic Area
56. Chau-Ram Park

Cherokee Lower Towns • 181

Miller moved to Eighteen Mile Creek near Pendleton and intended to become a farmer; however, ink was still in his blood and he started *Miller's Weekly Messenger* in 1795. The paper continued after Miller's death as *The Pendleton Messenger* and was later moved to Hartwell and became *The Hartwell Messenger*.

3. The Mavericks. Samuel Maverick was a successful Charleston businessman who moved to Pendleton when he married Elizabeth Anderson, daughter of Robert Anderson. He and his son, Gus, were opposed to nullification and secession and the younger Maverick was not inclined to remain in South Carolina. Gus went west to oversee family property in Alabama then traveled to see Texas, where he became involved in Texas independence and became a member of the Congress of the Republic of Texas. Gus became a large landowner and practiced law in San Antonio. His herd of unbranded cattle multiplied and ranged about San Antonio. Wild unbranded cattle became known as *mavericks*.

The Maverick home, Montpelier, is located outside of Pendleton on SC-88

4. Pendleton District Agriculture Museum. Farm implements and equipment, including an eighteenth century cotton gin are on display. Open by appointment only by calling (803) 646-3782. Located on US-76 south of Clemson.

5. Old Stone Church (c. 1800). This stone church is unusual in a region where people generally built frame churches. It was originally named Hopewell Presbyterian Church and was built by subscription of the leading families in the area. The cemetery contains the graves of many Revolutionary War veterans.

6. South Carolina State Botanical Garden. The botanical garden at Clemson University has been the official state garden of South Carolina since 1992 and has begun an impressive building program. New features include a conservatory, discovery center, and the Bob Campbell Geology Museum. The garden has many hiking trails that crisscross a stream where Oconee Bells bloom in mid-March. There is a woodland bog, camellia collection, hosta garden, native turf grasses, and an arboretum with 700 trees and shrubs. Interesting structures include the 1716 Hanover House, a pioneer homestead, and the outdoor sculpture collection. The vegetable garden features many favorite Southern garden crops and the commercially important varieties of cotton, indigo, sugar cane, and tobacco.

The South Carolina State Botanical Garden is located on Perimeter Road. Open everyday from dawn to dusk.

Hanover House. This historic home was built in 1716 by Paul de St. Julien, a French Huguenot pioneer of Berkeley County. The house was moved to Clemson in 1941 when Lake Moultrie was built. The chimney is inscribed with the phrase "peu a peu," which means *little by little* from a French saying that "little by little the little bird builds its nest." The upper portion of the chimney was moved intact 150 miles to preserve the inscription. St. Julien named his home Hanover in honor of King George I of England, Elector of Hanover. The home is furnished with authentic furniture and decorative elements of the 1700–1750 period. Hanover House is located near the heirloom vegetable garden at the South Carolina State Botanical Garden.

7. Hopewell-Keowee Monument. The Treaty Oak, site of the Hopewell Conference, is located on a hill near the Cherry Road bridge (Highway 37). Look for the historical marker at the pull-off and follow the hiking trail to the monument. The Hopewell Conference was named for the plantation of Andrew Pickens, which was located south of the historical marker.

Treaty of Hopewell. The Cherokees were weakened and impoverished from the seven years of almost continual warfare during the Revolution. They then suffered an outbreak of smallpox in 1783. On November 28, 1785, the Cherokees agreed to the Treaty of Hopewell, their first with the United States of America. Due to their misfortunes with smallpox and war with South Carolina, the Cherokees were in no position to make demands.

The conference was held on the east side of the Seneca River near the home of General Andrew Pickens and was attended by commissioners Colonel Benjamin Hawkins (North Carolina), General Andrew Pickens (South Carolina), Joseph Martin (Tennessee,) and General Lachlan McIntosh (Georgia). The speakers for the Cherokees were Old Tassel and Nancy Ward, niece of Attakullakulla. The Cherokees gave up all land east of the Blue Ridge and were restricted to their now historical national boundaries that included much of eastern Tennessee, north Georgia, western North Carolina, and the northeastern corner of Alabama. In return, regulations for trade were established and the Cherokees were promised protection by the United States.

Two other treaties were signed at Hopewell. A treaty with the Choctaws was signed on January 3, 1786, and one with the Chickasaws on January 10 of the same year.

8. Clemson University was established by Thomas Clemson in 1889 on land he inherited from his father in-law, John C. Calhoun. Thomas Clemson, like his father-in-law, was a president of the Pendleton Farmer's Society. He and the society's members had for many years considered the need for a college in upper South Carolina. Clemson's will provided that his fortune build a college of agricultural and mechanical sciences, leaving land and $80,000. Today Clemson University is well known for its research in forestry, marine sciences, technical education, and its beautiful setting at the foot of the Blue Ridge.

Clemson University Extension maintains an excellent web site that contains a wealth of information for southern gardeners. The Home and Garden Information Center is located at www.hgic.clemson.edu/.

Clemson University information may be obtained at Tillman Hall, located on the hill above US -93 as you enter the center of campus. Open Monday through Friday, 9 a.m.–5 p.m.; Saturday, 10 a.m.–4 p.m.; and Sunday, 2–5 p.m.

John C. Calhoun was born in the Long Cane area in 1782. His father, Patrick, came with his family to Pennsylvania from Donegal, Ireland, then to Virginia, the Waxhaws in South Carolina, then to Long Cane Settlement. Patrick's mother, Catherine, was killed during the Long Cane Massacre in 1760.

John Calhoun was educated at the Willington School run by his brother-in-law, Dr. Moses Waddel. Calhoun graduated from Yale in 1804 and returned to South Carolina to practice law in Abbeville. During his long career as a statesman he was a state representative, U.S. senator, U.S. secretary of war, secretary of state, and vice-president for John Quincy Adams and Andrew Jackson. He moved to Pendleton District in 1826 and bought the property of Fort Hill where he lived the later part of his life.

Fort Hill. John Calhoun named his home Fort Hill, for he could see the site of the old Fort Rutledge. The home is located on a hill in the central part of the Clemson campus; the oldest part of the house was built in 1803. It is a National Historic Landmark and a museum to the Calhoun and Clemson families. On the south side of Calhoun's office grows a healthy Franklinia, about twelve-feet tall and well-branched. It blooms at the end of July and beginning of August. The Calhoun house is open Monday through Saturday, 10 a.m.–5 p.m., and Sunday from 1–5 p.m.

---

*Cherokee Lower Towns**

Brass Town	Oustinare
Chauga	Seneca
Cheowee	Kulsage (Sugar Town)
Estatoe	Tomassee
Jocassee	Toxaway
Keowee	Tugaloo
Oconee	Warachy
Ostatoy	

*Towns occupied in 1775

Robert M. Cooper Library. The library of Clemson University contains over 1.5 million items and has a strong collection of agricultural and natural science literature.

Clemson City Library. Old Greenville Highway.

Clemson Visitors Center is located in the Chamber of Commerce offices at College Avenue and Strode Circle, just north of the Clemson campus.

Clemson Park and Recreation Area. Boat ramp, picnic area, and fitness trail. Located off College Avenue at the end of Mountain View Lane.

9. Site of Seneca. The Cherokee town of Seneca was a mile south of Clemson about where the university golf course is located and it occupied both sides of the Seneca River. It was settled by Senecas from New York who were friendly with the Cherokees. Seneca was burned by Colonel Montgomery in June 1760, and was partially rebuilt when Bartram visited.

In August 1776 Alexander Cameron, Tories, and Indian allies engaged the South Carolina militia at Seneca. Francis Salvador of Coronaca in Ninety Six District (Greenwood County) was wounded and died in this skirmish. As a member of the South Carolina Provincial Congress, Salvador was the first Jew in America to be elected as a representative of the people. At the conclusion of this campaign, Andrew Williamson had the houses on both sides of the Seneca River burned and then had his army erect Fort Rutledge on the east bank. Using Fort Rutledge as a base, Williamson's army destroyed all of the Cherokee towns east of the Blue Ridge and drove the inhabitants across the mountains.

Fort Rutledge. The Cherokees were instigated by British agents to attack white settlements in 1776. Andrew Williamson, Andrew Pickens, Thomas Sumter, and Robert Anderson invaded the Lower Towns and burned nearly all of the villages. Fort Rutledge was built on the east bank of the Seneca River near the site of Seneca Town as a base for military operations. In 1780 the fort was taken by Tories and destroyed. It stood on a hill that now overlooks the club house at the golf course.

10. Robert Anderson lived at his plantation Westville, which lay across the Seneca River from his friend Andrew Pickens. Anderson earlier lived in the Long Cane area and was one of the leading figures in the Revolution in South Carolina. He fought in the first Battle at Ninety Six, the Battle of Kettle Creek, Cowpens, and the recapture of Augusta. After the war he served in the legislature, as lieutenant governor, and as brigadier general of the South Carolina Militia. He died in 1813 and is buried at the Old Stone Church.

11. Oconee Point. U.S. Army Corps of Engineers recreation facility. Camping, boat ramp. Located at the end of South Friendship Road.

12. Coneross Park. U.S. Army Corps of Engineers recreation facility. CR-184, ten miles southeast of Seneca. Camping, boat ramp.

13. The Lunney Museum is the museum of Oconee County. It is foremost a house museum with a collection of turn-of-the-century furnishings, but also contains memorabilia of the history of Oconee County dating from the late seventeenth century. West First Street, Seneca. Open Thursday through Sunday, 1–5:30 p.m.

14. South Cove County Park. South Cove provides access to Lake Keowee for fishing and boating. Facilities are available for camping, picnicking, and family recreation area. SC-28, north of Seneca.

15. Newry is a historic industrial district centered around the 1890s mill town. The mill still stands immediately below the Little River Dam. The mill ceased operation in 1975.

16. Duke Power World of Energy, Keowee-Toxaway Center. The Duke Power visitor center displays information on the construction of the Oconee Nuclear Plant and exhibits on electric generation. The grounds and picnic area are an excellent place to see native plants used in a planned landscape. There is a 400-gallon aquarium containing local fish species. The Center is located on Rochester Highway, SC-130. Open Monday through Saturday, 9 a.m.–5 p.m. and on Sunday from 12–5 p.m. Closed on Thanksgiving, Christmas Eve, Christmas, and New Year's Day.

17. High Falls Park. The largest of the Oconee County parks, High Falls Park provides facilities for camping, fishing, handicap fishing pier, boating, and picnicking. Located on Lake Keowee, off SC-183.

18. Mile Creek Park. Mile Creek is so named because it is a mile from Keowee. This Pickens county park has campsites for RVs and tents, picnic shelters, boat ramps, and a bird sanctuary. Located off SC-133 north of Six Mile.

19. Keowee was the most important town of the Lower, or Underhill, Cherokee towns. Its name means *place of mulberries*. A trading post was established there in the early eighteenth century and the Keowee-Charleston Path connected Keowee with the English towns on the coast. The Virginia Path crossed the Keowee River a few miles above Keowee, adding to its importance in the regional economy. Keowee was burned by James Grant and South Carolina militia on June 1, 1760, and again by Andrew Williamson's forces on August 4, 1776.

The site of Keowee is underwater now, but it was located at the west side of the Old Nimmons Bridge. To view the area and historic marker turn east on Keowee Town Landing Road (Highway 98) and stop at the fork, right leads to the boat ramp and a view of the lake. The gated road to the left arrives at a parking area and the Keowee-Fort Prince George Marker.

20. Fort Prince George. At the beginning of the French and Indian War the frontier of South Carolina was alarmed by raids from Creeks, Cherokees, and Iroquois. In response Governor Glen embargoed the Cherokees, who had no other source for their manufactured goods. The Cherokees acquiesced and sent 160 leaders to meet Glen at Keowee. The Cherokees requested that a fort be built at Keowee, the capital of the Lower Towns. It was hoped that the presence of a garrison would deter mischief by Creeks, bandits, and renegades and protect the trading paths. The fort was constructed in 1753 on the site of Old Keowee, which was on the east side of the Keowee River opposite the new town.

The most infamous event at Fort Prince George occurred at the beginning of the Cherokee War when Captain Cotymore was lured outside the fort and killed on January 16, 1760. The soldiers murdered their Cherokee hostages, which comprised most of the headmen of the Lower Towns. The Cherokees besieged the fort for two months, retreating when it was learned that English troops and militia were gathering at Ninety Six. Fort Prince George was relieved in June when Colonel Archibald Montgomery arrived with his army.

When Bartram visited Keowee in 1775 most of the Cherokees had moved west to the Hiawassee River and Fort Prince George had become a trading post. The sepulchres that he saw were probably the graves of whites, not Indians. The site of the fort is now underwater.

21. Kulsage (Sugar Town) is an ancient Cherokee town. Its name in Cherokee is Kulsetsi'yi, meaning *honey locust place*. Kulsage appears to have always been located on Keowee River at Fall Creek until it was destroyed. Kulsage was burned in June 1760 during the Cherokee War and again by Major Williamson's militia on August 4, 1776. The town then moved to the Little Tennessee River across from Franklin, where it gave its name to the Cullasaja River.

22. Keowee-Toxaway State Park includes a thousand acres of wooded land on Lake Keowee. The streams are clear running mountain streams and the hiking trails cross cascades and

Whitewater Falls on a cold January day

rock outcrops. The Cherokee Interpretive Trail is on the south side of SC-11. Four outdoor exhibit kiosks depict the history of the Cherokees in the Lower Towns, their relationship to the traders and settlers of South Carolina, and the building of Fort Prince George. One interesting item is a list of trade goods and their price in deerskins. The Interpretive Center contains displays about the natural history of the South Carolina foothills.

Keowee-Toxaway Park has a camping area, cabin, picnic areas, and hiking trails. Located on SC-11 east of Lake Keowee. Open daily from 9 a.m.–9 p.m., April through October. Open 9 a.m.–6 p.m. during the remainder of the year.

23. Golden Creek Mill, c. 1825, is a reconstructed mill beautifully situated on Golden Creek northeast of Liberty. The mill is still operable and sells flour and meal. A country store, art museum, and picnic area are other features enjoyed by visitors, but tours of the mill must be prearranged. Located on Enon Church Road off SC-93.

24. Pickens County Museum contains art and historical exhibits of the Upcountry. Located at 307 Johnson Street in Pickens. Open Tuesday through Friday, 9 a.m.–5 p.m.

25. Glassy Mountain Heritage Preserve. Glassy Mountain is an excellent example of the impressive granite domes found throughout the South Carolina and Georgia Piedmont. The botanical communities found on these granite domes are similar to the granite flat rocks described by William Bartram.

26. Hagood Mill is the only grist mill in South Carolina with its original machinery. Operated by the Pickens County Museum. Located on US-178, two miles north of Pickens.

27. Cherokee Foothills Scenic Highway. SC-11 roughly follows the trading path that connected the Cherokee Lower Towns with Virginia, known as the Virginia Path. The highway skirts the foot of the Blue Ridge for 136 miles giving travelers sweeping views of the mountains and rolling farmland.

28. Table Rock State Park was created to protect the imposing Table Rock Mountain. A hiking trail winds its way to the top where visitors have a panoramic view of the Blue Ridge to the north and the Piedmont to the south. The remainder of the park is a resort with cabins and a popular restaurant. Camping and picnic areas are available. The lake is open for fishing and swimming.

29. Eastatoe Creek Heritage Preserve protects 373 acres of the upper Eastatoe Creek. This scenic area has a self-sustaining population of rainbow trout and several rare ferns. Eastatoe Gorge has an extremely humid microclimate that supports a habitat of temperate and tropical plants. Several of the ferns are not found anywhere else in America, including the bristle and Tunbridge ferns. Some of the mosses are more common to South American rain forests. The preserve is contained within a wildlife management area that allows for hunting and fishing. The hiking trail is 2.5 miles long, it begins on a logging road then follows the banks of Eastatoe Creek. Primitive camping is allowed at the end of the trail. Located on SC-237, off US-178.

30. Lake Jocassee is surrounded by a vast and botanically rich woodland. This 50,000-acre tract is the last large, unprotected portion of the Blue Ridge Escarpment and is being acquired by the state of South Carolina with help from environmental organizations.

Bad Creek Visitors Center. Bad Creek Reservoir is a pumped storage lake and is used to produce electricity during peak electric demand. The trail head to Coon Branch Natural Area begins at the parking lot of the Visitors Center. Located on SC-130. Open Thursday through Saturday, 10 a.m.–5 p.m., June through August. From September through October hours are 10 a.m.–5 p.m. on Saturday and 12–5 p.m. on Sunday.

31. Devils Fork State Park was created to protect the Oconee bells, a rare flower that grows in abundance along streams that are tributary to the Keowee River. This beautiful plant was first collected by André Michaux on December 8, 1788, near the junction of Whitewater and Toxaway rivers. The place was near the site of the abandoned town of Ellijah, now in the approximate center of Lake Jocassee.

Asa Gray found Michaux's specimen of Oconee bells (*Shortia galacifolia*) in the Michaux Herbarium in Paris in 1839. Gray began searching for the plant in the high mountains of North Carolina, at elevations above the plant's natural range. Though many searched, the plant was not rediscovered until 1877 when it was found by George Hyams on the Catawba River in McDowell County, North Carolina.

Though Oconee bells are found in Georgia and North Carolina, the greatest populations are concentrated around Lake Jocassee where it grows in association with mountain laurel along streams at elevations of 1,000–1,500 feet. It is very rare throughout the rest of its range. Its closest relatives all live in the Orient.

Devils Fork State Park provides recreational access to Lake Jocassee, certainly one of the most beautiful lakes in the Southeast. There are facilities for camping, picnicking, fishing, and swimming. The park has rental villas, a store, boat ramps, and nature trails. Open daily from 7 a.m.–9 p.m. Located on Highway 25 off SC-11.

32. Blue Ridge Escarpment and Gorges. The eastern edge of the Blue Ridge Mountains is marked by a steep and sudden rise from the Piedmont, which then becomes a 2,000–3,000-foot plateau from which peaks rise another 1,000–3,000 feet. The Cherokees called it the Blue Wall. The escarpment runs for almost sixty miles from Highlands to Asheville and features several dramatic drops of nearly 2,000 feet. The Blue Ridge is the oldest part of the Appalachians and is composed of basement rocks that have been uncovered by the erosion of several miles of mountain. Some of the gneiss is nearly a billion years old and predates any life-forms that could have left fossil records. The South's most dramatic gorges and waterfalls are created by rivers flowing down from this escarpment. The Blue Ridge has been under intense pressure for development in recent years.

The Blue Ridge, its escarpment, and gorges contain the most biologically diverse ecosystems in North America. Due to the position of the mountains with prevailing weather patterns, some parts of the southern Blue Ridge receive nearly eighty inches of rain each year. The ruggedness of the terrain has provided a haven for plants and amphibians. The Whitewater, Thompson, Horsepasture, and Toxaway rivers form the Keowee River and have carved deep ravines as they cascade down steep and ancient rock. The Thompson River Gorge is particularly remote and wild. The lower part of these rivers is home to the rare Oconee bells and numerous uncommon amphibians.

Much of this area was once owned by Duke Power but has now been purchased by North and South Carolina, environmental groups, and national agencies. The land is being converted into state parks and game lands. Part of the South Carolina purchase will become a heritage preserve.

Gorges State Park is the newest state park in North Carolina and encompasses the upper Toxaway River and its tributaries. The visitor center is located on NC-281 southeast of Sapphire. The park opens at 8 a.m. and closes at dusk.

Windy Falls Natural Area contains 103 acres of wilderness on Horsepasture River.

33. Lower Whitewater Falls and Upper Whitewater Falls form the steepest series of cascades in the eastern United States, falling over 800 feet. André Michaux visited the falls on December 9, 1778. The Cherokees thought the falls were inhabited by spirits for they told Michaux that at night fires could be seen among the cliffs. Lower Whitewater Falls is reached by a 3.4-mile hike from the Bad Creek Hydroelectric Station via the Foothills Trail and Waterfalls Overlook Trail. Hikers must register at the security gate.

34. Upper Whitewater Falls cascades 411 feet and is certainly one of the most scenic places in the South. It is popular with tourists because the view is easily available from the parking lot on SC-130. The Foothills Trail passes through the Whitewater Falls and Whitewater River area.

35. Coon Branch Natural Area is a preserve of fifteen acres of virgin forest located on Whitewater River at the state line. Coon Branch Natural Area is acknowledged as an excellent birding area in spring. The South Carolina champion Fraser magnolia grows at Coon Branch. It is six feet in diameter and eighty-six feet tall. The Coon Branch Natural Area is located in Duke Power forest land and is accessible from the Bad Creek Station on SC-107.

36. Whiteside Mountain (4,930 feet) is the highest sheer drop in the eastern United States. The peak rises 2,000 feet above the valley floor at Grimshawes and the southern side of Whiteside has a vertical face of 750 feet. Whiteside Mountain is the most prominent of the granite mountains surrounding Highlands. These domes were formed during the last Appalachian orogeny 350 million years ago as molten magma welled up into the existing rock. These structures were deep below the ancient Appalachians and have now been exposed by erosion. Whiteside Mountain has some of the oldest rock in the Appalachians. Interestingly, the exposed rock of the surrounding mountains is usually on the south side where the extremes of heat and cold cause more weathering of the rock. Peregrine falcons nest at the summit of Whiteside Mountain.

Devil's Courthouse is an extension on the northern slope of Whiteside Mountain. It has botanically rich cliffs and beautiful views of the surrounding mountains, but the trail is undeveloped and difficult. The Chatooga River begins as a spring on the north side.

The trail to Whiteside Mountain begins at the parking lot on Whiteside Mountain Road, off US-64 between Highlands and Cashiers.

37. Ellicott Rock Wilderness covers 9,015 acres within the states of Georgia, North Carolina and South Carolina and received its wilderness status in 1975. When Andrew Ellicott surveyed the boundary between Georgia and North Carolina in 1811, he set up the rock where the states have a common point with South Carolina. There are no roads into Ellicott Rock Wilderness. Access is from FS-1178 (Bull Pen Road), Burrell's Ford Road, and Walhalla Fish Hatchery. Sloan Bridge Trail enters from SC-107.

38. Walhalla Fish Hatchery. The hatchery raises over a million rainbow and native brown trout each year for the mountain streams of South Carolina and Georgia. The hatchery was built in the 1930s and has been modernized several times. The forest service operates the picnic area located in a grove of the largest hemlocks and white pines in South Carolina. A hiking trail leads to the East Fork of the Chatooga River and continues on to the Chatooga River. From there the Chatooga River Trail heads south to connect with the Bartram Trail. Another trail leads up the Chatooga River to Ellicott Rock Wilderness Area. Visitors may fish from a deck on the East Fork. Located off SC-107.

39. White Rock Scenic Area takes its name from the rock outcrops near Cherry Hill Campground. This scenic area remains remote and wild. Winding Stairs Trail follows an old stagecoach road that once crossed the mountains. Parking and access are from SC-107 north of Oconee State Park.

40. Burrell's Ford Recreation Area is popular with fishermen and hikers on the Chatooga River Trail. The Burrell's Ford area is noted for its beauty and has the only native population of Oconee bells in Georgia. Primitive camping, fishing, and hiking are popular activities. The area is accessible from SC-107 or SC-28 by taking Burrell's Ford Road (unpaved).

41. Foothills Trail is South Carolina's premier hiking trail. It is eighty-five miles long and traverses the eastern edge of the Blue Ridge. Foothills Trail covers some of the most varied and spectacular scenery in the southern Appalachians. It descends gorges in the Blue Ridge Escarpment, crosses valleys and mountains, ascends granite mountains, and follows mountain streams. The state parks of Oconee, Table Rock, Caesar's Head, and Jones Gap are all connected by the Foothills Trail. The trail is the only way to see the wilderness area of the Whitewater, Horsepasture, Thompson, and Toxaway gorges.

Almost forty miles of the trail was built by Duke Power Company to satisfy recreational requirements related to the construction of the Bad Creek pumping station. Information is available at the Duke Power Keowee-Toxaway Visitor Center, Highland Hiker in Highlands, and the Andrew Pickens District office of Sumter National Forest located on SC-107 in Mountain Rest. A book and trail maps are generally available at bookstores and outfitters throughout the region.

42. Cherry Hill Recreation Area is the only developed area within White Rock Scenic Area and is accessible from SC-107. Several hiking trails cross the area, including access to Winding Stairs Trail. Cherry Hill has developed campsites, a bathhouse, and a picnic area.

43. Chatooga River Trail follows the Chatooga River from Ellicott Rock to US-76. It coincides with the Foothills Trail and Bartram Trail for part of its distance.

44. Russell Homestead. The ruins of the 1867 Russell House is a National Forest Service historic site. Ganaway Russell and his large family grew corn, cattle, and hogs and they made soap, syrup, and coffins. The farm operated a blacksmith shop, shoe shop, and knitting machine. Later the house became an inn for travelers en route to Highlands. When the Cherokees gave up their last strip of land in South Carolina this property was part of a tract of land reserved for Walter Adair, perhaps the mixed-blood son of James Adair. The site of **Chatuga Old Town** occupied the site of the Russell Homestead and stretched along the Chatooga River above and below the SC-28 bridge. The U.S. Forest Service archaeologist determined that Chatuga Old Town has been occupied at various times beginning about 2,200 years ago

45. Oconee State Park is South Carolina's oldest state park, built in the 1930's by the Civilian Conservation Corps. It is located on a plateau between the Piedmont and the Blue Ridge. Originally the Bartram Trail began at Oconee State Park and connected to the Georgia Bartram Trail, though that is now not generally known. The first section of the Foothills Trail from Oconee State Park to the Chatooga River Trail is part of an unofficial Bartram Trail and there are several Bartram Trail signs remaining, one on SC-107 at Tamassee Road and another on the trail near Oconee State Park.

46. General Pickens Monument and Tomassee Town. The ancient Cherokee town of Tomassee[1] was abandoned from 1752 until just before Bartram's visit. In August 1776, Colonel Andrew Williamson sent Andrew Pickens into the area of Tomassee in search of Cherokee warriors. At Tamassee Creek Pickens and his soldiers were confronted by a party of Cherokees. The Americans used a cane patch for cover and held off the Cherokees until reinforcements arrived. Pickens was at Tomassee again in the summer of 1779 to engage an army of Cherokees. This time Pickens' men set fire to the canebrake. The popping sound of burning river cane lead the Cherokees to believe reinforcements had arrived and they retreated.

The Scottish-American propensity to move often is illustrated in the life of Andrew Pickens. Born in Pennsylvania to Scotch-Irish parents, he moved to Virginia then to the Waxhaw community (Lancaster) in South Carolina. Upon reaching adulthood Pickens married Rebecca Calhoun and moved again to be near her family in the Long Cane area of present-day Abbeville County and they lived at present-day Abbeville. After the Revolution he moved to his Hopewell property south of Clemson, then he moved to Tomassee where he ended his years. He is buried at the Old Stone Church near Pendleton.

As a young man Pickens fought in the Cherokee War. When the Revolution opened he commanded a patriot regiment from Ninety Six. Upon the fall of Charleston, with much of South Carolina again under British control, the militia surrendered and Pickens was paroled. For a time he was courted by the British to join his friend and former commander, Andrew Williamson, in aiding the British. Pickens remained steadfast and refused to break his parole until the loyalists plundered Long Cane Settlement. He then reunited his regiment and helped Daniel Morgan win the Battle of Cowpens.

Pickens was admired for his honesty and sobriety and after the Revolution he was voted into public office. He served in the state legislature, United States Congress, the commission to establish the new South Carolina capital, and the commission to settle boundary disputes between South Carolina and Georgia. He declined to accept the nomination for governor. He was appointed as a commissioner on Indian Affairs by George Washington. As a skilled Indian fighter he won the respect of the Cherokees who called him Border Wizard Owl, for they believed him to lead a charmed life.

At Hopewell and at Tamassee Pickens raised cattle and horses. The Andrew Pickens monument is located on a rise near the road at the intersection of Tamassee Knob Road and Jumping Branch Road.

47. Oconee Station State Park contains two historic buildings. The stone blockhouse is the oldest structure in Oconee County and one of the few remaining such buildings in the South. It was built about 1792 when the Cherokee boundary was not very many miles away. Blockhouses with thick timber or stone walls were cheaper to build and maintain than encompassing forts. The fact that the Oconee Station Block House was built of local stone with walls two feet thick has helped it survive the last two centuries. A well in the bottom floor provided essential water during a siege. The fortress was decommissioned in 1799 when the Cherokee boundary was moved farther into North Carolina and raids diminished.

The Richards House was built by William Richards in 1805 after he bought the property of Oconee Station. It was the first brick house built in this section of the state. Richards ran an Indian trading business and farm at Oconee Station for a number of years.

Oconee Station sponsors folklore and history workshops as well as a pioneer encampment in October. Open Thursday through Sunday from March through September. Tours are available on weekend afternoons. Located 2.5 miles from SC-11 on Oconee Station Road.

48. Station Cove Botanical Area has an impressive display of spring wildflowers and a sixty-foot waterfall. This rich woods is an interesting botanical area year-round and lies near the old path that William Bartram followed across Station Mountain. Showy spring flowers include trillium, bloodroot, anemone, jack-in-the-pulpit, and mayapple. The trail head begins at the parking area on Oconee Station Road just west of the entrance to Oconee Station State Park.

49. Oconee Town on Oconee Creek was abandoned before 1760 but apparently moved elsewhere in the area, probably farther south. Colonel Williamson marched on Oconee in August 1776, hoping to surprise Alexander Cameron and his Cherokee allies. Finding the town deserted, he burned the houses and corn and

---

1. The Cherokee town was spelled Tomassee but the modern place names are spelled Tamassee.

moved on to Tugaloo. The Cherokee Oconees, like other Lower Towns, left South Carolina after the war of 1776.

It is doubtful that the town of Oconee among the Lower Cherokees was related to the Hitchiti Oconees who were members of the Creek Confederacy. The Cherokee town has many spellings—Ukwunu, Ukwuni, Oconore, Acconee, Oakenni, Occounny, and Oakonowie—indicating many pronunciations. The name is probably derived from a Cherokee word that was corrupted by the English.

50. Blue Ridge Railroad Historical Trail. This seven-mile trail is built on sections of the bed of the never-completed Blue Ridge Railroad. The trail heads are located at Isaqueena Falls and at one-tenth mile west of the intersection of SR-181 (Pickett Post Road) and SR-174 (Earlstead Drive). For a complete description of the entire trail and points of access see *Hiking South Carolina Trails* by Allen de Hart.

The idea for the Blue Ridge Railroad began in 1836 when William H. Thomas and John C. Calhoun searched for a possible route over the Blue Ridge. Construction began in 1856 but in 1859 the South Carolina Legislature refused to appropriate more funds to the project, already having spent a million dollars on Stumphouse Tunnel alone. The railroad would have connected Charleston to Nashville and Cincinnati. A short section of White Cut Road, from Oconee Station to Pickett Post, follows the old railroad bed.

51. Stumphouse Tunnel was constructed as part of the Blue Ridge Railroad. The tunnel was never finished and is now closed to the public. Clemson University once used the tunnel to age their famous blue cheese. There is a picnic area and a trail that leads to Isaqueena Falls.

Isaqueena Falls is named for the Creek maiden who escaped her Cherokee captors by leaping to a rock ledge behind the falls. The Cherokees thought she had jumped to her death and ceased their pursuit. She is also known as Cateechee and is credited with having saved the settlement of Ninety-Six during the Cherokee War.

52. Sumter National Forest. Stumphouse Ranger Station is located on SC-28.

53. Walhalla was created in 1849–1850 by a group of German immigrants who settled on 30,000 acres of land purchased by the German Colonization Society of Charleston. The immigrants were of Saxon ancestry and spoke a dialect of German that was related to English. The name Walhalla refers to the home of the gods in Norse mythology. The Walhalla Okto-

Oconee Station blockhouse

berfest is becoming a popular fall weekend destination.

54. Buzzard Roost Heritage Preserve protects a marble outcrop that harbors smooth coneflower, stoneroot, bindweed, and several rare ferns. Old logging roads and trails provide access through the preserve. To reach Buzzard Roost follow SC-28 north six miles from downtown Walhalla, turn left on CR-193 (Whetstone Road), go .75 mile, then turn left on CR-290 (Stumphouse Road). Travel one mile then turn left on FS-744 (Rich Mountain Road). Travel another three miles then turn left on FS-744-I. The last road ends at a barricade, Buzzard Roost is to the east.

55. Chauga River Scenic Area. This seventeen mile section of the Chauga River is the best kept secret of the South Carolina mountains, perhaps overshadowed by the fame of the nearby Chatooga River. The Chauga River flows directly along the Brevard Fault that separates the Piedmont from the Blue Ridge. The ruggedness of the Chauga River Gorge is due to the fractured young rocks within the fault. Plant diversity is another attraction of the Chauga River, with Piedmont and montane plants growing together.

The lower section of the Chauga River, below Cobbs Bridge, is used by canoeists, and the section from Cassidy Bridge to Cobbs Bridge is whitewater. Numerous unpaved roads dead-end in the scenic area, particularly along Spy Rock Road.

56. Chau-Ram Park. Chauga Nature Trail brings hikers to the Chauga River for a view of the beautiful cascades. This is mountain-like country where one finds galax and rhododendron. The park includes facilities for camping, picnicking, fishing, kayaking, and hiking. Located off US-76 west of Westminster.

Counties

Oconee County. Oconee County was created from Pickens County in 1868. The Savannah River originally was defined at being the present Seneca and Keowee Rivers. For this reason Georgia claimed the land between the Chatooga, Tugaloo, and Keowee rivers, which included all of present-day Oconee County. Georgia even made land grants in the area. One such grant was a tract of 3,000 acres on the Tugaloo and Chauga rivers given in 1784 to Revolutionary War veteran Colonel Benjamin Cleveland. The boundary dispute with South Carolina was settled in 1787 at the Beaufort Conference where Georgia relinquished claim for this land and South Carolina gave up claim to the land between the Altamaha and St. Marys rivers.

Pickens County was created when Pendleton District was divided into Pickens and Anderson counties. It is named for General Andrew Pickens.

Itinerary

Miles	Directions
	Begin SC-187 at Portman Shoals and travel north
7.2	Left on US-76, Clemson Boulevard
.8	Right on SC-187, Mechanic Street
1.2	Downtown Pendleton, keep straight through town on Mechanic Street
2.6	Right on US-76
.1	Left on Perimeter Road
.6	Entrance for South Carolina State Botanical Garden
1.7	Approximate site of Seneca
2.5	Left on SC-93, Old Greenville Highway
1.4	Left on US-76
1.0	Right on CR-1, Old Clemson Highway
3.5	Right on SC-130
7.5	Bartram Trail Historical Marker
.3	SC-130, sharp right
2.9	Right on Nimmons Bridge Road
1.6	Right on Keowee Town Landing Road
.8	Park on the left and walk to the Keowee Town Monument *Return to Nimmons Bridge Road*
1.4	Keep left on Nimmons Bridge Road
1.9	Left on Shallowford Road
1.3	Left on Park Avenue
1.0	Left then immediate right on to Cherokee Path Road, becomes Crestwood Drive
.5	Bear right on Highway 73
1.0	Right on Flat Shoals Road
.9	Left on SC-11, Cherokee Foothills Scenic Highway
.8	Right on Dynamite Road
1.0	Left on Cheohee Valley Road
.3	Right on Tamassee Lane
.8	Straight on Kelly Road (gravel)
.3	Right on the paved road, George Todd Road
.4	Left on George Todd Road
.1	Right on Rocky Ford Road (gravel)
.4	Left on the gravel road, cross the creek
.2	Begin Oconee Station Road
1.3	Parking for Station Cove Trail
.2	Right on White Cut Road
3.8	Right on Pickett Post Road
1.3	Right on Playground Road
2.4	Right on SC-28
5.4	Keep left on SC-28
1.2	Left on Taylor Creek Road
.5	Left on Moorhead Place Road
.9	Right on Land Bridge Road
.4	Left on Chatooga Ridge Road
1.8	Right on Whetstone Road
4.0	Parking for Earl's Ford Area

Old Stecoe

The Cherokee town of Stecoe was located along Stekoa Creek at Clayton. It was a well-known intersection of several trails. One trail came from the Lower Towns in the east and one from Tugaloo in the south. Another trail went west to Hiawassee and the Valley Towns and yet another went north along the Little Tennessee River to the Middle Towns. The area was known as the Dividings because of the many diverging paths. The path traveling north passed through a break in the Blue Ridge at Rabun Gap and followed the Little Tennessee River.

The De Soto and Pardo expeditions entered the mountain home of the Cherokees across the headwaters of the Catawba, Nolichucky, and Holston rivers, home to the Cheraws (also called Sara by the English and Xuala by the Spanish). Subsequent Spanish expeditions, searching for gold and silver, no doubt entered the middle towns by way of the path across the Chatooga River. In the late seventeenth century the Charleston-Keowee Path and the Virginia Paths converged at Keowee, then crossed the Oconee Mountains, crossed the Chatooga River at Earl's Ford, and arrived at the Dividings.

The name Chatooga may be derived from a Cherokee word, *tsatu'gi*, which means we have crossed here. This area was part of the Cherokee land cession of July 8, 1817. This tract, and others in Tennessee, were given in exchange for an equal amount of land west of the Mississippi River in Arkansas Territory. Rabun County was organized on December 21, 1819 and the land lottery was held in 1820.

As happened with most treaties, thirty-one Eastern Cherokees signed a treaty that the United States government took to be binding to the whole nation even though sixty-seven leaders signed a memorial of dissent. Many of the Cherokees in western Georgia and eastern Alabama still clung to the old ways and desired to move west where they could carry on their hunting tradition. By the nineteenth century the mountain Cherokees were becoming settled farmers, little different from their white neighbors, and some even desired to become part of the United States. This division between the traditional and Americanized factions was to linger for years and even intensified after the Cherokee Nation was moved west.

Members of the North Carolina Bartram Trail Society enjoy the view from Scaly Mountain

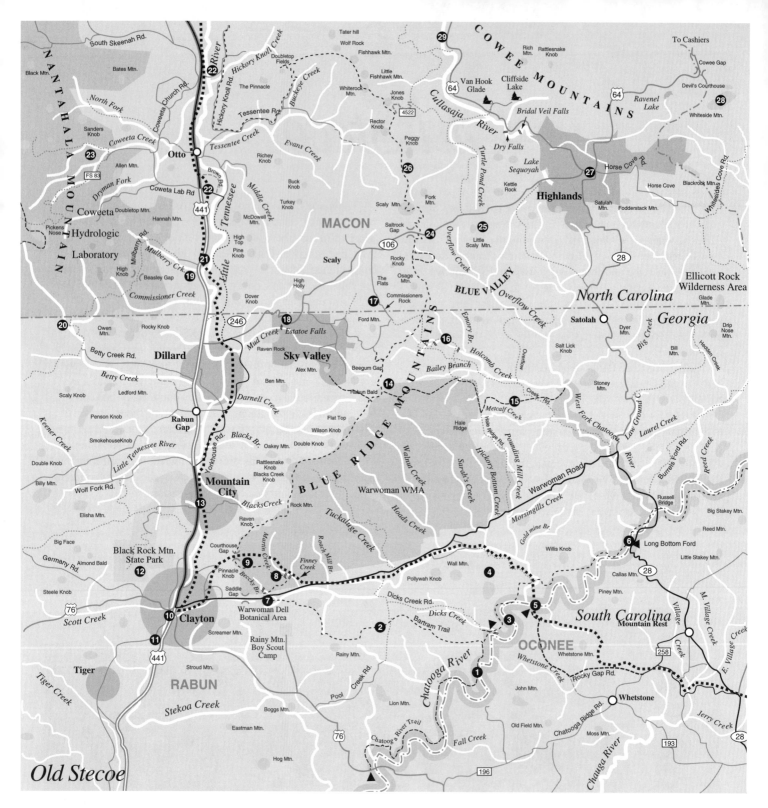

Legend

1. Chatooga River Trail
2. Bartram Trail
3. Chatooga Wild and Scenic River
4. Chattahoochee National Forest
5. Earl's Ford
6. Russell Homestead
7. Warwoman Dell
8. Martin Creek Falls
9. Pinnacle Knob
10. Clayton
11. Herbert's Savannah
12. Black Rock Mountain State Park
13. The Passover
14. Rabun Bald
15. Three Forks Trail
16. Holcomb Creek Trail
17. The Flats
18. Estatoe Falls
19. Huffman's Native Plants
20. Betty Creek Botanical Area
21. Second Battle of Echoe
22. Cherokee Victory at the Narrows (First Battle of Echoe)
23. Coweeta Hydrologic Laboratory
24. The Blue Ridge
25. Little Scaly Mountain
26. North Carolina Bartram Trail
27. Highlands
    Satulah Mountain
    Juan Pardo Expedition
    Highlands Nature Center
    Highlands Biological Station
    Highlands Botanical Garden
    Sunset Rock
    Nantahala National Forest Visitor Center
28. Whiteside Mountain
29. Cullasaja Gorge

William Bartram's Travels in Northeast Georgia

In May 1775 William Bartram traveled to the Cherokee Country. He crossed the Chatooga River at Earl's Ford on May 19, traveled up Warwoman Creek, crossed and recrossed the creek several times (Benjamin Hawkins crossed it nine times on his travels in 1796). Near Warwoman Dell the path ascended Finney Creek and Martin Creek (Bartram's Falling Creek), through Courthouse Gap, and down Norton Creek (Rattlesnake Creek to the Cherokees). Bartram's narrative becomes a little confusing here because he mentions Falling Creek two times, apparently before and after crossing the ridge at Pinnacle Knob. Bartram named the peak Mount Magnolia (Pinnacle Knob) where he found a new tree that he named *Magnolia auriculata*, now known as Fraser's magnolia (*Magnolia fraseri*).

Bartram passed through the old fields and site of Stecoe (Clayton) and then turned north, following the west bank of Stekoa Creek and through the narrow pass at Black Rock Mountain. He crossed the Blue Ridge Divide at Mountain City, called the Passover, and entered the headwaters of the Little Tennessee River and the Vale of Cowee (Rabun Gap). Bartram's path then followed closely the present York House Road. The two beautiful rivulets that enter the Little Tennessee River opposite one another are Betty Creek and Darnell Creek. Bartram's narrative seems to say that he crossed the Little Tennessee from east to west at Dillard, but this would put him too far away from a view of Eastotoe Falls. The pyramidal hill on his right must be Raven Rock and he must have crossed the river farther downstream, north of the North Carolina state line. This would place his path on the east side of Little Tennessee River, then he crossed the present Highlands Highway (GA-246/NC-106) closer to Mud Creek Valley where he viewed the *unparalleled falls* in the distance.

Bartram indicates he crossed the river again, which in The

Mountain City and the Blue Ridge Divide, view from Black Rock Mountain State Park looking east

Travels appears to mean from west to east. The trading path was by most accounts on the west side of the Little Tennessee River and indeed Bartram later says that …

> *After I left the graves, the ample vale soon offered on my right hand, through the tall forest trees, charming views, which exhibited a pleasing contrast, immediately out of the gloomy shades and scenes of death, into expansive, lucid, green, flowery fields, expanding between retiring hills, and turfy eminences, the rapid Tanase gliding through, as a vast serpent rushing after his prey.*[1]

This indicates that Bartram was traveling on the west side of the river at Otto. Probably Bartram crossed from the east to the west side of the Little Tennessee River near the graves of the fallen Cherokee warriors, just a mile or so north of the state line. The site is commemorated with a historical marker.

1. William Bartram, *Travels*, 346.

Sites

1. Chatooga River Trail follows the north side of the Chatooga River from US-76 to its intersection with the Bartram Trail at Dick's Creek. It is 10.7 miles long and most of it lies within the corridor of the Chatooga Wild and Scenic River.

2. Bartram Trail. The Bartram Trail in Georgia is thirty-seven miles long and begins at the SC-28 bridge on the Chatooga River. From there it generally follows the north side of the Chatooga River to Dick's Creek where it diverges from the Chatooga River Trail. The Bartram Trail then turns northwest and crosses the ridge to Rainy Mountain and descends to Warwoman Dell, then climbs along the southwest flank of Rabun Bald. From Rabun Bald the trail crosses Beegum Gap and joins the North Carolina Bartram Trail. Another section of trail in South Carolina is not so well known as the trails in Georgia and North Carolina. The Bartram Trail officially continues up the Chatooga River north of SC-28, coinciding with the Chatooga River Trail then turns southeast and ends at Oconee State Park. The last section is better known in South Carolina as the Foothills Trail.

3. Chatooga Wild and Scenic River. The Chatooga River is the dividing line between Georgia and South Carolina and rises at Whiteside Mountain near Highlands, North Carolina. Its name in Cherokee is *Tsatu'gi*, possibly meaning "I have crossed." The Chatooga River was the first river in the Southeast to be designated as a Wild and Scenic River, receiving Congressional approval in 1974. The Chatooga River is famous for its beauty and rugged rapids. Several outfitters operate whitewater guide services in the area. Boating is restricted to the section below SC-28. The protected area extends one-fourth mile on each side of the river.

The Chatooga River lies on a plateau called the 1600-foot level, which lies between

Fraser magnolia, discovered by William Bartram on the south slopes of Rabun Bald

the Blue Ridge and the Chatooga Escarpment. The Chatooga River was once a headwater of the Chattahoochee River but the Chatooga was captured by the Tugaloo and is now part of the Savannah River system. The West Fork is a particularly wild and inaccessible area that begins just below the steep Blue Ridge

Earl's Ford on the Chatooga River, the historical crossing of the trail from South Carolina to the Cherokee Nation

Escarpment in the Blue Valley. Native brown trout spawn in the waters of the West Fork.

The Chatooga River watershed and the steep flanks of the Blue Ridge to the north contain many special and diverse habitats. Uncommon plants making appearances in the Chatooga River basin include filmy fern, Stewartia, and ground juniper. On top of the balds we find unusual heaths and mosses. The Chatooga River Watershed Coalition is working to protect the old growth forests and roadless areas, to identify significant botanical sections, and change the National Forest Service logging policy for this important natural area.

4. Chattahoochee National Forest contains 750,000 acres of forest land in north Georgia and is contiguous with the Nantahala National Forest in North Carolina. The Chattahoochee, Nantahala, Pisgah, Sumter, and Jefferson National Forests along with the Great Smoky National Park protect the southern Appalachians—one of the most diverse ecosystems in the world. The National Forest Service visitor and information center for the Tallulah Ranger District is on US-441 in Clayton.

5. Earl's Ford. The historic Warwoman Trail from South Carolina to the Middle and Overhill Towns crossed the Chatooga River at Earl's Ford. William Bartram, André Michaux, and countless others crossed at Earl's ford during excursions to Cherokee Country. It was also a route for invasion as evidenced by the punitive expeditions of Montgomery, Grant, and Williamson.

44. Russell Homestead. The ruins of the 1867 Russell House is a National Forest Service historic site. Ganaway Russell and his large family grew corn, cattle, and hogs and made soap, syrup, and coffins. The farm operated a blacksmith shop, shoe shop, and knitting machine. Later the house became an inn for travelers en route to Highlands. The property was originally a tract reserved for Walter Adair, perhaps the mixed blood son of James Adair, when the Cherokees gave up their last strip of land in South Carolina.

The site of **Chatuga Old Town** occupied the Russell farm site beside the Chatooga River, above and below the SC-28 bridge. The U.S. Forest Service archaeologist determined that Chatuga Old Town has been occupied at various times beginning about 2,200 years ago.

7. Warwoman Dell is a botanically rich and beautiful recreation area near the head of Warwoman Creek. It may be named for Nancy Ward, one of the beloved women of the Cherokees who was known as Warwoman. Part of the Bartram Trail follows the bed of the unfinished Blue Ridge Railroad. There is a half-mile nature trail within the small recreation area. Warwoman Road and Warwoman Creek follow a geologic feature known as the Warwoman Shear.

The Cherokee Town of Tocoreche was probably located at one time on Warwoman Creek. The John Stuart map of the Cherokee Country shows the name of the upper portion of Warwoman Creek as Tuckaritche Creek. What he called Warwoman Creek now seems to be Sarah's Creek. Tuckaluge Creek, a tributary of Warwoman, is probably named for the town of Tocoreche. When Bartram visited Cherokee Country the Tocoreches was located on Tuckasegee River in North Carolina.

8. Martin Creek Falls is the Falling Creek of the *Travels*. It is a series of three cascades. To reach the falls from Warwoman Road, travel three-fourths of a mile east of Warwoman Dell, turn left at the game check station. The falls are a half-mile mile farther and a trail is on the west side of the creek.

9. Pinnacle Knob is William Bartram's Mount Magnolia.

10. Clayton is the county seat of Rabun County and occupies the site of Old Stecoe, which was located in the broad meadow of Stekoa Creek. The Rabun County Historical Society is located one block west of downtown at the corner of Church and Hiawassee streets.

11. Herbert's Savannah and Herbert's Spring. This noted place was marked on early maps of Cherokee Country and was located at the head of the Tugaloo River. John Herbert was a pioneer trader and around 1727 he became commissioner for regulating the Indian trade.

12. Black Rock Mountain State Park is the highest state park in Georgia at 3,640 feet. It covers three peaks on the Eastern Continental Divide and contains 1,500 acres. Most of the park is undeveloped and is accessible by back country trails. The park gets its name from the outcrops of biotite gneiss. Several overlooks have views of the surrounding valleys and on clear days the Great Smoky Mountains are visible. Black Rock Mountain has it all—rock outcrops, boulderfields, hardwood coves, waterfalls, wildflowers, and incredible views. Facilities include tent camping, RV hookups, picnic area, and camp store.

13. The Passover. Mountain City sits astride the Blue Ridge Divide, known in early days as the Passover. North of Mountain City is Bartram's *Vale of Cowee* (Rabun Gap). This was the route of the Upper Cherokee Path to the Middle Towns and became known as the Locust Stake Road when American settlers moved in.

14. Rabun Bald is 4,696 feet and is the second highest mountain in Georgia. William Bartram described Fraser magnolia, his *Magnolia auriculata*, on the slopes of Rabun Bald. The slopes of Rabun Bald and the adjoining escarpment contain patches of old growth forest and large roadless areas. The peak of Rabun Bald and the headwaters of Tuckaluge Creek are important botanical areas. From NC-106 follow Hale Ridge Road and Old Rabun Bald Road to parking at Beegum Gap.

15. Three Forks Trail. One section of Three Forks Trail traverses three miles from Rabun Bald to Hale Ridge Road. The more scenic section is the 1.2 miles of rugged trail from Overflow Road at John Teague Gap to the Three Forks where Holcomb, Overflow, and Big creeks meet to form the West Fork of the Chatooga River. The last section is in true wilderness country. The total length from Rabun Bald to Three Forks is eight miles.

16. Holcomb Creek Trail provides access to Holcomb Creek Falls and Ammon Creek Falls.

17. The Flats. The Southern Appalachians once contained high meadows and bogs such as the one at the Flats. The Atlanta Botanical Garden has recently re-established pitcher plants in this remnant bog (the property is privately owned.) **Commissioner's Rock** is nearby, marking the boundary between Georgia and North Carolina.

18. Estatoe Falls was mentioned by William Bartram as the *unparalleled falls* he viewed while traveling along the Little Tennessee River.

19. Huffman's Native Plants. John Huffman grows native azaleas from seed collected with the cooperation of the National Forest Service. He has other native plants for sale—Fothergilla, clethra, Franklinia, Carolina silver bell, and magnolias. Open most days, if the sign is out. Located on US-441 one mile north of the state line.

20. Betty Creek Botanical Area. Go to the end of Betty Creek Road and continue on FS-104 for a spectacular display of spring wildflowers, particularly trilliums.

21. Second Battle of Echoe. English Regulars under Colonel James Grant, South Carolina militia commanded by Thomas Middleton, and Chickasaw and Catawba warriors marched into Cherokee Country to punish the Cherokees for the massacre of the Fort Loudon garrison. The army defeated the Cherokees south of the town of Echoe on June 10, 1761, within two miles of Montgomery's defeat of the previous year. The army proceeded to the Middle Towns with difficulty and burned the houses and fields. Grant's mandate was total destruction, not even was he to spare women or children. However, the Cherokees had abandoned their towns and took refuge in the mountains. Grant was frustrated in finding no engagements where his army could make a definitive victory. The Cherokees capitulated rather than

Whiteside Mountain

face starvation that winter and the Cherokee War ended. A young Francis Marion, seeing his countrymen create so much destruction, pondered the reputation of Christians among the Cherokees.

22. Cherokee Victory at the Narrows (First Battle of Echoe). Archibald Montgomery and James Grant led South Carolina Rangers and a regiment of Highlanders against the Cherokees in 1760. They burned corn fields and many of the Lower Towns yet they met little resistance. The Cherokees preferred to abandon their villages and disappear into the forests and mountains. The British regulars and South Carolina militia marched on to the Middle Towns with the relief of the besieged garrison at Fort Loudon as their destination. On June 27 they were ambushed on the Little Tennessee River at a place called the *Narrows*, where the passage between the river and mountains was narrow and difficult. Above twenty of Montgomery's soldiers were killed and seventy wounded. The army marched on to Echoe but the militia and Rangers urged a retreat and began to depart. Montgomery had little choice but to give up his campaign and return to Charleston. The Cherokees were led that day by the Raven and Serowih (also known as Young Warrior).

23. Coweeta Hydrologic Laboratory encompasses 5,400 acres of the headwaters of Coweeta Creek. At the Lab scientists study the hydrology of the Appalachian forests and streams. Subtle changes in the water ecology can be detected, be it induced by insect infestation, farming, logging, or acid rain that has arrived from distant sources. Coweeta engineers have developed road designs and logging operations that dramatically reduce erosion and disturbance to the environment.

24. The Blue Ridge. The eastern Blue Ridge is a long ridge that stretches from Virginia to north of Atlanta, broken in only a few places before it reaches Clayton. The Blue Ridge was created when Africa and North America collided 230–300 million years ago in an event similar to the collision of India with Asia that is now thrusting up the Himalayas. During that time the Appalachians looked much like the Rockies do today. Over the ages erosion wore down those lofty peaks, very rapidly in the beginning due to the absence of vegetative cover. The rocks of the Blue Ridge contain no fossils since they were formed before marine life existed. Some of the oldest rocks in the Blue Ridge approach a billion years old. The linear feature of the Blue Ridge and the eastern Appalachians is apparent from satellite photographs. The rocks of the Blue Ridge are metamorphic gneiss, schists, and quartzites that exhibit the flowing folds caused by intense pressure and heat.

The southern Blue Ridge receives sixty to eighty inches of rain each year, which maintains the lush forests and coves. The thin soil soon washes away when cleared of vegetation, soil that has taken millions of years to form. Because the Blue Ridge and southern Appalachians were free of ice during the Pleistocene age they provided an avenue for the advance of plants and animals as the glaciers retreated northward. During that time flowering plants were developing and a great forest stretched across North America and Eurasia. Similarity of climate helped the forests of the southern

Appalachians and the mountains of the far East to remain botanically related while the intervening lands have changed. Thus the Southeast has in common with the Orient such species as fringe tree, sweet shrub, azaleas, rhododendrons, hemlock, witch hazel, and magnolias.

Today one may visit northern-type ecosystems by climbing to the summit of the taller mountains, especially on their north side. The summits are similar to true boreal landscapes with northern tree species and heath balds. There one finds heathers that cannot be found elsewhere in the Southeast. The richness of fauna is not lacking. The southern Appalachians contain the highest number of species of salamanders in the world, thirty-nine. The most unusual of these is the hellbender, a large amphibian with homely features that ranges from twelve to twenty inches in length.

25. Little Scaly Mountain is the first ascent of the North Carolina Bartram Trail and offers a view of the Chatooga River valley and Rabun Bald to the south. To the north are the Fish Hawks, the most scenic portion of the North Carolina Bartram Trail.

26. North Carolina Bartram Trail. See Chapter 22, Cherokee Middle Towns.

27. Highlands is the highest city in the eastern United States at 4,118 feet. Highlands was developed in the 1870s as a healthful place with a pleasant climate and it remains just such a place even today. Since the 1920s Highlands has become a popular resort town populated with many second homes, yet it has a vibrant downtown despite its seasonal population. A very healthy Franklinia grows in front of the Crosby Community Center at 348 South Fifth Street. Due to the elevation it blooms rather late, September and October.

Satulah Mountain lies within the city limits of Highlands. The top is a heath bald and harbors a number of unusual and rare plants. At the summit one has a 360° view of the Highlands Plateau and the Blue Ridge Escarpment.

Juan Pardo Expedition. When Governor Menéndez expelled the French from Florida and established Saint Augustine he sailed north and built Fort San Felipe at Santa Elena (Parris Island). On September 1, 1567, the captain of the garrison, Juan Pardo, set out to explore the interior of La Florida and claim all the land between Florida and Mexico.

The Pardo expedition traveled north and passed through the land of the Cherokees. They met resistance in northwest Georgia when the Coosas (remembering the De Soto expedition) united with the Yuchis, Koasatis, and Okalusas. The Pardo expedition turned back for Santa Elena. It was once thought that Pardo's route lay across the Highlands Plateau but new research places it farther to the northeast. The historical marker commemorating the expedition of Juan Pardo is located in downtown Highlands.

Highlands Nature Center and Highlands Biological Station contain exhibits on the botany and biology of the Highlands Plateau. Community programs educate the public to the unique biological treasures of the area and the Biological Station provides facilities for researchers and educators. Located on Horse Cove Road. Open 10 a.m.–5 p.m., Monday through Saturday, from Memorial Day to Labor Day.

Highlands Botanical Garden is located behind the Highlands Nature Center on Horse Cove Road (straight south through downtown). Numerous rare and exceptional mountain plants are on display, including Oconee bells, swamp pink, and Stewartia. The hiking trails are open daily.

Sunset Rock is an easy hike from the Highlands Biological Station and is a popular place to view sunsets. From Sunset Rock hikers have a breathtaking view westward along the Blue Ridge Escarpment.

Nantahala National Forest Visitor Center. Obtain information and maps about the Nantahala National Forest at the visitor center on Main Street in Highlands.

28. Whiteside Mountain. An unusual feature of the mountains surrounding the Highlands Plateau is the presence of numerous rock-faced cliffs. The finest example is Whiteside Mountain which is easily accessible from US-64 just east of Highlands. The sheer face of Whiteside, like most of the cliffs of the area, faces south and drops almost 2,000 feet to the valley below. The rock is very ancient, igneous Whiteside gneiss, indicating that this region was once far below the surface of the earth.

Although the view from the summit of Whiteside Mountain is spectacular, another excellent vista is looking up from Whiteside Cove Road in the valley below.

Whiteside Mountain is an excellent birding place. It was known to the Cherokees as *the sitting down place* because they liked to camp there when hunting in the area. The headwaters of the Chatooga River rise from a spring on the north side of the mountain.

Devil's Courthouse is the rock outcrop on the eastern side of Whiteside Mountain. A treacherous hiking trail leads to the Courthouse where the amateur botanist may find entertainment. Excellent views of Devil's Courthouse may be seen from US-64 just past Whiteside Mountain Road. This viewing area is especially crowded in the fall.

29. Cullasaja Gorge was cut into the Highlands Plateau by the Cullasaja River. This spectacular gorge is not the deepest in the eastern United States, but with only a short stone wall between US-64 and a sheer drop it is certainly one of the most unsettling. A number of waterfalls punctuate the Cullasaja River on its way from Highlands to the gorge.

The Cullasaja River is named for Kulsage, or Sugar Town, which was located at its mouth on the Little Tennessee River.

Itinerary

Begin at Earl's Ford and follow Whetstone Road back to Chatooga Ridge Road

Miles	Direction
4.2	Left on Chatooga Ridge Road
3.5	Left on SC-28
5.7	Russell Bridge and access to the Bartram Trail and Chatooga River Trail
2.2	Left on Warwoman Road
10.4	Finney Creek Road, access to Martin Creek Falls
.6	Entrance to Warwoman Dell
.2	Cross Bartram Trail
2.3	Left on Warwoman Road
	Cross US-441, becomes Savannah Street
.8	Right on Main Street
5.7	Left on US-441
1.5	Fox Fire Museum and Gift Shop (on the left)
.2	Blue Ridge Divide, Mountain City
1.1	Right on York House Road
2.0	Right on Kellys Creek Road
2.9	Left on Dillard-Franklin Highway, GA-246
1.0	Right on Lamb Road
1.0	Right on US-441

Counties

Rabun County was organized in 1819 and named for Governor William Rabun (1817–1719). Part of Habersham County was added in 1828.

Macon County was formed in 1828 from Haywood County and is named for Nathaniel Macon, speaker of the House of Representatives and U.S. Senator from North Carolina.

Cherokee Middle Towns

The Cherokees call themselves *Ani-Yunwiya*, which means real people, and *Ani-Kituwah*, the people of Kituwah. The original village from which the Cherokees spread out across the southern Appalachians was Kituwah on Tuckasegee River. *Cherokee* is a name that other tribes in the Southeast used for the Ani-Kituwah. It comes from a Muskhogean word and possibly means *strangers* or *people of the cave*. In the narrative of De Soto's expedition they appear as Chalaque but that name may not have applied to the speakers of the modern Cherokee language. It seems that the Cherokee encountered by De Soto were living in the town of Guasili on the Nolichucky River.

The Cherokees speak an Iroquoian language and are related linguistically to the Iroquois and Tuscaroras. The Cherokees lived on the upper Ohio River at one time but were driven out by the Delawares and the Iroquois. They migrated southward into the Southern mountains where they prospered and grew to become the largest of the Southeastern tribes. They displaced the Cowetas and Koasatis (Muscogees) from the valleys of the Tennessee River and became their enemies. When William Bartram visited the Cherokees they did not know who had built the mounds in their valleys though they themselves are possibly the creators of the earthworks in the Ohio Valley.

The Cherokees combined hunting and farming for their subsistence. They were tall and well-formed, lighter in complexion than other Southeastern tribes due to the fewer days of sunshine in their mountain home. Cherokee women were important members of the council and were included in peace missions. The capital of all the Cherokees was Chota. In 1775 there were about 10,000 Cherokees living in their large territory that included parts of Virginia, North and South Carolina, Georgia, Tennessee, Kentucky, and Alabama.

Cherokee basket weaver at Oconaluftee Village
Used by kind permission of the Cherokee Historical Association

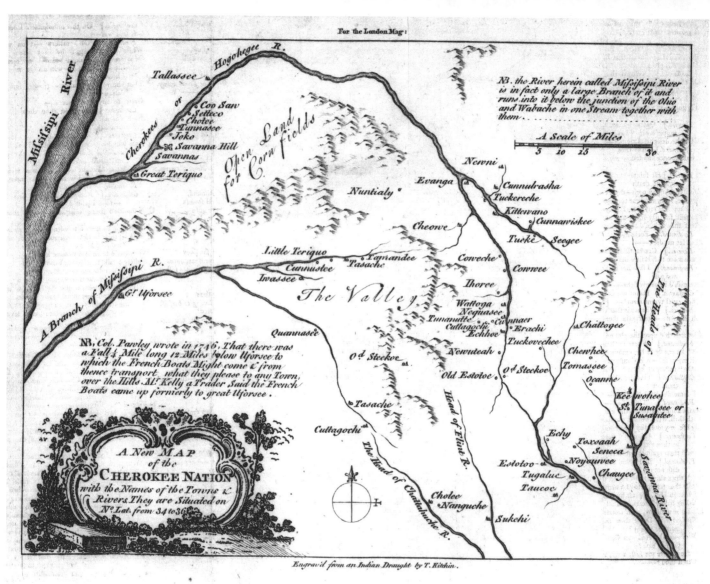

A map of the Cherokee Country, c. 1760, drawn by Thomas Kitchin
Courtesy of Hargrett Rare Book & Manuscript Library/University of Georgia Libraries

The first literary reference to the Cherokees is found in the accounts of the De Soto expedition. The next encounter between the Spanish and Cherokees occurred during the Juan Pardo Expedition of 1566. Little is known of the history of Spanish-Cherokee relations during the next century, except that the Spanish certainly operated mines in the Cherokee mountains. Cherokees encountered Virginians in the mid-1600s. The Cherokees were known to the Virginians as Rechahecrians from the Powhatan name for the Cherokees, Rickahockan. Virginians were trading with the Cherokees by the time Charleston was settled in 1670 and the Cherokees got their first guns around that time. The Cherokees and Carolinians had little contact until the early eighteenth century when the Cherokee headmen traveled to Charleston seeking a treaty and protection from slave raids.

The Cherokees were allies of Carolina during the Tuscarora War in 1711, but were their enemies at the outbreak of the Yamassee War in 1715. The Cherokees turned the tide of war when they switched sides and attacked the Creeks. The Cherokees then entered into a period of prosperity, safely protected by their mountains, such that James Adair estimated their population at around 16,000 in sixty-four towns in 1735. The Cherokees were able to play the French in the west against the English in the east to their advantage and keep the English on their best behavior. The arrival of a smallpox epidemic in South Carolina spread to the Cherokees in 1738 and killed nearly half the population. The Cherokees were enemies of all the tribes surrounding them and seemed to be constantly at war during the middle part of the eighteenth century. They were able to expand their empire into north Georgia and across Tennessee and Kentucky.

One of the most interesting episodes in the history of the Cherokees was the arrival of Christian Priber, who was said to be a Jesuit priest working in the interest of France. He quickly learned the Cherokee language and adopted their customs. He drew up a plan of government that would unify the Cherokees and create a new utopian society. He was obviously considered dangerous by the English who ordered his arrest but the Cherokees protected him. He was captured near Fort Toulouse in Alabama after living among the Cherokees for a number of years. Priber was taken to Frederica on Saint Simons Island where he died of natural causes while in custody. Priber wrote the first dictionary of the Cherokee language.

The Cherokees were allies of South Carolina and Virginia during the French and Indian War but suffered insults and murder at the hands of backcountry whites as their warriors passed to and from the northern theater of war. The young warriors were restrained with difficulty, but further insults by whites, official and unofficial, caused them to take their revenge by attacking frontier settlements in North and South Carolina, setting off the Cherokee War in 1760. Perhaps all could have been avoided if not for the inept diplomacy of South Carolina governor William Henry Lyttleton who displayed utter contempt for the Cherokees and their representatives. (See Chapter 10, *Upper Savannah Frontier*, and Chapter 20, *Cherokee Lower Towns*, for more details of the Cherokee War.)

On June 27, 1760, Colonel Archibald Montgomery marched toward the Middle Towns to subdue the Cherokees. As Montgomery's army reached a place on the Little Tennessee River called the Narrows they were ambushed by Cherokees. The Cherokees withdrew but the English had lost sixteen with sixty-six wounded. The provincial soldiers lost only three and had ten wounded. The provincials fought from behind trees rather than in formation as did the Regulars (Lieutenant Colonel James Grant wrote that the South Carolinians were cowardly fighters). Montgomery went on to Echoe but turned back for Fort Prince George, returned to Charleston, and abruptly departed for New York.

The following year Lieutenant Colonel James Grant led a regiment of South Carolina militia and 1,200 British Regulars into the mountains to bring an end to Cherokee raids. On June 10, 1761, they were attacked near the sight of Montgomery's engagement. This time the South Carolinians won the day by fighting guerrilla style. Lieutenant Francis Marion and his riflemen drove the Cherokees back. Grant's troops then marched into the Middle Towns on the Little Tennessee and Tuckasegee rivers, burning homes and crops and slaughtering livestock as they went. They could not continue on to the Overhill Towns and withdrew from the campaign. Francis Marion and Andrew Pickens were among the expedition and wrote of the cruelty the English brought down upon the Cherokees. Grant became the first British governor of East Florida, 1763–1770, and befriended John and William Bartram during their 1765–1766 expedition to Florida.

The Cherokees gave up their lands east of the Blue Ridge in Virginia and North Carolina at the Treaty of Augusta in 1763; and in a treaty in March 1775, they lost all land north of the Cumberland River. Although the Cherokees still maintained most of their towns, they had lost a great deal of important hunting ground. The loss of the Kentucky land was one of the causes of unrest that prevented William Bartram from continuing on to the Overhill Towns.

The Cherokees, as did most tribes, allied themselves with the British during the Revolution because the king and Parliament had tried to prevent the intrusion of white settlers into native lands. The Cherokees, with Alexander Cameron, attacked the frontier in concert with the British siege of Charleston in June 1776. During that fall General Griffith Rutherford

The Cherokee Gardens at Oconaluftee Village

lead the North Carolina militia into the Cherokee Country from the north and began destroying the Cherokee Middle Towns. General Andrew Williamson brought the South Carolina army from the southeast, destroyed the Lower Towns and crossed over the Blue Ridge. During these miserable times both sides took scalps and were rewarded financially for it; both sides killed women, children, and the helpless.

The Cherokees were overwhelmed and signed a treaty at DeWitt's Corner on May 20, 1777, where they bought peace with land. Dragging Canoe refused to associate with the Americans and took his followers to form the Chickamauga Band of the Cherokees. The Cherokees, especially the Chickamaugas, were again stirred to war when Georgia and South Carolina were retaken by the British. An army of frontiersmen under the command of John Sevier and Arthur Campbell marched on the Cherokee Nation and again the Cherokee Middle and Overhill Towns were burned. Peace between the Cherokees and the Americans coincided with the end of war with Britain

The Cherokees made their first treaty with the new United States government at Hopewell on November 28, 1785. The next decade saw numerous small wars and battles as conflict between the Cherokees and whites increased due to settlement pressures from surrounding states.

Removal

An effort to move all Native Americans to lands west of the Mississippi River began as early as 1802 when Thomas Jefferson suggested that a preserve be set aside for Indians. A group of Cherokees who became known as the Old Settlers voluntarily moved to Arkansas in 1817 and others moved to Texas as early as 1782. In the Treaty at the Cherokee Agency in 1817, the Cherokees gave up tracts of land in Georgia and Tennessee in exchange for tracts in Arkansas. This provided a home for Cherokees who had already moved west and for those who planned to do so in the future.

Another treaty concluded in Washington in 1818 further eroded the Cherokee boundaries in exchange for reserves in the west. The Treaty also began the modernization, or American-

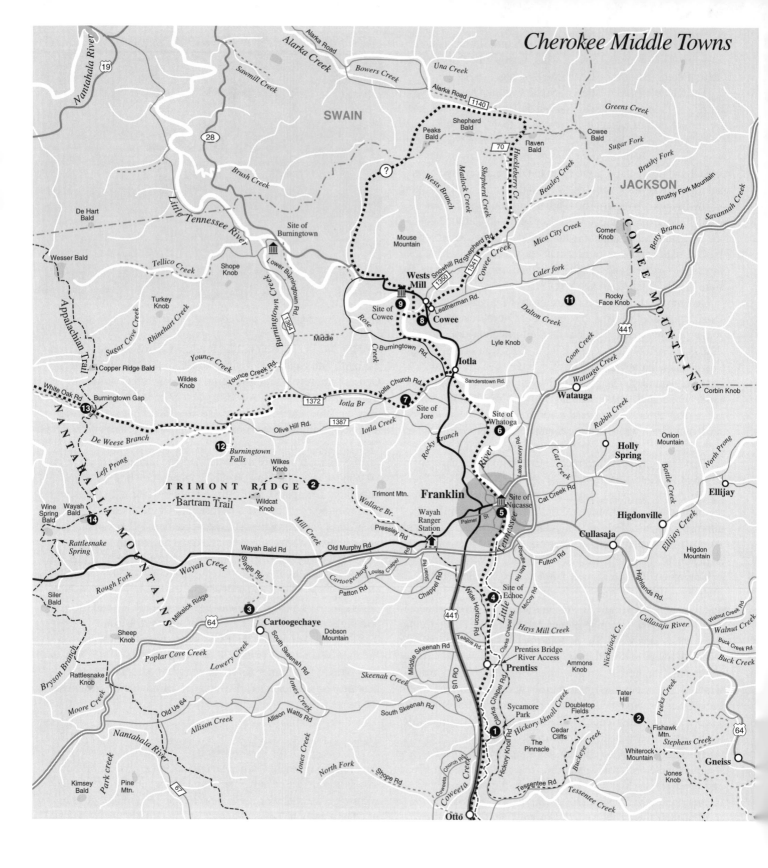

ization, of the Cherokees. They adopted a constitution and republican form of government modeled after the United States and established their capital at New Echota, near Calhoun, Georgia. John Ross was the principal officer of the government, a position he held from 1827 until his death in 1866. George Gist, known as Sequoyah, invented an alphabet for the Cherokee language and the *Cherokee Phoenix* began publishing at New Echota. Taxes were levied, rangers acted as a national police force, schools and missions were established. The golden age was not to last long.

The discovery of gold in 1828 on Cherokee lands in North Georgia attracted numbers of illegal American settlers. Georgia passed an act annexing all Cherokee land within the boundaries of the state, voiding all Cherokee laws, and denying to all Cherokees the legal rights enjoyed by any white citizen. There began a period of anarchy as bands of the worst sort of whites roamed with impunity and appropriated Cherokee property. The election of Andrew Jackson to the presidency in the same year meant the Cherokees and all Native Americans living east of the Mississippi could expect no support or relief from oppression.

Andrew Jackson authorized the Indian Removal Act in 1830. The act was met with opposition from Indians and Americans alike. In the Senate the opposition included senators Daniel Webster, Henry Clay, and David Crockett. The Cherokees challenged the Removal Act in court in 1831 with *Cherokee Nation vs. Georgia*. The Supreme Court dismissed the case, saying that the Cherokee Nation was not a foreign country in the strictest sense.

Using the Treaty of New Echota as justification for removal, Jackson sent the U.S. Army south to roundup the Cherokees and forcibly take them to Indian Territory. The Treaty of New Echota was signed in 1835 by a few hundred Cherokees who had no constitutional authority. They were led by John Ridge and Elias Boudinot and were known as the Treaty Party. They believed that removal was inevitable and sought to comply on the best possible terms. The Cherokees were disadvantaged by the disruption of their national government caused by the machinations of Georgia politicians, which included the suppression of the *Cherokee Phoenix* and the arrest of President John Ross on undeclared charges.

General John Wool arrived to enroll and disarm the Cherokees in 1836. General Winfield Scott and an army of 7,000 began the enforced removal of 17,000 reluctant Cherokees in 1838. Men were taken from the fields and families were interrupted at their dinner during the roundup. In the summer of 1838 about 2,000 Cherokees traveled by water to the Indian Territory but many became ill due to the heat of the season, then the water level of the Tennessee River dropped too low for navigation. The Cherokee leaders, desperately wishing to leave the unhealthy conditions of the stockades, did not want to wait until spring and sought permission to organize their own removal by an overland route. Fourteen-thousand Cherokees traveled 1,200 miles to Indian Territory in the winter of 1838–1839. They were given little protection by the American army and few provisions by the United States government. At least 4,000 Cherokees died as a result of removal.

The Trail of Tears National Historic Trail was created by the National Park Service in 1987. The modern driving trail from Chattanooga to Tahlequah, Oklahoma, is still being developed and will eventually include interpretative areas, commemorative sites, and developed parks created in cooperation with local, state, and national agencies. The water route is 1,226 miles long and follows the Tennessee River from Chattanooga to the Ohio and Mississippi rivers, then up the Arkansas River to south of Tahlequah, Oklahoma.

Creation of the Eastern Band

About 400 mountain Cherokees lead by Yonaguska had become U.S. citizens. They were not subject to removal and settled on Oconaluftee Creek. Hundreds of other Cherokees sought refuge in the rugged mountains of western North Carolina. The army ceased searching for them in 1842 when Scott agreed to allow the fugitives to remain in exchange for the surrender of Tsali and his sons, who had killed an American soldier. Tsali voluntarily gave his life in exchange for the release of his people and was executed near the mouth of Tuckasegee River.

William H. Thomas, a white trader and adopted son of Yonaguska, became the Eastern Cherokees' representative in dealings with the United States and North Carolina. He worked for years to secure a reservation for the 1,000 Eastern Cherokees and to have their share of compensation paid. His efforts were rewarded when North Carolina recognized the Eastern Band of Cherokees in 1848. The federal government recognized the Eastern Band as a separate tribe in 1868. The Eastern Band of Cherokees incorporated in 1889 in order to gain further legal protection.

Today 7,000 Cherokees live in several tracts south of Smoky Mountain National Park, the largest being Qualla Boundary. A joint council of the Eastern and Western Bands of Cherokees was held in 1984 to strengthen the bonds between the two groups.

William Bartram's Travels in Cherokee Country

William Bartram traveled north along the Little Tennessee River Valley and lodged at a trader's cabin near Skeenah Creek in the suburbs of present-day Franklin. He continued on through Echoe, Nikwasi, and arrived at Watauga where he was entertained by the headman whose name was Will. Bartram did not stay long but traveled on to Cowee, guided part way by his new friend, Will of Watauga. He visited with trader Patrick Galahan at Cowee, arriving there around May 22, 1775. The next day Bartram crossed to the east side of the Little Tennessee River and traveled with Galahan along Leatherman Creek and ascended the ridge of the Cowee Mountains. They descended the other side of the ridge, probably to the valley of Alarka Creek, where they encountered the Cherokee maidens gathering strawberries. Bartram wrote of the encounter in one of the most memorable and revealing passages of the *Travels*.

…enjoyed a most enchanting view, a vast expanse of green meadows and strawberry fields; a meandering river gliding through, saluting in its various turnings the swelling, green, turfy knolls,

embellished with parterres of flowers and fruitful strawberry beds; flocks of turkeys strolling about them; herds of deer prancing in the meads or bounding over the hills; companies of young, innocent Cherokee virgins, some busily gathering the rich fragrant fruit, others having already filled their baskets, lay reclined under the shade of floriferous and fragrant native bowers of Magnolia, Azalea, Philadelphus, perfumed Calycanthus, sweet Yellow Jessamine and cerulian Glycine frutescens, disclosing their beauties to the fluttering breeze, and bathing their limbs in the cool fleeting streams; whilst other parties, more gay and libertine, were yet collecting strawberries or wantonly chasing their companions, tantalising them, staining their lips and cheeks with the rich fruit.

This sylvan scene of primitive innocence was enchanting, and perhaps too enticing for hearty young men long to continue idle spectators.[1]

1. William Bartram, *Travels*, 354–355.

William Bartram and Galahan left Cowee around May 24 traveling west along Iotla Creek and through the town of Jore (Ayoree). Bartram called the Nantahalas the Jore Mountains after this village that lay in their shadow. This route corresponds to Olive Hill Road today. After crossing Iotla Gap he parted company with Galahan who took another path back, probably by way of Burningtown Creek. Today Galahan's return path would correspond to Younce Creek Road or Burningtown Road. William met the young Cherokee on the upper portion of Burningtown Creek. Bartram then continued up Burningtown Creek to Burningtown Gap where he left the path to climb Wayah Bald, the highest peak in that section of the Nantahala Mountains. The descent westward from Burningtown Gap on White Oak Road is indeed a gradual slope for a mile and a half as Bartram indicates.

Sites

1. Bartram Canoe Trail, Otto Access. The upper part of the Little Tennessee River from Otto to Franklin is designated as the Bartram Canoe Trail. Access to the river in Otto is at Sycamore Park.

2. North Carolina Bartram Trail. The North Carolina Bartram Trail Society grew out of the effort to commemorate William Bartram's travels and was organized in 1977. The Society is responsible for building and maintaining the eighty-mile Bartram Trail in North Carolina, which was recognized as a national recreation trail in 1997. The trail is marked with yellow blazes and parallels the actual route that Bartram took in 1775. From the ridge of the Cowee Mountains hikers can look down upon the Little Tennessee River Valley where Bartram traveled into Cherokee Country.

The Bartram Trail begins at Rabun Bald in Georgia and ends at Cheoah Bald near Robbinsville. The trail ranges from moderate to difficult. Beautiful sections are in the Fishhawk Mountains, at Wayah Bald, and the Nantahala Gorge. An old growth white oak forest lies just above White Rock Gap where the abundance of flame azaleas puts on a floral display in early June that must certainly rival what William Bartram saw in the wilderness. Around Franklin the trail has to take to the county roads and becomes a hiking and biking trail. The Trimont Ridge section is strenuous, but beautiful and secluded.

The North Carolina Bartram Trail Society has published maps of seven sections of the trail in great detail, including access points and descriptions of the natural areas. For information write the North Carolina Bartram Trail Society, PO Box 144, Scaly Mountain, NC 28775.

Abandoned apple orchard at Burningtown Gap

3. Sand Town Cherokees. Cherokees living near Cartoogeechay Creek in the early nineteenth century were befriended by Jacob Siler. He purchased land at the confluence of Muskrat Creek and Cartoogeechay Creek for his friends so that they did not have to move west. They became known as the Sand Town Cherokees and have since joined their kinsmen at the Qualla Reservation.

4. Echoe was located on the Little Tennessee River at the mouth of Cartoogeechay Creek several miles south of Franklin. It probably occupied both sides of the Little Tennessee River.

5. Franklin
Nikwasi. The Cherokee town Kikwasi was located on the Little Tennessee River at Franklin. The meaning of the name has been lost to memory. The town held about 480 people in 1761. Human occupation of the site of Nikwasi dates back 2,000 years. Nikwasi was burned in 1761 by Grant's army during the Cherokee War and again by General Rutherford in September 1776. During the Grant campaign the army used the council house at the mound as a hospital. In the 1880's the remains of Lieutenant Danyel Cryn, a member of Montgomery's army, were found in the bank of the river near the mound. He was captured at the Battle of the Narrows in 1760 and taken to Kikwasi where he either died of wounds or was executed.

Nikwasi Temple Mound is located in the middle of East Main Street near the Little Tennessee River and marks the site of the Cherokee town of Kikwasi. The mound was originally nearly 30-feet high and in the shape of a truncated pyramid. It is now only about fifteen-feet high. A remarkable legend surrounds the Nikwasi mound. It was believed that an eternal fire burned inside Nikwasi mound. Once when the town was under attack an army of spirit warriors known as the Nunnehi emerged from the mound, drove the enemy away, then returned to the mound. The site is owned by the Macon County Historical Society and is listed on the National Register of Historic Places.

Little Tennessee River Greenway. The Greenway is at present a work in progress. When finished, it will begin in downtown Franklin and follow the Little Tennessee River to the edge of town.

Franklin Museum & Visitor Center. Exhibits in the museum deal primarily with the American settlement of the area, the founding of Franklin, and local genealogy. The library contains a number of excellent books on the history of western North Carolina. Located at No. 6, West Main Street, downtown Franklin. Open 10 a.m.–4 p.m., Monday through Friday, and from 10 a.m.–12 p.m. on Saturday, May through October.

Franklin Gem Museum. The Old Macon County Jail is the home to the gem museum operated by the Franklin Gem Society. Franklin is the heart of a productive gem region, particularly the Cowee valley, which is known for its rubies. The States Room features specimens from each state of the union, and the North Carolina Room is devoted to the gems of the home state. An ultraviolet room shows off luminescent minerals. Located on West Main Street. Open daily 10 a.m.–4 p.m. and on Sunday from 1–4 p.m. Open only May 1 through October 31.

Scottish Tartan Museum. The American branch of the Scottish Tartans Society is headquartered at the Tartan Museum in Franklin. While the purpose of the museum is to display the history of Highland tartans and genealogy there are also excellent exhibits on the strong Scottish influence in Appalachia. The gift shop sells Scottish and Appalachian handicrafts, books, and tartan fabric. Each year the museum hosts a Scottish Heritage Week and a Tartans Symposium. Located downtown at 33 East Main Street.

Sir Alexander Cuming and the Crown of Tanase. Alexander Cuming was a self-appointed emissary who traveled into the Cherokee Country to win their allegience to the King of England. The Cherokees were being wooed by the French at the time and it appeared that they might join an alliance with the French and Creeks. Cuming persuaded Moytoy of Tellico to accept the Crown of Tanase so that as king of the Cherokees and representative of the many towns he could negotiate treaties with the British. At a talk in Nikwasi on April 4, 1730, the treaty was concluded, Moytoy received his crown of eagle tails, and the Cherokees received guns and ammunition.

Seven Cherokees accompanied Cuming on his return to England. They were entertained at Whitehall and renewed their alliance with the British. Though the Cherokee representatives were important young men and not powerful headmen there was among them the future leader Attakullakulla, then only a teenager. For all his efforts Cuming received no reward and was sent to debtor's prison in 1737.

6. Watauga, (Whatoga). The village of Watauga was located on the Little Tennessee River between Nikwasi (Franklin) and Iotla Creek.

7. Jore (Ayoree, Ihoree). The village of Jore was located on Iotla Creek probably in the area of the Macon County Airport. The valley of Iotla Creek is today a beautiful farming community.

8. Wedgewood Clay. Thomas Griffiths made an expedition to Cherokee Country in the fall of 1767 to collect clay samples for the famous Wedgewood factories in England. He arrived at Cowee in December and collected five tons of clay near West's Mill. He lost several horses on the slippery mountain paths returning to Keowee and with difficulty made his way back to Charleston and sailed for England in March 1768. He wrote an account of his expedition in *An Expedition in Search of Cherokee Clay, 1767–1768.*

9. Cowee was the capital of the Cherokee Middle Towns. The town occupied both sides of the Little Tennessee River around Cowee Creek at present-day West's Mill. Cowee was burned during the Revolution. The mound predates the Cherokee town of Cowee and still exists on private land about a mile and a half downriver from Cowee Creek. It's location is noted by a historical marker on NC-28.

10. Perry's Water Gardens is one of America's prominent suppliers of plants and material for water gardens. It was started by the famous hybridizer Perry Slocum during his retirement and was later operated by his stepson. The display gardens are on view for the public from May 20 through Labor Day. Perry's sponsors a Water Lily Festival each year around July 4th. Located on Leatherman Gap Road.

11. Nantahala National Forest. The land of the Cherokee Middle and Valley Towns is now included in the Nantahala National Forest. This national treasure covers over 500,000 acres of southern Appalachians and was established in 1920. Features include the Blue Ridge, Nantahala, and Cowee mountains; Ellicott Rock Wilderness; Joyce Kilmer-Slickrock Wilderness; Cullasaja and Nantahala gorges; Whiteside Mountain; and numerous rich botanical areas. The Nantahala Forest is traversed by many hiking trails including the Appalachian Trail and the Bartram Trail.

There are four ranger districts. Highlands District, includes much of Macon, Jackson, and Transylvania counties and has headquarters in Highlands. The Tusquitee District is the western portion of the forest and has offices in Murphy. The Wayah Ranger District has headquarters in Franklin and covers the central portion of the national forest adjacent to the Qualla Reservation. Cheoah District covers Graham and Swain counties, and offices are located at Lake Santeetlah near Robbinsville.

12. Burningtown Falls. Follow FS7-130 from Upper Burningtown Road.

13. Burningtown Gap. William Bartram crossed the Jore Mountains, now called the Nantahalas, at Burningtown Gap. The Appalachian Trail crosses the gap from Wayah Bald to Copper Ridge Bald. An old apple orchard occupies the saddle of the ridge, a particularly beautiful place in fall. The gap is accessible from the west by way of White Oak Road.

14. Wayah Bald. *Wayah* is the Cherokee word for wolf. Wayah Bald is known for the number of flame azaleas that bloom about the middle of June. The summit is an open field of several acres of native azaleas and mountain laurel. The fire tower provides a 360° view of the Nantahala Mountains. The North Carolina Bartram Trail and the Appalachian Trail intersect at Wayah Bald and coincide as far as Wine Spring Bald.

Nearby

Standing Indian and the Nantahala Basin. The Eastern Continental Divide separates the headwaters of the Nantahala River from those of the Tallulah River. The Nantahala River starts in Standing Indian Basin, surrounded on three sides by the Blue Ridge and Nantahala mountains, and flows in a northerly direction to the Little Tennessee River. The basin contains rare mountain bogs located along the Nantahala floodplain and is home to endangered and uncommon plants.

The Cherokee legend of the standing Indian tells the story of a giant winged monster who stole a child and took him to its lair in the mountains. The Cherokees prayed to the Great Spirit for aid in destroying the menace which was accomplished by a bolt of lightning that killed the monster and a Cherokee sentry. The Cherokee warrior was turned to stone and the top of the mountain was blasted clear of trees and vegetation. The Standing Indian has worn away and doesn't look much like the noble warrior anymore.

Standing Indian is located west of Franklin off US-64 on Old US-64. Facilities include wilderness hiking trails, access to the Appalachian Trail, camping, fishing for trout and Kokanee salmon. The Nantahala River has the only salmon run in the Southeast, though the fish were introduced and are not native.

Judaculla Rock is a large soapstone rock that is inscribed with petroglyphs of unknown origin. The Cherokees believed the markings were the footprints of the giant Judaculla. Located between Cashiers and Cullowhee on Caney Fork Road, three miles off NC-107.

Qualla Boundary encompasses the largest section of the reservation of the Eastern Band of Cherokees. It contains 56,000 acres of land and the largest community is the town of Cherokee.

Mountain Heritage Center, Western Carolina University, Cullowhee. The Mountain Heritage Center contains exhibits on the culture of the people who settled the southern Appalachians. There are Cherokee crafts on display and a permanent exhibit on the Scotch-Irish settlers of western North Carolina. Open Monday through

Friday, 8:00 a.m.–5 p.m., and 2–5 p.m. on Sundays from June through October.

Counties

Macon County was formed in 1828 from Haywood County. Named for Nathaniel Macon, speaker of the House of Representatives and U.S. Senator from North Carolina.

Itinerary

Miles	Distance
	Begin at the North Carolina state line and travel north on US-441
1.7	Historical marker for the Cherokee defeat in the Cherokee War
3.5	Historical Marker for the Cherokee victory in the Cherokee War
5.6	Intersection with West Main Street in Franklin *Turn right for downtown Franklin and Cowee, turn left for Wayah Bald and the Nantahala Mountains*

To Cowee

	Turn right on West Main Street
.1	Left on Harrison Avenue (NC 28)
4.3	Cross Little Tennessee River
2.2	Right on Cowee Road
.2	Right on Leatherman Gap Road
1.2	Left on Leatherman Gap Road
.8	Left on Leatherman Gap Road
1.2	Keep left on Leatherman Gap road
.7	Left on Huckleberry Creek Road (FS-70)
4.9	Arrive at Leatherman Gap, turn right for Cowee Bald, turn left on Deep Gap Road for Alarka

To the Nantahala Mountains

	Travel west on West Main Street at the intersection with US-441 (Palmer Street)
.6	Right on Palmer Street
.4	Palmer Street becomes Old Murphy Road
1.2	Right on Old Murphy Road
2.6	Right on Wayah Road
8.7	Arrive at Wayah Gap

Cherokee Overhill Towns

In 1540 the inhabitants of the lower Little Tennessee River were Koasatis, a Muskogean-speaking people, who were part of the Dallas cultural region. The Cherokees were at this time living on the Nolichucky and French Broad Rivers and did not occupy the extreme southern Appalachians. The De Soto expedition entered the region by way of the French Broad and Tennessee rivers, traveling southwestward. They passed through the town of Coste, on Bussell Island in the Tennessee River at the mouth of the Little Tennessee River. They crossed the Tennessee River and traveled a little way up the east side of the Little Tennessee to the town of Tali at the Toqua archaeological site. The Spaniards then continued south to the Hiawassee River and on to the Chiefdom of Coosa in present-day Northeast Georgia. Little is known of latter events on the Little Tennessee River until the English traders began traveling into Cherokee Country at the beginning of the eighteenth century. The Cherokees pushed the Creeks out of the Tennessee River valley after winning a victory at Talawi near Ball Ground, Georgia, in 1755.

The Cherokee Overhill Towns lined the lower part of the Little Tennessee River and the Tennessee River. The principal town was Chota (Echota) and it was considered the capital of the nation. Fort Loudon was built near Chota in 1756. It was besieged and destroyed by the Cherokees during the Cherokee War in 1760. The Overhill Towns were not ravaged as were the Lower and Middle Towns and was often a refuge for Cherokees who were driven from their homes by war with the Americans. It was not until the Revolution that the Overhill

Nantahala River

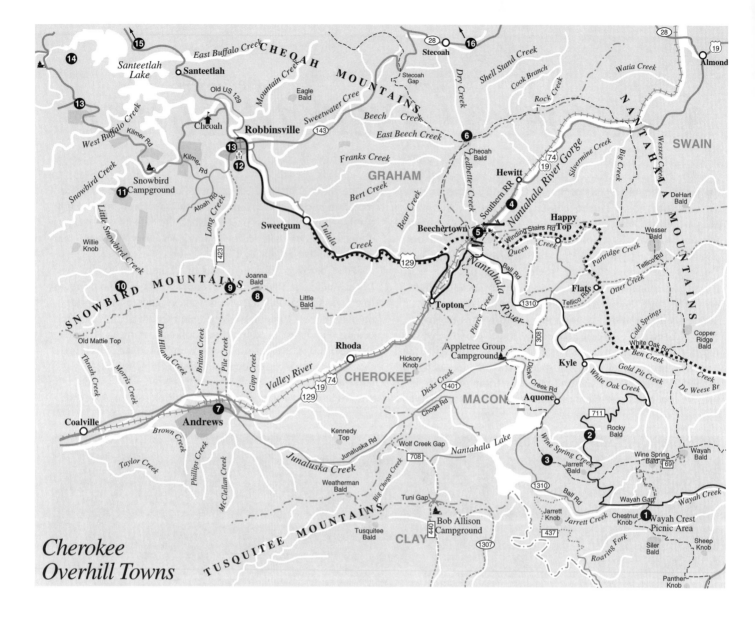

Cherokee Overhill Towns

Towns saw the destruction that had been visited upon her sister towns in the east.

On March 4, 1775, Oconostota, Attakullakula, and other headmen sold twenty million acres. Dragging Canoe, Attakullakula's son, was enraged and lead a faction in opposition to the established leadership. Dragging Canoe demanded the removal of squatters in Watauga. This discord among the Cherokees caused Bartram's fear of venturing on to the Overhill Towns that May. Dragging Canoe went on to found the Chickamauga branch of the Cherokees and moved west to the vicinity of present-day Chattanooga. When the Overhill Cherokees agreed to remain neutral in the war between England and the colonies, Dragging Canoe remained hostile and continued his association with Alexander Cameron.

In June 1776, Cherokee attacks on backcountry settlements were timed to coincide with the first British attack on Charleston. Cherokee warriors lead by Dragging Canoe, Old Abraham, and Raven attacked the settlements at Watauga and Holston River (in present-day northeastern Tennessee). The inevitable retaliation came in late July when Colonel William Christian and Virginia militia marched to the Little Tennessee River and burned Tuskegee and three other towns. By treaty at Long Island (Kingsport, Tennessee) on July 20, 1777, the Middle and Overhill Cherokees gave up all land east of the Blue Ridge and territory on the Watauga, Nolichucky, Holston, and New rivers—land that was already being settled by Americans. Elder Cherokee leaders agreed to break their

Legend

1. Wayah Crest Picnic Area
2. FS-711
3. North Carolina Bartram Trail
4. Nantahala Gorge
5. Attakullakulla
6. Cheoah Bald
7. Valleytown
8. Joanna Bald
9. Tatham Gap Road
10. Snowbird Mountains
11. Snowbird Cherokees
12. Junaluska's Grave
13. Cherohala Skyway
14. Joyce Kilmer Memorial & Slick Rock Wilderness
15. Fort Loudon and the Overhill Towns
16. Great Smoky Mountains National Park

allegiance with the British and take up no arms against the Americans. Dragging Canoe and the Chickamaugas refused to cease war against the Americans.

Colonel Evan Shelby led Virginia and North Carolina militia against Dragging Canoe and the Chickamaugas in April 1779 and burned eleven towns. The Chickamaugas moved their towns farther down the Tennessee River to present-day Chattanooga, a place that was easily defended. They were joined by Thomas Brown, the Florida Ranger who had become a deputy superintendent of Indian Affairs for the British. Brown continued to inflame the Cherokees against the Americans with an effort greater than even Cameron's. The Chickamaugas planned to attack the Watauga settlement in October 1780. The Americans were warned by Nancy Ward of the impending attack and the Cherokees were met by John Sevier, Arthur Campbell, and a force of Overmountain militia. This time, many Overhill Towns were destroyed in an effort to break the Cherokee antagonists. The only town that escaped damage was Talassee; even Chota was burned.

New settlers poured into Tennessee after the Revolution, creating new tension with the Cherokees. Unable to control the Overmountain settlers, North Carolina gave up any claim or responsibility for territory west of the mountains in exchange for cancelling its war debts to the national government. In 1784 the citizens of the Watauga settlements immediately organized themselves into a quasi-state they named Franklin. The Cherokees tried to remove illegal settlements and were punished repeatedly by John Sevier, president of Franklin.

When Attakullakulla and Oconostota died, Old Tassel became the new leader of the Overhill Towns. Although he was a capable leader, Tassel was unable to control the Chickamaugas or prevent Americans from entering Cherokee land. Old Tassel and Abraham, though friendly toward Americans, were spitefully, and cowardly murdered by Sevier's men while under a

A view of the Nantahala Mountains from Wayah Bald

flag of truce in 1788. This brutal act was so outrageous that Sevier lost his influence among the more civilized settlers in eastern Tennessee, and the state of Franklin dissolved. After the loss of their leaders, the Cherokees moved their capital to the Oostanoula River near present-day Calhoun, Georgia. The new leader, Hanging Maw, requested that the U.S. government construct a fort for the protection of Cherokees living in Tennessee, and Tellico Blockhouse was built in 1794.

The majority of the population of the Cherokee Nation moved out of the mountains and into southern Tennessee, upper Georgia, and Alabama. There they began the process of Americanization, building towns and farms, learning manufacturing skills, and establishing their national government. The Treaty of Washington in 1819 made the Nantahala Ridge the eastern boundary of the Cherokee Nation in North Carolina.

Nancy Ward

Nancy Ward was the daughter of Tame Doe who was a sister of Attakullakulla and Raven. Nancy is possibly the best known and most respected Native-American woman to have lived in the Southeast. She was a Beloved Woman of the Cherokees and was known as War Woman. As a young woman she took up the gun of her mortally wounded husband and rallied the Cherokees in a victory over the Creeks. She was thereafter a Beloved Woman, or *Ghigau*, of the Cherokees, which gave her a seat at the tribal council with influence and voting privileges. As head of the Women's Council she had power over prisoners and prepared the Black Drink for warriors.

Nancy Ward worked tirelessly to promote peace and amicable relations between Cherokees and American settlers. She was a participant at numerous conferences, including the Treaty of Long Island on the Holston (1781) and the Treaty of Hopewell (1985). Her presence and powers of oratory influenced both sides to moderate their rhetoric. She promoted modernization among the Cherokees and introduced dairying among her people.

Nancy Ward was born at Chota in 1738. She had two children by her first husband, a son named Five Killer and a daughter named Catherine. Following the French and Indian War she married trader Bryant Ward and they had a daughter, Betsy, who married Cherokee agent Joseph Martin. When her home was lost in a land cession to the United States Nancy moved to the Ocoee River near Benton, Tennessee, and operated an inn until her death in 1822. She is buried on a hill near her last home, just north of the intersection of US-64 and US-411.

Sites

1. Wayah Crest Picnic Area is a beautiful spot for botanizing as well as picnicking. Turn left off Wayah Bald Road at Wayah Gap.

2. FS-711 is a little-used paved road that winds along the west side of Wayah Bald. Travelers have access to the North Carolina Bartram Trail and stunning views of the Nantahala valley.

3. North Carolina Bartram Trail. This part of the North Carolina Bartram Trail descends westward from Wayah Bald, crosses the Nantahala River immediately below Nantahala Dam then follows the west side of the river. The trail crosses the river two more times at Beechertown Recreation Area near where William Bartram met Attakullakulla. The trail then ascends to Cheoah Bald, its western terminus. Maps are available from local outfitters or from the North Carolina Bartram Trail Society.

4. Nantahala Gorge. Nantahala comes from the Cherokee word *nundayeli*, which means

Attakullakulla

Attakullakulla was known as Little Carpenter because of his finesse at constructing political alliances and treaties. He was one of the principal leaders of the Cherokee Nation during the period between the French and Indian War and the coming of the Revolution. This venerable old gentleman whom Bartram met at the Nantahala River in May 1775 was on his way to Charleston to see his friend and Indian agent, John Stuart.

Attakullakulla was born Okoonaka, White Owl, in the very early 1700s on the French Broad River in Tennessee and died in 1780. His uncle was the powerful chief Connecorte (Old Hop) and his niece, Nancy Ward, became the most influential woman among the Cherokees in the post-Revolutionary period. His son was Dragging Canoe, leader of the Chickamaugas.

Attakullakulla entered the stage of world politics as a very young man when he and six of his countrymen accompanied Sir Alexander Cuming to London in 1730. There the Cherokees were honored by the press, Parliament, and King George II. A group portrait was painted and today remains the only image we have of Attakullakulla, who was surprisingly short of stature. During the tour of England, he began to learn English and saw that Cherokee success lay in friendship with Britain. Back in Cherokee country he was captured by the Ottawas and spent several years in Canada, then was returned home as an emissary. His travels among foreigners seem to have given him a particular advantage in diplomacy.

Attakullakulla was a renowned orator and prodégé of Connecorte, and in that he derived his power. By 1750 he had risen to the position as principal speaker for the Cherokees and Chief of Chota. During the Revolution, Attakullakulla and the Cherokee elders tried to maintain neutrality; but the Chickamaugas and the British agents, Alexander Cameron and Thomas Brown, continued harassing the frontier settlements, which brought reprisals from the Americans.

The Nantahala River at Beechertown Recreation area

midday sun. The gorge of the Nantahala River is very steep and runs south to north, therefore the sun reaches the bottom of the gorge in places for only a short period of time in the middle of the day. The river was home to Uktena, the giant serpent of Cherokee legend. The river is noted for its exceptional beauty and is a favorite among whitewater kayakers. An excursion train from Bryson City makes daily trips in the Nantahala River Gorge.

5. Attakullakulla and William Bartram met somewhere near the Beechertown Recreation Area on the Nantahala River.

6. Cheoah Bald is the western end of the North Carolina Bartram Trail and intersects the Appalachian Trail.

7. Valleytown. Andrews was once known as Valleytown to whites and Gunahitunyi to the Cherokees. The Cherokee name means *Long Place*, for it was at the head of a long valley where the Valley Towns were located. Paths from Valleytown crossed the mountains to the Middle and Overhill towns.

8. Joanna Bald was known to the Cherokees as the *Lizard Place* for at times they saw a great lizard sunning itself on the rocks.

9. Tatham Gap Road was built in 1838 by James Tatham under contract with General Winfield Scott. The road was needed to transport Cherokee captives from Fort Montgomery (Robbinsville) to Fort Delaney at Andrews and Fort Butler in Murphy. From Fort Butler they would be sent to embarkation points in the South to begin their journey to Oklahoma.

10. The Snowbird Mountains take their name from Little Snowbird Creek, *Tuti'yi* in Cherokee.

11. Snowbird Cherokees. The Cherokees in the Overhill Towns who were able to evade removal to Oklahoma have organized as the Snowbird Cherokees. They are a part of the Eastern Band and their many small reserves comprise the Cheoah Township.

12. Junaluska's Grave. Junaluska received his name, which means *one who tries but fails*, during the Creek War of 1814 because he boasted that he would destroy the Creeks, which he did not do. He once lived near Andrews on the creek that bears his name. He moved to Indian Territory in 1838 but returned to North Carolina when his wife and family died. North Carolina awarded citizenship and land to Junaluska for his service at the Battle of Horseshoe Bend during the Creek War. The graves of Junaluska and his second wife, Nicie, are in Robbinsville. Turn down Main Street at the Court House and go about one-fifth mile to the signs for the graves.

13. Cherohala Skyway. This recently opened scenic highway has been thirty years in the making. It is forty-eight miles long and connects Robbinsville, North Carolina, with Tellico Plains, Tennessee, through uninhabited mountainous terrain. Elevations at the highest point on the road reach five thousand feet. The eastern entrance is from Kilmer Road at Santeetlah Gap.

14. Joyce Kilmer Memorial & Slick Rock Wilderness. The memorial to Joyce Kilmer, author of the poem *Trees*, lies within an old growth forest and is abundantly carpeted with wildflowers in spring. Many trees are over 300 years old and much of the forest has been undisturbed. The wilderness area encompasses 3,800 acres of pristine forest.

15. Fort Loudon was built by the British in 1756 at the junction of the Tellico River and the Little Tennessee River near the principal town of Echota. The garrison was besieged by the Cherokees during the Cherokee War. When Montgomery and his army abandoned their campaign after their encounter at Echoe, the garrison at Fort Loudon was doomed without the prospect of relief. When food rations ran low, Captain Paul Demere accepted the offer to surrender the fort and guns in return for permission to travel to Fort Prince George. Finding guns destroyed and ammunition hidden, the angry Cherokees ambushed the soldiers on August 10, 1760, killed about thirty, and made prisoners of the others. Captain Demere was scalped and burned to death. Attakullakulla purchased Captain John Stuart from his captors, spirited him away, and rode with him to the Holston River settlement in an attempt to make peace.

William Bartram's destination in Cherokee

Country was Fort Loudon and the Overhill Towns but he realized that he could not safely travel while tensions were high. Had Bartram reached the Overhill Towns he possibly would have met at Tuskegee a thirteen-year-old boy named George Gist, or Sequoyah. In middle age Gist lived on the upper Coosa River in Alabama where he invented an alphabet for the Cherokee language, more remarkable for the fact that he could not read or write in any language other than that of his own invention. He moved to Arkansas in 1822 and died in 1843 while in Mexico looking for a lost tribe of Cherokees.

16. Great Smoky Mountains National Park. This popular national park contains over a half-million acres of land nestled in the southern Unaka (Unicoi) Mountains that straddle the North Carolina-Tennessee boundary. The Smokies contain many peaks and deep coves, including a dozen peaks rising over six thousand feet. However, the important natural resources are the many plants and animals that find refuge in the park—130 species of trees and more salamanders than anywhere else in the world. The Smoky Mountains are famous for the spring display of native wildflowers. The Great Smoky Mountain National Park contains the greatest biodiversity in all of North America and is an International Biosphere Reserve.

Counties

Swain was created in 1871 from surrounding counties and named for David L. Swain, governor and president of the University of North Carolina. Bryson City (originally named Charleston) is the county seat.

Cherokee was created in 1839 from Macon County. It honors the Cherokee Indians who originally inhabited the county. Murphy is the seat.

Graham was created in 1872 from Cherokee County and is named for William A. Graham, senator, governor, Secretary of the Navy, and Confederate States senator. Robbinsville is the seat.

Clay was created in 1861 from Cherokee County and named for Henry Clay. Hayesville is the seat.

Cherokee Overhill Towns*

Chilowhee	Tallassee	Toqua
Chota	Tanasi	Tuskegee
Citico	Tomatley	

Cherokee Valley Towns*

Chatiqui	Notteley
Cheoha	Quotecon
Great & Little Tellico	Toruro
Hiawassee	Tusquitee
Nehowee	Ustenary

*Names are taken from John Stuart's map of the Cherokee country.

Itinerary

Miles	Directions
	Begin at Wayah Gap and travel west on Wayah Road
1.6	Right on Forest Service Road 711
14.2	Left on White Oak Road (turn right to reach Burningtown Gap)
.5	Right on Long Branch Road
2.7	Right on Wayah Road
5.6	Left on US-19/74
2.1	Right on US-129
13.3	Robbinsville

The Great Trading Path

When the De Soto expedition reached the Oconee River near Milledgeville, they entered the province of Ocute, home of a Hitchiti speaking people. The Spaniards first visited a satellite village of the town of Altamaha then traveled upriver to Ocute. The paramount chief of the entire region was named Ocute and his empire included towns that stretched up the Oconee River from below Milledgeville northward to Scull Shoals in southwestern Oglethorpe County. Ocute's seat of government was located at Shoulderbone Creek near its mouth with the Oconee River. The Spaniards traveled from Ocute to Cofaqui, in northern Greene County at Dyar's Mound, now flooded by Lake Oconee. After the passing of the Europeans, these chiefdoms suffered from disease and were replaced by small towns of hunter-farmers who maintained a more egalitarian society. There are numerous mounds remaining in this area along the Oconee River, though they are much reduced in prominence.

When the English settled Charleston, Henry Woodward and the Carolina traders journeyed to the Creek Lower Towns over the Great Trading Path that followed the Fall Line across Georgia. This trail was also known as the White Path because the first whites from South Carolina traveled over it. The Great Trading Path became known as the Lower Creek Trading path as other trails emerged and grew in importance.

A group of Oconees moved from the Chattahoochee River and settled on the path where it crossed the Oconee River at Rock Landing and they gave their name to the river. After the Yamassee War in 1715, the Oconees moved back to the Chattahoochee River and lived near Hannahatchee Creek. The Cowetas moved to the Ocmulgee River about 1690 so as to be advantageously situated on the Great Trading Path, the conduit of excellent and inexpensive English goods. They, too, moved to the Chattahoochee River in the wake of the Yamassee War.

The land south of the Great Trading Path and east of the Ogeechee River was opened for settlement in the Treaty of Augusta in 1763, though not surveyed until 1768. In 1773 land north of the Trading Path was opened for settlement as the New Purchase but when William Bartram passed this way in 1775 few people had moved beyond Brier Creek. After the Revolution, settlers poured into this region as they did elsewhere in the northern parts of Georgia. Many were veterans taking up their bounty lands and a large number of the earliest settlers were Scotch-Irish from North and South Carolina. Very often, groups of related families and neighbors emigrated en masse and settled together in the new land. The first people to move to Saunders Crossroads (Sandersville) were all from Edgecombe County, North Carolina, and arrived in 1797.

After the close of the Revolutionary War, Georgia negotiated treaties with the Creeks that extended the western boundary of Georgia to the Oconee River. Treaties were signed at Augusta in 1783, at Galphinton in 1785, and at Shoulderbone Creek in 1786, but not enough important men were on hand to legitimate these documents. Alexander McGillivray declared the treaties to be invalid, but Georgia claimed otherwise. The Georgia Assembly passed a bill establishing Washington County in the Creek lands between the Ogeechee and Oconee rivers, bounded by the Cherokee Line in the north and extending to the confluence of the two rivers where they form the Altamaha. The Creek National Council declared war on Georgia and raided frontier settlements in what is known locally as the Oconee War.

The United States declared the treaties invalid because the Articles of Confederation and the new federal Constitution reserved all treaty-making power with the national government. The issue was resolved when McGillivray met with President Washington in New York in 1790.

The Treaty of New York attests to the power and statesmanship of Alexander McGillivray. He was made a U.S. brigadier general with an annual salary of $1,200; his trade monopoly was guaranteed and he forced the United States to treat the Creek Confederacy as a sovereign nation. The treaty set forth the proper conduct for dealing with white squatters, runaway slaves, and regulated the Indian trade. However, McGillivray was no more a representative of the Creek Confederacy than any of the previous signers. Indeed McGillivray claimed to speak for all Creeks, including the Seminoles in Florida who were the rightful owners of the Oconee River lands.

It took a number of treaties for Georgia to obtain the land between the Oconee and Ocmulgee—the Treaty of Fort Wilkinson in 1802, the Treaty of the Creek Agency in 1804, and the Treaty of Washington in 1805. In the 1805 treaty, the federal government obtained permission to build a road from Fort Wilkinson at Rock Landing on the Oconee River to Fort Mims on the Mobile River. In most of the land cessions, the Creeks were paid for the land and given annual stipends for their loss. It is not clear just how much the average Creek benefitted from these payments, since the powerful headmen tended to look out for themselves and their friends. Sometimes a leaders' power arose from his business interest in a trading post and it seems that much of the money received from sales of land went to line the pockets of those who already controlled the economy in the Creek Nation.

Land between of the Oconee and Ocmulgee rivers was the first to be organized under the Land Lottery Act of 1803 and was organized into Baldwin, and Wilkinson counties. Settlement was driven by the cotton boom as planters in older sec-

Shoals of the Ogeechee

tions of the South sought for new, rich land that could be obtained in large parcels and at cheap prices.

As good cotton land became scarce there was a great migration westward from many parts of the South. As wealthy farmers increased their holdings to provide for a steady source of new cotton land near their home the small farmer was priced out of the market and forced to seek cheaper land in new country. The younger sons of the wealthy planters were also inclined to move west with the intention of making fortunes and building empires as their fathers had done. The older cotton region of Piedmont Georgia and South Carolina provided many pioneer citizens for Alabama, Mississippi, and Texas—then known as the Old Southwest. The greatest migration out of the Old Southeast region occurred between 1825–1845. An excellent account of this migration is told by Tyrone Power who personally met many *cotton refugees* on the road to Alabama;

> *The rich alluvial lands of Alabama, recently belonging to the Indian reserves, and now on sale by government or through land-speculators, are attracting thousands of families from the washed-out and impoverished soil of the older Southern States: and, during this and the preceding season, the numbers moving along this and the other great lines towards the Southwest are incredible, when viewed in reference to the amount of population given to the countries whence the emigrants are chiefly derived.*[1]

Indeed one planter lamented that his community had been depopulated by the cotton fever disease and was not likely to recover its former vitality. The research and public relations of agricultural societies like the Hancock Planters Club and the commercial availability of guano beginning in 1850 encouraged planters to apply scientific methods to their farming and helped the old fields become productive again.

William Bartram's Travels on the Trading Path

When Francis Harper retraced the Bartram Trail in the late 1940s he felt that William Bartram followed the Upper Creek Path to Sparta where he turned southwest to the Rock Landing. Harper's location for the Flat Rock is one mile northwest of Camak on Lazenby Creek. By Bartram's own account it took him four days to reach the Flat Rock from the trader's plantation on the Savannah River, near Plum Branch. Travel-

---

1. *Impressions of America,* Tyrone Power. London, 1836. Reprinted by permission of the University of Georgia libraries.

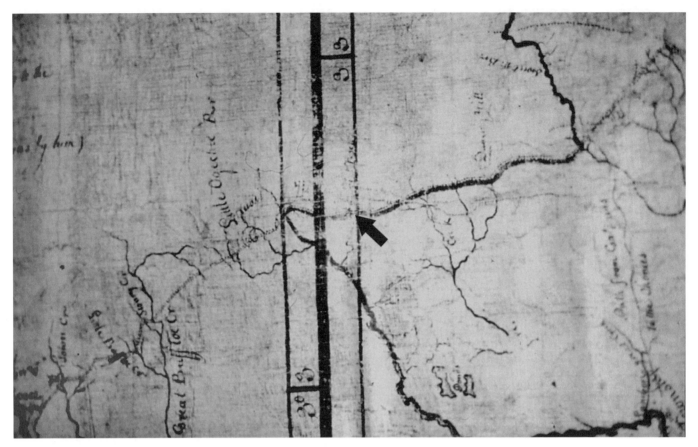

Detail showing the Lower Creek Trading Path between Augusta and the Oconee River. The arrow shows the location of Flat Rock lying on a branch east of the Ogeechee River. The map is titled A Map of West Florida, Part of East Florida, Georgia and Part of South Carolina *and was prepared for General Gage by John Stuart and Joseph Purcell. The condition of the map has deteriorated to the point that portions are barely readable.*

The original is located in the William L. Clements Library, Gates Collection. This image was reproduced from a photograph in the possession of Dr. Louis De Vorsey.

ing at a rate of fifteen to twenty miles per day the distance to Camak would account for two or three days. Harper surmised that Bartram and the traders must have stopped in Wrightsborough, possibly to gather supplies. Yet, it seems that if the party of traders had stopped at Wrightsborough William Bartram would have written of it in the *Travels*.

Dr. Louis DeVorsey has in his possession tracings of maps from the Public Record Office in London that clearly show a place called Flat Rock located on the Great Trading Path at a stream just east of the Ogeechee River. Additionally, the Joseph Purcell map located in the Gates Collection of the Clements Library at the University of Michigan shows Flat Rock lying on the Lower Creek Trading Path just east of Shoals on the Ogeechee River. Although this map is in poor condition the Flat Rock is just discernible. This place would be approximately seventy miles from the Plum Branch area, a more reasonable distance to cover in four days. The Flat Rock was important enough to be drawn on maps of the day and by Bartram's account it was a popular rendezvous for travelers.[2] Prior to the Revolution, the Lower Creek Trading Path was the most important route across Georgia. It seems more likely that William Bartram traveled by way of the Lower Creek Trading Path, possibly entering the trail near Dearing or Augusta and not passing through Wrightsborough, Warrenton, and Sparta as previously thought.

William Bartram, unfortunately, occasionally gets events out of sequence. The party of traders and travelers would not have camped by Rocky Comfort Creek after reaching the Flat Rock because Rocky Comfort is east of Flat Rock. Maybe Bartram meant to say Buffalo Creek, which they would have reached on June 28. The travelers must have reached Rocky Comfort on June 26. They crossed the Ogeechee River at Shoals or a little upriver at Jewell and proceeded along the county line between Hancock and Washington counties. The path deviated from the present-day county line near Linton but coincides again where Deepstep Road crosses Town Creek at O'Quinn's Pond. This place was described in the bill that created Hancock County as "where the lower trading road crosses Town Creek."

---

2. Flat Rock Creek is shown on these maps; Thomas Wright, 1763 (Cuming 333); Samuel Savory (Cumming 369); Bernard Romans (Cumming 370–A); Stuart-Purcell., c. 1773 (Cumming 438); and Stuart-Gage, 1773 (Cumming 440). There is no modern stream named Flat Rock Creek.

Also John H. Goff describes the Flat Rock as a well-known camping place on the Lower Creek Trading Path near Rocky Comfort Creek, *Place-names of Georgia*, p. 414.

Sites

1. Camak has its origins as a railroad depot and is named for the first president and a founder of the Georgia Railroad, James W. Camak of Athens. Francis Harper believed that the Flat Rock, where Bartram and the traders camped, was just northwest of Camak on the head of Lazenby Creek. (See the entry for Flat Rock below)

Georgia Railroad. The Georgia Railroad was organized in Athens on March 10, 1834, because local industrialists could not get heavy textile machinery delivered from Augusta over the muddy roads. The Georgia Railroad was the first railroad built in Georgia and the third in the nation. The natural disadvantages found in the Southern states, bad roads and long distances, helped spur the early development of railroads. The track was laid down on existing roads, much of which was part of the Upper and Lower Creek Trading Paths.

2. Bartram's Flat Rock was located on the Lower Creek Trading Path (see map, page 210). Although Bartram claimed it was a popular stopping place for travelers on the trading path it seems to have disappeared from local lore. John Goff tried to locate the site and thought it might be a rock outcrop on Storm Creek west of Stump Branch Church, about a quarter mile west of GA-80.

3. Happy Valley Road/County Line Road. The Lower Creek Trading Path branched off from other trails at Dearing and Harlem. It ran southwest to the junction of Sweetwater and Brier Creek. Maps of the mid-eighteenth century show the path once crossed Brier Creek farther south and passed through Savannah Town and Silver Bluff. This route probably became less important as Augusta grew in importance. From Brier Creek the Trading Path followed the modern Happy Valley Road, the Warren-Glascock County line, and the Hancock-Washington line. The path crossed the Oconee River at Rock Landing.

Upper Creek Trading Path (Oakfuskie Trail). The Upper Creek Trading Path forked into the Upper (or Oakfuskie) Creek Path and the Lower Cherokee Path. The Upper Creek Path passed through modern-day Warrenton, Eatonton, Indian Springs, and on to the Upper Creek town of Oakfuskie.

4. Shoals of Ogeechee was one of the most important crossings of the Lower Creek Path. The community of Georgetown grew up on the east side of the Ogeechee River where the trail crossed and Lexington was on the west side of the river. The place is now known simply as Shoals. The Bird Iron Works was constructed a little upstream and a gristmill was built at the shoals at the beginning of the nineteenth century. The millrace was made by building fires on the exposed granite, then pouring cold water on the hot rock to flake it away. Before the coming of the railroad, cotton was floated downriver from Shoals to the coast. Shoals was a thriving community for a number of years but little is left today. This is one of the most picturesque places in Georgia and deserves to be preserved.

5. Ogeechee River. The Ogeechee River has its headwaters near Union Point, at the southern edge of the Great Ridge that divides the Oconee and the Savannah rivers. The Ogeechee flows 245 miles to the Atlantic Ocean at its mouth between Wassaw and Ossabaw Islands. Ogeechee means *river of the Yuchi* because Yuchi Indians once lived on the river in present-day Taliaferro county. In 1773 the boundary between Georgia and the Creeks was the Ogeechee River from its source to a point just south of present-day Millen. From there the boundary traveled in a meandering line to Doctortown on the Altamaha river then to the St. Marys River. George Galphin had a cowpen on the Ogeechee River near present-day Louisville.

In *A Ranger's Report of Travels with General Oglethorpe, 1739–1742*, the unknown author reported on the method that traders and pack horse men used to ferry goods across rivers.

> We arrived at Great Ogeechee River which we swam our Horses over and The Packhorse Man got his Things over in a Leather Canoe which they carry for that Purpose and at every River where they are to use it, they stretch it with Stakes made on Purpose.
>
> July the 28th. The Things being all got over the River we set forward, The Indians killing plenty of Deer and Turkeys for our Refreshment, also several Buffaloes, of which there is great Plenty and they are very good Eating."[3]

When Bartram passed this way thirty-five years later the buffaloes were gone.

6. Ogeechee Wildlife Management Area is composed of several sections lying on Fulsome Road west of Mayfield, along Mayfield Road to the east of Mayfield, Jewell Road north of Jewell, Hamburg Road south of Jewell, and parcels on the east side of the Ogeechee River at Shoals. Information may be obtained at the check station on Jewell Road north of Jewell.

[3]. *Travels in the American Colonies*, edited by Newton D. Mereness for the National Society of the Colonial Dames of America. The MacMillan Company, New York, 1916.

7. Jewell is a picturesque Victorian mill village that began when William Shivers built Rock Factory in the early 1800s. In prehistoric times Native Americans built a fishdam on the Ogeechee River at Jewell. The settlement was first known as Kelly's Mill, then Rock Mill, then Shivers, and was later named Jewell after the owner who bought the mill in 1856. The site was a fording place during colonial times and a wagon road crossed there in the early 1800s. Renowned traveler Adam Hodgson lodged with the Shivers in March 1820.

8. Mayfield was settled around 1792, although it was then located about a mile northeast of the present community. Mayfield lies on the Upper Creek Path and the old Augusta-Milledgeville Stage Road. The famous Lamar Family lived on the Ogeechee River near Mayfield before moving to Putnam County. John Lamar had two sons, Lucius Quintus Cincinnatus and Mirabeau Buonaparte. LQC Lamar's son, also named LQC, was a senator, U.S. Secretary of the Treasury, and a Supreme Court Justice. Mirabeau Lamar was the founder of the *Columbus Enquirer* newspaper and became the second president of the Republic of Texas.

9. Powelton was the business center of Hancock County in the late eighteenth century. It declined when railroads bypassed the town.

11. Queensborough. With the 1763 Treaty of Augusta the Ogeechee River became the western boundary between Georgia and the Creeks and was opened for settlement. Andrew Lambert received a land grant between Big Creek, Spring Creek, and Ogeechee River that included Yuchi Old Town. George Galphin, realizing the importance of this location, bought Lambert's post and 1,400 acres in 1764. Galphin built a cowpen and trading post that became the most important settlement in the frontier until the founding of Wrightsborough. Old maps show Lambert's Creek (Big Creek) and a road leading from Galphin's Cowpen to Wrightsborough.

George Galphin had a tract of land near his cowpen set aside for Irish immigrants. The township was named Queensborough and later the town of Louisville was settled on part of this reserve. The site of Queensborough is two miles southeast of Louisville and Galphin's Cowpen, or Old Galphinton, was nine miles southeast.

Louisville was laid out in 1786 and named in honor of the French king who helped the Americans win independence. The capital of Georgia was at Louisville from 1795–1806. One of the oldest structures in the state is the Old Market at Louisville. It was supposedly built about 1758, but that would mean that it was built in Creek territory before many white

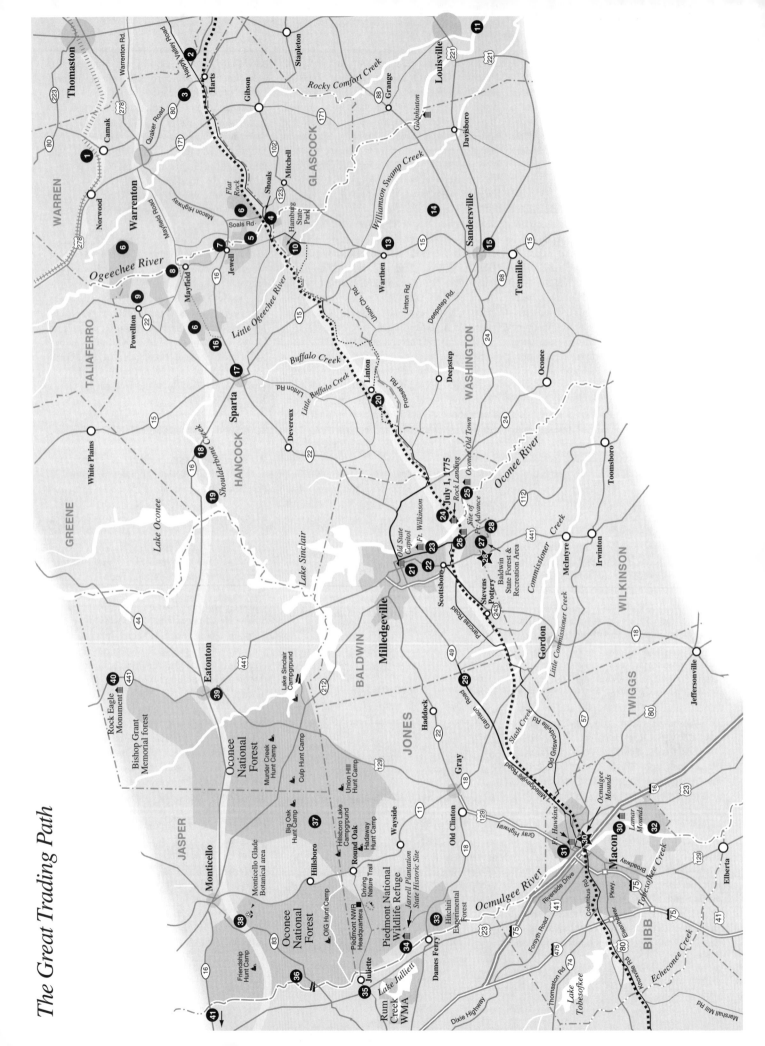

The Great Trading Path

settlers had arrived, unless it was built by George Galphin in anticipation of the creation of Queensborough.

The notorious **Yazoo Land Fraud** was organized while the capital was at Louisville. In this fiasco members of the Georgia Assembly passed a bill to sell lands in western Georgia between the Chattahoochee and Mississippi rivers at cheap prices and on easy terms to companies of land speculators. Some legislators even formed companies for the purpose of profiting from the sale while others were bribed for their vote. The Yazoo Act would have sold much of present-day Mississippi and Alabama, thirty-five million acres, for less than two cents per acre.

The outraged citizens of Georgia and the uncorrupted legislators demanded that the Yazoo Land Bill be rescinded in the next legislative session. The bill was retrieved from the state archives and burned in a solemn ceremony in front of the State House. The story is told that a magnifying glass was used to bring fire from the heavens to burn the documents. The careers of Governor Mathews and supporters of the Yazoo land sale were destroyed and those of the opposition grew. James Jackson and William H. Crawford became the leading statesmen of Georgia due in part to their role in nullifying the Yazoo land sale.

In 1802 the United States stepped in to clear up the confusion over lands already sold and settled. Georgia received $1,250,00 in return for giving up claim to land between the Chattahoochee and Mississippi rivers. The United States agreed to obtain for Georgia title to the Indian lands remaining within the present boundaries of the state.

12. Galphinton. George Galphin's sons, John and George, inherited 15,000 acres of land when their father died in 1780. They built a trading post on the west bank of the Ogeechee River opposite where their father had kept his cowpen. Both were patriots like their father and both served in the Burke County Rangers in 1781–1782. The trading enterprise had declined by the very early 1800s and the Galphins sold the land where they had their store, just northeast of Davisboro.

10. Hamburg State Park. Richard Warthen settled in Washington County in 1784 and built a sawmill, woolen mill, and cotton gin at this site on the fall line of the Little Ogeechee River. The mill was named for Hamburg, South Carolina.

The state park is built around the 1921 grist mill and 225-acre lake. The river below the dam is embellished with numerous rock outcrops. The lake provides for boating and fishing. There is a nature trail, museum of agricultural equipment, camping, and RV sites. The Fall Harvest Festival is held the third weekend of each September. Canoe trips on the Ogeechee are organized in April and May. Located on Hamburg Road. Open 7 a.m.–10 p.m. daily.

13. Warthen was the county seat of Washington County from 1784–1786 and is a National Historic District. The old log jail was built about 1784 and still stands today. Aaron Burr spent a night in the jail in 1807 while being transported to trial in Virginia.

14. Kaolin has replaced cotton as the economic base of Washington County. Kaolin is a fine, white clay found in the Fall Line Sand Hills that stretch from Augusta to Columbus. It is used in paints, plastics, medicine, insulators, and porcelain. Kaolin is formed by the weathering of mica and feldspar deposited from the mountains and Piedmont. Chemical weathering and leaching occurred during a period when the ocean had receded seventy million years ago. The waters returned and new sediments were laid down and helped preserve the kaolin. The kaolin shipped from Jefferson and Washington counties is among the finest in the world for coating paper. Kaolin is named for the Chinese province where it was first mined.

15. Sandersville grew up around the trading post of Mark Saunders that stood at the intersection of two Indian trading paths in an area originally known as White Ponds. The community was first called Saunders Crossroads and was renamed Sandersville when it became the county seat in 1796. The Kaolin Festival is held on the courthouse square the second Saturday of each October.

Washington County Museum. Located in the old jail on the courthouse square, corner of Jernigan and Jones streets. Open from 2–5 p.m. on Tuesdays and Thursdays.

Sandersville Library. 113 W. Haynes Street on the courthouse square. Open 10 a.m.–5:30 p.m., Monday through Friday and 10 a.m.–12:30 p.m. on Saturday.

Washington County Library. 114 Smith Street, Tennille. Open 12–6 p.m., Monday through Friday and 10 a.m.–4 p.m. on Saturday.

16. Richard Malcolm Johnston was the author of the such popular stories as *Georgia Sketches* written in 1864 and *Dukesborough Tales*, 1871. He was a long-time resident of Hancock County and established the respected Rockby Academy at his home three miles east of Sparta. He was a writer in the literary style of realism that was introduced by Augustus Baldwin Longstreet. Johnston's stories used small-town and country settings with average people whose characters were fully and realistically developed. He wrote in a straightforward, unembellished style. Dukesborough was

Legend

1. Camak
   Georgia Railroad
2. Bartram's Flat Rock
3. Happy Valley Road
   Upper Creek Trading Path
4. Shoals of Ogeechee
5. Ogeechee River
6. Ogeechee Wildlife Management Area
7. Jewell
8. Mayfield
9. Powelton
10. Hamburg State Park
11. Queensborough
    Louisville
    Yazoo Land Fraud
12. Galphinton
13. Warthen
14. Kaolin
15. Sandersville
    Washington County Museum
    Sandersville Library
    Washington County Library
16. Richard Malcolm Johnston
17. Sparta
    Sparta Female College
    Hancock Planters Club
18. Millmore
19. Shoulderbone Creek
20. Linton
21. Milledgeville
    Milledgeville Welcome Center
    Old State Capitol
    Old Governor's Mansion
    Flannery O'Conner
    Georgia College
22. Lockerly Arboretum
23. Fort Wilkinson
24. Rock Landing
25. Old Oconee Town
26. Trans-Oconee Republic
27. Baldwin State Forest
    Bartram Educational Forest
28. Bartram Trail Signs
29. Garrison Road
30. Ocmulgee National Monument
31. Fort Hawkins Replica
32. Bond Swamp National Wildlife Refuge
    Brown's Mount Educational Center
33. Piedmont Wildlife Management Area
    Hitchiti Nature Trail
34. Jarrell Plantation State Historical Site
35. Juliette
36. Ocmulgee River Trail
37. Oconee National Forest
38. Monticello Glade
39. Uncle Remus
40. Rock Eagle Mound
41. Indian Springs State Park

the literary name he used for the community of Powelton.

17. Sparta began as a trading post on a branch of the Upper Creek Path. Another trail turned southward from Sparta and joined the Lower Creek Path at Rock Landing on the Oconee River. The first settlers of the town were from Dinwiddie County Virginia. The settlement was called Sparta, after the classical Greek city, because the inhabitants were vigilant and showed courage against Creek raiders. In 1795 Sparta became the county seat for newly formed Hancock County. The stagecoach road to Milledgeville and the Old Federal Road passed through Sparta. Sparta was honored by a visit from Marquis de Lafayette in 1825 during his American tour. He was entertained by Major Charles Abercrombie at the Eagle Tavern, now called Hotel Lafayette.

Sparta Female College was organized around 1827 as one of the very first colleges for women in the country. Students were taught classical and practical courses by a method of instruction known as the Renselaer Plan, in which students participated in the instruction by researching a topic and presenting it to her classmates. For example, in botany class students prepared an herbarium that utilized the practical knowledge of plant identification learned from lecture. Each student then gave a lesson that was illustrated by her own collection of plants. The college was moved to Fort Gaines, Georgia, but several of the houses used to board students and faculty are still used today as private homes in Sparta.

Hancock Planters Club. Area planters became concerned with the depletion of cotton lands and the continual migration of people to new lands in Alabama, Mississippi, and Texas. The Hancock Planters Club was organized in 1837 to address these issues and improve the science of agriculture. The club discussed new farming techniques, performed experiments, and publicized their information. Terracing and contour plowing was introduced to Georgia farmers by Richard Hardwick of Hancock County. David Dickson experimented with commercial fertilizers and proved that undesirable pine barren land could be made productive with new scientific methods. The Hancock Planters Club held the first agricultural fair in Georgia in 1842.

18. Millmore. This operating grist mill was built about 1800. Located on Shoulderbone Creek just off GA-16. Open 9 a.m.–5 p.m., Monday through Friday.

19. Shoulderbone Creek has several important archaeological sites and mounds dating from the Mississippian period. The De Soto expedition visited the town of Ocute at Shoulderbone Creek on April 8, 1540. The chief of Ocute was the most powerful headman of a chiefdom that reached south to Shinholser Mound and north to Scull Shoals.

The **Treaty of Shoulderbone Creek** took place near the mouth of Shoulderbone Creek on November 3, 1786. This treaty between Georgia and the Creeks was an extension of two previous treaties, the 1783 Treaty of Augusta and the 1785 Treaty of Galphinton. The purpose of the Shoulderbone Creek treaty was to establish rules of behavior for both sides in consequence of the Oconee War and to reaffirm the western boundary of Georgia as being the Oconee River. However, without the express consent of Alexander McGillivray, the most powerful Creek leader, the treaties were not successful in stemming frontier tensions.

20. Linton community grew up around the Washington Institute, established in 1858.

21. Milledgeville was founded in 1807 as the capital of Georgia. It was laid out on the Savannah Plan with squares reserved for governmental offices and the streets named for the counties. Government Square was bounded by Green, Franklin, Tattnall, and Columbia streets and is now used for dormitories and an athletic complex for Georgia College. Statehouse Square was bounded by Greene, Franklin, Wayne, and Elbert streets and is now Georgia Military College. The main buildings of Georgia College are located on Penitentiary Square. The Marquis de Lafayette arrived in Milledgeville on March 20, 1825, and was entertained with a grand barbecue.

When the capital was moved to Atlanta in 1868 Milledgeville declined but today is enjoying a renaissance. The quiet years helped preserve dozens of grand homes that otherwise would have been lost to urban growth.

Milledgeville was named for Governor John Milledge, a grandson of one of the first colonists to arrive in Georgia. While in his late teens, Milledge was active as a member of the Committee of Safety during the stormy days leading up to the Revolution. He then fought in the major engagements along the Savannah River. After the war he served as a legislator and governor. Milledge was an early and ardent supporter for a state university and was a member of the committee that selected the site for the new college. He personally paid $4,000 for the land where now stands the University of Georgia and donated it to the Trustees. He was an opponent of the Yazoo Acts, which further increased his standing among the citizens of Georgia. He died at his home, Sand Hills, near Augusta in 1818. John Milledge was married to Martha Galphin, daughter of George Galphin of Silver Bluff, South Carolina.

Milledgeville Welcome Center. 200 West Hancock Street, at the intersection with Wilkinson Street. Open 8 a.m.–5 p.m., Monday through Friday and 10 a.m.–2 p.m. on Saturday.

Old State Capitol. Tradition has for many years held that the old statehouse was built upon an ancient Indian ceremonial mound, but no Indian town has been found at Milledgeville. The capitol was burned during the Civil War and was rebuilt to become part of Georgia Military College. The present building is a replica of the original Gothic revival styled capitol and is built on the original foundation. The gates on Jefferson and West Hancock streets were built in the 1860s. The Old Capitol served as the seat of the legislature from 1807–1868. It is now the main building of Georgia Military College and contains a museum of early Milledgeville and history of the college. 201 East Green Street.

Old Governor's Mansion. This fine Greek Revival home was completed in 1838 and served as the governor's home for thirty years. The lower floors are open for tours and the upper floors are offices for the president of Georgia College. 120 South Clark Street.

Flannery O'Connor lived in Milledgeville for most of her life and is buried in Cemetery Hill. She is Georgia's greatest author and her contribution to American literature is beyond debate. Her childhood home is at 311 West Greene Street, now a private residence. The Flannery O'Connor Room at the Georgia College Library contains manuscripts, memorabilia, and furnishings from her country home, Andalusia.

Georgia College campus covers forty-three acres near downtown Milledgeville. The college was founded in 1889 as Georgia Industrial and Normal College to train young women for teaching and industrial careers. It became Georgia State College for Women in 1922, and in 1967 it became a coed institution. Georgia College was renamed Georgia College and State University in 1996 and is the designated liberal arts college for the University of Georgia System. The visitor center is located on Montgomery Street in the College of Arts & Sciences Building.

22. Lockerly Arboretum. The Lockerly Arboretum is an outdoor laboratory used to test plants for suitability to the climate of Middle Georgia. The terrain here at the Fall Line contains environments from both the Piedmont and the Coastal Plain. Exhibition areas contain displays on the geology of the region and endangered and unusual plants. Collections include viburnums, conifers, camellias, azaleas, aquatic plants, hawthorns, hollies, and grasses. There are habitat displays of bogs, ponds, sand hills, and a climax forest. Located south of Milledgeville on US-441. Open 8:30 a.m.–4:30 p.m., Monday through Friday and 1–5 p.m. on Saturday.

23. Fort Wilkinson was built in 1797 and garrisoned until Fort Hawkins was constructed at Ocmulgee Old Fields (Macon) 1807. Fort Wilkinson was built on a hill overlooking the Oconee River and replaced Fort Fidius at nearby Rock Landing, which was thought to be an unhealthy site. Aaron Burr was imprisoned at Fort Wilkinson while enroute to trial in Virginia. The Treaty of Fort Wilkinson was signed June 16, 1802, and was the first step in Georgia's acquisition of the land between the Oconee and Ocmulgee Rivers. The treaty provided for Georgia's boundary to be fixed westward at Commissioner's Creek. The site of Fort Wilkinson is now a public park and is located at the end of Fort Wilkinson Drive, off GA-112 south of downtown Milledgeville.

24. Rock Landing. Though there are no rocks here it is thought a stone may once have marked the place of this historic crossing. The fording place of the Oconee River remained at Rock Landing until Milledgeville became settled. Fort Fidius, also known as Federal Town, was built near Rock Landing in 1793. The historical marker for Rock Landing is five miles north of the actual site and is located at the east side of the GA-22/24 bridge at downtown Milledgeville.

25. Oconee Old Town was about a mile southeast of Rock Landing. This is the historical home of the Oconee Indians, a Hitchiti-speaking people from whom the Oconee River takes its name. They moved to the Oconee River in the late seventeenth century and remained there until the Yamassee War when they moved to the Chattahoochee River. The Oconees began moving to Florida in the mid-1700s and formed the nucleus of the Seminole Tribe. The meaning of the word Oconee is unknown.

26. Trans-Oconee Republic. In 1794 General Elijah Clark and other adventurers attempted to establish a separate state to the west of the Oconee River. In June and July of that year they drafted a constitution and took control of a 120 mile section of the river and built three forts. Fort Advance was on the west side of the river across from Rock Landing and Old Fort Fidius (also known as Federal Town). This site is still marked on the official Baldwin County highway map as being at the intersection of Jesse Scott Road and GA-112. Fort Defiance was six miles north and Fort Winston was yet farther upriver at the crossing of the Lower Cherokee Path.

Settlement within the Creek territory by whites was illegal, therefore Governor Mathews was compelled to issue a warrant for Clark's arrest when he refused to disband his company. Generals Twiggs and Irwin were sent to persuade Clark to leave but failed. General Irwin and the militia invaded the Trans-Oconee settlements and burned the forts. Clark was induced to surrender rather than resist. He was not tried because no jury would sit in judgment against this popular Revolutionary War hero.

27. Baldwin State Forest is managed by the Georgia Forestry Commission for timber, wildlife, recreation, and a hundred acres are used as a pine seed orchard. Hunting is permitted during archery season and there are five fishing ponds. Located on US-441 four miles south of Milledgeville. Restrooms are available.

Bartram Educational Forest. The Georgia Forestry Commission established the Bartram Educational Forest as an outdoor classroom to teach students about natural history and conservation of natural resources. The forest was named in honor of William Bartram whose travels took him through this very property in July 1775. Located at 2892 US-441. Open 8 a.m.–4:30 p.m., Monday through Friday.

28. Bartram Trail Markers. In 1976 the Georgia Bartram Trail Conference began marking sections of the Bartram Trail with small green signs. Some are still in place around the state and there are two located just south of Milledgeville. One is near the Wilkinson County line on US-441 and another is on GA-112.

29. Garrison Road. GA-49 closely follows the old stage road from Milledgeville to Fort Hawkins, known as the Garrison Road. It was a section of the Old Federal Road.

30. Ocmulgee National Monument. When Georgia acquired the land between the Oconee and Ocmulgee rivers a section that included Ocmulgee Mounds was reserved for the Creeks. The Ocmulgee Old Fields was one of the early homes of the Muskogees but was occupied first by the Hitchitis. The Spanish burned Kasihta, Coweta, and other Muskhogean towns on the Chattahoochee River in 1686 in an attempt to drive out the English and turn the Muskogees away from their influence. The destruction of the towns and the building of Fort Apalachicola in 1789 actually drove the Muskogees into the arms of the English. The Kasihtas and the Cowetas moved to the Ocmulgee Old Fields on the Great Trading Path so as to be nearer the trade coming from Charleston. A trading post was built at the Old Fields around 1690 and the area was well populated until the disruptions of the Yamassee War. Then, the Muskogees moved back to the Chattahoochee River so as to be not so close to the English after all.

The Hitchitis living on the Ocmulgee river called their new Muskogee neighbors *Ochesee* and the Ocmulgee River was known as *Ochesee Creek*. The English called the people who lived along the Ocmulgee *Ochesee Creeks* or simply *Ochesee* or *Creeks*. This name was applied to all members of the loose confederation after they resettled on the Chattahoochee River. Ocmulgee is a Muskhogean word meaning "bubbling water."

Today at Ocmulgee National Monument the foundation of the old trading post is delineated, a Mississippian council house has been rebuilt on its original site, and part of the Great Trading Path is still visible. Seven mounds are located in the main park, including the Lesser and Greater Temple Mounds. The Greater Temple Mound is a truncated pyramid that offers a 360 degree view of the area, including downtown Macon. The Lamar Mounds are several miles downriver.

Inhabitation of this area began between 9,000 and 12,000 years ago and choice town sites such as this have seen recurring settlements through time. While the mounds within the main park date from the Mississippian Period, 900–1100 AD, the Lamar Mounds represent the Late Mississippian Period, 1350–1540. The Lamar Culture was first described from archaeological investigation of these mounds and is characterized by spiral temple mounds and decorated pottery. The De Soto expedition crossed the Ocmulgee River in March 1540 and met the Chief of Ichisi, whose seat of government was at the Lamar Mounds. The Spanish expedition brought the Lamar Culture to an end by the unknowing introduction of new diseases.

After contact with Europeans the Native American population of the Southeast plummeted, the balance of power between chiefdoms shifted, community life was disrupted, and the political systems changed as people lost faith in their leaders. A population of about 1.3 million for the Southeast in 1540 was reduced to about 200,000 by the end of the 1685.[4] In some areas nearly ninety percent of the population died out in a very short period of time. Certainly it must have seemed that the end of the world was at hand. Though these earlier mound sites would be inhabited again, the Indians of historical times had lost any memory of their construction.

The Ocmulgee Monument visitor center has an archaeological exhibit, an orientation film, and an excellent bookstore. The Bartram Trail historical marker is at the south end of the visitor center parking area. Ocmulgee National Monument is located at US-80/129 and Jeffersonville Highway. Open 9 a.m.–5 p.m. everyday except Christmas and New Year's Day.

31. Fort Hawkins was built in 1806 on the Lower Creek Trading Path as it approached the Ocmulgee River and was named for Indian

---

4. Charles Hudson, *Knights of Spain, Warriors of the Sun*; University of Georgia Press, 1997, p. 425.

agent Benjamin Hawkins. It was the western frontier of a land cession made by the Creeks in 1805. A replica of the Fort Hawkins blockhouse overlooks US-80 just west of the entrance to Ocmulgee Mounds.

32. Bond Swamp National Wildlife Refuge. Bond Swamp contains 6,500 acres of wetlands and floodplain along the Ocmulgee River. It was established as a wildlife refuge in 1989 and opened to general public use in 2000. The swamp was protected as a part of the Ocmulgee Heritage Greenway project and was established to provide for conservation, public recreation, and environmental education. Bond Swamp contains the highest concentration of winter waterfowl in Georgia, making it an ideal place for bird watchers. The area also protects habitat for fish, including the rare robust redhorse sucker.

Bond Swamp has two hiking trails with parking located on US-23. The Bond Swamp Visitor Center is located at the headquarters of the Piedmont National Wildlife Refuge on Jarrell Road in Jones County, between Round Oak and Juliette. Bond Swamp is open during daylight hours.

Brown's Mount Educational Center is an ecological and educational preserve of the Macon Museum of arts and Sciences. The Museum uses Brown's Mount as an outdoor classroom and is open only during organized classes, hikes, and programs. Regularly scheduled programs are held the second Saturday of each month. Contact the Museum or visit their web site for upcoming events. Brown's Mount is located west of US-23/129, just north of Bond Swamp National Wildlife Refuge.

33. Piedmont Wildlife Management Area. There are three nature trails at the Piedmont WMA visitor center. The Red Cockaded Woodpecker Trail takes hikers through a stand of trees that are home to a colony of the endangered woodpeckers. Look for the trees marked with a white band, then look for the telltale signs of running sap and the opening to the bird's nest as a cavity of the tree. Nest time for red cockaded woodpeckers is May and June. Another popular attraction is the Little Rock Wildlife Drive, a six-mile unpaved road that passes through the various habitats common to this area of the Piedmont. The visitor center is on the Juliette-Round Oak Road east of Juliette.

Hitchiti Nature Trail. The Hitchitis lived along the Ocmulgee River north of Macon. Hitchiti Nature Trail in the Oconee National Forest commemorates their name in their traditional homeland. The trail follows Falling Creek from the intersection of GA-18 and FS-908 to the Ocmulgee River. Information is available at nearby Jarrell Plantation

34. Jarrell Plantation State Historical Site. The oldest residence on the Jarrell Plantation was built in 1847 and was used as a home by Jarrell descendants until 1957. There are twenty historic structures on the farm, including a second home, barns, equipment, and tool sheds. The buildings, tools and furnishings span more than a century of farm life in the Georgia Piedmont. The Jarrells operated a grist mill, sawmill, syrup mill, planer, and cotton gin. There are some beautiful chickens, a pig, a milk cow, and a sheep. There is a very docile mule who has the envious job to stand by the fence and gets his head scratched. Jarrell Plantation sponsors a number of folklife events each year, the most popular being One Hundred years of Jarrell Clothing, the Fourth of July Celebration, Family Farm Day, and Labor Day on the Farm.

From Macon follow I-75 north to Exit 55, then travel north on US-23 to GA-18 East and follow the signs. Open 9 a.m.–5 p.m., Tuesday through Saturday and 2–5:30 p.m. on Sunday.

35. Juliette. After a tour of Jarrell Plantation, travelers must see the charming town of Juliette, made famous by the movie *Fried Green Tomatoes*. Juliette is a small mill town built on the Ocmulgee River. The abandoned flour mill stands as a somber sentinel over the town.

36. Ocmulgee River Trail begins at Ocmulgee Flats Hunt Camp on FS-1099.

37. Oconee National Forest was established during the Depression on worn-out and abandoned cotton land. The color of the Georgia red clay is due to the high iron content of the subsoil, and the reason we see so much of it is because several feet of topsoil was lost to cotton cultivation. This is especially true on the rolling ridges that are now growing millions of loblolly pines. The district ranger office is at 349 Forsyth Street in Monticello.

38. Monticello Glade lies adjacent to the marshy headwaters of Falling Creek. In mid-April several acres of atamasco lilies bloom among the open hardwood forest. The trail to the glade passes an interesting geological feature of the Piedmont called a *tors*, a naturally occurring pile of rocks. Look across the beaver pond and you will see several massive boulders lying at water's edge. The glade is reached by an unmarked hiking trail from FS-1030. Inquire at the ranger office in Monticello before heading out.

39. The *Uncle Remus* stories told by Joel Chandler Harris were learned from African Americans during his childhood growing up near Eatonton. Some of the stories were based on traditional African tales where animals figure prominently and exhibit the strengths and frailties of humans as well as their own species. Other stories were learned from the Creek Indians who, like other Native Americans, had a similar tradition of imbuing animals with human qualities, both valiant and ignoble. African and Native American stories were morality plays that demonstrated how one should live nobly and foretold the consequences for acting badly. The *Uncle Remus* stories were written in the vernacular of a Piedmont slave community.

The Uncle Remus Museum is located on US-441 in Eatonton, two blocks south of the Putnam County Courthouse.

40. Rock Eagle Mound is an earthwork of stones in the shape of a giant bird, measuring 120 feet across the wings and 102 feet in length. The effigy is believed to date from about 3,000 years ago. Rock Eagle Mound is located north of Eatonton at Rock Eagle 4-H Camp.

41. Indian Springs State Park. The inn at Indian Springs was originally owed by Chief William McIntosh. He and several other headmen signed the Treaty of Indian Springs in 1825, selling all Creek lands east of the Chattahoochee River. McIntosh was assassinated for this act.

Indian Springs State Park is Georgia's first state park, built in 1927. The spring still flows and the museum tells the history of the Creeks and American settlers who frequented the mineral springs. The park has a camping area, picnic facilities, hiking trail, and a fishing lake. A festival celebrating Southeastern Indian culture is held each June. Open 7 a.m.–10 p.m. daily. The museum is closed on Monday and certain holidays. Admission.

Counties

Jefferson County was created from Burke and Warren counties in 1796 and named for Thomas Jefferson.

Warren was created by the legislature on December 19, 1793 and was taken from Richmond County. It is named for General Joseph E. Warren, who was killed at the Battle of Bunker Hill.

Glascock was created in 1857 from other counties and named for militia General Thomas Glascock.

Hancock was organized in 1793 and named for John Hancock, President of the Continental Congress and signer of the Declaration of Independence.

Washington, organized in 1784, was the first county in the nation to bear the name of President George Washington. Washington County originally included all land below Cherokee Corner and between the Oconee and Ogeechee rivers.

Baldwin was organized by the Land Lottery Act of 1803. The original boundaries were the Ogeechee River on the east and Oconee River on the west. It is named for Abraham Baldwin, legislator, senator, first president of the University of Georgia and author of the University's charter.

Jones was created in 1807 and named for James Jones, congressman from Savannah.

Bibb was created in 1822 from other counties and named for Dr. William W. Bibb.

Wilkinson was created by the Land Lottery Act of 1803 and named for General James Wilkinson. The original area of the Wilkinson county was bounded by the Oconee River on the east, the Ocmulgee River on the west, and the fall line on the north. Jefferson Davis was captured at Irwinton, the county seat of Wilkinson.

Putnam was organized in 1807 and named for General Israel Putnam

Jasper was created in 1807 as Randolph County and renamed in 1812 to honor Revolutionary War hero Sergeant William Jasper who was killed at the Siege of Savannah.

Indian Paths

Etowah (Itawa) Trail is also known as the Lower Cherokee Path and Hightower Trail by whites, who mispronounced Etowah. The trail forked at Dearing into the Hightower Trail and the Lower Creek Trading Path. It forked again near Camak into the Upper Creek Path, or Oakfuskie Trail, running due west and the Hightower Trail running northwest. The Hightower trail passed through or near Crawfordville, Union Point, Greensboro, and Madison. It became the current boundary line between DeKalb and Gwinnett counties and crossed the Chattahoochee River at the Shallowford in Roswell. Portions of this historic trail are in use today and are still named Hightower Road and Shallowford Road.

Middle Cherokee Path. This trail ran from Augusta across the Little River to Washington, Lexington, Crawford, and crossed the Oconee River at Athens. From there it traversed Hall County then passed north of Atlanta and on to Chattanooga. The Middle Cherokee Path was an important route to the Tennessee towns and became part of the Cherokee Federal Highway that brought access to such faraway places as Knoxville and Nashville.

Upper Cherokee Path. The New Purchase survey party followed the Upper Cherokee Path as they traveled from the Tugaloo River back to Augusta in July 1773. It followed close to the Savannah River often within view of the river valley. From the junction of the Tugaloo and Seneca rivers at present-day Hartwell the trail ran up the western side of the Tugaloo to meet other important trails at a place called the Dividings, which is now the site of Clayton, Georgia.

Lower Creek Trading Path. The Hightower Trail and Lower Creek Trading Path forked at Dearing or near Harlem. The Lower Path then followed the county line between Warren-Glascock and Hancock-Washington. This trail was the most important and most traveled trade route in the Southeast during Colonial times. It was opened by the Cowetas and Charleston traders about 1670 and became known as the Great Trading Path, the Old Horse Path, and the White Path. It became the original route of the Federal Road to Mobile from Augusta and large sections became the Wire Road when the telegraph was strung from Washington, D.C., to New Orleans.

Oakfuskie Trail, Upper Creek Path. The Upper Creek Path was an important trade route from Augusta to the Creek towns lying on the upper Tallapoosa River. It diverged from the Lower Path near Harlem and the two trails ranged up to fifty miles apart before coming together again. The Hightower Trail branched northward from the Upper Creek Path near Sweetwater Creek. Parts of the Upper Path became the Old Milledgeville Road in McDuffie and Warren counties. The Oakfuskie Trail continued through Warrenton and over the Ogeechee River at Latimore's Mill just above Mayfield. It crossed the Oconee River above Milledgeville near the mouth of Shoulderbone Creek and continued on through Eatonton and Monticello.

Itinerary

Miles	Directions
	Begin at GA-17 and Happy Valley Road, south of Thomson, and travel west
3.9	Right on Purvis School Road
2.4	Cross GA-80/Old Quaker Road
	the itinerary now becomes County Line Road
4.6	Cross Rocky Comfort Creek
8.9	Right on GA-123
.6	Cross the Ogeechee River at Shoals
1.7	Left on Hamburg Road
3.0	Cross the Little Ogeechee River at Hamburg State Park
2.4	Right on Centralia-Rachels Road (unpaved)
3.5	Right on Sparta Davisboro Road
2.2	Right on GA-15N
.2	Left on unmarked county road, marked by a sign for Archer Grove Baptist Church and Balerma Baptist Church
2.1	Pavement ends
3.7	Keep left on Balerma Church Road
1.4	Right on Linton Road
2.2	Cross Buffalo Creek
.6	Left on Griffin Road (the county map names it Friendship-Nebo Road, becomes Prosser Road
9.1	Right on Deepstep Road
.6	Cross Town Creek
1.5	Right on GA-24
.6	Left on Kings Road
5.4	Left on GA-24
.2	Cross the Oconee River, notice the shoals to the north of the bridge
.6	Left on South GA-112, Elbert Street (becomes Vinson Highway)
2.6	Site of Fort Wilkenson is on the left
1.3	Intersection of Abatoir Road (public access to the Oconee River)
.7	Right on Carl Vinson Road
.2	Bartram Education Forest is on the left
1.4	Right on US-441
.5	Left on GA-243, Gordon Highway
2.0	Right on Pancras Road
4.4	Keep left on Pancras Road at the forks
3.3	Keep straight, Pancras Road becomes Union Hill Church Road
.8	Pavement ends
.2	Left on County Line Road
.4	Cross Commissioners Creek
.5	Right on Bethlehem Church Road
1.8	Right on GA-18
.5	Left on Old Griswoldville Road
1.8	Pavement ends
5.3	Pavement begins again, cross the paved road and continue on Griswoldville Road
3.5	Cross the railroad tracks
1.1	Left on GA-49
1.0	Left on Milledgeville Road
1.6	Right on Jeffersonville Road
.8	Left for Ocmulgee National Monument (cross Emery Highway)
.5	Ocmulgee National Monument visitor center and Bartram Trail historical marker

218 • *The Great Trading Path*

The Sand Hills

Prior to the English settlement of South Carolina, the region between the Ocmulgee and Chattahoochee rivers was sparsely settled. When the Creeks began trading with the English in Charleston, the Lower Creek Path became an important trade route across Georgia and several Indian towns moved to the Ocmulgee River to take advantage of the trade. The Lower Creek Trading Path followed the Fall Line Sand Hills, which Bartram called delightful and fruitful, although the ridge tops can be very dry and infertile. These hills are easily seen today along Averette Road northeast of Mauk where the sand is deep and the flora is mostly longleaf pine and turkey oak.

The Ocmulgee River was the traditional homeland of the Hitchitis and the Muskogees were latecomers. In the late seventeenth century there were Hitchiti and Muskogee towns on the Ocmulgee and Flint rivers, but most were relocated to the Chattahoochee River at the beginning of the eighteenth century in the wake of the Yamassee War. Between about 1680 and 1715 there was a trading post operating where the Lower Path crossed the Ocmulgee River, now Ocmulgee Mounds National Monument. The post was surrounded by a small village and was the staging ground for James Moore's invasion of Apalachee in 1703. By the time Bartram passed this way the area was again sparsely inhabited and used primarily as a Creek hunting preserve. When Benjamin Hawkins established the Creek Agency on the Flint River small villages of Creeks were attracted to the area and some families established small farms in the American fashion.

The Federal Road was opened for the general public in 1813 and followed almost exactly the Lower Creek Path. The road traveled from Hawkins' Creek Agency on the Flint River to Coweta on the Chattahoochee. The character of the Old

Cotton Avenue, Macon, Georgia

The Sand Hills

Legend

1. Macon
2. Macon Museum of Arts & Sciences
3. Wesleyan College
4. Tobesofkee and Echeconnee creeks
5. Bartram Trail Historical Marker
6. Oak-leaf hydrangea
7. Bartram Trail Historical Marker
8. Lone Star Flag
9. Old Federal Road
10. Museum of Southeastern Indians
11. Creek Agency
12. Flint River Crossings
13. Flint River Adventures
14. Patsiliga Creek
15. Timothy Barnard
16. Timpoochee Barnard
17. Fort Perry
18. Bartram Trail Historical Marker
19. The Bartram Trail Conference
20. Pasaquan

Federal Road as the link between the Southern states and the new American frontier is vividly illustrated in Adam Hodgson's *Letters from North America*. He described a night spent on the road somewhere in present-day Marion or Chattahoochee County. His party included an Alabama planter bringing his daughter home two-hundred miles from boarding school in Milledgeville. Camping nearby were immigrants from Georgia and South Carolina bound for the Alabama Black Belt. Within sight was a settlement of Creeks who were taking commercial advantage of traffic on the road. Hodgson's party was visited that night by Creeks who watched but did not speak and in the distance burned a forest fire. Hodgson admitted "The novelty of the scene, however, prevented my sleeping much."[1]

At the 1821 Treaty of Indian Springs, near present-day Jackson, Georgia, the Creeks sold their hunting lands between the Ocmulgee and Flint rivers. The area was organized into a land lottery that created the counties of Dooly, Houston, Monroe, and Henry. The remaining Creek land in Georgia was sold at the Second Treaty of Indian Springs in 1825 and the Treaty of Washington in 1826 and 1827.

The Treaty of Indian Springs brought upon General William McIntosh the disapproval and resentment of a large body of Upper Creeks because he had sold Creek lands without the express permission of all leaders, an act that was punishable by death. McIntosh had decided to move west and saw that the removal of the entire nation was inevitable. However, he was given a reserve on the Chattahoochee River near Whitesburg while others were being encouraged to move to Oklahoma.

1. Adam Hodgson, *Letters from North America,* vol. I; Hurst, Robinson, & Co., London, 1824.

There were suspicions that McIntosh and his friends, mostly Americanized Creeks from the Lower Towns, had personally profited by the treaty. Although Creek leaders traditionally used their position for personal gain the fact was used against McIntosh. He was condemned by the Creek National Council and assassinated in 1825 at his home north of Coweta in Alabama. He is buried at the McIntosh Reserve in Carroll County, Georgia. The McIntosh faction soon afterward moved to Fort Gibson on the Arkansas River.

Georgia Governor George Troup and William McIntosh were both related through the McIntosh clan of Darien, Georgia. Troup was incensed by the death of his cousin and began a concentrated effort to remove all Native Americans remaining within the boundaries of Georgia.

William Bartram's Travels in West Georgia

In the *Travels* William Bartram has his dates off by a year for he traveled to the Chattahoochee River in 1775. Bartram's Stony Creek is present-day Rocky Creek that flows through Macon. His route followed Columbus Road from Macon and then Knoxville Road along the south side of Sweetwater Creek. He passed by the south side of the Crawford County courthouse and through what was to become the Creek Agency on the Flint River. In present-day Taylor County his route passed northwest of Buena Vista on a series of sand ridges then he passed just north of Mauk and on to Fort Perry. From Fort Perry his path meandered along for some miles then passed along the south of Upatoi Creek in Chattahoochee County. First Division Road in the Fort Benning Reservation follows the Old Federal Road and the Lower Creek Trading Path.

Sites

1. Macon was surveyed in 1823 at the head of navigation on the Ocmulgee River. The Lower Creek Trading Path and the Old Federal Road evolved into Cotton Avenue, which still today cuts across the other streets at an angle. Macon was visited by many early professional travelers who made the perilous journey on the Federal Road and they published accounts of their travels. For descriptions of early Macon read Basil Hall, Sir Charles Lyell, James Silk Buckingham, and Tyrone Power.

Downtown Macon still retains the grace and beauty of its early days as a wealthy cotton town. Cotton was first shipped down the Ocmulgee River by barge. When the railroads came Macon boomed as a depot for shipping cotton to Savannah.

Macon hosts numerous popular festivals each year—the Georgia Pan-African Festival in early May, the Cherry Blossom Festival in mid-March, Sweet Georgia Jam music festival in September, the Georgia State Fair during the third week of October, and the Ocmulgee Indian Celebration every September.

A. Ocmulgee River Greenway. The ambitious Ocmulgee River Greenway is planned to extend thirty-five miles from Juliette to Warner Robins. Through downtown Macon the Greenway will occupy both sides of the river with access at Gateway Park on MLK Boulevard and on Riverside Drive. This is a work in progress that will expand to include trails to Central City Park, Rose Hill, and Ocmulgee National Monument.

B. The **Georgia Music Hall of Fame** is located at 200 Martin Luther King Boulevard, adjacent to Terminal Station. Macon is best known to outsiders as the birthplace of Rhythm and Blues and Dixie Rock. Macon was home to Otis Redding and Curtis Mayfield and James Brown began his recording career in Macon. In the 1970s Macon was the center of a rock music scene spawned by the Allman Brothers Band. The renowned blues singer Reverend Pearly Brown sang and played guitar on the streets of Macon for forty years. Open Monday–Saturday, 9 a.m.–5 p.m., and on Sunday, 1–5 p.m. Admission.

C. The **Macon Visitor Center** is located at Fifth and Cherry streets in Terminal Station, one of the grandest and largest railroad stations in the Southeast.

D. The **Harriet Tubman Historical and Cultural Museum** celebrates the history and culture of Macon's African-American community. An interesting exhibit is the collection of African-American inventions that includes the cash register, peanut butter, lawn mower, and Super Soaker water gun. Located at 340 Walnut Street. Open 9 a.m.–5 p.m., Monday through Friday, 10 a.m.–5 p.m. on Saturday, and on Sunday from 2–5 p.m. Admission.

E. Rose Hill Cemetery was designed in 1839 and is a fine example of the romantic landscape park. The cemetery is located on the banks of the Ocmulgee River and contains unusual and rare plants. There is a self-guided tour available. Located at 1091 Riverside Drive. Open during daylight hours.

F. The **African American Heritage Collection** of the **Washington Memorial Library** contains one of the largest collections of genealogy, archives, and biography in the Southeast. Located at 510 College Street.

G. Mercer University was founded in

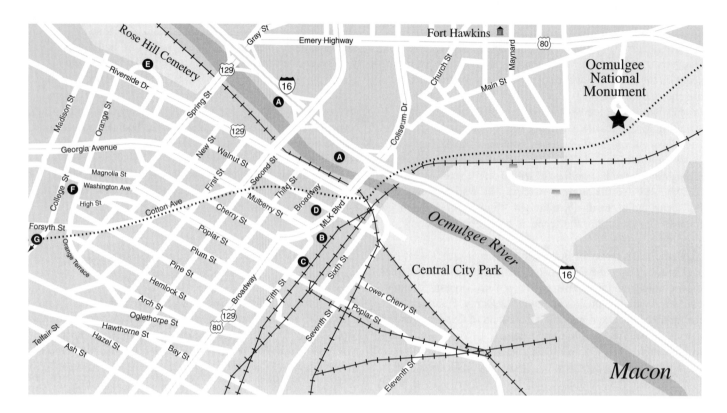

1833 by Baptist leader Jesse Mercer at Penfield in Greene County. The academy was moved to Macon in 1871 and has grown to include nine schools and campuses in Atlanta and four other cities in Georgia. Located on Coleman Avenue and College Street.

2. Macon Museum of Arts & Sciences. The Museum is a fine art and natural history museum with an excellent collection of gems, minerals, and fossils. There are several nature trails, an observatory, and a state of the art planetarium. 4182 Forsyth Road. Open Monday–Thursday, 9 a.m.-5 p.m.; Friday, 9 a.m.–9 p.m.; Saturday, 9 a.m.–5 p.m.; and Sunday, 1 p.m.–5 p.m. Admission.

3. Wesleyan College was the first Women's College in Georgia and the first to grant degrees to women. It was chartered as Georgia Female College on December 23, 1836 and is the oldest women's college in the world. Wesleyan College began classes in 1839 and, by absorbing nearby Clinton Female Institute, graduated the first class in July, 1840. Wesleyan College became associated with the Methodist Church in 1843. Wesleyan College is located at 4760 Forsyth Road.

4. Tobesofkee and **Echeconnee creeks** have been shown on maps since the early 1700s. Bartram's Little Tobesofkee was in actuality Echeconnee Creek, for the present-day Little Tobesofkee is farther north and was not crossed by the Lower Creek Trading Path. Tobesofkee means "I have lost (or spilled) my hominy." However, the original spellings were Togoso-

Benjamin Hawkins

Benjamin Hawkins was appointed Agent for Indian Affairs South of the Ohio River in 1796. He established his home on the Flint River on the Lower Creek Trading Path. His plantation became known as the Creek Agency and was a gathering place for Creeks who came to trade and do business with Americans. Hawkins was of one mind with William Bartram regarding the character of the Southeastern Indians. He was familiar with the *Travels,* although we do not know to what extent he was influenced by Bartram as he formulated his policies for Indian affairs. Hawkins respected the Indians and sought to help them become successful farmers, hoping they could adapt to modern life and thereby escape destruction as a people.

The Creeks were not inclined to the manual labor required to become modern agriculturists. The Creek men viewed farming as work for women and old men, hunting was the occupation of men. Also, the Creeks had become accustomed to receiving presents from the British, French, and Spanish in return for their political alliance, which further reduced the value of manual labor and entrepreneurial enterprises. Hawkins provided the Creeks with seeds, stock animals, and tools and established a four-acre demonstration garden at Coweta. He met with some successes and much resistance.

His successes in Americanizing the Lower Creeks helped divide the nation into traditional and modern factions that led to the Creek War of 1813–1814. Traditional Creek men were hunters but the Lower Creeks were becoming more like their American neighbors who raised cattle, hogs, corn, and cotton for home and market. These Americanized Creek families moved farther away from the towns and lived on independent farms. The conservative factions, mostly Upper Creeks, still hoped to maintain the traditional life of hunting and trading deerskins.

We can only guess what the future would have held if Benjamin Hawkins had been more successful in his efforts to settle the Creeks on farms. Could this have helped them resist being overwhelmed by Americans who were hot with cotton fever? Indeed, there were many Cherokees and Creeks who did not move to Oklahoma but remained behind as members of American communities and became U.S. citizens.

In his role as Indian Agent, Hawkins was deeply concerned with the welfare of the Native Americans. His influence among the Creeks is illustrated by the fact that he was able to talk them out of joining Tecumseh's war. He died in 1816 and is buried on the Flint River just off GA-128.

Detail from a wall at Pasaquan

hatchee and Tobosochte, which would have completely different meanings.

William Bartram crossed Echeconnee Creek at the bridge on Knoxville Road. A Bartram Trail historical marker is located on the Crawford County side of the bridge. Echeconnee means "deer trap." 2

5. Bartram Trail Historical Marker, located on Knoxville Road at Echeconnee Creek in Crawford County. The bridge is an excellent place to view the geological phenomenon known as the Fall Line. Look north from the bridge and one sees a rocky creek typical of the Piedmont. Look south and the creek becomes languid and sandy as it begins its journey over the Coastal Plain.

6. Oak-leaf hydrangea. William Bartram described the oak-leaf hydrangea from those specimens that he found on Tuesday, July 4, 1775, four miles east of Knoxville on Sweetwater Creek.3

7. Bartram Trail Historical Marker. The marker commemorating William Bartram's travels is located behind the Crawford County courthouse in Knoxville. Another plaque on the north side of the courthouse memorializes the travels of **Alexis de Tocqueville** over the Old Federal Road in January 1832.

---

2. Francis Harper fixed the place of discovery for oak leaf hydrangea as being on present day Culpepper Creek, a branch of the Flint. John Goff in *Placenames of Georgia* makes a better argument for Sweetwater Creek, a branch of Echeconnee Creek.

3. *Placenames of Georgia*, by John Goff. University of Georgia Press, Athens, 1975.

8. Lone Star Flag. A marker on the north side of the Crawford County courthouse commemorates Joanna Troutman of Knoxville who created a flag with a single blue star on a white silk background and presented it to the volunteers as they embarked on their fight for Texas independence. The flag was adopted as the national flag of the Republic of Texas. Many Georgians left for Texas to seek adventure and cheap land. It was said that the westward fever carried off much of the population of many older communities.

9. Old Federal Road. This early road followed the present highway from Roberta to the Flint River. It was later named the Wire Road when the telegraph line was built along it. The United States government had the road built and opened by 1813. It ran from Augusta to Warrenton and Sparta. Past that point there were no towns until the road reached Mobile after passing through the Creek Nation. Along that route new towns would grow—Macon and Columbus in Georgia, Montgomery and Greenville in Alabama.

Travel on the Federal Road was comfortless and dangerous. Many of the travelers of the early nineteenth century who published their accounts spoke of many narrow escapes from mishap and many encounters with colorful characters. In his second visit to the American South in 1846, British geologist Sir Charles Lyell wrote that upon leaving Macon for Columbus,

> *For the first time we remarked that our friends, on parting, wished us a safe journey, instead of a pleasant one, as usual.*4

---

4. *A Second Visit to the United States of North America*, Charles Lyell. New York, 1849.

The Federal Road was the great migration route for settlers leaving the Carolinas and Georgia and seeking new cotton land in Alabama and Mississippi. The coming of steamboats brought about the disuse of the section of the Federal Road between Montgomery and Mobile. Railroads and faster, more comfortable ocean-going vessels brought about the demise of much of the rest of the route. It was essentially abandoned, except locally, by the mid 1830s. Sections of the road are still in use and are often called Old Federal Road, even today.

10. Museum of Southeastern Indians. The museum exhibits artifacts and history of the Native Americans who inhabited this region. Open Wednesday through Saturday, 10 a.m.–5 p.m. Admission. Located on Julia Jordan Road, off US-80, west of Roberta.

11. Creek Agency. Benjamin Hawkins' plantation and the Agency for Southeastern Indian Affairs were located where the Old Federal Road crossed the Flint River. Land for the Agency Preserve was set aside on both sides of the river when the area was surveyed for the land lottery. Hawkins was succeeded as Indian agent by former governor David Mitchell who served in that office for only a short time and was replaced by Colonel John Crowell. Because Agent Crowell was a bachelor, it is believed that Lafayette stayed with the agent's brother, Captain Henry Crowell, across the river where there was a suitable hostess in residence. Fort Lawrence was located on the southwest side of the Flint River, directly opposite the Agency.

The town of Francisville was organized by Francis Bacon on the site of the Agency in 1825. He was married to Jeffersonia, Benjamin Hawkins' youngest daughter. Railroads bypassed the town when they were built through the area in the 1850s and the town died.

Benjamin Hawkins' grave overlooks the Flint River at the end of a dirt road off GA-128. The land is in private hands and very little archaeological work has been done at the site.

12. Flint River Crossings. The Flint River, Thronateeskee to the Muskogees, was crossed by several trails in a distance of twelve miles above the Creek Agency. The first crossing was immediately above the GA-128 bridge and was the most common ford during normal weather for travelers bound for Kasihta and Coweta and was called Chelocconeneauhasse. Four miles upriver, just below the mouth of Auchumpkee Creek, was Island Ford, or Otaulgaunene. This ford was used during high water to avoid the lower part of Patsiliga Creek. Three miles farther upriver was Buzzard Roost Ford, known as Sulenojuh. A Kasihta town lived at Buzzard Roost until 1787. The trail leading west from Buzzard Roost was called Smuteyes Trail.

The Sand Hills • 223

Echeconnee Creek, north of the bridge on the Old Knoxville Road, Bibb-Crawford county line. This is the southern edge of the Piedmont.

Echeconnee Creek, south of the bridge on the Old Knoxville Road. This is the beginning of the Coastal Plain.

13. Flint River Adventures is a unique recreation area that is privately owned and offers educational programs on the culture and history of the Southeastern Indians. Maxwell Duke, the owner, has taken the persona of Agent Benjamin Hawkins and uses the voice of Hawkins for several of the historical programs. Classes are available in flint shaping, pottery making, blowgun manufacture, Indian foods, archaeology, and Native-American myths and legends. Archaeological field trips can also be arranged. The centerpiece of the park is the replica of a sixteenth century Yuchi village.

The facilities are located on twenty acres in the fork of Auchumpkee Creek and Flint River. The entrance is at 1471 Minor Road (off US-80). Flint River Adventures is open to visitors by reservation only. Visit the web site for more information and reservations. Admission.

14. Patsiliga Creek has been drawn on maps since the 1760s. The name means *pigeon roost place*.

15. Timothy Barnard lived on the Flint River about a mile southeast of Oglethorpe in Macon County. He was the son of a Scotsman, Captain John Barnard, and nephew of George Galphin. In 1773 he was a Georgia Ranger and Justice of the Peace with jurisdiction over the newly purchased lands north and west of Augusta. During the Revolution Barnard moved to the Creek Nation and worked for the British, but after the war he was reconciled with the Americans. He continued to operate a trading post on the Flint River near Reynolds and became one of Benjamin Hawkins' deputies. He wife was Yuchi and one of their children was Timpoochee Barnard, the Yuchi leader who fought against the Red Stick faction in the First Creek War of 1813–1814.

16. Timpoochee Barnard was born in eastern Alabama, probably in Yuchi Town, during the Revolution when his father was a loyalist refugee. During the First Creek War he commanded Yuchi soldiers and attained the rank of major in the Georgia militia. Though an ally of Georgia he disapproved of the Treaty of Indian Springs and was part of the delegation that traveled to Washington to protest. He lived for years on the Flint River before moving to Fort Mitchell where he died and is buried.

17. Fort Perry was built in 1813 by General John Floyd during the First Creek War. The fort guarded the Federal Road as it passed through friendly Creek territory. The historical marker is located on GA-41 and another stone marker is a half mile east on Fort Perry Road.

18. Bartram Trail Historical Marker. The marker is located on GA-41 at Fort Perry Road and commemorates William Bartram's travels over the Lower Creek Trading Path.

19. The Bartram Trail Conference was created on November 4, 1975, at an organizational meeting in Talbotton. The purpose of the conference was to promote interest in developing a Bartram Trail in the eight participating states and to coordinate a regional approach to reaching that goal. The theme of the conference was the study, preservation, and interpretation of William Bartram's *Travels*. The Bartram Trail Conference contracted with the Bureau of Outdoor Recreation in the United States Department of the Interior to prepare a study of Bartram heritage sites and proposals to commemorate William Bartram's exploration of the Southeast. The conference published the *Bartram Heritage Report* in 1979.

Although it was determined that a national recreation trail connecting all eight states was unfeasible, the efforts of the Bartram Trail Conference did lead to the building of Bartram Trails in the Nantahala, Chattahoochee, DeSoto, and Tuskegee national forests. The Garden Clubs of the participating states were instrumental in erecting the historical markers commemorating Bartram's *Travels*.

The Bartram Trail Historical Marker commemorating the founding of the Bartram Trail Conference is located on US-80 in downtown Talbotton.

20. Pasaquan is the fantastic creation of visionary Eddie Owens Martin, better known as Saint EOM. Martin lived in New York for many years and while gripped by a fever during a severe illness he was visited by people from the future who instructed him to prepare for his role as a channel for their messages on creating peace and beauty in the world. He returned to his family farm in Marion County and as Saint EOM he recreated his visions in the physical world of Pasaquan. With paint, concrete, metal, and tile, he decorated his home and built walls and sculptures for the garden. It was said that he communicated with animals and that his home was protected by snakes. Visitors to Marion County should not miss the chance to visit the museum of one of the South's premier visionaries. Pasaquan is west of Buena Vista on Eddie Owens Martin Road, just off GA-26. Admission.

Counties

Crawford was created in 1822 as part of the land lottery from newly ceded Creek lands and named for William H. Crawford.

Taylor was created in 1852 from portions of other counties and named for Zachary Taylor.

Marion was created in 1827 and named for Revolutionary War hero General Francis Marion.

Talbot was created from Muscogee County in 1827. It is named for Matthew Talbot, member of the legislature and governor in 1819. An interesting bit of Talbot County history is the accomplishments of the Straus family, a Jewish family of Bavaria who settled in Talbotton in 1854. After the Civil War, Lazarus Straus moved to New York and established a crockery and glassware business that became part of Macy's Department Store. His son, Isidor Straus, was the head of Macy's during its growth into a world-class department store. Another son, Oscar, was prominent in government, and Nathan was a philanthropist and leader in health reform, including the move to pasteurize milk.

Itinerary

Miles	Directions
	Begin at Ocmulgee National Monument and turn left (west) on Emery Highway, US-80
.3	Turn left on Main Street
.1	Right on Main Street
.2	Intersection of Maynard Street (turn right to see the replica of Fort Hawkins)
.4	Right on Clinton Street then an immediate left onto Coliseum Drive
.3	Cross the Ocmulgee River (Coliseum Drive becomes Martin Luther King Boulevard)
.4	Turn right on Mulberry Street at the Georgia Music Hall of Fame
.3	Left on Second Street, then the next right on Cotton Avenue
.1	Right on Cherry Street, then the next left on First Street
.1	Right on Poplar Street
.1	Left on New Street
.1	Right on Forsyth Street (take the far right)
.4	Left on College Street
.5	Right on Coleman Avenue
.1	Left on Montpelier Avenue (becomes Columbus Road at Pio Nono Avenue)
2.0	Merge right onto Mercer University Drive (GA-74)
.8	Cross Rocky Creek
1.4	Left on Columbus Road at intersection
3.0	Left on Columbus Road
.2	Cross Tobesofkee Creek
.7	Left on Knoxville Road
.9	Left and Cross US-80 to keep on Knoxville Road
4.1	Cross Echeconnee Creek (Bartram Trail historical marker)
.7	Keep straight on Sutton Road
3.7	Left on Hamlin Road (may be unmarked)
1.5	Pavement ends
2.3.4	Right on Old Knoxville Road
2.1	Right on GA-42
.6	Crawford County Courthouse in Knoxville, keep straight on Agency Street Historical markers for the Bartram Trail, Alexis de Toqueville, Old Federal Road, Texas Lone Star Flag, and Crawford County
.8	Enter downtown Roberta, keep straight on Agency Street (GA-128) and cross US-341. The Benjamin Hawkins monument is located in downtown Roberta
6.6	Turn left to visit the grave of Benjamin Hawkins, keep straight for the itinerary
.3	Cross the Flint River
.4	Right on GA-137 for Butler
4.6	Right on GA-208 at Ficklin Mill
.6	Left on Wainwright Road, CR-254 (unmarked)
4.6	Left on US-19
3.6	Right on West Main Street, GA-96/137
.4	Left on GA-137
4.7	Turn right onto Currington Road after crossing Little Whitewater Creek
7.7	Right on GA-90, then left at Welcome Bruce Chapel Baptist Church
.5	Left onto the dirt road at the 4-way intersection
.1	Right on CR-33
2.4	Keep straight across GA-240
.5	Right on Fort Perry Road (paved)
4.8	Left on GA-41. Historical marker for Bartram Trail, Fort Perry, and Old Federal Road

Lower Creek Towns

Humans have inhabited the Chattahoochee Valley for at least 10,000 years. Clovis points of that era have been found at Bull Creek, which runs through the southern part of Columbus. Sandbars form on rivers below the rapids, creating a convenient crossing place for animals and humans who wish to avoid the dangerous rocks. The ford below the rapids of the Chattahoochee River was located at the Creek town of Coweta. It became one of the most important and well-traveled paths in historical times because of the strength of the Upper and Lower Creeks. Paths through their territory connected the tribes of the Gulf Coast with people on the Atlantic and in the Northeast.

Interesting artifacts found in the central Chattahoochee Valley, if authentic, point to a new source of immigration for Native Americans. A tablet was found near LaGrange that is inscribed with Sumerian cuneiform writing dating from 2040 B.C. A sandstone disk found south of Columbus contains Minoan writing of 3,500 years ago. A Carthaginian coin dating from 325 B.C. and Roman coins of the second century have been found in the area pointing to previously unknown trade routes if not immigration routes. The late Fortson Boyd of Swainsboro believed that these and other artifacts combined with the unusual and distinctive language of the Yuchis pointed to the ancient Minoans as their ancestors.

Evidence of Mississippian Culture exists in the Chattahoochee River floodplain at Rood Creek Mounds near Florence Landing State Park. There probably existed many more mounds that have been swept away by repeated spring floods and reclaimed by the plow. In the wake of the De Soto expedition, the surviving populations regrouped into new towns and societies and rejected centralized leadership. It was these new alliances that the Europeans encountered when they again entered the region more than a century after De Soto.

Creek legend tells that the river valley was originally occupied by Hitchitis and Apalachicolas. In the fourteenth century the Kasihtas, a Muskogean speaking people, arrived in the Chattahoochee Valley and attacked some of the settlements. The Apalachicolas were a peaceful people and persuaded the Kasihtas to join them in a confederation. Later the Cowetas, also Muskogean, settled on the west bank of the river. Thus Kasihta became the white, or peace, town and Coweta was the red, or war, town. The Creeks have since the time of initial European contact been a multicultural nation with several languages. The Lower Towns included speakers of the Muskogee, Yuchi, and Hitchiti languages. Historically, the Creek Confederacy has included more that fifty languages and dialects.

The Spanish province of Apalachicola extended from the confluence of the Chattahoochee and Flint rivers northward to the fall line. About 1672 future governor Salazar visited the province seeking trade and diplomatic relations. Bishop Cal-

Lower Creek Towns in 1775

Muskogee speaking: *Coweta, Kasihta, Lower Eufaula, Hothliwahali*

Hitchiti speaking: *Apalachicola, Chiaha, Hitchita, Oconee, Osochi, Okmulgee, Sowokli (Sabacola)*

Yuchi speaking: *Yuchi (Uchee)*

Historic mills and dam at Columbus, site of the Falls of Coweta

deron came from Cuba in 1674 to reinvigorate the missions of Florida and convert the Indians of the lower Chattahoochee and Apalachicola rivers. The only mission established in Apalachicola was Santa Cruz de Sabacola, located at the forks of the Chattahoochee and Flint rivers. Being a *visita*, an outstation served by an itinerant priest, it lasted only as long as the priest was in town. Santa Cruz de Sabacola was established first in 1674 and re-established about 1680. All Spaniards were expelled from the lower Apalachicola Province in 1681 by order of the cacique of Coweta. Efforts at establishing missions among the Apalachicolas, Cowetas, and Kasihtas became even more difficult as first the English then the French began to trade with the Creeks.[1] Two Franciscan friars visited Coweta again in 1690 but were expelled by the chief.

Dr. Henry Woodward arrived at Coweta in 1685 with packhorses laden with high-quality English goods and set up business. Spanish authorities in Saint Augustine grew alarmed at the growing influence of the English among the towns on the middle Chattahoochee River. To counter this English intrusion on Spanish territory, Governor Don Juan de Cabrera sent troops commanded by Antonio Matheos to evict the English from the Chattahoochee River and arrest Woodward. They destroyed Woodward's warehouse but the intrepid doctor had been forewarned and was long gone. When Matheos returned to Florida Woodward returned to Coweta, then began a game of cat and mouse between the English trader and the Spanish officer. Woodward would leave notes in the vacated villages offering his regrets for having not been in residence to receive the Spanish Lieutenant in a proper manner. An irate Matheos burned the towns of Tuskegee, Coweta, Kasihta, and Kolomoki on January 30, 1686.

Many Cowetas and Kasihtas moved to the Ocmulgee River about 1685 for convenience of trade with the English, which prompted the Carolinians to build a store at Ocmulgee Mounds. All of the towns on the Ocmulgee were abandoned following the Yamassee War and the people returned to the Chattahoochee River.

Spain knew she could hold Apalachicola only by building a permanent settlement and fort. In 1687 Don Enrique Primo de Rivera and a garrison of twenty soldiers were dispatched to build a blockhouse and earthen fort on the Chattahoochee River. They completed their task but were recalled to Saint Augustine two years later when the threat of a French invasion made it necessary that all forces be concentrated in the capital.

---

1. The name *Creeks* is derived from the original name for the Ocmulgee River, Ochesee Creek, upon which the Cowetas, Kasihtas, and Hitchitis lived at the time the English trading post was built at Ocmulgee Mounds. Ochesee was the Hitchiti name for the Muskogean-speaking Cowetas and Kasihtas. The English called these Indians *Ochesee Creeks, Ochesees,* or simply *Creeks.* The Creek Confederacy included speakers of many languages as noted in this chapter. Some modern scholars use the name Muscogulge to include Seminoles, Muskogees, Creeks, etc., and all the associated tribes regardless of language. We can use the term Muskogee only for those speaking that language.

Creek Titles

Mico, principal leader of a town, i.e., *Atasi Mico.*

Tastanagi, war leader.

Hillis haya, spiritual leader or shaman.

Yahola, a leader whose power is derived from his skills as an orator and as master of the black drink ceremony.

Heniha (Eneah), secondary man who advised the mico on domestic matters.

Isti atcagagi, a revered elderly leader who no longer took part in hunting or war.

Imathla (Imala), an advisor or assistant.

Spanish influence waned in the Southeast, except within the environs of Saint Augustine, as the British won the allegience of more and more native tribes.

The English brought with them an item of merchandise that the Spanish had steadfastly refused to trade, and that was the gun. The tame and unarmed Christian Indians of the Spanish mission provinces were no match against the raids of armed English and Indian slave catchers. In 1702 Carolina Governor James Moore led a devastating raid against the missions of Apalachee, even to the gates of Saint Augustine, and effectively removed Spanish influence from Greater Florida.

General James Edward Oglethorpe sponsored a conference at Coweta on August 8, 1739 and on August 21 a treaty was concluded that cemented the friendship between the Creeks and the young Georgia colony. The treaty helped take trade from the French and obtained a pledge that the Creek Confederacy would not join the Spanish nor fight against the English. Although they did not pledge to fight for the English, many young warriors fought with Oglethorpe during the invasion of Florida in 1740 and at the Battle of Bloody Marsh in 1742. The colony would have been lost without their help.

There was little conflict between Georgia and the Creek Nation until the 1760s when the English colony began to expand its boundaries by purchasing new land from her native neighbors. The Creek Confederacy was one of the most democratic societies in the New World, so much so that no treaty ever went uncontested regardless of how many headmen had signed. Europeans had difficulty understanding the diluted nature of Creek national policy. Quite often for the English, and particularly the Americans, any number of signatures was good enough. Not until the time of Alexander McGillivray did the Creek Confederacy appear to act in unison and even then there were dissenters, although they were usually controlled or nullified. During the Revolution the Creeks remained essentially neutral except for border skirmishes by small bands who acted independently.

After the Revolution the state of Georgia began to whittle away at Creek lands. During the Creek War of 1813–1814 the Lower Creek Towns were allied to Georgia and were a refuge for Upper Creeks who were targets of the Red Sticks. This First Creek War was a struggle between traditional and Americanized Creeks and was caused by a number of factors; the building of the Federal Road through Creek territory, the rise of the Tecumseh's Pan-Indian movement, British and Spanish influence in West Florida, the Americanization of the Creek economy, and the resulting loss of traditional cultural and economic values. The Lower Creeks were more closely tied to the economy of Georgia and the Americans. They were more likely to be involved in farming and trade and more likely to live independent of the towns.

Chief William McIntosh of Coweta, Big Warrior of Tuckabatchee, and 500 pro-American Creeks joined the Georgia Militia in a campaign against the Red Sticks in Alabama then fought

Lower Creek Towns

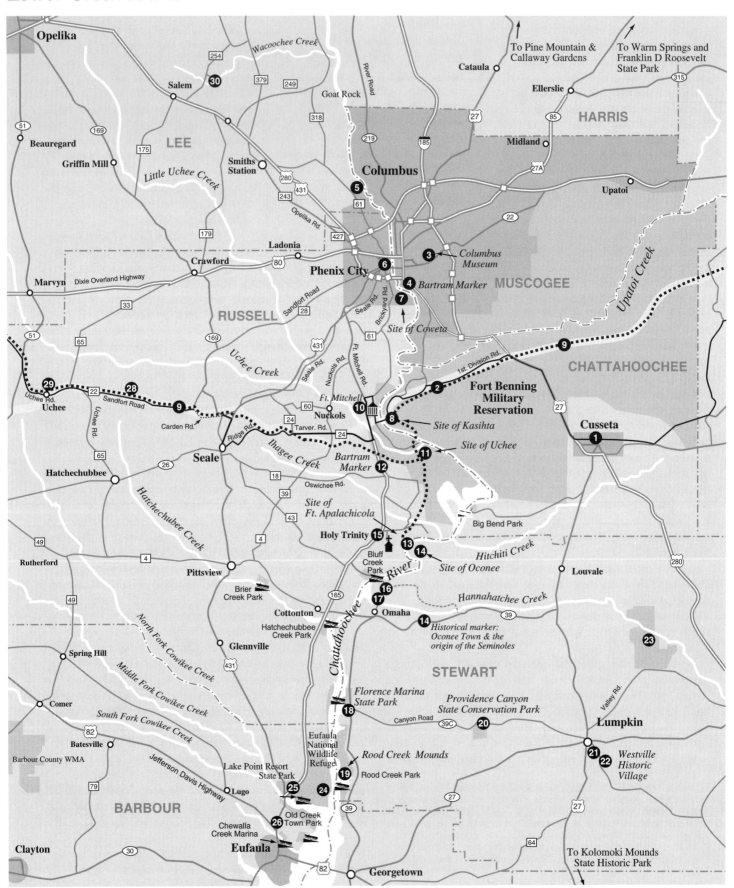

with Andrew Jackson at the Battle of Horseshoe Bend. The war ended in August, 1814 with the Treaty of Fort Jackson. Since most of the Red Stick opposition were either dead or had fled south Jackson dishonored his Creek allies by forcing them to sign the treaty. The Creeks gave up the western half of their territory and were left with a reserve in east central Alabama.

The Treaty of Indian Springs was held at Chief William McIntosh's tavern on February 12, 1825, and brought all Creek land east of the Chattahoochee River under Georgia jurisdiction (the Treaty of Washington, January 24, 1826, legitimized the land sale). William McIntosh, chief of the Cowetas, was assassinated in 1825 for signing the Treaty of Indian Springs and selling the Georgia lands, an act expressly forbidden by the Creek National Council and punishable by death. His cousin, Governor George Troup, was so outraged by McIntosh's death that he resolved to remove all Indians remaining within the boundaries of Georgia. The Indian Springs Land cession was organized into a land lottery in 1827.

The McIntosh faction moved west to Oklahoma beginning in 1827. Other Creeks who saw that their hold on their Alabama home was tenuous began moving soon afterward while others moved to Florida and joined the Seminoles. The United States Congress passed the Indian Removal Bill in 1830, which provided for relocating all Indians to the west of the Mississippi River. This bill affected the Southeast the most because few Indians remained in the Northeast and Midwest.

The Treaty of Cusseta, March 24, 1832, created individual land holdings for the Creeks remaining in Alabama and extended state jurisdiction over the former Creek Nation. For several years thereafter whites and Indians lived among one another, although uneasily. By 1836 many Creeks had sold their land and left for Oklahoma. Those Creeks who remained in Alabama were embittered because white and Indian speculators were falsely selling land, they suffered from increased racial violence, and they resisted being forced to move west. Their only recourse being vengeance, they went to war.

Many of the leaders and warriors of the Creek War of 1836 were non-Muskogees, predominantly Hitchitis and Yuchis. The most prominent leaders were Hitchitis—Jim Henry, Neamathla, and Neamico. The entire region of Alabama and Georgia south of the Federal Road became alarmed and 2,000 whites fled to Columbus for protection. Many farms were attacked and burned. In May 1836, the town of Roanoke in Stewart County, Georgia was attacked and burned by Jim Henry who then used the cotton warehouse as a fortress.

The few thousand Creek warriors were no match against General Winfield Scott and the 13,000 Georgians who joined the militia and swept into the Chattahoochee Valley. By the end of July 1836, the war ended with the capture of Neamathla by Thomas Woodward and Jim Henry's surrender at Fort Mitchell. Whole villages were marched to Fort Mitchell and sent to the west during the winter. Again, Florida became a refuge for those who chose to join the Seminoles.

Jim Henry's biography illustrates the paradoxical nature of the times. He was a mestizo whose mother was Hitchiti and whose father was white. Before taking command of the Creek Warriors, Henry had been a clerk in a mercantile business in Columbus. His path to war was due to racial injustice and violence against his mother's people.

William Bartram's Travels among the Lower Creeks

There were many trails coming to the Lower Creek Towns from Augusta—the Lower Creek Path, the Horse Path, Tom's Path, and numerous connector trails. William Bartram followed the Lower Creek Path that paralleled Upatoi Creek a mile to the south. Today this ancient route corresponds with First Division Road on the Fort Benning Military Reservation. The trail would have crossed the Chattahoochee River at the south end of Lawson Air Field and passed through the town of Yuchi, located at the mouth of Uchee Creek.

Bartram then traveled a few miles south to Apalachicola where he accompanied the resident trader to the ruins of the Spanish Fort Apalachicola. Although the fort was abandoned less than a hundred years earlier the Creeks had forgotten its history and believed it to have been built by an ancient people. The fort is on private property in the bend of the river near Holy Trinity Retreat. William Bartram discovered the bottlebrush buckeye on the banks of the Chattahoochee River in the vicinity of Apalachicola Town.

Resuming their journey to Mobile, Bartram and the traders traveled along the ridge on the south of Uchee Creek coinciding with the later Federal Road to the present-day community of Uchee. Beyond Uchee Bartram's route followed Slasheye Road, a curious name, that may be a remnant of the Indian path in Georgia known as Slosh-eye Trail.

Legend

1. Chattahoochee County Library & Archives
2. Fort Benning
3. Falls of Coweta
4. Columbus Museum
5. William McIntosh
6. Phenix City
7. Site of Coweta
8. Site of Kasihta
9. Federal Road
10. Fort Mitchell Chattahoochee Indian Heritage Center
11. Site of Yuchi Town
12. Bartram Trail Historical Marker
13. Fort Apalachicola
14. Origin of the Seminoles
15. Holy Trinity
16. Fort McCreary Reconstruction
1 . Creek Village Replica
1 . Florence Marina State Park
19. Rood Creek Mounds
20. Providence Canyon State Conservation Park
21. The Singer Company, 1838
22. Westville Historic Village
23. Hannahatchee Creek Wildlife Management Area
24. Eufaula National Wildlife Refuge Wingspread Wildlife Drive
25. Lakepoint State Park Resort
26. Tom Mann's Fish World
27. Eufaula
28. Sand Fort
29. Uchee
30. Salem-Shotwell Bridge

Sites

1. Chattahoochee County Library & Archives are located in the Old Jail just off Courthouse Square in Cusseta.

2. Fort Benning is the largest military installation in the world. The post contains numerous important archaeological sites, the most important being the site of Kasihta at Lawson Air Field. Kasihta was the principal peace town of the Muskogees and the Creek Confederation. First Division Road follows closely William Bartram's route over the Lower Creek Trading Path. With many thousands of acres of undeveloped land the Fort Benning post, like many military reserves, has been a boon to the preservation of native botanical and wildlife species. Red cockaded woodpeckers are closely studied at Fort Benning and the Nature Conservancy has completed a biological survey that found many other rare species. Fort Benning is named for General Henry Lewis Benning, a Confederate officer who lived in Columbus.

3. Falls of Coweta. A series of steep rapids marked the fall line of the Chattahoochee River. They extended for several miles upstream of the Dillingham Street Bridge but now are mostly obscured by the dams and impoundments that supplied water to the mills of Columbus. The falls were mentioned by early travelers and appear on early maps. American entrepreneurs realized the economic advantage of establishing a manufacturing city at the falls. On December 24, 1827, the Georgia General Assembly passed an act establishing the town of Columbus on a reserve of 1,200 acres.

The Creeks believed a giant serpent, the **Tie Snake**, lived in the rapids and played mischief on their people. This may explain why crossings were made upriver or downriver of the falls. Crossing over such extensive rapids was of course inherently hazardous but the danger was attributed to the monster who wrapped his coils around victims and pulled them into the churning waters. When the first steamboats began to service the Chattahoochee River in the early nineteenth century, accidents were attributed to the Tie Snake who had moved downstream from the falls to vanquish this new intruder.

4. Columbus Museum. This excellent regional museum features American art and the history of the Chattahoochee River Valley. Chattahoochee Legacy gallery contains exhibits of the natural history of the region and the history of the Lower Creek Towns. A 1791 edition of the *Travels* is on display. The museum has sponsored archaeological research of Native-American sites in the Chattahoochee River Valley.

Bottlebrush buckeye (Aesculus parviflora) *discovered by William Bartram on the banks of the Chattahoochee River. It occurs naturally in rich woods and bottomland from the Chattahoochee River to the Alabama River.*

1251 Wynnton Road. Open 10 a.m.–5 p.m., Tuesday through Saturday and on Sunday, 1–5 p.m.

5. William McIntosh was the chief of Coweta and had an extensive plantation on the Chattahoochee River north of Columbus. He was the son of Captain William McIntosh who worked among the Creeks as a British agent and commissary during the Revolution. After the war Captain McIntosh settled at Mallow Plantation among his relatives near Darien. General McIntosh's mother was of pure Muskogee blood.

McIntosh attained the office of general during the Creek War of 1813–1814 when he and Creek soldiers fought with Andrew Jackson against the Red Sticks. McIntosh was assassinated at his plantation near Whitesburg, Georgia, on May 1, 1825, for signing the Treaty of Indian Springs. His motives for signing the treaty are not entirely clear and he certainly knew that it was an illegal act condemned by the Creek National Council. He believed that the Creeks must eventually move west, possibly the sooner the better. Additionally, he gained financially from the sale of the land east of the Chattahoochee.

After the assassination of McIntosh his half-brother Roderick and his son Chilly lead the first large migration of Creeks to the West.

6. Phenix City was once called Sodom for its cultural similarities to the biblical city. Located on the edge of the Creek Nation and out of reach of Georgia law the early village was a refuge for renegades and fugitives. Tyrone Power visited Sodom in 1834 and had this to say,

On the Alabama side we found ourselves within a wild-looking village, scattered through the edge of the forest, bearing the unattractive name of Sodom; few of its denizens were yet stirring; they are composed chiefly of "minions o' the moon," outlaws from the neighbouring States. Gamblers, and other desperate men, here find security from their numbers, and from the vicinity of a thinly inhabited Indian country, whose people hold them in terror, yet dare not refuse them a hiding-place. These bold outlaws, I was informed, occasionally assemble to enjoy an evening's frolic in Columbus, on which occasions they cross the dividing bridge in force, all armed to the teeth: the warrants in the hands of the US Marshal are at such times necessarily suspended, since to execute a caption would require a muster greater than any within his command. If unmolested, the party usually proceed to the nearest hotel, drink deeply, make what purchases they require for the ladies of their colony, pay promptly, and, gathering the stragglers together, return peaceably into the territory, wherin their present rule is by report absolute.[2]

In the early 1950s Phenix City was again the scene of organized gambling, prostitution, vote fraud, extortion, and murder. Organized crime was fueled by the availability of young and reckless soldiers at nearby Fort Benning. The gangster element overstepped the bounds of tolerance among the people of Alabama when they assassinated Attorney General Albert Patterson and bombed the home of Hugh Bentley. Patterson's son, John, began a crusade to clean up Phenix city, which was brought under martial law. John Patterson became governor of Alabama in the late 1950s. Happily, Phenix City is today a peaceable and growing city, the seat of Russell County.

The southern part of Phenix City near the Dillingham Street Bridge was once the property of Paddy Carr, a noted Creek leader of the early nineteenth century. The river front has been made into a park with an amphitheater that provides a venue for open air concerts. Visitors can stroll along the river's edge and view the shoals once known as the Falls of Coweta.

7. Site of Coweta. The site of Coweta is just south of Phenix City in the area of the Alabama State Docks. Coweta was the red town of the Lower Creeks and provided leadership during times of war. Franciscan priests arrived at Coweta and the Lower Towns in 1690 to win converts and establish a mission. They met with little enthusiasm because Henry Woodward and the Carolina traders had completely won the allegiance of the Creeks.

General James Oglethorpe traveled to Coweta in the summer of 1739 to meet with representatives of the Creek, Choctaw and Chickasaw nations. He helped Britain repair

---

2. Tyrone Power, *Impressions of America*; London, 1836. Reprinted with the permission of the University of Georgia Libraries

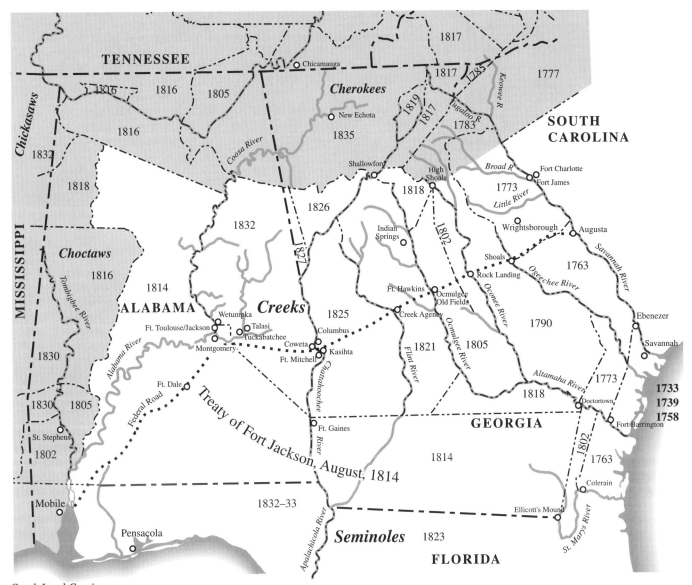

Creek Land Cessions

her damaged friendship with the Creeks and signed a treaty with them on August 21.

When Marquis de Lafayette crossed the Chattahoochee River on March 31, 1825, the young men of Coweta so revered the general that they pulled his carriage from the ferry barge to the top of the river bluff—so that Lafayette should not muddy his boots. He was greeted by Little Prince and entertained by a ball game. He met one of the prominent players, the young Chilly McIntosh, who had recently lost his father. Chilly expressed to Lafayette his belief that the proximity of civilization had brought few benefits but many vices and his hope that by moving farther west his people could maintain their cultural integrity.

Chigelley was the firstman of Coweta during the founding of Georgia and was a brother of Emperor Brim of Kasihta. Upon Brim's death around 1732, Chigelley held power until Brim's son, Malatchi, came of age in 1746.

Malatchi was apparently associated with Coweta, though his father was Emperor Brim of Kasihta. Malatchi was an important Creek leader during the early years of the Georgia colony and was a cousin to Mary Musgrove. He courted the French in 1749–1750 during a period when friction between the Creeks and Georgia was running high. He died in 1756 and his son Togulki took his place as headman.

Yahola Micco, was the leader of Eufaula Town and was the most noted orator of the Creek Confederacy during his lifetime. He traveled to Washington in 1825 to protest the Treaty of Indian Springs but later became an advocate for removal to the west. He died from the fatigue of travel when he and his town moved to Arkansas territory.

8. The site of **Kasihta** was located where Lawson Field is today. Kasihta furnished the chiefs for the Lower Towns by right of being the first town among the Muskogees. Kasihta was the White Town, or peace town, providing leadership during times of peace. When Oglethorpe signed the treaty with the Creeks on August 21, 1739, Georgians and Creeks had to cross the river from their meeting in Coweta to Kasihta because all such treaties had to be concluded at the peace town. First Division Road today follows the route of the Old Federal Road, and Lower Creek Trading Path, through Fort Benning to the site of Kasihta.

Emperor Brim was the most powerful Creek leader from 1700 to 1732. He was an accomplished diplomat, playing the French, Spanish, and English to the advantage of his people. In 1702 his warriors assisted the Carolinians in destroying the Spanish missions in Florida. He may have been responsible for instigating the Yamassees to attack the English without endangering his own warriors to any great extent. The Creeks then helped subdue and disperse the Yamassees when the war became overly disruptive to trade. His niece was Mary Musgrove, Oglethorpe's interpreter.

Broken Arrow was a Muskogee town that was immediately downriver of Coweta and was a satellite town to Coweta, although it had its own busk ground and separate identity. The Muskogee name for the town was Likatcka.

Little Prince was speaker of the Creek Nation in the early 1820s and a resident of Bro-

Lower Creek Towns • 231

Plumleaf Azalea (Rhododendron prunifolium)

ken Arrow, although his home town was Okchai on the Coosa River. He was also known as Bird Tail King, Mad Far Off Warrior, and Tustunnuggee Hopole. He married Hannah Hale, who was abducted from Taliaferro County, Georgia in 1777 and raised among the Creeks.

9. The Federal Road was begun in 1806 with a Congressional appropriation of $6,400 to construct a post road from Athens, Georgia to Fort Stoddert in Alabama. After crossing the Ocmulgee River at Ocmulgee Old Fields, the road entered the Creek Confederacy. Although the United States believed that the 1805 Treaty of Washington gave them permission to construct a road, the decentralized nature of the Creek government brought about delays in actual construction.

Impending war with Great Britain made evident the necessity of completing a road to connect the eastern seaboard with Louisiana. With the nature of the road now being military, the Creeks denied permission for it to pass through their territory. At a meeting in Tuckabatchee in September 1811, Benjamin Hawkins bluntly told the Creeks that the road was coming, with or without their permission.

When it officially opened in 1811, the Federal Road became one of the irritants that lead to the Creek War of 1813–1814. When the Americans gained title to the southern part of Alabama and all land east of the Chattahoochee River the Federal Road became the main immigration route through the Creek Nation for Americans bound for the fertile cotton lands of Alabama and Mississippi. By that time the road had extended in both directions to Augusta and Mobile. Many sections of the road are still being used today, including First Division Road in Fort Benning and Sandfort Road in Russell County, Alabama. When Columbus was surveyed the Federal Road was rerouted to run from Fort Perry through Talbotton and Columbus. The modern equivalent of the Old Federal Road is US-80 from Macon to Montgomery.

10. Fort Mitchell was constructed by General John Floyd and the Georgia Militia in November 1813 at the outbreak of the Creek War. Floyd constructed a string of forts along the Federal Road at a day's march from one another. After Fort Perry came Fort Mitchell, Sandfort, Fort Bainbridge, and Fort Hull. Fort Mitchell was named for the Georgia governor during the First Creek War, David Mitchell.

Fort Mitchell became a station on the Federal Road and in 1824 it was renovated and became the headquarters for the Indian agent to the Creeks. In 1822 the Asbury Indian School and Mission was built a mile to the north but closed in 1830 when the pupils were sent to Oklahoma. The Treaty of Fort Mitchell, signed on November 27, 1827, set into motion the events that eventually removed the Creeks to Oklahoma.

Fort Mitchell is today the site of a Russell County park that preserves the archaeological resources and interprets the role of the fort and the Federal Road in the history of East Alabama.

Chattahoochee Indian Heritage Center. The Creek Trail of Tears Memorial is a monument to the Creek families expelled in 1836. It is located on a hill in Fort Mitchell Park. The monument has four sections representing the four directions of the earth. Bronze slabs contain the names of the heads of families forcibly sent to Oklahoma between 1836 and 1838. A ball field lies just below the memorial where traditional ball games are played during special events. Plans include the construction of a visitor's center and reconstruction of Fort Mitchell and the Crowell Indian Agency.

The **Indian Cultural Festival** is held at Columbus College during the second weekend of October.

11. Site of Yuchi Town. William Bartram visited Yuchi Town around July 11, 1775 and found it to be a large and well-designed community. Yuchi Town was indeed one of the largest towns in the whole Southeast. Marquis de Lafayette, his son George, and his secretary Levasseur visited Yuchi and found it to be one of the most beautiful places they had visited and the inhabitants to be extraordinarily kind and generous. When the Frenchmen crossed Line Creek into Alabama a few days later, Levasseur was not so flattering in his description of the Americans who had settled on the edge of the Creek Nation.

12. Bartram Trail Historical Marker, AL-165 in Oswitchee, commemorates William Bartram's visit to the Lower Creek Towns in July, 1775. The marker incorrectly names William Bartram as botanist to King George III, a position held by his father, John Bartram.

13. Fort Apalachicola, 1689. Florida Governor Diego Quiroba y Losada realized that a permanent settlement in the upper part of Apalachicola was the only way to maintain Spain's claim on the frontier of Florida. He dispatched Captain Don Enrique Primo de Rivera to build a blockhouse and fort among the Creeks. Fort Apalachicola was completed in 1689 but Rivera was recalled to St. Augustine two years later because of the threat of a French assault on the capital. The fort fell into decline and the region was abandoned to the English. Francis Harper wrote that what Bartram believed to be the ancient city of Apalachicola was actually the ramparts of Fort Apalachicola. However, Frank Schnell of the Columbus Museum has visited the site of Fort Apalachicola and doesn't think that it fits the description given by Bartram. The Fort Apalachicola site is owned by Russell County but is not accessible to the public at this time. A historical marker is located on AL-165 at Terminal Road in Holy Trinity.

14. Origin of the Seminoles. During the time of Bartram's visit to the Lower Creek Towns the Oconees, a Hitchiti people, lived along the east side of the Chattahoochee River near Omaha and Hannahatchee Creek. In the mid-1700s a branch of the Oconees broke with the Creek Confederacy and traveled south to Alachua Savannah where they were called Seminoles. A historical marker commemorating this event is located on GA-39 where the ancient trail to Florida passed a few miles east of Omaha.

Earlier in the eighteenth century the Oconees were living on the Oconee River, which takes its name from their town. Oconee town was south of Milledgeville and above the mouth of Town Creek.

15. Holy Trinity. The Shrine of Holy Trinity is the original chapel of the Missionary Servants of the Most Blessed Trinity. The chapel was constructed by Father Thomas Augustine Judge when he began Catholic missionary work in the Southeast. Catholic Sisters arrived to assist in the missionary effort and lived temporarily in a remodeled chicken coop. A house was constructed in 1924 but burned in 1930. The property is now the Holy Trinity Retreat and contains the original chapel and living quarters. Visitors are welcome to visit the chapel and Emmaus Garden. A short woodland walk ends at an opening in the forest where benches are provided for meditation. Located off AL-165 on Terminal Road.

16. Fort McCreary Reconstruction. Fort McCreary blockhouse was built during the

Creek Indian War of 1836. A replica now stands on the site of the original structure. This hill once commanded a view of extensive open fields to the west but the view is now obstructed by pine trees.

17. Creek Village Replica. Members of the Suwannee Bend Creeks of White Springs, Florida, plan to re-create a Creek village near the site of the early eighteenth century town of Oconee, the mother town of the Seminoles. The village is a work in progress and is located just north of the town of Omaha near the replica of Fort McCreary.

18. Florence Marina State Park. Florence Marina is a recreation park with facilities for boating and fishing on Lake Walter F. George. The area is rich in Native-American heritage dating from prehistory. The park is just north of Rood Creek Mounds, a late Mississippian site on the banks of the Chattahoochee River. Part of the picnic area at Florence Marina was closed off in recent years because it was discovered to be a Native American burial site when bones were exposed in the river bank. A group of Georgia Creeks is rebuilding a Native-American village at the park.

The site of **Roanoke** is two miles south of Florence Marina. Roanoke was burned in 1836 by Jim Henry and his Hitchiti warriors. The Kirbo Interpretive Center has exhibits about the Creeks who lived in the area during the early part of the nineteenth century and the early white settlers of Stewart County. Display cases feature the reptiles, birds, mammals, and plants found near the park. Florence was a nineteenth century town that grew up near the site of Roanoke and prospered as a cotton depot. A wooden bridge once crossed the river at Florence but was destroyed by spring floods.

Florence Marina State Park is open 7 a.m.–10 p.m., daily. The office and interpretive center are open 8 a.m.–5 p.m. Located sixteen miles west of Lumpkin at the end of GA-39C.

19. Rood Creek Mounds. This Mississippian town site was inhabited from about 1000–1550 AD. It was the center of a chiefdom extending throughout the Chattahoochee Valley and contained as many as 3,500 people at the height of its occupation. The village site contains eight mounds that were surrounded by a moat and wooden palisade. The largest mound is a twenty-five-foot high pentagon but most of the mounds are circular and much smaller, only a few feet high. Rood Creek Mounds is located within Army Corps of Engineers property and is a protected site. The mounds may be visited only during guided tours conducted each Saturday by the park rangers at Florence Marina State Park. Tours leave the park office at 10 a.m.

Providence Canyon State Park

20. Providence Canyon State Conservation Park. Providence Canyon is one of the largest canyons east of the Mississippi River, but it didn't even exist before the middle of the last century. When white settlers moved into the Chattahoochee River Valley in the late 1820s they cleared the forests and planted cotton. Being located at the southern edge of the Fall Line Sandhills, the steep terrain increased the incidence of erosion. Once the gullies broke through the underlying layer of iron ore they grew deeper and became canyons. They continued to deepen until they reached a layer of sand and clay that was more resistant. The seven canyons are now growing wider rather than deeper. The layers of sand range in color from white to rust, yellow, and salmon.

There are a number of rare species that inhabit Providence Canyon, including the plumleaf azalea that grows along the braided streams at the floor of the canyon. This beautiful, bright red native azalea blooms in late July and early August when one would think it was too hot for such a display. Plumleaf azalea is found only in the central Chattahoochee Valley and is most abundant at Providence Canyon.

Providence Canyon State Park covers 1,108 acres. There is a seven-mile backcountry hiking trail and primitive camping sites. The interpretive center contains exhibits on the geology of the area and the plants and animals found in the park. Providence Canyon is open daily from 7 a.m.–6 p.m., September 15 through April 14 and 7 a.m.–9 p.m. during the rest of the year. Office and interpretive center hours are 8 a.m.–5 p.m. Located on GA-39C seven miles west of Lumpkin.

21. The Singer Company. The Singer Company is Georgia's oldest operating hardware store. It was established in 1838 as a shoe shop by German immigrant shoemaker Johann George Singer. After the Civil War the business developed into a general mercantile establishment. The business moved into the current location in 1894. The Singer Company still sells hardware but has added antiques and gifts for the tourist trade. Located on the courthouse square in Lumpkin.

22. Westville Historic Village. Time stands still in Westville, and the year is 1850. All of the buildings within the town are original to the era, although they have been moved from other locations. Employees and volunteers dressed in period costumes guide visitors through the homes and businesses. Craftsmen demonstrate skills during special events when the gin and cotton press are also in operation. Visitors learn how to make candles, syrup, soap, and dyes. The farm garden is planted seasonally and fresh-baked gingerbread is available in the kitchen.

Westville has a number of special-event weekends throughout the year. Extra special events are May Day, Fourth of July, and the Fall Fair held at the end of October and beginning of November. Open daily from 10 a.m.–5 p.m., except New Year's Day, Thanksgiving, Christmas, and most Mondays. Located on Mulberry Street a half mile from downtown Lumpkin.

23. Hannahatchee Creek Wildlife Management Area. Follow Valley Road from US-27 at the Lumpkin city limits or take the first paved road from GA-27 three miles west of Richland.

24. Eufaula National Wildlife Refuge was established to provide a stopover for migrating waterfowl in passage from the Tennessee Valley to the Gulf Coast. The refuge lies along the Chattahoochee River at Lake Walter F. George and Cowikee Creek.

Wingspread Wildlife Drive. This 7.5-mile nature drive provides access to Eufaula National Wildlife Refuge. The drive leads to impoundments, an observation tower, and the Chattahoochee River. Access is from AL-165, north of Eufaula.

25. Lakepoint State Park Resort is a comfortable resort park on the shores of Lake Eufaula. The park provides facilities for RV camping, tent camping, swimming, hiking, tennis, and picnicking. Lakepoint Park has a golf course, inn, cottages, store, gift shop, restaurant, and convention facilities. Park staff operate numerous wildlife programs throughout the year. Located on US-431, six miles north of Eufaula.

26. Tom Mann's Fish World, the world's largest freshwater aquarium, is located six miles north of Eufaula on US-41. Open daily. Admission.

27. Eufaula is named for a Lower Creek Town that was located nearby and is well known for its spring tour of homes.

28. Sand Fort was constructed during the Creek War of 1813–1814. It was located on Sandfort Road about halfway between Seale and Uchee.

29. Uchee. When you see Good Hope Church on AL-22 you are in the limits of the vanished town of Uchee. Uchee started as a stage stop on the Old Federal Road in the 1830s and grew into a thriving community until the railroad was built, bypassing Uchee and causing its decline.

30. Salem-Shotwell Bridge. Covered Bridge over Wacoochee Creek north in Lee County. Located north of US-280/432 just off CR-254.

Nearby

Museum of East Alabama, downtown Opelika.

Pine Mountain is sometimes thought to be the southernmost peak of the Appalachian Mountains but it lies entirely within the Piedmont. Its origin is unknown.

Franklin D. Roosevelt State Park is much more than the famous Little White House, it also includes much of the Pine Mountain Ridge. Picnic areas and a thirty-three-mile hiking trail have wonderful views of the countryside. Located on GA-190 off US-27, five miles east of Pine Mountain.

Callaway Gardens contains 14,000 acres of woodlands, lakes, and gardens. Mr. Cason Callaway purchased worn-out cotton land and created this educational and horticultural wonderland for public enjoyment. Facilities include the John A. Sibley Horticulture Center, Cecil B. Day Butterfly Center, and Mr. Cason's Vegetable Garden. Headquarters for Victory Garden South is at Callaway Gardens.

The Azalea Trail is Callaway Garden's best-known and most visited attraction. It displays one of the world's largest collections of azaleas with over 700 varieties. The Wildflower Trail features Virginia Callaway's favorites. Located on US-27, Pine Mountain, Georgia.

George T. Bagby State Park is a recreation park on Lake Walter F. Georgia. It is located on GA-39 north of Fort Gaines.

Fort Gaines Frontier Village. Fort Gaines was settled in 1814 around a frontier fort. Frontier Village contains pioneer log cabins from the area and a reproduction of the original blockhouse.

Kolomoki Mounds State Historic Park contains seven Mississippian mounds of the twelfth and thirteenth centuries, including the oldest great temple mound in Georgia. The museum houses artifacts of the period and explains the culture of the Swift Creek and Weeden Island people. The Kolomoki Indian Festival is held the second Saturday of October.

Itinerary

Miles	Directions
	Begin at the intersection of Fort Perry Road and GA-41 and travel south
1.7	Right at Oakland Church of God onto CR-55 (becomes CR-64)
6.5	Left on GA-355
3.9	Cross Pine Knot Creek
	Note: GA-255 makes several sharp turns to avoid the boundary of Fort Benning Reservation
10.3	Right on GA-26
8.6	Right on US-27
6.2	Left on First Division Road (turn at the Old Federal Road historical marker)
5.3	Left on Dixie Road
4.3	Right on Sunshine Road
1.9	Cross the Chattahoochee River
2.2	Left on AL-165
.8	Cross Uchee Creek
.8	Right on Russell-24 (Bradley Road)
	Becomes Tarver Road after crossing Nuckolds Road
5.2	Tarver Road becomes Ridge Road after the intersection
2.3	Pavement ends
2.7	The road bears right
.6	Right on Owichee Road
.6	Right on US-431
2.2	Left on N Al-169
.6	Left on Carden Road
2.8	Keep straight on Sandfort Road
5.5	Keep Right
6.0	Right on N Al-51
.5	Left on Slosh Eye Road (unpaved)

234 • *Lower Creek Towns*

The park has a recreation area with camping, picnic area, hiking trails, and lakes for fishing and boating. Located off US-27 north of Blakely.

Thronateeska Heritage Museum of History and Science. Natural history and the heritage of southwest Georgia are exhibited. Located at 100 Roosevelt Avenue, Albany.

Chehaw National Indian Festival is one of the major Indian festivals in the Southeast and celebrates the heritage of the Muskogee people. Traditional skills, dancing, crafts, food, storytelling, and lectures are featured in this three-day festival. The festival is held the third weekend of May at Chehaw Park in Albany.

Abbeville, Alabama, is the only colonial settlement in East Alabama.

Counties

Chattahoochee, GA. Created in 1854 and named for the Chattahoochee River.

Muscogee, GA. Created in 1825 and named for the principal people of the Creek Confederation.

Stewart, GA. Created in 1830 and named for Revolutionary War patriot General Daniel Stewart of Midway, Georgia.

Lee, AL. Created in 1866 and named for General Robert E. Lee.

Russell, AL. Created in 1832 and named for Colonel Gilbert C. Russell of Mobile.

Barbour, AL. Created in 1832 and named for Governor James Barbour.

Columbus

One of the earliest descriptions of Columbus is found in the writings of Captain Basil Hall, the renowned traveler who saw Columbus in March 1828 just as the lots for the new city were to be sold. He wrote,

*We arrived, fortunately, just in the nick of time to see the curious phenomenon of an embryo town—a city as yet without a name, or any existence in law or fact, but crowded with inhabitants, ready to commence their municipal duties at the tap of an auctioneer's hammer.*3

Whereas visitors to most cities are shown the great edifices and important historical sites, Basil and Margaret Hall were guided along a single raw road cut through the forest and told to imagine a great city where then existed only surveyor's stakes. Because the sale of lots was yet to happen, the small huts and box-like houses were built on trucks so that they could be moved when the owner knew the location of his property. Carpenters had pre-cut lumber stored in piles ready for buyers to order a house. A state official told Hall that 900 people were assembled and ready to take possession of lots and that 3,000–4,000 would be present on the day of the sale.

Charles Lyell visited Columbus in 1846 and wrote this remarkable statement,

Here, as at Milledgeville, the clearing away of the woods, where these Creek Indians once pursued their game, has caused the soil, previously level and unbroken, to be cut into by torrents, so that deep gullies may every where be

3. Basil Hall, *Travels in North America;* Edinburgh, 1829. Reprinted here by permission of the University of Georgia Library.

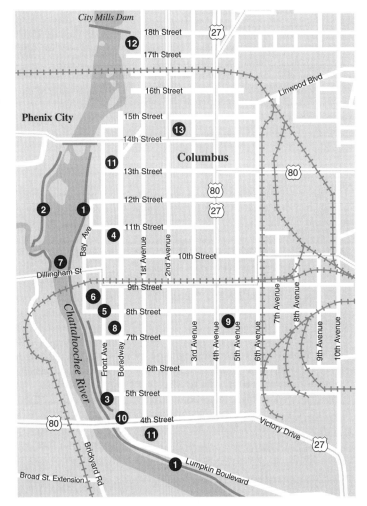

Columbus

1. Riverwalk Park
2. Chattahoochee River Park
3. Chattahoochee Promenade
4. Mirabeau Buonaparte Lamar
5. Center of the Sunbelt South
6. Columbus Iron Works Convention and Trade Center
7. Dillingham Street Bridge
8. Trader's Log Cabin
9. Columbus Black Heritage Tour
10. Bartram Trail Historical Marker
11. Confederate Naval Museum
12. Historic Mills
13. Uptown

seen; and I am assured that a large proportion of the fish, formerly so abundant in the Chattahoochee, have been stifled by the mud.[4]

The Georgia Assembly reserved a five mile square portion of the recent Creek cession to found a great town at the head of navigation on the Chattahoochee River. It was believed that a great manufacturing city would grow up at the falls and take its power from the river. Columbus indeed grew quickly and became an important mill town. The first mill built at Columbus was Jones Mills, which began as a grist mill in 1828 and was built on lot #1. It became City Mills and operated under that name for over a century. After the Civil War the Eagle Mill was rebuilt as the Eagle and Phenix Mills and by 1878 was the largest textile mill in the South. The Columbus riverfront is the largest nineteenth-century industrial complex remaining in the South.

The coming of the Civil War prevented the city from matching the industrial growth seen in Northern cities. Another problem for Columbus was finding a dependable labor force in a former slave territory where it was difficult to find skilled mechanics and operators. A white man could always find cheap land and lead an independent life as a farmer with the hopes of someday making a fortune with cotton. New sources of power developed in the late nineteenth century and allowed mills to be built where there were sources of labor rather than sources of falling water, and most new textile mills were built throughout the Piedmont. Unfortunately, some of the historic industrial structures in Columbus have been demolished recently when no buyers could be found.

4. Charles Lyell, *A Second Visit to the United States of North America;* New York, 1849. Reprinted here by permission of the University of Georgia Library.

Sites

1. Riverwalk Park follows the bank of the Chattahoochee River from the Fourteenth Street Dam to the Infantry Museum in Fort Benning. This elegant strolling park allows walkers to view the rapids and river. Historic markers note such historic places as the sites of Coweta and Kasihta, and events such as the crossings of James Oglethorpe and Lafayette. Among the notable writers and travelers who crossed the Chattahoochee River at Columbus were Lorenzo and Peggy Dow, Captain Basil and Margaret Hall, Sir Charles Lyell, Adam Hodgson, Louis Le Clerc Milfort, and Tyrone Power.

2. Chattahoochee River Park. The Phenix City riverfront has been developed into a park that extends from Dillingham Street Bridge to the Fourteenth Street Bridge. The park has a walking trail and amphitheater for outdoor events.

3. Chattahoochee Promenade begins on the river side of the Iron Works and follows the railroad tracks on the bluff above Riverwalk. Historical markers along the walk tell of historical events and commercial development of Columbus. The Founders Garden at Front and Fifth Streets features historical markers commemorating events in the history of Columbus.

4. Mirabeau Buonaparte Lamar was the founder of the *Columbus Enquirer* newspaper, which he began on May 29, 1828. Upon the death of his wife, he moved to Texas in 1835 and participated in the war for Texas independence. He succeeded Sam Houston as the second president of the Republic of Texas. Lamar was born near Louisville, Georgia and lived in Warren and Putnam counties before moving to Columbus. He was an accomplished poet, brother to L.Q.C. Lamar and uncle to L.Q.C. Lamar, II. His newspaper office was located near Broadway and Eleventh Street.

5. Center of the Sunbelt South. The geographic center of the Sunbelt is located in Columbus and is identified by a marker at the intersection of Eighth Street and Front Avenue, at the Columbus Iron Works.

6. Columbus Iron Works Convention and Trade Center, One Arsenal Place. This beautiful and historic building complex was once a foundry for cannons, armor, and engines for Confederate gunboats. The first breech-loading cannons were built at the Columbus Iron Works. The facility was begun in 1853 during a period when industry was booming in Columbus and it seemed that the city would fulfill its promise as an industrial center for the South. After the war the foundry manufactured implements and cast iron items for home and farm. From 1880 to the 1920s the Columbus Iron Works produced the world's most popular, and successful, ice machine.

The Iron Works complex is now the Columbus Convention Center, one of the largest and finest facilities in the South and one of the most beautiful industrial structures in Georgia. The second floor contains an exhibition area devoted to the history of the Iron Works.

7. Dillingham Street Bridge occupies the site of the first bridge to span the Chattahoochee River. The original bridge was built in 1832 by Horace King, a slave who became the most prominent bridge builder in the area. Original brickwork from King's bridge may be seen under the ramp of the present bridge on Riverwalk Park. The Dillingham Street Bridge is festooned with lights which adds a festive note to river in the evening.

8. Trader's Log Cabin is an authentic early nineteenth century log cabin that is of the kind used by traders and early settlers in the region. It is located in the historic district at 708½ Broadway.

9. Columbus Black Heritage Tour celebrates noted African-Americans who have called Columbus home. Among them is Ma Rainey, the pioneer blues singer. Her home is located on Fifth Avenue between Seventh and Eighth Streets. The African American Heritage Festival is held in early June each year.

10. Bartram Trail Historical Marker, Fourth Street and Broadway.

11. Confederate Naval Museum. This unique museum contains the remains of two gunboats armored and outfitted at Columbus and the *Virginia,* a Gulf Coast blockade runner. When Federal troops captured Columbus near the war's end the gunboats were set adrift and sank in the Chattahoochee River. They were salvaged from the river bottom in the 1960s. The Museum is located at 1000 Victory Drive. Open 10 a.m.–5 p.m., Tuesday through Friday and 1–5 p.m. on weekends.

12. Historic Mills. Columbus has the best surviving eighteenth century industrial complex in the South, although important structures located at City Mills Dam have been destroyed in recent years. Fieldcrest/Cannon Mills, at Broadway and Fourteenth Street, still operates in the buildings constructed in the late 1860s by the Eagle and Phenix Manufacturing Company.

13. Uptown. Elegant homes of early industrialists survive in the Uptown area. Many date from the mid- and late-nineteenth century.

Creek Treaties with Georgia, Great Britain, and the United States

Treaty of Savannah, May 21, 1733, allowed English settlers to occupy the coast as far inland as the tide reached and it established regulations for trade.

Treaty of Kasihta, August 21, 1739, reaffirmed friendship between Georgia and the Creeks and established trade regulations.

Treaty of Savannah, November 3, 1757, repaired relations between the Creeks and Georgia. Georgia gained the site of Yamacraw Town and land formerly reserved for Mary Musgrove—Ossabaw, Saint Catherines, and Sapelo islands.

Treaty of Augusta, 1763. The Creeks sold to Great Britain all land south of the Lower Creek Trading Path and east of the Ogeechee River, and another strip of land south of the Altamaha River. Boundary lines between the southern colonies and the Indian nations were delineated.

Treaty of Augusta, June 3, 1773. Georgia gained land north and west of Augusta in the New Purchase.

Treaty of Augusta, 1783
Treaty of Galphinton, 1785
Treaty of Shoulderbone Creek, 1786
These three treaties were an attempt by Georgia to purchase the land between the Ogeechee River and Oconee River. Alexander McGillivray invalidated the treaties because there were too few Creek leaders present at the proceedings.

Treaty of New York, August 7, 1790. The treaty promised protection to the Creeks and prevented U.S. citizens from squatting on Creek land. The treaty stipulated that $1,500 be paid annually to the Creek Nation. The boundary of Georgia was moved westward to the Oconee River and north to the Cherokee/Creek boundary. Alexander McGillivray received a general's commission from President Washington.

Treaty of Colerain, June 29, 1796. The Treaty of New York was reaffirmed and provided for the survey of the boundary line between Georgia and the Creek nation. The Creeks received $6,000 worth of tools and goods and two blacksmiths.

Treaty of Fort Wilkinson, June 16, 1802. The Creek Nation was promised $3,000 per year for this cession of land and each signing delegate was to receive $1,000 per year for ten years. The Creeks were to receive two blacksmiths for two years and $25,000 in goods, $10,000 of that was allocated to pay for debts to the factories and for property stolen from American citizens.

Treaty of Washington, November 14, 1805. The Creeks sold all land east of the Ocmulgee River except for a reserve of three by five miles surrounding Ocmulgee Old Fields. This treaty provided for the Federal Road to be built through the Creek Nation. The Creeks were to be paid $12,000 per year for eight years, in money or goods as desired by the Creeks, then $11,000 per year for the succeeding ten years. They were promised two blacksmiths for a period of eight years.

Treaty of Fort Jackson, August 9, 1814. The Treaty of Fort Jackson outlined the terms for ending the First Creek War. Half of the Creek territory was taken in reparation for expenses incurred by the United States during the war.

Treaty of the Creek Agency, January 22, 1818. The Creeks were paid a lump sum of $20,000 and then $10,000 annually for ten years for giving up title to two tracks of land. They also received two blacksmiths for a period of three years.

Treaty of the Indian Springs, January 8, 1821. All Creek land between the Ocmulgee River and Flint River was sold to the United States. Reserves for William MacIntosh and the various members of the Barnard family were set aside. The Creek Nation received $10,000 on the spot and $40,000 as soon as practicable. Other payments over the next 14 years totaled $150,000. The headmen of the Creek Nation were to receive payments over the succeeding five years, not exceeding $250,000. The Creeks could receive the payments in money or in goods as they desired. Property claims against the Creeks by Georgia citizens were relinquished. The first Treaty of Indian Springs provoked the Creek National Council to pass laws forbidding the sell of Creek land without the express consent of the council.

Treaty of Indian Springs, February 12, 1825. Leaders of the Lower Creek Towns sold the land remaining east of the Chattahoochee River in exchange for land west of the Mississippi River and payments totaling $400,000.

Broken Arrow Resolution, June 29, 1825. The associates of assassinated William McIntosh were pardoned by the Creek National Council and invited to return to their former lives among their people.

Treaty of Washington, January 24, 1826. This treaty voided the second Treaty of Indian Springs and renegotiated the sale of the remaining Creek land in Georgia. The Creeks were to be paid $217,600 plus an annuity of $20,000.

Supplementary Article to the 1826 Treaty of Washington, March 31, 1826. The northwestern boundary between the Creek Nation and Georgia was adjusted slightly and the Creeks were compensated with a payment of $30,000.

Treaty of the Creek Agency, November 15, 1827. When it was discovered that the Treaty of Washington had not taken in quite all of the Creek lands remaining in Georgia this treaty ceded the last strip. The Creeks were paid $27,491 with an additional $10,000 going toward the support of schools, internal improvements, and merchandise.

Treaty of Washington, March 24, 1832, commonly known as the Removal Treaty. The Creeks ceded all land east of the Mississippi River. Individual tracts of land were reserved for Creek families for five years, to be sold or retained by them. Thereafter the remaining land was to be sold. The Creeks were to receive $10,000 for relief of debts and suffering families. The Creek delegates were to receive $6,000 for the expense of traveling to Washington. Other payments were marked for internal improvements in Creek territory, education of children, and support of Creeks who chose to emigrate to the west.

Treaty of Fort Gibson, February 14, 1832, established the location of the Creek Reservation west of the Mississippi.

Upper Creek Towns

In the mid-sixteenth century the noble Tascaluza ruled an empire from his capital of Atahachi, south of present-day Montgomery. His domain reached up the Coosa River, down the Alabama to the Cahaba River, and up the Tallapoosa as far as the falls at Tallasee. Tascaluza was a giant, fully a foot-and-a-half taller than the Spaniards who would soon invade his nation, and his name meant *Black Warrior*. In early October 1540, Hernando De Soto and his army of adventurers entered Tazcaluza's empire. De Soto rewarded Tascaluza's hospitality by taking him hostage and demanding porters and women. Tascaluza provided four hundred porters but said the women would be provided only at Mabila, near present-day Selma. The Spaniards left Atahachi on October 12, traveling along the south side of the Alabama River and reached Mabila on the 18th.

Tascaluza's warriors were ready at Mabila and an allied force of Indians attacked the Spaniards. At the end of the day the town of Mabila was destroyed and over 2,000 Indians were dead. It had been a Pyrrhic victory for the Spaniards who lost all of their equipage and clothing, some horses and most of their treasure. The Spaniards lost only twenty-two members of their expedition but 148 were wounded, including De Soto. His men began to lose interest in continuing the expedition, but De Soto led them deeper into the continent rather than rendezvous with ships waiting at Pensacola Bay. From that point the De Soto expedition of conquest began to deteriorate. It has never been known if Tascaluza escaped or died in the battle. His name lives on in the names of the town of Tuscaloosa and Black Warrior River.

The Pardo expedition reached into central Alabama in 1567 from its base at Santa Elena. When the Tristan de Luna colony at Pensacola Bay lost their supplies in a hurricane an expedition traveled into the interior seeking food and a place to winter. They found the town of Nanipacana and sought refuge there in the winter of 1599.

The first Englishmen to visit and trade with the Upper Creeks were Virginians who arrived in the late 1670s. Carolina traders began penetrating into the region by the end of the seventeenth century. To the English the people living in Alabama and Georgia became known as Creeks. French influence extended into Alabama when Bienville established trade with the Indians living on the Alabama, Coosa, and Tallapoosa rivers. All of the Native Americans living in the region were known to the French as Alabamas. In 1717, at the request of the true

Confluence of the Tallapoosa and Coosa rivers

Alabamas, the French built Fort Toulouse at the confluence of the Tallapoosa and Coosa Rivers.

What is sadly lacking in the history of Alabama is an account by a Creek author. There were literate citizens in the Creek Nation, especially among the leadership, but it seems that writing down a history or autobiography was not as important to them as it was to European Americans. Creek archives continued to be an oral history until the early nineteenth century.

The Creek Confederacy

The Muskhogean-speaking towns were the principal people of the Creek Confederacy. At the close of the eighteenth century their towns lay on the Coosa and Tallapoosa rivers of Alabama; the Chattahoochee and Flint rivers of central Georgia; Savannah River and the Georgia coast; and even into present-day Tennessee. The earliest accounts of the Muskogees tell of two branches, the Coosas and Abihkas. Their founding towns were Coweta, Kasihta, Coosa, and Abihka. The origin of the Muskogee is to the west of the Mississippi River, either Texas or possibly northern Mexico. It may be that pressures caused by the Cortez conquest of Mexico caused them to move eastward.

The Creek Confederacy came into being in the years following the departure of the De Soto expedition as remnants of towns decimated by war and disease began to join with former neighbors and enemies for protection and survival. Although founded by the Muskogees and dominated by them, the confederation grew to include members of the Hitchiti, Alabama, Yuchi, Chickasaw, Natchez, and Shawnee-speaking peoples. The nation was divided into the Upper and Lower Creeks. The Upper Creeks lived in towns on the Coosa and Tallapoosa rivers in central Alabama with Tuckabatchee as their principal town. The Lower Creeks lived on the Chattahoochee River centered on the falls at Columbus with Kasihta as their principal town.

When the English began to settle South Carolina there were several Creek towns located on the Savannah River and the coast of Georgia. The Yamacraws lived at a bluff named for them and that later became the city of Savannah. Their chief was Tomochichi, a friend of Oglethorpe and benefactor of the colony of Georgia. As the Carolinians entered the Indian trade several Creek towns moved to the Ocmulgee River to be closer to the English and a trading post was established among them at Ocmulgee Old Fields.

The name of the Creeks is derived from an early name for the Ocmulgee River, Ochese Creek, Ochese being the Hitchiti name given to the Muskogees who invaded their country. The people living there were called Ochese Creek Indians by whites, then they were Ochese Creeks, then simply *Creeks*.

Members of weakened tribes such as the Natchez, Timucuans, Yamassees, and Apalachicolas sought refuge among the Muskogees in the late seventeenth and early eighteenth centuries and were absorbed into the Creek Confederacy. Thereafter, the term *Creeks* came to mean the loose organization of separate tribes speaking different languages and dialects. The European mind tried to unite the various members of the confederacy in a way that its members would not. Cowetas, Oconees, and Yuchis, though all were members of the Creek

Creek Towns on the Tallapoosa and Coosa rivers in 1775

Muskogee
Abihkutchi
Atasi
Chewockeleehatchee (Halfway House)
Coosa
Upper & Lower Eufaula
Fushatchee
Hilibi
Holiwahali
Kanhatki
Kealedji
Kolomi
Okchai
Upper & Lower Okfuskee
Saogahatchee
Sukaispoga

Great Talasi
Little Talasi (Hickory Ground)
Talishatchie
Talladega
Tallassehassee
Tuckabatchee
Wakokai

Alabama
Autauga
Ecunchate
Koasati (Coosada)
Muklasa
Witumpka

Shawnee, Savannuca

Natchez

Spellings for Creek towns are very inconsistent throughout history. These spellings are taken from John R. Swanton's *Early History of the Creek Indians & Their Neighbors* rather than use their modern English counterparts.

Confederacy, spoke different languages and saw themselves as separate people. For example, when a Tuckabatchee moved to Florida the whites called him a Seminole but he saw himself still a Tuckabatchee, though he may live among Hitchiti-speaking Seminoles. Creek identity was inherited from the mother's clan and town, not place of residence. The confederacy once encompassed as many as fifty languages and dialects.

The confederacy was too loosely organized to function efficiently against the Americans and it consistently lost territory to the expanding white population. Chiefs, or micos, were not absolute rulers, except possibly within their own town and even then the young warriors were not to be controlled. The pattern of events throughout the eighteenth and early nineteenth centuries was: a conflict between Americans and Indians provoked the warriors to attack white settlements and property, a war ensued with the Americans being the victors, a treaty was signed whereby the Creeks gave up land for peace and resumption of trade, then the warriors became angry at the lose of hunting land and attacked white settlements and property, and the cycle began again.

The most powerful leader among the Creeks was Alexander McGillivray who was able to play the Americans, British, and Spanish against one another. Being half Scottish and half Creek, he moved easily in both the white and Indian worlds. During his career the Creek Confederacy approached becoming a political entity for the first time. As the United States gained ascendancy in North America, diplomacy became more difficult for McGillivray because the Americans had less competition for the affection of the Creeks. Being more powerful than the Creeks, the Americans could more easily have their way. McGillivray died young and it is interesting to speculate

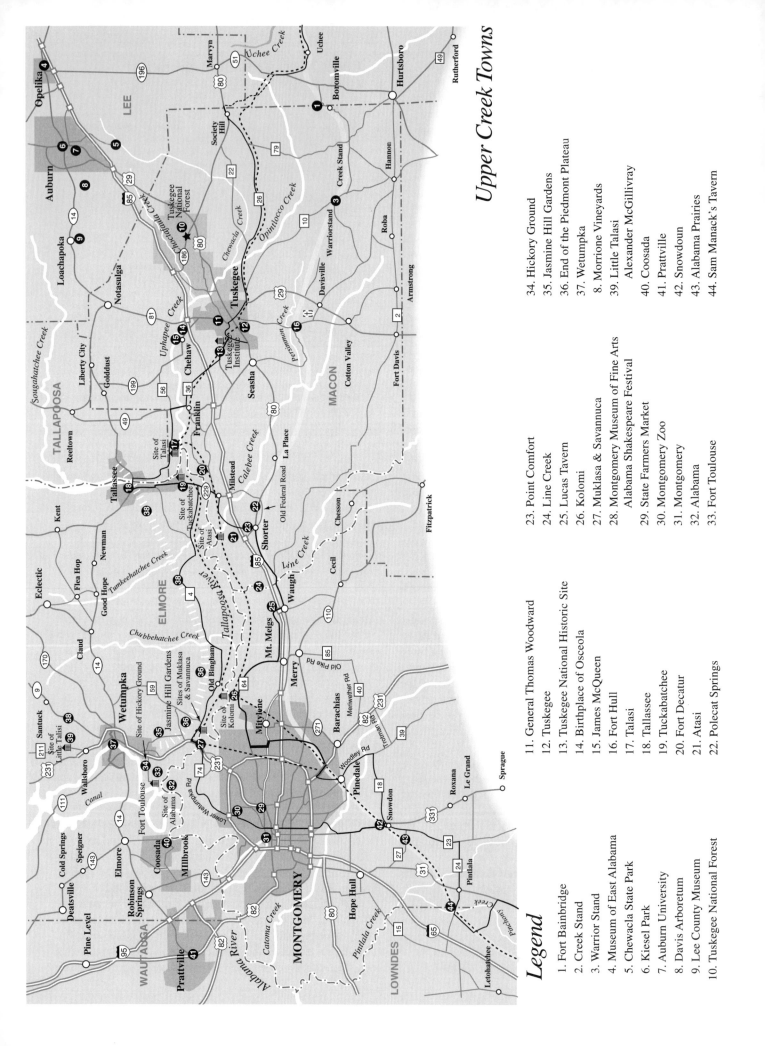

Upper Creek Towns

Legend

1. Fort Bainbridge
2. Creek Stand
3. Warrior Stand
4. Museum of East Alabama
5. Chewacla State Park
6. Kiesel Park
7. Auburn University
8. Davis Arboretum
9. Lee County Museum
10. Tuskegee National Forest
11. General Thomas Woodward
12. Tuskegee
13. Tuskegee National Historic Site
14. Birthplace of Osceola
15. James McQueen
16. Fort Hull
17. Talasi
18. Tallassee
19. Tuckabatchee
20. Fort Decatur
21. Atasi
22. Polecat Springs
23. Point Comfort
24. Line Creek
25. Lucas Tavern
26. Kolomi
27. Muklasa & Savannuca
28. Montgomery Museum of Fine Arts / Alabama Shakespeare Festival
29. State Farmers Market
30. Montgomery Zoo
31. Montgomery
32. Alabama
33. Fort Toulouse
34. Hickory Ground
35. Jasmine Hill Gardens
36. End of the Piedmont Plateau
37. Wetumpka
8. Morrione Vineyards
39. Little Talasi / Alexander McGillivray
40. Coosada
41. Prattville
42. Snowdoun
43. Alabama Prairies
44. Sam Manack's Tavern

what may have happened to the confederacy had he survived and succeeded in providing a centralized government to match that of his American neighbors.

The Stinkard language noted by Bartram was composed of dialects of Alabama, Koasati, and Hitchiti, which were all branches of the Muskhogean language stock. The Yuchi and Savannuca languages were not related as Bartram seemed to indicate; indeed, there was no known language related to Yuchi and the Savannucas were Shawnees.

The First Creek War, 1813–1814

The Creek War of 1813, also known as the War of the Red Sticks, was precipitated by the construction of the Federal Road through the Creek Nation, although tension had been building since the visit of Tecumseh in 1811. Many myths and stories have arisen from the exploits of participants on both sides—Sam Dale's canoe fight on the Alabama River, Weatherford's escape by jumping his horse, Arrow, into the Alabama River, and his later surrender to General Jackson. The war, however, brought out the worst of both whites and Indians with atrocities committed by all parties involved and ethnic hatred rising to new levels.

This war was essentially a civil war between traditional and Americanized factions of the Creeks. The traditionalists resented the erosion of their hunting economy by modern economic influences, loss of land to the Americans, and the building of the Federal Road. They were led in a return to traditional religious practices by a group of visionaries known as the Prophets and they embraced Tecumseh's Pan-Indian movement. During the war the traditionalists became known as the Red Sticks and were led by William Weatherford, Josiah Francis, Hillis Haya, and Peter McQueen. The majority of Red Sticks came from central Alabama where they were less involved in the economy of Georgia and more tied to Spanish West Florida.

In opposition, a new order of Creek society subscribed to the modernization programs sponsored by Agent Benjamin Hawkins and believed that accommodation of Americans was the key to the survival and prosperity of the Creeks as a nation. This opposing faction, predominantly Lower Creeks led by William McIntosh, became known as the Peace Party and they were assisted by Americans in subduing the Red Sticks. The McIntosh faction was much more intimately involved in the American economy than were the Red Sticks.

The Red Sticks began destroying the property of Americanized Creeks and sieged their towns, intending to destroy them. The Peace Party sought aid from Benjamin Hawkins and the Americans. General John Floyd's Georgia Militia and William McIntosh's warriors invaded from the east. General Andrew Jackson and his army marched south from Tennessee down the Coosa River. General Ferdinand Claiborne marched up the Alabama River from the south with his American, Chickasaw, and Choctaw volunteers.

The war officially started with the Red Stick attack on Fort Mims on August 30, 1813. The war ended with the defeat of the Red Sticks at Horseshoe Bend on March 27, 1814, by forces under General Andrew Jackson and General William McIntosh. A treaty was signed at Fort Jackson (Fort Toulouse) on August 9, 1814, which brought peace but punished both factions of Creeks by taking over half the territory of the Creek Nation. A line was run from the mouth of Line Creek to Eufaula and the new land to the west and south was opened for settlement. Many Creeks left the Upper Towns and found refuge among the Seminoles in Florida. Not being able to forgive the Americans nor forget their humiliation, the refugees were partially responsible, along with the British, for starting the First Seminole War in 1818.

The 1825 Treaty of Indian Springs, though illegal, was just what the United States needed to begin the removal of the Southeastern Indians. Indian land was taken out of the common and divided among the families as private property, which opened the way for loss of land by graft, fraud, bribery, and bankruptcy. Creeks began to sell their land to whites and move to Florida and the west. Others intended to remain and farm or carry on as best they could. Particularly among the Lower Creeks it seemed for a time as if the Creeks and Americans might just be able to live together, but increased white population brought institutionalized prejudice against their Indian neighbors. These whites would not distinguish between friendly and hostile Creeks and could never accept them as full participating citizens in American society. In reading Woodward's Reminiscences one learns that there were whites who were as ready to exact retribution upon innocent men, women and children, as was the upstart young Creek warrior.

The United States Congress passed the Indian Removal Act in 1830 with the blessing of Andrew Jackson. A contingent of Southeastern Indians traveled to Washington to stop the impending removal. Although the Supreme Court found in favor of the Creeks and Cherokees in their suit to retain their lands, there was a powerful force working against them. President Andrew Jackson refused to stop the removal and the courts could not, or would not, act against him. A majority of Americans began to believe that this was the best policy for both Americans and Indians. As was the case among the Cherokees there were many Creeks who had become Americanized and were able to remain in Alabama hidden among the whites. The last land cession by the Creek Confederacy was made on March 24, 1832.

Bartram's Travels in the Upper Creek Towns

Now we encounter another mystery regarding William Bartram's travels, his route from the present community of Uchee to Talasi. David Tait's map of 1772 shows that he took a path leading through Society Hill and Tuskegee, possibly passing through or near Tuskegee National Forest. In the early 1800s the Old Federal Road and another trail branched near Uchee, the latter trail headed northwest. The present-day Slasheye Road in Russell and Lee counties could possibly have been this path, connecting the Lower Creek Trading Path to another trail heading west from Coweta. In the early nineteenth century one of the Creek National Council Houses was not far from this path in the Little Uchee Creek Valley north of Crawford.

Another possible route to Talasi was by a path on the south side of Pintloco and Uphapee creeks that is shown on the William Bonar map of 1757. This route is the most direct, following Macon County Road 10 from Warrior Stand to Tuskegee. However, Bartram's brief description of his route seems to indicate the route through Society Hill, because it would cross more streams and cane swamps than if he had gone by way of Warrior Stand.

Bartram crossed Uphapee Creek near its mouth and arrived in Talasi on July 16, 1775. He then traveled downstream, keeping to the south side of the Tallapoosa River, passing through Atasi, then crossing the river to Kolomi. Kolomi had existed at different times on either side of the river. Bartram's description of hills with rocky cliffs overlooking the village could only be the north side of the Tallapoosa for the south side is very flat for many miles. James Germany's trading house still remained on the south side at the old town site.

When Bartram's band of travelers turned south for Mobile they passed through the Montgomery suburbs of Mitylene, Auburn University-Montgomery, and Pinedale. They crossed Catoma Creek and passed through Snowdoun and slightly above Pintlala. A section of the old Federal Road lies about a mile west of Pintlala on Pinchony Creek.

Here again the route indicated on old maps becomes ambiguous in its path from Pintlala to Fort Deposit. The old path may have passed through either Letohatchee or down the west side of Pinchony creek to Sandy Ridge.

William Bartram returned to Georgia through the Creek Nation, although he had intended to go through West Florida by way of Apalachee and Seminole Country. His recent illness and rising tensions between Americans and British may have compelled him to stay with the traders for protection. He arrived again at the Upper Creek Towns in early December 1775. He attended a wedding at Muklasa and dancing at Alabama. He went to Tuckabatchee to join a trading caravan bound for Augusta but they had departed so he returned to Muklasa and waited for the next group to leave. Before Bartram departed Muklasa and the Upper Creek Towns, he visited Kolomi and the plantation of James Germany, the senior trader in the region. Bartram crossed the river to reach Tuckabatchee. To reach Atasi, which was on the opposite side of the river and farther downstream, Bartram would have had to make yet another crossing of the Tallapoosa and double back to the west—not continue on upstream as he wrote. At Atasi he took part in a council and described the ceremonies in great detail. He left Atasi on January 2, 1776, in company of a group of traders and retraced his earlier path along Uchee creek.

Sites

1. Fort Bainbridge was located on the Macon-Russell county line northeast of Creek Stand. It was one of the string of forts built by General John Floyd and the Georgia Militia during the First Creek War. Big Warrior and his white son-in-law, Captain Kendall Lewis, kept an inn at Fort Bainbridge from 1816–1827. Lewis's Tavern was noted as the finest accommodations between Milledgeville and Mobile in the early days of the Federal Road. Among the famous writers and travelers who stayed at Lewis's Tavern were Adam Hodgson in 1820 and Lafayette in 1825. When George Featherstonhaugh visited in 1835 it had become Cook's Tavern.

2. Creek Stand was a stage stop on the old Federal Road but declined when traffic was diverted farther north through Columbus and Tuskegee.

3. Warrior Stand is named for Big Warrior, who lived there from 1805 until his death in 1825. He had lived earlier at Coosada on the Alabama River near Montgomery. Warrior Stand is now little more than a name on the map.

4. Museum of East Alabama. The items on exhibition date from the time of American settlement of East Alabama. Located at 121 South Ninth Street, Opelika. Open Tuesday through Friday, 10 a.m.–4 p.m.; and 2–5 p.m. on weekends, April through October. Open 2–4 p.m. on weekends during the remainder of the year.

5. Chewacla State Park. Though primarily a recreation area, Chewacla State Park has eight excellent nature trails on Moore's Mill Creek and Chewacla Creek. Two of the trails have a plant identification list and numbered stations. The park has a lake, campsites, cabins, picnic areas, tennis courts, and playground. Located south of I-85 in Auburn on Shell Toomer Parkway. Open every day, sunrise to sunset. Admission.

6. Kiesel Park is a day-use recreation park on 124 acres. Located on Chadwick Lane in Auburn. Open everyday, sunrise to sunset.

7. Auburn University was founded in 1856 as a land-grant college and is the largest university in Alabama.

8. Davis Arboretum. This rolling park contains 150 varieties of trees, many native to Alabama. The arboretum contains a pitcher-plant bog, vine arbor, reconstructed black belt prairie, and a coastal dune. The arboretum is a teaching facility and recreational area popular with Auburn students. Located on US-29 south of Auburn campus. Open during daylight hours.

9. Lee County Historical Society Museum. A log cabin, grist mill, and artifacts of mid-nineteenth century American settlement are featured. A historical fair and syrup festival are held each October. AL-14 west of Auburn in the Loachapoka Historic District. By appointment only. Call (334) 887–8747.

10. Tuskegee National Forest, like many national forests in the South, was purchased during the Depression under the Submarginal Land Program to help worn-out cotton land recover from abuse.

Bartram National Recreation Trail in Tuskegee National Forest commemorates the travels of William Bartram through eastern Alabama. This trail is eight and a half miles through a typical Piedmont forest and river bottom of Choctafaula Creek. The eastern end of the trail is at the Alliance community, believed to be the site of an Indian town.

Taska Recreational Area, located on US-29, has picnic facilities and a replica of the cabin in which Booker T. Washington was born. Tsinia Wildlife Viewing Area is located just east of Tuskegee on US-29. It has a variety of habitats, an interpretive trail, and an observation tower.

Primitive camping is allowed anywhere in the forest with a permit. The ranger office is open during regular business hours.

Bartram Trail Historical Marker. Located on the access road near the ranger station.

11. General Thomas Woodward. Possibly the best source for the history of East Alabama may be found in Thomas Woodward's reminiscences in *The American Old West*. This collection of letters to the *Montgomery Mail* recounts the life and times of the Creeks during the waning years of their nation in Alabama and the early white settlers who took their place.

Part of his writing may appear to be the sentimental yearnings of an elderly man for the excitement of his youth, but Woodward's stories ring with truth and he was a serious student of history. It is fascinating to read of his longing to visit Montgomery, "now it is a city, as I knew it forty years ago a forest."[1] His letters are a first person account of the closing of the last frontier east of the Mississippi, save deepest Florida. Woodward was particularly positioned to write on the subject authoritatively for he lived among the Creeks, fought with them and against them, and was one of the founders of Tuskegee and Macon County.

Thomas Woodward was born in Elbert County, Georgia, in 1794, and died in Louisiana about 1859. He joined the military at the beginning of the War of 1812. He fought in the Creek and Seminole wars, became Brigadier General in the Alabama Militia, and opened the first dancing school in Montgomery County. He was an adventurer and reckless in his younger days but eventually married and settled down to the planter's life in Macon County. Late in life he moved first to Arkansas where many of his family died. He spent his later years in Louisiana, where he wrote his published letters.

Although much has been made of Woodward's Native-American heritage, he was only one-sixteenth Indian and was raised and educated among whites. His penchant for dressing in buckskin and moving freely among the Creeks was due more to affinity of spirit than of blood. He was a colorful and controversial man who apparently took advantage of the turmoil in the Creek Nation during the 1830s to accumulate land. He was mostly unsuccessful in financial matters and admitted that ...

> *I managed my pecuniary matters badly most of the time; was very poor; was sold out twice by the sheriff; always voted on the weak side; was not very popular; often spoke too quickly and too freely; had a family that was interesting to me at least, consequently had often to submit to indignities or insults from a little short stock that under other circumstances I should have slapped a rod.*[2]

His life spanned the westward movement of the Southeastern frontier from the Oconee

1. Thomas S. Woodward, *The American Old West; Woodward's Reminiscences: A Personal Account of the Creek Nation in Georgia and Alabama.* Originally published in Montgomery in 1859. Republished in 1965 by Southern University Press for Graphics, Inc., Mobile.
2. *Ibid.*

Fort Toulouse

River to its closing in the 1830's and beyond. Woodward possibly was acquainted with every important personality on the frontier of the Old Southwest (Alabama and Mississippi). He personally knew Benjamin Hawkins and read his manuscripts. He knew William Weatherford, Osceola, Timpoochee Barnard, William McIntosh, Little Prince, Andrew Jackson, and others who figured large in the history of early Alabama. In 1825 he was one of Lafayette's escorts through the Creek Nation.

Woodward knew many of the leading Creek statesmen and judged their character fairly regardless of their position as friend or foe. He spoke highly of William Weatherford, although they fought on opposing sides during the Creek War of 1813–14. Woodward so regarded Osceola that he, his family, and several Creek friends planted cedars to mark the birthplace of the famous leader. Yet, he was a man of the times and looked upon slavery as a natural institution.

12. Tuskegee was settled in 1833 by immigrants from Georgia, Tennessee, and the Carolinas. The site for Tuskegee and the Macon County courthouse was selected by General Thomas Woodward, who told the history of the area in his collection of letters *The American Old West: A Personal Account of the Creek Nation in Georgia and Alabama.* The city of Tuskegee is named for Taskigi, an Alabama town located near Fort Toulouse. The name means *warrior* in the Alabama language.

13. Tuskegee National Historic Site. Tuskegee Institute was started by Booker T. Washington with $2,000 provided by Alabama for teachers' salaries. The first students arrived July 4, 1881, and the institute rapidly grew to become the leading black educational institute in the world. During the early years Tuskegee Institute educated teachers and provided practical and vocational education. Students built the campus and grew their own food as well as attended academic classes. In this century, Tuskegee evolved into a full college with a reputation for academic excellence.

The historic site encompasses the original main campus, including Washington's home and the Carver Museum. Located on Old Montgomery Road in Tuskegee.

George Washington Carver. Perhaps no other person's life exemplifies the spirit and character of William Bartram as does that of George Washington Carver, the internationally known scientist who taught for many years at Tuskegee Institute. Carver was a gentle and spiritual man whose interests included botany, science, agriculture, painting, and decorative arts.

During his youth Carver was raised by his former white owners, Moses and Susan Carver, on a successful farm in Missouri. Young George was not robust and less suited to farm work than his brother, Jim, so was most often found helping Susan with domestic work. He learned to cook, wash, sew, and garden. He was fascinated by plants and became known locally as a plant doctor. As kind as the Carvers were, young George longed for greater education and left home at age twelve to seek a better education. Although he wanted to become an artist, he believed that he was destined to become a teacher of his people and changed his studies to agriculture. In 1896 he

Upper Creek Towns • 243

earned a master's degree from Iowa Agricultural College and joined the faculty of Tuskegee Institute in October of the same year.

George Washington Carver was a deeply spiritual man, though his foster father was suspicious of organized religion and refused to attend church. Carver's spirituality was rooted in a natural mysticism that influenced his view of nature just as William Bartram's religious feelings influenced his career as botanist, artist, and writer.

Carver's interests knew no bounds. His list of accomplishments include the development of industrial and food products derived from peanuts and sweet potatoes and he developed new crop plants for Southern farmers. He manufactured paints, glues, and fibers from locally derived materials. Still, George Washington Carver considered himself an artist and continued painting throughout his life.

The Carver Museum on the campus of Tuskegee Institute is a gallery of the work of George Washington Carver and contains collections of his plants and products. Extensive exhibits depict the history of the Institute and the lives of Carver and Booker T. Washington. Open 9 a.m.–4 p.m.

Alexander McGillivray

Alexander McGillivray was the most able and powerful Creek leader of the eighteenth century. During his tenure as speaker the Creek Confederacy presented a more unified response to international affairs, which included diplomatic activity with the newly formed United States.

Alexander was born in 1759 to Lachlan McGillivray and Sehoy Marchand. At age thirteen he was sent to Charleston to be educated. With the coming of tensions during the Revolution, Lachlan fled to England and Alexander went to live with his mother's people, where he was made a headman while still a teenager.

McGillivray had the natural intelligence of a diplomat and successfully played the British, Spanish, and Americans against one another to the advantage of the Creek Confederacy. He saw the advantage of allying the Creeks with the new American nation. In 1790 he traveled to New York to sign a treaty and was given a general's commission by President Washington. There were several attempts by the British and Spanish to assassinate him after the Treaty of New York.

McGillivray's greatest diplomatic feat was probably his ability to keep the factions within the Creek Confederacy unified. He instituted laws that established punishments for crimes within the nation. Traders in the Creek Nation were allied with and subservient to McGillivray and he used this influence to keep the towns under control by threatening to halt trade. Although the Americans were able to put aside their own weak confederacy and create a stronger federal government, the Creeks were doomed to be torn apart by their decentralized government and factionalism after McGillivray's death.

McGillivray became a business partner of William Panton of Pensacola. McGillivray died of a fever on February 17, 1793, while visiting at Panton's home and was buried in Panton's Garden.

---

14. The Birthplace of Osceola is located in the vicinity of Chehaw near Uphapee Creek. Osceola was the grandson of James McQueen, one of the first traders in the Creek Nation. Osceola led the Seminoles in war against the United States during the Second Seminole War of the late 1830s. He was captured by General Thomas Jesup under a flag of truce and taken to Fort Moultrie near Charleston where he died and is buried. Osceola was admired by many Americans and found sympathy among his captors. His memoir was written by his guard at Fort Moultrie. Osceola was also known as Ussa Yoholo and Billy Powell.

15. James McQueen was one of the first English traders among the Creeks. He was born in Scotland in 1683 and arrived at Talasi around 1716 where he came to exercise much influence among the Talasis. He was the father of Peter McQueen and great-grandfather of Osceola. According to Woodward, McQueen died in 1811, making him 128 years old. He is buried in Macon County near Chehaw on Uphapee Creek.

16. Fort Hull was another of the forts built on the Federal Road during the First Creek War. Alexander Cornells, who fought with McIntosh against the Red Sticks, lived near Fort Hull.

17. Talasi (Tallasee, Talisi) was an important Muskogee town of the Upper Creeks and is synonymous with Tulsa, Talaxe, and Tallahassee. The Tulsas were a modern branch of the Coosas encountered by the De Soto expedition in northwest Georgia and northeast Alabama. In historic times, Talasi was located on the north side of Uphapee (Eufaubee) Creek on the Tallapoosa River and opposite Tuckabatchee. James McQueen was the first permanent white trader among the Talasis and was responsible for their move from the Coosa River to the Tallapoosa about 1756. Talasi means *old town*.

Hopothle Micco (Talasi King), was a powerful but controversial leader in the Creek Nation. He was on friendly terms with the Americans during the Revolution and was one of the signers of the 1783 Treaty of Augusta that ceded the remaining Creek hunting lands east of the Oconee River. He became disillusioned by the duplicity of the Americans and became hostile to the Georgians. Hopothle Micco was one of the dignitaries who traveled to New York with Alexander McGillivray in 1790. In 1798 Hopothle Micco halted the survey to establish the northern boundary of Spanish Florida. He became the leader of the Red Stick faction in 1812 and died the same year.

Peter McQueen was the son of James McQueen and leader of Talasi in the early 1800s. He joined the Red Sticks in the Creek War of 1813–1814 and was one of the victorious leaders at the Battle of Burnt Corn and the attack on Fort Mims. After the defeat of the Red Sticks, McQueen moved to Florida and revived his war as a leader of refugees and Seminoles in Florida. This lead to the First Seminole War with Peter McQueen and William McIntosh leading opposing Creek armies. McQueen was defeated at Econfinnah and sought refuge on an Atlantic Island off the coast of Florida where he died soon after.

18. Tallassee overlooks the falls of the Tallapoosa River and has been an important industrial city since its founding. The view of the Tallapoosa River from the bridge at Tallassee offers a rare sight, a dry river bed. The water is diverted by Thurlow Dam through the power plant so that during dry weather very little water flows across the exposed rocks downstream of the dam. Benjamin Fitzpatrick Bridge, connecting the east and west sides of Tallassee, curves gracefully and gently upriver, one of the longest bridges built with such a design.

Modern Tallassee was settled by Americans in 1835. One of the area's oldest surviving homes is the Patterson Log Cabin, c. 1845, in Carrville, just north of East Tallassee. The Confederate Carbine Factory was moved from Richmond to Tallassee in 1844 and is the only surviving Confederate armory.

Bicentennial Park is the site of the Tuckabatchee monument, which was moved from its original site in 1975. The monument originally stood south of West Tallassee at the site of the Council Tree where Tecumseh spoke to the Creek Nation.

Lake Talisi Park is located in West Tallassee. Continue west on Barnett Boulevard, turn right on Gilmer Avenue, then right on East Roosevelt Street.

19. Tuckabatchee (Tuckabatchi, Tuccabatchee, Tukabahchee) was the most powerful town among the Upper Creeks and the source of national speakers during the early nineteenth century. Tuckabatchee was a Muskogee town and one of the four foundation towns of the Creek Nation. The site of Tuckabatchee was south of West Tallassee near the Auburn University Experiment Station. It extended some distance up and down the river and was the largest Native-American town in the Southeast.

Tecumseh came to Tuckabatchee in 1811 and gave a great speech under the Council Tree. The Creeks hesitated to join the continental Indian confederacy, which provoked Tecumseh to announce that he would return to Ohio and stamp his feet so terribly that the earth would tremble in Tuckabatchee. It did just that a few days after Tecumseh left when a minor earthquake caused the town to tremble. Many took this as a sign to join in war against the Americans. Though Tecumseh lived among the Shawnees in Ohio his mother was a Tuckabatchee and Tecumseh may himself have been born in Alabama.

The Tuckabatchee Council Tree stood until felled by a storm in 1929. A monument was erected at the site in 1930 but was moved in 1975 to Bicentennial Park in West Tallassee.

Following are some of the noted leaders of Tuckabatchee.

Efau Hadjo (Mad Dog) became speaker for the Upper Creeks upon the death of Alexander McGillivray and held that position from the late 1790s until 1802. He was the principal speaker at the Treaty of Fort Wilkinson in 1802. In speaking of Efau Hadjo, Benjamin Hawkins touched on one of the problems lying at the heart of Creek culture that prevented them from entering American society as he hoped. Efau Hadjo was so habituated to receiving presents from the French, Spanish, or English that he saw it as his due. Although he had cattle, horses and slaves he did not look to them for support. His son was Little Prince, who was speaker of the Creek Nation in the 1820s.

Big Warrior (George Cornells) was speaker of the Upper Creeks beginning about 1812. Thomas Woodward remembered him as the largest man he ever knew. Big Warrior was born in Tuckabatchee in 1760 and was present at the Treaty of Colerain in 1796, Treaty of Fort Wilkinson in 1802, Treaty of Fort Jackson in 1814, and the Treaty of Indian Springs in 1821. During the tensions leading up to the Creek War, Big Warrior resisted the influence of Tecumseh and remained in the Peace Party, which counted only five of thirty-four Upper Creek towns. Big Warrior and six other leaders were condemned to death for their part in the execution of Little Warrior and his followers for murder, an act considered by Big

Alabama state capitol

Warrior's enemies to be an abuse of authority. Big Warrior and his followers were besieged at Tuckabatchee in the summer of 1813. They were rescued by Lower Creeks and escorted to safety at Coweta where he stayed during the ensuing war. Big Warrior was discredited by some for remaining with his family rather than join the war. He died in Washington in 1824 while lobbying against the Treaty of Indian Springs and removal to Oklahoma.

Davy Cornells (Efaw Tustanugga), was a son of trader Joseph Cornells. His Indian name means Dog Warrior and he was strongly anti-American. Davy was killed at a young age by a vengeful white as he approached Colerain under a flag of truce.

Opothleyaholo was the son of Davy Cornells, and was born near Tuckabatchee. He rose to become the speaker of the Upper Creeks sometime after the death of Big Warrior. At the Treaty of Indian Springs in February 1825, Opothleyaholo spoke out against the treaty and warned McIntosh and the other chiefs of the consequences for signing without the consent of the Creek National Council. He later led a delegation to Washington and lobbied for the nullification of the Treaty of Indian Springs. Although Opothleyaholo and other Creek leaders succeeded in having the Treaty of Indian Springs repealed, a new treaty was drawn up on January 26, 1826, in which all Creek land in the east was absorbed into Alabama and Georgia.

Opothleyaholo became the principal chief of the Creeks upon the death of Little Prince and helped bring an end to the hostilities of 1836 by subduing the insurgent towns of Sangahatchee and Hatchechubbee. Opothleyaholo moved west with his people and remained the principal chief. During the American Civil War the Creek Nation became divided by alliances to both sides of the conflict. Opothleyaholo sympathized with the United States and was forced to find refuge in Kansas in 1866, where he died the same year.

20. Fort Decatur was built during the Creek War in 1813 and was located near Milstead. General John Sevier of North Carolina, hero of King's Mountain, died at Fort Decatur in September 1815 while on a diplomatic trip among the Creeks and was buried there. His remains were removed to Knoxville in 1888.

21. Atasi (Autosse, Atosse, Attassee, Otassee), was associated with the Tuckabatchees and was located on Calabee Creek. James McQueen and T. Perryman were the traders there. William Bartram attended a council at "Autossee" during his visit among the Upper Creeks. Atasi was a Red Stick town and was destroyed by General Floyd on November 29, 1813. The people never rebuilt and either moved to Florida or were absorbed into other Creek towns.

Tustenuggee Emathla (Jim Boy, High Head Jim), was a chief of the Atasis and well known for his stature and noble bearing. During the First Creek War he fought on the side of the Red Sticks and was at the Battle of Burnt Corn where the Creeks defeated the Americans. After the war he settled near Polecat Springs and built a town called Thlopthlocco. He fought with McIntosh in the First Seminole War of 1818 and under General Jesup in the Second Seminole War in 1836.

The cruelty, duplicity, and obsession of the Americans, official and unofficial, in dealing

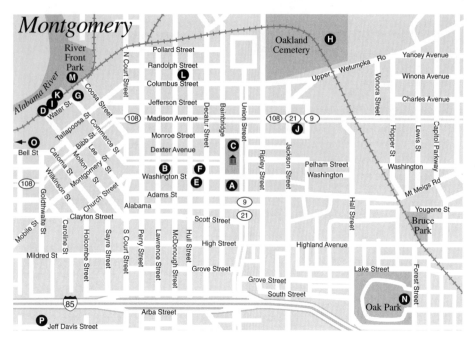

with the removal of the Creeks is sadly illustrated by the story of Jim Boy's family. When Jim Boy joined the war against the Seminoles in 1836 he was promised that his family and property would be protected in his absence and that he would be reimbursed for his expenses. But when Jim Boy returned to the Tallapoosa River in 1837 he found his family already removed to Oklahoma, his property taken or destroyed, and four of his nine children dead in the sinking of the steamboat, *Monmouth*. He and his wife, Hihethoye, lived out their years near Wetumka, Oklahoma.

22. Polecat Springs was the site of the Indian Agency after the death of Benjamin Hawkins. It was in operation between 1805 and 1836.

23. Point Comfort was the second home of Agent Benjamin Hawkins, two miles south of the Tallapoosa River near Shorter.

Shorter was an important community at the intersection of the Federal Road, Tuckabatchee Road, and Fort Jackson Road. William Walker ran a tavern nearby from 1816 to about the time of Creek Removal. He was a son-in-law of Big Warrior.

24. Line Creek is so named because it was the boundary between Alabama and the Creek Nation in the years 1814–1836. The boundary was established by the Treaty of Fort Jackson on August 14, 1814. Line Creek was originally known as Fawn Creek.

25. Lucas Tavern was located on the frontier when Lafayette stayed the night of April 2, 1825. The tavern was operated first by James Abercrombie then bought by Walter Lucas in 1821. It was the first American settlement encountered after crossing Line Creek from the Creek Nation. The Lucas Tavern is now located in Old Alabama Town in downtown Montgomery.

26. Kolomi (Coolome, Coloomee, Kulumi) was originally situated on the Chattahoochee River when Europeans first arrived. The Kolomis moved first to the Coosa River then to the Tallapoosa River. Kolomi occupied both sides of the river at a location that later became a white settlement known as Augusta in Montgomery County and Old Bingham in Elmore County. The community of Augusta later became known as Cook's Station. When Bartram visited the town it was located on the Elmore County side of the Tallapoosa River and James Germany was the trader. Members of the town moved to Florida in 1778 and settled near Suwannee Old Town. The rest of the town followed to Florida after the close of the Creek War in 1814.

27. Muklasa (Muclassee) was a town associated with the Alabamas and Koasatis. In 1775 it was located on the north side of the Tallapoosa River near US-231. Muklasa is not shown on maps after the end of the First Creek War in 1814, presumably because the people moved to Florida.

Wolf King was the best known of the Muklasa chiefs and speaker for the Upper and Lower Creeks at the Conference of Savannah in 1757. He was a friend of James Adair and remained a steady ally of the English. He is remembered for protecting the refugees after the massacre of the traders in 1760. At the Treaty of Augusta in 1763 Wolf King determined the new boundary between Georgia and the Creek lands.

Savannuca was a town of Savannahs, or Shawnees, located a little downstream of Muklasa and also on the north side of the Tallapoosa River in 1775. The town was also known as Little Shawnee and Sauwanogee. They were an Algonquian people who migrated from north of the Ohio River. Many Shawnees apparently moved freely between the two regions and they were great promoters of unity among the many Indian nations.

28. Montgomery Museum of Fine Arts. This regional museum features American paintings and prints and Southern Regional artists. The museum is located in Wynton M. Blount Cultural Park, which is also the home of the Alabama Shakespeare Festival and Montgomery Ballet. Located on Museum Drive just off Exit 6 of I-85. Open Tuesday through Saturday, 10 a.m.–5 p.m. and Sunday, noon–5 p.m. Open until 9 p.m. on Thursday. Closed Mondays, July 4th, Thanksgiving Day, Christmas, and New Year's Day.

Alabama Shakespeare Festival. This nationally known company is the fifth largest Shakespeare festival in the world. Productions range from classical to contemporary interpretations of Shakespeare and run year-round. Located on Festival Drive just off I-85. Call (800) 841-4ASF for schedule and information, or 271–5353 locally.

29. Alabama State Farmers Market. The state-sponsored market features regionally grown produce, fruit, and plants. The popular State Market Cafe serves up Southern-style home cooking for lunch and breakfast. Federal Drive and US-231N. Open daily, 7 a.m.–8 p.m., during spring and summer months and 8 a.m.–5 p.m. during the rest of the year.

30. Montgomery Zoo. North Boulevard between Coliseum Boulevard and Lower Wetumpka Road. Open daily, 9 a.m.–5 p.m. Admission.

31. Montgomery. The first American settlers in Montgomery moved in immediately after the Creeks lost the territory in 1814. In 1817 land in Montgomery County was offered for sale at the land office in Milledgeville. At first there were three settlements located near one another, New Philadelphia, Alabama, and East Alabama. In 1819 the towns were combined and incorporated as Montgomery. Steamboat service to Mobile was established in 1821. Lafayette visited Montgomery on April 3, 1825, and was honored with a ball in the evening at a tavern on the corner of Tallapoosa and Commerce streets. In 1846 the legislature voted to move the capital to Montgomery.

A. Alabama Department of Archives & History. The History Museum contains two floors of exhibits on the history of Alabama and a reference room for public access to genealogical and historical documents. Located at 624 Washington Avenue, immediately south of the Capitol. Open Monday through Friday, 8 a.m.–5 p.m., and on Saturday from 9 a.m.–5 p.m. The reference room is closed on Mondays.

B. Alabama Science Center. The Science Center is sponsored by Alabama Power and features hands-on exhibits and interactive learning programs for science students. Located at #2 N. Jackson Street. Open Tuesday through Friday, 9 a.m.–4:30 p.m.

C. Alabama State Capitol. The Capitol was built in 1850–1851 and is a National Historic Landmark. The government of the Confederate States of America was organized in the Alabama Capitol. The building has an impressive view of downtown Montgomery and the white marble is exceptionally beautiful on sunny, clear days. Open Monday through Saturday, 9 a.m.–4 p.m.

D. Black Heritage Trail. The history and culture of the black community in Montgomery and the struggle for civil rights is featured in this collection of sites. Information is available at the Montgomery Visitor Center.

E. The **Civil Rights Memorial** was created by renowned designer Maya Lin. This memorial commemorates the events of the Civil Rights Movement and the forty people who gave their lives for that cause. It is located at the Southern Poverty Law Center at the corner of Washington Avenue and Hull Street.

F. Dexter Avenue King Memorial Baptist Church. The Civil Rights Movement started in Montgomery when Rosa Parks refused to give up her seat to a white person and was arrested. The black community launched a boycott of the city busses and the center of organization was Dexter Avenue Baptist Church, the first church of the young Dr. Martin Luther King, Jr. Located at 454 Dexter Avenue. Tours are available at 10 a.m. And 2 p.m. Monday through Thursday, and at 2 p.m. on Friday. Donations welcomed.

G. Ecunchati (Ecunchata, Ecunchate) was an Alabama town and occupied the site of downtown Montgomery and. The name means *red ground*.

H. Hank Williams Memorial. Hank Williams was born on a farm near Georgiana in 1923. After his family moved into the town, Hank learned to play guitar from a music teacher and he learned songs from Uncle Teetot, a black street musician. The Williams family moved to Montgomery when Hank was fourteen and it was there that his musical career began when he won an amateur contest. Hank appeared on local radio, then the Louisiana Hayride, and in 1949 he joined the Grand Ole Opry. Hank dominated country music charts until his death in 1953 at age 29. His career marked the transition from country music based on traditional western, mountain, and ballad styles to one influenced by black gospel music and blues. The Hank Williams Memorial is located at the grave site of Hank and Audrey Williams in Oakwood Cemetery, Upper Wetumpka Road. Open daily from sunrise to sunset.

I. Hank Williams Museum features the life and music of Hank Williams, Sr. Exhibits include artifacts and memorabilia of his short but influential career. Located in Union Station, 300 Water Street. Open Monday through Friday, 10 a.m.–4 p.m.

J. Montgomery Curb Market. This popular market is filled with local produce, crafts, flowers, and food. Located at 1004 Madison Avenue. Open Tuesday, Thursday, and Saturday, 5 a.m.–1 p.m.

K. Montgomery Visitor Center. Located in Union Station, 300 Water Street. Open Monday through Friday, 8:30 a.m.–5 p.m.; Saturday, 9 a.m.–4 p.m.; Sunday, noon–4 p.m.

L. Old Alabama Town. The historic village of Old Alabama Town is a collection of thirty-five historic buildings that show Montgomery as it looked in the nineteenth century. The oldest structure is Lucas Tavern, built about 1817 at Waugh on the Federal Road. The Settlers' Cabin shows how the first white settlers lived when the area was a frontier. Other structures open for tours include the school, a corner grocery, shotgun house, cotton gin, Grange Hall, and town houses. In a working section of the town, artisans demonstrate skills of the past century. The gardens are typical of Southern gardens of the last century and include native and heirloom plants.

310 North Hull Street. Open Monday through Saturday, 9 a.m.–3.30 p.m., and on Sunday from 1 a.m.– 3:30 p.m. during warm months. The last tour is at 3 p.m. Admission.

M. Riverfront Park occupies the bluff where the Alabama town of Ecunchati was located. Riverboat cruises of the Alabama River embark from the park. Riverfront Park includes a picnic area, amphitheater, and the Amtrak station. Commerce and Coosa Street, next to Union Station.

N. Oak Park. Walking trails, Biblical garden, and a touch garden make a side trip to this city park worthwhile. It is also the home of the W. A. Gayle Planetarium.

O. Overlook Park. Located on Bell Street.

P. World Heritage Museum. The black and white heritage of Montgomery is told in exhibits. 119 W. Jeff Davis Avenue. By appointment only. 263–7229.

32. Alabama. The state and the river take their name from the Creek towns centered around the confluence of the Tallapoosa and Coosa rivers. These people were known as the Alibamous, Alibamons, or Alabamas. They were not a Muskhogean speaking people although they became part of the Creek Confederacy. Their language was more closely related to Choctaw. The Alabamas became French allies and requested that Fort Toulouse be constructed among their towns. When the French ceded their claim to land east of the Mississippi River and the English took control of trade, many Alabamas moved to Louisiana to remain close to their French allies or to Florida to join the Seminoles. Other Alabamas moved to Texas after the Revolution. William Bartram visited one of their towns just south of Baton Rouge when he traveled to the Mississippi River.

33. Fort Toulouse was built in 1717 during the governorship of Bienville in order to establish and protect French trade in the eastern part of Louisiana. The flight of English traders during the Yamassee War provided the French with an entrée to the Creek Nation. The fort was constructed at the invitation of the chief of the Alabamas and was located near their town in the fork of the Coosa and Tallapoosa rivers. The fort was originally named Fort aux Alibamos then was changed to Toulouse, to honor the son of Louis XIV who was commander of the French navy.

Fort Toulouse remained an isolated outpost during its existence. English traders soon returned because the Creeks preferred the English goods that were cheaper, of better quality, and more plentiful; therefore, French traders had little success. French support for the fort was minimal except for shipments of sugar, tea, and other imported goods. It was hoped that by purchasing provisions from the Indians the local economy would be more closely tied to the French. As it happened, the fort sometimes had to trade with the English for needed supplies. The Creeks took advantage of the contest for their affection to play one country against the other as it suited their needs.

Marchand became the second commander of Fort Toulouse, around 1722, and was killed by his soldiers during a mutiny. Lieutenant Villemont, second in command, pursued the deserters and executed them. Marchand had married an Indian princess with whom he had a daughter named Sehoy. As a young woman Sehoy married Lachlan McGillivray, a trader of Augusta. It has often been written that their son was Alexander who became the most powerful Creek leader. However, Thomas Woodward said that Alexander was born of McGillivray and a wife who was full-blood Tuckabatchee. The child of the first marriage with Sehoy must have been Alexander's older sister, Sophy.

After the French ceded their territory, the British garrisoned the fort for only a short period then abandoned it. During the Creek War in 1814, the fort was revived as Fort Jackson and was the site of the treaty that concluded that war. In 1819 it became the county seat for the original Montgomery County.

William Bartram visited the site of Fort Toulouse in December 1775, when the Alabamas still lived nearby. He wrote,

> *The trader obliged me with his company on a visit to the Alabama, an Indian town at the confluence of the two fine rivers, the Talapoose and Coosau, which here resign their names to the great Alabama, where are to be seen traces of the ancient French fortress, Thoulouse; here are yet lying, half buried in the earth, a few pieces of ordnance, four and six pounders.*[1]

When the French abandoned the fort they destroyed what they could not remove. While visiting at Cahaba, Lafayette was shown a French cannon from Fort Toulouse. He expressed melancholy feelings of sadness and pleasure at remembering his own country's presence in Alabama.

Fort Toulouse is now an Alabama State Park that is significant in that it is the site of two historic forts, three Mississippian mounds, and the William Bartram Arboretum. The Living History Program portrays the life of the French soldiers and settlers who lived at Fort Toulouse. The program is held the third weekend of each month from April through November. Special weekends include encampments of the French & Indian War and First Creek War.

Located off US-231, south of Wetumpka. Open daily except Thanksgiving, Christmas, and New Year's Day. Hours are 6 a.m.–9 p.m., April 1 through October 31; 8 a.m.–5 p.m., November 1 through March 31. Admission.

34. Hickory Ground, also known as Otciapofa, was a branch of the original Coosa town of Talasi. It was located in the lower part of present-day Wetumpka and near Fort Toulouse.

1. William Bartram, *Travels*, 445.

35. Jasmine Hill Gardens. The centerpiece of Jasmine Hill Gardens is the replica of the Temple of Hera. The temple sits in an open lawn with a view of the southernmost hills of the Piedmont. The gardens were built around replicas of Classical Greek sculpture that Benjamin and Mary Fitzpatrick collected on trips to Europe during the Depression. The walks, plantings, and sculpture are tastefully combined so as to complement one another.

36. End of the Piedmont Plateau. Topographic maps of the lower Tallapoosa River show a marked difference between the terrain south of the river and that north of the river. The Piedmont ends here and is dramatically visible from the visitor center on US-231, Wetumpka Road, just north of the river. Another interesting view is from the temple at Jasmine Hill Gardens, which appears almost mountainous with steep, forested hills and valleys. The Black Belt makes an arc from northwest to southeast around this lower end of the Piedmont.

37. Wetumpka was named for the Upper Creek town of the same name that was related to the Koasatis and Alabamas. The present town was settled soon after the Creeks gave up this land at the Treaty of Fort Jackson in 1814. It lies at the head of navigation of the Coosa River and the falls are visible below the dam. Hiking trails follow the river from Gold Star Park to the Bibb Graves Bridge and the downtown shopping district.

Elmore County Museum is located in the Old Farmer's Alliance Warehouse, built about 1820 as an Indian Trading Post. Located at 300 Wharf Street. Open the first Sunday of each month from 2–4 p.m.

38. Morrione Vineyards. This ambitious vineyard uses native muscadine grapes to make their wines. William Bartram found the muscadine everywhere he traveled during his Southern journey. The vineyards and tasting room are open Friday & Saturday, 8:15 a.m.–4:45 p.m.

39. Little Talasi, also known as Little Tulsa, was the plantation and home of Alexander McGillivray. The site is identified by a historical marker located on Highway 211 several miles north of Wetumpka. When McGillivray died, his family moved to Hickory Ground.

40. Coosada was the major town of the Koasatis who were close relatives of the Alabamas. Wetumpka and Koasati were sister towns and are more closely related to the Choctaws and Chickasaws than the Muskoghean members of the Creek Confederacy. Some of the Koasatis moved to Louisiana and Texas in the last half of the eighteenth century.

41. Prattville is unique in the South as a city founded upon and built by industry. The town was founded in 1836 by New Englander, Daniel Pratt. The city boasted a gin factory, cotton mills, grist mill, and a manufacturer of architectural millwork.

42. Snowdoun is the site of Bonham's Stand, a stage stop on the old Federal Road that was well known for its bad service.

43. Alabama Prairies. The rich calciferous prairie region south of Montgomery and Selma have been recognized since earliest times and became the richest cotton-producing land in the country. The prairies lie within a physiographic region known as the Black Belt, for the color of the soil. This geological formation runs from northern Mississippi, through Selma and south of Montgomery in a narrow crescent of about forty miles wide. The prairies were highly alkaline soils of low elevation that supported extensive grasslands and meadows with few trees. The area was intensely farmed for cotton and little is left to be seen of the prairies and in some areas the soil has eroded down to the underlying chalk.

44. Sam Moniac's Tavern (Manack's Tavern) was located on Pinchony Creek near Pintlala. Moniac's was the first licensed tavern in Alabama and was in operation from 1803 to 1816. Illustrious lodgers included Peggy and Lorenzo Dow and Aaron Burr. Sam Moniac was also called Sam Takkes-Hadjo Moniac, a Tuskegee Creek of mixed blood. His wife was Elizabeth Weatherford, sister of William Weatherford and daughter of Sehoy III and Charles Weatherford. Sam's sister, also named Elizabeth, married William Weatherford.

Sam and Elizabeth Moniac married in 1801 and their son, David Moniac, was the first Native American to graduate from West Point. David married Mary Powell, a cousin of Osceola, and settled among their Moniac relatives near Little River on the lower part of the Alabama River. David was killed at Wahoo Swamp in Florida during the Second Seminole. Moniac descendents are among the founding families of the Poarch Band Creeks.

Counties

Autauga is named for the Indian village of Atauga and was created November 21, 1818.

Elmore was created February 15, 1866 and named for John Archer Elmore, a Revolutionary War veteran from Virginia, member of the South Carolina legislature, Alabama settler, member of the Alabama legislature and general in the Alabama State Militia.

Lee, created December 15, 1866, was formed from other counties and named for General Robert E. Lee.

Lowndes was created January 20, 1830, in territory taken from several surrounding counties. It is named for South Carolina statesman William Lowndes.

Macon, created December 18, 1832, was formed out of the Creek land cession of March 24, 1832. The county was named for Nathaniel Macon, a member of congress from North Carolina.

Montgomery, was created December 6, 1816 by the legislature of Mississippi Territory. The county is named for Major Lemuel Putnam Montgomery of Tennessee who was killed at the Battle of Horse Shoe Bend.

Tallapoosa was created December 18, 1832 and was formed from the last large cession of Creek land and named for the Tallapoosa River.

Itinerary

Miles	Directions
	Begin at Good Hope Church in Uchee, Alabama, and travel west on North AL-51
2.2	Turn right on N Al-51
.5	Left on Slosh Eye Road (unpaved), which becomes CR-34 then CR-160
5.1	Left on US-80, Dixie Overland Highway
1.4	Left on Red Road, Macon CR-26
10.5	Left on Old Columbus Road, Macon CR-26
3.9	Keep straight on Main Street, US-29, in Tuskeegee
1.4	Downtown Tuskegee, keep straight on AL-81 past the Macon County courthouse
.3	Left on West Montgomery Road for Tuskegee University
.6	Enter Tuskegee University campus
1.3	Right at the intersection on Franklin Road at the National Park Service Headquarters sign
2.3	Right on Macon CR-36
4.4	Right on AL-49
	Cross Uphapee Creek
.8	Left on Lower Tuskegee Road, CR-56
5.1	Left on Lower Tuskegee Road, CR-51
2.4	Left on Central Boulevard, AL-14, in Tallassee
1.0	Left on Jordan Avenue, AL-229
3.0	Site of Tuckabatchee
3.3	Cross the Tallapoosa River
.6	Right on CR-40
4.4	Right on US-80, Jefferson Davis Highway
7.0	Right on AL-126, cross I-85
5.9	Right on Ware's Ferry Road in Mt. Meigs
8.4	Left on Burbank Drive
.8	Left on Atlanta Highway (US-80)
.4	Right on Bell Road (Montgomery-43)
5.9	Right on Troy Highway (US-82/231)
1.2	Left on Virginian Loop Road
1.9	Left on Woodley Road (Montgomery-39)
5.3	Right on Snowdoun-Chambers Road (Montgomery-18)
5.5	Right and keep straight across US-331 to Butler Mill Road
4.8	Right on Old Hayneville Road
2.5	Arrive at Pintlala, continue straight on Old Federal Road
1.1	Left on Old Federal Road (Montogomery-55)
1.3	Left on Tabernacle Road (Montgomery-53)
.7	Tabernacle Road makes a sharp left turn
1.1	Right on US-31
13.2	Right on AL-185
5.6	Arrive at Fort Deposit

The Mobile & Pensacola Path

There were no significant white settlements within the present boundaries of Alabama during the Colonial Period, except Mobile. The land between the Tombigbee and Alabama rivers was a kind of no-man's land separating the Creeks and Choctaws who were traditional enemies. The boundary between the two nations divided the headwaters of the two rivers. During the Revolution, refugees from the Southern colonies drifted southwestward into the land now contained within the counties of Baldwin, Clarke, and Washington.

The Mobile-Pensacola Path ran from the Upper Creek Towns to Mobile and followed high ground east of the Alabama River. It forked just south of Burnt Corn with one branch for Pensacola (called the Furrow Path), which joined with the Three Notch Road from Coweta somewhere near the Florida state line. The other branch lead to Mobile. The Mobile-Pensacola Path became a major route for trade among the Creeks and later, as the Spanish winked, a route for arms supplied by the British.

On April 7, 1798, Mississippi Territory was created out of Georgia's Yazoo Lands. The territory stretched from the Chattahoochee to the Mississippi rivers and from the 31st parallel to the Tennessee border. On June 4, 1800, the entire southern section was organized into Washington County with the government at McIntosh Bluff for a year before being moved to Wakefield then again to St. Stephens.

White traders who married Creek women were allowed to live in Creek territory and their children were allowed to own land. A number of mixed-blood families lived along the lower Alabama River away from the major Creek towns. The brothers John and William Weatherford lived in present-day Monroe County. William chose to live the life of his mother's people, the Creeks, and was a leading Red Stick warrior during the Creek War of 1813. John chose to live as a white, al-

The Alabama River at Claiborne

though he was able to live in Creek territory and operate a ferry near Claiborne. Conservative Creeks became increasingly alarmed at the erosion of their traditional culture, particularly the transition from a hunting to an agricultural economy as practiced by their mixed-blood brothers who owned businesses and farms. Whites in neighboring Georgia became jealous of the Creeks who lived on such large tracts of good cotton land.

Settlers from Georgia and South Carolina began moving into south Alabama soon after the Federal Road opened in 1811. The building of the road, the incursion of whites onto Creek hunting lands, and the passions aroused by the speeches of Tecumseh led to the Creek War of 1813. A number of the victims of the siege of Fort Mims were mestizo Creeks from the region. One of the survivors was the aunt of the Red Stick leader, William Weatherford.

In November 1813, General Ferdinand Claiborne marched from the south with American volunteers, Choctaw warriors, and his scout Sam Dale. They crossed the Alabama River and built a fort on the bluff near John Weatherford's ferry, which Claiborne named for himself. The army continued up the river and defeated William Weatherford's warriors at the Holy Ground. The lower Alabama River was then free of hostility while war continued on the Tallapoosa and Coosa rivers. When the Red Sticks were defeated in 1814 the Treaty of Fort Jackson appropriated over half of the Creeks' territory for white settlement, including all of the Alabama River. Immediately settlers began to pour in and they took up the rich new land along the river and in the Black Belt. Communities in the Carolinas and Georgia complained that they lost many good citizens to *Alabama fever*.

During the Removal of 1836–1838 many Creeks were able to remain in Alabama or they later quietly slipped back into the state and lived among the whites. Indeed, possibly as much as a third of the Creek population returned and as much as a fourth of the population of some lower Alabama counties claim some Creek blood.[1]

William Bartram's Travels on the Mobile and Pensacola Path

William Bartram followed the Pensacola and Mobile Trading Path from the Upper Towns and crossed Pintlala Creek near the site of Manack's Tavern, a well-known stop on the later Federal Road. The old Path passed through Fort Deposit and followed AL-185 past the site of the future Fort Dale. Bartram saw many vines of wild grapes and described how the Indians preserved them by turning them into raisins. His trail then followed Butler County 38 almost exactly. The extensive grove of dogwoods was possibly located in an area of Butler County known as the Flats, originally named Dogwood Flats. One suggestion for the existence of this grove is that a storm or tornado knocked down the tall pines and allowed the dogwoods to flourish and create a dense canopy.

The old Federal Road was built upon the existing trading path and became the county line between Monroe and Conecuh counties, still known today as the Old Stage Road. William Bartram probably followed this path to the Escambia County line. Francis Harper believes Bartram and his traveling companions may have traveled down the east side of the Big Escambia Creek and crossed farther downstream. This meant that they followed the Pensacola Path south into Escambia County, then turned and followed a connecting road to the Mobile Path. This connecting road is shown on the David Taitt map of 1772.

1. John Winterhawk Johnson, spiritual leader of the Creeks in Alabama, estimates that forty percent of the Creek population either did not leave or they returned from Oklahoma.

Sites

1. Remnant of the Old Federal Road. Located east of I-85 at Highway 24 and Pintlala Creek.

2. Fort Deposit grew up around a fort built by General Claiborne in 1813 during the Creek War. Settlers traveled there during times of tension for the protection offered by the garrison.

3. Holy Ground, called Ikanatchaka, was located on a bluff on the east bank of the Alabama River at Dutch Bend just below Powell's Ferry in Lowndes County. It was established by William Weatherford because the prophets had said no whites could approach this place without being destroyed. The town was surrounded by swamps and ravines that provided protection from attack. White and Creek prisoners were burned at Holy Ground in the public square. The Battle of Holy Ground took place on December 23, 1813. The inhabitants were surrounded by Claiborne's army but escaped into the swamps and crossed the river. Weatherford made a daring escape from his attackers. Myth has him riding his horse, Arrow, over the cliff and into the river, but he later told Thomas Woodward that he merely found a ravine and descended to the river. Claiborne's army burned the town.

4. Fort Dale was built in 1818 for defense of local settlers against attack in the aftermath of the murders of the Stroud and Ogle families. The blockhouse was built by Sam Dale and was located on the Federal Road.

Sam Dale is to Alabama what Daniel Boone is to Kentucky. He was a Georgian, over six feet tall and weighing 190 pounds. Dale earned his place in history at the famous Canoe Fight on the Alabama River at Weatherford's Ferry, near Claiborne. Dale, two friends, and the slave Ceasar, while crossing the river in advance of Claiborne's army, encountered nine Creeks coming downriver. The Americans met them and as Ceasar held the Indians' boat the Americans battled the Creeks with the butts of their rifles and overwhelmed them.

Although a fierce and renowned Indian fighter, Woodward said of Dale that he held no resentment once his enemy was conquered. Indeed, Sam Dale and William Weatherford developed a close friendship after the Creek War and Dale was chosen as best man when Weatherford married. Sam Dale lived near the site of Fort Dale and represented the area in the Alabama legislature. In 1820 he was visited by Adam Hodgson, although his name was not mentioned in the publication of Hodgson's *Letters from North America*.

5. The Ogle Massacre. One of Butler County's pioneer families was massacred on March 13, 1818, by Creeks led by Savannah Jack. Their home was immediately north of present-day Shiloh Church. Poplar Springs, shown on early maps of Alabama, arises in a gully near the church and the Ogle home site.

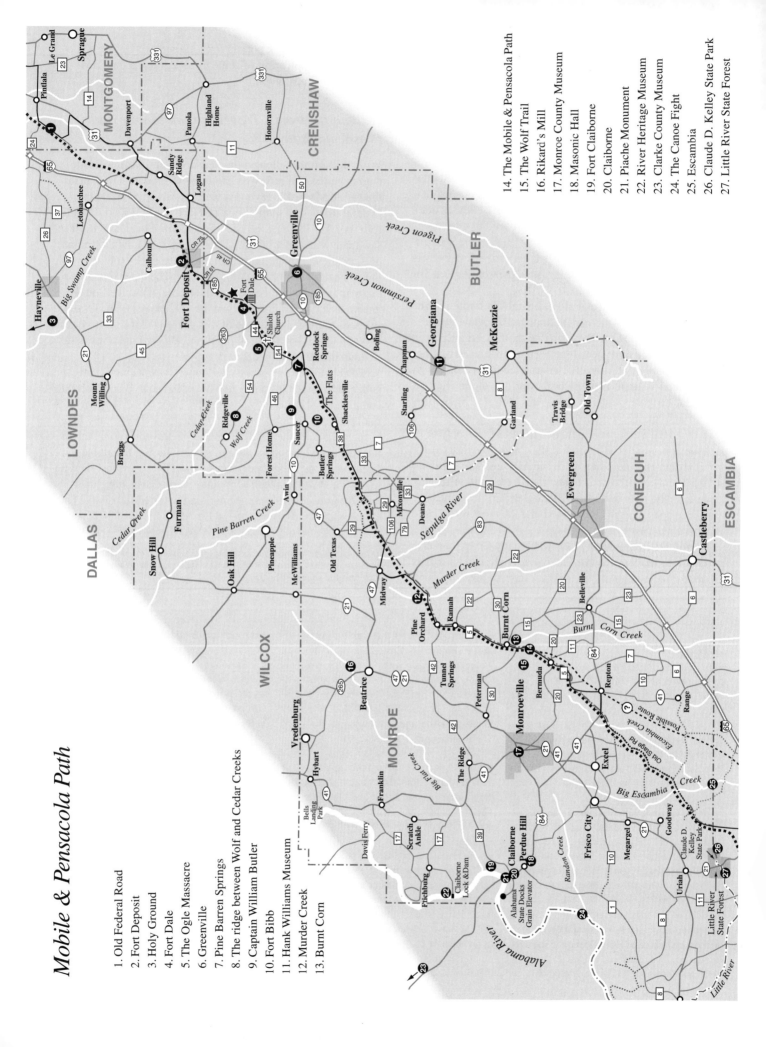

6. Greenville was settled in 1819 by immigrants from South Carolina and was originally named Buttsville then in 1822 was renamed Greenville in honor of Greenville, South Carolina, where many of the citizens originated. Greenville is the seat of Butler County,

7. Pine Barren Springs has been a landmark on maps since colonial times.

8. The ridge between Wolf and Cedar creeks is a remarkable terrain that rises 100–200 feet above the surrounding ravines.

9. Captain William Butler and companions were travelling to Fort Dale on March 20, 1818 with a message when they encountered Savannah Jack and a band of his followers on Pine Barren Creek. William Gardner and Daniel Shaw were killed and Butler and John Hinson were wounded. Hinson remounted his horse and hurried on to Fort Dale for help. When the detachment arrived next day, the bodies of Butler, Gardner, and Shaw had been mutilated.

10. Fort Bibb, 1818, Butler County.

11. Hank Williams Museum is housed in Hank Williams boyhood home where he lived from 1930–1934. 127 Rose Street, Georgiana. Admission.

12. Murder Creek received its chilling name from a murder that took place on the Pensacola Path. General Thomas Woodward told the story in his letters collected in *The American Old West*.

13. Burnt Corn received its name from a discarded batch of burned corn, thrown away by an Indian traveling on the Mobile and Pensacola Path. The spring at Burnt Corn Creek was a well-known camping spot on the old trading path to Pensacola. Several trails met at Burnt Corn. The Pensacola Path continued due south on the east side of Big Escambia Creek and the Mobile path followed the Monroe-Conecuh county line. The Wolf Trail traveled southwest through Monroe County then paralleled the Mobile River on the east bank. Another path traveled due west and crossed the Alabama River at Claiborne. The last trail became part of the early Federal Road that terminated at Saint Stephens. James Cornells, a mestizo Creek, lived at Burnt Corn in the early nineteenth century.

The Battle of Burnt Corn, July 27, 1813, was the first official engagement of the First Creek War. Peter McQueen of Talasi, Jim Boy of the Atasis, and Josiah Francis (Hillis Hadjo) of the Alabamas had traveled to Pensacola with their Red Stick warriors where they were being armed by the British. On their way south they had intimidated Indians who would not

Post office and general store in Burnt Corn, Alabama

follow the war talk. The news spread across southern Alabama and Mississippi that the Red Sticks were being armed and intended to sweep whites and mixed-blood Creeks from the Alabama River.

Militia from Washington, Clarke, and Baldwin counties marched over the Wolf Trail to intercept the Indians as they returned from Pensacola. The engagement took place below the ridge on Burnt Corn Creek. After surprising and dispersing the Creek warriors some of the American militiamen engaged themselves in stealing from the Indian packhorses rather than pursuing their foes. McQueen regrouped his men and attacked, causing the American militia to scatter in all directions. Their humiliation was such that there could be found no white man in Alabama who would admit to having fought at Burnt Corn.

14. The Mobile and Pensacola Path extended from the Alabama Towns, where Montgomery is located, to Burnt Corn. At that point the trail split with one path going to Mobile and the other to Pensacola. These trails became two of the most important paths into the Creek Nation and became part of the Federal Road. William Bartram traveled the trail to its fork at Burnt Corn then followed the Mobile Path to Tensaw.

When Adam Hodgson traveled over the Federal Road in April 1820, he remarked that somewhere south of Burnt Corn …

The only thing which attracted my attention during the morning, was a fingerpost of wood fastened to a tree and pointing down a grass path, and on which was written To Pensacola. *I felt more lonely and more distant from home at that moment, than at any time since I lost sight of my native shores.*[2]

2. Adam Hodgson, *Letters from North America*, vol. I; Hurst, Robinson, & Co., London, 1824.

15. The Wolf Trail traveled north from Tensaw along the east bank of the Mobile River, passed through south-central Monroe County, and connected with the Mobile-Pensacola Path at Burnt Corn.

16. Rikard's Mill was built in 1858 on Flat Creek near Beatrice, replacing a mill built in the early 1840s. The mill and ten acres of land are now a county park. The mill is operable and the miller grinds cornmeal and grits for visitors to purchase. Rural mills such as Rikard's were popular gathering places for families to picnic, visit, and catch up on neighborhood news. Cedar Swamp Trail follows along Flat Creek and other trails are planned for the future.

From Monroeville follow AL-21 north to Beatrice, then AL-265 until you see signs for Rikard's Mill. Open April through December, 11 a.m.–7 p.m., Thursday through Saturday.

17. Monroe County Museum. A large part of the exhibit area of the museum is devoted to the life and works of local residents Harper Lee and Truman Capote. Photographs from the filming of *To Kill a Mockingbird* are exhibited. A gift shop sells books of Alabama history. Located in the old courthouse in downtown Monroeville. Open 8 a.m.–12 noon, Monday through Friday and on Saturday from 9 a.m.–1 p.m.

18. Masonic Hall at Perdue Hill was built in 1824 at Claiborne. The structure was built by two slaves, Peter and Primus, and was the site of the festivities surrounding the visit of Lafayette. The hall was later used as a Baptist church and was the Monroe County courthouse until 1832. In 1884 the building was moved up the road to Perdue Hill.

William Barret Travis is best remembered for his martyrdom at the Alamo, yet his earlier life in Alabama was almost a typical American success story. He moved with his family from South Carolina to Conecuh County, Alabama, about 1818. He read law under Representative James Dellet, was admitted to the bar and began a practice at Claiborne. He published the *Claiborne Herald*, joined the Masonic Lodge, and was a member of the militia.

An otherwise blessed and successful young man of twenty-one, Travis's marriage was unfortunately not a happy one. Although the facts are unclear, Travis killed a man whom he suspected of being his wife's lover. Travis fled to Texas in early 1831 and became involved with the movement for Texas independence. He died with his soldiers at the siege of the Alamo in San Antonio, Texas, in 1836.

The Travis Cottage is located at Perdue Hill. This two-room building is thought to have been the law office of Travis when he lived at Claiborne.

19. Fort Claiborne was built by General Ferdinand Claiborne in 1813 and was located at the mouth of Limestone Creek.

20. Claiborne grew up near the site of Fort Claiborne on the bluff overlooking the Alabama River and became one of Alabama's most important cotton depots. Claiborne was incorporated in 1820 and provided the state with three governors and the first federal judge. Lafayette visited Claiborne for part of the afternoon of April 6, 1825.

Cotton was loaded onto steamboats by sliding the bales from the top of the bluff down a plank chute. By the time the cotton reached the deck of the boat it had gained significant momentum and provided great entertainment for steamboat travelers. Workers had to move fast to wrestle the 400-pound bales into place before the next one came speeding down the slide and bounding across the deck. Cotton was loaded according to the steamboat schedule even if that meant working in the middle of the night. Tyrone Power traveled on the Alabama River in 1834 and witnessed the loading of cotton in the dead of night.

> *Perpendicular, or nearly so: from the summit there is laid down in a slanting direction a slide or trough of timber, wide enough to admit of the passage of a cotton bale, at the bottom of the bluff this slide rests upon a platform of loose planks, alongside of which the boat is moored; the cotton-bag is guided into the slide at top, and thence, being launched, is left to find its own way to the bottom; if it keeps the slide until it strikes the platform, communicating with the vessel by a plane inclined according to circumstances, it is carried on board by its own impetus and the spring of the planks; but it often chances that through meeting a slight inequality on the slide, or from some unknown cause, the bale bounces off in its passage, either sticking amongst the trees by the way, or rolling headlong into the river. At any jutting intermediate stand of the precipice, Negroes are stationed to keep up the huge fires which afford light for the operation, as well as to forward such bales as may stick by the run ...*[1]

The slide at Claiborne was the longest in Alabama and was flanked by 365 steps. Later, cotton bales were lowered down the slide by an incline car rather than give them up to the unpredictable force of gravity. The steps may still be seen from the river.

The business opportunities at Claiborne attracted Jewish merchants from Mobile. They

[1]. Tyrone Power, *Impressions of America*; London, 1836. Reprinted with the permission of the University of Georgia Libraries

Rikard's Mill

established at Claiborne the second oldest Jewish organization and cemetery in Alabama. Claiborne began to decline after the Civil War due to yellow fever epidemics and loss of river freight to the railroads. By the early 1900s the once prosperous town was virtually abandoned. The only remaining buildings of Claiborne are the Travis Cottage and the Masonic Lodge, both have been moved a mile east of Claiborne to Perdue Hill.

The unpaved road that leads to the boat ramp at the bottom of the bluff is well worth a hike. Numerous indigenous plants grow on the steep bluff, including bottlebrush buckeye, a Bartram discovery.

21. Piache Monument. It was once believed that the Mississippian town of Piache visited by De Soto was located on the Alabama River near the dead town of Claiborne but recent research places it farther north near Selma. A monument to the town is located on US-84 at the east end of the Claiborne bridge.

22. River Heritage Museum contains samples of fossils from a section of the Alabama River that was studied by Charles Lyell. There are exhibits on the life and culture of Native Americans who lived along the river. The artifacts include tools, weapons, and textiles. The Museum is open Friday and Saturday, 9 a.m.– 4 p.m., and Sunday, 1–5 p.m., from mid-March through October. Admission.

23. Clarke County Museum. Located at the corner of highways US-43 and US-84 in Grove Hill. Open 9:30 a.m.–4 p.m., Monday through Thursday and on Friday until 2:30 p.m.

24. The Canoe Fight took place on November 12, 1813 at the mouth of Randon Creek. Sam Dale, several companions, and the slave Ceasar fought several Creeks who attacked the party as they crossed the Alabama River. Dale and his companions won the day though they were outnumbered and the event became an Alabama legend.

25. The name **Escambia** is derived from the Choctaw word Oskeambeha, meaning "cane therein" or simply a "canebrake." The Conecuh River and Big Escambia Creek join to become the Escambia River in Florida.

26. Claude D. Kelley State Park adjoins Little River State Forest and is located twelve miles north of Atmore. Claude D. Kelly State Park is known to some as Little River State Park. It offers facilities for camping, picnicking, hiking, and relaxing on the park's 960 acres. Blackshore Lake permits motorized boats and Anglers fish for bass, bream, and catfish. The Civilian Conservation Corps Trail and the Gazebo Trail cover six miles collectively and lead hikers through pine, dogwood, hickory, oak, and sweet gum forest. For overnight visitors there are five improved campsites, twenty-five primitive camping spots, and cottages for rent. Located on AL-21 at the Monroe-Escambia county line.

27. Little River State Forest. Camping, RV sites, fishing, picnicking, and hiking trails. Located on A-21 between Huxford and Uriah.

Counties

Butler County was created December 13, 1819, from Monroe and Conecuh counties. The county was named for Captain William Butler, a veteran of the War of 1813–14. He was one of the first settlers of the area and was killed on March 20, 1818, near Greenville. Early county court sessions and elections were held at Fort Dale.

Conecuh County. Created February 13, 1818, from Monroe County. It is named for the Conecuh River and is a Muskhogean word for "land of cane." The first seat of government was at Sparta, then it was moved to Evergreen in 1866.

Escambia County was created December 10, 1868, from Baldwin and Conecuh counties. It is named for the Escambia River, which begins at the confluence of Conecuh River and Big Escambia Creek.

Monroe County was created as a part of Mississippi Territory on June 29, 1815, and named for President James Monroe. The original boundaries of Monroe County included all land ceded by the Treaty of Fort Jackson in 1814. Monroe County was broken into several counties and reached its present limits in 1821. Fort Claiborne was the seat of government from 1815 to 1832, then the courthouse was moved to Monroeville.

Itinerary

Begin at Pintlala and drive west on Old Hayneville Road

Miles	Direction
1.1	Left on Old Federal Road (Montogomery-55)
1.3	Left on Tabernacle Road (Montogomery-53)
.7	Tabernacle Road makes a sharp left turn
1.1	Right on US-31
1.2	Right on AL-185
6.4	Left on AL-185 in Fort Deposit
8.3	Right on Butler-44
8.3	Left on Butler-42
.2	Right on Butler-54
3.6	Right on AL-10
2.0	Left on Butler-38
14.6	Right On Monroe-29
1.1	Right on Monroe-29
1.2	Left, then an immediate right
2.4	Right on CR-106
2.8	Left on AL-47
.2	Left on AL-83
3.1	Left on CR-5
12.8	Keep left on CR-5 in Burnt Corn
4.7	Left on CR-5
6.5	Right on US-84
2.0	Left on Old Stage Road
14	Left on CR-45
3.8	Right on Huxford Road (CR-30)

The Mobile & Pensacola Path

Mobile

The Mobile Delta has been inhabited for at least 10,000 years. Shell middens of the archaic Indians can be found along the bay and the rivers that thread through the delta. Most of these mounds do not seem to have been used ceremonially and are thought to be simply refuse piles. Mobile and the Mobile River take their name from the Mabila Indians who lived at the confluence of the Tombigbee and Alabama rivers during the late seventeenth century. The Mabilas spoke a variation of Choctaw and their dialect became the language of trade among the Gulf Coast Indians. The first mention of the Mabilas appears in the narratives of the De Soto expedition which reached Mabila on October 18, 1541. Mabila was then located at the mouth of the Cahaba River on the site of Old Cahaba.

The first European discovery of Mobile Bay was by Francisco de Garay, who sailed for Alonzo Alvarez de Pineda in 1519. Garay mapped the Gulf Coast as far west as Texas and gave the name of Río del Espiritu Santo to a large river, possibly Mobile Bay. Next came the struggling expedition of Pánfilo de Narváez in 1528, who encountered such hardships on their exploration of Florida that they built rafts and sailed the Gulf Coast in an attempt to reach Mexico. Near Galveston Bay, Narváez and all but eighty members of the expedition were lost at sea. The survivors began an overland march to Mexico by way of Texas and the Rocky Mountains, led by the amazing Alvar Núñez Cabeza de Vaca. Only five of the 400 members of the Narváez Expedition reached Mexico in 1536. In 1558, Guido de las Bazares sailed the Gulf Coast searching for a place to establish a colony. This was accomplished in the summer of 1559 when Tristán de Luna y Arellano made a settlement at Pensacola Bay. In 1561, that settlement was abandoned and there were no more attempts by the Spanish to colonize west Florida during the next century.

René Cavelier, Sieur de la Salle proclaimed the colony of Louisiana in 1782 but the first settlement was not made until 1699 when the Canadian Pierre le Moyne, Sieur de Iberville built Fort Maurepas on the Gulf coast. In 1702 Iberville explored Mobile Bay searching for a new site for the capital of Louisiana. His brother Jean Baptiste le Moyne, Sieur de Bienville constructed a new fort at Twenty-seven Mile Bluff on the Mobile River and named it Fort Saint-Louis de la Mobile. Bienville won the loyalty of many Indians tribes and resettled several towns near Mobile. The Apalachees were living where Blakeley Park is now, the Choctaws lived on the Dog River, the Tensaws at Stockton, and the Janaibes north of Mobile. The French settlement was moved downriver in 1710 to the site of present-day Mobile and a new fort was built and named Fort Saint-Louis de la Louisiane.

The French and Indian War (Seven Years War) was concluded with the Treaty of Paris on February 10, 1763. Great Britain gained control of all French land east of the Mississippi River, including Canada, and also received Florida from Spain in exchange for Cuba (Spain had joined France in the war against England just in time to have her jewel of the Caribbean captured by British forces). The French secretly ceded to Spain the Isle de Orleans and all Louisiana territory west of the Mississippi River as compensation for the loss of Florida and to keep this vast territory out of British hands. In reality, Louis XV and his court never fully committed themselves to the support of Louisiana. The French citizens of New Orleans did not know of their change in citizenship for some time, and Spain did not take control of Louisiana until 1766.

Mobile was turned over to the British on October 20, 1763 and Major Robert Farmar was the receiving officer. Fort Condé was renamed Fort Charlotte for the queen of George III. Half of the ninety-eight French families of Mobile chose to move to New Orleans in order to remain French citizens. The remaining inhabitants took the oath of allegiance to King George and generally retired to their plantations along the river to raise cattle.

During the British period, Mobile held a more important position as guardian of the Gulf Coast shipping lanes, as a supply point to the Mississippi River, and gateway to the Choctaw and Creek Nations. The colony of West Florida was established with its boundaries at the Apalachicola River on the east, the 31st parallel on the north, and the Mississippi River on the west. The southern boundary was the navigation route through Lake Pontchartrain, Lake Maurepas, and the Amite and Iberville rivers. Major Farmar was military commander at Fort Charlotte and the first governor was George Johnstone. The military was under the ultimate command of

Mobile Welcome Center

Audubon Bird Sanctuary, Dauphin Island

General Thomas Gage in New York, much to the dismay of the Royal Governor. The capital of West Florida was moved to Pensacola, which brought a decline in the fortunes of Mobile.

In June 1779, the Spanish government entered the American conflict as an ally to France and was thus able to help itself by aiding the American colonies. Louisiana governor Bernardo Governor Galvez learned of the alliance in August and began plans for an invasion of West Florida, to preempt the rumored and inevitable invasion of Louisiana by the British. After taking Fort Panmure at Natchez, Fort Bute on Bayou Manchac, and Fort New Richmond at Baton Rouge in September 1779, Galvez set his sights on Mobile. When Galvez arrived to take the city, most of the British garrison was too ill to resist. Mobile fell to Galvez and his troops on March 14, 1780, due to the superiority of the Spanish force and the failure of reinforcements from Pensacola to arrive in time. By the Treaty of Versailles on September 3, 1783, British West Florida was officially returned to Spanish ownership. The Pinckney Treaty of 1795 (Treaty of San Lorenzo) between Spain and the United States established the boundary between Spanish West Florida and the United States at the 31st parallel. Washington County was created in the southern part of Mississippi Territory in 1800.

After the West Florida Rebellion in 1810, rather than recognize the new state, President Madison directed Louisiana Governor Claiborne to occupy the Florida Parishes west of the Pearl River because the United States government had already made claim to the land south of the 31st parallel by virtue of the Louisiana Purchase and assumed it included all of the original Louisiana. The Spanish governor Juan Vicente Folch saw that he could not defend Mobile and offered to give it up if not supported by Spain. Congress authorized President Madison in 1811 to take possession of all of West Florida as far east as the Perdido River, but this was not done until General Wilkinson arrived in Mobile in April 1813 and politely asked Commandant Perez to retire to Pensacola. The Spanish having secretly allowed the British to use Florida ports during the War of 1812, prompted the Americans to make good their claims to West Florida in order to protect their backs. The Spanish garrison was provisioned and transported to Pensacola.

Alabama Territory was created on March 1, 1817 and included the existing counties of Washington and Mobile. The seat of government was established at Saint Stephens. President Monroe appointed William Wyatt Bibb, a senator from Georgia, as territorial governor.

William Bartram's Travels Around Mobile

William Bartram followed the path from Burnt Corn to Mobile, which took him through present-day Huxford, then he passed north of McCullough, and followed county road 47. This trail would later become the Federal Road, which officially ended at

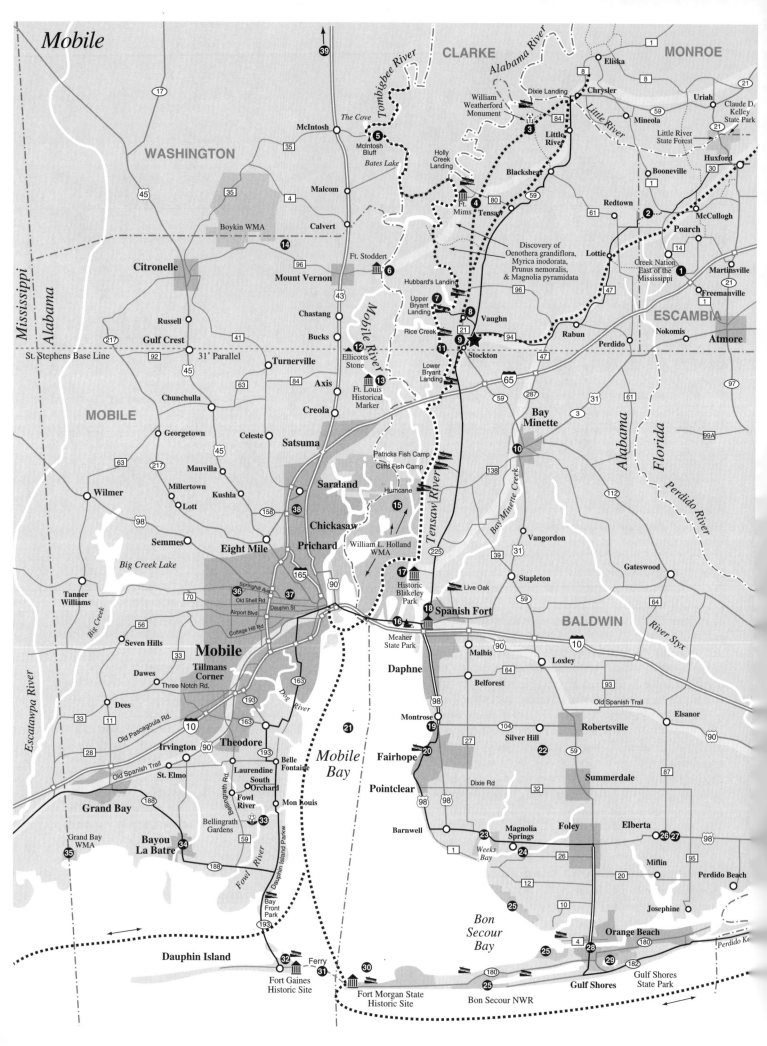

Fort Stoddert, but there were branches to points on Mobile Bay and the Tensaw River. The "Taensa" Bluff was located west of Stockton on the Tensaw River at present-day Lower Bryant Landing (Francis Harper placed it at Upper Bryant Landing). Bartram took a boat down the Tensaw River and arrived in Mobile near the end of July 1775, not 1778.

Bartram sailed from Mobile on August 5 and returned to Tensaw Bluff, where he visited Major Robert Farmar and family. Major Farmar's plantation was located between Lower Bryant Landing and Upper Bryant Landing, and west of Stockton. His home, Farm Hall, was probably located at Tensaw Bluff. William borrowed a canoe and explored up the Tensaw River for several days. During his excursion, he discovered *Myrica inodora, Oenothera grandiflora,* and *Magnolia pyramidata* on the upper reaches of the Tensaw River. He continued to ascend the river, stopping at convenient places that would become modern-day boat landings. He entered the Alabama River near the mouth of Major's Creek, then canoed the Alabama River Cutoff, and entered the Tombigbee River. His farthest point of travel on the Tombigbee was possibly a little above McIntosh Bluff. Bartram could not have seen the ruins of Fort Louis de la Mobile because it was farther south on the Mobile River.

Bartram had the early stages of a fever when he returned to the Farmar plantation. After a few days rest he, and one of Major Farmar's slaves, traveled by horseback north to the Little River in search of a particular medicinal plant. They may have gone as far as the present-day community of Mount Pleasant in Monroe County, near the intersection of Monroe County highways 8 and 1. They returned by a route farther back from the river so as not to retrace ground they had already explored.

The fever lingered; yet Bartram resolved to travel and he returned to Mobile in mid-August in the company of Dr. Michael Grant, physician to the British garrison at Mobile. On September 3, 1775, he sailed for Pensacola and returned to Mobile on the 6th. The fever now gripped him more strongly as he sailed for the Pearl River on the following day.

William returned to Mobile from Baton Rouge on November 16. He prepared his specimens and shipped them to London. He traveled a last time to Tensaw Bluff, said his good-byes to the Farmars, and departed for the Creek Nation on November 27.

Sites

1. The Creek Nation East of the Mississippi. About 800 descendants of the Creek Indians who were allied to the Americans during the Creek War live around Poarch and Atmore. Their claims go back to the Treaty of Fort Jackson in 1814 but were not settled until 1972. Their most important community event is Thanksgiving Day Homecoming when all Creeks living far and wide are welcomed. Creek Nation East of the Mississippi, Inc., Tribal Council Offices, Route 2, Box 243–A, Atmore, AL 36502.

2. Old Stagecoach Road. This remnant of the Old Federal Road may be retraced at the Baldwin-Escambia county line.

3. William Weatherford Monument. This small Baldwin County historic park contains the graves of William Weatherford, known as Red Eagle (Lumhe Chati), and his mother, Sehoy Tate Weatherford, a Tuskegee princess of the Wind Clan who was the third to bear the name of Sehoy. Sehoy was the daughter of Sehoy II and the chief of the Tuckabatchees, and she was a half-sister to Alexander McGillivray. Weatherford, like so many Creek leaders, was the son of a white father and a Creek mother. Sehoy's first husband was Colonel John Tate, the last British Indian Agent among the Creeks and their sons were David and John Tate. Colonel Tate died in Georgia and was buried near Kasihta. Sehoy then married Charles Weatherford and their son was William Weatherford. William's sister, Elizabeth (Betsey), married Sam Moniac, who ran the tavern on Pintlala Creek.

William Weatherford's first wife was Mary Moniac, Sam Moniac's sister. Mary died in 1804 and Weatherford next married Sopoth Thlanie in 1813. She was considered to be the most beautiful woman in the region and was renowned for her sweet singing voice. She died within the year shortly after their son was born. Weatherford next married Mary Stiggins in 1817 and Sam Dale was the best man at their wedding.

Although he was not a headman and only one-quarter Indian, Weatherford became a leader among the Red Sticks. He was with the Creeks at the attack on Fort Mims but left in disgust at the excess of young warriors who were inflamed by the speeches of Tecumseh.

Legend

1. Creek Indians East of the Mississippi
2. Old Stagecoach Road
3. William Weatherford Monument
4. Fort Mims Historic Site
5. McIntosh Landing
6. Site of Fort Stoddert
7. Byrne's Landing
8. Major Robert Farmar's Plantation
9. Stockton
10. Bay Minette Visitor Center
11. Bartram Canoe Trail
12. Ellicott's Stone
13. Fort Louis de la Louisiane
14. Mowa Band of Choctaw
15. Mobile Delta Bioreserve
16. Meaher State Park
17. Historic Blakeley Park
18. Spanish Fort Historic Overlook
19. Ecor Rouge
20. Fairhope Single Tax Colony
21. Mobile Bay
22. Minamac Wildflower Bog
23. Weeks Bay National Estuarine Reserve
24. Magnolia Springs
25. Bon Secour National Wildlife Refuge
26. Baldwin Heritage Museum
27. Biophilia Nature Center
28. Zooland Animal Park
29. Gulf State Park
30. Fort Morgan State Historic Site
31. Mobile Bay Ferry
32. Dauphin Island
    Audubon Sanctuary
    Dauphin Island Sea Lab and Estuarium
    Fort Gaines Historic Site
    Cadillac Square Park
    Prince Madoc ab Owain Gwnedd
33. Bellingrath Gardens
34. Bayou La Batre
35. Grand Bay National Wildlife Refuge
36. Mobile Botanical Gardens
    Mobile Museum of Art
37. Eichold-Heustis Medical Museum
    University of South Alabama Library and Archives
38. Grand Oak Wildlife Preservation Park
39. Saint Stephens

Major Robert Farmar

Robert Farmar was born in New Jersey in 1717 and rose through the ranks of the British military to command the 34th Regiment. He arrived in Mobile in 1763 to accept the transfer of that part of Louisiana that was to become attached to British West Florida. He was in charge of rebuilding Fort Condé, renamed Fort Charlotte, and organizing British government in Mobile. While he was military commander in Mobile, Farmar lived at the northeast corner of Government and St. Emanuel streets. The building was burned when Governor Bernardo Galvez captured Fort Condé. When William Bartram visited him in 1775, Robert Farmar had taken up residence across the Tensaw River as a private citizen and planter.

Farmar became embroiled in conflict with Governor Johnstone, who believed he had the power to direct the military as well as the civil government. Johnstone and Lieutenant Phillip Pittman brought thirty-five indictments against Farmar during a court-martial at Pensacola. Farmar was acquitted of twenty-five charges and the rest were dismissed as being without merit and too frivolous to pursue. Farmar asked for the governorship of West Florida as a sign of vindication and innocence but the office was given to Peter Chester. Though cleared of all charges, Farmar was deprived of his commission and traveled to London in an unsuccessful attempt to have it reinstated. The readings of the charges against Farmar are interesting and confusing. This was a time when public service and private gain were blurred by the fact that men in Farmar's position often spent their own money and resorted to tricks, ruses, and coercion to supply their troops and accomplish their mission.

Farmar was elected to the West Florida Assembly in 1769. He purchased land near the present-day town of Stockton with some of his lands extending above the Saint Stephens Base Line into Indian territory. The plantation where he had his residence, Farm Hall, was located west of Stockton. He tried growing indigo and rice then turned to lumber production during the Revolution. The Farmar plantation became a rendezvous point for traders traveling between Georgia and Mobile. Farmar also bought land at Natchez, Manchac, and other places in West Florida. By 1778 he owned over 65,000 acres of land scattered across West Florida. Major Farmar died on August 1, 1778.

When Governor Galvez of Louisiana captured Mobile in 1780, Mary Farmar and her family moved to Pensacola rather than take an oath of allegience to Spain. After Galvez captured Pensacola in 1781 the Farmar family was sent to New York, then Charleston, and in April 1782 they sailed for England.

Farmar's daughter Elizabeth returned to Mobile around 1813 and married Louis François le Gras de Vaubercey. In 1839 the United States confirmed the Farmar title to 400 acres known as the Island on the west side of the Mobile River just one mile above the city, now the site of the Alabama State Docks.

Ellicott's Stone marking the 31st parallel

Weatherford told Thomas Woodward many years later that he had hoped to guide the warriors into abandoning the attack and leaving in peace. After the Treaty of Fort Jackson ended the First Creek War, Weatherford walked into camp and surrendered to General Andrew Jackson. Jackson was so impressed with the character of his prisoner that Weatherford was paroled. Weatherford lived the remainder of his life on his plantation in Baldwin County and died there in 1826. Though he was a leader among the Red Sticks, William Weatherford became exactly what they had fought against—a gentleman, planter, and friend of the Americans.

4. Fort Mims Historic Site was the scene of the largest Indian Massacre of settlers in the United States. The massacre was the incident that precipitated the First Creek War in 1813–1814. Samuel Mims had in his youth been employed as a packhorse-man for George Galphin before moving to lower Alabama. Area settlers sought refuge at Mims' stockaded residence because parties of Red Sticks were on the move along the Mobile-Pensacola Path and Alabama River. In the wake of Tecumseh's visit to Tuckabatchee in 1811 disaffection began to grow in the Creek Nation. Resentment over the building of the Federal Road and British intrigue combined to create unrest that erupted with the Red Stick attack at Ft. Mims on August 30, 1813. The refugees were warned by James Cornells that hostiles were approaching, but commander Daniel Beasley, who was ripping drunk by midday, refused to believe that anyone would attack such a stronghold and ordered Cornells arrested. Cornells escaped and the Red Sticks attacked very soon afterwards. At their head was Red Eagle, William Weatherford, who lived in the area and was thought to be a friend of the Americans.

The siege might have been abandoned but the buildings caught fire and the Creeks, taking advantage of the settlers' distress, breached the walls and killed nearly 300. Among the victims of the massacre at Fort Mims were numerous wealthy mixed-blood citizens of Tensaw and Little River.

The Fort Mims area was known at the time as the Boat Yard. The site is now a Baldwin County park and the location of the fort and buildings are delineated with railroad ties. There is a re-enactment of the massacre on the last weekend of each August.

5. McIntosh Landing is the site of the principal town of the Tohome Indians. The landing was later the home of James McIntosh, interpreter for the British, and ancestor of Governor Troup of Georgia. In 1804, when the Mississippi Territory was organized out of the territory forfeited by Georgia, Washington was one of three original counties and had its seat of government at McIntosh Bluff during the first year. Washington County contained all land between the Pearl and Chattahoochee rivers and from the 31st parallel to 32° 28'. To reach McIntosh Landing travel north on US-43 then east on Washington County Road 35 in McIntosh. Bernard Romans noted during a visit to the landing in 1771 that the pine barrens reached to the edge of the bluff.

6. Site of Fort Stoddert. When the boundary line between Spanish West Florida and the United States was fixed at the 31st parallel the Americans constructed a fort near the line at Ward's Bluff on the Mobile River and named it after the Secretary of War. It was the official end of the Federal Road that began in Augusta. Beyond Fort Stoddert the Federal Road connected with established roads to Mobile, New Orleans, and Natchez. Located north of Mobile, turn right on Mobile County Road 96 in Mount Vernon.

7. Byrne's Landing is the only public landing on the Tensaw River, all others are private commercial landings and require a launch fee.

The private landings are a great place to get local information and many have campgrounds, weekend trailer parks, and sometimes a restaurant.

8. Major Robert Farmar's Plantation was located southwest of Stockton near Lower Bryant Landing. William Bartram visited with the Farmar family and met Dr. William Grant with whom he traveled about the area. A historical marker commemorating Major Farmar is one mile south of town and the **Bartram Trail Historical Marker** is located within the Stockton city limits near Old Stagecoach Road.

9. Stockton occupies land that Major Robert Farmar acquired after retiring from military service. During the 1790s Stockton was the second largest town in lower Alabama.

10. Bay Minette Visitor Center. Located on McMeans Avenue (AL-59) and West Third Street in Bay Minette.

11. Bartram Canoe Trail commemorates William Bartram's excursion on the Tensaw River. The trail begins at Hubbard Landing, ends at Live Oak Landing, and covers a total of twenty miles. Hubbard Landing is reached by going north of Stockton on AL-59, then turning left on Baldwin 96. Live Oak Landing is the first left going north of I-65 on AL-225.

12. Ellicott's Stone & the Saint Stephens Base Line represent the 31st parallel that became the boundary between Spanish West Florida and the United States as established by the 1795 Treaty of San Lorenzo (also called the Pinckney Treaty). The Saint Stephens Base Line became the southern boundary for the Mississippi Territory. The line was run by Andrew Ellicott beginning at the Mississippi River on April 11, 1798, and reaching the Mobile River on March 18, 1799. Ellicott's Stone marks the intersection of the Saint Stephens Meridian and Saint Stephens Base Line. This point is the base for surveying in southern Alabama. Located about eight miles north of I-65 on US-43 on the east side of the railroad grade.

13. Fort Louis de la Mobile was built by Bienville in 1702 at Twenty-seven Mile Bluff and was the first site of Mobile when it was the capital of Louisiana. The fort and town were moved to the present site of Mobile in 1711 when the river flooded the original settlement. The new fort was named Fort Louis de la Louisiane.

14. Citronelle is home to the **Mowa Band of Choctaw**, formally recognized in 1979. Their language is a mixture of English and French. The band has built a tribal center and are planning to construct a historic Choctaw village.

Bayou La Batre

15. Mobile Delta Bioreserve. The Mobile River delta is the largest inland river delta in the U.S. and encompasses 200,000 acres of marsh and wetland forest. Wildland Expeditions, based in Chickasaw, offers a two-hour educational boat tour of the Mobile delta where visitors can see the ancient shell mounds, points of historical interest, alligators, 250 species of birds, and maybe a black bear. Visit Wildland Expeditions at Chickasaw Marina on US-43 in Chickasaw. Admission.

16. Meaher State Park is located at the southern end of the Mobile Delta and provides easy access to the surrounding wetlands. It contains 1,327 acres and has a fishing pier, two nature trails, boat ramp and canoe rental. Meaher State Park is a day-use area, open 7 a.m.–4 p.m. The entrance is located on US-90.

17. Historic Blakeley Park. Blakeley has been a site of settlement for thousands of years. In the eighteenth century, the French established plantations in the area and the Apalachee Indians were settled there after being driven from Florida by the South Carolinians. The American town of Blakeley was chartered in 1814 and became the seat of government for Baldwin County. For a time it grew, but the citizens and commerce left for more healthy parts.

Historic Blakeley Park preserves a major Civil War Battle site and the Blakeley town site. The park is still being developed and will eventually have RV camping, a reconstructed courthouse, museum, an inn, and an interpretative village. Historic Blakeley Park has hiking trails, primitive camping, and Jacque Pate Nature Sanctuary.

18. Spanish Fort Historic Overlook occupies a high hill overlooking Mobile Bay. It was a celebrated resting place for travelers on the Old Spanish Trail as well as providing a strategic military position. When Galvez captured Mobile in 1780, his army constructed a fort on the overlook that gave the community its name. The entrance to the overlook is on AL-225 between I-10 and US-31 in Spanish Fort.

19. Ecor Rouge, at Montrose, has been noted on maps since the middle of the sixteenth century. The bluffs at Montrose are the highest point of land on the coast from Maine to Mexico. The British built a camp and military hospital at Ecor Rouge in the 1770s.

20. Fairhope Single Tax Colony was founded in 1894 by Midwesterners who were adherents of the philosophy of Henry George. They believed in public ownership of land and a single tax that came from leasehold fees. The fee is based on land use rather than value, ensuring an appropriate amount of public space, a thriving downtown shopping district, and a lack of urban sprawl. The Fairhope Community still operates as a single-tax community today. As you might surmise, such a community has attracted a different kind of citizen. The Bluffs at Fairhope Park overlook Mobile Bay and Fairhope Municipal Pier.

21. Mobile Bay is a submerged river valley that once extended to the Pleistocene seashore many miles farther into the Gulf. The Mobile Delta is the sixth largest watershed in the country, with five major rivers draining into the bay. Numerous mounds exist throughout the delta, the most significant is **Bottle Creek Mound** which is accessible only by boat. Many of the mounds appear to have been shell middens and had no ceremonial purpose. The estuaries of the bay and delta provide a livelihood for the fishing fleets at Bon Secour and Bayou La Batre. The greatest part of the seafood industry of Mobile Bay is shrimp. Brown shrimp are the first shrimp caught during the season and are usually caught at night. White shrimp are caught in September and October, closer to shore, and during the day. The white shrimp are preferred for their sweetness.

Jubilee! A strange phenomenon that seems to exist only at the eastern shore of Mobile Bay is signaled by the cry of *Jubilee!* Fish, crab, and shrimp move into the shallow water near shore and are so passive as to allow themselves to be scooped up by hand, net, and bucket. No one has successfully explained why this happens, and it may last from a few minutes to a few hours. Some years it happens again and again and some years it happens not at all.

22. Minamac Wildflower Bog is a five-acre private wildflower sanctuary that appeared after the owners built a pond in a wet, wooded area. Each year more and more flowers appeared and the family began control burning to encourage the native flowers—especially white top pitcher plants and orchids. With over 100 native flowers there is something blooming from April to October. Minamac Wildflower Bog, 13199 MacCartee Lane, Silverhill, AL 36576. Call ahead for a tour, (334) 947-3044 or 945-6157.

23. Weeks Bay National Estuarine Reserve. In Weeks Bay Estuary freshwater from the Fish and Magnolia rivers blends with brackish water to create a marine nursery that sustains the ecology of the bay and the local economy. Weeks Bay Sanctuary covers 3,000 acres of wetlands and coastal environment. The offices and Interpretive Center are located on US-98 at the west side of the Fish River Bridge. A nature trail and boardwalk make a loop through the adjacent wetland where trees and shrubs are labeled for identification. In June fragrant swamp lilies are in bloom. The extensive garden of native plants is worth a visit anytime from spring through fall. The interpretative center contains several aquariums of animals found in Weeks Bay and Mobile Bay. There is a cabinet of artifacts from several thousand years of human inhabitation. Open 8 a.m.–5 p.m., Monday through Friday.

24. Mail is still delivered by boat along **Magnolia Springs** as it has since 1916. The water route is twenty-five miles while the land route would be eighty-five, so mailboxes are located on the docks rather than on the roads.

25. Bon Secour National Wildlife Refuge covers over 6,000 acres of marsh and wetland along the south side of Bon Secour Bay. There are two hiking trails accessible from AL-180 and a freshwater lake for fishing and canoeing. Little Lagoon can be fished for trout, flounder, and crabs. Open year round, dawn to dusk.

26. Baldwin Heritage Museum has exhibits of farming practices and implements used by the settlers of Baldwin County. A historic village is planned for the five-acre site. Located on US-98 one mile east of Elberta. Open 10 a.m.–5 p.m., Friday and Saturday, 1–5 p.m. on Sunday.

27. Biophilia Nature Center displays the native plants of the Gulf Coast. Its features include a swamp, pitcher-plant bog, wildflower meadow, and butterfly conservatory. Open 8–10 a.m. on Wednesday and Saturday, 9 a.m.–5 p.m. on Sundays, and by appointment at other times. Located on Baldwin 95, three miles east of Elberta.

28. Zooland Animal Park has over 200 native and exotic animals. Located on AL-59 on the south side of the Intracoastal Waterway. Open at 9 a.m. everyday except Thanksgiving and Christmas.

29. Gulf State Park covers 6,000 acres and has over two miles of beach. There are hiking trails and a Nature Center. AL-135 in Gulf Shores.

30. Fort Morgan State Historic Site. Fort Morgan was completed in 1834 as part of the ambitious coastal defense system begun in 1819. This peninsula is a significant birding area in spring and fall. In October, monarch butterflies pass through on their way to wintering in Mexico. Located at the west end of AL-180. Open 8 a.m.–6 p.m., daily except Thanksgiving, Christmas, and New Year's Day. Admission.

31. Mobile Bay Ferry makes nine trips each day and takes thirty minutes to cross from Dauphin Island to Fort Morgan.

32. Dauphin Island was originally called Massacre Island by the French because they found a pile of human bones when they arrived. In 1711, Iberville renamed the island *Dauphine,* which is the title of the wife of the heir to the throne. The capital of Louisiana was at Dauphin Island temporarily in 1701 while Fort Louis was being constructed. Due to its excellent harbor, Dauphin Island remained the port for Mobile and the point of immigration for Louisiana. Dauphin Island became the capital again in 1713 when Antoine de la Mothe Cadillac became governor of Louisiana. The government was moved back to Biloxi in 1719 because the Dauphin harbor had become blocked by a sandbar during a hurricane.

Dauphin Island has quite a bit of developed real estate but there are public beaches, boat ramps, Fort Gaines Campground, and a running and bike path that parallels Bienville Boulevard.

Audubon Sanctuary. The Audubon Society owns a 160-acre preserve lying between Bienville Boulevard and the beach. Dauphin Island is the first landfall for birds migrating north from Central and South America, making it a popular birding area in the fall. Hiking trails guide visitors through a variety of habitats and end at the beach. Open during daylight hours.

Dauphin Island Sea Lab and Estuarium is a collection of aquariums filled with sealife of the Mobile delta, Mobile Bay, and Gulf of Mexico. Located at 101 Bienville Boulevard at the east end of Dauphin Island. Open 8 a.m.–5 p.m., Monday through Friday, June through December 15. Admission.

Fort Gaines Historic Site was the site of the Battle of Mobile in 1864 and is also the approximate site of Iberville's 1717 magazine and barracks. A French kitchen garden is maintained next to the officers' quarters. The fortress overlooks Mobile Bay.

Cadillac Square Park commemorates the governorship of Antoine de la Mothe Cadillac when the capital and port of Louisiana were at Dauphin Island. The park is located on the site of Governor Cadillac's home and is a popular picnic area. Open during daylight hours. Located on Bienville Boulevard.

Prince Madoc ab Owain Gwnedd was a Welsh explorer who some believe may have sailed to the New World and into Mobile Bay in 1170. A marker at Fort Gaines commemorates this legend.

33. Bellingrath Gardens is billed as one of the top five gardens in the United States. It is well known for its azalea display in early spring when over 25,000 plants are in bloom. Bellingrath has several theme gardens of tropical and subtropical plantings including a rose garden, oriental garden, and formal garden. Lying beside the Fowl River, the grounds of Bellingrath are also a good place to view local birds. 12401 Bellingrath Gardens Road. Open 8 a.m.–sunset everyday. Admission.

34. Bayou La Batre was made famous by the movie *Forrest Gump,* but is better known locally as the base for the Bayou La Batre shrimping fleet. The community was originally called Riviéré d'Erbane but received its present name from a battery maintained by the French that was located on the west bank of the Bayou. In 1786 Joseph Borsage of Poitiers, France, received the property in a Spanish land grant.

35. Grand Bay National Wildlife Refuge is accessible only by boat. The refuge protects salt marsh and estuary and provides a haven for water birds.

36. Mobile Botanical Gardens combines trails and native plants in a natural setting. Important features are the woodland trails, fern glade, magnolia grove, native azaleas, and community vegetable gardens. To reach the botanical gardens from downtown Mobile, follow Spring Hill Avenue, signs will indicate a left turn on Pixie Drive, then turn right on Museum Drive.

Mobile Museum of Art has a collection of art and artifacts that spans 2,000 years of culture in the Mobile delta. Museum Drive just off Spring Hill Avenue, 1 a.m.–5 p.m., Tuesday through Sunday.

37. Eichold-Heustis Medical Museum of the South. This interesting museum covers two centuries of medical history, much of it particular to the epidemic diseases and medical practices of the South. John Bartram's interest in botany started with an interest in medicine. Much of early botanical exploration and study was in search of new medicines as well as new foods. The Eichold-Heustis Medical Museum is not easy to find. It is located in the lobby of the University of South Alabama building at 1504 Springhill Avenue. Open 8 a.m.–5 p.m., Monday through Friday. The entrance is at Conception and Dauphin Streets.

University of South Alabama Library and Archives. 1504 Spring Hill Avenue. Photographic archives are located in room 0722.

38. Grand Oak Wildlife Preservation Park. Grand Oak Park includes exotic creatures as well as native wildlife and domestic animals. The Alabama champion live oak is the centerpiece of the park. Lectures, hiking trails, and day-camps are additional resources available at the park. 300 Industrial Parkway. Open 8 a.m. until two hours before dusk, everyday. Admission.

39. Saint Stephens was the capital of the Alabama Territory from 1817–1819 and was the southernmost port in the United States until the annexation of the Florida Parishes in 1810. Saint Stephens was established as an American military outpost and settlement on the Tombigbee River in the early 1790s and occupies the site of an earlier Spanish fort.

Saint Stephens Historical Park was established to protect the archaeological site of the town of Saint Stephens. The park provides recreational activities including fishing, hiking, birdwatching, bicycling, boating, swimming, and picnicking. From Mobile, travel north on US-43, turn left on Washington 34 in Leroy. Open sunrise to sunset daily; and 6 a.m.–4 p.m., November through January. Admission.

Itinerary

Miles	Directions
	Begin at the intersection of Escambia 45 and Old Stagecoach Road on the Conecuh-Monroe county line. Travel south on Escambia 45.
3.9	Right on Escambia 30 (keep left at the fork to McCullough)
8.2	Right on Old Booneville Road in McCullough, which become Escambia-1
2.4	Left on Taylor Circle (the road will make a sharp right turn)
1.8	Left on Stagecoach Road (unpaved)
2.2	Left on Pressley Road
.4	Right on Baldwin 61
.4	Left on Baldwin 47 (keep straight at the upcoming intersection)
13.3	Right on Baldwin 94
6.3	Left on Old Stagecoach Road
1.1	Left on AL-59, Bartram Trail historical marker on the left
.6	Right on AL-225, Historical Marker for Major Farmar's Plantation
24.4	Right on US-31 in Spanish Fort
.8	Right on US-90
7.8	Downtown Mobile, keep straight on Government Street
3.3	Left on Dauphin Island Parkway (AL-163)
9.5	Right on Hamilton Road (AL-163)
1.9	Left on Rangeline Road (AL-193)
3.6	Left on Laurendine Road (AL-193)
.8	Right on Dauphin Island Parkway (AL-193)
17.9	Arrive on Dauphin Island, left on Bienville Boulevard
.8	Cadillac Square, site of the Capital of Louisiana in 1715
1.6	Arrive at Dauphin Island Estuarium and Fort Gaines Return to the mainland by AL-193
10.3	Turn left on AL-188
8.6	Enter Bayou La Batre
2.6	Keep left on AL-188
6.6	Keep straight on two Mile Road where AL-188 turns sharply right
1.2	Left on US-90
2.7	Enter Mississippi

Tensaw Day Trip

Miles	Directions
	Begin at the intersection of AL-225 and AL-59 in Stockton and travel north on AL-225
1.7	Intersection with Baldwin 21 (left for Upper Bryant Landing, 3.7 miles)
3.9	Intersection with Hubbard Landing Road (left for Hubbard Landing, 2.2 miles)
7.8	Intersection with Boatyard Road (left for Fort Mims Historical Site, 3.55 miles)
10.7	Left on Dixie Landing Road (Baldwin-84)
2.2	Left on a dirt road
1.0	Grave of William Weatherford

Counties

Washington County, Alabama, was created in June 1800 and named for President George Washington. The original Washington County contained much of southern Alabama and Mississippi.

Mobile County, Alabama was created in 1812 and named for the city of Mobile and the Mabila Indians.

Baldwin County, Alabama was created in 1809 and named for Abraham Baldwin, Georgia senator and first president of the University of Georgia.

Escambia County, Florida was created in 1821 and named for the Escambia River.

Historic Mobile

When the government of Louisiana was moved from Old Biloxi to Mobile Bay in 1701, temporary headquarters were established on Dauphin Island while Bienville built a permanent settlement at Twenty-seven Mile Bluff. The new fort was completed in 1702 and named Fort Saint-Louis de la Mobile in honor of King Louis XIV. It was about 375 feet square and defended by six cannons. The civilian settlement was built a little upriver from the fort and was named Mobile for the Mabila Indians who lived near present-day Mount Vernon. Louisiana grew slowly; there were approximately 200 citizens in the colony in 1704 and almost 300 in 1708. The first French child born in Louisiana was Claude Jousset de la Loire, born in Mobile around 1703–1704. The colony was supported by shipments from France, hunting, fishing, and some farming. Fort Saint-Louis was moved downriver in 1710 to the present location of Mobile. The old site was low and marshy and valuable supplies had been lost to flooding.

Iberville left Louisiana in 1702 and was succeeded as governor by his brother Bienville who was assisted by Henri de Tonti. On September 14, 1712, Louisiana was granted to Antoine Crozat, Marquis de Chatel, as a proprietary colony for a period of fifteen years. Antoine de la Mothe Cadillac, founder of Detroit, was appointed governor and he made his capital at Dauphin Island. Cadillac was given a monopoly on trade in Louisiana and he brought in the first substantial numbers of African slaves to work the farms and help feed the colony. His control of the economy helped create a financial crisis and his authoritarian style of administration created widespread discontent. Cadillac was replaced in 1717 by Jean Michiele, Segneur de Lepinay et de la Longueville. Lepinay and Bienville soon were in disagreement and their conflict was about to divide the colony. Crozat gave up the colony and on September 12, 1717 Louisiana came under the control of the Company of the West. The harbor at Dauphin was made unusable by a hurricane that year and the capital of Louisiana was moved from Mobile Bay to Biloxi in 1719.

Though once the capital of the vast Louisiana colony that stretched from the Appalachian Mountains to the Rockies and from the Gulf of Mexico to the Great Lakes, Mobile became essentially an important military outpost when the focus of settlement and government moved to the Mississippi River. Mobile was strategically important because it was the entrepôt for the lucrative trade with the Alabamas. Like Pensacola to the east, the land around Mobile was not fertile enough to feed the city. Many of the early French settlers were not farmers but rather adventurers, soldiers, and traders.

The British occupied Mobile beginning in 1763 and incorporated it into West Florida. Mobile became an even more important center for the Indian trade because the British held more of the trade among the Creeks than had the French. Mobile was lost when Governor Bernardo Galvez of Louisiana seized the city on March 14, 1780. The Spanish held Mobile as part of Florida until they gave up the city to the Americans in 1813. Mobile was made a part of Mississippi Territory in that year.

Upon the close of the War of 1812 the United States con-

Fort Condé

trolled all lands east of the Mississippi River except Florida. Georgians, Carolinians, and Virginians poured into the Mississippi territory bringing cotton seed and slaves with them. After the Creek War of 1813 even more land opened up in the interior of Alabama for planters. Then came steamboats in 1821! Being the chief port on the river system that drained a large cotton growing region, Mobile entered a golden age. The city grew, fortunes were made, and the first mystic Mardis Gras societies were formed in the 1830s. Indeed, Mobile is the mother of Mardis Gras in North America, for Boeuf Gras (fattened ox) was celebrated at Fort Louis on the day before Ash Wednesday in 1703.

Sites

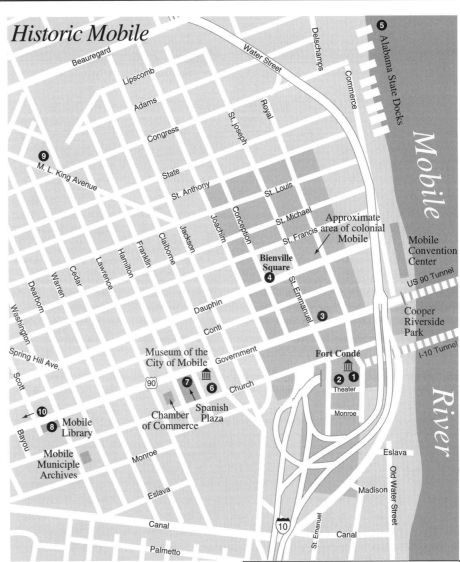

1. Fort Condé was constructed in 1724 on the site of the earlier Fort Saint Louis. The British made some changes and enlargements and renamed it Fort Charlotte. The walls stood until the 1820s when they were dismantled for the brick. The interior of the fortress was located approximately in the area bounded by Church, St. Emmanuel, Royal, and Theater streets. The current structure recreates the original French Fort Condé on its original ground and houses the Mobile Welcome Center and a museum that tells the history of Mobile from its founding by Iberville in 1702 to the most recent Mardis Gras balls. Located at 150 South Royal Street. Open 8 a.m.–5 p.m. every day.

2. Condé-Charlotte Museum House. The rooms are furnished in each of the national periods of Mobile—French Empire, English, American Federal, and Confederate. A walled Spanish garden completes the cycle. Located at 104 Theatre Street next to Fort Condé. Open 10 a.m.–4 p.m., Tuesday through Saturday. Admission.

6. Museum of the City of Mobile. The history of Mobile is displayed in the colony rooms for French, Spanish, British, and American periods. Located at 355 Government Street. Open 10 a.m.–5 p.m. Tuesday through Saturday and 1–5 p.m. on Sunday.

3. Major Robert Farmar's residence in Mobile was located at the corner of Saint Emmanuel and Government streets.

4. Bienville Square was dedicated in 1866 to honor Governor Bienville, founder of Mobile.

5. Alabama State Docks ranks eighth in the nation in exports. It is interesting to read the notices for goods being unloaded, including a great deal of bananas and coffee as one would suspect. The docks may be toured with professional guides. Part of this area was once owned by Major Robert Farmar.

8. Mobile Library. 701 Government Street.

7. Spanish Plaza honors the Spanish period of Mobile, 1780–1813, and Mobile's sister city, Malaga, Spain.

9. National African American Archives Museum. This important collection is housed in the library built for the black community when facilities were segregated. On display are memorabilia of Mobile's favorite son, Hank Aaron. Located at 564 Dr. Martin Luther King, Jr. Avenue. Open 10 a.m.–4 p.m., Tuesday through Saturday and from 2–4 p.m. on Sunday.

10. Azalea Trail. Mobile is internationally known for its public and private display of azaleas during the annual azalea pilgrimage. François Langlois brought the first azaleas to Mobile from Toulouse in 1754, but the largest plantings have been in the early part of this century.

Itinerary for Pensacola

Leave downtown Mobile and take US-90 cross the bay

Miles	Directions
7.7	US-90 keeps right
.8	Right on US-98
7.5	Right on US-98A for downtown Fairhope
2.1	US-98A turns right in downtown Fairhope
8.5	US-98A turns sharp left
4.6	Weeks Bay Visitor Center
9.4	Right on AL-59 in Foley
11.0	Left on AL-182 in Gulf Shores
2.0	Entrance for Gulf State Park
8.5	Alabama-Florida state line

Pensacola

The Panzacola Indians lived along the Gulf Coast during the time of earliest Spanish exploration. Diego Miruelo was the first European to see the bay at Pensacola when he cruised the Gulf in 1516. Diego Maldonado was probably the first European to actually explore Pensacola Bay when in the summer of 1540 he was to rendezvous with the De Soto expedition at Pensacola. However, De Soto turned his army northward and they never met Maldonado. De Soto's troops, suffering from their Pyrrhic victory against the Mabilas, were on the verge of deserting their expedition. To keep his troops in check, De Soto lead them deeper into the wilderness where they had only one another for support.

Tristán de Luna y Arellano and Angel de Villefañe made the first serious attempt to establish a colony north of Mexico. King Phillip, hoping to establish a credible claim to Florida and provide protection for Spanish treasure ships, instructed that a settlement be made at Santa Elena. Luna, however, sailed for Pensacola Bay, then called Ochuse Bay, where he planned to leave a settlement before traveling overland to Santa Elena. He arrived at Ochuse on August 14, 1559 with 1,000 settlers, 500 soldiers, horses, cattle, and food. A hurricane blew in, destroying supplies and hurling ships onto shore. The remaining undamaged ship was sent to Mexico for supplies.

During the next year the settlers suffered greatly, finally traveling inland to Nanipacana and Coosa to obtain food from the Indians. Luna became ill, the colonists became discouraged, and the soldiers lost faith in Luna's ability to command. Angel de Villafañe was appointed to replace Luna as Governor of Florida and by the end of 1561 everyone had been evacuated from Pensacola. In nearly all of the early attempts at exploration, conquest, or settlement in Florida the Spanish encountered their two nemeses—hunger and hurricanes. Spain ignored the Gulf Coast for the next century and concentrated her efforts on the strategically important Saint Augustine.

In 1683 Juan Enríques Barroto led an expedition in search of the La Salle colony and rediscovered Pensacola Bay. The report of its beauty and excellent harbor renewed interest in establishing a Spanish colony at Pensacola, no doubt due in part to the threat of a new French presence in the area. Five years later, the Crown decreed that a colony be established at Bahía de Santa María de Galvé (Pensacola Bay). On November 21, 1698, Spanish troops landed and set up camp at Barranca de Santo Tomé, the present site of Fort Barrancas. Another fort was constructed on the mainland and named Fort San Carlos de Austria in honor of Charles, heir apparent to the throne of Spain and son of Emperor Leopold I of Austria. A third fortification was built on the west end of Santa Rosa Island to guard the east side of the bay. Life in early Pensacola was often pathetic. The settlement was supported by outside shipments of food Because little could be grown on the sandy soil. When regular shipments did not arrive the people went hungry. During summer, heat and disease took a toll in lives. Forty convicts escaped into the wilderness but soon returned; a testament to the harshness and remoteness of Pensacola. The viceroys were reluctant to spend funds for building and improvements so life in Pensacola was destined to remain Spartan and isolated.

During the early eighteenth century, the French and Spanish aided one another during times of need, although trade was not sanctioned by either home government. When Spain was at war with the other European powers, the brothers Iberville and Bienville led an expedition from Mobile in May 1719 and captured Pensacola from Governor Juan Pedro Matamoras. The Spanish recaptured Pensacola immediately, then the French took it again and blew up Fort San Carlos. Pensacola was returned to Spain by treaty in 1722 and France renounced any claim to land east of the Perdido River.

The present city of Pensacola was established in 1752 when residents of Santa Rosa Island moved across Pensacola Bay to the San Miguel Mission, located where Seville Square is today. Presidio San Miguel de Panzacola was built to house the garrison.

The Treaty of Paris in 1763 ended the Seven Years War and gave Great Britain all of Florida in exchange for Cuba. The province was divided into East and West Florida, the fourteenth and fifteenth colonies. Pensacola became the capital of West Florida, an area that extended from the Apalachicola River to the Mississippi River and north to about the 32nd parallel (approximately Eufaula, Alabama, to Vicksburg, Mississippi). Most of the Spanish citizens left for New Orleans.

Pensacola was even more isolated than Mobile and, like Mobile, was little more than a military outpost. The first governor was George Johnstone who quarreled incessantly with the military leaders and elected assembly. He was recalled in 1767 and replaced with Lieutenant Governor Montfort Brown as interim governor. The newly appointed governor John Eliot arrived in the spring of 1769 and immediately committed suicide by hanging himself. The new streets were laid out by Elias Durnford, who became temporary governor when Montfort Brown was recalled. Peter Chester became governor in 1770 and continued the tradition of quarreling with the assembly, yet the colony grew during his tenure largely due to its importance as a haven for loyalists during the Revolution.

In 1781 Pensacola was defended by British regulars, German Waldecks, and American loyalists, many of whom had become ill. On March 8 of that year only 750 of 1,200 men were fit for duty when Bernardo de Galvez, governor of Louisiana, besieged Pensacola. Governor Chester and General John

Florida Scrub at Big Lagoon State Park

Campbell had been expecting the attack because Galvez had by then taken Baton Rouge, Natchez, and Mobile. Campbell was forced to surrender later in the day when a powder magazine blew up. Galvez diverted energy and troops from the main theater of war in the Carolinas and Virginia during the time that Cornwallis was campaigning.

The Spanish kept the British town layout for Pensacola but the streets were given the beautiful Spanish names that remain today. Very few English-speaking inhabitants chose to remain in Pensacola when it again became a Spanish colony. At the dawn of the nineteenth century, Pensacola was a government town with an annual stipend from Spain and the two main businesses were government affairs and Panton, Leslie & Company. The later enterprise was the authorized trading company to the Creek Confederacy and was owned by William Panton, John Leslie and other members of the Leslie family, John Forbes, and Alexander McGillivray was a silent partner

Andrew Jackson attacked Pensacola in 1814 because Governor Mateo Gonzales Manrique refused to surrender Creek warriors who had been involved in the Massacre of Fort Mims. The Spanish government also had allowed the presence of British soldiers at Fort Miguel and Fort Barrancas and the arming of Red Sticks through Panton, Leslie & Company. Jackson returned the city to the Spanish once the British were expelled. In 1818 Jackson again captured Pensacola because British agents were again arming the Indians and protecting runaway slaves. Realizing it would always be a struggle to hold onto Florida, Spain began negotiations to sell to the Americans. On February 22, 1820, the Adams-Onís Treaty was concluded and all of Florida became an American territory. Andrew Jackson was appointed provisional governor and received transfer of the former Spanish colony at Pensacola on July 17, 1820.

When the capital of Florida was moved to Tallahassee in 1824, Pensacola lost its traditional economic base, but the U.S. Navy moved in and the construction of numerous forts helped create a thriving brick industry. The coming of the railroad tied Pensacola to the great cotton country and immense pine forests of the interior.

William Bartram Travels to Pensacola

William Bartram was in Pensacola on September 4 and 5, 1775. He arrived late in the evening, spent the night sleeping on the beach and left at noon the next day. During that time he met Dr. Lorimer, Secretary Livingston, and Governor Peter Chester. Historical markers commemorating William Bartram's travels are located at Fort Pickens, Santa Rosa Island; Highway 98, Perdido River; Cypress and M Streets, Pensacola; the I–10 rest area east side of Escambia Bay; and Bartram Park between Pitt Slip Marina and Bayfront Parkway in downtown Pensacola.

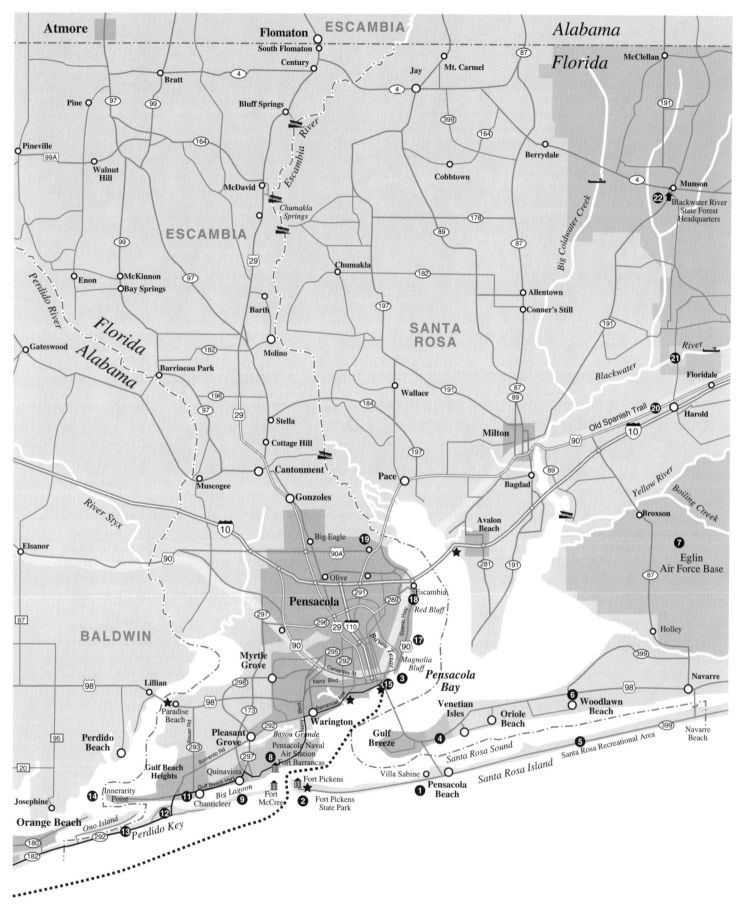

Pensacola

Sites

1. The Emerald Coast extends from Pensacola to Panama City in a series of bays and lagoons and is renowned for the white sand beaches. The emerald refers to the green water. The coast has become a popular vacation retreat and the beaches are strung with vacation condominiums and hotels, yet there are large areas where there is federal and state protection. The barrier islands of the Gulf are long and thin like those of North Carolina, created by wave action rather than tides, and unlike the sea islands of Georgia and South Carolina. The sugar beaches of fine white, squeaky sand are derived from the erosion of quartz from the ancient Appalachian Mountains.

2. Fort San Miguel was built on Santa Rosa Island about 1723. The Spanish settlement on Santa Rosa Island was destroyed by a hurricane in 1752 and relocated to the present site of Seville Square. The new settlement was protected by the Presidio San Miguel de Panzacola blockhouse.

Fort Pickens. The Fort Pickens area of Gulf Islands National Seashore includes the fort, two nature trails, boardwalks to the beach, picnic areas, camping, and fishing piers. Geronimo was imprisoned at Fort Pickens from 1886–1888.

3. Emanuel Point Shipwreck. This mid-sixteenth century wreck is believed to be the *Jesus*, the flagship of Tristán de Luña's fleet. On August 19, 1559 a hurricane blew in and destroyed several ships and supplies, which left the Luna colony in a weakened state. Over 5,000 items have been recovered by archaeologists from the University of West Florida. Because the fleet carried everything necessary to establish a community in a wilderness the variety of artifacts range from farm implements, food, and household goods to military gear.

4. Naval Live Oaks Reserve was established in 1828 to ensure a steady supply of live oak timbers to the naval shipyards. The preserve today still protects the live oaks and serves as the visitor center for the Florida District of the Gulf Islands National Seashore. The hiking trails give the visitor a glimpse of the Florida Scrub and an interpretative trail explains how the oaks were selected to make various braces and brackets for wooden sailing ships. The trails cross habitat that has remained little changed since the preserve was established. Naval Live Oaks Reserve is an excellent place to study the humid desert vegetation of the ancient sand hills. A remnant of Florida's first federal road, the 1824 Saint Augustine–Pensacola Mail Road, crosses along the northern portion of the reserve. Located on US-98 east of Gulf Breeze. Open 8 a.m.–5 p.m., daily.

5. Santa Rosa Day Use Area. This recreation area is open for picnicking, beachcombing, and swimming. There is a small visitor center in the main building that has exhibits and information. Boardwalks cross the dunes to the beach and another reaches back to Santa Rosa Sound. Located on Santa Rosa Island on Escambia 399 between Pensacola Beach and Navarre Beach. Open 8 a.m.–sunset, everyday.

6. The Zoo at Gulf Breeze. The zoo has exotic animals and a botanical garden with exotic and traditional southern landscape plants. Located at 5701 Gulf Breeze Parkway. Open 9 a.m.–5 p.m. in summer and 9 a.m.–4 p.m. in winter. Closed on Thanksgiving and Christmas. Admission.

7. Eglin Air Force Base began as Valparaiso Bombing and Gunnery Range in 1935. The immense, sparsely populated forests and the great open expanse of the Gulf of Mexico made it an ideal location for maneuvers. It was renamed Eglin Air Force Base in 1937 and became the site for aircraft armament testing at the outbreak of war in Europe in 1939. The Choctawhatchee National Forest was incorporated into the base in 1940, which made it the country's largest military base, with 800 square miles of pine forest on the Gulf Coast. The management of the forest has been exceptional and many habitats remain that might have disappeared had the land remained a national forest and therefore open to timbering.

Eglin Air Force Base has the largest longleaf pine forest in the world, containing fully ten percent of all remaining longleaf pines. It is home to numerous endangered species, most significant is the white-top pitcher-plant (*Sarracenia leucophylla*). The Eglin red-cockaded woodpecker colony is the third largest in the country. The Florida Natural Areas Inventory survey of Eglin Air Force Base found sixty-two rare species and twenty species found only in Florida.

8. Fort Barrancas occupies the site of the first Spanish fort, San Carlos de Austria, built about 1698. The site of the original settlement was discovered in 1998. Fort Barrancas is open to visitors and includes educational displays that tell the story of the earliest settlement of the Pensacola area. The present structure was built by the United States between 1839 and 1844. The Water Battery is an excellent place from which to view Santa Rosa Island and the entrance of Pensacola Bay.

The French captured Fort San Carlos in May 1719 during the European war between France and Spain. The expedition was organized by the brothers Iberville and Bienville and once the fort was taken another brother, Lemoyne de Chateagué, became commandant of Pensacola. However, the Spanish immediately recaptured the fort. In September the French again stormed the fort and destroyed it. France and Spain restored relations and agreed to form an alliance against England. Pensacola was returned to Spain in 1722.

9. Gulf Shores National Seashore, Perdido Key Area. Johnson Beach is a day-use area for swimming, picnicking, and beachcombing. The recreation area extends five miles beyond the end of the road and offers an excellent opportunity to hike on a barrier island in solitude. There is a boat ramp and a quarter-mile nature trail. Primitive camping is permitted in the roadless area and on the beach by prior arrangement.

Gulf Islands National Seashore in the Florida District includes Naval Live Oaks Reserve, Forts Barrancas, Advance Redoubt, the eastern end of Perdido Key, and the western end

Legend

1. The Emerald Coast
2. Fort San Miguel
   Fort Pickens
3. Emanuel Point Shipwreck
4. Naval Live Oaks Reserve
5. Santa Rosa Day Use Area
6. The Zoo at Gulf Breeze
7. Eglin Air Force Base
8. Fort Barrancas
9. Gulf Shores National Seashore
   Perdido Key
   Gulf Islands National Seashore
10. The Navy
11. Big Lagoon State Recreation Area
12. Perdido Bay Tribe Creek Cultural Center
13. Perdido Key State Recreation Area
14. Perdido Bay
15. Pensacola Convention and Visitor Information Center
16. Scenic Highway
17. Pensacola Bluffs
18. Old Chimney
19. University of West Florida
20. Old Spanish Trail
21. Blackwater River
    Blackwater River State Park
22. Blackwater River State Forest

of Santa Rosa Island. The park headquarters is located at Naval Live Oaks Reserve.

10. The Navy has been an important presence since the Tristan de Luna expedition arrived in 1559 to establish a settlement. It was important for the Spanish to have ships at Pensacola Bay to guard the Gulf Coast shipping lanes from pirates and protect the Spanish claim to Florida. During the British period Pensacola became a British military outpost. When Florida became a part of the United States, the American navy immediately established the Naval Live Oaks Reserve, built new forts, and established bases throughout the area.

11. Big Lagoon State Recreation Area is an excellent place to see relic beach dunes and learn about their natural history. The deep sand and harsh growing conditions cause the trees to remain stunted and gnarled. Much of this scrub at Big Lagoon was burned by a natural forest fire and has left a desolate landscape of dead, twisted trees on rolling hills of white sand—an eerie and beautiful landscape! There are also hiking trails along salt-marsh and freshwater marsh, wetlands, and sloughs. The park has camping, picnic areas, swimming, and a boat ramp. Big Lagoon State Recreation Area is located at 12301 Gulf Beach Highway. Open 8 a.m. until sunset everyday.

12. Perdido Bay Tribe Creek Cultural Center. Southeastern Lower Muskogee Creek Indians, Inc. 1410 Perdido Key Drive, Perdido Key.

13. Perdido Key State Recreation Area allows public access to beaches and secondary dunes on both sides of Perdido Key Drive.

14. Perdido Bay. Perdido means *lost* in Spanish and Perdido Bay received its name because it went undiscovered for a century and a half. Rumors of a large bay were known to the French at Mobile and the Spanish in Pensacola, but no one found an entrance until 1693 when Carlos Siquenza discovered it. He had difficulty finding the entrance due to the long strip of barrier island we know today as Perdido Key. Perdido Bay became the boundary between French Louisiana and Spanish Florida and is today the boundary between Alabama and Florida. Two-thirds of Perdido Key is protected by state and federal ownership.

15. Pensacola Convention and Visitor Information Center, north end of Pensacola Bay Bridge at Wayside Park. Open 8 a.m.–5 p.m., Monday through Friday; weekend hours are 9 a.m.–4 p.m.

Itinerary

Miles	Directions
	Begin at the Alabama-Florida state line on Perdido Key and travel east
5.7	Entrance to Perdido Key Area, Gulf Shores National Seashore
1.3	Right on Gulf Beach Highway
1.8	Entrance to Big Lagoon State Recreation Area
3.3	Right on West Access Road through Pensacola Naval Air Station
3.7	Fort Barrancas and Fort San Carlos
1.3	Left on Duncan Boulevard
2.3	Right on FL-292, Barrancas Avenue
2.6	Right on Barrancas avenue
.3	Right on West Main Street
1.7	Bartram Park and Seville Square

16. Scenic Highway hugs the bluff overlooking Pensacola Bay and Escambia Bay.

17. Pensacola Bluffs. Hikers can explore these high, colorful bluffs from boardwalks and hiking trails. Located on Scenic Highway, open during daylight hours.

18. Old Chimney is all that remains of the once thriving Pensacola brick industry. Clay for the bricks was dug from the bluffs of Pensacola Bay.

19. University of West Florida was established in 1963 and is located on University Parkway north of I-10. The university conducts research on marine biology and wetlands. There is a nature trail that loops around and crosses Thompson Bayou, the entrance is just west of the campus center.

20. Old Spanish Trail. This early trail connected Saint Augustine, Tallahassee, Pensacola, Mobile, New Orleans, and on through Texas to Mexico. Sections of the modern route are still named Old Spanish Trail, such as US-90 east of Pensacola. US-90 was the first paved road across Florida when it was finished in the 1920s. Sections of this old brick road are still visible a few miles east of Milton and a few feet north of the modern highway.

21. Blackwater River has become a popular canoeing river due to its beautiful sandy bottom and clean, tea-colored water.

Blackwater River State Park contains the last two miles of the Blackwater canoe trail. There are a variety of plant communities in the state park, including wiregrass flatwoods, hardwood bottomland, and upland pinewoods. Other canoe streams in the area are Sweetwater Creek, Big Coldwater Creek, and Juniper Creek. 7720 Deaton Bridge Road. Open 8 a.m. until sunset everyday.

22. Blackwater River State Forest is Florida's largest state forest at 183,000 acres. This forest and Conecuh National Forest is the largest contiguous longleaf pine-wiregrass ecosystem in the world. Longleaf pine-wiregrass is the natural habitat for the white top pitcher-plant, *Sarracenia leucophylla*. Blackwater River State Forest provides numerous launch points for paddlers on the Blackwater River. A program of prescribed fire maintains this unique forest, helps keep pitcher-plant bogs open, and provides habitat for cockaded woodpeckers. The twenty-five-mile Jackson Trail is a part of the Florida Trail and follows an old Indian path used by General Andrew Jackson when he marched to Pensacola in 1818. Forest headquarters is located on Santa Rosa CR-191 just south of FL-4 in Munson. Blackwater Forestry Center, 11650 Munson Highway.

Counties

Escambia County, created in 1821, is named for the Escambia River. Another suggestion is that the name is derived from the Spanish word for exchange, *cambiar*.

Santa Rosa County, created in 1842, is named for Rosa de Viterbo, a Catholic Saint.

Historic Pensacola

1. Plaza Ferdinand VII has been a public space since the first Spanish Period. Plaza Ferdinand is the site where the flag of Spain was exchanged for the Stars & Stripes on July 17, 1821.

2. Colonial Archaeological Trail. These open air exhibits show the foundations of the British Government House, bastions, and various outbuildings that date from the British and Second Spanish Period. Artifacts retrieved from the archaeological work are located on the second floor of the Wentworth Museum. A brochure and map of the archaeological trail are available at the Museum.

3. T. T. Wentworth, Jr. Florida State Museum. The history of West Florida and archaeology of the Pensacola area are exhibited at the Wentworth Museum. The Museum is located in the Pensacola Historical District at 330 S. Jefferson Street on Plaza Ferdinand. Hours of operation are 10 a.m.–4 p.m., Monday through Saturday. Admission.

4. Pensacola Museum of Art. 407 South Jefferson Street. Hours are 10 a.m.–5 p.m., Monday through Friday and 10 a.m.–4 p.m. on Saturday. Admission.

5. The Pensacola Historical Society Resource Center houses a collection of historical documents, maps, photographs, and genealogy of Pensacola. 117 East Government Street, enter from the rear. Hours are 10 a.m.–12 p.m. and 1–3 p.m., Tuesday, Wednesday, Thursday, and Saturday. Admission.

6. Historic Pensacola Preservation Board. The building at 120 Church Street houses an exhibition gallery and offices for the Pensacola Preservation Board. Located across from Jackson Park.

7. Historic Pensacola Village is a collection of historic homes and the *Museums of Industry and Commerce*. Homes and museums are open 10 a.m.–4 p.m., Monday through Saturday. Admission.

8. Pensacola Historical Museum. Exhibits interpret the culture of prehistoric Indians, colonial and recent history of the Pensacola area, maritime history, and the geology of Florida. The museum is located at 115 East Zaragosa Street. Open 10 a.m.–4:30, Monday–Saturday. Admission.

9. Museum of Industry. This nineteenth century warehouse is home to the museum of the industries that helped spur the growth of Pensacola. Displays include exhibits on the timber, naval stores, shipping, railroad, brickmaking, and seafood industries. Located on Taragona Street, between Church and Zaragoza streets. Open 10 a.m.–4 p.m., Monday through Saturday.

10. Museum of Commerce. The economic history of Pensacola is featured in the Museum of Commerce. Exhibits include displays on printing, automobiles, hardware, carriages, and other commercially important businesses. Located at 201 East Zaragoza Street. Open 10 a.m.–4 p.m., Monday through Saturday.

11. Bartram Park. The Bartram Trail historical marker is located in this small park lying between Bayfront Parkway and Pitts Slip Marina. When William Bartram visited Pensacola, he spent the night on the beach, which was at the time located about where the marker is now.

12. Seville Square is the heart of colonial Pensacola and contains the oldest existing buildings in the city.

13. Saint Michael's Cemetery occupies land deeded by the King of Spain for the purpose of a public burial ground. Many of the tombs are raised above ground and are called *ovans*, because of their resemblance to cooking ovens.

14. Seville District is a charming neighborhood of homes, shops, and museums that makes for an easy walking tour of Pensacola's history and culture. The first residential settlement of Pensacola was made around Seville Square in 1752, located just east of the fort. The British laid out the streets and the Spanish renamed the streets when Bernardo de Galvez captured Pensacola in 1781. The early wharves for the city were located at Pitts Slip just below the residential district. Alhough Pensacola has one of the longest histories of the United States, the oldest buildings date only from the early nineteenth century. Colonial homes were invariably built of wood, which was more abundant and cheaper than brick and mortar. The earliest buildings have long ago succumbed to rot and termites. Brick homes began to appear in Pen-

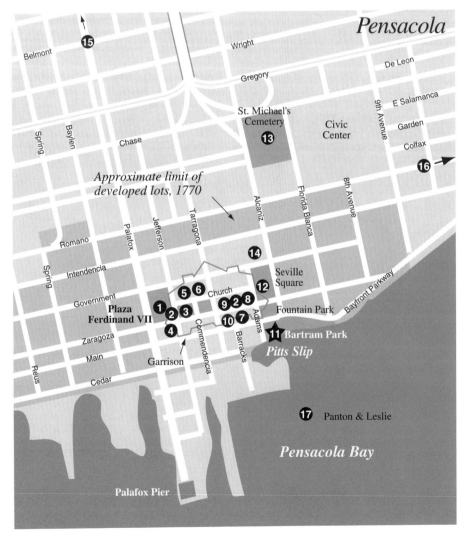

Commanding Officer's Compound, Pensacola Colonial Archaeological Trail

sacola when the brick industry was established in the early nineteenth century.

15. Fort George, 1778, was a British fort that was located at Palafox and LaRua Streets, on Gage Hill. The garrison numbered between 1,500 and 2,000 troops at the time of the Galvez conquest in 1781. The Spanish renamed it Fort San Miguel but allowed it to deteriorate. The last undeveloped parcel of the original site was preserved by the city in 1974.

16. Governor Chester's Villa overlooked Pensacola Bay and was located above the bluffs near the intersection of Romano Street and Bayfront Parkway.

17. Panton, Leslie & Co. William Panton was born in Aberdeenshire, Scotland. He emigrated to America and bought land in South Carolina and Georgia. As a loyalist he moved to Florida when the Revolution began and there built a thriving Indian trade based on his friendship with Alexander McGillivray, who was Chief of the Wind Clan and became a silent partner in Panton, Leslie & Company. The company was owned jointly with John Leslie and John Forbes. Panton moved to Pensacola in 1784 and was given a virtual monopoly of the Southeastern Indian trade for the Spanish. William Panton died at sea in 1801 and the trading company became John Forbes & Company. When Forbes retired in 1807, the company went to the Innerarity family.

Gulf Coast

Official Spanish exploration of the Gulf Coast began with the voyage of Francisco de Garay in 1519, sponsored by Jamaican governor Alonso Álvarez de Pineda. Garay mapped the northern Gulf coast and discovered the mouth of a river he named Río del Espíritu Santo, which may have been Mobile Bay or the Mississippi River. There were almost certainly unofficial and unrecorded voyages made by Spanish slavers and adventurers during the early sixteenth century. The struggling expedition of Pánfilo de Narváez sailed along the Gulf Coast in 1527. They entered the Pascagoula River and were at first welcomed by the Pascagoula Indians. The Pascagoulas abruptly attacked the expedition late in the day but the Spaniards were able to hold off their attackers and escape.

After the failure of their first settlement in the New World, the French concentrated their efforts in Canada, far from the Spanish in Florida. French Acadia was settled in 1604 and Champlain founded Quebec in 1608. As the Canadian fur trade grew, the French spread out along the Great Lakes and the Ohio River. René Robert Cavelier, Sieur de La Salle sailed down the Mississippi River in 1682 and claimed for France all of its drainage. Although French and Spanish relations in North America began with the murders of the Fort Caroline settlers, the two nations later carried on unsanctioned trade for the mutual benefit of the isolated and lonely settlements along the Mississippi River and Gulf Coast. In the eighteenth century the two Catholic nations found a common enemy in protestant England and became allies in the struggle to limit British influence in North America.

In 1699 Pierre le Moyne Sieur d'Iberville built the first fort and settlement in Louisiana at Fort Maurepas (la Fort du Biloxi) on the east side of Biloxi Bay in what is now Ocean Springs. The capital of Louisiana was moved to Dauphin Island in 1702. The government was moved back to Ocean Springs in 1719, then known as Old Biloxi, when the harbor at Dauphin Island became blocked by a sandbar. When part of Fort Maure-

Old Spanish Fort in Pascagoula

pas burned, Fort Louis was built on the west side of the bay and the capital of Louisiana was moved to New Biloxi in December 1720. Biloxi was the capital of Louisiana for only a short time because the seat of government was moved to New Orleans in 1722. The port of entry remained at Ship Island because the harbor could accommodate larger seafaring ships.

The Gulf Coast was at that time home to the Pascagoula and Biloxi Indians. The Biloxis and Pascagoulas were courted by Bienville in 1699 and thereafter remained friendly to the French. Both tribes were never numerous and have either become scattered or absorbed into other, larger tribes. The Biloxis spoke a Siouxian language and lived along the Gulf Coast and inland thirty to forty miles. They left the Gulf Coast at the beginning of the eighteenth century and settled near New Orleans. They returned to the Gulf Coast by mid-century and were thereafter closely associated with the Pascagoulas. Many Biloxis moved first to Texas and finally to Oklahoma.

The Pascagoulas lived farther inland on the river of the same name and, though evidence is scarce, it has been traditionally thought that they were related to the Choctaws. In the last half of the eighteenth century they moved to Louisiana and then to Oklahoma and Texas.

In the treaty of peace that concluded the French and Indian War, Britain exchanged Cuba for Florida. The British colony of West Florida extended from the Apalachicola River to the Mississippi River and north to a line running due east from the mouth of the Yazoo River. In the 1783 Treaty of Paris that concluded the Revolution, Florida was again returned to Spain. The Treaty of San Lorenzo in 1795 established the southern boundary of the United States at the 31st parallel. The area above the 31st parallel and between the Mississippi and Chattahoochee rivers was organized into Mississippi Territory in 1798. In 1800 Washington County was created in the lower part of Mississippi Territory. It extended from the Mississippi

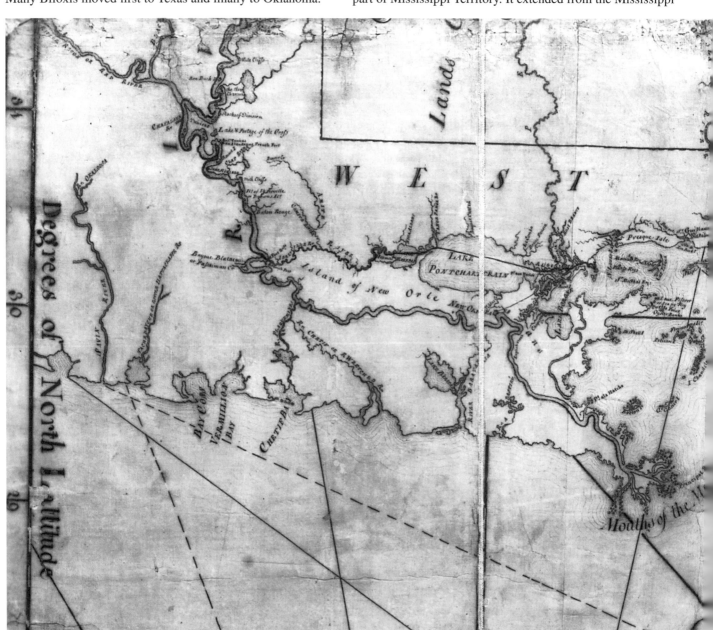

Detail of A Map of the Southern Indian District of North America, *c. 1778, by Joseph Purcell*
Reproduced from the Collections of the Library of Congress

River to the Chattahoochee River and extended northward eighty-eight miles.

In order to clear up contested land titles arising from the Yazoo Land Acts, Georgia gave up any claim to Mississippi Territory and the federal government agreed to settle the claims against Georgia. Spanish territory between the Pearl and Perdido rivers and below the 31st parallel was added to Mississippi Territory in early 1811 when Congress annexed the area. Governor Claiborne created two parishes; Biloxy from the Pearl to Biloxi River and Pascagoula which extended from the Biloxi River to Bayou la Batre. When the Spanish gave up Mobile in 1813 the territory between the Pearl and Perdido rivers was divided into Hancock, Jackson, and Mobile counties. Alabama Territory was created out of Mississippi Territory on March 1, 1817 and Mississippi was admitted to the union on December 10, 1817 as the twentieth state.

The present Gulf Coast counties of Mississippi were sparsely settled during the French period. Later, during the Revolution and the second Spanish period, West Florida became a refuge for loyalists who chose Spanish citizenship over American. There was a lack of willing Spanish immigrants, so the Spanish governors of Florida welcomed American settlers, which was to be their undoing. Because the lower coastal plain is not known for its fertility, growth of communities along the Gulf Coast had to wait for the coming of the railroad, steamboats, and wealthy urbanites looking for summer resorts. Steamboats had to stop along the coast at intervals for water and wood which helped spur the creation of coastal towns and ports. The growth of the nation brought a demand for forest products that are abundant in the Coastal Plain and the timber industry helped spur the building of railroads from inland towns to the ports on the Gulf. The seafood industry began to supply coastal towns with food and gave rise to a large canning and boat-building industry. The Mississippi Gulf Coast is

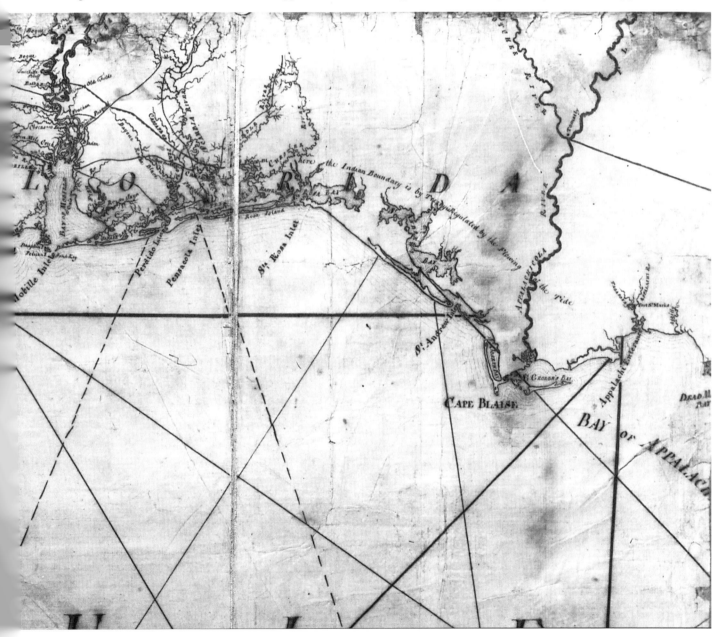

now a popular tourist destination, well-known for the gambling casinos and resorts. Nestled at each end of the hustle and bustle of Biloxi, Gulfport, and Pass Christian are the quiet and charming towns of Bay Saint Louis and Ocean Springs.

William Bartram's Travels on the Gulf Coast

William Bartram left Mobile by the middle of September 1775 on a trading ship bound for Manchac on the Mississippi River. The boat sailed the Gulf Coast and put in at a plantation in the mouth of the Pearl River, now the boundary between Mississippi and Louisiana. Bartram's illness returned with vigor and rendered him unable to see because bright light caused him so much pain. Bartram's host hurried him off to see Mr. Rumsey on Pearl Island for treatment. William Bartram left Baton Rouge about November 10, 1775 and arrived in Mobile around November 16. On his return to Mobile, Bartram again sailed along the Gulf Coast, the ship keeping between the islands and the shore.

Sites

1. Mississippi Welcome Centers are located on I-10 at Pearl River, I-59 near Picayune, and US-90 at the eastern state line.

2. Grand Bay National Wildlife Refuge contains one of the largest remaining pine savannah wetlands on the Gulf Coast. A second population of Mississippi sandhill cranes is being established there to augment the primary population at Mississippi Sandhill Crane NWR. Access is by boat with trail access being developed.

Grand Bay Savannah is a 150,000-acre preserve owned and administered by the Nature Conservancy. It lies in the Bang's Lake area between the National Wildlife Refuge and Pascagoula. The preserve protects some of the last undisturbed wet pine savannah on the Gulf Coast, which was once much more extensive than it is today.

3. Old Spanish Trail. When Spain owned Louisiana, the Old Spanish Trail connected Florida and Texas. The trail from Saint Augustine traveled through Tallahassee, Pensacola, Mobile, New Orleans to San Antonio and Mexico. Through the Gulf Coast it is most closely followed today by US-90 and Old Pass Christian Road. Older sections that are still named Old Spanish Trail run parallel to and south of US-90. The older sections of the Spanish Trail are by far the more scenic, interesting, and less hectic routes to travel.

4. Pascagoula is one of the world's largest builders of small work boats. Follow Beach Boulevard to its western end for parking and a view of the Gulf and shipyards.

5. Spanish Fort is the oldest documented building in the Louisiana territory, built in 1718. It is not a fort, nor is it of Spanish origin, but begins with a 1715 French land grant to Joseph Simon de la Pointe who had sailed with Iberville at a young age and was one of the first settlers at Fort Maurepas. The building known as Spanish Fort is the carpenter shop and only remaining structure of a fortified estate. The building is constructed of cypress and cedar with a fill of tabby. A daughter of de la Pointe married Hugo Ernestus Krebs and the Krebs family owned the property until the early twentieth century. The adjoining museum has exhibitions related to the Indian, French, Spanish, English, and American periods of Pascagoula. Open 10 a.m.–5 p.m., Monday through Saturday; and 12:30–4 p.m. on Sunday. Admission.

6. Moss Point was the largest pine lumber exporting port in the United States at the turn of the century.

7. Pascagoula River is called the *Singing River* because when all is quiet one can hear a humming sound like bees in flight. The legend is that Pascagoula Indians joined hands and walked into the river rather than be taken captive by an invading tribe. The singing is the chant of the Pascagoulas as they went to their death.

8. Ward Bayou Wildlife Management Area is a recent addition to the Mississippi public lands and has not had much development nor is much planned. The Army Corps of Engineers bought this area to mitigate for loss of wetlands during the construction of the Tennessee-Tombigbee Waterway and turned it over to the state of Mississippi. This management area protects the lower reaches of the Pasca-

Legend

1. Mississippi Welcome Center
2. Grand Bay National Wildlife Refuge
3. Old Spanish Trail
4. Pascagoula
5. Spanish Fort
6. Moss Point
7. Pascagoula River
8. Ward Bayou WMA
9. Pascagoula WMA
10. Black Creek
11. Scranton Floating Museum
12. Shepard State Park
13. Mississippi Sand Hill Crane NWR
14. Ocean Springs
   Ocean Springs Bicycle Route
   Walter Anderson Museum
15. Gulf Islands National Seashore
   Davis Bayou
16. Fort Maurepas
17. Ship Island
18. Biloxi
   Maritime & Seafood Industry Museum
   Gulf Marine State Park
   J. L. Scott Marine Education Center
   Biloxi Visitor Center
   The Old French House
   Indian mounds
   Beauvoir
   Fort Louis
   Cassette Girls
19. De Soto National Forest
   Black Creek Trail
   Tuxachanie Trail
   The Andrew Jackson Trail
20. Gulfport
   Marine Life Oceanarium
   James Hill Park Bayou Walk & Fishing Pier
   The Port of Gulfport
21. Pass Christian
22. Wolf River
23. Bay St. Louis
24. Buccaneer State Park
25. McLeod Water Park
26. John C. Stennis Space Center
27. Crosby Arboretum

goula River and is flooded in winter and spring. Access is north of Van Cleave by Ward Bayou Road.

9. Pascagoula Wildlife Management Area protects much of the bottomland of the magnificent Pascagoula River. The area is home to Mississippi's black bears and the endangered map turtle. As with most coastal river basins much of the area is underwater in winter and spring when canoes and boats are the best way to travel. During the rest of the year there is hiking and camping along public roads and streams, but be sure to have a map. Hunting and fishing are allowed. Black Creek, a tributary, is a noted canoeing stream.

10. Black Creek. Portions of Black Creek cross De Soto National Forest in an isolated region. The section of the Creek from Moody's Landing to Airley Bridge Landing is a National Wild and Scenic River. The upper reaches of Black Creek above Brooklyn are more challenging and scenic with gravel bars and haulouts. Information is available from De Soto National Forest and Black Creek Canoe Rental in Brooklyn.

Other canoeing streams on the Mississippi Gulf Coast are Red Creek, Hobolochitto Creek at Picayune, Leaf River, Big Biloxi River, and Homochito River. See descriptions in the *Trail Guide to the Delta Country*, published by New Orleans Sierra Club.

11. Scranton Floating Museum is a shrimp boat that has become a floating learning center with aquariums and hands-on exhibits. Located at River Side Park north of US-90 at the west end of the Pascagoula River Bridge.

12. Shepard State Park provides an opportunity for a naturalist looking for a quiet spot on the Gulf Coast. Bayou Lamotte extends into the park boundaries and there is a two-mile nature trail that crosses over the bayou into a pine maritime forest and then skirts the salt marsh. There are primitive campsites, picnic areas, and a boat launch. From US-90 or Old Spanish Trail, turn left on Ladnier Road and another left on Graveline Road. Open 8 a.m.–5 p.m. daily except Thanksgiving, Christmas, and New Year's Day. 1031 Graveline Road, Gautier.

13. Mississippi Sand Hill Crane National Wildlife Refuge was established in 1975 to protect the last remaining Mississippi sandhill cranes. These resident cranes are a little darker than the Florida sandhill cranes and greater sandhill cranes, both of which are much more abundant. The Mississippi sandhill cranes inhabit open wet savannah-pine areas that were unfit for farming but adequate for grazing. Because they do not migrate and their habitat along the Gulf Coast has been developed and planted in pine plantations, there are only about 120 sandhill cranes in the Refuge. Restoration of the refuge to make it compatible with the life-style of sandhill cranes has had the added benefit of creating a more diverse and natural wetland savannah where pitcher plants, sundews, bladderworts, and native orchids flourish.

Chances of seeing a sandhill crane on a visit are unlikely, because the only hiking trail is at the visitor center. In January and February, tours of observation blinds are available on Tuesday and Saturday. Part of the tour includes a visit to the rehabilitation area. The Visitor Center is open 8 a.m.–3 p.m., Monday through Friday. From US-90 in Gautier go north on Vancleave Avenue, pass under I-10, and take the next right to the Visitor Center.

14. Ocean Springs. Ocean Springs is the site of Fort Maurepas and Old Biloxi, the first French settlement in Louisiana. Fort Maurepas was named for Jérôme de Phélypeaux, Comte de Maurepas, the son of the Comte de Pontchartrain. Ocean Springs is a nice respite from the traffic and visual overload of the Biloxi casino strip. Washington Street is the heart of town and invites visitors to get out of their cars and walk.

Ocean Springs Bicycle Route covers fifteen miles of Ocean Springs streets in a round trip from the old L & N Depot to Davis Bayou. Maps are available at the Chamber of Commerce in the old depot at 1000 Washington Avenue.

Walter Anderson Museum has a collection of works by this mystical and eccentric artist who spent most of his last years painting on Horn Island. His paintings of the flora and wildlife of marsh and beach is colorful and outlandishly beautiful.

15. Gulf Islands National Seashore. The Gulf barrier islands stand six to twelve miles offshore and protect the coast and the Mississippi Sound from storms. They are an excellent laboratory for the evolution and migration of barrier islands. Petit Bois Island was once part of Dauphin Island but is now separated. All of the islands have been migrating westward since first being mapped by the French in the early 1700s. The Isle of Caprice appeared between West Ship and Horn islands in the early part of this century. It was developed as a resort and the vegetation, particularly sea oats, was disturbed by construction. The Island was completely reclaimed by the Gulf during a hurricane in 1947. The Mississippi section of Gulf Islands National Seashore include Ship, Horn, and Petit Bois islands. Shuttles operate from Biloxi and Gulfport to Ship Island, the only barrier island with visitor facilities. The other islands can be reached only by private or chartered boat.

Davis Bayou. The visitor center for Gulf Islands National Seashore in Mississippi is in Ocean Springs at Davis Bayou. Facilities include a boat ramp, boardwalks, nature trails, camping, and an interpretative center. Open year round. 3500 Park Road, Ocean Springs. From downtown Ocean Springs travel east on US-90, turn right on Park Road and follow the signs.

16. The Fort Maurepas replica is about a mile from its original site at Old Biloxi. Fort Maurepas was the first fortification built by the French in Louisiana territory and was completed in 1699. In 1702 a magazine and barracks were built on Ship Island, and Dauphin Island became the principal port and capital of Louisiana. When a hurricane filled the harbor at Dauphin Island the port of entry and government were moved back to Fort Maurepas temporarily in 1719, then to the present city of Biloxi in 1720 when Fort Louis was completed, then to New Orleans in 1722. To reach the fort take Washington Street south to the beach, turn right on Front Beach Drive and the replica will be about a block on the right. A colonial encampment is held each year in early October.

17. Ship Island was the site of the magazine and barracks for Fort Maurepas and was once the port of entry for Louisiana. Fort Massachusetts was built on Ship Island in 1866. Ship Island was cut in half by Hurricane Camille to form East and West Ship Island.

18. Biloxi. Although Biloxi claims to be the oldest settlement in the original Louisiana territory, the first settlement was actually in Ocean Springs at Fort Maurepas, which became known as Fort du Biloxi. When Fort Louis was constructed on the west side of the bay the name of the civilian settlement came with it and was for a time known as New Biloxi. The city is named for the Biloxi Indians who lived on the Gulf Coast and were a Choctaw people. In recent years the charm of this old Gulf Coast resort town and seafood center has been dramatically changed, for better or worse, by the casinos that have been built along Beach Boulevard.

The Maritime & Seafood Industry Museum showcases the history, artifacts, and implements of the seafood industry of Mississippi's Gulf Coast. There are exhibits on the history of French exploration and the Indians who lived on the Gulf Coast when the Europeans arrived. Photographs of turn-of-the-century Biloxi by the renowned photographer Lewis Hines are on display. Turn right on

Myrtle Street from US-90 just after crossing the Biloxi Bay Bridge. Open 9 a.m.–5 p.m., Monday through Saturday. Admission.

Gulf Marine State Park. Fishing piers and picnic pavilions. West end of US-90 bridge at Biloxi Bay.

J. L. Scott Marine Education Center & Aquarium is located at Point Cadet on the beach side of US-90 at the west end of the Biloxi Bay Bridge. There are forty-one aquariums featuring the native animals of the Gulf Coast from open water, marsh, and coastal rivers—including fish, turtles, alligators, and crustacea. The Scott Center is administered by the University of Mississippi as a research and education facility. For the public there is an auditorium and gift shop. Open 9 a.m.–4 p.m., Monday through Saturday. Admission.

Biloxi Visitors Center is open from 8 a.m.– 5 p.m., Monday through Friday and 9 a.m.– 4 p.m. on Saturday. Located on Beach Boulevard between Lameuse and Main streets on the Town Green.

The Old French House is believed to have been built about 1737, which makes it one of the oldest buildings remaining from French colonial Louisiana. The house is the centerpiece of the Mary Mahoney Restaurant complex. Located on the north side of US-90 between Ohr Street and Rue Magnolia.

Indian mounds, Moran's Art Studio, 110 Porter Avenue, north of Biloxi Lighthouse. 10 a.m.– 5 p.m., weekdays; 10 a.m.–1 p.m. Saturday.

Beauvoir is the last home of Jefferson Davis, president of the Confederate States of America. This historic site has a beautiful view of the Gulf and gardens for walking. The Jefferson Davis Museum and Library is under construction and will house Mississippi archives.

Fort Louis was the capital of Louisiana and seat of government for Bienville from 1720–1722. The fort was not completed before the government was moved to New Orleans. It was in the vicinity of the intersection of US-90 and I-110.

Cassette Girls. This historical marker on US-90 in Biloxi commemorates the arrival in 1721 of a group of young French women who became known as the Cassette Girls. France had trouble luring settlers to Louisiana, especially following the deportations and kidnappings that characterized the period of John Law's Company of the West, and men far outnumbered women. Governor Cadillac arranged for these young women of marriagable age and good character to be brought to Louisiana. They were called *la filles 'a la cassette* for each carried a small box containing her belongings. The young women were boarded with the Ursuline nuns in New Orleans and all were soon married. It became a point of distinction to be descended from a Cassette Girl.

19. De Soto National Forest. De Soto National Forest includes 502,000 acres and is administered by Chickasawhay, Black Creek, and Biloxi ranger districts. It covers a large section of what is called the Piney Woods by locals. De Soto National Forest contains two wilderness areas, Leaf and Black Creek, and the Black Creek National Wild and Scenic River.

The most noted feature of De Soto National Forest is the forty-one mile Black Creek Trail that was built as the National Bartram Historical Trail of Mississippi. It was originally supposed to cross the state and end at the Pearl River near Bogalusa but only the section through federally owned national forest was completed. This, unfortunately, has been the fate of many of the original plans to honor William Bartram in the land he explored and described. This is not surprising due to the large amount of private land in the Southeast that makes long trails very difficult to build.

Biloxi Ranger District Office is located on US-49 South of McHenry, the Black Creek Ranger District is in Wiggins, and Chickasawhay Ranger Office is in Laurel.

Black Creek Trail is a National Recreation Trail and passes through the Black Creek National Wild and Scenic River corridor.

Tuxachanie Trail is twenty-miles long and was built in the early 1970s, making it the oldest long trail in Mississippi. It covers a more varied landscape than the longer Black Creek Trail, and passes through sand hills, creek banks of mountain laurel, wet savannahs, and historic sites. Copeland Springs was home to James Copeland and the Copeland Clan, a band of outlaws who operated over an area from Texas to the Ohio Territory and even attacked the city of Mobile. Copeland was a portent of the unsavory characters who were to move steadily westward ahead of civilization to create the Wild West of the late 1800s. Moonshine was a major industry here during the Depression because of the seclusion of the Piney Woods and proximity to clandestine beaches. During World War II German prisoners were confined at the Old POW Camp, on a spur just off Tuxachanie Trail.

The Andrew Jackson Trail commemorates General Jackson's march to New Orleans along the Old Federal Road.

20. Gulfport.
Marine Life Oceanarium has demonstrations of trained dolphins and sea lions, underwater diving shows among sharks and stingrays, exhibitions, a touch pool, and listening post to eavesdrop on dolphins. Everything is contained under a dome that allows year-round events. Open 9 a.m.–sunset, shows end at 4 p.m. Admission. Intersection of US-90 and US-49.

James Hill Park Bayou Walk and Fishing Pier. This city recreation park has a short trail and a marsh boardwalk on Bernard Bayou. To reach the park, take Cowan Road north from Pass Christian, right on Magnolia Street and left on Pine.

The Port of Gulfport was opened in 1902 as a shipping terminus for railroads from the interior of Mississippi. It soon became an important shipping point for cotton and timber and today is a major banana port.

21. Pass Christian is named for Christian L'Adnier, an early settler who owned Cat Island in the early eighteenth century. The Pass Christian Historical Society is located on Scenic Drive in the old bank building.

22. Wolf River is a popular and accessible waterway. It is quiet and undeveloped with white sand bars and interesting clay banks. Canoes, shuttle service, and information are available from Wolf River Canoes in Long Beach, Mississippi.

23. Bay Saint Louis began as a popular summering place during the early nineteenth century for New Orleanians seeking relief from the heat and a place of respite from yellow fever epidemics. The Bay was named by Iberville for Saint Louis on his feast day in 1699. Turn left onto North Beach Boulevard from East US-90 just after crossing the bay bridge to reach Old Town and the public pier.

Hancock County Historical Society, 108 Cue Street, adjacent to the Hancock County Courthouse in Old Town. Open Monday through Friday, 8 a.m.–4 p.m.

24. Buccaneer State Park is a developed campground complete with a store, laundry, and deluxe RV camping sites. There are two hiking trails to the salt marshes of Grand Bayou and Mud Bayou, and another at the picnic area. There is a view of the Gulf and a boardwalk. 1150 South Beach Blvd., Waveland.

25. McLeod Water Park provides recreational access to the Jourdan River and Catahoula Creek. There is a mile-long nature trail, primitive and developed camping, and boat ramp. McLeod is a popular park with the local community and is crowded on holidays and warm weekends. 8100 Texas Flat Road in Kiln.

26. John C. Stennis Space Center is a rocket-testing facility for NASA. There are self-guided tours of the museum and guided tours of the testing facility. There are also a picnic area and gift shop. Open daily 9 a.m.–5 p.m. except on Christmas day. Admission.

27. Crosby Arboretum. There is no better place to learn about the natural history of the Gulf coastal plain than at Crosby Arboretum and Pinecote Educational Center in Picayune. The Arboretum encompasses over 1,000 acres

Itinerary

Miles	Description
	Begin US-90 at the Mississippi-Alabama state line and travel west
8.0	Enter Pascagoula
7.0	Left on Old Spanish Trail in Gautier
2.2	Ladnier Road intersection (left for Shepherd State Park)
5.9	Enter Sandhill Crane National Wildlife Refuge, Fontainbleau Unit (Old Spanish Trail becomes Government Street in Ocean Springs)
3.0	Intersection with Ocean Springs Road (right for Davis Bayou)
3.2	Right on Washington Avenue (left for beach and Fort Maurepas)
.2	Left on US-90
2.7	Biloxi city limits, US-90 is now called Scenic Drive
1.3	Biloxi Visitors Center and downtown Biloxi
12.4	Gulfport
10.1	Pass Christian
5.7	Left on North Beach Boulevard in Bay Saint Louis
11.0	Right on Lakeshore Road at direction sign for US-90
3.2	Left on Lower Bay/Pearlington Road
10.1	Left on US-90
4.0	Pearl River

of various plant communities with over 700 plant species on display in natural and enhanced settings. William Bartram Nature Trail was dedicated in 2002. The Pinecote Center is reached by taking Exit 4 on I-59. The arboretum is adjacent to the Mississippi Welcome Center.

1986 Ridge Road, Picayune. Open 10 a.m.–5 p.m. Wednesday through Sunday. Closed Thanksgiving, Christmas, and New Year's Day. Admission.

Counties

Jackson was created 1812 in Mississippi Territory and named for Andrew Jackson. The county seat is Pascagoula.

Harrison. The county seat is Biloxi.

Hancock was created in 1812 in Mississippi Territory and named for John Hancock. The county seat is Bay Saint Louis.

Pearl River was organized in 1872 from Mariona and Hancock counties and was named Pearl County. It was dissolved in 1878 due to the poor tax base and re-established in 1890 as Pearl River County. The county seat is Poplarville.

Lake Pontchartrain

That parishes of present-day Louisiana that were a part of British West Florida are called the Florida Parishes. At the end of the French and Indian War, Britain returned Cuba to Spain in exchange for East and West Florida. France ceded all of Louisiana west of the Mississippi River to Spain as a prize for having lost Florida and to keep the vast territory out of British hands. The western boundary of West Florida was extended to the Mississippi River and the eastern boundary was the Apalachicola River. The southern boundary was Bayou Manchac, Amite River, Lakes Maurepas and Pontchartrain, and the Rigolets. The northern boundary with the colony of Georgia was 32° 28' N, a line due west from the mouth of the Yazoo River (Vicksburg). After the Revolution, when West Florida was again under Spanish control, the Americans forced the boundary south to the 31st parallel by the Treaty of San Lorenzo in 1795.

When the French claimed Louisiana in 1699 it was inhabited by Indians related to the Choctaws and Creeks—they were Bayougoulas, Houmas, Acolapissas, Qinapisas, Okelousas, and Tangipahoas. There was little settlement of the Florida Parishes prior to British ownership when people began settling in the extreme western part of West Florida, along the Mississippi River, and along the north shore of Lake Pontchartrain.

West Florida was returned to Spain in 1783 at the Treaty of Paris. The Spanish governors allowed Americans to take up land grants and the Florida Parishes began to be well populated. The Florida Parishes were excluded from the transfer when Spain ceded Louisiana to France in 1802 and they were subsequently not a part of the Louisiana Purchase. Americans who had been enticed to settle the area longed to become a part of the United States and in 1810 they carried out the West Florida Rebellion which was more of a coup d'état than rebellion. The Republic of West Florida lasted for seventy-four days until President Madison directed Governor of Orleans William Claiborne to occupy the territory by right of the Louisiana Purchase. The Parishes of St. Tammany, St. Helena, East

Lake Pontchartrain, North Shore

Baton Rouge, and Feliciana were added to Louisiana Territory on April 14, 1812.

When the Florida Parishes became an American territory, settlers came in from the other Southern colonies. In the Antebellum era the northern coast of Lake Pontchartrain became known as the Ozone Belt because the air among the pines was thought to be healthful and the high ground was free of the miasmas of low, marshy land. Wealthy New Orleanians built summer homes at Mandeville and boats ferried people across Lake Pontchartrain to the new resorts. In the late 1800s the coming of railroads and timber companies brought prosperity to the piney woods.

William Bartram in the Florida Parishes

William Bartram remained at the Pearl River plantation for three days and was then carried to see Mr. Rumsey, who had medicines. Mr. Rumsey's Pearl Island is in actuality Prevost Island and not the present-day Pearl River Island. Mr. Rumsey's plantation was bounded on the east by West Pearl River, on the south by the Rigolets, and on the west by Lake Pontchartrain. It may have included Weems Island and Apple Pie Ridge. Bartram remained with Mr. Rumsey for about a month and as his health improved he began to explore the island. His daily excursions must have taken him over much of the plantation, which is now traversed by US-90. Bartram departed the Rumsey plantation in the middle of October 1775 and followed Salt Bayou to Lake Pontchartrain. Bartram and his traveling companions sailed along the northern shore of Lake Pontchartrain, probably keeping within sight of shore. They stopped at the mouth of the Tangipahoa River and bought provisions. The travelers entered the North Pass and spent the evening on high ground just north of its mouth with Lake Maurepas. Next morning they crossed Lake Maurepas and entered the Amite River.

Sites

1. Biloxi Wildlife Management Area. This 40,000-acre world of water and marsh provides habitat for waterfowl, fur-bearing mammals, alligators, fish, and shellfish. Hunting, boating, fishing, crabbing, shrimping, and birdwatching are popular recreational activities. Biloxi WMA is accessible only by boat.

2. Pearl River. The Pearl River Basin is fifty miles long, averages five miles wide, and contains numerous distributary streams. Half of the Pearl River Basin is publicly owned and most of it is covered with hardwood forest. There are boat launches and fishing spots at the bridgeheads. They are nice places for an early morning stroll and view of the river.

There are few hiking trails in the Pearl River Basin; however, the adventurous soul can explore at low water in summer and fall. Other times of the year this is canoe country. There are many canoe trails in the Pearl River Basin that are described in the *Trail Guide to the Delta Country*, published by the New Orleans Group of the Sierra Club. Louisiana requires all recreationists on state public land to purchase a hunting, fishing, or wildlife stamp. These stamps are only a few dollars and are available from any retailer that sells outdoor equipment.

Old River Wildlife Management Area, located northwest of Picayune, is administered by the Mississippi Department of Wildlife Conservation.

Bogue Chitto National Wildlife Refuge is a large bottomland hardwood forest containing extensive areas of bald cypress and tupelo. The refuge is reached by Sun River and Pearl River. Hiking trails follow the levees of the Pearl River Locks of the West Pearl River. Follow LA-41 north from Pearl River about nine miles to reach the turn for Lock #1. Lock #2 is about twenty miles north of the community of Pearl River via LA-41, near the town of Bush. The Bogue Chitto Refuge office is at 1010 Gause Boulevard, Building 936, Slidell.

Pearl River Game Management Area extends from I-59 to US-90 and is managed by the Louisiana Department of Wildlife and Fisheries.

3. Honey Island Swamp. For a close-up view of this extensive wetland, you might charter a boat tour with Dr. Wagner's Honey Island Swamp Tours. Dr. Wagner is a professional wetland ecologist and his tours focus on the natural history rather than historical and commercial aspects of the swamp. Honey Island Swamp Nature Trail can be found by exiting I-59 at the Honey Island Swamp exit after crossing the West Pearl River, keep east on Old US-41, then turn right onto Oil Well Road (gravel).

4. White Kitchen Wetlands & Chevron Boardwalk are located at the roadside picnic area on the north of US-90 at West Pearl River.

Legend

1. Biloxi WMA
2. Pearl River
3. Old River WMA
4. Bogue Chitto NWR
5. Pearl River Game Management Area
6. Honey Island Swamp
7. White Kitchen Wetlands
8. Fort Pike State Commemorative Area
9. Old Spanish Trail
10. Tammany Trace
11. Lacombe
12. Big Branch Creek NWR
13. Fontainbleu State Park
14. Mandeville
15. Northlake Museum and Nature Center
16. Lake Pontchartrain
17. Fairview-Riverside State Park
18. Madisonville
19. Bogue Falaya Park
20. Lake Ramsey WMA
21. Global Wildlife Park
22. Zemurrey Gardens
23. Loranger
24. Ponchatoula
25. Joyce WMA
26. Manchac WMA
27. Lake Maurepas
28. Gramercy Bonfires
29. Côte des Allemands
30. Great River Road
31. Bonnet Carré Spillway
32. Salvador WMA
33. Rivertown Harahan Trail
34. Bayou Segnette State Park
35. Audubon Park & Zoo
36. City Park & Botanical Garden
37. New Orleans
38. Louisiana Nature and Science Center
39. Jean Lafitte National Historic Park
40. St. Barnard State Park
41. Isleños Center
42. Bayou Savage Refuge

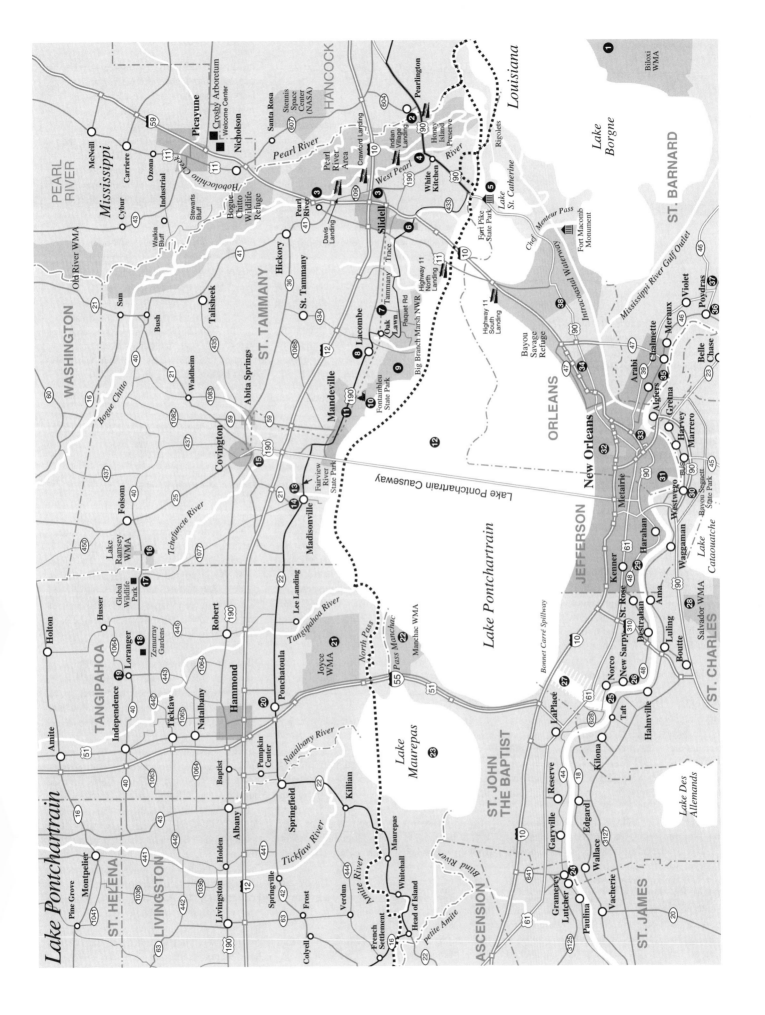

5. Fort Pike State Commemorative Area. Fort Pike was completed in 1827 to guard the Rigolets and was named for General Zebulon Pike. It was built on the site of the previous Fort Petites Coquilles and possibly an even earlier fort built in 1793 by Governor Francisco Carondelet. During the Seminole War of 1835, Fort Pike was a prison and gathering point for Seminole prisoners who were en route to Oklahoma. The fort overlooks Rigolets Pass.

6. Old Spanish Trail was the most important of a series of trails connecting Saint Augustine to Spanish Louisiana, Texas, and Mexico. In Louisiana, US-90 follows the general route of the Old Spanish Trail from Bay Saint Louis, across the Rigolets, through New Orleans, Houma, and Lafayette.

7. Tammany Trace is a Rails-to-Trails project that follows thirty-one miles of old railroad bed from Slidell to Covington. It provides recreation for hikers, bicyclists, and horseback riders. An eight mile section from Mandeville and Abita Springs is paved. It is wheelchair accessible along the completed portion and motorized vehicles are prohibited. The section from Mandeville to Lacombe will open in the near future. When complete, the Tammany Trace will be an unparalleled avenue through the natural history of the Florida Parishes. The Trace is open from 7 a.m. to dusk everyday. Entry to Tammany Trace is at Abita Springs Park and the Information Center at LA-59 and I-12.

8. Lacombe was established as a mission for the Choctaw Indians. The **Bayou Lacombe Museum** has artifacts of early colonial and native settlement. The museum is located one block from US-90, open Sunday 2–5 p.m., March through October; and the first Sunday of each month, November through February. The Bayou Lacombe Crab Festival is held during the last weekend of June.

9. Big Branch Marsh National Wildlife Refuge hugs Lake Pontchartrain and includes beach, brackish marsh, bottomland hammocks, and upland pine ridges. Endangered species include red-cockaded woodpeckers, bald eagles, and brown pelicans. The refuge also supports migratory waterfowl, wading birds, and neo-tropical birds. Opportunities for public recreation include bird watching, fishing, hunting, bicycling, hiking, and canoeing

To reach the refuge, take LA-434 south from I-12 in Lacombe. Another visitor area is reached by traveling east from Lacombe on US-190 for two and a half miles and turning south on Transmitter Road. Transmitter Road ends at Bayou Paquet Road, which runs through the refuge. Turn right and take your second left on Boy Scout Road, which dead ends at Bayou Lacombe.

Bernardo de Gálvez

The contribution of Bernardo de Gálvez and the Spanish to the success of the American Revolution is not well known, perhaps having been overshadowed by the fame of the Marquis de Lafayette and the importance of French assistance. Yet, the threat of attack from the southwest was removed and refugee loyalists lost a safe haven when in 1780 British West Florida was captured by the twenty-nine-year-old governor of Louisiana.

Bernardo de Gálvez was born in Spain in 1748, the son of Don Matias de Gálvez who had served as Viceroy of Mexico and Captain General of Guatemala. Young Gálvez joined the military at sixteen and came to Louisiana in 1776 as a colonel of the Louisiana Regiment, and soon became second in command. On January 1, 1777, he succeeded Luis de Unzaga as governor of Louisiana. During the Galvez administration, Louisiana and West Florida enjoyed growth and prosperity. Gálvez was well liked and admired by those who knew him and he had the affection of the citizens whom he governed. He encouraged immigration to Louisiana and ensured that those who came would receive tools and supplies to help during their first year. Gálvez was successful in cultivating the friendship of the Indians and maintaining peace. The population of Louisiana doubled during his governorship. He was succeeded by Colonel Don Esteban Rodriquez Miró as governor of Louisiana and West Florida in July 1785. Bernardo de Gálvez was then appointed Captain General of Cuba, Governor of Mexico, and Viceroy of New Spain. The career of this talented and competent statesman was cut short by his untimely death in 1786.

10. Fontainbleu State Park was once Fontainbleu Plantation, which was owned by Bernard de Marigny. A nature trail loop begins at the parking area for the sugar mill ruins. The trail passes a Pleistocene beach terrace and reaches the marsh at the edge of Lake Pontchartrain before turning back. There is also an unmarked trail along the banks of the lake that starts at the pavilion grounds and ends at the group campground. Facilities include a boat launch, primitive camping, developed campground, pavilion, pool, and bathhouse. Access is from US-190 south of Mandeville. Open 7 a.m.–8 p.m. daily from April 1 through September 30, and 8 a.m.–7 p.m. during the remainder of the year.

Cane Bayou runs along the east side of the park and can be canoed from the US-190 bridge to Lake Pontchartrain. It is an easy three-mile round trip, the upstream trip is difficult only during high water but at normal levels is an easy paddle.

11. Mandeville was developed by Bernard de Marigny who owned Fontainbleu Plantation and Sugar Mill. He was a descendant of Francis de Mandeville, Sieur de Marigny, a native of Bayeux, Normandy, who was one of Bienville's lieutenants and a commander at Fort Toulouse. In the nineteenth century Mandeville became a resort for New Orleanians who sought an escape from the suffocating and unhealthy summer heat in town and resorted to the pine woods on the north shore. The historic district is a collection of Victorian cottages dating from the turn of the century. Old Town Mandeville remains small, unpretentious, and folksy. The old commercial district faces Lake Pontchartrain and there is a lakefront walk for hikers. The oldest live oak in Louisiana, Seven Sisters Oak, grows on the Lake Pontchartrain shore (on private property).

The **Lake Pontchartrain Causeway** has its north end at Mandeville and at twenty-four miles is the longest bridge in the world.

Northlake Museum and Nature Center is on the right as you enter the city limits of Mandeville from the east. Hiking trails wind through the upland forest and along Bayou Castine. A boardwalk crosses a pond and provides a vantage to view waterfowl. An excellent guide to the trees is available at the parking area information board.

12. Lake Pontchartrain was named by Iberville in honor of Louis Phélypeaux, Count de Pontchartrain, Minister of the French Navy. Lake Pontchartrain is a brackish, shallow lake that was created when the Mississippi River built a delta eastward, overgrowing existing barrier islands and cutting off a bay from the Gulf of Mexico. The ancient island terraces, being higher ground and more stable for road building, can still be seen along the route of I-10. Lake Pontchartrain encompasses 635 square miles and averages only twelve-feet deep. North of Lake Pontchartrain are low flat hills of the pine land and savannah. South of the lake is the low lying delta of New Orleans. There has been recent concern regarding the ecology of Lake Pontchartrain. Commercial and residential growth along the north shore has increased sediment and chemical runoff. Additionally, the rivers draining the uplands have become contaminated by untreated sewage and waste from the dairy farms. The rivers that feed Lake Pontchartrain bear the romantic and exotic names of Tangipahoa, Tchefuncte, Abita, Bogue Lacombe, and Bogue Falaya. Several streams are designated scenic waterways and pollution control is currently underway to improve their water quality.

13. Fairview-Riverside State Park overlooks the Tchefuncte River near Madisonville. The park is primarily an RV campground but does have a short nature trail and the locally historic Otis House.

14. Madisonville was settled in the late eighteenth century and was originally known as Cokie, a corruption of coquille. The town was named in honor of the president in 1810. Madisonville was the embarkation point across Lake Pontchartrain for travelers on the Natchez Trace. The Madisonville Museum is located in the old courthouse and features exhibits on the wildlife, history, and Indian culture of the Tchefuncte River region. To reach the Museum turn right on LA-21 in Madisonville, left on LA-21 after four blocks, then right on Cedar Street. Open Saturday 10 a.m–4 p.m., and on Sunday from 12– 4 p.m.

15. Bogue Falaya Park is located on the Tchefuncte River in Covington. Facilities include a beach house, picnic shelters, nature trail, and access to fishing. New Hampshire Street, Covington.

16. Lake Ramsey Wildlife Management Area was established to protect one of Louisiana's largest remaining longleaf pine flatwood savannahs. The area encompasses 769 acres and eighteen rare plant species. Although controlled hunting is allowed, Lake Ramsey WMA is promoted as an education and recreation area for outdoor activities promoting conservation. Access is by foot travel only. Lake Ramsey is reached by way of Lake Ramsey Road west from LA-25, north of Covington.

17. Global Wildlife Park specializes in the protection of hoofed animals. Visitors to the park view the endangered wildlife from covered wagons. Global Wildlife Park is open daily, 10 a.m. until sunset, closed Christmas Day. To reach the park, exit I-12 at LA-445. Travel north ten and a half miles and turn right (east) on LA-40. It is one and a half miles to the entrance on your right. Admission.

18. Zemurrey Gardens is set among a seventy-five-acre pine forest featuring native and traditional non-native Southern plants. The gardens are open only for a few weeks from late March to mid-April. There are several nature trails. Admission.

New Orleans

Perhaps no other city in America exudes the ambience of a European city as does New Orleans. The city lots were surveyed in 1721 and the area is now called Vieux Carré, the Old Quarter. Not only has the old city survived intact, but it is inhabited by several thousand residents, belying the notion that the Quarter is simply a tourist destination. The architecture; the mixture of African, French, and English cultures; the Voodoo, the food, and the music—make New Orleans unique among American cities.

When Bienville's engineers cleared the site for New Orleans in 1719 they surveyed a natural levee fifteen feet above sea level; now, however, the city is below sea level. New Orleans is protected by the extensive man-made levees, Bonnet Carré spillway, and pumping stations.

Aquarium of the Americas. 10,000 species of fish, birds, and reptiles may be viewed at the aquarium. Located on Canal Street at the river. Open daily at 9:30 a.m., closing time varies by season. Admission.

Jean Lafitte National Historic Park, French Quarter Unit. The urban headquarters of this historic park features the history of the many cultures that have made New Orleans their home.

Jackson Square. The Place d'Armes military parade ground has been the center of Old New Orleans since the city was laid out in 1721. It was renamed in honor of General Andrew Jackson who defeated the British at the Battle of New Orleans. Jackson Square is flanked by the historic Pontalba Apartments and the Cabildo. The square is dominated by Saint Louis Cathedral, built in 1794.

Louisiana State Museum features exhibits on the history of Louisiana from earliest settlement through the Civil War. The Museum includes four historic buildings in the French Quarter. 701 Chartres Street.

Moon Walk. The promenade follows the levee at the French Market with views of the river and the Vieux Carré.

New Orleans Pharmacy Museum. John Bartram's interest in botany extended to the medicinal uses of plants and he was sought out by neighbors to act as physician.

New Orleans Voodoo Museum. This commercial museum and store explores the history of Voodoo in New Orleans and features the life of Marie Leveau, the first queen of Voodoo in America. 724 Dumaine Street.

Veux Carré is the historic district that includes the original 1721 city plan of New Orleans. It is bounded by the river, Canal, Esplanade, and Rampart streets.

Voodoo Spiritual Temple. Voodoo, or Voudun, is derived from the spiritual beliefs of Africa, particularly the Yoruba culture. Voodoo is not black magic or nefarious work but a way of dealing with the spirit world. Most Voodoo practitioners do not use their craft to cause harm but to help clients obtain good fortune and good health. Voodoo came to Louisiana from Haiti and is related to the Santaria faith of the Caribbean. Two spiritual advisors are available for consultation at the temple. 828 N. Rampart Street.

19. Loranger hosts Old Farmers Day the third weekend of October. This celebration features exhibits that portray farm life of the mid-eighteenth century and demonstrations of field work with horses and mules, syrup making, and cooking.

20. Ponchatoula received its name from a Choctaw word for Spanish moss, *Iti Shuma*, meaning tree hair. Ponchatoula is known for its number of antique shops and the strawberry festival that is held in early April. Ponchatoula is the center of the Louisiana strawberry industry and bills itself as the Strawberry Capital of the World.

21. Joyce Wildlife Management Area. This 15,000-acre preserve is predominantly cypress-Tupelo swamp but has an extensive maiden cane prairie in the northern portion. One of the prairies is located just north of the boardwalk on I-55. The Joyce area is located north of Pass Manchac and adjacent to I-55/US-51. The boardwalk is located at exit 22 on I-55 near the north end of the preserve. The rest of the preserve is accessible by boat from North Pass and Tangipahoa River. Waterfowl, particularly ducks, are abundant.

22. Manchac Wildlife Management Area is located immediately south of Pass Manchac. Most of the cypress has been logged, which has left an open freshwater marsh. The area is populated with alligators, muskrats, and numerous species of waterfowl. The headquarters is located on US-51 at Pass Manchac.

Southern Louisiana University maintains a biological research station on the northern side of Pass Manchac.

23. Lake Maurepas was named for Jérôme de Phélypeaux, Comte de Maurepas and the son of the Comte de Pontchartrain. Maurepas succeeded to his father's title and office as Minister of the French Navy and Secretary to the Royal Household. Lake Maurepas covers ninety-three square miles and averages only seven-feet deep. It was created soon after Lake Pontchartrain formed when part of the delta subsided. Lake Maurepas's tributaries are the Natalbany, Tickfaw, and Amite Rivers. Lake Maurepas drains into Lake Pontchartrain through Pass Manchac and the North Pass. William Bartram's boat took the North Pass from Lake Pontchartrain to Lake Maurepas, but the two passes do not reconnect as he wrote. I-55 and US-51 cross the neck of cypress swamp lying between Lake Maurepas and Lake Pontchartrain and provides access to Manchac and Joyce Wildlife Management Areas. Take US-51 south from Pontchatoula and exit at Manchac for views of the lake.

24. Gramercy Bonfires. Saint James parishioners prepare stacks of wood along the levee during the holiday season; they then ignite magnificent bonfires on Christmas Eve to light the way for Peré Noel, who travels by water in Louisiana. The bonfires have been a tradition of Gramercy since the 1700s, perhaps having its roots in ancient pagan rituals that lingered even after the coming of Christianity. The bonfires are constructed in elaborate and fanciful shapes. The Gramercy fire department oversees the whole event and benefits by selling gumbo and jambalaya to the crowds of onlookers.

25. Côte des Allemands (the German coast). The river north of New Orleans in Saint Charles and Saint John the Baptist parishes was settled by German farmers from Alsace, Rhineland, and Switzerland. They were enticed by false advertising published by John Law's Company of the West, which was chartered with developing Louisiana. Pamphlets portrayed Louisiana as extremely pleasant, the soil so rich it produced four to six crops per year, and the earth containing lead, silver, gold, and copper mines. Upwards of 9,000 German-speaking people entered Louisiana between 1717 and 1722. Although many died in the new environment, prosperous German communities soon began to appear upriver of New Orleans. These sober, hard-working farmers benefitted Louisiana by building homes, growing food crops, and providing a skilled work force. They helped stabilized the colony, unlike the fortune seekers and exiles who preceded them. The German names have disappeared with the language as families learned French and took French surnames.

26. Great River Road. The river roads hug the levee on both sides of the Mississippi River between New Orleans and Baton Rouge. Some of the richest farmland on the continent brought wealth to the French and German settlers who came in the eighteenth century. Fortunes made with sugar and cotton helped build the magnificent plantation homes that line the River Road—Destrehan (1787), San Francisco (1856), Oak Alley (1837), Tezcuco (1855), Houmas House (1840), Bocage (1801), L'Hermitage (1812), Reserve (1790), and Nottoway (1859). Many homes are still in excellent condition and open for public visitation. The river roads are LA-44 and LA-48 on the east bank, and LA-1 and LA-18 on the west bank. Driving maps and plantation guides are available at most visitor centers.

27. Bonnet Carré Spillway. Excess water in the Mississippi River is controlled by diversion through man-made spillways into other bodies of water. The Bonnet Carré Spillway diverts water into Lake Pontchartrain.

28. Salvador Wildlife Management Area covers over 30,000 acres of freshwater marsh and numerous ponds. The area is accessible only by boat. There are several stands of cypress in the northern portion where there are natural levees from old Mississippi River courses. Salvador WMA provides habitat for waterfowl, alligator, mink, bald eagle, deer, otter, and muskrat.

29. Rivertown is a collection of six museums operated by the city of Kenner and located in a renovated commercial district. Attractions include Jefferson Parish Mardi Gras Museum, Louisiana Wildlife and Fisheries Museum, and Kenner Historical Museum. LaSalle's Landing is a landscaped park that overlooks the Mississippi River. Located on the Mississippi River in Kenner. Open 8:30 a.m.–4:30 p.m., Tuesday through Saturday, and 1–5 p.m. on Sunday.

Harahan Trail follows the Mississippi River levee from Williams Boulevard in Kenner to Saint Charles Avenue in New Orleans. Harahan Trail is a multipurpose trail for horseback riding, hiking, and bicycling. The levee can be hiked as far as one desires in either direction. For information about hiking in the New Orleans area, see the *Trail Guide to the Delta Country,* published by the New Orleans Group of the Sierra Club.

30. Bayou Segnette State Park. Access to Barataria Basin, boat ramp, picnic area, and conference facilities. Westbank Parkway in Westwego.

31. Audubon Park & Zoo. In addition to Asian and African animals, Audubon Park Zoo has the very popular Louisiana Swamp exhibit where visitors can see native animals and sample Cajun food. Located on the Mississippi River at Magazine Street and Broadway. Audubon Park is accessible from the Aquarium by river taxi. Open at 9 a.m. every day except Thanksgiving, Christmas, Mardi Gras, and the first Friday in May.

32. City Park & Botanical Garden. At 1,500 acres, City Park is large enough to have lagoons for fishing and canoeing on Bayou St. John. City Park is the site of New Orleans Trace, where Bienville explored, and is home to the New Orleans Museum of Art. City Park was a popular dueling place for gentlemen in the nineteenth century. The ten-acre botanical garden has seasonal displays of subtropical native and introduced plants. The Garden supports botanical research and sponsors new plant introductions for the Gulf Coast region. Open daily with seasonal operating hours.

33. New Orleans. See page 285.

34. Louisiana Nature and Science Center. The Center has a planetarium, trails, and exhibits on native plants and animals. Three hiking trails traverse wetlands and surrounding forests. Located at Joe Brown Park on Read Boulevard, just off Forest Drive.

35. Jean Lafitte National Historical Park, Chalmette Unit. The Battle of New Orleans was fought at Chalmette Plantation on January 8, 1815 and the American victory helped bring an end to the War of 1812. The site is now preserved as a unit of Jean Lafitte National Historical Park. The Chalmette site includes a visitor center and museum, cemetery, and the Beauregard House. Located on St. Bernard Highway (LA-36). Open everyday except Christmas, New Year's Day, and Mardi Gras.

36. Saint Barnard State Park. Hiking trails, fishing, picnicking, and camping. Located on LA-39 near Poydras.

37. Isleños Center, Jean Lafitte National Historical Park and Preserve. The Isleños were Canary Islanders who emigrated to Louisiana in the late 1770s during the second Spanish period. Their history is told at the Isleños Museum, located on Bayou Road.

38. Bayou Savage Refuge lies between New Orleans and Chef Menteur Pass. The area is open for fishing, boating, and hiking. During the year over 340 species of birds use the refuge for breeding and feeding. Varying natural habitats include marsh, bottomland hardwood forests, chenieres (ancient beaches), bayous, and lagoons. The visitor center is located on US-90.

Nearby

Land Office Building in Greensburg was built in 1820 and was the office for the sale of land in the Florida Parishes until 1843. Located on LA-43 in Saint Helena Parish.

Louisiana Museum of Ancient Indian Culture and the **Bogue Lusa Pioneer Museum,** Cassidy Park, midtown Bogalusa. Both are open on weekends.

Lake Vista Nature Preserve Trail, ten miles east of Bogalusa.

Mile Branch Settlement, Franklinton, is a replica of a pioneer settlement of the late nineteenth century. The settlement is open during the Washington Parish Fair in mid-October when there are demonstrations of pioneer skills. It is open at other times by appointment.

Citrus Groves, Plaquemines Parish.

Parishes

Livingston was named for Edward Livingston, Louisiana statesman.

Orleans was created as a county in 1807 encompassing New Orleans and its precincts.

Saint Bernard was created as a county in 1807 and based on the Spanish ecclesiastical district of the same name.

Saint Helena was created from the original Feliciana County in 1810 and is named for St. Helena.

Saint Tammany was created from the original Feliciana County in 1810 and is named for Delaware Chief Tammany.

Tangipahoa was created in 1869 from surrounding parishes and is named for the Tangipahoa Indians.

Washington was created from Saint Tammany in 1819 and is named for President George Washington.

Itinerary

Miles	Directions
	Begin at the Pearl River drawbridge and travel west on US-90
1.0	Intersection of US-90 and US-190 in White Kitchen
	Keep left on US-90
4.8	Right on LA-433, becomes Old Spanish Trail
8.4	Enter Slidell, keep on LA-433, which becomes Bayou Liberty after the intersection with US-11 (Pontchartrain Drive)
.7	Keep left on LA-433, Bayou Liberty Road
3.9	Enter Bonfouca Community, cross Liberty Bayou
4.2	Left on Bayou Paquet Road (road closed at times; detour to US-190, if needed, by way of CC Road and Tranquility Road)
5.8	Dead end, right on Robert Avenue in Oaklawn, bear left at the intersection with Railroad Avenue
.7	Right on South Oaklawn Drive
.7	Left on US-190
1.4	Cross Bayou Lacombe
6.2	Entrance to Fontainbleau State Park
.9	Entrance to Northlake Museum & Nature Center
1.5	Intersection with Garrard Street (left for Old Mandeville and Lake Pontchartrain)
	Keep right on US-90 in Mandeville at Causeway intersection
5.1	Bear left on LA-22
3.8	Entrance to Riverside State Park
2.4	Cross Tchefuncte River to Madisonville
6.0	Enter Tangipahoa Parish
5.6	Cross Tangipahoa River
6.7	Enter downtown Pontchatoula
5.0	Enter Livingston Parish
.2	Sharp left turn on LA-22 in Springfield
4.0	Cross Tickfaw River
16.0	Old Amite River is on the right
5.0	Straight on LA-16
1.4	Cross Amite River and enter French Settlement
7.4	Left on LA-42

Mississippi River

The history of the Mississippi River is also the history of colonial Louisiana. Most early settlements were made along the river banks because of the extremely fertile land and to take advantage of trade and transportation opportunities. Farms were protected by the natural levee that is created when floodwaters deposit heavier sediment close to the river and finer particles drop out farther from the river. The French used a land survey system of long lots called *arpents*; each had some river frontage and extended back from the river. This system gave landowners access to river traffic at the front of the property, good farmland and pasture in the middle, and woodland for timber toward the back of the property. There was often some swamp at the back of the property that was a dependable source of wild game.

Spanish efforts at establishing settlements were concentrated on the Atlantic coast in order to protect their treasure fleets and they ignored the Mississippi River. The Narváez expedition may have been the first Europeans to see the Mississippi River Delta as they struggled toward Mexico in their small boats. Hernando De Soto came next and died somewhere between Natchez and Memphis and was buried in the river. The remainder of his army built boats and sailed down the Mississippi and returned to Mexico. Thereafter, the Spanish concentrated their efforts in Florida. Although the Spanish claimed all of North America, there was little attempt to make good their claim in the Mississippi River Valley and, indeed, they made little protest when the French claimed the region. The Spanish much preferred the French, to the English, as their neighbors.

The *Coureurs de bois,* Canadian fur traders, and Jesuit priests had by the late 1600s ranged from Canada down into the Ohio and upper Mississippi river valleys. René Robert Cavelier, Sieur de la Salle descended the Mississippi in 1682. He claimed the entire drainage basin in the name of Louis XIV of France and named the country in his honor. La Salle returned from France in the summer of 1684 with three ships, settlers, and soldiers to legitimate the French claim to Louisiana. Unfortunately, he missed the river's mouth and landed at Matagorda Bay on the Texas coast in January 1685. The *L'Aimable* was wrecked, the captain of *Le Joly* deserted with most of the supplies, then *La Belle* sank. In the winter of 1687 La Salle started out overland for Canada to secure aid for the suffering colony. On March 20 he was assassinated by his men and the colony was attacked by Indians. The only survivors were children who were taken captive by the Indians and who were rescued by a Spanish ship the next year. Recently La Salle's ship, *La Belle,* was discovered and has been recovered by the Texas Historical Commission. *La Belle* has yielded the greatest collection of trade goods, rigging, and implements yet found at a seventeenth century archaeological site in the New World.

The settlement of Louisiana briefly became urgent national policy for the French, who hoped to gain new possessions and contain the English, who were also beginning to have designs on the interior of the continent. The brothers Bienville and Iberville were chosen to oversee the exploration and settlement of Louisiana. Pierre le Moyne, Sieur de Iberville was a Canadian noble and a commandant in the French navy. He was appointed by the French government to explore the Mississippi River and establish settlements, forts, and create a colony. Iberville and his company set sail from La Rochelle, France in September 1698 and arrived at Santa Rosa Island in January 1699. They were received by the Spanish commander at Pensacola but were refused permission to enter Pensacola Bay. Iberville sailed westward exploring Mobile Bay, Dauphin Island, the Gulf Islands, and the Gulf Coast. Iberville's ships entered the Mississippi River on March 2, 1699 and sailed upstream, stopping at various points that included Baton Rouge, Pointe Coupee, and Tunica. The first French settlement in Louisiana was made at Fort Maurepas (Ocean Springs) in 1699, then Mobile in 1702, Saint Denis (Natchitoches) in 1714, and Biloxi in 1719. Iberville left Louisiana in 1702 and was succeeded in the governorship by his brother Bienville. In 1719 Bienville began building a capital on the Mississippi River, which was named for the Duc de Orleans.

France was unable to attract colonists to Louisiana and officially excluded many of the most willing and industrious colonists by barring Huguenots from immigrating into the colony. French Protestants settled instead in the British colonies and there they made invaluable contributions to the culture and economy. Louisiana was costing the crown a considerable sum of money in yearly maintenance so King Louis XIV granted the colony to Antoine Crozat in 1712 with a fifteen year charter in the hope that Crozat could develop Louisiana into a profitable business. Antoine de la Mothe Cadillac became the new governor in 1713. Cadillac was unpopular in Louisiana, quarrelled with Bienville, and was recalled in 1716. The new governor, Jean Michiele, Seigneur de Lepinay et de la Longueville, fared no better than Cadillac. Crozat, struggling with increased taxes and ineffective governors gave his charter back to the crown in 1717.

In 1716 John Law became head of the Royal Bank of France and director of the Company of the West, later renamed the Company of the Indies. In 1717 the company was given authority for developing Louisiana. During the company's control, prostitutes and petty criminals were given the choice of prison or passage to Louisiana. Soldiers were commissioned to take beggars and homeless persons from the streets of Paris who

Baton Rouge and the Mississippi River

were then sent to Louisiana. These *Bandoulliers de Mississippi* began to kidnap unwilling citizens in order to collect their bounty. Louisiana soon became known as a place to be feared and avoided. The company advertised among the German states for colonists and by false advertising enticed thousands of Germans and Swiss to emigrate. The Company of the West was built on speculation and the bubble burst in 1722, ending the period of intense immigration to Louisiana.

By 1728 there were a thousand people living in New Orleans. The Company of the Indies gave up their charter in 1731 and Bienville returned as governor. Bienville's fourth and last term was plagued by war with the Chickasaws and the disinterest of the Royal Court. The next governor, Pierre François de Rigaud Cavagnal, Marguis de Vaudreuil, attempted to establish a miniature version of French court life and allowed the colonial government of Louisiana to become corrupt. Louis Billouart, Chevalier de Kerlerec, became governor in 1752. Although Kerlerec was competent and determined to improve conditions in Louisiana, the Court at Versailles had become so self-absorbed that Louisiana was all but forgotten.

Louisiana was ceded to Spain in a secret agreement prior to the 1763 Treaty of Paris. The transfer of territory was partial restitution for Spain's loss of Florida but was also an unveiled attempt to keep a large part of North America out of the hands of the English. France had spent the better part of the century at war and could no longer afford to support Louisiana. Louis XV regretted the loss of Canada, but not of Louisiana.

The new Spanish governor, Don Antonio de Ulloa, arrived in 1766. He was not accepted by the Creole citizens nor did they like the new trade regulations he was instructed to implement. Ulloa was forced to leave Louisiana in 1768. Governor Don Alejandro O'Reilly arrived in August 1769 with an army and the determination that was lacking in Ulloa. O'Reilly executed the leaders of the rebellion that ousted Ulloa and reorganized the government around Spanish law. Don Luis de Unzaga y Amézaga governed from 1770 to late 1772 and was succeeded by Bernardo de Gálvez. Governor Gálvez was a popular and capable administrator. He encouraged immigration, and the population of Louisiana doubled during his office to nearly 30,000 in 1783. The Spanish governors had benefitted the Creoles of Louisiana more than had their own French government of Louis XV. The Spanish welcomed immigrants of numerous nationalities—Germans, Canary Islanders, Spaniards, English Loyalists, Americans, and French refugees from Santo Domingo. The greatest influx of Acadians occurred during the last quarter of the eighteenth century. Native populations of Louisiana were treated with respect and even allowed equal treatment in the courts.

When William Bartram visited the Mississippi River, the capital of Spanish Louisiana was at New Orleans. There were French settlements from Donaldsonville north to Pointe Coupee. North of New Orleans were Germans, north of them were the Bayougoula and Houma Indians, then the Acadians. Along the east side of the Mississippi River in West Florida, in what is now East Baton Rouge and West Feliciana Parishes, Great Britain had begun making land grants to British subjects. Many of the French inhabitants had chosen to move across the river to Spanish territory. Living between Bayou Manchac and the Baton Rouge plantations were a group of Alabama Indians who had settled near their French allies.

James Willing brought the Revolution to the Lower Mississippi River In 1778, though by his actions he alienated more of the French and British planters than he converted to the patriot cause. Willing was basically a freebooter who took advantage of the volatile political atmosphere. He burned plantations, including that of William Dunbar. Willing and his gang stole slaves with impunity and without regard for the diplomatic consequences with Spain. He never attracted many volunteers and was captured later in the year and imprisoned in New York.

During the Revolution, Governor Bernardo de Gálvez seized West Florida from the British. The Spanish government was much more involved in the welfare of Louisiana than the French had been. The Spanish were generous and accommodating in attracting new citizens to Louisiana and brought a period of prosperity to the colony. In 1800 Napoleon convinced Spain to return Louisiana to France (Treaty of Ildefonso, October 1, 1800). France did not take formal possession of Louisiana until Colonial Prefect Pierre Clement de Laussat arrived in New Orleans on March 24, 1803. Napoleon promptly sold Louisiana to the United States for $15,000,000. James Monroe and Robert Livingston signed the documents for the sale on April 30, 1803. Louisiana was admitted to the Union on April 30, 1812.

Acadian or Creole? There is a difference! The Creoles are descendants of the original French and Spanish settlers of Louisiana, the Gulf Coast, and Caribbean colonies. The Acadians are descended from the Canadian-born French citizens expelled from Acadia (Nova Scotia and New Brunswick) in the 1750s by the British.

The Acadians have their origins on the Celtic coast of France in the early seventeenth century where they were removed from the political and cultural center of activity. Breton fishermen were working the Grand Banks off Newfoundland as early as 1504. They began emigrating to Canada in 1604, three years before Jamestown was settled and a full century before many of the Louisiana Creoles arrived in New Orleans. The Acadians left Europe when France was much more provincial than it was to become during the reigns of the cosmopolitan Kings Louis XIV and XV in the eighteenth century. In isolation the Acadians retained much of their agrarian life, songs, music, and religious beliefs as their native France became a unified world power and entered the Industrial Revolution. Even when the Acadians emigrated to Louisiana they tended to settle in remote areas west of the Mississippi River.

The Creole citizens of Louisiana remained in contact with Europe and retained a much more urbane culture. The Creoles remained faithful Catholics, which encouraged the protestant French Huguenots to settle in the English colonies rather than Louisiana.

William Bartram at the Mississippi River

William Bartram sailed up the Amite River and Bayou Manchac (then called the Iberville River) as far as near present-day Kleinpeter. There, at the head of navigation, merchandise was loaded and unloaded at the warehouses. Bartram traveled on to Manchac by a road on the north side of Bayou Manchac. Upon arriving at Manchac, about October 21, 1775, he immediately went to the banks of the Mississippi River, the goal of his travels since leaving the Cherokee Nation.

At Manchac, Bartram met a gentleman who owned a plantation at New Richmond (Baton Rouge). This new friend was none other than William Dunbar, a Scotsman late of Jamaica and prosperous from supplying barrel staves to the Caribbean shipping industry. Dunbar was to become a prominent citizen of Natchez and correspondent of many learned men of the time, including Thomas Jefferson. The following day Bartram sailed with Dunbar in a private boat and stopped at Alabama Town on their way to Baton Rouge. They traveled farther upriver and spent the evening at a plantation. The following day Bartram and Dunbar visited at plantations as they made their way upriver to Dunbar's own home.

After resting for a day or two at Dunbar's home, William Bartram and his host decided to visit Pointe Coupee. On their way upriver they stopped at the White Cliffs, near Port Hudson. Governor Chester Brown owned land along the river at Port Hickey and inland to present-day Plains and Zachary. On August 27, 1775 (not 1787 as Bartram wrote), they traveled eastward from the river to see the White Plains, most certainly in the vicinity of present-day Plains. The area was later known

---

William Dunbar, 1749–1810

Although William Bartram did not mention William Dunbar by name in the *Travels,* we know from a letter Dunbar wrote to Jefferson that he befriended the botanist in 1775. It was Dunbar who was Bartram's host and companion during the sojourn at Baton Rouge from about October 22 to November 10, 1775. Dunbar became a well-known amateur naturalist who corresponded with Henry Muhlenberg, Benjamin Smith Barton, Benjamin Rush, and Alexander Wilson among others.

William Dunbar was born in Elgin, Scotland, of a noble family and was educated in mathematics and astronomy. He came to America in 1771 for health reasons and was soon engaged in the Indian trade at Pittsburg. He traveled down the Mississippi River to Louisiana in 1773 and took up a land grant at Baton Rouge where he built a profitable business manufacturing staves for the Caribbean trade. His plantation was plundered by Willing's Raiders in 1778 and by the troops of Governor Gálvez in 1779. Dunbar moved to Natchez in 1783 so that he could become an American citizen and he is now more closely associated with the history of Natchez than of Baton Rouge. His home was The Forest, nine miles south of Natchez. William Dunbar introduced the square cotton bale to the trade and was the first to extract cotton seed oil.

Dunbar's scientific observations brought him into contact with the learned men of the day with whom he corresponded on numerous topics. He was elected a member of the American Philosophical Society, assisted Andrew Ellicott in determining the 31st parallel at Bayou Sara, and was chosen by Jefferson to lead the Red River Expedition in 1804. His journal mentions a curious event seen at Baton Rouge when he and neighbors witnessed a ball of light and an explosion in the sky.

as Saint John's Plains and was the site of the West Florida Convention. On August 28, Bartram and Dunbar continued upriver and crossed to Pointe Coupee on the west bank, which was then Spanish territory. They visited a French planter who had been a refugee from the Natchez massacre of November 28, 1729.

On their return to Baton Rouge, Bartram and Dunbar stopped again at the White Cliffs where they observed a fossilized cypress forest, relic stumps that were then covered by many feet of earth with an entirely new forest growing above. William Bartram wondered at the forces that could have placed this ancient forest below ground level to be revealed many years later by the meandering Mississippi River. Sir Charles Lyell, having read Bartram's *Travels,* visited the same fossilized forest and in the memoirs of his travels in North America Lyell gives credit to William Bartram's powers of observation. Lyell articulated the *Theory of Uniformity* that states that the processes and forces we see acting on the Earth today have been operating consistently and unchanged throughout time. Lyell's prodigy, Charles Darwin, was influenced by the Theory of Uniformity while developing his own theory of the Origin of Species.

William Bartram left Baton Rouge on November 13, 1775, and returned to Mobile by the same route he had taken a month earlier.

Sites

1. Mississippi River. As it flows across the Louisiana delta, the Mississippi River is contained within levees that are now engineered but were once naturally occurring geologic features. Historically, when the river flooded and spread out across the delta, the heaviest soil particles were the first to settle nearest to the banks. From Bayou Manchac south to the mouth of the river the bank of the Mississippi was the highest land to be found anywhere in the Delta. The finest particles settled out much farther from the river banks and helped make the Delta the richest farm land in the nation. During the Antebellum era one half of America's millionaires lived on the Mississippi River between Natchez and New Orleans.

The best land in the delta is nearest the rivers where land is higher. Land then becomes increasingly swampy farther back from the natural levee. Due to these naturally occurring levees there are few streams entering the lower Mississippi; one encounters tributary streams only north of Baton Rouge. Waterways in the delta are *distributary* streams, meaning they distribute excess water rather than gather it.

The current course of the Mississippi River has by no means been its constant path. Seen through geologic time, the Mississippi would appear to be a writhing snake whipping back and forth across Louisiana. In the last several thousands years, it has at times coursed where the Bayou Teche and Bayou Lafource now flow; and if not for the work of the Army Corps of Engineers, the Mississippi would now choose the Atchafalaya, which is twelve feet lower in elevation. This continuous movement and looping can be seen clearly on state parish highway maps that show river meander lines of the past century. Boundaries of one parish cross the river and dip into another parish like a puzzle piece to follow an abandoned section of river or oxbow lake. The containment of the river, though protecting property and commerce, has interrupted the yearly cycle of flooding that created the delta and deposited the rich soil. In this century, significant amounts of land in the lower delta have subsided without this continual replenishment. New Orleans now averages fifteen feet below its original elevation and parts of the city are below sea level.

The French Coast. New Orleans was founded by Bienville in 1718 and became the capital of Louisiana in 1722. The first settlers were French immigrants and the focus of early settlement was the rich lowlands along the Mississippi River between New Orleans and Pointe Coupee. The French also settled on the Amite River during the Spanish period.

The Acadian Coast. In 1757 the first Acadians to arrive in Louisiana were settled along the Mississippi River south of Bayou Manchac in Saint James and Ascension Parishes. From there, they and later arrivals moved westward from the Mississippi River or followed the bayous northward from the Gulf. The oldest existing Catholic church in Louisiana is Saint Gabriel Catholic Church, built by Acadians in the 1770s.

The German Coast. The Company of the West, under the direction of John Law, lured German, Dutch, and Swiss farmers to Louisiana with tales of an earthly paradise. They settled along the Mississippi River north of New Orleans in Saint Charles and Saint John the Baptist Parishes. This area became known as the *Coté des Allemands,* the German Coast. Many settlers changed their names to French equivalents and they eventually ceased speaking German. Approximately 10,000 Germans emigrated to Louisiana between 1717 and 1722 and they can be credited with giving the floundering colony a sense of permanence and a foundation of industrious citizens.

The English. The parishes east of the Mississippi River, north of Lake Pontchartrain, and north of the Amite River are called the Florida Parishes because they were originally part of West Florida. The area was settled by the British after the end of the French and Indian War and by Americans after the close of the Revolution. The 1783 Treaty of Paris returned West Florida to Spain. Although the Spanish governed benevolently, American immigrants longed to become a part of the United States. On September 26, 1810, they proclaimed the area to be the Independent Republic of West Florida and petitioned President James Madison to annex the territory. Governor Claiborne took possession on December 10 and organized the land between the Mississippi River and Perdido River into Feliciana County; containing the parishes of Feliciana, East Baton Rouge, Saint Helena, and Saint Tammany. The Florida Parishes were annexed to Louisiana in 1812 during the process of statehood.

2. Atchafalaya Basin. Just an hour's drive from Baton Rouge is one of the most magnificent wetlands in the United States—the Atchafalaya Basin, the continent's largest riverine swamp. This extensive system of interlocking rivers, bayous, marshes, lakes, and swamps is thirty-five miles wide and 125 miles long and is the main distributary branch of the Mississippi River.

In the early 1800s the Atchafalaya River was a low area filled with numerous large lakes. A logjam at its source kept the Atchafalaya from taking too much water from the Mississippi River. In 1831, Captain Henry Miller Shreve dug a canal across Turnbull Bend to facilitate river traffic. A few years later he was authorized to clear logjams from the Red River and the Atchafalaya. The loop around Turnbull Bend was where the Red River entered the Mississippi and also where the Atchafalaya began. The result of Shreve's activity was that more of the Mississippi and most of the Red River flowed into the Atchafalaya River and transformed it into a much larger and sediment-laden river.

Since the mid-1800s the Atchafalaya River has filled its open lakes, built natural levees, and is building a delta in Atchafalaya Bay. During the flood of 1973, the Mississippi River would have diverted its course into the Atchafalaya Basin but for the Old River Control

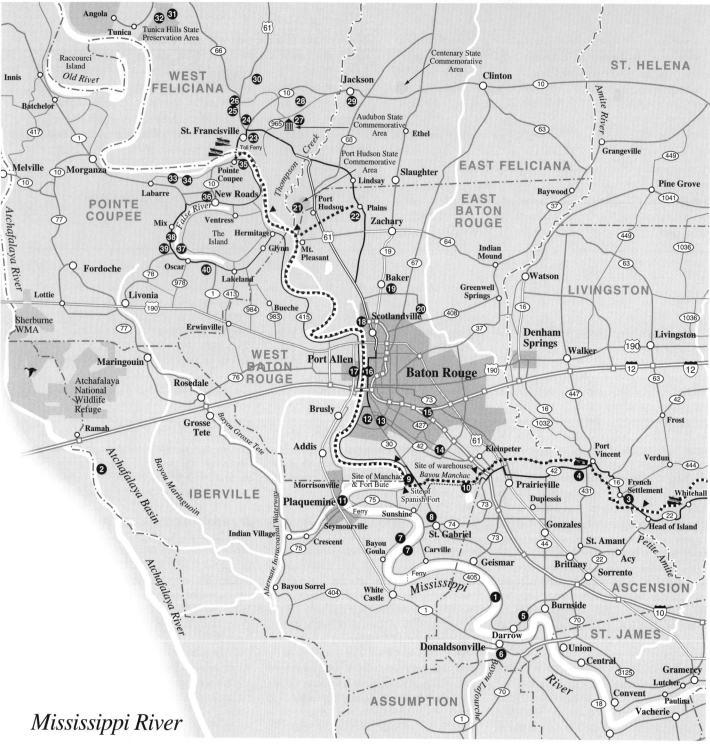

Mississippi River

Structure north of Angola. Recent agreements between the state of Louisiana and the Army Corps of Engineers will provide for restoration of the swamp, which has been badly damaged by channeling and clear-cutting of the cypress forest. The National Park Service has studied the Atchafalaya Basin for possible inclusion into the National Park System and much progress has been made in protecting this beautiful and mysterious wilderness.

The Sherbourne Wildlife Management Area and **Atchafalaya National Wildlife Refuge** lie between US-190 and I-10. Atchafalaya Basin tours can be arranged in Breaux Bridge and Henderson, St. Martin Parish. Public boat launches are located at Bayou Sorrell and Bayou Pigeon.

3. French Settlement was settled by French, German, and Italian immigrants around 1800. The Creole House Museum is located on LA-16 behind town hall. The museum is built in the French Creole style and contains memorabilia of the original settlers. It is open the third Sunday of the month from 2–4 p.m. A swamp boardwalk is located at Bayview Tavern.

4. Galveztown was established around 1778 by British and American loyalists fleeing the depredations of the renegade patriot Captain James Willing. The town was named in honor of their benefactor, Governor Gálvez of Spanish Louisiana. Galveztown was located at the confluence of Bayou Manchac and the Amite River near present-day Port Vincent. These English-speaking immigrants took an oath of allegiance to the King of Spain and changed their names to Spanish equivalents. The town is now gone, but a historical marker on LA–42 notes its site.

5. River Road African American Museum is located on LA-22, between Burnside and Darrow.

6. Donaldsonville, the third oldest city in Louisiana, was settled around 1750 by Indian traders at a village of Chitimacha Indians. In the 1760s Acadian refugees settled along the Mississippi River and Bayou Lafource. Donaldsonville was the capital of Louisiana in 1830 and 1831. The Sunshine Bridge at Donaldsonville honors Governor Jimmie Davis who wrote "You Are My Sunshine." It is the only bridge to cross the Mississippi River between New Orleans and Baton Rouge. The Ascension Parish Heritage Association Museum is located in the old Courthouse in Donaldsonville.

8. Saint Gabriel is just south of the site of the Spanish fort San Gabriel de Manchack. Saint Gabriel Catholic Church is the oldest Catholic Church in Louisiana, built by Acadians in the 1770s.

7. The River Roads hug the Mississippi River levee from New Orleans to Baton Rouge on the east bank, and from New Orleans to Pointe Coupee on the west bank. Scattered along LA-44, LA-18, LA-942, and LA-1 are the great Antebellum plantation homes built upon sugar fortunes.

9. Bayou Manchac was called the **Iberville River** in colonial times and was the boundary between British West Florida and Spanish Isle de Orleans. It was an important trade link between the Mississippi River and Lake Maurepas because the British did not control the Mississippi south of this point. Navigation was possible for only twelve river miles above its junction with the Amite River, a point at about Bayou Fountain. The boats were then unloaded and cargo was transported by horse to the settlement of Manchac. The road ran along the north side of the bayou. From Manchac, goods were transported upriver by boat. Manchac was established as a trading post and Fort Bute was built to guard the English navigation route. The fort was located just north of Bayou Manchac between LA-30 and the Mississippi River. The Spanish fort of **San Gabriel de Manchack** was directly south of Fort Bute and across Bayou Manchac. The chief merchant at Manchac was John Fitzpatrick who fled to Galveztown when the Willing raiders attacked Baton Rouge.

During Bartram's visit, Bayou Manchac was connected to the Mississippi River during periods of wet weather but its course was blocked by trees. Although there was an attempt by the British to clear Bayou Manchac, it never became a thoroughfare to the Mississippi and was completely cutoff when Andrew Jackson constructed a dike across the mouth in 1812 to prevent the British using it as a supply route.

10. Canoe access to Alligator Bayou and Spanish Lake is at the Bait Shop a half mile past the end of paved portion of Alligator Bayou Road.

Parlange

Legend

1. Mississippi River
   The French Coast
   The Acadian Coast
   The German Coast
   The English
2. Atchafalaya Basin
   Sherbourne WMA
   Atchafalaya NWR
3. French Settlement
4. Galveztown
5. River Road African American Museum
6. Donaldsonville
8. Saint Gabriel
7. The River Roads
9. Bayou Manchac
10. Alligator Bayou and Spanish Lake
11. Placquemine
12. Louisiana State University
13. Magnolia Mound Plantation
14. LSU Hill Top Aboretum
15. LSU Rural Life Museum
16. Baton Rouge
    Riverfront Park
    Louisiana Arts & Sciences Center
    Louisiana State Archives
    Louisiana State Capitol & Visitor Center
    Pentagon Barracks
    The Old Arsenal Museum
17. Port Allen
    West Baton Rouge Museum
18. Southern University
19. Greater Baton Rouge Zoo
20. Cohn Memorial Arboretum
21. Port Hudson State Commemorative Area
22. Governor Brown's White Plains
23. Saint Francisville
    Audubon Pilgrimage
    West Feliciana Historical Society Museum
    James R. Leake Memorial Park
    Bayou Sara
24. Rosedown Plantation & Gardens
25. Butler Greenwood Plantation
26. Afton Gardens
27. Audubon State Commemorative Area
28. Mary Ann Brown Preserve
29. West Florida Historical Association Museum
30. Locust Grove State Commemorative Area
31. Tunica Hills Wildlife Management Area
32. Tunica Hills State Preservation Area
33. Saint Francis of Assisi Chapel
34. Labatut House
35. Pointe Coupee
36. New Roads
37. False River
38. Pointe Coupee Museum and Visitor Center
39. Parlange
40. Riverlake Plantation

11. Plaquemine was one of the first areas to be settled by Acadians in the mid-eighteenth century. Plaquemine Locks Museum has an observation tower that overlooks downtown Plaquemine and the Mississippi River. Locks located at the mouth of Bayou Plaquemine connect the Mississippi River with the Alternate Intracoastal Waterway.

12. Louisiana State University was established in 1850 and the modern campus was completed in 1926. Hill Memorial Library has collections of Louisiana history and natural history. The Museum of Geoscience has changing exhibitions of geography, geology, and anthropology. The visitor and information center is located just past the entrance gates on Highland Road about one and a half miles south of downtown Baton Rouge.

LSU Mounds are among the oldest earthen mounds in the western hemisphere, dating to the Archaic period 5,000 years ago. The mounds are located on Dalrymple Road at Hill Memorial Library.

Museum of Natural Science. The LSU Museum of Natural Science has been designated as the state museum of natural history for Louisiana. Its extensive collections (over 2.5 million items) contain the fourth-largest university-based bird collection in the world. The museum has sixteen major collections including mammals, amphibians and reptiles, anthropology, archaeology, fish, and fossils. Several of the collections are housed at other sites—the Log Library, three herbaria, and the Textile and Costume Museum. The main museum is located in Foster Hall on Dalrymple Street. Open 8 a.m.–4 p.m., Monday through Friday; and 9:30 a.m.–1 p.m. on the last Saturday of each month.

13. Magnolia Mound Plantation. This Creole plantation home dates from 1790 and contains a visitor center, restored furnishings, vegetable gardens, seasonal demonstrations, and gift shop. The sixteen-acre site contains a Mississippian-era mound. 2161 Nicholson Drive Open Tuesday through Saturday, 10 a.m.–4 p.m., and on Sunday, 1–4 p.m. Admission

14. LSU Hill Top Arboretum is a twelve-acre urban forest that displays native trees and plants. Located at 11855 Highland Road. Open daily. Tours are available on Tuesdays from 8 a.m.–3:30 p.m., March, April, May, October, and November.

15. LSU Rural Life Museum is located on the Burden Research Plantation on Essen Lane just south of I-10. The outdoor museum is a reconstructed plantation complex of shops, slave cabins, overseer's house, sugar house, kitchen, and commissary. Authentic examples of an Acadian house, dogtrot house, shotgun house, pioneer cabin, and country church with painted "stained glass" represent the folk architecture of Louisiana. Artifacts of Louisiana history and rural life are on display in the Barn. Adjacent to the Rural Life Museum is **Windrush Gardens,** a semiformal twenty-five-acre garden planted with traditional southern landscape plants—crepe-myrtles, camellias, azaleas, live oaks, pines, and numerous shrubs. Open daily, 8:30 a.m.–5 p.m. Admission.

Louisiana State Capitol and grounds

16. Baton Rouge. Baton Rouge means *red stick* and refers to a post that marked the boundary between the Bayougoulas and Houmas. A monument that marks the site of the *baton rouge* is located on the campus of Southern University north of downtown. Settlement of Baton Rouge started as a land grant to the D'Artaguette family. Baton Rouge was not so much an actual town when Bartram arrived but rather a community of plantations surrounding Fort New Richmond. The first formal town plan was begun in 1805 and is the historic district now called Spanish Town. The capital of Louisiana was moved to Baton Rouge in 1849. Today Baton Rouge is the seat of government, home to the state university, and a working oil port.

Riverfront Park follows the levee in downtown Baton Rouge with views of the river and the old Capitol building. Markers tell the history of Baton Rouge.

Louisiana Arts & Sciences Center, Riverside Museum. The Riverside Museum contains rotating art exhibits and educational science displays. Located at the corner of North Boulevard and River Road. Open Tuesday through Friday, 10 a.m.–3 p.m.; Saturday, 10 a.m.–4 p.m.; and Sunday, 1–4 p.m. Admission.

Louisiana State Archives houses governmental and historical archives, exhibits, and a research room. Located in the Old State Capitol, 100 North Boulevard at River Road. Open Thursday through Saturday, 10 a.m.–4 p.m., and Sunday, 12–4 p.m. Admission.

Louisiana State Capitol & Visitor Information Center. The Louisiana State Capitol was built in 1934 by Governor Huey P. Long and is the tallest state capitol in America. Long was assassinated at the Capitol shortly after the building was completed. An observation deck on the 27th floor provides an astounding view of Baton Rouge and the Mississippi River. The Capitol is surrounded by twenty-seven acres of government buildings, gardens, and a Mississippian-era mound.

Pentagon Barracks. Visitor information for Baton Rouge and Louisiana is available at the Pentagon Barracks. Open 10 a.m.–4 p.m., Monday through Friday, and 1–4 p.m. on Saturday.

The Old Arsenal Museum contains artifacts and documents commemorating the French, Spanish, British, Republic of West Florida, and American periods of Louisiana history. Located in the Capitol Complex.

17. Port Allen is the port of Baton Rouge and the most inland deepwater port in the United States. The West Baton Rouge Tourist Commission is located at 2800 Frontage Road near the bridge in Port Allen.

West Baton Rouge Museum, 845 N. Jefferson Street in Port Allen.

18. Southern University was founded in 1880 to educate African-Americans. The library hosts exhibits on African-American heritage. The Red Stick monument is located on the campus and marks the site of the *baton rouge*. Southern University is located on Scenic Highway north of Baton Rouge.

19. Greater Baton Rouge Zoo is located on Thomas Road in Baker. Open 10 a.m.–5 p.m. daily and until 6 p.m. on weekends in summer. Closed during the week of Christmas. Admission.

20. Cohn Memorial Arboretum. This sixteen-acre Arboretum contains 250 varieties of native and introduced trees and shrubs. 12206 Foster Road, Open 8 a.m.–5 p.m. daily.

21. Port Hudson State Commemorative Area protects the site of an important Civil War battlefield. The area lies at the edge of a high flat terrace of the ancient Mississippi that is covered with deep loess. At Port Hudson the land near the river is deeply dissected into ravines. The White Cliffs at Port Hudson were significant in that William Bartram's description of the fossilized tree stumps prompted Charles Lyell to visit this site during his American tour in 1845. Lyell developed the Theory of Uniformity which influenced his protégé Charles Darwin in the development of a theory of species evolution. The White Cliffs were also known as Milk Cliffs and have changed considerably from what they were when Bartram visited the area. Governor Montfort Brown's West Florida property was located just south of Port Hudson Commemorative Area. William Bartram and William Dunbar explored Brown's estate on October 27, 1775.

The trails at Port Hudson Commemorative Area run throughout the park to the redoubts, ridges, and breastworks that figured in the Siege of Port Hudson in the summer of 1863. Here is an excellent opportunity to walk the same ground as William Bartram and view this historical area from three observation towers. The river bluffs are not accessible and visitors must stay on designated paths. Open Wednesday through Sunday, 9 a.m.–7 p.m., during summer months and 9 a.m.–5 p.m., during the rest of the year. Admission.

22. Governor Brown's White Plains was a prairie located on land owned by the former governor or West Florida. It was in the vicinity of Plains.

23. Saint Francisville was settled by American and British settlers after the Revolution. The town is named for the patron saint of the Capuchin monks of Pointe Coupee who established their cemetery on high ground at Saint Francisville. Although the Spanish maintained a congenial and accommodating government, many of the English-speaking immigrants were disappointed when Feliciana Parish was not included in the Louisiana Purchase. The West Florida Rebellion in 1810 established the Republic of West Florida when an army of seventy marched from Saint Francisville and captured Fort San Carlos at Baton Rouge with only two unfortunate Spanish soldiers killed. The republic existed for seventy-four days with the government meeting first at Saint Francisville then at Jackson. The flag of the West Florida Republic was a lone silver star on a field of blue.

The **Audubon Pilgrimage** is a celebration of the history and folklife of the Feliciana parishes and takes place each year in mid-March. Homes and gardens are opened for tours and the skills of eighteenth century daily life are demonstrated at the Rural Homestead.

West Feliciana Historical Society Museum. 11757 Ferdinand Street. Open daily 9 a.m.–5 p.m., and Sunday 9:30 a.m.–5 p.m. Free admission. The small **Mary Pipes Butler Garden** is located next door to the museum and contains native plants and popular introduced species.

Sugar cane field, East Baton Rouge Parish

James R. Leake Memorial Park. Feliciana Street in Saint Francisville. The Park contains 158 acres of undeveloped land with several hiking trails and a picnic area.

Bayou Sara. Bayou Sara is located at the bottom of the hill on the river below Saint Francisville. During its day in the early 1800s Bayou Sara was the largest cotton port between New Orleans and Memphis. The coming of the railroad diminished its importance as a cotton port and subsequent floods forced the citizens to move.

24. Rosedown Plantation & Gardens (1835). The original owners of Rosedown, Daniel and Martha Turnbull, established an extensive French-style garden around their plantation home and were among the first to import azaleas. The restoration was begun in 1956 using Martha Turnbull's meticulous records and the gardens have been returned to their former grandeur. Rosedown is now a bed and breakfast inn.

25. Butler Greenwood Plantation. Established in 1795, Butler Greenwood Plantation is still owned by descendants of the original owners. The extensive antebellum gardens are open to tours daily from 9 a.m.–5 p.m. and on Sunday, 1–5 p.m. The home is a bed and breakfast. Located at 8345 US-61. Admission charged to the gardens.

26. Afton Gardens. The plantation home at Afton Gardens burned in 1963 but the formal French-style gardens are still open to the public from March through October. US-61 north of Saint Francisville. Admission.

27. Audubon State Commemorative Area includes 100 acres surrounding the Oakley House where John James Audubon created eighty of his bird paintings. There are several miles of hiking trails and an available bird guide. Open 9 a.m.–5 p.m. daily, closed major holidays. Admission. Located on LA-965 three miles east of US-61.

Oakley House (1808). John James Audubon arrived in West Feliciana Parish in 1821 as tutor to young Eliza Pirrie of Oakley Plantation. He taught French, music, dance, drawing, and mathematics. Audubon was allowed half of each day to pursue his own study and painting. Audubon's employment lasted only four months due to conflicts with his pupil's mother so he returned to New Orleans. Audubon returned to West Feliciana Parish several times in the 1820s after his wife arrived from Cincinnati and was employed as a tutor at several plantations.

28. Mary Ann Brown Preserve is a 109-acre preserve of the Nature Conservancy. There are two miles of trails and gardens. Located on LA-965 east of US-61.

29. West Florida Historical Association Museum. Exhibits of the early settlement of the Florida Parishes include furniture, weapons, tools and Native American artifacts. Located on College Street in Jackson. Open 10 a.m.–5 p.m, Tuesday through Sunday.

30. Locust Grove State Commemorative Area is located on the site of Locust Grove Plantation and includes the cemetery where Jefferson Davis's first wife, Sarah, is buried. She was also the daughter of Zachary Taylor. Located on Locust Grove Road, just off US 61.

31. Tunica Hills Wildlife Management Area. LA-66 is called the **Tunica Trace** and is the historic road into the Tunica Hills, a region of steep red hills and hollows where plants grow that are more typical of the piedmont and mountains. During the ice ages the hills were covered with windblown loess that ranges from three to thirty-five feet thick. The management area provides opportunities for hunting, fishing, hiking, and horseback riding. Open year round. License required for entry into the area.

32. Tunica Hills State Preservation Area is the colonial home of the Tunica Indians who now live near Marksville, Louisiana. The Tunica Treasure, a cache of Indian and European artifacts, was discovered during excavation of the mounds at Tunica Hills. The Tunica Treasure is exhibited at Marksville Commemorative Area in Avoyelles Parish.

The Houma Indians occupied the Tunica Hills in 1682 when La Salle explored the Mississippi. In 1706 the Tunica Tribe, to escape depredations by the Chickasaws and Natchez, came to live among the peaceful Houmas but betrayed their allegiance and massacred many of their hosts. The surviving Houmas moved farther down river to Ascension Parish where they remained until the late eighteenth century. The Houmas were eventually joined by the Bayougoulas and Acolapissas. Their descendants now live in Lafource and Terrebonne Parishes and are centered around the town of Dulac.

The **Marksville Commemorative Area** in Avoyelles Parish is operated by the Tunica-Biloxi Tribe. Admission fees are charged for the annual Corn Festival and the Tunica Treasure Museum. The park contains numerous Mississippian-era mounds connected by hiking trails.

33. Saint Francis of Assissi Chapel was established in 1728 and the original chapel was built about 1760. The present structure was built in the late 1800s using the original timbers.

34. Labatut House (c. 1750), pronounced La-buh-too, sits between the highway and the river. It is privately owned and has not been renovated.

35. Pointe Coupee. The first French settlers arrived in Pointe Coupee in 1728, some to take up land grants, and others, like the old gentleman visited by William Bartram, were survivors of the massacre of Natchez. In 1775 the settlements of Pointe Coupee extended along the Mississippi River from east of Morganza to just south of False River.

36. New Roads is the government seat of Pointe Coupee Parish. New Roads takes its name from the new road that was built in 1822 to connect the False River to the settlement of Pointe Coupee.

Julien de Lallande Poydras (1746–1824) came to Louisiana as an immigrant peddler. He established a store at Pointe Coupee in 1769 and became a wealthy planter. As president of the territorial legislature and constitutional convention, Poydras helped guide Louisiana to statehood. He was elected to Congress in 1809 and traveled to Washington on horseback, a trip that took six weeks. He helped establish the first public schools in Louisiana. His grave is beneath his monument on the Poydras School grounds in New Roads. Poydras did not marry and upon his death he bequeathed his fortune as an endowment to provide education and dowries for young brides of limited means. Though not as large as it once was, his foundation still provides a stipend for Pointe Coupee brides.

37. False River was a oxbow of the Mississippi River until 1722 when the river cut through the narrow isthmus and the old channel became a crescent lake. False River is a very popular retreat for fishing and water sports.

38. Pointe Coupee Museum and Visitor Center was originally one of the Parlange Plantation structures. The building is representative of the life-style of a modest rural family and is furnished as it would have been during the time of Bartram's visit to Pointe Coupee. The building dates from about 1770 and is a fine example of two early French architectural styles. The oldest part of the structure is constructed of *piece sur piece*—hand-sawn timbers, stacked on edge and dovetailed at the corners. This is a method of construction brought to Louisiana by French Canadians. Another room was added in 1840 and is made of *bousillage*, mud and moss filled between timber framing and held in place with hand-split cypress lath.

The visitor center has a gift shop and is open Tuesday through Saturday, 10 a.m.–4 p.m. and on Sunday from 1–4p.m. Closed on Monday and holidays. Admission is free.

39. Parlange (c. 1750) is possibly the best-known French colonial home in Louisiana. It was built by Marquis Claude Vincent de Ternant on a land grant from King Louis XV. The bricks were made on site and the cypress timbers were cut from the estate's swamps. A gallery surrounds the house and French doors open to catch breezes. The family educated their children in France and visited Paris often during the nineteenth century.

Parlange is a working plantation owned by descendants of the builder. The Parlange family raise cattle, horses, sugar cane, corn, and soybeans. Mrs. Parlange offers tours of the home by appointment. Inquire at the museum about visiting hours. Parlange is a National Historic Landmark. Admission.

40. Riverlake Plantation (c. 1780) is the birth place of writer Earnest Gaines, author of *Autobiography of Miss Jane Pitman* and *A Gathering of Old Men*. Riverlake has a main floor of cypress and bousillage over a brick ground floor and is built on a French land grant.

Parishes

Ascension was created from old Acadia Parish in 1807 and named for the original Spanish ecclesiastical parish of the same name.

East Baton Rouge was created in 1810 from Spanish West Florida.

East Feliciana was created in 1824 from the original Feliciana County (1810).

Iberville is an original county created by the Legislative Council of the Territory of Orleans in 1805. It is based on the Spanish parish of Saint Gabriel and is named for Pierre le Moyne, Sieur d'Iberville, founder of Louisiana.

Livingston was created in 1832 from Saint Helena parish (1810). It is Named for Edward Livingston, Louisiana statesman and author of the state criminal code.

Pointe Coupee Is an original county created in 1805 by the Legislative Council of the Territory of Orleans and coincides with the Spanish parish of Saint Francis.

Saint James was created from Acadia Parish in 1807 and named for the original Spanish ecclesiastical parish of the same name.

Saint John the Baptist was created from the old German Coast County in 1807 and named for the original Spanish ecclesiastical parish.

West Feliciana was created in 1824 from Feliciana County (1810).

West Baton Rouge was created from Pointe Coupee County in 1807.

Itinerary

Miles	Description
	From Ponchatoula take LA-22 east
5.0	Enter Livingston Parish
0.2	Enter Springfield, LA-22 turns sharply left
4.0	Cross Tickfaw River
2.2	LA-22 bears left in Killian
16.0	LA-22 parallels Old Amite River
5.0	Straight on LA-16
1.35	Cross Amite River, enter French Settlement
7.45	Left on West LA-42
2.9	Galveztown historical marker
6.0	Right on US-61/LA-42
1.0	Left on Perkins Road/LA-427
1.25	Left at the sign for Saint Gabriel
0.8	Immediate right on the paved road (Alligator Bayou Road) Pavement ends after a half mile and begins Bayou Manchac Road
6.35	Pavement begins at Saint Gabriel town limit, Bayou Paul Lane
2.5	Right on LA-30, cross Bayou Manchac to East Baton Rouge Parish
3.2	Left on Spur LA-327 (to Burtville & Placquemine Ferry) then right at the stop sign on River Road/LA-327
11.1	Straight when LA-327 turns right
2.0	Downtown Baton Rouge

To Pointe Coupee

Miles	Description
	From downtown Baton Rouge follow US-61 north
19.3	Entrance to Port Hudson Commemorative Area
10.5	Left on LA-10 for St. Francisville
2.6	Cross the river on the ferry and turn right on LA-10
5.8	Right on LA-1
10.2	Left on LA-4116
7.1	Right on LA-415
15.3	Keep straight on North River Road
6.6	Right on Rosedale Road
.2	Left on North Jefferson Street in Port Allen
.8	Right on Court Street
.3	Left on LA-1
.9	Left on I-10 for downtown Baton Rouge

Santee

In 1521 Francisco Gordillo and Pedro Quejo made an expedition to the land of the Shakori (or Chicora) Indians. They enticed the inhabitants aboard their ship with food and gifts then lifted anchor and sailed for Santo Domingo with over a hundred hostages who were then sold as slaves. Lucas Vasquez de Ayllón, who sponsored the expedition, disapproved of the action of his lieutenants and won their release. One of the captives was named Francisco Chicora who became a friend of Ayllón. Francisco converted to Catholicism, learned Spanish, and visited Spain. He and Ayllón convinced the Council of the Indies to explore and colonize the land to the north of the Caribbean islands. Quejo again explored the coast of La Florida in the summer of 1525 and probably sailed into Chesapeake Bay and Delaware Bay

In 1526 Ayllón and 500 colonists made a settlement somewhere on the Southeastern coast. Although the exact location has been the subject of debate, possibly Parris Island, Saint Catherines Island, or Cape Fear, it is now acknowledged that the colony settled on the north shore of Winyah Bay and their name for the Waccamaw River was the Rio de Jordan. The colonists stayed for only a month before moving farther south and resettling either on the south side of the Altamaha River or near the mouth of the Savannah River. The colony met with starvation and came into conflict with the local Indians, Only about 150 of the original 500 settlers survived to return to Hispaniola. Ayllón himself became ill and died that October.

Jean Ribault founded the French colony of Charlesfort on Parris Island in 1562. The Spanish built Fort San Felipe at the same site in 566 and occupied Santa Elena for a decade before abandoning the area in favor of Saint Augustine. During the next century Spanish missions were maintained on the south Atlantic coast as far north as Santa Elena but other than one feeble attempt at establishing a mission somewhere near Chesapeake Bay Spanish authorities exhibited little interest in extending their occupation any farther north than present-day Beaufort, South Carolina. There were certainly Spanish reconnaissance missions along the coast but little of European activity took place on the beautiful Carolina coast until the founding of Charleston in 1670.

Seventeenth-century Carolina was divided into three colonies and the land from Awendaw Creek northward to Cape Fear was named Craven County. In the 1680s Craven county received a number of French Huguenot families of good character. The French Protestants were given grants along the Santee River as a line of defense against Indian, French, and Spanish invaders. English settlement was still localized in the low country around Charleston.

In 1700 there were over a hundred families in the Santee district and in 1705 they founded the town of Jamestown, named for their adopted English king. The French church at Jamestown held more than a hundred members at that time making it the largest Huguenot church outside Charleston. The Parish of Saint James, Santee, was created by the Church Act of 1706. The parish stretched from SC-41 to the ocean and from the Santee River to Awendaw, and the area became known as French Santee.

One of the first and most complete reports of the Santee River is found in John Lawson's *A New Voyage to Carolina*. In 1700 Lawson and some companions sailed from Charleston to the mouth of the Santee River. During the early eighteenth century, settlers were spreading up the coast as the older lands nearer Charleston became settled and incorporated into large plantations. Due to the success of rice growing around Charleston land grants on the Black, Pee Dee, Sampit, Waccamaw, and Santee rivers were made beginning in 1705. The rice planters quickly bought up the best land on the Pee Dee and Waccamaw rivers and built some of the most productive rice plantations in North America.

Prince George Winyah Parish was established north of the Santee River in 1721. An act providing for the improvement of roads in the Parish was passed in 1726 and at the request of local citizens Georgetown was authorized as a port in 1729. Exports from Prince George Winyah had reached such a level that shipping to Charleston for export to Europe became costly and inefficient. The economy was dominated by rice and indigo during the colonial period. Georgetown became the second-largest rice port in the world after Calcutta, and by 1840 it produced half of the rice consumed in the United States. Kingston (Conway) was authorized as one of twenty townships in 1730 and was surveyed in 1734. It became a port for inland communities and the Indian trade.

Guerin Creek as seen from Guerin Creek Bridge

Saint James Santee Church, 1768

At the outbreak of the Revolution, the Santee and Georgetown areas were sparsely populated because a large portion of desirable land was locked up in extensive landholdings owned by the aristocracy. When the low country between Charleston and Savannah was ravaged by the advancing British army, many women and children sought refuge at the plantations on the Santee River.

During the Revolution, the forest now bearing his name was the sanctuary from which Francis Marion (1732–1795) executed his guerilla raids. After making lightning raids on British convoys and patrols, Marion and his men would quickly disappear into the swamps along the Santee River and in Georgetown County. Marion was dubbed the Swamp Fox by Banastre Tarleton because of his cunning and evasive tactics. Marion escaped being captured at the fall of Charleston because he was recuperating from a broken ankle at his plantation on the Santee River. He continued to harass the British along the King's Road between Charleston and Georgetown until the Americans regained control of the Low Country near the end of the war.

Upon the fall of Charleston, Sir Henry Clinton commenced upon his attempt to reconquer South Carolina. Lord Cornwallis was dispatched to Camden and Banastre Tarleton was sent across the Santee to find Marion. The British believed that a large number of loyalists and uncommitted citizens could easily be reunited to the Crown but British command failed to agree upon a common approach in dealing with the rebellion. Lord Cornwallis believed that true rebels were in the minority and that the presence of his large army would unite the loyalists and dissolve opposition, thus bringing the wayward American children back into the family of the British citizenry.

Banastre Tarleton, on the other hand, believed that Americans must be dealt with harshly and punished severely. He used his cavalry as shock troops and practiced total war—burning houses, crops, and attacking civilians thought to be guilty of collusion with the rebels. After his slaughter of surrendering patriots at the Battle of the Waxhaws, Tarleton became known as *Bloody Tarleton* and it was his arrogance and brutality that converted many moderates into full-fledged patriots. *Tarleton's Quarter* came to mean accept no surrender and take no prisoners.

The British placed Georgetown under military rule in 1780, then retreated to Charleston the next summer in order to reinforce the capital as they began to lose control of the interior of South Carolina. Much of the Georgetown waterfront burned on August 2, 1781 when bombarded by a British privateer.

After the Revolution, rice continued to be the economic base for the Georgetown area; however, the fortunes were concentrated among the planter elite who were economically and socially tied to Charleston. Georgetown declined for a period as rice shipments bypassed her port and were sent directly to the new, large rice mills being built along the coast.

George Washington visited William and Mary Motte Alston at Clifton Plantation on Waccamaw River on April 29, 1791. Among the guests were former Governor William Moultrie, John Rutledge, Jr., and William Washington. On the morning of April 30, Washington and his entourage floated three miles downstream to Georgetown. Tradition has said that he stayed at the Stewart-Parker House, 1019 Front Street, while visiting Georgetown. In the afternoon, he was addressed by a committee representing the citizens of Georgetown, he was presented at an address in the Masonic lodge; he attended a public dinner, an afternoon tea, and a ball.

William Bartram's Travels at the Santee River

John and William Bartram left Ashwood on August 11, 1765 and began their trip to Charleston. That evening they lodged at Peake's, somewhere between Myrtle Beach and Murrell's Inlet. The next day they reached Georgetown and spent the evening. They continued on the King's Road and crossed the Santee River on Lynches Causeway and Cochran's Ferry. They dined at Cochran's and spent the evening of August 13 at Halsey's. The Bartram's traveled through Francis Marion National Forest then turned southeast to cross the Wando River at Guerin's Bridge.

In November 1775, William Bartram began his return trip home to Philadelphia after four years of traveling in the South. After leaving Charleston and crossing the Cooper River, he traveled along the north side of the Wando River first by a road that is now called Wambaw Creek Road, then on Willow Hall Road (FS-202). This brought him to Awendaw where his route then followed exactly the present-day Old Georgetown Road. Bartram crossed the Santee River a little below Hampton State Park at Cochran's Ferry. The old route followed fairly closely US-17 and Big Oaks Road to Belle Isle where he took the ferry over Winyah Bay. On the north side of Winyah Bay, one of the roads in Hobcaw Barony is still named King's Road. William Bartram continued up the Waccamaw Neck along River Road.

Sites

1. Capers Island Heritage Preserve. This undisturbed barrier island is administered by the South Carolina Nature Conservancy and the South Carolina Department of Natural Resources. It consists of 2,000 acres and contains a variety of habitats. Accessible by boat.

2. Bull Island was visited by John Lawson on December 30, 1700. It was owned at that time by Colonel Thomas Cary, who became deputy governor of North Carolina. Although it was winter, Lawson and his traveling companions were tormented by mosquitoes. The island is now part of Cape Romaine National Wildlife Refuge and is home to 250 species of birds during the year. There are sixteen miles of hiking trails and an unspoiled beach. The island is open for day use only and visitors must arrange ferry service at Moore's Landing.

3. Moore's Landing. Boat passage to Bull Island is from Moore's Landing. Reservations are not required but are advisable. Information is available at the Sewee Visitor Center.

4. Sewee Visitor and Environmental Education Center. The center contains exhibits on

Legend

1. Capers Island Heritage Preserve
2. Bull Island
3. Moore's Landing
4. Sewee Visitor and Environmental Education Center
5. I'on Swamp
6. Sewee Shell Mound Sewee Indians
7. Cape Romain NWR
8. Awendaw
9. Swamp Fox National Recreation Trail
10. Buck Hall Campground and Recreation Area
11. Francis Marion National Forest
12. Wambaw Swamp Wilderness
13. Little Wambaw Swamp Wilderness
14. Old Georgetown Road
15. Wambaw Ranger District Headquarters
16. Saint James Santee Episcopal Church
17. Carolina bays
18. Wambaw Creek Wilderness Area and Canoe Trail
19. Guilliard Lake Scenic Area
20. Jamestown
21. Hellhole Bay Wilderness
22. Hampton Plantation Old King's Road
23. The Wedge
24. Washo Preserve
25. Murphy Island & Santee Coastal Reserve WMA
26. Cedar Island
27. Santee Delta WMA
28. Hopsewee Plantation
29. Parson's Wax Myrtle Nursery
30. Roycroft Daylily Nursery
31. Yawkey Wildlife Center
32. Belle Isle Plantation and Battery White
33. Hobcaw Barony
34. Georgetown
35. Harbor Walk
36. Kaminski House
37. The Rice Museum.
38. Winyah Indigo Society Hall
39. Masonic Lodge
40. Prince George-Winyah Episcopal Church
41. Beth Elohim Cemetery
42. Morgan Park
43. Old Rice Fields
44. Bellefield Nature Center
45. Lafayette's Landing
46. Wallace Pate Research Center
47. Samworth WMA
48. Mansfield Plantation & Slave Village
49. Black River Canoe Trail
50. Brown's Ferry Vessel
51. Black River Swamp Preserve
52. Chicora Indian Tribe
53. Andrew's Museum

Items 35–43 are shown on the map of Georgetown, page 305

Hampton Plantation

the natural history of Francis Marion National Forest and Cape Romain National Wildlife Refuge. Educational programs and classrooms are available to visiting educational groups. As the center continues to develop it will include nature trails, live animal exhibits, and native plant gardens. Information about Francis Marion Forest and Cape Romain is available and a bookstore offers local guidebooks and nature publications. US-17. Open 9 a.m.–5 p.m., Tuesday through Sunday.

5. I'on Swamp is sometimes shown on maps as Iron Swamp, but it is named for Jacob Bond I'on who owned Fairlawn (later named Furman's) near the head of Wando River. The trail into I'on Swamp follows old rice field dikes dating from the very early eighteenth century. Parking is located on Iron Swamp Road (FS-228).

6. Sewee Shell Mound. The highlight of the Sewee Shell Mound Trail is the very ancient shell midden, but there are also views of the salt marsh and tidal creek. At low tide, hikers can explore the edge of the marsh where grow such salt-tolerant plants as glasswort, saltwort, and salt grass. The trail head is at the gate on Salt Pond Road, FS-243, which is reached by SC-432.

Sewee Indians. John Lawson related the sad story and tragic fate of the Sewee Indians. Desiring to open direct trade with England rather than depend on the unscrupulous traders, the Sewees attempted to sail for Europe in open boats, believing the trip would be a short one. Soon after they boats embarked, a storm scattered their boats and many were drowned. An English ship rescued the survivors and sold them into slavery in the Caribbean. Because most able-bodied adults were involved in the enterprise, this disaster left the Sewees a weakened and reduced nation, numbering only fifty-seven in 1715. They were a Siouan-speaking people and little is known of them other than what we learn from Lawson.

7. Cape Romain National Wildlife Refuge. The Cape Romain National Refuge includes 60,000 acres of salt marsh and barrier islands. Offices are located at the Sewee Visitor and Environmental Education Center on US-17.

Cape San Romano is shown on the earliest maps of La Florida and is remembered today as Cape Romain, though the exact location of the original name is open to speculation.

8. Awendaw. John Lawson wrote of camping near a deserted Indian village called Avendaughbough. During proprietary rule of South Carolina, land on Awendaw Creek was granted to Governor Nathaniel Johnson and Governor Robert Johnson. The land was sold to the Manigaults who named the plantation Awendaw Barony. Although the estate contained many thousands of acres, only a few hundred were planted in rice and corn. President Washington spent the evening of May 1, 1791, at Joseph Manigault's country house at Awendaw. Awendaw Creek was first known as Sewee River, named for the Sewee Indians who lived there.

9. Swamp Fox National Recreation Trail is named for Lieutenant Colonel Francis Marion. The trail is 27-miles long with parking on US-17 in Awendaw and at the Weatherbee District Office on Weatherbee Road. Hikers traverse all the varieties of coastal habitat. The longleaf pine forests are home to red-cockaded woodpeckers, deer, and turkeys. Wet uplands contain pitcher plants, orange milkwort, yaupon, and dahoon. The wetlands contain clethra, pondberry, fetterbush, and pond pines. The Swamp Fox Trail is part of the Palmetto Trail, which will connect the coast at McClellanville to the Foothills Trail at Oconee State Park in the mountains.

10. Buck Hall Campground and Recreation Area. Buck Hall includes a developed campground and a day-use area overlooking the Intracoastal Waterway.

11. Francis Marion National Forest was organized in 1936 with the purchase of neglected and cutover lands. Hurricane Hugo did a great deal of damage when it roared ashore in the early hours of September 21, 1989. The greatest damage was nearest the ocean, but many nest trees used by red-cockaded woodpeckers were blown down farther inland. The Forest Service created artificial cavities in new trees for the birds.

12. Wambaw Swamp Wilderness. 4,767 acres. Bounded on the North by SC-98.

13. Little Wambaw Swamp Wilderness. 5,154 acres. North of US-17 at Buck Hall.

14. Old Georgetown Road is an authentic, unaltered remnant of the King's Road that once connected the colonial seacoast communities stretching from Wilmington to Saint Augustine. William Bartram traveled this road in November, 1776, and George Washington traveled over this same section on May 1, 1791.

15. Wambaw Ranger District Headquarters. North Pinckney Street in McClellanville. Open 8 a.m.–5 p.m., Monday through Friday.

16. Saint James Santee Episcopal Church, also known as Wambaw Church, was built in 1768 to serve French Huguenots and English Anglicans. This beautiful church is no longer in service but is kept in excellent condition. The Chapel of Ease for Saint James Santee was Echaw Church, now in ruins, located at Honey Hill. Rebecca Motte presented an inscribed bible to the church in 1773, but the Bible was stolen by British soldiers during the Revolution. A friend of Mrs. Motte found the Bible in a London book shop, bought the book, and returned it to the church. Saint James is located on Old Georgetown Road.

17. Carolina bays are curious oblong depressions that are usually filled with water and have slight terraces around their perimeters. Carolina bays occur throughout the coastal areas of the Carolinas and Georgia and they are almost always oriented with their long axis pointing to the northwest. Their origin is still not fully understood. Some have thought that they were created by a large meteor shower.

They can be seen along the Old Georgetown Road in the Francis Marion National Forest.

18. Wambaw Creek Wilderness Area and Canoe Trail. An excellent way to experience a coastal wilderness is to canoe Wambaw Creek from SC-45 to FS-04. The wilderness area contains 1,937 acres along both sides of Wambaw Creek.

19. Guilliard Lake Scenic Area includes 925 acres of land on the Santee River. Old cypress and limestone outcrops are of interest to naturalists and there is an undeveloped campground. Located off FS-150.

20. Jamestown was the most important settlement of French Santee during the early eighteenth century. The area was settled by French Huguenots in the 1680s. They requested naturalization as English subjects in 1696 and in 1705 founded the town of Jamestown. The Huguenot Church at Jamestown was the largest outside of Charleston and is commemorated today by a rustic Huguenot cross. The Parish Act of 1706 created the Parish of Saint James Santee and the Huguenot Church was incorporated in the Anglican parish. Jamestown declined and Saint James Santee church was built in 1768 on the King's Road near the South Santee River to serve both French and English protestants. Jamestown is today a quaint little crossroads community.

21. Hellhole Bay Wilderness Area contains 2,180 acres of federal wilderness. It is accessible by canoe from FS-158, where there is a fire cut. The trail can be hiked during dry weather.

22. Hampton Plantation, c. 1736. Daniel Horry built this plantation home on land acquired by his father, Elias Horry. After Daniel's death, his wife, Harriott, continued to manage the plantation. In 1791, she and her mother, Eliza Lucas Pinckney, entertained George Washington at Hampton Plantation during his Southern tour. He recommended that they not remove the young live oak that stills stands today in front of the house. Harriott's brother, Thomas, lived three miles downriver at Fairfield. South Carolina poet laureate, naturalist, and writer Archibald Rutledge grew up at Hampton and restored the house and grounds in the 1930s.

The Old King's Road crossed the Santee River rice fields on Lynches Causeway, a cribbed road, just downriver from Hampton Plantation.

Hampton Plantation grounds are open Thursday through Monday, 9 a.m.–6 p.m. The house is open Saturday and Sunday, 1–4 p.m., and by appointment on other days.

The Sampit River at downtown Georgetown

Huguenots

The Huguenots were followers of John Calvin, who founded the Reformed Church in France around 1550. French Reformers who had become refugees in Geneva were called *Huguenots* by the Swiss, though the origin of the word is unknown. French Protestants immediately came into conflict with French Catholics and there ensued a series of seven wars from 1562 to 1598 between the two religious groups. Some of the leading families of France were Huguenots and were instrumental in the colonization effort in the New World. French Huguenots made settlements at Rio de Janeiro, Brazil, in 1555; Port Royal, South Carolina in 1562; and on the St. Johns River in Florida in 1564.

The protestant leaders were Louis de Condé, Gaspard de Coligny, and Henry de Navarre. The Catholics were led by the House of Guise, Catherine de Medici, and her sons. The most brutal of the seven Wars of Religion was the fourth, which was ignited by the Saint Bartholomew's Day Massacre of August 24, 1572, when Catherine de Medici and her son, King Charles IX, murdered nearly 8,000 Huguenots in a few days in Paris.

The Edict of Nantes in 1598 ended the wars and provided political and religious freedom for French Protestants. But, in the early seventeenth century Cardinal Richelieu captured Protestant leaders and stripped them of their political power. King Louis XIV revoked the Edict of Nantes on October 22, 1685, and the Huguenots became the object of official oppression. Nearly 200,000 French Protestants fled to Holland, England, and the Protestant German states. Of these 5,000–7,000 came to the British colonies in North America—New York, New England, Virginia, Pennsylvania, and the Carolinas. They, of course, were not welcome in Catholic French Canada. Most of the refugees came from the western provinces of France between the Loire and Gironde rivers where the Reformed Church was strong. LaRochelle was the point of departure for many.

Carolina was attractive to the Huguenots because the Lords Proprietors encouraged their immigration with land grants and the colony had the most liberal policy of religious tolerance. Several hundred Huguenot families settled in and around Charleston. They were educated and industrious, just what was needed by a young colony surrounded by wilderness and hostile populations. Many of the Huguenot families were settled along the Santee River in the area that became known as French Santee.

The Huguenots rejected their king and French citizenship and embraced their new home, becoming some of South Carolina's most successful and powerful families. Among the earliest French families to immigrate to South Carolina were Deloach, Dubose, Galliard, Guignard, Horry, Huger, Laurens, Legare, LeGrand, Manigault, Marion, Mazyck, Motte, Ravenel, and St. Julien.

Carolina Rice

The first grains of rice came to Charleston possibly as a gift from a ship captain to a local merchant. The first rice fields were built along river swamps and creeks and significant quantities of rice were being grown around Charles Town by the end of the seventeenth century. The rice was shipped to England and the West Indies. Later in the eighteenth century the largest market for Carolina rice was Northern Europe, where the staple supplemented the diet of humans and livestock during winter. Even then Carolina rice had to be shipped first to England for export to the continent.

With the success and profitability of rice culture assured in South Carolina, lawyers, merchants, and doctors turned their energies to establishing rice plantations. The first rice plantations used gravity to flood fields from stored water on impounded streams. It was not until the 1750s that tidal rice culture was perfected and provided for a more dependable supply of water. The South Atlantic coastal indentation is called the Georgia Bight and has an unusually high tide because the shape of the coast line acts as a funnel to gather and concentrate the tides. The tides powered the flow of water into and out of the rice fields and gave rise to the Rice Empire. Rice plantations were built along the tidal portion of every suitable river from the Waccamaw to the St. Marys River.

The rise of rice plantations and the growth of slavery are inextricably intertwined. Large-scale farming required labor in force not available in the colonial Southeast. The first slaves were Indians captured in war, but the Native Americans were too susceptible to European diseases and were temperamentally unsuited to such labor. Planters turned to the African slave trade to obtain labor for their fields, particularly seeking slaves from the rice-growing region of West Africa.

Building rice fields was monumental work and required many hands: swamps were laid out into fields, trees were cut and burned, banks were constructed, and ditches were dug by hand. During the second year the fields were laid out in quarter acres surrounded by ditches, and a system of drains and trunks were built so the fields could be alternately flooded and drained.

Once the fields were planted with rice in spring they could be flooded at times to control the growth of weeds. The incoming tide would push fresh water ahead of it, causing the river to cease flowing and back up. The rice trunks were opened, allowing the fresh water to flow into the ditches and fields. The trunks were closed before brackish water could enter the fields. When the fields needed to be worked, the trunks were opened as the tide went out and the fields were drained.

The coastal region became dominated by large rice plantations occupied by large communities of slaves and a few wealthy white families. The owners spent much of their time away from the fields, which were considered unhealthy for white people. Charleston and Savannah became the centers of social activity for these wealthy families during the cool months when the fields were fallow. The concentration of large amounts of land in the hands of a few landowners and the tendency of the aristocracy to live elsewhere meant the coastal areas were populated mostly by communities of slaves. Real economic development came only after the demise of rice culture in the last half of the nineteenth century.

The growing of rice declined after the Civil War because a large, cheap labor source was no longer ensured and a series of hurricanes brought several years of reduced production. Rice growing has moved in this century to Louisiana, Arkansas, and Texas where the fields can be worked by tractors and machinery and the rice is flooded with well water. The soft soil of the coastal rice fields of South Carolina and Georgia did not support machinery and had to be worked by hand. Today, rice is being grown in Jasper County, South Carolina, and on the Satilla River in Georgia, but in very small quantities and only as a hobby.

23. The Wedge is a research center for vector borne diseases. The property was a colonial rice plantation.

24. Washo Preserve is located within the Santee Coastal Reserve Management Area and is administered by the Nature Conservancy. A nature trail follows dikes, and a boardwalk reaches into an open pond for viewing water birds. Follow South Santee Road then Santee Gun Club Road to its end. There you will find an information board with a map of the Washo Reserve and adjacent section of the Santee Coastal Reserve.

25. Murphy Island & Santee Coastal Reserve Wildlife Management Area. Visitors enter Santee Coastal Reserve by Santee Gun Club Road. Much of the land was donated to the Nature Conservancy by the Santee Gun Club, and then turned over to the state for use as a wildlife management area. The Woodland Trail is located on the north side of the road as you approach the Santee River. On a June hike, I found numerous Jack-in-the-pulpits, scared up a couple of wild hogs, and was eaten alive by mosquitoes. In the southern part of the Reserve there is a bicycle/hiking trail and a canoe trail. Open February 1 through October 31.

As you approach the US-17 bridge that crosses the South Santee River, there is a parking area on the right for the Santee Coastal Reserve, South Side. There is a trail from the parking area to the river that follows an old dike. On the east side of US-17 as one approaches the bridge is Fairfield, the home of Thomas Pinckney (not open to the public). Pinckney was a Revolutionary War veteran, diplomat, and governor (1787–1789). His mother was Eliza Lucas Pinckney and his brother was Charles Cotesworth Pinckney. Thomas Pinckney negotiated the Treaty of San Lorenzo that established the boundary between Mississippi Territory and Spanish West Florida at 31° latitude.

26. Cedar Island, Santee Coastal Reserve Wildlife Management Area. Bob Joyner of the Yawkey Wildlife Center says that at one time a person could stand at the mouth of the Santee River as it flowed into the Atlantic and drink fresh water, such was the volume of its flow. Since the construction of the Santee-Cooper water project, the reduced flow of fresh water has allowed brackish water to reach several miles upstream. This has kept the cypress and gum swamp from returning and has provided habitat for birds.

27. Santee Delta Wildlife Management Area. The delta of the Santee River was one of the richest rice-producing lands in America during colonial times. Jonathan Lucas built the first rice mill on the Santee River which increased the profitability of growing rice. In 1700 John Lawson reported that the land from the mouth of the Santee to sixteen miles upstream was all swamp and pocosin. The vast swamps were cleared for rice fields during the eighteenth century. In this century, diversion of water for the Santee-Cooper project has reduced the flow of the Santee so that brackish water now reaches farther upstream and the old rice fields have been converted to salt marsh.

28. Hopsewee Plantation, c. 1740. Hopsewee was the home of Thomas Lynch, Jr. (1740–1779), signer of the Declaration of Independence. His father, Thomas Sr., designed the method of growing rice using tides to flood the fields. The elder Lynch lived on Wando River but had rice plantations scattered throughout the Santee Delta. Both Lynches were patriots and Thomas Lynch, Sr., was a member of the First and Second Continental

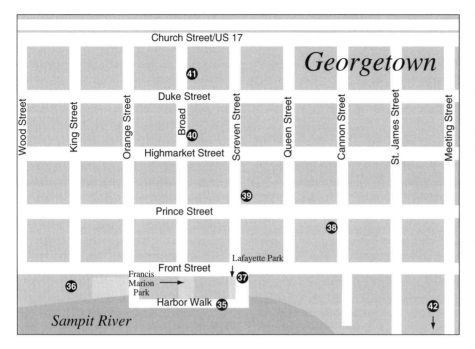

Congress. A half-mile trail follows the bank of the Santee River then circles back through a pine forest. The current owners open the house for tours Tuesday through Friday, March through October. The grounds are open everyday, admission is $2 by the honor system. Put your money in the box and pick up a brochure in the old kitchen.

29. Parson's Wax Myrtle Nursery is the world's largest grower of *Myrica cerifera*. Located on US-17.

30. Roycroft Daylily Nursery. Roycroft is one of the leading growers and breeders of daylilies in the country. They have an astounding display of *Hemerocallis* with hundreds of varieties for sale and a worldwide mail order business. Located on White Hall Avenue a half mile from South Island Road. Open Monday through Saturday, 9 a.m.–5:30 p.m.

31. Yawkey Wildlife Center. The Yawkey Wildlife Center was bequeathed to the State of South Carolina by Tom Yawkey. During his lifetime, Yawkey used this land as a private hunting preserve and wildlife refuge. The South Carolina Wildlife and Marine Resources Department operates a wildlife management area, a waterfowl reserve, and carries out research on wildlife management practices. The operation of the Yawkey Center is supported by the Yawkey Foundation Trustees and a $10 million trust fund. The number of resident and migratory birds and the lack of human presence distinguish the Yawkey Center.

The Yawkey Center is composed of North Island, South Island, and most of Cat Island. Much of the freshwater marshland was transformed into rice fields by Huguenot planters during the colonial period. Baron Johan DeKalb and Marquis de Lafayette first set foot on American soil on North Island and were entertained by Major Benjamin Huger.

Cat Island is accessible only by ferry, and tours of the Yawkey Wildlife Center must be arranged in advance. There is only one field trip each week, usually Tuesday or Wednesday. Write Tom Yawkey Wildlife Center, Route 2, Box 181, Georgetown, SC 29449, or call (803) 546–6814.

32. Belle Isle Plantation and **Battery White.** William Bartram crossed Winyah Bay at Belle Isle Plantation. The ferry landed where the Civil War fortification of Battery White was later built. The plantation of Belle Isle was originally owned by Peter Horry. Belle Isle is now a private resort, but visitors may see Battery White by stopping at the guard gate for a free pass. Follow the signs from South Island Road.

33. Hobcaw Barony. William Bartram landed at Frasier's point and continued through present-day Hobcaw Barony on the King's Road. The colonial road is still used by the staff of Hobcaw Barony and enters present-day US-17 at the entrance gates. The Bellefield Nature Center has natural history displays and fresh and saltwater aquariums. Hobcaw Barony is headquarters of the Baruch Forest Service Institute of Clemson University and the Belle W. Baruch Institute for Marine Biology and Coastal Research of the University of South Carolina.

San Miguel de Gualdape was the first European settlement attempted in North America and it was thought until recently to have been in the vicinity of Hobcaw Barony. New scholarship, however, places the colony on the coast of Georgia. In 1526 Lucas Vásquez de Ayllón settled 500 people on the Atlantic coast; but like many subsequent attempts at establishing settlements, the colonists suffered from hunger, fevers, and disillusionment. After the untimely death of Ayllón, the remaining 150 colonists returned to Santa Domingo. Lord Carteret was granted this land in 1718, hence the name Barony. John Roberts bought the land in 1730 and resold it to rice planters. Ditches running in straight lines from Winyah Bay eastward to the salt marshes divided the plantations one from the other and are still visible today.

In the early twentieth century Bernard Baruch acquired the land that once encompassed ten rice plantations. He used Hobcaw as a retreat for his family and entertained many distinguished personalities of the day, including Franklin Roosevelt and Winston Churchill. Baruch's daughter, Belle, bought Hobcaw from her father and created the Belle W. Baruch Foundation to administer the property and establish research and educational programs in natural history.

Tours of Hobcaw Barony are conducted on each Tuesday and Thursday. The tours are very popular and visitors are advised to make plans in advance. Contact Bellefield Nature Center, Route 5, Box 1003, Georgetown, SC 29440, (803) 546–4623. There is a $15 fee for a three-hour tour of Hobcaw Barony.

34. Georgetown. The Carolina Proprietors granted the first land in the Winyah Bay area in 1705. The historic district of Georgetown was laid out by Elisha Screven in 1729, making Georgetown the third-oldest city in South Carolina. Screven laid out the original town plan in a grid of five-by-seven blocks. Georgetown is located at the junction of the Pee Dee, Black, Sampit, and Waccamaw rivers and quickly became a center for river traffic and shipping. In 1732 the citizens of the area were successful in getting a port and customs office established at Georgetown. The first products shipped from the area were naval stores, timber, and beef.

An aristocratic society in Georgetown was built upon income earned from the production of indigo dye. As the market became glutted with Indian dye the planters of the coast turned to rice production. In the first half of the nineteenth century Georgetown became the leading rice port in this country and was second in the entire world only to Calcutta, India. Fortunes were made with Waccamaw Gold rice and the labor provided by slaves. In the early nineteenth century, rice planters began a resort community on Pawley's Island to escape summer fevers and malaria. They built mansions in Charleston where they spent winters and enjoyed the social season.

The emancipation of slaves and recurring hurricanes at the end of the nineteenth century brought an end to the profitability of rice farming in South Carolina. Machinery proved impractical in the soft mud of South Carolina and the use of rivers and tide to flood the fields is less predictable than the deep wells of Louisiana and Texas.

The Georgetown historic district has a number of colonial homes and churches. There are at least twenty-three that date from the colonial period. Visitor information is available at the Georgetown County Chamber of Commerce located at the corner of Front and Broad streets.

35. Harbor Walk, Sampit River. At the Georgetown waterfront ships loaded indigo and rice bound for England and unloaded the manufactured goods of the mother country. The Sampit River is named for the Sampit Indians.

36. Kaminski House (c. 1769) was built by Paul Trapier II, a prominent businessman. The house was donated to the city by the last owner, Mrs. Harold Kaminski, and is now a museum home. The grounds overlook the Sampit River and are free to the public for strolling and picnicking. Guided tours of the home are given on the hour Monday through Saturday, 10 a.m.–4 p.m., and on Sunday from 1–4 p.m. Located at 1003 Front Street. Admission.

37. The Rice Museum. Murals, dioramas, and artifacts from the days of rice culture are displayed at the Rice Museum in the Old Market Building. One of the workers has an interesting display of Chinaberry jewelry for sale. The museum is surrounded by Lafayette Park with displays of native plants and an herb garden. Front Street, open 9:30 a.m.–4:30 p.m., Monday through Saturday except major holidays. Admission.

38. Winyah Indigo Society Hall. Wealthy indigo planters formed this social organization to promote the culture of indigo. Members paid their dues in indigo and with the income they provided for the opening of a public school in 1757, the only school between Charleston and Wilmington. The present building dates from 1857.

39. Prince George's Masonic Lodge. The Masonic lodge in Georgetown dates from the 1700s. George Washington was honored by an address at the lodge on April 30, 1791.

40. Prince George-Winyah Episcopal Church. Consecrated in 1747, Prince George Winyah is still in service and in excellent condition. Located at the northwest corner of Broad and Highmarket streets. Open seasonally for tours.

41. Beth Elohim Cemetery (c. 1772) is one of the oldest Jewish cemeteries in the country. Several of Georgetown's mayors and civic leaders are buried there. The practice of religious tolerance in colonial South Carolina encouraged the immigration of adherents to many faiths. In 1800 there were more Jewish citizens in the South Carolina than in any other American colony.

42. Morgan Park. A boardwalk crosses a saltmarsh to an island in Winyah Bay. Picnic tables and grills are provided as well as a view of the bay. Travel east on Front Street, turn right on Meeting Street, then left on River Street.

43. Old Rice Fields can be seen along the Waccamaw River as travelers cross Harrell Siau Bridge (US-17). The ditches separated the plantations and helped flood the fields. Although each plantation extended from the Waccamaw River to the beaches on the Atlantic Ocean, rice could be grown only within a quarter mile of the river. The Waccamaw River is the northern limit of swamp lily (*Crinum americanum*), which is most common in North Florida and the Gulf Coast. The swamp lily is not known to grow wild anywhere else in South Carolina.

44. Bellefield Nature Center. Bellefield Nature Center is operated by Hobcaw Barony and is open to the general public. Exhibits include a salt water touch tank, terrarium, local plants and animals, and a slide presentation on the history of Hobcaw Barony and the Baruch family

The Bellefield Nature Center is open Monday through Friday, 10 a.m.–5 p.m., and on Saturdays, 1 p.m.–5 p.m. Admission is free.

45. Lafayette's Landing. The Marquis de Lafayette and Baron DeKalb came to America to aid the Patriot Revolution and landed at North Island on June 13, 1777. They were the guests of Benjamin Huger who had a summer home on the island. The marker on US-17 near Bellefield Nature Center commemorates their landing.

46. Wallace Pate Research Center. The Pate Foundation for Environmental Research and Education sponsors Clemson University research programs in coastal forest ecology. The foundation is building on North Island a center for education, outreach, and research. The new Pate Center will have nature trails and demonstration areas. Located on US-17 north of Bellefield Nature Center.

47. Samworth Wildlife Management Area is a waterfowl management area that originated with the donation of Thomas Samworth's Dirleton Plantation. Other purchases have increased the holdings to a total of 992 acres of wetland and 266 acres of upland. Dirleton House and grounds are open to the public Monday through Friday from 8 a.m.–5 p.m. Tours of the area may be arranged.

Samworth WMA is open for wildlife observation, bird watching, photography, and nature study from January 21 through October 31. The general public is restricted to designated areas at other times because of hunting activity. Observation points are marked on Butler Creek and the Big Pee Dee River. Fishing is open March 15 through August 31. There is a boat ramp with access to the Big Pee Dee River, only non-gasoline-powered boats are permitted within the Wildlife Management Area.

Samworth WMA is located off US-701 and is reached from Plantersville by way of Old Pee Dee River Road (SC-52) or from Carter's General Store at the Black River by Choppee Road (SC-4) and SC-52.

48. Mansfield Plantation & Slave Village. Mansfield Plantation is a private residence but features a self-guided tour of the slave village and an authentic rice-winnowing building. Open by chance, $2 per person. To arrange guided tours for groups of twelve or more call (803) 546–6961. Follow US-701 north from Georgetown, turn right on Pringle's Ferry Road then right on Beneventure Road.

49. Black River Canoe Trail. The Black River Canoe Trail begins at Scout Landing in Kingstree, Williamsburg County, and ends at Georgetown and Winyah Bay. It meanders eighty-one miles along pristine and undeveloped Black River. The trail begins in rocky limestone narrows and widens into black water river and cypress swamp.

For additional information contact Tide Water Trails, Georgetown County Chamber of Commerce, P.O. Box 1776, Georgetown, SC 29442.

Peters Creek. Canoe trail access on SC-4, two miles north of US-701.

Six Mile Creek. Located 6.5 miles north of Georgetown on US-701.

Pine Tree Landing and Pea House Landing. Follow SC-41 then turn right on SC-38.

50. Brown's Ferry Vessel, a river freighter of the 1730s, was raised from the Black River in 1976. The boat could be sailed, rowed, or poled and its flat bottom allowed landing on beaches. The Brown's Ferry Vessel is one of the oldest recovered vessels in America and is valuable in that it was a local duty merchant ship rather than a military or corporate sailing ship.

51. Black River Swamp Preserve. This Nature Conservancy preserve is composed of 1,276 acres of Black River floodplain. There are several species of rare plants protected here, sarvis holly, false dragonhead, and riverbank quillwort. The preserve is located on the east bank of the river and stretches 1.5 miles upstream from Pine Tree boat ramp and two miles downstream. Located off county road 38 northeast of Andrews.

52. Chicora Indian Tribe of South Carolina. The Chicorans were the first people encountered by Spanish and French explorers in the 1520s. They were diminished by war and disease, and in the 1740s many were forced to move to the Catawba reservation. The Chicora Tribe has recently been revived. Throughout the coastal area of Georgetown, Horry, Williamsburg, Marion, Clarendon, and Florence counties, people with Native-American heritage quietly lived in rural and isolated communities, living as whites though not being completely accepted by them. Twenty years ago, Chief Gene Martin began organizing Native-Americans in this region. He was elected chief in 1987 and the tribe has been granted a charter by South Carolina. The Chicora Tribe hosts a powwow each October for the public. Their office is in Andrews.

53. Andrews Museum. Andrews is a turn of the century lumber town, built on the railroad line. The museum is located in the Old Town Hall building. Located on Main Street (SC-521). Open Tuesday through Thursday, 10 a.m.–4 p.m.

Counties

Georgetown County is named for the city of Georgetown, which was named for King George II.

Itinerary

Miles	Directions
	Begin at the intersection of SC-41 and Wambaw Creek Road (Hwy. 100) and travel east on Wambaw Creek Road
1.4	Enter Francis Marion National Forest, the route is now called Halfway Creek Road
4.2	Right on Guerin's Bridge Road (unmarked paved road) and make an immediate left on Willow Hall Road (FS-202)
8.7	Right on Hwy 133/1032
1.9	Left on US-17 (*Alternate route:* Keep on Guerin's Bridge Road to US-17. Guerin's Creek Bridge has been an important route since early colonial times.)
3.3	Left on Old Georgetown Road at Buck Hall Recreation Area
1.3	Straight on Old Georgetown Road
3.4	Bear left at the forks, then straight through the 5-point intersection, keep to the right of the Cypress Bay sign
3.1	Keep straight across SC-45 on Old Georgetown Road
3.8	Saint James Santee Parish Church, 1768
1.9	Notice the Carolina bay on the left
.4	Right on Rutledge Road, Hwy 857
1.6	Left on US-17
1.1	Cross the South Santee River
1.8	Cross the North Santee River
6.9	Right on Whitehall Road. Turn when you see the Georgetown Marine Institute sign and Roycroft Daylily signs
2.7	Left on Island Road (Belle Isle Road and Belle Isle Gardens are straight ahead)
3.5	Right on US-17
1.7	Right on Front Street for historic downtown Georgetown
.8	Left on Queen Street
.4	Right on US-17

Long Bay

Horry County is known as the *Independent Republic of Horry*, owing to the independent nature of the inhabitants and its remoteness from Charleston. Horry County never had large numbers of plantations because the rivers were unsuited to growing rice and the upland soil was unsuited for growing cotton. Although the rest of coastal South Carolina came to be politically dominated by a wealthy aristocracy of slave owners, Horry County was home to self-reliant, though often poor, small farmers and their families. While eighty percent of the Georgetown County population were enslaved Africans, only 30 percent of Horry County were slaves.

Little River was the first settlement in the upper part of South Carolina. In the late seventeenth century, William Waties was operating an Indian trading post on the Little River Neck. By 1730 there were a few English and French families living in the Little River community. Governor Robert Johnson designated that Kingston Township be laid out on the inland side of the Waccamaw River as part of his 1730 township plan to settle the frontier portions of South Carolina. Kingston township was surveyed in 1732 and a town site was chosen. The town grew slowly, even at the outbreak of the Revolution, Kingston had only a few families and six or seven buildings.

Horry County was part of Georgetown Precinct of Craven County in the late Colonial period. What we today call the Grand Strand, between the Waccamaw River and the Atlantic Ocean, was All Saints Parish and Kingston was included in Prince George Parish. The ocean between Murrell's Inlet and Little River Neck was called the Long Bay. The remoteness of much of the district, filled with many large swamps and sectioned by numerous rivers, caused the region to become settled very slowly and kept the population culturally and politically isolated. Indeed many of the settlers came south from Cape Fear, North Carolina, rather than from South Carolina. In 1801 citizens of All Saints and Prince George parishes petitioned the South Carolina General Assembly to create Horry County with Kingston, renamed Conwayborough, as the seat of government.

In the early nineteenth century, the manufacture of naval stores and lumber became the economic base in Horry County as those industries moved south from North Carolina. Farmers began to grow tobacco near the end of the nineteenth century and Horry County is now the primary tobacco-growing area in South Carolina. Conway began to prosper after it became a tobacco market. Though the largest county east of the Mississippi River, Horry remained sparsely populated until the rise of tourism and development of the beaches in the twentieth

Myrtle Beach

century. The section of the Intracoastal Waterway through Horry County was the last to be completed and was opened in 1936.

William Bartram's Travels by the Long Bay

John and William Bartram passed through Horry County in 1765 as they traveled south from Ashwood to Charleston. They crossed into South Carolina on August 10 and lodged with Captain Ross in Little River. The next day they traveled on down the Long Bay, known today as the Grand Strand. Their route was the same then as it was for William in 1776 as he was traveling in the opposite direction, headed north from Charleston to Ashwood.

William followed the King's Road (US-17) up the Waccamaw Neck in late November 1776. Near present-day Myrtle Beach the road actually ran on the beach for fifteen miles, avoiding the deep and tiresome sand farther inland. The body of water lying between Murrell's Inlet and North Myrtle Beach was known then, and now, as Long Bay. William crossed Singleton Swash at the present-day Dunes Golf Club in Myrtle Beach. He continued on the King's Road around White Point Creek and the head of Little River, which was then only five miles in length. He passed through Little River and crossed into North Carolina at the Boundary House. William Bartram's journey along the coast of Horry County was the same route taken by President Washington's entourage in 1791. The President's diary contains much more detail about the region than does *The Travels*.

Sites

1. Pawley's Island was a 1711 land grant to Percival Pawley. This narrow barrier island has a number of historic summer homes dating from the first half of the nineteenth century. Amazingly, they have managed to survive hurricanes and modern development. Wealthy rice planters of the Waccamaw River built summer homes on Pawley's Island to be near the fresh, healthy salt air and to escape the summer fever and miasmas that bred in the still waters of the rice fields. Cypress timbers were cut, hewn, and numbered for fitting at the plantations then boated out to the island and assembled into houses. The causeway was built in 1846 by Governor Robert Allston.

2. Hagley Landing. Waccamaw River access, Georgetown County public boat ramp. Hagley's Point is a great place to watch sunsets over the Waccamaw River.

3. All Saints Parish Waccamaw Church (1767). The present building replaces the 1844 structure that burned in 1915 and is the fourth church to occupy the site. The exterior closely resembles the former building but the box pews and slave gallery are gone. Cypress and cedars in the beautifully landscaped cemetery shade the graves of many prominent citizens of the Waccamaw Neck. Grounds are open during daylight hours.

4. Waccamaw and Pee Dee River Plantations. Boat tours of the plantation district on the Waccamaw River can be arranged in Georgetown on Front Street and at Georgetown Marina.

5. Brookgreen Gardens was the winter home of Archer and Anna Huntington. The gardens were begun as a setting for the sculptures of Ms. Huntington, a renowned figurative sculptor, then expanded to contain a representative collection of American sculpture. The Huntingtons purchased Brookgreen in 1930, along with the former rice plantations, Laurel Hill, Springfield, and the Oaks. The Oaks was the home of Governor Joseph Alston and his wife Theodosia, beloved daughter of Aaron Burr. In 1812 Theodosia was bound for New York as a passenger on a schooner that never arrived and whose fate was never known. Was it lost in a storm or was it captured by pirates?

Brookgreen is the largest public sculpture garden in the nation in acreage and in number of works. The sculptures lend an architectural element to magnificent formal gardens filled with native plants. The masterpieces, however, are the 250-year-old live oaks that shade the main allée. The Wildlife Park has two aviaries, one for raptors unable to be released into the wild and one for birds of the cypress swamp, including white ibis, snowy egrets, and wood ducks. The Deer Savannah covers twenty-three acres. The Native Plant Garden has over seventy examples of regional plants and a pleasant walk guides visitors along the edge of a black water creek.

Brookgreen Garden is located on US-17 and is open 9:30 a.m.–5:30 p.m. Admission.

6. Huntington Beach State Park. Although officially a part of Brookgreen Gardens, the beach and marsh lying east of US-17 are managed by Huntington Beach State Park in partnership with the Brookgreen Gardens Foundation. The undeveloped beach and Atalaya, the Huntington's Moorish-style mansion, are the major attractions. For the naturalist there are the Sandpiper Pond and Sea Oats nature trails as well as a short unnamed trail located just behind the office. A canoe trail provides a close encounter with the salt marsh. A boardwalk and observation platforms present hikers with views of the salt marsh. An interesting feature of the park is the fresh water lagoon that allows an unusual side-by-side comparison between a fresh water habitat and that of the adjacent salt marsh separated only by a thin dike. There is a healthy population of alligators in the lagoon.

7. Murrell's Inlet is named for John Morrall who purchased the land in 1731. Like Pawley's Island, Murrell's Inlet was a resort for plantation families seeking to escape the heat and mosquitoes of summer. Today, Murrell's Inlet is a quiet residential community, contrasting pleasantly to busy Myrtle Beach, and is renowned for its number of fine seafood restaurants.

8. Northern limit of the large rice plantations. Though rice was grown as far north as the Cape Fear River, where it was grown in inland fields, the very large plantations that used tidal flooding extended only slightly north of Georgetown. North of Winyah Bay the tide diminishes in height and strength and the rivers lack the low swamp land necessary for building rice fields.

9. Waccamaw River Preserve. The Nature Conservancy owns 650 acres of tidal cypress-gum swamp at the confluence of the Waccamaw River and the Intracoastal Waterway. The preserve protects two rare fish species and twenty-eight rare plant species. The preserve is a refuge for black bears. The preserve is accessible only by boat.

10. Myrtle Beach State Park is an urban state park, nestled among the hustle and bustle of Myrtle Beach, and is one of the most popular state parks in South Carolina. Myrtle Beach State Park was the first state park to open in South Carolina and was built by the Civilian Conservation Corps in the early 1930s. The park has a campground, fishing pier, nature trails, cabins, nature programs, and beach access. The entrance is located on US-17 between Surfside Beach and Myrtle Beach. Open daily, 6 a.m.–10 p.m.

11. Myrtle Beach continues to grow as a vacation destination for families and golfers and

Legend

1. Pawley's Island
2. Hagley Landing
3. All Saints Waccamaw Parish Church
4. Waccamaw and Pee Dee River Plantations
5. Brookgreen Gardens
6. Huntington Beach State Park
7. Murrell's Inlet
8. Northern limit of the large rice plantations
9. Waccamaw River Preserve
10. Myrtle Beach State Park
11. Myrtle Beach
12. Hurl Rock Park coquina beds
13. Lewis Ocean Bay Heritage Preserve
14. Indian Camp Forest Trail
15. Horry County Museum
16. Chicora-Waccamaw Indians
17. Waccamaw River Heritage Preserve
18. Little River
19. Vereen Memorial Gardens
20. Boundary House Monument

Long Bay

South Carolina law provides for public use of all beaches below the high water mark. Most municipalities provide access at the end of streets, although parking may or may not be available. Additionally, all navigable waterways are open as public highways, although bank-side access is not ensured.

as a retirement community. Visitors were first attracted to the seashore for its recuperative qualities for the ill and it was thought that sea water and salt air were helpful in preventing disease. The area was known as New Town until 1900 when it was named Myrtle Beach for the abundance of wax myrtles (Conway was Old Town). The first hotel opened in 1901 and the Ocean Forest Hotel opened in 1929. Myrtle Beach became immensely popular after World War II and was the center of a dance and music scene. The community was nearly destroyed by Hurricane Hazel in 1954. Myrtle Beach was rebuilt and the new golf courses and tourist dollars have created an unprecedented amount of development.

12. Hurl Rock Park coquina beds are located at Twentieth Avenue South on the beach. These loosely consolidated rocks were described by William Bartram.

13. Lewis Ocean Bay Heritage Preserve. This 6,400-acre preserve contains over twenty Carolina bays and protects habitat for native orchids, Venus' fly-traps, pitcher plants, and black bears. The bays in Lewis Ocean Bay are filled with peat and organic matter which lies above an impervious layer of cemented sand. The bays do not appear to hold ponded water like those in Francis Marion National Forest because the water is absorbed by a deep layer of peat. Tannin leached from plant material creates an acidic environment that supports a plant community of heaths such as fetterbush, blueberry, huckleberry; and smilax, gallberry, pond pine, and loblolly bay. The Indians called such a place *pocosin*. A ridge of sand rims the pocosin and creates a drier environment dominated by longleaf pine, turkey oak, and dwarf live oak.

Insectivorous plants (Venus' flytrap, sundews, and pitcher plants) are found in savannahs, either where fire has removed surrounding vegetation or in ditches and powerline right-of-ways where mowing keeps the landscape open. The rare spoonflower, a member of the rhododendron family, is found in open water of the bays.

Lewis Ocean Bay Heritage Preserve is open during daylight hours, but call South Carolina Wildlife & Marine Resources Game Section before visiting during fall or winter hunting season (803/734–3886). For more information contact Nongame and Heritage Trust Section, SC Wildlife and Marine Resources Department, P.O. Box 167, Columbia, SC 29202.

14. Indian Camp Forest Trail. This nature trail is short, one-third mile, but contains a wide variety of trees and native flowers. The land belongs to the International Paper Company and is a cooperative project of the company and the Horry-Georgetown Technical Education Center. There is a guide to the sixty-six interpretive markers. Located on International Paper property a mile and a half south of University of South Carolina Coastal Campus. The trailhead is near the maintenance building. Open sunrise to sunset.

15. Horry County Museum. Museum exhibits tell the history of Native Americans in Horry County from prehistory to modern times and the story of Europeans during the last four centuries. The theme of the museum is everyday life during the last millennium. The Museum includes diverse collections of aboriginal artifacts, colonial items, farm implements, and modern commercial goods that were the staple of every country store. Visitors can also learn about the ecology of the forests and barrier islands. The museum is located at the corner of Fifth and Main Streets in downtown Conway. Open Monday through Saturday, from 10 a.m.–5 p.m.

16. Chicora-Waccamaw Tribe. People of Native-American ancestry living in Horry County chartered the Waccamaw Tribe in 1992, later adding the name Chicora to honor their ancestors who met the first Europeans to visit North America. Chicora was the name by which the Spanish knew the Carolina coast. The families that comprise the tribe lived originally around Dog Bluff, northwest of Conway. They are currently seeking federal recognition.

17. Waccamaw River Heritage Preserve. Much of the Waccamaw River floodplain is protected as a state heritage preserve and includes over 5,000 acres. The preserve contains a mature hardwood forest and protects several endangered and rare plants, including the dwarf fimbry. Canoeing, camping, fishing, hunting, and nature study are allowed in the preserve. The preserve is located along the Waccamaw River between SC-9 and County Road 31.

18. Little River is the oldest community in the upper part of the South Carolina coast. In the early 1700s William Waties operated an Indian trading post here and the area grew as a sparsely settled fishing community. The town of Little River developed in the 1840s as a port for shipping lumber and naval stores. George Washington dined at James Cochran's house in Little River on April 27, 1791. The house stood at the corner of Minneola Avenue and US-17.

19. Vereen Memorial Gardens. The Vereen family has lived in the Long Bay area since the early eighteenth century. Vereen Memorial Gardens contains the Vereen family cemetery. There are numerous hiking trails including one that follows the old King's Road.

Jeremiah Vereen lived on this property during the late eighteenth century and operated a public house for travelers.

20. Boundary House. The boundary line between North and South Carolina ran through a building that came to be known as Boundary House. It was built by the middle of the eighteenth century and became a well-known landmark, operating at times as a tavern, church and private residence. The Boundary House Monument is located in front of the Marsh Harbour Golf Links Clubhouse.

Counties

Horry County (pronounced Oree) was created from Georgetown District in 1801 and named for Peter Horry, Revolutionary soldier and representative from Prince George Winyah Parish. Horry County is the largest county east of the Mississippi River and larger even than the state of Rhode Island.

Itinerary

Miles	Directions
	Begin at Bellefield Nature Center and travel north on US-17
5.6	Left on King's River Road (Highway 255)
4.1	Right on Hawthorne Drive (Highway 569)
2.0	Right on Country Club Drive (Highway 535)
.2	Left on US-17, enter Litchfield Beach
4.5	Bear right on Business 17, enter Murrell's Inlet
15.8	Merge right on King's Highway (Business-17)
7.2	Merge right on US-17
11.2	Exit right for US-90
1.1	Keep right on US-17
2.8	Right on SC-179, the South Carolina Welcome Center is on the left and Vereen Memorial Gardens is on the right
1.0	Enter Brunswick County, North Carolina

Cape Fear

The first Europeans to visit the coast of North Carolina were members of the Spanish slave cartel of Havana who sailed north as early as 1519 searching for slaves to sell in the Caribbean islands. Their voyages were not recorded because they were not sanctioned and were therefore illegal. Francisco Gordillo, sailing under the sponsorship of Lucas Vásquez de Ayllón, explored the coast of North and South Carolina in 1521. The next visitors were the expedition of Giovanni da Verrazzano, sailing for Francis I of France. His ship anchored briefly off the mouth of Cape Fear in 1524 and a crew explored the mainland. In 1526 Ayllón landed his colony of 600 people on the Atlantic Coast but soon moved to a new location farther south. It was once thought that his first landing was at the Cape Fear River, but historians now believe that it was at Winyah Bay. One of the ships was lost and another had to be built. The colonists stayed only a month before moving to the Georgia Coast. It is now generally believed that the Ayllón colony, called San Miguel de Gualdape, was located either on Creighton Island in Sapelo Sound or at the mouth of the Savannah River.

The English were familiar with North America because their privateers had operated in the Caribbean and off the Atlantic coast where they attacked Spanish treasure ships. In the sixteenth century, pirating was sanctioned by Queen Elizabeth. The most successful of these privateers were from the noble class and they received knighthood for their service to the crown. Their number included Sir John Hawkins, Sir Humphrey Gilbert, and Sir Francis Drake. Gilbert received the first patent for colonizing North America but he failed, and his patent went to his half-brother, Walter Raleigh. Philip Amadas and Arthur Barlowe were dispatched to reconnoiter the coast in 1584. They returned with two North Carolina Indians, Wanchese and Manteo. They named the region Virginia in honor of Queen Elizabeth, the virgin queen.

The next voyage carried the first settlers to Virginia. They were settled on Roanoke Island in April 1585 with Ralph Lane as their governor. They suffered during the following year and were taken back to England the next summer by Sir Francis Drake, only days before Sir Richard Grenville arrived with supplies. Another colony was made in 1587 at the original settlement on Roanoke Island with John White as governor of 150 colonists, including women and children. White returned to England for supplies and was caught up in preparations for the impending conflict with Spain. White and Raleigh could not arrange for relief of the colonists because every available floating vessel was required for the defense of England. It was not until the great Spanish Armada was defeated that White could sail again. He arrived at Roanoke Island on August 15, 1590, to find the English colonists had disappeared. English interest in establishing colonies cooled for the next two decades and no attempt was made again until Jamestown was founded at Chesapeake Bay in 1607.

Governor White made watercolor paintings of the Indians during his brief stay on Roanoke Island in the summer of 1587. They were copied as engravings by Theodore de Bry and are an invaluable record of indigenous life at the time of contact with Europeans.

The original grant to the Virginia Company extended from 34° to 41° latitude, the southern limit was Cape Fear, well out of the range of the settled parts of Spanish Florida. Later in the seventeenth century, Cape Fear was to become the focus of the first English settlement south of Virginia (Albemarle was then considered part of Virginia), although it in fact became one of the last places on the Atlantic coast to be settled in the thirteen original colonies.

The English again cast their eyes upon the Cape Fear region in 1629 when Charles I granted the land from parallel 31° to 36° to Sir Robert Heath. Heath was not able to carry out his plans to settle the colony and turned his grant over to Lord Berkeley. Leaders of the Massachusetts Bay Colony engaged William Hilton to explore the Atlantic coast and find a suitable new home with a longer growing season. On October 4, 1662, Hilton successfully negotiated Frying Pan Shoals and explored the Cape Fear River for three weeks. A group of New Englanders came in 1663 but for unknown reasons returned to Massachusetts within a few months. The Lords Proprietors received the Heath Grant in 1663 and named the region Carolina in honor of King Charles I.

English Barbadians, also working with Hilton, petitioned the Lords Proprietors in August 1663 for permission to settle the Cape Fear River. John Vassall of Barbados brought the first settlers in May 1664 and chose a spot on the west bank of the river about twenty miles above the mouth. The settlement was named Charles Town, the river was named Charles River and the region was designated County Clarendon. Conditions in Barbados had become crowded and economic opportunities had become restricted for those who did not already own large plantations, so Carolina became the new promised land for the Barbadians.

The Cape Fear colony did not fare well. They were neglected by the Lords Proprietors and the system for granting lots did not make allowances for the untillable swamps and infertile pine barrens. Finally, attempts by the citizens of Clarendon County to enslave the local Indians brought war with their

Wilmington, North Carolina, and the Cape Fear River

neighbors. Most of the Cape Fear Barbadians left for Virginia and Massachusetts. The Cape Fear colony was abandoned by 1667 and the region between Albemarle Sound and Charleston Harbor was once again uninhabited by Europeans. The coastal region of North Carolina then became a haven for pirates to repair their ships and await opportunity. Stede Bonnet made the Cape Fear his base of operations for a time. He was captured in the Cape Fear River on September 27, 1718, by the combined effort of governors Alexander Spotswood of Virginia and Robert Johnson of South Carolina. Bonnett was hung in Charleston and buried at White Point.

The most notorious of all the pirates was Edward Teach, Blackbeard, who made his home at Bath, North Carolina. Although he had taken the King's pardon he could not resist returning to the pirate's life. Blackbeard enjoyed the tolerance and protection of some of the leading men of North Carolina who benefited from his trade. Again, it was up to the neighboring governors to bring him to justice. In November 1718, Teach was caught off Ocracoke Island by Captain Ellis Brand and Lieutenant Robert Maynard of Virginia. Blackbeard's men boarded Maynard's ship when the Virginians, who were below deck, emerged to surprise the pirates. Maynard and Blackbeard engaged in hand-to-hand combat and Blackbeard was killed. The remaining pirates fled or were captured and Maynard hung the head of Blackbeard from his bowsprit as a warning to other pirates. This effectively closed the era of piracy on the American seaboard. The remains of Blackbeard's flagship, *Queen Anne's Revenge*, have been discovered at Beaufort Inlet and are being recovered by the Underwater Archaeology Unit of the North Carolina Department of Archives and History.

John Hughes, Price Hughes, Thomas James, and Enoch Morgan received grants on the Cape Fear River where they planned to settle a community of Welsh immigrants. Price Hughes became involved in the Indian trade deep into the Southeast and was killed in Alabama. Thomas James seems to be the only grantee to take up residence on the Cape Fear River, but he was killed by Indians at the outbreak of the Yamassee War. With white settlement moving north from Charleston and south from Albemarle, it was only a matter of time before Cape Fear became permanently settled. Governor George Burington did much to encourage settlement of the area. In 1724–1725 he made an extensive survey of the Cape Fear River and charted the channels. He defied the instructions of the Proprietors and ignored boundary claims of South Carolina to begin making land grants in the Cape Fear basin in the summer of 1725.

Barbadian planters from the Goose Creek area near Charleston began taking up land grants on the Cape Fear River. The Moore brothers, James, Maurice, Roger, and Nathaniel, led the settlement of the area. They and their allies became so powerful that they were known simply as the Family. They were always independent and contentious of external authority. The governors found them to be formidable foes and their descendants were among the first to challenge the authority of Parliament. Maurice Moore founded Brunswick in 1726, which became the port for the region. The major exports were tar, pitch, and turpentine for the Royal Navy and British merchant fleet.

In July 1729, North Carolina passed from Proprietary rule to Crown rule and a boundary between the two Carolinas was fixed at a point south of Cape Fear. Representatives of North

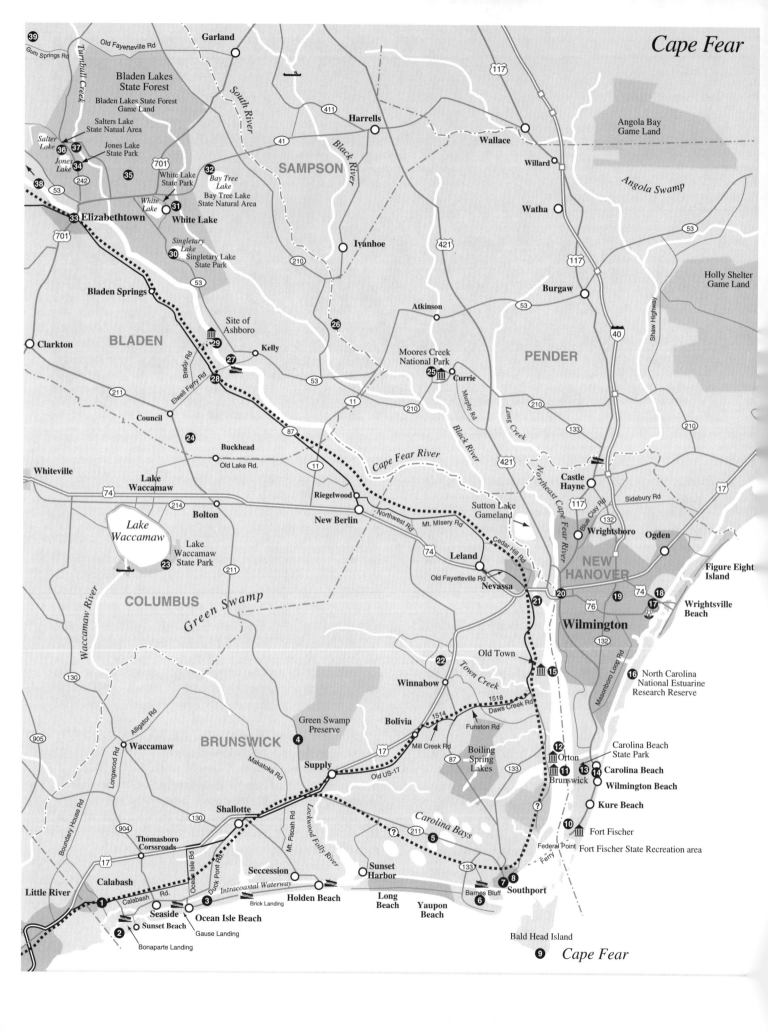

and South Carolina met on May 1, 1735 to begin surveying an actual boundary between the two colonies. They began at a point just a few yards above the mouth of the Little River and surveyed northwestward for seventy miles. Wilmington was established at the village of Newton in 1740 and became the official port in lower North Carolina.

Legend

1. Calabash
2. Bird Island
3. Museum of Coastal Carolina
4. Green Swamp Preserve
5. Carolina Bays
6. Oak Island Marshes
7. Fort Johnston
8. Southport Maritime Museum
9. Bald Head Island
10. Fort Fisher State Recreation Area
    Fort Fisher State Historic Site and Museum
    North Carolina Aquarium
    North Carolina Underwater Archaeology Center
11. Brunswick Town
12. Orton
13. Carolina Beach State Park
14. Old Town
15. Greenfield Gardens
16. North Carolina National Estuarine Research Reserve
17. New Hanover Arboretum
18. Airlie Gardens
19. University of North Carolina Wilmington
    Herbert Blumenthal Memorial Wildflower Preserve
    UNCW Arboretum
    UNCW Heritage Garden
20. Wilmington
21. Belville Boat Ramp
22. Ev-Henwood Nature Preserve
23. Lake Waccamaw State Park
24. Waccamaw-Siouan Indians
25. Moore's Creek National Battlefield
26. Black River
27. Elwell Ferry
28. Carver Creek Methodist Church
29. Ashwood
30. Singletary Lake State Park
31. White Lake
32. Bay Tree Lake State Natural Area
33. Elizabethtown
    Tory Hole Battleground
34. Jones Lake State Park
35. Bladen Lakes State Forest
36. Salters Lake State Natural Area
37. Turnbull Creek Educational State Forest
38. Harmony Hall
39. Horseshoe Lake

Governor Gabriel Johnston was a Highland Scot and he encouraged his countrymen to emigrate to North Carolina. Hard times in Scotland, the dissolution of the clans and the prospect of free or cheap land brought shiploads of Highlanders to the upper Cape Fear River. By the opening of the Revolution there were 20,000 Scots living along the Cape Fear River. Their movement northward into the Piedmont was blocked by the large tract of land owned by Lord John Carteret Granville, land that was not readily available for purchase or legal settlement.

The Cape Fear River region shipped flour, pork, beef, and indigo. The principal product of the area continued to be naval stores. Tar, pitch, and turpentine were floated downriver to Wilmington by tying barrels together to form large rafts. Indigo never became the successful cash crop that it was in South Carolina. Rice was grown along the river banks, but never in the quantities grown by South Carolina and it was of an inferior quality.

The Stamp Act brought a swift reaction from the citizens of Wilmington and the Cape Fear region. British ships entered the Cape Fear River and seized vessels lacking proper stamps. Wilmington citizens formed the Sons of Liberty and forced Dr. William Houston, the Stamp Receiver, to resign, though at the time he was unaware of his appointment. The leading men of North Carolina met with Governor William Tryon and received assurances from him that he hoped the act could be repealed, but until that time they must comply. The gentlemen refused on the grounds that the act was anathema to their interests and rights as English citizens and they were particularly displeased with the provision for trial of violators without a jury.

Without a stamp receiver to collect the stamp tax, trade began to stagnate. A thousand men marched on Governor Tryon's residence at Russellborough and presented a list of grievances. Tryon released the impounded ships and the collector of the port and comptroller of customs were forced to resign. This was the first overt act of defiance to the authority of Parliament in the American colonies. Unlike the Boston Tea Party participants of eight years later, the North Carolinians did not hide their identity but publicly presented their faces and signed their names.

Although the Stamp Act was repealed, the Townshend Acts and Tea Act brought new tension between the North Carolinians and Parliament. Cornelius Harnett, Jr., organized the Committee of Correspondence with the sister colonies in 1773. By June 1775, Governor Josiah Martin, fearing for his safety, took refuge at Fort Johnston.

The Scottish loyalists in the upper part of the Cape Fear River planned to march on Wilmington and put down the rebellion. They were met by patriots and defeated at Moore's Creek in February, 1776. On May 3, 1776, Commodore Peter Parker, Lord Cornwallis, and troop ships arrived off Cape Fear, landed and burned Brunswick. Because the loyalists had been dispersed, Sir Henry Clinton instructed Cornwallis to re-embark his troops and sail for Charleston. Wilmington was not occupied by the British until 1781. Cornwallis made his headquarters in Wilmington for several weeks before marching on to Virginia and meeting defeat.

Following the Revolution, Wilmington became the world's leading port for naval stores and grew to become the largest city in North Carolina in the early 1800s.

Site of Russellborough, home of Governor Dobbs and Tryon. Brunswick Town Historic Site

Cape Fear Indians

The Cape Fear Indians were a Siouan people, related to the Winyahs, Catawbas, and Waccamaws. Their name is not known to history except by the name bestowed upon them by Europeans. Because the Cape Fear was the last portion of coastal Carolina to become settled, the Cape Fear Indians were the last coastal tribe to be displaced. They harbored a dislike for whites due to their experience with the first Charles Town (North Carolina) settlers. They afterwards took advantage of shipwrecks and abused the survivors who reached shore. They were neither numerous nor powerful and sought the protection of the English against their enemies, entering into an agreement around 1696. Thereafter, they were known as kind and friendly and were allies of South Carolina during the Tuscarora War. However, they joined in the Yamassee War against South Carolina and were subdued by Colonel Maurice Moore. The remnants of the tribe, driven from their home by the Tuscaroras, drifted southward to join the Winyahs. For better security, they moved even closer to Charleston where they disappear from the records by the early nineteenth century.

Cape Fear River

The Cape Fear River was known to the native inhabitants as Sapona. It is a relatively new river, having formed only 75,000 years ago. The dangerous shoals created by the Cape Fear have been notorious since the first Europeans explored the coast of North America. The Cape Fear River is the only river in North Carolina to break through the Outer Banks. Its deposits are spread out twenty miles south of the mouth of the river in Frying Pan Shoals making it difficult for ships to take advantage of this open waterway.

John and William Bartram's Travels in the Cape Fear Region

John Bartram's parents, William and Elizabeth, moved to North Carolina about 1709, leaving John and Isaac in Pennsylvania. William was killed by Indians. Elizabeth and her two children, William II and James, were abducted then ransomed and returned to Philadelphia. As an adult, William II moved to North Carolina again and lived at Ashwood on the Cape Fear River where he was visited by John in 1760. William's nephew, William III, our botanist, ran his uncle's mercantile business there beginning in 1761. William was not very successful and joined his father on the expedition to Florida in 1765. While visiting at Ashboro, John and William Bartram explored Bladen County and visited Jones Lake, Singletary Lake, and Lake Waccamaw.

When another business venture in Philadelphia failed in 1770, William left town abruptly and fled to Ashwood. William loved his Uncle William and the Cape Fear River and found solace there. Unfortunately, his Uncle William and cousin Bill died very soon after William's arrival. While living with his uncle's family during the next year, William took stock of his life and prospects and determined to pursue the life of a botanist and artist, putting behind him forever the notion that he could be anything else. He arranged with Dr. John Fothergill to make another expedition to Florida and he left Ashwood either in late 1772 or early 1773. He returned to Philadelphia briefly to prepare for his journey.

On his return to Philadelphia in the winter of 1776 William Bartram visited again at Ashwood. He entered North Carolina at the Boundary House and traveled along the King's Road through present-day Calabash, Shallotte, Bolivia, and spent the evening at Old Town. There were two main roads that William could have taken through present-day Brunswick County. One went due east from Shalotte almost to Southport, corresponding to NC-211, then it turned northeastward and passed through Brunswick. The other road was a more direct route to Old Town, following present-day US-17 to Bolivia then turning east.

Bartram spent the next evening with a Mr. Lucas who lived near the community of Riegelwood above Livingston Creek and the next day he arrived at Ashwood. North Carolina had been William's second home for he had lived with his relatives at Ashwood during the years 1761–1765 and 1770–1772, and he dearly loved his Uncle William and his cousins. However, during William's brief visit in December 1776 the house must have been very lonely because Colonel William Bartram had died in a drowning accident in 1770, his wife had passed away in 1772, and their son Dr. William Bartram, Jr., had died in 1771. Two daughters remained, Sarah and Mary. William remained at Ashwood for about a week and a half before leaving on his return trip home to Philadelphia around December 12 or 13, 1776. He traveled up the western side of the Cape Fear River, passing through Elizabethtown and Fayetteville. He arrived in Alexandria, Virginia, at Christmas and reached Philadelphia in very early January 1777.

Sites

1. Calabash is famous for its seafood and has many excellent restaurants. A calabash is a dipper or bowl made from a gourd.

2. Bird Island is located just south of the town of Sunset Beach. It is a migrating island and has never been developed. The North Carolina Coastal Land Trust is working to preserve the island for loggerhead turtles and nesting birds. Seabeach amaranth, a threatened plant, grows on the island.

3. Museum of Coastal Carolina. The Museum contains exhibits on the natural and cultural history of the North Carolina coast. Learn about local animals, marine life, tides, and the Native-Americans who lived in Brunswick County. The Museum has a popular Reef Room and remnants of an eighteenth century shipwreck. Located on Ocean Isle Beach. Admission.

4. Green Swamp Preserve is a national natural landmark and contains over 15,000 acres of pine land, savannah, pocosins, and bay swamps. A number of rare plants are protected here, most significant are the carnivorous plants—pitcher plants, bladderworts, sundews, and naturally occurring Venus' flytrap. The preserve is also home to a number of red-cockaded woodpeckers. The entrance is on NC-211 about five miles north of Supply. The trails are primitive and access is restricted. Contact the Nature Conservancy, Southeast Coastal Plain Office, Building 4, Unit E, 2725 Old Wrightsboro Road, Wilmington, NC 28405, (910) 762-6277.

5. Carolina bays. The origin of Carolina bays is still a mystery. Some have said that they formed as sink holes, others suggest a meteor shower created the depressions. The Waccamaw-Siouan Indians of Bladen County have a belief that Lake Waccamaw was created by a ball of fire that plunged from the sky. Throughout the coastal area of Georgia and North and South Carolina there are nearly 500,000 of these distinctive geologic features. They are always oval shaped and ringed with a terrace of sand and they are oriented with their long axis running northwest-southeast. All Carolina bays began as lakes, but many have filled with peat and become boggy.

They are called bays because of the dominant tree that grows in the swampy parts of wholly or partially filled bays. The Indian name for a Carolina bay is pocosin, which means "swamp on a hill." Many bays have been logged for their valuable cypress and Atlantic white cedar. Fire suppression has accelerated the spread of fast growing trees and reduced the diversity of rare herbaceous plants.

The greatest concentration of pocosins is in North Carolina and the greatest number with open water are in Bladen County. Nearly eighty percent of existing bays occur in the Cape Fear region and forty-five percent of the land in Bladen County is occupied by bays. North Carolina has protected these bays since the early 1800s when a law was enacted claiming all lakes larger than 500 acres to be property of the state.

The best place to visit and hike a pocosin is in Bladen Lakes State Forest, Jones Lake State Park, and Horseshoe Lake in the Suggs Mill Pond Game Lands. The Nature Conservancy owns eight Carolina bays in Hoke, Robeson, and Scotland Counties and the North Carolina Chapter offers regular field trips. Contact the Nature Conservancy, Southeast Coastal Plain Office, Building 4, Unit E, 2725 Old Wrightsboro Road, Wilmington, NC 28405.

6. Oak Island Marshes contains 609 acres protected by the North Carolina Coastal Land Trust. A boardwalk over Davis Creek in Long Beach gives visitors a close up view of the marsh.

7. Fort Johnston, completed in 1764, was named for Governor Gabriel Johnston. Fort Johnston guarded the entrance to the Cape Fear River and stood until Fort Caswell was built nearby. The North Carolina Committee of Safety took possession of Fort Johnston in July 1776. A community grew up near the fort and was first named Smithville in 1792, then renamed Southport.

8. Southport Maritime Museum is devoted to the extensive nautical history of Cape Fear and the Cape Fear River. Artifacts range from remnants of a 2,000-year-old canoe to modern navigational devices. Located at 116 N. Howe Street in Southport. Open Tuesday through Saturday, 10 a.m.–4 p.m.

9. Bald Head Island. Landgrave Thomas Smith received Bald Head Island, then called Barren Island, as a land grant in 1713. Much of the island is privately owned, but the southern end has been protected by the North Carolina Coastal Land Trust. The 173-acre Bald Head Maritime Forest in the north-central part of the island is now state property. Bald Head Island is accessible by boat and ferry.

10. Fort Fisher State Recreation Area provides access to four miles of beach and opportunities for surf fishing, hiking, bicycling, and birdwatching. The Recreation Area is home to Fort Fisher State Historic Site, the North Carolina Aquarium, and the North Carolina Underwater Archaeology Center. Located on US-421 south of Kure Beach. Open daily and Sunday afternoons, closed Mondays.

Fort Fisher State Historic Site and Museum. Fort Fisher was one of the largest and most important fortifications in the Confederacy. The fort guarded Wilmington, the last port open to the Confederacy after the blockade began. The Union did not take Fort Fisher until January 1865, but it was the final stage in the total disruption of supplies and shipping for the confederacy.

North Carolina Aquarium. The Aquarium has exhibits of sharks, skates, alligators, and many more water creatures. The facilities include a picnic area, nature trails, and beach access. Located on US-401 at Fort Fisher State Recreation Area. Open Monday through Saturday, 9 a.m.–5 p.m., and on Sunday, 1–5 p.m. Closed on Thanksgiving, Christmas, and New Year's days.

North Carolina Underwater Archaeology Center is a department of the North Carolina Division of Archives and History. The Underwater Archaeology Center is located at Fort Fisher State Recreation Area and operates a small museum that contains exhibits on the marine history of the North Carolina coast. Open daily, 9 a.m.–4 p.m.

11. Brunswick Town. In 1726, Maurice Moore had a town laid out on his land grant near the mouth of the Cape Fear River. The town was named Brunswick in honor of the ancestral German home of King George I. In the early years Brunswick shipped naval stores and masts for the great British navy and merchant fleets. Brunswick was also the residence of governors Gabriel Johnston and Arthur Dobbs. Governor William Tryon lived there for several years until he moved the government to New Bern in 1770.

Tryon's move was precipitated by the Stamp Act disturbances of a few years earlier. The economy of Brunswick and the entire Cape Fear region was tied to exports to England and the necessity of paying cash for stamps was a hardship on the local businesses because currency was scarce. Ships lay in the Cape Fear River, unable to sail without stamps. Local citizens formed the Sons of Liberty and forced the Stamp Collector to resign. A thousand citizens marched on Brunswick to protest the seizure of ships for violation of the stamp tax. They forced the customs officials to swear not to enforce the stamp act then they marched to Governor Tryon's house, only a mile away, and held him hostage until the ships were released and he was presented with a list of grievances.

As Wilmington grew, Brunswick's importance diminished. There were 200 inhabitants in 1775. British soldiers occupied Brunswick in the spring of 1776 and burned what remained of the town. After the Revolution the town site became incorporated into Orton Plantation. The Confederacy constructed Fort Anderson on the site of Brunswick to protect the Cape Fear shipping channel.

Foundations of colonial homes are visible along the historic walk through the town. The ruins of Saint Philips Church, completed in 1760, lie at the edge of town. The visitor center has displays of artifacts from the colonial period. A cannon retrieved from the Cape Fear River is believed to be from the Spanish ship, *Fortuna*, which blew up during the failed invasion of 1748.

John and William Bartram visited with Governor Tryon at the governor's mansion, a mile from Brunswick at Russellborough, on August 8–9, 1765. Russellborough was the home of North Carolina governors from 1758–1770. The house was last owned by William Dry and was burned by British soldiers in 1776. William Bartram could have heard this news when he visited nearby Old Town in December of that year, giving him added encouragement to return home to Philadelphia as soon as possible.

12. Orton was the colonial home of Roger Moore and was built about 1725. Moore was a member of the powerful South Carolina family who helped settle the lower Cape Fear River. Orton was a rice and indigo plantation during the colonial period. In this century the Sprunt family planted extensive gardens and protected the famous heron rookery. The grounds are open to the public daily at 8 a.m., March through August, and at 10 a.m., September through November. Admission.

13. Carolina Beach State Park lies on the east bank of the lower Cape Fear River. It contains diverse habitats and has a natural population of Venus' fly trap. The park contains facilities for family and group camping, boating, fishing and picnicking. There are five miles of trails and excellent birdwatching sites. Carolina Beach State Park is located in Carolina Beach on Dow Road. Open at 8 a.m. Closing times range from 6–9 p.m. according to the season.

14. Old Town is the site of Charles Town, founded May 24, 1664. The colony was settled by John Vassal and Barbadians seeking new land for plantations; John Yeamans was the governor. The inhabitants, neglected by the Lords Proprietors, all deserted northward for Virginia and Albemarle County.

15. Greenfield Gardens. This public garden is operated by the town of Carolina Beach. It has facilities for picnicking, fishing, bicycling, hiking, and has a 180-acre cypress lake. Located on Carolina Beach Road, US-421.

Alyre Raffeneau DeLile

Alyre Raffeneau DeLile was appointed vice-consul to Wilmington by Napoleon and lived in Wilmington from 1801 to 1806. He was only twenty-four years old at the time but was already a respected scientist in France, where he was educated in botany, chemistry, and anatomy.

When only twenty-one years of age he was appointed to a scientific expedition to Egypt. His knowledge of the Greek language made him a valuable member of the party that included Boussard, who discovered the Rosetta Stone. DeLile was a founding member of the Institute of Egypt and was director of the Botanical Gardens of Cairo until the British took control of Egypt in 1801.

Soon after his career in Egypt ended DeLile was appointed to the post at Wilmington and was requested by Empress Josephine to collect plants that might be of interest in France. He also collected American grains for the botanist Palisot de Beauvois. DeLile befriended many prominent Americans during his visit, including Thomas Jefferson.

DeLile left Wilmington in 1806 and took a degree in medicine in New York. Upon his return to France he joined the faculty of Montpellier as botanist and director of the botanical garden. Under his direction, the garden became an agricultural experiment station. He produced more than sixty treatises on botany and medicine.

16. North Carolina National Estuarine Research Reserve has two units in the Wilmington Area—Masonboro Island and Zeke's Island. In addition to research, the reserve protects rare and endangered species such as seabeach amaranth and provides nesting sites for loggerhead and green sea turtles. Both units contain a wide variety of maritime habitats.

The Masonboro Island unit contains 5,097 acres and includes the island and salt marsh. Access is by boat only. There are no trails but camping is permitted, except on the dunes. Headquarters and the visitor center are located just off Myrtle Grove Loop Road in Myrtle Grove. Zeke's Island contains three islands and covers 1,160 acres. Parking and a boat ramp are located at the end of US-421. There are no trails but camping is permitted.

17. New Hanover County Arboretum. The Arboretum covers 6.5 acres and contains a wildflower garden, Japanese garden, vegetable and herb gardens, aquatic plants, and a greenhouse. The Arboretum displays native and introduced plants that are suitable for the North Carolina coastal area.

Located at 6206 Oleander Drive (US-76). Open during daylight hours. The office is open 8 a.m.–5 p.m., Monday through Friday.

18. Airlie Gardens was designed by R. A. Topel in the early part of this century. The garden has been in private hands until recently, when it was purchased by New Hanover County. The plantings were damaged by the hurricanes of 1996 but have been restored and the Gardens have reopened to the public. Located on Airlie Road just off US-74. Open Friday and Saturday, 9 a.m.–5 p.m. and on Sunday, 1–5 p.m.

19. University of North Carolina Wilmington. UNCW has been ranked among the top ten public undergraduate universities in the Southeast and has a world renowned marine biology program. Located at 601 South College Road.

Herbert Blumenthal Memorial Wildflower Preserve began as an informal nature trail for teaching botany and ecology and was formally established as a preserve in 1974 to prevent its loss to campus growth. The preserve is a haven for native plants and song birds, and provides biological diversity in the midst of the UNCW campus.

UNCW Arboretum. The entire UNCW campus is an urban arboretum and a microcosm of coastal North Carolina. The campus landscape plan includes thematic gardens and native plant communities that serve as outdoor laboratories for academic departments.

The master plan is divided into nine zones. The Academic area will contain several theme gardens; Butterfly Garden, Plant Pollinator Garden, Medicinal Herb Garden, Healing Garden, and a Fragrance Garden. The Gardens for the Arts area will contain gardens with literary themes and provide outdoor space for performances and exhibitions. This area will include Shakespeare's Garden, Monet's Flower Garden, Sculpture Garden, Drama Garden, Water lily Pond Garden, White Garden, and the Texture Garden. Other zones are The Entry Garden, Historic Core, the Preserve, Recreation and Residence, Maintenance and Support, Conservation Area, and Parking and Buffers.

UNCW Heritage Garden is located within the old quadrangle, bordered by the original campus buildings. The Garden contains traditional Southern landscape plants, old fashioned perennials, and an herb garden.

20. Wilmington. See page 321.

21. Belville Boat Ramp is located on NC-133 east of US-17, and provides access to the Brunswick River.

22. Ev-Henwood Nature Preserve is owned by the University of North Carolina Wilmington. It lies on Town Creek and contains 110 acres of varying coastal habitat that includes upland hardwoods, blackwater swamp, ponds, and old fields. The symbol of Ev-Henwood Preserve is stewartia, *Stewartia malacodendron*, also known as silky camellia. There are fifteen hiking trails that meander throughout the property.

The Preserve is open during daylight hours everyday. To reach the Preserve turn right onto Old Town Creek Road from US-17 when coming from Wilmington. Turn right at the intersection with Town Creek Road then left onto Rock Creek Road. The Preserve is located on Rock Creek Road.

23. Lake Waccamaw State Park. Lake Waccamaw is one of the largest Carolina Bays in the country. It covers 9,000 acres and has fourteen miles of shoreline. Its water is neutralized by limestone outcrops, allowing the lake to support a wide variety of wildlife. John and William Bartram visited Lake Waccamaw and found it fascinating and beautiful.

Lake Waccamaw is home to several of the state's rare plants—narrowleaf yellow pond-lily, water arrowhead, Venus-hair fern, greenfly orchid, and seven-angled pipewort. There are several endemic species found nowhere else—Waccamaw darter, Waccamaw silverside, Waccamaw killifish, and two species of snails.

Lake Waccamaw State Park has camping, hiking, nature trails, fishing, boating, and picnicking facilities. Hours of operation are 8 a.m.–9 p.m. during summer. Closing time is earlier when days are shorter. Closed Christmas Day.

24. Waccamaw-Siouan Indians. The Waccamaw Indians first appear in historical records as the Woccan who were visited by John Lawson in 1700. At the time they lived north of the Cape Fear River and south of the Tuscaroras. They moved into South Carolina to the area that is now Horry County sometime in the early eighteenth century. In 1749 they were at war with South Carolina and afterwards then sought refuge in the swamps around Lake Waccamaw. They now live in the communities of Saint James, Buck Head, Council, and Chadbourn. They were recognized as a tribe by North Carolina in 1971.

25. Moore's Creek National Battlefield. The important Battle of Moore's Creek took place on February 27, 1776. A force of 1,600 volunteers from Cross Creek was organized under Donald MacDonald. It included recently immigrated Scots, loyalists, and regulators. Their goal was to march to the coast and unite with a large force under Lord Cornwallis, Sir Henry Clinton, and Sir Peter Parker. Governor Joshiah Martin had worked in exile to organize the expedition and reconquer North Carolina.

The patriots, under the leadership of Alexander Lillington and Colonel Richard Caswell, built earth works on the east side of the bridge over Widow Moore's Creek, knowing the loyalists had to cross at that point. The patriots removed the decking on the bridge and greased the timbers before withdrawing behind their barricades. The loyalists were led that morning by Donald McLeod and Captain John Campbell and they unwisely decided to attack the patriots in their fortified position. The loyalists were overwhelmed and repulsed by the patriot fire. They lost thirty men dead and forty wounded, while the patriots lost only a single man.

During the next several weeks the participating loyalists were captured and paroled, with their weapons confiscated. The leaders were imprisoned or banished. The Battle of Moore's Creek was an important early victory for the patriots, who demonstrated their strength and resolve. Loyalist sentiment was dampened for a time in the Carolinas and the British force, arriving in May, moved on to Charleston where they were repulsed. The hope for a quick and lasting British conquest of the Carolinas disappeared. Historians believe that had the loyalists and British won at Moore's Creek and again at Charleston in 1776 the Revolution might not have materialized in the South.

The Moore's Creek National Battlefield Park contains eighty-six acres and includes the battle site and a replica of the bridge. The earthworks built by Lillington's patriots are still visible. The History Trail makes a circuit from the Visitor Center to the bridge site and passes monuments to the patriots, the loyalists, and the women of the Lower Cape Fear River who aided the patriot cause. The Tarheel Trail features exhibits that explain the production of naval stores, the primary industry of the Cape Fear River region during the colonial era.

The Park is open daily except New Year's Day and Christmas Day. Hours are 9 a.m.–5 p.m. Closing time from Memorial Day through Labor Day is 6 p.m. Located off NC-210.

26. Black River. The Black River is a popular canoe and kayak trail. The river is biologically diverse due to its clean water and is home to several rare fish species. The lower part of the river contains some of the oldest trees in the eastern United states, some cypresses are believed to be almost 1,700 years old. Roan Island, at the confluence of the Black and Cape Fear rivers, is owned by the Wildlife Resources Commission. Other portions of the river are owned by the Nature Conservancy or protected by conservation agreements with the landowners. Access is from NC-53 and at Ivanhoe.

27. Elwell Ferry is one of the few remaining cable ferries still in use. A boat ramp provides access to the Cape Fear River. Located at NC-87 and the Cape Fear River.

Lock and Dam #2. Boat ramp, fishing, picnic area, and restroom facilities.

28 Carver Creek Methodist Church was organized in 1790 by Bishop Francis Asbury. The current building dates from 1859. Located on NC-87.

29. Ashwood was the home of Colonel William Bartram, uncle to William Bartram, the botanist. The house site is on private property where some of the original foundation is still visible.

30. Singletary Lake State Park. Singletary Lake is one of the large Carolina bays protected by North Carolina. The park provides facilities for canoeing, swimming, camping, and hiking. The nature trail is a half-mile long and loops the lake. The park includes Turkey Oak Natural Area and is the headquarters for the State Lake Operations, which includes White Lake, Lake Waccamaw, and Baytree Lake.

Located on NC-53. Hours are 8 a.m.–5 p.m. daily. Closed on Christmas Day.

31. White Lake is one of North Carolina's most popular recreation areas and one of its most unusual lakes. White Lake has a bottom of white sand and perfectly clear water covering 1,065 acres. Unlike other bay lakes, White Lake is fed by underground springs and drains into the surrounding swamp while neighboring lakes are fed by water draining from the swamps and contain more tannic acid.

32. Bay Tree Lake State Natural Area is undeveloped public land protecting part of Bay Tree Lake, a large Carolina bay. Access is from NC-41.

33. Elizabethtown was laid out in 1773 and made the seat of Bladen County. Many of the early settlers of the Cape Fear River and Elizabethtown were Highland Scots. They and their descendants moved up the river and settled the counties northwest of Elizabethtown and founded Cross Creek, now Fayetteville.

Tory Hole Battleground. This historic site and recreation park occupies a ravine that connects Main Street in Elizabethtown with the

Cape Fear River. A battle took place at the ravine in August 1781 where Whigs broke the power of loyalists in Bladen County. Colonel Thomas Robeson and his seventy patriots surprised five times that number of loyalists one night. The patriots lined up to one side of their commander and fired. They quickly reloaded, rushed to the other side of the ravine and fired again. The loyalists believed that they were fighting many more men than were actually there and they panicked. Many of the loyalists escaped into the ravine and dispersed.

The park has a picnic shelter, playground, and exercise trail. Located adjacent to US-701 on the Cape Fear River.

34. Jones Lake State Park. Jones Lake is one of the largest Carolina bays in North Carolina. There are two trails; Jones Trail circles the lake and is 3.5 miles long, the nature trail is one mile long and passes through a bay forest.

Camping, picnicking, hiking, nature trail, boating, and swimming are activities enjoyed by visitors. Located on Highway 242 north of Elizabethtown. Open at 8 a.m. daily except Christmas Day. Closing time varies according to the season.

35 Bladen Lakes State Forest. This state reforestation project has interesting drives, trails, exhibits, and interpretative areas for the naturalist and recreationists. Trails are open from March through November.

36. Salters Lake State Natural Area adjoins Salters and Jones lakes. This area is maintained in its natural state for educational and scientific research. Tours may be arranged through the Jones Lake Park office.

37. Turnbull Creek Educational State Forest. This outdoor classroom has exhibits about the history and technology of the North Carolina forest and naval stores industry. Turnbull Creek Talking Tree Trail explains the natural history of a forest. A turpentine still and firefighting equipment are on display. Located on NC-242 north of Elizabethtown. Open mid-March through mid-November, 9 a.m.–5 p.m.

38. Harmony Hall (c. 1760). Harmony Hall is the colonial home of Colonel James Richardson. Lord Cornwallis used the house as a temporary headquarters near the end of the Revolution. Richardson's wife overheard the plans of General Cornwallis and had them relayed to her husband, who was serving with General Nathanael Greene in South Carolina. The Americans used the information to entrap the British at Yorktown.

The house has been restored to its 1760 appearance. The property also has a one-room school, general store, and a chapel. Harmony Hall contains almost 100 acres of land that lies on the east bank of the Cape Fear River. Located on NC-53 northwest of Elizabethtown near White Oak. Open Sundays, 2–4 p.m.

39. Horseshoe Lake is a black bear refuge and one of the nation's most extensive Carolina bay complexes. It is located in the Suggs Mill Pond Game Lands area. Camping, hiking, and hunting are permitted, please check regulations before entering. From NC-242 follow Gum Springs Road to Live Oak Church Road then look for the entrance.

Nearby

Lumberton is located on the Lumber River in Robeson County. The area was settled by Scottish, English, and Lumbee Indians. The Lumber River is designated a Natural and Scenic River. Lumberton hosts the Flora MacDonald Highland Games and an annual Revolutionary War battle re-enactment.

Lumbee Indians. The Lumbees are descendants of the Cheraw (Sara) tribe, a Siouan-speaking people. They are the largest tribe in the nation without a reservation and number about 40,000. They were generally ostracized from mainstream society during much of the nineteenth and twentieth centuries. Although they spoke English and were successful farmers. They lost much of their land because they had never held a legal title. In 1835, laws directed at controlling slaves came to apply to all non-whites and the Lumbees were denied the basic rights of citizenship.

During the Civil War they refused to fight for the Confederacy and many men took to the swamps. The times gave rise to the best known and most notorious Lumbee, Henry Berry Lowry. During the Civil War, he gathered about him a gang of exiled and refugee Lumbee Indians who raided prosperous plantations and gave their spoils to poor whites, blacks, and Indians. The band continued to operate until 1872 when Lowry disappeared from activity, never to be seen or heard from again.

Today, the Lumbees are achieving many political and social gains, reinvigorated by the civil rights movement of the 1950s and '60s. These proud and fearless people successfully drove the Ku Klux Klan from Robeson County during a Klan rally in January 1958. They then burned the Grand Wizard in effigy and the Klan never returned. Lumbee Tribe cultural activities are centered at the North Carolina Indian Cultural Center in Pembroke and at Pembroke State University.

Fayetteville. Fayetteville was called Cross Creek in early colonial times and was incorporated as Campbellton in 1762. It was settled by Scottish Highlanders who immigrated to America after the 1746 Battle of Culloden.

Museum of the Cape Fear. This regional museum tells the history of twenty southeastern counties in North Carolina. Located at the Fayetteville Arsenal. Open Tuesday through

Itinerary

Miles	Directions
	Begin at the North Carolina State Line in Calabash and travel east on NC-179.
2.3	Keep straight on Old Georgetown Road when 179 turns right
6.7	Left at the dead end onto Ocean Isle Beach Boulevard
1.9	Right on US-17
1.8	Right on Business 17 through Shallotte
4.0	Right on US-17
8.4	Right on Old Ocean Highway (Business US-17)
7.6	Right on US-17
.9	Right on Mill Creek Road
2.6	Left on George II Highway SE (NC-87)
.3	Right on Funston Road (becomes Dawes Creek Road)
7.0	Left on River Road (NC-133)
8.0	Keep straight across US-17 (right for Wilmington)
.2	Left on Old Fayetteville Road
1.7	Right on Andrew Jackson Highway (US-74)
2.4	Right on Mount Misery Road
13.0	Right on NC-87
16.1	Historic marker for Ashboro and the Bartram family

Saturday, 10 a.m.–5 p.m., and on Sunday, 1–5 p.m.

Cape Fear Botanical Garden. Located on US-301 at NC-24. Open daily 10 a.m.–5 p.m.

Clark Park and Nature Center. Located on the Cape Fear River at Sherman Drive.

Pauline Longest Nature Trail. Located at Methodist College, 5400 Ramsey Street.

Counties

Bladen County was formed in 1734 and named for Martin Bladen, Lord Commissioner of Trade and Plantations. Highland Scots began settling the Cape Fear River valley the same year. Bladen County originally covered a large area of southern North Carolina. It was later carved into fifty-five counties.

Brunswick County was formed in 1764 from New Hanover and Bladen. It is named for the ancestral German home of the King George I.

Columbus was formed in 1808 from Brunswick and Bladen. Named for Christopher Columbus.

New Hanover was named for the British royal family and the German state that was their ancestral home. Created in 1729 from Craven County.

Pender was formed in 1875 and named for Confederate General William D. Pender. The county seat is Burgaw and it is the heart of the North Carolina blueberry-growing region.

Sampson was formed in 1784 from Duplin County and named for Colonel John Sampson, a member of Governor Josiah Martin's council and first mayor of Wilmington.

Wilmington

Wilmington is named for Spencer Compton, Earl of Wilmington, patron of governor Gabriel Johnston. The community was first known as New Carthage, then New Liverpool, then New Town, and Newton. In 1735 Governor Johnston authorized that the community should become a town and he had streets surveyed. The offices of customs and naval officials were moved from Brunswick to Wilmington and Wilmington was made the port of entry. By the beginning of the Revolution Wilmington was the largest city in North Carolina with 1200 residents. Wilmington is located at the confluence of the Cape Fear River and the Northeast Cape Fear River, which made it an important port for products that were shipped from the interior of North Carolina.

One of the first acts of resistance to Parliament occurred in Wilmington in 1765 when citizens forced the stamp collector to resign. The same leaders and businessmen of Wilmington led North Carolina into the Revolution. British troops under the command of Major James Craig occupied Wilmington in November 1780. Lord Cornwallis marched into Wilmington in April 1781 and rested his troops there for eighteen days. He left Major James Craig in charge of the Cape Fear region which was the scene of several confrontations between patriot and loyalist militia. British troops evacuated Wilmington in November 1781 upon learning of the surrender of Cornwallis.

President Washington visited Wilmington in April 1791. He was honored with a ball by the townspeople. In the nineteenth century Wilmington became one of the largest ports in the world for shipping naval stores. The arrival of railroads in the 1840s brought growth and prosperity as inland products were shipped to Wilmington for export. Wilmington is now a center for film production and is home to the largest motion picture production facility east of Los Angeles. Wilmington's historic district includes 230 blocks and has undergone substantial revitalization during the last decade.

Easter weekend in Wilmington

Sites

1. Cape Fear Museum. This excellent regional museum has exhibits on the cultural and natural history of the Cape Fear River and coastal North Carolina. There are dioramas depicting life among the Cape Fear Indians before European contact and local industries that helped build Wilmington. One of the most extraordinary exhibits is the scale model of downtown Wilmington in 1863. The Discovery Gallery was built by native son, Michael Jordan. This exhibition area explains the natural history of the southeastern coast of North Carolina and the natural phenomena of weather, geology, and ecology. The Cape Fear Museum is the oldest historical museum in North Carolina, established in 1898.

Located at 814 Market Street. Open Tuesday through Saturday, 9 a.m.–5 p.m., and on Sunday from 2–5 p.m. Admission.

Sites

1. Cape Fear Museum
2. Saint James Cemetery
3. Saint James Episcopal Church,
4. Burgwin-Wright House
5. Lower Cape Fear Historical Society
6. Cape Fear Coast Convention Bureau and Visitors Information Center
7. New Hanover Public Library
8. Saint Johns Museum of Art
9. Mitchell-Smith-Anderson House
10. Dram Tree Park
11. Old City Market
12. Riverfront Visitor Information Center
13. Cotton Exchange
14. Wilmington Railroad Museum
15. Chamber of Commerce

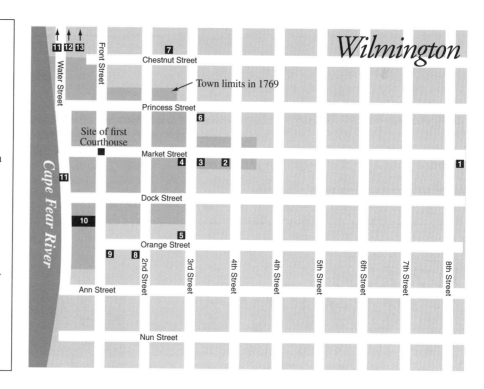

Wilmington

2. Saint James Cemetery was opened in 1745 and contains a number of graves dating from the eighteenth century. Saint James cemetery is the resting place of Cornelius Harnett, 1723–1781. Harnett was a major force in the Revolutionary movement in North Carolina and was a delegate to the Continental Congress from 1777 to 1780. He died of an illness that was complicated by his imprisonment during the British occupation of Wilmington. Saint James cemetery is located at the corner of Market and Fourth streets.

3. Saint James Episcopal Church was organized in 1729. The present church was constructed in 1840. Located at the corner of Market and Third streets.

4. Burgwin-Wright House, c. 1770, was built by John Burgwin, treasurer of North Carolina under Royal Governor Dobbs. The house was built on the foundation of the early town jail. While in Wilmington, General Lord Charles Cornwallis used the Burgwin House as his headquarters and used the basement as a prison. The parterre garden is planted in species that were typical of eighteenth century gardens. Located at 224 Market Street. Open Tuesday through Saturday, 10 a.m.–4 p.m. Admission.

5. Lower Cape Fear Historical Society. The Historical Society is housed in the Victorian-era Latimer House and contains archives and records for churches, cemeteries, property deeds, families, and diaries. The society operates a library of North and South Carolina history and a collection of maps, prints and photographs. While the house and gardens are open to the public the archives and library are reserved for historical society members, although membership fees are nominal. Located at 126 South Third Street. Open 10 a.m.–4 p.m., Tuesday through Saturday.

6. Cape Fear Coast Convention Bureau and Visitors Information Center. Information and maps are available at the visitors center and a twelve minute video introduces visitors to the Lower Cape Fear region. Located in the County Courthouse at Third and Princess streets. Open 8:30 a.m.–5 p.m., Monday through Friday; 9 a.m.–4 p.m. on Saturday; and 1–4 p.m on Sunday.

7. New Hanover Public Library. The library has a North Carolina Room that contains material for historical and genealogical research. Located at 201 Chestnut Street. Open Monday through Thursday, 9 a.m.–9 p.m.; Friday, 9 a.m.–6 p.m.; Saturday, 9 a.m.–5 p.m.; and Sunday 1–5 p.m.

8. Saint Johns Museum of Art. Exhibits include American and regional art from the past three centuries. The museum is housed in three adjacent historic buildings at 114 Orange Street. Open 10 a.m.–5 p.m., Tuesday through Saturday, and 12–4 p.m on Sunday.

9. Mitchell-Smith-Anderson House, 1740, is the oldest building in Wilmington. 102 Orange Street. Not open to the public.

10. Dram Tree Park provides access to the Cape Fear River and a view of the Wilmington riverfront. The Dram Tree was a large cypress that was a landmark for sailers coming up the Cape Fear River. Rum could be dispensed after passing the Dram Tree when arriving at Wilmington and put away at that point when leaving Wilmington. The tree stood until WW II when it was destroyed during construction. Located at Front Street immediately north of the US-17 bridge. Open during daylight hours.

11. Old City Market. The market has a variety of shops and vendors. Located at 119 South Water Street. Open at 10 a.m. and generally closes at 5 p.m. During summer months hours are 8 a.m.–6 p.m. on Friday and Saturday.

12. Riverfront Visitor Information Center. Located on the river near the foot of Market Street. Open daily, 9 a.m.–4:30 p.m., from April 1 through October 31.

13. Cotton Exchange. The Cotton Exchange building has been renovated and contains a mall of shops and restaurants. 300 North Front Street.

14. Wilmington Railroad Museum has rolling stock and railroading artifacts dating from the days of the Wilmington and Weldon Railroad in 1840. Located at the corner of Red Cross and Water streets. Open Monday through Saturday, 10 a.m.–5 p.m., and on Sunday, 1–5 p.m. Admission.

15. Wilmington Chamber of Commerce. Located on the river at One Estell Lee Place, just off Nutt Street. Open 8:30 a.m.–5 p.m., Monday through Friday.

Home Again

William Bartram remained at Ashwood in North Carolina during the early part of December 1776. He must have left his Uncle's home around December 12 or 13. Bartram wrote that he arrived at Alexandria, Virginia, on the day after Christmas. The distance of approximately 395 miles would have taken him two weeks if he traveled at thirty miles each day. His return to Philadelphia would have taken upwards of three weeks and he arrived home in very early January 1777, possibly around the second. Francis Harper researched and retraced Bartram's route in 1939 and 1940. In his book, *The Travels of William Bartram, Naturalist Edition*, Harper laid out a probable route from Ashwood to Philadelphia. Bartram was vague about much of the route, a distance of over 500 miles, and we must trust to the wisdom of Francis Harper in recreating the *Travels*. We can surmise that Bartram would have taken the more open, common roads because he was no longer on an exploratory journey. Much of the country through which Bartram traveled had been explored and described, just as he tells us, and there was nothing new to report.

We must believe that William Bartram also had a new goal in mind and that was to arrive home as soon as possible because the war was escalating and Philadelphia was threatened. General William Howe's British army captured New York in the fall of 1776 and swept across New Jersey during the winter of 1777. William arrived home at the Bartram Garden around January 2, 1777, and his father died in September just a few weeks before the British occupied Philadelphia.

William Bartram lived and worked at the Bartram Garden until his death on July 22, 1823. It is a curious fact that this enthusiastic and untiring traveler never again left the environs of

The Bartram House entrance lined with oakleaf hydrangea

Philadelphia. Although he did not venture out into the world, it seemed that for the next several decades the world came to him. Philadelphia was the center of American scientific research and education during Bartram's lifetime and many of America's first scientists made their pilgrimage to visit the humble botanist of Kingsessing. William Bartram was generous with his knowledge of natural history and unselfishly mentored the younger generation that laid the foundation of American natural science.

Philadelphia as seen from Bartram Gardens Park

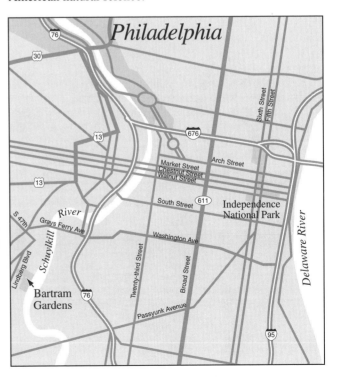

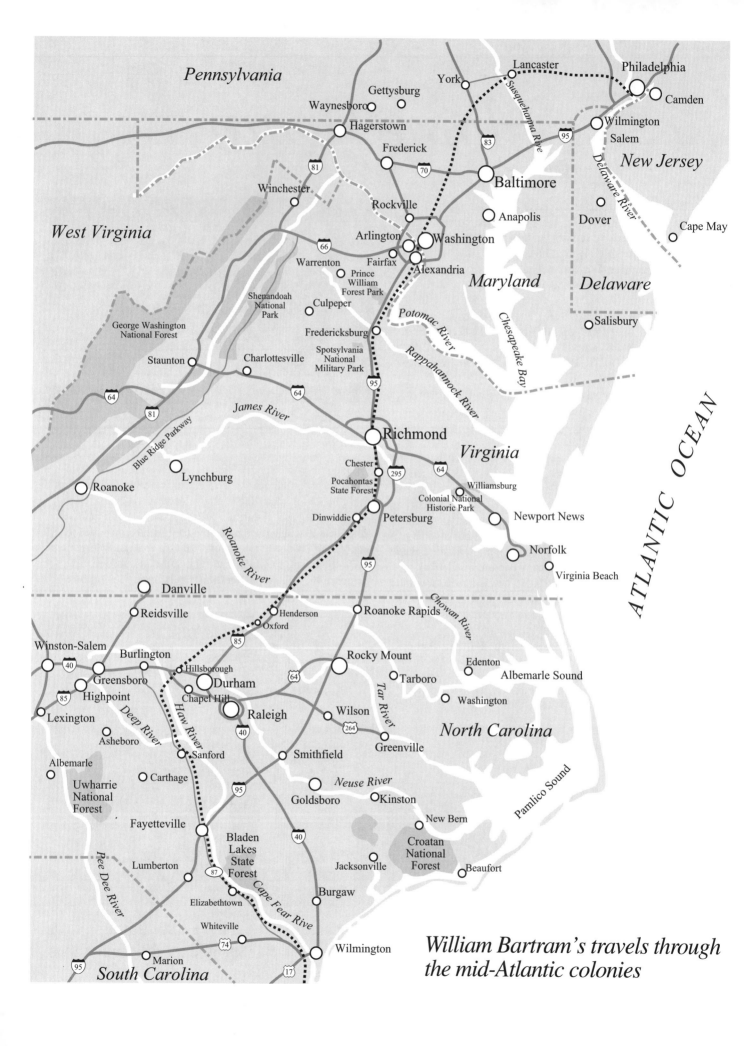

Appendix A

Timeline

Chronology of events relative to the lives of John and William Bartram

This timeline is intended to place into context the history of the Southern colonies and cultural events of England and the British colonies during the lifetime of John and William Bartram. Bartram entries are in bold.

1699   The Society for the Propagation for Christian Knowledge was founded by Reverend Thomas Bray.

Iberville began construction of Fort Maurepas at the site of Old Biloxi, now Ocean Springs, Mississippi. Old Biloxi was the capital of Louisiana until 1702 and again from 1719–20.

May 23, John Bartram was born in Darby, Pennsylvania.

1700   December 28, John Lawson began his travels through North and South Carolina.

1702   March 8, Queen Anne, second oldest child of James II, ascended the throne of England upon the death of William III.

October 1, South Carolina governor James Moore led an expedition of Indians and Carolinians against the Spanish missions in Florida. The invasion ended the Spanish mission system in Georgia. The invaders burned Saint Augustine but failed to subdue Castillo de San Marcos.

1702–13   Queen Anne's War, also known as the War of Spanish Succession, was the second of the Anglo-French conflicts known as the French and Indian Wars in North America.

1704   South Carolina destroyed most of the missions remaining outside the vicinity of Saint Augustine.

1705   The Navigation Laws were expanded to include molasses, rice, naval stores, and marine timber; requiring these products to be exported only to England.

1706   January 17, Benjamin Franklin was born in Boston.

1707   The Act of Union combined the legislative governments of England and Scotland. The union was thereafter known as the United Kingdom of Great Britain.

1711   Bienville built Fort Saint-Louis de la Mobile twelve miles north of present-day Mobile.

September 11, the Tuscarora War began in North Carolina and John Lawson was one of the first casualties.

1712   May 9, North and South Carolina were each given their own governor.

1713   March 23, the Tuscarora War ended and the Tuscaroras fled north to join the Iroquois League.

1714   Tea was introduced to the American colonies.

George I became King of England upon the death of Queen Anne.

1715   King Louis XIV died and Louis XV ascended the throne of France.

The Jacobite Rebellion began in Scotland in an attempt to restore the exiled James Francis Edward Stuart to the throne. James was to be King James VII of Scotland and James III of England.

April 14, The Yamassee War began at Pocotaligo in South Carolina.

1716   Combined South Carolina and Cherokee forces defeated the Yamassees at Pocotaligo, South Carolina.

1717   George Frederick Händel composed *Water Music* for King George I.

1717–18   The first wave of Ulster Scots emigrated from Ireland to the American colonies, numbering over 5,000 in the first year alone.

1718   Daniel Defoe wrote *Robinson Crusoe*.

San Antonio was settled in an attempt to check French influence on the Gulf Coast.

New Orleans was surveyed.

1719   The present-day city of Biloxi was founded.

1720   The Declaratory Act gave British Parliament power over Ireland.

The French Treasury was bankrupted by the Mississippi Bubble and collapse of stock values in the Company of the Indies.

1721   The first Germans settled in Louisiana north of New Orleans.

1722–25   Mark Catesby made botanical and biological explorations of South Carolina.

1722   May 23, Mark Catesby arrived in Charleston.

New Orleans became the capital of Louisiana.

1723   The first Dunkard Baptist Church was organized in Germantown, Pennsylvania.

John Bartram married Mary Maris.

1725   Roger Moore and Goose Creek families settled the lower Cape Fear River.

1725–29   Crop failures, excessive rents, and trade restraints forced the emigration of tens of thousands of Ulster Scots to the American colonies. The majority settled in Pennsylvania.

1726   Brunswick, North Carolina, was founded.

1727   George I died and George II became King of England.

Sir Isaac Newton died.

Mary Maris died.

1728   **John Bartram purchased the property that became the Bartram Garden.**

1729	Jonathan Swift published *A Modest Proposal*. Mark Catesby began work on the *The Natural History of Carolina, Florida, and the Bahama Islands* The Carolina Proprietors sold their patent to the Crown and North and South Carolina were separated. **October 10, John Bartram and Ann Mendenhall were married.**
1729	The Natchez War erupted in Louisiana. Georgetown, South Carolina, was surveyed.
1730	A quarter of the Cherokee population died of small pox. Nancy Ward was born.
1732	Benjamin Franklin began publishing *Poor Richard's Almanac*.
1732	Purrysburg, South Carolina, was settled by French and Swiss Protestants.
1733	February 12, James Edward Oglethorpe settled Savannah. **John Bartram began corresponding with Peter Collinson.**
1734	The Great Awakening began in England. Jonathan Edwards preached in Northampton, emphasizing man's sinful nature and the torments of eternal damnation.
1735	William Hogarth published his collection of prints titled "A Rake's Progress." Augustus Gootlieb Spangenberg established near Savannah the first Moravian community in America. They moved to Pennsylvania in 1741.
1736	February 5, John Wesley arrived in Savannah as spiritual leader of Georgia and missionary to the Creeks but returned to England within the year. **Spring, John Bartram began his travels in search of plants and seeds. His first excursion outside the environs of Philadelphia was to Cedar Swamp in New Jersey.** **Fall, John Bartram traveled toward the headwaters of the Schuylkill River in the Pennsylvania mountains.**
1737	**Fall, John Bartram traveled throughout the eastern shore of Maryland and Virginia.**
1738	**May, John Bartram discovered American ginseng on the Susquehanna River.** **September 25–October 26, John Bartram traveled to the western shore of Virginia, the Shenandoah Valley, and Blue Ridge Mountains.**
1739	The Philadelphia Academy was founded by Benjamin Franklin and associates. It was the first secular college in North America and was the first to offer a liberal arts education. It became the University of Pennsylvania in 1779. Oglethorpe established a presence on Amelia and Fort George islands in Florida and captured forts Picolata and Poppa on the Saint Johns River. George Whitefield became the spiritual leader of Georgia and brought the Great Awakening to the American Colonies. The War of Jenkins' Ear began and then merged with the War of Austrian Succession in Europe, also known as King George's War. It involved a dispute over the Georgia-Florida boundary and economic rivalry between Spain and England. **April 20, William and Elizabeth Bartram were born at Kingsessing on the Schuylkill River, west of Philadelphia. His date of birth was recorded as "2 mo. 9" which has been thought to mean February 9. By the old Quaker calendar that date is actually April 9, which is April 20 by the modern calendar.**
1740	Famine in northern Ireland caused the deaths of 400,000 people and initiated a third wave of emigration from Ulster that included a quarter of the population. Scotch-Irish settlers began flooding into the western part of Pennsylvania, Virginia, and North Carolina. February 25, Wilmington was incorporated and became the port of entry for the lower part of North Carolina
1740	**February, John Bartram began a correspondence with Mark Catesby.** *May 10*, Georgians and South Carolinians invaded Florida and besieged Saint Augustine but failed to take Castillo de San Marcos. **September, John Bartram explored north of Philadelphia, into the Blue Mountains, and to the Delaware Water Gap.**
1741	**May 20–early summer, John Bartram traveled to the Catskill Mountains and Albany, New York.** **July, John Bartram began a correspondence with Hans Sloane.**
1742	George Frederick Handel wrote *The Messiah*. July 7, Oglethorpe's Highland Regiment defeated the Spanish army at Bloody Marsh on Saint Simons Island.
1743	**Benjamin Franklin and John Bartram founded the American Philosophical Society.**
1745	July 1, Charles Edward Stuart, the grandson of James II, landed in Scotland and began his attempt to regain the throne of Great Britain.
1746	April 16, Scottish supporters of Prince Charles Edward Stuart were defeated at the Battle of Culloden Moor.
1748	September 1, Brunswick, North Carolina, was attacked by the Spanish ship *Fortuna*.
1749	October 26, slavery was officially sanctioned in Georgia. December 23, Mark Catesby died in London.
1750	**Fall, John Bartram traveled to the Delaware Water Gap.**
1751	The first sugarcane was grown in Louisiana. April 1, the Virginia House of Burgesses questioned the right of Parliament to interfere in colonial affairs.
1752	**William Bartram entered the Philadelphia Academy.** September 2, the Gregorian calender supplanted the Julian calender, the next day became September 14.
1753	**September, John and William Bartram traveled to the Catskill Mountains.**
1754	The French and Indian War began in North America. In Europe the conflict was known as the Seven Years War. July 4, George Washington surrendered Fort Necessity to the French. **Late Summer, John and William Bartram traveled to the Catskill Mountains and met Dr. Alexander Garden at the home of Cadwallader Colden.**
1755	Samuel Johnson's *Dictionary of the English Language* was published. **Benjamin Franklin offered to take William as a printer's apprentice, but John Bartram declined be-**

cause he thought the trade was too often unprofitable. Dr. Alexander Garden offered to take William as a physician's apprentice, but John Bartram declined that offer also because he felt that William was interested only because of Garden's botanical knowledge.

William Bartram's drawings were sent to Peter Collinson and shown to his circle of friends.

Late Summer–Fall, John and William Bartram traveled to New York and Connecticut.

October 8, the Acadians were expelled from Canada and dispersed throughout the British colonies.

November 27, Joseph Salvador purchased 100,000 acres near Ninety Six, South Carolina, and began the first Jewish settlement in America.

1756 May 17, Britain declared war on France and began the Seven Years War (1756-63). The conflict eventually involved most of the European powers.

William Bartram was apprenticed to merchant James Child.

1758 John Bartram was removed from membership of the Darby Meeting of Friends because he did not acknowledge the divinity of Jesus. He continued to attend meetings for the rest of his life.

1759 Voltaire wrote *Candide*.

The British Museum opened.

Late October, John Bartram and John Bartram, Jr., traveled to the Shenandoah Valley and the Blue Ridge Mountains of Virginia.

1760–62 The Cherokee War

1760 **March, John Bartram sailed to Charleston**

April, Bartram sailed to the Wilmington and traveled to his Brother William's home. He returned home through Virginia.

August 7, Fort Loudon was captured by the Cherokees.

September 8, The French surrendered Montreal to the British and ended the French and Indian War.

October 25, George III ascended the throne of England upon the death of his grandfather, George II.

1761 **Summer, William Bartram opened a mercantile business near his Uncle William's plantation on the Cape Fear River.**

September, John Bartram traveled to Pittsburg.

December 2, the Royal Governors were instructed to obtain permission from Parliament before purchasing Indian lands or making grants on Indian lands.

1762 **June, William Bartram returned to Philadelphia on business.**

August, John Bartram, William and Moses Bartram traveled through Virginia Piedmont and into North Carolina. At Yadkin, William and Moses traveled to Ashboro and John continued on into the South Carolina Piedmont beyond Camden.

December 3, France ceded Louisiana and Isle de Orleans to Spain.

1763 February 10, the Treaty of Paris officially ended the Seven Years War (French & Indian War). England obtained possession of East & West Florida from Spain in exchange for Cuba.

April, John Wilkes was arrested for writing an article in the *North Briton 45* that criticized the King and his hand-picked prime minister, the Earl of Bute. Wilkes became a cause célèbre, which lead to greater freedom of the press in England and the inclusion of that concept in the first amendment to the United States Constitution.

October 8, the Royal Proclamation forbade whites taking up lands west of a line demarcating the boundary of Indian lands.

1765 March 22, the Stamp Act received royal approval.

April 9, John Bartram was appointed His Majesty's Botanist in North America.

May 24, the Quartering Act became law and required the American colonies to house and feed British soldiers.

July 7, John Bartram arrived in Charleston.

July 16, Bartram left Charleston and traveled to Ashboro.

August 6, John and William Bartram returned to Charleston.

August 29, the Bartrams left Charleston.

September 4, the Bartrams arrived in Savannah. They lodged with James Habersham and met with Governor Wright. They left Savannah the next day and traveled north along the Augusta Road. On the way they visited Silver Bluff and Shell Bluff. They explored the Savannah River with George Galphin.

September 12, the Bartrams arrived in Augusta. They left Augusta on the 18th.

September 24, the Bartrams dined with Governor James Wright.

September 25, the Bartrams visited Bethesda.

September 29, the Bartrams spent the evening at Beverly, James Habersham's country home.

September 30, the Bartrams began their trip to East Florida and crossed the Ogeechee River. They lodged near Riceboro.

October 1, they reached Fort Barrington where they discovered Franklinia, fevertree, and Ogeechee lime.

October 5, the Bartrams left the Altamaha River and traveled south on the Old Post Road, then known as the Savannah to Saint Augustine Road.

October 7, the Stamp Act Congress met in New York and issued the Declaration of Rights and Grievances which claimed that the colonists were due the complete rights of English citizens. **The Bartrams crossed the Satilla River.**

October 11, the Bartrams arrived in Saint Augustine. They dined with Governor James Grant the next day. John contracted malaria.

November, the Stamp Act became effective law, colonial ports were closed because stamps were not available.

November 16, the Bartrams attended the Indian conference at Picolata.

December, the Sons of Liberty was organized in the colonies.

December 22, the Bartrams set out on their trip up the St. Johns River.

December 26, they visited Charlotia and Murphy Island.

December 31, they reached Spalding's Lower Store near Palatka.

1766 **January 12, the Bartrams reached their farthest point near the headwaters of the St. Johns River near Titusville. They started back downriver the next day.**

January 19, they arrived at Spalding's Upper Store.

Timeline 327

January 23, the Bartrams explored around Silver Glen Springs.

January 24, William Bartram discovered *Illicium floridanum*, star anise.

Early February, the Bartrams explored the lower St. Johns River.

Mid-February, the Bartrams returned to Saint Augustine. William decided to remain in Florida and become a planter. He took a land grant near Fort Picolata.

March 18, the Stamp Act was repealed. The Declaratory Act was passed, which stated that Parliament and the King had the right to make laws for the American colonies.

March 22, John Bartram arrived in Charleston and spent several weeks preparing his specimens for shipping. With the advice of Henry Laurens John purchased slaves, supplies, and seeds to send to William.

April 22, John Bartram arrived home in Philadelphia.

July 6, William Bartram was visited by Henry Laurens. Laurens reported to John Bartram that William's prospect as a planter looked dim and advised that John encourage his son to abandon the scheme. Sometime in the late summer William sold out and went to work for William De Brahm surveying the land for the colony of New Smyrna. Sometime around December William was shipwrecked just off the New Smyrna Beach.

1767   June 29, the Townshend Revenue Acts were passed to raise taxes in the American colonies. The revenue was to pay for governors and judges, retire debts arising from the French and Indian War, and to pay for defense of the colonies. Colonists were required to pay duty on tea, glass, oil, lead, paper, and paint colors.

Dr. John Fothergill became acquainted with William Bartram's work and ordered drawings of shells and turtles.

Fall, William Bartram returned to Philadelphia. He worked as a laborer for awhile then returned to the mercantile business in Philadelphia.

1768   The Royal Academy was founded.

The first edition of *Encyclopedia Britannica* was published.

Captain James Cook explored the Pacific Ocean.

April 11, Peter Collinson died.

February 11, the Massachusetts Lower House of Assembly wrote to the colonial legislatures requesting cooperation in seeking repeal of the Townshend Acts.

October 1, two regiments of British troops arrived in Boston to enforce the authority of Parliament.

1769   James Watt patented the steam engine.

April 26, John Bartram was elected to the Royal academy of Sciences of Stockholm.

1770   The College of Charleston was established, though classes did not commence until 1790.

The population of the British colonies in North America was 2,205,000.

Lord Frederick North became Prime Minister of England and began tightening control over the American colonies.

Richard Arkwright and associates built the first water powered spinning mill in Derbyshire, England, which started the factory system of manufacturing and fueled the industrial revolution in textile manufacture.

March 5, citizens of Boston taunted British soldiers who fired upon the crowd, killing five and wounding many others. The incident became known as the Boston Massacre.

April 12, the Townshend Revenue Acts were repealed, except for the tax on tea.

September, William was threatened by a creditor. He abruptly left Philadelphia and turned up at his uncle's home in North Carolina.

October 24, William Bartram's beloved Uncle William died.

1771–75   Over 50,000 Presbyterians emigrated from Ulster to North America and settled primarily in North and South Carolina, where they formed a majority of the backcountry population and became ardent patriots.

1772   Denis Diderot completed his *Encyclopedie*, which was the greatest collection of knowledge of the day and a monument to the Enlightenment.

Summer, William proposed that Dr. Fothergill fund a trip to Florida. That fall Fothergill authorized Dr. Lionel Chalmers of Charleston to allow Bartram a stipend of £50 and additional payments for each drawing. In return William would ship seeds and plants to Fothergill.

1773   The Watauga Association was organized by John Sevier and James Robertson to govern the trans-Appalachian settlements in present day eastern Tennessee.

January 12, the Charleston Museum was founded.

March 20, William Bartram departed Philadelphia.

March 31, Bartram arrived in Charleston to begin his travels in the South.

April 11 or 12, William Bartram arrived in Savannah.

April 16, he traveled to Midway, Sunbury, Darien, and Brunswick.

April 27, the Tea Act was passed in an effort to save the East India Company from bankruptcy. It enabled the company to undercut the prices of American tea merchants.

May 1, Bartram departed Darien with young John McIntosh as a traveling companion.

May 3, he arrived in Savannah.

May 5, he visited Ebenezer.

May 9, he crossed Savannah River to Silver Bluff and visited with George Galphin.

May 14, Bartram reached Augusta.

May 16–19, he visited Wrightsborough.

June 1, the Second Treaty of Augusta was concluded.

June 7, the survey party departed Augusta.

June 21, the survey party departed Wrightsborough and traveled up the north side of Little River to the Great Buffalo Lick, Cherokee Corner, and to the Tugaloo River.

Mid-July, William Bartram returned to Savannah.

Mid July 1773–March 1774, Bartram made excursions around Savannah and the Georgia coast. He was ill for several weeks during the summer of 1773 and recuperated at the home of Lachlan McIntosh in Darien.

December 16, the Boston Tea Party destroyed £18,000 worth of tea. Parliament began enacting a series of laws intended to punish Boston and subdue the democratic element and thus began the series of events leading to war.

1774   January 14, Coweta Creeks attacked settlers at Sherrill's Fort west of Wrightsborough.

January 29, in a Privy Council hearing to remove Massachusetts governor Thomas Hutchinson, Benjamin Franklin was publicly reprimanded and humiliated. That day he turned away from reconciliation and stated to Alexander Wedderburn, "I will make your master a little king for this."

March 31, the Coercive Acts were passed by Parliament in an effort to exert control over the colonies. The port of Boston was closed and the Massachusetts legislature lost some of its authority.

March, Bartram traveled to Frederica, then by boat to Cumberland Island and Amelia Island. He purchased a boat near present-day Jacksonville.

Mid-April he sailed up the St. Johns River, and arrived at Spalding's Lower Store near Palatka.

Late April, he traveled to Alachua Savannah (Gainesville) and Cuscowilla (Micanopy).

May 10, Louis XVI became King of France.

May 20, Parliament passed the Massachusetts Act which forbade public meetings in Massachusetts unless authorized by the governor.

May 20, the Administration of Justice Act provided that all British officials accused of capital crimes must be transported to England for trial.

Mid-May through early June, Bartram traveled to Lake George and Spalding's Upper Store. He had an encounter with the menacing alligators and visited Blue Springs

Mid-June–mid-July, he returned to Alachua Savannah, traveled to the Suwannee River, and explored Manatee Springs.

July 6, the First Provincial Congress of South Carolina met in Charleston.

August 10, Georgia Whigs met at Tondee's Tavern and drew up resolutions condemning British occupation of Boston and demanding equal rights as British citizens.

August 25, the first North Carolina Provincial Congress was convened at New Bern.

August–September, Bartram made an excursion up the St. John's River.

September 5, the First Continental Congress convened in Philadelphia.

September 17, the Suffolk Resolves of Massachusetts organized opposition to the Intolerable Acts.

November, Bartram departed East Florida.

November 10, he arrived at Broughton Island and prepared his specimens.

1775 Daniel Boone began cutting the Wilderness Road to Kentucky.

The Treaty of Sycamore Shoals opened up Kentucky for settlement.

Lord North extended the Restraining Act which forbade colonies from trading with any country other than Great Britain.

1775 January 11, Francis Salvador was elected to the South Carolina Provincial Congress and became the first Jew elected to public office in America.

March 25, Bartram arrived in Charleston.

March 26, the South Carolina Provincial Congress adopted a constitution and established an independent government with John Rutledge as president.

April 19, occurred the battles of Lexington and Concord.

April 22, Bartram departed Charleston for the Cherokee Nation.

May, John Stuart left Charleston and sought safety in Savannah.

Early May, Bartram traveled from Augusta to Fort James.

May 10, the Second Continental Congress began in Philadelphia.

May 10, Bartram left Fort James and crossed the Savannah River near Calhoun Falls. He traveled through Abbeville County and lodged with Alexander Cameron for several days.

May 15, he reached Seneca.

About May 19, he departed Fort Prince George and crossed Oconee Mountain. He crossed the Chatooga River at Earl's Ford and followed Warwoman Creek. He passed through Clayton and then traveled north along the Little Tennessee River.

May 20, the Mecklenburg Resolves were adopted in Charlotte. This document was the first declaration of independence from the authority of parliament. The Resolves suspended Royal officials from office in North Carolina, established a militia, and provided that all public income be received by the Resolves Committee.

May 22, William Bartram arrived at Cowee and explored the Cowee Mountains.

May 24, he departed Cowee and crossed the Nantahala Mountains at Burningtown Gap.

May 25, General William Howe, Sir Henry Clinton, General John Burgoyne, and British troops began the occupation of Boston.

May 27, Bartram returned to Cowee.

May 30, he returned to Fort Prince George.

Early June, he returned to Fort James and explored the Broad River.

June 15, George Washington was elected commander in chief of the Continental Army.

June 17, the Second Georgia Provincial Congress was held at Tondee's Tavern, Savannah.

June 22, Bartram left Fort James and crossed the Savannah River to Fort Charlotte where he joined a party of traders bound for Mobile. They traveled along the east side of the river and lodged near New Bordeaux at the farm of Jean Louis de Mesnil du St. Pierre. They crossed the Savannah River north of Augusta and entered the Lower Creek Trading Path.

June 27, they camped at Flat Rock.

July 1, they camped at Rock Landing on the Oconee River.

July 3, they crossed the Ocmulgee River.

July 5, they crossed the Flint River at site of the future Creek Agency.

July 11, Bartram arrived at Yuchi Town on the Chattahoochee River.

July 13, he departed the Lower Creek towns and traveled along the south side of Uchee Creek, passed through Tuskegee, and crossed Uphapee Creek to Talasi.

July 16(?), he traveled from Talasi to Kolomi.

July 19(?), he traveled through the Alabama prairies (Montgomery County).

July 20(?), he crossed Pintlala Creek near the present-day town of Pintlala.

July 21(?), he passed through Fort Deposit and followed the trading path that coincides with the present-day Conecuh-Monroe county boundary.

July 26(?), he arrived at Major Farmar's plantation on the Tensaw River.

July 30 or 31, William Bartram arrived in Mobile.

August 5, he returned to the Farmar plantation where he spent several days exploring the Tensaw River and made a trip upriver to the lower part of the Tombigbee River.

Mid-August, he explored Baldwin County to the north of Stockton.

September 4 & 5, he visited Pensacola and returned to Mobile on the 6th.

September 15, Royal Governor William Campbell dissolved the South Carolina Assembly and sought refuge aboard the *Tamar*.

September 7, Bartram became very ill yet sailed from Mobile on the 8th and reached the Pearl River in a day or two. He stayed at the home of a Frenchman for three days

Mid-September through the middle of October, Bartram recuperated from his illness at Mr. Rumsey's plantation.

About October 21, Bartram reached the Mississippi River at Manchac. He traveled to Baton Rouge in company of William Dunbar.

October 27, Bartram and Dunbar explored north of Baton Rouge and on the 28th they visited Pointe Coupee.

About November 10, he departed Baton Rouge.

November 27, he departed Mobile.

About December 4, he arrived on the Tallapoosa River. He visited Fort Toulouse, Alabama Town, Muklasa, Tuckabatchee, Kolomi, and Atasi.

1776   Adam Smith wrote *An Investigation into the Nature and Causes of the Wealth of Nations*.

January 2, Bartram departed the Upper Creek Towns.

January 14–18, he stayed in Augusta.

Late January, he arrived in Savannah.

February 11, Governor James Wright fled Savannah to a British ship anchored at the mouth of the Savannah River. Archibald Bulloch became President of Georgia.

March 3, a fleet of seven British ships and 200 soldiers sailed up the Savannah River with the possible intention of retaking Savannah or simply stealing rice. Lachlan McIntosh ordered the militia to fire upon the British and burn the merchant ships lying in the river. The British escaped with fourteen boatloads of rice and the incident became known as the Battle of the Rice Boats.

Spring and summer, Bartram explored the Georgia coast and traveled to the St. Mary's River where he had an encounter with the "intrepid Siminole."

April 12, North Carolina became the first British colony to advocate independence when the provincial congress adopted the Halifax Resolves instructing the North Carolina delegates to the Continental Congress to urge independence and cooperation among the American colonies.

June 28, the South Carolina army repulsed a British attack on Sullivan's Island.

July, William Bartram was involved in the defense of Georgia as a volunteer in the militia commanded by Lachlan McIntosh. During July McIntosh marched the militia to the St. Marys River to head off an expected invasion from Florida. Bartram probably engaged in reconnaissance for McIntosh and was not engaged in combat.

July 4, the Declaration of Independence was adopted in Philadelphia.

July 31, Bartram sailed up the Altamaha River.

Late October, he departed Darien for Savannah.

Early November, he Bartram left Savannah.

Early December, he arrived at Ashwood, on the Cape Fear River.

December 12 or 13, he departed Ashwood.

December 26, he arrived in Alexandria.

1777   **About January 2, William Bartram arrived home in Philadelphia**

September 22, John Bartram died.

September 26, The British began the occupation of Philadelphia.

1778   Voltaire died.

February 6, the Treaty of Commerce and Alliance brought France into the Revolution as an American ally.

June 18, The British army evacuated Philadelphia.

August 26, William Bartram signed the Affirmation of Allegiance and Fidelity to the government of Pennsylvania.

December 29, Savannah fell to Lt. Colonel Archibald Campbell.

1779   March 3, the Americans, led by General John Ashe, were defeated at the Battle of Briar Creek in Georgia. Three hundred Americans were killed or wounded and numerous others deserted. The defeat weakened enthusiasm for the patriot cause.

March 14, Pennsylvania became the first state to abolish slavery.

June 21, Spain declared war against Great Britain.

July 14, Royal Governor James Wright returned to British occupied Savannah.

September 21, Governor Bernardo de Gálvez of Louisiana captured Baton Rouge from the British.

October 9, French and American forces attacked but failed to take Savannah.

1780   March 14, Governor Gálvez captured Mobile

May 12, General Benjamin Lincoln surrendered Charleston to Sir Henry Clinton.

May 25, Thomas Brown and the King's Carolina Rangers occupied Augusta without opposition.

June 1, General Cornwallis established headquarters in Camden, South Carolina.

June 18, the British captured Ninety Six, South Carolina.

August 16, American forces under General Horatio Gates were defeated at the Battle of Camden by forces commanded by General Charles Cornwallis. Baron Johann de Kalb was fatally wounded.

October 7, British forces commanded by Major Patrick Ferguson were defeated at the Battle of King's Mountain, South Carolina. The American forces were commanded by Colonel William Campbell, Colonel Isaac Shelby, and Colonel Benjamin Cleveland.

December 26, John Fothergill died in London.

1781   Emmanuel Kant wrote *Critique of Pure Reason*.

January 17, General Daniel Morgan's militia and Continentals defeated Banastre Tarleton's dragoons and infantry at Cowpens, South Carolina. This marked the turning point of the war in the South in favor of the Americans.

March 1, the Articles of Confederation was ratified.

March 15, at the Battle of Guilford Courthouse General Cornwallis won a costly victory against General Nathaneal Greene. Cornwallis withdrew to Wilmington, North Carolina, and left much of the South without British reinforcements.

May 10, Governor Gálvez captured Pensacola.

	October 19, General Charles Cornwallis surrendered his army at Yorktown, Virginia.
	December 14, Charleston was returned to American control.
	July 11, British soldiers, officials, and loyalists evacuated Savannah.
	November 30, the preliminary meeting for the Treaty of Paris was held.
1782	**William Bartram was offered the position of professor of botany at the University of Pennsylvania. Though there are no records that he declined the position, he never lectured.**
1783	August 13, Charles Town, South Carolina, was incorporated as Charleston.
	September 3, The Treaty of Paris ended the American Revolution. The new American nation included all land from the Atlantic coast to the Mississippi River. England retained Canada and Spain held Louisiana and East and West Florida.
1784	**Ann Mendenhall Bartram died.**
	January 14, the Anglo-American Accord was ratified by Congress. The accord recognized the United States as a legitimate nation with a western boundary at the Mississippi River.
1785	**Humphrey Marshall, William Bartram's cousin, published *Arbustum Americanum*.**
	Edmund Cartwright patented the first power-driven loom.
	January 27, the University of Georgia was chartered. The first degree was awarded in 1804.
	March 19, the College of Charleston was chartered.
1786	**William Bartram fell from a cypress tree while gathering seeds and broke his leg. The fracture caused him continuing difficulty and limited his ability to travel. He was visited by André and François Michaux in September.**
	September 21, André and François Michaux arrived in Charleston.
1787	May 25, the Constitutional Convention convened in Philadelphia.
	June 10, George Washington visited the Bartram Garden.
	July 14, The Bartram Garden received a visit from Alexander Hamilton, James Madison, George Mason, John Rutledge, and other members of the Constitutional Convention.
	September 17, the Constitution was signed by the Constitutional Convention and presented to Congress.
	George Washington was elected president of the United States.
1789	**William Bartram wrote *Observations on the Creek and Cherokee Indians*. William Aiton published *Hortus Kewensis* in London and attributed twenty-one plant discoveries to William Bartram.**
	July 14, the Bastille was stormed by a Parisian mob and began the French Revolution.
	December, the University of North Carolina was chartered in Chapel Hill. The first degree was awarded in 1798.
1790	Samuel Slater built the first cotton spinning mill in Pawtucket, Rhode Island.
	April 17, Benjamin Franklin died in Philadelphia.
1791	**William Bartram's *Travels* was published in Philadelphia by James and Johnson. The copyright was recorded on August 26.**
	Slaves revolted in Santo Domingo, causing Creole planters to flee to Louisiana, Charleston, and Savannah.
	Summer, President George Washington traveled through the Southern states.
	October 1, the French National Legislative Assembly held its first meeting.
	December 5, Mozart died.
1792	Eli Witney built the first cotton gin at Mulberry Grove Plantation north of Savannah.
	September 21, the French National Assembly abolished the Monarchy.
	September 22, the French Republic was proclaimed.
1793	January 21, Louis XVI was executed.
	February 12, the Fugitive Slave Act became law.
	June 2, Robbespiere began the Reign of Terror during the formation of the French Republic.
1794	The Whiskey Rebellion erupted in western Pennsylvania; an armed protest against tax on distilled spirits. George Washington lead an army to Bedford and arrested leaders of the revolt. Washington's action established the authority of the federal government over state sovereignty and strengthened the legitimacy of the infant government in the eyes of European powers. This was the only time a sitting president of the United States commanded an army in the field.
1795	October 26, Napoleon Bonaparte became commander of the French Army.
1796	June 1, Tennessee was admitted to the Union.
1797	John Adams became the second president of the United States.
1800	The Library of Congress was established.
1801	Thomas Jefferson became the third president of the United States.
	Ireland became an official part of the United Kingdom.
1800	October 1, the Treaty of San Ildefonso returned Louisiana to France.
1802	**William Bartram befriended Alexander Wilson.**
1803	Benjamin Smith Barton published *Elements of Botany* which included illustrations by William Bartram.
	April 30, the Louisiana Purchase was concluded.
1804–06	The Corps of Discovery, lead by Meriwether Lewis and William Clark, explored the American West.
	William Bartram published "Anecdotes of an American Crow" and "Some Account of the Late Mr. John Bartram, of Pennsylvania" in the *Philadelphia Medical and Physical Journal*.
1806	Noah Webster published *A Compendious Dictionary of the English Language*.
	February, William Bartram declined President Thomas Jefferson's offer to serve as naturalist on the Red River expedition.

1808	Alexander Wilson published the first volume of *American Ornithology*.
1809	James Madison became the fourth president of the United States.
1810	October 27, The United States annexed the West Florida Republic.
	William Bartram began mentoring Thomas Say, his nephew, who published America's first book of entomology.
1812	**John Bartram, Jr. died. The Bartram Garden was left to his daughter Ann and her husband Robert Carr.**
	The Academy of Natural Sciences was founded in Philadelphia and William Bartram was elected to membership.
	April 30, Louisiana was admitted to the Union.
	May 14, Mississippi Territory was organized.
1813–14	First Creek War.
1813	April 15, the United States took possession of Mobile and all of West Florida lying west of the Perdido River
	August 30, Red Stick Creeks attacked Fort Mims and killed several hundred whites and mestizo Creeks.
1814	The first cotton spinning and weaving mill in the United States was built in Waltham, Massachusetts.
	August 9, the Treaty of Fort Jackson took over half of the Creek Nation's land.
	August 24–25, a British army invaded Washington D.C. and burned the White House and Capitol.
1815	January, Congress authorized $23,950 to purchase Thomas Jefferson's personal library of 6,487 books to replenish the Library of Congress collection burned by the British.
1817	James Monroe became the fifth president of the United States.
	March 3, Alabama Territory was created.
	December 10, Mississippi was admitted to the Union.
1818	The First Seminole War.
1819	December 14, Alabama was admitted to the Union.
1820	King George III died.
1821	Sequoyah completed his Cherokee alphabet. Within six months twenty-five percent of the Cherokee population had learned to read.
	February 22, the Adams-Onis Treaty completed the transfer of East Florida to the United States.
1822	March 30, Florida Territory was created.
	May, the Denmark Vesey slave revolt was discovered in Charleston.
1823	**July 22, William Bartram died at his home outside Philadelphia. He was buried the next day in an unmarked grave.**

Appendix B
Publications about John & William Bartram

Bartram, John. *Diary of a Journey through the Carolinas, Georgia, and Florida*. Annotated by Francis Harper. Philadelphia: American Philosophical Society, 1942.

Bartram, William. *Travels Through North and South Carolina. Georgia. East and West Florida, the Cherokee Country, the Extensive Territories of the Muscoculges, or Creek Confederacy, and the Country of the Chactaws*. Philadelphia: James and Johnson, 1791.

———. *Travels*. Introduction by Mark Van Doren. New York: Dover, 1928.

———. *Travels*. Introduction by James Dickey. New York: Viking Penguin, 1988.

———. *Travels*. Introduction by Gordon DeWolf. Facsimile of the 1792 London edition. Savannah: Beehive Press, 1973.

———. *William Bartram; Travels and Other Writings*. Edited by Thomas P. Slaughter. New York: The Library of America, 1996.

John and William Bartram's America. Selected passages and documents. New York: Devin-Adair, 1957.

Berkeley, Edmund, and Dorothy Smith Berkeley. *The Correspondence of John Bartram, 1734–1777*. Gainesville: University Presses of Florida, 1992.

Berkeley, Edmund, and Dorothy Smith Berkeley. *The Life and Travels of John Bartram: From Lake Ontario to the River St. John*. Tallahassee: University Presses of Florida, 1982.

Carr, Archie. *A Naturalist in Florida: a Celebration of Eden*. Edited by Marjorie H. Carr. New Haven: Yale University Press, 1994.

Cashin, Edward J. *William Bartram and the American Revolution on the Southern Frontier*. Columbia: University of South Carolina Press, 2000.

Cruickshank, Helen G., editor. *Bartram in Florida: 1774. The Adventures of the Great American Naturalist, Explorer, Artist*. Florida Federation of Garden Clubs, Inc., 1986.

Cutting, R. M. *John and William Bartram, William Byrd, and St. John de Crevecoueur: a Reference Guide*. 1976.

Earnest, Ernest P. *John and William Bartram, Botanists and Explorers*. Philadelphia: University of Pennsylvania Press, 1940.

Edwards, Jr., Elliott O. *Proceedings of the Symposium: Celebration of Travels, 1791*. Savannah: The Bartram Trail Conference, 1991.

Elman, Robert. *First in the Field: America's Pioneering Naturalists*. New York: Van Nostrand Reinhold, 1977.

Ewan, Joseph. *William Bartram: Botanical and Zoological Drawings*. 1756–1788. Philadelphia: Memoirs of the American Philosophical Society, Volume 74. 1968.

Fagin, N. Brylion. *William Bartram: Interpreter of the American Landscape*. Baltimore: Johns Hopkins University Press, 1933.

Harper, Francis. *The Travels of William Bartram: Naturalist Edition*. New Haven: Yale University Press, 1958.

———. *The Travels of William Bartram: Naturalist Edition*. Athens: The University of Georgia Press, 1998.

Herbst, Josephine. *New Green World: John Bartram and the Early Naturalists*. New York: Hastings House, 1954.

Kastner, Joseph. *A Species of Eternity*. New York: E. P. Dutton, 1977.

McInnes, Martha, et al. *Bartram Heritage: a Study of the Life of William Bartram*. Montgomery: The Bartram Trail Conference, 1979.

Porter, Charlotte M. *Eagle's Nest: Natural History and American Ideas. 1812–1842*. Tuscaloosa: University of Alabama Press, 1986.

Sanger, Marjory Bartlett. *Billy Bartram and His Green World*. New York: Farrar, Straus & Giroux, 1972.

Slaughter, Thomas P., editor. *William Bartram: Travels and Other Writings*. Includes the report to Dr. Fothergill and reproductions of his drawings. New York: The Library of America, 1996.

Slaughter, Thomas P. *The Natures of John and William Bartram*. New York: Alfred A. Knopf, 1996.

Waskelow, Gregory A., and Kathryn E. Holland Braund. *William Bartram on the Southeastern Indians*. Lincoln: University of Nebraska Press, 1995.

Appendix C

Organizations

The Bartram Trail Conference

The Bartram Trail Conference was created in 1975 with members from Alabama, Georgia, Florida, Louisiana, Mississippi, North Carolina, South Carolina, and Tennessee. The organization created the concept of "a string of pearls," a series of sites within a fifty-mile corridor that parallels William Bartram's most likely route. The Conference had three goals:

1. To identify William Bartram's contibution to American heritage and the heritage of the Southeast.

2. To develop a proposal for a heritage project to recognize and memorialize William Bartram's work.

3. To identify and describe other natural, historical, and cultural areas that would expand and complement the heritage project.

The Bartram Trail Conference published their report in *Bartram Heritage* in 1979. Many of the presently existing trails, historical markers, and Bartram commemoratives are a result of this significant work accomplished by the members of the conference. The report has been out of print for a number of years but is now available on the Bartram Trail Conference web site at **www.bartramtrail.org**.

The Bartram Trail Conference continues their work to honor and commemorate William Bartram. The Conference sponsors a biennial meeting where Bartram scholars and enthusiasts present current research about William Bartram, his science, his art, and his *Travels*. Members of the conference host field trips to Bartram sites in several of the states.

Historic Bartram's Garden

The home of John and William Bartram is a Philadelphia City park. It is home to the John Bartram Association and the restored public garden. The John Bartram Association was founded in 1893 by Bartram descendants to support and operate the garden.

The Historic Bartram's Garden occupies forty-four of the original 102 acres and contains the Bartram home, several outbuildings, restored garden, wildflower meadow, wetland area, exhibits, and library. Historic Bartram's Garden provides outreach and community programs on science, history, and nature. The grounds are open daily from dawn to dusk. The Historic Garden is open from 10 a.m.–5 p.m. daily except major holidays. The Bartram home is a museum house and is open Tuesday through Sunday at 12:10, 1:10, 2:10, and 3:10 p.m. The Museum Shop is open during times the Bartram home is open.

Visit their website at: **www.bartramsgarden.org**.

North Carolina Bartram Trail Society

The North Carolina Bartram Trail Society was created in 1977 to recognize William Bartram's contributions to American heritage and to build and maintain the hiking trail that bears his name in North Carolina. The society is very active and has completed over eighty miles of trail. Their web site is **www.ncbartramtrail.org**.
Direct inquiries to:
  North Carolina Bartram Trail Society
  P. O. Box 144
  Scaly Mountain, NC 28775

The Nature Conservancy

The Nature Conservancy preserves sensitive and endangered habitats by outright purchase and pursueing conservationa easements with private landowners. The work of the Nature Conservancy is particularly important in the Southeast where most land is privately owned. The Nature Conservancy works with governmental agencies by moving quickly on land purchases and holding it until public funds become available. Each state has a chapter of the Nature Conservancy and the chapters sponsor field trips to their preserves where visitors can learn about special natural areas. Nature Conservancy work parties are a popular event for members. Visit the web site for information and links to state chapters. **www.tnc.org**

The Sierra Club

The Sierra Club is America's oldest environmental organization and is distinguished by its work on national and local environmental issues. Because the Sierra Club has no tax exempt status the organization can endorse candidates in local and state elections and lobby Congress on important national legislation. Each state has a Sierra Club chapter and most urban areas have a local group. State and local Sierra Club organizations sponsor a wide variety of outings and service events. Visit the national web site for information and links to local Sierra Club groups.
www.sierraclub.org

The Audubon Society

The mission of the National Audubon Society is to conserve and restore natural ecosystems and to protect the Earth's biological diversity. Their particular interest is in preserving habitat for birds and other wildlife in over 100 sanctuaries. The Audubon Society was founded in 1905 and is named for John James Audubon. The Audubon Society has 550,00 members and 508 chapters in the western hemisphere. The Audubon Society has an office in each state and local chapters sponsor meetings, lectures, and outings. Their web site is **www.audubon.org**.

Appendix D
Historical Names for Rivers & Islands

Historical River Names

Indian	French	Spanish	English
Welaka	May	San Mateo and San Juan	St. Johns
Guasaca Esqui		San Juanito	Suwannee
		Barra de Santa Maria	Nassau
	Seine	San Pedro	St. Marys
	Somme	Barra de Ballenas	Satilla (St. Andrews Sound)
	Loire (?)	Barra de Guadalguini	Turtle (St. Simon Sound)
Utinahica (?)	Charente	Santa Isabel, Rio de Taleje	Altamaha
	Garonne	Barra de Espogue	Doboy Sound
Sapala (?)	Gironde	Barra de Sapala	Sapelo
	Belle	Barra de Azopo	St. Catherines Sound
		Barra de Aquadulce	Ogeechee
	Grande	Rio Dulce	Savannah (originally Westo River)
	Port Royal		Port Royal Sound
	Belle Voir	Barra de Santa Elena	St. Helena Sound
Kiawah		Rio San Jorge	Charleston Harbor
		San Lorenzo	Santee
		Jordan	Waccammaw
		Apalachicola	Chattahoochee
		Pedernales	Flint

Historical Island Names

Indian	French	Spanish	English
	Isle de la May	Isla de San Juan	Fort George
		Isla de Santa Maria	Amelia
Mocama and Tacatacuru	Isle de la Seine	Isla de San Pedro	Cumberland
	Isle de la Somme	Isla de Ballenas	Jekyll
Guadalquini	Isle de la Loire	Isla de Guadalquini	St. Simons
Sapala	Isle de la Garrone	Isla de Sapala	Sapelo
Guale	Isle de Gironde	Isla de Santa Catalina	St. Catherines
Azopo	Isle de la Rivère Belle	Isle de Azopo	Ossabaw
		Isla de los Osos	Hilton Head
	Port Royal	Santa Elena	St. Helena
	Isle de la Belle Voir		Edisto

Bibliography

Albu, Susan H., and Elizabeth Arndt. *Here's Savannah: A Journey through Historic Savannah & Environs*. Savannah: A & A Enterprises, 1994.

Alden, John Richard. *John Stuart and the Southern Colonial Frontier*. New York: Gordian Press, Inc., 1966.

Arredondo, Antonio de. *Arredondo's Historical Proof of Spain's Title to Georgia*. Edited by Herbert E. Bolton. Berkeley: University of California Press, 1925.

Baker, Pearl. *The Story of Wrightsboro, 1768–1964*. Thomson, Georgia: Wrightsboro Restoration Foundation, 1965.

Baldwin, III, William P. *Lowcountry Daytrips*. Greensboro, North Carolina: Legacy Publications, 1993.

Barnes, Ian. *The Historical Atlas of the American Revolution*. New York: Routledge, 2000.

Barnes, Judy; Jolane Edwards, Carolyn Lee Goodloe, and Laurel Wilson. *Coasting: an Expanded Guide to the Northern Gulf Coast*. Point Clear, Alabama, 1994

Bartram, John. *Diary of a Journey through the Carolinas, Georgia, and Florida*. Annotated by Francis Harper. Philadelphia: American Philosophical Society, 1942.

Bartram, William. *Travels in Georgia and Florida, 1773–74: A Report to Dr. John Fothergill*. Annotated by Francis Harper. Philadelphia: The American Philosophical Society, 1943.

———. *Travels of William Bartram*. Edited by Mark Van Doren. Reprint of the 1928 edition. New York: Dover Publications, Inc., 1955.

———. *Travels of William Bartram: Naturalist Edition*. Edited with commentary and an annotated index by Francis Harper. New Haven: Yale University Press, 1958.

———. *Travels of William Bartram: Naturalist Edition*. Edited with commentary and an annotated index by Francis Harper. Athens: University of Georgia Press, 1998.

———. *William Bartram: Travels and Other Writings*. Edited by Thomas P. Slaughter. New York: Library of America, 1996.

Berkeley, Edmund, and Dorothy Smith Berkeley. *The Life and Travels of John Bartram: From Lake Ontario to the River St. John*. Tallahassee: University Presses of Florida, 1982.

Beverley, Robert. *The Western North Carolina Almanac and Book of Lists*. Franklin, North Carolina: Sanctuary Press, 1991.

Bice, David A., et al. *A Panorama of Florida*. Charleston, West Virginia: Jalamap Publications, Inc. 1982.

Blackmun, Ora. *Western North Carolina: Its Mountains and Its People to 1880*. Boone, North Carolina: Appalachian Consortium Press, 1977.

Bonner, James C. *Milledgeville: Georgia's Antebellum Capital*. Athens: University of Georgia Press, 1978.

Bouwman, Robert Eldridge. *Traveler's Rest and the Tugaloo Crossroads*. Atlanta: State of Georgia Department of Natural Resources, 1980.

Bowen, John. *Adventuring Along the Southeast Coast*. San Francisco: Sierra Club Books, 1993.

Boyd, Brian. *The Highlands-Cashiers Outdoors Companion*. Clayton, Georgia: Fern Creek Press, 1995.

Brown, Fred. *Brown's I-95 Guide: the Sea Islands Coast*. Atlanta: CPM Group, Inc.

Brown, Fred, and Nell Jones, editors. *The Georgia Conservancy's Guide to the North Georgia Mountains*. Atlanta: Longstreet Press, 1991.

Bushnell, Amy Turner. *Situado and Sabana: Spain's Support System for the Presidio and Mission Provinces of Florida*. New York: American Museum of Natural History, 1994.

Cabell, Branch and A. J. Hanna. *The St. Johns: a Parade of Diversity*. New York: Rinehart & Co., Inc. 1943.

Cain, Cyril Edward. *Four Centuries on the Pascagoula*. Reprint of the 1953 edition. Spartanburg: the Reprint Company, Publishers, 1983.

Canouts, Celetta Kay. *Towards a Reconstruction of Creek and Pre-Creek Cultural Ecology*. Masters Thesis, Chapel Hill, NC, 1971.

Carlisle, Sharon. *George Washington's Guide to the Waccamaw Neck and Georgetown*. Pawley's Island, 1991.

Cashin, Edward J. and Heard Robertson. *Augusta & the American Revolution: Events in the Georgia Back Country, 1773–1783*. Augusta: Richmond County Historical Society, 1975.

Cashin, Edward J. *Colonial Augusta*. Macon: Mercer University Press, 1986.

———. *Lachlan McGillivray: Indian Trader*. Athens: University of Georgia Press, 1992.

———. *William Bartram and the American Revolution on the Southern Frontier*. Columbia: University of South Carolina Press, 2000.

Cashin, Joan E. *A Family Venture: Men and Women on the Southern Frontier*. New York and Oxford: Oxford University Press, 1991.

Cashman, Diane Cobb. *Cape Fear Adventure*. Woodland Hills, California: Windsor Publications, 1982.

Castiglioni, Luigi. *Luigi Castiglioni's Viaggio: Travels in the United States of North America, 1785–87*. Syracuse: Syracuse University Press, 1983.

Cate, Margaret Davis. *Our Todays and Yesterdays: a Story of Brunswick and the Coastal Islands*. Spartanburg: the Reprint Company, 1979

Catesby, Mark. *The Natural History of Carolina, Florida, and the Bahama Islands*. London, 1729–1747.

Cerulean, Susan and Ann Morrow. *Florida Wildlife Viewing Guide*. Helena, Montana: Falcon Press, 1993.

Cherokee Villages in South Carolina. Edited by Anne Sheriff. Easley, South Carolina: Forest Acres/McKissick Gifted Program, 1994.

Childs, Essie Jones. *They Tarried in Taylor (A Georgia County)*. Warner Robbins, Georgia: Central Georgia Genealogical Society, Inc., 1992.

Coulter, Ellis Merton. *Old Petersburg and the Broad River Valley of Georgia*. Athens: University of Georgia Press, 1965.

Cruickshank, Helen G. *Bartram in Florida, 1774*. Florida Federation of Garden Clubs, 1986.

———. *John and William Bartram's America*. Greenwich, Connecticut: Devin-Adair Publishers, 1957.

Darlington, William. *Memorials of John Bartram & Humphrey Marshall*. New York: Hafner Publishing Company, 1967.

Dau, Frederick W. *Florida Old and New*. New York: G. P. Putnam's Sons, 1934.

Davis, Edwin Adams. *Louisiana: a Narrative History*. Baton Rouge: Claitor's Publishing Division, 1976.

De Hart, Allen. *Adventuring in Florida*. San Francisco: Sierra Club Books, 1995.

———. *Hiking South Carolina Trails*. Old Saybrook, Connecticut: Glode Pequot Press, 1994.

Delorme Mapping, Yarmouth, Maine. *Alabama Atlas and Gazeteer*, 1998. *Florida Atlas and Gazeteer*, 1989. *Georgia Atlas and Gazeteer*, 1998. *Louisiana Atlas and Gazeteer*, 1998. *Mississippi Atlas and Gazeteer*, 1998. *North Carolina Atlas and Gazeteer*, 1992. *South Carolina Atlas and Gazeteer*, 1998.

De Vorsey, Louis. *De Brahm's Report of the General Survey in the Southern District of North America*. Columbia: University of South Carolina Press, 1971.

———. *The Indian Boundary in the Southern Colonies, 1763–1775*. Chapel Hill: University of North Carolina Press, 1961.

Dickinson, Jonathan. *Jonathan Dickinson's Journal, or God's Protecting Providence*. Edited by Evangeline Walker Andrews and Charles McLean Andrews. Port Salerno, Florida: Florida Classics Library, 1985.

Earnest, Ernest. *John and William Bartram: Botanists and Explorers*. Philadelphia: University of Pennsylvania Press, 1940.

Eaton, Clement. *The Growth of Southern Civilization: 1790–1860*. New York: Harper & Row, 1963.

———. *A History of the Old South*. New York: Macmillan Publishing Co., Inc.,1975.

Encyclopedia of Southern Culture. Edited by Charles Reagan Wilson and William Ferris. Two volumes. New York: Doubleday, 1989.

Evans, Virginia Fraser. *Liberty County, Georgia: A Pictorial History*. Liberty County Board of Commissioners, 1979.

Explorations, Descriptions, and Attempted Settlements of Carolina, 1584–1590. Edited by David Leroy Corbitt. Raleigh: North Carolina State Department of Archives and History, 1953.

Featherstonhaugh, George W. *Excursion Through the Slave States, from Washington on the Potomac to the Frontier of Mexico; with Sketches of Popular Manners and Geological Notices*. New York: Harper & Brothers, 1844.

Fagin, N. Bryllion. *William Bartram: Interpreter of the American Landscape*. Baltimore: John Hopkins Press, 1933.

Faragher, John Mack, editor. *The Encyclopedia of Colonial and Revolutionary America*. New York: De Capo Press, 1996.

Fleming, Thomas. *Liberty! The American Revolution*. New York: Viking, 1997.

Florida Trails, A Guide to Florida's Natural Habitats. Florida Department of Commerce, Division of Tourism.

Franklin, Benjamin. *The Autobiography of Benjamin Franklin*. New York: Macmillan Publishing Co., Inc., 1962.

Fraser, Walter J., *Charleston! Charleston!* Columbia: University of South Carolina Press, 1989.

Fretwell, Mark E. *This so Remote Frontier: The Chattahoochee Country of Alabama and Georgia*. Columbus, Georgia: Historic Chattahoochee commission, 1980.

Garrison, Webb. *Oglethorpe's Folly*. Lakemont, Georgia: Copple House Books, 1982.

Giffen, Morrison. *South Carolina: a Guide to Backcountry Travel & Adventure*. Asheville: Out There Press, 1997.

Godfrey, Michael A. *A Sierra Club Naturalist's Guide to the Piedmont*. San Francisco: Sierra Club Books, 1980.

Goins, Charles Robert and John Michael Caldwell. *Historical Atlas of Louisiana*. Norman: University of Oklahoma Press, 1995.

Goff, John H. *Placenames of Georgia*. Athens: University of Georgia Press, 1975.

Golden, Virginia Noble. *A History of Tallassee*. Reprint of the 1949 edition. Tallassee, Alabama: Tallassee Chamber of Commerce, 1990.

Gosse, Philip Henry. *Letters from Alabama, (U.S.): Chiefly Relating to Natural History*. Tuscaloosa: University of Alabama Press, 1993.

Hall, Basil. *Travels in North America in the Years 1827 and 1828*. London, 1829.

Hamilton, Peter Joseph. *Colonial Mobile*. Reprint of the 1910 edition. Tuscaloosa: University of Alabama Press, 1976.

Hatley, Tom. *The Dividing Paths: Cherokees and South Carolinians through the Revolutionary Era*. New York: Oxford University Press, 1995.

Hawkins, Benjamin. *A Sketch of the Creek Country*. Americus, Georgia: Americus Book Company, 1938

Heitzler, Michael J. *Historic Goose Creek, South Carolina, 1670–1980*. Easley, South Carolina: Southern Historical Press, 1983.

Hemperley, Marion R. and Edwin L. Jackson. *Georgia's Boundaries: The Shaping of a State*. Athens: Carl Vinson Institute of Government, University of Georgia, 1993.

———. *Indian Heritage of Georgia*. Garden Club of Georgia, 1994.

Herbst, Josephine. *New Green World*. New York: Hastings House Publishers, 1954.

Hines, Nell Womack. *A Treasure Album of Milledgeville and Baldwin County, Georgia*. L. W. Burke company, 1946.

Hodgson, Adam. *Letters from North America, Vol. I*. London: Hurst, Robinson, & Co., 1824.

Hodler, Thomas W. and Howard A. Schretter. *The Atlas of Georgia*. Athens: the Institute of Community and Area Development, University of Georgia, 1986.

Homan, Tim. *The Hiking Trails of North Georgia*. Atlanta: Peachtree Publishers, Ltd., 1980.

Houk, Rose. *Great Smoky Mountains National Park*. New York: Houghton Mifflin Company, 1993.

Hudson, Charles M. *Knights of Spain, Warriors of the Sun: Hernando De Soto and the South's Ancient Chiefdoms*. Athens: University of Georgia Press, 1997.

———. *The Southeastern Indians*. Knoxville: University of Tennessee Press, 1976.

Hudson, Charles, and Carmen Chaves Tesser, editors. *The Forgotten Centuries: Indians and Europeans in the American South, 1521–1704*. Athens: University of Georgia Press, 1994.

Iberville, Pierre LeMoyne, Sieur d.' *Iberville's Gulf Journals*. Translated and edited by Richebourg Gaillard McWilliams. Tuscaloosa: University of Alabama Press, 1981.

Jackson, Harvey H. *Lachlan McIntosh*. Athens: University of Georgia Press, 1979.

———. *Rivers of History: Life on the Coosa, Tallapoosa, Cahaba, and Alabama*. Tuscaloosa: University of Alabama Press, 1995.

Johannes, Jan H. *Yesterday's Reflections: Nassau County, Florida*. Callahan, Florida: Thomas O. Richardson, 1976.

Johnson, A Sydney; Hilburn O. Hillestad, Sheryl Fanning Shanholtzer, and G. Frederick Shanholtzer. *An Ecological Survey of the Coastal Region of Georgia*. National Park Service Scientific Monograph Series Number 3. Government Printing Office, Washington, D.C., 1974.

Jones, George Fenwick. *The Salzburger Saga: Religious Exiles and Other Germans Along the Savannah*. Athens: University of Georgia Press, 1984.

Jordan, Mary Alice; *Cotton to Kaolin: a History of Washington County, Ceorgia, 1784–1989*. Sandersville, Georgia: Washington County Historical Society, 1989.

Kahn, Jane G. and Buddy Kahn. *25 Bicycle Tours in Coastal Georgia and the Carolina Low Country*. Woodstock, Vermont: Backcountry Publications, 1995.

Kovacik, Charles F., and John J. Winberry. *South Carolina: the Making of a Landscape*. Columbia: University of South Carolina Press, 1897.

Krakow, Kenneth. *Georgia Place-Names*. Macon: Winship Press, 1975.

Lander, Jr., Ernest McPherson. *South Carolina: An Illustrated History of the Palmetto State*. Northridge, California: Windsor Publications, Inc., 1988.

Lane, Mills. *Savannah Revisited: A Pictorial History*. Savannah: The Beehive Press, 1973.

———. *The Rambler in Georgia*. Savannah: The Beehive Press, 1973.

Lawson, John. *A New Voyage to Carolina*. Edited by Hugh Talmage Lefler. Originally published in 1709. Chapel Hill: University of North Carolina Press, 1967.

Lee, Lawrence. *New Hanover County: a Brief History*. Raleigh: North Carolina Division of Archives and History, 1984.

LeLand, Jack. *62 Famous Houses of Charleston, South Carolina*. Charleston: Post-Courier, 1986.

Lenz, Richard J. *Longstreet High Road Guide to the Georgia Coast & Okefenokee*. Atlanta: Longstreet Press, Inc., 1999.

Lewis, Catherine H. *Horry County, South Carolina*. Columbia: University of South Carolina Press, 1998.

Leyburn, James G. *The Scotch-Irish: a Social History*. Chapel Hill: University of North Carolina Press, 1962.

Littlefield, Daniel C. *Rice and Slaves: Ethnicity and the Slave Trade in Colonial South Carolina*. Baton Rouge: Louisiana State University Press, 1981.

Lipscomb, Terry W. *South Carolina in 1791: George Washington's Southern Tour*. Columbia: South Carolina Department of Archives and History, 1993.

Logue, Victoria, and Frank Logue. *Georgia Outdoors*. Winston-Salem: John F. Blair, Publisher, 1995.

Lord, Jr., Clifton F., and Martha Jane K. Zachert. *The Botanical Garden of André Michaux Near Charleston, 1786–1802*. Presented to the Section on Historical Pharmacy, American Pharmaceutical Association Convention; Las Vegas, Nevada, March 7, 1962

Louisiana Tour Guide. Baton Rouge: Louisiana Travel Promotion Association.

Lyell, Charles. *A Second Visit to the United States of North America, Vol. I & II*. London: Harper & Brothers, 1849.

Mahan, Joseph B. *Columbus: Georgia's Fall Line Trading Town*. Northridge, California: Windsor Publications, Inc., 1986.

Manning, Phillip. *Afoot in the South: Walks in the Natural Areas of North Carolina*. Winston-Salem: John F. Blair, Publisher, 1993.

———. *Palmetto Journal: Walks in the Natural Areas of South Carolina*. Winston-Salem: John F. Blair, Publisher, 1995.

Marion, John Francis. *The Charleston Story: Scenes from a City's History*. Harrisburg, Pennsylvania: Stackpole Books, 1978.

McCullum, Jerry; Betsie Rothermel, and Chuck Rabolli. *Georgia Wildlife Viewing Guide*. Conyers, Georgia: Georgia Wildlife Press, 1996.

McGee, Gwen, ed. *A Guide to the Georgia Coast.* Savannah: Georgia Conservancy, 1993.

McGinnis, Helen. *Hiking Mississippi: a Guide to Trails and Natural Areas.* Jackson: University of Mississippi Press, 1994.

McInnes, Martha, et al. *Bartram Heritage: a Study of the Life of William Bartram.* Montgomery: The Bartram Trail Conference, 1979.

McWhiney, Grady. *Cracker Culture: Celtic Ways in the South.* Tuscaloosa: University of Alabama Press, 1988.

Meanley, Brooke. *Swamps, River Bottoms, and Canebrakes.* Barre, Massachussetts: Barre Publishers, 1972.

Meyer, Peter. *Nature Guide to the Carolina Coast.* Wilmington, North Carolina: Avian-Cetacean Press, 1994.

Milfort, Louis Le Clerc. *Memoirs or a Quick Glance at My Various Travels and My Sojourn in the Creek Nation.* Translated and Edited by Ben C. McCary. Savannah: Beehive Press, 1959.

Mooney, James. *History, Myths, and Sacred Formulas of the Cherokees.* Asheville: Bright Mountain Books, 1992.

Mowat, Charles Loch. *East Florida as a British Province, 1763–1784.* Gainesville: University of Florida Press, 1964.

Myers, Amy R., and Margaret Beck Pritchard. *Empire's Nature: Mark Catesby's New World Vision.* A collection of essays. Chapel Hill: University of North Carolina Press, 1998.

Nichols, John L. "Alexander Cameron; British Agent Among the Cherokee, 1764–1781." *South Carolina Historical magazine*, Vol. 97. No. 2, April, 1996.

O'Keefe, M. Timothy. *The Hiker's Guide to Florida.* Helena, Montana: Falcon Press, 1993.

Peck, Douglas T. "Lucas Vásquez de Ayllón's Doomed Colony of San Miguel de Gualdape." *The Georgia Historical Quarterly*, Vol. 85, No. 2 (Summer 2001), pp. 183–198. Savannah: Georgia Historical Society.

Perry, John, and Jane Greverus Perry. *The Sierra Club Guide to the Natural Areas of Florida.* San Francisco: Sierra Club Books, 1992.

Pinckney, Elise. *Thomas and Elizabeth Lamboll: Early Charleston Gardeners.* Charleston: Charleston Museum, 1969.

Pittman, Philip. *Present State of the European Settlements on the Mississippi.* Facsimile reproduction of the 1770 edition. Gainesville: University of Florida Press, 1973.

Pfitzer, Donald W. *The Hiker's Guide to Georgia.* Helena, Montana: Falcon Press, 1993.

Powell, William S. *North Carolina: A Bicentennial History.* New York: W. W. Norton & Co., Inc., 1977.

Power, Tyrone. *Impressions of America.* London, 1836.

Presley, Justine A. "The Establishing of the Indian Trade in Colonial Georgia." *Richmond County History*; Vol. 16, No. 1 (Winter 1984), pp. 22–29. Augusta, Georgia: Richmond County Historical Society.

Proctor, Samuel, editor. *Eighteenth-Century Florida and Its Borderlands.* Gainesville: University Presses of Florida, 1975.

Recreation Guide to District Lands. St. Johns River Water Management District. Palatka, Florida, 1995.

Rembert, David. H. "The Carolina Plants of André Michaux." *Castanea*, Vol. 4, No.2., June, 1979.

Reveal, James L. *Gentle Conquest: The Botanical Discovery of North America with Illustrations from the Library of Congress.* Washington: Starwood Publishing, Inc., 1992.

Rice, Dr. Thaddeus Brockett. *History of Greene County, 1786–1886.* Macon: J. W. Burke Company, 1961.

Rodgers, John. *The Tectonics of the Appalachians.* New York: John Wiley & Sons, Inc., 1970.

Ross, Malcolm. *The Cape Fear.* New York: Holt, Rinehart and Winston, 1965.

Rouse, Jr., Parke. *The Great Wagon Road: from Philadelphia to the South.* Richmond: Dietz Press, 1995.

Rowland, Lawrence S.; Alexander Moore and George C. Rogers, Jr. *The History of Beaufort County, South Carolina*, Vol. 1. Columbia: University of South Carolina Press, 1996.

Rozema, Vicki. *Footsteps of the Cherokees: a Guide to the Eastern Homelands of the Cherokee Nation.* Winston-Salem: John F. Blair, Publisher, 1995.

Rhyne, Nancy. *The Grand Strand.* Charlotte: Fast & McMillan Publishers, Inc., 1985.

———. *Touring the Coastal Georgia Backroads.* Winston-Salem: John F. Blair, Publisher, 1994.

———. *Touring the Coastal South Carolina Backroads.* Winston-Salem: John F. Blair, Publisher, 1992.

Ripley, Warren. *Battleground: South Carolina in the Revolution.* Charleston: Evening Post Publishing, 1983.

Rushton, William Faulkner. *The Cajuns: From Acadia to Louisiana.* New York: Farrar, Straus and Giroux, 1979.

Sakowski, Carolyn. *Touring the Western North Carolina Backroads.* Winston-Salem: John F. Blair, Publisher, 1910.

Savage, Jr., Henry, and Elizabeth J. Savage. *André and François André Michaux.* Charlottesville: University Press of Virginia, 1986.

Schoettle, Taylor. *A Naturalist's Guide to St. Simons Island.* St. Simons Island: Watermarks Printing Company, 1993.

Seaborn, Margaret Mills. *André Michaux's Journeys in Oconee County.* Walhalla, South Carolina: Oconee County Library, 1976.

Sieg, Edward Chan. *Eden on the Marsh:* An Illustrated History of Savannah. Northridge, California: Windsor Publications, Inc., 1985.

Simpson, Steven Alec. *Guide to Free Hunting Land in Georgia.* Albany, Georgia: Mossy Oak Publishing Company, 1989.

Slaughter, Thomas P. *The Natures of John and William Bartram.* New York: Alfred A. Knopf, 1996.

Smith, Carter, *editor. The Explorers and Settlers: A Sourcebook on Colonial Ameica.* Brookfield, Connecticut: Millbrook Press, 1991.

Smith, Elizabeth Wiley. *The History of Hancock County, Georgia: Vol. 1.* Washington, Georgia: Wilkes Publishing Company, Inc., 1974.

Smith, Florrie Carter. *The History of Oglethorpe County, Georgia*. Washington, Georgia: Wilkes Publishing Company, Inc., 1970.

South Carolina Public Beach & Coastal Access Guide. Columbia: South Carolina Department of Parks, Recreation & Tourism and South Carolina Coastal Council.

South Carolina Travel Guide. Columbia: South Carolina Department of Parks, Recreation & Tourism, 1994

Spearing, Darwin. *Roadside Geology of Louisiana*. Missoula, Montana: Mountain Press Publishing Company, 1995.

Sprunt, James. *Chronicles of the Cape Fear River, 1660–1916*. Reprint of the 1916 edition. Spartanburg: The Reprint Company, 1973.

Sternberg, Mary Ann. *The Pelican Guide to Louisiana*. Gretna, Louisiana: Pelican Publishing Company, 1993.

Stevens, William Bacon. *A History of Georgia from its First Discovery by Europeans to the Adoption of the Present Constitution in 1797*. Originally published in 1847 by D. Appleton and Company, New York. Savannah: The Beehive Press, 1972

Stockton, Robert P.; Sarah Fick, and John Laurens. *Historic Resources of Berkeley County South Carolina*. Berkeley County Historical Society, 1990.

Stokes, Thomas L. *The Savannah*. Reprint of the 1951 edition. Athens: University of Georgia Press, 1979.

Strutin, Michele, and Harry Middleton. *The Smithsonian Guide to Natural America: The Southeast*. New York: Random House/Smithsonian Books, 1997.

Swanton, John R. *Early History of the Creek Indians & Their Neighbors*. Gainesville: University of Florida Press, 1998.

———. *The Indians of the Southeastern United States*. Reprint of the 1949 edition. Washington: Smithsonian Institution Press, 1979.

Taylor, A. J. *A History of Dearing, McDuffie County, Georgia, from 1850–1904*. Dearing, Georgia: Published by Robert Printup, 1929.

Tebeau, Charlton W. *A History of Florida*. Coral Gables: University of Miami Press, 1971.

Temple, Sarah B., and Kenneth Coleman. *Georgia Journeys*. Athens: University of Georgia Press, 1961.

Thalimer, Carol, and Dan Thalimer. *Country Roads of Georgia*. Castine, Maine: Country Roads Press, 1995.

The Most Delightful Country of the Universe: Promotional Literature of the Colony of Georgia, 1717–1734. Introduction by Trevor R. Reese. Savannah: The Beehive Press, 1972.

The New Georgia Guide. A project of the Georgia Humanities Council. Athens: University of Georgia Press, 1996.

Thomas, David Hurst. *St. Catherines: An Island in Time*. Atlanta: Georgia Humanities Council, 1988.

Valentine, James. *Florida: Images of the Landscape*. Englewood, Colorado: Westcliffe Publishers, Inc., 1988.

Vignoles, Charles. *Observations upon the Floridas*. Facisimile reproduction of the 1823 edition. Gainesville: University Presses of Florida, 1977.

Wallace, David Duncan. *The Life of Henry Laurens*. New York: G. P. Putnam's Sons, 1915.

Weeks, Carl Solana. *Savannah in the Time of Peter Tondee*. Columbia: Summerhouse Press, 1997.

Weil, Tom. *Hippocrene USA Guide to America's South*. New York: Hippocrene Books, 1990.

Weir, Robert M. *Colonial South Carolina: a History*. Columbia: University of South Carolina Press, 1997.

Wells, Mary Ann. *A History Lover's Guide to Louisiana*. Baton Rouge: Quail Ridge Press, Inc., 1990.

Wharton, Charles H. *The Natural Environments of Georgia*. Bulletin 114. Atlanta: Department of Natural Resources, Environmental Protection Division, Georgia Geologic Survey, 1978.

Whitelaw, Robert, and Alice F. Levkoff. *Charleston: Come Hell or High Water*. Columbia: R. L. Bryan Company, 1975.

Willett, N. L. *Beaufort County, South Carolina*. Beaufort: Beaufort County Chamber of Commerce, 1953.

Willingham, Robert Marion. *We Have This Heritage: The History of Wilkes County, Georgia*. Washington, Georgia: Wilkes Publishing Co., 1969.

Wise, Lenna Smith. *The Story of Oglethorpe County*. Lexington, Georgia: Historic Oglethorpe County, Inc., 1980.

Woodmason, Charles. *The Carolina Backcountry on the Eve of the Revolution*. Chapel Hill: University of North Carolina Press, 1953.

Woodward, Thomas S. *The American Old West: Woodward's Reminiscences*. Mobile: Southern University Press for Graphics, Inc., 1965.

Worth, Johm E. *The Struggle for the Georgia Coast: an Eighteenth-Century Spanish Retrospective on Guale and Mocama*. New York: American Museum of Natural History, 1995.

Wright, Jr., J. Leitch. *Creeks and Seminoles*. Lincoln: University of Nebraska Press, 1990.

———. *Florida in the American Revolution*. Gainesville: University Presses of Florida, 1975.

Index

A

Aaron, Hank, 265
Abbeville, Ala., 235
Abbeville County, S.C., 8, 64, 72, 85, 175, 177, 186, 341; museum, 175
Abbeville, France, 176
Abbeville, S.C., 172, 174, 179, 182
Abbeville-Anderson county line, 170, 175
Abbott, James, 56
Abercorn, Ga., 17
Abercrombie, Charles, 214
Abercrombie, James, 246
Aberdeenshire, Scotland, 272
the Abihkas, 239
Abita River, 285
Abita Springs, La., 284
Abraham, Old, 204
Acadia, 105, 290
Acadian Coast, 291
Acadians, 50, 289–291, 293,
ACE Basin National Wildlife Refuge, 143, 169
the Acolapissas, 281, 296
Adair, James, 57, 186, 192, 196
Adair, Walter, 186, 192
Adams, John, 12, 157
Adams, John Quincy, 85, 182
Adams-Onís Treaty (1820), 267
Adventure, 145
Africa: Rice Coast, 34, 145
African American Museum of the Arts, DeLand, Fla., 117
African-Americans: arts and crafts, 148; birth of Civil Rights Movement, 247; education, 168; in Columbus, 236; in Louisiana, 264; in Macon, 221; in South Carolina, 139; in territorial Florida, 102; influence on Southern cooking, 137; influences in new Orleans, 285; isolated on rice plantations, 161; oral tradition, 216; population of Georgetown County, 308
Africans, 34, 137, 167
Afton Gardens, West Feliciana Parish, 295
Agency Preserve, 223
Agricultural Society of South Carolina, 146, 166
Ahaya (Cowkeeper), 122–123, 126
Aiken County, S.C., 72
Airlie Gardens, Wilmington, 318
Alabama: acquired by United States, 232; available farmland, 64; Black Belt, 221, 248; boundary, 246; central region, 238–242; Cherokee Nation, 182, 195, 205; Coosa Empire, 244; cotton migration, 209, 214, 232, 265; Creek homeland, 239, 243; East Alabama, 232, 242; extends jurisdiction over Creek territory, 229; governors, 257; immigration from Georgia and the Carolinas, 64; leaders, 248; Lower Alabama, 250; members of legislature, 251; militia, 243; Native Americans, 238; prairies, 248; Yazoo Land Fraud, 213
Alabama Department of Archives & History, 247
Alabama Fever, 251
Alabama River, 76, 242, 247, 251; Creek settlements, 250; empire of Tascaluza, 238; events of the First Creek War, 254, 260; Federal Road, 86; frontier, 250; American settlement, 251, 254, 256; the Canoe Fight, 254
Alabama Science Center, 247
Alabama Shakespeare Festival, 246
Alabama State Capitol, 247
Alabama State Docks, 230, 260, 265
Alabama State Farmers Market, 246
Alabama Territory, 257, 263, 275
Alabama Town, 239, 242, 247, 290
the Alabamas, 238, 246, 247, 248; language, 243; members of Creek Confederacy, 239; settled on the Mississippi River, 290; trade with the French, 264
Alachua, 8, 106, 109, 114, 122–125, 232; Alachua Savannah, 123, 126, 130, 132; Alachua Sink, 127
Alachua County, Fla., 123
Alachua Ferry, 111
Alamo, 253
Alarka Creek, 199
Albany, Duke of. *See* Hanover, Edward; Duke of York and Albany
Albemarle Point, 145
Albemarle Sound, 137, 313
Albemarle County, Va., 88, 312, 318
Albert Manucy Hall Museum, 107
Alcazar Hotel, 107
Aleck (Creek leader), 43
Alexander H. Stephens State Park, Ga., 82
Alexander Springs, Fla., 114; Alexander Springs Wilderness area, 109
Alexandria, Va., 316
Alfred A. Ring Park, Gainesville, Fla., 128
Algonquian language, 246
Alimacani (Fort George Island), 101
Alison, George, 161
Alison's Tavern, 166
All Saints Parish, S.C., 308
All Saints Parish Waccamaw Church, 309
Alliance, Ala., 242
alligator, 132, 133, 145, 164, 286
Alligator Bayou, La., 293
Alligator Creek, 53, 111
Alligator Creek Bridge, 15
Alligator Hole, 132
Allman Brothers Band, 221
Allston, Robert, 309
Alston, Theodosia Burr, 309
Alston, William and Mary Motte, 300
Altamaha (Hitchiti town), 160, 208
Altamaha Park, Ga., 43
Altamaha Province, 166
Altamaha River, 3, 7, 9, 12, 28, 34, 36, 37, 38, 40, 42, 43, 45, 51, 52, 160; as boundary, 237; boundary of Washington County, 208; claimed by South Carolina, 187; possible location of Ayllón colony, 298; Revolutionary activity, 70
Altamaha Wildlife Management Area, 38
Alternate Intracoastal Waterway, 294
Amadas, Philip, 312
Amatis, Martin, 24
Amelia Island, Fla., 40, 43, 45, 50, 53, 106; visited by William Bartram, 99; State Recreation Area, Fla., 53
American Academy of Natural Sciences, 7
American Beach, Fla., 102
American bison, 145
American Forests Famous & Historic Trees, Inc., 102
American Philosophical Society, 1, 6, 7, 144; members, 290
Americans: betrayal of the Creeks, 245; entrap Gen. Cornwallis, 320; fail to liberate Savannah, 161; relations with the Cherokees, 197, 205; relations with the Creeks, 239, 244; relations with the Seminoles, 123; settle eastern Tennessee, 204; settle Feliciana Parish, 295; settle Florida Parishes, 281, 291; tensions with Parliament, 139; welcomed by Spanish governors of Louisiana, 289
Amherst, Jeffrey, 49
Amite River, 9, 281, 286, 290, 291, 292, 256
Amity Recreation Area, Lake Hartwell, 66
amphianthus, 69
Amtrak, 247
Anabaptists, 138
Anastasia Island, Fla., 104, 106; State Recreation Area, 104; visited by William Bartram, 3
Andalusia, 214
Anderson County, S.C., 64, 85, 172, 176, 177; museum, 176
Anderson, Elizabeth, 182
Anderson, Robert, 95, 174, 176, 182, 183,
Anderson, S.C., 67, 171, 176, 179
Andrew, Benjamin, 8, 9, 15, 26, 29, 33
Andrew Jackson Highway, 132
Andrew Jackson Trail, 279
Andrews, N.C., 206
Andrews, S.C., 307
Andrews Wildlife Management Area, 125, 132
anemone, 186
Angel Oak Park, Charleston, 144
Anglicans, 138, 147, 151, 153, 302
Angola, Africa, 161
Angola, La., 292
anhinga, 143
anise, yellow, 114
Ann, 12, 20
Ansley, Thomas, 71
Ansley-Hodges Memorial Marsh Project, 38
Anson, George, 154
Ansonboro, Charleston, 156
Anthony Shoals, Ga., 89
Antreville, S.C., 172, 175
Apalache Province, 61, 106, 166, 242; English influence, 164; invaded by South Carolina, 219
Apalachees, 61, 130, 256, 261
Apalachicola, 8, 226, 229
Apalachicola Province, 226, 232
Apalachicola River, 256, 266, 274, 281
Apalachicolas, 26, 163; homeland, 226; join the Creek Confederacy, 239

Appalachian Mountains, 144, 185; biological diversity, 192; botanical areas, 193; boundary of Louisiana, 264; Cherokee homeland, 178, 203; erosion, 269; explored by Michaux, 182; orogeny, 185, 193; Pleistocene era, 193; white settlement, 73
Appalachian Trail, 201, 206
apple snail, 115
Appling, Ga., 65, 69
Aquarium of the Americas, 285
Archer, Fla., 125, 132
Argyle, Duke of, 1
Arkansas, 197, 243; rice, 304
Arkansas River, 199, 221
Arlington, Fla., 43, 99, 104; Lions Club Park, 103
Armstrong, James, 51
Army Corps of Engineers, 66, 112, 233, 277, 291
arpents, 288
Arredondo, Don Fernando de la Maza, 123, 127
Articles of Confederation, 208
Asa Gray Park, 119
Asbury Indian School and Mission, 232
Ascension Parish, La., 291, 296; Heritage Association Museum, 293
Ashe Island, S.C., 169
Ashe, John, 54, 56
Ashepoo Indians, 158
Ashepoo River, 160, 169
Ashley River, 143, 145, 147
Asheville, N.C., 185
Ashwood, 3, 4, 9, 300, 309, 316, 319, 323
Assembly House, Savannah, 25
Astor, Fla., 8, 109, 114
Atahachi, 238
Atalaya, 309
atamasco lily, 70, 87, 216
Atasi, 9, 242, 245
Atchafalaya National Wildlife Refuge, La., 292
Atchafalaya River, 291
Athens, Ga., 71, 79, 84, 85, 86, 173, 232
Athens Manufacturing Company, 82, 85
Atlanta Botanical Garden, 193
Atlanta, Ga., 69, 75, 76, 179, 214
Atlantic Coastal Highway, 29
Atlantic white cedar, 114, 317
Atmore, Ala., 254, 259
Attakullakulla, 8, 174, 178, 204, 206; biography, 206; death, 205; friendship with John Stuart, 154, 179; inability to prevent the Cherokee War, 179; meets William Bartram, 206; uncle to Nancy Ward, 182; visits England, 201
Auburn, Ala., 69, 242
Auburn University, 242; Experiment Station, 245
Auburn University-Montgomery, 242
Auchumpkee Creek, 223
Aucilla River, 130
Audubon, John James, 5, 7, 57, 115, 146, 295
Audubon Park & Zoo, La., 286
Audubon Pilgrimage, 295
Audubon Sanctuary, Ala., 262
Audubon Society, 58, 334
Audubon State Commemorative Area, La., 295
Audubon Swamp, S.C., 146
Augusta, Ala., 246
Augusta Baptist Institute, 75
Augusta Canal, 64, 70, 75, 76
Augusta Chronicle, 75
Augusta, Ga., 15, 54, 58, 60–65, 69–76, 242; American siege, 62; Augusta-Richmond County Museum, 75; Augusta-Richmond County Public Library, 75; Bartram Trail Bicentennial Committee, 70, beginning of Federal Road, 223, 232; British occupation, 83, 171; capital of Georgia, 64, 73; center of the Indian trade, 73; cotton market, 64, 70, 74; early settlement, 71; end of Great Wagon Road, 89, 170; falls to the British, 70, 83; first black kindergarten, 75; founded by Oglethorpe, 73; historic district, 73–74; Indian trails, 76, 91, 210; occupied by British, 84; railroads, 86; recaptured by patriots, 183; refuge for Tories, 83; Revolution, 73; Riverwalk, 74, 75; settled by Yuchis, 69; Stagecoach Road, 71; tobacco market, 64, 73; traders, 79, 80, 151; treaties, 237; visited by the Bartrams, 3; visited by William Bartram, 92; Welcome Center, 75
Augusta Gazette, 75
Augusta of Saxe-Gotha, 73
Augusta Road, 16, 17, 56
Augusta-Milledgeville Stage Road, 211
Augustine, Walter, 29
Austin, George, 157
Autauga County, Ala., 248
Autun, S.C., 181
Avendaughbough, 302
Avery Research Center for African-American History, 156
Avilés, Pedro Menéndez de, 11, 168
Avoyelles Parish, La., 296
Awendaw Barony, 302
Awendaw Creek, 298, 302
Awendaw, S.C., 298, 300, 302
Ayllón, Lucas Vasquez de, 11, 35, 135, 167, 298, 305
azalea, 87, 92, 194, 262

B

Bacon, Francis, 223
Bad Creek Visitor Center, S.C., 184
Bahamas: refuge for loyalists, 99, 106
Bahía de Santa María de Galvé, 266
Baillie, Kenneth, 32
Baillie, Robert, 29
Bain, Donald McIntosh, 29, 34
Baker Creek State Park, S.C., 67
Baker, John, 31
bald eagle, 115, 120, 125, 286
Baldhead Island, N.C., 317
Baldwin, Abraham, 85, 217, 263
Baldwin County, Ala., 250, 259, 262, 263
Baldwin County, Ga., 67, 217
Baldwin Heritage Museum, Ala., 262
Baldwin State Forest, Ga., 215
Baldwin, William, 5, 7, 50, 57
Ball, Eleanor, 157
Ball Ground, Ga., 203
Ball, John Coming, 157
Bandoulliers de Mississippi, 289
Bang's Lake, 277
Bank of South Carolina, 165
Banks County, Ga., 79
Baptist Church, 56
Baptists, 151, 166, 171
Barataria Basin, 286
Barbadians, 138, 147, 318, 312, 137, 138, 159, 164
Barbados, 138
Barbour County, Ala., 235
Bard, Peter, 50
Barlowe, Arthur, 312
Barnard, Edward, 80, 82, 84
Barnard, John, 224
Barnard, Timothy, 224
Barnard, Timpoochee, 224, 243
Barnard, William, 80
Barnet, Col.. *See* Barnard, Edward
Barnwell County, S.C., 58

Barnwell, John, 37, 160, 161
Barnwell Jr., John, 160
Barranca de Santo Tomé, 266
barrier islands, 50
Barrington Ferry, 39
Barrington Ferry Road, 29, 33
Barrington Park, Ga., 39
Barrington Road, 38
Barroto, Juan Enríques, 266
Barton, Benjamin Smith, 290
Bartram, Ann, 2
Bartram, Benjamin, 2
Bartram, Bill (cousin), 4
Bartram Canoe Trail, Tensaw River, 261
Bartram, Elizabeth (sister), 2
Bartram, Elizabeth (aunt), 1
Bartram, Elizabeth (grandmother), 1, 316
Bartram Forest, Ga., 215
Bartram Garden, 323. *See* Historic Bartram's Garden
Bartram Hall, 128
Bartram, Isaac, 2, 316
Bartram, James (brother of William), 2
Bartram, James (brother of John), 316
Bartram, John, 1–2, 3, 4, 7, 25, 38, 43, 54, 232, 333; appointed royal botanist, 2, 98; attitude toward Native Americans, 5; birth, 1; botanical explorations, 1; concerns for William, 2, 3; contracts malaria, 3; corresponds with Alexander Garden, 147; corresponds with Henry Laurens, 157; corresponds with Martha Logan, 155; death, 2, 5, 323; describes roads in Lowcountry, 161; discovers Ogeechee lime, 19; elected to Swedish Royal Academy of Sciences, 2; explores East Florida, 99; friendship with James Grant, 197; his Florida journal, 98; in Charleston, 142; in Savannah, 26; in South Carolina, 300; leaves William in Florida, 104; life, 1–2; lodges at Alison's Tavern, 166; Memorial, 85; parents, 316; patrons, 1; reaches source of the St. Johns River, 117, 120; travels through the upper coast of S.C., 309; travels to St. Augustine, 102; visits Blue Springs, 117; visits Galphin's Cowpen, 58; visits Gov. Tryon, 318; visits Henry Laurens, 149, 156; visits John Deas, 147; visits Lake Waccamaw, 319; visits Shell Bluff, 58; visits William Moultrie, 146
Bartram, John Jr., 2, 5
Bartram, Mary, 2
Bartram Memorial Highway, 104
Bartram Memorial Trail, Augusta, 70, 75
Bartram, Moses, 2
Bartram Park, Pensacola, 271
Bartram Trail, 17, 29, 191; Chattahoochee National Forest, 191; Clarks Hill Lake, 66; Fort Gordon Recreation Area, 66; in North Carolina, 17; Nantahala National Forest, 191; Northeast Georgia, 186, 192; Petersburg Campground, 66; South Carolina, 186; Western North Carolina, 194
Bartram Trail Conference, 82, 83, 215, 224, 334
Bartram Trail historical markers: Augusta, Ga., 74; Blue Sink, Fla., 132; Columbus, Ga., 236; Crawfordville, Ga., 215; Echeconee Creek, Ga., 223; Fort Perry, Ga., 224; Knoxville, Ga., 223; Lake Kanapaha, Fla., 125; Micanopy, Fla., 125; Mosquito Lagoon, Fla., 120; Ocmulgee National Monument, Ga., 215; Oswitchee, Ala., 232; Palatka, Fla., 111; Paynes Prairie, Fla., 125; Pensacola, Fla., 267, 271; Savannah, Ga., 24; Stockton, Ala., 261; Talbotton, Ga., 225; Tuskegee National Forest, Ala., 242; zebra butterfly, Fla., 120

342   Index

Bartram Trail Library, 83
Bartram Trail Roadside Park, Ga., 85
Bartram, William, 1–6; account of New Smyrna, 119; acquaintances, 7; aids the patriots, 99; the alligator battle, 6, 115; assisted by Henry Laurens, 157; association with Dr. Chalmers, 155; at Congress of Fort Picolata, 104; attitude towards Native Americans, 5, 222; attitude towards nature, 4; battles alligators, 4, 6; botanical discoveries, 165; business endeavors, 316; contracts fever, 259; criticism of, 1, 5, 6, 108; death, 6; departs Charleston for home, 143; early life, 3–6; employed by De Brahm, 109, 120; encounter with the wolf, 113; encounters storm on Lake Beresford, 109; establishes plantation at Picolata, 104; explores the Broad River, 93; friend to loyalists and patriots, 174; friendship with James Grant, 197; his fame, 6; his personality, 1, 4, 108; his spirituality, 4; honored in Mississippi, 279; illness, 277; incorrectly identified as King's botanist, 232; later years, 5; location of drawings, 7; location of specimens, 7; mentor to American scientists, 6; named Puc-Puggy, 112; plant discoveries, 68, 70, 146; reaches source of the St. Johns River, 117, 120; shipwrecked, 4, 99, 105, 117, 120; similarities to G. W. Carver, 243; spirituality, 4; the survey party, 92; the Travels, 4; works for De Brahm, 3, 16, 18

Descriptions: anhinga, 109; Estatoe Falls, 193; Fall Line Sandhills, 219; Florida Scrub, 113, 114; Florida sinkholes, 128; gopher tortoise, 114, 163; granite outcrops, 69, 184; limpkin, 115, 134; mound near New Smyrna, 120; rocks at Myrtle Beach, 311; royal palm, 109; scrub jay, 114

Discoveries: bottlebrush buckeye, 229, 254; Georgia plume, 165; fevertree, 50; Franklinia, 50; Fraser magnolia, 192; oak-leaf hydrangea, 223

Social encounters: Alexander Cameron, 171, 174; André Michaux, 144, 172; Attakullakulla, 205; Farmar family, 261; François Michaux, 144; French planter at Pointe Coupee, 296; Gov. James Wright, 26; Gov. William Tryon, 318; Henry Laurens, 149, 156; James Habersham, 25; John Stuart, 152; the Intrepid Seminole, 4

Travels: Alabama, 247; Alachua, 123, 126, 127; Ashley River, 145; Augusta, 17, 64, 73; Blue Sink, 132; Blue Springs, 117; Broad River, 92; Buffalo Lick, 84; Cape Fear to Charleston, 143; Charleston, 143, 151; Charlotia, 109, 112; Cherokee Corner, 85; Cherokee Middle Towns, 199; Cherokee Nation, 192, 195; Cherokee Path, 192; coastal South Carolina, 309; Cuscowilla, 126; East Florida, 2, 99; Flat Rock, 210; Ft. Apalachicola, 232; Ft. Charlotte, 173; Ft. James, 92; Ft. Moore, 71; Ft. Toulouse, 248; Galphin's Cowpen, 58; Georgia Coast, 15; Gov. Brown's Louisiana property, 295; Gulf Coast, 277; Baton Rouge, 294; Keowee, 183; King's Road, 169; Kolomi, 246; Lake Pontchartrain, 282; Lake Waccamaw, 319; Little Tennessee River, 193; Lower Alabama, 251; Lower Creek Trading Path, 208–210, 224; Manatee Springs, 132; Manchac, La., 293; Mississippi River, 290; Mobile, 257; Nantahala Mountains, 201; New Purchase, 73, 77, 80, 82, 84, 92; New Smyrna, 117; North Carolina, 316; Northeast Georgia, 189, 191; Oconee River, 87; Pensacola, 267, 271; Mobile & Pensacola Path, 253; Point Coupee, 289; return to Philadelphia, 323; Savannah, 14, 15, 24, 26; Savannah River, 89; Seneca, 172, 183; Shell Bluff, 58; Silver Glen Springs, 113; Sisters Ferry on Savannah River, 163; South Carolina, 161, 162, 171, 179, 186, 300; St. Augustine, 16, 102; St. Johns River, 109, 115; Suwannee River, 133; Upper Creek Towns, 241; Upper Savannah River, 95; West Georgia, 219–221; Winyah Bay, 305; Wrightsborough, 71; Yuchi Town, 83, 232

Bartram, William I (grandfather), 1, 316
Bartram, William II (uncle), 1, 2, 4, 316, 319
Baruch, Bernard, 305
Baruch Forest Service Institute, 305
basswood, 132
Bath, N.C., 313
Baton Rouge, La., 9, 257, 259, 267, 286, 288, 290, 291, 293–295
the Battery, 139, 151
Battery White, 305
Battle of Alligator Creek Bridge, 53, 99
Battle of Bloody Marsh, 13, 26, 42, 47. 160, 227
Battle of Brier Creek, 54, 57
Battle of Bunker Hill, 22, 72, 216
Battle of Burke County Jail, 57
Battle of Burnt Corn, 244, 245, 253
Battle of Chippewa, 22
Battle of Cowpens, 142, 183, 186
Battle of Culloden (1746), 50, 320
Battle of Echoe, 193
Battle of Econfinnah, 244
Battle of Fort Mims. *See* Fort Mims
Battle of Holy Ground, 251
Battle of Horseshoe Bend, 206, 241, 249
Battle of Kettle Creek, 67, 83, 183
Battle of King's Mountain, 62, 142, 245
Battle of Long Cane Creek, 174
Battle of Mobile, 262
Battle of Monterey, 22
Battle of Moore's Creek, 315, 319
Battle of New Orleans, 22, 285, 286
Battle of Ninety Six, 177, 183
Battle of Parker's Ferry, 169
Battle of Sorrell, 22
Battle of Sullivan's Island, 144
Battle of the Narrows, 193, 197, 200
Battle of the Waxhaws, 299
Baxter Mound, 121
Bay Minette, Ala., 261
Bay St. Louis, Miss., 279, 284
Bay Tree Lake State Natural Area, N.C., 319
Bayard Point Conservation Area, Fla., 104
Bayfront Parkway, Pensacola, 267
Bayou Fountain, La., 293
Bayou La Batre, Ala., 262, 275
Bayou Lacombe Museum, La., 284
Bayou Lafource, La., 291
Bayou Lamotte, La., 278
Bayou Manchac, La., 9, 257, 281, 290, 291, 292
Bayou Pigeon, La., 292
Bayou Placquemine, 294
Bayou Sara, La., 295
Bayou Savage Refuge, 286
Bayou Segnette State Park, La., 286
Bayou Sorrell, La., 292
Bayou Teche, La., 291
the Bayougoulas, 281, 289, 294, 296
Bazares, Guido de las, 256
Beach Institute African-American Cultural Center, 27
Beachwalker County Park, S.C., 143
BEAKS, 101
Beamer, James, 181
bear grass, 114
Bear Island Wildlife Management Area, S.C., 169
Beasley, Daniel, 260
Beatrice, Ala., 253

Beaufort Arsenal Museum, 167
Beaufort College, 165
Beaufort Conference (1787), 42, 187
Beaufort County, S.C., 138, 160, 161, 166
Beaufort Inlet, N.C., 313
Beaufort Library Society, 165
Beaufort Precinct, 18
Beaufort River, 161, 167
Beaufort, S.C., 12, 15, 28, 102, 140, 154, 160, 164, 166, 167, 171; cotton prosperity, 161; indigo economy, 160; site of Assembly in 1772, 140
Beauregard House, 286
Beauvoir, 279
Beauvois, Palisot de, 318
Beaverdam Creek, 56
Beaverdam Mound, 91, 95
Bedford, Duke of. *See* Russell, John, 4th Duke of Bedford
Beech Island, S.C., 60, 71
Beechertown Recreation Area, 205, 206
Bees Ferry Road, 143
Beet Island, S.C., 169
Belair Road, 65
Bellamy Road, 105, 128, 134
Belle Isle Plantation, 305
Belle Vista Plantation, 105
Belle W. Baruch Institute for Marine Biology, 305
Bellefield Nature Center, 306
Bellinger, William, 163
Bellingrath Gardens, 262
Bell's Ferry, 92
Beloved Woman, 205
Below Dam Recreation Area, Ga., 66
Belton, S.C., 171
Benavides, Antonio de, 106
Benjamin Fitzpatrick Bridge, 244
Benning, Henry Lewis, 230
Bentley, Hugh, 230
Benton, TN, 205
Beresford, Lord, 109, 117
Beresford Station, 109
Berkeley County Museum, 150
Berkeley County, S.C., 138, 146, 149, 150, 182
Berkeley, John; Baron of Stratton, 138, 312
Berkeley, Sir William, 138
Bermuda, 161
Best Friend of Charleston, 156
Beth Elohim Cemetery, Georgetown, 306
Bethany, Ga., 16, 54
Bethany, S.C., 67
Bethel Baptist Institutional Church, 102
Bethel Presbyterian Church, 169
Bethesda Gate, Savannah, 22, 26
Bethesda Orphanage, 17, 20, 24, 26
Bethesda Park, Fla., 103
Betty Creek, 191; Botanical Area, 193
Biafran Bight, 34
Bibb County, Ga., 217
Bibb, William Wyatt, 217, 257
Bicentennial Park, Tallassee, 244
Bienville, Jean Baptiste le Moyne, Sieur de, 256, 261, 266, 269, 289; becomes governor of Louisiana, 264; establishes Louisiana, 288; establishes trade with Creeks, 238; moves capital to New Biloxi, 279; surveys New Orleans, 286
Bienville Square, Mobile, 265
Big Bend Aquatic Preserve, Fla., 134
Big Bend Saltwater Paddling Trail, Fla., 134
Big Biloxi River, 278
Big Branch Marsh National Wildlife Refuge, La., 284
Big Creek, 211
Big Elk, 79

Big Escambia Creek, 253
Big Hart Campground, Ga., 66
Big Island, S.C., 169
Big Lagoon State Recreation Area, Fla., 270
Big Mortar Swamp, 29
Big Scrub, 113, 114
Big Spring, 87
Big Talbot Island, Fla., 43
Big Warrior, 50, 242, 245, 246
Biggins Church, 148
Biggins Creek, 150
Bignon, Poulain du, 49
Biloxi Bay, 273
Biloxi, Miss., 273, 278, 279, 280, 288; capital of Louisiana, 262, 278
Biloxi River, 275
Biloxi Wildlife Management Area, Miss., 282
the Biloxis, 274, 278
Biloxy Parish, Mississippi Territory, 275
bindweed, 187
Bird Iron Works, 211
Bird Island, N.C., 317
Bird Key-Stono Heritage Preserve, S.C., 144
bison, 126,
bitternut hickory, 69
Bivens Arm Nature Park, Gainesville, 127
black bear, 119, 125, 133, 145, 278, 309
Black Belt, 221
black cohosh, 92
Black Creek National Wild and Scenic River, Miss., 278–279
Black Creek Trail, 279
Black Heritage Trail, Montgomery, 247
Black River, S.C., 298, 305, 307; Black River Swamp Preserve, 307; Canoe Trail, S.C., 306
Black Rock Mountain State Park, Ga., 191, 192
Black Seminoles, 123
Black Warrior, 238
Black Warrior River, 238
Blackbeard. *See* Teach, Edward
Blackbeard Island National Wildlife Refuge, Ga., 35
Blackwater River, 270
Blackwater River Forest & State Park, Fla., 270
bladderwort, 278, 317
Bladen County, N.C., 316, 317, 319, 321
Bladen Lakes State Forest, N.C., 317, 320
Bladen, Martin, 321
Blakeley, Ala., 261
bloodroot, 68, 92, 186
Bloody Marsh, 28, 37
Blue Cypress Park, Fla., 103
Blue Ridge Escarpment, 184, 185, 186, 191, 194
Blue Ridge Gorges, 185
Blue Ridge Mountains, 89, 170, 182, 185, 193, 201; botanical areas, 192; boundary of Cherokee Nation, 182; explored by Dr. Alexander Garden, 153; geological features, 187, 189; recreation, 186
Blue Ridge Railroad, 187, 192; Historical Trail, 187
Blue Sink, Fla., 132
Blue Springs, Ga., 56; Blue Springs County Park, 56
Blue Springs State Park, Fla., 3, 8, 109, 117
Blue Valley, 191
Blue Wall, 185
blueberry, 311
Bluff Lake, 163
bluff oak, 132
Bluff Plantation, 148
Bluffton, S.C., 166
Blythe Island Regional Park, Ga., 49
Board of Trade and Plantations, 18, 37, 42, 49, 80

Boat Yard, Ala., 260
Bob Campbell Geology Museum, Clemson, 182
Bobby Brown State Park, Ga., 89
bobcat, 116, 133
Bocage Plantation, 286
Bogalusa, La., 279, 287
Bogue Chitto National Wildlife Refuge, 282
Bogue Falaya, La., 285; Bogue Falaya Park, 285
Bogue Lacombe, 284
Bogue Lusa Pioneer Museum, 287
Bolen's Bluff, 126
boll weevil, 71, 76, 165
Bolzius, Rev. Johann Martin, 18, 26
Bon Secour National Wildlife Refuge, Ala., 262
Bonar, William, 241
Bonaventure Cemetery, Savannah, 21
Bond Swamp National Wildlife Refuge, Ga., 216
Bonham's Stand, 248
Bonneau family, 147
Bonnet Carré Spillway, 285, 286
Bonnet, Stede, 139, 313
Boone, Daniel, 251
Boone Hall, 148
Boone, John, 148
Boone, Thomas, 61, 140
Boonesborough, S.C., 175
Bordeaux, France, 65
Border Wizard Owl, 186. *See also* Pickens, Andrew
Bosomworth, Thomas, 18, 31, 35
Boston, Mass., 14
botanical gardens: *Central Florida*: Lake Helen Garden Club, 119; Sugar Mill Gardens, 119; *Central Georgia*: Lockerly Arboretum, 214; *Coastal Georgia*: Chatham County Garden Center & Botanical Gardens, 21; Coastal Gardens, 19; LeConte-Woodmanston Plantation, 33; *Coastal North Carolina*: Airlie Gardens, 318; Burgwin-Wright House, 322; Greenfield Gardens, 318; New Hanover County Arboretum, 318; Orton Plantation, 318; *East Florida*: Sugar Mill Gardens, 119; *Eastern Louisiana*: Zemurrey Gardens, 285; *Georgetown*: Lafayette Park, 306; *Mississippi River*: Butler Greenwood Plantation, 295; City Park & Botanical Garden, 286; Mary Ann Brown Preserve, 295; Mary Pipes Butler Garden, 295; Rosedown Plantation & Gardens, 295; Windrush Gardens, 294; *Mobile*: Bellingrath Gardens, 262; Biophilia Nature Center, 262; Mobile Botanical Gardens, 263; Weeks Bay National Estuarine Reserve, 262; *North-central Florida*: Kanapaha Gardens, 128; *Pensacola*: Zoo at Gulf Breeze, 269; *Piedmont Georgia*: State Botanical Garden of Georgia, 85; *Upper South Carolina*: South Carolina State Botanical Garden, 182; *Western North Carolina*: Highlands Botanical Garden, 194
Botsford, Rev. Edward, 56
Bottle Creek Mound, 261
bottlebrush buckeye, 70, 229, 254
bottlenose dolphin, 133
Boudinot, Elias, 199
Boulware Springs Park, Gainesville, 127
boundary: between the colonies and Indian nations, 61, 154, 174; East Florida, 98, 104; Mississippi Territory, 250, 275; New Purchase, 79, 84; South Carolina and Cherokee Nation, 173, 175; South Carolina and North Carolina, 313–315; West Florida, 257, 274
Boundary House, N.C., 309, 311, 316
bounty land: East Florida, 98; Franklin County, Ga., 79; South Carolina Piedmont, 179; Washington County, Ga., 208

Bouquet, Henry, 2, 3
bousillage, 296
Bowlegs, 123
Bowman, Ga., 92
Boyd, Fortson, 226
Boyd, James, 83
Brailsford, William, 45
Brampton Plantation, 18, 26
Brand, Ellis, 313
Brandon, Ga., 61, 69
Brantley County, Ga., 42
Brass Town, 182
Bratton, William, 171
Braunsweig, Germany, 49
Bray, Rev. Dr. Thomas, 12
Bray, William, 160
Breaux Bridge, La., 292
Breintnall, Joseph, 3
Brevard Fault, 187
Brewton, Frances, 148
Brewton, Miles, 151
Brier Creek, 54, 56, 57, 61, 69, 208, 211
Brim, Emperor, 18, 166, 231
bristle fern, 184
Britain: allied to the Chickamaugas, 174; arms the Red Sticks, 253; civil war, 137; claims North America, 96; colonization efforts, 137, 159; conflict with the colonies, 14, 171; cotton imports, 161; creates the colony of Carolina, 159; declares war on Holland, 157; desires Southern colonies, 114; embargoed by Continental Congress, 160; enclosure laws, 175; exchanges Cuba for Florida, 266; exploration of North America, 312; first American minister, 145; gains control of Louisiana, 256; gains Florida, 98; gains Mobile, 264; gains St. Augustine, 106; government corruption, 181; in Queen Anne's War, 160; influence among the Creeks, 250; instigates Cherokee attacks, 183; intrigue among the Cherokees, 171; involvement in First Seminole War, 241; land grants in West Florida, 290; loses West Florida, 290; navy, 13; plans to invade Louisiana, 257; plot to incite the Cherokees, 174; preys upon Spanish shipping, 106; refuge for Huguenots, 303; relations with the Cherokees, 206; relations with the Creeks, 222, 231, 239, 244; relations with the Seminoles, 123; Southern strategy to end the Revolution, 299; tensions with United States, 232; textile industry, 76; trade goods, 18; trade with Creeks, 264; trade with the colonies, 76; treaty with Spain, 97; war with Spain, 104, 312

British military forces: 15, 32, 33; agents, 230; attack Charleston, 171; attacked by Francis Marion, 299; attempt to clear Bayou Manchac, 293; bombard Georgetown, 299; burn Brunswick, N.C., 318; burn Sheldon Church, 167; capture Jonathan Bryan, 18; confiscate rice in Lowcountry, 169; court Andrew Pickens, 186; defeat at King's Mountain, 176; defeat at New Orleans, 285; depart Spanish West Florida, 267; destroy Mepkin Plantation, 149; evacuate East Florida, 99; evacuate Savannah, 25; execute Isaac Haynes, 169; expelled from Spanish Florida, 267; garrison at Fort Toulouse, 248; headquartered in Brewton House, 151; imprison Charles Pinckney, 148; in East Florida, 99; in Florida, 15; in North America, 15, 29, 62, 140; in upper Georgia, 83; invade Georgia, 15, 29; lay waste to Lowcountry, 161; officers, 260; operate in Spanish West Florida, 257; planters alienated by Willing's Raiders, 290; ravage the Lowcountry, 299; Regulars, 56; rights of American citizens, 14; settle Feliciana

344   *Index*

Parish, 295; soldiers, 54; re-enactors, 177; surrender at Yorktown, 25; take Charleston, 142; threaten Charleston, 151; treaties with Cherokees, 201; withdraw from Augusta, 62
    Occupation: Augusta, 83; Beaufort, S.C., 161; Georgetown, 299; Georgia, 83; Savannah, 26, 160; Wilmington, 321;
British East Florida. *See* East Florida
British Government House, Pensacola, 271
British Museum, 1, 12, 165
British Royal Society, 13, 49
British West Florida. *See* West Florida
Broad River, 8, 33, 65, 79, 82, 88, 89, 92; cotton culture, 64; the survey party, 92; frontier, 80; population, 79, 89, 92; Revolutionary action, 62; settlement, 64, 79, 88, 89; tobacco, 89; Tories, 95
Broad River Camp, 89
Broad River Heritage Preserve, 92
Broken Arrow, 231
Broken Arrow Resolution, 1825, 237
Bronson, Fla., 125, 128
Brookgreen Gardens, 309
Brooklyn, Miss., 278
Broughton Island, Ga., 8, 38, 42, 43, 46, 157
Brown, Chester, 290
Brown, James, 221
Brown, Montfort, 266, 295
brown pelican, 284
Brown, Rev. Pearly, 221
Brown, Samuel, 73
Brown, Thomas, 15, 19, 51, 53, 59, 62, 99, 106, 171, 173, 174, 205, 206; biography, 70
Brown's Ferry Vessel, 307
Brown's Mount Educational Center, 216
Brunswick Canal, 45
Brunswick County, N.C., 321
Brunswick, Ga., 25, 42, 48, 89, 157
Brunswick, N.C., 3, 313, 315, 317, 321
Brunswick Pulp and Paper Company, 34, 49
Bryan, Andrew, 19
Bryan County, 21, 39
Bryan, Hugh, 18, 160, 168
Bryan, Jonathan, 15, 18, 21, 98, 168
Bryan, Joseph, 160, 168
Bryan, Katherine, 160
Bryson City, N.C., 206, 207
Buccaneer State Park, Miss., 279
Buck Hall Recreation Area, S.C., 302
Buck Head, N.C., 319
Buckingham, James Silk, 221
Buckman lock, 111
Buena Vista, Ga., 221
Buffalo Bluff, St. Johns River, 112
Buffalo Creek, 82, 210
Buffalo Lick. *See* Great Buffalo Lick
Buffalo Lick, at Philomath, 83
Buffalo Lick Monument, Union Point, 83
Buffalo Swamp Natural Heritage Preserve, 38
Bugnion family, 164
Bull, Burnaby, 160
Bull family, 151, 167
Bull Island, S.C., 300
Bull, John, 160
Bull, Stephen, 14, 160
Bull, Jr., William, 140, 168, 171
Bull, Mary, 160
Bull, Sr., William, 12, 21, 160, 167, 168
Bull Town Swamp, 34
Bulloch, Archibald, 14, 25, 26
Bulloch County, Ga., 57
bulrush, 148
Burden Research Plantation, 294
Burgaw, N.C., 321

Burgoyne, Gen. John, 147
Burgwin, John, 322
Burgwin-Wright House, 322
Burington, Gov. George, 313
Burke County, Ga., 29, 54, 165; courthouse, 57; during Revolution, 64; museum, 57
Burke County Rangers, 213
Burke, Edmund, 12, 54, 147, 157
Burks Mountain, 65, 69
Burningtown Creek, 200
Burningtown Falls, 201
Burningtown Gap, 8, 200, 201
Burnt Church, 169
Burnt Corn, Al, 250, 253
Burnt Fort, 50, 51
Burr, Aaron, 46, 213, 215, 309
Burrell's Ford Recreation Area, 185
Burton Mill, 89
Bushyhead family, 154
Bussell Island, 203
Bussey Point Wildlife Management Area, 66
Bute, Earl of. *See* Stuart, John, 3rd Earl of Bute
Butler County, Ala., 251, 253, 254
Butler Greenwood Plantation, 295
Butler Island, Ga., 37, 38
Butler, Pierce, 37, 46
Butler, William, 253, 254
Butler's Point, St. Simons Island, 46
Buzzard Roost Ford, 223
Buzzard Roost Heritage Preserve, 187
Byrne's Landing, 260

C

Cabbage Row, Charleston, 144
Cabbage Slough, 120
Cabeza de Vaca, Alvar Núñez, 256
Cabildo, New Orleans, 285
Cabrera, Don Juan de, 227
Cabretta Island, Ga., 35
Cabretta Research Project, 19
Cacique of Kiawah, 137
Cadillac, Antoine de la Mothe, 262, 264, 279
Cadillac Square Park, Dauphin Island, 262
Caesar's Head State Park, S.C., 186
Cahaba, Ala., 256
Cahaba River, 238, 256
Cainhoy, S.C., 148
Calabash, N.C., 316, 317
Calcutta, India, 298, 306
Calderon, Bishop, 227
Calhoun, Catherine, 173, 182
Calhoun Falls, S.C., 67, 171, 174
Calhoun Falls State Park, S.C., 174
Calhoun family, 170, 173
Calhoun, Ga., 199, 205
Calhoun, John C., 22, 155, 173, 182, 187
Calhoun Park, 173
Calhoun, Patrick, 171, 182
Calhoun, Rebecca, 186
Calhoun Square, Savannah, 22
Callahan, Fla., 53, 102
Callaway Gardens, 234
Callaway Plantation, 84
Calvin, John, 303
Camak, Ga., 76, 209, 217
Camak, James W., 211
Cambridge, S.C., 177
Camden County, Ga., 42, 53
Camden, Earl of. *See* Pratt, Charles, 1st Earl of Camden
Camden, S.C., 89, 91, 171, 178, 299
camellia, 33, 146
Cameron, Alexander, 8, 57, 171, 174, 197, 206; allied with Dragging Canoe, 204; Battle of Seneca, 183; incites the Cherokees, 179
Cameron, George, 174
Camp Pinckney, 42
Camp Pinckney Park, Ga., 51
Camp Tomahawk, 103
Campbell, Archibald, 15, 59, 62, 99
Campbell, Arthur, 197, 205
Campbell, John, 174, 266, 319
Campbell, Lord William, 140, 151, 171
Campbell, Martin & Son, 80
Campbellton, N.C., 320
Canada, 105, 288; fur traders, 288; obtained by Britain, 2; settled by French, 159
Canary Islanders, 289
Canaveral Marshes Conservation Area, Fla., 121
Canaveral National Seashore, 120
Candace R. Strawn-Lake Dias County Park, Volusia County, Fla., 114
Cane Bayou, 284
Cane Island, S.C., 168
Canoe Fight, 251, 254
Canoochee River, 19, 33
Cape Fear, 139, 165, 298, 308, 312–316
Cape Fear Botanical Garden, 321
Cape Fear Coast Visitors Information Center, 322
Cape Fear Indians, 316, 321
Cape Fear Museum, 321
Cape Fear River, 1, 3, 9, 143, 309, 312, 316, 321
Cape Romain National Wildlife Refuge, S.C., 300
Cape San Romano, 302
Capers Island Heritage Preserve, S.C., 300
Capote, Truman, 253
Capuchin monks, 295
Caravelle Ranch Conservation Area, Fla., 112
Cardross, Lord, 159, 167
Caribbean: patrolled by pirates, 105; route of African diseases, 145
CARL (Conservation and Recreation Lands), 112
Carl Duval Moore State Forest & Park, Fla., 111
Carlisle, Earl of. *See* Howard, Charles, Earl of Carlisle
Carlyle, Thomas, 1
Carnegie family, 50
Carney's Cowpen, 42
Carolina, 137; and religious freedom, 303; named for Charles IX of France, 96; trade with Creeks, 238
Carolina bays, 302, 317
Carolina Beach, N.C., 318
Carolina Beach State Park, N.C., 318
Carolina Gold Rice, 164, 304
Carolina Merchant (ship), 160
Carolina silverbell, 92, 153, 193
Carolinas: migration from, 64, 223, 243; migration into, 89; presence of Carolina bays, 302; refuge for Huguenots, 303
Carolinians: aid Georgians, 160; destroy Spanish missions, 97; Indian trade, 239; rivalry with Virginians, 79; settle Mississippi Territory, 265; trade with Creeks, 227
Carondelet, Francisco, 284
Carr, Ann, 6
Carr, Mark, 32
Carr, Robert, 6
Carroll County, Ga., 221
Carr's Hill, Athens, 82
Carrville, Ala., 244
Carteret, Sir George, 138, 305
Cartoogechay Creek, 200
Carver Creek Methodist Church, N.C., 319
Carver, George Washington, 243
Carver, Moses and Susan, 243
Carver Museum, 243

Cary State Forest, Fla., 102, 128
Cary, Thomas, 300
Cashiers, N.C., 201
Cassadega, Fla., 119
Cassette Girls, 279
Castiglioni, Luigi, 17
Castillo de San Marcos, 47, 97, 104, 106, 160
Caswell, Richard, 319
Cat Island, S.C., 168, 305
Catahoula Creek, 279
catalpa, 146
Catawba Reservation, 139
Catawba River, 139, 185, 189
Catawbas, 139, 166, 170, 307, 316; at Congress of Augusta, 61; in Cherokee War, 193; join Yamassee War, 138
Cateechee, 176, 187
Catesby, Mark, 2, 3, 20, 85, 146
Catesby trillium, 87
Cathead Creek, 29, 37; Cathead Creek Nature Preserve, 38
Cathedral Basilica of St. Augustine, 106
Catherine Street Fire Station, 102
Catholic Church, 82
Catholicism, 106
Catholics, 159, 175; among Native Americans, 106; at war with French Protestants, 96; banned from Southern colonies, 156; France and Spain allied against England, 273; in conflict with Huguenots, 303; in Louisiana, 290, 293, 296; Southern missionary work, 232
Catoma Creek, 242
Catskill Mountains, 1
Causton, Thomas, 25
Ceasar, the slave, 251, 254
Cedar Island, S.C., 304
Cedar Key, Fla., 53, 133
Cedar Key Scrub State Reserve. Fla., 133
Cedar Key State Museum, 133
Cedar Keys National Wildlife Refuge, 133
Cedar Shoals, Athens, 82, 86
Ceded Lands. *See* New Purchase
Center of the Sunbelt South, 236
Center of the World, 92
Central Florida Zoo, 119
Central of Georgia Railroad, 26
Chacala Lake, 126
Chadbourn, N.C., 319
Chalmers, Dr. Lionel, 2, 143, 154
Chalmette Plantation, 286
Champney River Park, Ga., 38
Chapman, Johnny "Appleseed", 102
Chapman oak, 114, 133
Charles I, King of England, 137, 312
Charles II, King of England, 137, 159
Charles IX, King of France, 96, 158, 303
Charles Pinckney National Historic Site, Charleston, 148
Charles Town, N.C., 312, 318
Charles Towne Landing, 137, 145
Charlesfort, Port Royal, 96, 105, 158, 167
Charleston, 2, 15, 20, 21, 29, 34, 56, 76, 99, 135–143, 151, 164, 166, 171, 298; aristocracy, 138, 161; attacked by Spanish, 160; British siege, 142; center of government, 171; City Market, 155; declines during Antebellum period, 142; during the Yamassee War, 160, 166; economic rivalry with Savannah, 64, 142; falls to the British, 15, 142, 169, 171, 177; fortifications, 16, 18; founding, 97, 137; gardening, 151; historic district, 151; Indian trade, 77, 163; Indian trails, 174, 175; Library Society, 154, 155; loyalists flee the City, 154; northern limit of Chicora, 168; port for rice and cotton, 76, 142; Queen City of the South, 151; railroads, 70, 142; Regulator movement, 171; site of Michaux's garden, 146; Symphony, 156; the Bartram's visit in 1765, 3; visited by John Bartram, 142; Visitor Center, 156
Charleston & Western Carolina Railroad, 174
Charleston County, S.C., 135–143, 149
Charleston Harbor, 135, 142, 148, 151, 156
Charleston Museum, 143, 156, 165
Charleston Neck, 142
Charleston Road, 177
Charleston Single House, 156
Charleston Tea Plantation, 143
Charleston Wagon Road, 175
Charleston-Hamburg Railroad, 70, 72, 74, 76, 156
Charleston-Keowee Path, 170, 171, 175, 177, 179, 181, 183, 189
Charlotia, Fla., 108, 111
Charlotte Harbor, Fla., 96
Charlotte, N.C., 89, 170
Charlotte, Queen of England, 173
chaste tree, 86
Chateagué, Lemoyne de, 269
Chatham County, Ga., 21, 22
Chatham, Earl of. *See* Pitt, William, 1st Earl of Chatham
Chatham Square, Savannah, 22
Chatooga Escarpment, 191
Chatooga River, 8, 185, 187, 191, 192, 194
Chatooga River Trail, 186, 191
Chatooga River Watershed Coalition, 192
Chattahoochee County, Ga., 221, 235; Library & Archives, 230
Chattahoochee Indian Heritage Center, 232
Chattahoochee National Forest, 192
Chattahoochee Promenade, Columbus, 236
Chattahoochee River, 8, 54, 60, 130, 137, 163, 226–229, 230, 236, 239; boundary between Creeks and Georgia, 216; boundary of Mississippi Territory, 250, 260, 274; Creek settlements, 246; cultural sites, 233; discovery of bottlebrush buckeye, 70; home of Muskogees and Hitchitis, 219; home of the Cowetas, 208; home of the Lower Creeks, 215; home of the Oconees, 123, 208, 215, 232; Oconee migration, 126; settled by Yuchis, 83; steamboats, 230
Chattahoochee River Park, 236
Chattahoochee Valley: cultural history, 226–229
Chattanooga, TN, 76, 199, 204
Chatuga Old Town, 186, 192
Chau-Ram Park, S.C., 187
Chauga Old Town, 181, 182
Chauga River, 176, 181, 187
Chechesee, 160
Chef Menteur Pass, 286
Chehaw, Ala., 244
Chehaw National Indian Festival, 235
Chelocconeneauhasse (trail), 223
Cheoah Bald, 200, 205, 206
Cheoah Ranger District, 201
Cheoah Township, 206
Cheowee, 182
Cheraw, S.C., 171
Cheraws, 166, 189, 320
Cherohala Skyway, 206
Cherokee Corner, 79, 82, 84, 85, 92, 216
Cherokee County, N.C., 207
Cherokee Federal Highway, 76
Cherokee Foothills Scenic Highway, 184
Cherokee Interpretive Trail, 184
Cherokee Line, 8, 79, 82, 175, 179, 208
Cherokee Lower Towns, 170, 175, 176, 178, 179, 183, 184, 203; abandoned permanently, 179; attacked by North and South Carolina, 179; destruction, 171, 183
Cherokee Middle Towns, 174, 179, 189, 192, 200, 203; absorb refuges from Lower Towns, 179; burned by South Carolina militia, 157; destroyed by Grant, 193, 197
Cherokee Nation, 37, 54, 92, 143, 172, 199; 201, 206; boundaries, 85, 186, 197, 205
Cherokee, N.C., 201
Cherokee Overhill Towns, 174, 203–205
Cherokee Phoenix, 199
Cherokee Recreation Area, Ga., 66
Cherokee Removal, 197–199
Cherokee Shoals, Savannah River, 94
Cherokee Valley Towns, 179, 201
Cherokee War, 147, 157, 173, 177, 178, 183, 186, 197
Cherokees, 5, 18, 25, 174, 178–181, 195–200; accept land in Arkansas Territory, 189; aid British, 62; allied to South Carolina, 138, 166, 177, 178, 196; Americanization, 199; and the New Purchase, 73, 80; association with Alexander Cameron, 174; at Congress of Augusta, 61, 64; attack frontier settlements, 140, 174, 179, 204; attack Sherril's Fort, 83; attack South Carolina frontier, 171, 173, 183; attack the Southern colonies, 171; besiege Fort Loudon, 179; capitulate in the war with South Carolina, 179; Chickamauga Band, 174, 197; conflict with Tennessee settlers, 205; debt to traders, 79; defeat at Echoe, 191, 193, 197; defeat the South Carolina militia, 197; defeated by James Grant, 98; destroy Fort Loudon, 203; disenfranchised by Georgia, 199; displace the Shawnees, 71; during the Revolution, 197; Eastern Band, 199, 201, 206; eastern towns destroyed during Revolution, 183; encounter the Spanish, 196; envoys to England, 201, 206; history, 178, 184, 195; in North Georgia, 176; language, 197, 199, 201, 207; Lower Cherokees, 178; national government, 199; obtain guns, 178; Old Settlers, 197; Overhill Towns, 203; peace with the Americans, 197; petition against Removal Act, 241; promised protection by the United States, 182; push Creeks from Tennessee River, 203; Qualla Boundary, 201; receive land in the West, 197; relations with the Scots, 73; relations with whites, 79, 174, 205; relationship to John Stuart, 154; release claim to all land east of the Blue Ridge, 182; release claim to South Carolina, 179; retribution, 179; sites, 92; small pox epidemic, 196; Snowbird Band, 206; trade embargo, 183; trade with South Carolina, 178; trade with Virginians, 196; trails, 67; Treaty Party, 199; victory at the Battle of the Narrows, 193; visited by William Bartram, 4; war with South Carolina, 193; Women's Council, 205
Cherry Hill Recreation Area, 186; Cherry Hill Campground, 185
Chesapeake Bay, Va., 312
Chesser Homestead, 51
Chester, Peter, 260, 266, 272
Chewacla State Park, Ala., 242
Chiaha, 226
Chichimecos, 48, 60, 106
Chickamaugas, 174, 197, 205, 206
Chickasaws, 57, 61, 71; allied to South Carolina, 166; at Congress of Augusta, 61, 73; in Cherokee War, 193; in First Creek War, 241; members of the Creek Confederacy, 239; related to Koasatis, 248; Treaty of Hopewell, 182; war against the Tunicas, 296; war with Louisiana, 289

Chicken, George, 147, 178
Chicora, 135
Chicora, Francisco, 298
Chicora Indian Tribe of South Carolina, 307
Chicora-Waccamaw Tribe, 311
Chicorans, 298, 307
Chiefland, Fla., 128, 132
Chiffelle, Philotheos, 160
Chigelley, 231
Chiluques, 106
Chinaberry, 151
chincona, 145
Chinese elm, 86
Chippewa Square, Savannah, 22
Chitimachas, 293
Chocolate Ruins, 36
Choctafaula Creek, 242
Choctawhatchee National Forest, 269
Choctaws, 174, 256, 274, 278, 281; at Congress of Augusta, 61, 73; boundaries, 250; disperse the Natchez, 148; in First Creek War, 241; join the Yamassee War, 138, 166; join war against Creeks, 251; Lacombe Mission, 284; language, 247, 254, 256, 285; MOWA Band, 261; related to Koasatis, 248; treaty of Hopewell, 182
Chota, 154, 195, 203, 205
Christ Church Parish, Ga., 21
Christ Church, St. Simons Island, 46
Christ Episcopal Church, Mt. Pleasant, S.C., 148
Christ Episcopal Church, Savannah, 25
Christian, William, 204
Christianity. *See individual denominations*
Christmas Park, Fla., 121
Christophe, Henri, 15
Chuck Lennon Park, Fla., 115
Church Act of 1706, 138, 298
Church of England, 20, 138, 159
Church of the Ascension, Savannah, 26
Church-Waddel-Brumby House, 86
Churchill, Winston, 305
Circular Congregation Church, Charleston, 155
Citronelle, Ala., 261
City Exchange, Savannah, 24
City Hall Gallery, 153
City Market: Charleston, 148; Savannah, 26; Wilmington, 322
City Mills Dam, Columbus, 236
City Park & Botanical Garden, New Orleans, 286
Civil Rights Memorial, 247
Civil Rights Movement, 177, 247
Civil War, 21, 83, 146; begins at Fort Sumter, 148; causes decline in rice planting, 148, 304; causes decline of Wrightsborough, 71; destruction caused by, 166; divides the Creek Nation, 245; effect on Columbus, 236; fortifications, 305; frees Southern slaves, 76; Georgia capitol burned, 214; in Charleston, 142; Lumbees refuse to fight, 320; Mulberry Grove destroyed, 18; museums, 83; on the Mississippi River, 294; sea islands abandoned, 168; Sheldon Church burned, 167
Civilian Conservation Corps, 68, 114, 186, 309
Claiborne, Ala., 251, 253, 254
Claiborne, Ferdinand, 241, 251, 254, 257
Claiborne Herald, 253
Clam Creek Picnic Area, Jekyll Island, 49
Clarenden County, S.C., 307
Clarendon County, N.C., 312
Clark, Elijah, 15, 51, 53, 54, 62, 64, 67, 79, 83, 89, 99, 215
Clark Park and Nature Center, Fayetteville, N.C., 321
Clark, William, 88
Clarke County, Ala., 89

Clarke County, Ga., 79, 80, 86, 87, 89
Clarke County Museum, Ala., 254
Clarke, John, 68
Clarks Hill Lake, 66, 69
Clarks Hill, S.C., 67
Claude D. Kelley State Park, Ala., 254
Clay County, N.C., 207
Clay, Henry, 84, 199, 207
Clay Hill Campground, 66
Clayton, Ga., 76, 189, 192, 193
Clayton, John, 2
Clements Ferry Road, 143
Clemson, S.C., 182–183
Clemson, Thomas, 182
Clemson University, 179, 182, 305, 306; Coastal Research & Education Center, 145; Extension service, 182; Urban Research and Demonstration, 145
clethra, 193, 302
Cleveland, Benjamin, 79, 176, 187
Clifton Plantation, 300
climbing hydrangea, 92
Clinton, Sir Henry, 99, 142, 299, 315, 319, 151
Clyo, Ga., 163
Coast Highway, 29
Coastal Gardens, Savannah, 19
Coastal Georgia Land Trust, 29
Coastal Heritage Society, 27
Coastal Plain, 56, 64, 70, 170, 214, 275
cochineal, 24
Cochran, James, 311
Cochran, John, 160
Cochran's Ferry, 300
Cockspur Island, Ga., 14, 21
Cofaqui, 87, 208
Coffer Creek, 173
Cofitachequi, 58, 60, 91
Cohn Memorial Arboretum, Baton Rouge, 294
Cokie, La., 285
Colby, George, 119
Colclough Hill Audubon Sanctuary, Gainesville, 127
Colden, Cadwallader, 2, 153
Colden, Jane, 3
Colerain, Ga., 42, 51, 164
Coleridge, Samuel Taylor, 5
Coligny, Gaspard de, 96, 158, 303
College of Charleston, 144, 156, 157, 165
College of Philadelphia, 3
Colleton County Historical and Preservation Society, 169
Colleton County Museum, 169
Colleton County, S.C., 138, 149, 161, 169
Colleton, Peter, 137, 150
Colleton, Sir. John, 138
Colleton State Park, S.C., 143
Collinson, Peter, 1, 2–4, 151
Colonel's Island, Ga., 29
Colonial Cemetery, Savannah, 26, 32, 47, 174
Colonsay, 82
Columbia County, Ga., 69, 70, 72
Columbia River, 88
Columbia Road, 64
Columbia Square, Savannah, 22
Columbia Theological Seminary, 84
columbine, wild, 92
Columbus Black Heritage Tour, 236
Columbus, Christopher, 321
Columbus County, N.C., 321
Columbus, Diego, 135
Columbus Enquirer, 211
Columbus, Ga., 223, 226–229, 229, 230, 235–236
Columbus Iron Works Convention and Trade Center, 236

Columbus Museum, 230, 232
Columbus Road, 221
Combahee Ferry, 168
Combahee Indians, 158, 168
Combahee River, 138, 143, 160, 161, 167, 168
Commissioner's Creek, 215
Commissioner's Rock, 193
Committee of Continental Association, 146
Committee of Correspondence, N.C., 315
Committee of Safety: Georgia, 27, 62, 214; North Carolina, 317
Commons House of Assembly, Georgia, 13, 14, 18, 25
Commons House of Assembly, S.C., 140, 142, 154, 157
Company of Barbadian Adventurers, 137, 159
Company of the Indies, 288
Company of the West, 264, 279, 286, 288, 291
Compton, Spencer, 321
Condé, Louis de, 303
Condé-Charlotte Museum House, 265
Conecuh County, Ala., 251, 255
Conecuh National Forest, 270
Conecuh River, 254
coneflower, smooth, 85, 187
Coneross Park, S.C., 183
Confederate Carbine Factory, 244
Confederate Council of War, 175
Confederate Naval Museum, 236
Confederate Powder Works, 70, 76
Confederate States of America, 83, 247, 279, 317
Conference of Savannah (1757), 246
Congarees, 166
Congo, 161
Congregation Beth Elohim, 156
Congregationalists, 22, 28, 29, 32, 138, 152, 155
Congress at Fort Picolata (1765), 104
Congress of Augusta (1763), 61, 73
Congress, US, 296
Connecorte, 177, 206
USS Constitution, 169
Constitution, US, 208; signers, 69, 75, 155
Constitutional Convention, 6, 46; members, 145, 148, 165
Continental Army, 15, 27, 51, 57, 64, 83; entrapped in Charleston, 142; officers, 147, 153
Continental Congress, 14, 29, 32, 33, 62, 75; delegates, 140, 157, 181; embargoes British goods, 160; members, 153, 216, 304; Second Continental Congress, 14, 164
Conway Cabal, 157
Conway, S.C., 298, 308
Conwayborough, S.C., 308
Cook, James, 4
Cooks Station, Ala., 246
Cook's Tavern, 242
Coon Branch Natural Area, S.C., 185
coontie, 115, 133
Cooper, Lord Anthony Ashley, 1st Earl of Shaftesbury, 137, 138
Cooper River, 135, 143, 149, 155, 300; plantations, 148, 157
Coosa Province, 203, 239, 266
Coosa River, 71, 238, 239, 246, 247
Coosada, Ala., 242, 248
Coosas, 239, 244
Coosaw River, 166
Coosawhatchie River, 161, 166; Coosawhatchie Bridge, 161
Coosawhatchie, S.C., 166
Copeland Clan, 279
Copeland, James, 279
Copper Ridge Bald, 201
coquina, 104

Index 347

coral honeysuckle, 70
cord grass, 148
coreopsis, whorled, 92
Cornelia, Ga., 92
Cornells, Alexander, 244
Cornells, Davy, 245
Cornells, James, 253, 260
Cornells, Joseph, 245
Cornwallis, Lord General Charles, 68, 142, 151, 171, 267, 299, 315, 319, 320–322; exchanged for Henry Laurens, 142, 157; surrenders, 169
Coronaca, S.C., 183
Cortez, Hernando, 239
Coste, 203
Côte des Allemands, 286
cotton, 24, 265; causes mass migrations, 208; factors in Savannah, 24; fortunes in Louisiana, 286; in Piedmont Georgia, 84; migration of planters, 209, 223; on Mississippi River, 295; prices, 24; shipping, 70, 221, 254
cotton belt, 76
Cotton Exchange; Augusta, 70; Savannah, 24; Wilmington, 322
Cotton Exchange Welcome Center, Augusta, 74
cotton gin, 17, 64, 71, 73, 76
Cotton Kingdom, 76
Cotymore, Captain, 179, 183
cougar, 145
Council Chamber, Charleston, 155
Council, N.C., 319
Council of Safety, Georgia, 14, 21, 26, 31, 75
Council of Safety, S.C., 142, 147
Council of the Indies, 159, 298
Countess of Huntington, 20
Couper, John, 45
Coureurs de bois, 288
Covington, La., 284, 285
Cow Ford, 101, 102
Cow Keeper, *see Ahaya*
cowboys, 82
Cowee, 8, 199, 201
Cowee Creek, 201
Cowee Mountains, 8, 199, 200, 201
Coweeta Creek, 193
Coweeta Hydrologic Laboratory, 193
Coweta, 57, 164, 219, 222, 226–229, 230, 231, 236, 239, 241; burned by Spanish, 215; conference of 1739, 227; refuge of Creek Peace Party, 245
Cowetas, 208, 226–229, 239; on Ocmulgee River, 215; on Tennessee River, 195
Cowikee Creek, 234
Cowpen Lake, 125
Crackers, 61, 80, 127, 178
Craig, Major James, 321
Craven County, Carolina, 298
Craven County, N.C., 321
Craven County, S.C., 138, 149, 308
Crawford Square, Savannah, 22
Crawford, Ala., 241
Crawford County, Ga., 221, 223, 225
Crawford, Ga., 76, 82, 84
Crawford, William H., 22, 64, 84, 92, 173, 213, 225
Crawfordville, Ga., 76, 86, 217
Creek Agency, 8, 219, 219–221, 221, 222, 223
Creek Confederacy, 239–241, 247, 248; 1739 treaty with Georgia, 227; as sovereign nation, 208; break with Oconees, 232; Federal Road, 232; Hitchitis, 123; last land cession, 241; national leaders, 244; nature of national policy, 229; origins, 163, 226; peace town, 230
Creek Indians, 3, 5, 12, 13, 18, 26, 42, 47, 51, 54, 61

Creek Nation, 8, 50, 56, 243; and traders, 65; Bartram's visits, 259; boundary, 246; four foundation towns, 245; frontier, 230, 232; route of Federal Road, 223; traders, 244; William Bartram's visit, 242
Creek Nation East of the Mississippi, 259
Creek Stand, Ala., 242
Creek Towns, Lower, *see Lower Creek Towns*
Creek Towns, Upper, *see Upper Creek Towns*
Creek Trail of Tears Memorial, 232
Creek Village Replica, 233
Creek War of 1813–14, 123, 206, 222, 224, 230, 233,–234, 241–244, 246, 251, 260; re-enactment, 248; caused by construction of Federal Road, 232; Creek territorial lose, 265
Creek War of 1836, 229, 234
Creeks, 160, 226–229, 281; absorb the Yamassees, 166; aid British, 62; allied to South Carolina, 122; Americanization, 222, 241; debt to traders, 80; and Federal Road, 232; and the New Purchase, 73, 79, 80; and trade ban, 79; as Georgia allies, 13; assassinated at Tugaloo, 178; at Congress of Augusta, 61, 64, 73; attack Sherrill's fort, 83; attacks on Southern frontier, 183; attempt to sell land in Seminole territory, 98; battle Yamassees in Florida, 109; betrayed by Cherokees, 196; boundaries, 211, 250; cede the Oconee River, 79; civil war, 241; Creek Agency, 219, 232; destroy Spanish missions, 106, 126; expelled from Tennessee River, 203; history, 243; in west Georgia, 221; join the Yamassee War, 166, 138; migrate to Florida, 122; migrate to the West, 230; mixed bloods, 250; myths and legends, 230; National Council House, 241; Ocmulgee Reserve, 215; on Chattahoochee River, 233; origin of the name, 215, 239; Peace Party, 241, 245; Poarch Tribe, 259; prophets, 241; raid Sparta, 214; Red Sticks armed by British, 267; relations with Georgia, 73, 83, 227; relations with Spain, 232; relations with whites, 222; removal, 222, 229, 232, 241, 246, 251; sell land east of Chattahoochee, 216; sell West Georgia, 221; Southeastern Lower Muscogee Creek Indians, 270; Suwannee Bend Creeks, 233; treaties, 208, 214 217, 237; visited by William Bartram, 4; war with Yamassees, 123

  National Council: 230, 245; condemns McIntosh, 221; declares war on Georgia, 208
Creeks, Lower, 51, 57, 226–229, 230; conflict with Georgia, 62; join Seminoles, 126; lead opposition in First Creek War, 241; modernization, 222; relations with whites, 241; rescue Tuckabatchees, 245
Creeks, Upper, 238–242; join Seminoles, 126; trade with English, 238
Creighton Island, Ga., 35
Creole House Museum, 292
Creoles, 279, 290
Crepe Myrtle, 86, 144, 146
Crescent City, Fla., 113
Crescent Lake, 103
Crèvecoeur, St. John de, 3
Crocket, David, 199
Crokatt, James, 157
Crooked River State Park, Ga., 50
Crosby Arboretum, Miss., 279
Cross & Sword Amphitheater, 104
Cross City, Fla., 125, 133
Cross Creek, N.C., 319, 320
Cross Florida Greenway, 112; Barge Canal, 112
Cross-Florida Railroad, 133
Crowell, Capt. Henry, 223
Crowell, Col. John, 223

Crowell Indian Agency, 232
Crown of Tanase, 201
Crozat, Antoine, 264
crying bird, 115
Cryn, Lt. Danyel, 200
Crystal Springs Road Park, Fla., 103
Cuba, 96, 104, 284; exchanged for Florida, 266, 274, 281; refuge for Christian Indians, 106; supplies St. Augustine, 105
Cubo Defense Line, 106
Cuckolds Creek, 143
Cucumber Tree, 92
Cullasaja Gorge, 194, 201
Cullasaja River, 183, 194
Cullowhee, N.C., 201
Cultural Arts Center/the DeLand Museum of Art, 117
Cumberland, Duke of. *See Hanover, William, Duke of Cumberland*
Cumberland Island, 8, 13, 40, 43, 47, 50
Cumberland River, TN, 71
Cuming, Alexander, 201, 206
Cummer Museum of Art, 103
Cummer Sanctuary, 133
Cunningham, Robert, 171
Curry, George, 73
Cusaboes, 11, 135, 143
Cuscowilla, 8, 125
Cusso Indians, 158
cypress, 38; dwarf cypress, 16; bald cypress, 150
Cypress Creek Wildlife Management Area, 166
Cypress Gardens, 149
cyrilla, 153

D

dahoon, 302
Dale, Sam, 241, 251, 254
Dallas Culture, 203
Daniel, John, 83
Daniel, Robert, 138
Darby, Earl of, 7
Darien, Ga., 8, 13, 29, 34, 36, 52, 230
Darien, Panama, 36
Darien oak, 86
Darlington, William, 7, 85
D'Artaguette family, 294
Dartmouth, Earl of. *See Legge, William; 2nd Earl of Dartmouth*
Dartmouth, Ga., 89
Darwin, Charles, 7, 291, 295
Daufuskie Island, S.C., 34, 165, 161
Dauphin Island, Ala., 262, 273, 278, 288
Dauphin Island Sea Lab and Estuarium, 262
Davis Bayou, Miss., 278
Davis, Jefferson, 83, 279
Davis, Jimmie, 293
Davis, Sarah Taylor, 295
Davisboro, Ga., 213
dawn redwood, 86
daylilies, 19
De Brahm, William Gerard, 3, 16, 18, 35, 98, 105; builds Charleston fortifications, 156; employs William Bartram, 99, 109, 120
de Bry, Theodore, 96, 312
de la Howe, Dr. John, 173
De la Howe School for the Blind, 173
de Lacy, Roger, 73
De Saussure, Daniel, 102, 160, 166
De Saussure, David, 166
De Soto Expedition, 60, 77, 87, 91, 130, 178, 194, 215, 226, 238, 299; aftermath of their passage, 239; at Mabila, 256; at Ocute, 208, 214; at Piache, 254; at the Mississippi River, 288;

Battle of Mabila, 238; encounter the Coosas, 244; in Cherokee territory, 189, 195, 203; of Altamaha, 166; weakened by war, 266
De Soto, Hernando, 38, 58
De Soto National Forest, Miss., 278, 279
De Treville, Captain, 161
Dean Hall Plantation, 149
Dearing, Ga., 65, 71, 76, 210, 211, 217
Deas, John, 142, 147
de Beaufain family, 164
Declaration of Independence, 22, 25, 26, 29, 32, 142, 155; signers, 75, 106, 142, 146, 152, 155, 166, 216, 304
Deep Creek, 114, 172, 176
deerskin trade, 75, 112, 138, 164
Deveaux, Jr., Andrew, 161
DeKalb, Baron Johan, 305, 306
DeKalb County, Ga., 217
DeLand Area
DeLand, Fla., 109, 117; DeLand House Museum, 117; Public Library, 117
the Delawares, 195
DeLeon Springs State Recreation Area, Fla., 115
DeLile, Alyre Raffeneau, 318
Dellet, James, 253
Deloach family, 303
Demere, Paul, 206
Demere, Raymond, 18, 46, 154
Den, James, 45
Dennis Wildlife Center, S.C., 149
d'Estaing, Jean Baptiste Charles Henri Hector, Comte, 15, 79
Destrehan Plantation, 286
DeVeaux, André, 144
Deveaux Bank Heritage Preserve, S.C., 143
Devil's Courthouse, 185, 194
Devils Fork State Park, S.C., 185
Devil's Millhopper State Geological Site, Fla., 128
devilwood, 114
DeVorsey, Dr. Louis, 82, 210
DeWitt's Corner, 171, 175; DeWitt's Store, 175
Dexter Avenue King Memorial Baptist Church, 247
diamorpha, 69
Dickerson Road, 143
Dick's Creek, 191
Dicks, Zachariah, 71
Dickson, David, 214
Diego Plains, Fla., 104
Dillard, Ga., 191
Dillenius, John, 2
Dillingham Street Bridge, 230, 236
Dinwiddie County, Va., 214
Dirleton Plantation, 306
diseases, 145, 215
Dividings, 8, 76, 189
Dixie-Levy-Gilchrist Greenway, Fla., 132
Dobbs, Arthur, 61, 317, 322
Dock Street Theater, 154
Doctortown, Ga., 52, 211
Dog Bluff, S.C., 311
dog fennel, 146
Donald family, 175
Donalds, S.C., 175
Donaldsonville, La., 293, 289
Donnelley Wildlife Management Area, S.C., 169
Dooly County, Ga., 221
Dooly, John, 62, 67, 79, 83, 79
Dorchester Academy, 32
Dorchester County, S.C., 148, 149
Dorchester Ga., 32
Dorchester, S.C., 28, 29, 31, 32, 147
Dow, Lorenzo, 56, 236

Dow, Peggy, 236
Dragging Canoe, 174, 197, 204, 205, 206
Drake, Sir Francis, 112, 105, 312
Drayton, Charles, 145
Drayton Hall, 143, 145
Drayton Island, Fla., 109
Drayton, John, 145
Drayton, Thomas, 138
Drayton, William Henry, 3, 56, 98, 140, 142, 171
Dry Creek, 82
Dry, William, 318
Dubose family, 303
Ducks Unlimited, 169
Due West, S.C., 171, 175
Duke, Maxwell, 224
Duke Power Company, 185, 183
Dukesborough, 213
Dulac, La., 296
Dunbar, George, 36
Dunbar, William, 290, 295; biography, 290
Dungannon Plantation, 143
Dungeness Plantation, 50
Dunk, George Montagu, Earl of Halifax, 49
Dunlop, William, 160
Dunns Creek Conservation Area, Fla., 112
Dupont, Cornelius, 160
Dupont, Gideon, 160
Duplin County, N.C., 321
Durnford, Elias, 266
Dutch: settlers in Louisiana, 291
Dutch Bend, 251
Duval County, Fla., 98
dwarf fimbry, 311
dwarf live oak, 311
dwarf pawpaw, 43
Dyar's Mound, 208
Dyars Pasture Conservation Area, 87
Dyers Bluff Botanical Area, 87
dysentery, 15, 27, 164

E

E. Dale Joyner Nature Preserve, Fla., 102
Eagle and Phenix Mills, 236
Eagle Tavern, 87
Earl's Ford, 189, 192
Early, Eleazar, 82
Early, Peter, 87
Earth Day Nature Trail, 49
East Baton Rouge Parish, La., 282, 289, 296
East Feliciana Parish, La., 296
East Florida, 2, 3, 18, 32, 33, 37, 39, 43, 51, 96–97, 97–99, 281; African militia, 104; as British colony, 114; boundary, 98; explored by the Bartrams, 3, 98; explored by William Baldwin, 4, 7; loyalist haven, 106; officials, 147, 197; population, 106; Revolutionary activity, 70; second Spanish period, 99; surveyor general, 117, 120
East Florida Rangers, 15, 19, 51, 53, 59, 70, 99, 160
East Palatka, Fla., 108
East Ship Island, Miss., 278
East Tallassee, Ala., 244
Eastatoe, 181
Eastatoe Creek Heritage Preserve, S.C., 184
Eastern Band of Cherokees. See Cherokees, Eastern Band
Eastern Continental Divide, 192, 201
Eastwick, Andrew, 7
Eatonton, Ga., 211, 216
Ebenezer Creek, 13, 54, 69
Ebenezer, Ga., 8, 17, 18, 20, 54, 61, 164
Ebo Landing, St. Simons Island, 46

Echaw Church, 302
Echeconnee Creek, 222
Echoe, 193, 199, 206
Echols Mill, 88
Echota. See Chota
Econlockhatchee River, 120
Ecor Rouge, Ala., 261
Ecunchati, 247
Ed Stone Park, Fla., 117
Edgar, James, 14
Edgecombe County, N.C., 208
Edgefield County, S.C., 69, 72, 177
Edgefield, S.C., 68, 72
Edict of Nantes (1598), 138, 303
Edisto Beach State Park, S.C., 143
Edisto Indian Tribe, 147
Edisto Island, S.C., 143
Edisto Nature Trail, 169
Edisto River, 139, 143, 160, 169; Canoe and Kayak Trail, 143
the Edistoes, 158
Edward, Mathew, 172
Edward Waters College, 102
Edwin Stantin School, 102
Efau Hadjo, 245
Effingham County, Ga., 15, 17, 21, 56
Effingham, Earl of, See Howard, Thomas
Egan, Stephen, 43, 99
Egan's Creek, 43, 99
Egg Island, Ga., 38, 46
Eglin Air Force Base, 269
Egmont, Earl of. See Perceval, John, 1st Earl of Egmont
egret, 115
egret, great, 143
egret, snowy, 165
Ehret, C. D., 3
Eichold-Heustis Medical Museum of the South, Mobile, 263
Elbert County Environmental Forest, 89
Elbert County, Ga., 64, 80, 90, 92, 93, 95, 243
Elbert, Samuel, 15, 26, 95, 99
Elberta, Ala., 262
Elberton, Ga., 69, 92, 93; Granite Museum, 93
Elfe, Thomas, 155
Elijah Clark State Park, 67
Eliot, John, 266
Elizabeth I, Queen of England, 312
Elizabethtown, N.C., 316, 319
elk, 145
Ellicott, Andrew, 185, 261, 290
Ellicott Rock Wilderness Area, 185, 186, 201
Ellicott's Stone, 261
Elliott, Grey, 32
Elliott, Jane Reily, 145
Elliott, John, 32
Elliott, Stephen, 57, 165
Elliott, William, 149
Elliottia racemosa, see Georgia Plume
Ellis, Henry, 13, 22, 25, 42, 49, 69, 153
Ellis, John, 2, 153
Ellis Square, Savannah, 22
Elmore County, Ala., 246, 248; Museum, 248
Elmore, John Archer, 248
the Elms, 147
Elwell Ferry, N.C., 319
Emancipation, 306
Emanuel A.M.E. Church, Charleston, 156
Emanuel Point Shipwreck, 269
Emerald Coast, 269
Emeralda Marsh Conservation Area, Fla., 116
Emmaus Garden, Holy Trinity, Ala., 232
Endeavor, Cook's ship, 49
indenture, 157

Index 349

England, 18, 24, 25, 26, 37, 96; refuge for Huguenots, 96; refuge for loyalists, 168
the English, 32, 36; and their Indian allies, 73; businesses, 76; control trade among the Creeks, 247; cruelty to the Cherokees, 197; encroach in Spanish Florida, 159; establish Carolina colony, 160, 164, 298; gentry, 157; influence among the Lower Creeks, 227; influences in New Orleans, 285; language, 261; privateers, 312; protect coastal tribes, 137, 316; Protestants, 175; relations with Cherokees, 167, 178, 196; relations with Creeks, 231245, ; settle the Florida Parishes, 291, 295; slave catchers, 227; trade goods, 208, 227; trade with Cherokees, 178; trade with Creeks, 215, 227, 232, 238, 239; trade with Indians, 12, 160
Enterprise, Ala., 76
Enterprise, Fla., 119
Enterprise Mill, 70, 76
Erskine College, 175
Escamaçu Indians, 158, 159
Escambia Bay, 270
Escambia County, Ala., 251
Escambia County, Fla., 255, 259, 263, 270
Escambia River, 251
Estatoe Falls, 191, 193
Estatoe Town, 179, 182
Etiwan Indians, 135
Etonia Creek, 105
Etowah Trail, 76, 217
Eufaula, Ala., 234, 241, 266
Eufaula National Wildlife Refuge, Ala., 234
Eufaula Town, 226
Euhaw (Yamassee town), 160
Euhaw Baptist Church, 166
Euhaw Settlement, 166
Eulonia, Ga., 29, 34
Eurasia, 193
Europeans: conflict with Native Americans, 168; contact with Native Americans, 226, 312; deerskin trade, 75; explore Cape Fear, 312; explore the Southeastern coast, 158; health problems in Charleston, 138; in South Carolina, 311; succumb to diseases, 145
Evangelical Movement, 46
Eveleigh, George, 151
Eveleigh, Samuel, 73
Everglades, 123
Evergreen, Ala., 255
Ezekiel Harris House, Augusta, 76

F

Factor's Walk, Savannah, 24
Fairfield Plantation, 303
Fairhope, Ala., 261
Fairview-Riverside State Park, La., 285
Fall Line, 208, 214, 223
Fall Line Sandhills, 213, 219, 233
Fall Pioneer Rendezvous, 67
Falling Creek, 191
Falls of Coweta, 230
false dragonhead, 307
False River, La., 296
Fanning Springs, Fla., 128, 133
Fanning Springs State Recreation Area, Fla., 132, 133
Farm Hall, 260
Farmar, Elizabeth, 260
Farmar, Mary, 260
Farmar, Robert, 256, 265, 261; biography, 260; visited by Bartram, 259
Farmers Hall, 181
Fatio, Francis Philip, 101, 104

Fauquier, Francis, 61
Faver-Dykes State Park, Fla., 105
Fayetteville, N.C., 316, 320
Featherstonhaugh, George, 176, 242
Federal Road, 86, 176, 214, 215, 219, 221, 223, 229, 231, 232, 241, 242, 244, 246, 247, 251, 257, 260, 279; causes First Creek War, 241; cotton migration, 251; creation and construction, 232; remnants, 242, 251, 259; travel conditions, 223
Federal Town, 215
Federalists, 64
Feliciana Parish, La., 282
Felicianas, 295
Ferguson, Patrick, 62, 161
Fernandina, Fla., 43, 53, 99, 133; Old Fernandina, 43, 52, 99
fetterbush, 302, 311
fevertree, 3, 7, 38, 145, 165
Few, James, 62
Few, William, 62, 69, 75
Filature, 14, 25
filmy fern, 192
Finizy, Ferdinand, 84
Finney Creek, 191
Fireproof Building, Charleston, 153
First African American Baptist Church, 19
First African Baptist Church, 26
First Baptist Church, Charleston, 151
First Bryan Baptist Church, 19, 26
First Creek War. *See* Creek War of 1813–14
First Division Road, 221, 229, 231, 232
First Presbyterian Church, Charleston, 152
Fish River, 262
Fishdam, 89
Fishhawk Mountains, 194, 200
Fitzpatrick, Benjamin and Mary, 248
Fitzpatrick, John, 293
Fitzwalter, Joseph, 19, 24
Five Fathom Hole, 142
Five Killer, 205
Flagler, Henry, 53
flame azalea, 7, 17, 200, 201
Flat Rock, 209, 211
Flats, 193
flax, 24
Flea Hill, Ga., 50
Fletchall, Thomas, 70, 171
Flint River, 8, 54, 130, 163, 219–223, 239
Flint River Adventures, 224
floating bladderwort, 146
Flora Caroliniana, 146
Florence County, S.C., 307
Florence, Fla., 233
Florence Marina State Park, Ga., 226, 233
Florida: becomes depopulated, 122; botany, 69; boundaries, 244, 270; divided into east and west colonies by Britain, 266; early trails, 250, 270; exploration, 194; first capital established at Santa Elena, 168; first Spanish settlement, 105; French colonization, 159; frontier, 243; Gulf Coast, 133; history, 96–101; history of West Florida, 267; intrigues of Citizen Genet, 68; invaded by Oglethorpe, 13; invaded by patriots, 14, 15, 99; loyalists, 83, 99, 102, 160; missions destroyed, 122, 160; natural features, 134; natural history, 133; northern boundary, 145; obtained by Britain, 2, 274; Old Spanish Trail, 277; purchased by the US, 102, 267; railroads, 133; refuge for Creeks, 229; refuge for Red Sticks, 241; Second Spanish Period, 61, 104, 274; Seminole War, 244; Spanish claim, 159; toured by Henry Laurens, 157; visited by Dr. Alexander Garden, 153

Florida Audubon Society, 127
Florida bear, 116
Florida clover, 70
Florida gooseberry, 68
Florida maple, 132
Florida Museum of Natural History, 128
Florida National Scenic Trail, 105, 109, 111, 112, 113, 120
Florida Natural Areas Inventory, 269
Florida panther, 102, 105, 133
Florida Parishes, 281, 295; annexed to Louisiana, 291; occupied by United States, 257; settled by English, 291
Florida Park Service, 126
Florida Power & Light, Putnam Plant, 108, 112
Florida Rangers, 177
Florida rosemary, 114, 125, 133
Florida sandhill crane, 278
Florida Sandhills, 125
Florida Scrub, 132, 133
Florida Southern Railroad, 125
Flowing Wells Spring, Augusta, 69
Floyd, John, 232, 241, 242, 245
Folch, Juan Vicente, 257
Folkston, Ga., 42, 51
Folly Beach County Park, S.C., 144
Fontainbleu State Park, La., 284
Foothills Trail, S.C., 186, 191, 302
Forbes, John & Co., 272
the Forest, 290
Fork Creek Roadside Park, Ga., 88
Forsyth Park, Savannah, 27
Fort Advance, 67, 215
Fort Alert, 51
Fort Anderson, 317
Fort Antonio de Anacape, 114
Fort Apalachicola, 215, 227, 229, 232
Fort Argyle, 19
Fort Augusta, 62, 75
Fort aux Alibamos, 247
Fort Bainbridge, 232, 242
Fort Barrancas, 266, 267, 269
Fort Barrington, 3, 29, 33, 39, 42, 43, 61, 99
Fort Barrington Ferry Road, 34
Fort Benning, 221, 229, 230, 231, 232
Fort Bibb, 253
Fort Bute, 9, 257, 293
Fort Butler, 206
Fort Caroline, 96, 97, 102, 103, 122, 159, 273
Fort Caroline National Memorial, 102
Fort Caswell, 317
Fort Charlotte, 65, 83, 89, 173, 256, 260, 265
Fort Christmas Museum, 121
Fort Claiborne, 251, 254, 255
Fort Clark, 87
Fort Clinch, 43, 99; State Park, Fla., 52
Fort Condé, 265; rebuilt, 260
Fort Cornwallis, 62, 70
Fort Dale, 251, 254
Fort Darien, 37
Fort Decatur, 245
Fort Defiance, 32, 67, 215
Fort Delaney, 206
Fort Deposit, Ala., 242, 251
Fort Diego, 104
Fort Discovery, 75
Fort du Biloxi, 278
Fort Fanning, 133
Fort Fidius, 215
Fort Fischer State Recreation Area, N.C., 317
Fort Fisher State Historic Site and Museum, 315, 317
Fort Frederica, 28, 42, 47
Fort Frederica National Monument, Ga., 46

Fort Frederick, 167
Fort Gaines, 262; Frontier Village, Ga., 234
Fort Gaines, Ga., 214
Fort Gaines Historic Site, Ala., 262
Fort Gates Ferry, 109
Fort George, 21, 272
Fort George Island, Fla., 40, 101, 102, 103, 106
Fort Gibson, 221
Fort Gordon, 74; Recreation Area, 66
Fort Greene, 21
Fort Hawkins, 214, 215
Fort Hill, 182
Fort Hull, 232, 244
Fort Independence, 174
Fort Jackson, 21, 248
Fort James, 8, 79, 89, 92; visited by William Bartram, 65
Fort Johnson, 140, 144
Fort Johnston, 315, 317
Fort King George, 37, 40, 48, 160
Fort Lawrence, 223
Fort Loudon, 16, 18, 154, 179, 193, 203, 206
Fort Louis, 278, 265
Fort Lyttleton, 161, 167
Fort Marion, 167
Fort Massachusetts, 278
Fort Matanzas, 105
Fort Maurepas, 273, 277, 278, 288
Fort McAllister State Historic Site, Ga., 19, 29
Fort McCreary, 232
Fort McIntosh, 51, 99
Fort Miguel, 267
Fort Mims, 208, 241, 251, 259, 260, 267; Fort Mims Historic Site, 260
Fort Mitchell, Ala., 224, 229, 232
Fort Montgomery, 206
Fort Moore, 56, 61, 71, 73, 173
Fort Morgan, Ala., 262
Fort Morris Historic Site, Ga., 32
Fort Mose, 104
Fort Moultrie, 142, 148, 244, 142
Fort New Richmond, 257, 294
Fort Palachacola, 160
Fort Panmure, 257
Fort Perry, 221, 224, 232
Fort Petites Coquilles, 284
Fort Pickens, 269
Fort Pickering, 51
Fort Picolata, 47, 98, 101, 104, 106
Fort Pike State Commemorative Area, La., 282
Fort Prince George, 8, 174, 178, 179, 183, 197, 206
Fort Pulaski National Monument, 21
Fort Rutledge, 172, 182, 183
Fort Saint-Louis de la Louisiane, 56, 261, 264, 265
Fort Saint-Louis de la Mobile, 256, 259, 261
Fort San Carlos de Austria, 266, 269, 295
Fort San Felipe, 159, 168, 194
Fort San Francisco de Poppa, 47, 104
Fort San Gabriel de Manchack, 293
Fort San Marcos (South Carolina), 159, 167
Fort San Mateo, 97, 112
Fort San Miguel, 269, 272
Fort Screven, 21
Fort St. George, 101
Fort St. Simons, 47, 48
Fort Stewart, 19, 33
Fort Stoddert, Ala., 86, 232, 258, 260
Fort Sumter National Monument, S.C., 148
Fort Tonyn, 43, 50, 160
Fort Toulouse, 9, 196, 239, 247, 284
Fort Washington, 84
Fort Wayne, 24
Fort Wilkinson, 51, 208, 215

Fort William, 43, 47, 50
Fort Winston, 215
Fortuna, ship, 318
Foster, Stephen, 133
Fothergill, Dr. John, 2, 3, 4, 6, 38, 43, 49, 154, 316; Bartram's report, 64, 132
Fothergilla, 193
Founders Garden, Columbus, 236
Fountain of Youth Archaeological Park, Fla., 106
Four Corners of Law, 153
Four Holes Swamp, 142, 148, 150
Fowl River, 262
Fowler, Jim, 45
Fowler's Bluff, 133
fox, 133
France: aid to the Americans, 15, 79, 157, 284; allied to the Alabamas, 247, 290; allied with Spain, 269; American ambassador, 22, 84, 92; American ministers, 145, 165; capture of Pensacola, 269; colonization efforts, 28, 114, 158; colonization of Canada, 105, 273, 290; employs Michaux to search for trees, 146; ends Seven Years War, 97; explores the Gulf Coast, 256; fur trade, 273; Indian trade, 73; influence among Catholics, 156; land survey system, 288; Louisiana; 256, 264, 266, 281, 273, 281, 288, 289; persecution of Protestants, 154; preys on Spanish shipping, 106; relations with Cherokees, 196, 200, 245; relations with Creeks, 13, 18, 57, 196, 222, 231, 238, 245; relations with Gulf Coast Indians, 274; relations with Spanish Florida, 273; religious wars, 96, 168, 303; Revolution, 15, 144; rivalry with Spain, 158; trade, 227, 238, 264; war with Chickasaws, 61, 71
Francis, Allen, 176
Francis Beidler Forest, 150
Francis I, King of France, 168, 312
Francis, Josiah, 241, 253
Francis Marion National Forest, 300, 302, 311; Witherbee Ranger District, 150
Franciscans, 40, 52, 227, 230
Francisco of Chicora, 135
Francisville, Ga., 223
Franklin, Benjamin, 2, 3, 20, 21, 22, 39; 147; 157; and John Bartram, 1; and William Bartram, 3
Franklin County, Ga., 61, 79; bounty lands, 79
Franklin D. Roosevelt State Park, Ga., 234
Franklin Gem Museum, 200
Franklin Museum & Visitor Center, 200
Franklin, N.C., 183, 199, 200
Franklin Square, Savannah, 22
Franklin, State of, 205
Franklinia, 3, 6, 7, 38, 182, 193, 194
Franklinton, La., 287
Fraser, John, 146
Fraser magnolia, 146, 185, 191, 192
Frederica, Ga., 8, 13, 42, 43, 46, 48, 197
Frederica River, 46, 47
Freeman, James, 2
the French, 18, 25, 35, 37; Acadians, 290; aid Spanish in Pensacola, 266; alienated by Willing's Raiders, 290; befriend the Saturiwas, 102; bring disease to the Southeast, 135; Cassette Girls, 279; Catholics, 298; colonists in Florida, 97; colonists in North America, 102; destroy Ft. San Carlos de Austria, 269; disperse the Natchez, 148; expelled from Florida, 194; explore the St. Johns River, 103; explorers in South Carolina, 307; Huguenots, 105, 298; Huguenots in South Carolina, 302; influence in new Orleans, 285; language, 261, 286; leave British West Florida, 290; on Dauphin Island, 262; protect the Apalachees at Mobile, 130;

Protestants, 138, 159, 164, 182, 303; settle Pointe Coupee Parish, 296; settlement of Parris Island, 167; settlements on Mobile Delta, 261; settlers in Louisiana, 286, 291; threat to St. Augustine, 232; welcomed by Spanish governors of Louisiana, 289
French and Indian War, 2, 25, 42, 54, 61, 73, 80, 154, 170, 177, 178, 183, 197, 206, 256, 266, 274, 281, 291; re-enactment, 177, 248. *See also* Seven Years War
French Broad River, 203, 206
French Coast, La., 291
French Garden. *See* Michaux's Garden
French Market, 285
French Protestant Church, Charleston, 154
French Santee, 298, 303
French Settlement, La., 292
Friendship Park, 102
fringe tree, 92, 194
Frogmore, S.C., 168
Frost, Dr. Henry, 153
Fruitland Cove, Fla., 3, 109
Fruitland, Fla., 113
Frying Pan Shoals, 312, 316
Fulton, Robert, 144
Fundamental Constitutions of Carolina, 137
fur trade, 273
Furrow Path, 250
Fury's Ferry, 65
Fuser, L. V., 32
Fushatchee Micco, 51

G

Gadsden, Christopher, 140, 157
Gage, Thomas, 256
Gaillard family, 147, 303
Gaines, Earnest, 296
Gainesville, Fla., 122–125, 123, 127–128, 130
Gainesville to Hawthorne Rail Trail, 127
Galahan, Patrick, 199
galax, 187
gallberry, 311
Galphin, George, 8, 56, 57, 58, 73, 80, 174, 211, 213, 224, 260
Galphin, John, 57, 213
Galphin, Martha, 214
Galphin's Cowpen, 211
Galphinton, Ga., 213
Gálvez, Bernardo de, 289; biography, 284; captures Mobile, 257, 260, 261, 264; captures Pensacola, 260, 266, 271; invades West Florida, 257, 290; provides refuge for loyalists, 292
Gálvez, Don Matias de, 284
Galvezton Bay, Texas, 256
Galveztown, La., 292
Garay, Francisco de, 256
Garden, Benjamin, 160, 167
Garden City, Ga., 15, 18
Garden Club of Georgia, 34
Garden Clubs of America, 82, 85, 86
Garden, Dr. Alexander, 2, 3, 147, 153; association with John Bartram, 1, 146, 153; biography, 153; visited by the Bartrams, 3
Garden II, Alexander, 147, 153
Gardens Corner, S.C., 167
Gardner, William, 253
Garnett, S.C., 164
Garrison Road, 215
Gascoigne Bluff, St. Simons Island, 47
Gascoigne, James, 48
Gavin, Michael, 79
Geechee, 34
Gemini Springs Park, Fla., 119

General Pickens Monument, 186
General's Cut, 38
General's Pond, 132
General's Road, 172, 175, 179
Genet, Citizen, 68, 144
George, Henry, 261
George I, 12, 50, 182, 206, 317, 321
George II, 26, 53, 307; visited by Tomochichi, 13
George III, 2, 12, 13, 36, 49, 53, 73, 140, 171, 173, 232, 256; appoints John Bartram as Royal botanist, 99
George T. Bagby State Park, Ga., 234
Georgetown County, S.C., 307
Georgetown Road. *See* Old Georgetown Road
Georgetown, S.C., 3, 171, 298, 299, 300, 305
Georgia, 73; 1812 invasion of Florida, 126; annexes Cherokee land, 199; Antebellum era, 86; army, 15; as British colony, 61; associated with Beaufort District, 160; attacks on Cherokee towns, 179; Baptists, 166; botanical areas, 186; boundaries, 68, 85, 186, 185, 193, 191, 211, 229, 281; bounty lands, 79, 208; capitals, 214; Cherokee Nation, 195, 205; colonial government, 13; controlled by patriots, 67; Coosa Empire, 203, 244; cotton empire, 209; cotton migration, 223, 243, 251; early trails, 208; established in Spanish territory, 106; Executive Council, 33, 62, 94; exploration, 19; explored by Ribault, 96; factionalism in the government, 64, 68; founding of the colony, 28, 97; friendship with Creeks, 227; Golden Isles, 40, 40–43; governors, 73, 75, 82; Governor's Council, 18; home of Cherokees, 182; home of the Creeks, 239; Indian trade, 73; invaded by the Spanish, 13; Militia, 67, 224; attacks Paynes' Town, 126; constructs Fort Mitchell, 232; invades the Creek Nation, 241, 242; Native Americans, 238; navy, 14, 142; northern parts settled, 208; patriots, 99; Piedmont, 92; population, 14; presence of Carolina bays, 302; protects Carolina frontier, 167; Provincial Congress, 26; provincial government, 73, 80; purchases last section of land, 229; Quakers, 69, 71; railroads, 211; Revolutionary activity, 29, 62, 99; royal governor, 13; rum outlawed, 164; Salzburgers, 17; Senate members, 89; Spanish exploration, 159; Spanish missions, 159, 168; surveyor general, 98; the Bartrams' visit in 1765, 3; toured by Henry Laurens, 157; treaties with the Creeks, 214, 237; University of Georgia, 85; upper coastal area, 28; William Bartram's travels, 4; Yazoo Lands, 250
    Assembly, 13, 22, 31, 84, 208, 213, 230 236; Lower House, 13, 61; Upper House, 13
Georgia Baptist Association, 88
Georgia Bight, 49, 304
Georgia Botanical Society, 19
Georgia College and State University, 214
Georgia D.A.R., 89
Georgia Department of Natural Resources, 35, 49
Georgia Endangered Plant Propagation Network, 85
Georgia Equal Rights Association, 75
Georgia Factory, Athens, 85
Georgia Guidestones, 93
Georgia Historical Society, 27
Georgia Industrial and Normal College, 214
Georgia, ironclad ship, 21
Georgia Medical Society, 21, 75
Georgia Military College, 214
Georgia Museum of Natural History, 86
Georgia Music Hall of Fame, 221
Georgia Pacific Railroad, 163
Georgia plume, 19, 33, 85, 165
Georgia Ports Authority, 18, 19
Georgia Railroad, 71, 86
Georgia Rangers, 104, 224
Georgia Sea Island Singers, 48
Georgia State Docks, 15, 18
Georgiana, Ala., 253
Georgians: and rum, 164; covet Creek land, 251; migrate to Texas, 223; migration to Florida, 123; migration to the Black Belt, 221; protect Carolina frontier, 160; relations with Creeks, 83; repulsed by King Payne, 123; settle Mississippi Territory, 265
German Coast, La., 291
German Colonization Society of Charleston, 187
Germans, 36; immigrates, 289; in Charleston, 155; in Georgia, 17, 164; in Louisiana, 286, 291; in South Carolina, 171; Palatines, 67; prisoners, 279; settle Walhalla, S.C., 187; welcomed to Spanish Louisiana, 289
Germany, James, 242, 246
Geronimo, 269
Gershwin, George, 144
Gettysburg, Pa., 89
Gibbe's Island, S.C., 168
Gibbes Museum of Art, 155
Gilbert, Sir Humphrey, 312
Gilcrest, Robert, 178
Gillespie Museum of Minerals, DeLand, 117
Gillisonville, S.C., 166
Gilmer, George Rockingham, 84, 89, 173
ginkgo, 144
Ginnie Springs, Fla., 134
ginseng, 1
Gist, George, 199, 207
Givhans Ferry, S.C., 143
Glascock County, Ga., 216
Glascock, Thomas, 216
Glascock, William, 62
glasswort, 302
Glassy Mountain Heritage Preserve, S.C., 184
Glenn, James, 177, 178, 183
Global Wildlife Park, La., 285
Gloucester, Duke of. *See* Hanover, William Henry; Duke of Gloucester
Glynn County, Ga., 42, 47, 53
Glynn, John, 53
Goat Island, Savannah River, 89
goat's beard, 146
Goddard, James, 12
Godfrey, Michael, 69
Goff, John, 211
Gola tribe, 34
gold, 199
Gold Star Park, Ala., 248
Golden Creek Mill, S.C., 184
Golden Grove, S.C., 174
Golden Isles Visitor Center, 49
Goldsmith, Oliver, 12
Goldwire, Benjamin, 25
Goodall House, 56
Goodall, Seaborn, 56
Goodby Creek, 101
Goodgion, Rae, Whitefield & Co., 80
Goodness Grows Nursery, 84
Goose Creek Faction, 138
Goose Creek Reservoir, 147
Goose Creek, S.C., 146, 147, 313
Goose Pond, Ga., 79, 88
gopher apple, 133
gopher tortoise, 33, 114, 116, 119, 132, 163
Gordillo, Francisco, 135, 298
Gordon, William, 22
gordonia, 153
Gores Landing River Trailhead, 115
Gouedy, Robert, 177
Gourgues, Dominique de, 97
Government House, Savannah, 14; St. Augustine, 106
Gracia Real de Santa Teresa de Mose, 104
Graham County, N.C., 201, 207
Graham, William A., 207
Grahamville, S.C., 166
Gramercy, La., 286
Grammont (pirate), 12
Grand Banks, Newfoundland, 290
Grand Bay National Wildlife Refuge, Miss. & Ala., 262, 277
Grand Oak Wildlife Preservation Park, Ala., 263
Grand Ole Opry, 247
Grand Strand, S.C., 308
granite outcrops, 69
Grant, Dr. William, 261
Grant, James, 18, 98, 179, 183, 193, 197, 200; meets the Bartrams, 3
Granville County, S.C., 138
Granville, Lord, 167, 315
Graves Mountain, Ga., 68
Gray, Asa, 185
Gray, Edmund, 42, 61, 69
Gray's Gang, 42, 69
Gray's Reef National Marine Sanctuary, Ga., 39
Great Buffalo Lick, 8, 64, 84
Great Creek Trading Path. *See* Lower Creek Trading Path
Great Ridge, 211
Great River Road, La., 286, 293
Great Smoky Mountains National Park, TN, 34, 192, 207
Great Swamp Wildlife Management Area, 166
Great Telico, 177
Great Valley, the, 170
Great Wagon Road, 89, 170
Greater Baton Rouge Zoo, 294
Greeks, 98, 120; Greek language, 318
green ash, 86
green sea turtle, 318
Green Shell Enclosure, 165
Green Springs, Fla., 119
Green Swamp Preserve, 317
green-fly orchid, 319
Greene, Catherine, 17, 18, 50
Greene County, Ga., 19, 77, 79, 83, 208
Greene, Nathanael, 17, 22, 50, 142, 147, 169, 177, 320
Greene Square, Savannah, 22
Greenfield Gardens, N.C., 318
Greensboro, Ga., 76, 86, 88, 217; burned by Creeks, 87
Greensboro, N.C., 170
Greenville, Ala., 8, 253; on Federal Road, 223
Greenville County, S.C., 64, 85
Greenville, S.C., 174
Greenwood County, S.C., 72, 177
Greenwood, S.C., 177
Gregg Shoals, Savannah River, 91, 95
Grenville, Sir Richard, 312
Grier, Robert, 82
Grier's Almanac, 82
Grierson, James, 80
Griffiths, Thomas, 172, 201
Grimke-Drayton, Rev. John, 146
Grimshawes, N.C., 185
Grinder's Stand, KY, 88
Gronovius, J. F., 3
Grove Creek, 174
Grove Hill, Ala., 254
Grovetown, Ga., 64
Guadalquini, 48
Guale, 11, 28, 34, 40, 48, 50, 61, 97, 106, 159, 166, 159

Guale Indians, 35
Guana River State Park, Fla., 104
Guana River Wildlife Management Area, 104
guano, 64, 209
Guasili, 195
Guerin's Bridge, 300
Guess, George, 199, 207
Guillebeau, Andre, and the Guillebeau House, 67
Guilliard Lake Scenic Area, S.C., 303
Gulf Breeze, Fla., 269
Gulf Coast, 269–270, 273–277; exploration, 256, 273, 288; historical trade routes, 226; Native American trade economy, 256
Gulf Hammock Wildlife Management Area, Fla., 134
Gulf Islands National Seashore, 269, 278
Gulf Marine State Park, Miss., 278
Gulf of Mexico, 105, 125, 262, 264
Gulf State Park, Ala., 262
Gulf Stream, 18, 159, 168
Gulfport, Miss., 278, 279
Gullah, 32, 34, 48, 156, 161, 165, 168
Gum Root Conservation Area, Fla., 127
Gunahitunyi, 206
guns, 227
Gwinnett, Button, 14, 31, 35, 56, 75; duel with Lachlan McIntosh, 32
Gwinnett County, Ga., 217

H

Habersham County, Ga., 92, 194
Habersham, Esther, 165
Habersham, James, 3, 14, 15, 25, 165
Habersham, Joseph, 14
Hackensack, New Jersey, 144
Hagood Mill, 184
Haines Institute, 75
hairy rattleweed, 85
Haiti, 15, 285
Half Moon Battery, 155
Halfway Pond, 125
Halifax, Earl of. *See* Dunk, George Montagu; Earl of Halifax
Hall, Basil, 31, 33, 221, 235, 236
Hall County, Ga., 76, 79
Hall, Lyman, 14, 29, 31, 33, 58, 75
Hall, Margaret, 235, 236
Hall's Knoll, 29
Hamburg Railroad. *See* Charleston-Hamburg Railroad
Hamburg, S.C., 64, 70, 213
Hamburg State Park, Ga., 213
Hamilton, Alexander, 6
Hamilton Branch State Park, S.C., 68
Hamilton, James Couper, 45
Hamilton Plantation, 46
Hammerer, Daniel, 172
Hammond, James, 71
Hammond, Le Roy, 80
Hampton Plantation, 37, 145, 303
Hampton State Park, S.C., 300
Hanahan, S.C., 146
Hancock County, Ga., 64, 77, 79, 87, 210, 211, 214, 216
Hancock County, Miss., 275, 279, 280
Hancock, John, 216, 280
Hancock Planters Club, 209, 214
Hanging Maw, 205
Hank Williams Museum, 247, 253
Hannahatchee Creek, 208, 232
Hannahatchee Creek Wildlife Management Area, Ga., 234
Hanover, Edward; Duke of York and Albany, 49

Hanover, Frederick Louis; Prince of Wales, 73
Hanover, George. *See* George I
Hanover House, 182
Hanover, Royal House of, 49
Hanover, William Henry; Duke of Gloucester, 49
Hanover, William; Duke of Cumberland, 12, 50
Happy Valley Road, 211
Harahan Trail, 286
Harbor Walk, Georgetown, 306
Hardee, Noble, 51
Hardeeville, S.C., 162, 164
Harden, William, 161, 169
Hardwick, Richard, 214
Hardwicke, Ga., 19, 29
Hargrett Library, 85
Harlem, Ga., 65, 76, 211
Harmony Hall, 320
Harnett, Jr., Cornelius, 315
Harper, Francis, 4, 8, 42, 51, 65, 82, 92, 105, 123, 132, 232, 251, 258, 323; and Buffalo Lick, 83; and Flat Rock, 211; retraces Bartram's Travels, 209; verifies Bartram's alligator story, 108
Harper, Roland, 51
Harrell Siau Bridge, 306
Harriet Tubman Historical and Cultural Museum, 221
Harrington, St. Simons Island, 34, 46
Harris, Joel Chandler, 216
Harris Neck National Wildlife Refuge, Ga., 34
Harrisburg (Augusta), 76
Harrison County, Miss., 280
Hart, Benjamin, 89
Hart County, Ga., 80, 95
Hart, John, 89
Hart, Nancy, 95
Hart State Park, Ga., 92
Hartwell Dam Visitor Center, 92
Hartwell, Ga., 76, 80
Hartwell Messenger, 182
Hatchechubbee, 245
Haunted Pillar, 75
Havana, Cuba, 97, 312
Haw Creek Conservation Area, Fla., 113
Hawe Creek Campground, 66
Hawkins, Benjamin, 51, 182, 191, 215, 219, 223, 224, 232, 241, 243, 245, 246; biography, 222
Hawkins, Jeffersonia, 223
Hawkins, Sir John, 312
Hawthorne, Fla., 125
Hayesville, N.C., 207
Hayne, Isaac, 142
Haywood County, N.C., 194, 201
Hazzards Neck Wildlife Management Area, Ga., 49
headright system, 79
Heard, Stephen, 67, 79, 91, 93
Heardmont, 91, 94, 95
Heard's Fort, 84
Heath, Sir Robert, 137, 312
Heggie's Rock, 69
hell bender, 194
Hell Hole Bay, 142
Hellhole Bay Wilderness Area, S.C., 303
hemlock, 194
hemp, 24
Henderson, La., 292
Heniha, 227
Henry County, Ga., 221
Henry, Jim, 229, 233
hepatica, 173
Herbert, John, 192; Herbert's Savannah, 192
heron, 115, 165
heron, great blue, 143
Hesters Ferry Campground, 66

Heyward, Daniel, 152, 160
Heyward, Dubose, 144, 155
Heyward, Jr., Thomas, 142; grave, 166
Heyward, Thomas, 106, 152, 160, 166
Heyward-Washington House, 152, 156
Hiawassee, 189
Hiawassee River, 203
hibiscus, 19
Hickory Ground, 248
Hickory Knob State Resort Park, S.C., 67
hickory, shagbark, 174
High Falls Park, S.C., 183
High Springs, Fla., 132
Highland clans, 50
Highland Hiker, 186
Highlander Monument, Darien, 37
Highlanders, 13, 28, 36, 37, 47; in North Carolina, 315; in the Revolution, 319; invasion of Florida, 104; settle Fayetteville, N.C., 320
Highlands, N.C., 185, 186, 191, 194; Highlands Biological Station, Botanical Garden, and Nature Center, 194
Highlands Plateau, 194
Highlands Ranger District, Nantahala National Forest, 201
Hightower Trail. *See* Etowah Trail
Hihethoye, 246
hiking trails, 69; *Central Alabama*: Wetumpka Riverfront, 248; William Bartram Arboretum, 248
  Central Florida: Alexander Springs Wilderness Trail, 115; Andrews Wildlife Management Area, 132; Austin Cary State Forest, 128; Backwood Nature Trail, 119; Beecher Springs Trail, 113; Boulware Springs Park, 127; Caravelle Ranch Conservation Area, 112; Cedar Key Scrub State Reserve, 133; Cross Florida Greenway, 112; Cummer Sanctuary, 133; DeLeon Springs, 115; Dixie-Levy-Gilchrist Greenway, 132; Emeralda Marsh, 116; Fanning Springs State Recreation Area, 132; Florida National Scenic Trail, 112; Gainesville to Hawthorne Rail Trail, 127; Gemini Springs Park, 119; Ginnie Springs, 134; Gores Landing River Trailhead, 115; Gum Root Conservation Area, 127; Haw Creek Conservation Area, 113; Hontoon Island State Park, 117; Ichetucknee Springs State Park, 134; Kratzert Conservation Area, 119; Lake Alice Wildlife Sanctuary, 128; Lake Ashby Park, 119; Lake Beresford Greenway, 117; Lake George Conservation Area, 113; Lake George State Forest, 114; Lake Monroe Park, 119; Little-Big Econ State Conservation Area, 120; Lochloosa Conservation Area, 125; Lower Suwannee River National Wildlife Refuge, 133; Manatee Springs State Park, 132; Marshall Swamp, 116; Merritt Island National Wildlife Refuge, 121; Morningside Nature Park, Gainesville, 127; Mud Spring Trail, 113; Ocala National Forest, 113; O'Leno State Park, 134; Orlando Wilderness Park, 121; Palatka–Navair Rail Trail, 109; Palatka-St. Augustine Rail Trail, 111; Poe Springs County Park, 134; Prairie Creek Conservation Area, 127; River Rise State Preserve, 134; Rock Springs Run State Reserve, 119; Salt Springs Trail, 113; San Felasco Hammock Preserve, 128; Seminole Ranch State Conservation Area, 120; Seneca Park, Cassadega, 119; South Lake Harney Conservation Area, 120; Spruce Creek Park, 119; St. Francis Trail, 115; St. Johns Loop Trail, 112; Tosohatchee State Reserve, 121; Tram Road, 112; Turnbull Hammock Conservation Area, 120; Wekiva Buffer

Conservation Area, 119; Wekiwa Springs State Park, 119

Chattahoochee River: Callaway Gardens, 234; Emmaus Garden, 232; Lakepoint State Park Resort, 234; Providence Canyon State Conservation Park, 233

Coastal Georgia: Ansley-Hodges Memorial Marsh Project, 38; Blythe Island Regional Park, 49; Crooked River State Park, 50; Cumberland Island National Seashore, 50; Earth Day Nature Trail, 49; Fort Frederica National Monument, 46; Fort McAllister State Historic Site, 29; Fort Morris Historic Site, 32; Harris Neck National Wildlife Refuge, 34; Hofwyl-Broadfield Plantation, 45; Jekyll Island, 49; Laura S. Walker State Park, 52; Little St. Simons Island, 46; Melon Bluff Nature Preserve, 33; Sapelo Island, 35; Stephen Foster State Park, 52; Suwannee Canal National Recreation Area, 52; Wesley Woodland Walk, 46

Coastal North Carolina: Bladen Lakes State Forest, 320; Brunswick Town, 317; Cape Fear Botanical Garden, 321; Carolina Beach State Park, 318; Fort Fischer State Recreation Area, 317; Greenfield Gardens, 318; Jones Lake State Park, 320; Moore's Creek National Battlefield Park, 319; New Hanover County Arboretum, 318; North Carolina Aquarium, 315, 317; Oak Island Marshes, 317; Pauline Longest Nature Trail, 321; Salters Lake State Natural Area, 320; Singletary Lake State Park, 319; Tory Hole Battleground, 319; Turnbull Creek Talking Tree Trail, 320; White Lake, 319

Coastal South Carolina: ACE Basin, 143; Audubon Swamp, 146; Charles Towne Landing, 145; Cypress Gardens, 149; Donnelley Wildlife Management Area, 169; Edisto Beach State Park, 143; Edisto Nature Trail, 169; Hunting Island State Park, 168; James Island County Park, 144; Palmetto Islands County Park, 148; Santee Canal State Park, 150; Wannamaker Park, 147

East Alabama: Bartram National Recreation Trail, 242; Chewacla State Park, 242; Davis Arboretum, 242; Kiesel Park, 242; Tsinia Wildlife Viewing Area, 242; Tuskegee National Forest, 242

Eastern Louisiana: Bayou Savage Refuge, 286; Big Branch Marsh, 284; Bogue Chitto National Wildlife Refuge, 282; Fairview-Riverside State Park, 285; Fontainbleu State Park, 284; Honey Island Swamp Nature Trail, 282; Joyce Wildlife Management Area, 285; Lake Ramsey Wildlife Management Area, 285; Lake Vista Nature Preserve Trail, 287; Northlake Museum and Nature Center, 284; Pearl River Basin, 282; Tammany Trace, 284; Zemurrey Gardens, 285

Georgia Piedmont: Anthony Shoals, 89; Cook's Trail, 87; Dyars Pasture, 87; North Oconee Greenway, 87; Oconee Forest Park, 86; Sandy Creek Park, 87; Scull Shoals Trail, 87; Watson Mill State Park, 88

Gulf Coast: Andrew Jackson Trail, 279; Black Creek Trail, 279; Buccaneer State Park, 279; Davis Bayou, 278; Gulf Islands National Seashore, 278; McLeod Water Park, 279; Mississippi Sand Hill Crane National Wildlife Refuge, 278; Pascagoula Wildlife Management Area, 278; Shepard State Park, 278; Tuxachanie Trail, 279

Lowcountry: Blue Heron Nature Trail, 166; Pinckney Island National Wildlife Refuge, 165; Sea Pines Forest Preserve, 165; Victoria Bluff Heritage Preserve, 165

Lower Alabama: Cedar Swamp Trail, 253; Claude D. Kelley State Park, 254

Middle Georgia: Hamburg State Park, 213; Hitchiti Nature Trail, 216; Lockerly Arboretum, 214; Millen Fish Hatchery, 57; Monticello Glade, 216; Ocmulgee National Monument, 215; Ocmulgee River Trail, 216; Piedmont Wildlife Management Area, 216; Red Cockaded Woodpecker Trail, 216

Mississippi River: Afton Gardens, 295; Audubon State Commemorative Area, 295; Cohn Memorial Arboretum, 294; Harahan Bridge, 286; James R. Leake Memorial Park, 295; Jean Lafitte National Historic Park, 286; Louisiana Nature and Science Center, 286; LSU Hill Top Aboretum, 294; Marksville Commemorative Area, 296; Mary Ann Brown Preserve, 295; Port Hudson State Commemorative Area, 294; St. Barnard State Park, 286; Tunica Hills State Preservation Area, 296; Tunica Hills Wildlife Management Area, 295

Mobile: Audubon Sanctuary, 262; Bon Secour National Wildlife Refuge, 262; Dauphin Island, 262; Gulf State Park, 262; Historic Blakeley Park, 261; Weeks Bay National Estuarine Reserve, 262

North Florida: Amelia Island State Recreation Area, 53; Bayard Point Conservation area, 104; Blackrock Trail, 101; Faver-Dykes State Park, 105; Fort Clinch State Park, 52; Jacksonville Nature Center, 104; Jennings State Forest, 104; Kathryn Abbey Hanna Park, 102; Saturiwa Trail, 101; Simpson Creek Trail, 101; Stokes Landing Conservation Area, 104

Northeast Georgia: Bartram Trail, 191; Black Rock Mountain State Park, 192; Chatooga River Trail, 186, 191; Ellicott Rock Wilderness, 185; Holcomb Creek Trail, 193; Three Forks Trail, 193; Warwoman Dell, 192

Pensacola: Big Lagoon State Recreation Area, 270; Blackwater River State Park, 270; Florida Trail, 270; Fort Pickens, 269; Jackson Trail, 270; Naval Live Oaks Reserve, 269; Pensacola Bluffs, 270; Perdido Key, 269; University of West Florida, 270

Santee Delta: Hopsewee Plantation, 304; I'on Swamp, 302; Palmetto Trail, 302; Sewee Shell Mound Trail, 302; Sewee Visitor and Environmental Education Center, 300; Swamp Fox National Recreation Trail, 302; Washo Preserve, 304; Woodland Trail, 304

Savannah: Ebenezer Nature Trail, 17; Fort McAllister State Historic Site, 19; Fort Pulaski National Monument, 21; Savannah River National Wildlife Refuge, 164; Savannah River Swamp Trail, 163; Savannah to Tybee Rails to Trails, 21; Savannah-Ogeechee Barge Canal, 19; Skidaway Institute of Oceanography, 20; Skidaway State Park, 20; Tillman Heritage Preserve, 163; Tybee National Wildlife Refuge, 21; Wormsloe State Historic Site, 20

South Carolina Piedmont: John De la Howe Interpretive Forestry Trail, 173; Long Cane Horse Trail, 174; Parson's Mountain, 174; Pine Grove Nature Trail, 176; South Carolina State Botanical Garden, 182; Turkey Creek, 68

South Carolina Upcountry: Blue Ridge Railroad Historical Trail, 187; Buzzard Roost Heritage Preserve, 187; Chatooga River Trail, 185; Chauga Nature Trail, 187; Chauga River Scenic Area, 187; Cherokee Interpretive Trail, 184; Cherry Hill Recreation Area, 186; Clemson Park and Recreation Area, 183; Coon Branch Natural Area, 185; Eastatoe Creek Heritage Preserve, 184; Foothills Trail, 186, 302; High Falls Park, 183; Hopewell-Keowee Monument, 182; Horn Creek, 68; Keowee-Toxaway State Park, 184; Lake Jocassee, 184; Mile Creek Park, 183; Oconee Bells Trail, 185; Oconee State Park, 186; Oconee Station State Park, 186; Station Cove Botanical Area, 186; Stevens Creek, 68; Stumphouse Tunnel, 187; Table Rock State Park, 184; Walhalla Fish Hatchery, 185; White Rock Scenic Area, 185; Whiteside Mountain, 185; Winding Stairs Trail, 185; Windy Falls Natural Area, 185

Upper Savannah River: Augusta Canal, 70, 75; Baker Creek Hiking Trail, 67; Beech Bluff Nature Trail, 92; Big Hart Campground, 66; Blue Hole Nature Trail, 174; Bobby Brown State Park, 89; Cedar Bluff Nature Trail, 174; Indian Mound Trail, 87; Lake Springs Recreation Area, 66; Modoc Campground, 66; Redcliffe Trail, 71; Tugaloo State Park, 95; Wild Mint Nature Trail, 67

Upper South Carolina Coast: Indian Camp Forest Trail, 311; Lewis Ocean Bay Heritage Preserve, 311; Myrtle Beach State Park, 309; Samworth Wildlife Management Area, 306; Sea Oats Nature Trail, 309; Vereen Memorial Gardens, 311

Western North Carolina: Appalachian Trail, 201; Bartram National Recreation Trail, 194, 200, 205; Coweeta Hydrologic Laboratory, 193; Highlands Botanical Garden, 194; Joyce Kilmer Memorial, 206; Nantahala National Forest, 201; Standing Indian, 201; Wayah Bald, 201; Whiteside Mountain, 194

Hill Memorial Library, 294
Hill, William, 171
Hill, Wills; Earl of Hillsborough, 49
Hillis Haya, 227, 241
Hillsboro, N.C., 71
Hillsborough, Earl of. *See* Hill, Wills
Hillsborough Township, 67
Hilton Head Island, S.C., 161, 165
Hilton, William, 137, 159, 165, 312
Hiltonia Sandhills, 57
Himely, J. J., 146
Hines, Lewis, 278
Hinesville, Ga., 33
Hinson, John, 253
Historic Augusta, Inc., 74
Historic Bartrams' Garden, 1, 6, 7, 102, 108, 334
Historic Beaufort Foundation, 167
Historic Blakeley Park, Ala., 261
Historic Charleston Foundation, 152, 154, 155, 166
Historic Charleston Reproduction Shop, 152
Historic Effingham Society, 15
Historic Pensacola Preservation Board, 271
Historic Pensacola Village, 271
Historic Railroad Shops, Savannah, 27
Historic Savannah Foundation, 22, 26
Hitchita, 226
Hitchiti Nature Trail, 216
Hitchitis, 135, 231, 232, 233, 239; homeland, 215, 219, 226; initiate Second Creek War, 229; language, 123, 163, 208, 215, 226
Hobcaw Barony, 300, 305, 306
Hobolochitto Creek, 278
Hodgson, Adam, 151, 211, 221, 236, 242, 251, 253
Hofwyl-Broadfield Plantation, 45, 52
Hog Hammock, Ga., 35
Holiday County Park, Ga., 66
Holland, 106, 303

Holston River, 189, 204
Holy Ground, 251
Holy Trinity Episcopal Church, Ridgeland, 164
Holy Trinity Retreat, Ala., 229, 232
Holzendorf family, 164
Homochito River, 278
Honea Path, S.C., 175
Honey Hill, S.C., 302
Honey Island Swamp, La., 282
Hontoon Island State Park, Fla., 117
Hontoon Landing, 109
Hop, Old. *See* Connecorte
Hopeton Plantation, 45
Hopewell, 172, 174, 186
Hopewell Conference, 182
Hopewell Factory, 89
Hopewell Presbyterian Church, 182
Hopewell-Keowee Monument, 182
Hopkins Prairie, 113
Hopothle Micco, 244
Hopsewee Plantation, 304
Horn Island, Miss., 278
Horry County, S.C., 307, 308, 311, 319
Horry, Daniel, 145, 303
Horry, Elias, 303
Horry, Harriott Pinckney, 145, 303
Horry, Peter, 311
Horry-Georgetown Technical Education Center, 311
Horse Path, 229
Horsepasture River Gorge, 186
Horseshoe Mud Lake, 109
Hotel Lafayette, 214
Hothliwahali, 226
Houlihan Bridge, 18
the Houmas, 281, 289, 294, 296
Houmas House Plantation, 286
Houmas, La., 284
House of Guise, 303
Houston County, Ga., 221
Houston, Dr. William, 315
Houston, John, 14
Houston, Sam, 236
Howard, Edward, 147
Howard, Thomas, Third Earl of Effingham, 21
Howe, Robert, 15, 99
Howe, William, 323
Hoya Indians, 158
Hubbard Landing, Tensaw River, 261
huckleberry, 311
Hudson, Charles, 178, 256
Hudson River, 92
Hudson's Ferry, 56
Huffman's Native Plants, 193
Huger, Benjamin, 306
Huger family, 149, 151, 303
Huger, Francis Kinloch, 151
Huger, S.C., 149
Hughes, John, 313
Hughes, Price, 313
Huguenin family, 164
Huguenot Memorial, 67
Huguenot Memorial Park, 102
Huguenots, 96, 102, 105, 138, 147, 157, 174, 182; associated with Anglicans, 138; barred from Louisiana, 288, 290; colonize Florida, 105; history, 303; in South Carolina, 148, 154, 298, 302, 303
Humboldt, Alexander Von, 7
Hunt, Dr. Kenneth, 146
Hunter, George, 170, 177
Hunting Island State Park, S.C., 168
Huntington, Archer and Anna, 309
Huntington Beach State Park, S.C., 309

Hurl Rock Park, Myrtle Beach, 311
Hurricane Camille, 278
Hurricane Hazel, 311
Hurricane Hugo, 148, 302
hurricanes, 33, 266, 269, 306, 309
Huspa, 160
Hutchinson Island, Ga., 19
Huxford, Ala., 254, 257
Hyams, George, 185
Hyde, Edward; Earl of Clarendon, 138

I

Iberville Parish, La., 296
Iberville, Pierre le Moyne, Sieur de, 297; builds Fort Maurepas, 278; captures Pensacola, 266, 269; establishes Louisiana colony, 273, 288; founds Mobile, 256, 265; names Dauphin Island, 262; names Lake Pontchartrain, 284
Iberville River, 9, 256, 290, 293
ibis, 115, 165
Ichetucknee Springs State Park, Fla., 128, 134
Idlewilde Point, 109
Ikanatchaka, 251
Ila, Ga., 80
Ile de la Loire, 48
Illinois, 2
Imathla, 227
Independent Republic of West Florida, *See* Republic of West Florida
Independent Presbyterian Church, Savannah, 26
Independent Republic of Horry, 308
Indian Camp Forest Trail, 311
Indian Removal Act, 199
Indian River, 120
Indian slave trade, 135
Indian Springs State Park, Ga., 211, 216
Indian trade, 73, 164, 219, 290, 298; between British and Creeks, 264; initiated by Henry Woodward, 159
Indian traders, 184, 199, 208, 210, 308, 313; abuse the Yamassees, 160; among the Cherokees, 203; among the Creeks, 250; on the Mississippi River, 293
Indians. *See also* Native Americans; Christians, 227; Christianized by Spain, 97; influence on food, 137; relations with the Scots-Irish, 175; threaten Charleston, 151; trade with Georgia, 73; trading at Augusta, 73
indigo, 24, 25, 139, 157, 160, 298, 306, 318
indigo snake, 114, 164
Industrial Revolution, 290
Infantry Museum, 236
Innerarity family, 272
Interlachen, Fla., 111, 114
International Biosphere Reserve, 207
International Paper Company, 311
Intracoastal Waterway, 43, 99, 302, 309
I'on, Jacob Bond, 302
I'on Swamp, S.C., 302
Iotla Creek, 8, 199
Iowa Agricultural College, 244
Irene Mound, 19
Irish, 61, 175
Iroquoian language, 195
Iroquois, 183
Iroquois Confederation, 1
Irwin, Jared, 215
Irwinton, Ga., 217
Isaac Haynes Tomb, 169
Isaqueena Falls, S.C., 187
Island Ford, 223
Island Ford Road, 177
Isle de Orleans, 256, 293

Isle of Caprice, Miss., 278
Isle of Hope, Ga., 20
Isleños Center, La., 286
Issaqueena, 176
Isti atcagagi, 227
Italian immigrants, 98, 120
Izard, Ralph, 147
Izard, Sarah, 140

J

J. L. Scott Marine Education Center & Aquarium, 279
J. Strom Thurmond Dam, 66
jack-in-the-pulpit, 186
Jackson, Andrew, 85, 102, 182, 199, 230, 241, 243, 279, 280, 285; accepts surrender of Weatherford, 260, 293; invades Pensacola, 267, 270; appointed territorial governor of Florida, 267; Indian Removal Act, 241
Jackson County, Ga., 79
Jackson County, Miss., 275, 280
Jackson County, N.C., 201
Jackson, Ga., 221
Jackson, James, 15, 21, 51, 64, 94, 213
Jackson, La., 295
Jackson Road, 64, 69
Jackson Square, New Orleans, 285
Jacksonboro, Ga., 56
Jacksonborough, S.C., 142, 169
Jacksonville Beach Wildlife Refuge, 104
Jacksonville, Fla., 101, 102; Black Heritage Trail, 102; Historical Center, 102; Nature Center, 104; Zoological Gardens, 102
Jacobites, 12, 36, 154
Jacque Pate Nature Sanctuary, 261
Jai, Ana Madgigine, 102
Jamaica, 99, 106
James Beamer House, 181
James Hill Park Bayou Walk & Fishing Pier, 279
James II. *See* Stuart, James II
James III, *See* Stuart, James III
James Island County Park, S.C., 144
James Island, S.C., 142, 151
James Jackson & Co., 80
James R. Leake Memorial Park, 295
James, Robert; 8th Baron Petre, 1
James, Thomas, 313
James Webb Nature Center, 163, 164
Jamestown, S.C., 298, 303
Jamestown, Va., 290, 312
Janaibes, 256
Jarrell Plantation State Historical Site, Ga., 216
Jarrett, Deveraux, 176
Jasmine Hill Gardens, 248
Jasper County, Ga., 67, 217
Jasper County, S.C., 148, 161, 166, 304
Jasper, William, 22, 148, 217
Jay, John, 157
Jay, William, 166
Jean Lafitte National Historic Park, 286
Jeanneret family, 164
Jefferson County, Ga., 213, 216
Jefferson Davis Museum and Library, 279
Jefferson National Forest, 192
Jefferson Parish Mardi Gras Museum, 286
Jefferson, Thomas, 6, 88, 148, 157, 290, 318
Jekyll Island Club, 49
Jekyll Island, Ga., 45, 49
Jekyll, Sir Joseph, 49
Jennings State Forest, 104
Jerusalem, 12
Jerusalem Church, 17
Jessie Ball Dupont Park, Fla., 103

Index 355

Jesuits, 28, 159
Jesup, Ga., 52
Jesup, Thomas, 244, 245
Jewell, Ga., 210, 211
Jews, 13, 27, 138, 183; in Alabama, 254; in Charleston, 156; in Georgetown, 306; in West Georgia, 225
Jim Boy, 245, 253
Joanna Bald, N.C., 206
Jocassee, 182
Joe Brown Park, New Orleans, 286
John C. Stennis Space Center, 279
John Mark Verdier House, 167
Johnson Beach, Fla., 269
Johnson, Robert, 12, 22, 139, 302, 308, 313
Johnson, Samuel, 12
Johnson Square, Savannah, 12, 22, 25
Johnston, Gabriel, 315, 317, 321
Johnston, James, 26
Johnston, Richard Malcolm, 213
Johnstone, George, 256, 260, 266
Jones Community, 34
Jones County, Ga., 67, 217
Jones family, 34
Jones Gap State Park, S.C., 186
Jones, James, 217
Jones Lake State Park, N.C., 316, 317, 320
Jones Mills, 236
Jones Narrows, 20
Jones, Noble, 12, 14, 20, 48
Jones, Noble Wimberly, 14, 20, 21
Jones Street, Savannah, 27
Jordan, Michael, 321
Jore, 199, 201
Joseph Manigault House, 156
Joseph's Town, 17
Jourdan River, 279
Jousset de la Loire, Claude, 264
Joyce Kilmer Memorial, 206
Joyce Kilmer-Slickrock Wilderness, 201
Joyce Wildlife Management Area, 285
Joyner, John, 160
Juan Pardo Expedition, 178, 196
Jubilee, 262
Judaculla Rock, 201
Judge, Father Thomas Augustine, 232
Juliette, Ga., 216
Junaluska, 206
Juniper Creek, 113
juniper (ground), 192
Juniper Springs, Fla., 114; Juniper Springs Recreation Area, Fla., 114

K

Kalm, Peter, 3
Kaminski House, 306
Kaminski, Mrs. Harold, 306
Kanapaha Gardens, Gainesville, 128
Kanapaha Prairie, 123, 132
kaolin, 213
Kaolin Festival, 213
karst, 132
Kasihta, 61, 226, 230, 231, 236, 239, 259; burned by Spanish, 215; capital of Lower Creek Towns, 239; leaders, 231
Kasihtas, 83, 226–229; on Ocmulgee River, 215; origin, 226
Kathryn Abbey Hanna Park, Mayport, Fla., 102
Keating, Edward, 80
Kelly's Mill, 211
Kelsall & Spalding, 48, 112
Kelsall, James, 114
Kelsall, Roger, 33, 46, 47, 48, 50, 114, 160

Kelsall Trading Co., 114
Kemble, Fanny, 37, 45, 46
Kenner Historical Museum, 286
Kenner, La., 286
Kentucky: Cherokee territory, 195; home of Shawnees, 71
Kenwood Campground, 112
Kenyon's Bluff, 73
Keowee, 174, 177, 178, 179, 182, 183
Keowee Path. See Charleston-Keowee Path
Keowee River, 8, 144, 176, 183, 185, 187
Keowee-Toxaway State Park, S.C., 183
Kerlerec, Louis Billouart; Chevalier de, 289
Kettle Creek Battle Site, 83
Kiawah River, 145
Kiawahs, 135, 159
King George's War, 13
King Hall Mill, 92
King, Henry, 48
King, Horace, 236
King, Jr., Dr. Martin Luther, 32, 247
King Mill, 76
King, of England, 13, 139, 164, 167, 171, 181, 171, 200. See also individual kings
King Payne, 123, 126
King, Roswell, 35
King Street, Charleston, 156
King-Tisdell Foundation, 27
King's Carolina Rangers, 62
King's Ferry, 19, 29, 42, 43, 50, 102
Kings Mountain, S.C., 176
King's Road, 3, 19, 29, 51, 105, 169, 299, 300, 302, 309, 311; at New Smyrna, 98, 120; in Florida, 102; in North Carolina, 316; in South Carolina, 303
Kingsley Creek, 99
Kingsley Plantation, 101, 102
Kingsley, Zephaniah, 102
Kingston, S.C., 298, 308
Kiokee Baptist Church, 69, 75
Kiokee Creek, 64
Kirbo Interpretative Center, 233
Kirkland, Moses, 171
Kissi tribe, 34
Kituwah, 195
Kleinpeter, La., 290
Knox, William, 14
Knoxville, Ga., 223
Knoxville Road, 221
Knoxville, TN, 76, 245
Koasatis, 194, 195, 203, 246, 248
Kolomi, 9, 242, 246
Kolomoki, 227
Kolomoki Mounds State Historic Park, 234
Kosciuszko, Thaddeus, 177
Kratzert Conservation Area, Fla., 119
Krebs, Hugo Ernestus, 277
Ku Klux Klan, 320
Kulsage, 179, 182, 183, 194
Kusso. See Cusabo

L

La Belle (La Salle's ship), 288
La Caroline, 102, 105
La Florida. See Florida
La Rochelle, France, 288, 303
La Salle, René Robert Cavelier, Sieur de, 266, 273, 288, 296
La Salle's Landing, 286
Labatut House, 296
Lachua Trail, 127
Lacombe, La., 284
lady lupine, 43

lady slipper, showy, 146
Lady's Island, S.C., 168
Lafayette, La., 284
Lafayette, Marquis de, 22, 147, 151, 214, 223, 232, 246–248, 253, 254, 284; arrives in America, 305, 306; in the Creek nation, 231, 242, 243
Lafayette Park, Georgetown, 306
Lafayette Square, Savannah, 22
Lafayette's Landing, 306
LaFourche Parish, La., 296
LaFrance, S.C., 181
LaGrange, Ga., 226
L'Aimable (ship), 288
Lake Alice Wildlife Sanctuary, S.C., 128
Lake Ashby Park, 119
Lake Beresford, 109
Lake Beresford Greenway, 117
Lake City, Fla., 109
Lake Colby County Park, Fla., 119
Lake County, Fla., 126
Lake Dexter, Fla., 8
Lake George Conservation Area, Fla., 113
Lake George County Conservation Area, Fla., 114
Lake George, Fla., 103, 109, 112, 113
Lake George State Forest, Fla., 114
Lake Harris Conservation Area, Fla., 116
Lake Hartwell State Park, Ga., 176
Lake Herrick, Athens, 86
Lake Jesup Conservation Area, Fla., 119
Lake Jocassee, S.C., 184, 185
Lake Kanapaha, Fla., 123, 125
Lake Keowee, S.C., 181, 184
Lake Lochloosa, Fla., 125
Lake Maurepas, La., 9, 256, 281, 286, 293
Lake Monroe Conservation Area, Fla., 119
Lake Monroe Park, Fla., 119
Lake Moultrie, S.C., 146, 182
Lake Oconee, Ga., 208
Lake Oklawaha, Fla., 125
Lake Pontchartrain, 9, 256, 284, 286, 291; boundary of West Florida, 281; British settlements, 281; Lake Pontchartrain Causeway, 284; resorts, 282
Lake Russell, Ga., 93, 94
Lake Santeetlah, N.C., 201
Lake Springs Recreation Area, Ga., 66
Lake Talisi Park, Talassee, 244
Lake Vista Nature Preserve Trail, 287
Lake Waccamaw, N.C., 316
Lake Waccamaw State Park, N.C., 319
Lake Walter F. George, Ga., 233
Lake Weir, 128
Lake Woodruff, Fla., 112; Lake Woodruff Wildlife Management Area, 115
Lakepoint State Park Resort, Ala., 234
Lamar Culture, 215
Lamar family, 211
Lamar, II, L.Q.C., 236
Lamar, John, 211
Lamar, L.Q.C., 211, 236
Lamar, Mirabeau Buonaparte, 211, 236
Lamar Mounds, 215
Lambert, Andrew, 211
Lambert's Creek, 211
Lamboll, Elizabeth, 2, 151; corresponds with John Bartram, 151; visited by John Bartram, 142
Lamboll, Thomas, 2, 112, 151; host to John Bartram, 142
Lancaster, Pa., 89
Lancaster, S.C., 69
Land Lottery Act (1803), 208, 217, 221, 229
Land Office Building, La., 287
Laney, Lucey Craft, 75

Langlois, François, 265
Lanier Oak, 49
Lanier, Sidney, 49
Large-flowered grass-of-Parnassus, 114
Latimer House, 322
Latimore's Mill, 76
Laudonnière, René de, 96, 103
Laura S. Walker State Park, Ga., 52
Laurel Hill Plantation, 309
Laurel Hill Wildlife Drive, 164
Laurens County, S.C., 177
Laurens, Eleanor, 149, 156
Laurens, Esther, 157
Laurens family, 303
Laurens, Henry, 2, 3, 38, 42, 43, 46, 57, 140, 149; assistance to William Bartram, 3, 99, 104, 143; biography, 157; captured by British, 142; describes William Bartram, 4; elected vice-president of South Carolina, 142; family, 153; meets the Bartrams, 3; residence, 156; tours East Florida, 3
Laurens, Jean, 157
Laurens, John, 149, 157
Laurens, Martha, 153, 157
Laurens, Mary Eleanor, 157
Laussat, Pierre Clement de, 290
Law, John, 279, 288, 291
Lawson Air Field, 229, 231
Lawson, John, 298, 300, 304, 319
Lazenby Creek, 209, 211
Le Moyne, Jacques, 96
Leaf River, 278
Leaf Wilderness Area, Miss., 279
Leatherman Creek, 199
Lebanon Station, Fla., 134
LeConte, John, 34
LeConte, John Eatton, 5, 33, 57, 108
LeConte, John Eatton II, 33
LeConte, Joseph, 34
LeConte, Louis, 31, 33
LeConte pear, 33
LeConte-Woodmanston Plantation, 29, 33
LeConte's sparrow, 34
Lee, Arthur: petitions Parliament, 147
Lee, Charles, 14
Lee County, Ala., 235, 249; museum, 242
Lee, Harper, 253
Lee, Harry, 62, 177
Lee, Richard Henry, 50
Lee, Robert E., 21, 50, 166, 235, 249
Legge, William; 2nd Earl of Dartmouth, 49
Leicester, Earl of, 1
Leigh, Judge Egerton, 157
Leitner Museum, 107
Lenape Indians, 7
Lennox, Charles; Duke of Richmond, 49, 62, 72
Leopold I, Emperor of Austria, 266
Lepinay, Jean Michiele, Segneur de, 264
Leroy's Ferry Campground, 66
Lesesne, Anne, 146
Leslie, John, 106
lesser rosebay, 7, 64, 92
Lethe Plantation, 173
Letohatchee, Ala., 242
Letters of Junius, 181
Levasseur, 232
Leveau, Marie, 285
Levy County Campground, 133
Lewis and Clark Expedition, 88
Lewis Island State Natural Area, Ga., 38
Lewis, Kendall, 242
Lewis, Meriwether, 7, 88
Lewis Ocean Bay Heritage Preserve, Fla., 311
Lewis' Tavern, 242

Lewisfield Plantation, 148
Lexington, Ga., 76, 84
L'Hermitage Plantation, 286
Liberty (ship of the Georgia Navy), 14
Liberty Boys, 26, 62
Liberty County, Ga., 33, 34, 39; Historical Society, 29
Liberty Hall, 83
Liberty Hill, S.C., 67
Liberty, S.C., 184
Liberty Square, Savannah, 22
Lick Fork Lake Recreation Area, S.C., 68
Life in the Wild Park, Brunswick, 45
Lightwood Log Creek, 92
Lillington, Alexander, 319
limpkin, 115, 116, 119, 134
Lin, Maya, 247
Lincoln, Benjamin, 15, 57, 72, 142, 160, 161, 177
Lincoln County, Ga., 33, 72, 80, 90
Lincoln County Historical Park, 68
Lincoln, Earl of, 1
Lincolnton, Ga., 68
Line Creek, 232, 241, 246
Lining, Dr. John, 153
Linnaeus, Carl, 1, 1–6, 2, 3, 4
Linnean System, 146
Linton, Ga., 76, 210, 214
Lisbon, Ga., 89
Literary and Philosophical Society of Charleston, 165
lithospermum tuberosum, 87
Little Carpenter. *See* Attakullakulla
Little Egg Island, Ga., 38
Little Lake George, Fla., 109, 112
Little Lake George Wilderness, 112
Little Ogeechee River, 213
Little Orange Creek, 125
Little Prince, 231, 243
Little Richard, 221
Little River, Ga., 61, 62, 66, 68, 69, 73, 76, 80, 82, 83, 91, 92; North Fork, 83
Little River Boat Ramp, 66
Little River Dam, 183
Little River Neck, S.C., 308
Little River, S.C., 3, 67, 170, 172, 173, 308, 311, 315
Little River State Forest, 254
Little Rock Wildlife Drive, 216
Little Scaly Mountain, N.C., 194
Little Shawnee, 246
Little St. Simons Island, Ga., 46
Little Talasi, 248
Little Tennessee River, 179, 183, 189, 191, 199, 200–201, 203; settlements, 194, 197; Greenway, 200
Little Uchee Creek, 241
Little Wambaw Swamp Wilderness, S.C., 302
Little Warrior, 245
Little Wekiva River, 119
Little-Big Econ State Conservation Area, Fla., 120
live oak, 20, 133, 144, 263, 269
Live Oak Landing, Tensaw River, 261
Livingston, Edward, 287, 297
Livingston Parish, La., 287, 296
Livingston, Robert, 290
Loachapoka Historic District, 242
loblolly bay, 311
loblolly pine, 216
Lochloosa Conservation Area, Fla., 125
Lochloosa Creek, 125
Locke, John, 137
Lockerly Arboretum, 214
Locust Grove State Commemorative Area, 295
Locust Stake Road, 192

Logan, James, 2, 3
Logan, Martha, 2, 155
loggerhead turtle, 19, 39, 121, 317, 318
London Courant, 181
London, England, 20, 49
London Evening Post, 181
Londonderry Township, S.C., 67
Lone Star Flag, 223
Long Bay, 3, 308–309, 311
Long Cane Creek, 67, 172, 173, 179
Long Cane Creek Recreation Area, S.C., 66
Long Cane Massacre, 173, 182
Long Cane Scenic Area, 174
Long Cane Settlement, 67, 170, 173–175, 178, 179, 186
Long County, Ga., 33
Long Creek, Ga., 84
Long, Huey P., 294
Long Pond, 132
Long Warrior, 112, 126
longleaf pine, 113, 148, 163, 269, 270, 302, 311
Longstreet, Augustus Baldwin, 173, 213
Lonnie C. Miller, Sr. Regional Park, Fla., 103
Loranger, La., 285
Lords Proprietors, 137, 138, 139, 159, 167, 303, 305, 312, 318
Lorimer, Dr., 267
Loughabber, 174, 179
Louis XIV, King of France, 138, 247, 264, 288, 290, 303
Louis XV, King of France, 256, 289, 290, 296
Louisiana, 144, 243, 281–282, 288–291; admitted to Union, 290, 291, 296; boundary with Florida, 270; ceded to Spain, 281, 289; colonial structures, 279; Delta, 291; early settlements, 278; fails to attract French colonists, 279, 288; Federal Road, 232; Florida Parishes, 281–282; Indian trade, 247; Koasatis, 248; natural areas, 285; Old Spanish Trail, 284; prospers under Gálvez, 284; rice, 304; schools, 296; Spain cedes Louisiana to France, 281, 290; Spanish period, 289; statehood, 296
 capitals: Baton Rouge, 294; Biloxi, 264; Dauphin Island, 262, 273; Mobile, 256
Louisiana Arts & Sciences Center, 294
Louisiana Hayride, 247
Louisiana Nature and Science Center, 286
Louisiana Purchase, 7, 88, 257, 281, 290, 295
Louisiana State Archives, 294
Louisiana State Capitol, Visitor Information Center, 294
Louisiana State Museum, 285
Louisiana State University, 294; Hill Top Aboretum, 294; Louisiana Museum of Ancient Indian Culture, 287; mounds, 294; Museum of Geoscience, 294; Museum of Natural Science, 294; Rural Life Museum, 294
Louisiana Territory, 282
Louisiana Wildlife and Fisheries Museum, 286
Louisville, Ga., 57, 211, 236; capital of Georgia, 64, 211
lousewort, 87
Lovelace Park, Fla., 103
Lowcountry, 158–162, 299
Lower Cape Fear Historical Society, 322
Lower Cherokee Path. *See* Etowah Trail
Lower Creek Towns, 26, 226–229; history, 230; visited by William Bartram, 232
Lower Creek Trading Path, 8, 58, 61, 64, 65, 71, 76, 208, 210, 211, 217, 219, 222–224, 230, 231, 237
Lower Long Cane Presbyterian Church, 173
Lower Suwannee River National Wildlife Refuge, 133

Index 357

Lower Wekiva River State Reserve, 119
Lower Whitewater Falls, 185
Lowland Scots, 37
Lowndes County, Ala., 249, 251
Lowndes, Rawlins, 140
Lowndes, William, 249
Lowndesville, S.C., 174
Lowry, Henry Berry, 320
loyalists, 53, 54, 77, 154; abandon Ninety Six, 177; attack Long Cane Settlement, 186; attacked by Cherokees, 174; defeated at Elizabethtown, N.C., 320; evacuate Charleston, 142; exiled to London, 153; flee Beaufort, 160; in Augusta, 62; in Bladen Co., N.C., 320; in Charleston, 153; in Florida, 14; in Georgia, 19; in Louisiana, 289, 292; in North Carolina, 315, 319; in South Carolina, 70, 171, 299; in South Carolina Upcountry, 171; in Southern colonies, 142; in the Cape Fear region, 321; in Pensacola, 266; in West Florida, 284, 275; militia, 171, 177; property confiscated, 169
Lucas, Eliza. *See* Pinckney, Eliza Lucas
Lucas, George, 139
Lucas, Jonathan, 148, 149, 304
Lucas, Lydia Simmons, 149
Lucas Tavern, 246, 247
Lucas, Walter, 246
Lucey Laney Museum, 75
Lumbees, 320
Lumber River, 320
Lumberton, N.C., 320
Lumpkin, Ga., 233
Lumpkin, Joseph, 84
Luna Colony, 238
Luna y Arellano, Tristán de, 256, 266, 269
Lunney Museum, 183
Lutheran Church of the Ascension, 26
Lyell, Sir Charles, 5, 7, 45, 46, 221, 223, 235, 236, 291, 295
Lynch, Jr., Thomas, 142, 304
Lynch, Sr., Thomas, 140, 304
Lynchburg, Va., 170
Lynches Causeway, 300, 303
lyonia, rusty, 165
Lyttleton, William Henry, 18, 139; escalates Cherokee War, 179, 197

M

Ma Rainey, 236
Mabila, 238
the Mabilas, 256, 263, 264
MacDonald, Donald, 319
MacDonald, Flora, 320
Mackay, Donald, 47
Mackay, Hugh, 36
Maclure, William, 5, 7, 57
Macon County, Ala., 243, 249
Macon County, Ga., 224
Macon County, N.C., 194, 202
Macon, Ga., 215, 221, 221–223, 232; Macon Museum of Arts & Sciences, 222; Washington Memorial Library, 221
Macon, Nathaniel, 194, 201, 249
Maddock, Joseph, 71
Madison County, Ga., 80, 90
Madison, Ga., 217
Madison, James, 6, 22, 257, 281
Madison Square, Savannah, 22
Madisonville, La., 285; Museum, 285
Madoc ab Owain Gwnedd, Welsh explorer, 262
Magnolia Bluff, Satilla River, 50, 51
Magnolia Gardens & Audubon Swamp Gardens, 145

Magnolia Mound Plantation, 294
Magnolia pyramidata, 259
Magnolia River, 262
Magnolia Springs State Park, Ga., 57
magnolias, 194; *Magnolia auriculata*, 192; Southern magnolia, 86
Maitland, John, 161
Malaga, Spain, 265
malaria, 15, 21, 27, 145, 164, 166
Malatchi, 231
Maldonado, Diego, 266
Mallow, 34
Mallow Plantation, 230
Manack, David. *See* Moniac, David
Manack, Elizabeth, 248
Manack, Sam, 248, 259
Manack's Tavern, 248, 251
manatee, 115, 117, 132, 133
Manatee Springs, 125, 128; State Park, 132
Manchac, La., 290, 293
Manchac Wildlife Management Area, La., 285
Mandarin Park, Fla., 103
Mandeville, Francis de, 284
Mandeville, La., 282, 284
mangrove, 120
Manigault family, 302, 303
Manigault, Joseph, 302
Manigault, Peter, 140
Manrique, Mateo Gonzales, 267
Mansfield Plantation & Slave Village, 306
Manteo, 312
map turtle, 278
Maple Leaf (ship), 102
Marchand, commander of Ft. Toulouse, 247
Marchand, Sehoy, 244
Mardis Gras, 265
Margravate of Azilia, 12
Marigny, Bernard de, 284
Marine Life Oceanarium, 279
Marineland, Fla., 105
Marion County, Ga., 221, 225
Marion County, Fla., Parks & Recreation Headquarters, 116
Marion County, S.C., 307
Marion family, 147, 303
Marion, Francis, 142, 150, 161, 169, 193, 197, 225, 299, 302
Marion Square, Savannah, 156
Maris, Mary, 1
Maritime & Seafood Industry Museum, Biloxi, 278
maritime forest, 21
Marjorie Kinnan Rawlings State Historic Site, Fla., 125
Marks family, 79
Marks, John, 88
Marksville Commemorative Area, La., 296
Marlborough, Duke of, 1
Marquéz, Don Thomas Menéndez, 111, 126
Marshall, Abraham, 19, 75, 101
Marshall, Humphrey, 6, 7, 85
Marshall, Moses, 5, 7
Marshall, Rev. Daniel, 62
Marshall Swamp Trailhead, 116
Martin, Betsy Ward, 205
Martin Creek, 191; Martin Creek Falls, 192
Martin, Eddie Owens, 225
Martin, Gene, 307
Martin, Joseph, 182, 205
Martin, Josiah, 315, 321
Marver, James, 111
Mary Ann Brown Preserve, Fla., 295
Mary Pipes Butler Garden, 295
Mary Ross Waterfront Park, 49

Mary Willis Library, Washington, Ga., 83
Maryland, 137
Mason, George, 6
Mason, Joseph, 7
Masonic Temple, 102
Massachusetts, 137, 140
Massachusetts Bay Colony, 312
Massacre Island. *See* Dauphin Island
Massingale Park, St. Simons Island, 48
Masters Tournament, 74
Matagorda Bay, Texas, 288
Matamoras, Juan Pedro, 266
Matanzas Inlet, Fla., 96, 97, 105
Matheos, Antonio, 227
Matheson Historical Center, 127
Mathews, George, 67, 79, 213, 215
Mauk, Ga., 219
Maverick, Gus, 182
Maverick, Samuel, 182
Maxwell, James, 32
May River, 166. *See* River May
Mayacans, 114
mayapple, 87, 186
Mayerhoffer family, 164
Mayfield, Ga., 76, 211
Mayhem Tower, 62
Maynard, Robert, 313
Mayon Indians, 158
Mayport, Fla., 102, 103
Mays, Dr. Benjamin E., 177
Mayson, James, 173
Mazariego, Governor of Cuba, 159
Mazyck family, 147, 303
McBean Creek, 56, 59
McBean, Lachlan, 73
McCalla Island Mounds, 94
McClellanville, S.C., 302
McCormick County, S.C., 69, 72, 177
McCormick, Cyrus, 67, 72
McCormick, S.C., 67
McCullough, Ala., 257
McDowell County, N.C., 185
McDuffie County, Ga., 72
McFie, T. G., 82
McGehee family, 79
McGillivray, Alexander, 208, 214, 229, 237, 239, 244, 248, 250, 254, 259, 272; biography, 244
McGillivray, Lachlan, 73, 244, 248
McGillivray, Sophy, 248
McGirth, Daniel, 59, 64, 70, 83, 99, 161, 171
McIntosh, Ann, 29
McIntosh Bluff, Ala., 250, 259
McIntosh, Capt. William (father of Chief William McIntosh), 230
McIntosh, Chilly, 230, 231
McIntosh County, Ga., 34, 39
McIntosh family, 28, 34, 39, 221
McIntosh, James, 260
McIntosh, John, 34, 37
McIntosh, John Mohr, 34, 36
McIntosh, John Houston, 50
McIntosh, Lachlan, 9, 14, 20, 26, 29, 31, 34, 37, 38, 43, 45, 47, 51, 79, 132, 157, 182; duel with Button Gwinnett, 32; employs William Bartram as a spy, 99; enemy of George Walton, 75; visited by William Bartram, 15
McIntosh Landing, Ala., 260
McIntosh, Lewis, 34
McIntosh, Margery, 26, 47
McIntosh Reserve, 221
McIntosh, Roderick, 34, 230
McIntosh, Sarah, 37
McIntosh Shouters, 48
McIntosh Sugar Mill, 50

McIntosh, William (Coweta chief), 34, 221, 229, 230, 241, 243; death, 221
McIntosh, William (brother of Lachlan), 47
McLatchy, Charles, 106, 112, 114
McLeod, Donald, 319
McLeod Water Park, Miss., 279
McQueen, James, 244, 245
McQueen, Peter, 241, 244, 253
meadow beauty, tall, 146
Meadow Garden, 70, 75
Meaher State Park, Ala., 261
Medical College of Georgia, 74; Old Medical College, 75
Medical College of South Carolina, 144, 165
Medici, Catherine de, 303
medicine, 145
Medway River, 29
Meigs, Josiah, 85
Melbourne, Fla., 103
Mellichamp, Dr. Joseph, 166
Melon Bluff Nature Preserve, Ga., 33
Memphis, TN, 73, 74, 288
Mende language, 34
Mendenhall, Ann, 3
Mendenhall family, 82
Menéndez de Avilés, Pedro, 28, 34, 96, 105, 126, 159, 194
Marqués, Pedro Menéndez, 159
Mepkin Abbey, 149
Mepkin Plantation, 148, 149, 157
Mercer University, 88, 221
Meriwether, Lucy, 88
Merritt Island National Wildlife Refuge, Fla., 120, 121
Meson Academy, 84
Meson, Francis, 84
Methodism, 24, 46
Methodist Church, 222
Mexico, 105, 168, 284; Old Spanish Trail, 277, 284; origin of the Creeks, 239; refuge for Catholic Indians, 106; trails from Florida, 270
Micanopy, Fla., 123, 125, 126, 132
Michaux, André, 7, 67, 144–146, 168, 171, 176, 179, 185, 192; visits William Bartram, 144
Michaux, François, 7, 39, 145, 146, 165; visits William Bartram, 144
Michaux Herbarium, 185
Michaux's Garden, 144, 146
mico, 227
Middle Cherokee Path, 76, 82, 85, 86, 217
Middle Oconee River, 85
Middle Towns. *See* Cherokee Middle Towns
Middleburg Plantation, 148, 149
Middleton, Arthur, 106, 142, 146, 147
Middleton, Edward, 138, 147
Middleton Family, 46
Middleton Gardens, 144
Middleton, Henry, 140, 146
Middleton Place, 146
Middleton, Thomas, 157, 160, 193
Middleton's Ferry, 65
Midway Cemetery, 31
Midway Congregational Church, 29, 31, 33
Midway, Ga., 22, 28, 29, 32, 33, 39, 99, 147, 235
Midway Museum and Visitors' Center, 31, 33
Mile Branch Settlement, 287
Mile Creek Park, 183
Miles Brewton House, 151
Milfort, Louis Le Clerc, 56, 61, 236
Military Road, St. Simons Island, 47
Mill Shoal Creek, 92
Milledge, John, 20, 214
Milledge, Richard, 20
Milledge, Thomas, 12

Milledgeville, Ga., 51, 60, 76, 123, 208, 214, 242, 247
Millen, Ga., 211
Millen National Fish Hatchery and Aquarium, 57
Miller, John, 181
Miller, Phineas, 18
Miller's Weekly Messenger, 181
Millionaire's Village, Jekyll Island, 49
Millmore, 214
Mill's Ferry, 51
Mills, Robert, 153
Milstead, Ala., 245
Milton, Fla., 270
mimosa, 144
Mims, Samuel, 260
Minamac Wildflower Bog, 262
mink, 286
Minoans, 226
Minorcan immigrants, 98, 120
Miranda, Gutierrez de, 159
Miró, Don Esteban Rodriquez, 284
Miruelo, Diego, 266
Mission Springs, 134
Missionary Servants of the Most Blessed Trinity, 232
missions, 97; destroyed by Carolinians and Indians, 106; in Apalachicola Province, 227; in South Carolina, 168
Mississippi, 243; admitted to the Union, 275; available farmland, 64; Black Belt, 248; cotton migration, 209, 214, 232; homeland of the Chickasaw185, s, 71; natural areas, 279; welcome centers, 277; Yazoo Land Fraud, 213
Mississippi River, 9, 199, 288–291, 291, 296; Alabama town, 247; as boundary, 98, 250,256, 261, 266, 274, 281; attractions, 286; British settlements, 281; Carolina trade, 167; events of the Revolution, 290; French exploration, 256, 288; French settlement, 164, 264; frontier, 243; natural history, 291; origin of the Creeks, 239; public roads, 286; Spanish exploration, 273; viewed by William Bartram, 289
Mississippi sandhill crane, 277, 278
Mississippi Territory, 250, 255, 257, 260, 264, , 265, 274, 280; boundary, 304
Mississippian Culture, 215, 226, 294; on Alabama River, 254; on Chattahoochee River, 233, 234
Missouri River, 88
Mistletoe State Park, Ga., 69
Mitchell, David, 223, 232
Mitchell-Smith-Anderson House, 322
Mitylene, Ala., 242
Mobile, Ala., 242, 250, 256–265, 275, 279, 288; Azalea Trail, 265; becomes part of Mississippi Territory, 264; Botanical Gardens, 263; capital of Louisiana, 261; captured by Gálvez, 257, 260, 267; center of French trade with Alabamas, 264; cotton port, 265; Federal Road, 86, 223, 232; historic district, 264–265; Library, 265; Museum of Art, 263; Old Spanish Trail, 270, 277; refuge for Apalachees, 130; Spain surrenders the city to United States, 259, 264; under British ownership, 260; Welcome Center, 265; William Bartram's visit, 259
Mobile Bay, 258, 261, 273; early exploration, 256, 288, 262
Mobile Bay Ferry, 262
Mobile County, Ala., 257, 263, 275
Mobile Delta, 256, 261, 262
Mobile River, 256–259, 260
Mocama, 12, 50
Mocama Indians, 40
Modoc Campground, S.C., 66
monarch butterfly, 262

Monck, Thomas, 150
Moncks Corner, S.C., 150
Moniac (Manack), David, 248
Monk, George; Duke of Albemarle, 138
Monroe County, Ala., 250, 251, 253, 255; Museum, 253
Monroe County, Ga., 221
Monroe, James, 255, 290
Monroeville, Ala., 255
Montagu, Lord Charles, 140
Monterey Square, Savannah, 22
Montgomery, Ala., 232, 223, 242, 246, 247–248, 253; Ballet, 246; Curb Market, 247; Museum of Fine Arts, 246; Visitor Center, 247; Zoo, 246
Montgomery, Archibald, 179, 183, 193, 197, 206
Montgomery County, Ala., 243, 246, 249
Montgomery, Lemuel Putnam, 249
Montgomery, Sir Robert, 160
Montiano, Manuel de, 47, 104
Monticello, Ga., 87, 216
Monticello Glade, 216
Montrose, Ala., 261
Montville, 58
Moon Walk, New Orleans, 285
Moore family, 79, 313
Moore, James, 71, 97, 106, 122, 130, 139, 147, 219, 227, 313
Moore, Maurice, 147, 178, 313, 316, 317
Moore, Nathaniel, 313
Moore, Roger, 313, 318
Moore's Creek National Battlefield, 319
Moore's Landing, S.C., 300
moorhen, 115
Moran, Mary, 34
Moravians, 13, 19
Morehouse College, 75, 177
Morgan County, Ga., 67
Morgan, Daniel, 186
Morgan, Enoch, 313
Morgan Park, Georgetown, 306
Morganza, La., 296
Mormon Branch, 114
Morningside Nature Park, Gainesville, 127
Morrall, John, 309
Morrione Vineyards, 248
Morris Museum of Art, 74
Morris, Thomas, 32
Morton, Joseph, 160
mosquito, 45
Mosquito Grove, 109
Mosquito Lagoon, 120
Mosquito River, 119
Moss Bluff Recreation Area, 116
Moss Point, Miss., 277
Motte family, 303
Motte, Isaac, 160
Motte, Jacob, 148
Motte, Rebecca, 151, 302
Moultrie family, 147
Moultrie, James, 3, 98
Moultrie, John, 3, 98, 147
Moultrie, William, 142, 144, 146, 148, 161, 300
Mount Carmel Park, 173
Mount Carmel, S.C., 67, 173
Mount Cornelia, 102
Mount Hope, 3, 109
Mount LeConte, 34
Mount Magnolia, 191, 192
Mount Pleasant (Yuchi), 54, 69
Mount Pleasant, Ala., 259
Mount Pleasant, Ga., 163
Mount Pleasant, S.C., 148
Mount Royal, 3, 109
Mountain City, Ga., 191

Index 359

Mountain Heritage Center, 201
mountain scullcap, 85
Mouse, Thomas and Lucy, 20
Mouzon map, 167
Mowa Band of Choctaw, 261
Moytoy, 201
Mt. Zion A.M.E. Church, 102
Mud Creek, 8, 191
Mud Spring Trail, 113
Muhlenberg, Henry, 165, 290
Muir, John, 21, 34, 166
Muklasa, 9, 242, 246
Mulberry Grove Plantation, Ga., 50
Mulberry Plantation, S.C., 22, 148
Mule Day Festival, 84
Munson, Fla., 270
Murder Creek, 253
Murphy Island, Fla., 3, 109, 112
Murphy Island, S.C., 304
Murphy, N.C., 201, 206, 207
Murray, Dr. John, 173
Murrell's Inlet, S.C., 300, 308, 309
Muscogee County, Ga., 235
Museum National D'Histoire Naturelle, 144
Museum of African-American History, Savannah, 27
Museum of Coastal History, St. Simons Island, 48
Museum of Commerce, Pensacola, 271
Museum of East Alabama, Opelika, 234, 242
Museum of Florida's Army, St. Augustine, 107
Museum of Historic St. Augustine, 106
Museum of Industry, Pensacola, 271
Museum of Natural History, London, 7, 146
Museum of Science and History, Jacksonville, 102
Museum of Southeastern Indians, Roberta, 223
Museum of the Cape Fear, Fayetteville, 320
Museum of the City of Mobile, 265
Museum of Weapons and Early American History, St. Augustine, 107
Museum on the Common, Mount Pleasant, S.C., 148
Musgrove, John, 12, 18
Musgrove, Mary, 12, 18, 31, 35, 231, 237
Musgrove Trading Post, 18
Muskhogean language, 17, 40, 123, 135, 158, 163, 195, 203, 226, 239, 255
Muskogees, 28, 135, 174, 239; attack Apalachicolas, 163; establish trade with S.C., 164; in French Louisiana, 281; join the Yamassee War, 160; on Ocmulgee River, 219
muskrat, 286
myrica inodora, 259
Myrtle Beach, S.C., 300, 309
Myrtle Beach State Park, S.C., 309
myrtle oak, 114

N

Nairne, Thomas, 138, 160, 166, 167
Nancy Hart Historical Park, Ga., 89
Nanipacana, 238, 266
Nantahala Gorge, 200, 201, 205
Nantahala Mountains, 8, 200, 201
Nantahala National Forest, 192, 201
Nantahala Ridge, 205
Nantahala River, 8, 201, 205
Napoleon (Bonaparte), 84, 290, 318
narrowleaf yellow pondlily, 319
Narváez Expedition, 273, 288
Narváez, Panfilo de, 256
Nashville, TN, 76
Nassau County, Fla., 53
Nassau, Germany, 53
Nassau River, 15

Nassau Sound, 43, 50, 99
Natalbany River, 286
Natchez Indians, 147, 239; in South Carolina, 148; language, 239; Massacre of French settlers, 291, 296
Natchez, Miss., 239, 257, 260, 288, 290, 291, 296; early roads, 260; taken by Gálvez, 267
Natchez Trace, 285
Natchitoches, La., 288
Nathaniel Russell House, 152
National African American Archives Museum, Mobile, 265
National Bartram Historical Trail of Mississippi, 279
National Forest Service, 192, 193
National Park Service, 148, 292
National Science Center, Augusta, 75
National Wild Turkey Federation, 69
Native Americans, 6; archaeology, 230, 233, 296; artifacts, 295; as slaves, 304; at Fort Mose, 104; Christian Indians disappear from Florida, 114; conflicts with colonists, 77; contact with Europeans, 312; decimated by disease, 208; deerskin trade, 75; enslaved by Carolinians, 312; history, 75, 128, 169; immigration routes, 226; in Horry County, S.C., 311; in South Carolina, 167, 307; myths and legends, 224; on the Gulf Coast, 274; oral traditions, 216; painted by Gov. White, 312; population, 215; raid white settlements, 84; removal, 221, 241
Nature Coast, 133
Nature Conservancy, 19, 33, 38, 69, 119, 133, 150, 163, 169, 230, 277, 300, 304, 307, 309
Navair, Fla., 109
Naval Live Oaks Reserve, 269
naval stores, 315
Navarre, Henry de, 303
Neamathla, 229
Neamico, 229
Negro Act, 139
Nelson, John, 84
Neptune Park, St. Simons Island, 48
New Biloxi, 278
New Bordeaux, S.C., 8, 65, 67
New Brunswick, 290
New Carthage, N.C., 321
New Dock Street Theater, 154
New Ebenezer, 56
New Echota, 199
New England, 76, 137, 161
New Englanders, 137
New Hanover County Arboretum, 318
New Hanover County, N.C., 321
New Hanover, Ga., 42, 61, 69
New Hanover Public Library, 322
New Hope Plantation, Ga, 42, 46, 52, 157
New Liverpool, N.C., 321
New Orleans, La., 286, 291; capital of Louisiana, 274, 278, 279, 289; colonial population, 289; early roads, 260; elevation, 291; founded by Bienville, 288; Great River Road, 286, 293; Museum of Art, 286; Old Spanish Trail, 270, 277, 284; Pharmacy Museum, 285; refuge for Spanish Floridians, 266; sites and public access, 285, 286; Voodoo Museum, 285
New Purchase, 8, 34, 37, 67, 68, 73, 77–82, 79, 80, 82, 90, 91; survey party, 92
New Richmond, La., 290
New River Landing, 165
New River, S.C., 161
New Roads, La., 296
New Savannah Town, 71
New Smyrna, Fla., 3, 98, 117, 120, 143; described by William Bartram, 109

New Switzerland Plantation, Fla., 104
New Town, N.C., 321
New York, NY, 303, 323
New York Zoological Society, 35
Newberry, Fla., 125, 132
Newberry, S.C., 89
Newbury Plantation, 168
Newcastle, Duke of. *See* Pelham, Thomas-Holles; Duke of Newcastle
Newnan, Daniel, 123, 126
Newnans Lake, 127
Newry, Ireland, 173
Newry, S.C., 183
Newton, N.C., 321
Nicholson, Francis, 139
Nikwasi, 199, 200
Ninety Six District, 72, 170, 299
Ninety Six National Historic Site, 177
Ninety Six, S.C., 89, 171, 176, 177, 178, 183, 186
Nisquesalla, 159
Nolichucky River, 189, 195, 203
Nombre de Dios, Mission de, 106
Non-importation Movement, 140
Norfolk, Duke of, 1
North America, 98, 193; claimed by Spain, 96; competition among European powers, 273
North Augusta, S.C., 70
North Carolina: Bartram family, 1; boundary with Georgia, 185, 193; boundary with South Carolina, 313; British attempt to re-establish authority, 319; Cherokee homeland, 182, 195; claims Cape Fear region, 313; coastal area, 317–321; during the Revolution, 315; governors, 73; haven for pirates, 313; history of the coastal region, 321; joins war against Cherokees, 179; land protection, 319; migration from the state, 67, 71, 79, 89, 92, 170; migration to Georgia, 208; militia, 171; Nantahala National Forest, 192; officials, 300; Piedmont settlement, 178; public lands, 185; relations with the Cherokees, 199; relinquishes western territory, 205; Revolution in the west, 62; Scots encouraged to immigrate, 315; search for Oconee bells, 185; settlement of frontier, 77; Spanish exploration, 159; war with the Chickamaugas, 205
North Carolina Aquarium, 315, 317
North Carolina Bartram Trail, 191, 194, 200, 201, 205
North Carolina Bartram Trail Society, 200, 205, 334
North Carolina Coastal Land Trust, 317
North Carolina Department of Archives and History, 313
North Carolina Indian Cultural Center, 320
North Carolina National Estuarine Research Reserve, 318
North Carolina Underwater Archaeology Center, 315, 317
North Carolinians, 79; settle Piedmont Georgia, 64, 84
North Chacan Plantation, 148
North Charleston, S.C., 146
North, Frederick (Lord North), 90
North Myrtle Beach, S.C., 309
North Newport River, 33
North Oconee River, 82, 85, 86, 87, 92
North Pass, La., 282, 286
North Street Aquarium, Beaufort, 167
North Wilkes Museum, Tignall, Ga., 84
Northeast Cape Fear River, 321
Northlake Museum and Nature Center, La., 284
Nottoway Plantation, La., 286
Nova Scotia, 290; refuge for loyalists, 99
nullification, 182

the Numbered Creeks, 176
Nunis, Dr. Samuel, 13
Nunnehi, 200
Nuttall, Thomas, 5, 7

O

Oak Alley Plantation, La., 286
Oak Island Marshes, N.C., 317
oak, scarlet, 86
oak-leaf hydrangea, 223
Oakfuskie, 211
Oakfuskie Trail. *See* Upper Creek Trading Path
Oakley Park, Edgefield, 68
Oakley Plantation, La., 295
Oaks Plantation, 309
Oakwood Cemetery, Montgomery, 247
Oatland Island Educational Center, Savannah, 21
Obediah's Okefenok, 52
O'Brien, Kennedy, 73
Ocala, Fla., 126
Ocala National Forest, 111, 114
Ocala Ridge, 113
Ocean Springs, Miss., 273, 278
Ochesee Creek, 215, 239
Ocmulgee Flats Hunt Camp, 216
Ocmulgee Mounds National Monument, 8, 215, 219, 227
Ocmulgee Old Fields, 214, 215, 232, 237, 239
Ocmulgee River, 8, 38, 50, 219, 227; boundary of Georgia, 215, 217; home of the Cowetas, 208; home of the Hitchitis, 219; home of the Muskogees, 239; Indian settlements, 219
Ocmulgee River Greenway, 221
Ocmulgee River Trail, 216
Ocoee River, 205
Oconee bells, 144, 182, 185, 186, 194
Oconee County, Ga., 87, 89
Oconee County, S.C., 42, 183, 186, 187
Oconee Forest Park, 86
Oconee Mountains, 8
Oconee National Forest, 87, 216
Oconee Old Town (Hitchiti), 215
Oconee River, 8, 38, 51, 60, 80, 85, 87, 123, 208, 211, 216, 243; boundary of, 77, 214, 217, 237, 244; boundary of Georgia, 79, 208, 215; boundary of Washington County, 208; bounty lands, 79; crossings, 76, 86, 214, 215; De Soto Expedition, 208; frontier, 80; home of the Oconees, 232; Mississippian Era, 87, 91; Trans-Oconee Republic, 67; visited by William Bartram, 82
Oconee River Greenway, 86
Oconee River Recreation Area, 87
Oconee State Park, S.C., 8, 186, 191, 302
Oconee Station State Park, 181, 186
Oconee Town (Cherokee), 182, 186, 226
Oconee War, 208, 214
Oconees, 208, 215, 232, 239; move to Florida, 123, 130
O'Conner, Flannery, 214
Oconostota, 174, 179, 204, 205
Ocracoke Island, N.C., 313
Ocute, 60, 87, 91, 160, 208, 214
Odum, Dr. Eugene, 58, 86
Oenothera grandiflora, 259
Ogeechee lime, 3, 19
Ogeechee Old Town, 83
Ogeechee River, 19, 28, 29, 45, 54, 57, 58, 61, 65, 70, 82, 83, 84, 210, 211, 213, 216; and the Yuchis, 69, 83; as boundary, 73, 80, 211, 237; boundary of Georgia, 208, 211; boundary of Washington County, 208; historic crossings, 76, 210

Ogeechee River Preserve, 19
Ogeechee Wildlife Management Area, 211
Ogle Massacre, 251
Oglethorpe County, Ga., 64, 84, 88, 89–90, 208; created from New Purchase, 79, 80; site of Great Buffalo Lick, 82
Oglethorpe, Ga., 224
Oglethorpe, James Edward, 13, 17, 18, 19, 20, 21, 22, 24, 26, 27, 28, 29, 34, 36, 38, 39, 40, 46, 47, 50, 53, 86, 89, 97, 120, 239; and Tomochichi, 26; assisted by William Bull, 167; biography, 12; conference at Coweta, 227, 230; founds Augusta, 73; invasion of Florida, 104, 106, 123; statue at Chippewa Square, 22
Oglethorpe oak, 37
Oglethorpe's House, 46
Ohio River, 199, 246, 256, 273
Ohio Territory, 279
Ohio Valley, 195
Okefenokee National Wildlife Refuge, 52–53
Okefenokee Swamp, 50, 51
Okelousas, 194, 281
Oklahoma, 206, 229; home of Biloxis and Pascagoulas, 274; Seminole settlers, 123, 284
Oklawaha Prairie Restoration Area, 116
Oklawaha River, 98, 109, 112, 116
Okmulgee Town, 226
Old Alabama Town, Montgomery, 246, 247
Old Arsenal Museum, Beaufort, 294
Old Biloxi, 278; capital of Louisiana, 264
Old Bingham, Ala., 246
Old Chimney, Pensacola, 270
Old City Gate, Charleston, 156
Old College, University of Georgia, 85
Old Dorchester State Park, S.C., 147
Old Edgefield District Archives, 68
Old Exchange and Provost Dungeon, Charleston, 140, 155
Old Farmers Day, 285
Old Federal Road. *See* Federal Road
Old French House, Biloxi, 279
Old Georgetown Road, 145, 300, 302
Old Governor's Mansion, Milledgeville, 214
Old Herb Shop, Savannah, 24
Old Hop. *See* Connecorte
Old House, S.C., 166
Old Jacksonborough Road, 143
Old Jail Museum, Springfield, 15
Old Market, Louisville, 211
Old Medical College. *See* Medical College of Georgia
Old Post Road, Ga., 42, 43, 53
Old Powder Magazine, Charleston, 155
Old River Control Structure, 291
Old River Wildlife Management Area, La., 282
Old Slave Mart, Charleston, 155
Old Spanish Trail, 105, 128, 261, 270; in eastern Louisiana, 284; in Mississippi, 277
Old Stage Road, Ala., 251
Old Stagecoach Road, Ala., 259, 261
Old State Capitol, Baton Rouge, 294
Old State Capitol, Milledgeville, 214
Old Stekoa, 8
Old Stone Church, Clemson, 182, 183
Old Tassel, 182
Old Town, Suwannee River, 123, 130, 133
Old Town, N.C., 316, 318
O'Leno State Park, Fla., 134
olives, 24
Olustee Battlefield, Fla., 102
Omaha, Ga., 126, 232
Onondago, 1
Oostanoula River, 205
Opelika, Ala., 242

Opothleyaholo, 245
Orange City, Fla., 117
Orange County, N.C., 71
Orange Lake, Fla., 122
orange milkwort, 302
Orange Springs, Fla., 112
Orange Springs Recreation Area, Fla., 112, 125
Orangeburg, S.C., 56, 171
Ord, George, 5, 7, 43, 57
O'Reilly, Don Alejandro, 289
Origin of Species, 291
Orista, 11, 158
Orlando Wilderness Park, Fla., 121
Orleans Parish, La., 287
Orleans Square, 22
The Orphan, 154
Ortega, Fla., 101
Ortega Stream Valley Park, Fla., 103
Orton Plantation, N.C., 317, 318
Osceola, 126, 148, 243, 244
Osgood, Rev. John, 147
Osochi, 226
osprey, 116, 120, 165
Ossabaw Island, Ga., 12, 29, 40, 211, 237
Ostatoy, 182
O'Sullivan, Florentia, 148
Otaulgaunene, 223
Otranto, 147, 153
Ottawas, 206
otter, 133, 145
Otter Island, S.C., 161, 169
Otto, N.C., 179, 191, 200
Outer Banks, N.C., 102, 316
Overhill Towns. *See* Cherokee Overhill Towns
Overlook Park, Brunswick, Ga., 49
Owen's Ferry, 42, 43
Oyotunji, S.C., 167
oysters, 165
Ozone Belt, 282

P

Pacific Ocean, 88
Palachacola, 56, 163
Palachucola Bluff, Savannah River, 19
Palachucola Wildlife Management Area, 163
Palatka, Fla., 101, 103, 108, 109, 111, 125, 128; Azalea Festival, 111
Palatka–Navair Rail to Trail, 109
Palatka–St. Augustine Rail to Trail, 111
Palm Point Nature Park, Gainesville, 127
Palm Valley, Fla., 104
Palmer, Elizabeth, 160
Palmer, John, 104, 160
palmetto, 133, 144, 148
Palmetto Islands County Park, Charleston, 148
palmetto, saw, 165
palmetto, scrub, 114
Palmetto Trail, S.C., 302
Pamlico geological era, 103
Panama City, Fla., 269
Panton, Leslie & Co., 109, 112, 114, 267, 272
Panton, William, 106, 112, 114, 244, 250, 272
Panzacolas, 266
Pardo Expedition, 189, 194, 238
Pardo, Juan, 97, 159, 168, 194
Parish Act (1706), 303
Park de Rambouilet, 146
Park Seed Company, 177
Parker, Sir Peter, 142, 147, 148, 315, 319
Parkers Ferry, S.C., 139, 169
Parksville Recreation Area, Ga., 66
Parlange Plantation, La., 296
Parliament, 12, 13, 14, 21, 25, 26, 62, 79, 138,

Index 361

313; and colonial economy, 76; and Indian affairs, 77, 79; bounty on indigo, 139; control of colonial governments, 13; control of White settlement, 197; corruption, 181; economic support of East Florida, 106; ends the war with the colonies, 142; hosts Cherokee visitors, 206; members, 80, 89, 112; observed by Henry Laurens, 157; ratifies 1773 Treaty of Augusta, 57; receives Tomochichi, 13; tensions with the colonies, 139, 147, 315; the Tax Acts, 321
Parmenter, Joseph, 160
Parmenter, Thomas, 160
Parris Island, S.C., 158, 159, 167, 298; Museum, 167
Parsons, George, 19
Parsons, James, 140
Parson's Mountain Recreation Area, 68, 174
Parson's Wax Myrtle Nursery, 305
Pasaquan, 225
Pascagoula, Miss., 277, 280
Pascagoula Parish, Mississippi Territory, 275
Pascagoula River, 273, 277
Pascagoula Wildlife Management Area, 278
Pascagoulas, 273, 277
Pass Christian, Miss., 279
Pass Manchac, La., 286
Pass Over, 191, 192
patriots, 15, 19, 25, 54, 77, 99, 140, 171, 181; and Thomas Brown, 70; attacked by Cherokees, 174; besiege Ninety Six, 177; build Ft. Independence, 174; control Beaufort District, 160; control of Georgia frontier, 83; defeat loyalists at Moores Creek, N.C., 315; first victory of the war, 148; in Boston, 14; in Georgia, 14, 15; in North Carolina, 319; in Savannah, 26; in South Carolina, 18, 120, 142, 171; in South Carolina Piedmont, 169; in the Cape Fear region, 321; in upper Georgia, 62, 83; Quakers, 71; regain control of South Carolina, 142; take fort Charlotte, 173
Pat's Hammock, Ocala National Forest, 113
Patsiliga Creek, 223, 224
Patterson, Albert, 230
Patterson, John, 230
Patterson Log Cabin, 244
Pauline Longest Nature Trail, 321
Pauline Pratt Webel Museum, 166
Pavey, Joseph, 73
Pawley, Percival, 309
Pawley's Island, S.C., 306, 309
Paynes Prairie, Fla., 8, 123, 125, 126
Paynes Prairie State Preserve, Fla., 126, 127
Payne's Town, 123
peaches, 24
Peacock Creek, 29, 33
Peake's, 300
Peale, Titian, 5, 7, 57
peanuts, 244
Pearis, Richard, 171, 179
Pearl Island, La., 282
Pearl River, 9, 257, 259, 260, 275, 279, 282; visited by William Bartram, 277
Pearl River County, Miss., 280
Pearl River Game Management Area, 282
Pearl River Island, 282
pecan, 86
Pee Dee River, 298, 305, 309
Pelham, Thomas, 49
Pelham, Thomas-Holles; Duke of Newcastle, 49
pelican, 144
Pellicer Creek Aquatic Preserve, Fla., 105
Pembroke, N.C., 320
Pembroke State University, 320
Pender County, N.C., 321

Pender, William D., 321
Pendleton County, S.C., 176
Pendleton District, 95, 176, 179, 181; Historical, Recreational and Tourism Commission, 181
Pendleton District Agriculture Museum, 182
Pendleton Factory, 181
Pendleton Farmer's Society, 179, 181, 182
The Pendleton Messenger, 182
Pendleton, S.C., 171, 179, 181; Library, 181; Female Academy, 181; Male Academy, 181
Penfield Academy, 88, 222
Penholloway Creek, 51
Penholloway Swamp, 43
Peninsular Railroad, 125
Penn Center, 168
Pennsylvania, 19, 20; home of Shawnees, 71; migration from, 170; refuge for Huguenots, 303
Penny Creek, 171, 174
Pensacola Bay, 238, 266, 269, 270, 288; exploration, 256, 266; Luna Colony, 238; rediscovered by Barroto, 266
Pensacola Bluffs, 270
Pensacola, Fla., 250, 253, 257, 264, 266–267; capital of West Florida, 256, 266; captured by Gálvez, 260; captured by Spanish, 99; Colonial Archaeological Trail, 271; Convention and Visitor Information Center, 270; exploration, 266; historic district, 271–272; Indian trade, 106, 114; invaded by Andrew Jackson, 267; loyalist refuge, 154, 174, 260; Old Spanish Trail, 277; Pensacola Historical Museum, 271; Pensacola Historical Society Resource Center, 271; Pensacola Museum of Art, 271; route to St. Augustine, 105; William Bartram's visit, 259
Pensacola Path, 250–251, 251, 253; Red Stick activity, 260
Pentagon Barracks, Baton Rouge, 294
Perceval, John; 1st Earl of Egmont, 12, 22, 49, 99
Percy, Walker, 84
Perdido Bay, 270
Perdido Bay Tribe Creek Cultural Center, 270
Perdido Key, Fla., 269
Perdido Key State Recreation Area, Fla., 270
Perdido River, 257, 275
Perdue Hill, Ala., 253, 254
peregrin falcons, 185
Perry Water Gardens, 201
persimmon, 132
persistent trillium, 85
Peters, Jesse, 19, 75
Petersburg boat, 64, 70, 75, 89
Petersburg Campground, 66
Petersburg, Ga., 64, 89
Petersburg Road, 65
Petigru, James, 67, 173
Petit Bois Island, Miss., 278
Petre, Lord. *See* James, Robert; 8th Baron Petre
Phélypeaux, Jérôme de; Comte de Maurepas, 278, 286
Phélypeaux, Louis; Comte de Pontchartrain, 278, 284, 286
Phenix City, Ala., 230, 236
Philadelphia Academy, 3
Philadelphia, Pa., 3, 89, 316, 323; threatened by British, 157
Phillippa (ship), 14
Philomath, Ga., 82, 83
Piache Monument, 254
Picayune, Miss., 277, 279, 282
Pickens, Andrew, 51, 54, 62, 83, 174, 176, 182, 187, 197, 299; breaks parole, 142; fight at Tomassee, 186; retaliation against Cherokees, 183; visited by André Michaux, 172

Pickens County Museum, 184
Pickens County, N.C., 187
Pickens County, S.C., 69
Pickens family, 170, 173
Pickens, S.C., 181
Picolata, Fla., 3, 99, 104, 128, 157
Picolata Indian Congress, 98
Piedmont, 19, 59; botanical communities, 69, 92; cotton empire, 209; cotton farming, 73, 76; cultural history, 216; frontier, 80; geography, 248; geology, 68, 69, 187, 213; immigration route, 73; in North Carolina, 315; last virgin forest, 173; migration from the region, 64, 178; natural features, 64, 69, 70, 84, 88, 92, 184, 185; natural history, 69, 214, 216; part of Cherokee territory, 178; population, 64, 77; recreation, 184; settled by Scots Irish, 175; settlements, 171; textile mills, 236
Piedmont National Wildlife Refuge, 87
Piedmont Plateau, 248
Piedmont Road, 89
Piedmont Wildlife Management Area, 216
Pierria, Captain Albert de la, 96, 158
Pike Expedition (1805), 6
Pike, Zebulon, 284
pin oak, 86
Pin Point, Ga., 34
Pinchony Creek, 242, 248
Pinckney, Charles, 139, 140, 145, 148, 157, 165; grave site, 155
Pinckney, Charles Cotesworth, 7, 145, 165, 304
Pinckney, Eliza Lucas, 144, 165, 303
Pinckney Island National Wildlife Refuge, 165
Pinckney, Thomas, 39, 51, 145, 303, 304
Pinckney Treaty. *See* Treaty of San Lorenzo
Pinckneya pubens, *See* fevertree
Pine Barren Springs, Ala., 253
pine lily, 146
Pine Mountain, Ga., 234
Pinecote Educational Center, 279
Pineda, Alonzo Alvarez de, 256
Pinedale, Ala., 242
Piney Woods, Miss., 279
pink lady slipper, 85
Pinnacle Knob, Chattahoochee National Forest, 192
Pintlala, Ala., 242, 248
Pintlala Creek, 251
Pintloco Creek, 241
Pioneer Settlement for the Creative Arts, 114
Pipemaker's Creek, 18, 19
pipewort, seven-angled, 319
pirates, 151
Pirates' House, Savannah, 24
Pirrie, Eliza, 295
Pisgah National Forest, 192
pitcher-plant, 302, 311
pitcher-plant, hooded, 47, 146
pitcher-plant, purple, 85
pitcher-plant, sweet, 146
pitcher-plant, white top, 269, 270
Pitt, William; 1st Earl of Chatham, 12, 21, 22
Pittman, Phillip, 98, 260
Pittsburg, Pa., 290
Place d'Armes, New Orleans, 285
Placquemine, La., 294
Plains, La., 291
Plaquemine Locks Museum, 294
Plaquemines Parish, La., 287
Plaza de la Constitution, 106
Plaza Ferdinand VII, 271
Pleistocene epoch, 103
Plum Branch, S.C., 65, 67, 209
plumleaf azalea, 233

Poarch, Ala., 259
Poarch Band, Creeks Indians, 256
Pocotaligo River, 161
Pocosabo, 160
pocosin, 304, 311, 317
Pocotaligo, S.C., 18, 166
Poe Springs County Park, Fla., 134
Point Comfort, Ala., 246
Point Peter, Ga., 50
Pointe Coupee, La., 9, 288–291, 293, 296
Pointe Coupee Parish, La., 296; Museum and Visitor Center, 296
Pointe, Joseph Simon de la, 277
Polecat Springs, Ala., 246
Pollards Corner, Ga., 65, 69
Pomona Park, Fla., 113
Pon Pon Chapel of Ease, 169
Ponce de Leon Inlet, 120
Ponce de Leon, Juan, 96, 104, 115
Ponchatoula, La., 285
pond pine, 302, 311
pond spice, 165
pondberry, 302
Pontalba Apartments, 285
Pontchartrain, Comte de. *See* Phélypeaux, Louis; Comte de Pontchartrain
Poplar Springs, Ala., 251
Poplarville, Miss., 280
Porgy and Bess, 144, 155
Port Allen, La., 294
Port Hickey, La., 290
Port Hudson State Commemorative Area, La., 290, 294, 295
Port Royal (ship), 137
Port Royal, S.C., 12, 37, 40, 105, 135, 137, 167, 303; defenses, 167; during the Revolution, 161; exploration, 158
Port Vincent, La., 292
Porter Shoals, 172
Portman Shoals, 176, 179
Post Road. *See* Old Post Road
the Potanoes, 122
Pottersville Museum, 68
Powell, Billy. *See* Osceola
Powell, Mary, 248
Powell's Ferry, 251
Powelton, Ga., 211, 213
Power, Tyrone, 209, 221, 236, 254; visits Sodom on Chattahoochee River, 230
Poydras, Julien, 296
Prairie Creek Conservation Area, Fla., 127
Pratt, Charles; 1st Earl of Camden, 53
Pratt, Daniel, 248
Pratt Memorial Library, 166
Prattville, Ala., 248
Presbyterian Church, 175
Presbyterian Meeting House, McIntosh County, 36
Presbyterian Theological Seminary, 84
Presbyterians, 138, 169; disdain for Baptists, 152; lack of ministers in Backcountry, 152; suppressed by Charles II, 159
Presidio San Miguel de Panzacola, 266
Presley, Elvis, 102
Prevost, Augustine, 15, 29, 56, 70, 161
Prevost, Mark, 32, 57, 99
Priber, Christian, 196
Price's Ferry, 65
Price's Store, 68
Prince George-Winyah Episcopal Church, 298, 306, 308, 311
Prince George's Masonic Lodge, 306
Prince of Wales, 73
Prince William Parish, S.C., 167

Princess Place Preserve, 105
Proclamation of 1763, 42, 73, 77, 79, 154, 170, 175
Protestants, 17; at war with French Catholics, 96; colonize Florida, 103; French, 298
Providence Canyon State Conservation Park, Ga., 233
Provincial Congress, Ga., 14, 29, 33, 62; members, 18, 21, 33
Provincial Congress, S.C., 142, 171; members, 147, 160, 183
Public Record Office, London, 82, 210
Puc-Puggy, 112
Pulaski, Count Kasimir, 15, 21, 22
Pulaski Square, Savannah, 22
Purcell, Joseph, 154
Puritans, 29
Purry, Charles, 164
Purry, David, 164
Purry, Jean Pierre, 164
Purrysburg Road, 161, 162
Purrysburg, S.C., 3, 160, 162, 164, 166
Putnam County, Ga., 67, 217, 236
Putnam Historic Museum, 111
Putnam, Israel, 217

Q

the Qinapisas, 281
Quaker Road, 54, 56, 57, 69
Quaker Springs, Ga., 61, 64, 69, 71
Quakers, 61, 69, 71, 80, 138; leave Georgia, 71
Qualla Boundary, 199, 201
Queen Anne's Revenge, Blackbeard's ship, 313
Queen Anne's War, 160
Queensborough, Ga., 57, 58, 61, 211
Quexos, Pedro, 158, 298
quillwort, mat forming, 85
Quiroba y Losada, Diego, 232

R

Rabun Bald, 191, 192, 194, 200; discovery of Fraser magnolia, 192
Rabun County, Ga., 189, 192, 194; Historical Society, 192
Rabun Gap, 189, 191
Rabun, William, 194
raccoon, 145
Rafinesque, Constantine, 7
ragwort, southern, 69
rail, 115
railroads, 64, 74, 76, 84; cause disuse of Old Federal Road, 223; in Alabama, 254; in Georgia, 221; in the Florida Parishes, 282; on the Gulf Coast, 275; Pensacola, 267; Wilmington, 321
Rails-to-Trails, 284
Rainy Mountain, Ga., 191
Raleigh, N.C., 179
Ralph E. Simmons Memorial State Forest, Fla., 52
Ramsay, Dr. David, 153, 157
Ranchero de la Chua, 126
Rattlesnake Island, Fla., 105
Raven (Cherokee leader), 193, 204, 205
Ravenel, S.C., 145
Ravine Gardens State Park, Palatka, 111
Rawdon, Lord, 177
Rawlings, Marjorie Kinnan, 113, 125
Raysville Campground, 66
Raytown, Ga., 82
Raytown-Sharon Garden Club, 82
Rechahecrians, 196
The Recruiting Officer, 154
Red Bluff, Ga., 17

Red Creek, 278
Red Eagle. *See* Weatherford, William
Red River, 291
Red River Survey of 1804, 6, 290
Red Sticks, 224, 230, 241, 244, 245; armed by British, 267; join Seminoles, 123; leaders, 251, 259
red-cockaded woodpecker, 19, 216, 230, 269, 270, 284, 302
redbud, 86
Redcliffe Plantation State Park, S.C., 71
Redding, Otis, 221
Reese Library, Augusta College, 76
Reform Jewish Congregation, Savannah, 27
Reform Society of Israelites, 156
Reformed Church, 303
Regulator movement, 71, 139
Regulators: in North Carolina, 319; in South Carolina, 70, 139, 171
Reid, Patrick, 154
relict trillium, 70
Rembert Mound, 92
Rembert's Bottom, 89, 95
Republic of West Florida, 281, 291, 295
Reserve Plantation, Mississippi River, 286
Retreat Plantation, St. Simons Island, 48
Revolution, 15, 22, 25, 26, 32, 33, 37, 47, 54, 61, 77, 84, 154, 155, 165, 229, 230, 274, 308; aided by Gov. Gálvez, 284; as civil war, 70, 83; British headquarters, 151; British influence among Creeks, 224; burning of Cherokee towns, 201; Catawbas join Americans, 139; Cherokee involvement, 182, 197; Creek involvement, 244; destruction of Ebenezer, 17; engagement at Ninety Six, 177; in Augusta, 73; in East Florida, 98–99, 99; in Florida, 18, 106; in Georgia, 14, 20, 21, 84; in Louisiana, 290; in North Carolina, 315, 319, 321; in South Carolina, 139, 173, 174, 183, 298; in the Lowcountry, 160, 167; in upper South Carolina, 186; loyalists, 153, 164, 250, 266, 272; neutrality of the Quakers, 71; on the Lower Mississippi River, 290; post-conflict era, 68, 75208, 295; post-war economy in S.C., 299; re-enactment, 177; tensions between loyalists and patriots, 154; veterans, 311
Reynolds, Ga., 224
Reynolds, John, 13, 19, 22, 24, 29, 42, 49, 61
Reynolds, Joshua, 12
Reynolds, R. J., 35
Reynolds Square, Savannah, 22, 25
Rhett, William, 139
rhododendron, 194
Ribault, Albert, 96
Ribault, Jean, 11, 18, 49, 103, 168; colonizes Florida, 96; death, 97, 105; founds colony of Carolana, 158
Ribault Monument, 102, 167
rice, 12, 25, 32, 33, 34, 38, 45, 157, 160, 298; Carolina Gold Rice, 164; exempted from embargo, 160; history and culture, 304; in Georgia, 28; in North Carolina, 315; in South Carolina, 139, 160, 161, 166; on Savannah River, 164; plantations of the Santee River, 304; rice economy of Georgetown, 305, 309; rice mills, 148
Rice Creek Natural Area, Fla., 109
Rice Hope Plantation, Charleston, 148
Rice Museum, Georgetown, 306
Riceboro, Ga., 33
Richard B. Russell Dam, 89, 91, 92, 94; visitor center, 89, 91, 95
Richard Russell State Park, Ga., 93
Richards, William, 186

Index 363

Richardson, James, 320
Richardson, Richard, 171
Richelieu, Cardinal, 303
Richmond County, Ga., 62, 64, 65, 72; during Revolution, 64; Historical Society, 76
Richmond, Duke of. *See* Lennox, Charles; Duke of Richmond
Richmond Hill, Ga., 19
Richmond, Va., 244
Ridge, John, 199
Ridge Road Campground, 66
Ridgeland, S.C., 162, 166
Ridgeville, Ga., 36
Riegelwood, N.C., 316
right whales, 50
Rigolets Pass, La., 281, 284
Rikard's Mill, 253
Riley, Alice, 19
Ringhaver Park, Gainesville, 103
Rio de Janeiro, Brazil, 303
Rio de San Pedro (St. Marys River), 50
Río del Espiritu Santo, 256, 273
Rio Dulce (Savannah River), 18
Rio San Juan, 103
Rio San Mateo, 103
river cane, 146
River Forest Campground, 115
River Forest Recreation Area, Ocala National Forest, 117
River May, 103, 168
River of Palms, 104
river otter, 116
River Rise State Preserve, Fla., 134
River Road African American Museum, La., 292
River Side Park, Pascagoula, 278
River Street, Savannah, 24
River Styx, 125
Rivera, Don Enrique Primo de, 227, 232
riverbank quillwort, 307
Rivercare 2000, 92
Riverfront Park, Baton Rouge, 294
Riverfront Park, Lake Monroe, Fla., 119
Riverfront Park, Montgomery, 247
Riverfront Plaza, Savannah, 24
Riverlake Plantation, 296
Rivertown, New Orleans, 286
Riverview Park, La., 70
Riverview Park, North Augusta, 70
Riverwalk Park, Columbus, 236
Rivière Grande (Savannah River), 18
Rivière May (St. Johns River), 96
Rivière Seine (St. Marys River), 49, 50
Roanoke, Ga., 137, 229, 233
Roanoke Island, N.C., 312
Roanoke, Va., 89
Robbinsville, N.C., 200, 201, 206, 207
Robert, John, 305
Robert M. Cooper Library, 183
Roberta, Ga., 223
Roberts, William, 98
Robeson County, N.C., 320
Robeson, Thomas, 320
Rock Eagle Mound, 216
Rock Factory, 211
Rock Hill, S.C., 139
Rock House, 71
Rock Landing, 8, 76, 123, 208, 209, 214, 215
rock spike moss, 69
Rock Springs Run State Reserve, Fla., 119
Rockby Academy, 213
the Rocks, near Augusta, 64, 69
Rockville, S.C., 143
Rocky Comfort Creek, 210
Rocky Creek, 221

Rocky River, 176
Rodman Reservoir, Palatka, 112; Rodman Campground, 112; Rodman Dam, 116
Rogas, Don Hernando de Manrique, 159
Rogel, Father Juan, 159
Rolle, Denys, 111
Rollestown, Fla., 3, 98, 111
Rollins Bird & Plant Sanctuary, 102
Romans, Bernard, 98, 260
Rood Creek Mounds, Chattahoochee River 226, 233
Roosevelt, Franklin D., 305
Rosario Line, St. Augustine, 106
Rose, Dr. William, 153
Rose Hill Cemetery, Macon, 221
roseate spoonbill, 120
Rosedown Plantation & Gardens, West Feliciana parish, 295
roses, 19
Ross, John, 199
Roswell, Ga., 217
Roy Croft Daylily Nursery, 305
Royal Academy of Sciences, Sweden, 2
Royal Bank of France, 288
Royal Carolina Rangers, 70
Royal Council, Ga., 13
Royal Governor's House, Savannah, 15, 22
Royal North Carolina Regiment, 99
Royal Proclamation. *See* Proclamation of 1763
Royal Society, 153
royalists, 138
Rucker's Bottom, 93, 95
Rucker's Bottom Mound, 91
rue anemone, 173
Rumsey, Mr., 277
Rush, Dr. Benjamin, 7, 153, 290
Russell County, Ala., 163, 232, 235, 241
Russell Dam. *See* Richard B. Russell Dam
Russell, Ganaway, 186, 192
Russell, Gilbert C., 235
Russell Homestead, 186, 192
Russell, John; 4th Duke of Bedford, 1
Russellborough, N.C., 315, 318
Rutherford, Griffith, 171, 197, 200
Rutledge, Archibald, 303
Rutledge, Edward, 106, 140; grave site, 155; signer of Declaration of Independence, 142
Rutledge, John, 6, 140, 142, 169
Rutledge, Jr., John, 300
Rutledge, Thomas, 160

S

Sabacola, 130
sabal palm, 133
Sadler Point, St. Johns River, 101
Sadlers Creek State Park, Fla., 176
SAL Railroad, 174
salamanders, 207
Salazar Expedition, 158
Salazar, Pablo de Hita, 226
Salazar, Pedro, 158
Salem, S.C., 181
Salem-Shotwell Bridge, 234
Salkehatchee, 160
salt marsh, 21
Salt Springs, Fla., 3, 109, 113
Salters Lake State Natural Area, N.C., 320
saltwort, 302
Saluda River, 60, 170, 174, 177, 178
Salvador, Francis, 183
Salvador Wildlife Management Area, La., 286
Salzburger Museum, 16, 17
Salzburgers, 13, 17, 54

Sampit Indians, 306
Sampit River, 298, 305
Sampson County, N.C., 321
Sampson, John, 321
Samuel P. Harn Museum of Art, Gainesville, 128
Samworth, Thomas, 306
Samworth Wildlife Management Area, 306
San Agustín, 96
San Antonio, Texas, 182, 253, 277
San Buenaventura de Guadalquini, Mission, 40, 48
San Diego de Salamototo, Mission, 104
San Domingo, Mission, 48
San Felasco Hammock State Preserve, Fla., 122, 128
San Felipe, Mission, 40
San Francisco de Potano, Mission, 122, 128, 130
San Francisco Plantation, 286
San Jorge River, 145
San Joseph de Sapala, Mission, 35
San Juan del Puerto, Mission, 40, 101, 103
San Mateo, Fla., 108, 112
San Miguel, mission, 266
San Miguel de Gualdape, Mission, 11, 31, 35, 305
San Pedro de Mocamo, Mission, 50
San Pedro Puturiba, Mission, 50
San Salvador de Mayaca, Mission, 114
Sand Fly, Ga., 34
Sand Fort, Ala., 234
sand live oak, 114, 133
sand pine, 113, 114, 133
sand skink, 114
Sand Town Cherokees, 200
Sandersville, Ga., 208, 213
Sandfort, 232
sandhill crane, 115, 116, 119, 120, 125, 126, 278
Sandhills, 214
Sandy Creek Park and Nature Center, Athens, 87
Sandy Hill Plantation, 145
Sandy Ridge, Ala., 242
Sanford, Robert, 137, 159, 164
Sangahatchee, 245
Sansavilla Bluff, Lower, 52
Sansavilla Bluff, Upper, 43
Sansavilla Wildlife Management Area, 42, 43
Santa Catalina de Guale, Mission, 34
Santa Cruz de Sabacola, Mission, 227
Santa Elena, 11, 28, 96, 97, 106, 158, 159, 167, 168, 194, 266
Santa Elena, La Punta de, 158
Santa Maria, Mission, 50
Santa Rosa County, Fla., 270
Santa Rosa Island, Fla., 269, 288; Spanish settlement, 266; Santa Rosa Day Use Area, 269
Santaria, 285
Sante Fe College Teaching Zoo, 128
Sante Fe River, 128, 134
Santee Canal Company, 146
Santee Canal State Park, S.C., 150
Santee Coastal Reserve Wildlife Management Area, 304
Santee Delta Wildlife Management Area, 304
Santee Gun Club, 304
Santee River, 135, 142, 145, 146, 150, 298, 303
the Santees, 166
Santeetlah Gap, 206
Santo Domingo, 289, 298
Santo Domingo de Talaje, Mission, 37
Sapelo Bridge, 29, 34
Sapelo Company, 36
Sapelo Island, Ga., 13, 34, 35, 40, 47, 49, 237
Sapelo Island Syndicate, 49
Sapelo Lighthouse, 36
Sapelo National Estuarine Sanctuary, 36
Sapona, 316

Sara Indians, 320
Sarah's Creek, 192
Sargent, Charles Sprague, 166
sarvis holly, 307
sassafras, 35
Satilla River, 42, 49, 51, 52, 69, 99, 304; exploration, 165
Satilla River Park, 50
Satonia Plantation, 101
the Saturiwas, 40, 97, 103
Saunders Crossroads, 208, 213
Saunders, Mark, 213
Savage Island, Ga., 19
Savannah, 11, 21, 22, 54, 57, 71, 99, 164, 239, 299; American and French siege, 21; aristocracy, 161; British occupation, 62, 83, 99, 160, 171; colonial city limits, 26; cotton market, 70, 76; Customs House, 24; economic rivalry with Charleston, 64, 142; founding, 12, 160; Governor's Mansion , 26; historic district, 22, 22–24; public squares, 22; railroads, 86; smuggling, 160; surrounding area, 12–15
Savannah Bluffs Heritage Preserve, S.C., 70
Savannah Highway, 143
Savannah History Museum & Visitor's Center, 26
Savannah Jack, 251
Savannah National Wildlife Refuge, 17, 161
Savannah Rapids Park, 70
Savannah River, 3, 8, 11–15, 17–19, 21, 26, 28, 40, 45, 54, 56, 57, 60, 68, 73, 75, 84, 135, 160, 191, 211; above Augusta, 91–92; archaeological sites, 89, 91, 94; as boundary, 92, 160, 187; at Augusta, 64; below Augusta, 54–56; during Revolution, 161; early roads, 161; frontier, 167; history, 74, 89; Indian trails, 73, 76, 91, 94, 162; industrial area, 164; limit of Spanish missions, 159; Muskogee towns, 239; Native American populations, 163, 164; natural history, 70, 163; prehistoric settlement, 19, 91; recreation, 66, 70, 89, 163; Revolutionary activity, 62; rice, 161; settled by Yuchis, 69, 83; settlement, 65, 67, 73, 79, 80, 160; Shawnee towns, 71; the survey party, 65, 92; Yamacraw Town, 166
Savannah River Ecology Laboratory, 58
Savannah River National Wildlife Refuge, 164
Savannah River Plant, S.C., 58
Savannah River Scenic Highway, 67
Savannah Road, 54, 166
Savannah to St. Augustine Road, 43
Savannah to Tybee Rails to Trails, 21
Savannah Town, 17, 61, 71, 211
Savannah Valley Railroad, 67
Savannah-Ogeechee Barge Canal Museum and Nature Center, 19
Savannuca language, 241
Savannuca Town, 246
Saxagotha, S.C., 171
Say, Thomas, 5, 7, 57
Sayle, William, 137
Scarborough (ship), 14
Scarbrough, William, 26
Scenic Highway, Pensacola, 270
Schnell, Frank, 232
Schuylkill River, 1
Scofieldites, 171
Scotch-Irish, 175, 179, 208
Scotland, 34, 36, 315
Scots, 47, 175, 186; as Indian traders, 73; Covenanters, 159; found Stuart Town, 159; settle North Carolina, 321; settle Wando River, 148; settle Western North Carolina, 200; trade with Cherokees, 178
Scott, Winfield, 199, 206, 229

Scottish Heritage Week, 201
Scottish Tartan Museum, Franklin, 201
Scranton Floating Museum, Pascagoula, 278
Screven County, Ga., 56
Screven, Elisha, 305
Screven, James, 31, 99
Screven, William, 151
scrub jay, 114, 119, 132, 133
scrub lizard, 114
Scrubby Bluff, 42, 50
Scull Shoals, GA, 77, 87, 208, 214; Scull Shoals Archaeological Site, 87
Sea Island cotton, 35, 42, 46, 143, 161, 165
Sea Island Festival, 48
Sea Islands, 32, 34
Sea Oats Nature Trail, Savannah, 309
Sea Pines Forest Preserve, Hilton Head, 165
sea turtles, 120
seabeach amaranth, 317, 318
Seabrook, Ga., 32, 34
Seagrove, Ann Zubly, 164
Seagrove, James, 50, 51, 164
Seagrove, Robert, 51
Seahorse Key, 133
Searles, Robert, 159, 164
secession, 182
Second Creek War. *See* Creek War of 1836
Sell, Jonathan, 71
Selma, Ala., 238, 248, 254
Seloy Town, 106
Seminole Ranch State Conservation Area, Fla., 120
Seminole State Forest, Fla., 119
Seminole Tribe, 126
Seminole Wars: First Seminole War (1818), 241, 243, 244, 245; Second Seminole War (1835–42), 111, 121, 123, 126, 244, 245, 248
Seminoles, 5, 18, 26, 51, 98, 120, 122–123, 229, 239, 244; absorb the Yamassees, 160, 166; and William Bartram, 4; claims on the Oconee River, 208; imprisoned in Louisiana, 284; joined by Alabamas, 247; joined by Creeks, 229; loot Spalding's Upper Store, 109; origins, 122, 215, 232, 233; provide sanctuary for Red Sticks, 241; settle in Florida, 106; tensions with Whites, 98; trade ban, 79
Semmes House, Washington, 83
Senauchi, wife of Tomochichi, 13
Seneca, 171, 179, 182, 183
Seneca Park, 119
Seneca River, 76, 79, 172, 174, 176, 179, 187
Sequoya. *See* Guess, George
Seven Sisters Oak, Mandeville, 284
Seven Years War. *See* French and Indian War
Sevier, John, 197, 205, 245
Seville Square, Pensacola, 266, 269, 271
Sewee River, 138, 302
Sewee Shell Mound, 302
Sewee Visitor and Environmental Education Center, 300
Sewees, 159, 302
Shaftesbury, Lord. *See* Cooper, Lord Anthony Ashley; Earl of Shaftsbury
Shaking Rock Park, Lexington, 84
Shallotte, N.C., 316
Shallowford on the Etowah Path, 217
Sharon, Ga., 82
Shaw, Charles, 160
Shaw, Daniel, 253
Shawnees, 18, 61, 71, 239, 245, 246
Sheftall, Benjamin, 20
Sheftall, Mordecai, 15, 27
Sheftall, Sheftall, 27
Shelby, Evan, 205

Sheldon Church, 167
Sheldon, S.C., 167
Shell Bluff, 3, 29, 58
shell rings, 35
Shellman Bluff, Ga., 34
Shem Creek Maritime Museum, Mt. Pleasant, S.C., 148
Shenandoah Valley, 89, 175
Shepard State Park, Miss., 278
Shepheard's Tavern, 154
Sherbourne Wildlife Management Area, La., 292
Sherman, William T., 32, 35
Sherrill, William, 83
Sherrill's Fort, 79, 83
Shinholser Mound, 214
Ship Island, Miss., 274, 278
Ships of the Sea Museum, Savannah, 24
Shivers, William, 211
Shoals, Ga., 210, 211
shoals spider lily, 64, 68, 70, 89
shooting stars, 68, 87
Shorter, Ala., 246
Shoulderbone Creek, 76, 77, 87, 208, 214
Shreve, Henry Miller, 291
shrimp, 262
Shrine of Holy Trinity, AL, 232
Shuck Pen Eddy, Savannah River, 89, 171
Sibley Mill, Augusta, 76
Siege of Savannah. *See* Savannah: American and French siege
Sierra Club, 69, 278, 282
Sierra Leone, 34
Signers Monument, Augusta, 29, 58, 75
Sile, Jacob, 200
silk, 17, 24, 25
Silk Hope Plantation, Charleston, 148
Silver Bluff Plantation Sanctuary, 58
Silver Bluff, S.C., 3, 8, 56, 57, 58, 211
Silver Glen Springs, Fla., 109, 113
Simons, Benjamin, 149
Singer Company, 233
Singer, Johann George, 233
Singing River, 277. *See also* Pascagoula River
Singletary Lake State Park, N.C., 316, 319
Singleton Swash, 309
Siouan language, 135, 139, 274, 302, 316, 320
Siquenza, Carlos, 270
Sisters Ferry, 163
Six and Twenty Creek, 172, 176, 179
Skee, Yamacraw warrior, 13
Skeenah Creek, 199
Skidaway Island, Ga., 20; including Skidaway Institute of Oceanography and Skidaway State Park
Skidaway Narrows, 20
Slasheye Road, 229, 241
slave catchers, 123
slave trade, 157; Africans, 60; Native Americans, 135
slavery, 37; legalized in Georgia, 28
slaves, 34, 71; and cotton culture, 17, 76; basket weaving, 148; dominate population of Lowcountry, 160; follow British army, 161; in Barbados, 147; in Georgia, 13, 18; in Louisiana, 264; in Mississippi Territory, 265; in South Carolina, 308; in the Lowcountry, 160; Indian slaves, 138; join Seminoles, 123; on rice plantations, 306; quarantine station, 148; rebellion, 156; religion, 18; rice culture, 139, 161, 304; seek refuge in St. Augustine, 106
Slick Rock Wilderness, 206
Slidell, La., 284
Sloane, Sir Hans, 1, 2, 12
Slocum, Perry, 201

Index   365

Slosh-eye Trail, 229
Small, Neptune, 48
smallpox, 138, 153, 179, 182, 196
Smalls, Sammy, 144
smilax, 311
Smith, Benjamin Barton, 7
Smith, Thomas, 317
Smoky Mountain National Park, 199
Smuteyes Trail, 223
Smyrna Dunes Park, Fla., 120
Smyrna, Turkey, 120
Snee Farm, Charleston, 148
Snoudoun, Ala., 242, 248
Snowbird Cherokees, 206
snowy egret, 309
Soap Creek County Park, Ga., 66
Society for the Promotion of Christian Knowledge, 12
Society for the Propagation of the Gospel in Foreign Parts, 12, 17
Society Hill, Ala., 241
Society of Friends, 71. *See also* Quakers
Solander, Dr. Daniel, 4, 6
Solomon's seal, 92, 146
Somerset, Henry, 160
Sons of Liberty, 315, 317
South Carolina, 42; aid to Georgia, 22; aristocracy, 160; artists, 155; Assembly: 138, 139, 142, 160, 165, 168, 169, 308; authorizes Blue Ridge Railroad, 187; Backcountry, 171; Baptists, 166; botanical areas, 186; boundaries, 160, 170, 191, 313; boundary dispute with Georgia, 186; British control, 299; builds defenses at Beaufort, 167; champion trees, 185; chapels of ease, 168; Cherokee territory, 195; Cherokee War, 179, 182; Chickasaws, 71; church laws, 138; conflicts with the royal governors, 139, Congregationalists, 147; cotton, 209, 251; delegates to Continental Congress, 160; destroys Spanish missions, 122, 126, 130; diseases, 164, 196; drive Apalachees from Florida, 261; early settlements, 311; education, 165, 182; emigration from South Carolina, 67, 79, 123, 208, 221; establishes provincial government, 142; exploration, 135; First Provincial Congress, 140, 157; frontier settlement, 173; General Assembly, 142, 147; governors, 71, 73, 145, 147, 148, 155; Governor's Council, 139, 140, 144; Indian trade, 73, 97, 164, 167, 178; indigo, 139; invasion of Florida, 104, 107; land grants, 302; Lowcountry, 158–162; members of the legislature, 186; militia, 14, 140, 177, 183, 193; navy, 142; objects to Georgia Indian trade regulations, 73; patriots, 142, 183; Piedmont history, 178, 184; post-Revolution government, 142; Presbyterians, 169; provincial army, 154; Provincial Congress, 171; public land, 184, 185; railroads, 74, 156; refuge for Georgia patriots, 83; relations with Native Americans, 138, 171; religious freedom, 137; religion, 155; represented at Parliament, 157; Revolution in Upcountry, 62; rice, 139, 164; rice and indigo economy, 298; Scottish settlement of Stuart Town, 160; settlement of the frontier, 77, 170; settlement of the Piedmont, 73, 170; settlement of the upper coast, 308; Spanish colonization, 96; Spanish exploration, 159; state flag, 144; state parks, 186; state printer, 181; statesmen, 153, 183; textile mills, 181; Upcountry, 145, 171; Upcountry regulators, 171; Upcountry settlements attacked by Cherokees, 179; war with Britain, 142; Yamassees, 28, 166
South Carolina Aquarium, 156
South Carolina Festival of Flowers, 177
South Carolina Gazette, 155
South Carolina Gazette and General Advertiser, 181
South Carolina General Assembly, 12, 104, 171, 174
South Carolina Historical Society, 153
South Carolina Marine Research Laboratory and National Fisheries Center, 144
South Carolina Medical Society, 98
South Carolina Railroad, 146
South Carolina Royalists, 99
South Carolina State Botanical Garden, 182
South Carolina State House, 153
South Carolina Wildlife and Marine Resources Department, 169
South Cove County Park, S.C., 183
South Dunes Picnic Area, Jekyll Island, 49
South Lake Harney Conservation Area, Fla., 120
South Newport, Ga., 29
Southbank Riverwalk, 103
Southern District for Indian Affairs, 174
Southern Poverty Law Center, 247
Southern red cedar, 133
Southern Review, 165
Southern University, 294
Southport, N.C., 316, 317; Southport Maritime Museum, 317
Sowokli, 226
Spain: abandons Santa Elena, 168; aids the French in Mobile, 266; allied with France, 257, 269; allows British intrigue in Florida, 267; American minister, 148; attacks South Carolina, 105, 137, 160, 167; attempts to settle the Gulf Coast, 266; bring prosperity to Louisiana, 290; claims Florida, 97, 270; claims south Georgia, 12; claims the Chattahoochee River, 232; colonizes Florida, 28; defeat at Bloody Marsh, 160; destroys Fort Caroline, 159; enters Seven Years War, 97; exploration of the Mississippi River, 288; explores South Carolina, 307; explores the St. Johns River, 103; Florida, 105, 274, 312; harasses Carolina, 137; influence among Catholics, 156; invades Georgia, 50, 48; Louisiana, 281, 284, 286, 287; military nature of her colonies, 159; missions, 35, 168; names the streets of Pensacola, 271; opposes slavery, 123; plagued by hurricanes, 158; protect the Yamassees, 166; recaptures Pensacola, 269; relations with Creeks, 222, 231, 239, 244, 250; relations with the French, 273; rescue remnants of La Salle's colony, 288; retaliates against the Potanoes, 122; rivalry with France, 158; sells Florida to the United States, 267; settlement of Parris Island, 167; supports Pensacola, 267; surrenders Mobile, 257; threat to British colonies, 12, 28, 137, 151; trade relations with US, 145; treasure ships, 105, 159, 266, 312; treaty with England, 97; treaty with United States, 257; war with England, 13, 19, 104, 312; welcomes settlers to West Florida, 275
Spalding & Co., 80
Spalding, James, 26, 33, 35, 43, 46, 47, 48, 108, 114; seeks refuge in Florida, 106; stores, 101, 106
Spalding, Phinizy, 84
Spalding, Thomas, 35
Spalding's Lower Store, 3, 8, 109, 112, 114
Spalding's Upper Store, 3, 8, 109, 112, 114
Spaniards, 47
the Spanish, 13, 25, 33, 37, 39, 40; and Henry Woodward, 137, 159, 164; bring disease to the Southeast, 135; coins, 77; encounter the Cherokees, 178, 196; in Apalachicola, 163; leave British West Florida, 266; ranchers, 126; relations with Blacks, 102; troops, 47
Spanish Armada, 312
Spanish Fort, Ala., 261, 277
Spanish moss, 70
Spanish Plaza, Pensacola, 265
Spanish Quarter Museum, 106
Spanish Trail. *See* Old Spanish Trail
Spanish West Florida, 260
Spark (ship), 114
Sparta Female College, 214
Sparta, Ga., 69, 209, 214, 223
Spartanburg County, S.C., 64
spartina, 20, 148
speculators, 79, 98
spiderwort, 173
Spinoza, Diego, 104
Spoleto Festival, 156
spoonflower, 311
Spotswood, Alexander, 313
Springfield Baptist Church, Augusta, 75
Springfield, Ga., 15, 17
Spruce Creek Park, Spruce Creek Preserve, Fla., 119
spruce pine, 146
St. Andrew Picnic Area, Jekyll Island, 49
St. Andrew's Cemetery, Darien, 37
St. Andrew's Parish Church, S.C., 145
St. Andrew's Parish, Ga., 33, 34
St. Andrews Society, 154
St. Augustine, 11, 26, 28, 32, 33, 34, 37, 40, 42, 43, 47, 51, 53, 71, 97, 105–106, 128, 227, 266; besieged by Oglethorpe, 13, 104, 123; besieged by Robert Searle, 159; British period, 15; as capital, 98, 159, 168; founding, 104, 105; French threat, 232; Greek population, 120; King's Road, 302; Old City Gates, 106; Old Spanish Trail, 270, 277, 284; Oldest House, 107; patriots imprisoned, 15, 21, 152; plundered by Robert Searles, 164; refuge for Catholic Indians, 122; refuge for loyalists, 70, 99, 154, 171; refuge for New Smyrna immigrants, 120; refuge for Rollestown colonists, 98; refuge for Yamassees, 166; road to New Smyrna, 120; roads to Pensacola, 105; visited by the Bartrams, 3; Visitor's Center, 106
St. Augustine Alligator Farm and Zoological Park, 104
St. Augustine–Pensacola Mail Road, 269
St. Barnard State Park, La., 286
St. Bartholomew's Day Massacre, 303
St. Bartholomew's Parish, S.C., 169
St. Catherines Island Foundation, 35
St. Catherines Island, Ga., 13, 18, 28, 34, 237, 298
St. Charles Parish, La., 286, 291
St. David's Parish, Georgia, 42, 53
St. Denis (Natchitoches), 288
St. EOM, 225
St. Francis, Fla., 109, 115
St. Francis of Assissi Chapel, 296
St. Francisville, La., 295
St. Gabriel, La., 293
St. George's Parish, Ga., 54, 61
St. Helena Episcopal Chapel of Ease, 168
St. Helena Island, S.C., 11, 29, 34, 161, 167, 168
St. Helena Parish, La., 281, 287
St. Helena Sound, 168
St. Helena Sound Heritage Preserve, 169
St. James Episcopal Church, Wilmington, 322
St. James Goose Creek Church, 147
St. James, N.C., 319
St. James Parish, La., 286, 291, 296
St. James Santee Episcopal Church, 302
St. James Santee Parish, S.C., 298, 303

St. John the Baptist Parish, La., 286, 291, 296
St. Johns Loop Trail, 111
St. Johns Lutheran Church, Charleston, 155
St. Johns Museum of Art, Wilmington, 322
St. Johns National Wildlife Refuge, 121
St. John's Parish, Ga., 14, 29, 33
St. John's Plains, La., 291
St. Johns River, 3, 6, 8, 15, 40, 42, 43, 47, 48, 50, 102–104, 303; boundary of East Florida, 98; exploration, 168; explored by William Bartram, 99, 109; French exploration and settlement, 96, 105, 159; natural areas, 102, 121; natural history, 102, 113; occupied by Yamassees, 114; orogeny, 103, 113; public lands, 109; recreation, 111, 112, 117; settlement, 157; the Bartrams' exploration in 1765, 3; tributaries, 112; upper St. Johns, 108–109
St. Joseph Bay, Fla., 79
St. Julian Square, Savannah, 15
St. Julien family, 147, 303
St. Julien, Paul de, 182
St. Louis Cathedral, New Orleans, 285
St. Marks, Fla., 106
St. Marks Lighthouse, 134
St. Marks Trail, 123, 128, 134
St. Martin Parish, La., 292
St. Mary's Catholic Church, Charleston, 156
St. Marys, Ga., 7, 25, 50, 53
St. Marys River, 9, 12, 28, 40, 42, 43, 45, 50, 51, 52, 53, 97, 102, 106, 164, 304; as boundary of Georgia and Florida, 98, 211; canoe Trail, 50, claimed by South Carolina, 187
St. Mathews Parish, Georgia, 21
St. Michael's Cemetery, Pensacola, 154, 271
St. Michael's Episcopal Church, Charleston, 153
St. Patricks Parish, 53
St. Paul's Episcopal Church, Augusta, 69, 75
St. Pauls Parish, Georgia, 61, 75, 79, 80
St. Philips Church, Brunswick, N.C., 318
St. Philip's Episcopal Church, Charleston, 155
St. Philip's Parish, S.C., 154
St. Phillip's Parish, Ga., 33
St. Pierre, Jean Louis de Mesnil, 65, 67
St. Simons Island, 13, 28, 34, 37, 40, 42, 43, 45, 46, 48, 49; library, 48, visitor center, 48
St. Stephens, Ala., 250, 253, 257, 263
St. Stephens Episcopal Church, Charleston, 148
St. Stephens Meridian (Baseline), 261
St. Tammany Parish, La., 281, 287
St. Thomas' Parish, Georgia, 42, 51, 53
Stagecoach Road, to Wrightsborough, 64, 71
staggerbush, 133, 146
Stagger Mud Lake, 115
Stalame Indians, 158
Stallings Island, Augusta, 60
Stamp Act, 14, 140, 315; protests, 157
Standing Indian, N.C., 201
Star Fort at Ninety Six, 177
Starved Gut Hall, 143
State Botanical Garden of Georgia, 85
State House, 142
Station Cove Botanical Area, 186
Station Mountain, 181
steamboats: cause disuse of Federal Road, 223; on Alabama River, 247, 254, 265; on the Gulf Coast, 275; on the St. Johns River, 114
Stecoe, 189–191, 192
Stekoa Creek, 191, 192
Stephen Foster State Park, 52
Stephens, Alexander H., 82, 83
Stephens, William, 13
Stetson, John, 117
Stetson University, 117
Stevens Creek, 68, 69

Stevens Creek Heritage Preserve, 68
Stevens, John, 32
Stevenson, Robert Louis, 25
Stewart, Prince Charles Edward, 50
Stewart County, Ga., 229, 233, 235
Stewart, Daniel, 31, 235
Stewart-Parker House, Georgetown, 300
stewartia, 192, 194
Stinkard language, 241
Stirk, Rev. Benjamin, 56
Stockton, Ala., 256, 258, 261
Stokes Bluff Landing, Savannah River, 163
Stokes Landing, 109
Stokes Landing Conservation Area, 104
Stone, John Nelson, 84
Stone Mountain, Ga., 69
stoneroot, 187
Stono River, 138, 144
Stork, Dr. William, 98
Storm Creek, 211
Straus family; Isidor, Lazarus, Nathan, Oscar, 225
Strawberry Chapel, 148
striped bass, 150
Stroud family, 251
Stuart, Dr. James, 168
Stuart family, 168
Stuart, Francis, 154
Stuart, Henry, 160, 168
Stuart House. See John Stuart House
Stuart, James II, 12
Stuart, James III, 12
Stuart, John, 3, 25, 61, 80, 98, 168, 171, 174, 192; biography, 154; escapes Fort Loudon, 179, 206; flees Charleston, 140, 160; house on Tradd St., 151, 152; implicated in Cherokee attacks, 140; imposes trade ban, 79; visited by William Bartram, 143
Stuart, John; 3rd Earl of Bute, 1, 3
Stuart, Sir John II, 152
Stuart Town, S.C., 160, 167
Stumphouse Tunnel, 187
styrax, 92
Submarginal Land Program, 242
sugar, 286
sugar cane, 120
Sugar Mill Gardens, 119
Sugar Mill Ruins Historic Site, 120
Sugar Party, 14
Sugar Town, 183, 194. See also Kulsage
Sulenojuh, 223
Sullivan's Island, S.C., 139, 142, 147, 148
Sumerian cuneiform, 226
Summerville, S.C., 147
Summerville-Dorchester Museum, 147
Sumter National Forest, 68, 192; Andrew Pickens District, 186; Long Cane District, 174; Stumphouse Ranger Station, 187
Sumter, Thomas, 142, 171, 183, 299
Sunbury, 14, 25, 28, 29, 32, 33, 38, 39
sundew, 278, 311, 317
Sunny Hill Restoration Area, 116
Sunset Rock, Highlands, 194
Sunshine Bridge, Mississippi River, 293
Sutherland Mill, Augusta, 76
Suwannee Bend Creeks, 233
Suwannee Canal National Recreation Area, 52
Suwannee Old Town, 246
Suwannee River, 8, 51, 109, 123, 128, 130–132
Swain County, N.C., 201, 207
Swain, David L., 207
Swamp Fox, 299
Swamp Fox National Recreation Trail, 302
swamp lily, 262, 306
swamp pink, 194

Swarbreck, Edward, 36
sweet grass and sweet grass baskets, 148
sweet potatoes, 244
sweet shrub, 194
Sweetwater Creek; Richmond Co., 76; Crawford Co., 211, 221
Sweetwater Park, 128
Swift Creek Culture, 234
Swiss: immigrate to Louisiana, 289; protestants, 164; settlers in Louisiana, 291
Switzerland, Fla., 101, 104
Sylph (ship), 114
Sylvania, Ga., 54

T

tabby, 20
Tabby Ruins, Darien, 37
Table Rock State Park, S.C., 184, 186
Tacatacuru, 40, 50
Tahlequah, Okla., 199
Taitt, David, 241, 251
Talahasochte, 8, 123, 128, 132, 133
Talasi, 8, 205, 241, 244, 248
Talawi, 203
Talaxe, 48, 244
Talbot County, Ga., 225
Talbot Islands State Park, Fla., 99, 101
Talbot, Matthew, 225
Talbotton, Ga., 224, 232
Tali, 203
Taliaferro, Benjamin, 89
Taliaferro County, Ga., 79, 80, 82, 89
Tallahassee, Fla., 105, 128, 166; becomes capital of Florida, 267; Old Spanish Trail, 270, 277
Tallahassee Town, 244
Tallapoosa County, Ala., 249
Tallapoosa River, 9, 239, 242, 244, 249; Creek settlements, 244, 246, 247; empire of Tascaluza, 238
Tallassee, Ala., 238, 244
tallow tree, 144
Tallulah Ranger District, 192
Tallulah River, 201
Tama, 38
Tamar (ship), 151
Tamassee Town, 182
Tamassee School, 181
Tame Doe, 205
Tammany, Chief, 287
Tammany Trace, 284
Tampa Bay, 128
Tangipahoa Parish, La., 287
Tangipahoa River, 282, 285
the Tangipahoas, 281, 287
Tarleton, Banastre, 83, 161, 299; his cruelty, 169
Tarleton's Quarter, 299
Tascaluza, 238
Taska Recreation Area, Tuskegee National Forest, 242
Taskigi, 243
Tassel, Old, 205
Tastanagi, 227
Tate, Davy, 259
Tate, John, 259
Tatham Gap Road, 206
Taylor County, Ga., 221, 225
Taylor, Zachary, 225, 295
Tchefuncte River, 285
tea, 144
Tea Act, 315
Teach, Edward, 35, 139, 313
Tecumseh, 222, 244, 251; inflames the young Creek warriors, 259; influence among Red

Sticks, 260; Visits the Creek Confederacy, 241
Telfair, Edward, 14
Telfair Museum, Savannah, 22, 26
Tellico Blockhouse, 205
Tellico Plains, TN, 206
Temple Mickve Israel, 27
Temple of Health, 172, 175
Temple of Hera, 248
Ten Mile, S.C., 146
Tennent, Rev. William, 171
Tennessee, 250; Cherokee Nation, 182, 195, 205; home of Shawnees, 71; home of the Creeks, 239; origin of the Yuchis, 69
Tennessee River, 199, 203; settlements, 195
Tennessee-Tombigbee Waterway, 277
Tensaw, Ala., 253
Tensaw Bluff, Ala., 259
Tensaw River, 258, 260; public access, 260
Tensaws, 256
Terminal Station, Macon, 221
Ternant, Marquis Claude Vincent de, 296
Terrebonne Parish, La., 296
Texas, 105, 182, 209, 236, 279; cotton migration, 214; flag, 223; home of Biloxis and Pascagoulas, 274; home to Alabamas, 247; independence, 253; Koasatis, 248; leaders, 211; Old Spanish Trail, 270, 277, 284; origin of the Creeks, 239; Republic of, 182, 223, 236; rice, 304, 306
Texas Historical Commission, 288
Tezcuco Plantation, Mississippi River, 286
Thames River, 32
Theodore Roosevelt Area, Fla., 102
Theory of Uniformity, 7, 291, 295
Thlopthlocco, 245
Thomas Center, Gainesville, 128
Thomas Elfe House, Charleston, 155
Thomas, Mary Lamboll, 143; hosts William Bartram, 151
Thomas, William H., 187, 199
Thompson Bridge, 57
Thompson River, 185, 186
Thomson, Charles, 5
Thomson, Ga., 71
Thoreau, Henry David, 5
Thorogood, Joseph, 147
Thorogood Plantation, 142, 147
Three & Twenty Creek, 172, 176
Three Brothers (ship), 137
Three Notch Road, 250
Three Sisters Ferry, 56, 162, 163
Thronateeska Heritage Museum of History and Science, 235
Thronateeskee (Flint River), 223
Thunderbolt, Ga., 21
Thursby House, Blue Springs, Fla., 117
Tick Island, Fla., 115
Tickfaw River, 286
Tie Snake, 230
Tiger Bay State Forest, Fla., 119
Tillman Heritage Preserve, S.C., 163
Tillman, S.C., 162
Tilly, Rev. William, 166
Timucuan Preserve, 101
Timucuan province, 50
Timucuans, 103, 117, 121; attacked by Carolina Scots, 160; capture Fontaneda, 114; European diseases, 122; join the Creek Confederacy, 239; language, 40, 126; Potanoes, 122; rebellion, 159; Utinas, 122
Titusville, Fla., 3, 117
tobacco, 64, 73, 84, 89, 308
tobacco roads, 65
Tobesofkee Creek, 222

Toccoa, Ga., 92
Tocoi, Fla., 101, 105
Tocoreche, 192
Tocqueville, Alexis de, 223
Tohomes, 260
Tolomato River, 104
Tom Mann's Fish World, Eufaula, 234
Tomassee Town, 186
Tomatly, 160
Tombigbee River, 89, 250, 256, 259
Tomochichi, 13, 22, 26, 166, 239
Tom's Path, 229
Tondee, Lucy, 26
Tondee, Peter, 20, 25, 26
Tondee's Tavern, 14, 21, 26, 62
Tonti, Henri de, 264
Tonyn, Patrick, 18, 70, 98, 120, 173
Toombs, Robert, 83
Toonahowi, 13, 26, 48, 50
Toqua, 203
Torah, in Savannah, 27
Tories, 47, 49, 54, 56. *See also* loyalists; atrocities, 62; attack South Carolina Upcountry, 174; banished from S.C., 169; burn Ft. Independence, 174; captured by Nancy Hart, 89, 95; destroy Lowcountry property, 161; in Augusta, 79; in Beaufort District, 161; in Georgia, 71; in South Carolina, 171; in South Carolina Upcountry, 171, 173; in Wilkes County, 83; leave Florida, 106; leave Savannah, 14
Torreya, 85
Tory Hole Battleground, 319
Tosohatchee State Reserve, Fla., 121
Toupa Indians, 158
Tower of London, 142
Town Creek, 210, 232
Townshend Acts of 1768, 14, 140, 315
Toxaway, 182
Toxaway River, 185, 186
traders, 79, 80; in Augusta, 73; relations with Cherokees, 174; relations with Native Americans, 73
Trader's Hill, Ga., 51, 98
Trader's Log Cabin, Columbus, 236
Trail of Tears National Historic Trail, 199
Trail Ridge, 50, 52
Trans-Oconee Republic, 67, 215
Transylvania County, N.C., 201
Trapier II, Paul, 306
Traveler's Rest State Historic Site, Ga., 176
Traveller, Lee's horse, 166
Travels, the, 1–6, 3, 64, 105, 117; account of East Florida, 98; account of Suwannee River, 132; account of the New Purchase survey, 79, 80, 82, 92; Alachua, 127; Bivens Arm, 127; Cherokee maidens, 199; chronology, 8; Falling Creek, 192; Fort James, 89; inaccuracy of dates, 221; influence on sir Charles Lyell, 7; influences, 5, 222; Little Tennessee River, 191; Mississippi River, 290; New Smyrna, 119; original edition, 230; plant discoveries, 146; publication of, 4, 6; study and commemoration, 225; the alligator battle, 108
Travis, William Barret, 253, 254
Treaty of the Cherokee Agency (1817), 197
Treaty Oak, 182
Treaty of Aix-la-Chapelle (1748), 13
Treaty of Augusta (1763), 197, 208, 211, 237, 246
Treaty of Augusta (1773), 25, 61, 64, 67, 73, 79, 80, 84, 89, 237
Treaty of Augusta (1783), 51, 79, 208, 214, 237, 244
Treaty of Colerain (1796), 51, 237, 245
Treaty of Coweta (1739), 230

Treaty of Cusseta (1832), 229
Treaty of Dewitt's Corner (1777), 175, 179, 197
Treaty of Fort Gibson (1832), 237
Treaty of Fort Jackson (1814), 237, 241, 245, 246, 248, 251, 255, 259, 260
Treaty of Fort Mitchell (1827), 232
Treaty of Fort Wilkinson (1802), 208, 215, 237, 245
Treaty of Galphinton (1785), 51, 79, 208, 214, 237
Treaty of Hopewell (1785), 79, 182, 197, 205
Treaty of Ildefonso (1800), 290
Treaty of Indian Springs (1821), 221, 237, 245
Treaty of Indian Springs (1825), 216, 221, 229, 230, 237, 241, 245
Treaty of Indian Springs (1835), 224
Treaty of Kasihta (1739), 237
Treaty of Long Island (1777), 204
Treaty of Long Island (1781), 205
Treaty of New Echota, 199
Treaty of New York (1790), 51, 208, 237, 244
Treaty of Paris (1763), 25, 42, 97, 256, 266, 289
Treaty of Paris (1783), 99, 106, 157, 274, 291
Treaty of San Lorenzo (1795), 145, 257, 261, 274, 281, 304
Treaty of Savannah (1733), 237
Treaty of Savannah (1757), 237
Treaty of Shoulderbone Creek (1786), 51, 79, 88, 208, 214, 237
Treaty of the Creek Agency (1804), 208
Treaty of the Creek Agency (1818), 237
Treaty of the Creek Agency (1827), 237
Treaty of Versailles (1783), 257
Treaty of Washington (1805), 208, 232, 237
Treaty of Washington (1818), 197
Treaty of Washington (1819), 205
Treaty of Washington (1826), 221, 237
Treaty of Washington (1827), 221
Treaty Tree, 85
Tree Hill, Jacksonville, 104
Tree that Owns Itself, Athens, 86
Trenton, Fla., 133
Treutlen, James, 56
trillium, 173, 186
Trimont Ridge, 200
Trotter Shoals, Savannah River, 89, 94
Troup, George, 22, 221, 229
Troup Square, Savannah, 22
trout lily, 68
Troutman, Joanna, 223
Trumbull, John, 153
Trustees, 12, 13, 19, 22, 24, 25, 27, 42, 49, 164; cattle, 19; Trustees' Garden, 24, 25; Trustees' Store, 22, 25
Tryon, William, 3, 71, 315, 317
Tsali, 199
Tsinia Wildlife Viewing Area, Tuskegee National Forest, 242
Tuckabatchee, 9, 50, 242, 244, 245; capital of Upper Creek Towns, 239; conference, 232; Council Tree, 245; visited by Tecumseh, 260
Tuckahoe WMA, 57
Tuckaluge Creek, 192
Tuckaritche Creek, 192
Tuckasee King, 56
Tuckasegee River, 192, 195, 197, 199
Tucker, Dan, 94
Tucker, Lord, 112
Tugaloo, 61, 76, 79, 91, 175, 178, 182, 189
Tugaloo River, 8, 76, 79, 84, 92, 176, 187, 191, 192
Tugaloo State Park, Ga., 95
Tullafinny River, 161
Tulsa, 244

Tunbridge fern, 184
Tunica, La.; explored by Iberville, 288; Tunica Hills State Preservation Area, La., 295–296; Tunica Hills Wildlife Management Area, 295; Tunica Trace, 295; Tunica Treasure, 296
Tunica Treasure Museum, 296
Tunica-Biloxi Tribe, 296
the Tunicas, 296
turkey, 133, 302
Turkey Creek, 172
turkey oak, 113, 114, 146, 163, 311
Turnbridge Plantation, S.C., 161, 164
Turnbull Bend, 291
Turnbull Creek Educational State Forest, N.C., 320
Turnbull, Daniel and Martha, 295
Turnbull, Dr. Andrew, 120
Turnbull, Dr. John, 98
Turnbull Hammock Conservation Area, Fla., 120
Turnbull, Nicholas, 46
turpentine, 320
Turtle Island Wildlife Management Area, 165
Turtle Mound, 120
Turtle River, 42, 157
Tuscage, 160
Tuscaloosa, Ala., 238
Tuscaney, 13
Tuscarora Jack. See Barnwell, John
Tuscarora War, 5, 196, 316
Tuscaroras, 195, 319
Tuskegee (Cherokee town), 204
Tuskegee, Ala., 241, 242, 243; Tuskegee Institute, 243, 244; Tuskegee National Historic Site, 243
Tuskegee (Creek town), 227
Tuskegee National Forest, 241, 242
Tusquitee Ranger District, Nantahala National Forest, 201
Tustenuggee Emathla, 245
Tuxachanie Trail, 279
Twenty-seven Mile Bluff, Mobile River, 256, 261
Twiggs, John, 59, 215
Tybee Island, 21, 158; Tybee Museum, 21; Tybee Lighthouse, 21; Visitors Center, 21
Tybee National Wildlife Refuge, 21, 165
Tyler Wildlife Management Area, Glynn Co., 43

U

Uchee, Ala., 229, 234, 241
Uchee Creek, Ala., 8, 229
Uchee Creek, Ga., 64, 69
Uchees. See Yuchis
Uchisees, 106
Uktena, 206
Ulloa, Don Antonio de, 289
Ulrica, Queen of Sweden, 1
Ulster, Ireland, 175
Ulster Scots, 37, 175
Unaka Mountains, 207
Uncle Remus Museum, Eatonton, 216
Unicoi Turnpike, 176
Uniformitarianism. See Theory of Uniformity
Union Point, Ga., 19, 65, 76, 82, 86, 211, 217
Union Society, 20, 26
United States: boundary with Florida, 261, 274; builds Federal Road through Creek Nation, 223; confirms title of Farmar family estate, 260; expands territory, 264; Indian removal, 241; navy, 270; relations with the Cherokees, 199; relations with the Creeks, 239, 244; settles Yazoo Fraud land claims, 213, 275; Submarginal Land Program, 242; treaties with the Creeks, 182, 208, 237
University of California, 34
University of Florida, 128
University of Georgia, 19, 34, 85, 173, 214, 217; Coastal Extension Center, 19; Franklin College of Arts and Sciences, 85; Georgia Museum of Natural History, 86; herbarium, 86; Institute of ecology, 86; libraries, 85; map room, 85; Marine Extension Center, 20; Marine Institute, 36; presidents, 263; School of Forest Resources, 86
University of Georgia System, 214
University of Mississippi, 279
University of North Carolina, 207
University of Pennsylvania, 6
University of South Alabama Library and Archives, 263
University of South Carolina, 34, 305; Coastal Campus, 311
University of West Florida, 269, 270
Unzaga y Amézaga, Don Luis de, 284, 289
Upatoi Creek, 221, 229
Upcountry, S.C., 171
Uphapee Creek, 241
Upper Cherokee Path, 65, 66, 76, 91, 92, 192, 217
Upper Creek Path, 65, 71, 76, 211, 214, 217
Upper Creek Towns, 9, 76. 238–241
Upper Creeks: capital, 245; condemn McIntosh, 221; joined by the Natchez, 148; national leaders, 245
Upper Three Runs Creek, 59
Upper Whitewater Falls, 185
Upson, Stephen, 84
Uriah, Ala., 254
Ursulines, 279
US Army Corps of Engineers, 89
US Congress: members, 186; passes Indian Removal Bill, 229, 241
US Fish & Wildlife Service, 19, 169
US Forest Service, 68, 186
US House of Representatives, 84, 86
US Marine Corps, 167
US Naval Hospital, 167
US Navy, 267
US Secretary of the Treasury, 84
US Senate, 85, 147; members, 194, 201
USDA Center for Forested Wetlands Research, 145
USS Constitution, 48
Ussa Yoholo. See Osceola
the Utinas, 122

V

Vale of Cowee, 191, 192
Valley Towns, 189
Valleytown, 206
Valparaiso Bombing and Gunnery, 269
Van Cleave, Miss., 278
vaquero, 82
Varennes Tavern, Anderson Co., 175
varnish tree, 144
Vassall, John, 312, 318
Vaubercey, Louis François le Gras de, 260
Vaudreuil, Pierre François de Rigaud Cavagnal, Mar, 289
Venus' fly-trap, 311, 317, 318
Venus-hair fern, 319
Vereen, Jeremiah, 311
Vereen Memorial Gardens, 311
Vernon, James, 12
Verrazano, Giovanni da, 168, 312
Versailles, Court of, 289
Vesey, Denmark, 156
Veux Carré, 285
Vicksburg, Miss., 266
Victoria Bluff Heritage Preserve, S.C., 165
Victoria Bryant State Park, Ga., 92
Vienna, S.C., 89, 173
Vignoles, Charles, 105, 112, 126, 128
Villafañe, Angel de, 158, 266
Village Creek, 181
Virginia, 137; Cherokee territory, 195; founding of the colony, 312; governors, 73; migration from, 64, 79, 88, 89, 92, 170; militia enters the Cherokee War, 179; origin of name, 312; refuge for Huguenots, 303; trade with Cherokees, 184; war with Chickamaugas, 205
Virginia (ship), 236
Virginia Path, 86, 181, 183, 184, 189
Virginians, 178; first encounter with Cherokees, 196; rivalry with Carolinians, 79; settle Mississippi Territory, 265; settle Piedmont Georgia, 64
Viterbo, Rosa de, 270
Volusia County, Fla., 3, 114, 119
Volusia, Fla., 109, 114, 128; Volusia Museum, 114
Von Reck, Baron Philipp Georg Friederich, 56
Voodoo, 285

W

W. A. Gayle Planetarium, Montgomery, 247
Waccamaw darter, 319
Waccamaw killifish, 319
Waccamaw Neck, S.C., 300, 309
Waccamaw River, 298, 305, 308; northern limit of rice culture, 304; plantations, 309; Waccamaw River Heritage Preserve, 309, 311
Waccamaw silverside, 319
Waccamaw-Siouan Indians, 317, 319
the Waccamaws, 316
Waccassassa Bay, 134; Waccassassa Bay State Preserve, Fla., 133
Waddel, Dr. Moses, 84, 85, 173, 182
Waddell Mariculture Center, 166
Wadsadler Campground, 92
Wadmalaw Island, S.C., 144
Wagon Road, Great, 73
Wakefield, Ala., 250
Walam Olum, 7
Walhalla Fish Hatchery, 185
Walhalla Oktoberfest, 187
Walhalla, S.C., 187
Walker, William, 246
Wallace Pate Research Center, S.C., 306
walnut, 86
Walpole, Horace, 147
Walter Anderson Museum, Ocean Springs, 278
Walter, Thomas, 146
Walterboro, S.C., 169
Walton, George, 14, 15, 29, 75, 79
Wambaw Creek Wilderness Area, S.C., 303
Wambaw Swamp Wilderness, S.C., 302
Wanchese, 312
Wando River, 143, 148, 300, 302
Wannamaker Park, Charleston, 147
Wansey, Henry, 108
Wanton, Fla., 126
Wappoo Cut, Charleston Co., 144
War Hill, Wilkes Co., 83
War of 1812, 151, 243, 257; American territorial gains, 264
War of Austrian Succession, 13
War of Jenkins' Ear, 13, 47, 97, 104, 106
War of the Red Sticks. See Creek War, 1813–14
War Woman, 205
Warachy, 182
Ward Bayou Wildlife Management Area, 277
Ward, Bryant, 205
Ward, John, 160

Ward, Nancy, 182, 192, 205, 206; biography, 205
Warren, Joseph, 72
Warren County, Ga., 72, 76, 90, 216, 236
Warren Island, S.C., 169
Warren, Joseph E., 22, 216
Warren Square, Savannah, 22
Warrenton, Ga., 76, 211, 223
Warrior Stand, Ala., 242
Warthen, Ga., 213
Warthen, Richard, 213
Warwoman Creek, 192
Warwoman Dell, 191, 192
Warwoman Shear, 192
Washington, Booker T., 242, 243, 244
Washington County, Ala., 250, 257, 260, 263; Washington County Museum, 213
Washington County, Ga., 79, 208, 210, 213, 217
Washington, DC, 88
Washington, Ga., 71, 76, 83, 84
Washington, George, 6, 22, 24, 25, 57, 83, 186, 237, 263, 287, 300, 302; authorizes arrest of Elijah Clark, 67; censures Citizen Genet, 144; dines at Cochran's, 311; dines at Snee Farm, 148; entertained at Hampton Plantation, 303; honored in Georgetown, 306; the Conway Cabal, 157; travels the S.C. coast, 309; visits Charleston, 153, 155; visits George Walton, 75; visits Hampton, 145; visits Wilmington, 321
Washington Monument, 153
Washington Oaks State Gardens, Fla., 105
Washington Parish, La., 287
Washington Square, Savannah, 22
Washington-Wilkes Museum, 83
Washington, William, 145, 300
Washo Preserve, S.C., 304
Wassaw Island, Ga., 19, 211; Wassaw Island Foundation, 19; Wassaw Island National Wildlife Refuge, Ga., 19; Wassaw Island Trust, 19
Watauga (Cherokee), 201
Watauga (white settlement), 204
Watauga District, North Carolina, 62
water arrowhead, 319
Water Lily Festival, 201
the Waterees, 166
Waterfront Park, Charleston, 155
Watermelon Pond, Alachua Co., 132
Waties, William, 308, 311
Watkinsville, Ga., 85, 87
Watsadler Campground, 93
Watson, John, 156, 157
Watson Mill State Park, Ga., 88
Watson, Samuel, 171
Waugh, Ala., 247
wax myrtle, 86, 133, 311
Wayah Bald, 17, 200, 201, 205; Wayah Crest Picnic Area, 205; Wayah Gap, 205
Wayah Ranger District, Nantahala National Forest, 201
Waycross, Ga., 52
Wayne, Anthony, 57
Waynesboro, Ga., 56, 57, 165
Weatherford, John, 250
Weatherford, Sehoy Tate, 259
Weatherford, William, 241, 243, 250, 259, 260
Webster, Daniel, 199
Webster's salamander, 68
the Wedge, 304
Wedgewood China, 172, 201
Weeden Island Culture, 234
Weeks Bay National Estuarine Reserve, Ala., 262
Weems Island, La., 282
Wekiva Buffer Conservation Area, Fla., 119
Wekiwa Springs State Park, Fla., 119
Welaka, Fla., 103, 112

Welaka National Fish Hatchery, 112
Wells, George, 94
Welsh immigrants, 313
Wentworth Museum, Pensacola, 271
Wereat, John, 62
Wesley, Charles, 13, 46
Wesley, John, 13, 22, 24, 25, 49
Wesley Woodland Walk, 46
Wesleyan College, 222
West Baton Rouge Parish, La., 296; West Baton Rouge Museum, 294
West Dam Recreation Area, Ga., 66
West Feliciana Parish, La., 289, 296; West Feliciana Historical Society Museum, 295
West Florida, 256, 260, 281, 291. *See also* Republic of West Florida; archaeology in Pensacola, 271; assembly quarrels with governor, 266; boundaries, 257, 274, 281, 293, 304; British period, 264, 271; captured by Gálvez, 284; Florida Parishes, 281; history, 271; refuge for loyalists, 275; returned to Spain, 257; settled by British and Americans, 281; Spanish boundaries, 260, 261; Spanish period, 264; West Florida Assembly, 260; West Florida Convention, 291; West Florida Rebellion, 281, 295; William Bartram's travels in, 4, 6
West Florida Historical Association Museum, 295
West Pearl River, 282
West Ship Island, Miss., 278
Westabou (Savannah River), 18
Western Carolina Land and Improvement Co, 174
Western Carolina University, 201
Westoes, 11, 48, 60, 71, 106, 137, 159, 168
West's Mill, 201
Westside Regional Park, Fla., 103
Westvaco Corporation, 169
Westville Historic Village, 183, 233
Wetumka, Okla., 246
Wetumpka, Ala., 248
Whatoga, 199
Whigs, 14, 62, 171; control Savannah, 160; establish government at Augusta, 62; in Georgia, 14, 71; in South Carolina, 171; in South Carolina Upcountry, 171
White Cliffs, 290
white ibis, 309
White, John, 312
White Kitchen Wetlands & Chevron Boardwalk, 282
White Lake, N.C., 319
white oak, 69
White Path, 208
White Plains, La., 291
White Point, Charleston, 137, 139, 151, 313
White Ponds, 213
White, Richard, 19
White Rock Gap, 200
White Rock Scenic Area, Sumter national Forest, 185, 186
White Sand Landing, St. Marys River, 42, 51
White Springs, Fla., 233
white-tailed deer, 145
White, William, 83
Whitefield, Rev. George, 17, 20, 24, 25, 166
Whitefield Square, Savannah, 24
Whitehall Bluffs, Clarke Co., 85
Whitehall Plantation, 172
Whitehall, S.C., 166, 177
whites: and tensions with Native Americans, 73; displaced by Yamassee War, 166; living in Creek territory, 241; population in South Carolina, 139; relations with Cherokees, 174, 197; retain Indian servants, 135; settle Alabama, 243; settle Chattahoochee River, 233; settle Indian lands, 79; settle the Piedmont, 79; settle upper Savannah River, 71; tensions with Seminoles, 98; trespass Creek land, 251; victims of the Second Creek War, 229

Whitesburg, Ga., 230
Whiteside Mountain, 185, 191, 194
Whitewater River, 185
Whitney & Miller Company, 18
Whitney, Eli, 17, 64, 73, 76
Wigan, Eleazer, 178
wild pine, 132
Wild Turkey Center, Edgefield, 68
Wildland Expeditions, 261
Wildwood County Park, Ga., 66
Wilkes County, Ga., 57, 62, 64, 72, 79, 80, 83, 89; as government of Georgia, 84; as Whig stronghold, 84; in the Revolution, 67
Wilkes, John, 80, 89, 140, 181
Wilkinson County, Ga., 208, 217
Wilkinson, James, 217, 257
Will of Watauga, 199
William and Sarah (ship), 27
Williams, Audrey, 247
Williams Creek, 61, 82
Williams, Hank, 247
Williamsburg County, S.C., 307
Williamson, Andrew, 142, 171, 172, 173, 174, 177, 179, 183, 186, 187, 197
Williamson Island, S.C., 21
Williamson, William, 160
Willing, James, 292
Willing's Raiders, 290
Willington Academy, 173, 182
Willington, S.C., 84
willow oak, 86
Willtown, S.C., 143, 161
Wilmington and Weldon Railroad, 322
Wilmington, Earl of, 321
Wilmington, N.C., 317; Chamber of Commerce, 322; King's Road, 143, 302; Riverfront Visitor Information Center, 322
Wilmington Railroad Museum, 322
Wilmington River, 21
Wilson, Alexander, 7, 57, 290
Wimbee Indians, 158
Wind Clan, 259, 272
Windrush Gardens, Baton Rouge, 294
Windsor, Conn, 147
Windsor Hill, 142
Windy Falls Natural Area, S.C., 185
Winfield Campground, 66
winged elm, 132
Wingspread Wildlife Drive, Ala., 234
Winterville, Ga., 80, 82, 86, 92
Winyah Bay, S.C., 35, 135, 298, 300, 309
Winyah Indigo Society Hall, 306
Winyahs, 316
Wire Road, 223
wiregrass, 163, 270
Wise, William, 19
Wistar, Caspar, 7
witch doctors, 168
witch hazel, 92, 194
Witcheough Indians, 158
Wolf Island National Wildlife Refuge, Ga., 38
Wolf King, 246
Wolf River, 279
Wolf Trail, 253
Woodbine, Ga., 50
wood duck, 309
Woodin, Rebekah, 173
Woodlawn Plantation, Oglethorpe Co., 85
Woodmason, Rev. Charles, 171
wood stork, 116, 119, 120, 125, 143, 165

Woodward, Dr. Henry, 18, 60, 71, 137, 208, 227; biography, 164
Woodward, Thomas, 123, 229, 242, 245, 248, 251, 260; *Reminiscences*, 241
Wool, John, 199
Wordsworth, William, 5
World Heritage Museum, Montgomery, 247
Wormsloe State Historic Site, Ga., 20
Wragg, William, 139
Wright, Elizabeth, 12
Wright, James, 14, 15, 25, 26, 29, 42, 49, 71, 80, 89; at Congress of Augusta, 61; Indian diplomacy, 62, 79; meets the Bartrams, 3; visited by William Bartram, 15
Wright, Jermyn, 42, 50
Wright Square, Savannah, 22, 26
Wright's Fort, 50
Wrightsborough, Ga., 8, 57, 61, 65, 71, 80, 210, 211; attacked by Native Americans, 79, 83; visited by William Bartram, 64, 69; Wrightsborough Academy, 71; Wrightsborough Methodist Church, 71
Wrightsborough Road, 64, 69, 71
Wynton M. Blount Cultural Park, Montgomery, 246

Y

Yahola, 227
Yahola Micco, 231
Yamacraw Bluff, Savannah, 12, 18, 26, 166
Yamacraw Town, 12, 15, 19, 26, 237
the Yamacraws, 12, 13, 15, 19, 26, 28, 239
Yamassee, 38
Yamassee War, 61, 71, 73, 83, 123, 143, 160, 163, 166, 178, 196, 208, 215, 219, 316; aftermath, 227; destroys Lowcountry cattle industry, 160; effect on Indian trade, 247; ends, 160; in North Carolina, 313
Yamassees, 26, 28, 166; attacked by Carolina militia, 160; burial ground, 109, 115; in South Carolina, 167; join the Creek Confederacy, 239; lower towns, 166; move to coastal South Carolina, 160; move to Upper St. Johns River, 114; their allies, 163; villages, 164; war with Creeks, 123; war with South Carolina, 138, 231
yaupon, 86, 133, 302
Yawkey, Tom, 305
Yawkey Wildlife Center, 305
Yazoo Act, 89, 213, 214
Yazoo Fraud, 213, 275
Yazoo Lands, 250; organized into Mississippi Territory, 260
Yazoo River, 274, 281
Yeamans, John, 147, 318
Yeamans, William, 137
Yellow Bluff Fort State Historical Site, Fla., 102
yellow fever, 33, 75, 138, 145, 254, 279
yellow-eyed grass, 146
yellowwood, 70, 153
Yesho Plantation, 153
yew, 86
Yonaguska, 199
York, Pa., 89
Yorktown, Va., 79, 320
Yorubas, 167, 285
yoshino cherry, 86
Young Warrior, 80
Younge, Philip, 68, 80, 82, 92
Yuchi Town, 8, 224, 229, 232
Yuchi Wildlife Management Area, Ga., 57
Yuchis, 54, 56, 61, 69, 83, 194, 224, 239; allied to the British, 114; conquer Mayaca Province, 114; in First Creek War, 224; initiate Second Creek War, 229; language, 226, 241; members of the Creek Confederacy, 239; origin, 226; settle on Savannah River, 163

Z

Zachary, La., 290
Zapala, 35
Zeke's Island, N.C., 318
Zemurrey Gardens, La., 285
Zéspedes, Manuel de, 99
Zoo at Gulf Breeze, 269
Zooland Animal Park, Gulf Shores, 262
Zubly, Anne Bard, 50
Zubly, Rev. Johannn Joachim, 50, 164
Zubly's Ferry, 17, 162, 164